Lecture Notes in Computer Science 13994

Advanced Research in Computing and Software Science
Subline of Lecture Notes in Computer Science

More information about this series at https://link.springer.com/bookseries/558

Sriram Sankaranarayanan ·
Natasha Sharygina
Editors

Tools and Algorithms for the Construction and Analysis of Systems

29th International Conference, TACAS 2023
Held as Part of the European Joint Conferences
on Theory and Practice of Software, ETAPS 2023
Paris, France, April 22–27, 2023
Proceedings, Part II

 Springer

Editors
Sriram Sankaranarayanan
University of Colorado
Boulder, CO, USA

Natasha Sharygina
University of Lugano
Lugano, Switzerland

ISSN 0302-9743   ISSN 1611-3349   (electronic)
Lecture Notes in Computer Science
ISBN 978-3-031-30819-2   ISBN 978-3-031-30820-8   (eBook)
https://doi.org/10.1007/978-3-031-30820-8

This Springer imprint is published by the registered company Springer Nature Switzerland AG
The registered company address is: Gewerbestrasse 11, 6330 Cham, Switzerland

ETAPS Foreword

Welcome to the 26th ETAPS! ETAPS 2023 took place in Paris, the beautiful capital of France. ETAPS 2023 was the 26th instance of the European Joint Conferences on Theory and Practice of Software. ETAPS is an annual federated conference established in 1998, and consists of four conferences: ESOP, FASE, FoSSaCS, and TACAS. Each conference has its own Program Committee (PC) and its own Steering Committee (SC). The conferences cover various aspects of software systems, ranging from theoretical computer science to foundations of programming languages, analysis tools, and formal approaches to software engineering. Organising these conferences in a coherent, highly synchronized conference programme enables researchers to participate in an exciting event, having the possibility to meet many colleagues working in different directions in the field, and to easily attend talks of different conferences. On the weekend before the main conference, numerous satellite workshops took place that attracted many researchers from all over the globe.

ETAPS 2023 received 361 submissions in total, 124 of which were accepted, yielding an overall acceptance rate of 34.3%. I thank all the authors for their interest in ETAPS, all the reviewers for their reviewing efforts, the PC members for their contributions, and in particular the PC (co-)chairs for their hard work in running this entire intensive process. Last but not least, my congratulations to all authors of the accepted papers!

ETAPS 2023 featured the unifying invited speakers Véronique Cortier (CNRS, LORIA laboratory, France) and Thomas A. Henzinger (Institute of Science and Technology, Austria) and the conference-specific invited speakers Mooly Sagiv (Tel Aviv University, Israel) for ESOP and Sven Apel (Saarland University, Germany) for FASE. Invited tutorials were provided by Ana-Lucia Varbanescu (University of Twente and University of Amsterdam, The Netherlands) on heterogeneous computing and Joost-Pieter Katoen (RWTH Aachen, Germany and University of Twente, The Netherlands) on probabilistic programming.

As part of the programme we had the second edition of TOOLympics, an event to celebrate the achievements of the various competitions or comparative evaluations in the field of ETAPS.

ETAPS 2023 was organized jointly by Sorbonne Université and Université Sorbonne Paris Nord. Sorbonne Université (SU) is a multidisciplinary, research-intensive and worldclass academic institution. It was created in 2018 as the merge of two first-class research-intensive universities, UPMC (Université Pierre and Marie Curie) and Paris-Sorbonne. SU has three faculties: humanities, medicine, and 55,600 students (4,700 PhD students; 10,200 international students), 6,400 teachers, professor-researchers and 3,600 administrative and technical staff members. Université Sorbonne Paris Nord is one of the thirteen universities that succeeded the University of Paris in 1968. It is a major teaching and research center located in the north of Paris. It has five campuses, spread over the two departments of Seine-Saint-Denis and Val d'Oise: Villetaneuse, Bobigny, Saint-Denis, the Plaine Saint-Denis and Argenteuil. The university has more than 25,000 students in different fields, such as health, medicine, languages, humanities, and science. The local organization team consisted of Fabrice Kordon (general co-chair), Laure Petrucci (general co-chair), Benedikt Bollig (workshops), Stefan Haar (workshops), Étienne André (proceedings and tutorials), Céline Ghibaudo (sponsoring), Denis Poitrenaud (web), Stefan Schwoon (web), Benoît Barbot (publicity), Nathalie Sznajder (publicity), Anne-Marie Reytier (communication), Hélène Pétridis (finance) and Véronique Criart (finance).

ETAPS 2023 is further supported by the following associations and societies: ETAPS e.V., EATCS (European Association for Theoretical Computer Science), EAPLS (European Association for Programming Languages and Systems), EASST (European Association of Software Science and Technology), Lip6 (Laboratoire d'Informatique de Paris 6), LIPN (Laboratoire d'informatique de Paris Nord), Sorbonne Université, Université Sorbonne Paris Nord, CNRS (Centre national de la recherche scientifique), CEA (Commissariat à l'énergie atomique et aux énergies alternatives), LMF (Laboratoire méthodes formelles), and Inria (Institut national de recherche en informatique et en automatique).

The ETAPS Steering Committee consists of an Executive Board, and representatives of the individual ETAPS conferences, as well as representatives of EATCS, EAPLS, and EASST. The Executive Board consists of Holger Hermanns (Saarbrücken), Marieke Huisman (Twente, chair), Jan Kofroň (Prague), Barbara König (Duisburg), Thomas Noll (Aachen), Caterina Urban (Inria), Jan Křetínský (Munich), and Lenore Zuck (Chicago).

Other members of the steering committee are: Dirk Beyer (Munich), Luís Caires (Lisboa), Ana Cavalcanti (York), Bernd Finkbeiner (Saarland), Reiko Heckel (Leicester), Joost-Pieter Katoen (Aachen and Twente), Naoki Kobayashi (Tokyo), Fabrice Kordon (Paris), Laura Kovács (Vienna), Orna Kupferman (Jerusalem), Leen Lambers (Cottbus), Tiziana Margaria (Limerick), Andrzej Murawski (Oxford), Laure Petrucci (Paris), Elizabeth Polgreen (Edinburgh), Peter Ryan (Luxembourg), Sriram Sankaranarayanan (Boulder), Don Sannella (Edinburgh), Natasha Sharygina (Lugano), Pawel Sobocinski (Tallinn), Sebastián Uchitel (London and Buenos Aires), Andrzej Wasowski (Copenhagen), Stephanie Weirich (Pennsylvania), Thomas Wies (New York), Anton Wijs (Eindhoven), and James Worrell (Oxford).

I would like to take this opportunity to thank all authors, keynote speakers, attendees, organizers of the satellite workshops, and Springer-Verlag GmbH for their support. I hope you all enjoyed ETAPS 2023.

Finally, a big thanks to Laure and Fabrice and their local organization team for all their enormous efforts to make ETAPS a fantastic event.

April 2023

Marieke Huisman
ETAPS SC Chair
ETAPS e.V. President

Preface

We are pleased to present the proceedings of TACAS 2023, the 29th edition of the International Conference on Tools and Algorithms for the Construction and Analysis of Systems held as part of the 26th European Joint Conferences on Theory and Practice of Software (ETAPS 2023), April 24–28, 2023 in Paris, France. TACAS brings together a community of researchers, developers, and end-users who are broadly interested in rigorous algorithmic techniques for the construction and analysis of systems. The conference is a venue that interleaves various disciplines including formal verification of software and hardware systems, static analysis, program synthesis, verification of machine learning/autonomous systems, probabilistic programming, SAT/SMT solving, constraint solving, static analysis, automated theorem proving and Cyber-Physical Systems.

There were five submission categories for TACAS 2023:

1. **Regular research papers** advancing the theoretical foundations for the construction and analysis of systems.
2. **Case study papers** describing the application of state-of-the-art research techniques on real-world applications.
3. **Regular tool papers** presenting a new tool, a new tool component, or novel extensions to an existing tool of interest to the community.
4. **Tool demonstration papers** focusing on the usage aspects of tools.
5. **SV-COMP competition tool papers** organized as a separate conference track.

Regular research, case study, and regular tool papers were restricted to a total of sixteen pages, and tool demonstration papers to six pages, exclusive of references.

This year 169 papers were submitted to TACAS, consisting of 119 regular research papers, 34 regular tool and case study papers, and 16 tool demonstration papers. Each paper was reviewed by three Program Committee (PC) members, who made use of sub-reviewers. As a result, the PC accepted in total 62 papers, among which there were 45 regular papers, 11 regular tool/case-study papers and 6 tool demonstration papers. The PC members were pleasantly surprised by an unusually large number of strong submissions. Almost all accepted papers had either all positive reviews or a "championing" program committee member who argued in favor of accepting the paper. Furthermore, all accepted papers had a positive average score. One paper was accepted conditionally and successfully "shepherded" by the PC.

Similarly to previous years, it was possible to submit an artifact alongside a paper, which was mandatory for regular tool and tool demonstration papers. An artifact might consist of tools, models, proofs, or other data required for validation of the results of the paper. The Artifact Evaluation Committee (AEC) reviewed the artifacts based on their documentation, ease of use, and, most importantly, whether the results presented in the corresponding paper could be accurately reproduced. The evaluation was carried out using a standardized virtual machine to ensure consistency of the results, except for 4 artifacts that had special hardware or software requirements. The evaluation had two rounds. The first round was carried out in parallel with the work of the PC and evaluated the artifacts for all the submitted regular tool and tool demo papers. The judgment of the AEC was communicated to the PC and weighed in their discussion (the PC rejected a total of 4 papers in this phase). The second round took place after the paper acceptance notifications were sent out so the authors of accepted research and case-study papers could submit their artifacts. In both rounds, the AEC provided 3 reviews per artifact and communicated with the authors to resolve apparent technical issues. In total, 69 artifacts were submitted (51 in the first round and 18 in the second), and the AEC evaluated a total of 64 artifacts regarding their availability, functionality, and/or reusability. Finally, among the 62 accepted papers, the AEC awarded 32 functional badges, 21 reusable badges, and 33 available badges. Such badges appear on the first page of each paper to certify the properties of each artifact.

As a separate conference track, TACAS 2023 hosted the 12th Competition on Software Verification (SV-COMP 2023). SV-COMP is the annual comparative evaluation of tools for automatic software verification and witness validation. The TACAS proceedings contain a selection of 13 short papers that describe participating verification systems and a report presenting the results of the competition. These papers were reviewed by a separate program committee (the competition jury); each of the papers was assessed by at least three reviewers. A total of 52 verification systems were systematically evaluated, with 34 developer teams from ten countries, including five submissions from industry. Two sessions in the TACAS program were reserved for the competition: presentations by the competition chair and the participating development teams in the first session and an open community meeting in the second session.

We would like to thank all the people who helped to make TACAS 2023 successful. First, we would like to thank the authors for submitting their papers to TACAS 2023. The PC members and additional reviewers did a great job in reviewing papers: they contributed informed and detailed reports and engaged in the PC discussions. We also thank the steering committee, and especially its chair, Joost-Pieter Katoen, for his valuable advice. Lastly, we would like to thank the overall organization team of ETAPS 2023.

April 2023

Sriram Sankaranarayanan
Natasha Sharygina
Grigory Fedyukovich
Sergio Mover
Dirk Beyer

Organization

Program Committee Chairs

Sriram Sankaranarayanan   University of Colorado Boulder, USA
Natasha Sharygina   University of Lugano, Switzerland

Program Committee

Christel Baier   TU Dresden, Germany
Haniel Barbosa   Universidade Federal de Minas Gerais, Brazil
Ezio Bartocci   TU Wien, Austria
Dirk Beyer   LMU Munich, Germany
Armin Biere   Freiburg, Germany
Nikolaj Bjørner   Microsoft, USA
Roderick Bloem   Graz University of Technology, Austria
Ahmed Bouajjani   IRIF, Université Paris Cité, France
Hana Chockler   King's College London, UK
Alessandro Cimatti   Fondazione Bruno Kessler, Italy
Rance Cleaveland   University of Maryland, USA
Javier Esparza   TU Munich, Germany
Chuchu Fan   MIT, USA
Grigory Fedyukovich   Florida State University, USA
Bernd Finkbeiner   CISPA Helmholtz Center for Information Security,
                             Germany
Martin Fränzle   Carl von Ossietzky Universität Oldenburg, Germany
Khalil Ghorbal   Inria, France
Laure Gonnord   Grenoble-INP/LCIS, France
Orna Grumberg   Technion - Israel Institute of Technology, Israel
Kim Guldstrand Larsen   Aalborg University, Denmark
Arie Gurfinkel   University of Waterloo, Canada
Ranjit Jhala   University of California, San Diego, USA
Laura Kovacs   TU Wien, Austria
Alexander Kulikov   St. Petersburg Department of Steklov Institute of
                             Mathematics, Russia
Bettina Könighofer   Graz University of Technology, Austria
Wenchao Li   Boston University, USA
Sergio Mover   Ecole Polytechnique, France
Peter Müller   ETH Zurich, Switzerland
Kedar Namjoshi   Nokia Bell Labs, USA
Aina Niemetz   Stanford University, USA
Corina Pasareanu   CMU, NASA, KBR, USA
Nir Piterman   University of Gothenburg, Sweden

Philipp Ruemmer	University of Regensburg, Germany
Krishna S.	Indian Institute of Technology Bombay, India
Cesar Sanchez	IMDEA Software Institute, Spain
Sharon Shoham	Tel Aviv University, Israel
Fabio Somenzi	University of Colorado Boulder, USA
Cesare Tinelli	University of Iowa, USA
Stavros Tripakis	Northeastern University, USA
Frits Vaandrager	Radboud University, Netherlands
Yakir Vizel	Technion, Israel
Tomas Vojnar	Brno University of Technology, Czechia
Naijun Zhan	Chinese Academy of Sciences, China
Lijun Zhang	Chinese Academy of Sciences, China
Florian Zuleger	Vienna University of Technology, Austria

Artifact Evaluation Committee Chairs

| Grigory Fedyukovich | Florida State University, USA |
| Sergio Mover | Ecole Polytechnique, France |

Artifact Evaluation Committee

Timothy A. Thijm	Princeton University, USA
Leonardo Alt	Ethereum Foundation, Germany
Pedro H. A. de Amorim	Cornell University, USA
Martin Blicha	University of Lugano, Switzerland
Alexander Bork	RWTH Aachen, Germany
Priyanka Darke	Tata Consultancy Services, India
Emanuele De Angelis	IASI-CNR, Rome, Italy
Jip J. Dekker	Monash University, Australia
Zafer Esen	Uppsala University, Sweden
Aleksandr Fedchin	Tufts University, USA
Hadar Frenkel	CISPA – Helmholtz Center for Information Security, Germany
Pamina Georgiou	Vienna University of Technology, Austria
Thomas Møller Grosen	Aalborg University, Denmark
Ahmed Irfan	SRI International, USA
Martin Jonas	Fondazione Bruno Kessler, Italy
Dongjoo Kim	Seoul National University, South Korea
Satoshi Kura	National Institute of Informatics, Japan
Denis Mazzucato	Ecole Normale Superieure, France
Baoluo Meng	GE Global Research, USA
Federico Mora	University of California, Berkeley, USA
Dmitry Mordvinov	Saint-Petersburg State University, JetBrains Research, Russia
Srinidhi Nagendra	Chennai Mathematical Institute, India
Andres Noetzli	Stanford University, USA

Jiří Pavela	FIT VUT, Czechia
Sumanth Prabhu	TRDDC, India
Felipe R. Monteiro	Amazon Web Services, USA
Olli Saarikivi	Microsoft Research, USA
Saeid Tizpaz Niari	University of Texas at El Paso, USA
Hari Govind Vediramana Krishnan	University of Waterloo, Canada
Jingbo Wang	University of Southern California, USA
Anton Xue	University of Pennsylvania, USA
Hansol Yoon	Republic of Korea Air Force, South Korea

Program Committee and Jury—SV-COMP

Dirk Beyer (Chair)	LMU Munich, Germany
Viktor Malík (2LS)	TU Brno, Czechia
Lei Bu (BRICK)	Nanjing University, China
Marek Chalupa (Bubaak)	ISTA, Austria
Michael Tautschnig (CBMC)	Queen Mary University London, UK
Henrik Wachowitz (CPAchecker)	LMU Munich, Germany
Hernán Ponce de León (Dartagnan)	Huawei Dresden Research, Germany
Fei He (Deagle)	Tsinghua University, China
Fatimah Aljaafari (EBF)	University of Manchester, UK
Rafael Sá Menezes (ESBMC-kind)	University of Manchester, UK
Martin Spiessl (Frama-C-SV)	LMU Munich, Germany
Falk Howar (GDart, GDart-LLVM)	TU Dortmund, Germany
Simmo Saan (Goblint)	University of Tartu, Estonia
William Leeson (Graves-CPA, Graves-Par)	University of Virginia, USA
Soha Hussein (Java-Ranger)	University of Minnesota, USA
Peter Schrammel (JBMC)	University of Sussex/Diffblue, UK
Gidon Ernst (Korn)	LMU Munich, Germany
Tong Wu (LF-checker)	University of Manchester, UK
Vesal Vojdani (Locksmith)	University of Tartu, Estonia
Lei Bu (MLB)	Nanjing University, China
Raphaël Monat (Mopsa)	Inria and University of Lille, France
Cedric Richter (PeSCo-CPA)	University of Oldenburg, Germany
Jie Su (PIChecker)	Xidian University, China
Marek Trtík (Symbiotic)	Masaryk University, Brno, Czechia
Levente Bajczi (Theta)	Budapest University of Technology and Economics, Hungary

Matthias Heizmann (UAutomizer)	University of Freiburg, Germany
Dominik Klumpp (UGemCutter)	University of Freiburg, Germany
Frank Schüssele (UKojak)	University of Freiburg, Germany
Daniel Dietsch (UTaipan)	University of Freiburg, Germany
Priyanka Darke (VeriAbs, VeriAbsL)	Tata Consultancy Services, India
Raveendra Kumar M. (VeriFuzz)	Tata Consultancy Services, India
HaiPeng Qu (VeriOover)	Ocean University of China, China

Steering Committee

Dirk Beyer	LMU Munich, Germany
Rance Cleaveland	University of Maryland, USA
Holger Hermanns	Universität des Saarlandes, Germany
Joost-Pieter Katoen (Chair)	RWTH Aachen, Germany and Universiteit Twente, Netherlands
Kim G. Larsen	Aalborg University, Denmark
Bernhard Steffen	Technische Universität Dortmund, Germany

Additional Reviewers

Abd Alrahman, Yehia
Ahmad, H. M. Sabbir
An, Jie
Asarin, Eugene
Azzopardi, Shaun
Bacci, Giorgio
Baier, Daniel
Balakrishnan, Gogul
Balasubramanian, A. R.
Baumeister, Jan
Becchi, Anna
Ben Shimon, Yoav
Berger, Guillaume
Beutner, Raven
Bily, Aurel
Blicha, Martin
Bombardelli, Alberto
Brieger, Marvin
Brizzio, Matías
Bunk, Thomas
Caillaud, Benoît
Cano Córdoba, Filip

Ceresa, Martin
Ceska, Milan
Chen, Mingshuai
Chen, Xin
Chen, Yilei
Chiari, Michele
Czerner, Philipp
Dardinier, Thibault
Dawson, Charles
De Masellis, Riccardo
Debrestian, Darin
Di Stefano, Luca
Egolf, Derek
Elad, Neta
Elashkin, Andrey
Esen, Zafer
Fazekas, Katalin
Feng, Shenghua
Ferres, Bruno
Fiedor, Jan
Fleury, Mathias
Fontaine, Pascal

Frenkel, Eden
Frenkel, Hadar
Froleyks, Nils
Fu, Feisi
Garcia-Contreras, Isabel
Garg, Kunal
Georgiou, Pamina
Gianola, Alessandro
Gigerl, Barbara
Goorden, Martijn
Gorostiaga, Felipe
Goyal, Srajan
Griggio, Alberto
Grosen, Thomas Møller
Gstrein, Bernhard
Gupta, Ashutosh
Habermehl, Peter
Hader, Thomas
Hadzic, Vedad
Hagemann, Willem
Hamza, Ameer
Haring, Johannes
Hausmann, Daniel
Havlena, Vojtěch
Hermo, Montserrat
Holík, Lukáš
Hozzová, Petra
Huang, Chao
Huang, Chengchao
Hyvärinen, Antti
Itzhaky, Shachar
Jacobs, Swen
Jaeger, Manfred
Jansen, David N.
Jensen, Nicolaj Østerby
Jha, Prabhat
Jonas, Martin
Junges, Sebastian
Kaki, Gowtham
Kaufmann, Daniela
Kenison, George
Kettl, Matthias
Khalimov, Ayrat
Kifetew, Fitsum
Kiourti, Panagiota
Klüppelholz, Sascha

Kröger, Paul
Käfer, Nikolai
Lal, Akash
Larrauri, Alberto
Larraz, Daniel
Lazic, Marijana
Le, Nham
Lee, Nian-Ze
Lengal, Ondrej
Li, Renjue
Lidell, David
Liu, Jiaxiang
Lopez-Miguel, Ignacio D.
Luttenberger, Michael
Macías, Fernando
Maderbacher, Benedikt
McClurg, Jedidiah
Meng, Yue
Metzger, Niklas
Michelland, Sebastien
Monniaux, David
Moosbrugger, Marcel
Nadel, Alexander
Nam, Seunghyeon
Nesterini, Eleonora
Neufeld, Emery
Nickovic, Dejan
Noetzli, Andres
Oliveira Da Costa, Ana
Otoni, Rodrigo
Parthasarathy, Gaurav
Paxian, Tobias
Pluska, Alexander
Poli, Federico
Pontiggia, Francesco
Prandi, Davide
Pranger, Stefan
Preiner, Mathias
Radanne, Gabriel
Rakow, Astrid
Rappoport, Omer
Rauh, Andreas
Rawson, Michael
Rebola Pardo, Adrian
Reynolds, Andrew
Riley, Daniel

Rodriguez, Andoni
Rogalewicz, Adam
Román Calvo, Enrique
Rubio, Rubén
Rutledge, Kwesi
Sallinger, Sarah
Sankaranarayanan, Sriram
Schlichtkrull, Anders
Schoisswohl, Johannes
Schultz, William
Schupp, Stefan
Schwammberger, Maike
Sextl, Florian
Siber, Julian
So, Oswin
Sogokon, Andrew
Spiessl, Martin
Steen, Alexander
Su, Yusen
Susi, Angelo
Síč, Juraj
Tappler, Martin
Thibault, Joan
Ting, Gan
Treml, Lilly Maria
Trivedi, Ashutosh

Turrini, Andrea
Varanasi, Sarat Chandra
Vediramana Krishnan, Hari Govind
Visconti, Ennio
Wachowitz, Henrik
Wand, Michael
Wardega, Kacper
Weininger, Maximilian
Wendler, Philipp
Wienhöft, Patrick
Wu, Hao
Wu, Haoze
Xue, Anton
Yadav, Drishti
Yang, Pengfei
Yang, Ruixiao
Yu, Chenning
Yu, Mingxin
Zavalia, Lucas
Zhan, Bohua
Zhang, Hanwei
Zhang, Songyuan
Zhou, Weichao
Zhou, Yuhao
Zimmermann, Martin
Zlatkin, Ilia

Contents – Part II

Tool Demos

EVA: a Tool for the Compositional Verification of AUTOSAR Models. 3
Alessandro Cimatti, Luca Cristoforetti, Alberto Griggio,
Stefano Tonetta, Sara Corfini, Marco Di Natale, and Florian Barrau

WASIM: A Word-level Abstract Symbolic Simulation Framework for
Hardware Formal Verification. 11
Wenji Fang and Hongce Zhang

Multiparty Session Typing in Java, Deductively 19
Jelle Bouma, Stijn de Gouw, and Sung-Shik Jongmans

PyLTA: A Verification Tool for Parameterized Distributed Algorithms 28
Bastien Thomas and Ocan Sankur

FuzzBtor2: A Random Generator of Word-Level Model Checking
Problems in Btor2 Format. 36
Shengping Xiao, Chengyu Zhang, Jianwen Li, and Geguang Pu

Eclipse ESCET™: The Eclipse Supervisory Control Engineering Toolkit. 44
W. J. Fokkink, M. A. Goorden, D. Hendriks, D. A. van Beek,
A. T. Hofkamp, F. F. H. Reijnen, L. F. P. Etman, L. Moormann,
J. M. van de Mortel-Fronczak, M. A. Reniers, J. E. Rooda,
L. J. van der Sanden, R. R. H. Schiffelers, S. B. Thuijsman,
J. J. Verbakel, and J. A. Vogel

Combinatorial Optimization/Theorem Proving

New Core-Guided and Hitting Set Algorithms for Multi-Objective
Combinatorial Optimization 55
João Cortes, Inês Lynce, and Vasco Manquinho

Verified reductions for optimization. 74
Alexander Bentkamp, Ramon Fernández Mir, and Jeremy Avigad

Specifying and Verifying Higher-order Rust Iterators. 93
Xavier Denis and Jacques-Henri Jourdan

Extending a High-Performance Prover to Higher-Order Logic............ 111
  Petar Vukmirović, Jasmin Blanchette, and Stephan Schulz

Tools (Regular Papers)

The WhyRel Prototype for Modular Relational Verification of Pointer
Programs.. 133
  Ramana Nagasamudram, Anindya Banerjee, and David A. Naumann

Bridging Hardware and Software Analysis with Btor2C:
A Word-Level-Circuit-to-C Translator............................ 152
  Dirk Beyer, Po-Chun Chien, and Nian-Ze Lee

CoPTIC: Constraint Programming Translated Into C.................... 173
  Martin Mariusz Lester

Acacia-Bonsai: A Modern Implementation of Downset-Based LTL
Realizability.. 192
  Michaël Cadilhac and Guillermo A. Pérez

Synthesis

Computing Adequately Permissive Assumptions for Synthesis 211
  *Ashwani Anand, Kaushik Mallik, Satya Prakash Nayak,
  and Anne-Kathrin Schmuck*

Verification-guided Programmatic Controller Synthesis 229
  Yuning Wang and He Zhu

Taming Large Bounds in Synthesis from Bounded-Liveness Specifications.... 251
  Philippe Heim and Rayna Dimitrova

Lockstep Composition for Unbalanced Loops........................ 270
  Ameer Hamza and Grigory Fedyukovich

Synthesis of Distributed Agreement-Based Systems with Efficiently-
Decidable Verification... 289
  *Nouraldin Jaber, Christopher Wagner, Swen Jacobs, Milind Kulkarni,
  and Roopsha Samanta*

LTL Reactive Synthesis with a Few Hints 309
  Mrudula Balachander, Emmanuel Filiot, and Jean-François Raskin

Timed Automata Verification and Synthesis via Finite Automata Learning 329
Ocan Sankur

Graphs/Probabilistic Systems

A Truly Symbolic Linear-Time Algorithm for SCC Decomposition 353
*Casper Abild Larsen, Simon Meldahl Schmidt, Jesper Steensgaard,
Anna Blume Jakobsen, Jaco van de Pol, and Andreas Pavlogiannis*

Transforming Quantified Boolean Formulas Using Biclique Covers 372
Oliver Kullmann and Ankit Shukla

Certificates for Probabilistic Pushdown Automata via Optimistic Value
Iteration 391
Tobias Winkler and Joost-Pieter Katoen

Probabilistic Program Verification via Inductive Synthesis of Inductive
Invariants 410
*Kevin Batz, Mingshuai Chen, Sebastian Junges,
Benjamin Lucien Kaminski, Joost-Pieter Katoen, and Christoph Matheja*

Runtime Monitoring/Program Analysis

Industrial-Strength Controlled Concurrency Testing for C# Programs with
Coyote 433
*Pantazis Deligiannis, Aditya Senthilnathan, Fahad Nayyar,
Chris Lovett, and Akash Lal*

Context-Sensitive Meta-Constraint Systems for Explainable Program
Analysis 453
Kalmer Apinis and Vesal Vojdani

Explainable Online Monitoring of Metric Temporal Logic 473
*Leonardo Lima, Andrei Herasimau, Martin Raszyk, Dmitriy Traytel,
and Simon Yuan*

12th Competition on Software Verification — SV-COMP 2023

Competition on Software Verification and Witness Validation:
SV-COMP 2023 495
Dirk Beyer

SYMBIOTIC-WITCH 2: More Efficient Algorithm and Witness Refutation
(Competition Contribution)..................................... 523
    Paulína Ayaziová and Jan Strejček

2LS: Arrays and Loop Unwinding (Competition Contribution)............ 529
    Viktor Malík, František Nečas, Peter Schrammel, and Tomáš Vojnar

BUBAAK: Runtime Monitoring of Program Verifiers
(Competition Contribution)..................................... 535
    Marek Chalupa and Thomas A. Henzinger

EBF 4.2: Black-Box Cooperative Verification for Concurrent Programs
(Competition Contribution)..................................... 541
    *Fatimah Aljaafari, Fedor Shmarov, Edoardo Manino, Rafael Menezes,
    and Lucas C. Cordeiro*

GOBLINT: Autotuning Thread-Modular Abstract Interpretation
(Competition Contribution)..................................... 547
    *Simmo Saan, Michael Schwarz, Julian Erhard, Manuel Pietsch,
    Helmut Seidl, Sarah Tilscher, and Vesal Vojdani*

Java Ranger: Supporting String and Array Operations in Java Ranger
(Competition Contribution)..................................... 553
    *Soha Hussein, Qiuchen Yan, Stephen McCamant, Vaibhav Sharma,
    and Michael W. Whalen*

KORN—Software Verification with Horn Clauses (Competition
Contribution) 559
    Gidon Ernst

Mopsa-C: Modular Domains and Relational Abstract Interpretation
for C Programs (Competition Contribution) 565
    Raphaël Monat, Abdelraouf Ouadjaout, and Antoine Miné

PIChecker: A POR and Interpolation based Verifier for Concurrent
Programs (Competition Contribution)............................. 571
    *Jie Su, Zuchao Yang, Hengrui Xing, Jiyu Yang, Cong Tian,
    and Zhenhua Duan*

Ultimate Taipan and Race Detection in Ultimate (Competition
Contribution) 577
    *Matthias Heizmann, Max Barth, Daniel Dietsch, Leonard Fichtner,
    Jochen Hoenicke, Dominik Klumpp, Mehdi Naouar, Tanja Schindler,
    Frank Schüssele, and Andreas Podelski*

Ultimate Taipan and Race Detection in Ultimate (Competition
Contribution) 582
  *Daniel Dietsch, Matthias Heizmann, Dominik Klumpp, Frank Schüssele,
  and Andreas Podelski*

VeriAbsL: Scalable Verification by Abstraction and Strategy Prediction
(Competition Contribution). 588
  *Priyanka Darke, Bharti Chimdyalwar, Sakshi Agrawal,
  Shrawan Kumar, R Venkatesh, and Supratik Chakraborty*

VeriFuzz 1.4: Checking for (Non-)termination (Competition Contribution) 594
  *Ravindra Metta, Prasanth Yeduru, Hrishikesh Karmarkar,
  and Raveendra Kumar Medicherla*

Author Index 601

Contents – Part I

Invited Talk

A Learner-Verifier Framework for Neural Network Controllers and
Certificates of Stochastic Systems   3
    Krishnendu Chatterjee, Thomas A. Henzinger, Mathias Lechner,
    and Đorđe Žikelić

Model Checking

Bounded Model Checking for Asynchronous Hyperproperties 29
    Tzu-Han Hsu, Borzoo Bonakdarpour, Bernd Finkbeiner,
    and César Sánchez

Model Checking Linear Dynamical Systems under Floating-point
Rounding 47
    Engel Lefaucheux, Joël Ouaknine, David Purser, and Mohammadamin
    Sharifi

Efficient Loop Conditions for Bounded Model Checking Hyperproperties 66
    Tzu-Han Hsu, César Sánchez, Sarai Sheinvald,
    and Borzoo Bonakdarpour

Reconciling Preemption Bounding with DPOR 85
    Iason Marmanis, Michalis Kokologiannakis, and Viktor Vafeiadis

Optimal Stateless Model Checking for Causal Consistency 105
    Parosh Abdulla, Mohamed Faouzi Atig, S. Krishna, Ashutosh Gupta,
    and Omkar Tuppe

Symbolic Model Checking for TLA+ Made Faster 126
    Rodrigo Otoni, Igor Konnov, Jure Kukovec, Patrick Eugster,
    and Natasha Sharygina

AutoHyper: Explicit-State Model Checking for HyperLTL 145
    Raven Beutner and Bernd Finkbeiner

Machine Learning/Neural Networks

Feature Necessity & Relevancy in ML Classifier Explanations   167
  Xuanxiang Huang, Martin C. Cooper, Antonio Morgado, Jordi Planes,
  and Joao Marques-Silva

Towards Formal XAI: Formally Approximate Minimal Explanations of
Neural Networks.   187
  Shahaf Bassan and Guy Katz

OccRob: Efficient SMT-Based Occlusion Robustness Verification of Deep
Neural Networks.   208
  Xingwu Guo, Ziwei Zhou, Yueling Zhang, Guy Katz, and Min Zhang

Neural Network-Guided Synthesis of Recursive List Functions   227
  Naoki Kobayashi and Minchao Wu

Automata

Modular Mix-and-Match Complementation of Büchi Automata.   249
  Vojtěch Havlena, Ondřej Lengál, Yong Li, Barbora Šmahlíková,
  and Andrea Turrini

Validating Streaming JSON Documents with Learned VPAs   271
  Véronique Bruyère, Guillermo A. Pérez, and Gaëtan Staquet

Antichains Algorithms for the Inclusion Problem Between ω-VPL   290
  Kyveli Doveri, Pierre Ganty, and Luka Hadži-Đokić

Stack-Aware Hyperproperties   308
  Ali Bajwa, Minjian Zhang, Rohit Chadha, and Mahesh Viswanathan

Proofs

Propositional Proof Skeletons   329
  Joseph E. Reeves, Benjamin Kiesl-Reiter, and Marijn J. H. Heule

Unsatisfiability Proofs for Distributed Clause-Sharing SAT Solvers   348
  Dawn Michaelson, Dominik Schreiber, Marijn J. H. Heule,
  Benjamin Kiesl-Reiter, and Michael W. Whalen

Carcara: An efficient proof checker and elaborator for SMT proofs in the
Alethe format.   367
  Bruno Andreotti, Hanna Lachnitt, and Haniel Barbosa

Constraint Solving/Blockchain

The Packing Chromatic Number of the Infinite Square Grid is 15 389
  Bernardo Subercaseaux and Marijn J. H. Heule

Active Learning for SAT Solver Benchmarking 407
  Tobias Fuchs, Jakob Bach, and Markus Iser

ParaQooba: A Fast and Flexible Framework for Parallel and Distributed
QBF Solving 426
  Maximilian Heisinger, Martina Seidl, and Armin Biere

Inferring Needless Write Memory Accesses on Ethereum Bytecode 448
  *Elvira Albert, Jesús Correas, Pablo Gordillo, Guillermo Román-Díez,
  and Albert Rubio*

Markov Chains/Stochastic Control

A Practitioner's Guide to MDP Model Checking Algorithms 469
  *Arnd Hartmanns, Sebastian Junges, Tim Quatmann,
  and Maximilian Weininger*

Correct Approximation of Stationary Distributions 489
  Tobias Meggendorfer

Robust Almost-Sure Reachability in Multi-Environment MDPs 508
  Marck van der Vegt, Nils Jansen, and Sebastian Junges

Mungojerrie: Linear-Time Objectives in Model-Free Reinforcement
Learning 527
  *Ernst Moritz Hahn, Mateo Perez, Sven Schewe, Fabio Somenzi,
  Ashutosh Trivedi, and Dominik Wojtczak*

Verification

A Formal CHERI-C Semantics for Verification 549
  Seung Hoon Park, Rekha Pai, and Tom Melham

Automated Verification for Real-Time Systems: via Implicit Clocks and an
Extended Antimirov Algorithm 569
  Yahui Song and Wei-Ngan Chin

Parameterized Verification under TSO with Data Types 588
Parosh Aziz Abdulla, Mohamad Faouzi Atig, Florian Furbach,
Adwait A. Godbole, Yacoub G. Hendi, Shankara N. Krishna,
and Stephan Spengler

Verifying Learning-Based Robotic Navigation Systems 607
Guy Amir, Davide Corsi, Raz Yerushalmi, Luca Marzari, David Harel,
Alessandro Farinelli, and Guy Katz

Make Flows Small Again: Revisiting the Flow Framework 628
Roland Meyer, Thomas Wies, and Sebastian Wolff

ALASCA: Reasoning in Quantified Linear Arithmetic 647
Konstantin Korovin, Laura Kovács, Giles Reger, Johannes Schoisswohl,
and Andrei Voronkov

A Matrix-Based Approach to Parity Games 666
Saksham Aggarwal, Alejandro Stuckey de la Banda, Luke Yang,
and Julian Gutierrez

A GPU Tree Database for Many-Core Explicit State Space Exploration 684
Anton Wijs and Muhammad Osama

Author Index 705

Tool Demos

EVA: a Tool for the Compositional Verification of AUTOSAR Models

Alessandro Cimatti[1] , Luca Cristoforetti[1] , Alberto Griggio[1] ,
Stefano Tonetta[1] , Sara Corfini[2(✉)] , Marco Di Natale[2,4],
and Florian Barrau[3]

[1] Fondazione Bruno Kessler, Trento, Italy
[2] Huawei Pisa Research Center, Pisa, Italy
s.corfini@huawei.com
[3] Huawei Grenoble Research Center, Grenoble, France
[4] Scuola Superiore Sant'Anna, Pisa, Italy

Abstract. We present EVA, a framework for the integration of modern verification tools in the context of AUTOSAR, a widely-used open standard for the development of automotive software systems. Our framework enables the automatic end-to-end verification of system-level properties using a compositional approach. It combines software model checking techniques for the verification of software components at the code level with a contract-based analysis for verifying their correct composition. In this paper, we present the tool through its application on a representative automotive case study, discussing the main functionalities provided and the results obtained.

1 Introduction

AUTOSAR [1] is a worldwide consortium of car manufacturers and component or service providers in the automotive domain, with the main goal of providing a standardized software architecture for the development and execution of software components. One of the fundamental challenges in designing software for the AUTOSAR platform is ensuring safety. To this end, the application of formal methods – and in particular automatic (or semi-automatic) techniques based on model checking and theorem proving – is receiving significant interest as a complement to more traditional V&V techniques. In this paper we present EVA, a framework for the integration of modern verification tools in the context of AUTOSAR. EVA adopts a model-based compositional verification that founds on the contract-based methodology in [8]. The tool allows the automatic end-to-end verification of system-level properties, and combines software model checking techniques for the verification of software components at the code level with a contract-based analysis for verifying their correct composition. EVA also implements all the features that are required for usability in a typical industrial context, including a front-end integrated in a standard AUTOSAR development environment [2] with a user-friendly (formal) property editor, the automatic generation of code stubs and other views and forms to help the user manage verification in an AUTOSAR environment.

© The Author(s) 2023
S. Sankaranarayanan and N. Sharygina (Eds.): TACAS 2023, LNCS 13994, pp. 3–10, 2023.
https://doi.org/10.1007/978-3-031-30820-8_1

4   A. Cimatti et al.

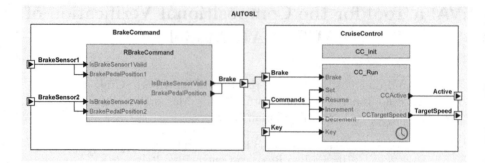

Fig. 1. BrakeCommand and CruiseControl components.

We present EVA through its application on a representative case study, which describes a simplified active safety automotive system containing some of the typical safety functions available in the modern vehicles (such as lane departure warning, cruise control and a fault-tolerant brake pedal system). The example is meant to show the potential of the tool as a driver for a more widespread adoption of formal methods and contract-based verification in the industrial automotive context. Specifically, we introduce the case study in §2 and we describe the typical verification workflow followed by a user of EVA in §3. Finally, in §4 we discuss the main verification results obtained.

2   A Case Study for Verification in AUTOSAR

AUTOSAR defines the reference architecture for the development of automotive systems and provides the language (meta-model) for describing their architectural models. An AUTOSAR application consists of a hierarchy of components connected through ports. *Provide* ports represent output ports and *require* ports correspond to the input ports. Connectors represent data flow from one port to another. An AUTOSAR port can be classified as sender-receiver or client-server and sender-receiver communications can be queued or non-queued (i.e., with no buffering and the receiver always accesses the last sent data). In this paper we assume that all ports are sender-receiver and non-queued.

An *atomic* software component consists of a set of runnables. A *runnable* is a sequence of operations started by the Run-Time Environment (RTE). The runnable is configured so that is triggered by an event that can be timing, data sent or received, operation invoked, return of a server call, mode switching or external events. A special *init* event is used for runnables that are executed when the RTE starts and initializes the software components.

We illustrate the basic notions above by means of a simple but representative case study, that we shall use to present the main features of EVA. Figure 1 overviews (a section of) the architecture of the sample application. It collects 22 atomic components (including sensors, controllers and actuators) plus one composite component (AUTOSL) that represents the whole system, and implements some of the typical safety functions available in the modern vehicles such as autonomous emergency braking, lane departure warning, crash preparation and cruise control. We implemented (the runnables of) 9 components, 7 have been coded manually and 2 have been generated from a Simulink model using the Embedded Coder Support Package for AUTOSAR. The other components are considered as stubs because their data come from lower levels (hardware sensors) and we assume that the values they provide are correct.

The case study considers various safety properties, both at the level of the whole system and at the level of the implementation of individual components or runnables. As an example, we describe here two properties, a system-level one and a component-level one, both concerning the behaviour of the cruise controller. Specifically, the cruise controller is expected to react to a brake input by disengaging itself within two execution steps. At the implementation level, the requirement relates the input and output ports of the CruiseControl periodic runnable, stating that whenever the CruiseControl CCActive port is true and the Brake input port is true, then the CCActive output port must become false in at most two steps. At the system level, instead, the same requirement relates the behaviour of the components BrakeCommand and CruiseControl, stating that the cruise control shall be disengaged if the user brakes, even when one of the two brake pedal sensors is faulty.

3   **EVA** Verification Workflow

EVA integrates the verification engines Kratos2 [6] and OCRA [5] into an analysis AUTOSAR toolchain. The ultimate goal is to automate the verification of formal properties (contracts) on AUTOSAR models. In its default configuration, EVA uses a portfolio of different state-of-the-art SAT- and SMT-based symbolic model checking algorithms (implemented in Kratos2 and OCRA) which include different variants of bit-level IC3 [10,12], IC3 with implicit abstraction [7], bounded model checking [3] and K-induction [11].

The typical workflow of the tool is sketched in Figure 2. At the beginning, the user creates an analysis project providing as input the AUTOSAR configuration of the system. The tool transforms the AUTOSAR configuration into an internal set of analysis models. Since the AUTOSAR standard deals neither with requirements nor with formal properties and their verification, EVA adopts the extended AUTOSAR metamodel defined in [4] to support such concepts.

The user then completes the configuration of the system and provides:

source code: the user imports into the analysis project the source code of the runnables and associates each runnable with its source files.

requirements: the user defines the (informal) properties of the system and their relationships. Specifically, the user can assign a requirement to a component, or to the system (modeled by a composite component) and refine it into other requirements. Considering the following examples of informal

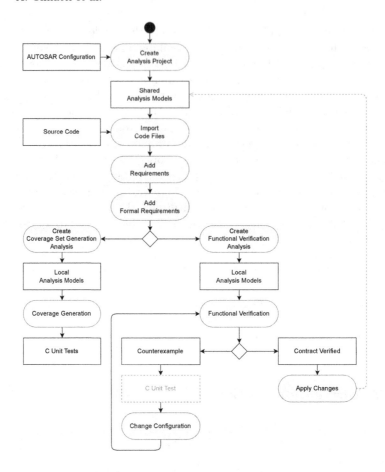

Fig. 2. The analysis workflow.

requirements for the case study of §2:

> *If the user brakes, the cruise control shall disengage within 2 steps*   (1)
>
> *The signals of the brake pedal sensors shall be merged*   (2)
>
> *Even if at most one brake pedal sensor is faulty*   (3)
> *if the user brakes, the cruise control shall disengage*

(1) and (2) are component-level requirements assigned to CruiseControl and BrakeCommand respectively, while (3) is a system-level requirement assigned to the composite AUTOSL and refined by (1) and (2).

contracts: the user formalizes the requirements into contracts. Precisely, a contract consists of (optional) assumptions (properties that shall be satisfied by the environment) and assertions (properties that the owner of the contract shall satisfy), expressed as formulas in Linear Temporal Logic (LTL) with some metric extensions (interpreted over discrete time). The user can assign a contract either to a runnable or to a (composite) component.

> **in the future within** [2,2]   (4)
> **it shall always_be that**
> > (CCActive **and** Brake **is_greater_than** 0) **implies**
> > **in the future within** [0,2] (**not next**(CCActive))
> **holds_true**

Contract (4) is the formal representation of requirement (1) and it is assigned to the periodic runnable of the CruiseControl component[5]. It is worth noting that EVA provides a *smart* contract editor that assists the user with context completion, syntax highlighting and error detection. Also, to aid readability of contracts, EVA uses some syntactic sugar to represent temporal operators, such as in the future for F or it shall always_be for G.

The user can create a new functional verification analysis, allowing to perform:

code verification: the user can check whether (the source code of) a runnable satisfies one of the contracts assigned to it. Let us consider again the periodic runnable of the CruiseControl component. The user can run code verification to check whether that runnable satisfies its assigned contract (4).

compositional verification: the user can check whether a contract assigned to a (composite) component is correctly refined by the contracts of the sub-components. Intuitively, the user can run compositional verification to check whether the system-level contract derived from requirement (3) and assigned to the composite AUTOSL, is refined by the contracts derived from requirements (1) and (2) and assigned to the runnables of components CruiseControl and BrakeCommand.

The result of both analyses can be that the contract is verified or violated. In case of contract violation, EVA returns a counterexample (and the corresponding test case, if the performed analysis is code verification). The user can fix the code or change the system configuration (refine requirements or scheduling runnables) and then execute the analysis again. The user can optionally apply local changes to the shared analysis models (typically after a contract has been verified).

In addition to the main features above, two further analyses are provided:

contract validation: the user can verify the consistency (and absence of logical contradictions) of the contracts of a component and of its sub-components.

coverage set generation: it combines model checking and random simulation to automatically generate unit tests (using the CUnit [9] framework) trying to cover all the branches of the C code of a given runnable.

4   Experimental Evaluation

In order to evaluate the effectiveness and performance of EVA, we applied it to the verification of all the 43 requirements (10 system-level, 33 component-level)

---

[5] We omit the contracts derived from (2) and (3) for lack of space (their formalization shall be included in the artifact accompanying this submission).

of the case-study application described in §2. Due to lack of space, we cannot report the results in detail and we shall limit our analysis to some qualitative considerations about the overall performance of EVA and the usefulness of the produced outputs. Full details on the obtained results will be included in the submitted artifact.

Performance considerations. We verified all the requirements on a PC running Ubuntu Linux 20.04, with a 2.6 GHz Intel Core I7-66000U CPU and 20 Gb of RAM. EVA was able to successfully perform 42 out of 43 verification tasks within the timeout (set to 1 hour), requiring less than one second in nearly half of the cases for component-level properties, and requiring less than one minute for all the remaining component-level tasks except one. For such problems, the main bottlenecks identified during the case study involved the use of complex floating-point operations, which are still handled inefficiently by the verification backend. Also the verification of the 10 system-level properties could be completed relatively efficiently, with EVA requiring less than one minute in 7 cases, and approximately 30 minutes for the hardest one. In this case, the main factor affecting performance (besides the expected ones such as the number of involved contracts and their complexity and length) are the constraints on the composition of components defined in the input model. In particular, performance is affected significantly in cases in which the contract under analysis involves periodic components with very different activation periods. The presence of periods that range from few milliseconds to seconds poses a conceptual/theoretical challenge because the reasoner must explore a large number of small steps of the more frequent tasks for each step of the slow ones. Optimizations targeting this issue are left as research directions for future works.

Issues discovered. During verification, several counterexamples have been discovered. Most of them turned out to be due to incorrect formalizations of requirements or missing environment assumptions, which could be easily fixed by examining the produced counterexamples. The analyses however revealed also a number of real bugs in the implementations of some of the software components as well as two issues due to wrong scheduling of components. The first was caused by a mismatch between the Simulink description of the CruiseControl periodic runnable and its C implementation in the AUTOSAR application. Specifically, the mismatch was due to different assumptions about the rate of execution of the step of the cruise control with respect to the rate of the change of the inputs, which caused the input values to be read only at even steps of the cruise controller. The second issue regarded the scheduling of the BrakeCommand runnable, which was set to be executed only upon changes in the input pedal positions. A counterexample in the contract refinement showed that the validity of these input signals could change value without the BrakeCommand running so that the pedal position was not propagated to the CruiseControl. The model was fixed by adding a trigger of the BrakeCommand also associated to the valid signal of the pedal positions. In both cases, the bugs could be fixed by analyzing the counterexamples generated by EVA.

5 Data Availability Statement

The artifact described in the paper is not publicly available due to internal policy. Any requests can be directed to the corresponding author.

References

1. https://www.autosar.org
2. Artop: The AUTOSAR Tool Platform, http://www.artop.org
3. Biere, A., Cimatti, A., Clarke, E.M., Zhu, Y.: Symbolic Model Checking without BDDs. In: Cleaveland, W.R. (ed.) 5th International Conference on Tools and Algorithms for the Construction and Analysis of Systems (TACAS). LNCS, vol. 1579, pp. 193–207. Springer (1999)
4. Cimatti, A., Corfini, S., Cristoforetti, L., Di Natale, M., Griggio, A., Puri, S., Tonetta, S.: A Comprehensive Framework for the Analysis of Automotive Systems. In: Syriani, E., Sahraoui, H.A., Bencomo, N., Wimmer, M. (eds.) ACM/IEEE 25th International Conference on Model Driven Engineering Languages and Systems (MODELS). pp. 379–389. ACM (2022)
5. Cimatti, A., Dorigatti, M., Tonetta, S.: OCRA: A Tool for Checking the Refinement of Temporal Contracts. In: Denney, E., Bultan, T., Zeller, A. (eds.) 28th IEEE/ACM International Conference on Automated Software Engineering (ASE). pp. 702–705. IEEE (2013)
6. Cimatti, A., Griggio, A., Micheli, A., Narasamdya, I., Roveri, M.: Kratos - A Software Model Checker for SystemC. In: Gopalakrishnan, G., Qadeer, S. (eds.) 23rd International Conference on Computer Aided Verification (CAV). LNCS, vol. 6806, pp. 310–316. Springer (2011)
7. Cimatti, A., Griggio, A., Mover, S., Tonetta, S.: Infinite-state Invariant Checking with IC3 and Predicate Abstraction. Formal Methods in System Design **49**(3), 190–218 (2016)
8. Cimatti, A., Tonetta, S.: Contracts-refinement proof system for component-based embedded systems. Science of Computer Programming **97**, 333–348 (2015)
9. CUnit: A Unit Testing Framework for C, cunit.sourceforge.net
10. Griggio, A., Roveri, M.: Comparing Different Variants of the ic3 Algorithm for Hardware Model Checking. IEEE Transactions on Computer-Aided Design of Integrated Circuits and Systems **35**(6), 1026–1039 (2016)
11. Sheeran, M., Singh, S., Stålmarck, G.: Checking Safety Properties Using Induction and a SAT-Solver. In: Hunt, W.A., Johnson, S.D. (eds.) 3rd International Conference on Formal Methods in Computer-Aided Design (FMCAD). LNCS, vol. 1954, pp. 108–125. Springer (2000)
12. Vizel, Y., Gurfinkel, A.: Interpolating Property Directed Reachability. In: Biere, A., Bloem, R. (eds.) 26th International Conference on Computer Aided Verification (CAV). LNCS, vol. 8559, pp. 260–276. Springer (2014)

WASIM: A Word-level Abstract Symbolic Simulation Framework for Hardware Formal Verification⋆

Wenji Fang[1]([✉]) [ID] and Hongce Zhang[1,2] [ID]

[1] The Hong Kong University of Science and Technology (Guangzhou),
Guangzhou, China
wfang838@connect.hkust-gz.edu.cn
[2] The Hong Kong University of Science and Technology,
Hong Kong, China
hongcezh@ust.hk

Abstract. This paper demonstrates the design and usage of WASIM, a word-level abstract symbolic simulation framework with pluggable abstraction/refinement functions. WASIM is useful in the formal verification of functional properties on register-transfer level (RTL) hardware designs. Users can control the symbolic simulation process and tune the level of abstraction by interacting with WASIM through its Python API. WASIM can be used to directly check formal properties on symbolic traces or to extract useful fragments from symbolic representations to construct safe inductive invariants as a correctness certificate. We demonstrate the utility of WASIM on the verification of two pipelined hardware designs. WASIM and the case studies are available under open-source license at: [9].

Keywords: Formal verification · symbolic simulation · abstraction refinement.

1 Introduction

Formal property verification (FPV) plays an essential role in hardware verification. Symbolic simulation is one of the model checking techniques used for FPV. It explores all paths of the design circuit simultaneously with symbolic values to work around the state explosion problem [6].

In this paper, we present WASIM, a word-level abstract symbolic simulation framework with customizable abstraction/refinement functions. In the practice of hardware formal verification, we consider the *guidance from human verification engineers* as the key to scaling formal techniques up for industrial-size designs. Therefore, in WASIM, we emphasize easy user-interaction that allows engineers to freely control the simulation process and plug-in their own

⋆ The work has been supported in part by Guangdong Basic and Applied Basic Research Fund no. 2022A1515110178; by Guangzhou-HKUST(GZ) Joint Funding Scheme no. SL2022A03J01288; and by Guangzhou Basic Research Project no. SL2022A04J00615.

S. Sankararayanan and N. Sharygina (Eds.): TACAS 2023, LNCS 13994, pp. 11–18, 2023.
https://doi.org/10.1007/978-3-031-30820-8_2

design-specific abstraction functions. WASIM can also ensure its trustworthiness through a certificate (an inductive invariant) constructed from the traces of symbolic simulation.

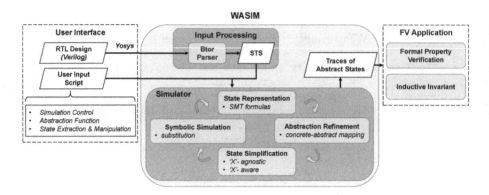

Fig. 1. Workflow of WASIM

Figure 1 demonstrates the workflow of WASIM. We highlight some of its features below:

1. WASIM has a full support for synthesizable Verilog through the integration with Yosys [17].
2. WASIM provides a set of Python API for rich user interactions.
3. WASIM performs symbolic simulation at the word level. It supports customizable abstraction refinement functions and has built-in state simplification functions to scale up for larger designs.
4. Users may freely extract symbolic state representations for various use cases (e.g., formal property verification).

The remainder of this paper is organized as follows. The next section demonstrates the functionalities of WASIM, followed by a short presentation of user interface in Sect. 3. Sect. 4 reports the results on case studies. Sect. 5 discusses related work. Finally, Sect. 6 concludes the paper.

2   WASIM Functionalities

The WASIM framework is built on top of PySMT [11], a unified interface for multiple SMT solvers. The functionalities are described below.

2.1   Input Processing.

The input Verilog circuits are initially processed by the open-source synthesis suite Yosys and transformed into the Btor2 format [15], an efficient word-level representation for a state transition system (STS). WASIM consumes Btor2 with a parser modified from CoSA (CoreIR Symbolic Analyzer) [14].

2.2   Representing Simulation States using SMT formulas.

The state in WASIM is represented using SMT formulas, with one for each state variable assignment. There are also assumptions (SMT formulas) associated with each state. The assumptions capture the additional constraints on a symbolic trace, for example, certain input combinations will never happen. The state is reachable (realizable) if all assumptions are satisfiable. The state representation may also include undetermined values ('X' values). We keep a special set of SMT variables to represent the 'X' values.

2.3   Symbolic Simulation.

Symbolic simulation is mainly achieved through substitution. Variables in the transition function of an STS are substituted by variable assignments from the previous cycle. Unassigned input or unknown state variables are replaced by 'X' values. WASIM can explore either the state in the next one cycle (single-step simulation) or traverse a set of states until no new (abstract) states are found (multi-step simulation). Expression simplification and abstraction are used in WASIM to reduce the size of the state representation.

2.4   Expression Simplification.

Expression simplification reduces the size of an SMT formula in the state representation through the combination of various techniques. The built-in rewriting functionality in SMT solvers serves as the 'X'-agnostic simplification step. After this first step, WASIM proceeds with 'X'-aware simplification that checks if any 'X' value can be reduced given the state assumptions. For example, an 'X' is reducible if it resides in the unreachable branch of an ITE (if-then-else) operator. WASIM traverses the abstract syntax tree of SMT expressions and heuristically guess-and-check reducible 'X' values. When confirmed, WASIM further rewrites the expression to syntactically eliminate the 'X' values. We design several patterns for common rewriting. For the most general case, WASIM will fall back to query the CVC5 [2] SyGuS solver [1] to synthesize a new expression without 'X'.

2.5   Abstraction Refinement.

We allow users to define abstraction functions that map a concrete state into an abstract domain. A simple example of such abstraction is to leave out certain registers in the symbolic state representation by replacing them with 'X' values. The abstraction could be design-specific — engineers familiar with the hardware microarchitecture may have better ideas on which registers to omit. Therefore, we give such freedom to the WASIM users and allow them to specify their own abstraction functions. Abstraction is also essential to the efficient state traversal because it is almost impossible to traverse the concrete state space of a large hardware design. When it is hard to pre-determine the best abstraction function, users can specify a refinement function and perform dynamic abstraction-refinement during symbolic simulation. An example of abstraction refinement function is demonstrated below in Sect. 3.2

3 User Interface

WASIM provides a Python interface to control the simulation, apply abstraction or refinement and manipulate the symbolic expressions in state representations.

3.1 Simulation Process Control.

WASIM provides a single-step simulation function `sim_one_step` for forward symbolic simulation of one clock cycle. Users can perform bounded-step simulation by using the function in a range-based loop.

On the other hand, there is often the need for unbounded simulation. WASIM provides an unbounded simulation function `traverse_all_states`. As its name suggests, this function instructs the simulator to search for all symbolic states that are reachable from the current state. Users may optionally provide a termination condition and the simulator will only search for reachable states before the condition becomes true. This is useful, for example, when searching for all symbolic states when an instruction is stalled in a certain pipeline stage.

3.2 Customizable Abstraction/Refinement Function.

Users may provide a callable Python object as the abstraction/refinement function. The abstraction function should transfer one symbolic state to its counterpart in the abstract domain, while the refinement function returns a list of states.

Here we give an example of user-specified dynamic abstraction refinement during symbolic simulation. In microprocessor verification, we can use symbolic simulation to check that the arithmetic processing pipeline is functionally correct by computing the output symbolic state from symbolic pipeline inputs. There are external signals coming into the pipeline that only affect latency rather than the arithmetic function. Abstraction can be applied to omit all external signals, however, the final abstract symbolic state might become too coarse. A refinement function can lazily bring back the external signals and branch the execution based on certain signal combinations, until the final symbolic states are sufficiently accurate to check for functional correctness. This example will require the simulator to have a pluggable interface for abstraction/refinement functions.

3.3 Symbolic State Extraction and Manipulation.

In order to use the result of symbolic simulation, WASIM allows users to freely extract and manipulate the symbolic expressions in a state representation. Simulation traces are available as Python lists. Users can collect all states in any simulation step and obtain the expressions of arbitrary state variable assignment. By checking the satisfiability of the conjunction of all variable assignments, the assumptions, and the negated property, users can check for property violations on a symbolic state. WASIM can also evaluate arbitrary functions over state variables given the variable assignment. This is useful to compute the symbolic value of wires in Verilog. Finally, users may re-assign an intermediate state and restart the simulation from that point.

Symbolic state extraction and manipulation enable two use cases: **formal property verification** and **inductive invariant construction**. Users can achieve formal property verification by checking the violation of properties on all abstract simulation states extracted from symbolic state traversal. Fragments of expressions in symbolic states are also helpful in the construction of inductive invariants, which could serve as the certificate for the abstract state traversal. For example,

$$(sv_1 = expr_1) \wedge (sv_2 = expr_2) \wedge ...$$

indicates that the STS resides in one (abstract) symbolic state where $sv_1, sv_2, ...$ are the state variables, and $expr_1, expr_2, ...$ are the symbolic expressions in state representation. By taking the disjunction of all such formulas of all reachable abstract symbolic states, we cover the whole abstract state space and therefore, the disjunction will constitute an inductive invariant for this STS. To certify a specific safety property is valid, one can build from this inductive invariant with additional expression fragments to create a safe inductive invariant.

4   Case Studies

We demonstrate the usage of WASIM with two verification case studies on pipelined hardware designs. The design statistics are shown in Table 1, including the number of state bits and logic gates.

Designs under verification. The first design is a simple arithmetic pipeline with two variants implemented with or without external stall signals. They share the same datapath that performs a multiply-accumulate (MAC) operation. The second design is a simple 3-stage pipeline that resembles the backend of a processor core. It contains data forwarding logic and the control logic to handle external stall signals. Verification in this case study checks if these hardware designs are implemented with the correct functions. Despite the relatively small size, some are already nontrivial for a symbolic model checker.

Users' input. For simple MAC without stall signals, users only need to provide a simulation script with bounded simulation steps. For all other designs, certain stages may be stalled by external signals for a period of time. The simulation script instructs the simulator to case-split based on the value of external stall signals and symbolically explore all stalled states in each step. The abstraction function only keeps the concrete representation in the downstream of the stalled stage, therefore, there are only a small number of stalled states in the abstract domain. Finally, users may check the given properties are valid on every symbolic path and the symbolic expressions in the state representations are used to construct parts of inductive invariants. The inductive invariants are further checked to ensure the correctness of simulation process given the user-provided abstraction functions.

Results of the experiment. In the experiments, we compare with the IC3/PDR symbolic model checking method implemented in Berkeley-ABC. The last three columns in Table 1 are the time of symbolic simulation, the time of checking

Table 1. Experimental Results

Design Statistics			IC3/PDR	WASIM		
Design name	#. state bit	#. logic gate	Time	Simulation-time	FPV-time	Inv-time
simple MAC no stall	27	180	0.03s	0.02	0.3s	0.09s
simple MAC + stall	27	234	0.03s	11min26s	1s	7s
3-stage-pipe-ADD		3153		1min57s	0.3s	2s
3-stage-pipe-NAND	199	2187	>72hr	1min57s	0.3s	2s
3-stage-pipe-SET		2681		1min21s	0.2s	0.8s
3-stage-pipe-NOP		2421		58s	0.1s	1s

functional properties on all traces and the time for checking the validity of inductive invariants. Results show that for the `3-stage-pipe-*` problems, with proper guidance from a human verification engineer, symbolic simulation can outperform autonomous model checking with order-of-magnitude speed-up. The results are obtained on a server running Ubuntu 20.04 with a 2.9 GHz Intel Xeon(R) Platinum 8375C CPU and 128G RAM.

5   Related Works

Apart from WASIM, VossII [16] is another tool for hardware symbolic simulation which implements the symbolic trajectory evaluation (STE) method [12,13]. VossII is mainly on the bit level using binary decision diagrams (BDDs) as the state representation. Several extensions to the original STE method have been proposed so far. For example, generalized STE (GSTE) enables unbounded property verification using assertion graphs [18], and the word-level STE (WSTE) achieves a higher level of abstraction with word-level variables in bit-fields [7]. These extensions are typically only available in a commercial STE implementation. Moreover, users must be fluent in a domain-specific functional programming language named `fl` in order to use VossII.

On the other hand, tools based on symbolic model checking are broadly available for hardware formal verification, for example, Berkeley-ABC [5], which is a powerful open-source tool implementing a collection of various model checking algorithms [3,4,8]. Unlike symbolic simulation, symbolic model checking runs autonomously to prove or falsify given properties without user interactions. However, without proper human guidance, model checking tools may suffer more from the scalability problem.

6   Conclusions

In this paper, we present the design and usage of WASIM, a word-level abstract symbolic simulation framework. WASIM is featured with a Python user interface and pluggable abstraction/refinement functions to facilitate human verification engineers to bring in their insights to better scale formal methods for hardware designs. Applications of WASIM include formal property verification and inductive invariant generation. Our case studies show that this strategy can be helpful for some problems that are hard for autonomous model checking.

Data Availability Statement

The data that support the findings of this study are openly available in WASIM: A Word-level Abstract Symbolic Simulation Framework for Hardware Formal Verification at `https://doi.org/10.5281/zenodo.7247147`, reference number [10]. The authors confirm that the data supporting the findings of this study are available within the article and its supplementary materials.

References

1. Alur, R., Bodik, R., Juniwal, G., Martin, M.M., Raghothaman, M., Seshia, S.A., Singh, R., Solar-Lezama, A., Torlak, E., Udupa, A.: Syntax-guided synthesis. FM-CAD 2013 Formal Methods in Computer–Aided Design p. 1
2. Barbosa, H., Barrett, C.W., Brain, M., Kremer, G., et al.: CVC5: A versatile and industrial-strength SMT solver. In: Tools and Algorithms for the Construction and Analysis of Systems, TACAS 2022, Held as Part of ETAPS 2022, Munich, Germany, April 2-7, 2022, Proceedings, Part I. Lecture Notes in Computer Science, vol. 13243, pp. 415–442. Springer (2022). https://doi.org/10.1007/978-3-030-99524-9_24, `https://doi.org/10.1007/978-3-030-99524-9_24`
3. Bradley, A.R.: Sat-based model checking without unrolling. In: International Workshop on Verification, Model Checking, and Abstract Interpretation. pp. 70–87. Springer (2011)
4. Bradley, A.R., Manna, Z.: Checking safety by inductive generalization of counterexamples to induction. In: Formal Methods in Computer Aided Design (FMCAD'07). pp. 173–180. IEEE (2007)
5. Brayton, R., Mishchenko, A.: ABC: An academic industrial-strength verification tool. In: International Conference on Computer Aided Verification. pp. 24–40. Springer (2010)
6. Bryant, R.E.: Symbolic simulation-techniques and applications. In: 27th ACM/IEEE Design Automation Conference. pp. 517–521. IEEE (1990)
7. Chakraborty, S., Khasidashvili, Z., Seger, C.J.H., Gajavelly, R., Haldankar, T., Chhatani, D., Mistry, R.: Word-level symbolic trajectory evaluation. In: International Conference on Computer Aided Verification. pp. 128–143. Springer (2015)
8. Eén, N., Mishchenko, A., Brayton, R.: Efficient implementation of property directed reachability. In: 2011 Formal Methods in Computer-Aided Design (FMCAD). pp. 125–134. IEEE (2011)
9. Fang, W., Zhang, H.: tacas23-wasim (2022), `https://github.com/fangwenji/tacas23-wasim`
10. Fang, W., Zhang, H.: WASIM: A word-level abstract symbolic simulation framework for hardware formal verification (artifact) (2022), `https://doi.org/10.5281/zenodo.7247147`
11. Gario, M., Micheli, A.: PySMT: a solver-agnostic library for fast prototyping of SMT-based algorithms. In: SMT workshop. vol. 2015 (2015)
12. Hazelhurst, S., Seger, C.J.H.: Symbolic trajectory evaluation. Formal hardware verification pp. 3–78 (1997)
13. Kaivola, R., Ghughal, E., et al.: Replacing testing with formal verification in intel® core™ i7 processor execution engine validation. In: International Conference on Computer Aided Verification. pp. 414–429. Springer (2009)

14. Mattarei, C., Mann, M., Barrett, C., Daly, R.G., Huff, D., Hanrahan, P.: CoSA: Integrated verification for agile hardware design. In: 2018 Formal Methods in Computer Aided Design (FMCAD). pp. 1–5. IEEE (2018)
15. Niemetz, A., Preiner, M., Wolf, C., Biere, A.: Btor2, btormc and boolector 3.0. In: International Conference on Computer Aided Verification. pp. 587–595. Springer (2018)
16. Seger, C.J.: The VossII hardware verification suite (2020), `https://github.com/TeamVoss/VossII`
17. Wolf, C.: Yosys open synthesis suite (2016), `https://github.com/YosysHQ/yosys`
18. Yang, J., Seger, C.J.: Introduction to generalized symbolic trajectory evaluation. IEEE transactions on very large scale integration (VLSI) systems **11**(3), 345–353 (2003)

Multiparty Session Typing in Java, Deductively

Jelle Bouma[1], Stijn de Gouw[1], and Sung-Shik Jongmans[1,2]([✉])

[1] Open University of the Netherlands, Heerlen, the Netherlands
ssj@ou.nl
[2] Centrum Wiskunde & Informatica (CWI), Amsterdam, the Netherlands

Abstract. Multiparty session typing (MPST) is a method to automatically prove safety and liveness of protocol implementations relative to specifications. We present BGJ: a new tool to apply the MPST method in combination with Java. The checks performed using our tool are purely static (all errors are reported early at compile-time) and resource-efficient (near-zero cost abstractions at run-time), thereby addressing two issues of existing tools. BGJ is built using VerCors, but our approach is general.

1 Introduction

Construction and analysis of distributed systems is hard. One of the challenges is this: given a specification S of the *roles* and the *protocols* an implementation I of *processes* and *communication sessions* should fulfil, can we prove that I is *safe* and *live* relative to S? Safety means "bad" communication actions never happen: if a channel action happens in I, <u>then</u> it is allowed by S. Liveness means "good" communication actions eventually happen (communication deadlock freedom). *Multiparty session typing* (MPST) [14,15] is a method to automatically prove safety and liveness of protocol implementations. The idea is shown in Figure 1:

1. First, a protocol among roles $r_1, \ldots, r_n$ is implemented as a session of processes $P_1, \ldots, P_n$ (concrete), while it is specified as a *global type* G (abstract). The global type models the behaviour of all processes together (e.g., "first, a number from Alice to Bob; next, a boolean from Bob to Carol").
2. Next, G is decomposed into local types $L_1, \ldots, L_n$ by *projecting* G onto every role. Each local type models the behaviour of one process alone (e.g., for Bob, "first, he receives from Alice; next, he sends to Carol").
3. Last, absence of communication errors is verified by *type-checking* every process P_i against its local type L_i. MPST theory assures that well-typedness at compile-time implies safety and liveness at run-time.

The following simple example demonstrates global types and local types in *Scribble* notation [28], as used in the Scribble tool [16,17] for the MPST method.

Example 1. The *Adder* protocol [12] consists of two roles: *Client* (c) and *Server* (s). Client either asks Server to add two numbers (Add-message with two Int-payloads) or tells Server goodbye (Bye-message). In the former case, Server tells Client the result (Res-message). This is repeated until Server is told goodbye.

© The Author(s) 2023
S. Sankaranarayanan and N. Sharygina (Eds.): TACAS 2023, LNCS 13994, pp. 19–27, 2023.
https://doi.org/10.1007/978-3-031-30820-8_3

global type G

projection

local types L_1 L_2 $\cdots$ L_n

type check

processes P_1 P_2 $\cdots$ P_n

Fig. 1: MPST method   Fig. 2: Example runs of Adder

```
1 global Adder(role C, role S) {          1 local Adder(role C, role S) at C {
2   choice at C {                         2   choice at C {
3     Add(Int, Int) from C to S;          3     Add(Int, Int) to S;   // send
4     Res(Int) from S to C;               4     Res(Int) from S;      // receive
5     do Adder(C, S); // recur            5     do Adder(C, S);
6   } or {                                6   } or {
7     Bye() from C to S; } }              7     Bye() to S; } }       // send
```

Fig. 3: Global type for Adder   Fig. 4: Local type for Client in Adder

Fig. 5: Workflow of API-generation-based tools for the MPST method

Figure 2 shows three example runs as sequence diagrams. Figure 3 shows the global type. Notation "$m(t_1,\ldots,t_n)$ from p to q" specifies the *communication* of a message of type m with payloads of types $t_1,\ldots,t_n$ from role p to role q. Notation "choice at r { G_1 } or $\cdots$ or { G_k }" specifies a *choice* among branches $G_1,\ldots,G_k$ made by role r. Figure 4 shows the local type for Client. The notation for local types resembles the notation for global types, except that communications are broken up into *sends* ("$m(t_1,\ldots,t_n)$ to q") and *receives* ("from p"). □

A premier approach to apply the MPST method in combination with mainstream programming languages is based on *API generation* (Figure 5); it is used in the majority of MPST tools, including Scribble [16,17], its extensions [32,5,25,22,8,23,9,27,35], StMungo [21], vScr [34], mpstpp [20], and Pompset [6]. The main ideas, first conceived by Deniélou/Hu/Yoshida and pursued in Scribble, follow two insights: **(a)** local types can be interpreted as *deterministic finite automata* (DFA) [10,11], where every transition models a send/receive action; **(b)** DFAs can be encoded as object-oriented *application programming interfaces* (API) [16,17], where classes and methods model states and transitions.

Example 2. Figure 6 shows the DFA and a Java API for Client in Adder (Example 1), in the style of Scribble. Transition labels of the form $q!m(t_1,\ldots,t_n)$ and $p?m(t_1,\ldots,t_n)$ in the DFA specify the send to q and the receive from p of a message of type m with payloads of types $t_1,\ldots,t_n$. Classes State1, State2, and State3 in the API correspond to states 1, 2, and 3 of the DFA; the methods of class State$i$ in the API correspond to the transitions from state i in the DFA.

Figure 7 shows a process for Client, using the Java API. The idea is to write method client that consumes an "initial state object" s1 as input and produces

```
1  class UseOnce { // superclass
2    boolean b = false;
3    void use() { if (b) throw new RuntimeException(); b = true; } }
4
5  class State1 extends UseOnce { // subclass
6    State2 sendAddToS(int x, int y) { use(); ... }
7    State3 sendByeToS()             { use(); ... } }
8
9  class State2 extends UseOnce { // subclass
10   State1 recvResFromS(int[] buff) { use(); ... } }
11
12 class State3 extends UseOnce { }
```

Fig. 6: DFA and Java API for Client in Adder (Scribble-style)

a "final state object" s3 as output. First, the only communication actions that can be performed, are those for which s1 has a method. When called, the communication action is performed and a fresh "successor state object" s2 (line 4) or s3 (line 8) is returned. Next, the only communication actions that can be performed, are those for which s2 or s3 has a method. And so on. By using state objects in this way, a run of method client simulates a run of the DFA.   □

However, existing API-generation-based tools that follow Example 2 in MPST practice, do not fully meet the promise of MPST theory, in two ways:

1. **Mixed static/dynamic checks:** To ensure safety and liveness, every non-final state object must be used *linearly* (exactly one method

```
1  State3 client(State1 s1) {
2    int x = 1; int y = 2;
3    while (x + y < 100) {
4      State2 s2 = s1.sendAddToS(x, y);
5      int[] buff = new int[1];
6      s1 = s2.recvResFromS(buff);
7      x = y; y = buff[0]; }
8    State3 s3 = s1.sendByeToS();
9    return s3; }
```

Fig. 7: Process for Client in Adder

call). However, the type systems of most mainstream programming languages are too weak to check linear usage statically. Instead, dynamic checks are needed (e.g., method use in Figure 6). As a result, MPST practice is weaker than MPST theory: in MPST practice, some errors are reported late at runtime, whereas in MPST theory, all errors are reported early at compile-time.

2. **Resource-inefficient checks:** Every time when a communication action is performed, a fresh state object is created. This costs time (allocation; garbage collection) and space. As a result, MPST practice is costlier at run-time than MPST theory: in MPST practice, API-encodings of DFA-interpretations of local types have a real footprint (proportionate to the number of communication actions), whereas in MPST theory, local types are zero cost abstractions.

In this paper, we present *BGJ*: a new API-generation-based tool to apply the MPST method in combination with Java. The checks performed using BGJ are purely static (all errors are reported early at compile-time) and resource-efficient (near-zero cost abstractions at run-time), thereby addressing the issues above. Instead of building a new static analyser from scratch, we leverage a state-of-the-art deductive verifier for Java, namely *VerCors* [2]. Under active development for years, VerCors has been used in industrial case studies, too [26,18,30]. We note that our approach is generic, though, while our current tool is VerCors-specific.

```
1  class DFA {                          12   //@ context  Perm(state, write);
2     int state;                        13   //@ requires state == 1;
3     //@ ensures Perm(state, write);   14   //@ ensures  state == 3;
4     //@ ensures state == 1;           15   void sendByeToS() {
5     DFA() { state = 1; }              16      state = 3; ... }
6                                       17
7     //@ context  Perm(state, write); 18   //@ context  Perm(state, write);
8     //@ requires state == 1;         19   //@ requires state == 2;
9     //@ ensures  state == 2;         20   //@ ensures  state == 1;
10    void sendAddToS(int x, int y) {  21   int recvResFromS() {
11       state = 2; ... }              22      state = 1; ... } }
```

Fig. 8: Java API for Client in Adder (BGJ-style)

2   Usage: BGJ in a Nutshell

BGJ follows the same workflow as in Figure 5. We explain the steps below.

Steps 1-3: global types; local types; DFAs. First, the programmer manually writes a global type in Scribble notation (e.g., Figure 3). Next, BGJ automatically projects the global type to local types, and it automatically interprets the local types as DFAs. This is standard and as usual [16,17].

Step 4: APIs. Next, BGJ automatically encodes the DFAs as APIs. Our approach is to encode a DFA of n states as an API of *a single* class instead of n classes (Figure 6). At run-time, only one instance of this class is created ("near-zero cost abstraction"); this instance allows any number of usages (method calls). To be able to check that these usages are proper, a key novelty of our approach is that BGJ also generates annotations for *method contracts*, Hoare-logic-style.

Example 3. Figure 8 shows the Java API for Client in Adder (Example 1), generated using BGJ (cf. Figure 6). Field state of class DFA identifies the current state; the methods of class DFA correspond to transitions. The annotations ("//@ ...") define for each method: a *precondition* ("requires"; what must be true before a call?), a *postcondition* ("ensures"; what will be true after?), and a *method invariant* ("context"; read/write permissions for which fields are needed?).   □

Step 5: processes. Last, the programmer manually writes processes using the APIs and automatically verifies proper usage with VerCors (i.e., methods are called only if the preconditions hold). These checks are purely static. If successful, safety relative to the global type and liveness (communication deadlock freedom) are assured; else, a bug is found ("all errors are reported early at compile-time").

```
1  //@ context  Perm(a.state, write)
2  //@ requires a.state == 1;
3  //@ ensures  a.state == 3;
4  void client(DFA a) {
5     int x = 1; int y = 2;
6     //@ loop_invariant a.state == 1;
7     while (x + y < 100) {
8        a.sendAddToS(x, y);
9        x = y; y = a.recvResFromS(); }
10    a.sendByeToS(); }
```

Fig. 9: Process for Client in Adder

Example 4. Figure 9 shows a process for Client in Adder (Example 1), using the Java API in Figure 8. It resembles Figure 7, except that method client and the loop are annotated with a simple contract and invariant. Using VerCors, we can verify that the methods are called only if the preconditions hold. Conversely, if we duplicate line 8, then VerCors reports an error: consecutively sending two Add-messages is forbidden. This can be detected only dynamically in Figure 7 (i.e., a RuntimeException would be thrown in UseOnce of Figure 6).   □

3   Implementation

BGJ is implemented in Java. It reuses the front-end of Scribble for global types, local types, and DFAs in steps 1-3 and, thus, supports the same features (including input branching). The encoder of DFAs as APIs in step 4 is new. It generates two versions of every API: concrete (e.g., Figure 8) and abstract (e.g., Figure 8 without "..."). The concrete API is for running a process. The abstract API, which omits all verification-irrelevant details, is for verifying a process.[3] At run-time, TCP is used to transport messages between processes.

Besides the APIs, BGJ also generates "skeletons" of process code. These skeletons represent the basic control flow (adapted from the DFAs) with send... and recv... method calls in the right places (guaranteed to pass verification). The skeletons can subsequently be filled in with the actual computations.

4   Preliminary Evaluation

We obtained first practical experience with BGJ to study its two improvements. Regarding "all errors are reported early at compile-time", we investigated how much time the verification step of VerCors takes for eight example protocols in Scribble's repository [13]. Figure 10 shows the results, averaged over thirty runs, using generated skeletons as process code. A preliminary conclusion is that the extra time can be low enough (worth the effort[4]) for our approach to be feasible.

Regarding "near-zero cost abstractions at run-time", we investigated run-time overhead of a Scribble-based process (e.g., Figure 6) vs. a BGJ-based process (e.g., Figure 8) for Client in Adder. We factored out code common to both versions (e.g., actual transport of messages over the wire), to be able to specifically measure the impact of the *differences* (methodology of Castro et al. [5]). Averaged over thirty runs, the Scribble-based process and the BGJ-based process

---

[3] The generated annotations are compatible with VerCors 1.0 and above; VerCors can be used as-is. A limitation of our approach is that VerCors supports only a subset of Java. This affects the set of Java features supported for processes.

[4] Usage of BGJ requires two kinds of effort. First, a method in hand-written process code needs to be annotated if the body uses a generated API. All the other code—typically the vast majority of the program (e.g., business logic, database access)—can be tagged to be skipped by VerCors. The few annotations to be added, are only about the state of the DFA at the beginning/ending of a method (pre/postconditions), or at the beginning of each iteration (loop invariants). This is similar to the effort of manually tracking state types when using the existing Scribble. Second, the validity of the annotations need to be checked by VerCors. This is fully automated.

protocol	#roles	time	$\frac{time}{\#roles}$	protocol	#roles	time	$\frac{time}{\#roles}$
Adder	2	15.1	7.6	HTTP	2	40.0	20.0
Booking	3	24.3	8.1	Negotiate	2	17.2	8.6
BuyerBrokerSupplier	4	30.4	7.6	SMTP	2	24.7	12.4
Fibonacci	2	14.9	7.5	TwoBuyer	3	22.8	7.6

Fig. 10: Time of VerCors (in seconds)

completed 2^{31} (`Integer.MAX_VALUE`) iterations in 5221ms and 974ms, respectively. Our preliminary conclusion is that our approach is indeed more resource-efficient.

5   Conclusion

Related work. The combination of the MPST method and deductive verification is largely unexplored territory. The only other work, by López et al. [24], uses deductive verifier VCC [7] to statically check safety and liveness of C+MPI protocol implementations relative to MPST-based specifications. Their approach is very different from ours, though, as it is not based on API generation.

The approach of encoding DFAs of n states as APIs of a single class was recently studied by Cledou et al. [6], by leveraging advanced features of the type system of Scala 3. Their approach does not address the issues in Section 1, though, whereas our approach does. Previous attempts to address the issue of "mixed static/dynamic checks" either target a programming language with a stronger type system (Rust) [22,8,23,9], or adopt callback-style APIs in the specific context of event-based programming [35,34]. In contrast, our approach does not rely on (the strength of) the type system of the targeted programming language, and it supports traditional procedural/object-oriented programming.

Closest to BGJ is StMungo [21]: the approaches of both tools are similar, but the underlying static analysis techniques differ. BGJ leverages method contracts and deductive verification, while StMungo is based on *typestate* [33]. A key advantage of using deductive verification is that it immediately opens the door to reasoning about functional correctness (next paragraph).

Future work. There are two next steps. First, now that we have the infrastructure to combine the MPST method and deductive verification, we are keen to explore their further integration to reason about *functional correctness* of distributed systems. VerCors is based on concurrent separation logic [29,4], so key capabilities to reason about concurrency are already in place. This is connected to work in which separation logic is used to control I/O operations (e.g., Penninckx et al. [31]). Second, while the usage of deductive verification is central to BGJ, our approach does not crucially depend on VerCors: we chose it because it is a fully automated, well-supported deductive verifier for Java, but other tools (e.g., KeY [1], VeriFast [19]) offer opportunities worth investigating, too.

Data Availability Statement

The artifact is available on Zenodo [3]. It contains: (a) our tool and its dependencies; (b) material to replicate the example in Section 2; (c) material to replicate the experiments in Section 4.

References

1. Ahrendt, W., Beckert, B., Bubel, R., Hähnle, R., Schmitt, P.H., Ulbrich, M. (eds.): Deductive Software Verification - The KeY Book - From Theory to Practice, Lecture Notes in Computer Science, vol. 10001. Springer (2016)
2. Blom, S., Huisman, M.: The vercors tool for verification of concurrent programs. In: FM. Lecture Notes in Computer Science, vol. 8442, pp. 127–131. Springer (2014)
3. Bouma, J., de Gouw, S., Jongmans, S.: Multiparty session typing in java, deductively (artifact) (2023). https://doi.org/10.5281/zenodo.7559175
4. Brookes, S.: A semantics for concurrent separation logic. Theor. Comput. Sci. **375**(1-3), 227–270 (2007)
5. Castro-Perez, D., Hu, R., Jongmans, S., Ng, N., Yoshida, N.: Distributed programming using role-parametric session types in Go: statically-typed endpoint APIs for dynamically-instantiated communication structures. Proc. ACM Program. Lang. **3**(POPL), 29:1–29:30 (2019)
6. Cledou, G., Edixhoven, L., Jongmans, S., Proença, J.: API generation for multiparty session types, revisited and revised using scala 3. In: ECOOP. LIPIcs, vol. 222, pp. 27:1–27:28. Schloss Dagstuhl - Leibniz-Zentrum für Informatik (2022)
7. Cohen, E., Dahlweid, M., Hillebrand, M.A., Leinenbach, D., Moskal, M., Santen, T., Schulte, W., Tobies, S.: VCC: A practical system for verifying concurrent C. In: TPHOLs. Lecture Notes in Computer Science, vol. 5674, pp. 23–42. Springer (2009)
8. Cutner, Z., Yoshida, N.: Safe session-based asynchronous coordination in rust. In: COORDINATION. Lecture Notes in Computer Science, vol. 12717, pp. 80–89. Springer (2021)
9. Cutner, Z., Yoshida, N., Vassor, M.: Deadlock-free asynchronous message reordering in rust with multiparty session types. In: PPoPP. pp. 246–261. ACM (2022)
10. Deniélou, P., Yoshida, N.: Multiparty session types meet communicating automata. In: ESOP. Lecture Notes in Computer Science, vol. 7211, pp. 194–213. Springer (2012)
11. Deniélou, P., Yoshida, N.: Multiparty compatibility in communicating automata: Characterisation and synthesis of global session types. In: ICALP (2). Lecture Notes in Computer Science, vol. 7966, pp. 174–186. Springer (2013)
12. GitHub, Inc: scribble-java/adder.scr at 02dbf9abd9993b17c809aa610311452ec4c76 3bc · scribble/scribble-java, accessed 22 January 2023, https://github.com/scribbl e/scribble-java/blob/02dbf9abd9993b17c809aa610311452ec4c763bc/scribble-dem os/scrib/tutorial/src/tutorial/adder/Adder.scr
13. GitHub, Inc: scribble-java/scribble-demos/scrib at ccb0e48d69c6e3088e74 6138099c3183ca1ac79b · scribble/scribble-java, accessed 22 January 2023, https://github.com/scribble/scribble-java/tree/ccb0e48d69c6e3088e746138099c 3183ca1ac79b/scribble-demos/scrib
14. Honda, K., Yoshida, N., Carbone, M.: Multiparty asynchronous session types. In: POPL. pp. 273–284. ACM (2008)

15. Honda, K., Yoshida, N., Carbone, M.: Multiparty asynchronous session types. J. ACM **63**(1), 9:1–9:67 (2016)
16. Hu, R., Yoshida, N.: Hybrid session verification through endpoint API generation. In: FASE. Lecture Notes in Computer Science, vol. 9633, pp. 401–418. Springer (2016)
17. Hu, R., Yoshida, N.: Explicit connection actions in multiparty session types. In: FASE. Lecture Notes in Computer Science, vol. 10202, pp. 116–133. Springer (2017)
18. Huisman, M., Monti, R.E.: On the industrial application of critical software verification with vercors. In: ISoLA (3). Lecture Notes in Computer Science, vol. 12478, pp. 273–292. Springer (2020)
19. Jacobs, B., Smans, J., Philippaerts, P., Vogels, F., Penninckx, W., Piessens, F.: Verifast: A powerful, sound, predictable, fast verifier for C and java. In: NASA Formal Methods. Lecture Notes in Computer Science, vol. 6617, pp. 41–55. Springer (2011)
20. Jongmans, S., Yoshida, N.: Exploring type-level bisimilarity towards more expressive multiparty session types. In: ESOP. Lecture Notes in Computer Science, vol. 12075, pp. 251–279. Springer (2020)
21. Kouzapas, D., Dardha, O., Perera, R., Gay, S.J.: Typechecking protocols with mungo and stmungo: A session type toolchain for java. Sci. Comput. Program. **155**, 52–75 (2018)
22. Lagaillardie, N., Neykova, R., Yoshida, N.: Implementing multiparty session types in Rust. In: COORDINATION. Lecture Notes in Computer Science, vol. 12134, pp. 127–136. Springer (2020)
23. Lagaillardie, N., Neykova, R., Yoshida, N.: Stay safe under panic: Affine rust programming with multiparty session types. In: ECOOP. LIPIcs, vol. 222, pp. 4:1–4:29. Schloss Dagstuhl - Leibniz-Zentrum für Informatik (2022)
24. López, H.A., Marques, E.R.B., Martins, F., Ng, N., Santos, C., Vasconcelos, V.T., Yoshida, N.: Protocol-based verification of message-passing parallel programs. In: OOPSLA. pp. 280–298. ACM (2015)
25. Miu, A., Ferreira, F., Yoshida, N., Zhou, F.: Communication-safe web programming in typescript with routed multiparty session types. In: CC. pp. 94–106. ACM (2021)
26. Monti, R.E., Rubbens, R., Huisman, M.: On deductive verification of an industrial concurrent software component with vercors. In: ISoLA (1). Lecture Notes in Computer Science, vol. 13701, pp. 517–534. Springer (2022)
27. Neykova, R., Hu, R., Yoshida, N., Abdeljallal, F.: A session type provider: compile-time API generation of distributed protocols with refinements in F#. In: CC. pp. 128–138. ACM (2018)
28. Neykova, R., Yoshida, N.: Featherweight scribble. In: Models, Languages, and Tools for Concurrent and Distributed Programming. Lecture Notes in Computer Science, vol. 11665, pp. 236–259. Springer (2019)
29. O'Hearn, P.W.: Resources, concurrency, and local reasoning. Theor. Comput. Sci. **375**(1-3), 271–307 (2007)
30. Oortwijn, W., Huisman, M.: Formal verification of an industrial safety-critical traffic tunnel control system. In: IFM. Lecture Notes in Computer Science, vol. 11918, pp. 418–436. Springer (2019)
31. Penninckx, W., Jacobs, B., Piessens, F.: Sound, modular and compositional verification of the input/output behavior of programs. In: ESOP. Lecture Notes in Computer Science, vol. 9032, pp. 158–182. Springer (2015)
32. Scalas, A., Dardha, O., Hu, R., Yoshida, N.: A linear decomposition of multiparty sessions for safe distributed programming. In: ECOOP. LIPIcs, vol. 74, pp. 24:1–24:31. Schloss Dagstuhl - Leibniz-Zentrum für Informatik (2017)

33. Strom, R.E., Yemini, S.: Typestate: A programming language concept for enhancing software reliability. IEEE Trans. Software Eng. **12**(1), 157–171 (1986)
34. Yoshida, N., Zhou, F., Ferreira, F.: Communicating finite state machines and an extensible toolchain for multiparty session types. In: FCT. Lecture Notes in Computer Science, vol. 12867, pp. 18–35. Springer (2021)
35. Zhou, F., Ferreira, F., Hu, R., Neykova, R., Yoshida, N.: Statically verified refinements for multiparty protocols. Proc. ACM Program. Lang. **4**(OOPSLA), 148:1–148:30 (2020)

PyLTA: A Verification Tool for Parameterized Distributed Algorithms

Bastien Thomas and Ocan Sankur[✉]

Univ Rennes, Inria, CNRS, Rennes, France
ocan.sankur@irisa.fr

Abstract. We present the tool PyLTA, which can model check parameterized distributed algorithms against LTL specifications. The parameters typically include the number of processes and a bound on faulty processes, and the considered algorithms are round-based and either synchronous or asynchronous.

1 Introduction

Distributed algorithms — algorithms that run on multiple communicating processes — are used in many domains including scientific computing, telecommunications and the Blockchain. Standard distributed algorithms typically perform relatively simple tasks such as consensus or leader election[17], but complexity arises from the lack of reliability of the network: some processes may crash, communications may be lost, faulty processes may send arbitrary messages (Byzantine faults)... In this setting, various automated verification techniques have been developped in order to provide guarantees on the executions of such algorithms. Notably, *parameterised* verification attempts to verify these algorithms for every possible number of processes and faults at once [4].

Threshold automata [14] (TA) are a formalism based on *counter abstraction* [18] that model asynchronous distributed algorithms with parameterised number of processes under crash and Byzantine faults. Verification can be performed using a complete encoding to SMT formulas [13]. The decidabililty of generalisations of these models was studied in [16] while [1] focuses on the complexity of the underlying problems. These algorithms were implemented in the Byzantine model checker ByMC [15]. However, algorithms based on threshold automata require bounding the diameter of the underlying transition system, either in the asynchronous case with bounded protocols (with only finitely many exchanged messages) in [14], or with unbounded messages but in the synchronous case, and for reachability properties only [20]. These techniques are therefore incomplete for threshold automata where such a bound does not exist.

In this article, we introduce PyLTA, a tool for fully verifying parameterised distributed algorithms both in the synchronous and asynchronous cases, without bounding the diameter of the state space or the number of exchanged messages. It is based on *layered threshold automata* (LTA), a formalism developed in [3] which can be thought of as some form of infinitely repeating threshold automata. These generalise the synchronous TAs used in [20] and can handle

© The Author(s) 2023
S. Sankaranarayanan and N. Sharygina (Eds.): TACAS 2023, LNCS 13994, pp. 28–35, 2023.
https://doi.org/10.1007/978-3-031-30820-8_4

both synchronous and asynchronous communication by exploiting some notions similar to *communication closure* [8]. This allows us to verify *any* LTL formula, including liveness properties, even on algorithms where processes may send unboundedly many messages (unlike [14] where only finite TAs and a fragment of LTL was considered).

Concretely, PyLTA takes as input the LTA description of a parameterised distributed algorithm as well as an LTL specification. It then verifies the specification under *all* parameter valuations, or finds a counterexample disproving the specification. The tool is meant to provide support for distributed algorithm designers. In fact, distributed algorithm design is not a single step process. In practice, the implemented versions of an algorithm often contain additional features or optimizations, and PyLTA can be used to automatically check these variants for counterexamples.

2   Modeling Distributed Algorithms

In order to illustrate the capabilities of PyLTA, we use the Phase King algorithm (Algorithm 1) [2]. In general, the algorithms that can be handled by PyLTA exhibit the following characteristics:

1. They are **parameterized**: in Algorithm 1, n denotes the number of processes and t a bound on the number of *Byzantine* faults. PyLTA verifies the algorithm for *all* the valuations of these parameters at once.
2. They can exchange **messages in an unbounded** domain: the indices $2i$ and $2i + 1$ in Algorithm 1 are not bounded by a constant.
3. They can be **synchronous** or **asynchronous** but must ensure *communication closure*: sent and received messages are tagged with indices ($2i$ and $2i+1$ in Algorithm 1) that can only increase with time. As noted in [8], communication closure appears both in synchronous and asynchronous algorithms in the literature.
4. The algorithms should use *threshold conditions*. This means that the conditions in branches on the algorithms should be arithmetic formulas comparing *numbers* of received messages and the values of parameters (see line 10).

Under these conditions, algorithms can be encoded in an LTA. The last two conditions can often be worked around. For example, we will show along this article how Algorithm 1 can be verified despite the fact that the condition on line 6 is not ameanable to counter abstraction as it uses the identity of processes which is lost in the abstraction.

Algorithm 1 uses the parameters n, and t with the condition $t < \frac{n}{4}$. We introduce an additional paramter $f \leq t$ which is the actual number of faulty processes: the algorithm does not have access to f, but it is used during verification. Communication closure yields a layered structure of our models: a *layer* indexed by $\ell \in \mathbb{N}$ models the portion of the program that deals with messages tagged with ℓ. In Algorithm 1, the layer $\ell = 2i$ corresponds to lines 3-5, while layer $\ell = 2i + 1$ corresponds to lines 6-12.

1 Process PhaseKing($n, t,$ id, v):
     Data: n processes, $t < \frac{n}{4}$ Byzantine faults, id $\in \{0 \ldots n-1\}$, $v \in \{0,1\}$.
2   **for** $i = 0$ *to* t **do**   `// Start of layer` $\ell = 2i$
3   broadcast $(2i, v)$ `// State` a_v, $v \in \{0,1\}$
4 $n_0 \leftarrow$ number of messages $(2i, 0)$ received
5 $n_1 \leftarrow$ number of messages $(2i, 1)$ received`// Start of layer` $\ell = 2i+1$
6   **if** $i ==$ id **then**   `// Current process is king`
7   **if** $n_0 \geq n_1$ **then** $v \leftarrow 0$ `// State` k_0
8   **else** $v \leftarrow 1$ `// State` k_1
9   broadcast $(2i+1, v)$
10   **else if** $n_0 > \frac{n}{2} + t$ **then** $v \leftarrow 0$ `// State` b_0
11   **else if** $n_1 > \frac{n}{2} + t$ **then** $v \leftarrow 1$ `// State` b_1
12   **else** $v \leftarrow v'$ where $(2i+1, v')$ is the king's message   `// State` $b_?$
13   **end**
14   **return** v;

Algorithm 1: The Phase King algorithm [2] is a synchronous algorithm that solves binary consensus under $t < \frac{n}{4}$ Byzantine faults. It executes $t+1$ rounds, and each round $i \in \{0 \ldots t\}$ is further decomposed into two layers (for round i, the layers are named $2i$ and $2i+1$). In layer $2i$, the processes broadcast their preferences v, and in layer $2i+1$, they update v either to the majority if it is strong enough, or to the preference of the process with id i, which is the king of the round i.

We use *counter abstraction* to model executions of the algorithm, meaning that we define a counter storing the number of processes at each state of the algorithm. Here, our approach differs from other works on threshold automata because we count the number of processes that *have been* through the state instead of those that are *currently* in it. It follows that the number of messages m sent during the execution can be accurately deduced from these counter values as the number of processes at states where messages m have been sent. The downside of counter abstraction is that the identities of the processes are lost. Notably, the condition on line 6 needs to be abstracted with a non deterministic choice.

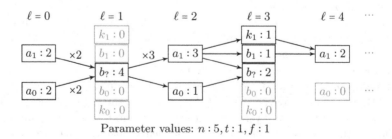

Parameter values: $n : 5, t : 1, f : 1$

Fig. 1: A configuration of the Phase King algorithm (Algorithm 1).

Configurations. PyLTA verifies properties on all reachable *configurations*. A configuration can be interpreted as a record of events that occured during an execution. An example is depicted in Fig. 1 which we now explain.

The configuration contains an instantiation of the parameter values (given on the bottom of the figure). Moreover, for each layer index, it specifies the number of *correct* (i.e. non-faulty) processes that were at a given state at that layer; as well as the number of correct processes that moved from one state to another between consecutive layers.

In Fig. 1, initially, 2 correct processes are at state a_1, and 2 are at a_0, for a parameter valuation $n = 5, t = 1, f = 1$. Recall that layers $2i$ and $2i + 1$ correspond to round i, and that the meaning of the states are given in Algorithm 1; in particular, a_x is the first line of an iteration where variable v has value x. All 4 correct processes go to $b_?$ at layer 1, which means that the Byzantine process was king at round 0. Then three of them go to a_1 at layer 3, and one of them goes to a_0, etc. This models the situation where the Byzantine process sent a message $(2 \times 0 + 1, 1)$ to the latter process but $(2 \times 0 + 1, 0)$ to the others. In the next layer, a correct process is king with value 1 (state k_1), and one correct process has received a majority of value 1 (state b_1), but not all correct processes have arrived to layer 4 yet. This configurations thus represents a finite prefix of an execution. When needed, LTL fairness assumptions can ensure that we only consider infinite configurations.

3   Input Format and Usage

The input format is based on layered threshold automata (LTA) defined in [3], which we illustrate on the running example. An input file needs to define three elements: *parameters*, *states* and *guards*.

In PyLTA, the set of parameters are declared as follows.

```
PARAMETERS: n, t, f
PARAMETER_RELATION: 4*t < n
```

The second line declares a constraint on these parameters, here $4t < n$, which is a necessary condition for the correctness of Algorithm 1.

As in our running example, the input format assumes that the states of the considered systems belong to layers. The following line defines two consecutive layers A, B, and specifies after layer B, we come back to layer A and loop.

```
LAYERS: A, B, A
```

In other terms, this results in the sequence of layers A, B, A, B, ... One can also specify lasso-shaped sequences; for instance, LAYERS: A, B, B would yield the sequence A, B, B, B, ... States can be declared by specifying the name of the layer and the name of the state separated by a period as below.

```
STATES: A.0, A.1
STATES: B.k0, B.0, B.u, B.1, B.k1
```

For instance, the first line defines the states a_0 and a_1 in Figure 1, and the second line is the rest of the states.

Transitions are defined by distinguishing cases for each state using guards. In Algorithm 1, a process needs to receive more than $\frac{n}{2} + t$ messages $(2i, 1)$ in order to move from state a_1 (line 3) to b_1 (line 11). These messages can either come from processes in state a_1 or from Byzantine processes. In PyLTA, this condition is called the *guard* from a_1 to b_1 and it is expressed with the formula $2(a_1 + f) > n + 2t$. State names correspond to the number of correct processes that have been at that state, so transitions are declared as follows.

```
FORMULA Afull: A.0 + A.1 + f == n
CASE A.1:
    IF Afull & 2*(A.1 + f) >= n THEN B.k1
    IF Afull & 2*(A.1 + f) >= n + 2*t THEN B.1
...
```

The formula `Afull` is used to enforce synchrony: no process can take a transition before every message was received. We present the other transitions for Algorithm 1 in Table 1. Note that `Afull` or an equivalent `Bfull` should also be added each time in order to avoid considering asynchronous executions.

The following instruction is used to declare an LTL specification to be verified on the configurations:

```
WITH
    A.initial: A.0 + A.1 + f == n
    A.one0: A.0 > 0
    B.not_two_kings: B.k0 + B.k1 <= 1
VERIFY: (A.initial & ! A.one0 & G(B -> B.not_two_kings)) -> G(A -> ! A.one0)
```

The instructions between `WITH` and `VERIFY` define predicates at given layers, which can be used in the subsequent LTL formula. Here, `A.one0` holds when at least one process is in state `A.0`; and `B.not_two_kings` is used to prevent executions where more than one king is present in a round. These predicates can then be used as propositions of the LTL formula that will be verified.

A layer type name (A or B) inside a formula indicates a predicate that only holds in the corresponding layers. An interpretation of the formula can therefore

Table 1: The guards of the transitions for Algorithm 1. The table on the left is for transitions leaving states of layers $\ell = 2i$, and the table on the right is for those with layer $\ell = 2i + 1$. Each cell is the guard of the transition from the state of the row to the state of the column.

$\ell = 2i$	k_0	b_0	$b_?$	b_1	k_1
a_0	$2(a_0 + f)$	$2(a_0 + f)$	$2a_0 \le n + 2t$	$2(a_1 + f)$	$2(a_1 + f)$
a_1	$\ge n$	$\ge n + 2t$	$\wedge 2a_1 \le n + 2t$	$\ge n + 2t$	$\ge n$

$\ell = 2i + 1$	a_0	a_1
k_0	true	false
b_0	true	false
$b_?$	$k_1 = 0$	$k_0 = 0$
b_1	false	true
k_1	false	true

be the following: "if there are n processes, and no process in A.0, and there is always at most one non-Byzantine king in layers of type B, then at all layers of type A, there is no process in A.0."

4 Tool Overview and Usage

PyLTA is written in Python. In addition to *counter abstraction* and *predicate abstraction*, PyLTA performs counter-example guided abstraction refinement [6]. Since we are working in an unbounded domain due to parameters, the tool uses an SMT solver to check the realizability of the traces, and refine the abstraction using interpolants produced by the solver [12]. The current version uses MathSAT [5] via PySMT [11]. We use Lark[19] for parsing.

The LTL specification is first negated, and then converted into a Büchi automaton using Spot [10]. The product between this automaton and the predicate abstraction is then built dynamically. We check the language emptiness of the resulting product automaton; if it is empty, then the specification holds. Otherwise, the abstract counterexample is checked for realizability using the SMT solver, and either the counterexample is confirmed, or the abstraction is refined.

We run PyLTA on an input file as follows.

```
python -m pylta [input_file]
```

The output on the file corresponding to our running example is the following:

```
VERIFYING R.initial & ! R.one0 & G (B -> B.not_two_kings) ...
Formula is Valid
```

More details such as the abstract counter examples encountered and the added predicates can be obtained by adding a -v flag. In this case, a single refinement was necessary, which added the predicate B.k0 + B.0 + B.u <= 0.

The verification algorithm does not require user interaction since abstractions are refined automatically. However, any predicate defined in the VERIFY instruction is used in the predicate abstraction, even if it does not appear in the formula. This behaviour provides a way to manually add predicates in order to help with the verification. The tool is distributed under the GNU GPL 3.0 licence and is available at https://gitlab.com/BastienT/pylta.

5 Conclusion

We have presented PyLTA, a tool for verifying parameterised distributed algorithms. Despite the undecidability barrier even in simple versions of the problem [20], PyLTA is able to verify complex properties on distributed algorithms, and unlike previous works, makes no assumptions on bounds on the state space or exchanged messages. As future work, one might explore the use of implicit predicate abstraction [21] to speed up the verification process. Another direction would be to integrate well ordered functions providing termination arguments [7] as used in [9] which could extend the usability of PyLTA.

References

1. A. R. Balasubramanian, Javier Esparza, and Marijana Lazić. Complexity of verification and synthesis of threshold automata. In *Proceedings of the 18th International Symposium on Automated Technology for Verification and Analysis (ATVA'20)*, volume 12302 of *Lecture Notes in Computer Science*, pages 144–160. Springer, 2020.
2. Piotr Berman and Juan A. Garay. Cloture votes: n/4-resilient distributed consensus in t+1 rounds. *Mathematical Systems Theory*, 26(1):3–19, 1993.
3. Nathalie Bertrand, Bastien Thomas, and Josef Widder. Guard automata for the verification of safety and liveness of distributed algorithms. In Serge Haddad and Daniele Varacca, editors, *32nd International Conference on Concurrency Theory, CONCUR 2021, August 24-27, 2021, Virtual Conference*, volume 203 of *LIPIcs*, pages 15:1–15:17. Schloss Dagstuhl - Leibniz-Zentrum für Informatik, 2021.
4. Roderick Bloem, Swen Jacobs, Ayrat Khalimov, Igor Konnov, Sasha Rubin, Helmut Veith, and Josef Widder. *Decidability of Parameterized Verification*. Synthesis Lectures on Distributed Computing Theory. Morgan & Claypool Publishers, 2015.
5. Alessandro Cimatti, Alberto Griggio, Bastiaan Schaafsma, and Roberto Sebastiani. The MathSAT5 SMT Solver. In Nir Piterman and Scott Smolka, editors, *Proceedings of TACAS*, volume 7795 of *LNCS*. Springer, 2013.
6. Edmund Clarke, Orna Grumberg, Somesh Jha, Yuan Lu, and Helmut Veith. Counterexample-guided abstraction refinement for symbolic model checking. *J. ACM*, 50(5):752–794, sep 2003.
7. Byron Cook, Andreas Podelski, and Andrey Rybalchenko. Termination proofs for systems code. In Michael I. Schwartzbach and Thomas Ball, editors, *Proceedings of the ACM SIGPLAN 2006 Conference on Programming Language Design and Implementation, Ottawa, Ontario, Canada, June 11-14, 2006*, pages 415–426. ACM, 2006.
8. Andrei Damian, Cezara Drăgoi, Alexandru Militaru, and Josef Widder. Communication-closed asynchronous protocols. In *Proceedings of the 31st International Conference on Computer Aided Verification (CAV'19)*, volume 11562 of *Lecture Notes in Computer Science*, pages 344–363. Springer, 2019.
9. Jakub Daniel, Alessandro Cimatti, Alberto Griggio, Stefano Tonetta, and Sergio Mover. Infinite-state liveness-to-safety via implicit abstraction and well-founded relations. In Swarat Chaudhuri and Azadeh Farzan, editors, *Computer Aided Verification - 28th International Conference, CAV 2016, Toronto, ON, Canada, July 17-23, 2016, Proceedings, Part I*, volume 9779 of *Lecture Notes in Computer Science*, pages 271–291. Springer, 2016.
10. Alexandre Duret-Lutz, Alexandre Lewkowicz, Amaury Fauchille, Thibaud Michaud, Etienne Renault, and Laurent Xu. Spot 2.0 — a framework for LTL and ω-automata manipulation. In *Proceedings of the 14th International Symposium on Automated Technology for Verification and Analysis (ATVA'16)*, volume 9938 of *Lecture Notes in Computer Science*, pages 122–129. Springer, October 2016.
11. Marco Gario and Andrea Micheli. Pysmt: a solver-agnostic library for fast prototyping of smt-based algorithms. In *SMT Workshop 2015*, 2015.
12. Thomas A. Henzinger, Ranjit Jhala, Rupak Majumdar, and Kenneth L. McMillan. Abstractions from proofs. In *Proceedings of the 31st ACM SIGPLAN-SIGACT Symposium on Principles of Programming Languages*, POPL '04, page 232–244, New York, NY, USA, 2004. Association for Computing Machinery.

13. Igor Konnov, Marijana Lazić, Helmut Veith, and Josef Widder. A short counterexample property for safety and liveness verification of fault-tolerant distributed algorithms. In *Proceedings of the 44th ACM SIGPLAN Symposium on Principles of Programming Languages (POPL'17)*, pages 719–734, 2017.
14. Igor Konnov, Helmut Veith, and Josef Widder. On the completeness of bounded model checking for threshold-based distributed algorithms: Reachability. *Information and Computation*, 252:95–109, 2017.
15. Igor Konnov and Josef Widder. Bymc: Byzantine model checker. In Tiziana Margaria and Bernhard Steffen, editors, *Leveraging Applications of Formal Methods, Verification and Validation. Distributed Systems - 8th International Symposium, ISoLA 2018, Limassol, Cyprus, November 5-9, 2018, Proceedings, Part III*, volume 11246 of *Lecture Notes in Computer Science*, pages 327–342. Springer, 2018.
16. Jure Kukovec, Igor Konnov, and Josef Widder. Reachability in parameterized systems: All flavors of threshold automata. In *Proceedings of the 29th International Conference on Concurrency Theory (CONCUR'18)*, volume 118 of *LIPIcs*, pages 19:1–19:17, 2018.
17. Nancy A. Lynch. *Distributed Algorithms*. Morgan Kaufmann, 1996.
18. Amir Pnueli, Jessie Xu, and Lenore D. Zuck. Liveness with (0, 1, infty)-counter abstraction. In *Proceedings of the 14th International Conference on Computer Aided Verification*, CAV '02, page 107–122, Berlin, Heidelberg, 2002. Springer-Verlag.
19. Erez Shinan. Lark. https://github.com/lark-parser/lark/, 2018-2022.
20. Ilina Stoilkovska, Igor Konnov, Josef Widder, and Florian Zuleger. Verifying safety of synchronous fault-tolerant algorithms by bounded model checking. In *Proceedings of the 25th International Conference on Tools and Algorithms for the Construction and Analysis of Systems (TACAS'19)*, volume 11428 of *Lecture Notes in Computer Science*, pages 357–374, 2019.
21. Stefano Tonetta. Abstract model checking without computing the abstraction. In Ana Cavalcanti and Dennis Dams, editors, *FM 2009: Formal Methods, Second World Congress, Eindhoven, The Netherlands, November 2-6, 2009. Proceedings*, volume 5850 of *Lecture Notes in Computer Science*, pages 89–105. Springer, 2009.

FuzzBtor2: A Random Generator of Word-Level Model Checking Problems in BTOR2 Format*

Shengping Xiao[1], Chengyu Zhang[2], Jianwen Li[1(✉)], and Geguang Pu[1,3(✉)]

[1] East China Normal University, Shanghai, China
spxiao@stu.ecnu.edu.cn, {jwli,ggpu}@sei.ecnu.edu.cn
[2] ETH Zurich, Zurich, Switzerland
chengyu.zhang@inf.ethz.ch
[3] Shanghai Trusted Industrial Control Platform Co., Ltd, Shanghai, China

Abstract. We present FuzzBtor2, a fuzzer to generate random word-level model checking problems in BTOR2 format. BTOR2 is one of the mainstream input formats for word-level hardware model checking and was used in the most recent hardware model checking competition. Compared to bit-level one, word-level model checking is a more complex research field at an earlier stage of development. Therefore, it is necessary to develop a tool that can produce a large number of test cases in BTOR2 format to test either existing or under-developed word-level model checkers. To evaluate the practicality of FuzzBtor2, we tested the state-of-the-art word-level model checkers AVR and Pono with the generated benchmarks. Experimental results show that both tools are buggy and not mature enough, which reflects the practical value of FuzzBtor2.

1 Introduction

Model checking plays an influential role in modern hardware design [4]. Its great success is inseparable from propositional methods such as Binary Decision Diagrams (BDDs) [10] and Boolean SATisfiability (SAT) solver [14]. Since BMC [6] was introduced, influential hardware model checking methods such as IMC [20], IC3 [9], and CAR [18] are all SAT-based. At the same time, many important efforts have been made to apply SAT-based model checking techniques to word-level verification tasks whose background theory are first-order logic [7,23,11,19,16]. These works all rely on more expressive reasoning techniques, i.e., Satisfiability Modulo Theories (SMT) [3] solvers. As the performance of the SMT solvers continues to improve [1,22], word-level hardware model checking has become a promising research area. Word-level reasoning is more powerful and opens up many possibilities for simplification [5]. It is strong evidence that a

* Jianwen Li is supported by National Natural Science Foundation of China (Grant #U21B2015 and #62002118) and Shanghai Pujiang Talent Plan (Grant #20PJ1403500). Geguang Pu is supported by National Key Research and Development Program (Grant #2020AAA0107800), and Shanghai Collaborative Innovation Center of Trusted Industry Internet Software.

S. Sankaranarayanan and N. Sharygina (Eds.): TACAS 2023, LNCS 13994, pp. 36–43, 2023.
https://doi.org/10.1007/978-3-031-30820-8_5

word-level model checker, AVR [17], achieved the best results in the most recent hardware model checking competition [2].

Implementing word-level reasoning tools such as SMT solvers and word-level model checkers is much more complex and difficult than bit-level tools. For word-level model checking, which is a developing and immature area, it is an urgent requirement to obtain a large number of diverse benchmarks that can be used for bug finding and performance evaluation. Responding to this requirement, we present FuzzBtor2, a fuzzing tool that can generate random word-level model checking problems. We choose BTOR2 [21] as the format of output files, which is simple, line-based, and easy to parse. BTOR2 is also the current official format for the hardware model checking competition [2]. Most of mainstream word-level model checkers support BTOR2 format directly (AVR and Pono [19]) or indirectly (nuXmv [11] and IC3ia [13]). To evaluate whether FuzzBtor2 is practical, we test two state-of-the-art word-level model checkers AVR and Pono that can read BTOR2 files directly via BTOR2 files generated by FuzzBtor2, and generated test cases trigger various errors of both checkers. We expect that FuzzBtor2 becomes infrastructure for the development of word-level model checkers.

2   Word-Level Model Checking and BTOR2 Format

We assume that the reader is familiar with standard first-order logic terminology [3]. *Words* generally refer to terms with bit-vector ranges, optionally combined with other theories. The background theory of BTOR2 is the Quantifier-Free theory of Bit Vectors with Arrays extension (QF_ABV), by which almost all computer system information can be encoded. And the invariant property is (one of) the most important property classes to verify.

A *model checking problem* consists of a transition system and a property to verify. A transition system is a tuple $S = (V, I, T)$ where

 – V and V' are sets of variables in the present state and next state respectively;
 – I is a set of formulas corresponding to the set of initial states;
 – T is a set of formulas over $V \cup V'$ for the transition relation.

Given a transition system $S = (V, I, T)$, its state space is the set of possible variable assignments. I and T determine the reachable state space of S. The bad property is represented by a formula $\neg P$ over V. A model checking problem can be defined as follows: either prove that P holds for any reachable states of S, or disprove P by producing a counterexample. In the former, the system is *safe*, and in the latter, the system is *unsafe*. There are input variables in some transition systems, which can be modeled as state variables whose corresponding next states are unconstrained. Assume that a BTOR2 file includes n_s state variables, n_c constraints, and n_b bad properties. Its initial state space consists of n_s init-formulas. The transition relation consists of n_s next-formulas and n_c constraint-formulas. And the bad property consists of n_b bad-formulas. The sorts of init-formulas and next-formulas should be consistent with the corresponding state variables, and constraint-formulas and bad-formulas are Boolean sort.

3   The FuzzBtor2 Tool

FuzzBtor2 is an open-source software consisting of approximately 2400 lines of C++11 code. FuzzBtor2 does not rely on specific libraries and it is self-contained. In this section we introduce the usage and architecture of FuzzBtor2. The tool is available at https://github.com/CoriolisSP/FuzzBtor2.

3.1   Usage

The command to execute FuzzBtor2 in Linux systems is ./fuzzbtor [options]. We present the usage and features of FuzzBtor2 along with the options here.

--seed INT This option is used to set the seed for the random number generator. Keeping other options, we could generate different test cases by changing the value of the random number seed. The default seed is 0.

--to-vmt Verification Modulo Theories (VMT) [12], which is an extension of SMT-LIB2 [3], is also used to represent symbolic transition systems and the properties to verify. vmt-tools [15] is a tool suite for VMT format, and it provides a translator from BTOR2 to VMT. However, vmt-tools supports only a subset of operators in BTOR2. By this option, the generated BTOR2 files only include the operators supported by vmt-tools, so that they can be translated into VMT format to test model checkers that take VMT files as input (e.g., IC3ia [13]).

--bv-states INT, --arr-states INT These options specify the numbers of bit-vector and array state variables. The default values are 2 and 0 respectively.

--max-inputs INT This option specifies the maximum number of input variables in the generated BTOR2 file. The actual number of input variables in the generated file may be smaller than the maximum. The default value is 1.

--bad-properties INT, --constraints INT These two options specify the numbers of bad properties and constraints in the generated BTOR2 file, and the default values are 1 and 0 respectively. The fuzzer currently does not support generating liveness properties and fairness constraints.

--max-depth INT A word-level model checking problem consisting of a transition system and properties to verify is essentially a set of first-order logic formulas. And formulas are represented by syntax trees in FuzzBtor2, so a word-level model checking problem corresponds to a set of syntax trees. This option specifies the maximum depth of these syntax trees. The default value is 4.

--candidate-sizes RANGE|SET FuzzBtor2 can get a set of positive integers from this option, which is used to specify sorts of variables. All sizes of indexes of array variables, elements of array variables, and sizes of bit-vector variables are in the set. The default set is $\{s \in \mathbb{Z} \mid 1 \leq s \leq 8\}$. Note that it does not allow to define a specific sort directly.

3.2   Architecture

The architecture of FuzzBtor2 consists of preprocessor, generator, and printer. Users of FuzzBtor2 only specify some arguments on the command line, and no other input is given. From command line arguments, the preprocessor sorts out

---

Algorithm 1: GenerateSyntaxTree

Input: A sort s of bit-vector or array, and a depth denoted by d
Output: A syntax tree of sort s with depth d

1   **if** $d = 1$ **then**
2      $leafType :=$ DecideLeafType()   // Decide the type of leaf node.
3   **if** $leafType = constant$ **then**
4   └ **return** a constant
5   **else if** $s \in candidateSort$ **then**
6   **if** $leafType = input$ **then**
7   **if** *there exists an input variable of sort* s **then**
8   └ **return** an existing input variable
9   **if** $existInputNum < MaxInputNum$ **then**
10   └ **return** an new input variable
11   **else if** $leafType = state$ **then**
            └ // Similar to the case of input variables, omitted here.
12   **return** $NULL$ // Construction fails.
13 $op :=$ DecideOperator(s)
14 $\langle n, depths, sorts \rangle :=$ DecideInformationOfSubtrees(op, d)
15 $tree :=$ NewTree(op)
16 **for** $i = 1 \ldots n$ **do**
17      $subTree :=$ GenerateSyntaxTree($sorts[i], depths[i]$)   // Recursion.
18   **if** $subTree = NULL$ **then**
19   └ **return** $NULL$
20   **else**
21   └ $tree$.AddSubTree($subTree$)
22 **return** $tree$

---

the information required by the generator and saves it as a configuration. According to the configuration, the generator constructs some syntax trees that satisfy requirements of the number and sorts as stated in Sec. 2. These syntax trees encode a set of first-order logic formulas, which essentially is a model checking problem independent of the BTOR2 format. At last, the printer outputs syntax trees constructed by the generator in BTOR2 format.

The generator is the key component of FuzzBtor2. The generator constructs a syntax tree recursively, that is, a syntax tree with a depth greater than 1 consists of sub-syntax trees, operators, and some possible parameters (only for indexed operators). When the recursive process reaches the base case, i.e., a leaf node of the syntax tree, it randomly decides to return a (state or input) variable or a constant based on a certain probability. Due to the limitation of the number and sort of variables, if the generator chooses to return a variable, it may encounter a situation where the required leaf node cannot be constructed. Therefore, FuzzBtor2 does not guarantee that the BTOR2 file can be successfully generated, and some parameters would cause the construction to fail. The overall process of constructing a syntax tree is described in Algorithm 1.

4   Experimental Evaluation

Tested Tools. In order to evaluate whether FuzzBtor2 is practical, we choose two state-of-the-art word-level model checkers AVR [17] and Pono [19] as tested tools. Both checkers can take BTOR2 as direct input format, and won the first and third place respectively in the 2020 Hardware Model Checking Competition [2].

Table 1: Overall results.

	Safe	Unsafe	Uniquely Solved	Error	Timeout
AVR (BV+ABV)	16 (11+5)	24 (11+13)	22 (13+9)	157 (78+79)	1 (0+1)
Pono (BV+ABV)	44 (20+24)	27 (13+14)	53 (24+29)	127 (67+60)	0

Table 2: Classification and statistics of error messages. The first type of error message of Pono has been confirmed by its developers.

	BV	ABV	Error Message
AVR	50	47	avr_word_netlist.cpp:912: static Inst* OpInst::create(OpInst::OpType, InstL, int, bool, Inst*, SORT): Assertion '0' failed.
	20	10	reach_y2.cpp:7367: void _y2::y2_API::inst2yices(Inst*, bool): Assertion '0' failed.
	1	3	reach_util.cpp:5785: void reach::Reach::check_correctness(): Assertion '0' failed.
	0	1	reach_y2.cpp:5365: virtual bool _y2::y2_API::get_assignment (Inst*, int&): Assertion 'e->get_sort_type() == bvtype' failed.
	2	3	reach_y2.cpp:7102: void _y2::y2_API::inst2yices(Inst*, bool): Assertion 'res != -1' failed.
	0	5	reach_y2.cpp:7113: void _y2::y2_API::inst2yices(Inst*, bool): Assertion 'res != -1' failed.
	1	3	Error: signal 11: build/bin/reach
	0	1	reach_y2.cpp:1784: void _y2::y2_API::add_gate_constraint (y2_expr &, y2_expr_ptr, std::string, Inst*, bool, bool): Assertion 'rhs != Y2_INVALID_EXPR' failed.
	0	1	reach_y2.cpp:6695: void _y2::y2_API::inst2yices(Inst*, bool): Assertion '0' failed.
	0	1	reach_y2.cpp:6002: y2_expr_ptr_y2::y2_API::create_y2_number (NumInst*): Assertion 'num->get_num() == 0' failed.
	4	3	reach_coi.cpp:943: bool reach::Reach::find_from_minset2 (Solver*, Inst*, InstS&, InstS&, std::set<std::__cxx11::basic_string<char> >&): Assertion 'ufType != "0"' failed.
	0	1	reach_util.cpp:5758: void reach::Reach::check_correctness(): Assertion '0' failed.
Pono	50	43	[boolector] boolector_slice: 'upper' must not be < 'lower'
	2	2	Segmentation fault (core dumped)
	7	7	free(): invalid pointer Aborted (core dumped)
	4	5	vector::_M_range_check: __n (which is 0) >= this->size() (which is 0)
	2	2	double free or corruption (out) Aborted (core dumped)
	2	1	[boolector] boolector_slice: 'upper' must not be >= width of 'exp'

Experimental Setups. We run FuzzBtor2 repeatedly with different parameters to generate a total of 200 test cases, in which 100 cases are array-free, i.e., without array variables (BV), and 100 cases include array variables (ABV). The command of FuzzBtor2 used for the former purpose is fuzzbtor2 --seed i --max-depth 4 --constraints 1 --bv-states 3 --arr-states 0 --max-inputs 3 --candidate-sizes 1..8. To generate BTOR2 models with array variables, the command is fuzzbtor2 --seed i --max-depth 4 --constraints 1 --bv-states 2 --arr-states 1 --max-inputs 3 --candidate-sizes 1..8. And i takes the value from 0 to 99. For every tested checker, the timeout to solve each instance is set to one hour.

Correctness. We use catbtor provided by btor2tools[4] [21] to verify the correctness of outputs of FuzzBtor2. All BTOR2 files generated by FuzzBtor2 pass the check of catbtor, which means all BTOR2 models generated by FuzzBtor2 are legal in syntax. Moreover, neither of the two tested tools (AVR or Pono) returns error messages that are relevant to the syntax issue of input BTOR2 files.

Results. We perform 200 calls to FuzzBtor2 and we get 100 BV test cases and 98 ABV test cases. Two calls for ABV test cases fail due to the situation discussed in sec. 3.2. The file sizes of the generated test cases are not large, with a maximum of 58 lines, a minimum of 22 lines, and an average of 39.2 lines. We use the generated 198 test cases to find bugs of AVR and Pono. All solving processes return results immediately, regardless of success or failure, except a situation where AVR timeouts on an ABV case. Table 1 presents overall statistical results. Neither AVR or Pono performs very well, since most of the test cases (157 vs. 127) trigger their bugs. And Table 2 presents the classification and statistics of error messages returned by tested tools. We encounter 12 and 6 different types of error messages for AVR and Pono respectively. It can be seen from Table 2 that ABV test cases trigger more types of errors than BV, which matches the fact that more code is covered in the process of solving a case in more complex theory. Considering both two tables, AVR performs worse than Pono in the experiments, where AVR solves fewer test cases and returns more types of error messages. Besides, the case where AVR timeouts is solved (Safe) by Pono, and is a BTOR2 file with only 43 lines, so we speculate that a performance issue occurs in AVR.

5   Conclusion

We have presented FuzzBtor2, an open-source tool for the generation of random BTOR2 files, by which the generated test cases can trigger various errors of state-of-the-art word-level model checkers. Several future works are being considered. First, if easy-to-trigger bugs of the tested tools are fixed, we could generate BTOR2 files of larger size and filter out benchmarks that can be used for performance evaluation through experiments. Second, there are some keywords (output, fair, and justice) of BTOR2 that are not supported by current FuzzBtor2, and we can extend the functionality of FuzzBtor2 to support them in future versions. Finally, as stated in sec. 3.2, the set of syntax trees constructed by the generator of FuzzBtor2 is essentially a model checking problem, independent of BTOR2 format. Therefore, it would be useful to print model checking problems randomly generated in other formats such as SMV [8] and VMT [12].

---

[4] https://github.com/boolector/btor2tools

Data-Availability Statement The artifact that supports the experimental results is available in Zenodo with the identifier `https://doi.org/10.5281/zenodo.7234681` [24].

References

1. International satisfiability modulo theories competition, `https://smt-comp.github.io/previous.html`
2. Hardware model checking competition 2020 (2020), `http://fmv.jku.at/hwmcc20/`
3. Barrett, C., Fontaine, P., Tinelli, C.: The SMT-LIB Standard: Version 2.6. Tech. rep., Department of Computer Science, The University of Iowa (2017), `www.SMT-LIB.org`
4. Bernardini, A., Ecker, W., Schlichtmann, U.: Where formal verification can help in functional safety analysis. In: 2016 IEEE/ACM International Conference on Computer-Aided Design (ICCAD). pp. 1–8. ACM (2016)
5. Biere, A.: Tutorial on world-level model checking. In: 2020 Formal Methods in Computer Aided Design. IEEE, Haifa, Israel (2020)
6. Biere, A., Cimatti, A., Clarke, E.M., Fujita, M., Zhu, Y.: Symbolic model checking using sat procedures instead of bdds. In: Proceedings of the 36th annual ACM/IEEE Design Automation Conference. pp. 317–320 (1999)
7. Bjesse, P.: Word level bitwidth reduction for unbounded hardware model checking. Formal Methods in System Design **35**(1), 56–72 (2009)
8. Bozzano, M., Cavada, R., Cimatti, A., Dorigatti, M., Griggio, A., Mariotti, A., Micheli, A., Mover, S., Roveri, M., Tonetta, S.: nuXmv 2.0. 0 user manual (2019)
9. Bradley, A.R.: Sat-based model checking without unrolling. In: International Workshop on Verification, Model Checking, and Abstract Interpretation. pp. 70–87. Springer (2011)
10. Bryant, R.E.: Graph-based algorithms for boolean function manipulation. Computers, IEEE Transactions on **100**, 677–691 (1986)
11. Cavada, R., Cimatti, A., Dorigatti, M., Griggio, A., Mariotti, A., Micheli, A., Mover, S., Roveri, M., Tonetta, S.: The nuxmv symbolic model checker. In: Proc. 26th Int. Conf. on Computer Aided Verification. pp. 334–342. Springer, Vienna, Austria (2014)
12. Cimatti, A., Griggio, A., Tonetta, S.: The vmt-lib language and tools. arXiv preprint arXiv:2109.12821 (2021)
13. Daniel, J., Cimatti, A., Griggio, A., Tonetta, S., Mover, S.: Infinite-state liveness-to-safety via implicit abstraction and well-founded relations. In: Proc. 28th Int. Conf. on Computer Aided Verification. pp. 271–291. Springer (2016)
14. Eén, N., Sörensson, N.: An extensible sat-solver. In: International conference on theory and applications of satisfiability testing. pp. 502–518. Springer (2003)
15. Embedded Systems Unit, Digital Industry Center, Fondazione Bruno Kessler: vmt-tools (2022), `http://es-static.fbk.eu/people/griggio/ic3ia/vmt-tools-latest.tar.gz`
16. Goel, A., Sakallah, K.: Model checking of verilog rtl using ic3 with syntax-guided abstraction. In: NASA Formal Methods Symposium. pp. 166–185. Springer (2019)
17. Goel, A., Sakallah, K.: Avr: Abstractly verifying reachability. In: Tools and Algorithms for the Construction and Analysis of Systems. pp. 413–422. Springer (2020)
18. Li, J., Zhu, S., Zhang, Y., Pu, G., Vardi, M.Y.: Safety model checking with complementary approximations. In: 2017 IEEE/ACM International Conference on Computer-Aided Design (ICCAD). pp. 95–100. IEEE (2017)

19. Mann, M., Irfan, A., Lonsing, F., Yang, Y., Zhang, H., Brown, K., Gupta, A., Barrett, C.: Pono: a flexible and extensible smt-based model checker. In: Proc. 33th Int. Conf. on Computer Aided Verification. pp. 461–474. Springer (2021)
20. McMillan, K.L.: Interpolation and sat-based model checking. In: International Conference on Computer Aided Verification. pp. 1–13. Springer (2003)
21. Niemetz, A., Preiner, M., Wolf, C., Biere, A.: Btor2 , btormc and boolector 3.0. In: Proc. 30th Int. Conf. on Computer Aided Verification. LNCS, vol. 10981, pp. 587–595. Springer, Oxford, UK (2018)
22. Weber, T., Conchon, S., Déharbe, D., Heizmann, M., Niemetz, A., Reger, G.: The smt competition 2015–2018. Journal on Satisfiability, Boolean Modeling and Computation **11**(1), 221–259 (2019)
23. Welp, T., Kuehlmann, A.: Qf bv model checking with property directed reachability. In: 2013 Design, Automation & Test in Europe Conference & Exhibition (DATE). pp. 791–796. IEEE (2013)
24. Xiao, S.: Artifact – FuzzBtor2: A Random Generator of Word-Level Model Checking Problems in Btor2 Format (2022). https://doi.org/10.5281/zenodo.7234681

Eclipse ESCET™: The Eclipse Supervisory Control Engineering Toolkit

W.J. Fokkink[1,2]($\boxtimes$), M.A. Goorden[3,4], D. Hendriks[5,6], D.A. van Beek[1], A.T. Hofkamp[1], F.F.H. Reijnen[7], L.F.P. Etman[1], L. Moormann[1], J.M. van de Mortel-Fronczak[1], M.A. Reniers[1], J.E. Rooda[1], L.J. van der Sanden[5], R.R.H. Schiffelers[1,8], S.B. Thuijsman[1], J.J. Verbakel[1], J.A. Vogel[4]

[1] Eindhoven University of Technology, Eindhoven, The Netherlands
[2] Vrije Universiteit Amsterdam, Amsterdam, The Netherlands
w.j.fokkink@vu.nl
[3] Aalborg University, Aalborg, Denmark
[4] Rijkswaterstaat, Utrecht, The Netherlands
[5] TNO-ESI, Eindhoven, The Netherlands
[6] Radboud University, Nijmegen, The Netherlands
[7] Vanderlande Industries, Veghel, The Netherlands
[8] ASML, Veldhoven, The Netherlands

Abstract. The Eclipse Supervisory Control Engineering Toolkit (ESCET™) is an open-source project to provide a model-based approach and toolkit for developing supervisory controllers , targeting their entire engineering process. It supports synthesis-based engineering of supervisory controllers for discrete-event systems, combining model-based engineering with computer-aided design to automatically generate correct-by-construction controllers. At its heart is supervisory controller synthesis, a formal technique for the automatic derivation of supervisory controllers from the unrestricted system behavior and system requirements. Vital for the future development of these techniques and tools is the ESCET project's open environment, allowing industry and academia to collaborate on creating an industrial-strength toolkit. We report on some crucial developments of the toolkit in the context of research projects with Rijkswaterstaat and ASML that have considerably improved its capability to deal with the complexity of real-life systems as well as its usability.

1 Introduction

A supervisory controller, supervisor for short, coordinates the behavior of a cyber-physical system according to discrete-event observations of its system behavior. Based on such observations, the supervisor decides which events the system can safely perform and which events must be disabled, because they would lead to violations of requirements or to a blocking state. Engineering of supervisors is a challenging task, due to the high complexity of real-life discrete-event systems.

Supervisory control theory [21] underpins a model-based technique for automatically deriving a model of a supervisor from models of the uncontrolled system behavior and the system's requirements, such as functional or safety-related requirements that intend to rule out all undesired behavior. This is achieved by

S. Sankaranarayanan and N. Sharygina (Eds.): TACAS 2023, LNCS 13994, pp. 44–52, 2023.
https://doi.org/10.1007/978-3-031-30820-8_6

disabling *controllable* (output) events, such as starting a motor. Supervisors exert no control over *uncontrollable* (input) events, such as sensor reports.

The Eclipse Supervisory Control Engineering Toolkit (ESCET^{TM}, pronounced *èsèt*) project,[1][2] provides a model-based approach and toolkit for the development of supervisors. It targets the entire engineering process for the development of supervisors, including modeling, synthesis, simulation-based validation and visualization, formal verification, real-time testing, and code generation. This entire process is supported by CIF [1],[3] featuring an automata-based modeling language for convenient specification of large-scale systems, and tools that support synthesis-based engineering (SBE). SBE is an engineering approach to design and implement supervisors that combines model-based engineering with computer-aided design to produce correct-by-construction controllers, by automating the engineering process as much as possible. While not detailed further in this paper, the ESCET project also comprises Chi [28], a hybrid language and toolset for modeling and simulation, developed by the same research group that developed CIF, and the ToolDef scripting language for the definition and execution of model-based toolchains, useful for combining different ESCET tools.[4]

The ESCET project, an Eclipse Foundation open-source project since 2020, builds upon decades of research and tool development at Eindhoven University of Technology. Vital for the evolvement from an academic into an industrially applicable toolkit are the years-long ongoing research collaborations with industry, including Rijkswaterstaat [7], ASML [27], and Vanderlande [29]. Rijkswaterstaat, part of the Dutch Ministry of Infrastructure and Water Management, is responsible for infrastructure in the Netherlands, including roads, bridges, tunnels, and waterway locks. ASML is an innovation leader in the semiconductor industry, providing chipmakers with all they need to mass produce patterns on silicon through lithography. Vanderlande is a market leader in logistic process automation for the warehousing, airport and parcel sectors. The quality of supervisory control software for such systems impacts their availability and reliability. Synthesis-based engineering allows for automation, modularization, and standardization, increasing quality and evolvability and decreasing life-cycle costs.

With the move to the Eclipse Foundation, and supported by the Eclipse Foundation's principles of transparency, openness, meritocracy and vendor-neutrality, the ESCET project aims to be an open environment and a growing community. It allows interested parties, such as academic and applied research institutes, industrial partners and tool vendors, to collaborate on and profit from further tool development for the model-based construction of supervisors. Furthermore, the project's open nature allows any vendor to develop commercial tool support.

We report on some crucial developments of the toolkit that have considerably improved its capability to deal with the complexity of real-life systems as well as its usability, as shown by the case studies reported in Section 5.

---

[1] See https://eclipse.org/escet.

[2] 'Eclipse', 'Eclipse ESCET' and 'ESCET' are trademarks of Eclipse Foundation, Inc.

[3] See https://eclipse.org/escet/cif.

[4] See https://eclipse.org/escet/chi and https://eclipse.org/escet/tooldef.

2   Supervisory Controller Synthesis

Figure 1 depicts the general system structure for supervisory control. A cyber-
physical system consists of mechanical
components to be controlled. Actuators
drive their operation, while sensors indicate their status. Resource control provides low-level control, often offering
more abstract actuator and sensor signals
for higher levels of control to use. Supervisors ensure actuator signals at lower
layers (the *plant*) that would violate requirements are disabled. Large systems
may be divided into (layers of) subsystems, and supervisors can be present at
each level, coordinating lower-level subsystems (only a single layer is depicted).
A (sub)system is often controlled by a
human operator through a graphical user
interface, or part of a larger system to
which it is connected by an interface.

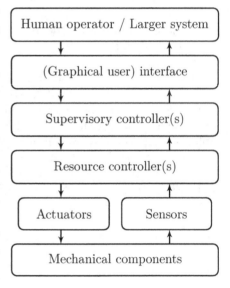

Fig. 1. Structure of supervisory control.

Supervisory controller synthesis [21,33] automatically generates a correct-by-
construction supervisor model for a discrete-event system, given precise descriptions of the behavior of the plant components as well as the (safety) requirements
for the overall plant behavior. These can be specified conveniently as extended finite automata (EFAs), i.e., automata with variables, guards and updates, possibly
carrying invariants that restrict the state space [13].

Synthesis considers the synchronous product of the plant automata together
with the requirement automata. That is, these automata synchronize on shared
events, meaning these events must be executed simultaneously. If an event is
missing in the local state of any plant automaton, or is restricted by a plant
invariant, it is absent from the overall system state, and it is considered physically
impossible. If, on the other hand, an event is missing only in the states of
requirement automata, or is restricted by a requirement invariant, it is physically
possible but must be disabled by the synthesized supervisor to ensure *safety*.

Controllable events (such as output signals to actuators) can be prevented
by a supervisor, but uncontrollable events (such as input signals from sensors)
cannot. To ensure *controllability*, if an uncontrollable event must be prevented,
the supervisor makes the system state where it occurs unreachable by disabling
all controllable events leading to it. Moreover, if an uncontrollable event leads to
such a state, the origin state of this event must be made unreachable too.

If safety of, for instance, a drawbridge is ensured by forcing it to remain raised
forever, it is useless for road traffic. Therefore states of the plant and requirement
EFAs can be marked, for instance states where the bridge deck is lowered, the
barriers are open, and the signals are green. A marked state in the synchronous

product means all individual plant components are in a marked local state, in this case allowing traffic to proceed over the bridge. The supervisor must guarantee that the plant can always reach a marked state, by disabling (events leading to) states that violate this property. Such a supervisor is said to be *nonblocking*.

Supervisory controller synthesis ensures *safety*, *controllability* and *nonblockingness* of a system with respect to its requirements, accounting for all possible behavior, also disabling events that lead to problems such as blocking behavior or requirement violations much later in the system's execution. It does so by restricting as little behavior as possible, thus ensuring *maximal permissiveness*.

Next to ESCET toolkit, other supervisory controller synthesis tools include DESTool [16], DESUMA [25], Supremica [12], and TCT [6]. For a comparison between these tools see [24]. The ESCET toolkit can be used to specify various different models during the entire development process, including simulation models, as it has a rich set of concepts. This prevents having to use multiple languages. It has a strong focus on industrial application, with, e.g., modeling convenience, efficient algorithms, and checking for common mistakes.

3   Synthesis-based Engineering Process

Figure 2 shows ESCET's synthesis-based engineering process. It starts with a model-based specification, consisting of plant and requirement models, modeled as EFAs and/or invariants. To these models, supervisory controller synthesis is applied, resulting in a model of the supervisor. The ESCET toolkit supports synthesis both with its own synthesis tools, and by a transformation to Supremica.

Synthesis ensures that all specified requirements are satisfied by the synthesized supervisor. Verification, such as model checking, supported through transformations to UPPAAL [2] and mCRL2 [3], can be used to check other requirements not yet supported by synthesis, including liveness guarantees or timing requirements. Validation, supported by ESCET's automated or interactive simulation and visualization, helps to determine whether the specified requirements, and thus the supervisor, achieve the desired system behavior.

An implementation of the controller can be obtained automatically from a model of the supervisor, by generating code for its control software. The ESCET toolkit supports code generation for multiple languages and platforms, including Java, C, Simulink, and PLC code (IEC standard 61131-3) for multiple vendors.

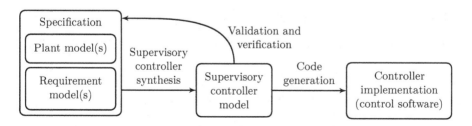

Fig. 2. Simplified representation of ESCET's synthesis-based engineering process.

4   Technical Improvements

We describe recent improvements and novel techniques that have been vital in making supervisory controller synthesis applicable to industrial-size cyber-physical systems. Some have already been integrated into the ESCET toolkit, while others are being integrated or are planned to be integrated.

Symbolic synthesis The ESCET toolkit is based on the symbolic supervisory controller synthesis algorithm from Ouedraogo et al. [19]. It iteratively strengthens guard predicates on transitions so that forbidden states become unreachable in the controlled plant. This represents a major step forward for the industrial applicability of supervisory controller synthesis, by allowing for synthesis of plants and requirements intuitively modeled as EFAs.

The use of EFAs also opens up the possibility to extract and represent the synthesized supervisor more compactly and intuitively [15]. The ESCET toolkit represents the supervisor model as the collection of the provided plant and requirement models together with the addition of a single EFA containing a strengthened guard for each controllable event.

BDD Data Structure The Binary Decision Diagram (BDD) data structure allows to efficiently and symbolically represent and manipulate predicates representing (parts of) state spaces [14]. Its use in ESCET's symbolic supervisory controller synthesis algorithm leads to major reductions of state space representations and computation times, which is essential for scalability.

Vital to the memory and running time characteristics of Reduced Ordered BDD representations and manipulations, as used by the ESCET toolkit, is the ordering of the Boolean variables [30]. Heuristic variable ordering algorithms that exploit the inherent structure of the system modeled as EFAs are able to significantly reduce the synthesis effort [11], especially for larger inputs, making synthesis applicable to more complex systems.

Multilevel Synthesis Contrary to monolithic synthesis, where only a single supervisor is synthesized, with multilevel synthesis [10] the plant components and requirements are grouped together into a hierarchical structure, and a separate supervisor is synthesized for each group. This allows to distribute the control problem over multiple cooperating supervisors, which together are significantly smaller than one monolithic supervisor. By encoding relations between plant components and requirements in a design structure matrix [5], and algorithmically reordering its rows and columns to place tightly coupled plant components side by side [32], a suitable multilevel structure can be obtained. Compared to monolithic synthesis, this can for certain systems substantially reduce synthesis effort [8], enabling synthesis for much larger variants of such systems.

Avoiding Nonblockingness Checks Although the local supervisors in multilevel synthesis are nonblocking, the overall supervisor may not be. A global nonblockingness check can be used to guarantee that all local supervisors can reach a marked state at the same moment in time, but is often expensive, nullifying much of the gains obtained through applying multilevel synthesis. However, in a dependency graph that encodes which plant components by means of requirements depend on state of other plant components to perform certain events, plant components do not give rise to blocking behavior if they are not part of an infinite path [9]. For certain systems, using such graphs, the global nonblockingness checks may be skipped entirely, or may be reduced to consider less subsystems.

Symmetry Reduction Real-life systems tend to contain a significant number of similar components, that for instance only differ by the instantiation of some of the parameters or their physical locations within the overall system. Such symmetries can be exploited to reduce the number of plant and requirement automata needed in the synthesis process, further reducing the synthesis effort [18].

5 Case Studies and Applications

Rijkswaterstaat Initially the collaboration with Rijkswaterstaat focused on generating control software with supervisory controller synthesis for bridges, waterway locks, and storm surge barriers. Notable case studies are the Algera complex, comprising a bascule bridge, a waterway lock and two storm surge barriers in the river Hollandse IJssel [22], and the Oisterwijksebaanbrug, a rotating bridge in Tilburg [23]. For the latter, a fault-tolerant controller was synthesized, from which PLC code was generated, which passed the regular site acceptance test.

Recent case studies target road tunnels, notably the Eerste Heinenoord tunnel [18] and the Swalmen tunnel [17], and roadside systems [31]. For the Swalmen tunnel, a digital twin, a 3D digital copy of a physical system, was conveniently constructed from the plant and requirement models. Combined with visualization, this allows simulation of the system in a setting close to real life.

ASML A prominent result of the collaboration with ASML is the use of the ESCET toolkit in a toolkit from another Eclipse Foundation open-source project, the Eclipse Logistic Specification and Analysis Toolkit (LSAT^{TM}) [26]. The LSAT toolkit is used at ASML to create fully calibrated models of subsystems of a wafer scanner, responsible for transporting wafers in and out of the scanner and performing preprocessing steps before the wafer is being exposed on the wafer stage subsystem. The LSAT toolkit exploits ESCET's supervisory controller synthesis to compute valid orderings of logistics activities, while maintaining the maximum freedom to subsequently perform scheduling on the synthesis result to compute a supervisor that optimizes productivity [20].

6 Conclusions

The ESCET project and toolkit support synthesis-based engineering to efficiently generate high-quality correct-by-construction supervisors. The toolkit is being applied to complex industrial systems in different domains. The project's open environment enables effective collaboration between industry, researchers and tool vendors. Owing to positive experiences with the ESCET toolkit, Rijkswaterstaat is seriously considering whether its document-based development process for control software could be adapted to one based on SBE with the ESCET toolkit.

7   Data-Availability Statement

The artifact that supports this paper is available at Zenodo under identifier doi:10.5281/zenodo.7296616 [4]. It contains Eclipse ESCET v0.7 for Linux. However, the authors prefer that the Eclipse ESCET toolkit is downloaded directly from the Eclipse Foundation, where the latest version of the toolkit is available for multiple platforms.[5]

References

1. van Beek, D.A., Fokkink, W.J., Hendriks, D., Hofkamp, A.T., Markovski, J., van de Mortel-Fronczak, J.M., Reniers, M.A.: CIF 3: Model-based engineering of supervisory controllers. In: Proc. 20th Conference on Tools and Algorithms for the Construction and Analysis of Systems (TACAS). LNCS, vol. 8413, pp. 575–580. Springer (2014). https://doi.org/10.1007/978-3-642-54862-8_48
2. Behrmann, G., David, A., Larsen, K.G., Håkansson, J., Pettersson, P., Yi, W., Hendriks, M.: UPPAAL 4.0. In: Proc. 3rd Conference on the Quantitative Evaluation of Systems (QEST). pp. 125–126. IEEE (2006). https://doi.org/10.1109/QEST.2006.59
3. Bunte, O., Groote, J.F., Keiren, J.J.A., Laveaux, M., Neele, T., de Vink, E.P., Wesselink, W., Wijs, A., Willemse, T.A.C.: The mCRL2 toolset for analysing concurrent systems - Improvements in expressivity and usability. In: Proc. 25th Conference on Tools and Algorithms for the Construction and Analysis of Systems (TACAS). LNCS, vol. 11428, pp. 21–39. Springer (2019). https://doi.org/10.1007/978-3-030-17465-1_2
4. Eclipse Foundation: Eclipse ESCET v0.7 for Linux (2022). https://doi.org/10.5281/zenodo.7296616
5. Eppinger, S.D., Browning, T.R.: Design Structure Matrix Methods and Applications. MIT Press (2012)
6. Feng, L., Wonham, W.M.: TCT: A computation tool for supervisory control synthesis. In: Proc. 8th Workshop on Discrete Event Systems (WODES). pp. 388–389. IEEE (2006). https://doi.org/10.1109/WODES.2006.382399
7. Fokkink, W.J., Goorden, M.A., van de Mortel-Fronczak, J.M., Reijnen, F.F.H., Rooda, J.E.: Supervisor synthesis: Bridging theory and practice. Computer **55**(10), 48–54 (2022). https://doi.org/10.1109/MC.2021.3134934
8. Goorden, M.A., van de Mortel-Fronczak, J.M., Reniers, M.A., Fokkink, W.J., Rooda, J.E.: Structuring multilevel discrete-event systems with dependence structure matrices. IEEE Transactions on Automatic Control **65**(4), 1625–1639 (2020). https://doi.org/10.1109/TAC.2019.2928119
9. Goorden, M.A., van de Mortel-Fronczak, J.M., Reniers, M.A., Fabian, M., Fokkink, W.J., Rooda, J.E.: Model properties for efficient synthesis of nonblocking modular supervisors. Control Engineering Practice **112**, 104830 (2021). https://doi.org/10.1016/j.conengprac.2021.104830
10. Komenda, J., Masopust, T., van Schuppen, J.H.: Control of an engineering-structured multilevel discrete-event system. In: Proc. 13th Workshop on Discrete Event Systems (WODES). pp. 103–108. IEEE (2016). https://doi.org/10.1109/WODES.2016.7497833

---

[5] See https://eclipse.org/escet/download.html.

11. Lousberg, S., Thuijsman, S.B., Reniers, M.A.: DSM-based variable ordering heuristic for reduced computational effort of symbolic supervisor synthesis. IFAC-PapersOnLine **53**(4), 429–436 (2020). https://doi.org/10.1016/j.ifacol.2021.04.058
12. Malik, R., Åkesson, K., Flordal, H., Fabian, M.: Supremica–An efficient tool for large-scale discrete event systems. IFAC-PapersOnLine **50**(1), 5794–5799 (2017). https://doi.org/10.1016/j.ifacol.2017.08.427
13. Markovski, J., van Beek, D., Theunissen, R., Jacobs, K., Rooda, J.: A state-based framework for supervisory control synthesis and verification. In: Proc. 49th IEEE Conference on Decision and Control (CDC). pp. 3481–3486 (2010). https://doi.org/10.1109/CDC.2010.5717095
14. McMillan, K.L.: Symbolic Model Checking. Springer (1993). https://doi.org/10.1007/978-1-4615-3190-6
15. Miremadi, S., Åkesson, K., Lennartson, B.: Extraction and representation of a supervisor using guards in extended finite automata. In: Proc. 9th Workshop on Discrete Event Systems (WODES). pp. 193–199. IEEE (2008). https://doi.org/10.1109/WODES.2008.4605944
16. Moor, T., Schmidt, K., Perk, S.: libFAUDES — An open source C++ library for discrete event systems. In: Proc. 9th Workshop on Discrete Event Systems (WODES). pp. 125–130. IEEE (2008). https://doi.org/10.1109/WODES.2008.4605933
17. Moormann, L., van Hegelsom, J., Maessen, P., van de Mortel-Fronczak, J.M., Fokkink, W.J., Rooda, J.E.: Advantages of using digital twins in the validation of road tunnel supervisory controllers. In: Proc. ITA/AITES World Tunnel Congress (WTC). pp. 573–578 (2022)
18. Moormann, L., van de Mortel-Fronczak, J.M., Fokkink, W.J., Maessen, P., Rooda, J.E.: Supervisory control synthesis for large-scale systems with isomorphisms. Control Engineering Practice **115**, 104902 (2021). https://doi.org/10.1016/j.conengprac.2021.104902
19. Ouedraogo, L., Kumar, R., Malik, R., Åkesson, K.: Nonblocking and safe control of discrete-event systems modeled as extended finite automata. IEEE Transactions on Automation Science and Engineering **8**(3), 560–569 (2011). https://doi.org/10.1109/TASE.2011.2124457
20. van Putten, B.J.C., van der Sanden, L.J., Reniers, M.A., Voeten, J.P.M., Schiffelers, R.R.H.: Supervisor synthesis and throughput optimization of partially-controllable manufacturing systems. Discrete Event Dynamic Systems **31**, 103–135 (2021). https://doi.org/10.1007/s10626-020-00325-x
21. Ramadge, P.J., Wonham, W.M.: Supervisory control of a class of discrete event processes. SIAM Journal on Control and Optimization **25**(1), 206–230 (1987). https://doi.org/10.1137/0325013
22. Reijnen, F.F.H., Goorden, M.A., van de Mortel-Fronczak, J.M., Rooda, J.E.: Modeling for supervisor synthesis - a lock-bridge combination case study. Discret. Event Dyn. Syst. **30**(3), 499–532 (2020). https://doi.org/10.1007/s10626-020-00314-0
23. Reijnen, F.F.H., Leliveld, E.B., van de Mortel-Fronczak, J.M., van Dinther, J., Rooda, J.E., Fokkink, W.J.: Synthesized fault-tolerant supervisory controllers, with an application to a rotating bridge. Computers in Industry **130**, 103473 (2021). https://doi.org/10.1016/j.compind.2021.103473
24. Reniers, M.A., van de Mortel-Fronczak, J.M.: An engineering perspective on model-based design of supervisors. IFAC-PapersOnLine **51**(7), 257–264 (2018). https://doi.org/10.1016/j.ifacol.2018.06.310
25. Ricker, L., Lafortune, S., Genc, S.: DESUMA: A tool integrating GIDDES and UMDES. In: Proc. 8th Workshop on Discrete Event Systems (WODES). pp. 392–393. IEEE (2006). https://doi.org/10.1109/WODES.2006.382402

26. van der Sanden, L.J., Blankenstein, Y., Schiffelers, R.R.H., Voeten, J.P.M.: LSAT: Specification and analysis of product logistics in flexible manufacturing systems. In: Proc. 17th Conference on Automation Science and Engineering (CASE). pp. 1–8. IEEE (2021). https://doi.org/10.1109/CASE49439.2021.9551412

27. van der Sanden, L.J., Reniers, M.A., Geilen, M.C.W., Basten, T., Jacobs, J., Voeten, J.P.M., Schiffelers, R.R.H.: Modular model-based supervisory controller design for wafer logistics in lithography machines. In: Proc. 18th Conference on Model Driven Engineering Languages and Systems (MODELS). pp. 416–425. IEEE (2015). https://doi.org/10.1109/MODELS.2015.7338273

28. Schiffelers, R.R.H., van Beek, D.A., Man, K.L., Reniers, M.A., Rooda, J.E.: A hybrid language for modeling, simulation and verification. IFAC Proceedings Volumes **36**(6), 199–204 (2003). https://doi.org/10.1016/S1474-6670(17)36431-5

29. Swartjes, L., van Beek, D.A., Fokkink, W.J., van Eekelen, J.A.W.M.: Model-based design of supervisory controllers for baggage handling systems. Simul. Model. Pract. Theory **78**, 28–50 (2017). https://doi.org/10.1016/j.simpat.2017.08.005

30. Thuijsman, S.B., Hendriks, D., Theunissen, R., Reniers, M.A., Schiffelers, R.R.H.: Computational effort of bdd-based supervisor synthesis of extended finite automata. In: Proc. 15th International Conference on Automation Science and Engineering (CASE). pp. 486–493 (2019). https://doi.org/10.1109/COASE.2019.8843327

31. Verbakel, J.J., Vos de Wael, M.E.W., van de Mortel-Fronczak, J.M., Fokkink, W.J., Rooda, J.E.: A configurator for supervisory controllers of roadside systems. In: Proc. 17th Conference on Automation Science and Engineering (CASE). pp. 784–791. IEEE (2021). https://doi.org/10.1109/CASE49439.2021.9551485

32. Wilschut, T., Etman, L.F.P., Rooda, J.E., Adan, I.J.B.F.: Multilevel flow-based Markov clustering for design structure matrices. Journal of Mechanical Design **139**(12) (2017). https://doi.org/10.1115/1.4037626

33. Wonham, W.M., Cai, K., Rudie, K.: Supervisory control of discrete-event systems: A brief history. Annual Reviews in Control **45**, 250–256 (2018). https://doi.org/10.1016/j.arcontrol.2018.03.002

Combinatorial Optimization/Theorem Proving

New Core-Guided and Hitting Set Algorithms for Multi-Objective Combinatorial Optimization

João Cortes ⓘ, Inês Lynce ⓘ, and
Vasco Manquinho[✉] ⓘ

INESC-ID - Instituto Superior Técnico, Universidade de Lisboa, Lisbon, Portugal
{joao.o.cortes,ines.lynce,vasco.manquinho}@tecnico.ulisboa.pt

Abstract. In the last decade, numerous algorithms for single-objective Boolean optimization have been proposed that rely on the iterative usage of a highly effective Propositional Satisfiability (SAT) solver. But the use of SAT solvers in Multi-Objective Combinatorial Optimization (MOCO) algorithms is still scarce. Due to this shortage of efficient tools for MOCO, many real-world applications formulated as multi-objective are simplified to single-objective, using either a linear combination or a lexicographic ordering of the objective functions to optimize.

In this paper, we extend the state of the art of MOCO solvers with two novel unsatisfiability-based algorithms. The first is a core-guided MOCO solver. The second is a hitting set-based MOCO solver. Experimental results in several sets of benchmark instances show that our new unsatisfiability-based algorithms can outperform state-of-the-art SAT-based algorithms for MOCO.

1 Introduction

Whenever facing a decision, there is often a set of objectives to optimize. For instance, when making a vacation plan with multiple destinations, one wants to minimize both the time spent in airports and the money spent on plane tickets. However, seldom can one obtain a solution that optimizes all objectives at once. It is usually the case that decreasing the value of an objective results in increasing the value of another. This occurs in many application domains [17,22,32].

In order to deal with multi-objective problems, we usually cast them into single-objective ones. For example, this can be achieved by defining a linear combination of the objective functions. Other option is to define a lexicographic order of the objectives [24], but this may result in unbalanced solutions where the first function is minimized while the remaining ones have a very high value.

In the multi-objective scenario, we are looking for *Pareto-optimal* solutions, i.e. all solutions for which decreasing the value of one objective function increases the value of another. After determining the set of all such solutions, known as *Pareto front*, one can select a representative subset and present it to the user [9].

Frameworks based on stochastic search have been developed to approximate the Pareto front of Multi-Objective Combinatorial Optimization (MOCO) problems [6,33]. Several algorithms were also proposed based on iterative calls to

© The Author(s) 2023
S. Sankaranarayanan and N. Sharygina (Eds.): TACAS 2023, LNCS 13994, pp. 55–73, 2023.
https://doi.org/10.1007/978-3-031-30820-8_7

a satisfiability checker, such as the Opportunistic Improvement Algorithm [8], among others [16]. Additionally, the Guided-Improvement Algorithm (GIA) [26] is implemented in the optimization engine of Satisfiability Modulo Theories (SMT) solver Z3 for finding Pareto optimal solutions of SMT formulas. New algorithms have also been proposed based on the enumeration of Minimal Correction Subsets (MCSs) [30] or P-minimal models [28]. A common thread to these algorithms is that they follow a SAT-UNSAT approach. A path diversification method has also been proposed where unsatisfiable cores are identified in order to cut the path generation procedure [31]. More recently, Maximum Satisfiability (MaxSAT) approaches have been used for MOCO [12,10], but the proposed algorithms are limited to two objective functions.

In this paper, we propose two new algorithms for MOCO. The first algorithm is a core-guided approach that relies on encodings of the objective functions to effectively cut the search space in each SAT call. Additionally, we also propose a hitting set-based approach where the previous core-guided algorithm is used to enumerate a multi-objective hitting set. Note that these are the first algorithms for MOCO that take full advantage of unsatisfiable core identification over several objectives, as well as the first MOCO algorithm based on an hitting set approach, taking advantage of the duality between Pareto-MCSs [30] and unsatisfiable cores over several objectives. Experimental results show that the new algorithms proposed in this paper are complementary to the existing SAT-based algorithms for MOCO, thus extending the state-of-the-art tools for MOCO based on SAT technology.

The paper is organized as follows. Section 2 defines the MOCO problem and the standard notation used in the remainder of the paper. Next, Sections 3 and 4 describe the new core-guided and hitting set-based algorithms for MOCO. Experimental results and comparisons with other SAT-based algorithms are provided in Section 5. Finally, conclusions are presented in Section 6.

2   Preliminaries

We start with the definitions that fall in the SAT domain. Next, we introduce the definitions specific to solving the MOCO problem.

Definition 1 (Boolean Satisfiability problem (SAT)). *Consider a set of Boolean variables $V = \{x_1, \ldots, x_n\}$. A literal is either a variable $x_i \in V$ or its negation $\neg x_i \equiv \bar{x}_i$. A clause is a set of literals. A Conjunctive Normal Form (CNF) formula ϕ is a set of clauses. A model ν is a set of literals, such that if $x_i \in \nu$, then $\bar{x}_i \notin \nu$ and vice versa.*

The truth value of ϕ, denoted by $\nu(\phi)$, is a function of ν, and is defined recursively by the following rules. First, the truth value of a literal is covered by $\nu(x_i) = \top$, if $x_i \in \nu$, $\nu(x_i) = \bot$, if $\bar{x}_i \in \nu$ and $\nu(\neg x_i) = \neg \nu(x_i)$. Secondly, a clause c is true iff it contains at least one literal assigned to true. Finally, formula ϕ is true iff it contains only true clauses,

$$\nu(\phi) \equiv \bigwedge_{c \in \phi} \nu(c), \quad \nu(c) \equiv \bigvee_{l \in c} \nu(l). \tag{1}$$

The model ν satisfies the formula ϕ iff $\nu(\phi)$ is true. In that case, ν is $(\phi\text{-})$feasible.

Given a CNF formula ϕ, the SAT problem is to decide if there is any model ν that satisfies it or prove that no such model exists.

Our algorithms require a SAT solver to be used as an Oracle. If the formula is satisfiable, then it returns a satisfiable assignment. Otherwise, the SAT solver returns with an explanation of unsatisfiability, called a *core*.

Definition 2 (Core κ). *Given a CNF formula ϕ, we say a formula κ is an* unsatisfiable core *of ϕ iff $\kappa \subseteq \phi$ and $\kappa \vDash \bot$.*

Definition 3 (SAT solver). *Let ϕ be a CNF formula and α a conjunction of unit clauses. We call ϕ the* main formula *and α the* assumptions*. A SAT solver solves the CNF[1] instance of the* working formula $\omega = \phi \cup \alpha$*, i.e. decides on the satisfiability of ω.*

A query to the solver is denoted by $\phi\text{-SAT}(\alpha)$. The value returned is a pair (ν, κ), containing a feasible model ν and a core of assumptions κ, i.e. a subset of the assumptions α contained in some core *of ω. If the working formula ω is not satisfiable, ν does not exist, and the call returns $(\emptyset, \bullet)$. If ω is satisfiable, the call returns $(\bullet, \emptyset)$.*

Definition 4 (Relaxing/Tightening a formula). *Given ϕ, a formula ψ is a* relaxation *of ϕ iff $\phi \vDash \psi$. We also say ψ relaxes ϕ. Conversely, ϕ tightens ψ.*

Next we review Pseudo-Boolean formulas and optimization and define the MOCO problem.

Definition 5 (Pseudo-Boolean function, clause, formula (PB)). *To any linear function $\{0, 1\}^n \to \mathbb{N}$, given by*

$$g(\boldsymbol{x}) = g(x_1 \ldots x_n) = \sum_i w_i x_i \quad w_i \in \mathbb{N}, \quad x_i \in V, \tag{2}$$

we call an (integer linear) PB function*. Expressions like $g(\boldsymbol{x}) \bowtie k$, $\bowtie \in \{\leq, \geq, =\}$, are called* PB clauses*. A* PB formula *is a set of PB clauses. For some model $\nu : V \to \{0, 1\}$, let $\boldsymbol{x}$ be the Boolean tuple $\nu(V) \equiv (\nu(x_1), \ldots, \nu(x_n))$. Given a formula ϕ, a model ν is said $(\phi\text{-})$feasible if it satisfies every clause in ϕ. The set of Boolean tuples $Z(\phi) = \{\boldsymbol{x} = \nu(V) \in \{0, 1\}^n : \nu(\phi)\}$ is called* feasible space *of the formula ϕ, and its elements $\boldsymbol{x}$ are called* feasible points*. Any subset of the feasible space is called a ϕ-feasible set.*

Definition 6 (Pseudo-Boolean Optimization (PBO)). *Let ϕ be a PB formula, and f be a PB function. Then, minimize the value of the objective f over the feasible space $Z(\phi)$ the formula ϕ. That is,*

$$\text{find } \underset{\boldsymbol{x} \in Z(\phi)}{\arg \min} f. \tag{3}$$

---

[1] We may use a PB formula (Definition 5) and assume it is translated to CNF.

Multi-objective optimization generalizes PBO and builds upon a criterion of comparison (or order) of tuples of numbers. The most celebrated one is called *Pareto order or dominance*.

Definition 7 (Pareto partial order ($\prec$)). *Let Y be some subset of $\mathbb{N}^n$. For any $\boldsymbol{y}, \boldsymbol{y}' \in Y$,*

$$\boldsymbol{y} \preceq \boldsymbol{y}' \iff \forall i, \boldsymbol{y}_i \leq \boldsymbol{y}'_i,$$
$$\boldsymbol{y} \prec \boldsymbol{y}' \iff \boldsymbol{y} \preceq \boldsymbol{y}' \wedge \boldsymbol{y} \neq \boldsymbol{y}'.$$

We say $\boldsymbol{y}$ dominates $\boldsymbol{y}'$ iff $\boldsymbol{y} \preceq \boldsymbol{y}'$. We say $\boldsymbol{y}$ strictly-dominates $\boldsymbol{y}'$ iff $\boldsymbol{y} \prec \boldsymbol{y}'$.

Given a tuple of objective functions sharing a common domain X, we can compare two elements $\boldsymbol{x}, \boldsymbol{x}' \in X$ by comparing the corresponding tuples in the objective space.

Definition 8 (Pareto Dominance ($\prec$)). *Let $F : X \to Y \subseteq \mathbb{N}^n$ be a multi-objective function, mapping the decision space X into the objective space Y. For any $\boldsymbol{x}, \boldsymbol{x}' \in X$,*

$$\boldsymbol{x} \prec \boldsymbol{x}' \iff F(\boldsymbol{x}) \prec F(\boldsymbol{x}'),$$
$$\boldsymbol{x} \preceq \boldsymbol{x}' \iff F(\boldsymbol{x}) \preceq F(\boldsymbol{x}').$$

We say $\boldsymbol{x}$ dominates $\boldsymbol{x}'$ iff $\boldsymbol{x} \preceq \boldsymbol{x}'$. We say $\boldsymbol{x}$ strictly-dominates $\boldsymbol{x}'$ iff $\boldsymbol{x} \prec \boldsymbol{x}'$.

Contrary to the single-objective case, the consequence of this comparison criterion is that many different *good* solutions are mapped to different points in the objective space. Therefore, the solution to the problem is actually a set called *Pareto front*.

Definition 9 (Fronts). *Given a a multi-objective function $F : X \to Y$ and a feasible space $Z \subseteq X$, the Pareto front of Z is a subset $P \subseteq Z$ containing all elements that are not strictly-dominated,*

$$P = \left\{ \boldsymbol{x} \in Z : \nexists \boldsymbol{x}' \in Z : \boldsymbol{x}' \prec \boldsymbol{x} \right\}.$$

We call img-front to the subset $\overline{Y} \subseteq Y$ which is the image of P by F,

$$\overline{Y} \equiv \operatorname{img front}_Z F = \left\{ \boldsymbol{y} \in Y : \exists \boldsymbol{x} \in P : \boldsymbol{y} = F(\boldsymbol{x}) \right\}.$$

Finally, we call arg-front of Z, or simply front of Z, to any subset $\overline{Z}$ of the Pareto Front P which is mapped by F into $\overline{Y}$ in a one-to-one fashion

$$\overline{Z} = \operatorname{front}_Z F.$$

Definition 10 (Multi-Objective Combinatorial Optimization (MOCO)). *Let $F : X \to Y \subseteq \mathbb{N}^n$ be a multi-objective PB function, mapping the decision space $X \subseteq \{0,1\}^n$ into the objective space Y. Let $Z \subseteq X$ be the feasible space of some PB formula ϕ, with variables in V. Then,*

$$\text{find } \operatorname{front}_{Z(\phi)} F. \tag{4}$$

An instance will be denoted by the triple $\langle \phi, V, F \rangle$.

Because the solutions of the problems are sets, bounds are now *bound sets* (Definition 13). In the single objective case, a bound is a value l such that $\forall y = f(x) : l \leq y$, or equivalently, $\nexists y = f(x) : l > y$. This equivalence is broken by the generalization. Each of the previous defining properties of a lower bound gives rise to a differently flavoured comparison of sets (Definitions 11 and 12).

Definition 11 (Set coverage). *Let A and B be subsets of some decision space X, equipped with a multi-objective function F. Then, A covers B iff every element of B is dominated by some element of A, i.e. $\forall b \in B, \exists a \in A : a \preceq b$, and A strictly covers B iff $\forall b \in B, \exists a \in A : a \prec b$.*

Definition 12 (Set non-inferiority). *Let A and B be subsets of some decision space X, equipped with a multi-objective function F. Then A is non-inferior to B iff there is no element of B that strictly-dominates an element of A, $\forall a \in A, b \in B : \neg(a \succ b)$, and A is strictly non-inferior to B iff $\forall a \in A, b \in B : \neg(a \succeq b)$.*

Note that in the single objective case, non-inferiority and coverage are the same. The next definition correctly generalizes the notion of lower bound.

Definition 13 (Bound sets). *$L \subseteq X$ is a (strictly) lower bound set of $Z \subseteq X$ iff L (strictly) covers and is (strictly) non-inferior to Z. If L is a lower bound set of Z, we say $L \preceq Z$. If it is a strictly lower bound set, we say $L \prec Z$.*

One way to generate a lower bound set of some Pareto front is to solve a related problem, where the formula is replaced by a relaxed version (Definition 4).

In our approach, we embed dominance relations into CNF formulas. We are interested in removing from the feasible space solutions that are dominated by some other known feasible solution. In order to do this, we make use of *unary counters* [3,13,14] that have been used to implement efficient *PB satisfiability solvers*.

Definition 14 (Unary Counter). *Let $f_i : \{0,1\}^n \to \mathbb{N}$ be a PB function and set V be an ordered set of variables that parametrize the domain of f_i,*

$$V = \{x_1, \ldots, x_n\}, f_i(\boldsymbol{x}) = f_i(x_1, \ldots, x_n) \qquad (5)$$

Consider the CNF formula $\widetilde{\phi}$ with variables $V \cup O$, where $O \cap V = \emptyset$ and O contains one variable $o_{i,k}$ for each value $k \in \mathbb{N} : \exists \boldsymbol{x} : k = f_i(\boldsymbol{x})$. The elements of O are the order variables. We call the tuple $\left\langle f_i, V, O, \widetilde{\phi} \right\rangle$ an unary counter of f_i iff all feasible models ν of $\widetilde{\phi}$ satisfy

$$f_i(\boldsymbol{x}) \geq k \implies o_{i,k}, \quad \boldsymbol{x} = \nu(V). \qquad (6)$$

3   Core-Guided Algorithm

Although core-guided algorithms for Maximum Satisfiability were initially proposed more than a decade ago [7,23,21,2,1], there is no such algorithm for MOCO. Hence, our goal is to take advantage of unsatisfiable cores identified by a SAT solver in order to lazily expand the allowed search space.

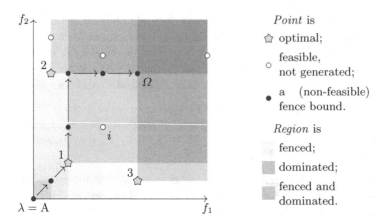

Fig. 1: Illustration of a run of `Core-Guided` (Algorithm 1) in the objective space. The img-front is the set $\{1, 2, 3\}$. The fence bound λ gets updated at each iteration of the while loop at line 6, starting at A and ending at Ω. The arrows are guided by the core κ (line 19). The green shading represents the evolution of the fence. Darker regions have been fenced for longer. The blue regions are blocked by optimal points. Darker regions are dominated by more points. We will be done in 7 iterations. After verifying that A is not feasible, we are instructed by the cores k to move along the diagonal twice. We find point 1 fenced. Therefore the associated $\boldsymbol{x}$ is copied into I and the dominated region is blocked. We extend λ twice, and find point 2. After moving once more, we find part of the fence blocked, and the point branded with i is never generated. The next movement stations λ at Ω. Point 3 is found. The Oracle acknowledges we are done, by returning $\kappa = \emptyset$ (line 15): she knows that no movement of λ will extend I.

3.1   Algorithm Description

Algorithm 1 presents the pseudo-code for an exact core-guided algorithm for MOCO. Figure 1 illustrates an abstract execution of the algorithm.

Let $\langle \phi, V, F \rangle$ be a MOCO instance. Recall that ϕ denotes the set of PB constraints, V is the set of variables and F denotes the list of m objective functions. First, the algorithm starts by building a working formula with the problem constraints and an *unary counter* for each objective function (lines 3-4). This is accomplished by the call to `EncodeOrder`. Next, a vector λ of size m is initialized with the lower bound of each objective function (line 5), assumed to be 0 for simplicity.

At each iteration of the main loop, the assumptions α are assembled from order variables o, chosen with the value of λ in mind (line 7). The call to `next`$(i, \lambda)^2$ returns the next smallest value belonging to the image of the objective i. Given the semantics of the order variables $o_{i,k}$ (Definition 14), the tuple λ *fences* the search space, i.e. ν satisfies α only if the corresponding tuple $\boldsymbol{x}$ satisfies $F(\boldsymbol{x}) \preceq \lambda$.

---

[2] May be replaced by $\lambda_i + 1$.

Algorithm 1: `Core-Guided MOCO solver`

    Input: $\langle \phi, V, F \rangle$ `// MOCO instance`
    Output: front$_\phi$ F `// one arg-front`

1   $m \leftarrow |F|$
2   $I \leftarrow \emptyset$
3   $(\widetilde{\phi}, \{O_i\}_{1 \leq i \leq m}) \leftarrow \texttt{EncodeOrder}(F, V)$
4   $\widetilde{\phi} \leftarrow \widetilde{\phi} \cup \phi$
5   $\lambda \leftarrow \langle 0, 0, \ldots, 0 \rangle$ `// initialize fence`
6   **while** *true* **do**
7      $\alpha \leftarrow \{\{\neg o_{i, \text{next}(i, \lambda)}\} : i \in 1 \ldots m\}$
8      $(\nu, \kappa) \leftarrow \widetilde{\phi}\text{-}\texttt{SAT}(\alpha)$
9   **while** $\nu \neq \emptyset$ **do**
10        $\boldsymbol{x} \leftarrow \nu(V)$
11        $I \leftarrow I \setminus \{\boldsymbol{x}' \in I : \boldsymbol{x} \preceq \boldsymbol{x}'\} \cup \{\boldsymbol{x}\}$
12        $\beta \leftarrow \left\{ \bigvee\limits_{i=1}^{m} \neg o_{i, f_i(\boldsymbol{x})} \right\}$
13        $\widetilde{\phi} \leftarrow \widetilde{\phi} \cup \beta$ `// block dominated`
14        $(\nu, \kappa) \leftarrow \widetilde{\phi}\text{-}\texttt{SAT}(\alpha)$
15   **if** $\kappa = \emptyset$ **then**   `// if fence exhausted,`
16   **return** I
17   **else**
18   **foreach** $\{\neg o_{i,k}\} \in \kappa$ **do**   `// expand fence`
19           $\lambda_i \leftarrow k$

If the SAT call (line 10) returns a solution (i.e. $\nu \neq \emptyset$), $\boldsymbol{x}$ is stored in and all dominated solutions are removed from I (line 11). Moreover, one can readily block all feasible solutions dominated by $\boldsymbol{x}$ using a single clause (line 13) [28].

Usually, there are several feasible fenced solutions. This occurs because the algorithm may increase multiple entries of λ at once. In any case, the inner while loop (lines 9-14) collects all such solutions.

When the working formula $\widetilde{\phi}$ becomes unsatisfiable, the SAT solver provides a core κ. If κ is empty (line 15), then the unsatisfiability does not depend on the assumptions, i.e. it does not depend on temporary bounds imposed on the objective functions. At that point, we can conclude that no more solutions exist that are both satisfiable and not dominated by an element of I. As a result, the algorithm can safely terminate (line 16). Otherwise, the literals in κ denote a subset of the fence walls λ_i that may be too restrictive, in the sense that unless we increment them (line 19) no new non-dominated solutions can be found.

3.2 Algorithm Properties

Lemma 1. *The* img-front $\overline{Y}$ *of* $I \cup Z(\widetilde{\phi})$ *(Definition 9) is not changed by the inner loop (lines 9-14).*

Proof. Consider some particular iteration of the internal loop. Line 11 and line 13 remove all elements of $I \cup Z(\widetilde{\phi})$ that are dominated by the feasible point x. Line 11 filters the explicit set I, line 13 filters the implicit set $Z(\widetilde{\phi})$. Solutions that are strictly dominated by x cannot be mapped into an element of $\overline{Y}$. The other solutions x' that are filtered out must attain the same objective vector attained by x, $F(x') = F(x)$. Because x is also inserted at line 11, removing x' will not disturb $\overline{Y}$.

Lemma 2. *At the start of each iteration of the external loop (lines 6-19), every solution in I is optimal, and no two elements of I attain the same objective vector.*

Proof. We prove this by contradiction. Assume that there is a non-optimal solution $x \in I$ at the start of the external loop (line 6). In the first iteration, this does not occur because I is empty. Hence, this can only occur if the inner loop (lines 9-14) finishes with a non-optimal solution $x \in I$.

The inner loop (lines 9-14) enumerates solutions inside the fence defined by λ. We know that $F(x) \preceq \lambda$ because it is inside the fence and the entries of λ never decrease. If x is non-optimal, then there must be an optimal solution x' such that $F(x') \prec F(x)(\preceq \lambda)$. Hence, x' is also inside the fence. As a result, x' must be found before the inner loop finishes, since at each iteration only dominated solutions are blocked (line 13). If x is found before x', then x is excluded from I (line 11) when x' is found. Otherwise, if x' is found first, then x is not found by the SAT solver (blocked at line 13) because it is dominated by x'. Therefore, we cannot have a non-optimal solution $x \in I$ at the end of the inner loop or at the start of each iteration of the external loop (lines 6-19). Furthermore, no two elements of I attain the same objective vector since when a solution x is found, all other solutions x' such that $F(x) = F(x')$ are also blocked (line 13).

Lemma 2 establishes a weaker form of *anytime optimality*. The elements of the incumbent list I are not necessarily optimal at anytime, but they are optimal immediately after completing the inner loop. It is easy enough to make it anytime optimal. This could be achieved if the algorithm refrains from adding solutions directly to I in the inner loop and maintain a secondary list, where it stores the solutions that are still not necessarily optimal. This list takes the role of I inside the inner loop. After completing the inner loop, all elements of the secondary list are optimal, and can be safely transferred to the main list I.

Proposition 1. *Algorithm 1 is sound.*

Proof. If the algorithm returns, $Z(\widetilde{\phi} \wedge \alpha) = \emptyset$. Because κ is empty, no core of the unsatisfiable formula $\widetilde{\phi} \wedge \alpha$ intersects α, and $\widetilde{\phi}$ is also unsatisfiable, $Z(\widetilde{\phi}) = \emptyset$. Using Lemma 1 both at the end and at the start of the course of the algorithm, the img-front of I is the img-front of $Z(\widetilde{\phi})$, with $\widetilde{\phi}$ given by line 4. Because the order variables are only restricted by the unary counter formula, the img-front of $Z(\widetilde{\phi})$ is the img-front of $Z(\phi)$. Therefore I must contain an arg-front of the problem. Using Lemma 2, every element of I is optimal, and there is no pair

$x, x' \in I$ such that $F(x) = F(x')$. Therefore, I is an arg-front of the MOCO instance.

Proposition 2. *Algorithm 1 is complete.*

Proof. The inner loop will always come to fruition, because in the worst case it will generate every feasible solution dominated by the current λ once, and the feasible space is finite.

   If the algorithm does not return for some particular instance, then κ is never empty. In that case, every iteration of the external loop starting at line 6 will increase at least one of the entries of λ. Eventually, one entry i must achieve the upper limit of f_i, and the order variable retrieved by o_{i,λ_i+1} will not exist. Because the evolution of λ_i is monotonous, the assumptions will contain at most $m - 1$ variables, from that point on. By the same token, the assumptions α will eventually be empty, and so must be $\kappa \subseteq \alpha$, contradicting the assumption that the algorithm never terminates.

4   Hitting Set-based Algorithm

This section proposes a MOCO solver based on the enumeration of hitting sets. The main idea is to compute a sequence of relaxations ψ of the formula ϕ, and solve the corresponding problems. The front $\overline{T}$ of the relaxed problem gets incrementally closer to the desired front $\overline{Z}$, and will eventually reach it.

4.1   Algorithm Description

Algorithm 2 contains the pseudo-code for our hitting set-based algorithm for MOCO. Figure 2 illustrates an abstract execution of the algorithm.

   The algorithm starts by setting the *relaxed formula* ψ to empty (line 1). The main loop that starts at line 2 hones the relaxation until we get the desired result. At each iteration, we solve the current relaxed formula ψ at line 4. This is accomplished by using some MOCO solver. Because this amounts to computing a lower bound set, the Core-Guided algorithm, previously described, is a good choice for the task. We anticipate that it performs well for problems whose front is in the vicinity of the origin, given that by construction, the focus of its search is biased to that region. Notice that the first relaxation's arg-front is the set that contains the origin only (assuming all literals in the objective functions are positive). We expect that the first few relaxations will stay close to it.

   Next, for each element x in $\overline{T}$ (the Pareto-front of ψ), we check the ϕ-feasibility of $\nu : \nu(V) = x$, using the assumptions mechanism, and return a (possibly empty) core of assumptions κ. The assumptions α_x built at line 6 are a set of unit clauses whose polarity is inherited from ν,

$$\nu(x_i) \implies x_i \in \alpha, \quad \neg\nu(x_i) \implies \neg x_i \in \alpha. \tag{7}$$

   Assuming ϕ is satisfiable, the returned core κ will be void iff $\alpha_x \wedge \phi$ is satisfiable. In this case, x corresponds to an optimal solution.

Algorithm 2: Hitting-Sets MOCO solver

   Input: $\langle \phi, V, F \rangle$ `// MOCO instance`
   Output: $\text{front}_\phi F$ `// one arg-front`
1   $\psi \leftarrow \emptyset$ `// relaxed formula` ψ
2   **while** *true* **do**
3      $\Delta \leftarrow \emptyset$
4      $\overline{T} \leftarrow \text{front}_\psi F$ `// use auxiliar solver`
5   **foreach** $x \in \overline{T}$ **do**   `// diagnose` $\overline{T}$
6          $\alpha_x \leftarrow \{\{l\}, l \in \nu : \nu(V) = x\}$
7          $(\bullet, \kappa) \leftarrow \phi\text{-}\mathsf{SAT}(\alpha_x)$
8   **if** $\kappa \neq \emptyset$ **then**
9             $\Delta \leftarrow \kappa \cup \Delta$

10   **if** $\Delta = \emptyset$ **then**   `// if` $\overline{T}$ `is fine`
11   **return** $\overline{T}$

12   **foreach** $\kappa \in \Delta$ **do**
13        $\psi \leftarrow \psi \cup \{\neg l, \{l\} \in \kappa\}$ `// tighten` ψ

The *diagnosis* Δ is central for the algorithm. Intuitively, it reports if and why the relaxed problem's solution is different from the true Pareto solution. We add every non-empty κ to the diagnosis Δ (line 9). In the end, Δ is empty iff every element of the relaxed front $\overline{T}$ is ϕ-feasible. At that point, we have found a ϕ-feasible lower bound set. All such sets are arg-fronts, and so the algorithm terminates (line 11). Otherwise, if Δ is not empty, then the found cores are added to the relaxed formula ψ (line 13). This step ensures all tentative points produced in line 4 hit all previously found unsatisfiable cores, and that the algorithm advances in a monotonous fashion towards the solution.

4.2 Algorithm Properties

Given a MOCO instance $\langle \phi, V, F \rangle$, the formula ϕ encodes the feasible space Z implicitly, which in turn defines the desired front $\overline{Z}$. This is a many to one correspondence, in the sense that there are many different values of ψ that encode the same Pareto front. It may happen that some of the counterpart instances are easier to solve than the original one, which begs the question: given ϕ, can we effectively find a simpler formula ψ with the same Pareto front? This is the motto of the proposed algorithm. It is done by iteratively honing a *relaxed formula* (Definition 4).

The main idea is to compute a sequence of relaxations that get incrementally tighter. In that case, the corresponding front $\overline{T}$ gets incrementally closer to the desired front $\overline{Z}$,

$$\phi \quad \Longrightarrow \quad \psi_n \quad \Longrightarrow \quad \ldots \quad \Longrightarrow \quad \psi_1, \quad (8)$$

$$\overline{Z} \quad \succeq \quad \overline{T}_n \quad \succeq \quad \ldots \quad \succeq \quad \overline{T}_1, \quad (9)$$

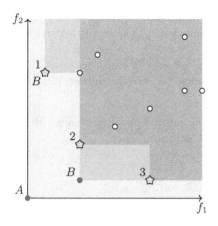

Point is

☆ optimal;

○ feasible, not generated;

● non-feasible.

Fig. 2: Illustration of a run of the `Hitting-Sets` (Algorithm 2) in the objective space. The Pareto front is the set $\{1, 2, 3\}$, and the feasible solutions are marked by o. For each iteration of the main while loop at line 2 we get a narrower lower bound $\overline{T}$ (line 4), culminating in the solution. We are done in 3 iterations, marked by A, B and ☆. The shading represents the number of iterations whose freshly found points dominate the region. The lighter tone was painted by A, the darker one by all three. We start with the empty formula (line 1) and get A. Because the only point in A is not feasible, we tighten the relaxation (line 13). Iteration B generates one feasible point, 1, which is therefore optimal. Note that the region dominated by 1 can be pruned from now on. The other point is used to tighten the formula once more. Lastly, the lower bound contains the feasible points 2 and 3 in addition to 1, which was already found, and the algorithm stops.

where $\overline{Z}$ is one of the desired arg-fronts, and $\overline{T}_i$ is an arg-front of ψ_i.

Lemma 3. *Consider some multi-objective function $F : X \to Y$. Let Z, T be subsets of X, such that $T \subseteq Z$. Then, any arg-front of T is a lower bound set of any arg-front of Z (Definition 13), i.e. $T \subseteq Z \implies \overline{T} \preceq \overline{Z}$.*

Lemma 3 is true because optimizing over a superset of some feasible space always returns a (non-strict) lower bound set. In a sense, the optimization can only be more extreme when applied to the superset. In particular, the feasible space of a relaxed formula is a superset of the original one. This is why the chain of $\preceq$ relations in Equation (9) is correct.

Lemma 4. *Let ϕ be a formula, $Z \subseteq X$ be its feasible space and $F : X \to Y$ be some multi-objective function. Let L be a lower bound set of the Pareto front of Z. Then, any element $x \in L$ that is feasible belongs to the Pareto front, $L \cap Z \subseteq P$. If all elements $\boldsymbol{x} \in L$ are feasible, then L is an arg-front.*

Lemma 4 implies that every lower bound set with only feasible elements must be itself an arg-front (this is an exact analogy with the single-objective case, where *lower bound set* is replaced by *infimum* and *arg-front* by *arg-min.*) By construction of the diagnosis Δ, this is equivalent to the condition used in Algorithm 2 to decide if it can terminate.

To ensure the sequence gets to $\overline{Z}$ in a finite number of steps, we need more than a string of relaxations. Each entry ψ' must be strictly tighter than the predecessor ψ.

Lemma 5. *Consider Algorithm 2. Let ψ be the relaxed formula at some iteration, and ψ' be the relaxed formula at the next iteration. Then,*

1. *ψ relaxes ψ', i.e. $\psi' \vDash \psi$;*
2. *Both ψ and ψ' relax ϕ, i.e. $\phi \vDash \psi, \phi \vDash \psi'$;*
3. *ψ' does not relax ψ, i.e. $\psi \nvDash \psi'$;*

Proof. Each statement will be proven in turn.

The first is true because $\psi \subseteq \psi'$, by construction (line 13).

We prove the second by induction on the number of iterations. Initially, ψ is empty. Therefore, ψ relaxes any formula, in particular ϕ. Assume $\phi \vDash \psi$ for some iteration. Consider one of the clauses $\neg\kappa$ added at line 13. We know that $\phi \wedge \kappa$ is unsatisfiable. Therefore, $\phi \wedge \kappa \vDash \bot \implies \neg(\phi \wedge \kappa) \vDash \top \iff \phi \vDash \neg\kappa$. Given the assumption $\phi \vDash \psi$, we get $\phi \vDash \psi \wedge \neg\kappa$. Repeating the process for the other added clauses $\neg\kappa_i$, we get $\phi \vDash \psi \wedge \neg\kappa_1 \ldots \wedge \neg\kappa_n \equiv \psi'$.

Assume ψ' is a relaxation of ψ. Then, any ψ-feasible model ν is also ψ'-feasible. We will prove there is at least one model that violates this. To start, note that it only makes sense to consider ψ' if there is some non-empty core κ in the diagnosis Δ; otherwise, the algorithm would have terminated before updating ψ into ψ'. Let κ be one element of Δ, generated at line 7 while ψ is current. Consider the Boolean tuple $\boldsymbol{x} \in \overline{T}$ used to build the assumptions of the query that generated κ. Let $\nu : \nu(V) = \boldsymbol{x}$. The model ν is ψ-feasible, because it is part of the arg-front of ψ. The model ν satisfies κ because $\kappa \subseteq \alpha_{\boldsymbol{x}}$ and the way $\alpha_{\boldsymbol{x}}$ is constructed (line 6, Equation (7)). Therefore, ν does not satisfy $\neg\kappa$. Because $\neg\kappa \subseteq \psi'$, ν cannot satisfy ψ', i.e. there is at least one ψ-feasible model that is not ψ'-feasible.

Proposition 3. *Algorithm 2 is sound.*

Proof. By Lemma 5, ψ relaxes ϕ and therefore $\overline{T}$ solves a relaxation of the original problem. By Lemma 3, it is a lower bound set of $\overline{Z}$. When the algorithm returns, all elements of $\overline{T}$ are feasible. By Lemma 4, $\overline{T}$ must be an arg-front.

Proposition 4. *Algorithm 2 is complete.*

Proof. Assume Algorithm 2 never ends, implying $\overline{T}$ is never completely feasible (i.e. $\overline{T} \nsubseteq Z$). The number of relaxed feasible spaces T is finite. If Algorithm 2 does not end, it will enumerate all of them, never repeating any: at any iteration, the updated relaxed formula effectively blocks the reappearance of any feasible space seen before, because by Lemma 5 the updated value ψ' strictly tightens ψ. Then, this sequence is necessarily finite, and so must be the number of iterations. But in that case, Algorithm 2 must end, and we have a contradiction.

Consider the sequence whose entries are the value of $F(\overline{T})$ computed at the beginning of each iteration of the main loop at line 2. The last element of this sequence is the solution. It may happen that for some i, the entries indexed by i and $i+1$ are the same. Therefore, the sequence may include blocks of contiguous entries that share the same value. In the worst case scenario, there are many different arg-fronts for the same img-front, and the algorithm ends up enumerating all of them without any movement in the objective space. We expect the algorithm will be effective whenever a few of the relaxed problems are enough to get to the full solution. Otherwise, we can end up solving an exponential number of problems.

5 Experimental Results

This section evaluates the performance of the algorithms proposed [3] in Sections 3 and 4. These algorithms are compared against other SAT-based MOCO solvers.

5.1 Algorithms and Implementation

The `Core-Guided` algorithm proposed in Algorithm 1 uses the selection delimiter encoding [14] that has been shown to be more compact. Next, the selection delimiter encoding is extended to produce a unary encoding for each objective function. Additionally, an order encoding [29] is also used. We refer the interested reader to the literature for further details on this and other encodings [27,13,14,15]. Observe that any unary encoding from PB into CNF can be used.

The `Hitting-Sets` algorithm implements Algorithm 2. This hitting set-based approach uses Algorithm 1 to find the relaxed arg-front (line 4 of Algorithm 2).

The `P-Minimal` algorithm implements a SAT-UNSAT approach based on the enumeration of P-Minimal models [28]. This algorithm is implemented with the same PB to CNF encoding as the `Core-Guided`. Finally, the `ParetoMCS` is based on the stratified enumeration of Minimal Correction Subsets. We used the publicly available implementation of `ParetoMCS`[4].

5.2 Experimental Setup and Benchmark Sets

The following MOCO problems are considered: the multi-objective Development Assurance Level (DAL) Problem [5], the multi-objective Flying Tourist Problem (FTP) [22], the multi-objective Set Covering (SC) Problem [4,28] and the multi-objective Package Upgradeability (PU) Problem [11]. All instances are publicly available from previous research work or were generated from real-world data.

The DAL benchmark set (95 instances) encodes different levels of rigor in the development of a software or hardware component of an aircraft. The development assurance level defines the assurance activities aimed at eliminating

---

[3] Available at https://gitlab.inesc-id.pt/u001810/moco
[4] https://gitlab.ow2.org/sat4j/moco

design and coding errors that could affect the safety of an aircraft. The goal is to allocate the smallest DAL to functions to decrease the development costs [18].

The FTP benchmark set (129 instances) encodes the problem of a tourist that is searching for a flight travel route to visit n cities. The tourist defines her home city, the start and end of the route. She specifies the number of days d_i to be spent on each city c_i ($1 \leq i \leq n$) and also a time window for the complete trip. The problem is to find the route that minimizes the time spent on flights and the sum of the prices of the tickets[5].

The SC benchmark set (60 instances) is a generalization of the set covering problem and was used in previous research work [28]. Let X be some ground set and A a cover of X. Each element in A has an associated cost tuple. The goal is to find a cover of X contained in A that Pareto-optimizes the overall cost.

The PU benchmark set (687 instances) were generated from the Package Upgradeability benchmarks [19] from the Mancoosi International Solver Competition [20]. The `packup` tool [25] was used to generate these benchmarks that contain between two and five objectives to optimize.

All results were obtained on an Intel Xeon Silver 4110 CPU @ 2.10GHz, with 64 GB of RAM. Each tool was executed on each instance with a time limit of 1 hour and 10 GB of RAM memory limit.

5.3   Results and Analysis

Table 1 shows the number of instances whose Pareto front is completely enumerated, for each algorithm and benchmark set. Overall, the new unsatisfiability-based algorithms proposed in the paper completely solve more instances than the `ParetoMCS` and the `P-Minimal` algorithms. Note that the `ParetoMCS` is the one that solves fewer instances since it needs to enumerate all MCSs. The `Core-Guided` and `Hitting-Sets` converge faster to the Pareto front due to their UNSAT-SAT approach, while the `P-Minimal` is slower to converge. Overall, the `Core-Guided` algorithm is able to solve more instances than the other algorithms.

All tested algorithms are exact, but in some cases only an approximation of the Pareto front could be found within the time limit. However, the partial solution that is returned may still be valuable. In order to evaluate the quality of the approximations provided by each tool, we use the Hypervolume (HV) [34] indicator. HV is a metric that measures the volume of the objective space dominated by a set of points in the objective space, up to a given *reference point*. The coordinates of the reference point chosen are the maximal values of each objective. Regions that are not dominated by a *reference front* are discarded (we combined the results for each algorithm in order to produce the reference front). Larger values are preferred. A normalization procedure is carried out so that the values of HV are always between 0 and 1.

Figure 3 shows a cactus plot of the HV for all tools on each benchmark set. The `P-Minimal` provides better quality approximations of the Pareto front in the DAL (Figure 3a) and PU (Figure 3d) benchmarks since it uses a SAT-UNSAT

---

[5] Instances generated from flights in Europe between October and December 2019.

Table 1: Number of MOCO instances whose complete solution is found and certified per algorithm and benchmark set. Best results are **in bold**.

Algorithm	Benchmark Set				Total
	DAL	FTP	SC	PU	
	95	129	60	687	971
ParetoMCS	24	**76**	0	279	379
P-Minimal	47	**76**	17	473	613
Core-Guided	**58**	**76**	26	**497**	**657**
Hitting-Sets	47	**76**	**29**	392	544

approach. Hence, it is faster to find an approximation to the Pareto front. Moreover, since some of the instances in these sets have higher optimal values on the objective functions, the `Core-Guided` and `Hitting-Sets` take many interactions until they reach the feasible part of the search space. Despite performing an unsatisfiability-based search, `Core-Guided` and `Hitting-Sets` algorithms are still able to provide good quality solutions since when these algorithms find solutions, these are in the Pareto front. Moreover, observe that even in these sets of instances, `Core-Guided` is still able to find all the Pareto front in more instances.

The `ParetoMCS` is able to provide good quality approximations in the FTP (Figure 3b) and PU (Figure 3d) benchmarks. Note that `ParetoMCS` does not use an explicit representation of the objective functions. The FTP instances have several large coefficients in the objective functions, but the representation used in `Core-Guided` is still effective for these instances. Observe that the performance of both algorithms is similar in the FTP dataset.

The `Hitting-Sets` finds poor approximations for all datasets. A common feature of this algorithm is the need to enumerate many hitting sets before being able to find feasible solutions. Hence, in several instances it is unable to provide good approximations. However, it is still able to prove optimality for more instances in the SC benchmark set than the `P-Minimal` algorithm.

Overall, the `Core-Guided` is the best performing algorithm being able to find the complete Pareto frontier in more instances. This is due to the fact that in many cases, it does not need to relax all variables to find solutions in the Pareto front. Moreover, when evaluating the quality of the approximations, it is still able to outperform the other approaches on the FTP and SC benchmark sets, despite applying an unsatisfiability-based approach.

6   Conclusions

This paper proposes two new algorithms for Multi-Objective Combinatorial Optimization (MOCO). The first is a core-guided approach, while the second is

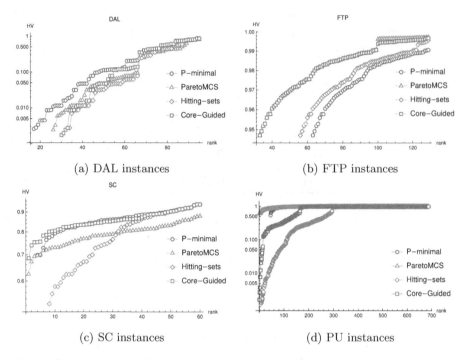

Fig. 3: Comparison of the *HV* results for each set of instances. Each series is sorted independently, smaller values first. Vertical scale is logarithmical.

based on the enumeration of hitting sets. These are the first SAT-based algorithms that fully integrate these strategies into a MOCO solver.

Experimental results on different sets of benchmark instances show that the new core-guided approach results in a robust algorithm that outperforms other SAT-based algorithms for MOCO. Using unary counters to express Pareto dominance in CNF proved to be an effective way to harness the power of SAT solvers in solving MOCO. The ability to express concepts related to dominance makes the algorithms conceptually simple.

Overall, the new algorithms are able to completely enumerate the Pareto front for more instances than previous SAT-based approaches. Moreover, despite following an unsatisfiability-based approach, the newly proposed algorithms are also able to provide good quality approximations even when they are unable to completely enumerate the Pareto front. Hence, these new unsatisfiability-based algorithms extend the state of the art for MOCO solvers by complementing and improving upon the existing tools based on queries to SAT Oracles.

Acknowledgements This work was supported by Portuguese national funds through FCT under projects UIDB/50021/2020, PTDC/CCI-COM/2156/2021, 2022.03537.PTDC and project ANI 045917 funded by FEDER and FCT.

References

1. Ansótegui, C., Bonet, M.L., Gabàs, J., Levy, J.: Improving WPM2 for (weighted) partial maxsat. In: International Conference Principles and Practice of Constraint Programming. LNCS, vol. 8124, pp. 117–132. Springer (2013), https://doi.org/10.1007/978-3-642-40627-0_12

2. Ansótegui, C., Bonet, M.L., Levy, J.: Solving (weighted) partial maxsat through satisfiability testing. In: International Conference Theory and Applications of Satisfiability Testing. LNCS, vol. 5584, pp. 427–440. Springer (2009), https://doi.org/10.1007/978-3-642-02777-2_39

3. Bailleux, O., Boufkhad, Y.: Efficient CNF encoding of boolean cardinality constraints. In: Rossi, F. (ed.) International Conference on Principles and Practice of Constraint Programming (CP). Lecture Notes in Computer Science, vol. 2833, pp. 108–122. Springer (2003), https://doi.org/10.1007/978-3-540-45193-8_8

4. Bergman, D., Ciré, A.A.: Multiobjective optimization by decision diagrams. In: International Conference on Principles and Practice of Constraint Programming (CP). LNCS, vol. 9892, pp. 86–95. Springer (2016), https://doi.org/10.1007/978-3-319-44953-1_6

5. Bieber, P., Delmas, R., Seguin, C.: Dalculus - theory and tool for development assurance level allocation. In: International Conference on Computer Safety, Reliability, and Security. LNCS, vol. 6894, pp. 43–56. Springer (2011), https://doi.org/10.1007/978-3-642-24270-0_4

6. Deb, K., Agrawal, S., Pratap, A., Meyarivan, T.: A Fast Elitist Non-dominated Sorting Genetic Algorithm for Multi-objective Optimisation: NSGA-II. In: International Conference on Parallel Problem Solving from Nature. pp. 849–858. Springer (2000)

7. Fu, Z., Malik, S.: Extracting logic circuit structure from conjunctive normal form descriptions. In: International Conference on VLSI Design. pp. 37–42. IEEE Computer Society (2007), https://doi.org/10.1109/VLSID.2007.81

8. Gavanelli, M.: An algorithm for multi-criteria optimization in csps. In: European Conference on Artificial Intelligence. pp. 136–140. IOS Press (2002)

9. Guerreiro, A.P., Manquinho, V.M., Figueira, J.R.: Exact hypervolume subset selection through incremental computations. Comput. Oper. Res. **136**, 105471 (2021), https://doi.org/10.1016/j.cor.2021.105471

10. Jabs, C., Berg, J., Niskanen, A., Järvisalo, M.: Maxsat-based bi-objective boolean optimization. In: International Conference on Theory and Applications of Satisfiability Testing. LIPIcs, vol. 236, pp. 12:1–12:23. Schloss Dagstuhl - Leibniz-Zentrum für Informatik (2022), https://doi.org/10.4230/LIPIcs.SAT.2022.12

11. Janota, M., Lynce, I., Manquinho, V.M., Marques-Silva, J.: Packup: Tools for package upgradability solving. J. Satisf. Boolean Model. Comput. **8**(1/2), 89–94 (2012), https://doi.org/10.3233/sat190090

12. Janota, M., Morgado, A., Santos, J.F., Manquinho, V.M.: The seesaw algorithm: Function optimization using implicit hitting sets. In: International Conference on Principles and Practice of Constraint Programming. LIPIcs, vol. 210, pp. 31:1–31:16. Schloss Dagstuhl - Leibniz-Zentrum für Informatik (2021), https://doi.org/10.4230/LIPIcs.CP.2021.31

13. Joshi, S., Martins, R., Manquinho, V.M.: Generalized totalizer encoding for pseudo-boolean constraints. In: International Conference Principles and Practice of Constraint Programming. LNCS, vol. 9255, pp. 200–209. Springer (2015), https://doi.org/10.1007/978-3-319-23219-5_15

14. Karpinski, M., Piotrów, M.: Encoding cardinality constraints using multiway merge selection networks. Constraints **24**(3-4), 234–251 (2019), https://doi.org/10.1007/s10601-019-09302-0

15. Karpinski, M., Piotrów, M.: Incremental encoding of pseudo-boolean goal functions based on comparator networks. In: International Conference on Theory and Applications of Satisfiability Testing. LNCS, vol. 12178, pp. 519–535. Springer (2020), https://doi.org/10.1007/978-3-030-51825-7_36

16. Legriel, J., Guernic, C.L., Cotton, S., Maler, O.: Approximating the pareto front of multi-criteria optimization problems. In: Esparza, J., Majumdar, R. (eds.) International Conference on Tools and Algorithms for the Construction and Analysis of Systems, (TACAS), Held as Part of the Joint European Conferences on Theory and Practice of Software (ETAPS). Lecture Notes in Computer Science, vol. 6015, pp. 69–83. Springer (2010), https://doi.org/10.1007/978-3-642-12002-2_6

17. Li, R., Zheng, Q., Li, X., Yan, Z.: Multi-objective optimization for rebalancing virtual machine placement. Future Gener. Comput. Syst. **105**, 824–842 (2020), https://doi.org/10.1016/j.future.2017.08.027

18. Development Assurance Level Benchmark Set from the LION Challenge. https://www.lifl.fr/LION9/challenge.php

19. Benchmarks from the Mancoosi International Solver Competition 2011. http://data.mancoosi.org/misc2011/problems/

20. Mancoosi international solver competition 2011. https://www.mancoosi.org/misc-2011/index.html

21. Manquinho, V.M., Silva, J.P.M., Planes, J.: Algorithms for weighted boolean optimization. In: International Conference on Theory and Applications of Satisfiability Testing. LNCS, vol. 5584, pp. 495–508. Springer (2009), https://doi.org/10.1007/978-3-642-02777-2_45

22. Marques, R., Russo, L.M.S., Roma, N.: Flying tourist problem: Flight time and cost minimization in complex routes. Expert Syst. Appl. **130**, 172–187 (2019), https://doi.org/10.1016/j.eswa.2019.04.024

23. Marques-Silva, J., Planes, J.: On using unsatisfiability for solving maximum satisfiability. CoRR **abs/0712.1097** (2007), http://arxiv.org/abs/0712.1097

24. Marques-Silva, J., Argelich, J., Graça, A., Lynce, I.: Boolean lexicographic optimization: Algorithms & applications. Ann. Math. Artif. Intell. **62**, 317–343 (07 2011). https://doi.org/10.1007/s10472-011-9233-2

25. packup package upgradeability solver webpage. http://sat.inesc-id.pt/$\sim$mikolas/sw/packup/

26. Rayside, D., Estler, H.C., Jackson, D.: The guided improvement algorithm for exact, general-purpose, many-objective combinatorial optimization. Tech. Rep. Technical Report MIT-CSAIL-TR-2009-033, MIT Massachusetts Institute of Technology (2009)

27. Roussel, O., Manquinho, V.M.: Pseudo-boolean and cardinality constraints. In: Handbook of Satisfiability, Frontiers in Artificial Intelligence and Applications, vol. 185, pp. 695–733. IOS Press (2009), https://doi.org/10.3233/978-1-58603-929-5-695

28. Soh, T., Banbara, M., Tamura, N., Berre, D.L.: Solving multiobjective discrete optimization problems with propositional minimal model generation. In: International Conference Principles and Practice of Constraint Programming. LNCS, vol. 10416, pp. 596–614. Springer (2017), https://doi.org/10.1007/978-3-319-66158-2_38

29. Tamura, N., Banbara, M.: Sugar: A CSP to SAT translator based on order encoding. Proceedings of the Second International CSP Solver Competition pp. 65–69 (2008)
30. Terra-Neves, M., Lynce, I., Manquinho, V.M.: Introducing pareto minimal correction subsets. In: International Conference on Theory and Applications of Satisfiability Testing. LNCS, vol. 10491, pp. 195–211. Springer (2017), https://doi.org/10.1007/978-3-319-66263-3_13
31. Tian, N., Ouyang, D., Wang, Y., Hou, Y., Zhang, L.: Core-guided method for constraint-based multi-objective combinatorial optimization. Appl. Intell. **51**(6), 3865–3879 (2021), https://doi.org/10.1007/s10489-020-01998-5
32. Yuan, Y., Banzhaf, W.: ARJA: automated repair of java programs via multi-objective genetic programming. IEEE Trans. Software Eng. **46**(10), 1040–1067 (2020), https://doi.org/10.1109/TSE.2018.2874648
33. Zhang, Q., Li, H.: MOEA/D: A Multiobjective Evolutionary Algorithm Based on Decomposition. IEEE Transactions on Evolutionary Computation **11**(6), 712–731 (2007)
34. Zitzler, E.: Evolutionary Algorithms for Multiobjective Optimization: Methods and Applications. Ph.D. thesis, University of Zurich, Zürich, Switzerland (1999)

Verified Reductions for Optimization

Alexander Bentkamp[1,2]($\boxtimes$) (ID), Ramon Fernández Mir[3] (ID), and Jeremy Avigad[4] (ID)

[1] Heinrich-Heine-Universität Düsseldorf, Düsseldorf, Germany
bentkamp@gmail.com
[2] State Key Laboratory of Computer Science, Institute of Software,
Chinese Academy of Sciences, Beijing, China
[3] School of Informatics, University of Edinburgh, Edinburgh, UK
[4] Carnegie Mellon University, Pittsburgh, PA, USA

Abstract. Numerical and symbolic methods for optimization are used extensively in engineering, industry, and finance. Various methods are used to reduce problems of interest to ones that are amenable to solution by these methods. We develop a framework for designing and applying such reductions, using the Lean programming language and interactive proof assistant. Formal verification makes the process more reliable, and the availability of an interactive framework and ambient mathematical library provides a robust environment for constructing the reductions and reasoning about them.

Keywords: convex optimization · formal verification · interactive theorem proving · disciplined convex programming

1 Introduction

Optimization problems and constraint satisfaction problems are ubiquitous in engineering, industry, and finance. These include the problem of finding an element of $\mathbb{R}^n$ satisfying a finite set of constraints or determining that the constraints are unsatisfiable; the problem of bounding the value of an objective function over a domain defined by such a set of constraints; and the problem of finding a value of the domain that maximizes (or minimizes) the value of an objective function. Linear programming, revolutionized by Dantzig's introduction of the simplex algorithm in 1947, deals with the case in which the constraints and objective function are linear. The development of interior point methods in the 1980s allows for the efficient solution of problems defined by convex constraints and objective functions, which gives rise to the field of convex programming [10,36,43]. Today there are numerous back-end solvers for convex optimization problems, including MOSEK [30], SeDuMi [41], and Gurobi [23]. They employ a variety of methods, each with its own particular strengths and weaknesses. (See [1, Section 1.2] for an overview.)

Using such software requires interpreting the problem one wants to solve in terms of one or more associated optimization problems. Often, this is straightforward; proving the safety of an engineered system might require showing that a certain quantity remains within specified bounds, and an industrial problem might require determining optimal or near-optimal allocation of certain

S. Sankaranarayanan and N. Sharygina (Eds.): TACAS 2023, LNCS 13994, pp. 74–92, 2023.
https://doi.org/10.1007/978-3-031-30820-8_8

resources. Other applications are less immediate. For example, proving an interesting mathematical theorem may require a lemma that bounds some quantity of interest (e.g. [4]). Once one has formulated the relevant optimization problems, one has to transform them into ones that the available software can solve, and one has to ensure that the conditions under which the software is designed to work correctly have been met. Mathematical knowledge and domain-specific expertise are often needed to transform a problem to match an efficient convex programming paradigm. A number of modeling packages then provide front ends that apply further transformations so that the resulting problem conforms to a back-end solver's input specification [15,20,26,17,42]. The transformed problem is sent to the back-end solver and the solver produces a response, which then has to be reinterpreted in terms of the original problem.

Our goal here is to develop ways of using formal methods to make the passage from an initial mathematical problem to the use of a back-end solver more efficient and reliable. Expressing a mathematical problem in a computational proof assistant provides clarity by endowing claims with a precise semantics, and having a formal library at hand enables users to draw on a body of mathematical facts and reasoning procedures. These make it possible to verify mathematical claims with respect to the primitives and rules of a formal axiomatic foundation, providing strong guarantees as to their correctness. Complete formalization places a high burden on practitioners and often imposes a standard that is higher than users want or need, but verification is not an all-or-nothing affair: users should have the freedom to decide which results they are willing to trust and which ones ought to be formally verified.

With respect to the use of optimization software, the soundness of the software itself is one possible concern. Checking the correctness of a solution to a satisfaction problem is easy in principle: one simply plugs the result into the constraints and checks that they hold. Verifying the correctness of a bounding problem or optimization problem is often almost as easy, in principle, since the results are often underwritten by the existence of suitable certificates that are output by the optimization tools. In practice, these tasks are made more difficult by the fact that floating point calculation can introduce numerical errors that bear on the correctness of the solution.

Here, instead, we focus on the task of manipulating a problem and reducing it to a form that a back-end solver can handle. Performing such transformations in a proof assistant offers strong guarantees that the results are correct and have the intended meaning, and it enables users to perform the transformations interactively or partially, and thus introspect and explore the results of individual transformation steps. Moreover, in constructing and reasoning about the transformations, users can take advantage of an ambient mathematical library, including a database of functions and their properties.

In Section 3, we describe the process that CVXPY and other systems use to transform optimization problems expressed in the *disciplined convex program* (DCP) framework to conic form problems that can be sent to solvers like MOSEK [30]. In Section 4, we explain how our implementation in the Lean programming language and proof assistant [33,32] augments that algorithm so that it at the same time produces a formal proof that the resulting reduction is correct. DCP relies on a library of basic atoms that serve as building blocks for reductions, and in Section 5, we explain how our implementation makes it possible to add new atoms in a verified way. In Section 6, we provide an example of the way that one can further leverage the power of an interactive theorem prover to justify the reduction of a problem that lies outside the DCP framework to one that lies within, using the mathematical library to verify its correctness. In Section 7, we describe our interface between Lean and an external solver, which transforms an exact symbolic representation of a problem into a floating point approximation. Related work is described in Section 8 and conclusions are presented in Section 9.

We have implemented these methods in a prototype, CvxLean.[5] We offer more information about the implementation in Section 9. A preliminary workshop paper [6] described our initial plans for this project and the reduction framework presented here in Section 2.

2 Optimization Problems and Reductions

The general structure of a minimization problem is expressed in Lean 4 as follows:

```
structure Minimization (D R : Type) :=
  (objFun : D → R)
  (constraints : D → Prop)
```

Here the data type D is the *domain* of the problem and R is the data type in which the objective function takes its values. The field objFun represents the objective function and constraints is a predicate on D, which, in Lean, is represented as a function from D to propositions: for every value a of the domain D, the proposition constraints a, which says that the constraints hold of a, is either true or false. The domain D is often $\mathbb{R}^n$ or a space of matrices, but it can also be something more exotic, like a space of functions. The data type R is typically the real numbers, but in full generality it can be any type that supports an ordering. A maximization problem is represented as a minimization problem for the negation of the objective function.

A *feasible point* for the minimization problem p is an element point of D satisfying p.constraints. Lean's foundational framework allows us to package the data point with the condition that it satisfies those constraints:

```
structure FeasPoint {D R : Type} [Preorder R] (p : Minimization D R) :=
  (point : D)
  (feasibility : p.constraints point)
```

The curly and square brackets denote parameters that can generally be inferred automatically. A *solution* to the minimization problem p is a feasible point, denoted point, such that for every feasible point y the value of the objective function at point is smaller than or equal to the value at y.

---

[5] https://github.com/verified-optimization/CvxLean

```
structure Solution {D R : Type} [Preorder R] (p : Minimization D R) :=
  (point : D)
  (feasibility : p.constraints point)
  (optimality : ∀ y : FeasPoint p, p.objFun point ≤ p.objFun y.point)
```

Feasibility and bounding problems can also be expressed in these terms. If the objective function is constant (e.g. the constant zero function), a solution to the optimization problem is simply a feasible point. Given a domain, an objective function, and constraints, the value b is a strict lower bound on the value of the objective function over the domain if and only if the feasibility problem obtained by adding the inequality `objFun x ≤ b` to the constraints has no solution.

Lean 4 allows us to implement convenient syntax for defining optimization problems. For example, the following specifies the problem of maximizing $\sqrt{x - y}$ subject to the constraints $y = 2x - 3$ and $x^2 \leq 2$:

```
optimization (x y : ℝ)
  maximize sqrt (x - y)
  subject to
    c1 : y = 2*x - 3
    c2 : x^2 ≤ 2
    c3 : 0 ≤ x - y
```

The third condition, c3, ensures that the objective function makes sense and is concave on the domain determined by the constraints. In some frameworks, like CVXPY, this constraint is seen as implicit in the use of the expression `sqrt (x - y)`, but we currently make it explicit in CvxLean. Problems can also depend on parameters and background conditions. For example, we can replace c1 above by `y = a*x - 3` for a parameter a, and we can replace the objective function by `b * sqrt (x - y)` with the background assumption `0 < b`.

In Section 6, we will consider the covariance estimation for Gaussian variables, which can be expressed as follows, for a tuple of sample values y:

```
optimization (R : Matrix (Fin n) (Fin n) ℝ)
  maximize (∏ i, gaussianPdf R (y i))
  subject to
    c_pos_def : R.posDef
```

Here `Matrix (Fin n) (Fin n) ℝ` is Lean's representation of the data type of $n \times n$ matrices over the reals, `gaussianPdf` is the Gaussian probability density function defined in Section 6, and the constraint `R.posDef` specifies that R ranges over positive definite matrices.

If p and q are problems, a *reduction* from p to q is a function mapping any solution to q to a solution to p. The existence of such a reduction means that to solve p it suffices to solve q. If p is a feasibility problem, it means that the feasibility of q implies the feasibility of p, and, conversely, that the infeasibility of p implies the infeasibility of q. We can now easily describe what we are after: we are looking for a system that helps a user reduce a problem p to a problem q that can be solved by an external solver. (For a bounding problem q, the goal is to show that the constraints with the negated bound are infeasible by finding a reduction from an infeasible problem p.) At the same time, we wish to verify the correctness of the reduction, either automatically or with user interaction. This will ensure that the results from the external solver really address the problem that the user is interested in solving.

This notion of a reduction is quite general, and is not restricted to any particular kind of constraint or objective function. In the sections that follow, we explain how the notion can be applied to convex programming.

3   Reduction to Conic Form

Disciplined Convex Programming (DCP) is a framework for writing constraints and objective functions in such a way that they can automatically be transformed into problems that can be handled by particular back-end solvers. It aims to be flexible enough to express optimization problems in a natural way but restrictive enough to ensure that problems can be transformed to meet the requirements of the solvers. To start with, the framework guarantees that expressions satisfy the relevant curvature constraints [1,21], assigning a *role* to each expression:

- Constant expressions and variables are affine.
- An expression $f(\mathsf{expr}_1, \ldots, \mathsf{expr}_n)$ is affine if f is an affine function and for each i, expr_i is affine.
- An expression $f(\mathsf{expr}_1, \ldots, \mathsf{expr}_n)$ is convex if f is convex and for each i, one of the following conditions holds:
  - f is increasing in its ith argument and expr_i is convex.
  - f is decreasing in its ith argument and expr_i is concave.
  - expr_i is affine.
- The previous statement holds with "convex" and "concave" switched.

An affine expression is both convex and concave. Some functions f come with side conditions on the range of arguments for which such curvature properties are valid; e.g. $f(x) = \sqrt{x}$ is concave and increasing on the domain $\{x \in \mathbb{R} \mid x \geq 0\}$.

A minimization problem is amenable to the DCP reduction if, following the rules above, its objective function is convex and the expressions occurring in its constraints are concave or convex, depending on the type of constraint. For example, maximizing $\sqrt{x - y}$ requires minimizing $-\sqrt{x - y}$, and the DCP rules tell us that the latter is a convex function of x and y on the domain where $x - y \geq 0$, because $x - y$ is affine, $\sqrt{\cdot}$ is concave and increasing in its argument, and negation is affine and decreasing in its argument.

CvxLean registers the properties of atomic functions $f(\bar{a})$ in a library of *atoms*. Each such function f is registered with a formal representation $\mathsf{expr}_f(\bar{a})$ using expressions, like x * log x or log (det A), that can refer to arbitrary functions defined in Lean's library. The atom also registers the relevant properties of f. The curvature of f, curv_f, has one of the values convex, concave, or affine, and the monotonicity of the function in each of its arguments is tagged as increasing, decreasing, or neither. CvxLean also allows the value auxiliary, which indicates an expression that serves as a fixed parameter in the sense that it is independent of the variables in the optimization problem. Atoms can also come with *background conditions* $\mathsf{bconds}_f(\bar{a})$, which are independent of the domain variables, and *variable conditions* $\mathsf{vconds}_f(\bar{a})$, which constrain the domain on which the properties hold. Notably, the atoms also include *proofs* of properties that are needed to justify the DCP reduction.

By storing additional information with each atom, a DCP framework can use the compositional representation of expressions to represent a problem in a form appropriate to a back-end solver. For example, solvers like MOSEK expect problems to be posed in a certain *conic form* [30]. To that end, CVXPY stores a *graph implementation* for each atomic function f, which is a representation of f as the solution to a conic optimization problem. By definition, the graph implementation of an atomic function f is an optimization problem in conic form, given by a list of variables $\bar{v}$, an objective function $\mathsf{obj}_f(\bar{x}, \bar{v})$, and a list of constraints $\mathsf{constr}_f(\bar{x}, \bar{v})$, such that the optimal value of the objective under the constraints is equal to $f(\bar{x})$ for all $\bar{x}$ in the domain of validity. For example, for any $x \geq 0$, the concave function $\sqrt{x}$ can be characterized as the maximum value of the objective function $\mathsf{obj}(x, t) = t$ satisfying the constraint $\mathsf{constr}(x, t)$ given by $t^2 \leq x$. Once again, a notable feature of CvxLean is that that the atom comes equipped with a formal proof of this fact.

The idea is that we can reduce a problem to the required form by iteratively replacing each application of an atomic function by an equivalent characterization in terms of the graph implementation. For example, we can replace a subexpression $\sqrt{x - y}$ by a new variable t and add the constraint $t^2 \leq x - y$, provided that the form of the resulting problem ensures that, for any *optimal* solution to the constraints, t will actually be *equal* to $\sqrt{x - y}$. Given a well-formed DCP minimization problem, CvxLean must perform the reduction and construct a formal proof of the associated claims. In this section we describe the reduction, and in the next section we describe the proofs. A more formal description of both are given in an extended version of this paper [7].

Let e be a well-formed DCP expression. CvxLean associates to each such expression a tree T whose leaves are expressions that are affine with respect to the variables of the optimization problem. For example, this is the tree associated with the expression `-sqrt (x - y)`:

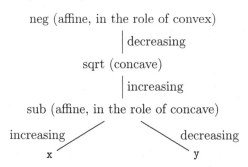

Alternatively, we could use a single leaf for `x - y`. Denoting the variables of the optimization problem by $\bar{y}$, we can recursively assign to each node n a subexpression $\mathsf{oexpr}_n(\bar{y})$ of e that corresponds to the subtree with root n. In the example above, the subexpressions are x, y, x - y, sqrt (x - y), and -sqrt (x - y). To each internal node, we assign a curvature, convex, concave, or affine, subject to the rules of DCP. An expression that is affine can be viewed as either convex or concave. Equalities and inequalities are also atoms; for example, $e_1 \leq e_2$ describes a convex set if and only if e_1 is convex and e_2 is concave. A formalization of the DCP rules allows us to recursively construct formal proofs of these curvature claims, modulo the conditions and assumptions of the problem. We elaborate on this process in the next section.

Now consider a well-formed DCP minimization problem with objective function o and constraints $c_1, \ldots, c_n$. We call these expressions the *components* of the problem. Recall the following example from the previous section, recast as a minimization problem:

```
optimization (x y : ℝ)
  minimize -sqrt (x - y)
  subject to
    c1 : y = 2*x - 3
    c2 : x^2 ≤ 2
    c3 : 0 ≤ x - y
```

Here the components are -sqrt (x - y), y = 2*x - 3, x^2 ≤ 2, and 0 ≤ x - y.

First, we assign to each component c an atom tree T_c as described above. If $\bar{y}$ are the variables of the original problem, the variables of the reduced problem are $\bar{y} \cup \bar{z}$, where $\bar{z}$ is a collection of variables consisting of a fresh set of variables for the graph implementation at each internal node of each tree, for those atoms whose graph implementations introduce new variables. To each node n of each atom tree, we assign an expression $\mathsf{rexpr}_n(\bar{y}, \bar{z})$ in the language of the reduced problem representing the expression $\mathsf{oexpr}_n(\bar{y})$ in the original problem. At the leaves, $\mathsf{rexpr}_n(\bar{y}, \bar{z})$ is the same as $\mathsf{oexpr}_n(\bar{y})$. At internal nodes we use the objective function of the corresponding atom's graph implementation, applied to the interpretation of the arguments. The objective of the reduced problem is the expression assigned to the root of T_o.

As far as the constraints of the reduced problem, recall that each internal node of the original problem corresponds to an atom, which has a graph implementation. The graph implementation, in turn, is given by a list of variables $\bar{v}$, an objective function $\mathsf{obj}_f(\bar{a}, \bar{v})$, and a list of constraints $\mathsf{constr}_f(\bar{a}, \bar{v})$. These constraints, applied to the expressions representing the arguments, are part of the reduced problem. Moreover, the constraints of the original problem, expressed in terms of the reduced problem, are also constraints of the reduced problem, with one exception. Recall that atoms can impose conditions $\mathsf{vconds}_f(\bar{a})$, which are assumed to be among the constraints of the original problem and to be *implied* by the graph implementation. For example, the condition $0 \leq x$ is required to characterize $\sqrt{x}$ as the maximum value of a value t satisfying $t^2 \leq x$, but, conversely, the existence of a t satisfying $t^2 \leq x$ implies $0 \leq x$. So a constraint $0 \leq x$ that is present in the original problem to justify the use of sqrt x can be dropped from the reduced problem.

In the example above, there is a tree corresponding to each of the components -sqrt (x - y), x^2 ≤ 2, 0 ≤ x - y, and y = 2*x - 3. As n ranges over the nodes of these trees, $\text{oexpr}_n(x, y)$ ranges over all the subexpressions of these components, namely, x, y, x - y, sqrt (x - y), -sqrt (x - y), x^2, 2, x^2 ≤ 2, and so on. The only atoms whose graph implementations introduce extra variables are the square root and the square. Thus, CvxLean introduces the variable t.0, corresponding to the expression sqrt (x - y), and the variable t.1, corresponding to the expression x^2. The values of $\text{rexpr}_n(x, y, t_0, t_1)$ corresponding to some of the expressions above are as follows:

$\text{oexpr}_n(x, y)$	x - y	sqrt (x - y)	-sqrt (x - y)	x^2
$\text{rexpr}_n(x, y, t_0, t_1)$	x - y	t.0	-t.0	t.1

The constraints c1 and c2 of the original problem translate to cone constraints c1' and c2' on the new variables, the constraint c3 is implied by the graph representation of x^2, and the graph representations of sqrt (x - y) and x^2 become new cone constraints c4' and c5'. Thus the reduced problem is as follows:

```
optimization (x y t.0 t.1 : ℝ)
  maximize t.0
  subject to
    c1' : zeroCone (2*x - 3 - y)        -- 2*x - 3 - y = 0
    c2' : posOrthCone (2 - t.1)         -- 2 - t.1 ≥ 0
    c4' : rotatedSoCone 0.5 (x - y) ![t.0]   -- x - y ≥ t.0^2
    c5' : rotatedSoCone t.1 0.5 ![x]         -- t.1 ≥ x^2
```

Here, ![t.0] and ![x] denote singleton vectors and the meaning of the cone constraints is annotated in the comments. For a description of the relevant conic forms, see the MOSEK modeling cookbook [31].

4   Verifying the Reduction

The reduction described in the previous section is essentially the same as the one carried out by CVXPY. The novelty of CvxLean is that it provides a formal justification that the reduction is correct. The goal of this section is to explain how we manage to construct a formal proof of that claim. In fact, given a problem P with an objective function f, CvxLean constructs a new problem Q with an objective g, together with the following additional pieces of data:

- a function φ from the domain of P to the domain of Q such that for any feasible point x of P, $\varphi(x)$ is a feasible point of Q with $g(\varphi(x)) \leq f(x)$
- a function ψ from the domain of Q to the domain of P such that for any feasible point y of Q, $\psi(y)$ is a feasible point of P with $f(\psi(y)) \leq g(y)$.

These conditions guarantee that if y is a solution to Q then $\psi(y)$ is a solution to P, because for any feasible point x of P we have

$$f(\psi(y)) \leq g(y) \leq g(\varphi(x)) \leq f(x).$$

This shows that ψ is a reduction of P to Q, and the argument with P and Q swapped shows that φ is a reduction of Q to P. Moreover, whenever y is a solution to Q, instantiating x to $\psi(y)$ in the chain of inequalities implies $f(\psi(y)) = g(y)$. Similarly, when x is a solution to P, we have $g(\varphi(x)) = f(x)$. So the conditions above imply that P has a solution if and only if Q has a solution, and when they do, the minimum values of the objective functions coincide. Below, we will refer to the data (φ, ψ) as a *strong equivalence* between the two problems.

To construct and verify such a strong equivalence between the original problem and the result of applying the transformation described in Section 3, we need to store additional information with each atom. Specifically, for each atomic function $f(\bar{a})$, that atom must provide solutions $\mathsf{sol}_f(\bar{a})$ to the graph implementation variables $\bar{v}$, as well as formal proofs of the following facts:

- The function $f(\bar{a})$ satisfies the graph implementation: for each $\bar{a}$ satisfying the conditions $\mathsf{vconds}_f(\bar{a})$, we have:
  - *solution feasibility:* $\mathsf{sol}_f(\bar{a})$ satisfies the constraints $\mathsf{constr}_f(\bar{a}, \mathsf{sol}_f(\bar{a}))$
  - *solution correctness:* we have $\mathsf{obj}_f(\bar{a}, \mathsf{sol}_f(\bar{a})) = \mathsf{expr}_f(\bar{a})$, where $\mathsf{expr}_f(\bar{a})$ is the expression representing f.
- The function $f(\bar{a})$ is the *optimal* solution to the graph implementation, in the following sense. Write $\bar{a}' \bigtriangleup \bar{a}$ to express the assumptions that $a'_i \geq a_i$ for increasing arguments to f, $a'_i \leq a_i$ for decreasing arguments, and a'_i and a_i are syntactically identical for other arguments. If f is convex and $\bar{a} \bigtriangleup \bar{a}'$, we require $\mathsf{obj}_f(\bar{a}, \bar{v}) \geq \mathsf{expr}_f(\bar{a}')$ for any $\bar{v}$ such that $\mathsf{constr}_f(\bar{a}, \bar{v})$ holds. If f is concave and $\bar{a}' \bigtriangleup \bar{a}$, we require $\mathsf{obj}_f(\bar{a}, \bar{v}) \leq \mathsf{expr}_f(\bar{a}')$ for any $\bar{v}$ such that $\mathsf{constr}_f(\bar{a}, \bar{v})$ holds. For affine atoms, we require both.

Finally, as noted in the previous section, the graph implementation implies the conditions needed for the reduction. Under the assumptions on $\bar{a}$ and $\bar{a}'$ in the second case above, we also require a proof of $\mathsf{vconds}_f(\bar{a}')$. We refer to this as *condition elimination*.

For a concrete example, consider the atom for the concave function $\sqrt{a}$. In that case, $\mathsf{vconds}(a)$ is the requirement $a \geq 0$, and $\mathsf{expr}(a)$, the Lean representation of the function, is given by Lean's `sqrt` function. The graph implementation adds a new variable v. The only constraint $\mathsf{constr}(a, v)$ is $v^2 \leq a$, and the objective function is $\mathsf{obj}(a, v) = v$. The solution function $\mathsf{sol}(a)$ returns $\sqrt{a}$ when a is nonnegative and an arbitrary value otherwise. The atom for $\sqrt{\cdot}$ stores Lean proofs of all of the following:

- solution feasibility: $\forall$ a, 0 $\leq$ a $\rightarrow$ (sqrt a)^2 $\leq$ a
- solution correctness: $\forall$ a, 0 $\leq$ a $\rightarrow$ sqrt a = sqrt a
- optimality: $\forall$ v a a', a $\leq$ a' $\rightarrow$ v^2 $\leq$ a $\rightarrow$ v $\leq$ sqrt a'
- condition elimination: $\forall$ v a a', a $\leq$ a' $\rightarrow$ v^2 $\leq$ a $\rightarrow$ 0 $\leq$ a'.

More precisely, the atom stores the representation of the graph of the square root function as a cone constraint, and the properties above are expressed in those terms. These properties entail that `sqrt` is concave, but we do not need to prove concavity explicitly.

Let the variables $\bar{y}$ range over the domain of the original problem, P, and let the variables $\bar{y}, \bar{z}$ be the augmented list of variables in the reduced problem, Q. We wish to construct a strong equivalence between P and Q. To that end, we need to define a forward map φ and a reverse map ψ. The definition of ψ is easy: we simply project each tuple $\bar{y}, \bar{z}$ to $\bar{y}$. The definition of the forward map, φ, is more involved, since we have to map each tuple $\bar{y}$ of values to an expanded tuple $\bar{y}, \bar{z}$. The values of $\bar{y}$ remain unchanged, so the challenge is to define, for each new variable z, an expression $\mathsf{interp}_z(\bar{y})$ to interpret it.

Recall that for each subexpression $\mathsf{oexpr}_n(\bar{y})$ in the original problem, corresponding to a node n, there is an expression $\mathsf{rexpr}_n(\bar{y}, \bar{w})$ involving new variables from the reduced problem. Suppose a node n corresponds to an expression $f(u_1, \ldots, u_n)$ in the original problem, and the graph implementation of f introduces new variables $\bar{v}$. For each v_j, we need to devise an interpretation $\mathsf{interp}_{v_j}(\bar{y})$. To start with, sol_f provides a solution to v_j in terms of the arguments $u_1, \ldots, u_n$. For each of these arguments, rexpr provides a representation in terms of the variables $\bar{y}$ and other new variables. Composing these, we get an expression $\mathsf{e}(\bar{y}, w_1, \ldots, w_\ell)$ for v_j in terms of the variables $\bar{y}$ of the original problem and new variables $w_1, \ldots, w_\ell$. Recursively, we find interpretations $\mathsf{interp}_{w_k}(\bar{y})$ of each w_k, and define $\mathsf{interp}_{v_j}(\bar{y})$ to be $\mathsf{e}(\bar{y}, \mathsf{interp}_{w_1}(\bar{y}), \ldots, \mathsf{interp}_{w_\ell}(\bar{y}))$. In other words, we read off the interpretation of each new variable of the reduced problem from the intended solution to the graph equation, which may, in turn, require the interpretation of other new variables that were previously introduced.

In the end, the forward map φ is the function that maps the variables $\bar{y}$ in the original problem to the tuple $(\bar{y}, \mathsf{interp}_{z_1}(\bar{y}), \ldots, \mathsf{interp}_{z_m}(\bar{y}))$, where $z_1, \ldots, z_m$ are the new variables. To show that (φ, ψ) is a strong equivalence, we must show that for any feasible point $\bar{y}$ of the original problem, $\varphi(\bar{y})$ is a feasible point of the reduced problem. This follows from the solution correctness requirement above. We also need to show that if $f(\bar{y})$ is the objective function of the original problem and $g(\bar{y}, \bar{z})$ is the objective function of the reduced problem, $g(\varphi(\bar{y})) \leq f(\bar{y})$. In fact, the solution correctness requirement enables us to prove the stronger property $g(\varphi(\bar{y})) = f(\bar{y})$. Finally, we need to show that for any feasible point $\bar{y}, \bar{z}$ of the reduced problem, the tuple $\bar{y}$ is a feasible point of the original problem and $f(\bar{y}) \leq g(\bar{y}, \bar{z})$. To do that, we recursively use the optimality requirement to show $\mathsf{rexpr}_n(\bar{y}, \bar{z}) \geq \mathsf{oexpr}_n(\bar{y})$ whenever the node n marks a convex expression or an affine expression in the role of a convex expression, and $\mathsf{rexpr}_n(\bar{y}, \bar{z}) \leq \mathsf{oexpr}_n(\bar{y})$ whenever the node n marks a concave expression or an affine expression in the role of a concave expression.

A proof that the maps φ and ψ constructed above form a strong equivalence can be found in the extended version of this paper [7], but it is helpful to work through the example from Section 3 to get a sense of what the proof means. For this example, the forward map is $\varphi(x, y) = (x, y, \sqrt{x - y}, x^2)$ and the reverse map is $\psi(x, y, t_0, t_1) = (x, y)$. Assuming that (x, y) is a solution to the original problem, the fact that $\varphi(x, y)$ satisfies c1' follows from c1, the fact that it satisfies c2' follows from c2, the fact that it satisfies c4' and c5' follows from the fact that $\sqrt{x - y}$ and x^2 are correct solutions to the graph implementation constraints. In this direction, $g(\varphi(x,y)) = -\sqrt{x-y} = f(x,y)$. In the other direction, assuming that (x, y, t_0, t_1) is a solution to the reduced problem, the fact that (x, y) satisfies c1 follows from c1', that fact that it satisfies c2 follows from c2' and c5', and the fact that is satisfies c3 follows from c4'. Here we have $f(\psi(x, y, t_0, t_1)) = -\sqrt{x-y}$ and $g(x, y, t_0, t_1) = -t_0$, and the fact that the former is less than or equal to the latter follows from c4'.

5 Adding Atoms

One important advantage to using an interactive theorem prover as a basis for solving optimization problems is that it is possible to extend the atom library in a verified way. In a system like CVXPY, one declares a new atom with its graph implementation on the basis of one's background knowledge or a pen-and-paper proof that the graph implementation is correct and that the function described has the relevant properties over the specified domain. In CvxLean, we have implemented syntax with which any user can declare a new atom in Lean and provide formal proofs of these facts. The declaration can be made in any Lean file, and it becomes available in any file that imports that one as a dependency. Lean has a build system and package manager that handles dependencies on external repositories, allowing a community of users to share such mathematical and computational content.

For example, the declaration of the atom for the logarithm looks as follows:

```
declare_atom log [concave] (x : ℝ)+ : log x :=
  conditions (cond : 0 < x)
  implementationVars (t : ℝ)
  implementationObjective t
  implementationConstraints (c_exp : expCone t 1 x)
  solution (t := log x)
  solutionEqualsAtom by ...
  feasibility (c_exp : by ...)
  optimality by ...
  conditionElimination (cond : by ...)
```

The ellipses indicate places that are filled by formal proofs. Proof assistants like Lean allow users to write such proofs interactively in an environment that displays proof obligations, the local context, and error messages, all while the user types. For example, placing the cursor at the beginning of the optimality block displays the following goal:

```
x t : ℝ
c_exp : expCone t 1 x
⊢ ∀ (y : ℝ), x ≤ y → t ≤ log y
```

In other words, given real values x and t and the relevant constraint in terms of the exponential cone, we need to prove that for every $y \geq x$, we have $t \leq \log(y)$.

For the example we present in the next section, we had to implement the *log-determinant* atom [10, Example 9.5], whose arguments consist of a natural number n and a matrix $A \in \mathbb{R}^{n \times n}$. This function is represented in Lean by the atom expression $\mathsf{expr}_{log\text{-}det} = \texttt{log (det A)}$, where the parameter n is implicit in the type of A. The curvature is specified to be concave, the monotonicity in n is auxiliary because we do not support the occurrence of optimization variables in this argument, and the monotonicity in A is neither because the value of $\log(\det A)$ is neither guaranteed to increase nor guaranteed to decrease as A increases. (The relevant order here on matrices is elementwise comparison.) The correctness of the reduction requires the assumption that A is positive definite. Following CVXPY, we used the following graph implementation:

$$\begin{aligned}
&\text{maximize} && \sum_i t_i \\
&\text{over} && t \in \mathbb{R}^n,\ Y \in \mathbb{R}^{n \times n} \\
&\text{subject to} && (t, 1, y) \in \text{expcone} \\
& && \begin{pmatrix} D & Z \\ Z^T & A \end{pmatrix} \text{ positive semidefinite}
\end{aligned}$$

Here y is the diagonal of Y; Z is obtained from Y by setting all entries below the diagonal to 0; and D is obtained from Y by setting all entries off the diagonal to 0. Here, saying that the tuple $(t, 1, y)$ is in the exponential cone means that $e^{y_i} \geq t_i$ for each i. Our implementation in CvxLean required proving that this graph implementation is correct. To do so, we formalized an argument in the MOSEK documentation.[6] This, in turn, required proving properties of the Schur complement, triangular matrices, Gram-Schmidt orthogonalization, and LDL factorization. Moreover, the argument uses the subadditivity of the determinant function, for which we followed an argument by Andreas Thom on MathOverflow.[7]

6   User-defined Reductions

An even more important advantage of using an interactive proof assistant as a framework for convex optimization is that, with enough work, users can carry out *any* reduction that can be expressed and justified in precise mathematical terms. As a simple example, DCP cannot handle an expression of the form $exp(x)exp(y)$ in a problem, requiring us instead to write it as $exp(x + y)$. But in CvxLean, we have the freedom to express the problem in the first form if we prefer to and then verify that the trivial reduction is justified:

```
reduction red/prob :
  optimization (x y : ℝ)
    maximize x + y
    subject to
```

[6] https://docs.mosek.com/modeling-cookbook/sdo.html#log-determinant
[7] https://mathoverflow.net/questions/65424/determinant-of-sum-of-positive-definite-matrices/65430#65430

```
    h : (exp x) * (exp y) ≤ 10 := by
conv_constr => rw [←Real.exp_add]
```

Here the expression `rw [←Real.exp_add]` supplies the short formal proof that $exp(x + y)$ can be replaced by $exp(x)exp(y)$.

Of course, this functionality becomes more important as the reductions become more involved. As a more substantial example, we have implemented a reduction needed to solve the the covariance estimation problem for Gaussian variables [10, pp. 355]. In this problem, we are given N samples $y_1, \ldots, y_N \in \mathbb{R}^n$ drawn from a Gaussian distribution with zero mean and unknown covariance matrix R. We assume that the Gaussian distribution is nondegenerate, so R is positive definite and the distribution has density function

$$p_R(y) = (2\pi)^{-n/2} \det(R)^{-1/2} \exp(-y^T R^{-1} y/2).$$

We want to estimate the covariance matrix R using maximum likelihood estimation, i.e., we want to find the covariance matrix that maximizes the likelihood of observing $y_1, \ldots y_N$. The maximum likelihood estimate for R is the solution to the following problem:

$$\text{maximize} \ \prod_{k=1}^{N} p_R(y_k) \ \text{over} \ R \ \text{subject to} \ R \ \text{positive definite.}$$

As stated, this problem has a simple analytic solution, namely, the sample covariance of $y_1, \ldots, y_n$, but the problem becomes more interesting when one adds additional constraints, for example, upper and lower matrix bounds on R, or constraints on the condition number of R (see [10]). We can easily reduce the problem to maximizing the logarithm of the objective function above, but that is not a concave function of R. It is, however, a concave function of $S = R^{-1}$, and common constraints on R translate to convex constraints on S. We can therefore reduce the problem above to the following:

$$\text{maximize} \ \log(\det(S)) - \sum_{k=1}^{N} y_k^T S y_k \ \text{over} \ S \ \text{subject to} \ S \ \text{positive definite,}$$

possibly with additional constraints on S. We express the sum using the sample covariance $Y = \frac{1}{N} \sum_{k=1}^{N} y_k y_k^T$ and the trace operator:

$$\text{maximize} \ \log(\det(S)) - N \cdot \text{tr}(Y S^T) \ \text{over} \ S$$
$$\text{subject to} \ S \ \text{positive definite}$$

The problem can then be solved using disciplined convex programming. The constraint that S is positive definite is eliminated while applying the graph implementation of $\log(\det(S))$.

We have formalized these facts in Lean and used them to justify the reduction. An example with an additional sparsity constraints on R can be found in `CvxLean/Examples` in our repository.

7   Connecting Lean to a Conic Optimization Solver

Once a problem has been reduced to conic form, it can be sent to an external back-end solver. At this point, we must pass from the realm of precise symbolic representations and formal mathematical objects to the realm of numeric computation with floating point representations. We traverse our symbolic expressions, replacing functions on the reals from Lean's mathematical library with corresponding numeric functions on floats, for example associating the floating point exponential function `Float.exp` to the real exponential function `Real.exp`. Our implementation makes it easy to declare such associations with the following syntax: `addRealToFloat : Real.exp := Float.exp`.

This is one area where more verification is possible. We could use verified libraries for floating point arithmetic [2,9,19,44], we could use dual certificates to verify the results of the external solver, and we could carry out formal sensitivity analysis to manage and bound errors. Our current implementation is only designed to verify correctness up to the point where the problem is sent to the back-end solver, and to facilitate the last step, albeit in an unverified way.

We have implemented a `solve` command in CvxLean which takes a an optimization problem `prob` in DCP form and carries out the following steps:

1. It applies the `dcp` procedure to obtain a reduced problem, `prob.reduced`, and a reduction `red : Solution prob.reduced -> Solution prob`.
2. It carries out the translation to floats, traversing each expression and applying the registered translations.
3. It extracts the numerical data from the problem. At this point, we have scalars, arrays and matrices associated to every type of constraint.
4. It writes the problem to an external file in the conic benchmark format.[8]
5. It calls MOSEK and receives a status code in return, together with a solution, if MOSEK succeeds in finding one. The problem status is added to the environment and if it is infeasible or ill-posed, we stop.
6. Otherwise, the `solve` command interprets the solution so that it matches the shape of the variables of `prob.reduced`. It also expresses these values as Lean reals, resulting in an approximate solution `p` to `prob.reduced`. It declares a corresponding `Solution` to `prob.reduced`, using a placeholder for the proofs of feasibility and optimality (since we simply trust the solver here).
7. It then uses the reduction from `prob` to `prod.reduced`, again reinterpreted in terms of floats, to compute an approximate solution to `prob`.

Finally, the results are added to the Lean environment. In the following example, the command `solve sol` results in the creation of new Lean objects `sol.reduced`, `sol.status`, `sol.value`, and `sol.solution`. The first of these represents the conic-form problem that is sent to the back-end solver, while the remaining three comprise the resulting solution.

```
noncomputable def sol :=
```

---

[8] https://docs.mosek.com/latest/rmosek/cbf-format.html

```
optimization (x y : ℝ)
  maximize sqrt (x - y)
  subject to
    c1 : y = 2*x - 3
    c2 : x^2 ≤ 2
    c3 : 0 ≤ x - y

solve sol
#print sol.reduced     -- shows the reduced problem
#eval sol.status       -- "PRIMAL_AND_DUAL_FEASIBLE"
#eval sol.value        -- 2.101003
#eval sol.solution     -- (-1.414214, -5.828427)
```

8   Related Work

Our work builds on decades of research on convex optimization [10,36,39,43], and most directly on the CVX family and disciplined convex programming [15,17,20,21,42]. Other popular packages include Yalmip [26].

Formal methods have been used to solve bounding problems [18,38], constraint satisfaction problems [16], and optimization problems [25]. This literature is too broad to survey here, but [14] surveys some of the methods that are used in connection with the verification of cyber-physical systems. Proof assistants in particular have been used to verify bounds in various ways. Some approaches use certificates from numerical packages; Harrison [24] uses certificates from semidefinite programming in HOL Light, and Magron et al. [27] and Martin-Dorel and Roux [28] use similar certificates in Coq. Solovyev and Hales use a combination of symbolic and numeric methods in HOL Light [40]. Other approaches have focused on verifying symbolic and numeric algorithms instead. For example, Muñoz, Narkawicz, and Dutle [34] verify a decision procedure for univariate real arithmetic in PVS and Cordwell, Tan, and Platzer [13] verify another one in Isabelle. Narkawicz and Muñoz [35] have devised a verified numeric algorithm to find bounds and global optima. Cohen et al. [11,12] have developed a framework for verifying optimization algorithms using the ANSI/ISO C Specification Language (ACSL) [5].

Although the notion of a convex set has been formalized in a number of theorem provers, we do not know of any full development of convex analysis. The Isabelle [37] HOL-Analysis library includes properties of convex sets and functions, including Carathéodory's theorem on convex hulls, Radon's theorem, and Helly's theorem, as well as properties of convex sets and functions on normed spaces and Euclidean spaces. A theory of lower semicontinuous functions by Grechuk [22] in the Archive of Formal Proofs [8] includes properties of convex functions. Lean's mathlib [29] includes a number of fundamental results, including a formalization of the Riesz extension theorem by Kudryashov and Dupuis and a formalization of Jensen's inequality by Kudryashov. Allamigeon and Katz have formalized a theory of convex polyhedra in Coq with an eye towards applications to linear optimization [3]. We do not know of any project that has formalized the notion of a reduction between optimization problems.

9 Conclusions

We have argued that formal methods can bring additional reliability and interactive computational support to the practice of convex optimization. The success of our prototype shows that it is possible to carry out and verify reductions using a synergistic combination of automation and user interaction.

The implementation of CvxLean is currently spread between two versions of Lean [32,33]. Lean 3 has a formal library, mathlib [29], which comprises close to a million lines of code and covers substantial portions of algebra, linear algebra, topology, measure theory, and analysis. Lean 4 is a performant programming language as well as a proof assistant, but its language is not backward compatible with that of Lean 3. All of the substantial programming tasks described here have been carried out in Lean 4, but we rely on a binary translation of the Lean 3 library and some additional results proved there. This arrangement is not ideal, but a source-level port of the Lean 3 library is already underway, and we expect to move the development entirely to Lean 4 in the near future.

There is still a lot to do. We have implemented and verified all the atoms needed for the examples presented in this paper, but these are still only a fraction of the atoms that are found in CVXPY. The DCP transformation currently leaves any side conditions that it cannot prove for the user to fill in, and special-purpose *tactics*, i.e. small-scale automation, could help dispel proof obligations like monotonicity. Textbooks often provide standard methods and tricks for carrying out reductions (e.g. [10, Section 4.1.3]), and these should also be supported by tactics in CvxLean. Our project, as well as Lean's library, would benefit from more formal definitions and theorems in convex analysis and optimization. We need to implement more efficient means of extracting numeric values for the back-end solver, and it would be nice to verify more of the numeric computations and claims. Finally, and most importantly, we need to work out more examples like the ones presented here to ensure that the system is robust and flexible enough to join the ranks of conventional optimization systems like CVXPY.

Acknowledgements Seulkee Baek did some preliminary experiments on connecting Lean 3 to external optimization solvers. Mario Carneiro and Gabriel Ebner advised us on how to formalize optimization problems and on Lean 4 metaprogramming. Steven Diamond helped us understand the world of convex optimization. We also had helpful discussions with Geir Dullerud, Paul Jackson, Florian Jarre, John Miller, Balasubramanian Narasimhan, Ivan Papusha, and Ufuk Topcu. Diamond, Jackson, and Parth Nobel provided helpful feedback on a draft of this paper. This work has been partially supported by the Hoskinson Center for Formal Mathematics at Carnegie Mellon University. Bentkamp has received funding from a Chinese Academy of Sciences President's International Fellowship for Postdoctoral Researchers (grant No. 2021PT0015). We thank the anonymous reviewers for their corrections and suggestions.

References

1. Agrawal, A., Verschueren, R., Diamond, S., Boyd, S.: A rewriting system for convex optimization problems. J. Control and Decision **5**(1), 42–60 (2018)
2. Akbarpour, B., Abdel-Hamid, A.T., Tahar, S., Harrison, J.: Verifying a synthesized implementation of IEEE-754 floating-point exponential function using HOL. Comput. J. **53**(4), 465–488 (2010). https://doi.org/10.1093/comjnl/bxp023
3. Allamigeon, X., Katz, R.D.: A formalization of convex polyhedra based on the simplex method. J. Autom. Reason. **63**(2), 323–345 (2019)
4. Bachoc, C., Vallentin, F.: New upper bounds for kissing numbers from semidefinite programming. J. Amer. Math. Soc. **21**(3), 909–924 (2008). https://doi.org/10.1090/S0894-0347-07-00589-9
5. Baudin, P., Cuoq, P., Filliâtre, J.C., Marché, C., Monate, B., Moy, Y., Prevosto, V.: Acsl: ANSI / ISO c specification language (2020), https://frama-c.com/html/acsl.html, version 1.17
6. Bentkamp, A., Avigad, J.: Verified optimization (work in progress) (2022), Formal Mathematics for Mathematicians (FMM) workshop, 2021
7. Bentkamp, A., Fernández Mir, R., Avigad, J.: Verified reductions for optimization (2023), https://arxiv.org/abs/2301.09347
8. Blanchette, J.C., Haslbeck, M.W., Matichuk, D., Nipkow, T.: Mining the archive of formal proofs. In: Kerber, M., Carette, J., Kaliszyk, C., Rabe, F., Sorge, V. (eds.) Intelligent Computer Mathematics (CICM) 2015. pp. 3–17. Springer (2015)
9. Boldo, S., Filliâtre, J.: Formal verification of floating-point programs. In: 18th IEEE Symposium on Computer Arithmetic (ARITH-18) 2007, 25-27 June 2007, Montpellier, France. pp. 187–194. IEEE Computer Society (2007). https://doi.org/10.1109/ARITH.2007.20
10. Boyd, S.P., Vandenberghe, L.: Convex Optimization. Cambridge University Press (2014), https://web.stanford.edu/~boyd/cvxbook/
11. Cohen, R., Davy, G., Feron, E., Garoche, P.L.: Formal verification for embedded implementation of convex optimization algorithms. IFAC-PapersOnLine **50**(1), 5867–5874 (2017), 20th IFAC World Congress
12. Cohen, R., Feron, E., Garoche, P.: Verification and validation of convex optimization algorithms for model predictive control. Journal of Aerospace Information Systems **17**(5), 257–270 (2020)
13. Cordwell, K., Tan, Y.K., Platzer, A.: A verified decision procedure for univariate real arithmetic with the BKR algorithm. In: Cohen, L., Kaliszyk, C. (eds.) Interactive Theorem Proving (ITP) 2021. LIPIcs, vol. 193, pp. 14:1–14:20. Schloss Dagstuhl - Leibniz-Zentrum für Informatik (2021)
14. Deshmukh, J.V., Sankaranarayanan, S.: Formal techniques for verification and testing of cyber-physical systems. In: Al Faruque, M.A., Canedo, A. (eds.) Design Automation of Cyber-Physical Systems. pp. 69–105. Springer, Cham (2019)
15. Diamond, S., Boyd, S.: CVXPY: A Python-embedded modeling language for convex optimization. J. Machine Learning Research **17**(83), 1–5 (2016)
16. Fränzle, M., Herde, C., Teige, T., Ratschan, S., Schubert, T.: Efficient solving of large non-linear arithmetic constraint systems with complex Boolean structure. J. Satisf. Boolean Model. Comput. **1**(3-4), 209–236 (2007). https://doi.org/10.3233/sat190012
17. Fu, A., Narasimhan, B., Boyd, S.: CVXR: An R package for disciplined convex optimization. Journal of Statistical Software **94**(14), 1–34 (2020)

18. Gao, S., Avigad, J., Clarke, E.M.: δ-complete decision procedures for satisfiability over the reals. In: Gramlich, B., Miller, D., Sattler, U. (eds.) Automated Reasoning (IJCAR) 2012. pp. 286–300. Springer (2012)

19. Goodloe, A., Muñoz, C.A., Kirchner, F., Correnson, L.: Verification of numerical programs: From real numbers to floating point numbers. In: Brat, G., Rungta, N., Venet, A. (eds.) NASA Formal Methods (NFM) 2013. pp. 441–446. Springer (2013). https://doi.org/10.1007/978-3-642-38088-4_31

20. Grant, M., Boyd, S.: CVX: Matlab software for disciplined convex programming, version 2.1. http://cvxr.com/cvx (Mar 2014)

21. Grant, M., Boyd, S., Ye, Y.: Disciplined convex programming. In: Global optimization, pp. 155–210. Springer (2006)

22. Grechuk, B.: Lower semicontinuous functions. Archive of Formal Proofs (Jan 2011), https://isa-afp.org/entries/Lower_Semicontinuous.html, Formal proof development

23. Gurobi Optimization, LLC: Gurobi Optimizer Reference Manual (2022), https://www.gurobi.com

24. Harrison, J.: Verifying nonlinear real formulas via sums of squares. In: Schneider, K., Brandt, J. (eds.) Theorem Proving in Higher Order Logics (TPHOLs) 2007. pp. 102–118. Springer (2007)

25. Kong, S., Solar-Lezama, A., Gao, S.: Delta-decision procedures for exists-forall problems over the reals. In: Chockler, H., Weissenbacher, G. (eds.) Computer Aided Verification (CAV) 2018, Part II. pp. 219–235. Springer (2018)

26. Löfberg, J.: Yalmip : A toolbox for modeling and optimization in matlab. In: Computer Aided Control System Design (CACSD) 2004. pp. 284–289 (2004)

27. Magron, V., Allamigeon, X., Gaubert, S., Werner, B.: Formal proofs for nonlinear optimization. J. Formaliz. Reason. **8**(1), 1–24 (2015). https://doi.org/10.6092/issn.1972-5787/4319

28. Martin-Dorel, É., Roux, P.: A reflexive tactic for polynomial positivity using numerical solvers and floating-point computations. In: Bertot, Y., Vafeiadis, V. (eds.) Certified Programs and Proofs (CPP) 2017. pp. 90–99. ACM (2017). https://doi.org/10.1145/3018610.3018622

29. Mathlib Community: The Lean mathematical library. In: Blanchette, J., Hritcu, C. (eds.) Certified Programs and Proofs (CPP) 2020. pp. 367–381. ACM (2020)

30. MOSEK ApS: Introducing the MOSEK Optimization Suite (2022), https://docs.mosek.com/latest/intro

31. MOSEK ApS: MOSEK Modeling Cookbook (2022), https://docs.mosek.com/modeling-cookbook

32. de Moura, L., Ullrich, S.: The Lean 4 theorem prover and programming language. In: Platzer, A., Sutcliffe, G. (eds.) Automated Deduction (CADE) 2021. pp. 625–635. Springer (2021). https://doi.org/10.1007/978-3-030-79876-5_37

33. de Moura, L.M., Kong, S., Avigad, J., van Doorn, F., von Raumer, J.: The Lean theorem prover (system description). In: Felty, A.P., Middeldorp, A. (eds.) Conference on Automated Deduction (CADE) 2015. pp. 378–388. Springer (2015)

34. Muñoz, C.A., Narkawicz, A.J., Dutle, A.: A decision procedure for univariate polynomial systems based on root counting and interval subdivision. J. Formaliz. Reason. **11**(1), 19–41 (2018). https://doi.org/10.6092/issn.1972-5787/8212

35. Narkawicz, A., Muñoz, C.A.: A formally verified generic branching algorithm for global optimization. In: Cohen, E., Rybalchenko, A. (eds.) Verified Software: Theories, Tools, Experiments (VSTTE) 2013. pp. 326–343. Springer (2013)

36. Nesterov, Y.: Lectures on convex optimization. Springer, Cham (2018). https://doi.org/10.1007/978-3-319-91578-4, second edition

37. Nipkow, T., Paulson, L.C., Wenzel, M.: Isabelle/HOL - A Proof Assistant for Higher-Order Logic. Springer (2002)
38. Ratschan, S., She, Z.: Safety verification of hybrid systems by constraint propagation-based abstraction refinement. ACM Trans. Embed. Comput. Syst. **6**(1), 8 (2007). https://doi.org/10.1145/1210268.1210276
39. Rockafellar, R.T.: Convex analysis. Princeton University Press, Princeton, N.J. (1970)
40. Solovyev, A., Hales, T.C.: Formal verification of nonlinear inequalities with Taylor interval approximations. In: Brat, G., Rungta, N., Venet, A. (eds.) NASA Formal Methods (NFM) 2013. pp. 383–397. Springer (2013)
41. Sturm, J.F.: Using Sedumi 1.02, a Matlab toolbox for optimization over symmetric cones. Optimization methods and software **11**(1-4), 625–653 (1999)
42. Udell, M., Mohan, K., Zeng, D., Hong, J., Diamond, S., Boyd, S.: Convex optimization in Julia. SC14 Workshop on High Performance Technical Computing in Dynamic Languages (2014)
43. Vishnoi, N.: Algorithms for Convex Optimization. Cambridge University Press (2021)
44. Yu, L.: A formal model of IEEE floating point arithmetic. Archive of Formal Proofs (July 2013), https://www.isa-afp.org/entries/IEEE_Floating_Point.shtml

Specifying and Verifying Higher-order Rust Iterators

Xavier Denis and Jacques-Henri Jourdan(✉)

Université Paris-Saclay, CNRS, ENS Paris-Saclay, Laboratoire Méthodes Formelles,
91190, Gif-sur-Yvette, France
jacques-henri.jourdan@cnrs.fr

Abstract. In Rust, programs are often written using *iterators*, but these pose problems for verification: they are *non-deterministic*, *infinite*, and often *higher-order*, *effectful* and built using *adapters*. We present a general framework for specifying and reasoning with Rust iterators in first-order logic. Our approach is capable of addressing the challenges set out above, which we demonstrate by verifying real Rust iterators, including a higher-order, effectful `Map`. Using the CREUSOT verification platform, we evaluate our framework on clients of iterators, showing it leads to efficient verification of complex functional properties.

Keywords: Rust · Deductive verification · Iterators · Closures

1 Introduction

The Rust language aims to empower systems software programmers by offering them safe and powerful linguistic abstractions to solve their problems. The most notorious of these abstractions, Rust's *borrowing* mechanism, enables safe usage of pointers without a garbage collector or performance penalty. A close second is perhaps Rust's *iterator* system, through which Rust provides composable mechanisms to express the traversal and modification of collections. Iterators also underlie Rust's `for` loop syntax, and are thus the primary manner Rust developers write loops or interact with data structures. It is therefore essential for a verification tool for Rust to provide good support for iterators.

Rust iterators generate sequences of values. Most importantly, they are objects providing a method `fn next(&mut self) -> Option<Self::Item>`. This method takes a *mutable reference* (`&mut self`) to the iterator, allowing it to change its internal state, and optionally returns a value of type `Self::Item`, the type of the values generated by the iterator. If, instead of returning such a value, the iterator returns `None`, it means iteration has finished for now, though it may resume again later. Rust's `for` loops are just syntactic sugar for repeatedly calling `next` at the beginning of each iteration, until such a call returns `None`. For example, the following two pieces of code present a Rust loop for iterating over integers between 0 (included) and `n` (excluded), using a *range* iterator:

© The Author(s) 2023
S. Sankaranarayanan and N. Sharygina (Eds.): TACAS 2023, LNCS 13994, pp. 93–110, 2023.
https://doi.org/10.1007/978-3-031-30820-8_9

```
                                    let mut iter = 0..n;
                                    loop { match iter.next() {
for i in 0..n { <body> }               None => break,
                                       Some(i) => <body>
                                    } }
```

The piece of code on the left-hand side uses an idiomatic `for` loop, while the other shows its desugared version.

Iterators present unique challenges for verification tools: indeed, because the use of iterators is pervasive in Rust, it is necessary to allow verification of code using iterators with as little interaction as possible. In particular, most common patterns such as iterating over integers in a given range or reading the elements of a vector should not need any annotation other than the loop invariants the user would write if not using iterators. On the other hand, Rust's iterator library is complex, with many features representing as many challenges for verification: iterators can be built from various data structures and modified through *iterator adapters*, which make it possible to create iterators from simpler ones, by, e.g., skipping the first few elements or applying a given function to each of the elements.

Consider the example below:

```
1  let mut cnt = 0;
2  let w = vec![1,2,3].iter().map(|x|{cnt += 1; x + 1}).collect();
3  assert_eq!(w, vec![2,3,4]);  assert_eq!(cnt, 3);
```

On line 2, quite a lot happens at once. First, we produce an iterator over the elements of the vector `vec![1,2,3]` with the syntax `.iter()`, which we transform through a call to `map`. The method `map` is an *iterator adapter*: it returns a new iterator that calls the given closure on each of the elements generated by the underlying iterator, and forwards the value returned by the closure. Interestingly, the closure we pass to `map` *captures mutable state*: it modifies the variable `cnt`. Finally, the method `collect` gathers the elements generated into a new vector `w`.

We aim at requiring only lightweight annotations for verifying this kind of code: the appeal of *iterator chains* like on line 2 are the ergonomics, they are compact and highly-readable. For verification of iterator-based code to be successful, it must preserve this ergonomics. However, despite its apparent simplicity, this piece of code is challenging to verify: it combines higher-order functions and mutable state, uses potentially overflowing integers, and assertions on line 3 check full functional behavior.

More generally, to support iterators, a verification tool for Rust needs to provide a specification scheme that both provides good ergonomics and overcomes the following technical challenges:

- *Strong Automation*: for verification to be used, it must require little to no user interaction and lead to good verification performance.
- *Interruptibility*: iterators can produce infinite sequences of values and can be interrupted before completion, thus specification and verification must happen as the iterator is used, and not at completion.

- *Non-Determinism*: iterators can feature both specification or implementation non-determinism, so the sequence of known values might not be known in advance to the verifier. For example, the order of elements generated by an iterator over a hash table may be left unspecified for a client.
- *Compositionality*: iterators can be consumed by *adapters*, so their specifications need to follow a general pattern which make them *composable*. For example, the specification of a adapter such as `skip(n)`, which skips the first n elements of a given iterator, should accept the specification of any iterator, and provide a sound and useful specification for the combined iterator.
- *Higher-Order & Effects*: some iterator adapters, such as `map`, are *higher-order*, they take a closure as parameter. To verify programs using these adapters, a verification tool should overcome the challenges of higher-order functions, which potentially capture mutable state.

1.1 Contributions

In order to reach this goal, we propose a new specification scheme for iterators in Rust. Our contributions can be summarized as follows:

- In Section 3, we provide a general specification scheme for Rust iterators in first-order logic. It supports possibly non-deterministic, infinite and interruptible iterators. It is inspired by Filliâtre and Pereira's specification of iterators in Why3 [5], but it is adapted to our style of specification using a *prophetic mutable value semantics* [13] for Rust. This style of specification is particularly well suited to handle mutable values (of which iterators are an instance), by leveraging the non-aliasing guarantees provided by Rust's type system.
- In Section 4.1, we show that this scheme can be trivially instantiated for basic iterators such as a range of integers.
- In Section 4.2, we show how this scheme can be instantiated to give full functional specification to *mutating iterators*. These iterators allow to mutate the content of a data structure by iterating over mutable references *pointing to the content of the data structure*.
- In Section 4.3, we show that our specification scheme is *composable*, so that it can be used to specify iterator adapters transforming arbitrary iterators into more complex ones. We give two examples: `take`, which truncates an iterator to at most a given number of elements, and `skip`, which skips a given number of elements at the beginning of iteration.
- To support higher-order iterator adapters, we provide a specification mechanism for *closures* in Section 5. This mechanism distinguishes the three kinds of closures of Rust (`Fn`, `FnMut` and `FnOnce`), and allows specifying the side effects a closure may have on its environment by making explicit the effect of a call on the state of the closure. It allows reducing the verification conditions for closures to *first-order logic*, enabling usage of off-the-shelf automation.
- In Section 6, we explain how we can combine the techniques presented in previous sections to specify higher-order iterator adapters, by taking `map` as

an example. This provides a way to verify the functional correctness of programs using higher-order iterators, while requiring lightweight annotations.

- We provide a freely available[1] implementation of our proposal in CREUSOT [4]. This tool is a state-of-the-art verification platform for safe Rust code, allowing users to verify programs by adding *contracts* to their functions. This implementation extends CREUSOT's handling of `for` loops to benefit from *structural invariants* provided by the specification of iterators. We evaluate it in Section 7 on several benchmarks.

2   Specifications in Rust Programs

Before explaining the specification of iterators, we introduce the style of specification we use in this paper. One important aspect of specifications of imperative programs is their *memory model*, that is the way they handle pointers and mutations performed through them. Following previous work [7, 8, 4], we choose to leverage the non-aliasing guarantees of Rust's type system. Because of the non-aliasing guarantees, a given memory location can be mutated through at most one reference at a given point in time, excluding all "spooky actions at a distance" that are customary with pointer aliasing. Therefore, it is possible to give a *mutable value semantics* [13] to Rust programs, meaning that, even though Rust programs can perform mutation of memory, they can be reasoned about in a purely applicative manner. As a result, the Rust type `Box<T>` of heap-allocated pointers, and the Rust type `&T` of read-only references are simply modeled by wrappers over values of type `T` in our specifications. As shown in previous work [4, 7, 8], this interpretation of Rust programs is key to verifying complex Rust programs, because it avoids the use of any kind of separation logic or dynamic frames, which are challenging to automate.

The handling of mutable references `&mut T` requires caution. Such references represent the temporary *borrow* of ownership of a memory location, so that mutations through such a reference will be observed by the initial owner once the borrow ends. To correctly model the propagation of mutations from the mutable reference to the borrowed variable, this style of specification models a mutable reference `r: &mut T` as a *pair* of a current value `*r` of type `T` (representing the current value pointed to by the reference) and of a *prophecy* `^r`, representing the value the reference *will point to when the borrow ends*.

This prophetic interpretation makes it possible to give precise specifications to functions that manipulate mutable references. For example, the function `push` adding a new element at the end of a vector in place can be specified as follows:

```
#[ensures(@^self == (@*self).concat(Seq::singleton(v)))]
fn push(&mut self, v: T);
```

Here, we use the operator `@` to refer to the *model* of a vector, i.e., the mathematical sequence of its elements. The postcondition thus ensures that the content of

---

[1]   https://github.com/xldenis/creusot/

the final vector pointed to by `self`, denoted by `^self`, is modeled by the sequence of elements of the initial vector `*self`, concatenated with the new element `v`.

We sometimes use purely mathematical functions and predicates, annotated with the `#[logic]` and `#[predicate]` attributes.

We use Rust *traits* to give composable specifications to iterators. They are analogous to Haskell's typeclasses, enabling *ad-hoc polymorphism*. For example, an order relation can be specified as a trait containing both a mathematical order relation with its *laws* (reflexivity, antisymmetry and transitivity), and a program function specified as returning the value prescribed by the logical predicate.

To aid in specification and verification of code, we use *ghost code*, code which exists only during verification and has no influence on runtime behavior.

3   Reasoning on Iteration

In this section, we present the general mechanism we use to specify iterators (Section 3.1), and how this kind of specification is used in a `for` loop (Section 3.2).

3.1   Specifying Iterators

In Rust, the mechanism of iterators is captured by a *trait* named `Iterator`, whose simplified definition can be given as:

```
trait Iterator { type Item;  fn next(&mut self) -> Option<Self::Item>;  }
```

This trait describes the *interface* an iterator should implement: an iterator should give a type `Item` of generated elements, and should implement a method `next` which optionally returns the next generated element, and possibly mutates in place the internal state of the iterator through the mutable reference `&mut self`.

As can be seen in Figure 1, we extend[2] the iterator trait with the purely logical *predicates* `produces` and `completed`. We require that any implementation of this trait satisfies the *laws* `produces_refl` and `produces_trans`: such laws are lemmas stated as specifications of purely logical functions (i.e., the preconditions should imply the postconditions). The `next` method is then specified thanks to the two predicates. Any implementation of the `Iterator` trait needs to give a logical definition of `produces` and `completed` predicates, prove the laws, give a program definition for `next` and finally prove that it satisfies its specification.

Iterators are specified as *state machines*: a value of an iterator type is seen as a state; $produces(a, s, b)$ defines the transition relation (noted $a \overset{s}{\rightsquigarrow} b$), and the predicate `completed` (noted $completed(\cdot)$) give the set of final states. The `completed` predicate takes a mutable reference `&mut self`, which allows us to

---

[2] In our implementation, to keep better compatibility with existing Rust code, we choose to define the iterator specification as a sub-trait of the `Iterator` trait from Rust's standard library, and to give the specification of `next` using CREUSOT's `extern_spec!` mechanism. For simplicity, we present it here as a unique trait: the main idea of the specification is the same.

```
1   trait Iterator {
2     type Item;
3     #[predicate] fn completed(&mut self) -> bool;
4     #[predicate] fn produces(self, visited: Seq<Self::Item>, _: Self)
5                         -> bool;
6     #[law]    // I.e., ∀a, a ↝ᵉ a
7     #[ensures(a.produces(Seq::EMPTY, a))]
8     fn produces_refl(a: Self);
9
10    #[law]    // I.e., ∀a b c, a ↝ᵛ b ∧ b ↝ʷ c ⇒ a ↝ᵛ·ʷ c
11    #[requires(a.produces(ab, b) && b.produces(bc, c))]
12    #[ensures(a.produces(ab.concat(bc), c))]
13    fn produces_trans(a: Self, ab: Seq<Self::Item>,
14                      b: Self, bc: Seq<Self::Item>, c: Self);
15
16    #[ensures(match result {
17        None => self.completed(),
18        Some(v) => (*self).produces(Seq::singleton(v), ^self)})]
19    fn next(&mut self) -> Option<Self::Item>;
20  }
```

Fig. 1. Iterator trait extended with specification.

specify mutations that happen when an iterator returns None[3]. This added expressivity in the specification allows us to express properties of *unfused* iterators which may intermittently produce None during iteration. The produces transition relation is annotated with *sequences* of generated values rather than with unique values so that a user can reason about interesting properties of *sequences* as a whole rather than directly reasoning about the notion of transitive closure, which automated solvers do not handle well. The price to pay is the laws of reflexivity and transitivity which the implementers have to prove.

3.2   Structural Invariant of for Loops

Part of the appeal of for loops is the *structure* they provide over the looping process. When a programmer sees a for, they can conclude that the body will be executed once for each element in the iterator. Unlike with while loops, it is not possible to decrement the loop index or otherwise perform unpredictable looping patterns. This informal reasoning can be formalized as a loop invariant, provided *structurally* by the for loop itself. The iterator at the i-th iteration is the result of calling next exactly i times on some initial state. In our formalism, given an initial iterator state initial and a current iterator state iter, we can state this

---

[3] The predicate completed does not perform any side effects; it should rather be seen as a two-state predicate.

invariant as $\exists p$, initial $\overset{p}{\leadsto}$ iter. This invariant holds for *any* for loop over *any* iterator: it can be derived from the laws `produces_refl` and `produces_trans`.

When using our extension to CREUSOT, every for loop benefits from this structural invariant: we change the way these loops are desugared into the more primitive `loop` construct, by adding ghost variables `init_iter` and `produced` and the new invariant `init_iter.produces(produced, iter)`. More precisely, a simple for loop `for x in iter {<body>}` is desugared into:

```
let init_iter = ghost! { iter };
let mut produced = ghost! { Seq::EMPTY };
#[invariant(structural, init_iter.produces(produced, iter))]
loop { match iter.next() {
  None => break,
  Some(x) => {
    produced = ghost! { produced.concat(Seq::singleton(x)) };
    <body> },
} }
```

Interestingly, the ghost variable `produced` can be referred to in a user invariant to relate the state of the loop with the iteration state. In the piece of code in Figure 2, we use a variable `count` to count the number of elements generated by an iterator, and use such an invariant to verify its intended meaning.

```
let mut count = 0;
#[invariant(count_is_n, @count == produced.len())]
for i in 0..n { count += 1; assert!(0 <= i && i < n); }
assert!(n < 0 || count == n);
```

Fig. 2. A simple for loop using ranges.

4 Examples of Specifications of Simple Iterators

In Section 3, we have presented a general framework to specify iterators and use them in for loops. In this section, we present several simple examples of iterators defined in this framework.

4.1 The Range Iterator

We start with a simple `Range` iterator, whose purpose is to iterate over the integers in a given range. The notation `a..b` used idiomatically in Rust is a syntactic sugar for this kind of iterators. The original definition from the Rust standard library is generic over the type of integers used, but, for the sake of simplicity, we use a monomorphic version here:

```
struct Range { start: usize, end: usize }
```

If `self.start` $\geq$ `self.end`, the `next` method returns `None`. Otherwise, it increments `self.start` and returns the initial value of `Some(self.start)`. Note that the upper bound of the range, `end`, is *excluded* in the iteration.

In order to instantiate our iterator specification scheme with `Range`, we use the `produces` and `completed` predicates defined by:

$$r \overset{v}{\leadsto} r' \quad \triangleq \quad |v| = r'.\text{start} - r.\text{start} \wedge r.\text{end} = r'.\text{end}$$
$$\wedge \; |v| > 0 \Rightarrow r'.\text{start} \leq r'.\text{end}$$
$$\wedge \; \forall i \in [0, |v| - 1], \; v[i] = r.\text{start} + i$$
$$completed(r) \quad \triangleq \quad *r = \hat{\ }r \wedge (*r).\text{end} \geq (*r).\text{start}$$

Transitivity and reflexivity are easily verified.

Rust's standard library also contains ranges whose upper bound is included rather than excluded, and ranges without an upper bound. They can all be specified using similar techniques.

Note that with these definitions, the structural invariant of `for` loops directly implies that the loop index (the last produced value) is in the range. In addition, if the range is non-empty, one can deduce that the last iterated value is $\text{end} - 1$. These two properties usually require an additional invariant if the loop is encoded using the `while` construct. For an illustration consider Figure 2.

4.2 IterMut: Mutating Iteration Over a Vector

Our approach to iterators can be used to iterate over elements of a vector. But instead of presenting the simple case of a *read-only* vector iterator, we study a more general iterator, `IterMut`, permitting to both *read and write* vector elements while iterating; the simpler case of the read-only iterator uses the same ideas.

This iterator produces mutable references for each element of a vector in turn. The state of this iterator is a mutable reference to the *slice* (i.e., a fragment of a vector) of elements that remain to be iterated:

```
struct IterMut<'a, T> { inner: &'a mut [T] }
```

To define the production relation of `IterMut`, we use a helper function tr, which transposes a mutable reference to a slice into a *sequence* of mutable references to its elements. Its defining property is:

$$|tr(s)| = |s| \; \wedge \; \forall i \in [0, |s| - 1], \, tr(*s)[i] = *s[i] \; \wedge \; tr(\hat{\ }s)[i] = \hat{\ }s[i]$$

With the help of tr, the `produces` and `completed` relations of `IterMut` are simple to express:

$$it \overset{v}{\leadsto} it' \quad \triangleq \quad tr(it.\text{inner}) = v \cdot tr(it'.\text{inner})$$
$$completed(it) \quad \triangleq \quad *r = \hat{\ }r \wedge |*r| = 0$$

It means that the iterator it produces a sequence of mutable references, which must be the initial segment of $tr(it.\text{inner})$, into a final state it' such that

$tr(it.\text{inner})$ is the sequence of mutable references that are left to be generated. Such an iterator is completed when the inner slice is empty.

This compact specification is enough to reason about mutating through the returned pointers as in the following example:

```
#[invariant(all_zero, forall<i: Int> 0 <= i && i < produced.len()
                        ==> @^produced[i] == 0)]
for x in v.iter_mut() { *x = 0; }
assert!{ forall<i: Int> 0 <= i && i < (@v).len() ==> @(@^v)[i] == 0 }
```

That is, we are able to prove with a simple loop invariant that this loop sets to 0 all the elements of the vector.

The reasoning that occurs to prove this program is as follows. First, at the end of a loop iteration, we know that the final value of the borrow x is equal to 0 since we have just written 0 and this value will not change since x goes out of scope. Together with the invariant of the preceding iteration, this is enough to prove that the invariant is maintained. Second, after the loop has executed, the final iterator state is empty, so we know produced contains the complete sequence of borrows to elements of v. But, thanks to the loop invariant, the prophetic value of each of these borrows is 0. So we can deduce that the final content of v is a sequence of zeros.

4.3 Iterator Adapters

Because all iterators implement the same trait Iterator which gives them a specification, we can easily build adapters which wrap and transform the behavior of an iterator.

It is important to note that, following Rust's standard library, these adapters are generic over the *type* of the underlying iterator; individual values of a type cannot have different predicates. While the verification tool cannot know the concrete definitions of produces or completed for the wrapped iterator, it knows it must satisfy the Iterator trait interface.

The simplest example is Take<I> (where I is another iterator), which truncates an iterator to produce at *most* n elements. The state of Take<I> is a record with two fields: a counter n for the remaining elements to take and an iterator iter to take from. The specification predicates of Take<I> are defined as follows:

$$it \overset{v}{\leadsto} it' \quad \triangleq \quad it.\text{iter} \overset{v}{\leadsto} it'.\text{iter} \wedge it.\text{n} = it'.\text{n} + |v|$$

$$completed(it) \quad \triangleq \quad (*it).\text{n} = 0 \wedge *it = {}^{\wedge}it$$
$$\vee \ (*it).\text{n} > 0 \wedge (*it).\text{n} = ({}^{\wedge}it).\text{n} + 1 \wedge completed(it.\text{iter})$$

The subtle definition here is that of $completed(it)$: if the counter is 0, then next does nothing. But, following Rust's implementation, if the counter is not 0, then it is first decremented even if the call to the underlying iterator returns None.

Again, when instantiated to a specific underlying iterator *type*, we can substitute the definitions of $(\leadsto)$ and $completed(-)$ for the underlying iterator, to get a concrete definition of these predicates for Take<I>, which are easier to handle by automated solvers.

Another adapter is Skip<I>, whose goal is to *skip* the first n elements of an iterator. Similarly to Take<I>, the state is a record with two fields: a number n of elements to skip and an underlying iterator iter.

The $\rightsquigarrow$ relation of Skip<I> is defined as follows:

$$it \overset{v}{\rightsquigarrow} it' \quad \overset{\Delta}{=} \quad v = \varepsilon \wedge it = it'$$

$$\vee \; it'.\text{n} = 0 \wedge |v| > 0 \wedge \exists w, \; |w| = it.\text{n} \wedge it.\text{iter} \overset{w \cdot v}{\rightsquigarrow} it'.\text{iter}$$

The first disjunct is needed to ensure reflexivity of ($\rightsquigarrow$). The second disjunct describes what happens after a non-empty sequence of calls. If we produced some sequence of elements v, then we must have been able to skip n elements first, which we existentially quantify over.

If the Skip<I> iterator is completed, the underlying iterator has also completed, but potentially after having generated some skipped elements that we existentially quantify over:

$$completed(it) \quad \overset{\Delta}{=} \quad \exists w \; i, \; (\hat{\ }it).\text{n} = 0 \wedge |w| \leq (*it).\text{n}$$

$$\wedge \; (*it).\text{iter} \overset{w}{\rightsquigarrow} *i \wedge completed(i) \wedge \hat{\ }i = (\hat{\ }it).\text{iter}$$

Using Skip<I> and Take<I> we are able to prove an algebraic property of iterators: if we take n elements and then skip n elements from that iterator, we must necessarily get the empty iterator.

```
assert!(iter.take(n).skip(n).next().is_none())
```

This property is easy to prove from the composition of both production relations.

5 Closures in Rust

Unlike traditional functional languages, Rust has no function type for closures. Two closures, even with identical bodies, are not of the same type: closures are each given a unique, anonymous type representing the captured environment. This design is motivated by the need to fully resolve closures during compilation: the compiler is always able to identify exactly which piece of code is used at every call site. To abstract over closures and write higher-order functions, Rust provides three traits that the closure type may implement: FnOnce, FnMut, and Fn. They describe the different ways a closure's environment can be passed during a call: by ownership, by mutable reference or by immutable reference. The compiler automatically provides the relevant instances when a user writes a closure.

Traditionally, verifying higher-order code with mutable state has needed *seperation logic* or *dynamic frames*, but because of Rust's mutable value semantics we can avoid these tools. Instead, we provide a specification for higher-order functions in first-order logic, which generates simple verification conditions (see code of Section 7). Specifically, we extend FnOnce, FnMut, and Fn with logical predicates that capture the pre- and post- conditions of closures. We begin by considering the simplest case, FnOnce:

```
pub trait FnOnce<Args> {
    #[predicate] fn precondition(self, a: Args) -> bool;
    #[predicate] fn postcondition_once(self, a: Args, res: Self::Output)
                          -> bool;
    #[requires(self.precondition(args))]
    #[ensures(self.postcondition_once(args, result))]
    fn call_once(self, args: Args) -> Self::Output;
}
```

The predicates `precondition` and `postcondition_once` refer to the specification added to the `call_once` method used to call the closure.

A call to a `FnOnce` closure *consumes* it. On the other hand, `FnMut` allows a mutable closure to be called multiple times. Here is our extended `FnMut` trait:

```
pub trait FnMut<Args> : FnOnce<Args> {
    #[predicate] fn unnest(self, _: Self) -> bool;
    #[ensures(self.unnest(self))]
    #[law] fn unnest_refl(self);
    #[requires(self.unnest(b) && b.unnest(c))]
    #[ensures(self.unnest(c))]
    #[law] fn unnest_trans(self, b: Self, c: Self);
    #[predicate] fn postcondition_mut(&mut self, _: Args, _: Self::Output)
                          -> bool;
    #[requires((*self).precondition(arg))]
    #[ensures(self.postcondition_mut(arg, result))]
    fn call_mut(&mut self, arg: Args) -> Self::Output;
[...] }
```

Because every `FnMut` closure is also an `FnOnce` closure, we can reuse the precondition predicate to specify `call_mut`. However, we need a new predicate for the richer postconditions that become possible: since the closure is called using a mutable borrow, the postcondition specify changes made to captured variables.

Rust compiles closures via closure conversion, the state of each closure becomes a struct holding references to all captured variables. However, this struct can only be modified in a restricted fashion: we can only mutate the values pointed by the captures, and not the captures themselves. In particular, this means the *prophecies* of captures remain constant. We capture this property in an *unnesting* predicate `F::unnest(a, b)`. It expresses that the prophecies in the state of type `F` have not changed from a to b. This property is both reflexive and transitive which we capture via laws. The unnesting predicate is essential to link the states of a closure throughout repeated calls. Without it we would lose track of the contained prophecies.

In addition to these predicates, our `FnMut` trait contains laws we elided: `unnest` is implied by `postcondition_mut`, and `postcondition_mut` is linked to the `postcondition` predicate of the `FnOnce` trait.

Finally, `Fn` imposes that the closure is immutable. Each call upholds the postcondition and leaves the state intact. Again, in the following, we elided laws relating `postcondition`, `postcondition_mut` and `postcondition_once`:

```
pub trait Fn<Args> : FnMut<Args> {
```

```
#[predicate] fn postcondition(&self, _: Args, _: Self::Output) -> bool;

#[requires((*self).precondition(arg))]
#[ensures(self.postcondition(arg, result))]
fn call(&self, arg: Args) -> Self::Output;
[...] }
```

6   A Higher-order Iterator Adapter: Map

The challenge with the specification of Map is proving the preconditions of the closure being called. Map treats the closure opaquely, it cannot tell what the concrete pre- and post- conditions are, the justification for the precondition must come from elsewhere. To help work through this, we use a thought experiment where we see Map implemented as a loop with a yield instruction to generate elements, in the style of e.g., Python generators:

```
fn map<I : Iterator, B, F: FnMut(I::Item) -> B>(iter: I, func: F) {
    for a in iter { yield (f)(a) }
}
```

To verify it, we need f.precondition(a) to be true at each iteration, so we need an invariant which implies it. This exposes the key property that must be true of our closure: the postcondition at iteration n must be able to establish the precondition for iteration $n + 1$. In the vocabulary of iterators:

$$it \overset{s \cdot e_1 \cdot e_2}{\rightsquigarrow} i' \wedge pre(*f, e_1) \wedge post(f, e_1, r) \Rightarrow pre(\hat{} f, e_2)$$

This expresses that if we eventually produce an element e_1 which satisfies the precondition of the initial closure $*f$, then combined with the postcondition of f, we must be able to establish the precondition for the final closure $\hat{} f$ with the following element e_2. Quantifying over a prefix s in the iteration from a known initial state i ensures this property holds for all possible subsequent iterations.

To encode this property in Map, we use a *type invariant*, which allows specifying a property that values of a type must uphold. Values of type Map are records with two fields: field func contains the closure state, and field iter contains the underlying iterator. The invariant states that (1) the precondition for the next call will be verified; (2) the preservation property above holds for the current state it; (3) these two invariants are reestablished if the underlying iterator returns None (this is usually trivial since the underlying iterator often is fused: it cannot generate new elements once it returns None); and (4) the type invariant of the underlying iterator holds.

These invariants are initially required as a precondition of the map method used to create the Map iterator. In order to be tackled by automated solvers, this verification condition need to be unfolded: it is therefore crucial that closures and their pre- and post- conditions are statically resolved thanks to the unique anonymous closure types in Rust.

The specification predicates for Map can now be stated:

$$it \overset{v}{\leadsto} it' \triangleq \exists v' fs, |v'| = |fs| = |v| \land it.\texttt{iter} \overset{v'}{\leadsto} it'.\texttt{iter}$$
$$\land\, (it.\texttt{func} = *fs[0] \land \hat{}fs[0] = *fs[1] \land .. \land \hat{}fs[n] = it'.\texttt{func})$$
$$\land\, \forall i \in [0, |v| - 1],\ pre(*fs[i], v'[i]) \land post(fs[i], v'[i], v[i])$$
$$\land\, unnest(it.\texttt{func}, it'.\texttt{func})$$
$$completed(it) \triangleq completed(it.\texttt{iter}) \land (*it).\texttt{func} = (\hat{}it).\texttt{func}$$

In $\leadsto$, we quantify existentially over two pieces of information: the sequence of values v' produced by the underlying iterator and the sequence of *mutable references* of states fs that the closure traverses. We require that fs forms a chain, the final state of each element being the same as the current value of the following one. Finally, we require the closure pre- and post- conditions for every iteration, and that the first and last state are related by the unnesting relation. The definition of $completed(-)$, on the other hand, straightforwardly states that the underlying iterator is completed.

Interestingly, the user of this specification can use the precondition of the closure to encode closure invariants that she wishes to maintain along the iteration (as with loop invariants). This specification for Map allows us to specify many use cases, so long as the supplied closure is "history-free": its specification does not depend on the sequence of previously generated values, like in x.map(|a : u32| a + 5). While this is certainly the most common usage of map, we sometimes need a more powerful specification.

Extending Map With Ghost Information. If we attempt to use the previous specification of Map to verify the counter example of Section 1, we will rapidly encounter an issue: to establish that cnt properly counts the number of iterations would require a (manual) induction on the iterated sequence. While the prior specification allows the closure to specify the impact of an immediate call, it has no way of reasoning on the position in the iteration. In our prior thought experiment using a generator, we have no way of writing an invariant which depends on produced, as we allowed for usual for loops.

To make the verification of this kind of code simpler, we extend the signature of Map to provide to the closure the sequence of elements generated by the underlying iterator since the creation of the mapping iterator object. This information does not change the behavior of the program: we make it *ghost*, so it can only be used in specifications.

The extended version, MapExt, is thus given an additional ghost field, produced, containing this sequence. The relation ($\leadsto$) is extended to account for this ghost information, by adding a conjunct stating that $it'.\texttt{produced} = it.\texttt{produced}{\cdot}v'$ and passing the additional ghost parameter $it.\texttt{produced}{\cdot}v'[0..i{-}1]$ to the pre- and post- conditions. The $completed()$ relation is extended by adding the conjunct $(\hat{}it).\texttt{produced} = \varepsilon$ (the produced field is reset when the iterator returns None). The type invariants are adapted accordingly.

This extra information avoids the need for an explicit induction after the fact to establish that we have properly counted the number of iterations: the postcondition of the last call to `next` is enough. This mechanism is useful in a wide variety of situations, beyond reasoning on the length of the sequence.

7   Evaluation

In this section we measure the performance of both the proofs of iterators and their clients, using the CREUSOT [4] tool for verification of Rust programs. It allows for verification of Rust programs, and requires some annotations to verify the functional correctness of Rust programs. Verification is performed by translating annotated Rust code into a pure, first-order functional program. Then, CREUSOT uses Why3 [15] to generate verification conditions, which are discharged using automated solvers such as CVC5, Z3 or Alt-Ergo.

The results in Figure 3, were gathered using a Macbook Pro with an M1 Pro CPU and 32 GB of RAM, running macOS 12.2. Why3 was limited to using four provers simultaneously among Z3 4.11.2, CVC5 1.0.2, and Alt-Ergo 2.4.1.

WHY3 supports *proof transformations*: manual tactics which can be used in combination with automated solvers. Because we wish to obtain ergonomic specifications which work well with automation, we minimize their use. Nevertheless, certain complex proofs required minor manual work, which we clearly indicate.

Iterator	LOC	Spec	Time	Fully auto.	Benchmark	LOC	Spec	Time	Fully auto.
Range	13	39	0.40	✓	all_zero	5	3	0.43	✓
IterMut	12	34	0.61	✓	skip_take	3	2	0.40	✓
Map	23	46	0.89	✗	counter	12	4	0.55	✓
MapExt	42	115	1.06	✗	concat_vec	3	3	0.41	✓
Skip<I>	20	53	0.51	✗	decuple_range	9	3	0.64	✓
Take<I>	17	43	0.40	✓	hillel	89	109	0.86	✓
Fuse	29	51	0.52	✗	knights_tour	89	55	1.15	✓

Fig. 3. Selected evaluation results. "LOC" counts the lines of program code, while "Spec" counts specification code and assertions. "Time" measures in seconds the time taken to solve the proofs. "Fully auto." determines whether manual tactics were used.

The left table in Figure 3 contains a selection of the iterators and adapters we have verified. The `Range`, `IterMut`, `Skip` and `Take` iterators are implementations of the iterators described in Sections 4.1 to 4.3. The `Fuse` adapter is responsible for transforming any iterator into a *fused* one, which will always return `None` after the first, never resuming iteration. Two versions of `Map` are provided, the first is the standard library `Map`, which is restricted to closures whose preconditions are 'history-free', the version in `MapExt` is provided with ghost information about previous calls as explained in Section 6.

Some manual proof steps were required to prove several iterators. For `Skip<I>` and `Fuse`, the manual tactics consist only of telling Why3 to access lemmas about sequences. For `Map` and `MapExt`, tactics were used to instantiate quantifiers within the production relation. We think that the use of ghost variables and of the SMT theory of sequences could lift the use of manual tactics.

We also verified several clients of iterators, sometimes featuring combinations of several iterators. The example `decuple_range` maps a `Range`, multiplying elements by 10, collecting the results into a vector and verifying functional correctness; `counter` is an annotated version of the example in the introduction, verifying that we can use mutable state to count the elements of an iterator; `concat_vec` uses `extend` to append an iterator to the end of a vector; `all_zero` uses `IterMut` to zero every cell of a vector; `take_skip` checks that if we truncate an iterator to the first n elements and then skip them, the resulting iterator must be empty. We have larger scale examples where iterators are used in the context of a larger verified development: `hillel` is a port of a prior CREUSOT solution to Hillel Wayne's verification challenges [16]; `knights_tour` is the same for the Knight's Tour problem. In both of these cases, updating the code to use `for`-loops and iterators actually *reduced* the number of lines of specification.

Because our lines of specification include the assertions which test functional properties, we believe the resulting overhead is reasonable, especially in our client examples. Additionally, our specifications for iterators seem to have low impact on verification times. We compared `hillel` and `knights_tour` with alternative versions that only differ by using traditional `while` loops instead of iterators, verification times are 0.91 and 1.14 respectively. This provides evidence that integrating our iterators does not cause prohibitive increases in verification time.

8   Related and Future Work

RUSTHORN [7] and RUSTHORNBELT [8] show how the non-aliasing guarantees of Rust can be used for reducing the verification of Rust programs into the proof of first-order logic formulas. These works serve as theoretical foundations for CREUSOT [4], which we use to evaluate our specification scheme for iterators.

PRUSTI [1] is a semi-automatic verifier for Rust built on the Viper [10] separation logic verification platform. PRUSTI models mutable borrowing and ownership using separation logic permissions, unlike our choice of using a prophetic mutable value semantics. This leads to differences in the specification languages: whereas Creusot uses the `^` operator to reason about borrows, PRUSTI uses a notion called *pledges*. Pledges are assertions which must be true at the end of a specific lifetime. At the time of writing, pledges are not fully first-class in PRUSTI's specification logic: they are used through a kind of postcondition. In particular a ghost predicate like `produces` cannot contain a pledge. The `^` operator can be used anywhere in specifications, which allows us to give a natural specification to mutating iterators like `IterMut` (Section 4.2).

The verification of higher-order programs has been studied by Régis-Gianas and Pottier [14], who verify them using higher-order logic. PRUSTI supports closures by modeling them in Viper's separation logic [17]. Like our approach, PRUSTI transforms specifications of higher-order programs into first-order verification conditions, but in separation logic. They introduce several constructs to specify closures: *history invariants*, *specification entailment*, and *call descriptions*. We instead enable users to refer to pre- and post- conditions of closures via a *trait*. While we not have the constructs PRUSTI provides primitively for closures, we believe these constructs can be encoded using our primitives, at the cost of lower ergonomics. Our approach is more expressive: unlike PRUSTI's call descriptions, we can distinguish the *order* of calls (see Section 6). Also, Prusti's approach for borrows makes it difficult to handle iterators such as IterMut.

Like us, AENEAS [6] verifies Rust programs by translation to a functional language, and targets traditional proof assistants such as COQ, or F*. They use a technique called *backward functions* to interpret mutable borrows. To our knowledge, AENEAS supports neither closures nor iterators.

The formalization of iterators is a well-studied subject with implementations in a variety of imperative and functional languages: WhyML [5], Eiffel [11], Java [9], and OCaml [12]. Of particular relevance is the approach developed by Filliâtre and Pereira [5], which specifies iterators in WhyML using a ghost field `visited : seq 'a` and two predicates `permitted : cursor 'a -> bool` and `completed : cursor 'a -> bool` where `cursor 'a` is an iterator for values of type `'a`. This work leverages Why3's regions system to distinguish individual cursors over time. In contrast, in our context, we lose *object identity*: there is no way to identify that two iterator values are two successive states of the same iterator. We thus generalize this approach to our setting by explicitly providing pre- and post- states in `produces`. Our work is also more expressive: we specify and verify higher-order iterators using potentially mutable closures, which are ruled out by Why3's region system. The framework of iteration described by Polikarpova, Tschannen, and Furia [11] is limited to finite, deterministic iteration: the user must provide up front the sequence of abstract values the iterator will produce. Pottier [12] presents an implementation of iterators for a hash map written in OCaml. They do this by working in the separation logic CFML [2], utilizing Coq's powerful but manual reasoning mechanisms for theorem proving. While Pottier does not provide a general specification of iterators (*cascades*) with mutable state, CFML should permit it, though usage may require a challenging proof.

Future Work. While we have specified and proved key iterators, many more remain. The `filter` adapter is interesting as each call to `next` may make an unbounded number of steps with the underlying iterator using the provided *mutable* closure. Rust provides a hierarchy of traits that further refine iterators like `DoubleEndedIterator`, and `ExactSizeIterator`. The recent integration of *generic associated types* enables new, more flexible forms of iteration like *lending iterators*. We believe these would naturally integrate into our framework, but remain to be done. Finally, while we believe we have developed a correct, and simple approach to specify closures, the ergonomics leave much room for improvement. Improving this will help make our specifications more concise and user-friendly. In particular, we would like to explore automatic inference of pre- and post-conditions of simple closures.

Data availability

The implementation of Creusot and the examples that we used to evaluate our methodology in Section 7 form an artifact available [3] on Zenodo with DOI 10.5281/zenodo.7305463.

References

[1]   Vytautas Astrauskas et al. "The Prusti Project: Formal Verification for Rust". In: *NASA Formal Methods*. Vol. 13260. LNCS. 2022. DOI: 10.1007/978-3-031-06773-0_5.

[2]   Arthur Charguéraud. "Characteristic formulae for the verification of imperative programs". In: *ICFP*. 2011. DOI: 10.1145/2034773.2034828.

[3]   Xavier Denis and Jacques-Henri Jourdan. *Artifact for Paper "Specifying and Verifying Higher-order Rust Iterators"*. DOI: 10.5281/zenodo.7305463.

[4]   Xavier Denis, Jacques-Henri Jourdan, and Claude Marché. "Creusot: A Foundry for the Deductive Verication of Rust Programs". In: *ICFEM*. Vol. 13478. LNCS. 2022. DOI: 10.1007/978-3-031-17244-1_6.

[5]   Jean-Christophe Filliâtre and Mário Pereira. "A Modular Way to Reason About Iteration". In: *NASA Formal Methods*. Vol. 9690. LNCS. 2016. DOI: 10.1007/978-3-319-40648-0_24.

[6]   Son Ho and Jonathan Protzenko. "Aeneas: Rust Verification by Functional Translation". In: *ICFP*. 2022. DOI: 10.1145/3547647.

[7]   Yusuke Matsushita, Takeshi Tsukada, and Naoki Kobayashi. "RustHorn: CHC-based verification for Rust programs". In: *TOPLAS* 43.4 (2021), pp. 1–54. DOI: 10.1145/3462205.

[8]   Yusuke Matsushita et al. "RustHornBelt: A Semantic Foundation for Functional Verification of Rust Programs with Unsafe Code". In: *PLDI*. 2022. DOI: 10.1145/3519939.3523704.

[9]   João Mota, Marco Giunti, and António Ravara. *On Using VeriFast, VerCors, Plural, and KeY to Check Object Usage*. 2022. URL: http://arxiv.org/abs/2209.05136.

[10] Peter Müller, Malte Schwerhoff, and Alexander J. Summers. "Viper: A Verification Infrastructure for Permission-Based Reasoning". In: *VMCAI*. Vol. 9583. LNCS. 2016. DOI: 10.1007/978-3-662-49122-5_2.

[11] Nadia Polikarpova, Julian Tschannen, and Carlo A. Furia. "A Fully Verified Container Library". In: *Formal Aspects of Computing* 30.5 (2018). DOI: 10.1007/s00165-017-0435-1.

[12] François Pottier. "Verifying a Hash Table and Its Iterators in Higher-Order Separation Logic". In: *CPP*. 2017. DOI: 10.1145/3018610.3018624.

[13] Dimitri Racordon et al. "Implementation Strategies for Mutable Value Semantics." In: *J. Object Technol.* 21.2 (2022), pp. 2–1.

[14] Yann Régis-Gianas and François Pottier. "A Hoare Logic for Call-by-Value Functional Programs". In: *MPC*. Vol. 5133. LNCS. 2008.

[15] The Why3 development team. *The Why3 verification platform*. URL: https://why3.lri.fr/.

[16] *The Great Theorem Prover Showdown*. Hillel Wayne. Apr. 25, 2018. URL: https://www.hillelwayne.com/post/theorem-prover-showdown/ (visited on 10/14/2022).

[17] Fabian Wolff et al. "Modular Specification and Verification of Closures in Rust". In: *OOPSLA*. 2021. DOI: 10.1145/3485522.

Extending a High-Performance Prover to Higher-Order Logic

Petar Vukmirović[1], Jasmin Blanchette[1,2]([⊠]), and Stephan Schulz[3]

[1] Vrije Universiteit Amsterdam, Amsterdam, The Netherlands
petar.vukmirovic2@gmail.com, j.c.blanchette@vu.nl
[2] Université de Lorraine, CNRS, Inria, LORIA, Nancy, France
[3] DHBW Stuttgart, Stuttgart, Germany
stephan.schulz@dhbw-stuttgart.de

Abstract. Most users of proof assistants want more proof automation. Some proof assistants discharge goals by translating them to first-order logic and invoking an efficient prover on them, but much is lost in translation. Instead, we propose to extend first-order provers with native support for higher-order features. Building on our extension of E to λ-free higher-order logic, we extend E to full higher-order logic. The result is the strongest prover on benchmarks exported from a proof assistant.

1 Introduction

In the last few decades, proof assistants have become indispensable tools for developing trustworthy formal proofs. They are used both in academia to verify mathematical theories [17] and in industry to verify the correctness of hardware [21] and software [16,22,24]. However, due to the lack of strong built-in proof automation, proving seemingly simple goals can be a tedious manual task. To mitigate this, many proof assistants include a subsystem such as CoqHammer, HOL(y)Hammer, or Sledgehammer [9] that translates higher-order goals to first-order logic and passes them to efficient first-order automatic provers. If a first-order prover succeeds, the proof is reconstructed and the goal is closed.

Unfortunately, the translation of higher-order constructs is clumsy and leads to poor performance on goals that require higher-order reasoning. Using native higher-order provers such as Satallax [10] as backends is not always a good solution because they are much less efficient than their first-order counterparts [37]. To bridge this gap, in 2016 we proposed to develop a new generation of higher-order provers that extend the arguably most successful first-order calculus, superposition, to higher-order logic, starting from a position of strength.

Our research has focused on three milestones: supporting λ-free higher-order logic, adding λ-terms, and adding first-class Boolean terms. In 2019, we extended the state-of-the-art first-order prover E [32] with a λ-free superposition calculus [42], obtaining a version of E called Ehoh, as a stepping stone towards full higher-order logic. Together with Bentkamp, Tourret, and Waldmann, we have since developed calculi, called λ-*superposition*, corresponding to the other two milestones [5,4] and implemented them in the experimental superposition prover

© The Author(s) 2023
S. Sankaranarayanan and N. Sharygina (Eds.): TACAS 2023, LNCS 13994, pp. 111–129, 2023.
https://doi.org/10.1007/978-3-031-30820-8_10

Zipperposition [14]. This OCaml prover is not nearly as efficient as E. Nevertheless, it has won the higher-order division of the CASC prover competition [39] in 2020, 2021, and 2022, ending nearly a decade of Satallax domination.

We now fulfill a four-year-old promise: We present the extension of Ehoh to full higher-order logic (Sect. 2) based on incomplete variants of λ-superposition. We call this prover λE. In λE's implementation, we used the extensive experience with Zipperposition to choose a set of effective rules that could easily be retrofitted into an originally first-order prover. Another guiding principle was *gracefulness*: Our changes should not impact the strong first-order performance of E and Ehoh.

One of the main challenges we faced was retrofitting λ-terms in Ehoh's term representation (Sect. 3). Furthermore, Ehoh's inference engine assumes that inferences compute a most general unifier. We implemented a higher-order unification procedure [41] that can return multiple unifiers (Sect. 4) and integrated it in the inference engine. Finally, we extended and adapted the superposition rule, resulting in an incomplete, pragmatic variant of λ-superposition (Sect. 5).

We evaluated λE on a selection of proof assistants benchmarks as well as all higher-order theorems in the TPTP library [38] (Sect. 6). λE outperformed all other higher-order provers on the proof assistant benchmarks; on the TPTP benchmarks, it ended up second only to the cooperative version of Zipperposition, which employs Ehoh as a backend. An arguably fairer comparison without the backend puts λE in first place for both benchmark suites. We also compared the performance of λE with E on first-order problems and found that no overhead has been introduced by the extension to higher-order logic.

λE is part of the E prover's development repository and will be part of E 3.0. It can be enabled by passing the option `--enable-ho` to the `configure` script. E and λE's source code is freely available online.[1]

2   Logic

Our target logic is monomorphic classical higher-order logic with Hilbert choice. The following text is partly based on Vukmirović et al. [40, Sect. 2].

Terms s, t, u, v are inductively defined as free variables $F, X, \ldots$, bound variables $x, y, z, \ldots$, constants $\mathsf{f}, \mathsf{g}, \mathsf{a}, \mathsf{b}, \ldots$, applications $s\,t$, and λ-abstractions $\lambda x.\,s$. Bound variables may be *loose* (e.g., y in $\lambda x.\,y\,\mathsf{a}$) [27].

We let $s\,\bar{t}_n$ stand for $s\,t_1 \ldots t_n$ and $\lambda \bar{x}_n.\,s$ for $\lambda x_1 \ldots \lambda x_n.\,s$. Every β-normal term can be written as $\lambda \bar{x}_m.\,s\,\bar{t}_n$, where s is not an application; we call s the *head* of the term. If s is a free variable, we call the term *flex*; otherwise, the term is *rigid*. A term of type o, where o is the distinguished Boolean type, is called a *formula*. A term whose type is of the form $\tau_1 \to \cdots \to \tau_n \to o$ is called a *predicate*. Logical symbols are part of the signature and may thus occur within terms. We write them in bold: $\bot, \top, \neg, \wedge, \vee, \rightarrow, \leftrightarrow, \forall, \exists, \approx$.

On top of the terms, we define some clausal structure. This structure is needed by λ-superposition. A literal l is an equation $s \approx t$ or a disequation $s \not\approx t$. A clause is a finite multiset of literals, interpreted and written disjunctively: $l_1 \vee \cdots \vee l_n$.

---

[1] https://github.com/eprover/eprover.git

3   Terms

E is designed around perfect term sharing [25], a principle that we kept in Ehoh and λE: Any two structurally identical terms are guaranteed to be the same object in memory. This is achieved through term *cells*, which represent individual terms. Each cell has (among other fields) (1) f_code, an integer corresponding to the symbol at the head of the term (negative if the head is a free variable, positive otherwise); (2) num_args, corresponding to the number of arguments applied to the head; and (3) args, an array of size num_args of pointers to argument terms. We use the notation $f(s_1, \ldots, s_n)$ to denote a cell whose f_code corresponds to f, num_args equals n, and args points to the cells for $s_1, \ldots s_n$.

Like Leo-III [33, Sect. 4.8], Ehoh represents λ-free higher-order terms using a flattened, spine notation [12]. Thus, the terms f, f a, and f a b are represented by the cells f, f(a), and f(a, b). To ensure that free variables are perfectly shared, Ehoh treats applied free variables differently: Arguments are not applied directly to a free variable, but using a distinguished symbol @ of variable arity. For example, the term X a b is represented by the cell @(X, a, b). This ensures that two different occurrences of the free variable X correspond to the same object, which makes substitutions more efficient [42].

Representation of λ-Terms. To support full higher-order logic, Ehoh's λ-free cell data structure must be extended to support the λ binder. We use the locally nameless representation [13]: De Bruijn indices represent (possibly loose) bound variables, whereas we keep the current representation for free variables.

Extending the term representation of Ehoh with a new term kind involves intricate manipulation of the cell data structure. De Bruijn indices must be represented like other cells with either a negative or a positive f_code, but the code must clearly identify that the cell is a De Bruijn index.

Apart from during β-reduction, De Bruijn indices mostly behave like constants. Therefore, we choose to represent De Bruijn indices using positive f_codes: The De Bruijn index i will have f_code i. To ensure that De Bruijn indices are not mistaken for function symbols, we use the cell's properties bitfield, which holds precomputed properties. We introduce the property IsDBVar to denote that the cell represents a De Bruijn index. De Bruijn indices are systematically created through a dedicated function that sets the IsDBVar property. When given the same De Bruijn index and type, this function always returns the same object. Finally, we guard all the functions and macros that manipulate function codes to check if the property IsDBVar is set. To ensure perfect sharing of De Bruijn indices, arguments to De Bruijn indices are applied like for free variables, using @.

Extending cells to support λ-abstraction is easier. Each λ-abstraction has the distinguished function code LAM as the head symbol and two arguments: (1) a De Bruijn index 0 of the type of the abstracted variable; (2) the body of the λ-abstraction. Consider the term $\lambda x. \lambda y. f\,x\,x$, where both x and y have the type ι. This term is represented as $\lambda\lambda f\,\mathbf{1}\,\mathbf{1}$ in locally nameless representation, where bold numbers represent De Bruijn indices. In λE, the same term is represented by the cell $\text{LAM}(\mathbf{0}, \text{LAM}(\mathbf{0}, f(\mathbf{1}, \mathbf{1})))$, where all De Bruijn variables have type ι.

The first argument of LAM is redundant, since it can be deduced from the type of the λ-abstraction. However, basic λ-term manipulation operations often require access to this term. We store it explicitly to avoid creating it repeatedly.

Efficient β-Reduction. Terms are stored in βη-reduced form. As these two reductions are performed very often, they ought to be efficient. Ehoh performs β-reduction by reducing the leftmost outermost β-redex first. To represent β-redexes, E uses the @ symbol. Thus, the term $(\lambda x. \lambda y. (x\,y))$ f a is represented by @(LAM(0, LAM(0, @(1, 0))), f, a). Another option would have been to add arguments applied to λ-terms directly to the λ representation (as in LAM(0, LAM(0, @(1, 0)), f, a)), but this would break the invariant that LAM has two arguments. Furthermore, replacing free variables with λ-abstractions (e.g., replacing X with $\lambda x. x$ in @(X, a)) would require additional normalization.

A term can be β-reduced as follows: When a cell @(LAM(0, s), t) is encountered, the field **binding** (normally used to record the substitution for a free variable) of the cell **0** is set to t. Then s is traversed to instantiate every loose occurrence of **0** in s with **binding**, whose loose De Bruijn indices are shifted by the number of λ binders above the occurrence of **0** in s [20]. Next, this procedure is applied to the resulting term and its subterms, in leftmost outermost fashion.

λE's β-normalization works in this way, but it features a few optimizations. First, given a term of the form $(\lambda \overline{x}_n. s)\,\overline{t}_n$, λE, like Leo-III [34], replaces the bound variables x_i with t_i in parallel. Avoiding the construction of intermediate terms reduces the number of recursive function calls and calls to the cell allocator.

Second, in line with the gracefulness principle, we want λE to incur little (or no) overhead on first-order problems and to excel on higher-order problems with a large first-order component. If β-reduction is implemented naively, finding a β-redex involves traversing the entire term. On purely first-order terms, β-reduction is then a waste of time. To avoid this, we use Ehoh's perfectly shared terms and their **properties** field. We introduce the property HasBetaReducibleSubterm, which is set if a cell is β-reducible. Whenever a new cell that contains a β-reducible term as a direct subterm is shared, the property is set. Setting of the property is inductively continued when further superterms are shared. For example, in the term $t = $ f a (g(($\lambda x. x$) a)), the cells for $(\lambda x. x)$ a, g (($\lambda x. x$) a), and t itself have the property HasBetaReducibleSubterm set. When it needs to find β-reducible subterms, λE will visit only the cells with this property set. This further means that on first-order subterms, a single bit masking operation is enough to determine that no subterm should be visited.

Along similar lines, we introduce a property HasDBSubterm that caches whether the cell contains a De Bruijn subterm. This makes instantiating De Bruijn indices during β-normalization faster, since only the subterms that contain De Bruijn indices must be visited. Similarly, some other operations such as shifting De Bruijn indices or determining whether a term is closed (i.e., it contains no loose bound variables) can be sped up or even avoided if the term is first-order.

Efficient η-Reduction. The term $\lambda x. s\,x$ is η-reduced to s whenever x does not occur unbound in s. Observing that a term cannot be η-reduced if it contains no λ-abstractions, we introduce a property HasLambda that notes the presence of λ's in a term. Only terms with λ's are visited during η-reduction.

λE performs parallel η-reduction: It recognizes terms of the form $\lambda \overline{x}_m . s \, \overline{x}_m$ such that none of the x_i occurs unbound in s. If done naively, reducing terms of this kind requires up to m traversals of s to check if each x_i occurs in s. In λE, exactly one traversal of s is required. More precisely, when η-reducing a cell LAM$(0, s)$, λE considers all λ binders in s as well. In general, the cell will be of the form LAM$(0, \ldots, \text{LAM}(0, t) \ldots)$, where t is not a λ-abstraction, and l is the number of LAM symbols above t. Then λE breaks the body t down into a decomposition $u \, (n-1) \ldots 1 \, 0$ where u is not of the form $\ldots n$; such a decomposition is unique. If $n = 0$, the cell is not η-reducible. Otherwise, u is traversed to determine the minimal index j of a loose De Bruijn index, taking $j = \infty$ if no such index exists. λE can then remove the $k = \min\{j, l, n\}$ rightmost outermost λ binders in LAM$(0, \ldots, \text{LAM}(0, t) \ldots)$ and replace t by the variant of $u \, (n-1) \ldots (k+1) \, k$ obtained by shifting the loose De Bruijn indices down by k.

To illustrate this convoluted De Bruijn arithmetic, we consider the term $\lambda x. \lambda y. \lambda z. f \, x \, x \, y \, z$. This term is represented by the cell LAM$(0, \text{LAM}(0, \text{LAM}(0, f(2, 2, 1, 0))))$. λE splits $f(2, 2, 1, 0)$ into two parts: $u = f \, 2$ and the arguments $2, 1, 0$. Since the minimal index in u is 2, we can omit the De Bruijn indices 1 and 0 and their λ binders, yielding the η-reduced cell LAM$(0, f(0, 0))$.

Parallel η-reduction both speeds up η-reduction and avoids creating intermediate terms. For finding the minimal loose De Bruijn index, optimizations such as the HasDBSubterm property are used.

Representation of Boolean Terms. E and Ehoh represent Boolean terms using cells whose f_codes are reserved for logical symbols. Quantified formulas are represented by cells in which the first argument is the quantified variable and the second one is the body of the quantified formula. For example, the term $\forall x. p \, x$ corresponds to the cell $\forall(X, p(X))$, where X is a free variable. This representation is convenient for parsing and clausification, which is what E and Ehoh use it for, but in full higher-order logic, it is problematic during proof search: Booleans can occur as subterms in clauses, as in $q(X) \vee p(\forall(X, r(X)))$, and instantiating X in the first literal should not affect X in the second literal.

To avoid this issue, in λE we use λ binders to represent quantified formulas, as is customary in higher-order logic [1, §51]. Thus, $\forall x. s$ is represented by $\forall (\lambda x. s)$. Quantifiers are then unary symbols that do not directly bind the variables. Since λE represents bound variables using De Bruijn indices, this solves all α-conversion issues. However, this solution is incompatible with thousands of decades-old lines of clausification code that assumes E's representation of quantifiers. Therefore, λE converts quantified formulas only after clausification, for Boolean terms that occur in a higher-order context (e.g., as argument to a function symbol).

New Term Orders. The λ-superposition calculus is parameterized by a term order that is used to break symmetries in the search space. We implemented the versions of the Knuth–Bendix order (KBO) and lexicographic path order (LPO) for higher-order terms described by Bentkamp et al. [4]. These orders encode

λ-terms as first-order terms and then invoke the standard KBO or LPO. For efficiency, we implemented separate KBO and LPO functions that compute the order directly, intertwining the encoding and the order computation.

Ehoh cells contain a `binding` field that can be used to store the substitution for a free variable. Substitutions can then be applied by following the `binding` pointers, replacing each free variable with its instance. Thus, when Ehoh needs to perform a KBO or LPO comparison of an instantiated term, it needs only follow the `binding` pointers. In full higher-order logic, however, instantiating a variable can trigger a chain of $\beta\eta$-reductions, changing the shape of the term dramatically. To prevent this, λE computes the $\beta\eta$-reduced instances of the terms before comparing them using KBO or LPO.

4   Unification, Matching, and Term Indexing

Standard superposition crucially depends on the concept of a most general unifier (MGU). In higher-order logic, the concept is replaced by that of a complete set of unifiers (CSU), which may be infinite. Vukmirović et al. [41] designed an efficient procedure to enumerate a CSU for a term pair. It is implemented in Zipperposition, together with some extensions to term indexing. In λE, we further improve the performance of this procedure by implementing a terminating, incomplete variant. We also introduce a new indexing data structure.

The Unification Procedure. The unification procedure works by maintaining a list of unification pairs to be solved. After choosing a pair, it first normalizes it by β-reducing and instantiating the heads of both terms in the pair. Then, if either head is a variable, it computes an appropriate binding for this variable, thereby approximating the solution.

Unlike in first-order and λ-free higher-order unification, in the full higher-order case there may be many bindings that lead to a solution. To reduce this mostly blind guessing of bindings, the procedure features support for *oracles* [41]. These are procedures that solve the unification problem for a subclass of higher-order terms on which unification is decidable and, for λE, unary. Oracles help increase performance, avoid nontermination, and avoid redundant bindings.

Vukmirović et al. described their procedure as a transition system. In λE, the procedure is implemented nonrecursively, and the unifiers are enumerated using an iterator object that encapsulates the state of the unifier search. The iterator consists of five fields: (1) *constraints*, which holds the unification constraints; (2) *bt_state*, a stack that contains information necessary to backtrack to a previous state; (3) *branch_iter*, which stores how far we are in exploring different possibilities from the current search node; (4) *steps*, which remembers how many different unification bindings (such as imitation, projection, and identification) are applied; and (5) *subst*, a stack storing the variables bound so far.

The iterator is initialized to hold the original problem in *constraints*, and all other fields are initially empty. The unifiers are retrieved one by one by calling the function FORWARDITER. It returns TRUE if the iterator made progress, in which case the unifier can be read via the iterator's *subst* field. Otherwise, no more unifiers can be found, and the iterator is no longer valid. The function's pseudocode is given below, including two auxiliary functions:

function NORMALIZEHEAD(t) **is**
 if $t.head = @ \wedge t.args[0].is\_lambda()$ **then**
  reduce the top-level β-redex in t
  return NORMALIZEHEAD(t)
 else if $t.head.is\_var() \wedge t.head.binding \neq$ NIL **then**
  $t.head \leftarrow t.head.binding$
  return NORMALIZEHEAD(t)
 else
  return t

function BACKTRACKITER($iter$) **is**
 if $iter.bt\_state.empty()$ **then**
  clear all fields in $iter$
  return FALSE
 else
  pop ($constraints, branch\_iter, steps, subst$) from $iter.bt\_state$
  set the corresponding fields of $iter$
  return TRUE

function FORWARDITER($iter$) **is**
 $forward \leftarrow \neg iter.constraints.empty() \vee$ BACKTRACKITER($iter$)
 while $forward \wedge \neg iter.constraints.empty()$ **do**
 $(lhs, rhs) \leftarrow$ pop pair from $iter.constraints$
 $lhs \leftarrow$ NORMALIZEHEAD(lhs)
 $rhs \leftarrow$ NORMALIZEHEAD(rhs)
 normalize and discard the λ prefixes of lhs and rhs
 if $\neg lhs.head.is\_var() \wedge rhs.head.is\_var()$ **then**
 swap lhs and rhs
 if $lhs.head.is\_var()$ **then**
 $oracle\_res \leftarrow$ FIXPOINT($lhs, rhs, iter.subst$)
 if $oracle\_res =$ NOTINFRAGMENT **then**
 $oracle\_res \leftarrow$ PATTERN($lhs, rhs, iter.subst$)
 if $oracle\_res =$ NOTUNIFIABLE **then**
  $forward \leftarrow$ BACKTRACKITER(ITER)
 else if $oracle\_res =$ NOTINFRAGMENT **then**
  $n\_steps, n\_branch\_iter, n\_binding \leftarrow$
   NEXTBINDING($lhs, rhs, iter.steps, iter.branch\_iter$)
  if $n\_branch\_iter \neq$ BINDEND **then**
   push pair (lhs,rhs) back to $iter.constraints$
   push quadruple ($iter.constraints, n\_branch\_iter$,
    $iter.steps, iter.subst$) onto $iter.bt\_state$
   extend $iter.subst$ with $n\_binding$

$iter.steps \leftarrow n\_steps$
$iter.branch\_iter \leftarrow$ BindBegin
else if $lhs.head = rhs.head$ **then**
    create constraint pairs of arguments of lhs and rhs
    and push them to $iter.constraints$
    $iter.branch\_iter \leftarrow$ BindBegin
else if $lhs.head = rhs.head$ **then**
    create constraint pairs of arguments of lhs and rhs
    and push them to $iter.constraints$
else
    $forward \leftarrow$ BacktrackIter($iter$)
return $forward$

FORWARDITER begins by backtracking if the previous attempt was successful (i.e., all constraints were solved). If it finds a state from which it can continue, it takes term pairs from *constraints* until there are no more constraints or it is determined that no unifier exists. The terms are normalized by instantiating the head variable with its binding and reducing the potential top-level β-redex that might appear. This instantiation and reduction process is repeated until there are no more top-level β-redexes and the head is not a variable bound to some term. Then the term with shorter λ prefix is expanded (only on the top level) so that both λ prefixes have the same length. Finally, the λ prefix is ignored, and we focus only on the body. In this way, we avoid fully substituting and normalizing terms and perform just enough operations to determine the next step of the procedure.

If either term of the constraint is flex, we first invoke oracles to solve the constraint. λE implements the most efficient oracles implemented in Zipperposition: fixpoint and pattern [41, Sect. 6]. An oracle can return three results: (1) there is an MGU for the pair (UNIFIABLE), which is recorded in *subst*, and the next pair in *constraints* is tried; (2) no MGU exists for the pair (NOTUNIFIABLE), which causes the iterator to backtrack; (3) if the pairs do not belong to the subclass that oracle can solve (NOTINFRAGMENT), we generate possible variable bindings—that is, we guess the approximate form of the solution.

λE has a dedicated module that generates bindings (NEXTBINDING). This module is given the current constraint and the values of *branch_iter* and *steps*, and it either returns the next binding and the new values of *branch_iter* and *steps* or reports that all different variable bindings are exhausted. The bindings that λE's unification procedure creates are imitation, Huet-style projection, identification, and elimination (one argument at a time) [41, Sect. 3]. A limit on the total number of applied binding rules can be set, as well as a limit on the number of individual rule applications. The binding module checks whether limits are reached using the iterator's *steps* field.

Computing bindings is the only point in the procedure where the search tree branches and different possibilities are explored. Thus, when λE follows the branch indicated by the binding module, it records the state to which it needs to return should the followed branch be backtracked. The state consists of the values of *constraints*, *steps*, and *subst* before the branch is followed and the value of *branch_iter* that points past the followed branch. The values of *branch_iter* are either BINDBEGIN, which denotes that no binding was created, intermediate values that NEXTBINDING uses to remember how far through bindings it is, and BINDEND, which indicates that all bindings are exhausted.

If all bindings are exhausted, the procedure checks whether the pair is flex–flex and both sides have the same head. If so, the pair is decomposed and constraints are derived from the pair's arguments; otherwise, the iterator backtracks. If the pair is rigid–rigid, for unification to succeed, the heads of both sides must be the same. Unification then continues with new constraints derived from the arguments. Otherwise, the iterator must be backtracked.

Matching. In E, the matching algorithm is mostly used inside simplification rules such as demodulation and subsumption [29]. As these rules must be efficiently performed, using a complex matching algorithm is not viable. Instead, we provide a matching algorithm for the pattern class of terms [27] to complement Ehoh's λ-free higher-order matching algorithm [42, Sect. 4]. A term is a *pattern* if each of its free variables either has no arguments (as in first-order logic) or is applied to distinct De Bruijn indices.

To help determine whether to use the pattern or λ-free algorithm, we introduce a cached property `HasNonPatternVar`, which is set for terms of the form $X \bar{s}_n$ where $n > 0$ and either there exists some s_i that is not a De Bruijn index or there exist indices $i < j$ such that $s_i = s_j$ is a De Bruijn index. This property is propagated to the superterms when they are perfectly shared. This allows later checks if a term belongs to the pattern class to be performed in constant time.

We modify the λ-free higher-order matching algorithm to treat λ prefixes as above in the unification procedure—by bringing the prefixes to the same length and ignoring them afterwards. This ensures that the algorithm will never try to match a free variable with a λ-abstraction, making sure that β-redexes never appear. We also modify the algorithm to ensure that free variables are never bound to terms that have loose bound variables. This algorithm cannot find many complex matching substitutions (matchers), but it can efficiently determine whether two terms are variable renamings of each other or whether a simple matcher can be used, as in the case of $(X (\lambda x. x) \mathsf{b}, \mathsf{f} (\lambda x. x) \mathsf{b})$, where $X \mapsto \mathsf{f}$ is usually the desired matcher. If this algorithm does not find a matcher and both terms are patterns, pattern matching is tried.

Indexing. E, like other modern theorem provers, efficiently retrieves unifiable or matchable pairs of terms using indexing data structures. To find terms unifiable with a query term or instances of a query term, it uses *fingerprint indexing* [30]. Vukmirović et al. extended this data structure to support full higher-order terms in Zipperposition [41, Sect. 6]. We use the same approach in λE, and we extend feature vector indices [31] in the same way.

E uses *perfect discrimination trees* [26] to find generalizations of the query term (i.e., terms of which the query term is an instance). This data structure is a trie that indexes terms by representing them in a serialized, flattened form. The left branch from the root in Figure 1 shows how the first-order terms $\mathsf{f}\,\mathsf{a}\,X$

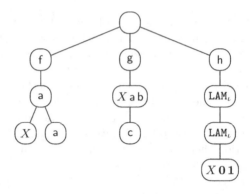

Fig. 1. First-order, λ-free higher-order, and higher-order pattern terms in a perfect discrimination tree

and f a a are stored. In Ehoh, this data structure is extended to support partial application and applied variables [42].

In λE, we extend this structure to support λ-abstractions and the higher-order pattern matching algorithm. To this end, we change the way in which terms are serialized. First, we require that all terms are fully η-expanded (except for arguments of variables applied in patterns). Then, when the term is serialized, we use a single node for applied variable terms $X\,\bar{s}_n$, instead of a node for X followed by nodes for the arguments $\bar{s}_n$. We serialize the λ-abstraction $\lambda x.\,s$ using a dedicated node LAM_τ, where τ is the type of x, followed by the serialization of s. Other than these changes, serialization remains as in Ehoh, following the gracefulness principle. Figure 1 shows how $\mathsf{g}\,(X\,\mathsf{a}\,\mathsf{b})\,\mathsf{c}$ and $\mathsf{h}\,(\lambda x.\,\lambda y.\,X\,y\,x)$ are serialized. Since the terms are stored in serialized form, it is hard to manipulate λ prefixes of stored terms during matching. Performing η-expansion when serializing terms ensures that matchable terms have λ prefixes of the same length.

We have dedicated separate nodes for applied variables because access to arguments of applied variables is necessary for the pattern matching algorithm. Even though arguments can be obtained by querying the arity n of the variable and taking the next n arguments in the serialization, this is both inefficient and inelegant. As for De Bruijn indices, we treat them the same as function symbols.

Following the notation from the extension of perfect discrimination trees to λ-free higher-order logic [42], we now describe how enumeration of generalizations is performed. To traverse the tree, λE begins at the root node and maintains two stacks: `term_stack` and `term_proc`, where `term_stack` contains the subterms of the query term that have to be matched, and `term_proc` contains processed terms that are used to backtrack to previous states. Initially, `term_stack` contains the query term, the current matching substitution σ is empty, and the successor node is chosen among the child nodes as follows:

A. If the node is labeled with a symbol ξ (where ξ is either a De Bruijn index or a constant) and the top item t of `term_stack` is of the form $\xi\,\bar{t}_n$, replace t by n new items $t_1,\ldots,t_n$, and push t onto `term_proc`.

B. If the node is labeled with a symbol LAM_τ and the top item t of `term_stack` is of the form $\lambda x.\,s$ and the type of x is τ, replace t by s, and push t onto `term_proc`.

C. If the node is labeled with a possibly applied variable $X\,\bar{s}_n$ (where $n \geq 0$), and the top item of `term_stack` is t, the matching algorithm described above is run on $X\,\bar{s}_n$ and t. The algorithm takes into account σ built so far and extends it if necessary. If the algorithm succeeds, pop t from `term_stack`, push it onto `term_proc`, and save the original value of σ in the node.

Backtracking works in the opposite direction: If the current node is labeled with a De Bruijn index or function symbol node of arity n, pop n terms from `term_stack` and move the top of `term_proc` to `term_stack`. If the node is labeled with LAM_τ, pop the top of `term_stack` and move the top of `term_proc` to `term_stack`. Finally, if the node is labeled with a possibly applied variable, move the top of the `term_proc` to `term_stack` and restore the value of σ.

As an example of how finding a generalization works, when looking for generalizations of $\mathsf{g\,(f\,a\,b)\,c}$ in the tree of Figure 1, the following states of stacks and substitutions emerge, from left to right:

	ϵ	g	$\mathsf{g}.(X\,\mathsf{a\,b})$	$\mathsf{g}.(X\,\mathsf{a\,b}).\mathsf{c}$
`term_stack`	$[\mathsf{g\,(f\,a\,b)\,c}]$	$[\mathsf{f\,a\,b,c}]$	$[\mathsf{c}]$	$[]$
`term_proc`	$[]$	$[\mathsf{g\,(f\,a\,b)\,c}]$	$[\mathsf{f\,a\,b},\mathsf{g\,(f\,a\,b)\,c}]$	$[\mathsf{c},\mathsf{f\,a\,b},\mathsf{g\,(f\,a\,b)\,c}]$
σ	$\emptyset$	$\emptyset$	$\{X \mapsto \mathsf{f}\}$	$\{X \mapsto \mathsf{f}\}$

5   Preprocessing, Calculus, and Extensions

Ehoh's simple λ-free higher-order calculus performed well on Sledgehammer problems and formed a promising stepping stone to full higher-order logic [42]. When implementing support for full higher-order logic, we were guided by efficiency and gracefulness with respect to Ehoh's calculus rather than completeness. Whereas Zipperposition provides both complete and incomplete modes, λE only offers incomplete modes.

Preprocessing. Our experience with Zipperposition showed the importance of flexibility in preprocessing the higher-order problems [40]. Therefore, we implemented a flexible preprocessing module in λE.

To maintain compatibility with Ehoh, λE can optionally transform all λ-abstractions into named functions. This process is called λ-*lifting* [19]. λE also removes all occurrences of Boolean subterms (other than $\bot, \top$, and free variables) in higher-order contexts using a FOOL-like transformation [23]. For example, the formula $\mathsf{f}(\mathsf{p} \wedge \mathsf{q}) \approx \mathsf{a}$ becomes $(\mathsf{p} \wedge \mathsf{q} \to \mathsf{f}(\top) \approx \mathsf{a}) \wedge (\neg\,(\mathsf{p} \wedge \mathsf{q}) \to \mathsf{f}(\bot) \approx \mathsf{a})$.

Many TPTP problems use the `definition` role to identify the definitions of symbols. λE can treat definition axioms as rewrite rules, and replace all occurrences of defined symbols during preprocessing. Furthermore, during SInE [18] axiom selection, it can always include the defined symbol in the trigger relation.

Calculus. λE implements the same superposition calculus as Ehoh with three important changes. First, wherever Ehoh requires the MGU of terms, λE enumerates unifiers from a finite subset of the CSU, as explained in Sect. 4. Second, λE uses versions of the KBO and LPO orders designed for λ-terms.

The third difference is more subtle. One of the main features of Ehoh is *prefix optimization* [42, Sect. 1]: a method that, given a demodulator $s \approx t$, makes it possible to replace both applied and unapplied occurrences of s by t by traversing only the first-order subterms of a rewritable term. In a λ-free setting, this optimization is useful, but in the presence of $\beta\eta$-normalization, the shapes of terms can change drastically, making it much harder to track prefixes of terms. This is why we disable the prefix optimization in λE. To compensate for losing this optimization, we introduce the argument congruence rule AC in λE and enable positive and negative functional extensionality (PE and NE) by default:

$$\frac{s \approx t \vee C}{s\, X \approx t\, X \vee C}\, \text{AC} \qquad \frac{s \not\approx t \vee C}{s\, (\text{sk}\, \overline{X}) \not\approx t\, (\text{sk}\, \overline{X}) \vee C}\, \text{NE} \qquad \frac{s\, X \approx t\, X \vee C}{s \approx t \vee C}\, \text{PE}$$

AC and NE assume that s and t are of function type. In NE, $\overline{X}$ denotes all the free variables occurring in s and t, and sk is a fresh Skolem symbol of the appropriate type. PE has a side condition that X may not occur in s, t, or C.

Saturation. E's saturation procedure assumes that each attempt to perform an inference will either result in a single clause or fail due to one of the inference side conditions. Unification procedures that produce multiple substitutions break this invariant, and the saturation procedure needed to be adjusted.

For Zipperposition, Vukmirović et al. developed a variant of the saturation procedure that interleaves computing unifiers and scheduling inferences to be performed [40]. Since completeness was not a design goal for λE, we did not implement this version of the saturation procedure. Instead, in places where previously a single unifier was expected, λE consumes all elements of the iterator used for enumerating a unifier, converting them into clauses.

Reasoning about Formulas. Even though most of the Boolean structure is removed during preprocessing, formulas can reappear at the top level of clauses during saturation. For example, after instantiating X with $\lambda x.\, \lambda y.\, x \wedge y$, the clause $X\, \mathsf{p}\, \mathsf{q} \vee \mathsf{a} \approx \mathsf{b}$ becomes $(\mathsf{p} \wedge \mathsf{q}) \vee \mathsf{a} \approx \mathsf{b}$. λE converts every clause of the form $\varphi \vee C$, where φ has a logic symbol as its head, or it is a (dis)equation between two formulas different than T, to an explicitly quantified formula. Then, the clausification algorithm is invoked on the formula to restore the clausal structure. Zipperposition features more dynamic clausification modes, but for simplicity we decided not to implement them in λE.

The λ-superposition calculus for full higher-order logic [4] includes many rules that act on Boolean subterms, which are necessary for completeness. Other than Boolean simplification rules, which use simple tautologies such as $\mathsf{p} \wedge \mathsf{T} \leftrightarrow \mathsf{p}$ to simplify terms, we have implemented none of the Boolean rules of this calculus in λE. First, we have observed that complicated rules such as FLUIDBOOLHOIST and

FLUIDLOOBHOIST are hardly ever useful in practice and usually only contribute to an uncontrolled increase in the proof state size. Second, simpler rules such as BOOLHOIST can usually be simulated by pragmatic rules that perform Boolean extensionality reasoning, described below.

To make up for excluding Boolean rules, we use an incomplete, but more easily controllable and intuitive rule, called *primitive instantiation*. This rule instantiates free predicate variables with approximations of formulas that are ground instances of this variable. We use the approximations described by Vukmirović and Nummelin [43, Sect. 3.3].

λE's handling of the Hilbert choice operator is inspired by Leo-III's [35]. λE recognizes clauses of the form $\neg P X \vee P(f P)$, which essentially denote that f is a choice symbol. Then, when subterm f s is found during saturation, s is used to instantiate the choice axiom for f. Similarly, Leibniz equality [43] is eliminated by recognizing clauses of the form $\neg P$ a $\vee P$ b $\vee C$. These clauses are then instantiated with $P \mapsto \lambda x. x \approx$ a and $P \mapsto \lambda x. x \not\approx$ b, which results in a $\approx$ b $\vee C$.

Finally, λE treats induction axioms specially. Like Zipperposition [40, Sect. 4], it abstracts literals from the goal clauses and instantiates induction axioms with these abstractions. Since Zipperposition supports dynamic calculus-level clausification, induction axioms are instantiated during saturation, when the axioms are processed. In λE, this instantiation is performed immediately after clausification. After λE has collected all the abstractions, it traverses the clauses and instantiates those that have applied variable of the same type as the abstraction.

Extensionality. λE takes a pragmatic approach to reasoning about functional and Boolean extensionality: It uses *abstracting* rules [5] which simulate basic superposition calculus rules but do not require unifiability of the partner terms in the inference. More precisely, assume a core inference needs to be performed between two β-reduced terms u and v, such that they can be represented as $u = C[s_1, \ldots, s_n]$ and $v = C[t_1, \ldots, t_n]$, where C is the most general "green" [5] common context of u and v, not all of s_i and t_j are free variables, and for at least one i, $s_i \neq t_i$, s_i and t_i are not possibly applied free variables, and they are of Boolean or function type. Then, the conclusion is formed by taking the conclusion D of the core inference rule (which would be created if s and t are unifiable) and adding literals $s_1 \not\approx t_1 \vee \cdots \vee s_n \not\approx t_n$.

These rules are particularly useful because λE has no rules that dynamically process Booleans in FOOL-like fashion, such as BOOLHOIST. For example, given the clauses f (p$\wedge$q) $\approx$ a and g (f p) $\not\approx$ b, the abstracting version of the superposition rule would result in g a $\not\approx$ b $\vee$ (p $\wedge$ q) $\not\approx$ p. In this way, the Boolean structure bubbles up to the top level and is further processed by clausification. We noticed that this alleviates the need for the other Boolean rules in practice.

6 Evaluation

We now try to answer two questions about λE: *How does λE compare against other higher-order provers (including Ehoh)? Does λE introduce any overhead* *compared with Ehoh?* To answer these questions, we ran provers on problems from the TPTP library [38] and on benchmarks generated by Sledgehammer (SH) [28]. The experiments were carried out on StarExec Miami [36] nodes equipped with Intel Xeon E5-2620 v4 CPU clocked at 2.10 GHz. For the TPTP part, we used the CASC 2021[2] time limits: 120 s wall-clock and 960 s CPU. For SH benchmarks and to answer the other question, we used Sledgehammer's default time limit: 30 s wall-clock and CPU. The raw evaluation data is available online.[3]

Comparison with Other Provers. To answer the first question, we let λE compete with the top contenders in the higher-order division of CASC 2021: cvc5 0.0.7 [2], Ehoh 2.7 [42], Leo-III 1.6.6 [35], Vampire 4.6 [8], and Zipperposition 2.1 [40]. We also included Satallax 3.5 [10]. We used all 2899 higher-order theorems in TPTP 7.5.0 as well as 5000 SH higher-order benchmarks originating from the Seventeen benchmark suite [15]. On SH benchmarks, cvc5, Ehoh, λE, Vampire, and Zipperposition were run using custom schedules provided by their developers, optimized for single-core usage and low timeouts. Otherwise, we used the corresponding CASC configurations.

Although it internally does not support λ-abstractions, Ehoh 2.7 can parse full higher-order logic using λ-lifting. We included two versions of Zipperposition: *coop* uses Ehoh 2.7 as a backend to finish proof attempts, whereas *uncoop* does not. Both Ehoh and λE were run in the automatic scheduling mode. Compared with Ehoh, λE features a redesigned module for automatic scheduling, it can exploit multiple CPU cores, and its heuristics have been more extensively trained on higher-order problems.

The results are shown in Figure 2. λE dramatically improves E's higher-order reasoning capabilities compared with Ehoh. It solves 20% more TPTP benchmarks and 7% more SH benchmarks. The reason for the higher performance increase for TPTP is likely that TPTP benchmarks tend to require more higher-order reasoning than SH benchmarks, which often have a large first-order component and for which Ehoh was already very successful.

λE was envisioned as an efficient backend to proof assistants. As such, it excels on SH benchmarks, outperforming the competition. On TPTP, it outperforms all higher-order provers other than Zipperposition-coop. If Zipperposition's Ehoh backend is disabled, λE outperforms Zipperposition by a wide margin. This comparison is arguably fairer; after all, λE does not use an older version of Zipperposition as a backend. These results suggest that λE already implements most of the necessary features for a high-performance higher-order prover but could benefit from the kind of fine-tuning that Zipperposition underwent in the last four years.

Remarkably, the raw evaluation data reveals thats λE solves 181 SH problems and 24 TPTP problems that Zipperposition-coop does not. The lower number of uniquely solved TPTP problems is likely because Zipperposition was heavily optimized on the TPTP.

---

[2] http://www.tptp.org/CASC/28/
[3] https://doi.org/10.5281/zenodo.6389849

	TPTP	SH
cvc5	1931	2577
Ehoh	2105	2611
λE	2533	**2804**
Leo-III	2282	1601
Satallax	2320	1719
Vampire	2203	2240
Zipperposition-coop	**2583**	2754
Zipperposition-uncoop	2483	2181

Fig. 2. Comparison of higher-order provers

	TPTP
Ehoh FO	535
Ehoh HO	538
λE FO	537
λE HO	**541**

Fig. 3. Evaluation of λE's overhead

Comparison with the First-Order E. Both Ehoh and λE can be compiled in a mode that disables most of the higher-order reasoning. This mode is designed for users that are interested only in E's first-order capabilities and care a lot about performance. To answer the second evaluation question, about assessing overhead of λE, we chose all the 1138 unique problems used at CASC from 2019 to 2021 in the first-order theorem division and ran Ehoh and λE both in this first-order (FO) mode and in higher-order (HO) mode.

We fixed a single configuration of options, because Ehoh's and λE's automatic scheduling methods could select different configurations and we would not be measuring the overhead but the quality of the chosen configurations. We chose the *boa* configuration [42, Sect. 7], which is the configuration most often used by E 2.2 in its automatic scheduling mode. The results are shown in Figure 3.

Counterintuitively, the higher-order versions of both provers outperform the first-order counterparts. However, the difference is so small that it can be attributed to the changes to memory layout that affect the order in which clauses are chosen. Similar effects are visible when comparing the first-order versions.

CASC Results. λE also took part in CASC 2022. In the TPTP higher-order division, λE finished second, after Zipperposition, as expected. In the Sledge-hammer division, λE tied with Ehoh for first place, a disappointment. The likely explanation is that λE used a wrong configuration in this division, as we found out afterwards. We expect better performance at CASC 2023.

7   Discussion and Related Work

On the trajectory to λE, we developed, together with colleagues, three super-position calculi: for λ-free higher-order logic [6], for a higher-order logic with λ-abstraction but no Booleans [5], and for full higher-order logic [5]. These milestones allowed us to carefully estimate how the increased reasoning capabilities of each calculus influence its performance.

Extending first-order provers with higher-order reasoning capabilities has been attempted by other researchers as well. Barbosa et al. extended the SMT solvers CVC4 (now cvc5) and veriT to higher-order logic in an incomplete way [3]. Bhayat and Reger first extended Vampire to higher-order logic using combinatory unification [8], an incomplete approach, before they designed and implemented a complete higher-order superposition calculus based on SKBCI combinators [7]. The advantage is that combinators can be supported as a thin layer on top of λ-free terms. This calculus is also implemented in Zipperposition. However, in informal experiments, we found that λ-superposition performs substantially better, corroborating the CASC results, so we decided to make a more profound change to Ehoh and implement λ-superposition.

Possibly the only actively maintained higher-order provers built from the bottom up as higher-order provers are Leo-III [35] and Satallax's [10] successor Lash [11]. A further overview of other traditional higher-order provers and the calculi they are based on can be found in the paper about Ehoh [42, Sect. 9].

8   Conclusion

In 2019, the reviewers of our Ehoh paper [42] were skeptical that extending Ehoh with support for full higher-order logic would be feasible. One of them wrote:

> A potential criticism could be that this step from E to Ehoh is just extending FOL by those aspects of HOL that are easily in reach with rather straightforward extensions (none of the extensions is indeed very complicated), and that the difficult challenges of fully supporting HOL have yet to be confronted.

We ended up addressing the theoretical "difficult challenges" in other work with colleagues. In this paper, we faced the practical challenges pertaining to the extension of Ehoh's data structures and algorithms to support full higher-order logic and demonstrated that such an extension is possible. Our evaluation shows that this extension makes λE the best higher-order prover on benchmarks coming from interactive theorem proving practice, which was our goal. λE lags slightly behind Zipperposition on TPTP problems. One reason might be that Zipperposition does not assume a clausal structure and can perform subtle formula-level inferences. It would be useful to implement the same features in λE. We have also only started tuning λE's heuristics on higher-order problems.

Acknowledgment. Ahmed Bhayat and Martin Suda provided Vampire configurations optimized for Sledgehammer. Andrew Reynolds did the same for cvc5. Jannis Limperg helped us debug the submission artifact. Simon Cruanes, Wan Fokkink, Mark Summerfield, and the anonymous reviewers suggested several textual improvements. We thank them all.

This research has received funding from the European Research Council (ERC) under the European Union's Horizon 2020 research and innovation program (grant agreement No. 713999, Matryoshka). Vukmirović and Blanchette have received funding from the Netherlands Organization for Scientific Research (NWO) under the Vidi program (project No. 016.Vidi.189.037, Lean Forward).

References

1. Andrews, P.B.: An Introduction to Mathematical Logic and Type Theory: To Truth Through Proof (2nd Ed.), Applied Logic, vol. 27. Springer (2002)
2. Barbosa, H., Barrett, C.W., Brain, M., Kremer, G., Lachnitt, H., Mann, M., Mohamed, A., Mohamed, M., Niemetz, A., Nötzli, A., Ozdemir, A., Preiner, M., Reynolds, A., Sheng, Y., Tinelli, C., Zohar, Y.: cvc5: A versatile and industrial-strength SMT solver. In: Fisman, D., Rosu, G. (eds.) TACAS 2022. LNCS, vol. 13243, pp. 415–442. Springer (2022)
3. Barbosa, H., Reynolds, A., El Ouraoui, D., Tinelli, C., Barrett, C.W.: Extending SMT solvers to higher-order logic. In: CADE. LNCS, vol. 11716, pp. 35–54. Springer (2019)
4. Bentkamp, A., Blanchette, J., Tourret, S., Vukmirović, P.: Superposition for full higher-order logic. In: Platzer, A., Sutcliffe, G. (eds.) CADE. LNCS, vol. 12699, pp. 396–412. Springer (2021)
5. Bentkamp, A., Blanchette, J., Tourret, S., Vukmirović, P., Waldmann, U.: Superposition with lambdas. J. Autom. Reason. 65(7), 893–940 (2021)
6. Bentkamp, A., Blanchette, J.C., Cruanes, S., Waldmann, U.: Superposition for lambda-free higher-order logic. In: Galmiche, D., Schulz, S., Sebastiani, R. (eds.) IJCAR. LNCS, vol. 10900, pp. 28–46. Springer (2018)
7. Bhayat, A., Reger, G.: Restricted combinatory unification. In: Fontaine, P. (ed.) CADE. LNCS, vol. 11716, pp. 74–93. Springer (2019)
8. Bhayat, A., Reger, G.: A combinator-based superposition calculus for higher-order logic. In: Peltier, N., Sofronie-Stokkermans, V. (eds.) IJCAR (1). LNCS, vol. 12166, pp. 278–296. Springer (2020)
9. Blanchette, J.C., Kaliszyk, C., Paulson, L.C., Urban, J.: Hammering towards QED. J. Formaliz. Reason. 9(1), 101–148 (2016)
10. Brown, C.E.: Satallax: An automatic higher-order prover. In: Gramlich, B., Miller, D., Sattler, U. (eds.) IJCAR. LNCS, vol. 7364, pp. 111–117. Springer (2012)
11. Brown, C.E., Kaliszyk, C.: Lash 1.0 (system description). In: Blanchette, J., Kovács, L., Pattinson, D. (eds.) IJCAR 2022. LNCS, vol. 13385, pp. 350–358. Springer (2022)
12. Cervesato, I., Pfenning, F.: A linear spine calculus. J. Log. Comput. 13(5), 639–688 (2003)
13. Charguéraud, A.: The locally nameless representation. J. Autom. Reason. 49(3), 363–408 (2012)
14. Cruanes, S.: Extending Superposition with Integer Arithmetic, Structural Induction, and Beyond. PhD thesis, École Polytechnique (2015)
15. Desharnais, M., Vukmirović, P., Blanchette, J., Wenzel, M.: Seventeen provers under the hammer. In: Andronick, J., de Moura, L. (eds.) ITP. LIPIcs, vol. 237, pp. 8:1–8:18. Schloss Dagstuhl (2022)
16. Gu, R., Shao, Z., Chen, H., Wu, X.N., Kim, J., Sjöberg, V., Costanzo, D.: CertiKOS: An extensible architecture for building certified concurrent OS kernels. In: Keeton, K., Roscoe, T. (eds.) OSDI. pp. 653–669. USENIX Association (2016)
17. Hales, T.C., Adams, M., Bauer, G., Dang, D.T., Harrison, J., Hoang, T.L., Kaliszyk, C., Magron, V., McLaughlin, S., Nguyen, T.T., Nguyen, T.Q., Nipkow, T., Obua, S., Pleso, J., Rute, J., Solovyev, A., Ta, A.H.T., Tran, T.N., Trieu, D.T., Urban, J., Vu, K.K., Zumkeller, R.: A formal proof of the Kepler conjecture. CoRR abs/1501.02155 (2015)

18. Hoder, K., Voronkov, A.: Sine qua non for large theory reasoning. In: Bjørner, N., Sofronie-Stokkermans, V. (eds.) CADE. LNCS, vol. 6803, pp. 299–314. Springer (2011)

19. Hughes, R.J.M.: Super combinators: A new implementation method for applicative languages. In: Park, D.M.R., Friedman, D.P., Wise, D.S., Jr., G.L.S. (eds.) LFP. pp. 1–10. ACM (1982)

20. Kamareddine, F.: Reviewing the classical and the de Bruijn notation for λ-calculus and pure type systems. J. Log. Comput. 11(3), 363–394 (2001)

21. Kern, C., Greenstreet, M.R.: Formal verification in hardware design: A survey. ACM Trans. Design Autom. Electr. Syst. 4(2), 123–193 (1999)

22. Klein, G., Andronick, J., Elphinstone, K., Heiser, G., Cock, D., Derrin, P., Elkaduwe, D., Engelhardt, K., Kolanski, R., Norrish, M., Sewell, T., Tuch, H., Winwood, S.: seL4: Formal verification of an operating-system kernel. Commun. ACM 53(6), 107–115 (2010)

23. Kotelnikov, E., Kovács, L., Suda, M., Voronkov, A.: A clausal normal form translation for FOOL. In: Benzmüller, C., Sutcliffe, G., Rojas, R. (eds.) GCAI. EPiC, vol. 41, pp. 53–71. EasyChair (2016)

24. Leroy, X.: Formal verification of a realistic compiler. Commun. ACM 52(7), 107–115 (2009)

25. Löchner, B., Schulz, S.: An evaluation of shared rewriting. In: de Nivelle, H., Schulz, S. (eds.) IWIL. pp. 33–48. Max-Planck-Institut für Informatik (2001)

26. McCune, W.: Experiments with discrimination-tree indexing and path indexing for term retrieval. J. Autom. Reason. 9(2), 147–167 (1992)

27. Nipkow, T.: Functional unification of higher-order patterns. In: Best, E. (ed.) LICS. pp. 64–74. IEEE Computer Society (1993)

28. Paulson, L.C., Blanchette, J.C.: Three years of experience with Sledgehammer, a practical link between automatic and interactive theorem provers. In: Sutcliffe, G., Schulz, S., Ternovska, E. (eds.) IWIL. EPiC, vol. 2, pp. 1–11. EasyChair (2012)

29. Schulz, S.: E—a brainiac theorem prover. AI Commun. 15(2-3), 111–126 (2002)

30. Schulz, S.: Fingerprint indexing for paramodulation and rewriting. In: Gramlich, B., Miller, D., Sattler, U. (eds.) IJCAR. LNCS, vol. 7364, pp. 477–483. Springer (2012)

31. Schulz, S.: Simple and efficient clause subsumption with feature vector indexing. In: Bonacina, M.P., Stickel, M.E. (eds.) Automated Reasoning and Mathematics— Essays in Memory of William W. McCune. LNCS, vol. 7788, pp. 45–67. Springer (2013)

32. Schulz, S., Cruanes, S., Vukmirović, P.: Faster, higher, stronger: E 2.3. In: Fontaine, P. (ed.) CADE. LNCS, vol. 11716, pp. 495–507. Springer (2019)

33. Steen, A.: Extensional paramodulation for higher-order logic and its effective implementation leo-iii. Künstliche Intell. 34(1), 105–108 (2020)

34. Steen, A., Benzmüller, C.: There is no best \beta -normalization strategy for higher-order reasoners. In: Davis, M., Fehnker, A., McIver, A., Voronkov, A. (eds.) LPAR-20 2015. LNCS, vol. 9450, pp. 329–339. Springer (2015)

35. Steen, A., Benzmüller, C.: Extensional higher-order paramodulation in Leo-III. J. Autom. Reason. 65(6), 775–807 (2021)

36. Stump, A., Sutcliffe, G., Tinelli, C.: StarExec: A cross-community infrastructure for logic solving. In: Demri, S., Kapur, D., Weidenbach, C. (eds.) IJCAR. LNCS, vol. 8562, pp. 367–373. Springer (2014)

37. Sultana, N., Blanchette, J.C., Paulson, L.C.: LEO-II and Satallax on the Sledgehammer test bench. J. Applied Logic 11(1), 91–102 (2013)

38. Sutcliffe, G.: The TPTP problem library and associated infrastructure—from CNF to TH0, TPTP v6.4.0. J. Autom. Reason. 59(4), 483–502 (2017)

39. Sutcliffe, G.: The 10th IJCAR automated theorem proving system competition—CASC-J10. AI Commun. 34(2), 163–177 (2021)
40. Vukmirović, P., Bentkamp, A., Blanchette, J., Cruanes, S., Nummelin, V., Tourret, S.: Making higher-order superposition work. In: Platzer, A., Sutcliffe, G. (eds.) CADE. LNCS, vol. 12699, pp. 415–432. Springer (2021)
41. Vukmirović, P., Bentkamp, A., Nummelin, V.: Efficient full higher-order unification. In: Ariola, Z.M. (ed.) FSCD. LIPIcs, vol. 167, pp. 5:1–5:17. Schloss Dagstuhl (2020)
42. Vukmirović, P., Blanchette, J.C., Cruanes, S., Schulz, S.: Extending a brainiac prover to lambda-free higher-order logic. In: Vojnar, T., Zhang, L. (eds.) TACAS. LNCS, vol. 11427, pp. 192–210. Springer (2019)
43. Vukmirović, P., Nummelin, V.: Boolean reasoning in a higher-order superposition prover. In: Fontaine, P., Korovin, K., Kotsireas, I.S., Rümmer, P., Tourret, S. (eds.) PAAR+SC^2. CEUR Workshop Proceedings, vol. 2752, pp. 148–166. CEUR-WS.org (2020)

Tools (Regular Papers)

The WhyRel Prototype for Modular Relational Verification of Pointer Programs

Ramana Nagasamudram[1] ([✉]), Anindya Banerjee[2], and David A. Naumann[1]

[1] Stevens Institute of Technology, Hoboken, USA
{rnagasam,dnaumann}@stevens.edu
[2] IMDEA Software Institute, Madrid, Spain
anindya.banerjee@imdea.org

Abstract. Verifying relations between programs arises as a task in various verification contexts such as optimizing transformations, relating new versions of programs with older versions (regression verification), and noninterference. However, relational verification for programs acting on dynamically allocated mutable state is not well supported by existing tools, which provide a high level of automation at the cost of restricting the programs considered. Auto-active tools, on the other hand, require more user interaction but enable verification of a broader class of programs. This article presents WhyRel, a tool for the auto-active verification of relational properties of pointer programs based on relational region logic. WhyRel is evaluated through verification case studies, relying on SMT solvers orchestrated by the Why3 platform on which it builds. Case studies include establishing representation independence of ADTs, showing noninterference, and challenge problems from recent literature.

Keywords: local reasoning · relational verification · auto-active verification · data abstraction.

1 Introduction

Relational properties encompass conditional equivalence of programs (as in regression verification [28]), noninterference (in which a program is related to itself via a low-indistinguishability relation), and other requirements such as sensitivity [6]. The problem we address concerns tooling for the modular verification of relational properties of heap-manipulating programs, including programs that act on differing data representations involving dynamically allocated pointer structures.

Modular reasoning about pointer programs is enabled through local reasoning using frame conditions, procedural abstraction (i.e., reasoning under hypotheses about procedures a program invokes), and data abstraction, requiring state-based encapsulation. For establishing properties of ADTs such as representation independence, encapsulation plays a crucial role, permitting implementations to rely on invariants about private state hidden from clients. Relational verification also involves a kind of compositionality, the *alignment* of intermediate execution steps, which enables use of simpler relational invariants and specs (see e.g. [29,17,25]).

© The Author(s) 2023
S. Sankaranarayanan and N. Sharygina (Eds.): TACAS 2023, LNCS 13994, pp. 133–151, 2023.
https://doi.org/10.1007/978-3-031-30820-8_11

We aim for auto-active verification [19], accessible to developers, as promoted by tools such as Dafny and Why3. Users are expected to provide specifications, annotations such as loop invariants and assertions, and, for relational verification, alignment hints. The idea is to minimize or eliminate the need for users to manually invoke tactics for proof search.

Automated inference of specs, loop invariants, or program alignments facilitates automated verification, and is implemented in some tools. But in the current state of the art these techniques are restricted to specs and invariants of limited forms (e.g., only linear arithmetic) and seldom support dynamically allocated objects. So inference is beyond the scope of this paper.

What is in scope is use of strong encapsulation, to hide information in the sense that method specs used by clients do not expose internal representation details, and to enable verification of modular correctness of a client, in the sense that its behavior is independent from internal representations. Achieving strong encapsulation for pointer programs, without undue restriction on data and control structure, is technically challenging. Auto-active tools rely on extensive axiomatization for the generation of *verification conditions (VCs)*; for high assurance the VCs should be justified with respect to a definitional operational semantics of programs and specs.

In this article, we describe WhyRel, a prototype for auto-active verification of relational properties of pointer programs. Source programs are written in an imperative language with support for shared mutable objects (but no subtyping), dynamic allocation, and encapsulation. The assertion language is first-order and, for expressing relational properties, includes constructs that relate values of variables and pointer structures between two programs. WhyRel is based on relational region logic [1], a relational extension of region logic [4,2]. Region logic provides a flexible approach to local reasoning through the use of *dynamic frame* conditions [15] which capture *footprints* of commands acting on the heap. Verification involves reasoning explicitly about regions of memory and changes to them as computation proceeds; flexibility comes from being able to express notions such as parthood and separation in the same first-order setting.

Encapsulation is specified using a kind of dynamic frame, called a *dynamic boundary*: a footprint that captures a module's internal locations. Enforcing encapsulation is then a matter of ensuring that clients don't directly modify or update locations in a module's boundary. There are detailed soundness proofs for the relational logic [1], of which our prototype is a faithful implementation.

WhyRel is built on top of the Why3 platform[3] for deductive program verification which provides infrastructure for verifying programs written in WhyML, a subset of ML [7] with support for ghost code and nondeterministic choice. The assertion language is a polymorphic first-order logic extended with support for algebraic data types and recursively and inductively defined predicates [11]. Why3 generates VCs for WhyML which can then be discharged using a wide array of theorem provers, from interactive proof assistants such as Coq and Isabelle, to first-order theorem provers and SMT solvers such as Vampire, Alt-Ergo and Z3.

---

[3] The Why3 distribution can be found at: `https://why3.lri.fr/`.

Primarily, WhyRel is used as a front end to Why3. Users provide programs, specs, annotations, and for relational verification, relational specs and alignment specified using a specialized syntax for product programs. WhyRel translates source programs into WhyML, performing significant encoding so as to faithfully capture the heap model and fine-grained framing formalized in relational region logic. VCs pertinent to this logic are introduced as intermediate assertions and lemmas for the user to establish. Verification is done using facilities provided by Why3 and the primary mode of interaction is through an IDE for viewing and discharging verification conditions.

Our approach is evaluated through a number of case studies performed in WhyRel, for which we rely entirely on SMT solvers to discharge proof obligations. The primary contribution is the development of a tool for relational verification of heap manipulating programs which has been applied to challenging case studies. Examples formalized demonstrate the effectiveness of relational region logic for alignment, for expressing heap relations, and for relational reasoning that exploits encapsulation.

Organization. Sec. 2 highlights aspects of specifying programs and relational properties in WhyRel using a stack ADT example. Sec. 3 discusses examples of program alignment. Sec. 4 gives an overview of the design of WhyRel and Sec. 5 provides highlights on experience using the tool. Sec. 6 discusses related work and Sec. 7 concludes.

2 A tour of WhyRel

Programs and specifications. WhyRel provides a lightweight module system to organize definitions, programs, and specs. Developments are structured into interfaces and modules that implement interfaces. In addition, for relational verification, WhyRel introduces the notion of a *bimodule*, described later, to relate method implementations between two (*unary*) modules.

We'll walk through aspects of specification in WhyRel using the STACK interface shown in Fig. 1, which describes a stack of boxed integers with push and pop operations. The interface starts by declaring global variables, pool and capacity, and client-visible fields of the Cell and Stack classes. Variable pool has type rgn, where a *region* is a set of references, and is used to describe objects notionally owned by modules implementing the stack interface; capacity has type int and describes an upper bound on the size of a stack. The Cell class for boxed integers is declared with a single field, val, storing an int. The Stack class is declared with three fields: rep of type region keeps track of objects used to represent the stack, size of type int stores the number of elements in the stack, and the ghost field abs of type intlist (list of mathematical integers) keeps track of an abstraction of the stack, used in specs. Class definitions can be refined later by modules implementing the interface: e.g., a module using a linked-list implementation might extend the Stack class with a field head storing a reference to the list.

Heap encapsulation is supported at the granularity of modules through the use of *dynamic module boundaries* which describe locations internal to a module. A

```
interface STACK =
  public pool:rgn /* rgn: a set of references */  public capacity:int
  class Cell {val:int}  class Stack {rep:rgn; size:int; ghost abs:intlist}

  /* encapsulated locations */
  boundary {capacity, pool, pool'any, pool'rep'any}

  public invariant stkPub = ∀ s: Stack ∈ pool. 0 ≤ s.size ≤ capacity
    ∧ (∀ t: Stack ∈ pool. s ≠ t ⇒ s.rep ∩ t.rep ⊆ {null}) ∧ ...

  meth Cell(self: Cell) : unit ...    meth getVal(self: Cell) : int ...
  meth Stack(self: Stack) : unit ensures {self ∈ pool} ...

  meth push(self: Stack, k: int) : unit
    requires {self ∈ pool ∧ self.size < capacity}
    ensures  {self.abs = cons(k,old(self.abs)) ∧ ...}
    /* allowed heap effects of implementations */
    effects  {rw {self}'any, self.rep'any, alloc; rd self,capacity}

  meth pop(self: Stack) : Cell
    requires {self ∈ pool ∧ self.size > 0}
    ensures  {self.size = old(self.size)-1}
    ensures  {result.val = hd(self.abs) ∧ self.abs = tl(old(self.abs))}
```

Fig. 1: WhyRel interface for the Stack ADT

location is either a variable or a heap location $o.f$, where o is an object reference and f is its field. In WhyRel, module boundaries are specified in interfaces and clients are enforced to not directly read or write locations described by the boundary except through the use of module methods. For our stack example, the dynamic boundary is capacity, pool, pool'any, pool'rep'any; expressed using image expressions and the any datagroup. Given a region G and a field f of class type, the *image expression* $G'f$ denotes the region containing the locations $o.f$ of all non-null references o in G, where f is a valid field of o. If f is of type region, $G'f$ is the union of the collection of reference sets $o.f$ for all o in G. For f of primitive type, such as int or intlist, $G'f$ is the empty region. The *datagroup* any is used to abstract from concrete field names: the expression pool'any is syntactic sugar for pool'val,...,pool'abs. Intuitively, the dynamic boundary in Fig. 1 says that clients may not directly read or write capacity, pool, any fields of objects in pool, and any fields of objects in the rep of any Stack in pool.

While encapsulation is specified at the level of modules, separation or locality at finer granularities can be specified using module invariants. The stack interface defines a public invariant stkPub which asserts that the rep fields of all Stack objects in pool are disjoint. This idiom can be used to ensure that modifying one object has no effect on any locations in the representation of another. Clients can rely on public invariants during verification, but modules implementing the interface must ensure they are preserved by module methods. Additionally, modules may define private invariants that capture conditions on internal state; provided these refer only to encapsulated locations, i.e., the designated boundary *frames* these invariants, clients are exempt from reasoning about them [14].

```
module Client =
  meth prog (n: int) : int
    requires { 0 ≤ n < capacity ∧ ... }
    effects  { rw alloc, pool, pool'any, pool'rep'any; rd n, capacity }
  = var i: int in var c: Cell in
    var stk: Stack in stk := new Stack; Stack(stk);
    while (i < n) do push(stk,i); i:=i+1 done; i := 0;
    while (i < n) do c:=pop(stk); result:=result+getVal(c); i:=i+1 done;

  meth prog (n: int|n: int) : (int|int)   /* Relational spec for prog */
    requires { n ≐ n ∧ Both(0 ≤ n < capacity ∧ ... ) }
    ensures  { result ≐ result }
```

Fig. 2: Example client for STACK and relational spec for equivalence

Finally, the STACK interface defines specs for initializers (methods Cell and Stack) and public specs for client-visible methods getVal, push, and pop. Notice that the stack initializer ensures self is added to the boundary (through post self ∈ pool) and stack operations require self to be part of the boundary (through pre self ∈ pool). Specs for push and pop are standard, using "old" expressions to precisely capture field updates. WhyRel's assertion language is first-order and includes constructs such as the points-to assertion $x.f = e$ and operations on regions such as subset and membership. In addition to pre- and post-conditions, each method is annotated with a frame condition in an effects clause that serves to constrain heap effects of implementations. Allowable effects are expressed using read/write (rw) or read (rd) of locations or location sets, described by regions. For example, the effects clause for push says that implementations may read/write any field of self and any field of any objects in self.rep. The distinguished variable alloc is used to indicate that push may dynamically allocate objects.

In our development, we build two modules that implement the interface in Fig. 1: one using arrays, ArrayStack and another using linked-lists, ListStack. Both rely on private invariants on encapsulated state that capture constraints on their pointer representations and its relation to abs, the mathematical abstraction of stack objects. The private invariant of ListStack, for example, says that Cell values in the linked-list of any Stack in pool are in correspondence with values stored in abs.

Example client, equivalence spec, and verification. We now turn attention to an example client, prog, shown in Fig. 2. This program computes the sum $\Sigma_{i=0}^{n} i$, albeit in a roundabout fashion, using a stack. The frame condition of prog mentions the boundary for STACK, but this is fine since the client respects WhyRel's encapsulation discipline, modifying encapsulated locations solely through calls to methods declared in the STACK interface. For this client, our goal is to establish equivalence when linked against either implementations of STACK. Let the *left* program be the client linked against ArrayStack, and the *right* the client linked against ListStackEquivalence is expressed using the relational spec shown in Fig. 2. For brevity, we omit frame conditions when describing relational specs.

```
meth prog (n: int | n: int) : (int | int)
= var i: int | i: int in var c: Cell | c: Cell in
  var stk: Stack in ⌊ stk := new Stack ⌋; ⌊ Stack(stk) ⌋;
  while (i < n) | (i < n) do ⌊ push(stk,i) ⌋; ⌊ i:=i+1 ⌋ done; ⌊ i:=0 ⌋;
  while (i < n) | (i < n) do ⌊ c:=pop(stk) ⌋;
    ⌊ result:=result+getVal(c) ⌋; ⌊ i:=i+1 ⌋ done;
```

Fig. 3: Alignment for example stack client

This relational spec relates two versions of prog; the notation (n:int | n:int) is used to declare that both versions expect n as argument. The pre-relation requires equality of inputs: n $\overset{.}{=}$ n says that the value of n on the left is equal to the value of n on the right. We use ($\overset{.}{=}$), instead of (=) to distinguish between values on the left and the right[4]. The relational spec requires the two states being related to satisfy the unary precondition for the client, as indicated by Both(...). The post-relation, result $\overset{.}{=}$ result, asserts equality on returned values. In WhyRel, relational specs capture a ∀∀ termination-insensitive property: *terminating executions of the programs being related, when started in states related by the pre-relation, will result in states related by the post-relation.*

WhyRel supports two approaches to verifying relational properties. The first reduces to proving functional properties of the programs involved. For instance, equivalence of the client when linked against the two stack implementations is immediate if we prove that prog indeed computes the sum of the first n nonnegative integers.

However, this approach neither lends well to more complicated programs and relational properties, nor does it allow us to exploit similarities between related programs or reason modularly using relational specs. The alternative is to prove the relational property using a convenient alignment of the two programs. Alignments are represented syntactically in WhyRel using *biprograms* which pair points of interest between two programs so that their effects can be reasoned about in tandem. If the chosen alignment is *adequate* in the sense of capturing all pairs of executions of the related programs, relational properties of the alignment entail the corresponding relation between the underlying programs.

The biprogram for prog is shown in Fig. 3. The alignment it captures is maximal: every control point in one version of the client is paired with itself in the other version. The construct (C|C') pairs a command C on the left with a command C' on the right, and the *sync* form ⌊C⌋ is syntactic sugar for (C|C); e.g., the biprogram for prog aligns the two allocations using ⌊stk := new Stack⌋. Further, this biprogram aligns both loops in *lockstep*, indicated using the syntax while e|e' do ... done. This alignment pairs a loop iteration on the left with a loop iteration on the right and requires the loop guards be in agreement: here, that i < n on the left is true just when i < n on the right is. Calls to stack operations are aligned in the loop body using the sync construct to facilitate

---

[4] Note in particular that $x \overset{.}{=} y$ is not the same as $y \overset{.}{=} x$

```
bimodule REL_STACK (ArrayStack | ListStack) =
  coupling stackCoupling = ∀ s: Stack ∈ pool | s: Stack ∈ pool.
    s ≐ s ⇒ s.abs ≐ s.abs ∧ ...

  meth Stack(self: Stack | self: Stack) : (unit | unit)
    ensures {self ≐ self ∧ ...} = /* biprogram for Stack */
  meth push(self: Stack | self: Stack) : (unit | unit)
    requires {self ≐ self ∧ ... }
    ensures   {self.abs ≐ self.abs ∧ ... } = /* biprogram for push */
  meth pop(self:Stack | self:Stack) : (Cell | Cell)
    requires {self ≐ self ∧ Both (self ∈ pool) ∧ Both (self.size > 0)}
    ensures   {... ∧ result.val ≐ result.val} = /* biprogram for pop */
```

Fig. 4: Bimodule for Stack; excerpts

modular verification of relational properties by indicating that relational specs for push and pop are to be used.

To prove the spec (in Fig. 2) about the biprogram in Fig. 3 we reason as follows: after allocation stk on both sides is initialized to be the empty stack. The first lockstep aligned loop which pushes integers from $0, \ldots, n$ maintains as invariant equality on i and on the mathematical abstractions the two stacks represent, i.e., $i \doteq i \wedge \texttt{stk.abs} \doteq \texttt{stk.abs}$. The second lockstep aligned loop which pops the stacks and increments result maintains as invariant agreement on the stack abstractions and result, the key conjunct being $\texttt{result} \doteq \texttt{result}$. This is sufficient to establish the desired post-relation. Importantly, the loop invariants are simple to prove—they only contain equalities between variables—and we don't have to reason about the exact contents of the two stacks involved.

Relational specs for Stack and verification. The reasoning described above relies on knowing the method implementations in ArrayStack and ListStack are equivalent. We need relational specs for push which state that given related inputs, the contents represented by the two stacks are the same; and for pop, which state that given related inputs, the values of the returned Cells are the same.

Fig. 4 shows a bimodule, REL_STACK, relating the two implementations of STACK. It includes relational specs for the stack operations along with biprograms used for verification. The bimodule maintains a *coupling* relation which relates data representations used by the two stack implementations. Concretely, the coupling here states that related stacks in pool represent the same abstraction. Note that quantifiers in relation formulas bind pairs of variables; and the equality $s \doteq s$ in stackCoupling is not strict pointer equality, but indicates correspondence. Strict pointer equality is too strong as it would not allow for modeling allocation as a nondeterministic operation or permit differing allocation patterns between programs being related. Behind the scenes, WhyRel maintains a partial bijection π between allocated references in the two states being related. The relation $x \doteq y$, where x and y are pointers, states that x in the left state is in correspondence with y in the right state w.r.t π, i.e., $\pi(x) = y$.

The relational spec for the initializer Stack ensures $\texttt{self} \doteq \texttt{self}$, which is required in the specs for push and pop. Like other invariants, coupling relations

```
meth mult(n: int, m: int) =          meth mult(n:int, m:int) =
  i := 0;                              i := 0;
  while (i < n) do j:=0;               while (i < n) do
    while (j < m) do                     result := result+m;
      result := result+1; j := j+1       i := i+1
    done; i := i+1 done;               done;
```

Fig. 5: Two versions of a simple multiplication routine

are meant to be framed by the boundary and are required to be preserved by module methods being related. Encapsulation allows for coupling relations to be hidden so that clients are exempt from reasoning about them.

The steps taken to complete the Stack development and verify equivalence of two versions of its client are as follows: (i) build the STACK interface in WhyRel, with public invariants clients can rely on and a boundary that designates encapsulated locations; (ii) develop two modules refining this interface, ArrayStack and ListStack, and verify that their implementations conform to STACK interface specs, relying on any private invariants that capture conditions on encapsulated state; (iii) provide a bimodule relating the two stack modules and prove equivalence of stack operations, relying on a coupling relation that captures relationships between pointer structures used by the two modules; (iv) verify the client with respect to specs given in STACK and prove it respects WhyRel's encapsulation regime; and finally (v) develop a bimodule for the client and verify equivalence using relational specs for stack methods.

3   Patterns of alignment

Well chosen alignments help decompose relational verification, allowing for the use of simple relational assertions and loop invariants. In this section, we'll look at examples of biprograms that capture alignments that aren't maximal, unlike the STACK client example in Sec. 2. We don't formalize the syntax of biprograms here, but we show representative examples. When discussing examples, we'll omit frame conditions and other aspects orthogonal to alignment.

Differing control structures. Churchill et al. [8] develop a technique for proving equivalence of programs using state-dependent alignments of program traces. They identify a challenging problem for equivalence checking, shown in Fig. 5, which compares two procedures for multiplication with different control flow. For automated approaches to relational verification, their example is challenging because of the need to align an unbounded number m of loop iterations on the left with a single iteration on the right.

To prove equivalence, we verify the biprogram shown in Fig. 6 with respect to a relational spec with pre-relation $n \stackrel{.}{=} n \wedge m \stackrel{.}{=} m$ and post-relation result $\stackrel{.}{=}$ result; i.e., agreement on inputs results in agreement of outputs. Unlike the stack client biprogram shown in Fig. 3, the alignment embodied here is not maximal—indeed, such alignment would not be possible due to the differing

```
meth mult(n: int, m: int | n: int, m: int) : (int | int) =
  ⌊ i := 0 ⌋;
  while (i < n) | (i < n) do  invariant { i ≐ i ∧ result ≐ result }
  ( j := 0; while (j < m) do result := result+1; j := j+1 done
  | result := result+m );
  assert { ⟨result = old(result)+m⟩ };
  ⌊ i := i+1 ⌋ done;
```

Fig. 6: Biprogram for example in Fig. 5

```
meth sumpub (l: List) : int =         meth sumpub (l: List | l: List) : int =
  p:=l.head; s:=0;                      ⌊ p:=l.head ⌋; ⌊ s:=0 ⌋;
  while (p ≠ null) do                   while (p ≠ null) | (p ≠ null) .
    if p.pub then                       ⟨ ¬ p.pub ⟨ | ⟩ ¬ p.pub ⟩ do
      s:=s+p.val                        ( if p.pub then s:=s+p.val end;
    end;                                  p:=p.nxt
    p:=p.nxt                            | if p.pub then s:=s+p.val end;
  done;                                   p:=p.nxt)
  result:=s;                           done; ⌊ result:=s ⌋;
```

Fig. 7: Summing up public elements of a linked list: program and alignment

control structure. Similarities are still exploited by aligning the outer loops in lockstep and the left inner loop with the assignment to result on the right.

A simple relational loop invariant which asserts agreement on i and result is sufficient for proving equivalence. To show this is invariant, we need to establish that the inner loop on the left has the effect of incrementing result by m, thereby maintaining equality on result after the inner loop. In Fig. 6 this is indicated by the assertion after the left inner loop. The notation ⟨P⟨ (resp. ⟩P⟩) is used to state that the unary formula P holds in the left (and resp. right) state.

Conditionally aligned loops. Examples so far have concerned lockstep aligned loops, requiring a one-to-one correspondence between loop iterations. However, this condition is often too restrictive. WhyRel provides for other patterns of loop alignment, including those that account for conditions on data values. Consider for example the program shown in Fig. 7 which traverses a linked list and computes the sum of all elements marked public, indicated in each element's pub field. The program satisfies the following noninterference property, with relational spec:

```
meth sumpub(l: List | l: List) : (int | int)
  requires { Both(listpub(l,xs)) ∧ xs ≐ xs }
  ensures { result ≐ result }
```

Here listpub(l,xs) is a predicate which asserts that the *sequence* of public values reachable from the list pointer l is realized in xs, a mathematical list of integers. Intuitively, this specification captures the property that the result of sumpub does not depend on the values of nonpublic elements in the input list l. Showing the program computes exactly the sum of public elements: result = sum(xs) would imply the desired noninterference property. However, to showcase support

WhyRel offers for non-lockstep alignments, we'll establish noninterference by conditionally aligning the loops in the two copies of sumpub (see Fig. 7).

The alignment is as follows: if p is a nonpublic node on one side, perform a loop iteration on that side, pausing the iteration on the other; and if p on both sides is public, perform lockstep iterations of both loops. This has the effect of incrementing s exactly when both sides are visiting public nodes, the values of which are guaranteed to be the same by the relational precondition. The biprogram expresses this alignment through the use of additional annotations, called *alignment guards* which are general relation formulas and express conditions that lead to left-only, right-only, or lockstep iterations. The left alignment guard ⟨¬ p.pub| indicates that left-only loop iterations are to be performed when p on the left is not public. The right alignment guard expresses a similar condition when p on the right is not public. Iterations proceed in lockstep when both alignment guards are false, i.e., when Both(p.pub) is true.

This biprogram maintains $\exists$ xs|xs. Both(listpub(p,xs)) $\wedge$ xs$\stackrel{\cdot}{=}$xs $\wedge$ s$\stackrel{\cdot}{=}$s as loop invariant, which implies the desired post-relation. This invariant states that p on both sides points to the same sequence of public values as captured by listpub(p,xs) and that there is agreement on the sum s computed so far. During verification, we must establish that left-only, right-only, and lockstep iterations of the aligned loops preserve this invariant. Due to the alignment, the value of s is only updated during lockstep iterations and its straightforward to show preservation. For one-sided iterations, reasoning relies on knowing that the sequence of public values pointed to by p remains the same.

4 Encoding and design

We implement WhyRel in OCaml, relying on a library provided by Why3 for constructing WhyML parse trees. Source programs are parsed and typechecked before being translated to WhyML. Prior to translation, WhyRel performs a variety of checks and transformations: primary among these is a check that clients respect encapsulation and that any biprograms provided by users are adequate. Proof obligations pertinent to relational region logic are generated in the form of intermediate assertions in WhyML programs and lemmas for the user to prove. In this section, we provide an overview of some aspects of our implementation, focusing on the translation to WhyML.

Encoding program states. References are represented using an abstract WhyML type reference with a distinguished element, null. The only operation supported on reference values is equality; WhyRel does not deal with pointer-arithmetic. Regions are encoded as ghost state, using a library for mathematical sets provided by Why3. Set operations on regions are inherently supported, and we axiomatize image expressions: for each field f, WhyRel generates a Why3 function symbol img_f along with an axiom that captures the meaning of $G`f$.

Program states are encoded using WhyML records. An example is shown in Fig. 8. The state type includes at least two mutable components called alloct

```
                          type reftype = Cell | Node (*class names*)
                          type heap = {
                            mutable val: map reference int;
/* class defs */            mutable ghost rep : map reference Rgn.t;
class Cell {                mutable curr: map reference reference;
  val: int;                 mutable nxt: map reference reference }
  ghost rep: rgn; }       type state = {
                            mutable alloct: map reference reftype;
class Node {                mutable heap: heap;
  curr: Cell;               mutable ghost pool: rgn }
  nxt: Node; }            invariant {¬(Map.mem null alloct) ∧ ...}

/* global vars */         (* axiomatization of G'nxt *)
public pool : rgn         function img_nxt : state → Rgn.t → Rgn.t
                          axiom img_nxt_ax : ∀ s, r, p.
                            Rgn.mem p (img_nxt s r) ⇔ ∃ q.
                              s.alloct[q] = Node ∧ Rgn.mem q r
                          ∧ p = s.head.nxt[q]
```

Fig. 8: State encoding: WhyRel source on left, encoding in WhyML on right.

and `heap`. The component `alloct` stores a map from references to object types and keeps track of allocated objects; `heap` is itself a record with one mutable component per field in the source program that stores a map from references to values. The set of values includes references, Why3 mathematical types such as arrays and lists, regions, and primitive types such as `int` and `bool`. In addition, the `state` type contains one mutable field per global variable in the source program, storing a value of the appropriate type. The `state` type is annotated with a WhyML invariant that captures well-formedness. This invariant includes conditions such as `null` never being allocated, no dangling references, and typing constraints: for example, the `nxt` field of a `Node` is itself a `Node`.

Translating unary programs and effects. WhyRel translates unary programs into WhyML functions that act on our encoding of states. Commands that modify the heap are modeled as updates to an explicit state parameter, and local variables, parameters, and the distinguished `result` variable are encoded using WhyML reference cells. Object parameters are modeled using the `reference` type and a typing assumption. Translation of control flow statements is straightforward. For programs with loops, WhyRel additionally adds a `diverges` clause to the generated WhyML function: this indicates that the function may potentially diverge, avoiding generation of VCs for proving termination. While Why3 supports reasoning about total correctness, we're only concerned with partial correctness. Fig. 9 shows an example translation.

Translation of frame conditions requires care given our encoding of states. As an example, the writes for method m shown in Fig. 9 would include rw {c}'val due to the write to, and read of, field `val` of object c. Correspondingly, in the Why3 translation, component `val` of `s.heap` is updated; so specifying the function in Why3 requires adding `writes {s.heap.val}` as annotation. However, this isn't the granularity we want since it implies the field `val` of any reference can be

```
meth m (c: Cell, i: int) : int
  requires { c.val ≥ 0 }
= while (i ≥ 0) do
    invariant { c.val ≥ 0 }
    c.val := c.val+i;
    i := i-1
  done;
  result := c.val
```

```
let m (s:state) (c:reference) (i:int)
  : int diverges
  requires { s.alloct[c] = Cell }
  requires { s.heap.val[c] ≥ 0 }
= let result = ref 0 in
  let c = ref c in
  let i = ref i in
  while (!i ≥ 0) do
    invariant { s.heap.val[!c] ≥ 0 }
    (* c.val := c.val + i *)
    s.heap.val ← Map.add !c
      (s.heap.val[!c]+!i) s.heap.val;
    i := !i-1
  done;
  result := s.heap.val[!c]; !result
```

Fig. 9: Program translation example: WhyRel program on the left, WhyML translation on the right; frame conditions omitted.

written. Hence, WhyRel generates an additional postcondition for method m:
wr_framed_val (old s) s (Rgn.singleton c), where

predicate wr_framed_val (s: state) (t: state) (r: rgn) = ∀ p: reference.
  s.alloct[p] = Cell ∧ p ∉ r ⇒ s.heap.val[p] = t.heap.val[p]

With this postcondition, callers of m (in WhyML) can rely on knowing that the val fields of only references in {c} are modified.

Biprograms. WhyRel translates biprograms into product programs; specifically, WhyML functions that act on a pair of states[5]. Before translation, it performs an adequacy check to ensure the biprogram is well-formed. Recall that adequacy here means that all computations of the underlying unary programs are covered by their aligned biprogram. Adequacy ensures that a relational judgment about the biprogram entails the expected relation between the underlying unary programs. The check WhyRel performs is syntactic and defined using projection operations on biprograms. Given a biprogram CC, the left projection $\overleftarrow{CC}$ (and resp. the right projection $\overrightarrow{CC}$) extracts the unary program on the left (and resp. the right). As an example, the left projection of ⌊c.f:=g⌋; (x:=c.f | skip) is c.f:=g; x:=c.f and its right projection is c.f:=g. For adequacy, given unary programs C and C' and their aligned biprogram CC, it suffices to check whether $\overleftarrow{CC} \equiv C$ and $\overrightarrow{CC} \equiv C'$ [1].

Translation of biprograms is described in Fig. 10. The translation function $\mathcal{B}$ takes a biprogram and a pair of contexts (Γ_l, Γ_r) to a WhyML program. In addition to mapping WhyRel identifiers to WhyML identifiers, contexts store information about the state parameters on which the generated WhyML program

---

[5] In reality, generated WhyML functions act on a pair of states and a bijective renaming of references allocated in these states. This is to cater for relation formulas such as $x \doteq y$ where x and y are references. However, this additional parameter is not important to our discussion here, so we avoid mentioning it.

$$\mathcal{B}[\![\texttt{C}\,|\,\texttt{C'}]\!](\varGamma_l, \varGamma_r) \quad\triangleq\quad \mathcal{U}[\![\texttt{C}]\!](\varGamma_l);\ \mathcal{U}[\![\texttt{C'}]\!](\varGamma_r)$$

$$\mathcal{B}[\![\lfloor\texttt{m(x}\,|\,\texttt{y)}\rfloor]\!](\varGamma_l, \varGamma_r) \quad\triangleq\quad apply(\varPhi(\texttt{m}), [\varGamma_l.\texttt{st};\ \varGamma_r.\texttt{st}; \mathcal{E}[\![\texttt{x}]\!](\varGamma_l); \mathcal{E}[\![\texttt{y}]\!](\varGamma_r)])$$

$$\mathcal{B}[\![\lfloor\texttt{C}\rfloor]\!](\varGamma_l, \varGamma_r) \quad\triangleq\quad \mathcal{B}[\![\texttt{C}\,|\,\texttt{C}]\!](\varGamma_l, \varGamma_r)$$

$$\mathcal{B}[\![\texttt{C};\ \texttt{C'}]\!](\varGamma_l, \varGamma_r) \quad\triangleq\quad \mathcal{B}[\![\texttt{C}]\!](\varGamma_l, \varGamma_r);\ \mathcal{B}[\![\texttt{C'}]\!](\varGamma_l, \varGamma_r)$$

$$\mathcal{B}[\![\texttt{var x:T}\,|\,\texttt{x:T' in CC}]\!](\varGamma_l, \varGamma_r) \quad\triangleq\quad \texttt{let } x_l = \texttt{def(T) in let } x_r = \texttt{def(T') in}$$
$$\mathcal{B}[\![\texttt{CC}]\!]([\varGamma_l \mid \texttt{x} : x_l], [\varGamma_r \mid \texttt{x} : x_r])$$

$$\mathcal{B}[\![\texttt{if E}\,|\,\texttt{E' then CC else DD}]\!](\varGamma_l, \varGamma_r) \quad\triangleq\quad \texttt{assert } \{\mathcal{E}[\![\texttt{E}]\!](\varGamma_l) = \mathcal{E}[\![\texttt{E'}]\!](\varGamma_r)\};$$
$$\texttt{if } \mathcal{E}[\![\texttt{E}]\!](\varGamma_l) \texttt{ then } \mathcal{B}[\![\texttt{CC}]\!] \texttt{ else } \mathcal{B}[\![\texttt{DD}]\!]$$

$$\mathcal{B}[\![\texttt{while E}\,|\,\texttt{E' do DD}]\!](\varGamma_l, \varGamma_r) \quad\triangleq\quad \texttt{while } \mathcal{E}[\![\texttt{E}]\!](\varGamma_l) \texttt{ do}$$
$$\texttt{invariant } \{\mathcal{E}[\![\texttt{E}]\!](\varGamma_l) = \mathcal{E}[\![\texttt{E'}]\!](\varGamma_r)\}$$
$$\mathcal{B}[\![\texttt{CC}]\!](\varGamma_l, \varGamma_r)$$

$$\mathcal{B}[\![\texttt{while E}\,|\,\texttt{E'.}\ \mathcal{P}\,|\,\mathcal{P} \texttt{ do DD}]\!](\varGamma_l, \varGamma_r) \quad\triangleq\quad$$
$$\texttt{while } (\mathcal{E}[\![\texttt{E}]\!](\varGamma_l) \vee \mathcal{E}[\![\texttt{E'}]\!](\varGamma_r)) \texttt{ do invariant } \{\mathcal{A}\}$$
$$\texttt{if } (\mathcal{E}[\![\texttt{E}]\!](\varGamma_l) \wedge \mathcal{F}[\![\mathcal{P}]\!](\varGamma_l, \varGamma_r)) \texttt{ then } \mathcal{U}[\![\overleftarrow{\texttt{CC}}]\!](\varGamma_l)$$
$$\texttt{else if } (\mathcal{E}[\![\texttt{E'}]\!](\varGamma_r) \wedge \mathcal{F}[\![\mathcal{P'}]\!](\varGamma_l, \varGamma_r)) \texttt{ then } \mathcal{U}[\![\overrightarrow{\texttt{CC}}]\!](\varGamma_r) \texttt{ else } \mathcal{B}[\![\texttt{CC}]\!](\varGamma_l, \varGamma_r)$$
$$\texttt{where } \mathcal{A} \equiv (\mathcal{E}[\![\texttt{E}]\!](\varGamma_l) \wedge \mathcal{F}[\![\mathcal{P}]\!](\varGamma_l, \varGamma_r)) \vee (\mathcal{E}[\![\texttt{E'}]\!](\varGamma_r) \wedge \mathcal{F}[\![\mathcal{P'}]\!](\varGamma_l, \varGamma_r)) \vee$$
$$(\neg\mathcal{E}[\![\texttt{E}]\!](\varGamma_l) \wedge \neg\mathcal{E}[\![\texttt{E'}]\!](\varGamma_r)) \vee (\mathcal{E}[\![\texttt{E}]\!](\varGamma_l) \wedge \mathcal{E}[\![\texttt{E'}]\!](\varGamma_r))$$

Fig. 10: Translation of biprograms, excerpts

acts. Similar to $\mathcal{B}$, the function $\mathcal{U}$ translates unary programs to WhyML programs, $\mathcal{E}$, expressions to WhyML expressions, and $\mathcal{F}$, a restricted set of relation formulas to WhyML expressions. Biprograms don't require the underlying unary programs to act on a disjoint set of variables; however, this means that WhyRel has to perform appropriate renaming during translation. Renaming is manifest in the translation of variable blocks (var x:T|x:T' in CC), where the context $\varGamma_l$ (and resp. $\varGamma_r$) is extended, $[\varGamma_l \mid \texttt{x} : x_l]$, mapping x to a renamed copy x_l (and resp. $\varGamma_r$ is extended with the binding x : x_r).

In translating $(C\,|\,C')$, the unary translations of C and C' are sequentially composed. Syncs $\lfloor C \rfloor$ are handled similarly, as syntactic sugar for $(C\,|\,C)$, except for the case of method calls. Procedure-modular reasoning about relational properties is enabled by aligning method calls which indicates that the relational spec associated with the method is to be exploited. WhyRel will translate these to calls to the appropriate WhyML product program, using a global method context ($\varPhi$ in Fig. 10). Since translated product programs act on pairs of states, the generated WhyML call takes $\varGamma_l$.st and $\varGamma_r$.st, names for left and right state parameters, as additional arguments.

Product constructions for control flow statements require generating additional proof obligations. For aligned conditionals, WhyRel introduces an assertion that the guards are in agreement. Lockstep aligned loops are dealt with similarly; guard agreement must be invariant. For conditionally aligned loops, the generated loop body captures the pattern indicated by the alignment guards $\mathcal{P}\,|\,\mathcal{P'}$: if the left (resp. right) guard is true and $\mathcal{P}$ (resp. $\mathcal{P'}$) holds, perform a left-only (resp. right-only) iteration; otherwise, perform a lockstep iteration. Adequacy is ensured by requiring the condition $\mathcal{A}$ to be invariant. This condition states that until both sides terminate, the loop can perform a lockstep or a one-sided iteration. In relational region logic, the alignment guards $\mathcal{P}$ and $\mathcal{P}'$ can be any relational formula. However, the encoding of conditionally aligned loops is in terms of a conditional that branches on these alignment guards. In Why3, this only works if $\mathcal{P}$ and $\mathcal{P}'$ are restricted; for example, to not contain quantifiers. WhyRel supports alignment guards that include agreement formulas, one-sided points-to assertions, one-sided boolean expressions, and the usual boolean connectives.

Proof obligations for encapsulation. To ensure sound encapsulation, WhyRel performs an analysis on source programs. This analysis includes two parts: a static check to ensure client programs don't directly write to variables in a module's boundary; and the generation of intermediate assertions that express disjointness between the footprints of client heap updates and regions demarcated by module boundaries. For modules with public/private invariants, WhyRel additionally generates a lemma which states that the module's boundary frames the invariant, i.e., the invariant only depends on locations expressed by the boundary. The same is done with coupling relations, for which we need to consider boundaries of both modules being related. A technical condition of relational region logic requiring boundaries grow monotonically as computation proceeds is also ensured by introducing appropriate postconditions in generated programs.

5   Evaluation

We evaluate WhyRel via a series a case studies, representative of the challenge problems highlighted at the outset of this article. Examples include representation independence, optimizations such as loop tiling [5], and others from recent literature on relational verification (including [9] and [21]). Some, like those described in Sec. 3, deal with reasoning in terms of varying alignments including data-dependent ones. Our representation independence examples include showing equivalence of Dijkstra's single-source shortest-paths algorithm linked against two implementations of priority queues, which requires reasoning about fine-grained couplings between pointer structures; and Kruskal's minimum spanning tree algorithm linked against different modules implementing union-find, which requires couplings equating the partitions represented by the two versions. For all examples, VCs are discharged using the SMT solvers Alt-Ergo, CVC4, and Z3. Replaying proofs of most developments using Why3's saved sessions feature takes less than 30 minutes on a machine with an Intel Core i5-6500 processor and 32 gigabytes of RAM.

A primary goal of this work is to investigate whether verifying relational properties of heap manipulating programs can be performed in a manner tractable to SMT-based automation, and for the most part, we believe WhyRel provides a promising answer. The tool serves as an implementation of relational region logic and demonstrates that even its additional proof obligations for encapsulation can be encoded using first-order assertions. In fact, exploration of case studies using WhyRel was instrumental in designing proof rules of relational region logic.

Reasoning about heap effects à la region logic is generally simple and VCs get discharged quickly using SMT. However, technical lemmas WhyRel generates which pertain to showing that module boundaries frame private invariants and couplings require considerable manual effort to prove. These lemmas usually involve reasoning about image expressions, which involve existentials and nontrivial set operations on regions. Given our encoding of states and regions, SMT solvers seem to have difficulties solving these goals. Manual effort involves applying a series of Why3 transformations (or proof tactics) and introducing intermediate assertions. We conjecture that the issue can be mitigated by using specialized solvers [23] or different heap encodings [24].

Another issue with our encoding of typed program states is the generation of a large number of VCs related to well-formedness of states. These account for a substantial fraction of proof replay time. Why3 programs act directly on our minimally-typed state representation and each heap update needs to preserve an invariant that specifies constraints on the types of allocated references (see Fig. 8). Using Why3's support for module abstraction [12] may ameliorate this issue. An alternative is to use assumptions, which can be justified by correctness of the WhyRel type checker and translator.[6]

Apart from these challenges related to verification, we note that specs in region logic tend to be verbose when compared to other formalisms such as separation logic [4].

6   Related work

WhyRel is closely modeled on relational region logic, developed in [1]. That paper provides a high-level overview of WhyRel, using a small set of examples verified in the tool to motivate aspects of the formal logic; but it doesn't give a full presentation of the tool or go into details about the encoding. The paper provides comprehensive soundness proofs of the logic and shows how the VCs WhyRel generates and the checks it performs correspond closely to obligations of relational proof rules. The paper builds on a line of work on region logic [4,2,3]. The VERL tool implements an early version of unary region logic without encapsulation and was used to evaluate a decision procedure for regions [23].

For local reasoning about pointer programs, separation logic is an effective and elegant formalism. For relational verification, ReLoC [13], based on the Iris separation logic and built in the Coq proof assistant supports, apart from many others, language features such as dynamic allocation and concurrency. However, we are unaware of auto-active relational verifiers based on separation logic.

Alignments for relational verification have been explored in various contexts. In WhyRel, the biprogram syntax captures alignment based on control flow, but also caters to data-dependent alignment of loops through the use of alignment guards (as discussed in Sec. 3). Churchill et al. [8] develop a technique for equivalence checking by using data dependent alignments represented by control

---

[6] The Boogie verification language provides "free requires" and "free ensures" syntax for just such assumptions.

flow automata which they use to prove correctness of a benchmark of vectorizing compiler transformations and hand-optimized code. Unno et al. [30] address a wide range of relational problems including k-safety and co-termination, expressing alignments and invariants as constraint satisfaction problems they solve using a CEGIS-like technique. Their work is applied to benchmarks proposed by Shemer et al. [25] who develop a technique for equivalence and regression verification. Both the above works represent alignments as transition systems and perform inference of relational invariants and alignment conditions. Inference relies on solvers and therefore programs need to be restricted so they are amenable to these solvers. A promising approach by Barthe et al. [6] reduces relational verification to proving formulas in trace logic, a multi-sorted first-order logic using first-order provers. In trace logic, conditions can be expressed on traces including relationships between different time points without recourse to alignment per se.

Sousa and Dillig develop Descartes [26] for reasoning about k-safety properties of Java programs automatically using implicit product constructions and in a logic they term Cartesian Hoare logic. Their work is furthered by Pick et al. [22] who develop novel techniques for detecting alignments. The REFINITY [27] workbench based on the interactive KeY tool can be used to reason about transformations of Java programs; heap reasoning relies on dynamic frames and relational verification proceeds by considering *abstract programs*. Other related tools include SymDiff [18] which is based on Boogie and can modularly reason about program differences in a language-agnostic way, and LLRêve [16] for regression verification of C programs. Eilers et al. [10] develop an encoding of product programs for noninterference that facilitates procedure-modular reasoning. They verify a large collection of benchmark examples using the VIPER toolchain.

7   Conclusion

In this paper we present WhyRel, a prototype for relational verification of pointer programs that supports dynamic framing and state-based encapsulation. The tool faithfully implements relational region logic and demonstrates how its proof obligations, including those related to encapsulation, can be encoded in a first-order setting. We've performed a number of representative examples in WhyRel leveraging support Why3 provides for SMT, and believe these demonstrate the amenability of region logic, and its relational variant, to automation.

Acknowledgments We thank the anonymous TACAS reviewers and artifact evaluators for their thorough feedback and suggestions which have led to major improvements in this paper. We thank Seyed Mohammad Nikouei who built an initial version of WhyRel which helped guide the design of the current version. Nagasamudram and Naumann were partially supported by NSF award 1718713. Banerjee's research was based on work supported by the NSF, while working at the Foundation. Any opinions, findings, and conclusions or recommendations expressed in this article are those of the authors and do not necessarily reflect the views of the NSF.

Data Availability Statement Sources for WhyRel and all examples performed using the tool are available in Zenodo with the identifier `https://doi.org/10.5281/zenodo.7308342` [20].

References

1. Banerjee, A., Nagasamudram, R., Naumann, D.A., Nikouei, M.: A relational program logic with data abstraction and dynamic framing. ACM Transactions on Programming Languages and Systems **44**(4), 25:1–25:136 (2022). `https://doi.org/10.1145/3551497`
2. Banerjee, A., Naumann, D.A.: Local reasoning for global invariants, part II: Dynamic boundaries. Journal of the ACM **60**(3), 19:1–19:73 (2013). `https://doi.org/10.1145/2485981`
3. Banerjee, A., Naumann, D.A., Nikouei, M.: A logical analysis of framing for specifications with pure method calls. ACM Transactions on Programming Languages and Systems **40**(2), 6:1–6:90 (2018)
4. Banerjee, A., Naumann, D.A., Rosenberg, S.: Local reasoning for global invariants, part I: Region logic. Journal of the ACM **60**(3), 18:1–18:56 (2013). `https://doi.org/10.1145/2485982`
5. Barthe, G., Crespo, J.M., Kunz, C.: Beyond 2-safety: Asymmetric product programs for relational program verification. In: Logical Foundations of Computer Science, International Symposium. Lecture Notes in Computer Science, vol. 7734, pp. 29–43 (2013)
6. Barthe, G., Eilers, R., Georgiou, P., Gleiss, B., Kovács, L., Maffei, M.: Verifying relational properties using trace logic. In: Formal Methods in Computer Aided Design. pp. 170–178 (2019). `https://doi.org/10.23919/FMCAD.2019.8894277`
7. Bobot, F., Filliâtre, J.C., Marché, C., Paskevich, A.: Why3: Shepherd your herd of provers. In: Boogie 2011: First International Workshop on Intermediate Verification Languages. pp. 53–64 (2011)
8. Churchill, B.R., Padon, O., Sharma, R., Aiken, A.: Semantic program alignment for equivalence checking. In: ACM Conf. on Program. Lang. Design and Implementation. pp. 1027–1040 (2019)
9. Eilers, M., Müller, P., Hitz, S.: Modular product programs. In: Programming Languages and Systems, European Symposium on Programming. pp. 502–529 (2018)
10. Eilers, M., Müller, P., Hitz, S.: Modular product programs. ACM Trans. Program. Lang. Syst. **42**(1), 3:1–3:37 (2020). `https://doi.org/10.1145/3324783`
11. Filliâtre, J.C.: One Logic To Use Them All. In: CADE. Springer (2013)
12. Filliâtre, J.C., Paskevich, A.: Abstraction and genericity in Why3. In: Leveraging Applications of Formal Methods, Verification and Validation: Verification Principles. pp. 122–142. Springer International Publishing (2020)
13. Frumin, D., Krebbers, R., Birkedal, L.: ReLoC: A mechanised relational logic for fine-grained concurrency. In: IEEE Symp. on Logic in Computer Science. pp. 442–451 (2018)
14. Hoare, C.A.R.: Proofs of correctness of data representations. Acta Informatica **1**, 271–281 (1972). `https://doi.org/10.1007/BF00289507`
15. Kassios, I.T.: Dynamic frames: Support for framing, dependencies and sharing without restrictions. In: Formal Methods. Lecture Notes in Computer Science, vol. 4085, pp. 268–283 (2006). `https://doi.org/10.1007/11813040_19`

16. Kiefer, M., Klebanov, V., Ulbrich, M.: Relational program reasoning using compiler IR: Combining static verification and dynamic analysis. J. Automated Reasoning **60**, 337–363 (2018)
17. Kovács, M., Seidl, H., Finkbeiner, B.: Relational abstract interpretation for the verification of 2-hypersafety properties. In: ACM CCS (2013)
18. Lahiri, S.K., Hawblitzel, C., Kawaguchi, M., Rebêlo, H.: SYMDIFF: A language-agnostic semantic diff tool for imperative programs. In: Computer Aided Verification. pp. 712–717 (2012). https://doi.org/10.1007/978-3-642-31424-7_54
19. Leino, K.R.M., Moskal, M.: Usable auto-active verification. In: Ball, T., Shankar, N., Zuck, L. (eds.) Usable Verification Workshop (2010), http://fm.csl.sri.com/UV10/submissions/uv2010_submission_20.pdf
20. Nagasamudram, R., Banerjee, A., Naumann, D.A.: The WhyRel Prototype for Modular Relational Verification of Pointer Programs (Nov 2022). https://doi.org/10.5281/zenodo.7308342
21. Naumann, D.A.: Thirty-seven years of relational Hoare logic: Remarks on its principles and history. In: 9th International Symposium On Leveraging Applications of Formal Methods, Verification and Validation (ISOLA), Part II. Lecture Notes in Computer Science, vol. 12477, pp. 93–116 (2020), https://doi.org/10.1007/978-3-030-61470-6_7, extended version at https://arxiv.org/abs/2007.06421.
22. Pick, L., Fedyukovich, G., Gupta, A.: Exploiting synchrony and symmetry in relational verification. In: Computer Aided Verification. pp. 164–182 (2018)
23. Rosenberg, S., Banerjee, A., Naumann, D.A.: Decision procedures for region logic. In: Int'l Conf. on Verification, Model Checking, and Abstract Interpretation. Lecture Notes in Computer Science, vol. 7148, pp. 379–395 (2012)
24. Schmid, G.S., Kuncak, V.: Proving and disproving programs with shared mutable data. CoRR **abs/2103.07699** (2021), https://arxiv.org/abs/2103.07699
25. Shemer, R., Gurfinkel, A., Shoham, S., Vizel, Y.: Property directed self composition. In: Computer Aided Verification. pp. 161–179 (2019)
26. Sousa, M., Dillig, I.: Cartesian Hoare Logic for verifying k-safety properties. In: ACM Conf. on Program. Lang. Design and Implementation. pp. 57–69 (2016)
27. Steinhöfel, D.: REFINITY to model and prove program transformation rules. In: Asian Symposium on Programming Languages and Systems APLAS. Lecture Notes in Computer Science, vol. 12470, pp. 311–319 (2020). https://doi.org/10.1007/978-3-030-64437-6_16
28. Strichman, O., Godlin, B.: Regression verification - a practical way to verify programs. In: Verified Software: Theories, Tools, Experiments (VSTTE), pp. 496–501 (2008)
29. Terauchi, T., Aiken, A.: Secure information flow as a safety problem. In: Static Analysis Symposium (SAS). Lecture Notes in Computer Science, vol. 3672, pp. 352–367 (2005)
30. Unno, H., Terauchi, T., Koskinen, E.: Constraint-based relational verification. In: Computer Aided Verification. Lecture Notes in Computer Science, vol. 12759, pp. 742–766. Springer (2021). https://doi.org/10.1007/978-3-030-81685-8_35

Bridging Hardware and Software Analysis with Btor2C: A Word-Level-Circuit-to-C Translator

Dirk Beyer, Po-Chun Chien, and Nian-Ze Lee

LMU Munich, Munich, Germany

Abstract. Across the broad research field concerned with the analysis of computational systems, research endeavors are often categorized by the respective models under investigation. Algorithms and tools are usually developed for a specific model, hindering their applications to similar problems originating from other computational systems. A prominent example of such a situation is the area of formal verification and testing for hardware and software systems. The two research communities share common theoretical foundations and solving methods, including satisfiability, interpolation, and abstraction refinement. Nevertheless, it is often demanding for one community to benefit from the advancements of the other, as analyzers typically assume a particular input format. To bridge the gap between the hardware and software analysis, we propose Btor2C, a translator from word-level sequential circuits to C programs. We choose the Btor2 language as the input format for its simplicity and bit-precise semantics. It can be deemed as an *intermediate representation* tailored for analysis. Given a Btor2 circuit, Btor2C generates a behaviorally equivalent program in the language C, supported by many static program analyzers. We demonstrate the use cases of Btor2C by translating the benchmark set from the Hardware Model Checking Competitions into C programs and analyze them by tools from the Intl. Competitions on Software Verification and Testing. Our results show that software analyzers can complement hardware verifiers for enhanced quality assurance: For example, the software verifier VeriAbs with Btor2C as preprocessor found more bugs than the best hardware verifiers ABC and AVR in our experiment.

Keywords: Hardware compilation · Word-level circuit · Intermediate representation · Formal verification · Testing · Btor2 · SMT · SAT

1 Introduction

Computational systems have become more and more ubiquitous in our daily life and manifest themselves in various contexts, including VLSI circuits, software programs, and cyber-physical systems. To construct reliable systems, quality assurance has become an indispensable research topic. Numerous endeavors have been invested for different computational systems. Because of the ever-increasing system complexity and applications in safety-critical missions, it is of vital importance to take advantage of all available solutions for different types of systems to guarantee the quality and correctness.

© The Author(s) 2023
S. Sankaranarayanan and N. Sharygina (Eds.): TACAS 2023, LNCS 13994, pp. 152–172, 2023.
https://doi.org/10.1007/978-3-031-30820-8_12

Formal verification and testing are two active fields of research to analyze and assure the quality of computational systems. The former decides with mathematical rigorousness whether a system conforms to a specification. The latter aims at generating input patterns and executing a system on a test suite to observe irregular output responses. Studies for formal verification or testing usually focus on a specific computational model, especially a sequential circuit (hardware) or a program (software). Tool competitions are also established based on modeling languages for input instances, such as the language BTOR2 [64] used in the Hardware Model Checking Competitions (HWMCC) [28, 29], or the language C assumed by the Competitions on Software Verification (SV-COMP) [11, 14] and Testing (Test-Comp) [12, 13]. Unfortunately, such distinction erects a barrier between the two closely related research communities.

1.1 Our Motivations and Contributions

For the hardware community to easily benefit from state-of-the-art software-analysis techniques, we aim at *developing a lightweight yet effective translation flow to bridge the gap between hardware and software analysis*. There have been several attempts [48, 62] to compile hardware designs into software, mostly using the language Verilog as the input format. Verilog is a general-purpose hardware description language, and thus, a comprehensive frontend for Verilog requires tremendous engineering effort. Moreover, Verilog has rather complicated syntax and semantics, which might increase the burden on the translation flow.

To address the complexity in the frontend design, we resort to the language BTOR2 [64], proposed recently to model word-level sequential circuits. A suite BTOR2TOOLS [63] of utility tools is also provided for conveniently parsing, simulating, and bit-blasting (to the bit-level format AIGER [26]) BTOR2 circuits. We emphasize the following two benefits of using BTOR2 as the translation frontend over Verilog. First, BTOR2 provides simple yet sufficient operations over bit-vectors and arrays. The simplicity makes it an appropriate *intermediate representation* for formal verification and testing, as the operations are suitable for the underlying satisfiability solvers. Second, BTOR2 is the input format used in the HWMCC. Many hardware model checkers support this format, and a large collection of benchmarking tasks is available for empirical evaluation. In practice, a Verilog circuit can be translated to BTOR2 via YOSYS [70], an open-source Verilog synthesis tool. Therefore, using BTOR2 as frontend does not restrict the applicability of the translation flow.

Having settled down the frontend choice, our next question is: Should we make software analyzers support BTOR2, or should we implement a standalone translator that does the job for all tools? We take the latter approach such that any software analyzer (from 76 available [25]) can in principle be used for hardware analysis. As opposed to using Verilog as frontend, the simplicity of the BTOR2 language helps to generate C programs suitable for the backend analysis, as will be shown in Sect. 5 via comparison with the Verilog-to-C translator v2c [62].

Once a handy translator is viable, we are enthusiastic about *empirically comparing hardware and software analyzers on a large scale*. Similar experiments have been carried out for bounded [60] and unbounded [61] formal verification on a

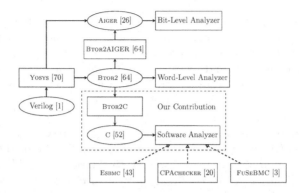

Fig. 1: Software analysis made readily available for hardware designs

small set of circuits. By building a translator on top of the BTOR2 language, more than a thousand benchmarking tasks from the HWMCC are at our immediate disposal. To draw a more reliable conclusion on the performance comparison of state-of-the-art hardware and software analyzers, we evaluate bit-level and word-level hardware model checkers from HWMCC, software verifiers from SV-COMP, and software testers from Test-Comp, on the HWMCC benchmark set.

Our contributions in this paper are summarized below:

Novelty. (1) To bridge the gap between hardware and software analysis, we design and implement BTOR2C, the first hardware-to-software compiler taking the format BTOR2 [64] as input. Specifically, BTOR2C accepts a BTOR2 circuit and produces a behaviorally equivalent C program. Given a Verilog design, BTOR2C (with the help of YOSYS) makes off-the-shelf software verifiers and testers readily available for its analysis. In addition to bit-level and word-level analyzers, hardware developers will be equipped with more tool choices to perfect their designs, as shown in Fig. 1. (2) BTOR2C makes it easy to construct new hardware analyzers by prepending the translator in front of any software analyzer. (3) Applying BTOR2C to the HWMCC benchmark set, we submitted 1224 new tasks[1] to sv-benchmarks, the benchmark collection used by many researchers, including SV-COMP and Test-Comp. Developers of software analyzers can now assess their tools using the hardware-analysis counterparts as a new baseline.

Significance. (1) We conduct a large-scale evaluation involving hardware model checkers, software verifiers, and software testers on the HWMCC benchmark set. Our results show that software-analysis techniques can complement hardware model checkers. (2) The proposed lightweight translator makes software analyzers more accessible to the entire research community, as BTOR2 can be used as an intermediate representation for analysis, not limited to hardware designs.

1.2   Example

Figure 2 illustrates the proposed translator BTOR2C on an example. A circuit whose state is a bit-vector of width 3 is given in BTOR2 format in Fig. 2a. The

---

[1] Some tasks used in this paper were excluded due to license issues.

```
1  extern void abort(void);
2  extern unsigned char nondet_uchar();
3  void main() {
4    typedef unsigned char SORT_1;
5    typedef unsigned char SORT_11;
6    const SORT_1 var_2 = 0b000;
7    const SORT_1 var_7 = 0b001;
8    const SORT_1 var_10 = 0b111;
9    SORT_1 input_5;
10   SORT_1 state_3 = var_2;
11   for (;;) {
12     input_5 = nondet_uchar();
13     input_5 = input_5 & 0b111;
14     SORT_11 var_12 = state_3 == var_10;
15     SORT_11 bad_13 = var_12;
16     if (bad_13) {
17       ERROR: abort();
18     }
19     SORT_1 var_6 = state_3 + input_5;
20     var_6 = var_6 & 0b111;
21     SORT_1 var_8 = var_6 - var_7;
22     var_8 = var_8 & 0b111;
23     state_3 = var_8;
24   }
25 }
```

```
1 sort bitvec 3
2 zero 1
3 state 1
4 init 1 3 2
5 input 1
6 add 1 3 5
7 one 1
8 sub 1 6 7
9 next 1 3 8
10 ones 1
11 sort bitvec 1
12 eq 11 3 10
13 bad 12
```

(a) BTOR2 circuit   **(b)** C program (simplified for demo)

Fig. 2: An example BTOR2 circuit (a) and its translated C program (b)

bit-vector is initialized to 0 (lines 2-4). In every iteration, the value of the bit-vector will be incremented by the value of the external input (lines 5-6) and then decremented by 1 (lines 7-8). The circuit reaches a bad state (i.e., violates the safety property) if the value of the bit-vector equals 0b111 (lines 12-13). The translated C program is shown in Fig. 2b. BTOR2C first looks for the sorts used in the input BTOR2 file. In this example, bit-vectors of 3 bits and 1 bit are used, and BTOR2C encodes them with the shortest possible unsigned integer type unsigned char (lines 4-5). After sort declarations, BTOR2C defines constants, declares inputs, and initializes circuit states (lines 6-10). An infinite loop is created to simulate the behavior of a sequential circuit. At the beginning of the loop, the safety property is evaluated. If the property is violated (namely, variable bad_13 evaluates to *true*), the program reaches the error location at line 17. Otherwise, the next-state value (stored in variable var_8) is computed and assigned to the current state (lines 19-23), and another loop iteration follows. After the translation, we can apply software verifiers to the translated program in Fig. 2b to check whether the circuit in Fig. 2a conforms to the specified safety property.

2 Related Work

2.1 Compiling Hardware to Software

Several research efforts [48, 68] have been invested into representing a circuit as a program, whose primary goal is to accelerate hardware simulation. The most related work to ours is the Verilog-to-C translator v2c [62], used to translate hardware circuits into software programs for bounded [60] and unbounded [61] formal verification. Unlike v2c, our translator uses as frontend the BTOR2 language, which is simple to parse and suitable for analysis. In Sect. 5, we compare the performance of software analyzers on C programs generated by V2C and our tool BTOR2C.

2.2 Compiling Hardware to Intermediate Representation

Another line of research related to our work is the compilation of hardware to an intermediate representation that eases the burden of analysis. The motivation of these works is to interface real-world designs and problems described in a more abstract language with tools that use a primitive model representation. Our tool BTOR2C shares a similar spirit because it interfaces problems in hardware analysis with software techniques. Among other tools, VERILOG2SMV [51] and VER2SMV [59] translate a Verilog circuit into SMV format [34, 56], which can be verified by tools like NUXMV [33]. QUTERTL [71] translates a register-transfer-level hardware design (usually in Verilog or VHDL) to BTOR [31], an earlier version of BTOR2. EBMC [55] generates SMT formulas in SMT-LIB 2 format [8], which encode the bounded model checking or k-induction problems of a Verilog circuit. YOSYS [70], which translates a Verilog circuit into the AIGER or BTOR2 formats, also serves the same purpose. Recently, there has been an interest to develop an intermediate language for the model-checking research community [67]. The project aims at providing an expressive frontend language as well as an efficient interface with backend model checkers.

3   Background

3.1   The BTOR2 Language

BTOR2 is a bit-precise modeling language for word-level sequential circuits. It can be seen as a generalization of the bit-level AIGER format [26]. The essential ingredients of BTOR2 relevant to our discussion in Sect. 4 will be introduced below. For the complete syntax, please refer to the BTOR2 publication [64].

Each line in a BTOR2 file starts with a unique number, used by other lines to identify the entity defined in this line. Such an entity can be either a *sort* or a *node*. A sort is either a bit-vector type of an arbitrary width w, denoted by $\mathcal{B}^w$, or an array type. An array type whose indices and elements are bit-vector types $\mathcal{I}$ and $\mathcal{E}$, respectively, is denoted by $\mathcal{A}^{\mathcal{I} \to \mathcal{E}}$. A node can be an *input*, a *state*, or a *result* of an operator over other inputs, states, or results. Inputs are external stimuli given to the BTOR2 circuit. Memory elements of the circuit are modeled by states. Usually, inputs have bit-vector types, and states can be of either bit-vector or array types.

Operators are the building blocks of a BTOR2 circuit. They take arguments of the prescribed types and guarantee a specific type for the result. The general signature for a BTOR2 operator is as follows: `<node id> <op> <sort id0> <node id1> [<node id2 [node id3]>]`, which defines a node to be the computation result of the operator `op` on node `id1` and optionally `id2` and `id3`. The result will have type `id0` and can be accessed by `id`. The operators in BTOR2 will be introduced later in Sect. 4 alongside the translation process of BTOR2C.

BTOR2 also provides constructs like `init`, `next`, and `bad` to describe the safety-reachability problem for sequential circuits. Initial and bad states can be defined by `init` and `bad`, respectively. The transition from one state to another is captured by next. In the following, we briefly recap sequential circuits and their model-checking formulation.

3.2 Sequential Circuits and Hardware Model Checking

A sequential circuit is a computational model widely used in the design and analysis of hardware. It consists of a combinational circuit and memory elements. The combinational circuit is in charge of the computation, and the memory elements store the circuit's state. The combinational circuit is a directed acyclic graph whose vertices are logic gates and edges are wires connecting the gates. If the output pin of gate u is connected to an input pin of gate v, we say that u is a *fan-in* of v, and v is a *fan-out* of u.

The computation of sequential circuits is segmented into consecutive time frames. Before the first time frame starts, the memory elements are typically reset (described by init). At the beginning of each time frame, the combinational circuit reads the values stored in the memory elements and receives stimuli from the environment. The former is called the *current state* of the circuit, and the latter is called the *external input* in this time frame. Propagating the current state and external input through its logic gates, the combinational circuit computes the output response and the new values to be stored in the memory elements (namely, *next-state values*, described by next). At the end of the time frame, the next-state values are saved into the memory elements, which become the current state for the next time frame.

The model-checking problem of *reachability safety* for hardware is formulated as follows: Given a sequential circuit and a safety property (usually encoded as an output of the sequential circuit's combinational part, described by bad), decide whether the safety property holds on all executions of the sequential circuit. If the property does not hold on some execution, a hardware model checker generates an input sequence to trigger the output, and the sequential circuit is deemed unsafe with respect to the property. Otherwise, the sequential circuit is considered safe, and a model checker might additionally generate (an overapproximation of) the set of reachable states as correctness witness.

3.3 Software Model Checking

The reachability-safety problem for software is formulated similarly as hardware model checking. Given a program and a safety property (usually labeled as an error location in the program), determine whether there is an executable program path that reaches the error location. Although, unlike hardware, software model checking is in general undecidable, many research efforts have been invested into automated solutions to this problem [10, 19, 53], including predicate abstraction [5, 42, 47, 50], counterexample-guided abstraction refinement (CEGAR) [6, 36], and interpolation [49, 58]. The verification of industry-scale software such as operating-systems code [4, 7, 23, 32, 37, 54] is made feasible together by these solutions and the advances in SMT solving [9]. It is our research enthusiasm to explore how these concepts work on hardware.

4   Translating BTOR2 to C

This section describes the proposed translator BTOR2C[2], implemented in the language C with approximately 1600 lines of code. We first describe the general idea of using C programs to simulate sequential circuits, whose behavior is intrinsically concurrent. The implementations of various BTOR2 operators and optimizations in BTOR2C are discussed later.

4.1   Simulating Sequential Circuits with C Programs

Sequential circuits work in a concurrent manner: The external input and current state propagate in parallel through the combinational circuitry to produce circuit outputs and next-state values. In contrast, the C programming language is imperative, and hence C programs are generally executed line-by-line.

To capture the behavior of sequential circuits in the context of reachability safety, BTOR2C generates C programs with the generic single-loop program in Fig. 3 as a template. In the generic program, the sorts and constants used in the sequential circuit are defined at the beginning of the `main()` function. Second, the program initializes the circuit's states. An endless loop is then used to mimic the state-transition behavior of the circuit throughout time frames: When a loop

```
void main() {
  // Define sorts and constants
  // Initialize states
  for (;;) {
    /* Evaluate safety property
    if (bad) {
      ERROR: abort();
    } */
    // Compute and assign next states
  }
}
```

Fig. 3: A generic program to imitate sequential circuits for reachability safety

iteration begins, the safety property is evaluated over the current state and external input. If the property is violated, the program exits with an error. Otherwise, the next-state values are computed and stored into the state variables. This generic program reflects the reachability safety for sequential circuits.

The commented blocks in the generic program have to be replaced by C instructions to encode the concurrent computation of the sequential circuit. BTOR2C assigns every node in the input BTOR2 circuit a unique variable in the translated C program. Nodes used for state initialization, state transition, or safety properties, are specified by keywords **init**, **next**, or **bad**, respectively. For such a node, a backward depth-first traversal is applied to collect its transitive fan-in cone to avoid irrelevant signals regarding model checking. Multiple **bad** keywords in a BTOR2 file are translated to multiple error labels in the C program.

4.2   Variable Naming

We use the unique identification numbers for lines in a BTOR2 file to name their corresponding variables in the translated C program. Suppose the unique ID of a line is n. If the line defines a sort, it is named SORT_n in the C file. If the line defines a state or an input, it is named state_n or input_n, respectively. If the line defines a node used for state initialization, transition, or property evaluation,

---
[2] https://gitlab.com/sosy-lab/software/btor2c

it is named `init_n`, `next_n`, or `bad_n`, respectively, to honor the keywords `init`, `next`, or `bad`. For the rest of the nodes, we name their variables `var_n` in the C file.

4.3 Expressing BTOR2 Sorts in C

The language BTOR2 supports two sorts: bit-vectors and arrays. Whenever possible, BTOR2C represents a bit-vector type $\mathcal{B}^w$ by the shortest unsigned-integer type whose number of bits is greater than or equal to w. For example, a $\mathcal{B}^3$ type with sort ID n is encoded by `typedef SORT_n unsigned char;`, and a $\mathcal{B}^{20}$ type with sort ID m is encoded by `typedef SORT_m unsigned int;`. A BTOR2 bit-vector type can have an arbitrary width. If a BTOR2 circuit uses a bit-vector type longer than 64 bits, BTOR2C cannot translate it to a C program, because no C type can accommodate the bit-vector[3]. The missing capability to handle bit-vectors longer than 64 bits is a restriction of BTOR2C, but the sacrifice is worthy: By encoding bit-vectors with integer variables, native C operators can be directly applied to implement BTOR2 operators, which greatly simplify the analysis of translated programs. As can be seen in Sect. 5, the state-of-the-art software verifiers and testers have a decent performance on the translated programs. In practice, only 20 % of the collected BTOR2 benchmarking circuits have bit-vectors longer than 64 bits, so we consider the restriction acceptable.

For BTOR2 arrays, BTOR2C represents them by static arrays. Suppose the sort ID for an array type $\mathcal{A}^{\mathcal{I} \to \mathcal{E}}$ is n. Let its index type $\mathcal{I}$ be $\mathcal{B}^w$ and element type $\mathcal{E}$ be encoded by `SORT_m`. Then $\mathcal{A}^{\mathcal{I} \to \mathcal{E}}$ is encoded by the following C instruction: `typedef SORT_m SORT_n[1 << w];`, which means `SORT_n` is an array with 2^w objects of type `SORT_m`.

4.4 Implementing BTOR2 Operators in C

The language BTOR2 provides various operations, most of which can be easily implemented by the corresponding C operators. Recall that we extend to the next unsigned-integer type to encode a bit-vector type $\mathcal{B}^w$. As a result, there might be some spare most-significant bits (MSBs) in an unsigned-integer variable. Normally, these bits have to be set to zeros (namely, the computation result is modulo 2^w) after each operation to guarantee the precision. Later in Sect. 4.5, we discuss the possibility of performing the modulo operation to results lazily only when needed, instead of applying it eagerly after each operator. Such laziness helps to generate shorter C programs and provides an opportunity for software analyzers to work more efficiently. In the evaluation, we will also compare the effects of these two translation schemes. Next, we follow the order of Table 1 in the BTOR2 paper [64] to introduce the BTOR2 operators and their implementations in C.

Indexed Operators. Unsigned- and signed-extension operators `uext` and `sext` can be implemented by type casting during the variable assignment. The bit-slicing operator `slice` is implemented by first right-shifting the number of sliced least-significant bits and masking the spare MSBs to zeros.

---

[3] We stick to the ISO C18 standard [52]; GNU C offers an unsigned `__int128` type, but not every software analyzer supports it. Recently, there is a proposal to support arbitrary-width integers in ISO C23, which will further simplify the translation.

Unary Operators. The bitwise negation operator not is implemented by its counterpart ~ in C. The arithmetic operators inc, dec, and neg are implemented using the ++, −−, and − operators in C. The reduction operator redand (resp. redor) is implemented by comparing the operand to $2^w - 1$ (resp. 0) for an operand of type $\mathcal{B}^w$. As there is no native support in C to compute the sum of all bits modulo 2 (parity) in an integer variable, the reduction operator redxor is implemented by repeatedly shifting and XOR-ing the variable with itself, such that the result will end up in the least-significant bit.

Binary Operators. For bit-vectors, the (in)equality operators eq, neq, gt, gte, lt, and lte are implemented by the corresponding C operators. For arrays, the equality operator is implemented by looping the two input arrays to find a different element. Bitwise operators and, or, and xor[4] and arithmetic operators add, mul, div, rem (remainder), and sub are all supported in C and can be directly implemented using the respective C operators. In the language BTOR2, the result of division-by-zero is defined to be the maximum number of the operands' sort. Our translation takes this specification into account to generate equivalent C programs. Otherwise, division-by-zero would be considered as undefined behavior in C.

Shifting operators sll (logical left shift) and srl (logical right shift) are implemented by the left- and right-shifting operators in C, respectively. According to the ISO C18 standard [52], the result of right-shifting a negative value is implementation-defined. Therefore, to ensure the intended behavior of the arithmetic right-shift operator sra, we always pad ones directly to the resulting value if the given operand is negative (i.e., MSB equals 1). In this way, we do not have to assume any specific implementation of the software verifiers.

Concatenating and rotating operators concat, rol (rotating left), and ror (rotating right), are not natively supported in C. We implemented them by shifting and bitwise disjunction. For example, in order to concatenate node n_1 of type $\mathcal{B}^3$ and node n_2 of type $\mathcal{B}^5$, we use var_1 << 5 | var_2, assuming var_1 and var_2 are of type unsigned char.

The read operator for array types, which takes an array and an index, is simply implemented by C's syntax to access an array.

Ternary Operators. The if-then-else operator ite works both for bit-vectors and arrays. It is implemented by the ternary operator exp1 ? exp2 : exp3 in C.

The write operator takes an array, an index for where to write, an element for what to write, and returns an updated array. It is implemented using the standard syntax in C to modify the content of an array.

Note that in a BTOR2 file, a line with operator write essentially creates a new copy of the original array with one updated element. The original array is not replaced, because it might also be referred to by other lines. In principle, if no lines access the original array after a write operation, the operation could modify the element in place without allocating a new array. For now, BTOR2C always copies a new array during a write operation for simplicity.

---

[4] The operators nand, nor, and xnor are implemented with the bitwise NOT operator.

4.5   Applying Modulo Operations Lazily

Observe that there are some operators that can work correctly without precise operand values, which offers us the opportunity to apply modulo operations lazily and save some computations in translated programs. For instance, consider the addition operator. If $a_1 \equiv a_2 \pmod{n}$ and $b_1 \equiv b_2 \pmod{n}$, we conclude that $a_1 + b_1 \equiv a_2 + b_2 \pmod{n}$ according to modular arithmetic. In other words, the addition operator does not need precise operands and works correctly for modular numbers (i.e., equivalence classes modulo n). By contrast, other operators might yield different results for modular numbers. For example, $a + kn > b$ does not guarantee $a > b$ when $k > 0$. Therefore, performing the modulo operation to the result of an operator is only necessary where the result is used in another operator that requires precise operand values.

BTOR2C provides an option for the lazy application of modulo operations. If the option is turned on, BTOR2C analyzes whether the precise value is required for each node by looking at the node's fan-outs. If any of its fan-outs needs the precise computation result of the node, the modulo operation will be applied to it. Otherwise, the modulo operation will be skipped, and the result could be a modular number of the precise value. Operators that require precise operand values mainly include inequalities as well as indices for reading and writing arrays. As an example, if we enable the lazy behavior to translate the BTOR2 circuit in Fig. 2a, the modulo operations in line 13 and line 20 of the program in Fig. 2b can be omitted, because `input_5` and `var_6` are used only in addition and subtraction, which do not need precise operand values.

4.6   Discussion

Correctness of the Translation. As will be seen in Sect. 5, the reliability of BTOR2C is empirically validated over a large input set: Most software verifiers obtain consistent answers on the translated C programs as the hardware verifiers. For BTOR2 models that violate the safety property, the violation witness generated by software verifiers can be transformed to that of the original BTOR2 circuit as a certificate of the translation process. The BTOR2TOOLS utility suite offers a simulator to check the transformed witness against the BTOR2 model.

Limitations. The current version of BTOR2C has no support yet for the translation of fairness constraints (keyword `fair`), liveness properties (keyword `justice`), and overflow detection (keywords `addo`, `divo`, `mulo`, and `subo`). In our evaluation, only supported keywords appear in the collected BTOR2 circuits.

5   Evaluation

We evaluate the claims presented in Sect. 1.1 using the following research questions:

- **RQ1**: How do software analyzers perform on hardware-verification tasks?
- **RQ2**: Can software analyzers complement hardware model checkers?
- **RQ3**: What is the effect of the optimization in Sect. 4.5 on the verification of the translated C programs?
- **RQ4**: How effective is the proposed translator BTOR2C in comparison with the Verilog-to-C translator v2c [62]?

To answer the above research questions, we evaluated the state of the art of hardware and software analyzers over a large benchmark set consisting of more than thousand hardware-verification tasks.

5.1 Benchmark Set

We collected hardware-verification tasks in both BTOR2 and Verilog formats from various sources, including the benchmark suites used in the 2019 and 2020 Hardware Model Checking Competitions [29] and the explicit-state model-checking tasks derived from the BEEM project [65]. The whole benchmark set as well as a complete list of sources are available in the reproduction artifact [16] of this paper. We also contributed a set of verification tasks to the sv-benchmarks collection, the largest freely available benchmark set of the verification and testing community.

As the proposed translator BTOR2C uses BTOR2 as frontend, we translated tasks in Verilog to BTOR2 with YOSYS [70]. An aggregate of 1912 BTOR2 tasks were collected. We excluded 414 tasks with bit-vectors longer than 64 bits, because BTOR2C cannot translate these tasks into standard ISO C18 programs. Out of the remaining 1498 BTOR2 tasks, 1341 use only bit-vector sorts, and the remaining 157 tasks manipulate both bit-vector and array sorts. The bit-vector category contains 473 unsafe tasks (with a known specification violation) and 868 safe tasks (for which the specification is satisfied). The array category contains 17 unsafe and 140 safe tasks.

We translated the remaining 1498 BTOR2 tasks into C programs by the proposed tool BTOR2C (tag `tacas23-camera`), assuming the LP64 data model. The 1341 tasks in the bit-vector category are also translated to AIGER by the translator BTOR2AIGER, which is provided in the BTOR2TOOLS utility suite. The original BTOR2 models as well as the translated C programs and AIGER circuits are available in the reproduction package [16] and online[5].

Unfortunately, BTOR2AIGER does not translate BTOR2 circuits with array sorts to AIGER. In our benchmark set, translating a BTOR2 file to either a C program or an AIGER circuit took less than a second. Therefore, we ignore the translation time in the run-time of compared tools. An input task with the required format is directly given to each tool. To facilitate the comparison with v2c, we additionally gathered 22 C programs translated by v2c from its repository[6].

5.2 State-of-the-Art Hardware and Software Analysis

To adequately reflect the state of the art of hardware and software analysis, we evaluated the most competitive tools from the Hardware Model Checking Competitions and Competitions on Software Verification and Testing. A wide range of analysis techniques implemented in these tools were investigated in our experiment. Due to space limitation, Sect. 5.4 will show the best configuration of each tool on our benchmark set.

Hardware Model Checkers. For hardware analysis, we selected the state-of-the-art bit-level model checker ABC [30] (commit `a9237f5`[7]) and AVR [46] version 2.1,

---

[5] https://gitlab.com/sosy-lab/research/data/word-level-hwmc-benchmarks
[6] https://github.com/rajdeep87/verilog-c
[7] https://github.com/berkeley-abc/abc

a word-level hardware model checker that won HWMCC 2020. The former takes AIGER circuits as input, and the latter directly consumes BTOR2 models. We evaluated the implementations of bounded model checking (BMC) [27] and property directed reachability (PDR) [41, 45] in both ABC and AVR. Interpolation-based model checking (IMC) [57] in ABC and k-induction (KI) [69] in AVR were also assessed.

Software Analyzers. For software verifiers, we enrolled the first, second, and fourth ranked verifiers VERIABS [2], CPACHECKER [20], and ESBMC [43] of category *ReachSafety* in SV-COMP 2022. The 3rd ranked verifier PESCO [66] was omitted because it selects algorithms from the CPACHECKER framework. All verifiers were downloaded from the archiving repository[8] of the competition. (For ESBMC, the performance of an earlier version in SV-COMP 2021 was better than the latest version on our benchmark set, so we used the older version instead.) We tried the implementations of loop abstraction (LA) [38] in VERIABS; predicate abstraction (PA) [18, 50], IMPACT [24, 58], and IMC [21] in CPACHECKER; BMC and KI [17, 18, 39, 44] in both CPACHECKER and ESBMC.

For software testers, the overall winner FUSEBMC [3] of Test-Comp 2022, which implements fuzz testing (fuzzing), was picked. We also experimented with other testers from the competition, but they failed to generate test suites on our benchmark set. FUSEBMC was downloaded from the archiving repository[9] of the competition.

In the following discussion, we use ⟨tool⟩-⟨algorithm⟩ to denote the implementation of a specific algorithm in a particular tool. For example, AVR-KI refers to the k-induction implementation in AVR.

5.3   Experimental Setup

All experiments were conducted on machines running Ubuntu 22.04 (64 bit), each with a 3.4 GHz CPU (Intel Xeon E3-1230 v5) with 8 processing units and 33 GB of RAM. Each task was limited to 2 CPU cores, 15 min of CPU time, and 15 GB of RAM. We used BENCHEXEC[10] [22] to ensure reliable resource measurement and reproducible results.

5.4   Results

RQ1: Solving HW-Verification Tasks with SW Analyzers. To study the performance of software analyzers on hardware-verification tasks, we compared the selected software tools against the state-of-the-art hardware model checkers. The results are summarized in Table 1.

Note that some software verifiers are good at finding bugs in these tasks. VERIABS found most correct alarms in the experiment, and ESBMC also detected more bugs than AVR. By contrast, hardware model checkers were better at computing correctness proofs. Even the best software configuration CPACHECKER-PA for proving correctness only achieved fewer than a half of the proofs for

---

[8] https://gitlab.com/sosy-lab/sv-comp/archives-2022/-/tree/svcomp22
[9] https://gitlab.com/sosy-lab/test-comp/archives-2022/-/tree/testcomp22
[10] https://github.com/sosy-lab/benchexec

Table 1: Summary of the results for hardware and software verifiers (suffixes *-e* and *-l* stand for applying modulo operations eagerly or lazily, respectively)

Tool		ABC	AVR	CPACHECKER		ESBMC		VERIABS	
Algorithm		PDR	PDR	Pred. Abs.		k-Induction		Loop Abs.	
Input	Tasks	AIGER	BTOR2	C-e	C-l	C-e	C-l	C-e	C-l
Correct results	1498	**862**	736	274	280	401	**410**	392	393
BV proofs	868	**524**	458	188	**189**	88	93	53	49
BV alarms	473	**338**	233	86	91	311	315	337	**342**
Array proofs	140	–	45	0	0	0	0	0	0
Array alarms	17	–	0	0	0	2	2	2	2
Wrong proofs		0	0	0	0	0	0	2	2
Wrong alarms		0	0	0	0	0	0	1	1
Timeouts		479	559	924	922	554	551	1049	1042
Out of memory		0	3	9	7	543	537	3	4
Other inconclusive		0	200	291	289	0	0	51	56

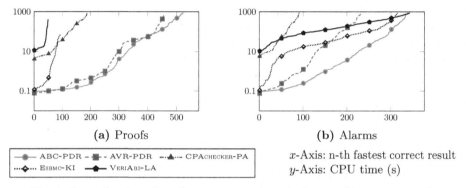

(a) Proofs   (b) Alarms

—●— ABC-PDR –■– AVR-PDR ··▲·· CPACHECKER-PA
···◇··· ESBMC-KI —◆— VERIABS-LA

x-Axis: n-th fastest correct result
y-Axis: CPU time (s)

Fig. 4: Quantile plots for all correct proofs and alarms of bit-vector tasks

bit-vector tasks. In the array category, AVR delivered 45 correct proofs, whereas the software verifiers cannot solve any of them. Our results may inspire tool developers to investigate and alleviate the performance difference. Since we have contributed a category *ReachSafety-Hardware* of verification tasks to the common benchmark collection, the 2023 competition results of SV-COMP include evaluations of all participating tools on those new tasks.

The quantile plots of correct proofs and alarms for bit-vector tasks are shown in Fig. 4a and Fig. 4b, respectively. A data point (x, y) in the plots indicates that there are x tasks correctly solvable by the respective tool within a CPU time of y seconds. In our experiments, ABC is the most efficient and effective tool in producing proofs, and VERIABS is the best for bug hunting. While the number of alarms found by ESBMC is more than AVR and close to ABC, it spent more time in finding bugs in general.

In our evaluation, we observe that PDR is the most competitive algorithm for both hardware model checkers, whereas software verifiers show diverse strengths in different approaches. To account for the difference in algorithms, we also compare implementations of the same algorithm in various analyzers.

BMC is one of the most popular formal approaches to detect errors. It is implemented by most of the evaluated tools. Software testers are also able to

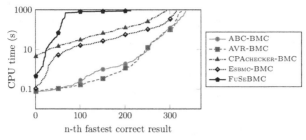

Fig. 5: Quantile plot comparing bug hunting (with BMC) on bit-vector tasks

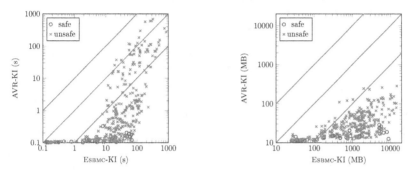

Fig. 6: CPU time (left) and memory (right) consumption of AVR-KI and Esbmc-KI

hunt bugs, and hence we include FuSeBMC, a derivative of Esbmc that combines BMC and fuzzing, into the comparison. Figure 5 shows the quantile plot of correct alarms for unsafe bit-vector tasks. Note that the performance of BMC implementations in software verifiers are close to those in hardware verifiers. However, FuSeBMC performed not as well as other competitors, indicating that fuzzing might not be fruitful for our benchmark set.

We also performed a head-to-head comparison of the k-induction implementations in AVR and Esbmc over the bit-vector and array tasks. Both tools rely on SMT solving for formula reasoning, so the confounding variables are fewer than other combinations. Figure 6 shows the scatter plots for the CPU time and memory usage of AVR and Esbmc to produce correct results. A data point (x, y) in the plots indicates the existence of a task correctly solved by both tools, for which Esbmc took x units of the computing resource and AVR took y units. AVR was often more efficient than Esbmc, but the latter solved 13 tasks that the former cannot solve.

RQ2: Complementing HW Model Checkers with SW Analyzers. Overall, hardware model checkers performed better than software analyzers on our benchmark set, which is expected since they have been heavily optimized for hardware-verification tasks. However, comparing the results of the tools for Table 1, we observed 43 tasks that were uniquely solved by software verifiers. Interestingly, 39 of these uniquely solved tasks have a violated property. Combining BMC with loop unwinding heuristics, e.g., the technique implemented in VeriAbs [2], is helpful to find bugs in these tasks. This phenomenon demonstrates that software-

Table 2: Results for 22 programs generated by BTOR2C and v2c

Tool	CPACHECKER		ESBMC		VERIABS	
Algorithm	Pred. Abs.		k-Induction		Loop Abs.	
translated by	BTOR2C	v2c	BTOR2C	v2c	BTOR2C	v2c
Correct results	15	11	16	13	12	7
proofs	13	8	11	11	7	3
alarms	2	3	5	2	5	4
Wrong results	0	0	0	1	0	0
Errors & Unknown	7	11	6	8	10	15

analysis techniques are able to complement hardware model checkers, which is facilitated by the proposed BTOR2C translator. Some potential reasons affecting the effectiveness and efficiency of software analyzers will be discussed in Sect. 5.5.

RQ3: Optimization in BTOR2C. Section 4.5 presented an optimization technique that performs modulo operations to intermediate results lazily, in order to generate shorter C programs. To assess whether this technique benefits the downstream software analysis, we compared the performance of the selected software verifiers, CPACHECKER, ESBMC, and VERIABS, on C programs translated by BTOR2C with or without this optimization (namely, applying modulo operations lazily or eagerly, respectively).

The results of the best-performing algorithm for each tool in terms of the number of correct answers are summarized in Table 1, whose right panel also shows the results of the verifiers on these 2 sets of C programs. (CPACHECKER-BMC actually solved more tasks than CPACHECKER-PA, but it was mainly for bug hunting. Therefore, we reported the second best configuration, predicate abstraction, for CPACHECKER.) If modulo operations are applied lazily instead of eagerly, the numbers of overall correct results are increased by roughly 2.2 % for both CPACHECKER and ESBMC, and by 0.3 % for VERIABS. Although VERIABS found 4 fewer correct proofs if modulo operations are applied lazily, it reported 5 more correct alarms. Therefore, we conclude that generating shorter C programs by reducing modulo operations is an effective optimization in BTOR2C. From now on, BTOR2C enables this optimization by default.

RQ4: Comparison with v2c. BTOR2C is a lightweight tool, whose compiled binary is smaller than 0.25 MB. By contrast, the precompiled v2c executable downloaded from its web archive[11] is 5.7 MB. While such difference is negligible given the capability of modern computers, we believe that a simple frontend language benefits tool implementation.

Besides implementation complexity, we also investigated the efficiency of the translation process. As mentioned in Sect. 5.1, BTOR2C took less than a second to translate any BTOR2 model in the benchmark set. Unfortunately, neither the v2c executable in the archive was runnable, nor was its source code compilable[12]. Therefore, we were not able to directly compare the translation efficiency of BTOR2C and v2c.

---

[11] https://www.cs.ox.ac.uk/people/rajdeep.mukherjee/tacas16_v2c.tar.gz
[12] https://github.com/rajdeep87/verilog-c/issues/6

As an alternative, we collected 22 C programs from v2c's benchmark repository and manually adapted them to the syntax rules used in SV-COMP. The original Verilog circuits of these C programs were translated to BTOR2 by YOSYS and further translated by BTOR2C into another set of C programs. We compare the performance of the evaluated software verifiers on these two sets of 22 verification tasks in Table 2. Observe that the three verifiers produced more correct results on the C programs generated by BTOR2C, showing the benefit of using YOSYS +BTOR2 as frontend in the translation flow.

5.5 Discussion

From the experimental results shown above, we observe a notable performance difference between software and hardware analyzers. There are several possibilities to explain this outcome: First, the tasks were encoded in different formats for software and hardware analyzers. BTOR2C encoded bit-vectors with unsigned integer types, which may contain some spare bits that complicate software analysis. Second, each analyzer uses a different backend logical solver. ABC encodes queries in propositional logic and uses SAT solving, while other tools resort to first-order formulas and SMT solving. (In our experiments, AVR used YICES2 [40], CPACHECKER used MATHSAT5 [35] for predicate abstraction and BOOLECTOR3 [64] for BMC, and ESBMC used BOOLECTOR3.) The ability of solvers may affect the analyzers' performance. Third, the internal modeling used by the analyzers varies. Software verifiers typically represent a program as a control-flow graph, which might be unnecessarily complex when the problem at hand is merely a state-transition system. Despite the above reasons, software verifiers were able to solve 43 tasks that the considered hardware model checkers cannot solve.

6 Conclusion

Assuring the correctness of computational systems is challenging yet imperative. Therefore, we should embrace every opportunity to analyze our systems by removing the barriers between research communities. We implemented the lightweight and open-source tool BTOR2C for translating sequential BTOR2 circuits to C programs, to enable the application of off-the-shelf software analyzers to hardware designs. We conducted a large-scale experiment including more than thousand verification tasks. State-of-the-art bit-level and word-level model checkers as well as software verifiers and testers were evaluated empirically. Thanks to the simplicity of the BTOR2 language, software analyzers performed decently on the translated programs and complemented the hardware model checkers by detecting more bugs and uniquely solving 43 tasks in our experiment. Our translator BTOR2C demonstrates a new spectrum of analysis options to hardware developers and verification engineers. The translator also simplifies the construction of a new set of hardware analyzers, because any software analyzer can now be used to solve hardware-verification tasks, with BTOR2C as preprocessing. In the future, we wish to bridge the gap from the other direction. That is, we aim at translating programs into circuits and apply hardware analyzers to solve software problems.

Data-Availability Statement. To enhance the verifiability and transparency of the results reported in this paper, all used software, verification tasks, and raw experimental results are available in a supplemental reproduction package [16]. A previous version [15] of the reproduction package was reviewed by the Artifact Evaluation Committee. The updated version [16] fixes issues found by reviewers of the paper and the artifact. For convenient browsing of the data, interactive result tables are also available at `https://www.sosy-lab.org/research/btor2c/`.

Funding Statement. This project was funded in part by the Deutsche Forschungs-gemeinschaft (DFG) – 378803395 (ConVeY).

Acknowledgements. We thank the SV-COMP community and an anonymous reviewer for pointing out the division-by-zero issue.

References

1. IEEE Standard for Verilog Hardware Description Language (2006). `https://doi.org/10.1109/IEEESTD.2006.99495`
2. Afzal, M., Asia, A., Chauhan, A., Chimdyalwar, B., Darke, P., Datar, A., Kumar, S., Venkatesh, R.: VERIABS: Verification by abstraction and test generation. In: Proc. ASE. pp. 1138–1141 (2019). `https://doi.org/10.1109/ASE.2019.00121`
3. Alshmrany, K.M., Aldughaim, M., Bhayat, A., Cordeiro, L.C.: FUSEBMC: An energy-efficient test generator for finding security vulnerabilities in C programs. In: Proc. TAP. pp. 85–105. Springer (2021). `https://doi.org/10.1007/978-3-030-79379-1_6`
4. Ball, T., Cook, B., Levin, V., Rajamani, S.K.: SLAM and Static Driver Verifier: Technology transfer of formal methods inside Microsoft. In: Proc. IFM. pp. 1–20. LNCS 2999, Springer (2004). `https://doi.org/10.1007/978-3-540-24756-2_1`
5. Ball, T., Majumdar, R., Millstein, T., Rajamani, S.K.: Automatic predicate abstraction of C programs. In: Proc. PLDI. pp. 203–213. ACM (2001). `https://doi.org/10.1145/378795.378846`
6. Ball, T., Rajamani, S.K.: Boolean programs: A model and process for software analysis. Tech. Rep. MSR Tech. Rep. 2000-14, Microsoft Research (2000), `https://www.microsoft.com/en-us/research/wp-content/uploads/2016/02/tr-2000-14.pdf`
7. Ball, T., Rajamani, S.K.: The SLAM project: Debugging system software via static analysis. In: Proc. POPL. pp. 1–3. ACM (2002). `https://doi.org/10.1145/503272.503274`
8. Barrett, C., Stump, A., Tinelli, C.: The SMT-LIB Standard: Version 2.0. Tech. rep., University of Iowa (2010), `https://smtlib.cs.uiowa.edu/papers/smt-lib-reference-v2.0-r10.12.21.pdf`
9. Barrett, C., Tinelli, C.: Satisfiability modulo theories. In: Handbook of Model Checking, pp. 305–343. Springer (2018). `https://doi.org/10.1007/978-3-319-10575-8_11`
10. Beckert, B., Hähnle, R.: Reasoning and verification: State of the art and current trends. IEEE Intelligent Systems **29**(1), 20–29 (2014). `https://doi.org/10.1109/MIS.2014.3`
11. Beyer, D.: 11th Intl. Competition on Software Verification (SV-COMP 2022). `https://sv-comp.sosy-lab.org/2022/`, accessed: 2023-01-29
12. Beyer, D.: 4th Intl. Competition on Software Testing (Test-Comp 2022). `https://test-comp.sosy-lab.org/2022/`, accessed: 2023-01-29

13. Beyer, D.: Advances in automatic software testing: Test-Comp 2022. In: Proc. FASE. pp. 321–335. LNCS 13241, Springer (2022). https://doi.org/10.1007/978-3-030-99429-7_18
14. Beyer, D.: Progress on software verification: SV-COMP 2022. In: Proc. TACAS (2). pp. 375–402. LNCS 13244, Springer (2022). https://doi.org/10.1007/978-3-030-99527-0_20
15. Beyer, D., Chien, P.C., Lee, N.Z.: Reproduction package for TACAS 2023 submission 'Bridging hardware and software analysis with BTOR2C: A word-level-circuit-to-C translator'. Zenodo (2022). https://doi.org/10.5281/zenodo.7303732
16. Beyer, D., Chien, P.C., Lee, N.Z.: Reproduction package for TACAS 2023 article 'Bridging hardware and software analysis with BTOR2C: A word-level-circuit-to-C translator'. Zenodo (2023). https://doi.org/10.5281/zenodo.7551707
17. Beyer, D., Dangl, M., Wendler, P.: Boosting k-induction with continuously-refined invariants. In: Proc. CAV. pp. 622–640. LNCS 9206, Springer (2015). https://doi.org/10.1007/978-3-319-21690-4_42
18. Beyer, D., Dangl, M., Wendler, P.: A unifying view on SMT-based software verification. J. Autom. Reasoning **60**(3), 299–335 (2018). https://doi.org/10.1007/s10817-017-9432-6
19. Beyer, D., Gulwani, S., Schmidt, D.: Combining model checking and data-flow analysis. In: Handbook of Model Checking, pp. 493–540. Springer (2018). https://doi.org/10.1007/978-3-319-10575-8_16
20. Beyer, D., Keremoglu, M.E.: CPACHECKER: A tool for configurable software verification. In: Proc. CAV. pp. 184–190. LNCS 6806, Springer (2011). https://doi.org/10.1007/978-3-642-22110-1_16
21. Beyer, D., Lee, N.Z., Wendler, P.: Interpolation and SAT-based model checking revisited: Adoption to software verification. arXiv/CoRR **2208**(05046) (July 2022). https://doi.org/10.48550/arXiv.2208.05046
22. Beyer, D., Löwe, S., Wendler, P.: Reliable benchmarking: Requirements and solutions. Int. J. Softw. Tools Technol. Transfer **21**(1), 1–29 (2019). https://doi.org/10.1007/s10009-017-0469-y
23. Beyer, D., Petrenko, A.K.: Linux driver verification. In: Proc. ISoLA. pp. 1–6. LNCS 7610, Springer (2012). https://doi.org/10.1007/978-3-642-34032-1_1
24. Beyer, D., Wendler, P.: Algorithms for software model checking: Predicate abstraction vs. IMPACT. In: Proc. FMCAD. pp. 106–113. FMCAD (2012), https://www.sosy-lab.org/research/pub/2012-FMCAD.Algorithms_for_Software_Model_Checking.pdf
25. Beyer, D., Podelski, A.: Software model checking: 20 years and beyond. In: Principles of Systems Design. pp. 554–582. LNCS 13660, Springer (2022). https://doi.org/10.1007/978-3-031-22337-2_27
26. Biere, A.: The AIGER And-Inverter Graph (AIG) format version 20071012. Tech. Rep. 07/1, Institute for Formal Models and Verification, Johannes Kepler University (2007). https://doi.org/10.35011/fmvtr.2007-1
27. Biere, A., Cimatti, A., Clarke, E.M., Zhu, Y.: Symbolic model checking without BDDs. In: Proc. TACAS. pp. 193–207. LNCS 1579, Springer (1999). https://doi.org/10.1007/3-540-49059-0_14
28. Biere, A., van Dijk, T., Heljanko, K.: Hardware model checking competition 2017. In: Proc. FMCAD. p. 9. IEEE (2017). https://doi.org/10.23919/FMCAD.2017.8102233
29. Biere, A., Froleyks, N., Preiner, M.: 11th Hardware Model Checking Competition (HWMCC 2020). http://fmv.jku.at/hwmcc20/, accessed: 2023-01-29

30. Brayton, R., Mishchenko, A.: ABC: An academic industrial-strength verification tool. In: Proc. CAV. pp. 24–40. LNCS 6174, Springer (2010). https://doi.org/10. 1007/978-3-642-14295-6_5

31. Brummayer, R., Biere, A., Lonsing, F.: Btor: Bit-precise modelling of word-level problems for model checking. In: Proc. SMT/BPR. pp. 33–38. ACM (2008). https: //doi.org/10.1145/1512464.1512472

32. Calcagno, C., Distefano, D., Dubreil, J., Gabi, D., Hooimeijer, P., Luca, M., O'Hearn, P.W., Papakonstantinou, I., Purbrick, J., Rodriguez, D.: Moving fast with software verification. In: Proc. NFM. pp. 3–11. LNCS 9058, Springer (2015). https://doi. org/10.1007/978-3-319-17524-9_1

33. Cavada, R., Cimatti, A., Dorigatti, M., Griggio, A., Mariotti, A., Micheli, A., Mover, S., Roveri, M., Tonetta, S.: The NUXMV symbolic model checker. In: Proc. CAV. pp. 334–342. LNCS 8559, Springer (2014). https://doi.org/10.1007/ 978-3-319-08867-9_22

34. Cimatti, A., Clarke, E.M., Giunchiglia, E., Giunchiglia, F., Pistore, M., Roveri, M., Sebastiani, R., Tacchella, A.: NuSMV 2: An open-source tool for symbolic model checking. In: Proc. CAV. pp. 359–364. LNCS 2404, Springer (2002). https: //doi.org/10.1007/3-540-45657-0_29

35. Cimatti, A., Griggio, A., Schaafsma, B.J., Sebastiani, R.: The MATHSAT5 SMT solver. In: Proc. TACAS. pp. 93–107. LNCS 7795, Springer (2013). https://doi. org/10.1007/978-3-642-36742-7_7

36. Clarke, E.M., Grumberg, O., Jha, S., Lu, Y., Veith, H.: Counterexample-guided abstraction refinement for symbolic model checking. J. ACM 50(5), 752–794 (2003). https://doi.org/10.1145/876638.876643

37. Cook, B.: Formal reasoning about the security of Amazon web services. In: Proc. CAV (2). pp. 38–47. LNCS 10981, Springer (2018). https://doi.org/10.1007/ 978-3-319-96145-3_3

38. Darke, P., Chimdyalwar, B., Venkatesh, R., Shrotri, U., Metta, R.: Over-approximating loops to prove properties using bounded model checking. In: Proc. DATE. pp. 1407–1412. IEEE (2015). https://doi.org/10.7873/DATE.2015.0245

39. Donaldson, A.F., Haller, L., Kröning, D., Rümmer, P.: Software verification using k-induction. In: Proc. SAS. pp. 351–368. LNCS 6887, Springer (2011). https: //doi.org/10.1007/978-3-642-23702-7_26

40. Dutertre, B.: YICES 2.2. In: Proc. CAV. pp. 737–744. LNCS 8559, Springer (2014). https://doi.org/10.1007/978-3-319-08867-9_49

41. Eén, N., Mishchenko, A., Brayton, R.K.: Efficient implementation of property directed reachability. In: Proc. FMCAD. pp. 125–134. FMCAD Inc. (2011), http: //dl.acm.org/citation.cfm?id=2157675

42. Flanagan, C., Qadeer, S.: Predicate abstraction for software verification. In: Proc. POPL. pp. 191–202. ACM (2002). https://doi.org/10.1145/503272.503291

43. Gadelha, M.R., Monteiro, F.R., Morse, J., Cordeiro, L.C., Fischer, B., Nicole, D.A.: ESBMC 5.0: An industrial-strength C model checker. In: Proc. ASE. pp. 888–891. ACM (2018). https://doi.org/10.1145/3238147.3240481

44. Gadelha, M.Y., Ismail, H.I., Cordeiro, L.C.: Handling loops in bounded model checking of C programs via k-induction. Int. J. Softw. Tools Technol. Transf. 19(1), 97–114 (February 2017). https://doi.org/10.1007/s10009-015-0407-9

45. Goel, A., Sakallah, K.: Model checking of Verilog RTL using IC3 with syntax-guided abstraction. In: Proc. NFM. pp. 166–185. Springer (2019). https://doi.org/10. 1007/978-3-030-20652-9_11

46. Goel, A., Sakallah, K.: AVR: Abstractly verifying reachability. In: Proc. TACAS. pp. 413–422. LNCS 12078, Springer (2020). https://doi.org/10.1007/978-3-030-45190-5_23

47. Graf, S., Saïdi, H.: Construction of abstract state graphs with Pvs. In: Proc. CAV. pp. 72–83. LNCS 1254, Springer (1997). https://doi.org/10.1007/3-540-63166-6_10

48. Greaves, D.J.: A Verilog to C compiler. In: Proc. RSP. pp. 122–127. IEEE (2000). https://doi.org/10.1109/IWRSP.2000.855208

49. Henzinger, T.A., Jhala, R., Majumdar, R., McMillan, K.L.: Abstractions from proofs. In: Proc. POPL. pp. 232–244. ACM (2004). https://doi.org/10.1145/964001.964021

50. Henzinger, T.A., Jhala, R., Majumdar, R., Sutre, G.: Lazy abstraction. In: Proc. POPL. pp. 58–70. ACM (2002). https://doi.org/10.1145/503272.503279

51. Irfan, A., Cimatti, A., Griggio, A., Roveri, M., Sebastiani, R.: VERILOG2SMV: A tool for word-level verification. In: Proc. DATE. pp. 1156–1159 (2016), https://ieeexplore.ieee.org/document/7459485

52. ISO/IEC JTC 1/SC 22: ISO/IEC 9899-2018: Information technology — Programming Languages — C. International Organization for Standardization (2018), https://www.iso.org/standard/74528.html

53. Jhala, R., Majumdar, R.: Software model checking. ACM Computing Surveys **41**(4) (2009). https://doi.org/10.1145/1592434.1592438

54. Khoroshilov, A.V., Mutilin, V.S., Petrenko, A.K., Zakharov, V.: Establishing Linux driver verification process. In: Proc. Ershov Memorial Conference. pp. 165–176. LNCS 5947, Springer (2009). https://doi.org/10.1007/978-3-642-11486-1_14

55. Kroening, D., Purandare, M.: EBMC. http://www.cprover.org/ebmc/, accessed: 2023-01-29

56. McMillan, K.L.: Symbolic Model Checking. Springer (1993). https://doi.org/10.1007/978-1-4615-3190-6

57. McMillan, K.L.: Interpolation and SAT-based model checking. In: Proc. CAV. pp. 1–13. LNCS 2725, Springer (2003). https://doi.org/10.1007/978-3-540-45069-6_1

58. McMillan, K.L.: Lazy abstraction with interpolants. In: Proc. CAV. pp. 123–136. LNCS 4144, Springer (2006). https://doi.org/10.1007/11817963_14

59. Minhas, M., Hasan, O., Saghar, K.: VER2SMV: A tool for automatic Verilog to SMV translation for verifying digital circuits. In: Proc. ICEET. pp. 1–5 (2018). https://doi.org/10.1109/ICEET1.2018.8338617

60. Mukherjee, R., Kroening, D., Melham, T.: Hardware verification using software analyzers. In: Proc. ISVLSI. pp. 7–12. IEEE (2015). https://doi.org/10.1109/ISVLSI.2015.107

61. Mukherjee, R., Schrammel, P., Kroening, D., Melham, T.: Unbounded safety verification for hardware using software analyzers. In: Proc. DATE. pp. 1152–1155. IEEE (2016), https://ieeexplore.ieee.org/document/7459484

62. Mukherjee, R., Tautschnig, M., Kroening, D.: v2c: A Verilog to C translator. In: Proc. TACAS. pp. 580–586. LNCS 9636, Springer (2016). https://doi.org/10.1007/978-3-662-49674-9_38

63. Niemetz, A., Preiner, M., Wolf, C., Biere, A.: Source-code repository of BTOR2, BTORMC, and BOOLECTOR 3.0. https://github.com/Boolector/btor2tools, accessed: 2023-01-29

64. Niemetz, A., Preiner, M., Wolf, C., Biere, A.: BTOR2, BTORMC, and BOOLECTOR 3.0. In: Proc. CAV. pp. 587–595. LNCS 10981, Springer (2018). https://doi.org/10.1007/978-3-319-96145-3_32

65. Pelánek, R.: BEEM: Benchmarks for explicit model checkers. In: Proc. SPIN. pp. 263–267. LNCS 4595, Springer (2007). https://doi.org/10.1007/978-3-540-73370-6_17
66. Richter, C., Hüllermeier, E., Jakobs, M.C., Wehrheim, H.: Algorithm selection for software validation based on graph kernels. Autom. Softw. Eng. **27**(1), 153–186 (2020). https://doi.org/10.1007/s10515-020-00270-x
67. Rozier, K.Y., Shankar, N., Tinelli, C., Vardi, M.: An open-source, state-of-the-art symbolic model-checking framework for the model-checking research community. https://www.aere.iastate.edu/modelchecker/, accessed: 2023-01-29
68. Snyder, W.: Verilator. https://www.veripool.org/verilator/, accessed: 2023-01-29
69. Wahl, T.: The k-induction principle (2013), http://www.ccs.neu.edu/home/wahl/Publications/k-induction.pdf
70. Wolf, C.: Yosys open synthesis suite. https://yosyshq.net/yosys/, accessed: 2023-01-29
71. Yeh, H., Wu, C., Huang, C.R.: QuteRTL: Towards an open source framework for RTL design synthesis and verification. In: Proc. TACAS. pp. 377–391. LNCS 7214, Springer (2012). https://doi.org/10.1007/978-3-642-28756-5_26

CoPTIC: Constraint Programming Translated Into C

Martin Mariusz Lester[✉]

University of Reading, Reading, United Kingdom
`m.lester@reading.ac.uk`

Abstract. Constraint programming systems allow a diverse range of problems to be modelled and solved. Most systems require the user to learn a new constraint programming language, which presents a barrier to novice and casual users. To address this problem, we present the CoPTIC constraint programming system, which allows the user to write a model in the well-known programming language C, augmented with a simple API to support using a *guess-and-check* paradigm. The resulting model is at most as complex as an ordinary C program that uses naive brute force to solve the same problem.

CoPTIC uses the bounded model checker CBMC to translate the model into a SAT instance, which is solved using the SAT solver CaDiCaL. We show that, while this is less efficient than a direct translation from a dedicated constraint language into SAT, performance remains adequate for casual users. CoPTIC supports constraint satisfaction and optimisation problems, as well as enumeration of multiple solutions. After a solution has been found, CoPTIC allows the model to be run with the solution; this makes it easy to debug a model, or to print the solution in any desired format.

Keywords: constraint programming · bounded model checking · C programming language

1 Introduction

Constraint programming is a form of declarative programming. A constraint program or *model* typically declares some variables and asserts a certain relationship that must hold between them. A *constraint solver* automatically finds values of the variables that satisfy the constraints.

There is a broad body of research in constraint programming, which explores different kinds of constraints, different languages for expressing them, and different methods for solving them. If you know you are likely to become a frequent user of constraint programming, it is relatively easy to take advantage of this. After making the effort to learn a standardised constraint language, such as *MiniZinc*, you have easy access to a range of common constraints and solvers.

But what if you are a casual user, who encounters a single problem that is too complex or time-consuming to solve by hand, but might be easy with the

© The Author(s) 2023
S. Sankaranarayanan and N. Sharygina (Eds.): TACAS 2023, LNCS 13994, pp. 173–191, 2023.
https://doi.org/10.1007/978-3-031-30820-8_13

assistance of a computer? You may be tempted to prototype a solution using a simple technique such as brute force or backtracking search. This may well work, but it is easy to make an error when writing such a program. Or the problem may turn out to be computationally harder than expected. Alternatively, you may try to learn a constraint programming language, but if the effort required is high and the process is error-prone, you may be deterred. Furthermore, if you do not need to use the language again for months or years, you may well have forgotten it by then, meaning that much of the effort is wasted.

To meet the needs of this kind of user, we introduce the *CoPTIC* (Constraint Programming Translated Into C) system for constraint programming. CoPTIC reduces the effort needed to write a model by allowing the user to write it in a declarative style as a C program. It achieves this by using the existing program verification tool CBMC, which in turn uses a SAT solver.

In outline, the C program must first declare all variables in the constraint problem and assign them a *nondeterministic* value. Next, it *assumes* that all of the constraints hold; paths where they do not hold should be ignored. Finally, it *asserts* false; that is, it is an error if the program reaches its end.

We can pass the program to CBMC and ask it to verify that the assertion cannot be violated. CBMC tries to find a resolution of the nondeterminism that leads to an assertion violation; it does this by encoding the problem as a SAT instance and solving it with a SAT solver. It reports back a counterexample trace to the verification problem. By construction, the values of the variables in this trace satisfy the constraints.

This idea is fairly straightforward for someone familiar with CBMC to apply in an ad-hoc way to a particular problem. However, a usable constraint programming system needs more than this. The contributions of this paper are the implementation, description and experimental evaluation of the CoPTIC system, which automates and extends the process outlined above.

We illustrate how to write constraint models in the *guess-and-check* paradigm outlined above with examples and explain how CoPTIC solves these models using CBMC in Section 2. We show how CoPTIC makes it easy for a user to:

- import constraint data from an external source, such as a JSON or CSV file;
- solve constraint satisfaction and optimisation problems;
- enumerate distinct solutions to a problem;
- export a solution in a suitable format; and
- maintain consistency between the constraints, validation and output as the model evolves by keeping the whole model in a single file written in one programming language.

In particular, CoPTIC reads resolved nondeterministic choices from CBMC's counterexample trace and constructs a C function that replays them when the program is compiled and run with an ordinary compiler. A similar construction has been used by Beyer and others to produce tests from verification witnesses [3], but CoPTIC uses it to display the solution to the constraint model.

We discuss debugging constraint models, efficiency of the SAT encoding and some other practical considerations in Section 3. Next, we evaluate CoPTIC empirically on problems from CSPLib in Section 4, considering both solver performance and the size of the models. The software artifact accompanying this paper [15] contains the source code for CoPTIC, which is released under the MIT License, as well as the models and scripts needed to reproduce our experiments. In Section 5 we discuss related work in constraint programming and automated verification, before concluding in Section 6.

2   The Guess-and-Check Paradigm

CoPTIC constraint models are C programs that mix the language's conventional imperative style with a declarative guess-and-check paradigm. To illustrate how the system is used and how it works, we now consider some worked examples. First, we will see that the code in the CoPTIC models is similar to a naive attempt to solve the problems using brute force or backtracking search (but often faster in execution). We argue that this makes the system easy to learn and to use for programmers with little knowledge or experience of constraint programming. Then we will see how to extend the approach to solution enumeration and optimisation.

Many finite-domain constraint problems are in the complexity class NP. NP problems can be characterised as those that:

1. have a certificate verifiable in deterministic polynomial-time; or
2. can be translated into SAT in polynomial-time.

CoPTIC exploits this equivalence constructively. Given a *guess-and-check* program that verifies a certificate, we can view CoPTIC as compiling the program into SAT with CBMC, which executes the nondeterministic program with a SAT solver. CoPTIC extracts the certificate, hard-codes it into the program to make it deterministic, then compiles it with a normal compiler and executes it deterministically.

2.1   Constraint Satisfaction: Magic Square

Let us consider the well-known problem of finding a normal 3×3 magic square. A normal $n \times n$ magic square is an $n \times n$ grid of integers from 1 to n^2, where every row, every column and both diagonals have the same sum.

Suppose we try to solve this problem using brute force. We write the simple program shown on the left side of Figure 1, which iterates through all possible assignments of integers to each grid cell. The program checks each assignment to see if it meets all the required constraints. As soon as one does, it prints it out and terminates.

We are pleased to see that, after a few minutes, the program finds a solution. Next we try with a larger square. We will be dismayed, as the running time of the program increases drastically.

How could we solve this problem more efficiently? The right side of Figure 1 shows the program adapted for use with CoPTIC. The program begins by

```
#define N 3                              #define N 3
#define MAX (N * N)                      #define MAX (N * N)
#define TARGET ((((N*N)+1)*N)/2)         #define TARGET ((((N*N)+1)*N)/2)

#include <stdio.h>                       #include "coptic.h"

int main() {                            int main() {
  int grid[N][N];                         int grid[N][N];

  for (int x = 0; x < N; x++) {           for (int x = 0; x < N; x++) {
    for (int y = 0; y < N; y++) {           for (int y = 0; y < N; y++) {
      grid[x][y] = 1;                         grid[x][y] = GUESS_INT();
    }                                         CHECK(grid[x][y] > 0 &&
  }                                                 grid[x][y] <= MAX);
                                            }
  int ok;                                 }
  do { // Try all cell values.
                                          // No need to search for the right
    grid[0][0]++;                         // cell values explicitly. CBMC's
    int x = 0;                            // embedded SAT solver will find
    int y = 0;                            // them for us.
    while (grid[x][y] > MAX) {
      grid[x][y] = 1;                     // When using CBMC, we will roughly
      if (++x == N) {                     // set the following macros:
        x = 0;                            // GUESS_INT() -> nondet_int()
        y++;                              // CHECK(X)    -> assume(X)
      }                                   // SATISFY()   -> assert(0)
      grid[x][y]++;                       // OUTPUT(X)   -> { }
    }       // Until we find a
    ok = 1; // valid magic square.

    // Check cells all different.        // Check cells all different.
    for (int x = 0; x < N; x++) {        for (int x = 0; x < N; x++) {
    for (int y = 0; y < N; y++) {        for (int y = 0; y < N; y++) {
    for (int x2 = 0; x2 < N; x2++) {     for (int x2 = 0; x2 < N; x2++) {
    for (int y2 = 0; y2 < N; y2++) {     for (int y2 = 0; y2 < N; y2++) {
      ok &= ((x==x2) && (y==y2)) ||        CHECK(((x==x2) && (y==y2))
      (grid[x][y]!=grid[x2][y2]);          || (grid[x][y]!=grid[x2][y2]));
    } } }                                } } }

    // Check column sums correct.        // Check column sums correct.
    for (int x = 0; x < N; x++) {        for (int x = 0; x < N; x++) {
      int sum = 0;                         int sum = 0;
      for (int y = 0; y < N; y++) {        for (int y = 0; y < N; y++) {
        sum += grid[x][y];                   sum += grid[x][y];
      }                                    }
      ok &= (sum == TARGET);               CHECK(sum == TARGET);
    }                                    }

    // 3 similar checks omitted.         // 3 similar checks omitted.
  } while (!ok);                         SATISFY();

  // Print out the solution.             OUTPUT(
  for (int y = 0; y < N; y++) {            for (int y = 0; y < N; y++) {
    for (int x = 0; x < N; x++) {            for (int x = 0; x < N; x++) {
      printf("%d ", grid[x][y]);                printf("%d ", grid[x][y]);
    }                                        }
    printf("\n");                            printf("\n");
  }                                        }
                                          )
}                                       }
```

Fig. 1. Left: A brute force program to find a magic square. Right: A CoPTIC model to solve the same problem. Note the absence of code for explicit search.

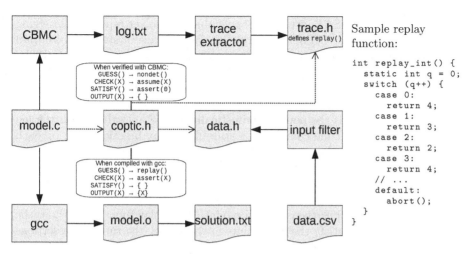

Fig. 2. The architecture of the CoPTIC system. Solid arrows indicate data flow. Dashed arrows indicate inclusion of a C header file.

including the `coptic.h` header file. Now, instead of iterating through each possible assignment explicitly, the program *GUESS*es the values of the grid cells. The checks are much the same as before, but use CoPTIC's *CHECK* macro. The call to *SATISFY* indicates that we want to find any solution that satisfies all the constraints, while the code in the *OUTPUT* block is run only when a solution is found. We run the modified program with CoPTIC and are once again pleased as it finds a solution in a few seconds.

2.2 CoPTIC Architecture

Now let us consider how CoPTIC produces the solution. Figure 2 shows the architecture of the system. After using the C compiler *gcc* to syntax-check and type-check the program (not shown), it runs the bounded model-checker CBMC on the program, asking it to verify absence of assertion violations. CBMC transforms the problem of finding an assertion violation in the program into a giant SAT instance and attempts to solve it using a SAT solver.

The header file `coptic.h` supplies definitions of *GUESS, CHECK, SATISFY* and *OUTPUT* that behave as follows: *GUESS* tells CBMC to pick a value nondeterministically and log it. *CHECK* takes a condition and tells CBMC to ignore program paths where the condition is false. *SATISFY* violates a trivial assertion; this tells CBMC to report failed verification and an accompanying program trace if there is a program path that reaches the assertion. *OUTPUT* takes a block and ignores it.

If the SAT instance is unsatisfiable, the solver reports this to CBMC. Then CBMC reports to CoPTIC that program verification was successful, as no assertion violation could be found. CoPTIC in turn reports that the constraints in the model were unsatisfiable.

Conversely, if the SAT instance is satisfiable, the solver reports a satisfying assignment to CBMC. CBMC converts this into a trace of steps of execution through the program that lead to the assertion violation. It reports to CoPTIC that program verification was unsuccessful and logs the trace that led to the assertion violation. Now CoPTIC can report that the constraints in the model are satisfiable, but it still has to show how.

To do this, it reads the nondeterministically *GUESS*ed values from the log and writes a C header file containing a stateful `replay` function that, on each successive call, returns these values in the same order. It compiles the model with gcc, but uses a preprocessor macro to set a flag that changes the behaviour of `coptic.h`. Now *GUESS* calls the replay function, *CHECK* becomes a run-time assertion, *SATISFY* does nothing and *OUTPUT* executes the supplied block.

Finally, CoPTIC runs the compiled model. The replay function provides the variable values that satisfy the constraints in the model, the run-time assertions pass and the *OUTPUT* code prints the solution. Because the *OUTPUT* code can be arbitrary C code, it is easy to format the solution and display it in any reasonable format.

Many constraint models represent not just a single problem, but a family of similar instances. For example, instances for our magic square model might involve completing partially filled magic squares of different sizes. In this case, CoPTIC allows instance data to be imported from an external source, such as a JSON or CSV file. To achieve this, the user needs to specify a filter program that translates the instance data into definitions in a C header file; `coptic.h` will then include this header file. The filter can be written in any language and the CoPTIC distribution includes some examples.

2.3   Planning: Knight's Tour

In the magic square example, the CoPTIC model began by guessing all the values in the square and the rest of the program was deterministic. However, this need not be the case, and we can often express a model more naturally or succinctly by mixing declarative and imperative programming. This is particularly useful for planning problems.

To demonstrate the flexibility of this approach, let us consider another well-known problem: finding a knight's tour on a chessboard. An open knight's tour is a sequence of moves made by a knight on a chessboard that visits each square exactly once. The top of Figure 3 shows a simple program to find a knight's tour on a 5×5 board using a recursive implementation of a backtracking search. Most of the implementation's complexity comes from using recursion to manage backtracking and from enumerating all the possible moves of a knight from a particular square.

The bottom of Figure 3 shows how we can remove this complexity in a CoPTIC model. Instead of using recursion and backtracking, we now use a simple loop that nondeterministically guesses the next move at each step. Instead of enumerating possible moves explicitly, we guess a position where the x-ordinate differs by 2 and the y-ordinate differs by 1 or vice versa.

```
#define M 5
#define N 5

#include <stdio.h>

int board[M][N] = {0};

int search(int x, int y, int d);

int search(int x, int y, int d) {
    if (x < 0 || x >= M || y < 0 || y >= N || board[x][y]) {
        return 0; // Check the square is on the board and unvisited.
    }

    d--; // Stop when all squares visited.
    if (d == 0) {
        printf("(%d,%d)\n", x, y);
        return 1;
    }

    board[x][y] = 1; // Don't visit this square again.

    if (search(x-2, y-1, d) || search(x+2, y-1, d) || // Try all valid
        search(x-2, y+1, d) || search(x+2, y+1, d) || // knight's moves
        search(x-1, y-2, d) || search(x+1, y-2, d) || // in sequence.
        search(x-1, y+2, d) || search(x+1, y+2, d)) {
        printf("(%d,%d)\n", x, y); // Unwind recursion on success,
        return 1;                  // printing moves in reverse.
    }

    board[x][y] = 0; // Backtrack on failure.
    return 0;
}

int main() {
    search(0, 0, (M*N)); // Start the search, beginning in a corner.
}
```

```
#define M 5
#define N 5

#include "coptic.h"

int main() {
    int board[M][N] = {0};
    int x0 = 0; // Begin in a corner.
    int y0 = 0;
    printf("(0,0)\n");

    for (int d = 1; d < M*N; d++) { // Find a sequence of M*N moves.
        int x = GUESS_INT(); // Pick the next move.
        int y = GUESS_INT();
        // Check the square is on the board and unvisited.
        CHECK(!(x < 0 || x >= M || y < 0 || y >= N || board[x][y]));
        CHECK((abs(x-x0) == 2 && abs(y-y0) == 1) || // Check it's a valid
              (abs(x-x0) == 1 && abs(y-y0) == 2)); // knight's move.
        board[x][y] = 1; // Don't visit this square again.
        OUTPUT(
            printf("(%d,%d)\n", x, y); // Print the move.
        )
        x0 = x; // The square we picked becomes the new position.
        y0 = y;
    }

    SATISFY();
}
```

Fig. 3. Top: A backtracking program to find an open Knight's Tour (with moves listed in reverse order). Bottom: A CoPTIC model to solve the same problem (with moves listed in order).

```
#include "coptic.h"                  // Trie generated for this model:

int main() {                         void trie(int x) {
    int x = GUESS_INT();               switch (_trie) {
    // (x-2)(x-5) = x^2 - 7x + 10       case 0:
    CHECK((x*x) - (7*x) + 10 == 0);       switch (x) {
    DECLARE(x);                             case 5: _trie = 1; break;
    ENUMERATE();                            case 2: _trie = 2; break;
    OUTPUT(printf("%d\n", x);)              default: _trie = -1; break;
}                                           }
                                          break;
// Rough definitions when using CBMC:     default: _trie = -1; break;
// DECLARE(X) -> log(X); trie(X)         }
// ENUMERATE() -> assert(_trie==leaf); }
```

Fig. 4. A CoPTIC model to enumerate integer solutions to a quadratic equation.

Knight's Tour can be solved efficiently using a program implementing back-tracking search with the additional heuristic of preferring the move that leaves fewest options for the following move. Our CoPTIC model cannot compete with this in speed of execution (or with a custom encoding in SAT [21]), but it has the advantages that it is shorter and does not require specialist knowledge of the problem, so is significantly easier to implement.

2.4   Enumeration: Integer Quadratics

Next we turn our attention to constraint problems that require not only satisfying a set of constraints, but also finding an optimal solution (as measured by some objective function) or enumerating all solutions. Both of these involve making multiple calls to CBMC.

For solution enumeration, we consider the example of finding integer solutions to an equation. Figure 4 shows a CoPTIC model to find all integer solutions to a quadratic equation. This model introduces *ENUMERATE*, which instructs CoPTIC to enumerate all solutions.

This is not as straightforward as it might first seem. While CBMC generates a SAT instance and some SAT solvers support an option that enumerates all solutions to an instance, this would not help much here, as a model may guess and check auxiliary values that do not contribute to the solution, and these need not be unique. So we need a way for a model to indicate which values are significant, in the sense that a difference in one of these values is sufficient to make a solution distinct; this is what *DECLARE* does.

We also need a way, within the C program, to *assume* that one of these values is different. In this case, we could use a single assumption to check x is not equal to the solution already found. But in general, a solution may comprise multiple values and we cannot simply check all of them at once, as they might not all be in scope simultaneously. (Consider the Knight's Tour model, where the variable holding the current position is overwritten on each iteration of the loop.) The solution CoPTIC adopts is to construct a trie of *DECLARE*d values for each solution, then within the model to trace progress through the trie as the program

```
#define ORDER 4
#define BETTER(A,B) (A < B)

#include "coptic.h"

int main() {
    int a[ORDER];

    a[0] = 0;
    for (int n = 1; n < ORDER; n++) {
        a[n] = GUESS_INT();
        CHECK(a[n] > a[n-1]);
        // DECLARE(a[n]);
        OUTPUT(printf("%d ", a[n]);)
    }
    OUTPUT(printf("\n");)

    for (int i1 = 0; i1 < ORDER; i1++) {
        for (int j1 = i1+1; j1 < ORDER; j1++) {
            for (int i2 = 0; i2 < ORDER; i2++) {
                for (int j2 = i2+1; j2 < ORDER; j2++) {
                    CHECK(((i1==i2)&&(j1==j2)) || (a[j1]-a[i1]!=a[j2]-a[i2]));
                }
            }                // Rough definition when using CBMC on 1st run:
        }                    // OPTIMIZE(X) -> log(X); assert(0)
    }                        // Rough definition when using CBMC on 2nd run:
                             // OPTIMIZE(X) -> log(X); assert(!BETTER(X, BEST))
    OPTIMIZE(a[ORDER-1]);    // where BEST is best objective found so far.
}
```

Fig. 5. A CoPTIC model for finding an optimal Golomb ruler.

executes. Finally, *ENUMERATE* asserts that the current trie node is terminal; if it is not, then the solution is novel. This approach is not very efficient, as each use of *DECLARE* (after any loops have been unrolled) leads to another copy of the trie's "next node" function in CBMC's SAT encoding. But it does work even when there are multiple paths through a program and when the number of *DECLARE*d values varies between solutions. For situations where the number of values is constant and they are all available at a single point in the program, CoPTIC supports a form of *DECLARE* with multiple arguments.

One usually considers the problem of finding solutions to polynomial equations in the context of real numbers, not integers. So one might wonder whether CoPTIC supports *GUESS*ing values of types other than int. Indeed it does: all primitive C types are supported. However, while (in contrast to many other constraint solvers) floating point types are supported, CBMC's implementation depends on an encoding in SAT, which does not perform very well.

2.5   Optimisation: Golomb Rulers

Finally, to illustrate optimisation, we consider the Golomb ruler problem of finding a sequence of n increasing integers, starting from 0, such that the differences between all pairs taken from the sequence are unique. For a given n, an *optimal* Golomb ruler minimises the last number in the sequence. For $n = 4$, the only optimal solution is $0, 1, 4, 6$.

Figure 5 shows a CoPTIC model for finding an optimal Golomb ruler. The model guesses a sequence of n integers and checks that the sequence is increasing, and that all differences between pairs are unique. (Ignore the commented line for the moment.) Instead of calling *SATISFY*, this model calls *OPTIMIZE* with the last element of the sequence, which is our objective that we wish to minimise.

When CoPTIC passes this model to CBMC, it uses an implementation of *OPTIMIZE* that does two things. Firstly, it logs the objective, so that CoPTIC can read it afterwards. Secondly, if it has already found a feasible value of the objective, it asserts that the objective is not *BETTER* than that previously found. CoPTIC calls CBMC repeatedly until it is unable to find a better objective, at which point, the best found so far must be optimal.

By allowing *BETTER* to be defined as part of the model, CoPTIC supports not only maximisation and minimisation of numerical objectives, but also more complex objectives, such as lexicographic minimisation of a pair of values.

Returning to the problem of finding an optimal Golomb Ruler, for $n = 7$, there are multiple solutions. We can use CoPTIC to find them all by uncommenting the *DECLARE* line and replacing *OPTIMIZE* with *ENUMERATE_OPTIMAL*. CoPTIC treats *ENUMERATE_OPTIMAL* the same as *OPTIMIZE* until it has found an optimal solution, after which it behaves as *ENUMERATE* with the extra restriction that solutions must be optimal.

3   Practical Considerations

Now that we have seen how the *guess-and-check* paradigm is used for modelling and how it is implemented by CoPTIC for constraint satisfaction, optimisation and enumeration, we turn our attention to some practical details of usability and performance.

3.1   Debugging Constraint Models

In program verification, a common concern is not only whether a program meets its specification, but also whether the specification is correct. In constraint programming, a similar concern applies. It is easy to under-specify a model, resulting in solutions to the model that are not solutions to the intended problem. In this case, a useful approach is to add extra logging to the model as *OUTPUT*. It is also easy to over-specify a model, resulting in a model with no solutions, even though the intended problem has solutions. This is harder to diagnose, but one helpful method is to comment out *CHECK*s until the model has a solution.

Another important concern in verification is whether the verification tool has accurately modelled the behaviour of the program being verified. Similarly, in constraint programming, we may worry whether the solution found by a solver really does satisfy the constraints. CoPTIC addresses this by turning *CHECK*s into assertions when running the model with nondeterminism resolved. On the occasions when the compiled program does violate one of these assertions, we have usually found that it results from an erroneous out-of-bounds array access in the model, which is undefined behaviour. A particular problem that results from CBMC's bit-level modelling of two's complement integer arithmetic is that CoPTIC may find solutions to a model that involve very large integers that overflow when added together, leading to an erroneous negative objective value. This is usually easy to avoid by *CHECK*ing an upper bound on *GUESS*ed integers in the model. It may also improve performance, especially for optimisation problems, where it may reduce the number of calls to CBMC.

CoPTIC keeps all files it produces during solution in a temporary directory. This includes log files from CBMC, header files for replaying nondeterminism, and output from the compiled programs (of which there may be several in the case of optimisation or enumeration). In the event of any problems, this makes it easy for a user to examine exactly what has happened.

One occasional problem is that CBMC is unable to translate the model into a SAT instance. General program verification is undecidable, so there are necessarily limits to the kinds of programs CBMC can handle. For example, it may be unable to infer a bound on the number of executions of a loop. In this case, CoPTIC will hang and CBMC's log file will show the loop in question being unrolled repeatedly, so the cause will be clear. However, we recommend that it is best to avoid this problem in the first place by using simple for loops with obvious statically computable bounds wherever possible. We also suggest that, while use of arrays, functions and structs is fine, unbounded recursion, heap memory allocation and pointer arithmetic should be avoided. CBMC should always be able to handle programs satisfying these restrictions.

3.2   Performance

CoPTIC's target audience is casual users of constraint programming. Therefore performance need not be outstanding, but it should still be acceptable. In constraint programming, performance often depends more on modelling decisions than on the efficiency of the solver, so an important factor in this regard is that different ways of modelling a problem should be easily expressible. We argue that CoPTIC's ability to mix imperative with declarative programming helps here.

Clearly there will be some overhead introduced by CBMC's translation into SAT, when compared with a translation from a dedicated constraint programming language directly into SAT. An obvious example might be use of fixed bit-width integers in the C program that are larger than necessary for the range of values taken by a variable in the model. But if these wasted high bits do not materially participate in any constraints, they will rarely lead to a conflict during SAT solving, so the SAT solver may be able to ignore them much of the time.

CBMC aims for bit-precise verification of C programs running on conventional microprocessors, so it uses a two's complement encoding for integers. This is acceptable, but Zhou and Kjellerstrand found that a sign-magnitude encoding worked better when developing PicatSAT [23]. Furthermore, for many problems where variables range over small domains, a one-hot encoding works better than a binary encoding.

4   Evaluation on CSPLib Problems

We claim that CoPTIC is easy to write models in and that its performance is adequate for many problems. To evaluate these claims empirically, we developed and benchmarked CoPTIC models for problems from *CSPLib* [12].

CSPLib is "a library of test problems for constraint solvers" expressed in natural language. The problems are drawn from a variety of domains, including operations research, combinatorial mathematics and puzzle games. Most problems include sample models written in constraint programming languages, such as *MiniZinc* or *Essence*. Some problems consist of a single instance; some consist of several similar instances. Some problems are constraint satisfaction problems; some are optimisation problems. CSPLib now contains 95 problems and has served as a focus for research in constraint programming over the past two decades [13]. For our evaluation, we restrict our attention to the 14 problems in the original 1999 release. This gives us a reasonable sample of the different kinds of problem, although there are no solution enumeration problems; see the artifact for some examples of enumeration [15].

For each CSPLib problem, we wrote a CoPTIC model. Where present in CSPLib, we also selected a MiniZinc model and an Essence model for the same instance. Where a problem included several instances, we picked one we considered to be representative. Mostly, we chose the example given in the problem specification, but in some cases these were very easy, so we chose harder instances to make the differences in performance clearer. For problem 6, we chose the largest instance listed as having multiple solutions. For problem 10, we used the hardest instance solved using SAT by Triska and Musliu [19]. For problems 12 and 13, we picked the hardest instances in CSPLib.

To benchmark performance, we ran our models using CoPTIC and recorded time taken to solve them. We measured times with two different builds of CBMC 5.57.0: one using MiniSat 2.2.1 as the solver (the standard configuration) and the other using CaDiCaL 1.4.1 (a supported compile-time option). For comparison, we also ran the MiniZinc models and the Essence models using SAT-based solvers. Note that, while these models encode the same problem, they may do so with quite different formalisations, which can have a big impact on solution time. This is fine for our purposes, as in evaluating the whole CoPTIC system, the ease with which we can write good models is at least as important as the speed of solution.

To run the MiniZinc models, we used MiniZinc 2.6.3 to convert them into FlatZinc, then PicatSAT in Picat 3.3#3 to solve them. PicatSAT uses the SAT solver Kissat 1.0.3. PicatSAT won 2nd place in the Free track of the MiniZinc Challenge 2022; Kissat won the Main track of the SAT Competition 2020. We also benchmarked a version of PicatSAT patched to use CaDiCaL 1.4.1.

To run the Essence models, we used Conjure 2.3.0 to compile to EssencePrime, then SavileRow 1.9.1 to solve using CaDiCaL 1.4.1 as the SAT solver (instead of the shipped solver CaDiCaL 1.3.0).

Table 1 shows our results. All benchmarks were run on a Debian Linux 10 machine with a 3.4 GHz Intel Core i5-7500 CPU and 64 GB of RAM, using a time limit of 1 hour. It is clear that dedicated constraint modelling languages

Table 1. Solution times for different CSPLib problem instances with different models and solvers. All values are times rounded to the nearest second. The time limit was 1 hour of CPU time. Times are from a single run; problems 4 and 10 showed some variation on repetition.

# Instance	CoPTIC (MiniSat)	CoPTIC (CaDiCaL)	Essence (CaDiCaL)	MiniZinc (CaDiCaL)	MiniZinc (Kissat)
1 sample	0	0	3	**0**	0
2 catfood 3	3563	324	timeout	23	**16**
3 QG4, non-ID	0	0	2	0	**0**
4 sample	**28**	99			
5 n=17	118	74	**4**		
6 n=11	timeout	2718	memout	**582**	699
7 n=12	1	1	2	**0**	0
8 sample	1	1	6	**0**	0
9 n=21, size=112	78	**9**	timeout		
10 g=8, s=4, w=7	63	93	**30**	timeout	timeout
11 sample	163	**31**			
12 soccer player	6	7	memout	**0**	0
13 Ian10	18	25	**7**		
14 sample	9	7		**0**	**0**

and solvers generally perform better than CoPTIC, as one would expect. But the majority of problems are still solvable within a reasonable amount of time. Therefore this is not a problem for our intended user, who would normally be happy to trade an increase in solution time for a decrease in time and effort needed to learn how to write a model. In fact, comparing directly with just the Essence models or just the MiniZinc models, we see that the CoPTIC models led to more solutions within our time limit, although this is somewhat dependent on our choice of time limit and hardness of problem instances.

Using CBMC built with CaDiCaL rather than MiniSat slows down some models, but mostly results in more consistent performance. CaDiCaL is much better at proving unsatisfiability, which makes a big difference for the optimisation problems (2, 5 and 6), where unsatisfiability demonstrates optimality.

During our benchmarking, we discovered that there were some errors in the Essence models in CSPLib. The model for problem 2 (template design) omits the limit on the total number of designs in a template, so the solution it gives is infeasible. We fixed the model by adding the missing constraint. The model for problem 8 (vessel loading) has a subtle error resulting from the semantics of evaluating a function outside its defined domain, so it can never be solved. We fixed the model by changing a guard in an implication. We also found that the EssencePrime solver SavileRow ran out of memory very quickly on some problems; we suspect this is a bug in the translation to SAT.

It is difficult to evaluate ease of writing models quantitatively, although perhaps this could be done through a controlled trial with undergraduate students. But what we can do is measure the size of the models we produced in terms

Table 2. Number of lines of code and resulting SAT instance sizes (thousands of variables/clauses) for modelling different CSPLib problems in different languages. Blank lines, comments, input data and formatting are excluded from SLoC totals.

CSPLib Problem				Instance size (kvars/kclauses)		
# Name	C.	Ess.	MZ	CoPTIC	Essence	MiniZinc
1 Car Sequencing	22	15	34	4 / 17	29 / 145	0 / 2
2 Template Design	27	12	60	13 / 54	/	3 / 25
3 Quasigroup Existence	35	8	44	11 / 38	1 / 4	1 / 9
4 Mystery Shopper	44			90 / 134	/	/
5 Low Autocorrelation	18	4		74 / 361	2 / 53	/
6 Golomb Rulers	21	10	12	85 / 360	/	10 / 87
7 All Interval	23	7	19	27 / 77	2 / 6	0 / 4
8 Vessel Loading	33	32	33	24 / 109	8 / 47	1 / 5
9 Perfect Square	26	12		23 / 89	174 / 1046	/
10 Social Golfers	38	8	33	175 / 480	41 / 153	366 / 4541
11 ACC Basketball	146			84 / 755	/	/
12 Nonograms	49	52	84	102 / 317	/	5 / 18
13 Progressive Party	56	14		78 / 251	6 / 43	/
14 Solitaire Battleships	119		85	94 / 403	/	6 / 46

of source lines of code (SLoC). While there are many criticisms of SLoC, it is widely used as a metric to estimate the amount of effort needed to develop a program. Table 2 shows the size of our CoPTIC models, compared with the MiniZinc and Essence models. As is conventional, we do not count blank lines or comments. We have also chosen not to count lines used for any input data or for formatting output. For input data, this is because the formats are very similar, but conventions on line breaks may differ between them, so it is not meaningful to compare them. For formatting, Essence does not appear to support custom formatting in the models, so including formatting code would inflate the line counts for CoPTIC and MiniZinc. Furthermore, for some problems, the output format may differ significantly between the CoPTIC and MiniZinc models. For example, output for a problem involving laying out rectangles in a grid could consist of co-ordinates of the rectangles or a rendering in ASCII art.

Again, it is clear that models written in the dedicated modelling languages tend to be smaller, as one would expect, However, the CoPTIC models are of similar size to and occasionally smaller than the MiniZinc models. The Essence models are particularly succinct because they include more complex, higher-level modelling constructs. For example, in the model for the Progressive Party problem, one of the constraints is encoded in the Essence model using universal quantification, function preimage and function composition, while the CoPTIC model expresses the same constraint using a for loop and nested array lookup. From the perspective of a casual user, while the latter is more verbose, it may be easier to write and comprehend.

Table 2 also shows the number of variables and clauses in the SAT instances generated from each model. While this is a poor metric of the difficulty of a SAT instance, it is useful here in demonstrating the extra overhead introduced by using CoPTIC, compared with a dedicated modelling language and encoding.

5 Related Work

The key underlying technology in CoPTIC is the bounded model checker CBMC [7], which in turn relies on the SAT solvers MiniSat and CaDiCaL. In typical operation, CBMC aims to verify the universally quantified property that, for all paths of execution of a C program, there is no assertion violation. It does this by using a SAT solver to solve the existential problem of finding a path containing an assertion violation. If the SAT solver finds a path, CBMC reports failed verification with the path as a counterexample; if not, CBMC reports successful verification. In CoPTIC, we typically use CBMC to solve the existential problem of finding values of variables that satisfy constraints.

In the field of automated verification, bounded model checkers have been successful because of their ability to verify (or find bugs in) large programs with bit-level accuracy and minimal user annotation. Other successful bounded model checkers include SMACK [18], which uses the LLVM toolchain with Boogie as the solver, and ESBMC [8], which uses SMT solvers rather than a SAT solver.

Most modern SAT solvers use a variant of Conflict-Driven Clause Learning (CDCL). MiniSat [9] won the SAT Race 2006. Because of its good performance and publicly available, easily editable source code, it became the default choice for developers of applications that needed a SAT solver. The more modern solver CaDiCaL [4] won several tracks in the 2017 and 2018 competitions and has since also become a popular choice. The recent editions of the SAT Competition have been dominated by Kissat, Biere's rewrite of CaDiCaL in C.

Constraint programming encompasses a wide range of modelling languages and solution techniques. Because the ability of a technique to handle a problem efficiently depends significantly on how the problem is expressed, modelling of constraint problems, including the choice of modelling language, remains a big concern. Significant milestones in modelling include the release of CSPLib in 1999 [12] and the MiniZinc modelling language in 2007 [17]. Whilst MiniZinc is the most broadly supported language and has a long-running associated competition, there are many others, including Essence [11] (which supports higher-level types, such as functions), Picat [24] (which adopts a logic programming paradigm) and XCSP3 [1] (which aims to be a kind of intermediate language).

There are several constraint programming toolkits such as Gecode [6] that provide an API through which a constraint solver can be invoked from within a C program. However, these either require that the constraints be written in a separate modelling language, or that the model be built through a sequence of API calls that resembles a transliteration of a constraint program written in the solver's native language. The system closest to ours is CoJava [5], which adopts a similar guess-and-check paradigm in Java; there is a custom translation into

MiniZinc [10]. As it does not use an existing, well-tested verification tool, there may be concerns about the correctness of its translation.

The main techniques implemented in general-purpose constraint solvers are backtracking search and local search, both of which can be improved by good choice of heuristics and constraint propagation. However, in recent years, translation into SAT has become a leading technique for solving constraint problems. PicatSAT [22] won the main tracks in the XCSP3 Competition 2019 and 2022, and has ranked highly in every MiniZinc Challenge since 2016.

The idea of solving a constraint problem by translating it into C and using a C program verification tool, such as CBMC, is not new, but CoPTIC automates part of this process. Verma and Yap translated XCSP3 problems into C programs [20] and used them to benchmark symbolic execution tools such as KLEE. Lester used a similar translation as the basis for Exchequer [2], which won the Mini Solver track in the XCSP3 Competition 2022. Lester has also shown how to solve the planning problem of completing an interactive fiction game by applying CBMC to a modified version of the source code [14]. Meanwhile, in the SAT Competition 2022, Manthey submitted a set of benchmarks based around using CBMC to solve the puzzle Summle [16].

6   Conclusion

We have presented the CoPTIC system for constraint programming, which allows a user to write constraint models in C and solve them by translation to SAT using the bounded model checker CBMC. Our system is freely available online and easy to install, with only standard dependencies. CoPTIC supports not only constraint satisfaction problems, but also optimisation and enumeration.

These features make CoPTIC an attractive system for casual users of constraint programming. In time, it may serve as a gateway language for some to learn dedicated constraint programming languages. As well as being a useful system in its own right, CoPTIC showcases the power of automated verification tools and SAT solvers, which have advanced massively in the last two decades.

In many cases, a CoPTIC model for solving a problem will perform better than a C program that uses brute force or heuristic search. Even when it does not, we should recall that in the world of programming, it is received wisdom that "premature optimisation is the root of all evil", as it wastes development effort and increases the risk of introducing bugs. Thus the CoPTIC approach is still preferable, as it reduces development effort.

This argument also applies at the meta level. For occasional users of constraint programming, it is better to write constraint programs in a language one already knows than to expend time and effort learning a dedicated constraint programming language, even if the dedicated language ultimately allows one to write more succinct models and supports more efficient solvers. For regular users of constraint programming, the dedicated language is a clear winner, but for casual users, CoPTIC achieves an acceptable balance of ease of learning, ease of use and performance.

Data Availability Statement

The source code and constraint models that support the findings of this study are available in Zenodo: https://doi.org/10.5281/zenodo.7313351 [15]. The constraint models were derived from CSPLib: https://www.csplib.org/.

References

1. Audemard, G., Boussemart, F., Lecoutre, C., Piette, C., Roussel, O.: Xcsp³ and its ecosystem. Constraints An Int. J. **25**(1-2), 47–69 (2020). https://doi.org/10.1007/s10601-019-09307-9, https://doi.org/10.1007/s10601-019-09307-9
2. Audemard, G., Lecoutre, C., Lonca, E.: Proceedings of the 2022 XCSP3 competition. CoRR **abs/2209.00917** (2022). https://doi.org/10.48550/arXiv.2209.00917, https://doi.org/10.48550/arXiv.2209.00917
3. Beyer, D., Dangl, M., Lemberger, T., Tautschnig, M.: Tests from witnesses - execution-based validation of verification results. In: Dubois, C., Wolff, B. (eds.) Tests and Proofs - 12th International Conference, TAP@STAF 2018, Toulouse, France, June 27-29, 2018, Proceedings. Lecture Notes in Computer Science, vol. 10889, pp. 3–23. Springer (2018). https://doi.org/10.1007/978-3-319-92994-1_1, https://doi.org/10.1007/978-3-319-92994-1_1
4. Biere, A., Fazekas, K., Fleury, M., Heisinger, M.: CaDiCaL, Kissat, Paracooba, Plingeling and Treengeling entering the SAT Competition 2020. In: Balyo, T., Froleyks, N., Heule, M., Iser, M., Järvisalo, M., Suda, M. (eds.) Proc. of SAT Competition 2020 – Solver and Benchmark Descriptions. Department of Computer Science Report Series B, vol. B-2020-1, pp. 51–53. University of Helsinki (2020), https://helda.helsinki.fi/handle/10138/318450
5. Brodsky, A., Nash, H.: Cojava: Optimization modeling by nondeterministic simulation. In: Benhamou, F. (ed.) Principles and Practice of Constraint Programming - CP 2006, 12th International Conference, CP 2006, Nantes, France, September 25-29, 2006, Proceedings. Lecture Notes in Computer Science, vol. 4204, pp. 91–106. Springer (2006). https://doi.org/10.1007/11889205_9, https://doi.org/10.1007/11889205_9
6. Cipriano, R., Dovier, A., Mauro, J.: Compiling and executing declarative modeling languages to gecode. In: de la Banda, M.G., Pontelli, E. (eds.) Logic Programming, 24th International Conference, ICLP 2008, Udine, Italy, December 9-13 2008, Proceedings. Lecture Notes in Computer Science, vol. 5366, pp. 744–748. Springer (2008). https://doi.org/10.1007/978-3-540-89982-2_69, https://doi.org/10.1007/978-3-540-89982-2_69
7. Clarke, E.M., Kroening, D., Lerda, F.: A tool for checking ANSI-C programs. In: Jensen, K., Podelski, A. (eds.) Tools and Algorithms for the Construction and Analysis of Systems, 10th International Conference, TACAS 2004, Held as Part of the Joint European Conferences on Theory and Practice of Software, ETAPS 2004, Barcelona, Spain, March 29 - April 2, 2004, Proceedings. Lecture Notes in Computer Science, vol. 2988, pp. 168–176. Springer (2004). https://doi.org/10.1007/978-3-540-24730-2_15, https://doi.org/10.1007/978-3-540-24730-2_15
8. Cordeiro, L.C., Fischer, B., Marques-Silva, J.: Smt-based bounded model checking for embedded ANSI-C software. IEEE Trans. Software Eng. **38**(4), 957–974 (2012). https://doi.org/10.1109/TSE.2011.59, https://doi.org/10.1109/TSE.2011.59

9. Eén, N., Sörensson, N.: An extensible sat-solver. In: Giunchiglia, E., Tacchella, A. (eds.) Theory and Applications of Satisfiability Testing, 6th International Conference, SAT 2003. Santa Margherita Ligure, Italy, May 5-8, 2003 Selected Revised Papers. Lecture Notes in Computer Science, vol. 2919, pp. 502–518. Springer (2003). https://doi.org/10.1007/978-3-540-24605-3_37, https://doi.org/10.1007/978-3-540-24605-3_37

10. Francis, K., Brand, S., Stuckey, P.J.: Optimisation modelling for software developers. In: Milano, M. (ed.) Principles and Practice of Constraint Programming - 18th International Conference, CP 2012, Québec City, QC, Canada, October 8-12, 2012. Proceedings. Lecture Notes in Computer Science, vol. 7514, pp. 274–289. Springer (2012). https://doi.org/10.1007/978-3-642-33558-7_22, https://doi.org/10.1007/978-3-642-33558-7_22

11. Frisch, A.M., Grum, M., Jefferson, C., Hernández, B.M., Miguel, I.: The design of ESSENCE: A constraint language for specifying combinatorial problems. In: Veloso, M.M. (ed.) IJCAI 2007, Proceedings of the 20th International Joint Conference on Artificial Intelligence, Hyderabad, India, January 6-12, 2007. pp. 80–87 (2007), http://ijcai.org/Proceedings/07/Papers/011.pdf

12. Gent, I.P., Walsh, T.: Csp$_{lib}$: A benchmark library for constraints. In: Jaffar, J. (ed.) Principles and Practice of Constraint Programming - CP'99, 5th International Conference, Alexandria, Virginia, USA, October 11-14, 1999, Proceedings. Lecture Notes in Computer Science, vol. 1713, pp. 480–481. Springer (1999). https://doi.org/10.1007/978-3-540-48085-3_36, https://doi.org/10.1007/978-3-540-48085-3_36

13. Gent, I.P., Walsh, T.: Csplib: Twenty years on. CoRR abs/1909.13430 (2019), http://arxiv.org/abs/1909.13430

14. Lester, M.M.: Solving interactive fiction games via partial evaluation and bounded model checking. CoRR abs/2012.15365 (2020), https://arxiv.org/abs/2012.15365

15. Lester, M.M.: CoPTIC: Constraint programming translated into C (Nov 2022). https://doi.org/10.5281/zenodo.7313351, https://doi.org/10.5281/zenodo.7313351

16. Manthey, N.: Solving summle.net with SAT. In: Balyo, T., Heule, M., Iser, M., Järvisalo, M., Suda, M. (eds.) Proc. of SAT Competition 2022 – Solver and Benchmark Descriptions. Department of Computer Science Report Series B, vol. B-2022-1, pp. 70–71. University of Helsinki (2022), http://hdl.handle.net/10138/318450

17. Nethercote, N., Stuckey, P.J., Becket, R., Brand, S., Duck, G.J., Tack, G.: Minizinc: Towards a standard CP modelling language. In: Bessiere, C. (ed.) Principles and Practice of Constraint Programming - CP 2007, 13th International Conference, CP 2007, Providence, RI, USA, September 23-27, 2007, Proceedings. Lecture Notes in Computer Science, vol. 4741, pp. 529–543. Springer (2007). https://doi.org/10.1007/978-3-540-74970-7_38, https://doi.org/10.1007/978-3-540-74970-7_38

18. Rakamaric, Z., Emmi, M.: SMACK: decoupling source language details from verifier implementations. In: Biere, A., Bloem, R. (eds.) Computer Aided Verification - 26th International Conference, CAV 2014, Held as Part of the Vienna Summer of Logic, VSL 2014, Vienna, Austria, July 18-22, 2014. Proceedings. Lecture Notes in Computer Science, vol. 8559, pp. 106–113. Springer (2014). https://doi.org/10.1007/978-3-319-08867-9_7, https://doi.org/10.1007/978-3-319-08867-9_7

19. Triska, M., Musliu, N.: An improved SAT formulation for the social golfer problem. Ann. Oper. Res. **194**(1), 427–438 (2012). https://doi.org/10.1007/s10479-010-0702-5, https://doi.org/10.1007/s10479-010-0702-5

20. Verma, S., Yap, R.H.C.: Benchmarking symbolic execution using constraint problems - initial results. In: 31st IEEE International Conference on Tools with Artificial Intelligence, ICTAI 2019, Portland, OR, USA, November 4-6, 2019. pp. 1–9. IEEE (2019). https://doi.org/10.1109/ICTAI.2019.00010, https://doi.org/10.1109/ICTAI.2019.00010

21. Zhou, N.: In pursuit of an efficient SAT encoding for the hamiltonian cycle problem. In: Simonis, H. (ed.) Principles and Practice of Constraint Programming - 26th International Conference, CP 2020, Louvain-la-Neuve, Belgium, September 7-11, 2020, Proceedings. Lecture Notes in Computer Science, vol. 12333, pp. 585–602. Springer (2020). https://doi.org/10.1007/978-3-030-58475-7_34, https://doi.org/10.1007/978-3-030-58475-7_34

22. Zhou, N., Kjellerstrand, H.: The picat-sat compiler. In: Gavanelli, M., Reppy, J.H. (eds.) Practical Aspects of Declarative Languages - 18th International Symposium, PADL 2016, St. Petersburg, FL, USA, January 18-19, 2016. Proceedings. Lecture Notes in Computer Science, vol. 9585, pp. 48–62. Springer (2016). https://doi.org/10.1007/978-3-319-28228-2_4, https://doi.org/10.1007/978-3-319-28228-2_4

23. Zhou, N., Kjellerstrand, H.: Optimizing SAT encodings for arithmetic constraints. In: Beck, J.C. (ed.) Principles and Practice of Constraint Programming - 23rd International Conference, CP 2017, Melbourne, VIC, Australia, August 28 - September 1, 2017, Proceedings. Lecture Notes in Computer Science, vol. 10416, pp. 671–686. Springer (2017). https://doi.org/10.1007/978-3-319-66158-2_43, https://doi.org/10.1007/978-3-319-66158-2_43

24. Zhou, N., Kjellerstrand, H., Fruhman, J.: Constraint Solving and Planning with Picat. Springer Briefs in Intelligent Systems, Springer (2015). https://doi.org/10.1007/978-3-319-25883-6, https://doi.org/10.1007/978-3-319-25883-6

Acacia-Bonsai: A Modern Implementation of Downset-Based LTL Realizability

Michaël Cadilhac[1]([✉]) [ID] and Guillermo A. Pérez[2] [ID]

[1] DePaul University, Chicago, USA
michael@cadilhac.name
[2] University of Antwerp – Flanders Make, Antwerp, Belgium
guillermo.perez@uantwerp.be

Abstract. We describe our implementation of downset-manipulating algorithms used to solve the realizability problem for linear temporal logic (LTL). These algorithms were introduced by Filiot et al. in the 2010s and implemented in the tools Acacia and Acacia+ in C and Python. We identify degrees of freedom in the original algorithms and provide a complete rewriting of Acacia in C++20 articulated around genericity and leveraging modern techniques for better performance. These techniques include compile-time specialization of the algorithms, the use of SIMD registers to store vectors, and several preprocessing steps, some relying on efficient Binary Decision Diagram (BDD) libraries. We also explore different data structures to store downsets. The resulting tool is competitive against comparable modern tools.

Keywords: LTL synthesis · C++ · downset · antichains · SIMD · BDD

1 Introduction

Nowadays, hardware and software systems are everywhere around us. One way to ensure their correct functioning is to automatically synthesize them from a formal specification. This has two advantages over alternatives such as testing and model checking: the design part of the program-development process can be completely bypassed and the synthesized program is correct by construction.

In this work we are interested in synthesizing *reactive systems* [17]. These maintain a continuous interaction with their environment. Examples of reactive systems include communication, network, and multimedia protocols as well as operating systems. For the specification, we consider *linear temporal logic* (LTL) [27]. LTL allows to naturally specify time dependence among events that make up the formal specification of a system. The popularity of LTL as a formal specification language extends to, amongst others, AI [15,8,16], hybrid systems and control [6], software engineering [21], and bio-informatics [1].

The classical doubly-exponential-time synthesis algorithm can be decomposed into three steps: 1. *compile* the LTL formula into an automaton of exponential size [32], 2. *determinize* the automaton [29,26] incurring a second exponential blowup, and 3. determine the winner of a *two-player zero-sum game*

© The Author(s) 2023
S. Sankaranarayanan and N. Sharygina (Eds.): TACAS 2023, LNCS 13994, pp. 192–207, 2023.
https://doi.org/10.1007/978-3-031-30820-8_14

played on the latter automaton [28]. Most alternative approaches focus on avoiding the determinization step of the algorithm. This has motivated the development of so-called Safra-less approaches, e.g., [20,11,10,31]. Worth mentioning are the on-the-fly game construction implemented in the Strix tool [24] and the *downset*-based (or "antichain-based") on-the-fly bounded determinization described in [13] and implemented in Acacia+ [5]. Both avoid constructing the doubly-exponential deterministic automaton. Acacia+ was not ranked in recent editions of SYNTCOMP [18] (see http://www.syntcomp.org/) since it is no longer maintained despite remaining one of the main references for new advancements in the field (see, e.g., [12,33,30,22,2]).

Contribution. We present the Acacia approach to solving the problem at hand and propose a new implementation that allows for a variety of optimization steps. For now, we have focused on *(Büchi automata) realizability*, i.e., the decision problem which takes as input an automaton compiled from the LTL formula and asks whether a controller satisfying it exists. In our tool, we compile the input LTL formula into an automaton using Spot [9]. We entirely specialize our presentation on the technical problem at hand and strive to distillate the algorithmic essence of the Acacia approach in that context. The main algorithm is presented in Section 3.4 and the different implementation options are listed in Section 4. Benchmarks are included in Section 6.

All benchmarks were executed on the revision of the software that can be found at: https://github.com/gaperez64/acacia-bonsai/tree/SYNTCOMP22.

2 Preliminaries

Throughout this paper, we assume the existence of two alphabets, I and O; although these stand for input and output, the actual definitions of these two terms is slightly more complex: An *input* (resp. *output*) is a boolean combination of symbols of I (resp. O) and it is *pure* if it is a *conjunction* in which *all* the symbols in I (resp. O) appear exactly once; e.g., with $I = \{i_1, i_2\}$, the expressions $\top$ (true), $\bot$ (false), and $(i_1 \vee i_2)$ are inputs, and $(i_1 \wedge \neg i_2)$ is a pure input. Similarly, an *IO* is a boolean combination of symbols of $I \cup O$, and it is *pure* if it is a conjunction in which all the symbols in $I \cup O$ appear exactly once. We use i, j to denote inputs and x, y for IOs. Two IOs x and y are *compatible* if $x \wedge y \neq \bot$.

A *Büchi automaton* $\mathcal{A}$ is a tuple (Q, q_0, δ, B) with Q a set of states, q_0 the initial state, δ the transition relation that uses IOs as labels, and $B \subseteq Q$ the set of Büchi states. The actual semantics of this automaton will not be relevant to our exposition, we simply note that these automata are usually defined to recognize infinite sequences of pure IOs. We assume, throughout this paper, the existence of some automaton $\mathcal{A}$.

We will be interested in valuations of the states of $\mathcal{A}$ that encode the number of visits to Büchi states—again, we do not go into details here. We will simply speak of *vectors over* $\mathcal{A}$ for elements in $\mathbb{Z}^Q$, mapping states to integers. We will write $\vec{v}$ for such vectors, and v_q for its value for state q. In practice, these vectors will range into a finite subset of $\mathbb{Z}$, with -1 as an implicit minimum value (meaning that $(-1) - 1$ is still -1) and an upper bound provided by the problem.

For a vector $\vec{v}$ over $\mathcal{A}$ and an IO x, we define a function that takes one step back in the automaton, decreasing components that have seen Büchi states. Write $\chi_B(q)$ for the function mapping a state q to 1 if $q \in B$, and 0 otherwise. We then define $\mathrm{bwd}(\vec{v}, x)$ as the vector over $\mathcal{A}$ that maps each state $p \in Q$ to:

$$\min_{\substack{(p,y,q)\in\delta \\ x \text{ compatible with } y}} (v_q - \chi_B(q)) \ ,$$

and we generalize this to sets: $\mathrm{bwd}(S, x) = \{\mathrm{bwd}(\vec{v}, x) \mid \vec{v} \in S\}$. For a set S of vectors over $\mathcal{A}$ and a (possibly nonpure) input i, define:

$$\mathrm{CPre}_i(S) = S \cap \bigcup_{\substack{x \text{ pure IO} \\ x \text{ compatible with } i}} \mathrm{bwd}(S, x) \ .$$

It can be proved that iterating CPre with any possible pure input stabilizes to a fixed point that is independent from the order in which the inputs are selected. We define $\mathrm{CPre}^*(S)$ to be that set.

All the sets that we manipulate will be *downsets*: we say that a vector $\vec{u}$ dominates another vector $\vec{v}$ if for all $q \in Q$, $u_q \geq v_q$, and we say that a set is a downset if $\vec{u} \in S$ and $\vec{u}$ dominates $\vec{v}$ implies that $\vec{v} \in S$. This allows to implement these sets by keeping only dominating elements, which form, as they are pairwise nondominating, an *antichain*. In practice, it may be interesting to keep more elements than just the dominating ones or even to keep all of the elements to avoid the cost of computing domination.

Finally, we define Safe_k as the downset $\{i \mid i \leq k\}^Q$, i.e., all vectors with values bounded by k. We are now equipped to define the computational problem we focus on:

BackwardRealizability
- **Given:** A Büchi automaton $\mathcal{A}$ and an integer $k > 0$,
- **Question:** Is there a $\vec{v} \in \mathrm{CPre}^*(\mathrm{Safe}_k)$ with $v_{q_0} \geq 0$?

We note, for completeness, that (for sufficiently large values of k) this problem is equivalent to deciding the realizability problem associated with $\mathcal{A}$: the question has a positive answer if and only if the *output player* wins the Gale-Stewart game with payoff set the *complement* of the language of $\mathcal{A}$.

3 Realizability algorithm

The problem admits a natural algorithmic solution: start with the initial set, pick an input i, apply CPre_i on the set, and iterate until all inputs induce no change to the set, then check whether this set contains a vector that maps q_0 to 0. We first introduce some degrees of freedom in this approach, then present a slight twist on that solution that will serve as a canvas for the different optimizations.

3.1   Boolean states

This opportunity for optimization was identified in [4] and implemented in Acacia+, we simply introduce it in a more general setting and succinctly present the original idea when we mention how it can be implemented in Section 4.2. We start with an example. Consider the Büchi automaton from Figure 1 with $q_0, q_1 \notin B$.

Fig. 1. Small automaton with $q_0, q_1 \notin B$.

Recall that we are interested in whether the initial state can carry a non-negative value, after CPre has stabilized. In that sense, the crucial information associated with q_0 is boolean in nature: is its value positive or -1? Even further, this same remark can be applied to q_1 since q_1 being valued 6 or 7 is not important to the valuation of q_0. Hence the set of states may be partitioned into integer-valued states and boolean-valued ones. Naturally, detecting which states can be made boolean comes at a cost and not doing it is a valid option.

3.2   Actions

For each IO x, we will have to compute $\mathrm{bwd}(\vec{v}, x)$ oftentimes. This requires to refer to the underlying Büchi automaton and checking for each transition therein whether x is compatible with the condition. It may be preferable to precompute, for each x, what are the relevant pairs (p, q) for which x can go from p to q. We call the set of such pairs the *io-action* of x and denote it io-act(x); in symbols:

$$\mathrm{io\text{-}act}(x) = \{(p, q) \mid (\exists(p, y, q) \in \delta)[x \text{ is compatible with } y]\} \ .$$

Further, as we will be computing $\mathrm{CPre}_i(S)$ for inputs i, we abstract in a similar way the information required for this computation. We use the term *input-action* for the set of io-actions of IOs compatible with i and denote it i-act(i); in symbols:

$$\mathrm{i\text{-}act}(i) = \bigcup_{\substack{x \text{ an IO} \\ \text{compatible with } i}} \mathrm{io\text{-}act}(x) \ .$$

In other words, actions contain exactly the information necessary to compute CPre. Note that from an implementation point of view, we do not require that the actions be precomputed. Indeed, when iterating through pairs $(p, q) \in \mathrm{io\text{-}act}(x)$, the underlying implementation can choose to go back to the automaton.

3.3 Sufficient inputs

As we consider the transitions of the Büchi automaton as being labeled by boolean expressions, it becomes more apparent that some pure IOs can be redundant. For instance, consider a Büchi automaton with $I = \{i\}, O = \{o_1, o_2\}$, but the only transitions compatible with i are labeled $(i \wedge o_1)$ and $(i \wedge \neg o_1)$. Pure IOs compatible with the first label will be $(i \wedge o_1 \wedge o_2)$ and $(i \wedge o_1 \wedge \neg o_2)$, but certainly, these two IOs have the same io-actions, and optimally, we would only consider $(i \wedge o_1)$. However, we should not consider $(i \wedge o_2)$, as it induces an io-action that is not induced by a pure IO. We will thus allow our main algorithm to select certain inputs and IOs and introduce the following notion:

Definition 1. *An IO (resp. input) is* valid *if there exists any pure IO (resp. input) with the same io-action (resp. input-action). A set X of valid IOs is* sufficient *if it represents all the possible io-actions of pure IOs: $\{$io-act$(x) \mid x \in X\} = \{$io-act$(x) \mid x$ is a pure IO$\}$. A sufficient set of inputs is defined similarly with input-actions.*

3.4 Algorithm

We solve **BackwardRealizability** by computing CPre* explicitly:

Algorithm 1 Main algorithm

Input: A Büchi automaton $\mathcal{A}$, an integer $k > 0$
Output: Whether $(\exists \vec{v} \in \text{CPre}^*(\text{Safe}_k))[v_{q_0} \geq 0]$

1 Possibly remove some useless states in $\mathcal{A}$
2 Split states of $\mathcal{A}$ into boolean and nonboolean
3 Let `Downset` be a type for downsets using a vector type that possibly has a boolean part
4 Let $S = \text{Safe}_k$ of type `Downset`
5 Compute a sufficient set E of inputs
6 Compute the input-actions of E
7 **while** true **do**
8 $\quad$ Pick an input-action a of E
9 $\quad$ **if** no action is returned **then**
10 $\quad\quad$ **return** whether a vector in S maps q_0 to a nonnegative value
11 $\quad$ $S \leftarrow \text{CPre}_a(S)$

Our algorithm requires that the "input-action picker" used in line 8 decides whether we have reached a fixed point. As the picker could check whether S has changed, this is without loss of generality.

The computation of CPre$_a$ is the intuitive one, optimizations therein coming from the internal representation of actions. That is, it is implemented by iterating through all io-actions compatible with a, applying bwd on S for each of them, taking the union over all these applications, and finally intersecting the result with S.

4   The many options at every line

The main computational costs of the algorithm are in finding input-actions and computing CPre$_a$. For the former, reducing the number of candidates is crucial (by considering a good set of sufficient inputs). For the latter, reducing the size of the automaton (hence the dimension of the vectors) and providing efficient data types for downsets is key. Additionally, for the "input-action picker" to return an input that *will* make progress, it has to explore S in some way — this can again be a costly operation that would be sped up by better data structures for downsets. Let us now review these potential optimizations line by line.

4.1   Preprocessing of the automaton (line 1)

In this step, one can provide a heuristic that removes certain states that do not contribute to the computation. We provide an optional step that detects *surely losing states*, as presented in [14].

4.2   Boolean states (line 2)

We provide an implementation of the detection of boolean states, in addition to an option to not detect them. Our implementation is based on the concept of *bounded state*, as presented in [4]. A state is *bounded* if it cannot be reached from a Büchi state that lies in a nontrivial strongly connected component. This can be detected in several ways, although it is not an intrinsically costly operation.

4.3   Vectors and downsets (line 3)

The most basic data structure in the main algorithm is that of a vector used to give a value to the states. We provide a handful of different vector classes:

- Standard C++ vector and array types (`std::vector`, `std::array`). Note that arrays are of fixed size; our implementation pre-compiles arrays of different sizes (up to 300 by default), and defaults to vectors if more entries are needed.
- Vectors and arrays backed by SIMD[3] registers. This makes use of the type `std::experimental::simd` and leverages modern CPU optimizations.

Additionally, all these implementations can be glued to an array of booleans (`std::bitset`) to provide a type that combines boolean and integer values. These types can optionally expose an integer that is compatible with the partial order (here, the sum of all the elements in the vector: if $\vec{u}$ dominates $\vec{v}$, then the sum of the elements in $\vec{u}$ is larger than that of $\vec{v}$). This value can help the downset implementations in sorting the vectors.

Downset types are built on top of a vector type. We provide:

---

[3] SIMD: Single Instruction Multiple Data, a set of CPU instructions & registers to compute component-wise operations on fixed-size vectors.

- Implementations using sets or vectors of vectors, either containing only the dominating vectors, or containing explicitly all the vectors;
- An implementation that relies on k-d trees, a space-partitioning data structure for organizing points in a k-dimensional space; [3]
- Implementations that store the vectors in specific bins depending on the information exposed by the vector type.

4.4   Selecting sufficient inputs (line 5)

Recall our discussion on sufficient inputs of Section 3.3. We introduce the notion of *terminal* IO following the intuition that there is no restriction of the IO that would lead to a more specific action:

Definition 2. *An IO x is said to be* terminal *if for every compatible IO y, we have* io-act$(x) \subseteq$ io-act(y). *An input i is said to be* terminal *if for every compatible input j we have* i-act$(i) \subseteq$ i-act(j).

Our approaches to input selection focus on efficiently searching for a sufficient set of terminal IOs and inputs. The key property of terminal inputs is that they are automatically valid, while still being more general than pure inputs.

Proposition 1. *Any pure IO and any input is terminal. Any terminal IO and any terminal input is valid.*

Proof. Any pure IO is terminal.   Consider a pure IO x and a compatible IO y. If $(p,q) \in$ io-act(x), then there is a transition $(p,z,q) \in \delta$ such that x is compatible with z, and thus $x \wedge z = x$. Consequently, $x \wedge z \wedge y = x \wedge y \neq \bot$, hence y and z are compatible and $(p,q) \in$ io-act(y). This shows that io-act$(x) \subseteq$ io-act(y) and that x is terminal.

Any pure input is terminal.   Consider now a pure input i and a compatible input j. Let io-act$(x) \in$ i-act(i). It holds that x is compatible with i, hence $i \wedge x \neq \bot$. Since i is pure, $i \wedge j = i$, thus $i \wedge j \wedge x \neq \bot$, and x is also compatible with j, implying that io-act$(x) \in$ i-act(j). This shows that i-act$(i) \subseteq$ i-act(j) and that i is terminal.

Any terminal IO and input is valid.   We prove the case for inputs, the IO case being similar. Let i be a terminal input and j be a compatible pure input (at least one exists), then i-act$(i) \subseteq$ i-act(j). Since j is pure, it is also terminal, hence i-act$(j) \subseteq$ i-act(i). Hence i-act$(i) =$ i-act(j) and i is valid.   □

We present a simple algorithm for computing a sufficient set of terminal IOs. This is done by iteratively refining a set P of terminal IOs, starting by assuming that $\{\top\}$ is such a set and using any counterexample to split the IOs:

Algorithm 2 Computing a sufficient set of terminal IOs

Input: A Büchi automaton $\mathcal{A}$
Output: A sufficient set of terminal IOs

$P \leftarrow \{\top\}$
for every label x in the automaton **do**
    for every element y in P **do**
        if $x \wedge y \neq \bot$ **then**
            Delete y from P
            Insert $x \wedge y$ in P
            if $\neg x \wedge y \neq \bot$ **then** insert $\neg x \wedge y$ in P
return P

We provide 3 implementations of input selection:

- No precomputation, i.e., return pure inputs/IOs;
- Applying Algorithm 2 twice: for IOs and inputs;
- Use a pure BDD approach to do the previous algorithm; this relies on extra variables to have the loop "**for** *every element* y *in* P" iterate *only* over elements y that satisfy $x \wedge y \neq \bot$.

4.5 Precomputing actions (line 6)

Since computing CPre_i for an input i requires to go through i-act(i), possibly going back to the automaton and iterating through all transitions, it may be beneficial to precompute this set. We provide this step as an optional optimization that is intertwined with the computation of a sufficient set of IOs; for instance, rather than iterating through labels in Algorithm 2, one could iterate through all transitions, and store the set of transitions that are compatible with each terminal IO on the fly.

4.6 Main loop: Picking input-actions (line 8)

We provide several implementations of the input-action picker:

- Return each input-action in turn, until no change has occurred to S while going through all possible input-actions;
- Search for an input-action that is certain to change S. This is based on the concept of *critical input* as presented in [4]. This is reliant on how input-actions are ordered themselves, so we provide multiple options (using a priority queue to prefer inputs that were recently returned, randomize part of the array of input-actions, and randomize the whole array).

4.7 When are we done?

The main algorithm answers either "yes, the formula is realizable" or "don't know." Indeed, for the value of k to provide an exact value, it has to be very large and reaching a fixed point in the computation becomes impossible in practice. However, it is not necessary to restart the whole algorithm with larger values of k in order to converge towards the correct answer: one can just increase all the components of all the vectors in S (our main set), and go back to the main loop. There are thus two parameters that can be adjusted: the starting value of k and the increment to S each time the loop is restarted.

5   Checking unrealizability of LTL specifications

As mentioned in the preliminaries, for large values of k the **BackwardRealizability** problem is equivalent to a non-zero sum game whose payoff set is the complement of the language of the given automaton. More precisely, for small values of k, a negative answer for the **BackwardRealizability** problem does not imply that the output player does not win the game. Instead, if one is interested in whether the output player wins, a property known as determinacy [23] can be leveraged to instead ask whether a complementary property holds: does the input player win the game?

We thus need to build an automaton $\mathcal{B}$ for which a positive answer to the **BackwardRealizability** translates to the previous property. To do so, we can consider the negation of the input formula, $\neg\phi$, and inverse the roles of the players, that is, swap the inputs and outputs. However, to make sure the semantics of the game is preserved, we also need to have the input player play first, and the output player *react* to the input player's move. To do so, we simply need to have the outputs moved *one step forward* (in the future, in the LTL sense). This can be done directly on the input formula, by putting an X (neXt) operator on each output. This can however make the formula much more complex.

We propose an alternative to this: Obtain the automaton for $\neg\phi$, then push the outputs one state forward. This means that a transition $(p, \langle i, o \rangle, q)$ is translated to a transition (p, i, q), and the output o should be fired from q. In practice, we would need to remember that output, and this would require the construction to consider every state (q, o), augmenting the number of states tremendously. Algorithm 3 for this task, however, tries to minimize the number of states (q, o) necessary by considering nonpure outputs that maximally correspond to a pure input compatible with the original transition label.

Algorithm 3 Modifying $\mathcal{A}$ so that the outputs are shifted forward

Input: A Büchi automaton $\mathcal{A}$ with initial state q_0 and transition set δ
Output: The states S and transitions Δ of the Büchi automaton $\mathcal{B}$
$S, V \leftarrow \{(q_0, \top)\}$
$\Delta \leftarrow \{\}$

```
while V is nonempty do
    Pop (p, o) from V
    for every (p, x, q) ∈ δ do
        y ← x
        while y ≠ ⊥ do        // Iterating through x's minterms focusing on inputs
            Let i be a pure input compatible with y
            o' ← ∃I.x ∧ i        // Extract nonpure output compatible with i
            Add (⟨p, o⟩, o ∧ i, ⟨q, o'⟩) to Δ
            If (q, o') is not in S, add it to S and V
            y ← y ∧ ¬i
return S, Δ
```

6   Benchmarks

6.1   Protocol

For the past few years, the yardstick of performance for synthesis tools is the SYNTCOMP competition [19]. The organizers provide a bank of nearly a thousand LTL formulas, and candidate tools are run with a time limit of one hour on each of them. The tool that solves the most instances in this timeframe wins the competition.

To benchmark our tool, we relied on the 930 LTL formulas that were used in the 2021 SYNTCOMP competition, of which about 60% are realizable. Notably, 864 of all the tests were solved in less than 20 seconds by some tool during the competition, and among the 66 tests left out, 50 were not solved by any tool. This showcases a usual trend of synthesis tools: either they solve an instance fast, or they are unlikely to solve it at all. To better focus on the fine performance differences between the tools, we set a timeout of 60 seconds for all tests.

We compared Acacia-Bonsai against itself using different choices of options, and against Acacia+ [5], Strix [24], and ltlsynt [9,25]. The benchmarks were completed on a Linux computer with the following specifications:

- CPU: Intel® Core™ i7-8700 CPU @ 3.20GHz. This CPU has 6 hyper-threaded cores, meaning that 12 threads can run concurrently. It supports Intel® AVX2, meaning that it has SIMD registers of up to 256 bits.
- Memory: The CPU has 12 MiB of cache, the computer has 16 GiB of DDR4-2666 RAM.

We present some of these results in the form of survival plots (also called cactus plots). They indicate how many instances can be solved within a set time, where the time limit is for each instance. As a rule of thumb, the lower the curve, the better. Since the tool tend to solve a lot of instances under one second, we elected to present these graphics with a logarithmic y-axis.

6.2   Results

The options of Acacia-Bonsai. We compared 25 different configurations of Acacia-Bonsai, in order to single out the best combination of options. We elected to start with some sensible defaults and test each parameter by diverging from the defaults by a single option each time.

- Preprocessing of the automaton (Section 4.1). This has little impact, although a handful of tests saw an important boost. Overall, the performance was slightly worse with automaton preprocessing, owing to the cost of computing the surely loosing states. We elected to deactivate this option in our best configuration, as this allowed four more tests to pass.
- Boolean states (Section 4.2). This step allowed solving about 5% more tests when activated, globally.
- Vectors and downsets (Section 4.3). Despite a wealth of different implementations, only the k-d tree implementation really stands out, in that it solves 5% fewer tests than the rest. The impact on using SIMD vectors and tailoring downset algorithms to leverage SIMD operations appears to be minimal. This is likely caused by two factors: 1. The increasing ability for modern compilers to automatically identify where SIMD instructions can benefit performances; 2. The relative uselessness of pointwise vector operations in the task at hand.
- Precomputing a sufficient set of inputs and IO (Section 4.4). Computing that set using Algorithm 2 turned out to offer the best performance, solving 23 more tests than using the pure inputs/IOs. The pure BDD approach for this step was slightly more costly.
- Picking input-actions (Section 4.6). The approaches performed equivalently, with a slight edge for the choice of critical inputs without randomizing or priority queue.
- Initial value and increments of k (Section 4.7). We compared several combinations, which had little impact on overall performance, with the best one solving 3 more tests than the worst.
- Unrealizability (Section 5). The following figure shows how the formula-based and the automaton-based approaches to unrealizability compare. We only show the unrealizable tests and add the configuration we use in practice: start two threads, one for each option, and stop as soon as one returns.

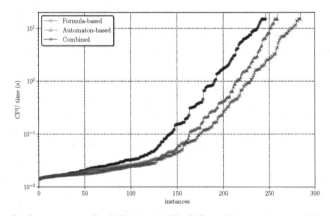

Fig. 2. Reducing unrealizability to realizability. Timeout set at 20 seconds.

Despite the automaton-based approach showing better overall results, we note that this approach provides a larger automaton than the formula-based approach in about 99.5% of the tests. Additionally, the automaton-based approach offers better performances even when looking at the running time *without* the formula-to-automaton part of the process. This seems to indicate that the automaton that is produced is somewhat simpler for the main algorithm.

Acacia-Bonsai and foes. The following plot shows the performance of the tools together. Within our parameters, Acacia-Bonsai solves 699 tests, while Acacia+ solves 560, ltlsynt 703, and Strix 770.

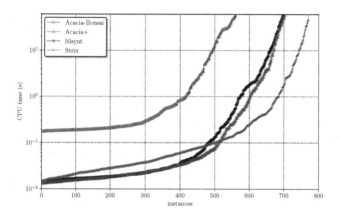

Fig. 3. Survival plot for SYNTCOMP tools and Acacia-Bonsai

Instances solved by one tool but not the other. To better understand the intrinsic algorithmic competitiveness of the different tools, we study which instances were solved by our tool but not the others, and conversely:

- *ltlsynt.* This tool solves 4 more instances than Acacia-Bonsai overall. It solves 61 instances on which Acacia-Bonsai times out, with less than a third of them being unrealizable instances. It would be interesting to implement, within ltlsynt, the unrealizability techniques we describe in Section 5.
- *Strix.* This tool solves 71 more instances than Acacia-Bonsai overall. It solves 124 instances on which Acacia-Bonsai times out, 58% of which are unrealizable. For 90% of these 124 instances, Strix answers in less than 2 seconds. Conversely, of the instances on which Acacia-Bonsai answers while Strix times out, three quarters are solved within two seconds. This naturally hints at the possibility of combining the approaches of the two tools, using parallelization.

7   Conclusion

We provided multiple degrees of freedom in the main algorithm for downset-based LTL realizability and implemented options for each of these degrees. In this paper, we presented the main ideas behind these. Experiments show that this careful reimplementation surpasses the performance of the original Acacia+, making Acacia-Bonsai competitive against modern LTL realizability tools. Along with implementing some optimizations present in previous implementations, we introduced several new ones: reduction of the input-output alphabet, alternative antichain data structures, different strategies for input-picking, and constructing a "shifted automaton" to test unrealizability.

A somewhat disappointing conclusion of our experiments concerns code that makes explicit use of SIMD registers, i.e., large CPU registers that support pointwise vector operations. Our experiments indicate that downset-based algorithms and downset data structures are not able to take full advantage of SIMD. In the future, we plan on investigating data structures for downsets that delay some of their computations in order to better leverage vectorized operations. Such a data structure would not provide better theoretical performances, but would potentially outperform our other data structures.

One surprise that prompts for further investigation is brought by our approach to unrealizability (Section 5): we provided two options for processing the input LTL formula into an automaton that expresses a realizable game iff the original formula was *un*realizable. Although one option consistently produces larger automata than the other, it appears that the downset-based realizability algorithm performs better on the larger automata. A close study of the resulting automata may help in identifying salient features of automata that are easier for the Acacia algorithm.

Lastly, we should note that this reimplementation of Acacia+ is not complete, since a few options of Acacia+ have not yet been included in Acacia-Bonsai yet. One such option consists in decomposing LTL formulas that are conjunctions of subformulas into smaller instances of the realizability problem. We plan on implementing this before the next edition of SYNTCOMP.

Acknowledgements. We would like to thank Véronique Bruyère for recommending the use of k-d trees as a data structure to store and manipulate downsets as well as Clément Tamines for useful conversations on these and alternative data structures. This research was partially funded by the FWO G030020N project "SAILor".

Data-Availability Statement The software presented in this article and the analysed dataset are available as [7]. In addition, the version under study is tagged in the GitHub repository of this software as:
https://github.com/gaperez64/acacia-bonsai/tree/TACAS23

References

1. Ahmed, Z., Benqué, D., Berezin, S., Dahl, A.C.E., Fisher, J., Hall, B.A., Ishtiaq, S., Nanavati, J., Piterman, N., Riechert, M., Skoblov, N.: Bringing LTL model checking to biologists. In: VMCAI. Lecture Notes in Computer Science, vol. 10145, pp. 1–13. Springer (2017)
2. Bansal, S., Li, Y., Tabajara, L.M., Vardi, M.Y.: Hybrid compositional reasoning for reactive synthesis from finite-horizon specifications. In: AAAI. pp. 9766–9774. AAAI Press (2020)
3. de Berg, M., Cheong, O., van Kreveld, M.J., Overmars, M.H.: Computational geometry: algorithms and applications, 3rd Edition. Springer (2008), https://www.worldcat.org/oclc/227584184
4. Bohy, A.: Antichain based algorithms for the synthesis of reactive systems. Ph.D. thesis, University of Mons (2014)
5. Bohy, A., Bruyère, V., Filiot, E., Jin, N., Raskin, J.: Acacia+, a tool for LTL synthesis. In: Madhusudan, P., Seshia, S.A. (eds.) CAV. LNCS, vol. 7358, pp. 652–657. Springer (2012). https://doi.org/10.1007/978-3-642-31424-7_45
6. Bombara, G., Vasile, C.I., Penedo, F., Yasuoka, H., Belta, C.: A decision tree approach to data classification using signal temporal logic. In: HSCC. pp. 1–10. ACM (2016)
7. Cadilhac, M., Pérez, G.A.: Acacia-Bonsai (TACAS'23 version) (Nov 2022). https://doi.org/10.5281/zenodo.7296659
8. Camacho, A., McIlraith, S.A.: Learning interpretable models expressed in linear temporal logic. In: ICAPS. pp. 621–630. AAAI Press (2019)
9. Duret-Lutz, A., Lewkowicz, A., Fauchille, A., Michaud, T., Renault, E., Xu, L.: Spot 2.0 - A framework for LTL and ω-automata manipulation. In: ATVA. Lecture Notes in Computer Science, vol. 9938, pp. 122–129 (2016)
10. Esparza, J., Kretínský, J., Raskin, J., Sickert, S.: From LTL and limit-deterministic büchi automata to deterministic parity automata. In: TACAS (1). Lecture Notes in Computer Science, vol. 10205, pp. 426–442 (2017)
11. Esparza, J., Kretínský, J., Sickert, S.: From LTL to deterministic automata - A Safraless compositional approach. Formal Methods Syst. Des. **49**(3), 219–271 (2016). https://doi.org/10.1007/s10703-016-0259-2
12. Faymonville, P., Finkbeiner, B., Rabe, M.N., Tentrup, L.: Encodings of bounded synthesis. In: Legay, A., Margaria, T. (eds.) TACAS. LNCS, vol. 10205, pp. 354–370 (2017). https://doi.org/10.1007/978-3-662-54577-5_20
13. Filiot, E., Jin, N., Raskin, J.: An antichain algorithm for LTL realizability. In: CAV. Lecture Notes in Computer Science, vol. 5643, pp. 263–277. Springer (2009)
14. Geeraerts, G., Goossens, J., Stainer, A.: Synthesising succinct strategies in safety and reachability games. In: Ouaknine, J., Potapov, I., Worrell, J. (eds.) RP. LNCS, vol. 8762, pp. 98–111. Springer (2014). https://doi.org/10.1007/978-3-319-11439-2_8
15. Giacomo, G.D., Vardi, M.Y.: LTL_f and LDL_f synthesis under partial observability. In: IJCAI. pp. 1044–1050. IJCAI/AAAI Press (2016)
16. Gutierrez, J., Najib, M., Perelli, G., Wooldridge, M.J.: Automated temporal equilibrium analysis: Verification and synthesis of multi-player games. Artif. Intell. **287**, 103353 (2020). https://doi.org/10.1016/j.artint.2020.103353
17. Harel, D., Pnueli, A.: On the development of reactive systems. In: Apt, K.R. (ed.) Logics and Models of Concurrent Systems - Conference proceedings, Colle-sur-Loup (near Nice), France, 8-19 October 1984. NATO ASI Series, vol. 13, pp. 477–498. Springer (1984). https://doi.org/10.1007/978-3-642-82453-1_17

18. Jacobs, S., Basset, N., Bloem, R., Brenguier, R., Colange, M., Faymonville, P., Finkbeiner, B., Khalimov, A., Klein, F., Michaud, T., Pérez, G.A., Raskin, J., Sankur, O., Tentrup, L.: The 4th reactive synthesis competition (SYNTCOMP 2017): Benchmarks, participants & results. In: SYNT@CAV. EPTCS, vol. 260, pp. 116–143 (2017)

19. Jacobs, S., Pérez, G.A., Abraham, R., Bruyère, V., Cadilhac, M., Colange, M., Delfosse, C., van Dijk, T., Duret-Lutz, A., Faymonville, P., Finkbeiner, B., Khalimov, A., Klein, F., Luttenberger, M., Meyer, K.J., Michaud, T., Pommellet, A., Renkin, F., Schlehuber-Caissier, P., Sakr, M., Sickert, S., Staquet, G., Tamines, C., Tentrup, L., Walker, A.: The reactive synthesis competition (SYNTCOMP): 2018-2021. CoRR **abs/2206.00251** (2022). https://doi.org/10.48550/arXiv.2206.00251

20. Kupferman, O., Piterman, N., Vardi, M.Y.: Safraless compositional synthesis. In: CAV. Lecture Notes in Computer Science, vol. 4144, pp. 31–44. Springer (2006)

21. Lemieux, C., Park, D., Beschastnikh, I.: General LTL specification mining (T). In: ASE. pp. 81–92. IEEE Computer Society (2015)

22. Luttenberger, M., Meyer, P.J., Sickert, S.: Practical synthesis of reactive systems from LTL specifications via parity games. Acta Informatica **57**(1-2), 3–36 (2020). https://doi.org/10.1007/s00236-019-00349-3

23. Martin, D.A.: Borel determinacy. Annals of Mathematics **102**(2), 363–371 (1975), http://www.jstor.org/stable/1971035

24. Meyer, P.J., Sickert, S., Luttenberger, M.: Strix: Explicit reactive synthesis strikes back! In: CAV (1). Lecture Notes in Computer Science, vol. 10981, pp. 578–586. Springer (2018)

25. Michaud, T., Colange, M.: Reactive synthesis from LTL specification with Spot. In: Proceedings of the 7th Workshop on Synthesis, SYNT@CAV 2018. Electronic Proceedings in Theoretical Computer Science (2018)

26. Piterman, N.: From nondeterministic Büchi and Streett automata to deterministic parity automata. Log. Methods Comput. Sci. **3**(3) (2007). https://doi.org/10.2168/LMCS-3(3:5)2007

27. Pnueli, A.: The temporal logic of programs. In: 18th Annual Symposium on Foundations of Computer Science, Providence, Rhode Island, USA, 31 October - 1 November 1977. pp. 46–57. IEEE Computer Society (1977). https://doi.org/10.1109/SFCS.1977.32

28. Pnueli, A., Rosner, R.: On the synthesis of a reactive module. In: Conference Record of the Sixteenth Annual ACM Symposium on Principles of Programming Languages, Austin, Texas, USA, January 11-13, 1989. pp. 179–190. ACM Press (1989). https://doi.org/10.1145/75277.75293

29. Safra, S.: On the complexity of omega-automata. In: 29th Annual Symposium on Foundations of Computer Science, White Plains, New York, USA, 24-26 October 1988. pp. 319–327. IEEE Computer Society (1988). https://doi.org/10.1109/SFCS.1988.21948

30. Shi, Y., Xiao, S., Li, J., Guo, J., Pu, G.: Sat-based automata construction for LTL over finite traces. In: 27th Asia-Pacific Software Engineering Conference, APSEC 2020, Singapore, December 1-4, 2020. pp. 1–10. IEEE (2020). https://doi.org/10.1109/APSEC51365.2020.00008

31. Tomita, T., Ueno, A., Shimakawa, M., Hagihara, S., Yonezaki, N.: Safraless LTL synthesis considering maximal realizability. Acta Informatica **54**(7), 655–692 (2017). https://doi.org/10.1007/s00236-016-0280-3

32. Vardi, M.Y., Wolper, P.: Automata theoretic techniques for modal logics of programs (extended abstract). In: DeMillo, R.A. (ed.) Proceedings of the 16th Annual ACM Symposium on Theory of Computing, April 30 - May 2, 1984, Washington, DC, USA. pp. 446–456. ACM (1984). https://doi.org/10.1145/800057.808711
33. Zhu, S., Tabajara, L.M., Li, J., Pu, G., Vardi, M.Y.: A symbolic approach to safety LTL synthesis. In: Strichman, O., Tzoref-Brill, R. (eds.) HVC. LNCS, vol. 10629, pp. 147–162. Springer (2017). https://doi.org/10.1007/978-3-319-70389-3_10

Synthesis

Computing Adequately Permissive Assumptions for Synthesis [*]

Ashwani Anand[1], Kaushik Mallik[2], Satya Prakash Nayak[1]([⊠]),
and Anne-Kathrin Schmuck[1]

[1] Max Planck Institute for Software Systems, Kaiserslautern, Germany
{ashwani,sanayak,akschmuck}@mpi-sws.org
[2] Institute of Science and Technology Austria, Klosterneuburg, Austria
kaushik.mallik@ist.ac.at

Abstract. We automatically compute a new class of environment assumptions in two-player turn-based finite graph games which characterize an "adequate cooperation" needed from the environment to allow the system player to win. Given an ω-regular winning condition Φ for the system player, we compute an ω-regular assumption Ψ for the environment player, such that (i) every environment strategy compliant with Ψ allows the system to fulfill Φ (sufficiency), (ii) Ψ can be fulfilled by the environment for every strategy of the system (implementability), and (iii) Ψ does not prevent any cooperative strategy choice (permissiveness). For parity games, which are canonical representations of ω-regular games, we present a polynomial-time algorithm for the symbolic computation of *adequately permissive assumptions* and show that our algorithm runs faster and produces better assumptions than existing approaches—both theoretically and empirically. To the best of our knowledge, for *ω-regular* games, we provide the first algorithm to compute sufficient and implementable environment assumptions that are also *permissive*.

Keywords: Synthesis · Two-player Games · Parity · Permissiveness.

1 Introduction

Two-player ω-regular games on finite graphs are the core algorithmic components in many important problems of computer science and cyber-physical system design. Examples include the synthesis of programs which react to environment inputs, modal μ-calculus model checking, correct-by-design controller synthesis for cyber-physical systems, and supervisory control of autonomous systems.

These problems can be ultimately reduced to an abstract two-player game between an *environment player* and a *system player*, respectively capturing the external unpredictable influences and the system under design, while the game captures the non-trivial interplay between these two parts. A *solution of the*

[*] S. P. Nayak and A.-K. Schmuck are supported by the DFG project 389792660 TRR 248-CPEC. A. Anand and A.-K. Schmuck are supported by the DFG project SCHM 3541/1-1. K. Mallik is supported by the ERC project ERC-2020-AdG 101020093.

S. Sankaranarayanan and N. Sharygina (Eds.): TACAS 2023, LNCS 13994, pp. 211–228, 2023.
https://doi.org/10.1007/978-3-031-30820-8_15

game is a set of decisions the system player needs to make to satisfy a given ω-regular temporal property over the states of the game, which is then used to design the sought system or its controller.

Traditionally, two-player games over graphs are solved in a zero-sum fashion, i.e., assuming that the environment will behave arbitrarily and possibly adversarially. Although this approach results in robust system designs, it usually makes the environment too powerful to allow an implementation for the system to exist. However in reality, many of the outlined application areas actually account for some cooperation of system components, especially if they are co-designed. In this scenario it is useful to understand how the environment (i.e., other processes) needs to cooperate to allow for an implementation to exist. This can be formalized by environment assumptions, which are ω-regular temporal properties that restrict the moves of the environment player in a synthesis game. Such assumptions can then be used as additional specifications in other components' synthesis problems to enforce the necessary cooperation (possibly in addition to other local requirements) or can be used to verify existing implementations.

For the reasons outlined above, the automatic computation of assumptions has received significant attention in the reactive synthesis community. It has been used in two-player games [8,6], both in the context of monolithic system design [11,19] as well as distributed system design [18,13].

All these works emphasize two desired properties of assumptions. They should be (i) *sufficient*, i.e., enable the system to win if the environment obeys its assumption and (ii) *implementable*, i.e., prevent the system from falsifying the assumption to vacuously win the game by not even respecting the original specification. In this paper, we claim that there is an important third property — *permissiveness*, i.e. the assumption retains all cooperatively winning plays in the game. This notion is crucial in the setting of distributed synthesis, as here assumptions are generated *before* the implementation of every component is fixed. Therefore, assumptions need to retain *all* feasible ways of cooperation to allow for a distributed implementation to be discovered in a decentralized manner.

While the class of assumptions considered in this paper is motivated by their use for distributed synthesis, this paper focuses only on their formalization and computation, i.e., given a two-player game over a finite graph and an ω-regular winning condition Φ for the system player, we automatically compute an *adequately permissive ω-regular assumption* Ψ for the environment player that formalizes the above intuition by being (i) sufficient, (ii) implementable, and (iii) permissive. The main observation that we exploit is that such *adequately permissive assumptions* (APA for short) can be constructed from three simple templates which can be directly extracted from a cooperative synthesis game leading to a polynomial-time algorithm for their computation. By observing page constrains, we postpone the very interesting but largely orthogonal problem of contract-based distributed synthesis using APAs to future work.

To appreciate the simplicity of the assumption templates we use, consider the game graphs depicted in Fig. 1 where the system and the environment player control the circle and square vertices, respectively. Given the specification $\Phi =$

(a)   (b)   (c)

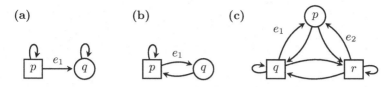

Fig. 1: Game graphs with environment (squares) and system (circles) vertices.

$\Diamond\Box\{p\}$ (which requires the play to eventually only see vertex p), the system player can win the game in Fig. 1 (a) by requiring the environment to fully disable edge e_1. This introduces the first template type—a *safety template*—on e_1. On the other hand, the game in Fig. 1 (b) only requires that e_1 is taken finitely often. This is captured by our second template type—a *co-liveness template*—on e_1. Finally, consider the game in Fig. 1 (c) with the specification $\Phi = \Box\Diamond\{p\}$, i.e. vertex p should be seen infinitely often. Here, the system player wins if whenever the source vertices of edges e_1 and e_2 are seen infinitely often, also one of these edges is taken infinitely often. This is captured by our third template type—a *live group template*—on the edge-group $\{e_1, e_2\}$.

Contribution. The main contribution of this paper is to show that APAs can always be composed from the three outlined assumption templates and can be computed in polynomial time.

Using a set of benchmark examples taken from SYNTCOMP [1] and a prototype implementation of our algorithm in our new tool SIMPA, we empirically show that our algorithm is both faster and produces more desirable solutions than existing approaches. In addition, we apply SIMPA to the well known 2-client arbiter synthesis benchmark from [21], which is known to only allow for an implementation of the arbiter if the clients' moves are suitably restricted. We show that applying SIMPA to the unconstrained arbiter synthesis problem yields assumptions on the clients which are less restrictive but conceptually similar to the ones typically used in the literature.

Related Work. The problem of automatically computing environment assumptions for synthesis was already addressed by Chatterjee et al. [8]. However, their class of assumptions does in general not allow to construct *permissive* assumptions. Further, computing their assumptions is an NP-hard problem, while our algorithm computes APAs in $\mathcal{O}(n^4)$-time for a parity game with n vertices. The difference in the complexity arises because Chatterjee et al. require minimality of the assumptions. On the other hand, we trade minimality for permissiveness which allows us to utilize cooperative games, which are easier to solve.

When considering cooperative solutions of non-zerosum games, related works either fix strategies for both players [7,14], assume a particularly rational behavior of the environment [4] or restrict themselves to safety assumptions [18]. In contrast, we do not make any assumption on how the environment chooses its strategy. Finally, in the context of specification-repair in zerosum games multiple automated methods for repairing environment models exist, e.g., [22,15,16,20,8]. Unfortunately, all of these methods fail to provide permissiveness. A recent work by Cavezza et al. [6] computes a minimally restrictive set of assumptions but only for GR(1) specifications, which are a strict subclass of the problem considered in our work. To the best of our knowledge, we propose the first fully automated algorithm for computing *permissive* assumptions for general ω-regular games.

2   Preliminaries

Notation. We use $\mathbb{N}$ to denote the set of natural numbers including zero. Given two natural numbers $a, b \in \mathbb{N}$ with $a < b$, we use $[a; b]$ to denote the set $\{n \in \mathbb{N} \mid a \leq n \leq b\}$. For any given set $[a; b]$, we write $i \in_{even} [a; b]$ and $i \in_{odd} [a; b]$ as short hand for $i \in [a; b] \cap \{0, 2, 4, \ldots\}$ and $i \in [a; b] \cap \{1, 3, 5, \ldots\}$ respectively. Given two sets A and B, a relation $R \subseteq A \times B$, and an element $a \in A$, we write $R(a)$ to denote the set $\{b \in B \mid (a, b) \in R\}$.

Languages. Let Σ be a finite alphabet. The notations Σ^* and Σ^ω denote the set of finite and infinite words over Σ, respectively, and Σ^∞ is equal to $\Sigma^* \cup \Sigma^\omega$. For any word $w \in \Sigma^\infty$, w_i denotes the i-th symbol in w. Given two words $u \in \Sigma^*$ and $v \in \Sigma^\infty$, the concatenation of u and v is written as the word uv.

Game graphs. A *game graph* is a tuple $G = (V, E)$ where (V, E) is a finite directed graph with *vertices* V and *edges* E, and $V = V^0 \uplus V^1$ be a partition of V. Without loss of generality, we assume that for every $v \in V$ there exists $v' \in V$ s.t. $(v, v') \in E$. For the purpose of this paper, the *system* and the *environment* players will be denoted by *Player* 0 and *Player* 1, respectively. A *play* is a finite or infinite sequence of vertices $\rho = v_0 v_1 \ldots \in V^\infty$. A *play prefix* $\mathrm{p} = v_0 v_1 \cdots v_k$ is a finite play.

Winning conditions. Given a game graph G, we consider winning conditions specified using a formula Φ in *linear temporal logic* (LTL) over the vertex set V, that is, we consider LTL formulas whose atomic propositions are sets of vertices V. In this case the set of desired infinite plays is given by the semantics of Φ over G, which is an ω-regular language $\mathcal{L}(\Phi) \subseteq V^\omega$. Every game graph with an arbitrary ω-regular set of desired infinite plays can be reduced to a game graph (possibly with an extended set of vertices) with an LTL winning condition, as above. The standard definitions of ω-regular languages and LTL are omitted for brevity and can be found in standard textbooks [3].

Games and strategies. A *two-player (turn-based) game* is a pair $\mathcal{G} = (G, \Phi)$ where G is a game graph and Φ is a *winning condition* over G. A strategy of *Player* i, $i \in \{0, 1\}$, is a partial function $\pi^i \colon V^* V^i \to V$ such that for every $\mathrm{p}v \in V^* V^i$ for which π is defined, it holds that $\pi^i(\mathrm{p}v) \in E(v)$. Given a strategy π^i, we say that the play $\rho = v_0 v_1 \ldots$ is *compliant* with π^i if $v_{k-1} \in V^i$ implies $v_k = \pi^i(v_0 \ldots v_{k-1})$ for all $k \in dom(\rho)$. We refer to a play compliant with π^i and a play compliant with both π^0 and π^1 as a π^i-*play* and a $\pi^0\pi^1$-*play*, respectively. We collect all plays compliant with π^i, and compliant with both π^0 and π^1 in the sets $\mathcal{L}(\pi^i)$ and $\mathcal{L}(\pi^0\pi^1)$, respectively.

Winning. Given a game $\mathcal{G} = (G, \Phi)$, a strategy π^i is (surely) *winning for Player* i if $\mathcal{L}(\pi^i) \subseteq \mathcal{L}(\Phi)$, i.e., a *Player* 0 strategy π^0 is winning if *for every Player* 1 strategy π^1 it holds that $\mathcal{L}(\pi^0\pi^1) \subseteq \mathcal{L}(\Phi)$. Similarly, a fixed strategy profile (π^0, π^1) is *cooperatively winning* if $\mathcal{L}(\pi^0 \pi^1) \subseteq \mathcal{L}(\Phi)$. We say that a vertex $v \in V$ is *winning for Player i* (resp. *cooperatively winning*) if there exists a winning strategy π^i (resp. a cooperatively winning strategy profile (π^0, π^1)) s.t. $\pi^i(v)$ is defined. We collect all winning vertices of *Player i* in the *Player i winning region* $\langle\!\langle i \rangle\!\rangle \Phi \subseteq V$ and all cooperatively winning vertices in the *cooperative winning region* $\langle\!\langle 0, 1 \rangle\!\rangle \Phi$. We note that $\langle\!\langle i \rangle\!\rangle \Phi \subseteq \langle\!\langle 0, 1 \rangle\!\rangle \Phi$ for both $i \in \{0, 1\}$.

3 Adequately Permissive Assumptions for Synthesis

Given a two-player game $\mathcal{G}$, the goal of this paper is to compute assumptions on *Player 1* (i.e., the environment), such that both players cooperate *just enough* to fulfill Φ while retaining all possible cooperative strategy choices. Towards a formalization of this intuition, we define winning under assumptions.

Definition 1. *Let $\mathcal{G} = (G = (V, E), \Phi)$ be a game and Ψ be an LTL formula over V. Then a Player 0 strategy π^0 is winning in $\mathcal{G}$ under assumption Ψ, if for every Player 1 strategy π^1 s.t. $\mathcal{L}(\pi^1) \subseteq \mathcal{L}(\Psi)$ it holds that $\mathcal{L}(\pi^0 \pi^1) \subseteq \mathcal{L}(\Phi)$. We denote by $\langle\!\langle 0 \rangle\!\rangle_\Psi \Phi$ the set of vertices from which such a Player 0 strategy exists.*

We remark that the 'winning-under-assumption' strategies π^0 from Def. 1 satisfy two simple but interesting properties — *anti-monotonicity* (if π^0 is winning under an assumption, then it is so under every stronger assumption), and *conjunctivity* (if π^0 is winning under two different assumptions, then it is so under their conjunction). However, it does not satisfy *disjunctivity* (see [2, Sec. 3.1] for an example). In addition, we remark that the definition of 'winning-under-assumption' in terms of plays (rather than strategies) might seem more natural to some readers. We refer these readers to the full version of the paper [2, Sec. 3.1] for an in-depth discussion on the differences of these definitions.

We now see that the assumption Ψ introduced in Def. 1 *weakens* the strategy choices of the environment player (*Player 1*). We call assumptions *sufficient* if this weakening is strong enough to allow *Player 0* to win from every vertex in the cooperative winning region.

Definition 2. *An assumption Ψ is* sufficient *for (G, Φ) if $\langle\!\langle 0 \rangle\!\rangle_\Psi \Phi \supseteq \langle\!\langle 0, 1 \rangle\!\rangle \Phi$.*

Unfortunately, sufficient assumptions can be abused to change the given synthesis problem in an unintended way. Consider for instance the game in Fig. 2 (left) with $\Phi = \Box\Diamond\{v_0\}$ and $\Psi = \Box\Diamond e_1$. Here, there is no strategy π^1 for *Player 1* such that $\mathcal{L}(\pi^1) \subseteq \mathcal{L}(\Psi)$ as the system can always falsify the assumption by simply not choosing e_1 infinitely often in v_1. Therefore, any *Player 0* strategy is winning under assumption even if Φ is violated. The assumption Ψ, however, is trivially sufficient, as $\langle\!\langle 0 \rangle\!\rangle_\Psi \Phi = V$. In order to prevent sufficient assumptions to be falsifiable and thereby enabling vacuous winning, we define the notion of *implementability*, which ensures that Ψ solely restricts *Player 1* moves.

Definition 3. *An assumption Ψ is* implementable *for (G, Φ) if $\langle\!\langle 1 \rangle\!\rangle \Psi = V$.*

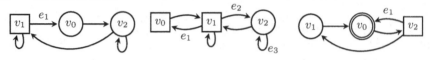

Fig. 2: Two-player games with *Player* 1 (squares) and *Player* 0 (circles) vertices.

A sufficient and implementable assumption ensures that the cooperative winning region of the original game coincides with the winning region under that assumption, i.e., $\langle\!\langle 0\rangle\!\rangle_{\Psi}\Phi = \langle\!\langle 0,1\rangle\!\rangle\Phi$. However, all cooperative strategy choices of both players might still not be retained, which is ensured by the notion of *permissiveness*.

Definition 4. *An assumption Ψ is* permissive *for (G,Φ) if $\mathcal{L}(\Phi) \subseteq \mathcal{L}(\Psi)$.*

This notion of permissiveness is motivated by the intended use of assumptions for compositional synthesis. In the simplest scenario of two interacting processes, two synthesis tasks—one for each process—are considered in parallel. Here, generated assumptions in one synthesis task are used as additional specifications in the other synthesis problem. Therefore, permissiveness is crucial to not "skip" over possible cooperative solutions—each synthesis task needs to keep all allowed strategy choices for both players intact to allow for compositional reasoning. This scenario is illustrated in the following example to motivate the considered class of assumptions. Formalizing assumption-based compositional synthesis in general is however out of the scope of this paper.

Example 1. Consider the (non-zerosum) two-player game in Fig. 2 (middle) with two different specifications for both players, namely $\Phi_0 = \Diamond\Box\{v_1, v_2\}$ and $\Phi_1 = \Diamond\Box\{v_1\}$. Now consider two candidate assumptions $\Psi_0 = \Diamond\Box\neg e_1$ and $\Psi_0' = (\Box\Diamond v_1 \implies \Box\Diamond e_2)$ on *Player* 1. Notice that both assumptions are sufficient and implementable for (G, Φ_0). However, Ψ_0' does not allow the play $\{v_1\}^{\omega}$ and hence is not permissive whereas Ψ_0 is permissive for (G, Φ_0). As a consequence, there is no way *Player* 1 can satisfy both her objective Φ_1 and the assumption Ψ_0' even if *Player* 0 cooperates, since $\mathcal{L}(\Phi_1) \cap \mathcal{L}(\Psi_0') = \emptyset$. However, under the assumption Ψ_0 on *Player* 1 and assumption $\Psi_1 = \Diamond\Box\neg e_3$ on *Player* 0 (which is sufficient and implementable for (G, Φ_1) if we interchange the vertices of the players), they can satisfy both their own objectives and the assumptions on themselves. Therefore, they can collectively satisfy both their objectives.

We also remark that for this example, the algorithm in [9] outputs Ψ_0' as the desired assumption for game (G, Φ_0) and their used assumption formalism is not rich enough to capture assumption Ψ_0. This shows that the assumption type we are interested in is not computable by the algorithm from [9].

Definition 5. *An assumption Ψ is called* adequately permissive *(an APA for short) for (G, Φ) if it is sufficient, implementable and permissive.*

4   Computing Adequately Permissive Assumptions (APA)

In this section, we present our algorithm to compute *adequately permissive assumptions* (APA for short) for *parity games*, which are canonical representations of ω-regular games. For a gradual exposition of the topic, we first present algorithms for simpler winning conditions, namely safety (Sec. 4.2), Büchi (Sec. 4.3), and Co-Büchi (Sec. 4.4), which are used as building blocks while presenting the algorithm for parity games (Sec. 4.5). All proofs omitted can be found in the full version [2]. Let us first introduce some preliminaries.

4.1 Preliminaries

We use symbolic fixpoint algorithms expressed in the μ-calculus [17] to compute the winning regions and to generate assumptions in simple post-processing steps.

Set Transformers. Let $G = (V = V^0 \uplus V^1, E)$ be a game graph, $U \subseteq V$ be a subset of vertices, and $a \in \{0, 1\}$ be the player index. Then we define two types of predecessor operators:

$$\mathsf{pre}_G(U) = \{v \in V \mid \exists u \in U. \ (v, u) \in E\} \tag{1}$$

$$\mathsf{cpre}_G^a(U) = \{v \in V^a \mid v \in \mathsf{pre}_G(U)\} \cup \{v \in V^{1-a} \mid \forall (v, u) \in E. \ u \in U\} \tag{2}$$

$$\mathsf{cpre}_G^{a,1}(U) = \mathsf{cpre}_G^a(U) \cup U \tag{3}$$

$$\mathsf{cpre}_G^{a,i}(U) = \mathsf{cpre}_G^a(\mathsf{cpre}_G^{a,i-1}(U)) \cup \mathsf{cpre}_G^{a,i-1}(U) \text{ with } i \geq 1 \tag{4}$$

The predecessor operator $\mathsf{pre}_G(U)$ computes the set of vertices with at least one successor in U. The controllable predecessor operators $\mathsf{cpre}_G^a(U)$ and $\mathsf{cpre}_G^{a,i}(U)$ compute the set of vertices from which *Player a* can force visiting U in *at most one* and i steps respectively. In the following, we introduce the attractor operator $\mathsf{attr}_G^a(U)$ that computes the set of vertices from which *Player a* can force at least a single visit to U in *finitely many but nonzero*[3] steps:

$$\mathsf{attr}_G^a(U) = \left(\bigcup_{i \geq 1} \mathsf{cpre}^{a,i}(U)\right) \backslash U \tag{5}$$

When clear from the context, we drop the subscript G from these operators.

Fixpoint Algorithms in the μ-calculus. μ-calculus [17] offers a succinct representation of symbolic algorithms (i.e., algorithms manipulating sets of vertices instead of individual vertices) over a game graph G. The formulas of the μ-calculus, interpreted over a 2-player game graph G, are given by the grammar

$$\phi := p \mid X \mid \phi \cup \phi \mid \phi \cap \phi \mid pre(\phi) \mid \mu X.\phi \mid \nu X.\phi$$

where p ranges over subsets of V, X ranges over a set of formal variables, *pre* ranges over monotone set transformers in $\{\mathsf{pre}, \mathsf{cpre}^a, \mathsf{attr}^a\}$, and μ and ν denote, respectively, the least and the greatest fixed point of the functional defined as $X \mapsto \phi(X)$. Since the operations $\cup, \cap$, and the set transformers *pre* are all monotonic, the fixed points are guaranteed to exist, due to the Knaster-Tarski Theorem [5]. We omit the (standard) semantics of formulas (see [17]).

A μ-calculus formula evaluates to a set of vertices over G, and the set can be computed by induction over the structure of the formula, where the fixed points are evaluated by iteration. The reader may note that pre, cpre and attr can be computed in time polynomial in number of vertices.

---

[3] In existing literature, usually $U \subseteq \mathsf{attr}^a(U)$, i.e., $\mathsf{attr}^a(U)$ contains vertices from which U is visited in zero steps. We exclude U from $\mathsf{attr}^a(U)$ for a technical reason.

4.2 Safety Games

A safety game is a game $\mathcal{G} = (G, \Phi)$ with $\Phi := \Box U$ for some $U \subseteq V$, and a play fulfills Φ if it never leaves U. APAs for safety games disallow every *Player 1* move that leaves the cooperative winning region in G w.r.t. *Safety(U)*. This is formalized in the following theorem.

Theorem 1. *Let* $\mathcal{G} = (G = (V, E), \Box U)$ *be a safety game,* $Z^* = \nu Y.U \cap \mathsf{pre}(Y)$, *and* $S = \{(u, v) \in E \mid (u \in V^1 \cap Z^*) \wedge (v \notin Z^*)\}$. *Then* $Z^* = \langle\!\langle 0, 1 \rangle\!\rangle \Box U$ *and* [4]

$$\Psi_{\text{UNSAFE}}(S) := \Box \bigwedge\nolimits_{e \in S} \neg e, \tag{6}$$

is an APA for the game $\mathcal{G}$. *We denote by* $\text{UNSAFEA}(G, U)$ *the algorithm computing* S *as above, which runs in time* $\mathcal{O}(n^2)$, *where* $n = |V|$.

We call the LTL formula in (6) a *safety template* and assumptions that solely use this template *safety assumptions*.

4.3 Live Group Assumptions for Büchi Games

Büchi games. A Büchi game is a game $\mathcal{G} = (G, \Phi)$ where $\Phi = \Box \Diamond U$ for some $U \subseteq V$. Intuitively, a play is winning for a Büchi game if it visits the vertex set U infinitely often. We first recall that the cooperative winning region $\langle\!\langle 0, 1 \rangle\!\rangle \Box \Diamond U$ can be computed by a two-nested symbolic fixpoint algorithm [10]

$$\text{BÜCHI}(G, U) := \nu Y.\mu X. \ (U \cap \mathsf{pre}(Y)) \cup (\mathsf{pre}(X)). \tag{7}$$

Live group templates. Given the standard algorithm in (7), the set X^i computed in the i-th iteration of the fixpoint variable X in the last iteration of Y actually carries a lot of information to construct a very useful assumption for the Büchi game $\mathcal{G}$. To see this, recall that X^i contains all vertices which have an edge to vertices which can reach U in at most $i - 1$ steps [10, sec. 3.2]. Hence, for all *Player 1* vertices in $X^i \setminus X^{i-1}$ we need to assume that *Player 1* always eventually makes progress towards U by moving to X^i. This can be formalized by a so called live group template.

Definition 6. *Let* $G = (V, E)$ *be a game graph. Then a live group* $H = \{e_j\}_{j \geq 0}$ *is a set of edges* $e_j = (s_j, t_j)$ *with source vertices* $src(H) := \{s_j\}_{j \geq 0}$. *Given a set of live groups* $H^\ell = \{H_i\}_{i \geq 0}$ *we define a live group template as*

$$\Psi_{\text{LIVE}}(H^\ell) := \bigwedge_{i \geq 0} \Box \Diamond src(H_i) \implies \Box \Diamond H_i. \tag{8}$$

---

[4] We use $e = (u, v)$ in LTL formulas as a syntactic sugar for $u \wedge \bigcirc v$, where $\bigcirc$ is the LTL *next* operator. A set of edges $E' = \{e_i\}_{i \in [0;k]}$, when used as atomic proposition, is a syntactic sugar for $\bigvee_{i \in [0;k]} e_i$.

The live group template says that if some vertex from the source of a live group is visited infinitely often, then some edge from this group should be taken infinitely often. We will use this template to give the assumptions for Büchi games.

Remark 1. Note that the assumptions computed by Chatterjee et al. [8] uses *live edges*, i.e., singleton live groups, and hence, they are less expressive. In particular, there are instances of Büchi games, where the permissive assumptions can not be expressed using live edges but they can be using live groups, e.g., in Fig. 1 (c) the live edge assumption $\Box\Diamond e_1 \wedge \Box\Diamond e_2$ is sufficient but not permissive, whereas the live group assumption $\Box\Diamond src(H) \implies \Box\Diamond H$ with $H = \{e_1, e_2\}$ is an APA.

In the context of the fixpoint computation of (7), we can construct live groups $H^\ell = \{H_i\}_{i\geq 0}$ where each H_i contains all edges of *Player* 1 which originate in $X^i \setminus X^{i-1}$ and end in X^{i-1}. Then the live group assumption in (8) precisely captures the intuition that, in order to visit U infinitely often, *Player* 1 should take edges in H_i infinitely often if vertices in $src(H_i)$ are seen infinitely often. Unfortunately, it turns out that this live group assumption is not *permissive*. The reason is that it restricts *Player* 1 also on those vertices from which she will anyway go towards U. For example, consider the game in Fig. 2 (right). Here defining live groups through computations of (10), will mark e_1 as a live group, but then $(v_2 v_1 v_0)^\omega$ will be in $\mathcal{L}(\Phi)$ but not in the language of the assumption. Here the permissive assumption would be $\Psi = \text{TRUE}$.

Accelerated fixpoint computation. In order to provide permissiveness, we use a slightly modified fixpoint algorithm that computes the same set Z^* but allows us to extract *permissive* assumptions directly from the fixpoint computations. Towards this goal, we introduce the *together predecessor operator*.

$$\text{tpre}_G(U) = \text{attr}_G^0(U) \cup \text{cpre}_G^1(\text{attr}_G^0(U) \cup U). \tag{9}$$

Intuitively, tpre adds all vertices from which *Player* 0 does not need any cooperation to reach U in every iteration of the fixpoint computation. The interesting observation we make is that substituting the inner pre operator in (7) by tpre does not change the computed set but only accelerates the computation. This is formalized in the next proposition and visualized in Fig. 3.

Proposition 1. *Let* $\mathcal{G} = (G, \Box\Diamond U)$ *be a Büchi game and*

$$\text{TB\"{u}chi}(G, U) = \nu Y.\mu X. (U \cap pre(Y)) \cup (tpre(X)). \tag{10}$$

Then $\text{TB\"{u}chi}(G, U) = \text{B\"{u}chi}(G, U) = \langle\!\langle 0, 1\rangle\!\rangle \Box\Diamond U.$

Prop. 1 follows from the correctness proof of (7) by using the observation that for all $U \subseteq V$ we have $\mu X. U \cup pre(X) = \mu X. U \cup \text{tpre}(X)$.

Computing live group assumptions. Intuitively, the operator tpre_G computes the union of (i) the set of vertices from which *Player* 0 can reach U in a finite number of steps with no cooperation from *Player* 1 and (ii) the set of *Player* 1 vertices from which *Player* 0 can reach U with at most *one-time* cooperation from *Player* 1. Looking at Fig. 3, case (i) is indicated by the dotted line,

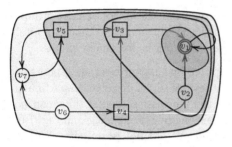 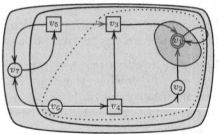

Fig. 3: Computation of $\mu X.\; U \cup \mathsf{pre}(X)$ (left) and $\mu X.\; U \cup \mathsf{tpre}(X)$ (right). Each colored region describes one iteration over X. The dotted region on the right is added by the attr part of tpre, and this allows only the vertex v_5 to be in $front(\{v_1\})$. Each set of the same colored edges defines a live transition group.

while case (ii) corresponds to the last added *Player* 1 vertex (e.g., v_5). Hence, we need to capture the cooperation needed by *Player* 1 only from the vertices added last, which we call the *frontier* of U in G and are formalized as follows:

$$front(U) := \mathsf{tpre}_G(U) \setminus \mathsf{attr}^0_G(U). \tag{11}$$

It is easy to see that, indeed $front(U) \subseteq V^1$, as whenever $v \in front(U) \cap V^0$, then it would have been the case that $v \in \mathsf{attr}^0_G(U)$ via (10).

Defining live groups based on frontiers instead of all elements in X^i indeed yields the desired permissive assumption for Büchi games. By observing that we additionally need to ensure that *Player* 1 never leaves the cooperative winning region by a simple safety assumption, we get the following result, which is the main contribution of this section.

Theorem 2. *Let* $\mathcal{G} = (G = (V, E), \Phi = \Box\Diamond U)$ *be a Büchi game with* $Z^* = \mathrm{TB\ddot{u}CHI}(G, U)$ *and* $H^\ell = \{H_i\}_{i \geq 0}$ *s.t.*

$$\emptyset \neq H_i := (front(X^i) \times (X^{i+1} \setminus front(X^i))) \cap E, \tag{12}$$

where X^i *is the set computed in the* i-*th iteration of the computation over* X *and in the last iteration of the computation over* Y *in* $\mathrm{TB\ddot{u}CHI}$. *Then* $\Psi = \Psi_{\mathrm{UNSAFE}}(S) \wedge \Psi_{\mathrm{LIVE}}(H^\ell)$ *is an APA for* $\mathcal{G}$, *where* $S = \mathrm{UNSAFEA}(G, U)$. *We write* $\mathrm{LIVEA}(G, U)$ *to denote the algorithm to construct live groups* H^ℓ *as above, which runs in time* $\mathcal{O}(n^3)$, *where* $n = |V|$.

In fact, there is a faster algorithm for computation of APAs for Büchi games, that runs in time linear in the size of the graph, which we present in the full version [2]. We chose to present the μ-calculus based algorithm here, because it provides more insights into the nature of live groups.

4.4 Co-Liveness Assumptions in Co-Büchi Games

A co-Büchi game is the *dual* of a Büchi game, where a winning play should visit a designated set of vertices only finitely many times. Formally, a co-Büchi game is a tuple $\mathcal{G} = (G, \Phi)$ where $\Phi = \Diamond\Box U$ for some $U \subseteq V$. The standard symbolic algorithm to compute the cooperative winning region is as follows:

$$\text{CoBüchi}(G, U) := \mu X.\nu Y. \ (U \cap \text{pre}(Y)) \cup (\text{pre}(X)). \tag{13}$$

As before, the sets X^i obtained in the i-th computation of X during the evaluation of (13) carry essential information for constructing assumptions. Intuitively, X^1 gives precisely the set of vertices from which the play can stay in U with *Player* 1's cooperation and we would like an assumption to capture the fact that we do not want *Player* 1 to go further away from X^1 infinitely often. This observation is naturally described by so called co-liveness templates.

Definition 7. *Let $G = (V, E)$ be a game graph and $D \subseteq V \times V$ a set of edges. Then a* co-liveness template *over G w.r.t. D is defined by the LTL formula*

$$\Psi_{\text{COLIVE}}(D) := \Diamond\Box \bigwedge_{e \in D} \neg e. \tag{14}$$

The assumptions employing co-liveness templates will be called co-liveness assumptions. With this, we can state the main result of this section.

Theorem 3. *Let $\mathcal{G} = (G = (V, E), \Diamond\Box U)$, $Z^* = \text{CoBüchi}(G, U)$ and*

$$D = \big(\ [(X^1 \cap V^1) \times (Z^* \setminus X^1)] \ \cup [\bigcup_{i>1}(X^i \cap V^1) \times (Z^* \setminus X^{i-1})]\big) \cap E, \tag{15}$$

where X^i is the set computed in the i-th iteration of fixpoint variable X in CoBüchi. *Then $\Psi = \Psi_{\text{UNSAFE}}(S) \wedge \Psi_{\text{COLIVE}}(D)$ is an APA for $\mathcal{G}$, where $S = $* UnsafeA$(G, U)$. *We write* CoLiveA$(G, U)$ *to denote the algorithm constructing co-live edges D as above which runs in time $\mathcal{O}(n^3)$, where $n = |V|$.*

We observe that X_1 is a subset of U such that if a play reaches X^1, *Player* 0 and *Player* 1 can cooperatively keep the play in X^1. To do so, we ensure via the definition of D in (15) that *Player* 1 can only leave X^1 finitely often. Moreover, with the other co-live edges in D, we ensure that *Player* 1 can only go away from X^1 finitely often, and hence if *Player* 0 plays their strategy to reach X^1 and then stay there, the play will be winning. The permissiveness of the assumption comes from the observation that if co-liveness is violated, then *Player* 1 takes a co-live edge infinitely often, and hence leaves X^1 infinitely often, implying leaving U infinitely often.

We again present a faster algorithm that runs in time linear in size of the graph for computation of APAs for co-Büchi games in the full version [2].

4.5   APA Assumptions for Parity Games

Parity games. Let $G = (V, E)$ be a game graph, and $C = \{C_0, \ldots, C_k\}$ be a set of subsets of vertices which form a partition of V. Then the game $\mathcal{G} = (G, \Phi)$ is called a *parity game* if

$$\Phi = Parity(C) := \bigvee_{i \in \text{odd}[0;k]} \Box\Diamond C_i \implies \bigvee_{j \in \text{even}[i+1;k]} \Box\Diamond C_j. \tag{16}$$

The set C is called the *priority set* and a vertex v in the set C_i, for $i \in [1; k]$, is said to have *priority* i. An infinite play ρ is winning for $\Phi = Parity(C)$ if the highest priority appearing infinitely often along ρ is even.

Conditional live group templates. As seen in the previous sections, for games with simple winning conditions which require visiting a fixed set of edges infinitely or only finitely often, a single assumption (conjoined with a simple safety assumption) suffices to characterize APAs, as there is just one way to win. However, in general parity games, there are usually multiple ways of winning: for example, in parity games with priorities $\{0, 1, 2\}$, a play will be winning if either (i) it only infinitely often sees vertices of priority 0, or (ii) it sees priority 1 infinitely often but also sees priority 2 infinitely often. Intuitively, winning option (i) requires the use of co-liveness assumptions as in Sec. 4.4. However, winning option (ii) actually requires the live group assumptions discussed in Sec. 4.3 to be *conditional* on whether certain states with priority 1 have actually been visited infinitely often. This is formalized by generalizing live group templates to *conditional live group templates*.

Definition 8. *Let $G = (V, E)$ be a game graph. Then a* conditional live group *over G is a pair (R, H^ℓ), where $R \subseteq V$ and H^ℓ is a live group. Given a set of conditional live groups $\mathcal{H}^\ell$, a* conditional live group template *is the LTL formula*

$$\Psi_{\text{COND}}(\mathcal{H}^\ell) := \bigwedge_{(R, H^\ell) \in \mathcal{H}^\ell} \left(\Box \Diamond R \implies \Psi_{\text{LIVE}}(H^\ell) \right). \tag{17}$$

Again, the assumptions employing conditional live group templates will be called conditional live group assumptions. With the generalization of live group assumptions to *conditional* live group assumptions, we actually have all the ingredients to define an APA for parity games as a conjunction

$$\Psi = \Psi_{\text{UNSAFE}}(S) \wedge \Psi_{\text{COLIVE}}(D) \wedge \Psi_{\text{COND}}(\mathcal{H}^\ell) \tag{18}$$

of a safety, a co-liveness, and a conditional live group assumptions. Intuitively, we use (i) a safety assumption to prevent *Player* 1 to leave the cooperative winning region, (ii) a co-live assumption for each winning option that requires seeing a particular *odd* priority only finitely often, and (iii) a conditional live group assumption for each winning option that requires seeing an *even* priority infinitely often if certain *odd* priority have been seen infinitely often. The remainder of this section gives an algorithm (Alg. 1) to compute the actual safety, co-live and conditional live group sets S, D and $\mathcal{H}^\ell$, respectively, and proves that the resulting assumption Ψ (as in (18)) is actually an APA for the parity game $\mathcal{G}$.

Computing APAs. The computation of unsafe, co-live, and conditional live group sets S, D, and $\mathcal{H}^\ell$ to make Ψ in (18) an APA is formalized in Alg. 1. Alg. 1 utilizes the standard fixpoint algorithm $\text{PARITY}(G, C)$ [12] to compute the cooperative winning region for a parity game $\mathcal{G}$, defined as

$$\text{PARITY}(G, C) := \tau X_d \cdots \nu X_2 \, \mu X_1 \, \nu X_0. \bigcup_{i \in [0; d]} (C_i \cap \text{pre}(X_i)), \tag{19}$$

where τ is ν if d is even, and μ otherwise. In addition, Alg. 1 involves the algorithms UNSAFEA (Thm. 1), LIVEA (Thm. 2), and COLIVEA (Thm. 3) to

Algorithm 1 PARITYASSUMPTION

Input: $G = (V, E)$, $C : V \rightarrow \{0, 1, \ldots\}$
Output: Ψ
1: $Z^* \leftarrow$ PARITY(G, C)
2: $S \leftarrow$ UNSAFEA(G, Z^*)
3: $G \leftarrow G|_{Z^*}$, $C \leftarrow C|_{Z^*}$
4: $(D, \mathcal{H}^\ell) \leftarrow$ COMPUTESETS$((G, C), \emptyset, \emptyset)$
5: **return** $S, D, \mathcal{H}^\ell$

6: **procedure** COMPUTESETS$((G, C), D, \mathcal{H}^\ell)$
7:     $d \leftarrow \max\{i \mid C_i \neq \emptyset\}$
8:     **if** d is odd **then**
9:         $W_{\neg d} \leftarrow$ PARITY$(G|_{V \setminus C_d}, C)$
10:        $D \leftarrow D \cup$ COLIVEA$(G, W_{\neg d})$
11:     **else**
12:        $W_d \leftarrow$ BÜCHI(G, C_d), $W_{\neg d} \leftarrow V \setminus W_d$
13:        **for all** odd $i \in [0; d]$ **do**
14:           $\mathcal{H}^\ell \leftarrow \mathcal{H}^\ell \cup (W_d \cap C_i,$ LIVEA$(G|_{W_d}, C_{i+1} \cup C_{i+3} \cdots \cup C_d))$
15:     **if** $d > 0$ **then**
16:        $G \leftarrow G|_{W_{\neg d}}$, $C_0 \leftarrow C_0 \cup C_d$, $C_d \leftarrow \emptyset$
17:        COMPUTESETS$((G, C), D, \mathcal{H}^\ell)$
18:     **else**
19:        **return** $(D, \mathcal{H}^\ell)$

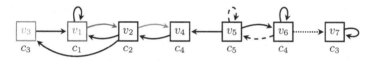

Fig. 4: A parity game, where a vertex with priority i has label c_i. The dotted edges are the unsafe edges, the dashed edges are the co-live edges, and every similarly colored vertex-edge pair forms a conditional live group.

compute safety, live group, and co-liveness assumptions in an iterative manner. In addition, $G|_U := (U, U^0, U^1, E')$ s.t. $U^0 := V^0 \cap U$, $U^1 := V^1 \cap U$, and $E' := E \cap (U \times U)$ denotes the restriction of a game graph $G := (V, V^0, V^1, E)$ to a subset of its vertices $U \subseteq V$. Further, $C|_U$ denotes the restriction of the priority set C from V to $U \subseteq V$.

We illustrate the steps of Alg. 1 by an example depicted in Fig. 4. In line 1, we compute the cooperative winning region Z^* of the entire game, to find that the parity condition cannot be satisfied from vertex v_7 even with cooperation, i.e., $Z^* = \{v_1, \ldots, v_6\}$. So we put the edge (v_6, v_7) in a safety template, restrict the game to $G = G|_{Z^*}$ and run COMPUTESETS on the new restricted game.

In the new game G the highest priority is odd ($d = 5$), hence we execute lines 9-10. Now a play would be winning only if eventually the play does not see v_5 any more. Hence, in step 9, we find the region $W_{\neg 5} = \{v_1, \ldots, v_4, v_6\}$ of the restricted graph $G|_{V \setminus C_5}$ (only containing nodes v_i with priority $C(v_i) < 5$) from where we can satisfy the parity condition without seeing v_5. We then make sure that we do not leave $W_{\neg 5}$ to visit v_5 in the game G infinitely often by executing COLIVEA$(G, W_{\neg 5})$ in line 10, making the edges (v_5, v_5) and (v_6, v_5) co-live.

Once we restrict a play from visiting v_5 infinitely often, we only need to focus on satisfying parity without visiting v_5 within $W_{\neg 5}$. This observation allows us to further restrict our computation to the game $\mathcal{G} = \mathcal{G}|_{W_{\neg 5}}$ in line 16, where we also update the priorities to only range from 0 to 4. In our example this step does not change anything. We then re-execute COMPUTESETS on this game.

In the restricted graph, the highest priority is 4 which is even, hence we execute lines 12-14. One way of winning in this game is to visit C_4 infinitely often, so we compute the respective cooperative winning region W_4 in line 12. In our example we have $W_4 = W_{\neg 5} = \{v_1, \ldots, v_4, v_6\}$. Now, to ensure that from the vertices from which we can cooperatively see 4, we actually win, we have to make sure that every time a lower odd priority vertex is visited infinitely often, a higher priority is also visited. This can be ensured by conditional live group fairness as computed in line 14. For every odd priority $i < 4$, (i.e, for $i = 1$ and $i = 3$) we have to make sure that either 2 or 4 (if $i = 1$) or 4 (if $i = 3$) is visited infinitely often. The resulting live groups $\mathcal{H}_i^{\ell} = (R_i, H_i^{\ell})$ collect all vertices in W_4 with priority i in R_i and all live groups allowing to see even priorities j with $i < j \leq 4$ in H_i^{ℓ}, where the latter is computed using the fixed-point algorithm LIVEA to compute live groups. The resulting live groups for $i = 1$ (blue) and $i = 3$ (red) are depicted in Fig. 4 and given by $(\{v_1\}, \{(v_1, v_2)\})$ and $(\{v_3\}, \{(v_2, v_4)\}, \{(v_1, v_2)\})$, respectively.

At this point we have $W_{\neg 4} = \emptyset$, making the game graph computed in line 16 empty, and the algorithm eventually terminates after iteratively removing all priorities from C by running COMPUTESETS (without any computations, as $\mathcal{G}$ is empty) for priorities 3, 2 and 1. In a different game graph, the reasoning done for priorities 5 and 4 above can be repeated for lower priorities if there are other parts of the game graph not contained in W_4, from where the game can be won by seeing priority 2 infinitely often. The main insight into the correctness of the outlined algorithm is that all computed assumptions can be conjoined to obtain an APA for the original parity game.

With Alg. 1 in place, we now state the main result of the entire paper.

Theorem 4. *Let $\mathcal{G} = (G, Parity(C))$ be a parity game such that $(S, D, \mathcal{H}^{\ell}) = $ PARITYASSUMPTION(G, C). Then $\Psi = \Psi_{\text{UNSAFE}}(S) \wedge \Psi_{\text{COLIVE}}(D) \wedge \Psi_{\text{COND}}(\mathcal{H}^{\ell})$ is an APA for $\mathcal{G}$. Moreover, Alg. 1 terminates in time $\mathcal{O}(n^4)$, where $n = |V|$.*

5   Experimental Evaluation

We have developed a C++-based prototype tool SIMPA[5] computing **S**ufficient, **I**mplementable and **P**ermissive **A**ssumptions for Büchi, co-Büchi, and parity games. We first compare SIMPA against the closest related tool GIST [9] in Sec. 5.1. We then show that SIMPA gives small and meaningful assumptions for the well-known 2-client arbiter synthesis problem from [21] in Sec. 5.2.

---

[5] Repository URL: https://gitlab.mpi-sws.org/kmallik/simpa

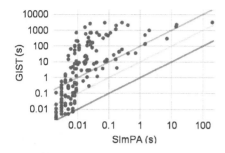

	SIMPA	GIST
Mean-time	64.8s	1079.0s
Non-timeout mean-time	64.8s	209.2s
Timeouts (1hr)	0(0%)	59(26%)
No assumption generated	0(0%)	20(9%)
Faster	230(100%)	0(0%)

Fig. 5: Running times of SIMPA vs GIST (in seconds, log-scale)

Table 1: Summary of the experimental results

5.1 Performance Evaluation

We compare the effectiveness of our tool against a re-implementation of GIST [9], which is not available anymore [6]. GIST originally computes assumptions only enabling a particular initial vertex to become winning for *Player* 0. However, for the experiments, we run GIST until one of the cooperatively winning vertices is not winning anymore. Since GIST starts with a maximal assumption and shrinks it until a fixed initial vertex is not winning anymore, our modification makes GIST faster as the modified termination condition is satisfied earlier. Owing to the non-dependence of our tool and dependence of GIST on a fixed vertex, this modification allows a fair comparison.

We compared the performance and the quality of the assumptions computed by SIMPA and GIST on a set of parity games collected from the SYNTCOMP benchmark suite [1], with a timeout of one hour per game. All the experiments were performed on a computer equipped with Intel(R) Core(TM) i5-10600T CPU @ 2.40GHz and 32 GiB RAM.

We provide all details of the experimental results in the full version [2] and summarize them in Table 1. In addition, Fig. 5 shows a scatter plot, where every instance of the benchmarks is depicted as a point, where the X and the Y coordinates represent the running time for SIMPA and GIST (in seconds), respectively. We see that SIMPA is computationally much faster than GIST in every instance (all dots lie above the lower red line) – most times by one (above the middle green line) and many times even by two (above the upper orange line) orders of magnitude.

Moreover, in some experiments, GIST fails to compute a sufficient assumption (in the sense of Def. 2), whereas SIMPA successfully computes an APA (see the row labeled 'no assumption generated' in Table 1). This is not surprising, as the class of assumptions used by GIST are only unsafe edges and live edges (i.e., singleton live groups) which are not expressive enough to provide sufficient assumptions for all parity games (see Fig. 1(b) for a simple example where there is no sufficient assumption that can be expressed using live edges). Furthermore,

---

[6] The link provided in the paper is broken, and the authors informed us that the implementation is not available.

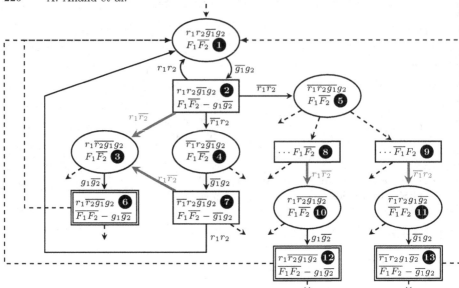

Fig. 6: Illustration of a relevant part of the game graph for the 2-client arbiter. Rectangles and circles represent *Player* 1 and *Player* 0 vertices, respectively. The labels of the *Player* 0 states indicate the current status of the request and grant bits, and in addition, remember if a request is currently *pending* using the atomic propositions F_1, F_2. The double-lined vertices are Büchi vertices, i.e., ones with no pending requests.

we note that in all cases where the assumptions computed by GIST are actually APAs, SIMPA computes the same assumptions orders of magnitudes faster.

5.2   2-Client Arbiter Example

We consider the 2-client arbiter example from the work by Piterman et al. [21], where clients $i \in \{1, 2\}$ (*Player* 1) can request or free a shared resource by setting the input variables r_i to true or false, and the arbiter (*Player* 0) can set the output variables g_i to true or false to grant or withdraw the shared resource to/from client i. The game graph for this example is implicitly given as part of the specification (as this is a GR(1) synthesis problem [21]). The goal of the arbiter is to ensure that always eventually the requests are granted. This can be depicted by a Büchi game, part of which is presented in Fig. 6. It is known that *Player* 0 can not win the game without constraining moves of *Player* 1.

Running SIMPA (took 0.01s) on this example yields two live groups (edges of one live group are indicated by thick red arrows in Fig. 6) that ensures that the play eventually moves to vertices where the *Player* 0 can force a visit to a Büchi vertex. These assumptions are similar to the ones used to restrict the clients' behavior in [21], but are more permissive. Furthermore, running GIST (took 6.44s) yields several live edges (e.g., **2**–**3**, **7**–**1**), which again is less permissive than ours. It turns out that an APA for this example will unavoidably require live groups — singleton live edges, as computed by GIST, will not suffice. For a detailed discussion, we refer the reader to the full version [2].

References

1. The reactive synthesis competition. http://www.syntcomp.org
2. Anand, A., Mallik, K., Nayak, S.P., Schmuck, A.K.: Computing adequately permissive assumptions for synthesis (2023), https://arxiv.org/abs/2301.07563
3. Baier, C., Katoen, J.P.: Principles of model checking. MIT press (2008)
4. Brenguier, R., Raskin, J.F., Sankur, O.: Assume-admissible synthesis. Acta Informatica (2017)
5. Bronisław Knaster, A.T.: Un théorème sur les fonctions d'ensembles. Annales de la Société polonaise de mathématique **6** (1928)
6. Cavezza, D.G., Alrajeh, D., György, A.: Minimal assumptions refinement for realizable specifications. In: Formal Methods in Software Engineering (2020)
7. Chatterjee, K., Henzinger, T.A.: Assume-guarantee synthesis. In: TACAS (2007)
8. Chatterjee, K., Henzinger, T.A., Jobstmann, B.: Environment assumptions for synthesis. In: CONCUR (2008)
9. Chatterjee, K., Henzinger, T.A., Jobstmann, B., Radhakrishna, A.: Gist: A solver for probabilistic games. In: CAV (2010)
10. Chatterjee, K., Henzinger, T.A., Piterman, N.: Algorithms for büchi games (2008), https://arxiv.org/abs/0805.2620
11. Chatterjee, K., Horn, F., Löding, C.: Obliging games. In: International Conference on Concurrency Theory. pp. 284–296. Springer (2010)
12. Emerson, E., Jutla, C.: Tree automata, μ-calculus and determinacy. In: FOCS (1991)
13. Finkbeiner, B., Metzger, N., Moses, Y.: Information flow guided synthesis. In: Proceedings of 34th International Conference on Computer Aided Verification (CAV 22) (2022)
14. Fisman, D., Kupferman, O., Lustig, Y.: Rational synthesis. In: TACAS (2010)
15. Gaaloul, K., Menghi, C., Nejati, S., Briand, L., Parache, Y.I.: Combining genetic programming and model checking to generate environment assumptions. TSE (2021)
16. Gaaloul, K., Menghi, C., Nejati, S., Briand, L.C., Wolfe, D.: Mining assumptions for software components using machine learning. In: ESEC/FSE (2020)
17. Kozen, D.: Results on the propositional μ-calculus. In: ICALP. Springer (1982)
18. Majumdar, R., Mallik, K., Schmuck, A.K., Zufferey, D.: Assume–guarantee distributed synthesis. IEEE TCAD (2020)
19. Majumdar, R., Piterman, N., Schmuck, A.K.: Environmentally-friendly gr (1) synthesis. In: International Conference on Tools and Algorithms for the Construction and Analysis of Systems. pp. 229–246. Springer (2019)
20. Maoz, S., Ringert, J.O., Shalom, R.: Symbolic repairs for GR(1) specifications. In: ICSE (2019)
21. Piterman, N., Pnueli, A., Sa'ar, Y.: Synthesis of reactive(1) designs. In: Proceedings of the 7th International Conference on Verification, Model Checking, and Abstract Interpretation. p. 364-380. VMCAI'06, Springer-Verlag, Berlin, Heidelberg (2006)
22. Schmelter, D., Greenyer, J., Holtmann, J.: Toward learning realizable scenario-based, formal requirements specifications. In: REW (2017)

Verification-guided Programmatic Controller Synthesis

Yuning Wang and He Zhu$^{(\boxtimes)}$

Rutgers University, New Brunswick NJ, USA
{yw895,hz375}@cs.rutgers.edu

Abstract. We present a verification-based learning framework VEL that synthesizes safe programmatic controllers for environments with continuous state and action spaces. The key idea is the integration of program reasoning techniques into controller training loops. VEL performs abstraction-based program verification to reason about a programmatic controller and its environment as a closed-loop system. Based on a novel verification-guided synthesis loop for training, VEL minimizes the amount of safety violation in the proof space of the system, which approximates the *worst-case* safety loss, using gradient-descent style optimization. Experimental results demonstrate the substantial benefits of leveraging verification feedback for synthesizing provably correct controllers.

1 Introduction

Controller search is commonly used to govern cyber-physical systems such as autonomous vehicles, where high assurance is particularly important. Reinforcement Learning (RL) of neural network controllers is a promising approach for controller search [19]. State-of-the-art RL algorithms can learn motor skills autonomously through trial and error in simulated or even unknown environments, thus avoiding tedious manual engineering. However, well-trained neural network controllers may still be unsafe since the RL algorithms do not provide any formal guarantees on safety. A learned controller may fail occasionally but catastrophically, and debugging these failures can be challenging [46].

Guaranteeing the correctness of an RL controller is therefore important. Principally, given an environment model, the correctness of a controller can be verified by reachability analysis over a closed-loop system that combines the environment model and the controller. Indeed, the use of formal verification techniques to aid the design of reliable learning-enabled autonomous systems has risen rapidly over the last few years [43,28,41,18,17]. A natural extended question is that in case verification fails, can we exploit verification feedback in the form of counterexamples to synthesize a verifiably correct controller? This turns out to be a very challenging task due to the following reasons.

Verification Scalability. A counterexample-guided controller synthesizer has to *iteratively* conduct reachability analysis and controller optimization as each

S. Sankaranarayanan and N. Sharygina (Eds.): TACAS 2023, LNCS 13994, pp. 229–250, 2023.
https://doi.org/10.1007/978-3-031-30820-8_16

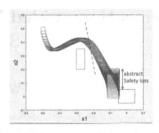

if $28.33x_1 + 4.23x_2 + 4.16 \geq 0$
then $6.79x_1 - 8.56x_2 + 0.35$
else $11.01x_1 - 13.50x_2 + 8.71$

(a) Oscillator Programmatic Controller   (b) Oscillator Reachability Analysis

Fig. 1: An oscillator programmatic controller and its reachability analysis. In Fig. 1b, the red region represents the oscillator unsafe set $(-03, -0.25) \times (0.2, 0.35)$, and the blue region depicts the target set $[-0.05, 0.05] \times [-0.05, 0.05]$. The initial state set of oscillator is $[-0.51, -0.49] \times [0.49, 0.51]$.

iteration may discover a new counterexample. However, repeatedly calculating the reachable set of a nonlinear system controlled by a neural network controller over a long horizon is computationally challenging. For example, consider designing a controller for the Van der Pol's oscillator system [49]. The oscillator is a 2-dimensional non-linear system whose state transition can be expressed by the following ordinary differential equations:

$$\dot{x}_1 = x_2 \qquad \dot{x}_2 = (1 - x_1^2)x_2 - x_1 + u \qquad (1)$$

where (x_1, x_2) is the system state variables and u is the control action variable. A feedback controller $\pi(x_1, x_2)$ measures the current system state and then manipulates the control input u as needed to drive the system toward its target. The initial set of the control system is $(x_1, x_2) \in [-0.51, -0.49] \times [0.49, 0.51]$. As depicted in Fig. 1b, the controlled system is expected to reach the target region in blue while avoiding the obstacle region in red within 120 timesteps (i.e. control steps). In our experience, even for this simple example, using Verisig [28] and ReachNN* [18] (two state-of-the-art verification tools for neural network controlled systems) to calculate the reachable set of a simple 2-layer neural network feedback controller $\pi_{NN}(x_1, x_2)$ costs more than 100s each. It is even more a costly process to repeatedly conduct reachability analysis of a complex neural network controller in a counterexample-guided learning loop.

Recently, programmatic controllers emerge as a promising solution to address the lack of interpretability problem in deep reinforcement learning [47,27,44,38] by training controllers as *programs*. A programmatic controller to control the oscillator environment learned by a programmatic reinforcement learning algorithm [38] is depicted in Fig. 1a. We depict the decision boundary of the program's conditional statement ($28.33x_1 + 4.23x_2 + 4.16 = 0$) in solid dash in Fig. 1b. The program can be interpreted as a decomposition of the reach-avoid learning problem into two sub-problems — the linear controller in the *else* branch first pushes the system away from the obstacle and next the linear controller in the *then* branch takes over to make the system reach the target. As we show in this paper, the compact and structured representation of a programmatic controller lends itself amenable to off-the-shelf hybrid or continuous system reachability tools e.g. [10,20]. Compared with verifying a deep neural network controller, reasoning about a programmatic controller is more feasible. However, the question remains when verification fails – rather than retraining a new controller, how can we leverage verification feedback to construct a verifiably correct controller?

Proof Space Optimization. The other main challenge of verification-guided controller synthesis is that when verification fails, the counterexample path may provide little help or even be spurious due to estimated approximation errors. This is because reachability analyses typically overapproximate the true reachable sets using a computationally convenient representation such as polytopes [20] or Taylor models [10]. This overapproximation leads to quick error accumulation over time, known as the wrapping effect. Even a well-trained controller may fail verification because of approximation errors. For example, we adapted a state-of-the-art reachability analyzer Flow* [10] to conduct reachability analysis of the closed-loop system combined by the programmatic controller in Fig. 1a and the oscillator environment (Equation 1) to compute a reachable state set between each time interval within the episode horizon (the controller is applied to generate a control action at the start of each time interval). The result is depicted in Fig. 1b. Although the programmatic controller empirically succeeds reaching the goal on extensive test simulations, the reachability analysis cannot determine whether the target region can always be reached as it computes a larger reachable region that keeps expansion, which may be an overestimation caused by over-approximation.

We hypothesize that verification failures can be caused by (1) true counterexample of unsafe states, (2) states caused by approximate errors, and (3) states in between the time interval of each control step (RL algorithms only sample states at the start and the end of a time interval). The latter two kinds of states cannot be observed by an RL algorithm during training in the concrete system state space. Thus, counterexample-guided controller synthesis may not work well if counterexamples are in the form of paths within the concrete state space.

To address this challenge, we propose synthesizing controllers in the proof space of a reachability analyzer. Controller synthesis in the proof space is critical to learning a verified controller because it can leverage verification feedback on either true unsafe counterexample states or approximation errors introduced by the verification procedure for searching a provably correct controller. A counterexample detected by a reachability analyzer is a *symbolic rollout* of abstract states of the closed-loop system that combines a (fixed) environment model and a (parameterized) programmatic controller. An abstract state (e.g. depicted as a green region in Fig. 1b) at a timestep over-approximates the set of concrete states reachable during the time interval of the timestep. VEL quantifies the safety and reachability property violation by the abstract states, e.g. there is an *abstract* loss between the approximative abstract state and the target region at the last control step. The loss approximates the *worst-case* reachability loss of any concrete state subsumed by the abstraction. We introduce lightweight gradient-descent style optimization algorithms to optimize controller parameters to effectively minimize the amount of correctness property violation to zero to refute any verification counterexamples.

Contributions. The main contribution of this paper is twofold. First, we present an efficient controller synthesis approach that integrates formal verification within a programmatic controller learning loop. Second, instead of synthesizing a programmatic controller from *concrete* state and action samples, we optimize the controller using *symbolic rollouts* with abstract states obtained by reachability analysis in the verification proof space. We implement the proposed ideas in a tool called VEL and present a detailed experimental study over a range of reinforcement learning systems. Our experiments demonstrate the benefits of integrating formal verification as part of the training objective and using verification feedback for controller synthesis.

2   Problem Setup

Environment Models. An environment is a structure $M^\delta[\cdot] = (S, A, F : \{S \times A \to S\}, R : \{S \times A \to \mathbb{R}\}, \cdot)$ where S is an infinite set of *continuous real-vector* environment states which are valuations of the state variables $x_1, x_2, \ldots, x_n$ of dimension n ($S \subseteq \mathbb{R}^n$); and A is a set of *continuous real-vector* control actions which are valuations of the action variables $u_1, u_2, \ldots, u_m$ of dimension m. F is a state transition function that emits the next environment state given a current state s and an agent action a. We assume that F is defined by an ordinary differential equation (ODE) in the form of $\dot{x} = f(x, u)$ and the function $f : \mathbb{R}^m \times \mathbb{R}^n \to \mathbb{R}^m$ is Lipschitz continuous in x and continuous in u. $R(s, a)$ is the immediate reward after transition from an environment state $s \in S$ with action $a \in A$. An environment $M^\delta[\cdot]$ is parameterized with an (unknown) controller.

Controllers. An agent uses a controller to interact with an environment $M^\delta[\cdot]$. We explicitly model the deployment of a (learned) controller $\pi : \{S \to A\}$ in $M^\delta[\cdot]$ as a *closed-loop* system $M^\delta[\pi]$. The controller π determines which action the agent ought to take in a given environment state. Specifically, it is invoked every δ time period at a timestep. π reads the environment state $s_i = s(i\delta)$ at time $t = i\delta$ ($i = 0, 1, 2, \ldots$) or timestep i, and computes a control action as $a_i = a(i\delta) = \pi(s(i\delta))$. Then the environment evolves following the ODE $\dot{x} = f(x, a(i\delta))$ within the time period $[i\delta, (i + 1)\delta]$ and obtain the state $s_{i+1} = s((i + 1)\delta)$ at the next timestep $i + 1$. In the oscillator example from Sec. 1, the duration δ of a timestep is $0.05s$ and the time horizon is $6s$ (i.e. 120 timesteps).

For environment simulation, given a set of initial states S_0, we assume the existence of a flow function[1] $\phi(s_0, t) : S_0 \times \mathbb{R}^+ \to S$ that maps some initial state s_0 to the environment state $\phi(s_0, t)$ at time t where $\phi(s_0, 0) = s_0$. We note that ϕ is the solution of the ODE $\dot{x} = f(x, a(i\delta))$ in the state transition function F during the time period $[i\delta, (i + 1)\delta]$ and $a(i\delta) = \pi(\phi(s_0, i\delta))$.

---

[1] ϕ may be implemented using scipy.integrate.odeint (or scipy.integrate.solve_ivp).

Reinforcement Learning (RL). Given a set of initial states S_0 and a time horizon $T\delta$ ($T > 0$) with δ as the duration of a timestep, a T-timestep rollout ζ of a controller π is denoted as $(\zeta = s_0, a_0, s_1, \ldots, s_T) \sim \pi$ where $s_i = s(i\delta)$ and $a_i = a(i\delta)$ are the environment state and the action taken at timestep i such that $s_0 \in S_0$, $s_{i+1} = F(s_i, a_i)$, and $a_i = \pi(s_i)$. The aggregate reward of π is

$$J^R(\pi) = \mathbb{E}_{(\zeta = s_0, a_0, \ldots, s_T) \sim \pi}[\sum_{t=0}^{T} \beta^t R(s_i, a_i)] \qquad (2)$$

where β is the reward discount factor ($0 < \beta \leq 1$). Controller search via RL aims to produce a controller π that maximizes $J^R(\pi)$.

Controller Correctness Specification. A correctness specification of a controller is a logical formula specifying whether any rollout ζ of the controller accomplishes the task without violating safety properties and reachability properties. To define safety and reachability over rollouts, the user first specifies a set of atomic predicates over environment states s.

Definition 1 (Predicates). *A predicate φ is a quantifier-free Boolean combinations of linear inequalities over the environment state variables x:*

$$\langle\varphi\rangle ::= \langle P\rangle \mid \varphi \wedge \varphi \mid \varphi \vee \varphi;$$

$$\langle P\rangle ::= \mathcal{A} \cdot x \leq b \text{ where } \mathcal{A} \in \mathbb{R}^{|x|}, b \in \mathbb{R};$$

A state $s \in S$ satisfies a preciate φ, denoted as $s \models \varphi$, iff $\varphi(s)$ is true.

The correctness requirement of a controller goes beyond from predicates over environment states s to specifications over controller rollouts ζ.

Definition 2 (Rollout Specifications). *The syntax of our correctness specifications for RL controllers is defined as:*

$$\psi ::= \varphi_I \text{ reach } \varphi_1 \text{ ensuring } \varphi_2$$

In a rollout specification, φ_I reach φ_1 enforces reachability - the controlled agent should eventually reach some goal states evaluated true by the predicate φ_1 from an initial state that satisfies φ_I. For instance, the agent should achieve some goals from an initial state. The constraint ensuring φ_2 additionally enforces safety - any rollout of the controller should only visit safe states evaluated true by the predicate φ_2. For example, the agent should remain within a safety boundary or avoid any obstacles throughout a rollout. Formally, the semantics of a rollout specification ψ is defined as follows:

$$[\![\varphi_I \text{ reach } \varphi_1 \text{ ensuring } \varphi_2]\!](\zeta_{0:T}) = \varphi_1(s_T) \wedge (\forall\, 0 \leq i \leq T.\ \varphi_2(s_i))$$

where $\zeta_{0:T} = s_0, s_1, \ldots, s_T$ is a rollout such that $s_0 \in \varphi_I$ and $T > 0$ denotes the total number of timesteps. Our specification implicitly requires that if the target region is reached before the T timestep of a rollout, the controlled agent does not leave the target region at the end of the rollout.

Given a time horizon $T\delta$ $(T > 0)$, a controller π is correct for an environment $M^\delta[\cdot]$ with respect to a rollout specification $\psi ::= \varphi_I$ **reach** φ_1 **ensuring** φ_2 iff for any rollout $\zeta_{0:T} = s_0, s_1, \ldots s_{T-1}, s_T$ of $M^\delta[\pi]$ such that $\varphi_I(s_0)$ holds, $[\![\psi]\!](\zeta_{0:T})$ is true. Notice that this definition does not consider any states of the continuous environment occurring within the time period of a timestep.

Example 1 *Continue the oscillator example. Assume an oscillator initial state is from $x_1, x_2 \in [-0.51, -0.49] \times [0.49, 0.51]$. Specify the initial state constraint:*

$$\varphi_I(x_1, x_2) \equiv -0.51 \le x_1 \le -0.49 \wedge 0.49 \le x_2 \le 0{,}51$$

The unsafe set of oscillator is $(-03, -0.25) \times (0.2, 0.35)$ (depicted as the red region in Fig. 1b). The safety φ_{safe} of the system is specified as:

$$\varphi_{safe}(x_1, x_2) \equiv x_1 \le -0.3 \vee x_1 \ge -0.25 \vee x_2 \le 0.2 \vee x_2 \ge 0.35$$

For this example, the target region is $[-0.05, 0.05] \times [-0.05, 0.05]$ (the blue region in Fig. 1b). The reachability of the system φ_{reach} is specified as:

$$\varphi_{reach}(x_1, x_2) \equiv -0.05 \le x_1 \le 0.05 \wedge -0.05 \le x_2 \le 0.05$$

The target region should be eventually reached by the end of a control episode while avoiding the unsafe state region. We express the rollout specification as:

$$\varphi_I(x_1, x_2) \; \textbf{\textit{reach}} \; \varphi_{reach}(x_1, x_2) \; \textbf{\textit{ensuring}} \; \varphi_{safe}(x_1, x_2)$$

The following specification formulates that a desired controller stabilizes the oscillator around the target region over an infinite time horizon:

$$\varphi_{reach}(x_1, x_2) \; \textbf{\textit{reach}} \; \varphi_{reach}(x_1, x_2) \; \textbf{\textit{ensuring}} \; \varphi_{safe}(x_1, x_2)$$

3   Programmatic Controllers

Programmatic controllers have emerged as a promising solution to address the lack of interpretability in deep reinforcement learning [47,38,27,8] by learning controllers as programs. This paper focuses on programmatic controllers structured as *differentiable* programs [38].

Our programmatic controllers follow the high-level context-free grammar depicted in Fig. 2 where E is the start symbol, θ represents real-valued parameters of the program. The nonterminals E and B stand for program expressions that evaluate to action values in $\mathbb{R}^m$ and Booleans, respectively, where m is the action dimension size, $\theta_1 \in \mathbb{R}$ and $\theta_2 \in \mathbb{R}^n$. We represent a state input to a programmatic controller as $s = \{x_1 : \nu_1, x_2 : \nu_2, \ldots, x_n\}$ where n is the state dimension size and $\nu_i = s[x_i]$ is the value of x_i in s. As usual, the unbounded variables in $\mathcal{X} = [x_1, x_2, \ldots, x_n]$ are assumed to be input variables (i.e., state variables). C is a low-level affine controller that can be invoked by a programmatic controller where $\theta_3, \theta_c \in \mathbb{R}^m, \theta_4 \in \mathbb{R}^{m \cdot n}$ are controller parameters. Notice that C can be as simple as some (learned) constants θ_c.

$$E ::= C \mid \textbf{if } B \textbf{ then } C \textbf{ else } E$$
$$B ::= \theta_1 + \theta_2^T \cdot \mathcal{X} \geq 0$$
$$C ::= \theta_3 + \theta_4 \cdot \mathcal{X} \mid \theta_c$$

Fig. 2: A context-free grammar for programmatic controllers.

The semantics of a programmatic controller in E is mostly standard and given by a function $[\![E]\!](s)$, defined for each language construct. For example, $[\![x_i]\!](s) = s[x_i]$ reads the value of a variable x_i in a state s. A controller may use an **if-then-else** branching construct. To avoid discontinuities for differentiability, we interpret its semantics in terms of a smooth approximation:

$$[\![\textbf{if } B \textbf{ then } C \textbf{ else } E]\!](s) = \sigma([\![B]\!](s)) \cdot [\![C]\!](s) + (1 - \sigma([\![B]\!](s))) \cdot [\![E]\!](s) \quad (3)$$

where σ is the sigmoid function. Thus, any controller programmed in this grammar is a differentiable program. During execution, a programmatic controller invokes a set of low-level affine controllers under different environment conditions, according to the activation of the B conditions in the program.

Programmatic Reinforcement Learning. We use the programmatic reinforcement learning algorithm [38] to learn a programmatic controller. Compared with other programmatic reinforcement learning approaches [27,47], this algorithm stands out by jointly learning both program structures and program parameters. Empirical results show that learned programmatic controllers achieve comparable or even better reward performance than deep neural networks [38].

4 Proof Space Optimization

The main challenge of using a verification procedure to guide controller synthesis is that verifiers are in general incomplete. When verification fails, it does not necessarily mean the system under verification has a true counterexample as the verifier may introduce states caused by over-approximation errors, commonly seen in reachability analysis. Even a well-trained controller may fail verification because of approximation errors. In our context, for soundness, reachability analysis of continuous or hybrid systems additionally takes environment states in between the time interval of a timestep into account. Both of these kinds of states cannot be observed by RL agents during training in the concrete state space, which renders the importance of controller optimization in the proof space of verification. In the following, Sec. 4.1 defines a verification procedure for environment models governed by programmatic controllers. Sec. 4.2 encodes verification feedback as a loss function of controller parameters over the verification proof space. Finally, Sec. 4.3 defines an optimization procedure that iteratively minimizes the loss function for correct-by-construction controller synthesis.

4.1   Controller Verification

We formalize controller synthesis as a verification-based controller optimization problem. A synthesized controller π is certified by a formal verifier against an environment model $M^\delta[\cdot]$ and a rollout specification ψ (Definition 2). The verifier returns true if π can be verified correct.

Reinforcement learning algorithms typically discretize a continuous environment model $M^\delta[\cdot]$ to sample environment states every δ time period (as a timestep) for controller learning (Sec. 2). For soundness, in verification our approach instead considers all states reachable by the original continuous system. Formally, given a set of initial states S_0, we use S_i ($i > 0$) to represent the set of reachable concrete states during the time interval of $[(i-1)\delta,\ i\delta]$:

$$S_i = \{\phi(s_0, t) \mid \forall s_0 \in S_0, \forall t \in [(i-1)\delta,\ i\delta]\}$$

where ϕ is the flow function for environment state transition defined in Sec. 2. Our algorithm uses abstract interpretation to soundly approximate the set of reachable states S_i at each time step by reachability analysis.

Definition 3 (Symbolic Rollouts). *Given an environment model* $M^\delta[\pi] = (S, A, F, R, \pi)$ *deployed with a controller* π, *a set of initial states* S_0, *and an abstract domain* $\mathcal{D}$, *a symbolic rollout of* $M^\delta[\pi]$ *over* $\mathcal{D}$ *is* $\zeta^{\mathcal{D}} = S_0^{\mathcal{D}}, S_1^{\mathcal{D}}, \ldots$ *where* $S_0^{\mathcal{D}} = \alpha(S_0)$ *is the abstraction of the initial states* S_0 *in* $\mathcal{D}$. *Each symbolic state* $S_i^{\mathcal{D}} = F^{\mathcal{D}}[\pi](S_{i-1}^{\mathcal{D}})$ *over-approximates* S_i - *the set of reachable states from the initial state* S_0 *during the time interval* $[(i-1)\delta, i\delta]$ *of the timestep* i. $F^{\mathcal{D}}$ *is an abstract transformer for* $M^\delta[\pi]$*'s state transition function* F.

Our implementation of the abstract interpreter $F^{\mathcal{D}}$ is based on Flow* [10], a reachability analyzer for continuous or hybrid systems, where the abstract domain $\mathcal{D}$ is Taylor Model (TM) flowpipes. Formally, for reachability computation at each timestep i (where $i > 0$), we firstly use Flow* to evaluate the TM flowpipe $\hat{S}_{i-1}$ for the reachable set of states at time $t = (i-1)\delta$. To obtain a TM representation for the output set of the programmatic controller at timestep i, we use TM arithmetic to evaluate a TM flowpipe $\hat{A}_{i-1}$ for $[\![\pi]\!](s)$ for all states $s \in \hat{S}_{i-1}$. Here $[\![\pi]\!]$ encodes the semantics of π (Equation 3). For example, the semantics of the oscillator controller in Fig. 1a is:

$$\sigma(28.33x_1 + 4.23x_2 + 4.16) \times (6.79x_1 - 8.56x_2 + 0.35)$$
$$+ (1 - \sigma(28.33x_1 + 4.23x_2 + 4.16)) \times (11.01x_1 - 13.50x_2 + 8.71)$$

where the sigmoid function σ can be handled by TM arithmetic. The resulting TM representation $\hat{A}_{i-1}$ can be viewed as an overapproximation of the controller's output at timestep i. Finally, we use Flow* to construct the TM flowpipe overapproximation $S_i^{\mathcal{D}}$ for all reachable states during the time period at timestep i by reachability analysis over the ODE dynamics of the transition function $\dot{x} = f(x, a)$ for δ time period with initial state $x(0) \in \hat{S}_{i-1}$ and the control action $a \in \hat{A}_{i-1}$.

Verification Procedure. Given a closed-loop system $M^\delta[\pi]$, a time horizon $T\delta$ ($T > 0$), and a rollout specification $\psi ::= [\![\varphi_I \text{ reach } \varphi_1 \text{ ensuring } \varphi_2]\!]$, we obtain the symbolic rollout of $M^\delta[\pi]$ as $\zeta^{\mathcal{D}}_{0:T} = S^{\mathcal{D}}_0, S^{\mathcal{D}}_1, \ldots, S^{\mathcal{D}}_T$ where $S^{\mathcal{D}}_0$ is the abstraction of all states in φ_I in the abstract domain $\mathcal{D}$. For formal verification, we extend the semantics definition of the rollout specification $[\![\psi]\!]$ over concrete rollouts (Definition 2) to support symbolic rollouts. Formally, $[\![\psi]\!](\zeta^{\mathcal{D}}_{0:T})$ holds iff:

$$\forall s \in \gamma(S^{\mathcal{D}}_T). \; \varphi_1(s) \; \bigwedge \; \forall \, 0 \leq i \leq T, \; s \in \gamma(S^{\mathcal{D}}_i). \; \varphi_2(s)$$

where γ is the concretization function of the abstract domain $\mathcal{D}$. The closed-loop system $M^\delta[\pi]$ satisfies ψ, denoted as $M^\delta[\pi] \models \psi$, iff $[\![\psi]\!](\zeta^{\mathcal{D}}_{0:T})$ holds. The abstract domain $\mathcal{D}$ is the proof space of controller verification.

Example 2 *To verify the closed-loop system composed by the oscillator ODE in Eq. 1 and the learned controller in Fig. 1a, we have conducted reachability analysis to overapproximate the reachable state set during the time period of each timestep within the episode horizon. The result of the TM flowpipes are depicted as a sequence of green regions in Fig. 1b. The verification procedure cannot guarantee that the target be reached eventually due to the approximation errors.*

4.2   Correctness Property Loss in the Proof Space

To facilitate controller optimization in the presence of verification failures, our approach measures the amount of correctness property violation as verification feedback. To this end, we firstly define correct property violation over the concrete environment state space and then lift this definition to the proof space of controller verification.

We note that a controller rollout that fails correctness property verification violates desired properties at some states. The following definition characterizes a correctness loss function to quantify the correctness property violation of a state.

Definition 4 (State Correctness Loss Function). *For a predicate φ over states $s \in S$, we define a non-negative loss function $\mathcal{L}(s, \varphi)$ such that $\mathcal{L}(s, \varphi) = 0$ iff s satisfies φ, i.e. $s \models \varphi$. We define $\mathcal{L}(s, \varphi)$ recursively, based on the possible shapes of φ (Definition 1):*

- $\mathcal{L}(s, \mathcal{A} \cdot x \leq b) := \max(\mathcal{A} \cdot s - b, 0)$
- $\mathcal{L}(s, \varphi_1 \wedge \varphi_2) := \max(\mathcal{L}(s, \varphi_1), \mathcal{L}(s, \varphi_2))$
- $\mathcal{L}(s, \varphi_1 \vee \varphi_2) := \min(\mathcal{L}(s, \varphi_1), \mathcal{L}(s, \varphi_2))$

Notice that $\mathcal{L}(s, \varphi_1 \wedge \varphi_2) = 0$ iff $\mathcal{L}(s, \varphi_1) = 0$ and $\mathcal{L}(s, \varphi_2) = 0$, and similarly $\mathcal{L}(\varphi_1 \vee \varphi_2) = 0$ iff $\mathcal{L}(\varphi_1) = 0$ or $L(\varphi_2) = 0$.

Our objective is to use verification feedback to improve controller safety. To this end, we lift the correctness loss function over concrete states (Definition 4) to an *abstract correctness loss* function over abstract states.

Definition 5 (Abstract State Correctness Loss Function). *Given an abstract state $S^\mathcal{D}$ and a predicate φ, we define an abstract correctness loss function:*

$$\mathcal{L}_\mathcal{D}(S^\mathcal{D}, \varphi) = \max_{s \in \gamma(S^\mathcal{D})} \mathcal{L}(s, \varphi)$$

where γ is the concretization function of the abstract domain $\mathcal{D}$. The abstract correctness loss function applies γ to obtain all concrete states represented by an abstract state $S^\mathcal{D}$. It measures the worst-case correctness loss of φ among all concrete states subsumed by $S^\mathcal{D}$. Given an abstract domain $\mathcal{D}$, we can usually approximate the concretization of an abstract state $\gamma(S^\mathcal{D})$ with a tight interval $\gamma_I(S^\mathcal{D})$. As exemplified in Fig. 1b, it is straightforward to represent Taylor model flowpipes as intervals in Flow*. Based on the possible shape of φ, we redefine $\mathcal{L}_\mathcal{D}(S^\mathcal{D}, \varphi)$ as:

- $\mathcal{L}_\mathcal{D}(S^\mathcal{D}, \mathcal{A} \cdot x \leq b) := \max_{s \in \gamma_I(S^\mathcal{D})} \left(\max(\mathcal{A} \cdot s - b, 0) \right)$
- $\mathcal{L}_\mathcal{D}(S^\mathcal{D}, \varphi_1 \wedge \varphi_2) := \max(\mathcal{L}_\mathcal{D}(S^\mathcal{D}, \varphi_1), \mathcal{L}_\mathcal{D}(S^\mathcal{D}, \varphi_2))$
- $\mathcal{L}_\mathcal{D}(S^\mathcal{D}, \varphi_1 \vee \varphi_2) := \min(\mathcal{L}_\mathcal{D}(S^\mathcal{D}, \varphi_1), \mathcal{L}_\mathcal{D}(S^\mathcal{D}, \varphi_2))$

Theorem 1 (Abstract State Correctness Loss Function Soundness). *Given an abstract state $S^\mathcal{D}$ and a predicate φ, we have:*

$$\mathcal{L}_\mathcal{D}(S^\mathcal{D}, \varphi) = 0 \implies \forall s \in \gamma_I(S^\mathcal{D}) \ s \models \varphi.$$

We further lift the definition of the correctness loss function over abstract states (Definition 5) to a correctness loss function over symbolic rollouts.

Definition 6 (Symbolic Rollout Correctness Loss). *Given a rollout specification $\psi := \varphi_I$ reach φ_1 ensuring φ_2 and a symbolic rollout $\zeta_{0:T}^\mathcal{D} = S_0^\mathcal{D}, \ldots, S_T^\mathcal{D}$ where $S_0^\mathcal{D}$ is the abstraction of all states in φ_I in the abstract domain $\mathcal{D}$, we define an abstract safety loss function $\mathcal{L}_\mathcal{D}(\zeta_{0:T}, \psi)$ measuring the degree to which the rollout specification is violated:*

$$\mathcal{L}_\mathcal{D}(\zeta_{0:T}, \ \varphi_I \textbf{ reach } \varphi_1 \textbf{ ensuring } \varphi_2) = \max(\mathcal{L}_\mathcal{D}(S_T^\mathcal{D}, \varphi_1), \max_{0 < i \leq T}(\mathcal{L}_\mathcal{D}(S_i^\mathcal{D}, \varphi_2)))$$

Definition 6 enables a quantitative metric for the correctness loss of a controller in the verification proof space. Given a closed loop system $M^\delta[\pi]$, a time horizon $T\delta$, a rollout specification ψ, and the corresponding symbolic rollout $\zeta_{0:T}^\mathcal{D}$ of $M^\delta[\pi]$, the correctness loss of $M^\delta[\pi]$ with respect to ψ, denoted as $\mathcal{L}_\mathcal{D}(M^\delta[\pi], \psi)$, is defined over the symbolic rollout i.e. $\mathcal{L}_\mathcal{D}(M^\delta[\pi], \psi) = \mathcal{L}_\mathcal{D}(\zeta_{0:T}^\mathcal{D}, \psi)$.

Example 3 *In Fig. 1b, there is a correctness loss (depicted as a red arrow) between the abstract state at the last timestep of the oscillator symbolic rollout and the desired reachable region φ_{reach} defined in Example 1. We characterize it as an abstract state correctness loss. The whole symbolic rollout has the same correctness loss with respect to the rollout specification defined in Example 1.*

Theorem 2 (Symbolic Rollout Correctness Soundness). *Given an environment $M^\delta[\cdot]$ deployed with a controller π and a rollout specification ψ, we have*

$$\mathcal{L}_\mathcal{D}(M^\delta[\pi], \psi) = 0 \implies M^\delta[\pi] \models \psi.$$

Algorithm 1 VEL: **V**erification-based l**e**arning framework for controller synthesis. In line 8, ω_k is a Gaussian noise and ν is a small positive real number.

Require: Environment model $M^{\delta}[\cdot]$, rollout specification ψ, initial controller π_{θ} trained using the programmatic RL algorithm [38].
Ensure: Optimized controller π_{θ} such that $M^{\delta}[\pi_{\theta}] \models \psi$.

1: **procedure** VEL
2:     $\theta \leftarrow$ all parameters in π_{θ} for optimization
3:     **while true do**
4:         $\ell_{\mathcal{D}} \leftarrow \mathcal{L}_{\mathcal{D}}(M^{\delta}[\pi_{\theta}], \psi)$
5:         **if** $\ell_{\mathcal{D}} = 0$ **then**
6:             Dump π_{θ} to a verified controller list
7:         **end if**
8:         $\nabla_{\theta} \mathcal{L}_{\mathcal{D}} \leftarrow \frac{1}{N} \sum_{k=1}^{N} \frac{\mathcal{L}_{\mathcal{D}}(M^{\delta}[\pi_{\theta+\nu\omega_k}], \psi) - \mathcal{L}_{\mathcal{D}}(M^{\delta}[\pi_{\theta-\nu\omega_k}], \psi)}{\nu} \omega_k$
9:         $\theta \leftarrow \theta - \eta \cdot \nabla_{\theta} \mathcal{L}_{\mathcal{D}}$ where η is a learning rate
10:    **end while**
11: **end procedure**

4.3   Controller Synthesis

The unique feature of our controller synthesis algorithm is that it leverages verification feedback on either true unsafe states or overapproximation errors introduced by verification to search for a provably correct controller.

Controller Synthesis in the Proof Space. We deem a programmatic controller π with trainable parameters θ (e.g. from the grammar in Fig. 2) as π_{θ}. Given a closed-loop system $M^{\delta}[\pi_{\theta}]$, the correctness loss function $\mathcal{L}_{\mathcal{D}}(M^{\delta}[\pi_{\theta}], \psi)$ is essentially a function of π_{θ}'s parameters θ. To reduce the correctness loss of π_{θ} over the proof space $\mathcal{D}$, we leverage a gradient-descent style optimization to update θ by taking steps proportional to the negative of the gradient of $\mathcal{L}_{\mathcal{D}}(M^{\delta}[\pi_{\theta}], \psi)$ at θ. As opposed to standard gradient descent optimization, we optimize π_{θ} based on symbolic rollouts in the proof space $\mathcal{D}$, favouring the abstract interpreter (i.e. Flow*) directly for verification-guided controller updates.

Black-box Gradient Estimation. Directly deriving the gradients of $\mathcal{L}_{\mathcal{D}}$, however, requires the controller verification procedure be differentiable, which is not supported by reachability analyzers such as Flow*. To overcome this challenge, our algorithm effectively estimates the gradients of $\mathcal{L}_{\mathcal{D}}$ based on random search [34]. Given a closed-loop environment $M^{\delta}[\pi_{\theta}]$, at each training iteration, we obtain perturbed systems $M^{\delta}[\pi_{\theta+\nu\omega}]$ and $M^{\delta}[\pi_{\theta-\nu\omega}]$ where we add sampled Gaussian noise ω to the current controller π_{θ}'s parameters θ in both directions and ν is a small positive real number. By evaluating the abstract correctness losses of the symbolic rollouts of $M^{\delta}[\pi_{\theta+\nu\omega}]$ and $M^{\delta}[\pi_{\theta-\nu\omega}]$, we update θ with a finite difference approximation along an unbiased estimator of the gradient:

$$\nabla_{\theta} \mathcal{L}_{\mathcal{D}} \leftarrow \frac{1}{N} \sum_{k=1}^{N} \frac{\left(\mathcal{L}_{\mathcal{D}}(M^{\delta}[\pi_{\theta+\nu\omega_k}], \psi) - \mathcal{L}_{\mathcal{D}}(M^{\delta}[\pi_{\theta-\nu\omega_k}], \psi)\right)}{\nu} \omega_k$$

We update controller parameters θ as follows where η is a learning rate:

$$\theta \leftarrow \theta - \eta \cdot \nabla_\theta \mathcal{L}_\mathcal{D}$$

Our high-level controller synthesis algorithm is depicted in Algorithm. 1. The algorithm takes as input an environment model $M^\delta[\cdot]$, a rollout specification ψ, and a programmatic controller π learned using the programmatic reinforcement learning technique [38]. When verification fails (line 4), it uses the correctness loss of the symbolic rollout of $M^\delta[\pi]$ for optimization (line 8-9). The algorithm repeatedly performs the gradient-based update until a verified controller is synthesized. As the controller verification procedure is undecidable in general, it is possible that Algorithm 1 converges with a nonzero correctness loss. Our empirical results in Sec. 5 demonstrate that the algorithm works well in practice.

5 Experimental Results

We have implemented the verification-guided controller synthesis technique in Algorithm 1 in a tool called VEL (**VE**rification-based **L**earning) [50]. Given an environment and a rollout specification ψ (Definition 2), VEL uses the programmatic reinforcement learning algorithm [38] to learn a programmatic controller π. The controller π is trained to satisfy the safety and reachability requirements as set by ψ. We do so by shaping a reward function that is consistent with ψ - this function rewards actions leading to goal states and penalizes actions leading to unsafe states. As the RL algorithm does not provide any correctness guarantees and the verification procedure may introduce large approximation errors, even well-trained controllers may fail verification. In case of verification failures, VEL applies Algorithm 1 to optimize π based on the verification feedback.

We evaluated VEL on several *nonlinear* continuous or hybrid systems taken from the literature. These are problems that are widely used for evaluating state-of-the-art verification tools for learning-enabled cyber-physical systems. Benchmarks B1 - B5 were introduced by [18]; adaptive cruise control (ACC) was presented in [43]; mountain car (MC) and quadrotor with model-predictive control (QMPC) were introduced by [28]; Pedulum and CartPole were taken from [29]; Tora and Unicyclecar were presented in the ARCH-COMP21 competition on formal verification of Artificial Intelligence and Neural Network Control Systems (AINNCS). We present the dynamics and the detailed description of each benchmark in [50]. The rollout specifications (Definition 2) are depicted in Table 1. The specifications define for each benchmark the initial states, the goal regions to reach, and the safety properties describing the safety boundary or the obstacles to avoid. On three benchmarks we verify the controller correctness over an infinite horizon. For the classic control problem Pendulum, to verify that the pendulum does not fall in an infinite time horizon, the rollout specification requires that any rollout starting from the region $x_1, x_2 \in [-0.1, 0.1]$ (representing pendulum angle and angular velocity) eventually turns back to it and any rollout states must be safe (including those that temporarily leave this region). Similarly, Tora models a moving cart attached to a wall with a spring.

Table 1: Benchmark Rollout Specifications ($\mathcal{T}$ represents True).

Tasks	Rollout Specifications
B_1	$x_1 \in [.8, .9] \wedge x_2 \in [.5, .6]$ **reach** $x_1 \in [0, .2] \wedge x_2 \in [.05, .3]$ **ensuring** $x_1, x_2 \in [-1.5, 1.5]$
B_2	$x_1 \in [.7, .9] \wedge x_2 \in [.7, .9]$ **reach** $x_1 \in [-.3, .1] \wedge x_2 \in [-.35, .5]$ **ensuring** $x_1, x_2 \in [-1.5, 1.5]$
B_3	$x_1 \in [.8, .9] \wedge x_2 \in [.4, .5]$ **reach** $x_1 \in [0, .2] \wedge x_2 \in [.05, .3]$ **ensuring** $\mathcal{T}$
B_4	$x_1, x_3 \in [.25, .27] \wedge x_2 \in [.08, .1]$ **reach** $x_1 \in [-.3, .1] \wedge x_2 \in [-.35, .5]$ **ensuring** $\mathcal{T}$
B_5	$x1 \in [.38, .4] \wedge x_2 \in [.45, .47] \wedge x_3 \in [.25, .27]$ **reach** $x_1 \in [0, .2] \wedge x_2 \in [.05, .3]$ **ensuring** $\mathcal{T}$
Oscillator$_{\text{inf}}$	$x_1 \in [-.51, -.49] \wedge x_2 \in [.49, .51]$ **reach** $x_1, x_2 \in [-.05, .05]$ **ensuring** $x_1 \leq -.3 \vee x_1 \geq -.25 \vee x_2 \leq .2 \vee x_2 \geq .35,$ $x_1, x_2 \in [-.05, .05]$ **reach** $x_1, x_2 \in [-.05, .05]$ **ensuring** $x_1 \leq -.3 \vee x_1 \geq -.25 \vee x_2 \leq .2 \vee x_2 \geq .35$
ACC	$x_1 \in [90, 110] \wedge x_2 \in [32, 32.05] \wedge x_4 \in [10, 11] \wedge x_5 \in [30, 30.05]$ **reach** $-x_1 + x_4 - 102 \leq 0$ **ensuring** $-x_1 + 1.4 \cdot x_2 + x_4 + 10 \leq 0$
MountainCar	$x_1 \in [-.6, -.4]$ **reach** $x_1 > .45$ **ensuring** $x_1 \leq .15 \vee x_2 \geq .25 \vee x_2 \geq .02$
QMPC	$.025 \leq x_1 \leq .05 \wedge 0 \leq x_2 \leq .025$ **reach** $\mathcal{T}$ **ensuring** $-.32 \leq x_1, x_2, x_3 \leq .32$
Pendulum$_{\text{inf}}$	$x_1, x_2 \in [-.1, .1]$ **reach** $x_1, x_2 \in [-.1, .1]$ **ensuring** $x_1, x_2 \in [-\frac{\pi}{2}, \frac{\pi}{2}]$
CartPole	$x_1, x_2, x_3, x_4 \in [-.05, .05]$ **reach** $\mathcal{T}$ **ensuring** $x_1 \in [-2.4, 2.4] \wedge x_2 \in [-.21, .21]$
UnicycleCar	$x_1 \in [9.5, 9.55] \wedge x_2 \in [-4.5, -4.45] \wedge x_3 \in [2.1, 2.11] \wedge x_4 \in [1.5, 1.51]$ **reach** $x_1 \in [-.6, .6] \wedge x_2 \in [-.2, .2] \wedge x_3 \in [-.06, .06] \wedge x_4 \in [-.3, .3]$ **ensuring** $\mathcal{T}$
Tora	$x_1 \in [-.77, -.75] \wedge x_2 \in [-.45, -.43] \wedge x_3 \in [.51, .54] \wedge x_4 \in [-.3, -.28]$ **reach** $x_1 \in [-.1, .2] \wedge x_2 \in [-.9, .6]$ **ensuring** $x_1, x_2, x_3, x_4 \in [-1.5, 1.5]$
Tora$_{\text{inf}}$	$x_1, x_2, x_3, x_4 \in [-.1, .1]$ **reach** $x_1, x_2, x_3, x_4 \in [-.1, .1]$ **ensuring** $x_1, x_2, x_3, x_4 \in [-1.5, 1.5]$

On Tora$_{\text{inf}}$, we prove that the controller for the arm of the cart connecting to the spring can stabilize the cart over an infinite horizon while maintain safety around the origin. On Oscillator$_{\text{inf}}$, we verify that the controller can stabilize the oscillator around a target region over an infinite horizon while the process of reaching the target region from the initial states is safe.

The experimental results are given in Table 2. VEL synthesized provably correct programmatic controllers for all the benchmarks. Table 2 shows the total time spent on each benchmark (T.T) as well as the verification time of the final controller (V.T). Half of the benchmarks can be directly verified with the initial programmatic controller (in Table 2, T.T for these benchmarks is empty as they only need one pass of verification in V.T). The other half must go through the verification-guided controller learning loop due to approximation errors in verification although these controllers achieved satisfactory test performance. We depict the learning performance of VEL on these benchmarks in Fig. 3 averaged over 5 random seeds. The results show that VEL can robustly and reliably reduce the correctness loss over symbolic rollouts (i.e. the verification feedback) to zero.

Table 2: Experiment Results. Depth shows the height of the abstract syntax tree of a programmatic controller. T.T shows the overall execution time of VEL including both the time for reachability analysis and verification-guided controller synthesis. V.T measures only the verification time for the final controller. If a controller can be verified directly without verification-guided optimization, the value of T.T is empty. The execution times for ReachNN* and Verisig measure the cost of verifying a neural network controlled system (NNCS). The notation of the size ($n \times k$) indicates a neural network (with sigmoid activations) with n hidden layers and k neurons per layer. If a property could not be verified, it is marked as Unknown. N/A means that the tool is not applicable to a benchmark.

	VEL (ours)			NNCS		
Task	Depth	V.T	T.T	Size	ReachNN*	Verisig
B_1	2	27.32s	86.57s	2×20	69s	49s
B_2	2	0.25s	-	2×20	32s	Unknown
B_3	2	1.96s	-	2×20	130s	47s
B_4	2	0.63s	-	2×20	20s	12s
B_5	2	0.64s	2.01s	3×100	31s	196s
Oscillator$_{inf}$	2	1.74s	25.72s	2×20	Unknown	Unknown
ACC	3	5.56s	196.03s	3×20	Unknown	1512s
MountainCar	3	233.45s	-	2×16	N/A	52s
QMPC	5	2.21s	16.54s	2×20	N/A	697s
Pendulum$_{inf}$	2	0.95s	-	3×64	57s	Unknown
CartPole	3	8.97s	-	2×64	Unknown	Unknown
Unicycle	3	0.75s	16.52s	3×20	N/A	Unknown
Tora	2	3.71s	-	3×20	Unknown	83s
Tora$_{inf}$	2	0.86s	150.86s	3×20	Unknown	Unknown

Table 2 also shows the results of verifying the benchmarks as neural network controlled systems (NNCS) using two state-of-the-art verification tools ReachNN* [18] and Verisig [28] where the controllers are trained as neural networks. We note that VEL is designed for *programmatic* controllers and uniquely has a verification-guided learning loop. Here our intention is not to compare the tools' performance. Instead, Table 2 demonstrates that integrating verification in training loops for programmatic controllers is more tractable than for neural network controllers. It shows that programmatic controller verification (column V.T) has a much lower computation cost compared to verifying neural network controllers using ReachNN* and Verisig except for MountainCar[2]. When ReachNN* and Verisig produces Unknown, the tools are not able to verify the rollout specification due to the large estimated approximation errors in verification. On Tora, ReachNN* spent over 13000s to produce imprecise flowpipes with large approximation errors that cannot be used for verification. In this case, repeatedly conducting neural network controller verification in a learning loop is

---

[2] MountainCar is a hybrid system model. VEL is not yet optimized for hybrid system verification.

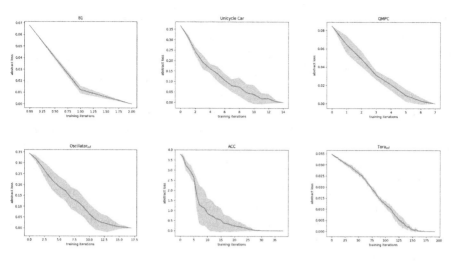

Fig. 3: Learning Performance of Verification-guided Controller Synthesis on B1, UnicycleCar, QMPC, Oscillator, ACC, and $Tora_{inf}$. The y-axis records the correctness loss of symbolic rollouts over abstract states. The results are averaged over 5 random seeds. VEL reliably reduces the symbolic rollout correctness loss to zero across the learning loop iterations (the x axis) for each benchmark.

computationally infeasible. On the other hand, VEL makes verification-guided controller synthesis feasible as evidenced in Table 2 and Fig. 3. It efficiently uses the programmatic controller verification feedback to reduce the correctness loss over the abstraction of controller reachable states to 0 in the verification proof space (even if the abstraction may introduce approximation errors).

6 Related Work

Robust Machine Learning. Our work on using abstract interpretation [14] for controller synthesis is inspired by the recent advances in verifying neural network robustness, e.g. [23,5,40,51]. These approaches apply abstract interpretation to relax nonlinearity of activation functions in neural networks into convex representations, based on linear approximation [52,51,39,40,55] or interval approximation [26,35]. Since the abstractions are differentiable, neural networks can be optimized toward tighter concertized bounds to improve verified robustness [35,7,55,48,33]. Principally, abstract interpretation can be used to verify the reachability properties of nonlinear dynamics systems [30,37,4]. Recent work [43,28,41,18,17,29,13] has already achieved initial results about verifying neural network controlled autonomous systems by conducting reachability analysis. However, these approaches do not attempt to leverage verification feedback for controller synthesis within a learning loop partially because of the high computation demand of repeatedly verifying neural network controllers. VEL demonstrates the substantial benefits of using verification feedback in a proof space for learning correct-by-construction programmatic controllers. Related works [25,16] conduct trajectory planning from temporal logic specifications but do not provide formal correctness guarantees. Extending VEL to support richer logic specifications is left for future work.

Safe Reinforcement Learning. Safe reinforcement learning is a fundamental problem in machine learning [36,45]. Most safe RL algorithms form a constraint optimization problem by specifying safety constraints as cost functions in addition to reward functions [1,9,15,31,42,54,53]. Their goal is to train a controller that maximizes the accumulated reward and bound the aggregate safety violation under a threshold. However, aggregate safety costs do not support reachability constraints in the Safe RL context. In contrast, VEL ensures that a learned controller be formally verified correct and can better handle reachability constraints beyond safety. Model-based safe learning is combined with formal verification in [22] where an environment model is updated as learning progresses to take into account the deviations between the model and the actual system behavior. We leave combing VEL and model-based learning in future work.

Safe Shielding. The general idea of shielding is to use a backup controller to enforce the safety of a deep neural network controller [3]. The backup controller is less performant than the neural controller but is safe by construction using formal methods. The backup controller runs in tandem with the neural controller. Whenever the neural controller is about to leave the provably safe state space governed by the backup controller, the backup controller overrides the potentially unsafe neural actions to enforce the neural controller to stay within the certified safe space [2,11,21,22,24,56,6,32]. In contrast, VEL directly integrates formal verification into controller learning loops to ensure that learned controllers are correct-by-construction and hence eliminates the need for shielding.

7   Conclusion

We present VEL that bridges formal verification and synthesis for learning correct-by-construction programmatic controllers. VEL integrates formal verification into a controller learning loop to enable counterexample-guided controller optimization. VEL encodes verification feedback as a loss function of the parameters of a programmatic controller over the verification proof space. Its optimization procedure iteratively reduces both controller correctness violation by true counterexamples and overapproximation errors caused by abstraction. Our experiments demonstrate that controller updates based on verification feedback can lead to provably correct programmatic controllers. For future work, we plan to extend VEL to support controller safety during exploration in noisy environments. When a worst-case environment model is provided, this can be achieved by repeatedly leveraging the verification feedback on safety violation to project a controller back onto the verified safe space [12] after each reinforcement learning step taken on the parameter space of the controller.

Data-Availability Statement VEL is available at the repository [50]. The instructions for reproducing our experiment results are included in this repository.

Acknowledgments This work was supported in part by NSF CCF-2007799 and NSF CCF-2124155.

References

1. Achiam, J., Held, D., Tamar, A., Abbeel, P.: Constrained policy optimization. In: Precup, D., Teh, Y.W. (eds.) Proceedings of the 34th International Conference on Machine Learning, ICML 2017, Sydney, NSW, Australia, 6-11 August 2017. Proceedings of Machine Learning Research, vol. 70, pp. 22–31. PMLR (2017)
2. Akametalu, A.K., Kaynama, S., Fisac, J.F., Zeilinger, M.N., Gillula, J.H., Tomlin, C.J.: Reachability-based safe learning with gaussian processes. In: 53rd IEEE Conference on Decision and Control, CDC 2014, Los Angeles, CA, USA, December 15-17, 2014. pp. 1424–1431. IEEE (2014)
3. Alshiekh, M., Bloem, R., Ehlers, R., Könighofer, B., Niekum, S., Topcu, U.: Safe reinforcement learning via shielding. In: McIlraith, S.A., Weinberger, K.Q. (eds.) Proceedings of the Thirty-Second AAAI Conference on Artificial Intelligence, (AAAI-18), New Orleans, Louisiana, USA, February 2-7, 2018. pp. 2669–2678. AAAI Press (2018)
4. Althoff, M.: An introduction to cora 2015. In: Proc. of the Workshop on Applied Verification for Continuous and Hybrid Systems (2015)
5. Anderson, G., Pailoor, S., Dillig, I., Chaudhuri, S.: Optimization and abstraction: a synergistic approach for analyzing neural network robustness. In: Proceedings of the 40th ACM SIGPLAN Conference on Programming Language Design and Implementation, PLDI 2019, Phoenix, AZ, USA, June 22-26, 2019. pp. 731–744 (2019)
6. Anderson, G., Verma, A., Dillig, I., Chaudhuri, S.: Neurosymbolic reinforcement learning with formally verified exploration. In: Larochelle, H., Ranzato, M., Hadsell, R., Balcan, M., Lin, H. (eds.) Advances in Neural Information Processing Systems 33: Annual Conference on Neural Information Processing Systems 2020, NeurIPS 2020, December 6-12, 2020, virtual (2020)
7. Balunovic, M., Vechev, M.T.: Adversarial training and provable defenses: Bridging the gap. In: 8th International Conference on Learning Representations, ICLR 2020, Addis Ababa, Ethiopia, April 26-30, 2020. OpenReview.net (2020)
8. Bastani, O., Pu, Y., Solar-Lezama, A.: Verifiable reinforcement learning via policy extraction. In: Bengio, S., Wallach, H.M., Larochelle, H., Grauman, K., Cesa-Bianchi, N., Garnett, R. (eds.) Advances in Neural Information Processing Systems 31: Annual Conference on Neural Information Processing Systems 2018, NeurIPS 2018, 3-8 December 2018, Montréal, Canada. pp. 2499–2509 (2018)
9. Berkenkamp, F., Turchetta, M., Schoellig, A.P., Krause, A.: Safe model-based reinforcement learning with stability guarantees. In: Guyon, I., von Luxburg, U., Bengio, S., Wallach, H.M., Fergus, R., Vishwanathan, S.V.N., Garnett, R. (eds.) Advances in Neural Information Processing Systems 30: Annual Conference on Neural Information Processing Systems 2017, 4-9 December 2017, Long Beach, CA, USA. pp. 908–918 (2017)

10. Chen, X., Ábrahám, E., Sankaranarayanan, S.: Flow*: An analyzer for non-linear hybrid systems. In: Sharygina, N., Veith, H. (eds.) Computer Aided Verification - 25th International Conference, CAV 2013, Saint Petersburg, Russia, July 13-19, 2013. Proceedings. Lecture Notes in Computer Science, vol. 8044, pp. 258–263. Springer (2013)

11. Chow, Y., Nachum, O., Duéñez-Guzmán, E.A., Ghavamzadeh, M.: A lyapunov-based approach to safe reinforcement learning. In: Bengio, S., Wallach, H.M., Larochelle, H., Grauman, K., Cesa-Bianchi, N., Garnett, R. (eds.) Advances in Neural Information Processing Systems 31: Annual Conference on Neural Information Processing Systems 2018, NeurIPS 2018, 3-8 December 2018, Montréal, Canada. pp. 8103–8112 (2018)

12. Chow, Y., Nachum, O., Faust, A., Duéñez-Guzmán, E.A., Ghavamzadeh, M.: Safe policy learning for continuous control. In: Kober, J., Ramos, F., Tomlin, C.J. (eds.) 4th Conference on Robot Learning, CoRL 2020, 16-18 November 2020, Virtual Event / Cambridge, MA, USA. Proceedings of Machine Learning Research, vol. 155, pp. 801–821. PMLR (2020)

13. Christakis, M., Eniser, H.F., Hermanns, H., Hoffmann, J., Kothari, Y., Li, J., Navas, J.A., Wüstholz, V.: Automated safety verification of programs invoking neural networks. In: Silva, A., Leino, K.R.M. (eds.) Computer Aided Verification - 33rd International Conference, CAV 2021, Virtual Event, July 20-23, 2021, Proceedings, Part I. Lecture Notes in Computer Science, vol. 12759, pp. 201–224. Springer (2021)

14. Cousot, P., Cousot, R.: Abstract interpretation: A unified lattice model for static analysis of programs by construction or approximation of fixpoints. In: Conference Record of the Fourth ACM Symposium on Principles of Programming Languages, Los Angeles, California, USA, January 1977. pp. 238–252 (1977)

15. Dalal, G., Dvijotham, K., Vecerík, M., Hester, T., Paduraru, C., Tassa, Y.: Safe exploration in continuous action spaces. CoRR **abs/1801.08757** (2018)

16. Dawson, C., Fan, C.: Robust counterexample-guided optimization for planning from differentiable temporal logic. In: IEEE/RSJ International Conference on Intelligent Robots and Systems, IROS 2022, Kyoto, Japan, October 23-27, 2022. pp. 7205–7212. IEEE (2022)

17. Dutta, S., Chen, X., Sankaranarayanan, S.: Reachability analysis for neural feedback systems using regressive polynomial rule inference. In: Ozay, N., Prabhakar, P. (eds.) Proceedings of the 22nd ACM International Conference on Hybrid Systems: Computation and Control, HSCC 2019, Montreal, QC, Canada, April 16-18, 2019. pp. 157–168. ACM (2019)

18. Fan, J., Huang, C., Chen, X., Li, W., Zhu, Q.: Reachnn*: A tool for reachability analysis of neural-network controlled systems. In: Hung, D.V., Sokolsky, O. (eds.) Automated Technology for Verification and Analysis - 18th International Symposium, ATVA 2020, Hanoi, Vietnam, October 19-23, 2020, Proceedings. Lecture Notes in Computer Science, vol. 12302, pp. 537–542. Springer (2020)

19. François-Lavet, V., Henderson, P., Islam, R., Bellemare, M.G., Pineau, J.: An introduction to deep reinforcement learning. Foundations and Trends® in Machine Learning **11**(3-4), 219–354 (2018)

20. Frehse, G., Guernic, C.L., Donzé, A., Cotton, S., Ray, R., Lebeltel, O., Ripado, R., Girard, A., Dang, T., Maler, O.: Spaceex: Scalable verification of hybrid systems. In: Gopalakrishnan, G., Qadeer, S. (eds.) Computer Aided Verification - 23rd International Conference, CAV 2011, Snowbird, UT, USA, July 14-20, 2011.

Proceedings. Lecture Notes in Computer Science, vol. 6806, pp. 379–395. Springer (2011)

21. Fulton, N., Platzer, A.: Safe reinforcement learning via formal methods: Toward safe control through proof and learning. In: McIlraith, S.A., Weinberger, K.Q. (eds.) Proceedings of the Thirty-Second AAAI Conference on Artificial Intelligence, (AAAI-18), New Orleans, Louisiana, USA, February 2-7, 2018. pp. 6485–6492. AAAI Press (2018)

22. Fulton, N., Platzer, A.: Verifiably safe off-model reinforcement learning. In: Vojnar, T., Zhang, L. (eds.) Tools and Algorithms for the Construction and Analysis of Systems - 25th International Conference, TACAS 2019, Held as Part of the European Joint Conferences on Theory and Practice of Software, ETAPS 2019, Prague, Czech Republic, April 6-11, 2019, Proceedings, Part I. Lecture Notes in Computer Science, vol. 11427, pp. 413–430. Springer (2019)

23. Gehr, T., Mirman, M., Drachsler-Cohen, D., Tsankov, P., Chaudhuri, S., Vechev, M.T.: AI2: safety and robustness certification of neural networks with abstract interpretation. In: 2018 IEEE Symposium on Security and Privacy, SP 2018, Proceedings, 21-23 May 2018, San Francisco, California, USA. pp. 3–18 (2018)

24. Gillula, J.H., Tomlin, C.J.: Guaranteed safe online learning via reachability: tracking a ground target using a quadrotor. In: IEEE International Conference on Robotics and Automation, ICRA 2012, 14-18 May, 2012, St. Paul, Minnesota, USA. pp. 2723–2730. IEEE (2012)

25. Gilpin, Y., Kurtz, V., Lin, H.: A smooth robustness measure of signal temporal logic for symbolic control. IEEE Control. Syst. Lett. $5(1)$, 241–246 (2021)

26. Gowal, S., Dvijotham, K., Stanforth, R., Bunel, R., Qin, C., Uesato, J., Arandjelovic, R., Mann, T.A., Kohli, P.: On the effectiveness of interval bound propagation for training verifiably robust models. CoRR **abs/1810.12715** (2018)

27. Inala, J.P., Bastani, O., Tavares, Z., Solar-Lezama, A.: Synthesizing programmatic policies that inductively generalize. In: 8th International Conference on Learning Representations, ICLR 2020, Addis Ababa, Ethiopia, April 26-30, 2020. OpenReview.net (2020)

28. Ivanov, R., Weimer, J., Alur, R., Pappas, G.J., Lee, I.: Verisig: verifying safety properties of hybrid systems with neural network controllers. In: Ozay, N., Prabhakar, P. (eds.) Proceedings of the 22nd ACM International Conference on Hybrid Systems: Computation and Control, HSCC 2019, Montreal, QC, Canada, April 16-18, 2019. pp. 169–178. ACM (2019)

29. Jin, P., Tian, J., Zhi, D., Wen, X., Zhang, M.: Trainify: A cegar-driven training and verification framework for safe deep reinforcement learning. In: Shoham, S., Vizel, Y. (eds.) Computer Aided Verification - 34th International Conference, CAV 2022, Haifa, Israel, August 7-10, 2022, Proceedings, Part I. Lecture Notes in Computer Science, vol. 13371, pp. 193–218. Springer (2022)

30. Koller, T., Berkenkamp, F., Turchetta, M., Krause, A.: Learning-based model predictive control for safe exploration. In: 57th IEEE Conference on Decision and Control, CDC 2018, Miami, FL, USA, December 17-19, 2018. pp. 6059–6066. IEEE (2018)

31. Le, H.M., Voloshin, C., Yue, Y.: Batch policy learning under constraints. In: Chaudhuri, K., Salakhutdinov, R. (eds.) Proceedings of the 36th International Conference on Machine Learning, ICML 2019, 9-15 June 2019, Long Beach, California, USA. Proceedings of Machine Learning Research, vol. 97, pp. 3703–3712. PMLR (2019)

32. Li, S., Bastani, O.: Robust model predictive shielding for safe reinforcement learning with stochastic dynamics. In: 2020 IEEE International Conference on Robotics

and Automation, ICRA 2020, Paris, France, May 31 - August 31, 2020. pp. 7166–7172 (2020)

33. Lin, X., Zhu, H., Samanta, R., Jagannathan, S.: Art: Abstraction refinement-guided training for provably correct neural networks. In: 2020 Formal Methods in Computer Aided Design, FMCAD 2020, Haifa, Israel, September 21-24, 2020. pp. 148–157. IEEE (2020)

34. Mania, H., Guy, A., Recht, B.: Simple random search of static linear policies is competitive for reinforcement learning. In: Bengio, S., Wallach, H.M., Larochelle, H., Grauman, K., Cesa-Bianchi, N., Garnett, R. (eds.) Advances in Neural Information Processing Systems 31: Annual Conference on Neural Information Processing Systems 2018, NeurIPS 2018, 3-8 December 2018, Montréal, Canada. pp. 1805–1814 (2018)

35. Mirman, M., Gehr, T., Vechev, M.T.: Differentiable abstract interpretation for provably robust neural networks. In: Dy, J.G., Krause, A. (eds.) Proceedings of the 35th International Conference on Machine Learning, ICML 2018, Stockholmsmässan, Stockholm, Sweden, July 10-15, 2018. Proceedings of Machine Learning Research, vol. 80, pp. 3575–3583. PMLR (2018)

36. Moldovan, T.M., Abbeel, P.: Safe exploration in markov decision processes. In: Proceedings of the 29th International Conference on Machine Learning, ICML 2012, Edinburgh, Scotland, UK, June 26 - July 1, 2012. icml.cc / Omnipress (2012)

37. Oulamara, M., Venet, A.J.: Abstract interpretation with higher-dimensional ellipsoids and conic extrapolation. In: Kroening, D., Pasareanu, C.S. (eds.) Computer Aided Verification - 27th International Conference, CAV 2015, San Francisco, CA, USA, July 18-24, 2015, Proceedings, Part I. Lecture Notes in Computer Science, vol. 9206, pp. 415–430. Springer (2015)

38. Qiu, W., Zhu, H.: Programmatic reinforcement learning without oracles. In: The Tenth International Conference on Learning Representations, ICLR 2022, Virtual Event, April 25-29, 2022. OpenReview.net (2022)

39. Singh, G., Gehr, T., Mirman, M., Püschel, M., Vechev, M.T.: Fast and effective robustness certification. In: Bengio, S., Wallach, H.M., Larochelle, H., Grauman, K., Cesa-Bianchi, N., Garnett, R. (eds.) Advances in Neural Information Processing Systems 31: Annual Conference on Neural Information Processing Systems 2018, NeurIPS 2018, 3-8 December 2018, Montréal, Canada. pp. 10825–10836 (2018)

40. Singh, G., Gehr, T., Püschel, M., Vechev, M.T.: An abstract domain for certifying neural networks. Proc. ACM Program. Lang. 3(POPL), 41:1–41:30 (2019)

41. Sun, X., Khedr, H., Shoukry, Y.: Formal verification of neural network controlled autonomous systems. In: Ozay, N., Prabhakar, P. (eds.) Proceedings of the 22nd ACM International Conference on Hybrid Systems: Computation and Control, HSCC 2019, Montreal, QC, Canada, April 16-18, 2019. pp. 147–156. ACM (2019)

42. Tessler, C., Mankowitz, D.J., Mannor, S.: Reward constrained policy optimization. In: 7th International Conference on Learning Representations, ICLR 2019, New Orleans, LA, USA, May 6-9, 2019. OpenReview.net (2019)

43. Tran, H., Yang, X., Lopez, D.M., Musau, P., Nguyen, L.V., Xiang, W., Bak, S., Johnson, T.T.: NNV: the neural network verification tool for deep neural networks and learning-enabled cyber-physical systems. In: Lahiri, S.K., Wang, C. (eds.) Computer Aided Verification - 32nd International Conference, CAV 2020, Los Angeles, CA, USA, July 21-24, 2020, Proceedings, Part I. Lecture Notes in Computer Science, vol. 12224, pp. 3–17. Springer (2020)

44. Trivedi, D., Zhang, J., Sun, S.H., Lim, J.J.: Learning to synthesize programs as interpretable and generalizable policies. In: Beygelzimer, A., Dauphin, Y., Liang, P., Vaughan, J.W. (eds.) Advances in Neural Information Processing Systems (2021)

45. Turchetta, M., Berkenkamp, F., Krause, A.: Safe exploration in finite markov decision processes with gaussian processes. In: Lee, D.D., Sugiyama, M., von Luxburg, U., Guyon, I., Garnett, R. (eds.) Advances in Neural Information Processing Systems 29: Annual Conference on Neural Information Processing Systems 2016, December 5-10, 2016, Barcelona, Spain. pp. 4305–4313 (2016)
46. Uesato, J., Kumar, A., Szepesvári, C., Erez, T., Ruderman, A., Anderson, K., Dvijotham, K.D., Heess, N., Kohli, P.: Rigorous agent evaluation: An adversarial approach to uncover catastrophic failures. In: 7th International Conference on Learning Representations, ICLR 2019, New Orleans, LA, USA, May 6-9, 2019. OpenReview.net (2019)
47. Verma, A., Murali, V., Singh, R., Kohli, P., Chaudhuri, S.: Programmatically interpretable reinforcement learning. In: Dy, J.G., Krause, A. (eds.) Proceedings of the 35th International Conference on Machine Learning, ICML 2018, Stockholmsmässan, Stockholm, Sweden, July 10-15, 2018. Proceedings of Machine Learning Research, vol. 80, pp. 5052–5061. PMLR (2018)
48. Wang, S., Chen, Y., Abdou, A., Jana, S.: Mixtrain: Scalable training of formally robust neural networks. CoRR **abs/1811.02625** (2018)
49. Wang, Y., Huang, C., Wang, Z., Wang, Z., Zhu, Q.: Design-while-verify: correct-by-construction control learning with verification in the loop. In: Oshana, R. (ed.) DAC '22: 59th ACM/IEEE Design Automation Conference, San Francisco, California, USA, July 10 - 14, 2022. pp. 925–930. ACM (2022)
50. Wang, Y., Zhu, H.: VEL: Verification-guided Programmatic Controller Synthesis. https://doi.org/10.5281/zenodo.7574512, **https://github.com/ RU-Automated-Reasoning-Group/VEL**
51. Weng, T., Zhang, H., Chen, H., Song, Z., Hsieh, C., Daniel, L., Boning, D.S., Dhillon, I.S.: Towards fast computation of certified robustness for relu networks. In: Dy, J.G., Krause, A. (eds.) Proceedings of the 35th International Conference on Machine Learning, ICML 2018, Stockholmsmässan, Stockholm, Sweden, July 10-15, 2018. Proceedings of Machine Learning Research, vol. 80, pp. 5273–5282. PMLR (2018)
52. Wong, E., Kolter, J.Z.: Provable defenses against adversarial examples via the convex outer adversarial polytope. In: Dy, J.G., Krause, A. (eds.) Proceedings of the 35th International Conference on Machine Learning, ICML 2018, Stockholmsmässan, Stockholm, Sweden, July 10-15, 2018. Proceedings of Machine Learning Research, vol. 80, pp. 5283–5292. PMLR (2018)
53. Yang, C., Chaudhuri, S.: Safe neurosymbolic learning with differentiable symbolic execution. In: The Tenth International Conference on Learning Representations, ICLR 2022, Virtual Event, April 25-29, 2022. OpenReview.net (2022)
54. Yang, T., Rosca, J., Narasimhan, K., Ramadge, P.J.: Projection-based constrained policy optimization. In: 8th International Conference on Learning Representations, ICLR 2020, Addis Ababa, Ethiopia, April 26-30, 2020. OpenReview.net (2020)
55. Zhang, H., Chen, H., Xiao, C., Gowal, S., Stanforth, R., Li, B., Boning, D.S., Hsieh, C.: Towards stable and efficient training of verifiably robust neural networks. In: 8th International Conference on Learning Representations, ICLR 2020, Addis Ababa, Ethiopia, April 26-30, 2020. OpenReview.net (2020)
56. Zhu, H., Xiong, Z., Magill, S., Jagannathan, S.: An inductive synthesis framework for verifiable reinforcement learning. In: McKinley, K.S., Fisher, K. (eds.) Proceedings of the 40th ACM SIGPLAN Conference on Programming Language Design and Implementation, PLDI 2019, Phoenix, AZ, USA, June 22-26, 2019. pp. 686–701. ACM (2019)

Taming Large Bounds in Synthesis from Bounded-Liveness Specifications *

Philippe Heim$^{(\boxtimes)}$ and Rayna Dimitrova

CISPA Helmholtz Center for Information Security, Saarbrücken, Germany
{philippe.heim, dimitrova}@cispa.de

Abstract Automatic synthesis from temporal logic specifications is an attractive alternative to manual system design, due to its ability to generate correct-by-construction implementations from high-level specifications. Due to the high complexity of the synthesis problem, significant research efforts have been directed at developing practically efficient approaches for restricted specification language fragments. In this paper we focus on the `Safety LTL` fragment of Linear Temporal Logic (LTL) syntactically *extended with bounded temporal operators*. We propose a new synthesis approach with the primary motivation to solve efficiently the synthesis problem for specifications with bounded temporal operators, in particular those with large bounds. The experimental evaluation of our method shows that for this type of specifications it outperforms state-of-art synthesis tools, demonstrating that it is a promising approach to efficiently treating quantitative timing constraints in safety specifications.

1 Introduction

Reactive synthesis [8] has the goal of automatically generating an implementation from a formal specification that describes the desired behavior of a reactive system. The system requirements are typically specified using temporal logics such as Linear Temporal Logic (LTL). Temporal logics are expressive, high-level specification languages capable of describing rich properties, such as, for example, robotic missions [16]. Specifications of reactive systems often include requirements of the form "something good eventually happens". These can be expressed in LTL via the temporal operators $\mathcal{U}$ ("until") and $\Diamond$ ("eventually"). "Eventually" is an abstraction for the existence of some unknown time point in the future of a system execution when some property holds true. While this abstraction is useful for avoiding over-specification, there are many situations in which there are practical bounds on the time within which a requirement must be met. In such cases, it is vital that the synthesis procedure checks if the timing requirements are realizable, and synthesizes an implementation that adheres to these bounds.

As a simple example, consider a specification of the desired behavior of a controller for the front door of an office building. Our specification states that the

---

* Philippe Heim carried out this work as PhD candidate at Saarland University, Germany.

© The Author(s) 2023
S. Sankaranarayanan and N. Sharygina (Eds.): TACAS 2023, LNCS 13994, pp. 251–269, 2023.
https://doi.org/10.1007/978-3-031-30820-8_17

door must always be locked at night, and unlocked otherwise. It also stipulates that in the event of a fire the door should eventually open. Formulated like this, the specification is realizable. However, in case of a fire during night the synthesized implementation will only open the door at the start of the day. Clearly, this is not the behavior we intended! We can specify the actual desired behavior in LTL by using the temporal operator $\bigcirc$ ("next"), which allows us to state that a property should hold at the next time step. However, we would need to use nested $\bigcirc$ operators in order to express the required time bounds. This can quickly become inconvenient, especially if we need to specify various different time bounds, some of them large. This modeling inconvenience and the increase of specification size are easily avoided by adding bounded versions of the temporal operators as syntactic sugar, without increasing expressiveness.

Due to their practical significance, fragments of LTL in which the formulas (in negation normal form) include only bounded versions of the $\mathcal{U}$ and $\Diamond$ operators have attracted considerable attention. The most prominent such fragment is **Safety LTL** the until-free fragment of LTL in negated normal form. Since **Safety LTL** is a syntactic fragment of LTL, it can express bounded liveness properties only via nested next operators. Another notable example is the logic Extended Bounded Response LTL (LTL$_{EBR}$) [9], which is a fragment of LTL that includes bounded temporal operators as well as unbounded universal temporal operators (i.e., "globally" and "release"). While every LTL$_{EBR}$ formula can be expressed in **Safety LTL**, one significant advantage of LTL$_{EBR}$ is that the bounds of the temporal operators are represented in binary, which allows for exponentially more succinct formulas. However, in the course of the synthesis procedure presented in [9] these bounds are expanded into nested "next" operators. Keeping bounds symbolic is identified in [9] as an interesting direction for future developments. Indeed, in many practically relevant cases large bounds are unavoidable due to requirements on the same system across different time-scales.

In this paper we address this challenge by proposing a synthesis procedure for an extension of **Safety LTL** with bounded operators. We develop dedicated techniques for handling the temporal bounds symbolically and efficiently.

Contribution. We propose a synthesis method for specifications expressed in a fragment of LTL which is a syntactic extension of **Safety LTL** with bounded temporal operators. The distinguishing characteristic of our method is a reduction to a dedicated game model, called *countdown-timer games* in which the temporal operators' bounds are treated symbolically via the introduction of *timers*. Further features of the translation are techniques for on-the-fly pruning of edges in the constructed game and reduction of the number of introduced timers. We present an abstraction-based method for solving the resulting games. We have developed a prototype implementation of our approach, and the experimental evaluation demonstrates that it is indeed capable of handling efficiently safety specifications with large bounds. We demonstrate that on a set of benchmarks featuring bounded temporal operators with large bounds, our technique outperforms state-of-the-art tools for LTL$_{EBR}$ and LTL synthesis.

Related Work. *The synthesis problem for* Safety *LTL* has attracted significant interest due to its algorithmic simplicity compared to general LTL synthesis [25]. For instance, the symbolic approach presented in [25] is shown to outperform the state-of-the-art LTL synthesis tools at the time. For LTL_{EBR}, [9] proposes a synthesis algorithm based on a fully symbolic translation to deterministic safety automata. A key difference between our approach and the above techniques is that our countdown-timer game construction does not expand upfront the bounded temporal operators, but treats them symbolically instead. Furthermore, the authors of [25] point out that for large Safety LTL formulas the construction of the deterministic safety automaton presents a performance bottleneck. Our safety game constriction makes use of pruning in order to alleviate this problem by eliminating on-the-fly parts of the game graph that need not be explored.

Parameterized temporal logics, such as PLTL [1] enable the specification of parametric lower and upper bounds on the satisfaction time of the "globally" operator and the wait time of "eventually". In the logic PROMPT-LTL [17], only eventualities are parameterized by upper bounds. The bounds of the temporal operators in these logics are unknown parameters, while in the case that we consider, the bounds are given integer constants. The goal of our work is to develop a synthesis method that treats constant bounds efficiently.

In the *real-time setting*, temporal logics that allow for limiting the time scope of temporal operators have been extensively studied. Notable logics are Metric Temporal Logic (MTL) [15], and its fragment Metric Interval Temporal Logic (MITL) [2]. Compared to the untimed setting, synthesis from real-time logic specifications poses additional challenges. Controller synthesis is undecidable for MTL [4], for MITL [5,11], and even for the safety fragment of MTL [5]. Decidability is regained by fixing the resources (clocks and guards) of the controller [5,12]. The key challenge stems from the fact that synthesis requires deterministic automata, and it is not generally possible to construct deterministic timed automata for MITL. To circumvent this problem, the assumption of bounded variability is commonly made. Under this assumption, [20] proposes a synthesis algorithm for bounded response properties, and a translation from MTL to deterministic timed automata is presented in [23]. With respect to tool support, sound but incomplete synthesis methods for fragments of MTL have been proposed in [6] and [18], and implemented in toolchains that employ UPPAAL-TIGA [3] for timed games solving. A tool for MTL controller synthesis via translation to alternating timed automata was presented in [14]. In the case when the real-time synthesis problem is given as a timed game and the specification is a state-based winning condition, the problem of computing a control strategy is decidable [21]. Efficient on-the-fly algorithms for timed games have been developed [7], and successfully implemented in UPPAAL-TIGA [3] and UPPAAL-STRATEGO [10].Since we are interested in discrete-time systems, we circumvent the additional challenges present in the dense-time setting by remaining the realm of discrete time and focusing on efficiently treating quantitative timing constraints there.

2   Preliminaries

Reactive Synthesis Let $\mathcal{I}$ be a finite set of uncontrollable environment *input Boolean propositions* and $\mathcal{O}$ be a finite set of controllable *output Boolean propositions*. A *reactive system* is a tuple (C, c_0, γ) where C is a set of *control states*, $c_0 \in C$ the *initial control state*, and $\gamma : C \times 2^{\mathcal{I}} \to C \times 2^{\mathcal{O}}$ is the *transition function*. A *specification* is a language $\mathcal{L} \subseteq \left(2^{\mathcal{I} \cup \mathcal{O}}\right)^{\omega}$ of infinite words over $\mathcal{I} \cup \mathcal{O}$.

A system (C, c_0, γ) *realizes* a specification $\mathcal{L}$ if for all infinite sequences of environment inputs $i \in \left(2^{\mathcal{I}}\right)^{\omega}$ it yields an output sequence $o \in \left(2^{\mathcal{O}}\right)^{\omega}$ defined by $(c_{t+1}, o_t) = \gamma(c_t, i_t)$ for $t \in \mathbb{N}$, such that $i \cup o \in \mathcal{L}$. *Reactive synthesis* is the problem of finding a realizing implementation for a given specification.

Safety LTL with Bounded Liveness Operators We consider specifications expressed using temporal logic, more concretely, in a fragment of LTL [24], which we denote by $SafeLTL_B$. The fragment $SafeLTL_B$ is a syntactic extension of Safety LTL [25] and defined by the following grammar:

$$\varphi, \psi := ap \mid \neg ap \mid \varphi \wedge \psi \mid \varphi \vee \psi \mid \bigcirc[n]\varphi \mid \Diamond[n]\varphi \mid \varphi \, \mathcal{W}[n]\psi \mid \varphi \, \mathcal{W} \, \psi$$

for $ap \in \mathcal{I} \cup \mathcal{O}$ and $n \in \mathbb{N}$. $SafeLTL_B$ extends Safety LTL by bounded operators with bounds encoded in binary. While all bounded operators have equivalent Safety LTL formulas (e.g. $\Diamond[n]\varphi \equiv \bigvee_{i \in \{0...n\}} \bigcirc^i \varphi$) these have exponentially larger encoding. The constants $\top$ (true), $\bot$ (false), the "globally" operator $\Box$ and "bounded until" $\mathcal{U}[n]$ can be derived as $\top := a \vee \neg a$, $\bot := a \wedge \neg a$, $\Box \varphi := \varphi \, \mathcal{W} \, \bot$, $\Box[n]\varphi := \varphi \, \mathcal{W}[n] \bot$, and $\varphi \mathcal{U}[n]\psi := (\varphi \, \mathcal{W}[n]\psi) \wedge \Diamond[n]\psi$, respectively.

The satisfaction of a formula $\Phi \in SafeLTL_B$ by infinite word $w = w_0 w_1 \ldots \in \left(2^{\mathcal{I} \cup \mathcal{O}}\right)^{\omega}$ at time point $k \in \mathbb{N}$ is denoted as $w \vDash_k \Phi$ and is defined follows:

$$
\begin{aligned}
&w \vDash_k a &&:\Leftrightarrow a \in w_k &\qquad &w \vDash_k \neg a &&:\Leftrightarrow a \notin w_k \\
&w \vDash_k \varphi \wedge \psi &&:\Leftrightarrow (w \vDash_k \varphi) \wedge (w \vDash_k \psi) &\qquad &w \vDash_k \varphi \vee \psi &&:\Leftrightarrow (w \vDash_k \varphi) \vee (w \vDash_k \psi) \\
&w \vDash_k \Diamond[n]\varphi &&:\Leftrightarrow \exists i \leq n. \; w \vDash_{k+i} \varphi &\qquad &w \vDash_k \bigcirc[n]\varphi &&:\Leftrightarrow w \vDash_{k+n} \varphi
\end{aligned}
$$

$$w \vDash_k \varphi \, \mathcal{W}[n]\psi :\Leftrightarrow (\forall i \leq n. w \vDash_{k+i} \varphi) \vee (\exists j \leq n. w \vDash_{k+j} \psi \wedge \forall i < j. w \vDash_{k+i} \varphi)$$

$$w \vDash_k \varphi \, \mathcal{W} \, \psi :\Leftrightarrow (\forall i. w \vDash_{k+i} \varphi) \vee (\exists j. w \vDash_{k+j} \psi \wedge \forall i < j. w \vDash_{k+i} \varphi).$$

The language of $\Phi \in SafeLTL_B$ is defined as $\mathcal{L}(\Phi) := \{w \in \left(2^{\mathcal{I} \cup \mathcal{O}}\right)^{\omega} \mid w \vDash_0 \Phi\}$.

Two-Player Safety Games The synthesis problem for temporal logic specifications can be solved by translating the specification into a two-player game between the system and the environment, and then solving the game to determine the winning player. If the system wins, an implementation can be extracted.

A *game structure* is a tuple $G = (S, S_0, \mathcal{I}, \mathcal{O}, \rho)$, where S is a set of *states*, $S_0 \subseteq S$ is a set of *initial states*, $\mathcal{I}$ and $\mathcal{O}$ are sets of propositions as defined earlier, and $\rho : S \times 2^{\mathcal{I}} \times 2^{\mathcal{O}} \to S$ is a *transition function*. A game on G is played by two players, the system and the environment. In a given state $s \in S$, the environment chooses some input $i \subseteq \mathcal{I}$, then the system chooses some output $o \subseteq \mathcal{O}$, and these choices determine the next state $s' := \rho(s, i, o)$. The game then continues from s'. The resulting infinite sequence $\pi = s_0, s_1, s_2, \ldots$ of states is called a *play*. Formally, a play is a sequence $\pi = s_0, s_1, s_2, \ldots \in S^{\omega}$ such that

$s_0 \in S_0$ and for every $t \in \mathbb{N}$, $s_{t+1} = \rho(s_t, i, o)$. A *system strategy* is a function $\sigma : S^+ \times 2^{\mathcal{I}} \to 2^{\mathcal{O}}$. An *environment strategy* is a function $\pi : S^+ \to 2^{\mathcal{I}}$. Given a state $s \in S$, a system strategy σ and an environment strategy π, we denote with $Outcome(s, \pi, \sigma)$ the unique play $s_0, s_1, s_2, \ldots$ such that $s_0 = s$, and for all $k \in \mathbb{N}$, $s_{k+1} = \rho(s_k, i_k, \sigma((s_0, s_1 \ldots, s_k), i_k))$, where $i_k = \pi((s_0, s_1 \ldots, s_k))$.

A *safety game* is a tuple $(G, UNSAFE)$ where $UNSAFE \subseteq S$ are unsafe states. The system wins the safety game if it has a strategy σ such that for all environment strategies π, $s_0 \in S_0, k \in \mathbb{N}$, it holds that $Outcome(s_0, \pi, \sigma)_k \notin UNSAFE$. Such strategy is called a *winning strategy* for the system. Intuitively, the system has to avoid the unsafe states no matter what the environment does. The environment wins if it can enforce a visit to $UNSAFE$, i.e., when there exist environment strategy π and $s_0 \in S_0$ such that for every system strategy σ there exists $k \in \mathbb{N}$ such that $Outcome(s_0, \pi, \sigma)_k \in UNSAFE$.

3 $SafeLTL_B$ Synthesis with Countdown-Timer Games

$SafeLTL_B$ Synthesis We consider the realizability and synthesis problems for the fragment $SafeLTL_B$. We focus on the challenge of handling efficiently specifications with large bounds in the bounded temporal operators, and propose a new synthesis method towards achieving this goal. The proposed approach proceeds in two stages. In the first stage, the given $SafeLTL_B$ formula is transformed into a kind of safety game, in which bounds are treated symbolically. We term these games *countdown-timer games*, introduced later in this section. The second stage of our synthesis algorithm is the solving of the generated countdown-timer game in order to determine the winning player and answer the realizability question. We propose in Section 5 a method that employs symbolic representation and approximations in order to efficiently solve such games in practice.

Countdown-Timer Games Intuitively, countdown-timer games are like safety games but with additional *countdown-timers*. Countdown-timers are discrete timers that always start with an assigned duration and are decremented by one with every transition in the game. Once a timer reaches zero it times out, and the transition relation of the countdown-timer game may depend on this information for determining the successor state. A countdown-timer can be reset to the duration associated with it. In addition, countdown-timers with the same duration can swap their values, which we will later use when generating timer-games to avoid unnecessary blowup in the number of timers.

Definition 1 (Countdown-Timer Games). *A countdown-timer game structure is a tuple $G_T = (\mathcal{T}, d, L, L_0, \mathcal{I}, \mathcal{O}, \delta)$ where $\mathcal{T}$ is a finite set of countdown timers, $d : \mathcal{T} \to \mathbb{N}$ associates a duration with each timer, L is a finite set of game locations, $L_0 \subseteq L$ is the set of initial locations, $\mathcal{I}, \mathcal{O}$ are finite sets of uncontrollable environment input propositions and controllable system propositions, respectively, and $\delta : L \times 2^{\mathcal{I}} \times 2^{\mathcal{O}} \times 2^{\mathcal{T}} \to L \times \mathcal{E}$ is the transition relation. $\mathcal{E} := \mathcal{T} \to (\mathcal{T} \cup \{RESET\})$ is the set of effects where for all $e \in \mathcal{E}$:*
1. for all $t \in \mathcal{T}$ either $e(t) = RESET$, or $e(t) \in \mathcal{T}$ and $d(e(t)) = d(t)$ and,

2. *for* $t_1, t_2 \in \mathcal{T}$ *with* $t_1 \neq t_2$ *we have* $e(t_1) \neq e(t_2)$ *or* $e(t_1) = e(t_2) = RESET$.
A countdown-timer game is a pair $(G_T, UNSAFE_L)$ *where* $UNSAFE_L \subseteq L$ *is a set of* unsafe locations.

The effects $\mathcal{E}$ capture the resets and remapping of timers that can occur upon transitions. Condition (1) states that each timer is either reset or remapped to a timer with the same duration. Condition (2) requires the remapping to be injective, i.e. no two timers are mapped to the same timer. When timers are not reset and not remapped to other timers, they are simply mapped to themselves.

The semantics of a countdown-timer game is the safety game generated by explicitly expanding the possible valuations of the timers. Intuitively, each state of the game structure is a pair $s = (l, v)$ of a location $l \in L$ and a timer valuation v. Initially, each timer t is set to its associated duration $d(t)$. The transition relation updates the values of the timers by first decrementing them and then applying the effect e of the corresponding transition in G_T. The relevant transition in G_T is determined by the location l, the input and output sets i and o, and the set of timers whose value has become 0 after the decrementation.

Definition 2 (Countdown-Timer Games Semantics). *In the context of Definition 1, let* $\mathcal{V} := \{v : \mathcal{T} \to \mathbb{N} \mid \forall t \in \mathcal{T}.\ v(t) \leq d(t)\}$ *be the space of all possible timer valuations. Let* $G = (L \times \mathcal{V}, L_0 \times \{\lambda t.d(t)\}, \mathcal{I}, \mathcal{O}, \rho)$ *be a game structure where* $\rho((l, v), i, o) := trans(l, step(v), i, o)$ *with*

$$step(v) := \lambda t.\max\{0, v(t) - 1\}$$

$$trans(l, v, i, o) := \begin{cases} \left(l', \lambda t. \begin{cases} v(e(t)) & \text{if } e(t) \in \mathcal{T} \\ d(t) & \text{if } e(t) = RESET \end{cases} \right), \\ \text{where } (l', e) := \delta(l, i, o, \{t \in \mathcal{T} \mid v(t) = 0\}). \end{cases}$$

The semantics of the countdown-timer game $(G_T, UNSAFE_L)$ *is the safety game* $(G, UNSAFE_L \times \mathcal{V})$. *The system (environment) wins the countdown-timer game if and only if it wins the safety game representing its semantics.*

4   Countdown-Timer Game Construction

We now present the first phase of our synthesis algorithm, namely the translation of a *SafeLTL$_B$* formula to a countdown-timer game. Our construction is based on expansion rules. For example, the formula $\Diamond[50]a$ is equivalent to $a \vee \bigcirc \Diamond[49]a$. If a is true, then the whole formula is true. Otherwise, in the next step $\Diamond[49]a$ has to hold. Interpreted as a state of a safety game, $\Diamond[50]a$ has a transition to $\top$ on $a = \top$ and to $\Diamond[49]a$ on $a = \bot$. This can be repeated on $\Diamond[49]a$ and so on. Once we reach $\Diamond[0]a$ we expand it to $a \vee \bigcirc \bot$, and hence, $a = \bot$ leads to $\bot$ which is the unsafe state. This construction works for safety formulas, as rejection can be decided with a finite prefix. As we show later, generating a game structure in this way has the advantage that it can be pruned using information from the formula.

However, this explicit expansion yields a sequence of formulas that is linear in the bound, and hence, exponential in the description of the formula. Instead of explicit bounds, we use countdown-timers representing multiple values. In the above example, we do not generate all the expansions $\Diamond[50]a, \ldots, \Diamond[0]a$, but instead a timer t with duration 51 to represent all expansions from 50 to 0 in the single location $a \vee \Diamond[t]a$. If t times out, $\Diamond[t]$ has reached the end of the expansion and is transformed to $\bot$. Hence, instead of having $\Diamond[50]a, \ldots, \Diamond[0]a$, $\top$ and $\bot$ as states of a safety game we only have locations $a \vee \Diamond[t]a$, $\top$ and $\bot$ in a countdown-timer game. We now describe this construction formally.

4.1   Construction of a Countdown-Timer Game from $SafeLTL_B$

The locations of the generated countdown-timer games are $SafeLTL_B$ formulas with, additionally, timers as bounds of the temporal operators. We denote the set of these formulas as $SafeLTL_B^t$. Given a set of timers $\mathcal{T}$, the grammar of $SafeLTL_B^t$ is the grammar of $SafeLTL_B$ but in $\Diamond[n]$, $O[n]$, and $\mathcal{W}[n]$ we have $n \in \mathbb{N} \cup \mathcal{T}$. For $\varphi \in SafeLTL_B^t$, $Timers(\varphi) \subseteq \mathcal{T}$ denotes all timers appearing in φ.

Game Structure Let $\varPhi$ be a $SafeLTL_B$ formula over input propositions $\mathcal{I}$ and output propositions $\mathcal{O}$. We construct a countdown-timer game structure $(\mathcal{T}, d, L, L_0, \mathcal{I}, \mathcal{O}, \delta)$ as follows. The set of timers

$$\mathcal{T} := \{t_i^d \mid O[d], \Diamond[d-1], \text{ or } \mathcal{W}[d-1] \text{ occurs in } \varPhi, 0 \leq i \leq d\}$$

consists of timers t_i^d with index i and durations $d(t_i^d) := d$ for $0 \leq i \leq d$. The duration of a timer determines the bounds of the temporal operators in $\varPhi$ for which it can be used, and the indices are used for distinguishing multiple timers of the same duration (introduced at different points of the expansion).

Let $L := PositiveBooleanCombinations(cl(\varPhi))$ (i.e., built from $cl(\varPhi)$ using $\wedge, \vee$) be the set of locations, where cl is the *closure* operator defined as:

$$
\begin{aligned}
cl(l) &:= \{l, \top, \bot\} & l &\in \{ap, \neg ap\}\\
cl(\varphi \, o \, \psi) &:= cl(\varphi) \cup cl(\psi) & o &\in \{\wedge, \vee\}\\
cl(O[n]\varphi) &:= cl(\varphi) \cup \{O[t_i^n]\varphi \mid 0 \leq i \leq n\}\\
cl(\Diamond[n]\varphi) &:= cl(\varphi) \cup \{\Diamond[t_i^{n+1}]\varphi \mid 0 \leq i \leq n+1\}\\
cl(\varphi \, \mathcal{W}[n]\psi) &:= cl(\varphi) \cup cl(\psi) \cup \{\varphi \, \mathcal{W}[t_i^{n+1}]\psi \mid 0 \leq i \leq n+1\}\\
cl(\varphi \, \mathcal{W} \, \psi) &:= cl(\varphi) \cup cl(\psi) \cup \{\varphi \, \mathcal{W} \, \psi\}.
\end{aligned}
$$

Intuitively, the closure contains all possible temporal-operator sub-formulas and literals that can appear during expansion. The locations L then represent the expanded formulas, which, intuitively, correspond to the current obligations of the system. Thus, the initial location will correspond to obligation $\varPhi$. Note that $L \subseteq SafeLTL_B^t$. We apply simplifications to the generated formulas to ensure that L is finite. Since by definition $cl(\varPhi)$ is finite, we can ensure that $|L| \leq 2^{|cl(\varPhi)|}$.

In the construction of the initial location and the transition function we use two helper functions, $introExp : SafeLTL_B^t \to SafeLTL_B^t$, which performs expansion and introduces new timers, and $opt : SafeLTL_B^t \to L$, which performs simplifications that ensure that L is finite. We let $L_0 := \{opt(introExp(\varPhi))\}$ and

$$\delta(\varphi, i, o, T) := (opt(introExp(\psi)), e) \text{ where } (e, \psi) := squeeze(to(T, tree(\varphi, i, o))).$$

Here, we use the additional functions $tree : SafeLTL_B^t \times 2^\mathcal{I} \times 2^\mathcal{O} \to SafeLTL_B^t$, which performs the input and outputs choices, $to : 2^\mathcal{T} \times SafeLTL_B^t \to SafeLTL_B^t$, which handles time-outs, and $squeeze : SafeLTL_B^t \to \mathcal{E} \times SafeLTL_B^t$, which determines remapping and reset of timers. Below, we describe these functions in detail.

Remark: Note that for $\bigcirc[b]$ we use timers of duration b, while for $\Diamond[b]$ and $\mathcal{W}[b]$ we use timers of duration $b+1$. The reason for this is that for the latter we consider the last step as part of the timing as this simplifies the game structure.

Before describing the functions, we illustrate them on a simple example.

Example 1. Let $\mathcal{I} = \{r\}$, $\mathcal{O} = \{g\}$, and consider the $SafeLTL_B$ formula $\Phi = (\square[100]\neg g) \wedge \bigcirc[10](r \to \Diamond[100]g)$. Φ states that the system should not give a grant during the first 100 steps, and, if at step 10 there is a request, then a grant should be given within the following 100 steps. We show how to construct the initial location and some of the transitions in a countdown-timer game for Φ.

Initial state $\varphi_0 = opt(introExp(\Phi))$

The initial state is computed from Φ by expanding the formula and introducing any necessary timers. This is done by the function $introExp$. The subformula $\square[100]\neg g$ expands to $\neg g \wedge \square[t_0^{101}]\neg g$, reflecting the semantics of the operator $\square[100]$. This introduces the timer t_0^{101} with duration 101 and index 0. The subformula $\bigcirc[10](r \to \Diamond[100]g)$ expands to $\bigcirc[t_0^{10}](r \to \Diamond[100]g)$, which introduces the timer t_0^{10} for $\bigcirc[10]$. The durations 101 and 10 of the timers correspond to the respective bounds in $\square[100]$ and $\bigcirc[10]$, and the index 0 is the smallest index of a currently unused timer of the respective duration. No timer is introduced at this step for $\Diamond[100]$ as it is guarded by a $\bigcirc$ operator. Thus, the initial state is the expanded formula $\varphi_0 = \neg g \wedge (\square[t_0^{101}]\neg g) \wedge \bigcirc[t_0^{10}](r \to \Diamond[100]g)$.

Determining transition $\delta(\varphi_0, \emptyset, \{g\}, \emptyset) = (\varphi_1, e_1)$

We apply $tree(\varphi_0, \emptyset, \{g\})$ which computes the effect of the input $\emptyset$ and output $\{g\}$ on the formula in the current step, and thus substitutes g with $\top$ in φ_0. This results in $tree(\varphi_0, \emptyset, \{g\}) = \bot$, meaning that this transition leads to location $\bot$.

Determining transition $\delta(\varphi_0, \emptyset, \emptyset, \{t_0^{10}\}) = (\varphi_2, e_2)$

Again, we first compute $tree(\varphi_0, \emptyset, \emptyset) = (\square[t_0^{101}]\neg g) \wedge \bigcirc[t_0^{10}](r \to \Diamond[100]g)$, which now substitutes $\bot$ for g. To the result we apply the function to that handles time-outs, here $\{t_0^{10}\}$, which means that the timer t_0^{10} times out at the current step. As a result, the subformula $\bigcirc[t_0^{10}](r \to \Diamond[100]g)$ is replaced by $r \to \Diamond[100]g$, meaning that the formula $r \to \Diamond[100]g$ becomes part of the obligation at the next step, since the timer t_0^{10} has run out. Thus, we obtain $to(\{t_0^{10}\}, (\square[t_0^{101}]\neg g) \wedge \bigcirc[t_0^{10}](r \to \Diamond[100]g)) = (\square[t_0^{101}]\neg g) \wedge (r \to \Diamond[100]g)$. After that, we apply function $squeeze$ that takes care of timers that might have become unused upon time-out. This is reflected in the effect e_2 that resets all timers that do not appear in the current formula. Thus, in e_2 the timer t_0^{10} that just timed out is mapped to $RESET$, and the timer t_0^{101} that is still present is mapped to itself. The final step is to apply function $introExp$ that performs expansion on the current formula and introduces any new timers that might be needed. The subformula $\square[t_0^{101}]\neg g$ expands to $\neg g \wedge \square[t_0^{101}]\neg g$. The subformula $r \to \Diamond[100]g$ expands to $r \to (g \vee \Diamond[t_1^{101}]g)$, which introduces the timer t_1^{101} for $\Diamond[100]$. Note that since the formula already contains the timer t_0^{101} of duration 101, the newly introduced timer t_1^{101} has index 1. The functions *to* and *squeeze* ensure that the order between the indices of timers of the same duration represents the order in which these timers will time out. After computing $introExp((\Box[t_0^{101}]\neg g) \wedge (r \to \Diamond[100]g))$ we obtain $\varphi_2 = \neg g \wedge (\Box[t_0^{101}]\neg g) \wedge (r \to (g \vee \Diamond[t_1^{101}]g))$.

Construction We construct the sets of locations, timers, and transitions, by exploring the reachable parts of L from L_0. We describe several pruning mechanisms that we use in order to maintain the set of reachable locations small.

Construction Invariants. To ensure correctness and keep the game generation efficient, we maintain the following invariants for each reachable location:

1. For every reachable location φ we have (1.a) all literals and bounded operators not guarded by a "next" operator appear on the Boolean top-level, and (1.b) all bounded operators at the top-level are instantiated with a timer.
2. For every duration d, the values of the timers are ordered by index, i.e. $t_0^d < t_1^d < \ldots t_j^d = \ldots t_d^d = d$. The order is strict for timers whose value is not d.
3. In location φ, for any d and $i > 0$, if $t_i^d \in Timers(\varphi)$, then $t_{i-1}^d \in Timers(\varphi)$.

Invariant (1) is needed for correctness, and for ensuring that all literals that are relevant in the current step are considered, and that all relevant bounded operators are tracked by timers. Invariant (2) ensures that we never need more than the available d timers. This holds since the timers are strictly ordered when running, and once we would introduce t_{d+1}^d, t_0^d would have timed out. Furthermore, ordering the timers reduces the possible combinations of time-outs. Invariant (3) prevents having unused timers that are between used ones according to the above order, thus reducing the possible combinations of equivalent locations.

Function *tree*: *Selection of Inputs and Outputs.* The function $tree(\varphi, i, o)$ computes the effect of the input i and output o on the formula in the current step. With invariant (1) it suffices to consider literals on the Boolean top-level, i.e. literals that are not sub-formulas of a temporal operator. When assigning the literals in φ according to i and o, we prune and select some "obvious choices" which can immediately be decided, using the fact that we are generating a game. This pruning is an important part of our approach, as in practice it can prune a significant portion of the possible locations. Function *tree* applies recursively a set of rules. We now describe these rules in the order in which they are applied in each recursion step. Figure 1 provides a formal description.

1. With top-level disjunct c that is output literal, the system wins by making the formula $\top$. The opposite choice for the system can be safely pruned.
2. With top-level conjunct u that is input literal, the environment wins by making the formula $\bot$. The opposite choice can be safely pruned.
3. If an output proposition appears either with only positive or with only negative polarity, it suffices for the system to pick the literal with the respective polarity, as for the other choice the generated formula is subsumed.
4. If an input proposition appears either with only positive polarity or only negative polarity, it suffices to consider the case where the environment picks the negated literal, as this case is strictly more difficult to realize (i.e. one formula implies the other) and every strategy for this case works also for the other.

$$tree(c \lor \psi, i, o) := [\![c \in o]\!] \tag{1}$$

$$tree(u \land \psi, i, o) := \bot \tag{2}$$

$$tree(\psi, i, o) := \begin{cases} tree(\psi[c/\top]_T) & \text{if } c \in o \\ \bot & \text{if } c \notin o \end{cases} \qquad c \in ActL(\psi), \neg c \notin ActL(\psi) \tag{3}$$

$$tree(\psi, i, o) := tree(\psi[u/\bot]_T) \qquad u \in ActL(\psi), \neg u \notin ActL(\psi) \tag{4}$$

$$tree(\psi, i, o) := \psi[u/[\![u \in i]\!]]_T \qquad u, \neg u \in ActL(\psi) \tag{5}$$

$$tree(\psi, i, o) := \psi[c/[\![c \in o]\!]]_T \qquad c, \neg c \in ActL(\psi) \tag{6}$$

Figure 1: Let $u \in \mathcal{I}$ and $c \in \mathcal{O}$. For simplicity of the presentation we leave out the commutative and associative cases and negative literals. $ActL(\psi)$ denotes the set of literals appearing in the Boolean top-level of ψ. The formula $\psi[ap/v]_T$ is obtained from ψ by replacing ap by $v \in \{\top, \bot\}$ for all occurrences of ap at the Boolean top-level, but only there. After each replacement we simplify the formula by doing constant folding. $[\![x \in X]\!]$ is $\top$ if $x \in X$ and $\bot$ if $x \notin X$.

5. If no "early decision" or "worst case-decision" can be made, we apply the environment choice, as the environment moves first in the game.
6. If no environment choices are left, we generate the branching for the system.

Function to: Handling Time-out. A consequence of invariant (2) is that only timers with index 0, i.e., of the form t_0^d, can time out since the timers are ordered. In addition, timers that do not appear inside a formula should not time out (this is enforced by *squeeze*) as we show later. Note that this does not apply to timers with duration 1 as these time out immediately. We direct impossible time-outs to $\top$ since they do not occur. Hence, $to(T, \varphi) := \top$ if for some $t_i^d \in T$ we have that $i \neq 0$, or $d > 1$ and $t_i^d \notin Timers(\varphi)$. Otherwise, $to(T, \varphi)$ is defined by applying the following transformations on all subformulas of φ and timing out timers $t \in T$: We transform $\Diamond[t]\psi \rightsquigarrow \bot$, $\Box[t]\psi \rightsquigarrow \psi$, and $\phi \mathcal{W}[t]\psi \rightsquigarrow \top$. After applying *to* we do constant folding as parts of the formula may become irrelevant.

Function squeeze: Determining remapping and reset of timers. When applying the functions *tree* and *to* some timers might become unused. Hence, we have to ensure that invariant (3) holds and, as stated in the previous paragraph, reset all timers that do not appear in the formula. We define $squeeze(\varphi) := (e, \psi)$ as follows: For each duration d, let $t_{i_j}^d \in Timers(\varphi)$ with indices $i_0 < i_1 < i_2 < \ldots$ be the remaining timers with sorted indices i_j. Then set $e(t_j^d) := t_{i_j}^d$ if i_j exists and $e(t_j^d) := RESET$ otherwise. ψ is obtained by replacing the timers $t_{i_j}^d$ by t_j^d.

Function introExp: Expansion and Timer Introduction. The function *introExp* performs the formula expansion and introduces new timers if necessary. The expansion guarantees that invariant (1) holds afterwards. When introducing new timers, invariant (2) and invariant (3) have also to be maintained. This is achieved by assigning for each bound b with associated duration d, the timer with the next unused index, i.e. $t_j^d \notin Timers(\varphi)$ where $t_0^d, \ldots, t_{j-1}^d \in Timers(\varphi)$. Let $I(d) := \max\{i \mid t_i^d \in Timers(\varphi)\} + 1$ be the next unused index. In addition, as timers t_i^d with $i > d$ do not exist by invariant (2), expansions generating them are redirected to $\top$. Hence, we define $introExp(\varphi) := rd(iE_I(\varphi))$ where $rd(\varphi) := \top$ if for some $i > d$ we have $t_i^d \in Timers(\varphi)$, and $rd(\varphi) = \varphi$ otherwise. The function iE_I performing the expansion is defined by

$$
\begin{aligned}
iE_I(l) &:= l & iE_I(\varphi \circ \psi) &:= iE_I(\varphi) \circ iE_I(\psi) \\
iE_I(\Diamond[n]\varphi) &:= iE_I(\varphi) \vee \Diamond[t_{I(n+1)}^{n+1}]\varphi & iE_I(\Diamond[t]\varphi) &:= iE_I(\varphi) \vee \Diamond[t]\varphi \\
iE_I(\bigcirc[n]\varphi) &:= \bigcirc[t_{I(n)}^n]\varphi & iE_I(\bigcirc[t]\varphi) &:= \bigcirc[t]\varphi \\
iE_I(\varphi\,\mathcal{W}[n]\psi) &:= iE_I(\psi) \vee iE_I(\varphi) \wedge & iE_I(\varphi\,\mathcal{W}[t]\psi) &:= iE_I(\psi) \vee iE_I(\varphi) \\
&\quad\;\; (\varphi\,\mathcal{W}[t_{I(n+1)}^{n+1}]\psi) & &\quad\;\; \wedge (\varphi\,\mathcal{W}[t]\psi) \\
iE_I(\varphi\,\mathcal{W}\,\psi) &:= iE_I(\psi) \vee iE_I(\varphi) \wedge (\varphi\,\mathcal{W}\,\psi)
\end{aligned}
$$

where $l \in \{ap, \neg ap\}$, $o \in \{\wedge, \vee\}$, $n \in \mathbb{N}$ and $t \in \mathcal{T}$.

Function *opt*: *Formula Simplification*. The function opt ensures that the constructed set of locations L is finite, by simplifying the formulas in order to avoid introducing infinitely many logically equivalent formulas. Since we must maintain the invariants, the simplification does not guarantee uniqueness modulo equivalence. Nevertheless, it ensures finiteness of L and performs optimizations.

Definition of *UNSAFE* and Correctness To complete the construction of the countdown-timer game, we define the set of unsafe locations as $UNSAFE_L = \{\bot\}$. The proof of the correctness theorem below is given in the full version [13].

Theorem 1. *Let $\Phi \in SafeLTL_B$ and G be the countdown-timer game structure constructed from Φ as described above. Then there exists a system realizing $\mathcal{L}(\Phi)$ if and only if the system wins in the countdown-timer game $(G, UNSAFE_L)$.*

We augment the construction with several extensions to improve its efficiency and expand its scope. For instance, we combine explicit expansion with timer-based implicit expansion, which allows us to handle directly operators like single $\bigcirc$. We also use approximation to handle simple assumptions of the form $\Box\psi$ where ψ is fully bounded, i.e., without $\mathcal{W}$. Details can be found in the full version [13].

5   Solving Countdown-Timer Games

We now describe the second phase of our synthesis algorithm, namely the solving of the countdown-timer game generated from the $SafeLTL_B$ specification. In a countdown-timer game, the durations of the timers, which correspond to the bounds of the temporal operators in the specification, are encoded in binary. Hence, the set $\mathcal{V}$ of timer valuations and thus also the safety game defined in Section 3 grow exponentially in the size of the countdown-timer game. Since our goal is to efficiently solve countdown-timer games with large durations, explicitly constructing and solving the semantic safety game is not desired. We note, however, that in the worst case it is not possible to avoid this blowup. This is stated in the next theorem, the proof of which is given in the full version [13].

Theorem 2. *Solving countdown-timer games is EXPTIME-complete.*

This means that solving countdown-timer games efficiently requires an approach that manipulates sets of timer valuations symbolically, in order to avoid, if possible, explicit enumeration. We propose a symbolic algorithm for solving countdown-timer games that additionally employs an iteratively refined approximation. The method is applicable to generic symbolic representations of the set of timer valuations. We present an instantiation of the method with a representation composed of intervals of timer values and partial orders on timers.

Symbolic Game Solving The standard way to solve a safety game is to compute the set of states from which the environment can enforce reaching an unsafe state, and check if it intersects with the set of initial states. If this is the case, then the environment wins the game, and otherwise the system wins.

For a game (G, UNSAFE) with $G = (S, S_0, \mathcal{I}, \mathcal{O}, \rho)$, the set of states from which the environment can enforce reaching UNSAFE is called *environment attractor* and is defined as $\mathit{AttrE}_G(\mathit{UNSAFE}) = \{s \in S \mid \exists \pi : \text{env. strategy}. \forall \sigma : \text{sys. strategy}. \exists k \in \mathbb{N}.\ \mathit{Outcome}(s, \pi, \sigma)_k \in \mathit{UNSAFE}\}$. The environment wins the safety game if and only if $\mathit{AttrE}_G(\mathit{UNSAFE}) \cap S_0 \neq \emptyset$.

We solve the countdown-timer game by computing a symbolic representation of the attractor of the environment player to the unsafe locations. We assume a symbolic representation Rep of the space of timer valuations $2^{\mathcal{V}}$. For each $R \in \mathit{Rep}$ we denote with $[\![R]\!] \subseteq \mathcal{V}$ the subset of $\mathcal{V}$ represented by R. We represent subsets of the state space $L \times \mathcal{V}$ of the semantic safety game using functions from $L \to \mathit{Rep}$ where $U \in (L \to \mathit{Rep})$ represents $\{(l, v) \mid v \in [\![U(l)]\!]\}$.

The symbolic enforceable predecessor for the environment $\mathit{CPreE}_{symb} : (L \to \mathit{Rep}) \to (L \to \mathit{Rep})$ is defined as follows. For $U \in (L \to \mathit{Rep})$, we let

$$\mathit{CPreE}_{symb}(U) := \lambda l. \bigcup_{i \subseteq \mathcal{I}} \bigcap_{o \subseteq \mathcal{O}} \bigcup_{T \subseteq \mathcal{T}} \mathit{symTrans}(\delta(l, i, o, T), T, U), \text{ where}$$

$$\mathit{symTrans}((l', e), T, U) := \mathit{inc}(\mathit{effTO}(T, \mathit{remap}(e, \mathit{effReset}(e, U(l')))))$$

is the symbolic backward application of transition $\delta(l, i, o, T)$ to the target set $[\![U(l')]\!]$. The operations that $\mathit{symTrans}$ requires, from last to first, are as follows.

- $\mathit{inc} : \mathit{Rep} \to \mathit{Rep}$ performs the backward increment of the timers, formally, $[\![\mathit{inc}(R)]\!] = \{\lambda t.\ v(t) + 1 \in \mathcal{V} \mid v \in [\![R]\!]\}$.
- $\mathit{effTO} : 2^{\mathcal{T}} \times \mathit{Rep} \to \mathit{Rep}$ models the effect of time-outs: $[\![\mathit{effTO}(T, R)]\!] = \{v \in [\![R]\!] \mid \forall t \in \mathcal{T}.(t \in T \to v(t) = 0) \land (t \notin T \to v(t) \in [1, d(t)])\}$.
- $\mathit{remap} : \mathcal{E} \times \mathit{Rep} \to \mathit{Rep}$ models the effect of remapping: $[\![\mathit{remap}(e, R)]\!] = \{v \in \mathcal{V} \mid \exists v' \in [\![R]\!]. \forall t \in \mathcal{T} \text{ s.t. } e^{-1}(t) \text{ is defined. } v(t) = v'(e^{-1}(t))\}$.
- $\mathit{effReset} : \mathcal{E} \times \mathit{Rep} \to \mathit{Rep}$ models the effect of timer resets: $[\![\mathit{effReset}(e, R)]\!] = \{v \in [\![R]\!] \mid \forall t \in \mathcal{T}.e(t) = \mathit{RESET} \to v(t) = d(t)\}$. Note that $e^{-1}(t)$, the timer mapped to t by effect e is unique, since the effect is injective for values different from RESET, and can thus be inverted if defined.

We also require that we can preform set operations $\cup$, $\cap$, and equality checking between elements of Rep, in order to perform the computation.

We employ the symbolic enforceable predecessor operator $CPreE_{symb}$ to compute a symbolic representation of the environment attractor $AttrE_{symb}$ as follows. We set $AttrE^0_{symb} := (\lambda l.$ if $l \in UNSAFE_L$ then $\mathcal{V}$ esle $\emptyset)$, and then for $n \in \mathbb{N}$ we let $AttrE^{n+1}_{symb} := AttrE^n_{symb} \cup CPreE_{symb}(AttrE^n_{symb})$.

Proposition 1. *If* $(G_T, UNSAFE_L)$ *is a countdown-timer game with* $G_T = (\mathcal{T}, d, L, L_0, \mathcal{I}, \mathcal{O}, \delta)$ *and the safety game* $(G, UNSAFE_L \times \mathcal{V})$ *with* $G = (L \times \mathcal{V}, L_0 \times \{\lambda t.d(t)\}, \mathcal{I}, \mathcal{O}, \rho)$ *is its semantics, then for the symbolic attractor computed above it holds* $[\![AttrE_{symb}(l)]\!] = \{v \in \mathcal{V} \mid (l, v) \in AttrE_G\}$ *for every* $l \in L$.

Approximation of Timer Valuations As the symbolically represented statespace described above might still lead to exploring a large number of sets, we perform an over- and under-approximation of the attractor of explored states.

We use a *threshold* $k \in \mathbb{N}$ to control the precision of the abstraction. Intuitively, when approximating for $t \in \mathcal{T}$ we would like to treat exactly timer values at the "border", i.e. timer values in $[0, k]$ and $[d(t) - k, d(t)]$, since these matter for timeouts and resets. Our approximations $over : Rep \to Rep$ and $under : Rep \to Rep$ treat the intermediate values $[k, d(t) - k]$ like a single value-block. The over-approximation $over(R)$ adds all intermediate values if one value from R is inside $[k, d(t) - k]$ and the under-approximation $under(R)$ removes all intermediate values if one value from R is not inside. Formally:

$$approx_k(t, I) := (I \cap [k, d(t) - k] \neq \emptyset) \wedge ([k, d(t) - k] \not\subseteq I)$$

$$[\![over(R)]\!] := \left\{ \lambda t. \begin{cases} v(t) \cup [k, d(t) - k] & \text{if } approx_k(t, v(t)) \\ v(t) & \text{otherwise} \end{cases} \middle| v \in [\![R]\!] \right\}$$

$$[\![under(R)]\!] := \left\{ \lambda t. \begin{cases} v(t) \setminus [k, d(t) - k] & \text{if } approx_k(t, v(t)) \\ v(t) & \text{otherwise} \end{cases} \middle| v \in [\![R]\!] \right\}$$

The attractor computation is now done as follows: We start with $k := 1$. For the current k we compute the environment attractor once using under- and once using over-approximation at each symbolic state in the computation. If the environment wins in the under-approximation, it wins the concrete game. If the system wins in the over-approximation, it wins the concrete game. If neither holds, we set $k := 2 \cdot k$ and repeat. This always terminates since for $k > d(t)/2$ the approximations become exact, and hence, one player wins for sure.

Example 2. Consider a countdown-timer game, some transitions of which are depicted in Fig. 2a. From the depicted transitions, only the transition from l_2 to

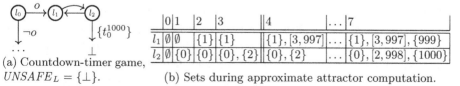

(a) Countdown-timer game, $UNSAFE_L = \{\bot\}$.

	0	1	2	3	4	...	7
l_1	$\emptyset$	$\emptyset$	$\{1\}$	$\{1\}$	$\{1\}, [3, 997]$	...	$\{1\}, [3, 997], \{999\}$
l_2	$\emptyset$	$\{0\}$	$\{0\}$	$\{0\}, \{2\}$	$\{0\}, \{2\}$	...	$\{0\}, [2, 998], \{1000\}$

(b) Sets during approximate attractor computation.

Figure 2: Example demonstrating the effect of approximation of timer valuations.

$\bot$ has a non-empty time-out set, $\{t_0^{1000}\}$. Since the timer t_0^{1000} has duration 1000, computing $AttrE_{symb}$ for the locations l_1 and l_2 precisely would require 1000 iterations. Employing over-approximation with threshold $k = 3$, on the other hand, reaches a fixed point in 7 iterations, as shown in Fig. 2b. This is helpful in cases like the one in the game in Fig. 2a, where the choice of transition in location l_0 is controlled by the system (via the output o). Here, the overapproximation allows the solving algorithm to quickly determine that the choice of transition to l_1 is loosing, while the system can win via the alternative transition.

Symbolic Representation using Boxes As a symbolic domain we chose an interval representation augmented with partial orders over timers $Rep := 2^{PartialOrder(\mathcal{T}) \times 2^{Rec}}$ where $Rec := \{\, i \in (\mathcal{T} \to \mathbb{N} \times \mathbb{N}) \mid \forall t \in \mathcal{T}, (a, b) = i(t).0 \le a \le b \le d(t)\}$ are the intervals in the form of a hyper-cube. Intuitively, we have a set of partial-orders and for each of them we have a set of hyper-cubes. Formally:

$$[\![R]\!] := \bigcup_{(p,C) \in R} \left(\{v \in \mathcal{V} \mid \forall (t_1 \sim t_2) \in p : v(t_1) \sim v(t_2)\} \cap \bigcup_{r \in C} \lambda t.[r(t)_1, r(t)_2] \right)$$

where $r(t)_i$ is the i-th projection of $r(t)$. It remains to define the necessary operations: *inc*, *effReset*, *effTO*, and *remap* are mostly straightforward according to their definition, as they can be performed by modifying and inspecting all intervals individually or just reordering timers. Additionally, *effReset* uses the partial order to derive bounds on timers that are in relation with a timer that is reset. *effTO* refines the partial order, since on time-out T, all timers in T are smaller than $\mathcal{T} \backslash T$. Also the approximations can be performed point-wise on the intervals, as an approximate interval is again an interval.

We chose this domain since it is simple, and, at the same time, due to the use of partial orders, well suited for the type of problem we are solving. Our solving algorithm is generic and can accommodate other, more sophisticated domains.

6   Evaluation

We implemented[1] and evaluated our approach. We compare our prototype implementation to `ebr-ltl-synth` introduced in [9] which performs synthesis for LTL$_{EBR}$. We also compare to the state-of-the-art LTL synthesis tool `strix` version 21.0.0 [19, 22]. In the following, we present the benchmarks we used, the experiments, and the results. We ran all experiments on an Intel Core i7-1165G7 processor with 16GB RAM and a single core available. All times are wall-clock times. A detailed description of the benchmarks is given in the full version [13].

Bounded Response Benchmarks In our first set of experiments we evaluate the tools on LTL$_{EBR}$ formulas from [9], and on 23 SYNTCOMP 2021 benchmarks[2] that fall into LTL$_{EBR}$ and are used for a similar comparison in [9]. Figure 3 and

---

[1] Available at: https://github.com/phheim/lisynt
[2] https://github.com/SYNTCOMP/benchmarks

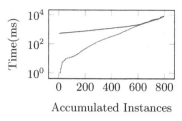
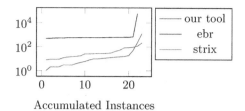

Figure 3: Execution times in milliseconds on the benchmarks [9].

Figure 4: Execution times in milliseconds on the LTL$_{\mathrm{EBR}}$ SYNTCOMP benchmarks.

Figure 4 show the runtimes with a time-out of one minute, respectively. Unfortunately, for roughly half of the benchmarks from [9] `strix` did not accept the input formula for being too long, since the bounded operators must be expanded explicitly upon input. We therefore left `strix` out for this comparison. Figure 3 shows that on the benchmarks from [9] both our implementation and `ebr-ltl-synth` have roughly the same runtime, ignoring different startup times. Figure 4 shows that on the selected SYNTCOMP benchmarks all three tools are comparable.

These experiments evaluate our implementation on relevant benchmarks that are partially not designed in the spirit of the problem that our approach targets. The results show that our implementation is comparable to existing tools.

Adaption of Real-Time Benchmarks In our second set of experiments, we took MTL synthesis problems from [14] and adapted them to *SafeLTL$_B$* formulas. The

Name	$|L|$	$|\mathcal{T}|$	τ_{Gen}	k	Win.	τ_Σ	$\tau_{\mathtt{strix}}$	Name	$|L|$	$|\mathcal{T}|$	τ_{Gen}	k	Win.	τ_Σ	$\tau_{\mathtt{strix}}$
$Clean(1)$	8	2	0.01	1	S	0.01	3.56	$Clean_H(1)$	3	2	0.02	512	E	0.07	1.61
$Clean(2)$	16	3	0.02	1	S	0.03	7.99	$Clean_H(2)$	3	2	0.02	512	E	0.07	2.63
$Clean(3)$	41	4	0.06	8	S	0.33	21.4	$Clean_H(3)$	3	2	0.02	512	E	0.07	4.99
$Clean(4)$	123	5	0.22	8	S	1.45	97.3	$Clean_H(4)$	3	2	0.02	512	E	0.07	5.64
$Clean_C(1)$	10	4	0.03	1	S	0.05	189	$Clean_N(1)$	23	4	0.07	1	S	0.12	TO
$Clean_C(2)$	22	5	0.08	16	S	617	TO	$Clean_N(2)$	32	4	0.10	1	S	0.27	TO
$Clean_C(3)$	61	6	0.32	-	-	TO	TO	$Clean_N(3)$	48	4	0.15	8	S	7.47	TO
$Clean_C(4)$	205	7	1.30	-	-	TO	TO	$Clean_N(4)$	75	4	0.26	8	S	13.7	TO
$Coffee(1)$	14	4	0.03	1	S	0.04	TO	$Coffee_C(1)$	46	6	0.16	1	S	0.88	F
$Coffee(2)$	44	5	0.12	2	S	0.33	TO	$Coffee_C(2)$	151	7	0.59	1	S	5.51	F
$Coffee(3)$	175	6	0.55	2	S	3.53	TO	$Coffee_C(3)$	613	8	2.73	1	S	62.9	F
$Coffee(4)$	418	7	1.34	2	S	10.2	TO	$Coffee_C(4)$	1634	9	6.82	1	S	191	F
conv-belt	9	3	0.01	1	S	0.02	F	rail(4,8)	647	7	2.53	1	S	3.96	TO
robo-cam	22	5	0.04	1	S	0.19	F	rail(8,8)	647	7	2.60	1	S	4.03	TO
rail(2,2)	647	6	2.60	1	S	3.93	TO	rail(1,1,1)	3111	7	27.8	-	-	TO	TO
rail(2,4)	647	6	2.58	1	S	4.05	TO	rail(2,1,1)	9179	9	89.1	1	S	220	TO
rail(2,8)	647	6	2.62	1	S	3.97	TO	rail(2,2,2)	9179	9	93.7	1	S	225	TO
rail(4,4)	647	7	2.67	1	S	4.10	TO								

Table 1: Results on the office-robot and adapted real-time benchmarks. $|L|$ and $|\mathcal{T}|$ are the numbers of locations and timers in the generated countdown-timer game. τ_{Gen} is the runtime of the game generation in seconds. k is the approximation threshold on which the solving terminated. Win. shows whether the system (S) or the environment (E) wins. τ_Σ is the total runtime including the game generation and solving, where TO means a time-out after 15 minutes. $\tau_{\mathtt{strix}}$ is the runtime of `strix`. For some benchmarks `strix` rejects the input for being too long (F) which is due to expanding the bounded operators when using `strix`.

benchmarks include a conveyor belt (conv-belt), a robot camera (robo-cam), and several parametrized instances of a multiple railroad-crossings controller (rail). We discretized the real-time bounds. The benchmarks use up to 19 propositions and 16 bounded operators, and bounds between 60 and 4000. Detailed results can be found in Table 1. ebr-ltl-synth was not applicable to these benchmarks as we had to use assumptions (which cannot be captured by the specifications in the LTL$_{EBR}$ fragment) to model the timed environment.

These experiments show that *SafeLTL$_B$* can express interesting requirements from the real-time domain by appropriate discretization. We did not compare directly to the tool in [14], as the underlying modeling formalism is different, and hence we adapted the benchmarks. However, a superficial comparison of our results to those in [14] shows that our tool compares well (and is in some cases better). Furthermore, on these benchmarks our tool clearly outperforms strix.

Office Robot Benchmarks Our last set of experiments considers benchmarks we created ourselves. They consists of a number of specifications describing tasks for a robot in an office building with four rooms. The benchmarks are parametrized by the number of rooms that have to be serviced. They use up to 11 propositions and 14 bounded temporal operators, and bounds between 10 and 21600. Detailed results can be found in Table 1. ebr-ltl-synth was either not applicable due to use of assumptions (4 benchmarks) or timed out (25 benchmarks).

The results show that *SafeLTL$_B$* can express meaningful synthesis tasks, and that our approach is viable for solving them. Furthermore, they show that our method indeed fulfills its purpose: for specifications requiring large bounds in the temporal operators our method clearly outperforms the state-of-the-art tools.

Overall Analysis Table 1 shows that the countdown-timer game generation is very efficient compared to the solving. As we expect to be able to improve the solving by more sophisticated symbolic techniques, we expect the countdown-timer game based approach to be viable for even more complex properties. In most cases the solver terminated with a low approximation threshold, which shows the usefulness of approximation. In our experience, without approximation solving the benchmarks with large bounds becomes infeasible with our current technique.

7   Conclusion

We presented a new synthesis approach for specifications expressed in an extension of Safety LTL with bounded temporal operators. A distinguishing feature of our method is that it is specifically targeted at efficiently solving the synthesis problem for specifications with bounded temporal operators, in particular those with large bounds. Our evaluation results show that our technique performs very well on a range of benchmarks featuring such timing requirements. The key to this success is a novel translation to a safety game with symbolically represented bounds, whose efficiency is due to the use of effective pruning techniques. We observe that our method for solving the generated game is viable, as shown by the evaluation. However, it has potential for further improvement by employing more performant symbolic representations and abstraction techniques.

Data-Availability Statement

The datasets generated during and/or analysed during the current study are available in the Zenodo repository, https://doi.org/10.5281/zenodo.7505914.

References

1. Alur, R., Etessami, K., Torre, S.L., Peled, D.A.: Parametric temporal logic for "model measuring". ACM Trans. Comput. Log. **2**(3), 388–407 (2001). https://doi.org/10.1145/377978.377990, https://doi.org/10.1145/377978.377990
2. Alur, R., Feder, T., Henzinger, T.A.: The benefits of relaxing punctuality. J. ACM **43**(1), 116–146 (1996). https://doi.org/10.1145/227595.227602, https://doi.org/10.1145/227595.227602
3. Behrmann, G., Cougnard, A., David, A., Fleury, E., Larsen, K.G., Lime, D.: Uppaal-tiga: Time for playing games! In: Damm, W., Hermanns, H. (eds.) Computer Aided Verification, 19th International Conference, CAV 2007, Berlin, Germany, July 3-7, 2007, Proceedings. Lecture Notes in Computer Science, vol. 4590, pp. 121–125. Springer (2007). https://doi.org/10.1007/978-3-540-73368-3_14, https://doi.org/10.1007/978-3-540-73368-3_14
4. Bouyer, P., Bozzelli, L., Chevalier, F.: Controller synthesis for MTL specifications. In: Baier, C., Hermanns, H. (eds.) CONCUR 2006 - Concurrency Theory, 17th International Conference, CONCUR 2006, Bonn, Germany, August 27-30, 2006, Proceedings. Lecture Notes in Computer Science, vol. 4137, pp. 450–464. Springer (2006). https://doi.org/10.1007/11817949_30, https://doi.org/10.1007/11817949_30
5. Brihaye, T., Estiévenart, M., Geeraerts, G., Ho, H., Monmege, B., Sznajder, N.: Real-time synthesis is hard! In: Fränzle, M., Markey, N. (eds.) Formal Modeling and Analysis of Timed Systems - 14th International Conference, FORMATS 2016, Quebec, QC, Canada, August 24-26, 2016, Proceedings. Lecture Notes in Computer Science, vol. 9884, pp. 105–120. Springer (2016). https://doi.org/10.1007/978-3-319-44878-7_7, https://doi.org/10.1007/978-3-319-44878-7_7
6. Bulychev, P.E., David, A., Larsen, K.G., Li, G.: Efficient controller synthesis for a fragment of $mtl_{0,\infty}$. Acta Informatica **51**(3-4), 165–192 (2014). https://doi.org/10.1007/s00236-013-0189-z, https://doi.org/10.1007/s00236-013-0189-z
7. Cassez, F.: Efficient on-the-fly algorithms for partially observable timed games. In: Raskin, J., Thiagarajan, P.S. (eds.) Formal Modeling and Analysis of Timed Systems, 5th International Conference, FORMATS 2007, Salzburg, Austria, October 3-5, 2007, Proceedings. Lecture Notes in Computer Science, vol. 4763, pp. 5–24. Springer (2007). https://doi.org/10.1007/978-3-540-75454-1_3, https://doi.org/10.1007/978-3-540-75454-1_3
8. Church, A.: Logic, arithmetic and automata. In: International congress of mathematicians. pp. 23–35 (1962)
9. Cimatti, A., Geatti, L., Gigante, N., Montanari, A., Tonetta, S.: Reactive synthesis from extended bounded response LTL specifications. In: 2020 Formal Methods in Computer Aided Design, FMCAD 2020, Haifa, Israel, September 21-24, 2020. pp. 83–92. IEEE (2020). https://doi.org/10.34727/2020/isbn.978-3-85448-042-6_15, https://doi.org/10.34727/2020/isbn.978-3-85448-042-6_15

10. David, A., Jensen, P.G., Larsen, K.G., Mikucionis, M., Taankvist, J.H.: Uppaal stratego. In: Baier, C., Tinelli, C. (eds.) Tools and Algorithms for the Construction and Analysis of Systems - 21st International Conference, TACAS 2015, Held as Part of the European Joint Conferences on Theory and Practice of Software, ETAPS 2015, London, UK, April 11-18, 2015. Proceedings. Lecture Notes in Computer Science, vol. 9035, pp. 206–211. Springer (2015). https://doi.org/10.1007/978-3-662-46681-0_16, https://doi.org/10.1007/978-3-662-46681-0_16

11. Doyen, L., Geeraerts, G., Raskin, J., Reichert, J.: Realizability of real-time logics. In: Ouaknine, J., Vaandrager, F.W. (eds.) Formal Modeling and Analysis of Timed Systems, 7th International Conference, FORMATS 2009, Budapest, Hungary, September 14-16, 2009. Proceedings. Lecture Notes in Computer Science, vol. 5813, pp. 133–148. Springer (2009). https://doi.org/10.1007/978-3-642-04368-0_12, https://doi.org/10.1007/978-3-642-04368-0_12

12. D'Souza, D., Madhusudan, P.: Timed control synthesis for external specifications. In: Alt, H., Ferreira, A. (eds.) STACS 2002, 19th Annual Symposium on Theoretical Aspects of Computer Science, Antibes - Juan les Pins, France, March 14-16, 2002, Proceedings. Lecture Notes in Computer Science, vol. 2285, pp. 571–582. Springer (2002). https://doi.org/10.1007/3-540-45841-7_47, https://doi.org/10.1007/3-540-45841-7_47

13. Heim, P., Dimitrova, R.: Taming large bounds in synthesis from bounded-liveness specifications (full version) (2023). https://doi.org/10.48550/ARXIV.2301.10032, https://arxiv.org/abs/2301.10032

14. Hofmann, T., Schupp, S.: Tacos: A tool for MTL controller synthesis. In: Calinescu, R., Pasareanu, C.S. (eds.) Software Engineering and Formal Methods - 19th International Conference, SEFM 2021, Virtual Event, December 6-10, 2021, Proceedings. Lecture Notes in Computer Science, vol. 13085, pp. 372–379. Springer (2021). https://doi.org/10.1007/978-3-030-92124-8_21, https://doi.org/10.1007/978-3-030-92124-8_21

15. Koymans, R.: Specifying real-time properties with metric temporal logic. Real Time Syst. $2(4)$, 255–299 (1990). https://doi.org/10.1007/BF01995674, https://doi.org/10.1007/BF01995674

16. Kress-Gazit, H., Fainekos, G.E., Pappas, G.J.: Temporal-logic-based reactive mission and motion planning. IEEE Trans. Robotics $25(6)$, 1370–1381 (2009). https://doi.org/10.1109/TRO.2009.2030225, https://doi.org/10.1109/TRO.2009.2030225

17. Kupferman, O., Piterman, N., Vardi, M.Y.: From liveness to promptness. Formal Methods Syst. Des. $34(2)$, 83–103 (2009). https://doi.org/10.1007/s10703-009-0067-z, https://doi.org/10.1007/s10703-009-0067-z

18. Li, G., Jensen, P.G., Larsen, K.G., Legay, A., Poulsen, D.B.: Practical controller synthesis for $mtl_{0,\infty}$. In: Erdogmus, H., Havelund, K. (eds.) Proceedings of the 24th ACM SIGSOFT International SPIN Symposium on Model Checking of Software, Santa Barbara, CA, USA, July 10-14, 2017. pp. 102–111. ACM (2017). https://doi.org/10.1145/3092282.3092303, https://doi.org/10.1145/3092282.3092303

19. Luttenberger, M., Meyer, P.J., Sickert, S.: Practical synthesis of reactive systems from LTL specifications via parity games. Acta Informatica $57(1-2)$, 3–36 (2020). https://doi.org/10.1007/s00236-019-00349-3, https://doi.org/10.1007/s00236-019-00349-3

20. Maler, O., Nickovic, D., Pnueli, A.: On synthesizing controllers from bounded-response properties. In: Damm, W., Hermanns, H. (eds.) Computer Aided Ver-

ification, 19th International Conference, CAV 2007, Berlin, Germany, July 3-7, 2007, Proceedings. Lecture Notes in Computer Science, vol. 4590, pp. 95–107. Springer (2007). https://doi.org/10.1007/978-3-540-73368-3_12, https://doi.org/10.1007/978-3-540-73368-3_12

21. Maler, O., Pnueli, A., Sifakis, J.: On the synthesis of discrete controllers for timed systems (an extended abstract). In: Mayr, E.W., Puech, C. (eds.) STACS 95, 12th Annual Symposium on Theoretical Aspects of Computer Science, Munich, Germany, March 2-4, 1995, Proceedings. Lecture Notes in Computer Science, vol. 900, pp. 229–242. Springer (1995). https://doi.org/10.1007/3-540-59042-0_76, https://doi.org/10.1007/3-540-59042-0_76

22. Meyer, P.J., Sickert, S., Luttenberger, M.: Strix: Explicit reactive synthesis strikes back! In: Chockler, H., Weissenbacher, G. (eds.) Computer Aided Verification - 30th International Conference, CAV 2018, Held as Part of the Federated Logic Conference, FloC 2018, Oxford, UK, July 14-17, 2018, Proceedings, Part I. Lecture Notes in Computer Science, vol. 10981, pp. 578–586. Springer (2018). https://doi.org/10.1007/978-3-319-96145-3_31, https://doi.org/10.1007/978-3-319-96145-3_31

23. Nickovic, D., Piterman, N.: From mtl to deterministic timed automata. In: Chatterjee, K., Henzinger, T.A. (eds.) Formal Modeling and Analysis of Timed Systems - 8th International Conference, FORMATS 2010, Klosterneuburg, Austria, September 8-10, 2010. Proceedings. Lecture Notes in Computer Science, vol. 6246, pp. 152–167. Springer (2010). https://doi.org/10.1007/978-3-642-15297-9_13, https://doi.org/10.1007/978-3-642-15297-9_13

24. Pnueli, A.: The temporal logic of programs. In: 18th Annual Symposium on Foundations of Computer Science, Providence, Rhode Island, USA, 31 October - 1 November 1977. pp. 46–57. IEEE Computer Society (1977). https://doi.org/10.1109/SFCS.1977.32, https://doi.org/10.1109/SFCS.1977.32

25. Zhu, S., Tabajara, L.M., Li, J., Pu, G., Vardi, M.Y.: A symbolic approach to safety LTL synthesis. In: Strichman, O., Tzoref-Brill, R. (eds.) Hardware and Software: Verification and Testing - 13th International Haifa Verification Conference, HVC 2017, Haifa, Israel, November 13-15, 2017, Proceedings. Lecture Notes in Computer Science, vol. 10629, pp. 147–162. Springer (2017). https://doi.org/10.1007/978-3-319-70389-3_10, https://doi.org/10.1007/978-3-319-70389-3_10

Lockstep Composition for Unbalanced Loops

Ameer Hamza[ID] and Grigory Fedyukovich[✉][ID]

Florida State University, Tallahassee, FL, USA,
ahamza@fsu.edu, grigory@cs.fsu.edu

Abstract. Equivalence checking of two programs is often reduced to
the safety verification of a so-called product program that aligns the
programs in lockstep. However, this strategy is not applicable when programs have arbitrary loop structures, e.g., the numbers of loops vary. We
introduce an automatic iterative abstraction-refinement-based technique
for checking equivalence of a single-loop program and a program which
has a series of consecutive loops. Our approach decomposes the single
loop into a sequence of separate loops thus reducing the main problem
to a series of equivalence-checking problems for pairs of loops. Since due
to the decomposition, these problems become abstract, our approach iteratively refines the decomposed loops and lifts useful information across
them. Our second contribution is a procedure for the alignment of loops
with counters and explicit bounds that cannot be composed in lockstep.
We have implemented the approach and successfully evaluated it on two
suites, one with benchmarks containing different numbers of loops and
the other containing benchmarks that need alignment.

1 Introduction

To gain performance benefits, optimizing compilers perform program transformations such as loop peeling, loop unrolling, and loop unswitching. The reliance
on many transformations lowers the trust in the computation and motivates us
to use automated SMT-based verification to *verify equivalence* of the program
before and after the transformation. Specifically, one should prove that for any
equal inputs to both programs, their outputs are equal too. The problem is often reduced to construction of a *product program* by *aligning* (or merging) the
instructions in lockstep and then determining if the product program meets a
safety specification represented by the original relational specification. While effective for many pairs of programs that are relatively close to each other, this
strategy may be insufficient for pairs of loopy programs with arbitrary control
flow. We target the verification of pairs of programs in which the source program
has a single loop, and the target program has a sequence of non-nested loops.
Such programs have been extensively studied in the literature [4,23,31] but still
are challenging for automated reasoning.

Before proving equivalence, our approach decomposes the loop in the source
program into multiple loops such that the structure of this new program exactly
matches the one in the target program. With two structurally similar programs

S. Sankaranarayanan and N. Sharygina (Eds.): TACAS 2023, LNCS 13994, pp. 270–288, 2023.
https://doi.org/10.1007/978-3-031-30820-8_18

at hand, our approach targets pairs of loops and creates a lockstep composition for each pair. This lets us break our equivalence checking problem into smaller isolated problems, and if each such problem is successfully solved, then the given programs are indeed equivalent. An obvious downside of decomposition is the loss of context: if a program property is defined before the first loop, it may not be available for the second and later loops. For that reason, we have to *refine* the decomposition by extracting the requested properties in the previously considered pairs of loops and pulling them to the currently-considered loops. Technically, this process is driven by counterexamples.

Moreover, when attempting to create a lockstep composition for loops that have different numbers of iterations, we might need to *align* them. When our method can compute an exact number of iterations of both the source and the target, it rearranges the control flow in the source by grouping the iterations in the loop, and extracting selected iterations to either before the loop or after. Such rearranging helps with programs where the number of iterations of one loop is a multiple of other, or is off by few iterations, which is common for optimizations including loop vectorization and loop peeling.

We implemented our equivalence checking algorithm, along with the algorithms to refine and align the loops, in a tool called ALIEN. On many commonly used public benchmarks [23], ALIEN is an order of magnitude faster than the most recent (to our knowledge) state-of-the-art tool COUNTER [14]. ALIEN can prove equivalence of pairs of user-written programs and it is not bound to any particular compiler unlike many related tools based on translation validation.

We proceed with an overview of the related work in Sect. 2 and a motivating example in Sect. 3. Then, we formally introduce our problem in Sect. 4. The main ingredients of our algorithm are then discussed in Sect. 5, and in Sect. 6. The evaluation is reported in Sect. 7, and conclusion in Sect. 8.

2   Related Work

Relational verification aims at analyzing two different programs or two executions of the same program. This research field has been extensively studied, but since it reduces to safety verification, it is known to be undecidable in general. Relational verification has applications in checking program equivalence, information-flow leakage, incremental verification, etc. To reduce to safety, it is a common practice to convert the programs into a product. The product can be used for relational verification tasks by providing appropriate relational precondition and postcondition. This research trend is pioneered by Barthe et al. [3] who used product programs in Hoare-style proving. More recently, there has been a rise of automated product construction techniques. e.g., [7, 16, 25, 26].

Creating product program requires that the two programs can be composed in some way, which is usually assumed to be trivial (e.g., lockstep), or provided to the verifier in some form. However, it is not always possible to get the trivial composition. The technique presented by Strichman et al. [36] extends the work of Godlin et al. [12] and it attempts to prove equivalence of two recursive functions having different base-cases and no lockstep composition, by creating an alignment between them. However, the alignment is done using unrolling factors, which are manually provided by the user, for both programs. The technique presented in [34] targets self-composition. It computes a scheduler for an asynchronous execution of both programs using counterexamples and a selection of predicates (e.g., from the user). A more recent work [38] is also a scheduler-driven but mainly targets mutual termination rather than full functional equivalence.

Translation validation techniques, [9, 17, 20, 22, 27, 28, 32, 35, 39], relate the source programs with their compiler outputs to check equivalence. However, it is usually the case that the compiler provides the manner of composition. Many data-driven techniques for proving equivalence, like [5, 33], rely on finding a trace alignment between concrete executions of the programs. Such techniques might perform inefficiently when sufficient number of execution traces are not available. They might also require a lot of time for the data runs. The work in [22] performs bounded translation validation at the level of LLVM intermediate representation. The technique looks for a subset of behaviors of the source program in the target to infer equivalence. As the technique is bounded, it may not be sound.

The work by Gupta et al. [14] presents a counterexample-guided algorithm for translation validation of given programs. It explores the space of potential products to find a bisimulation relation between intermediate program locations of the two programs. and prove it via the generation of strong enough inductive invariants. Again, while making the approach flexible, reliance on counterexamples makes it slower, and as we will see from our evaluation (Sect. 7), this approach does not scale well in the cases an alignment needs larger unrollings.

Many techniques use relational verification for regression verification, where two versions of a program are compared for equivalence checking [1, 2, 11, 13, 15, 19, 24, 30, 36, 37]. Such techniques usually assume that two programs are closely related, hence the analysis is usually reduced by either pruning out or abstracting common parts of the programs. Many techniques simplify the process of equivalence checking. Some assume a static relationship between the number of iterations of two loops, in order to prove equivalence [6, 11, 21, 29, 33]. Other techniques create finite unrollings of loops and prove equivalence until a certain bound, e.g., [1,18,22,30]. Our work makes an attempt to relax such assumptions.

3 Illustration on Example

Fig. 1 gives two C programs, the source program contains a single loop and the optimized target programs contains two sequential loops. Our approach aims at proving the equivalence of the source and the target, that is, if variables are initially given equal values (b = d, M = X, K = Y), then their values at the end are equal toothen outputs are equal too to, i.e., a = c, b = d. A *lockstep composition* on the programs in Fig. 1 is challenging to construct: 1) it is difficult to compare one loop with two sequential loops, and 2) there are different numbers of iterations taken by programs.

Our method decomposes the source loop into two loops to make it easier to create a product program. It creates two copies of the loop in the source with the same

```
1  int M = nondet(), K = nondet(),        1  int X = nondet(), Y = nondet(),
2  a = 0, N = 2*M+1+K, b = 2*M+1;          2  c = 1, d = 2*X+1;
3  assume(M >= 0 && K >= 0);               3  assume(X >= 0 && Y >= 0);
4  while(a != N) {                         4  while(c < 2*X+1) c+=2;
5      b = (a >= b) ? b + 1 : b;           5  while(c != 2*X+1+Y) {
6      a++;                                6      d++;
7  }                                       7      c++;
                                           8  }
```

Fig. 1: Source (left) and target (right) programs.

```
1   int M = nondet(), K = nondet(),       1   int M = nondet(), K = nondet(),
2   a = 0, N = 2*M+1+K, b = 2*M+1;         2   a = 0, N = 2*M+1+K, b = 2*M+1;
3   assume(M >= 0 && K >= 0);              3   assume(M >= 0 && K >= 0);
4   while(a != N && a < 2*M+1) {           4   b = (a >= b) ? b + 1 : b; a++;
5       b = (a >= b) ? b + 1 : b;          5   while(a != N && a < 2*M+1) {
6       a++;                               6       b = (a >= b) ? b + 1 : b; a++;
7   }                                      7       b = (a >= b) ? b + 1 : b; a++;
8   while(a != N) {                        8   }
9       b = (a >= b) ? b + 1 : b;          9   assume(N == 2*M+1+K && b == 2*M+1);
10      a++;                               10  while(a != N) {
11  }                                      11      b = (a >= b) ? b + 1 : b;   a++; }
```

Fig. 2: Decomposed (left) and refined (right) source programs.

loop body but different loop guards, shown in Fig 2 (left). Specifically, it uses the loop guard for the first loop in the target program, i.e. c < 2*X+1, to create a < 2*M+1 and add it to the guard of the first source loop. It then checks the equivalence of pairs of loops from the decomposed source and the target. However, the first pair of loops (lines 4-7 in the decomposed source, line 4 in the target) is not in lockstep, as for each iteration of the target, the source is expected to iterate twice. Thus, we attempt to construct a lockstep composition by grouping two iterations of the first loop in the decomposed source. However, this results in some residual iterations to be processed before the loop in the decomposed source. After conducting an analysis on the initial states of both loops and the body of the source loop, our approach moves one iteration to before the loop in the source. This is sufficient to complete the lockstep composition and prove that the first pair of loops are equivalent.

Similarly, the approach considers the second pair of loops (lines 8-11 in the decomposed source, lines 5-8 in the target). To prove that the loops are in lockstep and for equivalence we are missing the information that N = 2*M+1+K and b = 2*M+1, which is available at the beginning of the program, but not in the middle of it. We say that these equalities *refine* the composition of the second loops, and they are added as an assumption before the start of the second loop (the refined source program is given in Fig. 2 (right)). The refinement makes it possible to both create the lockstep composition and prove the equivalence of both pairs of loops. The analysis terminates with the verdict that both programs are equivalent.

4 Preliminaries

We follow the *Satisfiability Modulo Theories* (SMT) background and notation to present the contributions. The goal of SMT is either to find an assignment to variables of a first-order logic formula that makes it true (written $m \models \varphi$, where m is a model, and φ is a formula), or prove its non-existence (also called unsatisfiability, denoted $\varphi \implies \bot$). For formulas φ, ψ, if every model of φ satisfies ψ, we say that φ is logically stronger than ψ (written $\varphi \implies \psi$). We write *ite* for an if-then-else.

4.1   Constrained Horn Clauses

Throughout the paper, we use the notion of *Constrained Horn Clauses (CHCs)* as a mean to represent the programs containing arbitrary number of loops.

Definition 1. A *Constrained Horn Clause C* over a set of uninterpreted relation symbols R is a (universally quantified, implicitly) formula in first-order logic that has the form of one of the three implications (namely a fact, an inductive clause and a query, respectively):

$$\phi(V_1) \implies L_1(V_1) \qquad L_1(V_1) \wedge \ldots \wedge L_n(V_n) \wedge \psi(V_1, \ldots, V_{n+1}) \implies L_{n+1}(V_{n+1})$$
$$L_1(V_1) \wedge \ldots \wedge L_k(V_k) \wedge \pi(V_1, \ldots, V_k) \implies \bot$$

where for all i, $L_i \in R$ are uninterpreted predicate symbols, V_i are implicitly quantified vectors of variables, and some L_i and L_j might be the same. All formulas ϕ, ψ, π are fully interpreted.

Throughout, we assume that each single loop is represented by two CHCs, e.g.:

$$Init(V) \implies L(V) \qquad L(V) \wedge GTr(V, V') \implies L(V')$$

where, *Init* represents the initial state of the loop, $GTr(V, V')$ represents one iteration of the loop, which we call a *guarded transition*. For convenience, we split $GTr(V, V')$ to $Tr(V, V') \wedge G(V)$, where G encodes a guard over the variables at the beginning of transition, and Tr has no additional guard.

Definition 2. Given a set R of uninterpreted predicates and a set H of CHCs over R, we say that H is *satisfiable* if there exists an interpretation for every $L \in R$ that makes all implications in H valid.

Solutions for CHC systems are called *inductive invariants*. If a CHC system is unsatisfiable, there exists a counterexample showing a bad state is reachable.

4.2   Relational Verification

The problems of equivalence checking and lockstep composability are the instances of a more general problem of *relational verification*. In this section, we introduce it in a simple case for two systems containing a single loop each.

Definition 3. Given two single-loop CHC systems over $L_{\{1,2\}} \in R$ with initial states $Init_{\{1,2\}}$ and guarded transition bodies $GTr_{\{1,2\}}$, resp., a relational precondition *pre* and a relational postcondition *post*, the problem of *relational verification* can be formulated as the satisfiability of the following CHC system:

$$Init_1(V) \implies L_1(V, V) \qquad\qquad Init_2(V) \implies L_2(V, V)$$
$$L_1(V_0, V) \wedge GTr_1(V, V') \implies L_1(V_0, V') \qquad L_2(V_0, V) \wedge GTr_2(V, V') \implies L_2(V_0, V')$$
$$pre(V_0, W_0) \wedge L_1(V_0, V) \wedge L_2(W_0, W) \wedge \neg post(V, W) \implies \bot$$

Here, both loop systems are augmented with an additional variable (at the first argument of $L_{\{1,2\}}$) to keep track of the initial values of variables.

To solve the problem, formulated as a complex nonlinear CHC, we need to find *individual* invariants for both loops, which is difficult [7,25]. Instead, we aim at simplifying the problem for certain classes of programs. Specifically, it often can be reduced to safety verification via so-called *lockstep composition*.

Definition 4 (Lockstep-composability). Given two single-loop CHC systems and a relational precondition *pre*, a *lockstep composition* exists if 1) the following CHC system is satisfiable:

$$pre(V_1, V_2) \land Init_1(V_1) \land Init_2(V_2) \implies L_{1,2}(V_1, V_2)$$
$$L_{1,2}(V_1, V_2) \land GTr_1(V_1, V'_1) \land GTr_2(V_2, V'_2) \implies L_{1,2}(V'_1, V'_2)$$
$$L_{1,2}(V_1, V_2) \land G_1(V_1) \neq G_2(V_2) \implies \bot$$

where $L_{1,2} \in R$ is an uninterpreted predicate symbol, an interpretation of which corresponds to a *relational invariant*, and G_1 and G_2 represent the loop guards and 2) the body of the first CHC is satisfiable.

Intuitively, the first CHC constrains the values of input variables to be related through *pre* (and also, *pre* should be consistent with both *Init*-s.). The second CHC encodes a synchronous computation of both loops. The third CHC ensures that inside the product loop both G_1 and G_2 should be true, and outside the loop both G_1 and G_2 should be false. This implies that the numbers of steps in two lockstep-composable programs under some *pre* are the same.

The following lemma lets us reduce a relational verification problem to a safety verification problem computed after *merging* the loops and then use existing invariant generation techniques for solving relational verification problems. Note that due to the lockstep, both loop guards are always equal, so it is enough to conjoin the negation of only one of the loop guards to the query.

Lemma 1. *Given a relational verification problem over two systems over $L_{\{1,2\}} \in R$ representing single loops, pre, and post, if the systems are lockstep-composable under pre, and the following CHC problem is satisfiable, then post holds at the end of these loops.*

$$pre(V_1, V_2) \land Init_1(V_1) \land Init_2(V_2) \implies L_{1,2}(V_1, V_2)$$
$$L_{1,2}(V_1, V_2) \land GTr_1(V_1, V'_1) \land GTr_2(V_2, V'_2) \implies L_{1,2}(V'_1, V'_2)$$
$$L_{1,2}(V_1, V_2) \land \neg G_1(V_1) \land \neg post(V_1, V_2) \implies \bot$$

The problem of proving program equivalence is a special case of the relational verification problem where *pre* = *post* is a pairwise equality over V_1 and V_2.

5   Equivalence Checking for Unbalanced Loops

In this section, we present our novel equivalence checking algorithm designed for the cases when the source and the target programs have different structures. We first describe a class of the input CHC systems that we target in Sect. 5.1. We then provide a procedure to decompose the source such that we can break the problem of equivalence checking under our limitations into a sequence of smaller problems in Sect. 5.2. We then finalize our core abstraction-refinement schema for equivalence checker in Sect. 5.3.

5.1   Input Limitations and Auxiliary Definitions

We support pairs of programs where the source contains a single loop, and the target possibly contains an arbitrary number of sequential loops. A CHC system of the latter sort that has n loops is called a *flat n-sequence* of loops further in the paper. Here and throughout, we assume that G_S and G_i encode the loop guard for the source loop and the ith loop in the target, and that Tr_S and Tr_i encode respective loop bodies without the corresponding guards. Specifically, the shape of a source program that we consider is defined over a single predicate symbol S, and we thus refer to this system as S-system later in the text:

$$Init_S(V_S) \implies S(V_S) \qquad S(V_S) \wedge G_S(V_S) \wedge Tr_S(V_S, V'_S) \implies S(V'_S)$$

The flat n-sequence is defined over n predicate symbols $T_1, \ldots, T_n$, and is referred to as T-system in the paper:

$$Init_T(V_T) \implies T_1(V_T) \qquad T_1(V_T) \wedge G_1(V_T) \wedge Tr_1(V_T, V'_T) \implies T_1(V'_T)$$
$$T_1(V_T) \wedge \neg G_1(V_T) \implies T_2(V_T) \qquad T_2(V_T) \wedge G_2(V_T) \wedge Tr_2(V_T, V'_T) \implies T_2(V'_T)$$
$$\cdots$$
$$T_{n-1}(V_T) \wedge \neg G_{n-1}(V_T) \implies T_n(V_T) \qquad T_n(V_T) \wedge G_n(V_T) \wedge Tr_n(V_T, V'_T) \implies T_n(V'_T)$$

There is one *fact* CHC, in which $Init_T$ represents the initial state of the program. There are n *inductive* clauses, i.e., for each $i \in [1, n]$, the ith inductive clause has occurrence of symbol T_i on both sides of the implication. There are also $n - 1$ non-inductive clauses that encode transitions between adjacent loops, so $\neg G_i$ represents the condition when loop i exits.

Example 1. The source in Fig. 1 is encoded to CHCs as follows:
$$a = 0 \wedge N = 2*M+1+K \wedge b = 2*M+1 \wedge M \geq 0 \wedge K \geq 0 \implies S(a, b, M, K, N)$$
$$S(a, b, M, K, N) \wedge a \neq N \wedge a' = a+1 \wedge b' = ite(a \geq b, b+1, b) \implies S(a', b', M, K, N)$$

Example 2. The CHC encoding of the target program in Fig 1 is given as:
$$c = 1 \ \wedge d = 2*X + 1 \wedge X \geq 0 \wedge Y \geq 0 \implies T_1(c, d, X, Y)$$
$$T_1(c, d, X, Y) \wedge c < 2*X + 1 \ \wedge c' = c + 2 \implies T_1(c', d, X, Y)$$
$$T_1(c, d, X, Y) \wedge c \geq 2*X + 1 \implies T_2(c, d, X, Y)$$
$$T_2(c, d, X, Y) \wedge c \neq 2*X + 1 + Y \ \wedge c' = c+1 \ \wedge d' = d+1 \implies T_2(c', d', X, Y)$$

We introduce a concept needed for the presentation in the next section, where by $A[B/C]$, we denote expression A with all instances of C replaced by B:

Definition 5. Given a CHC system H over predicate symbols $L_1, \ldots, L_n$, an L_i-projection of H (denoted $H \mid_i$) is defined as $\{C[\top / L_j(\cdot)] \mid C \in H, j \neq i\}$.

That is, our projection replaces all applications of all predicate symbols except of L_i by true. Clearly, some CHCs then can be simplified to true, and we assume that they are removed from the projection.

Example 3. Let H be a T-system from Example 2, then $H \mid_2$ has two CHCs:

$$c \geq 2*X + 1 \implies T_2(c, d, X, Y)$$
$$T_2(c, d, X, Y) \wedge c \neq 2*X + 1 + Y \wedge c' = c+1 \wedge d' = d+1 \implies T_2(c', d', X, Y)$$

5.2 Equivalence Checking by Decomposition

Our main insight on checking equivalence of a source loop and a flat n-sequence is that if the source breaks into n distinct loop-chunks, and if each of these chunks is equivalent to the corresponding loop from the n-sequence, then the actual programs are equivalent too. We thus present a decomposition of the source into a sequence of n new loops that gives us the basis for comparing the two CHC systems. A decomposition of S-system into an n-flat sequence is done by:

1. introducing n fresh predicate symbols $S_1, \ldots, S_n$,
2. cloning the inductive CHC n times and replacing S with S_i in each clone,
3. creating $n - 1$ non-inductive CHCs between S_i and S_{i+1}, and
4. introducing additional guard predicates $P_1, \ldots, P_{n-1}$ to schedule chunks of iterations of the S-loop to either of the new n loops. To sum up:

$$Init_S(V_S) \implies S_1(V_S)$$
$$S_1(V_S) \wedge G_S(V_S) \wedge P_1(V_S) \wedge Tr_S(V_S, V'_S) \implies S_1(V'_S)$$
$$S_1(V_S) \wedge \neg(G_S(V_S) \wedge P_1(V_S)) \implies S_2(V_S)$$

$$\cdots$$

$$S_n(V_S) \wedge G_S(V_S) \wedge Tr_S(V_S, V'_S) \implies S_n(V'_S)$$

For *any interpretation* of $P_1, \ldots, P_{n-1}$, the CHC system constructed above is equivalent to the S-system, for the following three reasons. First, no matter how many iterations the first $n - 1$ loops conduct, all the remaining ones will be conducted in the last loop. Second, all n loops still use the original guard G, and if it is exceeded in some ith loop, then all the remaining $i+1$th, $\ldots$, nth loops will be just skipped. Lastly, all these loops perform exactly the same operations as the original loop since Tr_S is copied to all of them. We will instantiate all the P-predicates on demand in our CounterExample Guided Abstraction Refinement (CEGAR) loop.

The CEGAR loop for our equivalence checking problem is outlined in Alg. 1. It begins with decomposing the S-system into a flat n-sequence, as defined above. The P-predicates are created from G_i guards in T-system by rewriting T-variables to S-variables, $i \in [1, n-1]$:

$$P_i(V) \stackrel{\text{def}}{=} \exists V'. G_i(V') \wedge pre(V, V')$$

Algorithm 1: DECOMPOSEANDCHECK(S, T, *Pre*, *Post*)

Input: S-system, T-system, relational pre and post-conditions
$Pre = \langle pre_1, pre_2, \ldots, pre_n \rangle$ and $Post = \langle post_1, post_2, \ldots, post_n \rangle$
Output: $res \in \langle$EQUIV, UNKNOWN$\rangle$

1 $S' \leftarrow$ DECOMPOSE(S, n);
2 **for** $i \leftarrow 1; i \leq n; i \leftarrow i+1$ **do**
3 $\quad S_i \leftarrow S' \mid_i; T_i \leftarrow T \mid_i;$
4 $\quad$ **while** *true* **do**
5 $\quad\quad$ *aligned* $\leftarrow \perp$; *refined*$_{1,2} \leftarrow \perp$;
6 $\quad\quad ST_i \leftarrow$ GETPRODUCT(S_i, T_i, pre_i);
7 $\quad\quad$ Let *Init* be the body of the fact CHC in ST_i;
8 $\quad\quad res \leftarrow$ CHECKSAT(*Init*);
9 $\quad\quad$ **if** *res* **then**
10 $\quad\quad\quad \langle inv, cex \rangle \leftarrow$ CHECKSAT($ST_i \cup \{L \wedge (G_s \wedge P_i) \neq G_i \implies \perp\}$);
11 $\quad\quad$ **if** $\neg res \vee cex \notin \varnothing$ **then**
12 $\quad\quad\quad \langle aligned, S_i \rangle \leftarrow$ ALIGNCHCS(S_i, T_i, pre_i);
13 $\quad\quad\quad$ **if** *aligned* **then continue**;
14 $\quad\quad$ **else**
15 $\quad\quad\quad \langle inv, cex \rangle \leftarrow$ CHECKSAT($ST_i \cup \{L \wedge \neg G_i \wedge \neg post_i \implies \perp\}$);
16 $\quad\quad\quad$ **if** $cex \in \varnothing$ **then break**;
17 $\quad\quad \langle refined_1, S_1, \ldots, S_i \rangle \leftarrow$ REFINE($S_1, \ldots, S_i, cex$);
18 $\quad\quad \langle refined_2, T_1, \ldots, T_i \rangle \leftarrow$ REFINE($T_1, \ldots, T_i, cex$);
19 $\quad\quad$ **if** $\neg(refined_1 \vee refined_2 \vee aligned)$ **then return** UNKNOWN;
20 **return** EQUIV;

Note that the relational precondition *pre* is assumed to be a conjunction of equalities. This gives us two flat n-sequences, which lets us consider pairs of loops (line 2) from both systems separately. Each such CHC system is created by applying the projection from Def. 5. In a sense, this is an *abstraction* of the original system since by isolating one loop (say, i^{th}), we lose the state computed all the way from the entry to the program by iterating $i - 1$ loops. Aiming to check equivalence for each pair of projections, the algorithm first figures out how/if a lockstep-composition is applicable. We write: $res \leftarrow$ CHECKSAT(fla) to denote a satisfiability check for a (first order) formula fla, and we write:

$$\langle inv, cex \rangle \leftarrow \text{CHECKSAT}(ST_i \cup \{L \wedge \ldots \implies \perp\})$$

to denote this check for the CHC-product ST_i over predicate symbol L with respect to the query written in $\{\ldots\}$. The check returns either an inductive invariant (i.e., an interpretation of L) or a counterexample. Before checking for lockstep, the compatibility of the initial states needs to be checked, i.e., if the body of the fact is satisfiable (line 8). If it succeeds, each check of the lockstep-composability is reduced by Def. 4 to a CHC satisfiability check, and it uses both guards in the CHC query (line 9). If either the initial-states check or the lockstep check fails, the algorithm uses a method for alignment of projections discussed in detail in Sect. 6. If aligned, we continue with the next iteration of the loop, attempting to prove lockstep composition and equivalence of the projections.

Algorithm 2: REFINE$(Q_1, \ldots, Q_i, cex)$

Input: Set of i CHC systems $Q_1, \ldots, Q_i$ over L; and counterexample cex
Output: $res \in \langle\langle\bot, \cdot\rangle, \langle\top, \text{refined systems } Q_1, \ldots, Q_i\rangle\rangle$

1 **if** $i = 1$ **then return**$\langle\bot, \cdot\rangle$;
2 **while** $cex \notin \varnothing$ **do**
3 $\quad \langle inv, cex' \rangle \leftarrow$ CHECKSAT$(Q_{i-1} \cup \{L(V) \wedge \neg G_{i-1}(V) \wedge \bigwedge_{v \in V} v = cex(v) \Longrightarrow \bot\})$;
4 $\quad$ **if** $cex' \in \varnothing$ **then**
5 $\quad\quad$ **assert**$(inv \notin \varnothing)$;
6 $\quad\quad$ $Fact \leftarrow \{C \in Q_i \mid C \text{ has form } Init(V) \Longrightarrow L(V)\}$;
7 $\quad\quad$ $Q_i \leftarrow Q_i \setminus \{Fact\} \cup \{Init(V) \wedge inv(V) \Longrightarrow L(V)\}$;
8 $\quad\quad$ **return**$\langle\top, Q_1, \ldots, Q_i\rangle$;
9 $\quad$ **else**
10 $\quad\quad$ $\langle res, Q_1, \ldots, Q_{i-1} \rangle \leftarrow$ REFINE$(Q_1, \ldots, Q_{i-1}, cex')$;
11 $\quad\quad$ **if** $\neg res$ **then return**$\langle\bot, \cdot\rangle$;

Example 4. Recall CHC systems defined in Examples 1 and 2. In the first iteration, Alg. 1 considers the first pair of loops. The initial-states check at line 8 fails, and thus the loops are aligned at line 12 (to be explained in Example 8).

Whenever two CHC systems are in lockstep, the algorithm utilizes Lemma 1 and checks the product system computed for two isolated loops (line 15) for safety. The success of the check lets the algorithm to continue with the next pair of loops. Otherwise, we receive a counterexample, which might be spurious because of the abstraction. Our refinement procedure then searches for a strengthening of either of the CHC systems (lines 17-18), which is described in more details in the next subsection. If it cannot refine further using the given technique, it returns UNKNOWN (line 19).

5.3 Refinement

Due to the decomposition presented in the previous section, there could be sensitive information that is available in the earlier parts of the programs, but not in the later parts. Alg. 2 gives a refinement procedure needed to propagate useful properties about the programs towards queries. Intuitively, we have to strengthen our relational preconditions, thus improving the chances to prove the safety of the ith CHC product. Recall that in Alg. 1, refinement is invoked for each counterexample which is technically an assignment to the variables at the initial state of either of the programs being composed into the product CHC.

The key idea is to check if the counterexample is spurious by constructing a scenario in which the $i - 1^{\text{th}}$ system can eventually reproduce the values from the counterexample at the end of its execution (line 3). This is reduced to a satisfiability check of the corresponding CHC system w.r.t. the "negation" of the counterexample. If it succeeds, then an inductive invariant can be used to strengthen (line 7) the ith system. Otherwise, the algorithm might recursively descend to refining the $i - 1^{\text{th}}$ system via finding an invariant for the $i - 2^{\text{nd}}$

product, and so on (line 10). For this reason, the algorithm has the while-loop (line 2) that lets to repeat the satisfiability check for some (already strengthened) systems, and it continues till the current system has been refined.

Example 5. Continuing with Example 4, in the second iteration of Alg. 1, the lockstep check[1] does not succeed:

$$a = c \wedge b = d \wedge M = X \wedge Y = K \wedge (a = N \vee a \geq 2*M + 1) \wedge c \geq 2*X + 1 \implies L_2(V)$$

$$L_2(V) \wedge a \neq N \wedge a' = a + 1 \wedge b' = ite(a \geq b, b + 1, b) \wedge$$
$$c \neq 2*X + 1 + Y \wedge c' = c + 1 \wedge d' = d + 1 \implies L_2(V')$$
$$L_2(V) \wedge (a \neq N) \neq (c \neq 2*X + 1 + Y) \implies \bot$$

For the CHC system above, a counterexample could be $cex = \{a, c, b, d \mapsto 110, M, K \mapsto 50, N \mapsto 0, X, Y \mapsto 50\}$ because we miss that $N = 2*M + 1 + K$, hence lockstep is not possible. Alg. 2 then confirms that this counterexample is spurious by learning this inductive invariant. After adding it to the fact CHC of S_2 and recomputing the product system ST_2, it becomes satisfiable. We then add the following query for equivalence check:

$$L_2(V) \wedge c = 2*X + 1 + Y \wedge (a \neq c \vee b \neq d \vee M \neq X \vee K \neq Y) \implies \bot$$

which fails because of missing invariant $b = 2*M + 1$. After adding it to the fact CHC of S_2 and recomputing the product CHC system, it becomes satisfiable.

As can be seen from this example, the refinement procedure is beneficial for both the lockstep-composability and the equivalence checks in Alg. 1, thus the inner loop in the algorithm can iterate multiple times before terminating with a positive verdict. We note that inductive invariants are in general tricky for finding. Thus, our approach has essential limitations and cannot prove equivalence of programs that require complicated (e.g., quantified) inductive invariants.

6   Aligning Unbalanced Loops

In this section, we present an algorithm for creating alignment between two single-loop CHC systems that have different number of loop iterations. Our new method of *alignment* of an S-projection and a T-projection is based on restructuring the former to become lockstep-composable with the latter. The algorithm identifies if any iterations of the former have to be extracted and placed before the loop and if any iterations have to be grouped and performed at once. These numbers (called *alignment bounds* in the rest of the section) are identified if exact loop bounds of both projections are computable.

6.1   Finding the Number of Iterations

We aim first at computing a function that returns the exact number of iterations of a single loop in terms of input variables, based on the CHC representation.

---

[1] We abbreviate $\langle a,b,M,K,N,c,d,X,Y \rangle$ with V, and $\langle a',b',M,K,N,c',d',X,Y \rangle$ with V'.

In the technique presented below, the input systems need to have a counter variable that monotonically increments between two extremes that do not change in the loop.[2] Focusing on a single-loop CHC system with initial states $Init$ and guarded transition body $G \wedge Tr$ where G encodes a guard over the variables at the beginning of the transition, and Tr has no additional guard, we wish to find the exact number of the iterations of the corresponding loop. In general, for that, we could consider an augmented CHC system with a fresh decrementing counter.

Definition 6. The exact number of iterations is an interpretation of the function symbol $\mathcal{N}$ that makes the augmented CHC system satisfiable:

$$Init(V) \wedge j = \mathcal{N}(V) \implies L(V, j)$$
$$L(V, j) \wedge G(V) \wedge Tr(V, V') \wedge j' = j - 1 \implies L(V', j')$$
$$L(V, j) \wedge \neg G(V) \wedge j \neq 0 \implies \bot$$

For an arbitrary loop, finding $\mathcal{N}$ is difficult and often not possible (e.g., for problems with nondeterminism in the loop). However, for some CHC systems encoding *range-based* loops, i.e., that already have counters, we can attempt to synthesize $\mathcal{N}$ from the information obtained from syntax of CHCs. Specifically, we assume that formula $Init$ has the form $i = \mathcal{S}(V) \wedge Init'(V, i)$ for some variable i and some function $\mathcal{S}$, We also assume that the guard of the transition has the form $i < \mathcal{F}(V) \wedge G'(V, i)$ for some function $\mathcal{F}$, and Tr has the form $i' = i + \mathcal{D} \wedge Tr'(V, i, V', i')$ for some positive constant $\mathcal{D} > 0$.

Definition 7. A *range-based* CHC system is the one that has the following form

$$Init'(V, i) \wedge i = \mathcal{S}(V) \implies T(V, i)$$
$$T(V, i) \wedge i < \mathcal{F}(V) \wedge i' = i + \mathcal{D} \wedge G'(V, i) \wedge Tr'(V, i, V', i') \implies T(V', i')$$

such that for some inductive invariant inv the following hold:

$$Tr'(V, i, V', i') \wedge inv(V, i) \implies \mathcal{S}(V) = \mathcal{S}(V') \tag{1}$$
$$Tr'(V, i, V', i') \wedge inv(V, i) \implies \mathcal{F}(V) = \mathcal{F}(V') \tag{2}$$
$$i < \mathcal{F}(V) \wedge inv(V, i) \implies G'(V, i) \tag{3}$$

To guarantee soundness of our construction, the constraints in the definition above ensure that $\mathcal{S}$ and $\mathcal{F}$ are the tightest bounds for the counter variable i. Specifically, (1) and (2) ensure that i has the lower and the upper bound that do not change throughout the execution, and (3) ensures that the loop does not break before i exceeds $\mathcal{F}(V)$. An invariant inv could in simple cases be just $\top$ but often it needs to bring important information from an initial state to an arbitrary iteration. For instance, if a loop has two counters with their own upper and lower bounds, then our analysis can proceed only when we can prove that

---

[2] A similar technique for a *decrementing counter* is straightforward but omitted for brevity of presentation.

either of the counters exceeds its upper bound *always faster* than another does so. Our running example makes another use of (3), to ensure that the residual guard $G'(V, i)$ is weaker than $i < \mathcal{F}(V)$ strengthened by the invariant.

Example 6. Recall the first loop of the decomposed source of Example 1. It has the guard $a \neq N \wedge a < 2{*}M + 1$. We can find invariant $N = 2{*}M + 1 + K \wedge K \geq 0$. Clearly, since $N = 2{*}M + 1 + K \wedge K \geq 0 \wedge a < 2{*}M + 1 \implies a \neq N$, then $\mathcal{F}(M) \stackrel{\text{def}}{=} 2{*}M + 1$ satisfies (3). With no invariant, $a < 2{*}M + 1 \not\Rightarrow a \neq N$.

Lemma 2. *An integer function $\mathcal{N}$ computes the exact number of iterations for a range-based CHC system:*

$$\mathcal{N} \stackrel{\text{def}}{=} (\mathcal{F} - \mathcal{S}) \ \textit{div} \ \mathcal{D} + (\textit{if} \ ((\mathcal{F} - \mathcal{S}) \ \textit{mod} \ \mathcal{D} = 0) \ \textit{then} \ 0 \ \textit{else} \ 1)$$

In practice, the approach is limited to the invariant generation capabilities. If a sufficient invariant for Def. 7 (and thus, Lemma 2) is found, the approach proceeds to align loops. Otherwise, it returns UNKNOWN.

6.2   Identifying Unrolling Depths

If the numbers of iterations can be computed, the approach proceeds to finding alignment bounds ℓ and m that define respectively the number of iterations to be extracted and placed before the loop and the number of iterations to be grouped and performed at once in the loop. These bounds are obtained from the following ingredients:

1. functions $\mathcal{N}_S$ and $\mathcal{N}_T$ to compute the numbers of iterations of the S-projection and the T-projection, respectively;
2. fresh integer variable v_ℓ to represent (a yet unknown) number of iterations to be moved out of the loop in the S-projection,
3. fresh integer variable v_m to represent (a yet unknown) number of iterations to be grouped inside the loop for the S-projection.

Values ℓ and m can be directly taken from a satisfying assignment to variables v_ℓ and v_m for the following SMT query. Intuitively, it equates the total numbers of iterations in the S-projection and the T-projection:

$$Q_{ST} \stackrel{\text{def}}{=} \exists v_\ell, v_m \, . \, \forall V_S, V_T \, . \, (v_\ell \geq 0 \wedge v_m > 0) \wedge pre(V_S, V_T) \implies$$
$$\mathcal{N}_S(V_S) - v_\ell = v_m * \mathcal{N}_T(V_T)$$

Thus, the SMT formula has the form of implication: if *pre* holds, then the number of iterations of one program can be expressed over the number of iterations of another program (and vice versa). If $\mathcal{M} \models Q_{ST}$, then $\ell \stackrel{\text{def}}{=} \mathcal{M}(v_\ell)$, and $m \stackrel{\text{def}}{=} \mathcal{M}(v_m)$.

Example 7. For the first projections in the decomposed source and the target, we generate the following (simplified) SMT query:

$$Q_{ST} = \exists v_\ell, v_m \, . \, (v_\ell \geq 0 \wedge v_m > 0) \wedge M = X \implies 2{*}M + 1 - v_\ell = v_m * X$$

and the solver generates model $\mathcal{M} = \{v_\ell \mapsto 1, v_m \mapsto 2\}$, and $\ell = 1$, and $m = 2$.

6.3 Rearrangement of the Source Projection

Finally, we present the restructuring of the S-projection based on two alignment bounds, ℓ and m, computed in the previous section. The former represents the number of iterations to be moved before the loop, and the latter represents the number of iterations to make a batch inside the loop.[3] We assume that an S-projection is defined using the following two CHCs over a single predicate symbol L: $Init_S(V) \implies L(V)$ and $L(V) \wedge GTr(V,V') \implies L(V')$.

We define an auxiliary predicate $U(u,V,V')$ that allows us to create an unrolling of arbitrary length: if $u = 0$, the result is the identity formula, otherwise we create u unrollings of the system (GTr_S conjoined u times), then define $Init_S^{(\ell)}$ and $GTr_S^{(m)}$, as follows:

$$U(u,V,V') \stackrel{\text{def}}{=} ite(u = 0,\ V' = V,$$
$$\exists V'',\ldots,V^{(u)}.\ GTr_S(V,V'') \wedge \ldots \wedge GTr_S(V^{(u)},V'))$$
$$Init_S^{(\ell)}(V') \stackrel{\text{def}}{=} \exists V.\ Init_S(V) \wedge U(\ell,V,V')$$
$$GTr_S^{(m)}(V,V') \stackrel{\text{def}}{=} U(m,V,V')$$

Finally, we are ready to define the aligned CHC product used in Alg. 1 (ALIGN-CHCs(S,T,pre)).

Definition 8. Let S and T be two range-based CHC systems, as defined in Def. 7. Let $\mathcal{M} \models Q_{ST}(\mathcal{N}_S,\mathcal{N}_T,v_\ell,v_m,pre)$, as defined in Sect. 6.2. Then, the rearranged system S_R is defined as follows:

$$Init_S^{(\mathcal{M}(v_\ell))}(V) \implies L(V) \qquad L(V) \wedge GTr_S^{(\mathcal{M}(v_m))}(V,V') \implies L(V')$$

Note that S^R and T are in lockstep, and S^R is equivalent to S, both by construction. Thus, after such alignment, our Alg. 1 will proceed to checking the equivalence of S and T by means of checking equivalence of S^R and T.

Example 8. For the first projections in the decomposed source and the target, the lockstep check does not succeed because the body of the fact is unsatisfiable:

$$a = c \wedge b = d \wedge M = X \wedge Y = K \wedge a = 0 \wedge N = 2*M+1+K \wedge b = 2*M+1 \wedge M \geq 0 \wedge$$
$$K \geq 0 \wedge c = 1 \wedge d = 2*X+1 \wedge X \geq 0 \wedge Y \geq 0 \implies L_1(a,b,M,K,N,c,d,X,Y)$$

With the bounds computed in Example 7, we compute the following product:

$$a = 0 \wedge N = 2*M + 1 + K \wedge b = 2*M + 1 \wedge M \geq 0 \wedge K \geq 0 \wedge$$
$$a \neq N \wedge a < 2*M+1 \wedge a' = a+1 \wedge b' = ite(a \geq b, b+1, b) \wedge$$
$$c = 1\ \wedge d = 2*X + 1 \wedge X \geq 0 \wedge Y \geq 0 \wedge a' = c \wedge b' = d \wedge M = X \wedge Y = K$$
$$\implies L_1(a',b',M,K,N,c,d,X,Y)$$
$$L_1(a,b,M,K,N,c,d,X,Y) \wedge a \neq N \wedge a < 2*M+1 \wedge a' = a+1\ \wedge\ b' = ite(a \geq b, b+1, b) \wedge$$
$$a' \neq N \wedge a' < 2*M+1 \wedge a'' = a'+1 \wedge b'' = ite(a' \geq b', b'+1, b') \wedge$$
$$c < 2*X+1\ \wedge c' = c+2 \implies L_1(a'',b'',M,K,N,c',d,X,Y)$$

---

[3] In practice, it could also be required to move some iterations to after the loop (and our implementation supports it). Then, we split m into $m_1 + m_2$ heuristically and move m_1 iterations to before the loop, and m_2 to after the loop.

7   Evaluation

We have implemented the algorithm for equivalence checking in a tool called ALIEN[4] on top of the invariant synthesizer FREQHORN that supports integers and arrays (over integers) [10]. ALIEN takes as input an S-system and a T-system, automatically decomposes the former, creates a sequence of product programs, and delegates the inductive invariant generation to FREQHORN. For solving SMT queries, it uses Z3 [8]. We considered two benchmark suites:

- Test Suite of Vectorization Compilers (TSVC) [23], preprocessed in the way suggested by [5]. TSVC has 152 benchmarks, and 48 of which are either not vectorizable, contain floating point operations, intrinsic functions, or need some extra processing like loop rerolling. We thus experimented on a set of remaining 104 remaining benchmarks. We check equivalence of these programs w.r.t. their optimized versions, both translated to CHCs.
- A subset of 24 multi-phase benchmarks taken from [4,31] in which the phases can be "extracted" from the loops. The optimized versions of these benchmarks have more than one loop, thus necessitating to use our decomposition.

We considered the state-of-the-art tools LLREVE [16], an equivalence checker by Churchill et al. [5], COUNTER [14], and CHC-PRODUCT [25]. However, only COUNTER was able to solve some of our benchmarks in reasonable time: Churchill et al. report that the minimum time any benchmark takes to solve is around 2 hours, and it was largely outperformed by COUNTER in [14].

We thus evaluate our ALIEN against COUNTER for both benchmark suites. To run COUNTER on a pair of manually provided C programs[5], it was configured to apply no optimization to any of the programs. For TSVC benchmarks, we manually pass an unrolling factor 8 required by each benchmark (compare to our approach in which the tool automatically identifies this number). For ALIEN, we provide two CHC encodings of the program before and after the optimization. We specified a timeout of 15 minutes for both tools.

ALIEN solved 103 out of 104 TSVC benchmarks. ALIEN times out on the s279 benchmark because its invariant synthesizer struggles with finding a helper invariant. Benchmark s113 requires the approach to automatically synthesize an extra lemma (i.e., $cnt>0$), in addition to the variable equalities. ALIEN took 3.7 seconds to solve a benchmark on average: from 1.3 in the best case to 27.4 in the worst case. Among all, 26 (resp. 2) benchmarks require moving iterations before (resp. after) the loop. COUNTER proved equivalence for 15 benchmarks, it failed to prove equivalence for 9 benchmarks, while the rest (81 benchmarks) timed-out. Its minimum running time is 50.2 seconds, maximum 704 seconds and average 117.4 seconds.

---

[4] The tool and benchmarks are available at https://github.com/a-hamza-r/aeval/tree/equiv-check.

[5] We consulted https://github.com/compilerai/counter to run tool in our setting. Note that in their paper, the authors evaluated COUNTER only on compiler-optimized targets. Our case study is different, and it shows that checking equivalence between two arbitrary programs is a harder problem for COUNTER.

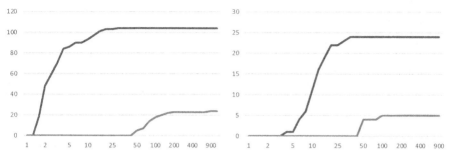

Fig. 3: Cactus plots (left: for TSVC benchmarks, right: for multi-phase benchmarks) comparing running times of ALIEN (blue line) and COUNTER (orange line).

For 24 multi-phase benchmarks, ALIEN proved all of them. COUNTER proved equivalence for 5 benchmarks, it failed to prove equivalence for 3 benchmarks, while the remaining benchmarks timed-out. The minimum, maximum and average times are 3.2, 32.6, and 11.5 seconds, respectively for ALIEN; and 43.8, 106.9, and 56.2 seconds respectively for COUNTER.

A larger picture on the experimental results is given in Fig. 3. The horizontal axes in the cactus plots represent time limit (logarithmic scale), and the vertical axes represent the numbers of benchmarks (linear scale) solved within the corresponding time limits. Intuitively, the plots demonstrate that COUNTER is an order of magnitude slower than our novel approach.

8   Conclusion

We have presented a novel CEGAR-based approach for checking equivalence of two programs containing possibly different number of loops. The technique involves automatic decomposition of one of the programs to match the loops structure of the other, so that the task of equivalence checking of two given programs can be split into a sequence of tasks of equivalence checking of single loops, each of which is solved easier. Since such decomposition comes at a cost of possible loss of information, we developed a refinement schema that is intuitively based on propagation of lemmas on demand. Moreover, in case we deal with loops with provably-different number of iterations, our technique automatically rearranges the iterations in the loops making them lockstep-composable for each subtask. We developed the ALIEN tool and empirically demonstrated that our approach to equivalence checking is more efficient than state-of-the-art on two classes of public benchmarks. In future, it would be interesting to extend these techniques to more general program structures, e.g., where both programs have multiple and possibly nested loops.

Acknowledgments The work is supported in parts by a gift from Amazon Web Services and by the National Science Foundation grant 2106949.

References

1. J. D. Backes, S. Person, N. Rungta, and O. Tkachuk. Regression verification using impact summaries. In *SPIN*, volume 7976 of *LNCS*, pages 99–116. Springer, 2013.
2. S. Badihi, F. Akinotcho, Y. Li, and J. Rubin. Ardiff: scaling program equivalence checking via iterative abstraction and refinement of common code. In *ESEC/FSE*, pages 13–24. ACM, 2020.
3. G. Barthe, J. M. Crespo, and C. Kunz. Relational verification using product programs. In *FM*, volume 6664 of *LNCS*, pages 200–214. Springer, 2011.
4. M. Blicha, G. Fedyukovich, A. E. J. Hyvärinen, and N. Sharygina. Transition Power Abstractions for Deep Counterexample Detection. In D. Fisman and G. Rosu, editors, *Tools and Algorithms for the Construction and Analysis of Systems*. Springer Berlin Heidelberg, 2022.
5. B. R. Churchill, O. Padon, R. Sharma, and A. Aiken. Semantic program alignment for equivalence checking. In *PLDI*, pages 1027–1040. ACM, 2019.
6. B. R. Churchill, R. Sharma, J. F. Bastien, and A. Aiken. Sound loop superoptimization for google native client. In *ASPLOS*, pages 313–326. ACM, 2017.
7. E. De Angelis, F. Fioravanti, A. Pettorossi, and M. Proietti. Relational Verification Through Horn Clause Transformation. In *SAS*, volume 9837 of *LNCS*, pages 147–169. Springer, 2016.
8. L. M. de Moura and N. Bjørner. Z3: An Efficient SMT Solver. In *TACAS*, volume 4963 of *LNCS*, pages 337–340. Springer, 2008.
9. S. Dutta, D. Sarkar, A. Rawat, and K. Singh. Validation of loop parallelization and loop vectorization transformations. In *ENASE*, pages 195–202. SciTePress, 2016.
10. G. Fedyukovich, S. Prabhu, K. Madhukar, and A. Gupta. Quantified Invariants via Syntax-Guided Synthesis. In *CAV, Part I*, volume 11561 of *LNCS*, pages 259–277. Springer, 2019.
11. D. Felsing, S. Grebing, V. Klebanov, P. Rümmer, and M. Ulbrich. Automating regression verification. In *ASE*, pages 349–360. ACM, 2014.
12. B. Godlin and O. Strichman. Inference rules for proving the equivalence of recursive procedures. *Acta Informatica*, 45(6):403–439, 2008.
13. B. Godlin and O. Strichman. Regression verification: proving the equivalence of similar programs. *Softw. Test. Verification Reliab.*, 23(3):241–258, 2013.
14. S. Gupta, A. Rose, and S. Bansal. Counterexample-guided correlation algorithm for translation validation. *Proc. ACM Program. Lang.*, 4(OOPSLA):221:1–221:29, 2020.
15. M. Jakobs. PEQCHECK: localized and context-aware checking of functional equivalence. In S. Bliudze, S. Gnesi, N. Plat, and L. Semini, editors, *9th IEEE/ACM International Conference on Formal Methods in Software Engineering, FormaliSE@ICSE 2021, Madrid, Spain, May 17-21, 2021*, pages 130–140. IEEE, 2021.
16. V. Klebanov, P. Rümmer, and M. Ulbrich. Automating regression verification of pointer programs by predicate abstraction. *Formal Methods Syst. Des.*, 52(3):229–259, 2018.
17. S. Kundu, Z. Tatlock, and S. Lerner. Proving optimizations correct using parameterized program equivalence. In *PLDI*, pages 327–337. ACM, 2009.
18. S. K. Lahiri, C. Hawblitzel, M. Kawaguchi, and H. Rebêlo. SYMDIFF: A language-agnostic semantic diff tool for imperative programs. In *CAV*, volume 7358 of *LNCS*, pages 712–717. Springer, 2012.

19. S. K. Lahiri, K. L. McMillan, R. Sharma, and C. Hawblitzel. Differential assertion checking. In *FSE*, pages 345–355. ACM, 2013.
20. J. P. Lim, V. Ganapathy, and S. Nagarakatte. Compiler optimizations with retrofitting transformations: Is there a semantic mismatch? In *PLAS@CCS*, pages 37–42. ACM, 2017.
21. J. P. Lim and S. Nagarakatte. Automatic equivalence checking for assembly implementations of cryptography libraries. In *CGO*, pages 37–49. IEEE, 2019.
22. N. P. Lopes, J. Lee, C. Hur, Z. Liu, and J. Regehr. Alive2: bounded translation validation for LLVM. In S. N. Freund and E. Yahav, editors, *PLDI '21: 42nd ACM SIGPLAN PLDI, Virtual Event, Canada, June 20-25, 2021*, pages 65–79. ACM, 2021.
23. S. Maleki, Y. Gao, M. J. Garzar, T. Wong, D. A. Padua, et al. An Evaluation of Vectorizing Compilers. In *2011 PACT*, pages 372–382. IEEE, 2011.
24. V. Malík and T. Vojnar. Automatically checking semantic equivalence between versions of large-scale C projects. In *14th IEEE Conference on Software Testing, Verification and Validation, ICST 2021, Porto de Galinhas, Brazil, April 12-16, 2021*, pages 329–339. IEEE, 2021.
25. D. Mordvinov and G. Fedyukovich. Synchronizing Constrained Horn Clauses. In *LPAR*, volume 46 of *EPiC Series in Computing*, pages 338–355. EasyChair, 2017.
26. D. Mordvinov and G. Fedyukovich. Property Directed Inference of Relational Invariants. In *FMCAD*, pages 152–160. IEEE, 2019.
27. K. S. Namjoshi and A. Xue. A self-certifying compilation framework for webassembly. In F. Henglein, S. Shoham, and Y. Vizel, editors, *VMCAI - 22nd International Conference, VMCAI 2021, Copenhagen, Denmark, January 17-19, 2021, Proceedings*, volume 12597 of *LNCS*, pages 127–148. Springer, 2021.
28. G. C. Necula. Translation validation for an optimizing compiler. In *PLDI*, pages 83–94. ACM, 2000.
29. N. Partush and E. Yahav. Abstract semantic differencing for numerical programs. In *SAS*, volume 7935 of *LNCS*, pages 238–258. Springer, 2013.
30. S. Person, M. B. Dwyer, S. G. Elbaum, and C. S. Pasareanu. Differential symbolic execution. In *FSE*, pages 226–237. ACM, 2008.
31. D. Riley and G. Fedyukovich. Multi-phase invariant synthesis. In A. Roychoudhury, C. Cadar, and M. Kim, editors, *Proceedings of the 30th ACM Joint European Software Engineering Conference and Symposium on the Foundations of Software Engineering, ESEC/FSE 2022, Singapore, Singapore, November 14-18, 2022*, pages 607–619. ACM, 2022.
32. T. A. L. Sewell, M. O. Myreen, and G. Klein. Translation validation for a verified OS kernel. In *PLDI*, pages 471–482. ACM, 2013.
33. R. Sharma, E. Schkufza, B. R. Churchill, and A. Aiken. Data-driven Equivalence Checking. In *OOPSLA*, pages 391–406. ACM, 2013.
34. R. Shemer, A. Gurfinkel, S. Shoham, and Y. Vizel. Property directed self composition. In *CAV, Part I*, volume 11561, pages 161–179. Springer, 2019.
35. M. Stepp, R. Tate, and S. Lerner. Equality-based translation validator for LLVM. In *CAV*, volume 6806 of *LNCS*, pages 737–742. Springer, 2011.
36. O. Strichman and M. Veitsman. Regression verification for unbalanced recursive functions. In *FM*, volume 9995 of *LNCS*, pages 645–658, 2016.
37. A. Trostanetski, O. Grumberg, and D. Kroening. Modular demand-driven analysis of semantic difference for program versions. In *SAS*, volume 10422 of *LNCS*, pages 405–427. Springer, 2017.

38. H. Unno, T. Terauchi, and E. Koskinen. Constraint-based relational verification. In A. Silva and K. R. M. Leino, editors, *CAV - 33rd International Conference, CAV 2021, Virtual Event, July 20-23, 2021, Proceedings, Part I*, volume 12759 of *LNCS*, pages 742–766. Springer, 2021.
39. A. Zaks and A. Pnueli. Covac: Compiler validation by program analysis of the cross-product. In *FM*, volume 5014 of *LNCS*, pages 35–51. Springer, 2008.

Synthesis of Distributed Agreement-Based Systems with Efficiently-Decidable Verification

Nouraldin Jaber[1]([⊠]), Christopher Wagner[1], Swen Jacobs[2], Milind Kulkarni[1], and Roopsha Samanta[1]

[1] Purdue University, West Lafayette, USA
{njaber,wagne279,milind,roopsha}@purdue.edu
[2] CISPA Helmholtz Center for Information Security, Saarbrücken, Germany
jacobs@cispa.de

Abstract. *Distributed agreement-based* (DAB) systems use common distributed agreement protocols such as leader election and consensus as building blocks for their target functionality. While automated verification for DAB systems is undecidable in general, recent work identifies a large class of DAB systems for which verification is *efficiently-decidable*. Unfortunately, the conditions characterizing such a class can be opaque and non-intuitive, and can pose a significant challenge to system designers trying to model their systems in this class.

In this paper, we present a synthesis-driven tool, CINNABAR, to help system designers building DAB systems ensure that their intended designs belong to an efficiently-decidable class. In particular, starting from an initial *sketch* provided by the designer, CINNABAR generates sketch completions using a counterexample-guided procedure. The core technique relies on compactly encoding root-causes of counterexamples to varied properties such as efficient-decidability and safety. We demonstrate CINNABAR's effectiveness by successfully and efficiently synthesizing completions for a variety of interesting DAB systems including a distributed key-value store and a distributed consortium system.

1 Introduction

Distributed system designers are increasingly embracing the incorporation of formal verification techniques into their development pipelines [8,10,13,31]. The formal methods community has been enthusiastically responding to this trend with a wide array of modeling and verification frameworks for prevalent distributed systems [29,17,15,32]. A desirable workflow for a system designer using one of these frameworks is to (1) provide a framework-specific model and specification of their system, and (2) *automatically* verify if the system model meets its specification.

However, the problem of algorithmically checking if a distributed system is correct for an *arbitrary* number of processes, i.e., the *automated parameterized verification problem*, is undecidable, even for finite-state processes [5,34]. To circumvent undecidability, the system designer must be involved, *one way*

© The Author(s) 2023
S. Sankaranarayanan and N. Sharygina (Eds.): TACAS 2023, LNCS 13994, pp. 289–308, 2023.
https://doi.org/10.1007/978-3-031-30820-8_19

or another, in the verification process. *Either* the designer may choose a semi-automated verification approach and use their expertise to "assist" the verifier by providing inductive invariants [32,25,15,36]. *Or,* the designer may choose a fully-automated verification approach that is only applicable to a restricted class of system models [16,17,24,7] and use their expertise to ensure that the model of their system belongs to the decidable class. This begs the question—*for each workflow, how can we further simplify the system designer's task?* While effective frameworks have been developed to aid the designer in discovering inductive invariants for the first workflow (e.g., Ivy [29], I4 [26]), there has been little emphasis on aiding the designer to build *decidability-compliant* models of their systems for the second workflow.

In this paper, we present a synthesis-driven approach to help system designers using the second workflow to build models that are *both* decidability-compliant and correct. Thus, our approach helps designers to construct models that belong to a decidable class for automated, parameterized verification, and can be automatically verified to be safe for any number of processes.

In particular, we instantiate this approach in a tool, CINNABAR, that targets an existing framework, QUICKSILVER, for modeling and automated verification of *distributed agreement-based (DAB) systems* [17]. Such systems use *agreement protocols* such as leader election and consensus as building blocks. QUICKSILVER enables modular verification of DAB systems by providing a modeling language, MERCURY, that allows designers to model *verified* agreement protocols using inbuilt language primitives, and identifying a class of MERCURY models for which the parameterized verification problem is *efficiently decidable.*

Unfortunately, this *efficiently-decidable* class of MERCURY models is characterized using conditions that are rather opaque and non-intuitive, and can pose a significant challenge to system designers trying to model their systems in this class. The designer is responsible for understanding the conditions, and manually modifying their system model to ensure it belongs to the efficiently-decidable class of MERCURY. This process can be both tedious and error-prone, even for experienced system designers.

CINNABAR demonstrates that synthesis can be used to automatically build models of DAB systems that belong to the efficiently-decidable fragment of MERCURY and are correct.

Contributions. The key contributions of this paper are:

1. *A synthesis-driven method for building efficiently-decidable, correct* MER-CURY *models* (Sec. 3). Starting from an initial *sketch* of the system design provided by the designer, CINNABAR generates a *sketch completion* that (i) belongs to the efficiently-decidable class of MERCURY *and* (ii) is correct.
2. *A counterexample-guided synthesis procedure that leverages an efficient, extensible, multi-stage architecture* (Sec. 4). We present a procedure that involves a learner that proposes completions of the MERCURY sketch, and a teacher that checks if the completed model belongs to the efficiently-decidable class of MERCURY and is correct. To enable efficient synthesis using this procedure, we propose an architecture that proceeds in stages.

The initial stages focus on checking if a completed model is in the efficiently-decidable class while the latter stages focus on checking if a completed model is also correct. To enable efficiency, when a candidate completion fails at any stage, the architecture helps the learner avoid " similar" completions by *extracting* a *root-cause* of the failure and *encoding* the root-cause as an additional constraint for the learner. Each stage is equipped with a counterexample extraction strategy tailored to the *property* checked in that stage. The encoding procedure, on the other hand, is property-agnostic—it is able to encode the root-cause of any failure regardless of the stage that extracts it. The separation of the counterexample extractions and the encoding allows the architecture to be extensible—one can add a new stage with a new counterexample extraction strategy, and leverage the existing encoding.

3. *The* CINNABAR *tool* (Sec. 5). We develop a tool, CINNABAR, to help system designers build MERCURY models of DAB systems. CINNABAR employs QUICKSILVER as its teacher and the Z3 SMT solver as its learner. CINNABAR is able to successfully and efficiently complete MERCURY sketches of various interesting distributed agreement-based systems.

2   The MERCURY Parameterized Synthesis Problem

We first briefly review the syntax and semantics of MERCURY [17], a modeling language for distributed systems that build on top of verified agreement protocols such as leader election and consensus. Then, we formalize the synthesis problem.

2.1   Review: MERCURY Systems

MERCURY *Process Definition.* A MERCURY system is composed of an arbitrary number of n identical MERCURY system processes with process identifiers $1, \ldots, n$ and one environment process. The programmer specifies a system process definition P that consists of (i) a set V of *local variables* with finite domains, (ii) a set E of *events* used to communicate between processes, and (iii) a set of *locations* that the processes can move between. Each event e in E incarnates an *acting action* $A(e)$ and a *reacting action* $R(e)$ (e.g., for a rendezvous event, the acting (resp.

```
process DistributedStore
variables
  int[1,5] cmd
events
  env rz doCmd : int[1,5]
initial location Candidate
  on partition<elect>(All, 1)
    win: goto Leader
    lose: goto Replica
location Leader
  on recv(doCmd) do
    cmd := doCmd.payld
    if(cmd = 3) goto Return
    else goto RepCmd
  ...
```

reacting) action is the send (resp. receive) of that event. All processes start in a location denoted **initial**. Each location contains a set of *action handlers* a process in that location can execute. Each handler has an associated action, a Boolean guard over the local variables, and a set of update statements. A partial process definition is depicted on the right.

The language supports five different types of events, namely, broadcast, rendezvous, partition, consensus, and internal. The *synchronous* broadcast (resp.

rendezvous) *communication* event type is denoted br (resp. rz) and indicates an event where one process synchronously communicates with all other processes (resp. another process). The *agreement* event type partition, denoted partition, indicates an event where a set of processes agree to partition themselves into winners and losers. For instance, in the figure, partition<elect> (All,1) denotes a leader election round with identifier elect where All processes elect 1 winning process that moves to the Leader location, while all other losing processes move to the Replica location. The *agreement* event type consensus, denoted consensus, indicates an event where a set of processes, each proposing one value, reach consensus on a given set of decided values. For instance, consensus<vcCmd>(All,1,cmd) denotes a consensus round with identifier vcCmd where All processes want to agree on 1 decided value from the set of proposed values in the local variable cmd. Finally, the internal event indicates an event where a process is performing its own internal computations. For a communication event, the acting action is a send, while the reacting action is a receive. For a partition event, the acting action is a win, while the reacting action is a lose. Finally, for a consensus event, the acting action is proposing a winning value, while the reacting action is proposing a losing value. We denote by $A(E)$ and $R(E)$ the set of all acting and reacting actions, respectively.

The updates in an action handler may contain send, assignment, goto, and/or conditional statements. Assignment statements are of the form lhs := rhs where lhs is a local variable and rhs is an expression of the appropriate type. The goto statement goto ℓ causes the process to switch to location ℓ (i.e., it can be thought of as the assignment statement $v_{loc} := \ell$, where v_{loc} is a special "location variable" that stores the current location of the process). The conditional statements are of the expected form: if(cond) then...else.... We denote by H the set of all handlers in the process, and for each handler $h \in H$ we denote its action, guard, and updates as $a(h)$, $g(h)$, and $u(h)$, respectively.

Local Semantics. The local semantics $[\![P]\!]$ of a process P is expressed as a state-transition system (S, s_0, E, T), where S is the set of local states, s_0 is the initial state, E is the set of events, and $T \subseteq S \times \{A(E) \cup R(E)\} \times S$ is the set of transitions of $[\![P]\!]$. A state $s \in S$ is a valuation of the variables in V. We let $s(v)$ denote the value of the variable v in state s.

The set of action handlers associated with all acting and reacting actions of all events induces the transitions in T. In particular, a transition $t = s \xrightarrow{a} s'$ based on action handler h over action a is in T iff the guard $g(h)$ evaluates to *true* in s and s' is obtained by applying the updates $u(h)$ to s.

Global Semantics. The global semantics $[\![P, n]\!]$ of a MERCURY system $P_1 || \ldots || P_n || P_e$ consisting of n identical processes $P_1, \ldots, P_n$ and an environment process P_e (with local state space S_e) is expressed as a transition system (Q, q_0, E, R), where $Q = S^n \times S_e$ is the set of global states, q_0 is the initial global state, E is the set of events, and $R \subseteq Q \times E \times Q$ is the set of global transitions of $[\![P, n]\!]$.

The set of events E induce the transitions in R. As is the case for events, there are five types of global transitions: broadcast, rendezvous, partition, consensus, and internal. In particular, a transition $r = q \xrightarrow{e} q'$ for some broadcast event e

is in R iff the send local transition $q[i] \xrightarrow{A(e)} q[i]'$ is in T for some process P_i, and the receive local transition $q[j] \xrightarrow{R(e)} q[j]'$ is in T for every other process P_j with $j \neq i$. The remaining global transitions can be formalized similarly.

A trace of a MERCURY system is a sequence $q_0, q_1, \ldots$ of global states such that for every $i \geq 0$, the global transition $q_i \xrightarrow{e} q_{i+1}$ for some event e is in R. A global state q is *reachable* if there is a trace that ends in it.

Permissible Safety Specifications. QUICKSILVER targets parameterized verification for a class of properties called *permissible* safety specifications that disallow global states where m or more processes, for some fixed number m, are in some subset of the local states. We denote by $\phi_s(n)$ the permissible safety specifications provided by the designer for a system with n processes. A MERCURY system is safe if there are no reachable error states in its global semantics. We denote that as $[\![P, n]\!] \models \phi_s(n)$.

The Efficiently-Decidable Fragment. QUICKSILVER identifies a fragment of MERCURY for which the parameterized verification problem of a large class of safety properties is *efficiently-decidable*. In particular, a pair $\langle P, \phi \rangle$ of a MERCURY process P and a safety specification ϕ is in the efficiently-decidable fragment of MERCURY if it satisfies *phase-compatibility* and *cutoff-amenability* conditions. For such a pair, a *cutoff* number c of processes can be computed and the parameterized verification problem can be reduced to the verification of the cutoff-sized system (i.e., $\forall n : [\![P, n]\!] \models \phi_s(n) \Leftrightarrow [\![P, c]\!] \models \phi_s(c)$).

During verification, QUICKSILVER computes a set of *phases* that an execution of the system goes through. On a high level, the phase-compatibility conditions ensure that the system moves between phases through "globally-synchronizing" events (i.e., broadcast, partition, or consensus), and that all processes in the same phase can participate in further globally-synchronizing events. This ensures that the system's ability to move between phases is *independent* of the number of processes in the system. The cutoff-amenability conditions ensure that an error state, where m processes are in a subset of the local states violating some safety specification, is reachable in a system of any size iff it is reachable in a system with exactly m processes. If any of these conditions fails, the designer must modify the process definition manually and attempt the verification again. We denote by $[\![P]\!] \models \phi_{pc}$ (resp. $[\![P]\!] \models \phi_{ca}$) that the MERCURY process P with local semantics $[\![P]\!]$ satisfies phase-compatibility (resp. cutoff-amenability) conditions.

2.2 MERCURY Process Sketch

Let us extend MERCURY's syntax to allow process *sketches* that can be completed by a synthesizer. In particular, we allow the process definition to include a set of *uninterpreted functions* that can replace various expressions in MERCURY such as the Boolean expression `cond` in the `if(cond) then ... else ...`, the target locations of `goto` statements, and the `rhs` of assignments. [3] As is standard, each uninterpreted function f is equipped with a signature determining its

---

[3] Such uninterpreted functions are sufficient to be a building block for more complex expressions and statements (See, for instance, the SKETCH Language [33]).

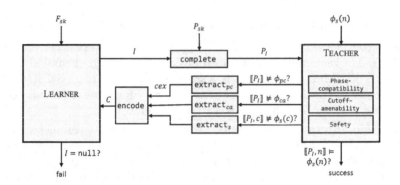

Fig. 1: Overview of CINNABAR's architecture.

list of named, typed parameters and its return type. A valid list of arguments arg for some function f is a list of values with types that match the function's parameter list. Applying a function f to a valid list of arguments arg is denoted by $f(\text{arg})$. Additionally, we define a *function interpretation* $I(f)$ of an uninterpreted function f as a mapping from every valid list of arguments of f to a valid return value.

A MERCURY process definition P that contains one or more uninterpreted functions is called a *sketch*, and is denoted P_{sk}. We denote by F_{sk} the set of all uninterpreted functions in a sketch P_{sk}. An interpretation I of the set F_{sk} of uninterpreted functions is then a mapping from every uninterpreted function $f_{sk} \in F_{sk}$ to some function interpretation $I(f_{sk})$.

For some process sketch P_{sk} and some interpretation I of the set F_{sk} of uninterpreted functions in P_{sk}, we denote by P_I the *interpreted process sketch* obtained by replacing every uninterpreted function $f_{sk} \in F_{sk}$ in the sketch P_{sk} with its function interpretation $I(f_{sk})$ according to the interpretation I.

2.3   Problem Definition

We now define the parameterized synthesis problem for MERCURY systems.

Definition 1 (MERCURY Parameterized Synthesis Problem (MPSP)). *Given a process sketch P_{sk} with a set of uninterpreted functions F_{sk}, an environment process P_e, and permissible safety specification $\phi_s(n)$, find an interpretation I of uninterpreted functions in F_{sk} such that the system $P_{I,1}||\ldots||P_{I,n}||P_e$ is safe for any number of processes, i.e., $\forall n : [\![P_I, n]\!] \models \phi_s(n)$.*

3   Constraint-Based Synthesis for MERCURY Systems

Architecture. To solve MPSP, we propose a multi-stage, counterexample-based architecture, shown in Fig. 1, with the following components:

- LEARNER: a constraint-solver that accepts a set C of *constraints* over the uninterpreted functions F_{sk} and generates interpretations I satisfying these constraints (i.e., $I \models C$). Specifically, a constraint $\mathsf{c} \in C$ is a well-typed Boolean formula over uninterpreted function applications.
- TEACHER: a component capable of checking phase-compatibility, cutoff-amenability, safety, and *liveness*[4] of MERCURY systems. We refer to these four conditions as *properties*.
- complete: a component that builds an interpreted process sketch P_I from a process sketch P_{sk} and an interpretation I provided by the learner.
- extract$_{prop}$: a *property-specific* component to extract a counterexample cex, capturing the root cause of a violation, if the TEACHER determines that a property $prop$ from the above-mentioned properties is violated.
- encode: a novel *property-agnostic* component that encodes counterexamples generated by extract components into additional constraints for the learner.

Synthesis Procedure. CINNABAR instantiates this architecture as shown in Algo. 1. The algorithm starts with an empty set of constraints, C (Line 2) over the set F_{sk} of uninterpreted functions in the process sketch P_{sk}. In each iteration, it checks if there exists an interpretation I of the uninterpreted functions that satisfies all the constraints collected so far (Line 4). If such an interpretation is found, it is used to obtain an interpreted process sketch P_I (Line 6). Then, the algorithm checks if the system described by P_I is phase-compatible and cutoff-amenable. If so, a cutoff c is computed (Line 13) and the c-sized system is checked to be safe. The cutoff-amenability stage is similar to phase-compatibility and is hence omitted from the algorithm. At any stage, if the process fails

---

Algorithm 1: Solving MPSP.

---

1 **procedure** Synth$(P_{sk}, \phi_s(n), \phi_l(c))$
2 | $C = \varnothing$
3 | **while** *true* **do**
4 | | $I = \mathtt{interpret}(F_{sk}, C)$
5 | | **if** $I \neq null$ **then**
6 | | | $P_I = \mathtt{complete}(P_{sk}, I)$
7 | | | $[\![P_I]\!] = \mathtt{buildLS}(P_I)$
8 | | | $cex_p = \mathtt{findPhCoCE}([\![P_I]\!])$
9 | | | **if** $cex_p \neq null$ **then**
10 | | | | $C = C \cup \neg \mathtt{encode}(cex_p)$
11 | | | | **Continue**
12 | | | ... ▷ check cutoff-amenability
13 | | | $c = \mathtt{compCutoff}(P_I, \phi_s(n))$
14 | | | $[\![P_I, c]\!] = \mathtt{buildGS}(P_I, c)$
15 | | | $cex_s = \mathtt{findSaCE}([\![P_I, c]\!], \phi_s(c))$
16 | | | **if** $cex_s \neq null$ **then**
17 | | | | $C = C \cup \neg \mathtt{encode}(cex_s)$
18 | | | | **Continue**
19 | | | **return** P_I
20 | | **else**
21 | | | **return null**

---

to satisfy any of these properties (e.g., a counterexample cex_p to phase-compatibility is found on Line 8), the root-cause of the failure is extracted and encoded into a constraint for the learner to rule out the failure (e.g., Line 10).

---

[4] While MPSP targets permissible safety specifications, in order to improve the *quality* of the interpreted process sketch P_I, we extend MERCURY with *liveness* specifications to help rule out trivial completions that are safe. We emphasize that such specifications are only used as a tool to improve the quality of synthesis, and are only guaranteed for the cutoff-sized system, as opposed to safety properties that are guaranteed for any system size.

Note that these stages are checked sequentially due to the inherent dependency between them: (i) the system can only be cutoff amenable if it is phase compatible, and (ii) one can only check safety after a cutoff has been computed.

Lemma 1. *Assuming that the teacher is sound and the learner is complete for finite sets of interpretations, Algo. 1 for solving MPSP is sound and complete.*

Proof. Soundness follows directly from the soundness of the teacher. Completeness follows from that the encoding and extraction procedures ensure progress by eliminating at least the current interpretation at each iteration, and the finiteness of the set of interpretations. Finiteness follows from (i) the finite number of uninterpreted functions in a sketch P_{sk}, (ii) the finiteness of the domain of each local variable, and (iii) the finiteness of the number of local variables in P_{sk}.

In the remainder of this section, we describe the property-agnostic encode component in Algo. 1. In the following section, we describe our implementation of our synthesis procedure specialized to a QUICKSILVER-based teacher and property-specific extraction procedures.

Property-Agnostic Counterexample Encoding Procedure

We first describe the necessary augmentation of local semantics with *disabled transitions* needed for CINNABAR's counterexample extraction and encoding. While such transitions are not relevant when reasoning about a "concrete" process definition (i.e., one with no uninterpreted functions), they are quite important when extracting an *explanation* for why some conditions (e.g., phase-compatibility) fail to hold on $[\![P]\!]$.

Augmented Local Semantics of the MERCURY *Process* P_I. We extend the definition of the local semantics of a MERCURY interpreted process sketch P_I to be $[\![P_I]\!] = (S_I, s_0, E, T_I, T_I^{dis})$ where S_I, s_0, E, and T_I are defined as before and T_I^{dis} is the set of *disabled transitions* under the current interpretation I. In particular, a disabled transition $t = s \xrightarrow{a} \bot$ based on action handler h over action a is in T_I^{dis} iff the guard $g(h)$ evaluates to *false* in s. The symbol $\bot$ here indicates that no local state is reachable, since the guard is disabled.

Additionally, we say a transition $t = s \xrightarrow{a} s'$ based on action handler h over action a is a *sketch transition* if h contains no uninterpreted functions in its guard or updates. A local state $s \in S_I$ is *concrete* if (i) s is the initial state s_0, or (ii) there exists a sketch transition $s' \rightarrow s$ where s' is concrete. In other words, a local state s is concrete if there exists a path from the initial state s_0 to s that is composed purely of sketch transitions and hence is always reachable regardless of the interpretation we obtain from the learner.

We now formalize counterexamples for phase-compatibility and cutoff amenability properties then present an encoding procedure for such counterexamples. The encoding is *exact* in the sense that a generated constraint c corresponding to some counterexample *cex* rules out exactly all interpretations I where an interpreted process sketch P_I exhibits *cex* (as opposed to an over-approximation where c would rule out interpreted process sketches that do not exhibit *cex*, or an under-approximation where c would allow interpreted process sketches that do exhibit *cex*). Additionally, the encoding is *property-agnostic* in the sense that it can handle counterexamples for any property failure.

Counterexamples. Recall that a candidate process P_I based on some process sketch P_{sk} and interpretation I has the local semantics $[\![P_I]\!] = (S_I, s_0, E, T_I, T_I^{dis})$. A counterexample *cex* to phase-compatibility (resp. cutoff-amenability) is a "subset" of the local semantics $[\![P_I]\!]$ such that *cex* $\not\models \phi_{pc}$ (resp. *cex* $\not\models \phi_{ca}$). We say that *cex* is a subset of $[\![P_I]\!]$, denoted *cex* $\subseteq [\![P_I]\!]$, when it has a subset of its enabled and disabled transitions, i.e., *cex* $= (S_I, s_0, E, T_I' \subseteq T_I, T_I'^{dis} \subseteq T_I^{dis})$.

Encoding Counterexamples. Let C be the set of all well-typed constraints that the learner accepts. The encoding of counterexample *cex* $= (S_I, s_0, E, T_I, T_I^{dis})$ w.r.t. interpretation I is a formula $\langle\!\langle cex \rangle\!\rangle_I \in C$ defined as:

$$\langle\!\langle cex \rangle\!\rangle_I = \Big(\bigwedge_{t_{en} \in T_I} \langle\!\langle t_{en} \rangle\!\rangle_I \Big) \wedge \Big(\bigwedge_{t_{dis} \in T_I^{dis}} \langle\!\langle t_{dis} \rangle\!\rangle_I \Big),$$

where $\langle\!\langle t_{en} \rangle\!\rangle_I$ (resp. $\langle\!\langle t_{dis} \rangle\!\rangle_I$) is an encoding of an enabled (resp. disabled) local transition. Note that $\langle\!\langle cex \rangle\!\rangle_I$ is satisfied under interpretation I (i.e., $I \models \langle\!\langle cex \rangle\!\rangle_I$) and implies that *cex* $\subseteq [\![P]\!]$. An encoding of some enabled transition $t_{en} = s \xrightarrow{a} s'$ based on action handler h over action a is defined as:

$$\langle\!\langle s \xrightarrow{a} s' \rangle\!\rangle_I = \langle\!\langle s \rangle\!\rangle_I \wedge \langle\!\langle a : s \rangle\!\rangle_I \wedge \langle\!\langle s' : s, a \rangle\!\rangle_I,$$

where:

1. the predicate $\langle\!\langle s \rangle\!\rangle_I$ indicating that the source state s is reachable from the initial state s_0 under interpretation I. If s is concrete, $\langle\!\langle s \rangle\!\rangle_I$ is simply *true* (i.e., s is always reachable regardless of I). Otherwise, $\langle\!\langle s \rangle\!\rangle_I$ is defined as follows. Let $\mathcal{P}$ be the set of all paths from the initial state s_0 to state s. Then, $\langle\!\langle s \rangle\!\rangle_I := \bigvee_{p \in \mathcal{P}} \langle\!\langle p \rangle\!\rangle_I$, where $\langle\!\langle p \rangle\!\rangle_I$ for some path p consisting of local transitions $t_1, \ldots, t_i$ is defined as $\langle\!\langle t_1 \rangle\!\rangle_I \wedge \ldots \wedge \langle\!\langle t_i \rangle\!\rangle_I$.

2. the predicate $\langle\!\langle a : s \rangle\!\rangle_I$ indicating that the process can perform action a from state s. The predicate $\langle\!\langle a : s \rangle\!\rangle_I$ is defined as follows: $\langle\!\langle a : s \rangle\!\rangle_I := (g(h)[s(V)/V] = true)$, where $g(h)[s(V)/V]$ is the guard $g(h)$ with each local variable $v \in V$ replaced by its value $s(v)$ in state s.

   Example. Let $\mathtt{uf}(x, y)$ be an uninterpreted function over local $\mathtt{int}$ variables x and y. Let the local state $s := \{v_{loc} = \mathtt{F}, x = 1, y = 2\}$, and let the local guard of action handler h over action a in location $\mathtt{F}$ be $g := \mathtt{uf}(x, y) > 7 \vee x = 2$. Then $\langle\!\langle a : s \rangle\!\rangle_I = ((\mathtt{uf}(s(x), s(y)) > 7 \vee s(x) = 2) = true))$ which is $((\mathtt{uf}(1, 2) > 7 \vee 1 = 2) = true)$ which simplifies to $\mathtt{uf}(1, 2) > 7$.

3. the predicate $\langle\!\langle s' : s, a \rangle\!\rangle_I$ indicating that s goes to s' on action a. The predicate $\langle\!\langle s' : s, a \rangle\!\rangle_I$ is defined as follows. Let $u(h)$ denote the set of updates of the form $\mathtt{lhs} := \mathtt{rhs}$ of handler h over action a. Then, $\langle\!\langle s' : s, a \rangle\!\rangle_I := \bigwedge_{\mathtt{lhs}:=\mathtt{rhs} \in u(h)} s'(\mathtt{lhs}) = \mathtt{rhs}[s(V)/V]$.

   Example. Let the set of updates have the single update $x := \mathtt{uf}(y, z)$ and s, s' be $\{v_{loc} = \mathtt{F}, x = 1, y = 2, z = 3\}$ and $\{v_{loc} = \mathtt{D}, x = 5, y = 2, z = 3\}$. Then $\langle\!\langle s' : s, a \rangle\!\rangle_I$ is: $s'(x) = \mathtt{uf}(s(y), s(z))$ which is $\mathtt{uf}(2, 3) = 5$.

An encoding of some disabled transition $t_{dis} = s \xrightarrow{a} \perp$ in cex is defined as $\langle\!\langle t_{dis} \rangle\!\rangle_I = \langle\!\langle s \rangle\!\rangle_I \wedge \langle\!\langle \neg a : s \rangle\!\rangle_I$ where $\langle\!\langle s \rangle\!\rangle_I$ is as before and the predicate $\langle\!\langle \neg a : s \rangle\!\rangle_I$, indicating that the process cannot perform action a from state s, is defined as follows: $\langle\!\langle \neg a : s \rangle\!\rangle_I := (g(h)[s(V)/V] = false)$.

The intuition behind breaking a transition's encoding to various predicates is that some phase-compatibility conditions leave parts of a transition unspecified. For instance, the predicate "the local state s can react to event e" corresponds to a local transition $s \xrightarrow{R(e)} * \in T_I$ with encoding $\langle\!\langle s \rangle\!\rangle_I \wedge \langle\!\langle R(e) : s \rangle\!\rangle_I$.

Finally, to rule out any interpretation I that exhibits cex, we add the constraint $c = \neg\langle\!\langle cex \rangle\!\rangle_I$ to the learner.

Encoding Counterexamples to Safety Properties. Similar to the local semantics, we extend the definition of the global semantics $[\![P_I, n]\!]$ of a MERCURY system $P_{I,1} \|\ldots\| P_{I,n} \| P_e$ to be $[\![P_I, n]\!] = (Q_I, q_0, E, R_I, R_I^{dis})$, where Q_I, q_0, E, and R_I are defined as before and R_I^{dis} is the set of *disabled global transitions* under the current interpretation I. Then, a counterexample cex to safety is a "subset" of the *global* semantics $[\![P_I, c]\!]$ such that $cex \not\models \phi_s(c)$. Encoding of such a counterexample cex is formalized as before, with the encoding of an enabled global transition r in cex being a formula $\langle\!\langle cex \rangle\!\rangle_I \in \mathcal{C}$ computed as follows. For some global transition $r = q \xrightarrow{e} q'$, we denote by $active(r)$ the local transitions that processes in q locally use to end in q'. That is, $active(r) = \{t \in T_I \mid \exists P_{I,i} : t = q[i] \xrightarrow{A(e)} q'[i] \vee t = q[i] \xrightarrow{R(e)} q'[i]\}$ We then define the encoding $\langle\!\langle r \rangle\!\rangle_I$ as: $\langle\!\langle r \rangle\!\rangle_I = \bigwedge_{t \in active(r)} \langle\!\langle t \rangle\!\rangle_I$.

Note that the predicates $\langle\!\langle q \rangle\!\rangle_I$, $\langle\!\langle e : q \rangle\!\rangle_I$, $\langle\!\langle q' : q, e \rangle\!\rangle_I$, and $\langle\!\langle \neg e : q \rangle\!\rangle_I$ as well as the encoding for the global disabled transitions can be defined similar to their counterparts discussed earlier.

4   Counterexample Extraction

Our tool specializes the synthesis procedure in Algo. 1 by using QUICKSILVER as the teacher to check phase-compatibility, cutoff-amenability, and safety. For the remainder of this section, we will refer to phase-compatibility and cutoff-amenability conditions as *local* properties and safety (and liveness) specifications as *global* properties.

Local Properties. Given a local property ϕ expressed as first-order logic formulas over the local semantics of a MERCURY process, CINNABAR extracts a counterexample cex according to Algo. 2.

First, we negate the property and express in disjunctive normal form (DNF):

Algorithm 2: Counterexample Extraction.

---

1 **procedure** Extract(P_I, ϕ)
2    $\phi' = makeDNF(\neg\phi)$
3    $W = \varnothing$
4   **foreach** $c \in cubes(\phi')$ **do**
5   **if** $[\![P_I]\!] \models c$ **then**
6        $cw = \varnothing$
7   **foreach** $l \in literals(c)$ **do**
8          $lw = \text{witness}(l)$
9          $cw = cw \cup \{lw\}$
10        $W = W \cup \{cw\}$
11    $cex = pickMinimal(W)$
12   **return** cex

$\phi' = \neg\phi = c_1 \vee c_2 \vee \ldots$, where each cube $c_i = l_1 \wedge l_2 \wedge \ldots$ is a conjunction of literals (Line 2). Then, for each cube c satisfied under $[\![P_I]\!]$ (Line 5), extract a cube *witness* cw that is a subset of the local semantics $[\![P_I]\!]$ such that $[\![P_I]\!] \models cw$ (Lines 7 - 9). This is done by extracting, for each literal l in c, a minimal subset lw of $[\![P_I]\!]$ such that $lw \models l$ (Line 8). We say lw is a *minimal witness* of l if any strict subset of lw cannot be a witness for l (i.e., $\forall lw' \subset lw : lw' \not\models l$). Finally pick a minimal (in terms of size) cube witness of some cube c as a *cex* (Line 11). Since $cex \models c$ and $c \Rightarrow \neg\phi$, we know that $cex \models \neg\phi$ (or equivalently, $cex \not\models \phi$).

In this work, we carefully analyzed the phase-compatibility and cutoff amenability conditions and incorporated procedures to compute witnesses for their literals (i.e., the `witness` calls on Line 8). We refer the interested reader to the extended version [19] of this paper for complete details, and illustrate one such counterexample extraction procedure using an example.

Example. We present a simplified phase-compatibility condition and demonstrate the above procedure on it. Let the set of broadcast, partition, and consensus events be called the *globally-synchronizing* events, denoted $E_{\texttt{global}}$. Let $ph(s)$ be the set of all "phases" containing local state s. The condition states that: for each internal transition $s \rightarrow s'$ that is accompanied by a reacting transition $s' \xrightarrow{R(\texttt{f})} s''$ for some globally-synchronizing event $\texttt{f}$, and for each state t in the same phase as s, state t must have a reacting transition of event $\texttt{f}$. Formally:

$$\forall \texttt{f} \in E_{\texttt{global}}, s, s' \in S :$$

$$\left(s \rightarrow s' \in T \wedge s' \xrightarrow{R(\texttt{f})} * \in T\right) \Rightarrow \left(\forall X \in ph(s), t \in X : \exists t \xrightarrow{R(\texttt{f})} * \in T\right).$$

This condition is an example of a local property ϕ we want to extract counterexamples for when it fails. The procedure is applied as follows:
Step (1): We first simplify ϕ to the following:

$$\forall \texttt{f} \in E_{\texttt{global}}, s, s', t \in S, X \in ph(s) :$$

$$\left(s \rightarrow s' \in T \wedge s' \xrightarrow{R(\texttt{f})} * \in T \wedge inPhase(X, s, t)\right) \Rightarrow \left(\exists t \xrightarrow{R(\texttt{f})} * \in T\right),$$

where $inPhase(X, s, t)$ indicates that states s and t are in phase X together. We then obtain the negation $\neg\phi$:

$$\exists \texttt{f} \in E_{\texttt{global}}, s, s', t \in S, X \in ph(s) :$$

$$s \rightarrow s' \in T \wedge s' \xrightarrow{R(\texttt{f})} * \in T \wedge inPhase(X, s, t) \wedge \neg\exists t \xrightarrow{R(\texttt{f})} * \in T.$$

Step (2): The formula $\neg\phi$ is in DNF, and there is a cube for each instantiation of event $\texttt{f} \in E_{\texttt{global}}$, states $s, s', t \in S$, and phase X that satisfies the formula $\neg\phi$. There are 4 literals. The literals "$s \rightarrow s' \in T$" and "$s' \xrightarrow{R(\texttt{f})} * \in T$" can be witnessed by the corresponding transitions $s \rightarrow s'$ and $s' \xrightarrow{R(\texttt{f})} *$, respectively. The literal "$\neg\exists t \xrightarrow{R(\texttt{f})} * \in T$" can be witnessed by the *disabled* transition $t \xrightarrow{R(\texttt{f})} \bot$. The witness for the literal $inPhase(X, s_a, s_b)$ for some phase X and local states s_a and s_b is more involved. It depends on the *nature* of that phase. We analyzed the phase construction procedure given in [17] and distilled it as follows. For each event $e \in E_{\texttt{global}}$, we define its source (resp. destination) set to be the set of states in S from (resp. to) which there exists a transition in T labeled with an acting or reacting action of event e. Let *corePhases* be the set of all source and destination sets of all globally-synchronizing actions. Then, two states s_a and s_b are in the same phase if:

(a) they are part of some core phase, i.e., $\exists X \in \textit{corePhases} : s_a, s_b \in X$, or,

(b) they are in different core phases that are connected by an internal path, i.e., $\exists A, B \in \textit{corePhases} : s_a, s'_a \in A \wedge s_b, s'_b \in B \wedge s'_a \rightsquigarrow s'_b$, where $s'_a \rightsquigarrow s'_b$ is an internal path from s'_a to s'_b.

If X is a core phase (i.e., case (A) holds), the counterexample extraction procedure returns the phase itself. Otherwise, case (B) holds and the two core phases are recursively extracted as well as the internal path connecting them.

Step (3) The final step is to build a subset of the local semantics that include the extracted witnesses for all 4 literals.

Global Properties. If a candidate process P_I meets its phase-compatibility and cutoff-amenability conditions, then it belongs to the efficiently-decidable fragment of MERCURY, and a cutoff c exists. It then remains to check if the system $P_{I,1}||\ldots||P_{I,n}||P_e$ is safe (i.e., $[\![P_I, c]\!] \models \phi_s(c)$).

Safety properties $\phi_s(n)$ are specified by the system designer as (Boolean combinations of) permissible safety specifications. Such properties are invariants that must hold in every reachable state in $[\![P_I, c]\!]$.

A counterexample $cex \subseteq [\![P_I, c]\!]$ to a safety property $\phi_s(c)$ is a finite trace from the initial state q_0 to an error state q_e. Such traces are extracted while constructing $[\![P_I, c]\!]$.

5   Implementation and Evaluation

5.1   Implementation

Our tool, CINNABAR[5], implements the architecture illustrated in Fig. 1. Additionally, it incorporates a liveness checker into the teacher. Liveness properties $\phi_l(c)$ ensure that the system makes progress and eventually reacts to various events. We refer the interested reader to the extended version [19] for details on specifying liveness properties as well as extracting and encoding counterexamples to such properties.

5.2   Evaluation

In this section, we investigate CINNABAR's performance. We study the impact of CINNABAR's counterexample extraction and encoding, as well as the choice of uninterpreted functions, on performance. Finally, we examine how CINNABAR's iterations are distributed across the different types of counterexamples.

---

[5] CINNABAR is publicly available on Zenodo [18].

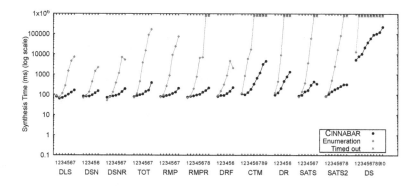

Fig. 2: CINNABAR's performance compared to enumeration-based synthesis. The systems studied are: Distributed Store (DS), Consortium (CTM), Distributed Lock Service (DLS), Distributed Register (DR), Two-Object Tracker (TOT), Distributed Robot Flocking (DRF), variants Small Aircraft Transportation System Landing Protocol (SATS, SATS2), variants of Distributed Sensor Network (DSN, DSNR), and variants of Robotics Motion Planner (RMP, RMPR). For each benchmark, the i-th point denotes the average runtime for all variants with i uninterpreted functions.

Benchmarks. The benchmarks we use are process sketches based on the benchmarks presented in [17]. We refer the reader to the extended version [19] for (i) a description of each benchmark's functionality, its safety and liveness specifications, and the unspecified functionality in the sketch, and (ii) an example MERCURY sketch and its completion.

Experimental Setup. To ensure that our reported results are not dependent on a particular choice of uninterpreted functions, we create a set of *variants* for each benchmark as follows. For each benchmark, we first pick a set ue of "candidate uninterpreted functions", corresponding to expressions that a designer might reasonably leave unspecified. Then, for each subset e in the set $\mathcal{P}(ue)$ of all non-empty subsets of ue, we create a variant of the benchmark where the uninterpreted functions in e are included in the sketch. We set a timeout of 15 minutes when running any variant and conduct our experiments on a MacBook Pro with 2 GHz Quad-Core Intel Core i5 and 16 GB of RAM.

Effect of Counterexample Extraction and Encoding. As our baseline, we consider a synthesis loop where the learner enumerates interpretations until a correct interpretation is found. If some interpreted process sketch P_I fails a property at any stage, we add the constraint $c = \neg I$ to the learner. This effectively eliminates one interpretation at a time, as opposed to all interpretations that exhibit the given counterexample at a time (as done by our encoder). In Fig. 2, we present a comparison of CINNABAR's runtime compared to this enumeration-based baseline. We make the following observations. While the runtimes of both enumeration-based synthesis and CINNABAR grow exponentially when increasing the number of uninterpreted functions, CINNABAR outperforms

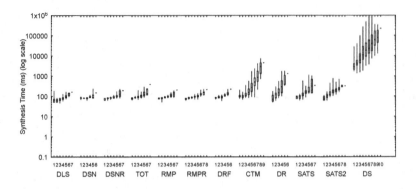

Fig. 3: Effect of the choice of uninterpreted functions on synthesis time. For some benchmark and some number m of uninterpreted functions, the m-th box-and-whiskers plot presents, from bottom to top, the minimum, first quartile, median, third quartile, and maximum synthesis run time across the run times of all variants of that benchmark with m uninterpreted functions.

enumeration-based synthesis in almost all scenarios. Only for variants with a single uninterpreted function we observed cases where enumeration-based synthesis found a correct solution faster than CINNABAR (e.g., as in DSNR with one uninterpreted function). This is due to the additional time spent extracting and encoding counterexamples. However, the value of the counterexample extraction and encoding becomes clearly apparent with larger number of unspecified expressions as the number of interpretations grows much larger and it becomes infeasible to just enumerate them. Furthermore, CINNABAR is able to perform synthesis for any variant of our benchmarks in under 9 minutes.

Effect of the Choice of Uninterpreted Functions. In Fig. 3, for each benchmark, we examine the variation of synthesis runtime across variants with the same number of uninterpreted functions. As shown in the figure, in some cases (e.g., CTM and DS), the variation is more noticeable. The main factor contributing to this is that uninterpreted functions present different overhead on synthesis based on their nature. For instance, an uninterpreted function corresponding to a `lhs` of some assignment expression is more expensive to synthesize compared to an uninterpreted function corresponding to a target of some `goto` statement, as the latter has a smaller search space.

Counterexample Distribution on Iterations. In Fig. 4, we illustrate the different types of counterexamples encountered throughout CINNABAR's iterations. We make the following observations. First, CINNABAR spends most of its iterations ruling out phase-compatibility violations. This is expected as checking phase-compatibility is the first stage in our synthesis loop. Since a phase-compatible system moves in a structured way between its phases, this stage rules out all arbitrary completions that prohibit processes from advancing through the phases. Furthermore, there are fewer safety violations than any other type of violations. Once an interpreted process sketch is in the efficiently-decidable fragment

Fig. 4: A property-based visualization of CINNABAR's iterations for a representative subset of the variants. Each line corresponds a CINNABAR's execution of a synthesis variant of a benchmark. From left to right, each line starts with iteration 1, ends with the iteration where a correct interpretation was found, and is colored to indicate nature of violations encountered throughout the execution. For instance, the line ▭■■■ would indicate that CINNABAR encountered a phase-compatibility violation in iteration 1, then a cutoff-amenability in iteration 2, ..., and finally was able to find a correct interpretation in iteration 6.

of MERCURY, it is more likely to be safe. There are two factors that contribute to this: (i) phase-compatible systems move in a structured way and are more likely to be "closer" to a correct version of the system, and (ii) because cutoff-amenability depends on the safety specification, satisfying cutoff-amenability means the interpreted process sketch is more likely to be correct with respect to the safety property already. Finally, eliminating liveness violations ensures that CINNABAR is able to synthesize higher-quality completions. As shown in the figure, liveness violations are often encountered in the very first iteration, as the SMT-based learner tends to favor interpretations with disabled guards that trivially satisfy phase-compatibility, cutoff-amenability, and safety properties.

Usability. If CINNABAR fails to synthesize a correct completion, the designer can *replace* existing expressions in the sketch with uninterpreted functions, allowing CINNABAR to explore a larger set of possible candidate completions.

Finally, while the supported uninterpreted functions may not correspond to large segments of the code or complex control-flow constructs, they are the main "knobs" that the designer needs to turn to ensure that their systems belong to the efficiently-decidable fragment of MERCURY.

6   Related Work

Aiding System Designers via Decidable Verification. Ivy [29] adopts an interactive approach to aid the designer in searching for inductive invariants for their systems. Ivy translates the system model and its invariant to EPR [30], and looks for a *counterexample-to-induction* (CTI). The designer adjusts the invariant to eliminate that CTI and Ivy starts over. I4 [26] builds on Ivy by first considering a fixed system size, automatically generating a potential inductive invariant, and using Ivy to check if that invariant is also valid for any system size. The approach in [11] identifies a class of asynchronous systems that can be reduced to an equivalent synchronized system modeled in the Heard-Of Model [9]. The designer manually annotates the asynchronous system to facilitate the reduction, and encodes the resulting Heard-Of model in the $\mathbb{CL}$ [14] logic which has a semi-decision procedure. These approaches differ from ours in two ways. First, the designer needs to manually provide/manipulate inductive invariants and/or annotations to eventually enable decidable verification. Second, these approaches are "verification only": they require a *fully-specified* model that either meets or violates its correctness properties and the designer is responsible for adjusting the model if verification fails. CINNABAR, on the other hand, accepts a sketch that is then completed to meet its properties.

Parameterized Synthesis. Jacobs and Bloem [20] introduced a general approach for parameterized synthesis based on cutoffs, where they use an underlying fixed-size synthesis procedure that is required to guarantee that the conditions for cutoffs are met by the synthesized implementation. Our approach can be seen as an instantiation of this approach, as one of the stages in our multi-stage counterexample-based loop ensures that cutoff-amenability conditions hold on any candidate process. Other approaches that tackle the parameterized synthesis problem without cutoff results are more specialized. For instance, the approach in [24] adopts a CEGIS-based synthesis strategy where the designer provides a threshold automaton with some parameters unspecified. Synthesis completes the model and uses the parameterized model checker in [23] to check the system. A similar idea, but based on the notion of well-structured transition systems, is used for the automatic *repair* of parameterized systems in [21]. The approach in [22] targets parameterized synthesis for self-stabilizing rings, and shows that the problem is decidable even when the corresponding parameterized verification problem is not. The designer provides a set of legitimate states and the size of the template process, and the procedure yields a completed self-stabilizing template. A similar approach for more general topologies is presented in [28]. Bertrand et al. [6] target systems composed of an unbounded number of agents that are fully specified and one underspecified controller process. The synthesis goal is to synthesize a controller that controls all agents uniformly and guides them to a specific desired state. Markgraf et al. [27] also target synthesis of controllers by posing the problem as an infinite-duration 2-player game and utilize regular model checking and the L* algorithm [4] to learn correct-by-design controllers. These approaches are not applicable to our setup as they do not admit distributed agreement-based systems (modeled in MERCURY).

Synthesis of Distributed Systems with a Fixed Number of Processes. Various approaches focus on automated synthesis of distributed systems with a *fixed* number of processes [3,2,1,12,35]. While such approaches deploy a similar counterexample-guided strategy to complete a user-provided sketch, they do not provide parameterized correctness guarantees nor the necessary agreement primitives needed to model distributed agreement-based systems.

Data availability. The artifact and related data that support the findings of this work are publicly available on Zenodo [18].

References

1. Alur, R., Martin, M., Raghothaman, M., Stergiou, C., Tripakis, S., Udupa, A.: Synthesizing finite-state protocols from scenarios and requirements. In: Yahav, E. (ed.) Hardware and Software: Verification and Testing. pp. 75–91. Springer International Publishing, Cham (2014)
2. Alur, R., Raghothaman, M., Stergiou, C., Tripakis, S., Udupa, A.: Automatic completion of distributed protocols with symmetry. In: Kroening, D., Păsăreanu, C.S. (eds.) Computer Aided Verification. pp. 395–412. Springer International Publishing, Cham (2015)
3. Alur, R., Tripakis, S.: Automatic synthesis of distributed protocols. SIGACT News **48**(1), 55–90 (Mar 2017). https://doi.org/10.1145/3061640.3061652, https://doi.org/10.1145/3061640.3061652
4. Angluin, D.: Learning regular sets from queries and counterexamples. Inf. Comput. **75**(2), 87–106 (nov 1987). https://doi.org/10.1016/0890-5401(87)90052-6, https://doi.org/10.1016/0890-5401(87)90052-6
5. Apt, K.R., Kozen, D.C.: Limits for automatic verification of finite-state concurrent systems. Information Processing Letters **22**(6), 307–309 (1986). https://doi.org/https://doi.org/10.1016/0020-0190(86)90071-2, https://www.sciencedirect.com/science/article/pii/0020019086900712
6. Bertrand, N., Dewaskar, M., Genest, B., Gimbert, H., Godbole, A.A.: Controlling a population. arXiv preprint arXiv:1807.00893 (2018)
7. Bloem, R., Jacobs, S., Khalimov, A., Konnov, I., Rubin, S., Veith, H., Widder, J.: Decidability of Parameterized Verification. Synthesis Lectures on Distributed Computing Theory, Morgan & Claypool Publishers (2015)
8. Bornholt, J., Joshi, R., Astrauskas, V., Cully, B., Kragl, B., Markle, S., Sauri, K., Schleit, D., Slatton, G., Tasiran, S., Van Geffen, J., Warfield, A.: Using lightweight formal methods to validate a key-value storage node in amazon s3. In: Proceedings of the ACM SIGOPS 28th Symposium on Operating Systems Principles. p. 836–850. SOSP '21, Association for Computing Machinery, New York, NY, USA (2021). https://doi.org/10.1145/3477132.3483540, https://doi.org/10.1145/3477132.3483540
9. Charron-Bost, B., Schiper, A.: The Heard-of Model: Computing in Distributed Systems with Benign Faults. Distributed Computing **22**(1), 49–71 (2009). https://doi.org/10.1007/s00446-009-0084-6
10. Cook, B.: Formal reasoning about the security of amazon web services. In: Chockler, H., Weissenbacher, G. (eds.) Computer Aided Verification. pp. 38–47. Springer International Publishing, Cham (2018)
11. Damian, A., Dragoi, C., Militaru, A., Widder, J.: Communication-closed Asynchronous Protocols. In: International Conference on Computer Aided Verification (2019)
12. Damm, W., Finkbeiner, B.: Automatic Compositional Synthesis of Distributed Systems. In: International Symposium on Formal Methods. pp. 179–193. Springer (2014)

13. Dill, D., Grieskamp, W., Park, J., Qadeer, S., Xu, M., Zhong, E.: Fast and reliable formal verification of smart contracts with the move prover. In: Fisman, D., Rosu, G. (eds.) Tools and Algorithms for the Construction and Analysis of Systems. pp. 183–200. Springer International Publishing, Cham (2022)

14. Drăgoi, C., Henzinger, T.A., Veith, H., Widder, J., Zufferey, D.: A Logic-based Framework for Verifying Consensus Algorithms. In: International Conference on Verification, Model Checking, and Abstract Interpretation. pp. 161–181. Springer (2014)

15. Hawblitzel, C., Howell, J., Kapritsos, M., Lorch, J.R., Parno, B., Roberts, M.L., Setty, S., Zill, B.: Ironfleet: Proving practical distributed systems correct. In: Proceedings of the 25th Symposium on Operating Systems Principles. p. 1–17. SOSP '15, Association for Computing Machinery, New York, NY, USA (2015). https://doi.org/10.1145/2815400.2815428, https://doi.org/10.1145/2815400.2815428

16. Jaber, N., Jacobs, S., Wagner, C., Kulkarni, M., Samanta, R.: Parameterized verification of systems with global synchronization and guards. In: Lahiri, S.K., Wang, C. (eds.) Computer Aided Verification. pp. 299–323. Springer International Publishing, Cham (2020)

17. Jaber, N., Wagner, C., Jacobs, S., Kulkarni, M., Samanta, R.: Quicksilver: Modeling and parameterized verification for distributed agreement-based systems. Proc. ACM Program. Lang. 5(OOPSLA) (oct 2021). https://doi.org/10.1145/3485534, https://doi.org/10.1145/3485534

18. Jaber, N., Wagner, C., Jacobs, S., Kulkarni, M., Samanta, R.: Synthesis of Distributed Agreement-Based Systems with Efficiently-Decidable Verification (Artifact) (Apr 2023). https://doi.org/10.5281/zenodo.7497463, https://doi.org/10.5281/zenodo.7497463

19. Jaber, N., Wagner, C., Jacobs, S., Kulkarni, M., Samanta, R.: Synthesis of distributed agreement-based systems with efficiently-decidable verification (extended version) (2023). https://doi.org/10.48550/ARXIV.2208.12400, https://arxiv.org/abs/2208.12400

20. Jacobs, S., Bloem, R.: Parameterized Synthesis. Logical Methods in Computer Science 10(1) (2014)

21. Jacobs, S., Sakr, M., Völp, M.: Automatic repair and deadlock detection for parameterized systems. In: FMCAD 2022. pp. 225–234

22. Klinkhamer, A.P., Ebnenasir, A.: Synthesizing parameterized self-stabilizing rings with constant-space processes. In: Dastani, M., Sirjani, M. (eds.) Fundamentals of Software Engineering. pp. 100–115. Springer International Publishing, Cham (2017)

23. Konnov, I., Lazić, M., Veith, H., Widder, J.: A Short Counterexample Property for Safety and Liveness Verification of Fault-tolerant Distributed Algorithms. ACM SIGPLAN Notices 52(1), 719–734 (2017)

24. Lazic, M., Konnov, I., Widder, J., Bloem, R.: Synthesis of Distributed Algorithms with Parameterized Threshold Guards. In: Aspnes, J., Bessani, A., Felber, P., Leitão, J. (eds.) OPODIS. LIPIcs, vol. 95, pp. 32:1–32:20. Schloss Dagstuhl - Leibniz-Zentrum fuer Informatik (2017)

25. Leino, K.R.M.: Dafny: An automatic program verifier for functional correctness. In: Clarke, E.M., Voronkov, A. (eds.) Logic for Programming, Artificial Intelligence, and Reasoning. pp. 348–370. Springer Berlin Heidelberg, Berlin, Heidelberg (2010)

26. Ma, H., Goel, A., Jeannin, J.B., Kapritsos, M., Kasikci, B., Sakallah, K.A.: I4: Incremental inference of inductive invariants for verification of distributed protocols. In: Proceedings of the 27th ACM Symposium on Operating Systems Principles. p. 370–384. SOSP '19, Association for Computing Machinery, New York, NY, USA (2019). https://doi.org/10.1145/3341301.3359651, https://doi.org/10.1145/3341301.3359651

27. Markgraf, O., Hong, C.D., Lin, A.W., Najib, M., Neider, D.: Parameterized synthesis with safety properties. In: Oliveira, B.C.d.S. (ed.) Programming Languages and Systems. pp. 273–292. Springer International Publishing, Cham (2020)

28. Mirzaie, N., Faghih, F., Jacobs, S., Bonakdarpour, B.: Parameterized synthesis of self-stabilizing protocols in symmetric networks. Acta Informatica **57**(1-2), 271–304 (2020)

29. Padon, O., McMillan, K.L., Panda, A., Sagiv, M., Shoham, S.: Ivy: Safety verification by interactive generalization. In: Proceedings of the 37th ACM SIGPLAN Conference on Programming Language Design and Implementation. p. 614–630. PLDI '16, Association for Computing Machinery, New York, NY, USA (2016). https://doi.org/10.1145/2908080.2908118, https://doi.org/10.1145/2908080.2908118

30. Piskac, R., de Moura, L., Bjørner, N.: Deciding Effectively Propositional Logic Using DPLL and Substitution Sets. Journal of Automated Reasoning **44**(4), 401–424 (2010)

31. Reid, A., Flur, S., Church, L., de Haas, S., Johnson, M., Laurie, B.: Towards making formal methods normal: meeting developers where they are. In: HATRA 2020: Human Aspects of Types and Reasoning Assistants (2020), https://arxiv.org/abs/2010.16345

32. Sergey, I., Wilcox, J.R., Tatlock, Z.: Programming and proving with distributed protocols. Proc. ACM Program. Lang. **2**(POPL) (Dec 2017). https://doi.org/10.1145/3158116, https://doi.org/10.1145/3158116

33. Solar-Lezama, A., Tancau, L., Bodik, R., Seshia, S., Saraswat, V.: Combinatorial Sketching for Finite Programs. In: Proceedings of the 12th International Conference on Architectural Support for Programming Languages and Operating Systems. pp. 404–415. ASPLOS XII, ACM (2006)

34. Suzuki, I.: Proving properties of a ring of finite-state machines. Inf. Process. Lett. **28**(4), 213–214 (Jul 1988). https://doi.org/10.1016/0020-0190(88)90211-6, https://doi.org/10.1016/0020-0190(88)90211-6

35. Udupa, A., Raghavan, A., Deshmukh, J.V., Mador-Haim, S., Martin, M.M., Alur, R.: TRANSIT: Specifying Protocols with Concolic Snippets. ACM SIGPLAN Notices **48**(6), 287–296 (2013)

36. Wilcox, J.R., Woos, D., Panchekha, P., Tatlock, Z., Wang, X., Ernst, M.D., Anderson, T.: Verdi: A framework for implementing and formally verifying distributed systems. In: Proceedings of the 36th ACM SIGPLAN Conference on Programming Language Design and Implementation. p. 357–368. PLDI '15, Association for Computing Machinery, New York, NY, USA (2015). https://doi.org/10.1145/2737924.2737958, https://doi.org/10.1145/2737924.2737958

LTL Reactive Synthesis with a Few Hints

Mrudula Balachander[1]([✉]), Emmanuel Filiot, and Jean-François Raskin

Université libre de Bruxelles, Brussels, Belgium
mbalacha@ulb.be

Abstract. We study a variant of the problem of synthesizing Mealy machines that enforce LTL specifications against all possible behaviours of the environment, including hostile ones. In the variant studied here, the user provides the high level LTL specification φ of the system to design, and a set E of examples of executions that the solution must produce. Our synthesis algorithm first generalizes the user-provided examples in E using tailored extensions of automata learning algorithms, while preserving realizability of φ. Second, it turns the (usually) incomplete Mealy machine obtained by the learning phase into a complete Mealy machine realizing φ. The examples are used to guide the synthesis procedure. We prove learnability guarantees of our algorithm and prove that our problem, while generalizing the classical LTL synthesis problem, matches its worst-case complexity. The additional cost of learning from E is even polynomial in the size of E and in the size of a symbolic representation of solutions that realize φ, computed by the synthesis tool ACACIA-BONZAI. We illustrate the practical interest of our approach on a set of examples.

1   Introduction

Reactive systems are notoriously difficult to design and even to specify correctly [1,13]. As a consequence, formal methods have emerged as useful tools to help designers to built reactive systems that are correct. For instance, model-checking asks the designer to provide a model, in the form of a Mealy machine $\mathcal{M}$, that describes the reactions of the system to events generated by its environment, together with a description of the *core correctness properties* that must be enforced. Those properties are expressed in a logical formalism, typically as an LTL formula φ_{CORE}. Then an algorithm decides if $\mathcal{M} \models \varphi_{\text{CORE}}$, i.e. if all executions of the system in its environment satisfy the specification. Automatic reactive synthesis is more ambitious: it aims at automatically generating a model from a high level description of the "*what*" needs to be done instead of the "*how*" it has to be done. Thus the user is only required to provide an LTL specification φ and the algorithm automatically generates a Mealy machine $\mathcal{M}$ such that $\mathcal{M} \models \varphi$ whenever φ is *realizable*. Unfortunately, it is most of the time not sufficient to provide the core correctness properties φ_{CORE} to obtain a Mealy machine $\mathcal{M}$ that is useful in practice, as illustrated next.

Example 1. [Synthesis from φ_{CORE} - Mutual exclusion] Let us consider the classical problem of *mutual exclusion*. In the simplest form of this problem, we need to design an arbiter that receives requests from two processes, modeled

© The Author(s) 2023
S. Sankaranarayanan and N. Sharygina (Eds.): TACAS 2023, LNCS 13994, pp. 309–328, 2023.
https://doi.org/10.1007/978-3-031-30820-8_20

by two atomic propositions r_1 and r_2 controlled by the environment, and that grants accesses to the critical section, modeled as two atomic propositions g_1 and g_2 controlled by the system. The core correctness properties (the *what*) are: (*i*) mutual access, i.e. it is never the case that the access is granted to both processes at the same time, (*ii*) fairness, i.e. processes that have requested access eventually get access to the critical section. These core correctness specifications for mutual exclusion (ME) are easily expressed in LTL as follows: $\varphi_{CORE}^{ME} \equiv \Box(\neg g_1 \vee \neg g_2) \wedge \Box(r_1 \rightarrow \Diamond g_1) \wedge \Box(r_2 \rightarrow \Diamond g_2)$. Indeed, this formula expresses the core correctness properties that we would model check no matter *how* $\mathcal{M}$ implements mutual exclusion, e.g. Peterson, Dedekker, Backery algorithms, etc. Unfortunately, if we submit φ_{CORE}^{ME} to an LTL synthesis procedure, implemented in tools like ACACIA-BONZAI [11], BoSY [17], or STRIX [25], we get the solution $\mathcal{M}$ depicted in 1-(left) (all three tools return this solution). While this solution is perfectly correct and realizes the specification φ_{CORE}^{ME}, the solution ignores the inputs from the environment and grants access to the critical sections in a round robin fashion. Arguably, it may not be considered as an efficient solution to the mutual exclusion problem. This illustrates the limits of the synthesis algorithm to solve the design problem by providing *only* the core correctness specification of the problem, i.e. the *what*, only. To produce useful solutions to the mutual exclusion problem, more guidance must be provided.

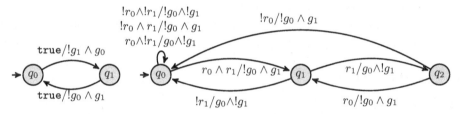

Fig. 1: (Left) The solution of Strix to the mutual exclusion problem for high level specification φ_{LOW}^{ME}. Edge labels are of the form φ/ψ where φ: Boolean formula on input atomic propositions (Boolean variables controlled by environment) and ψ: maximally consistent conjunction of literals over set of output propositions (Boolean variables controlled by system). (Right) A natural solution that could be drawn by hand, and is automatically produced by our learning/synthesis algorithm for the same specification plus with two simple examples.

The main question is now: *how should we specify these additional properties* ? Obviously, if we want to use the "plain" LTL synthesis algorithm, there is no choice: we need to reinforce the specification φ_{CORE}^{ME} with additional lower level properties φ_{LOW}^{ME}. Let us go back to our running example.

Example 2. [Synthesis from φ_{CORE}^{ME} and φ_{LOW}^{ME}] To avoid solutions with *unsolicited grants*, we need to reinforce the core specification. The Strix online demo website proposes to add the following 3 LTL formulas φ_{LOW}^{ME} to φ_{CORE}^{ME} (see Full arbitrer $n = 2$, at https://meyerphi.github.io/strix-demo/): (1) $\bigwedge_{i \in \{1,2\}} \Box((g_i \wedge \Box \neg r_i) \rightarrow \Diamond \neg g_i)$, (2) $\bigwedge_{i \in \{1,2\}} \Box(g_i \wedge \bigcirc(\neg r_i \wedge \neg g_i) \rightarrow \bigcirc(r_i R \neg g_i))$, and (3) $\bigwedge_{i \in \{1,2\}} (r_i R \neg g_i)$. Strix, on the specification $\varphi_{CORE}^{ME} \wedge \varphi_{LOW}^{ME}$, provides us with a better solution, but it is more complex than needed (it has 9 states: refer [5]) and clearly does not look like an optimal solution to our mutual exclusion problem. E.g., the model of Fig. 1-(right) is arguably more natural. How can we get this model without coding it into the LTL specification, which would diminish greatly the interest of using a synthesis procedure in the first place?

In general, higher level properties are properties that need to be met by all implementations, e.g. safety-critical properties. In contrast, lower level properties are more about a specific implementation, its expected behaviour and efficiency. At this point, it is legitimate to question the adequacy of LTL as a specification language for *lower level* properties, and so as a way to guide the synthesis procedure towards relevant solutions to realize φ_{CORE}. In this paper, we introduce an alternative to guide synthesis toward useful solutions that realize φ_{CORE}: we propose to use examples of executions that illustrate behaviors of expected solutions. We then restrict the search to solutions that *generalize* those examples. Examples, or scenarios of executions, are accepted in requirement engineering as an adequate tool to elicit requirements about complex systems [12]. For reactive system design, examples are particularly well-suited as they are usually much easier to formulate than full blown solutions, or even partial solutions. It is because, when formulating examples, the user controls *both* the inputs *and* the outputs, avoiding the main difficulty of reactive system design: having to cope with *all* possible environment inputs. We illustrate this on our running example.

Example 3. [Synthesis from φ_{CORE}^{ME} and examples] Let us keep, as the LTL specification, φ_{CORE}^{ME} only, and let us consider the following simple prefix of executions that illustrate how solutions to mutual exclusion should behave:

(1) $\{!r_1, !r_2\}.\{!g_1, !g_2\}\#\{r_1, !r_2\}.\{g_1, !g_2\}\#\{!r_1, r_2\}.\{!g_1, g_2\}$

(2) $\{r_1, r_2\}.\{g_1, !g_2\}\#\{!r_1, !r_2\}.\{!g_1, g_2\}$

These trace prefixes prescribe reactions to typical *fixed* finite input sequences: (1) if there is no request initially, then no access is granted (note that this excludes already the round robin solution), if process 1 and 2 request subsequently, process 1 is granted first and then process 2 is granted after, (2) if both process request simultaneously, then process 1 is granted first and then process 2 is granted after. Given those two simple traces together with φ_{CORE}, our algorithm generates the solution of Fig. 1-(right). Arguably, the solution is now simple and natural.

Contributions First, we provide a synthesis algorithm SYNTHLEARN that, given an LTL specification φ_{CORE} and a finite set E of prefixes of executions, returns a Mealy machine $\mathcal{M}$ such that $\mathcal{M} \models \varphi_{CORE}$, i.e. $\mathcal{M}$ realizes φ_{CORE}, and $E \subseteq \mathsf{Prefix}(L(\mathcal{M}))$, i.e. $\mathcal{M}$ is compatible with the examples in E, if such a machine $\mathcal{M}$ exists. It returns *unrealizable* otherwise. Additionally, we require SYNTHLEARN to *generalize* the decisions illustrated in E. This learnability requirement is usually formalized in automata learning with a *completeness criterium* that we adapt here as follows: for all specifications φ_{CORE}, and for all Mealy machines $\mathcal{M}$ such that $\mathcal{M} \models \varphi_{CORE}$, there is a small set of examples E (polynomial in $|\mathcal{M}|$) such that $L(\text{SYNTHLEARN}(\varphi_{CORE}, E)) = L(\mathcal{M})$. We prove this completeness result in Theorem 4 for safety specifications and extend it to ω-regular and LTL specifications in Section 4, by reduction to safety.

Second, we prove that the worst-case execution time of SYNTHLEARN is 2EX-PTIME (Theorem 7), and this is worst-case optimal as the plain LTL synthesis problem (when $E = \emptyset$) is already known to be 2EXPTIME-COMPLETE [27]. SYNTHLEARN first *generalizes* the examples provided by the user while maintaining realizability of φ_{CORE}. This generalization leads to a Mealy machine with possibly missing transitions (called a preMealy machine). Then, this preMealy machine is extended into a (full) Mealy machine that realizes φ_{CORE} against all behaviors of the environment. During the completion phase, SYNTHLEARN reuses as much as possible decisions that have been generalized from the examples. The generalization phase is essential to get the most out of the examples. Running classical synthesis algorithms on $\varphi_{\text{CORE}} \wedge \varphi_E$, where φ_E is an LTL encoding of E, often leads to more complex machines that fail to generalize the decisions taken along the examples in E. While the overall complexity of SYNTH-LEARN is 2EXPTIME and optimal, we show that it is only polynomial in the size of E and in a well-chosen symbolic representation a set of Mealy machines that realize φ_{CORE}, see Theorem 6. This symbolic representation takes the form of an antichain of functions and tends to be compact in practice [19]. It is computed by default when ACACIA-BONZAI is solving the plain LTL synthesis problem of φ_{CORE}. So, generalizing examples while maintaining realizability only comes at a marginal polynomial cost. We have implemented our synthesis algorithm in a prototype, which uses ACACIA-BONZAI to compute the symbolic antichain representation. We report on the results we obtain on several examples.

Related works Scenarios of executions have been advocated by researchers in requirements engineering to elicit specifications, see e.g. [12,14] and references therein. In [28], learning techniques are used to transform examples into LTL formulas that generalize them. Those methods are complementary to our work, as they can be used to obtain the high level specification φ_{CORE}.

In non-vacuous synthesis [8], examples are added automatically to an LTL specification in order to force the synthesis procedure to generate solutions that are non-vacuous in the sense of [23]. The examples are generated directly from the syntax of the LTL specification and they cannot be proposed by the user. This makes our approach and this approach orthogonal and complementary. Indeed, we could use the examples generated automatically by the non-vacuous approach and ask the user to validate them as desirable or not. Our method is more flexible, it is semi-automatic and user centric: the user can provide any example he/she likes and so it offers more flexibility to drive the synthesis procedure to solutions that the user deems as interesting. Furthermore, our synthesis procedure is based on learning algorithms, while the algorithm in [8] is based on constraint solving and does not offer guarantees of generalization, unlike our algorithm (see Thm 4).

Supplementing the formal specification with additional user-provided information is at the core of the *syntax-guided synthesis* framework (SyGuS [3]), implemented for instance in *program by sketching* [31]: in SyGuS, the specification is a logical formula and candidate programs are syntactically restricted by a

user-provided grammar, to limit and guide the search. The search is done by using counter-example guided inductive synthesis techniques (CEGIS) which rely
on learning [32]. In contrast to our approach, examples are not user-provided
but automatically generated by model-checking the candidate programs against
the specification. The techniques are also orthogonal to ours: SyGuS targets programs syntactically defined by expressions over a decidable background theory,
and heavily relies on SAT/SMT solvers. Using examples to synthesise programs
(*programming by example*) has been for instance explored in the context of string
processing programs for spreadsheets, based on learning [30], and is a current
trend in AI (see for example [26] and the citations therein). However this approach only relies on examples and not on logical specifications.

[4] explores the use of formal specifications and scenarios to synthesize distributed protocols. Their approach also follows two phases: first, an incomplete
machine is built from the scenarios and second, it is turned into a complete one.
But there are two important differences with our work. First, their first phase
does not rely on learning techniques and does not try to generalize the provided
examples. Second, in their setting, all actions are controllable and there is no
adversarial environment, so they are solving a satisfiability problem and not a
realizability problem as in our case. Their problem is thus computationally less
demanding than the problem we solve: PSPACE versus 2EXPTIME for LTL specs.

The synthesis problem targeted in this paper extends the LTL synthesis
problem. Modern solutions for this problem use automata constructions that
avoid Safra's construction as first proposed in [24], and simplified in [29,18], and
more recently in [16]. Efficient implementations of Safraless constructions are
available, see e.g. [9,17,25,15]. Several previous works have proposed alternative
approaches to improve on the quality of solutions that synthesis algorithms can
offer. A popular research direction, orthogonal and complementary to the one
proposed here, is to extend the formal specification with quantitative aspects,
see e.g. [6,10,22,2], and only synthesize solutions that are optimal.

The first phase of our algorithm is inspired by automata learning techniques
based on state merging algorithms like RPNI [21,20]. Those learning algorithms
need to be modified carefully to generate partial solutions that preserve realizability of φ_{CORE}. Proving completeness as well as termination of the completion
phase in this context requires particular care.

2   Preliminaries on the reactive synthesis problem

Words, languages and automata An alphabet is a finite set of symbols. A
word u (resp. ω-word) over an alphabet Σ is a finite (resp. infinite sequence) of
symbols from Σ. We write ϵ for the empty word, and denote by $|u| \in \mathbb{N} \cup \{\infty\}$
the length of u. In particular, $|\epsilon| = 0$. For $1 \leq i \leq j \leq |u|$, we let $u[i{:}j]$ be the
infix of u from position i to position j, both included, and write $u[i]$ instead of
$u[i{:}i]$. The set of finite (resp. ω-) words over Σ is denoted by Σ^* (resp. Σ^ω). We
let $\Sigma^\infty = \Sigma^* \cup \Sigma^\omega$. Given two words $u \in \Sigma^*$ and $v \in \Sigma^\infty$, u is a *prefix* of v,
written $u \preceq v$, if $v = uw$ for some $w \in \Sigma^\infty$. The set of prefixes of v is denoted by
Prefs(v). Finite words are linearly ordered according to the length-lexicographic

order $\preceq_{ll}$, assuming a linear order $<_\Sigma$ over Σ: $u \preceq_{ll} v$ if $|u| < |v|$ or $|u| = |v|$ and $u = p\sigma_1 u'$, $v = p\sigma_2 v'$ for some $p, u', v' \in \Sigma^*$ and some $\sigma_1 <_\Sigma \sigma_2$. In this paper, whenever we refer to the order $\preceq_{ll}$ for words over some alphabet, we implicitly assume the existence of an arbitrary linear order over that alphabet. A *language* (resp. ω-language) over an alphabet Σ is a subset $L \subseteq \Sigma^*$ (resp. $L \subseteq \Sigma^\omega$).

In this paper, we fix two alphabets $\mathcal{I}$ and $\mathcal{O}$ whose elements are called inputs and outputs respectively. Given a word $u \in (\mathcal{IO})^\infty$, we let $\mathsf{in}(u) \in \mathcal{I}^\infty$ be the word obtained by erasing all $\mathcal{O}$-symbols from u. We define $\mathsf{out}(u)$ similarly and naturally extend both functions to languages.

Automata over ω-words A *parity automaton* is a tuple $\mathcal{A} = (Q, Q_{\mathsf{init}}, \Sigma, \delta, d)$ where Q is a finite non empty set of states, $Q_{\mathsf{init}} \subseteq Q$ is a set of initial states, Σ is a finite non empty alphabet, $\delta : Q \times \Sigma \to 2^Q \setminus \{\emptyset\}$ is the transition function, and $d : Q \to \mathbb{N}$ is a parity function. The automaton $\mathcal{A}$ is *deterministic* when $|Q_{\mathsf{init}}| = 1$ and $|\delta(q, \sigma)| = 1$ for all $q \in Q$. The transition function is extended naturally into a function $\mathsf{Post}^* : Q \times \Sigma^* \to 2^Q \setminus \{\emptyset\}$ inductively as follows: $\mathsf{Post}^*(q, \epsilon) = \{q\}$ for all $q \in Q$ and for all $(u, \sigma) \in \Sigma^* \times \Sigma$, $\mathsf{Post}^*(q, u\sigma) = \bigcup_{q' \in \mathsf{Post}^*(q,u)} \delta(q', \sigma)$.

A *run* of $\mathcal{A}$ on an ω-word $w = w_0 w_1 \ldots$ is an infinite sequence of states $r = q_0 q_1 \ldots$ such that $q_0 \in Q_{\mathsf{init}}$, and for all $i \in \mathbb{N}$, $q_{i+1} \in \delta(q_i, w_i)$. The run r is said to be *accepting* if the minimal colour it visits infinitely often is even, i.e. $\liminf(d(q_i))_{i\geq 0}$ is *even*. We say that $\mathcal{A}$ is a *Büchi automaton* when $\mathsf{dom}(d) = \{0, 1\}$ (1-coloured states are called accepting states), a *co-Büchi automaton* when $\mathsf{dom}(d) = \{1, 2\}$, a *safety automaton* if it is a Büchi automaton such that the set of 1-coloured states, called *unsafe states* and denoted Q_{usf}, forms a *trap*: for all $q \in Q_{\mathsf{usf}}$, for all $\sigma \in \Sigma$, $\delta(q, \sigma) \subseteq Q_{\mathsf{usf}}$, and a *reachability automaton* if it is $\{0, 1\}$-coloured and the set of 0-coloured states forms a trap.

Finally, we consider the existential and universal interpretations of nondeterminism: under the *existential (resp. universal) interpretation*, a word $w \in \Sigma^\omega$ is in the language of $\mathcal{A}$, if there exists a run r on w such that r is accepting (resp. for all runs r on w, r is accepting). We denote the two languages defined by these two interpretations $L^\exists(\mathcal{A})$ and $L^\forall(\mathcal{A})$ respectively. Note that if $\mathcal{A}$ is deterministic, then the existential and universal interpretations agree, and we write $L(\mathcal{A})$ for $L^\forall(\mathcal{A}) = L^\exists(\mathcal{A})$. For a deterministic automaton $\mathcal{A}$, the initial state is fixed to the singleton $\{q\}$.

For a *co-Büchi automaton*, we also define a strengthening of the acceptance condition, called K-co-Büchi, which requires, for $K \in \mathbb{N}$, that a run visits at most K times a state labelled with 1 to be accepting. Formally, a run $r = q_0 q_1 \ldots q_n \ldots$ is *accepting* for the K-co-Büchi acceptance condition if $|\{i \geq 0 \mid d(q_i)) = 1\}| \leq K$. The language defined by $\mathcal{A}$ for the K-co-Büchi acceptance condition and universal interpretation is denoted by $L_K^\forall(\mathcal{A})$. Note that this language is a *safety* language because if a prefix of a word $p \in \Sigma^*$ is such that $\mathcal{A}$ has a run prefix on p that visits more than K times a states labelled with color 1, then all possible extensions $w \in \Sigma^\omega$ of p are rejected by $\mathcal{A}$.

(Pre)Mealy machines Given a (partial) function f from a set X to a set Y, we denote by $\mathsf{dom}(f)$ its domain, i.e. the of elements $x \in X$ such that $f(x)$ is defined. A *preMealy machine* $\mathcal{M}$ on an input alphabet $\mathcal{I}$ and output alphabet

$\mathcal{O}$ is a triple $(M, m_{\text{init}}, \Delta)$ such that M is a non-empty set of states, $m_{\text{init}} \in M$ is the initial state, $\Delta : Q \times \mathcal{I} \to \mathcal{O} \times M$ is a partial function. A pair (m, i) is a hole in $\mathcal{M}$ if $(m, i) \notin \text{dom}(\Delta)$. A *Mealy machine* is a preMealy machine such that Δ is total, i.e., $\text{dom}(\Delta) = M \times \mathcal{I}$.

We define two semantics of a preMealy machine $\mathcal{M} = (M, m_{\text{init}}, \Delta)$ in terms of the languages of finite and infinite words over $\mathcal{I} \cup \mathcal{O}$ they define. First, we define two (possibly partial functions) $\text{Post}_{\mathcal{M}} : M \times \mathcal{I} \to M$ and $\text{Out}_{\mathcal{M}} : M \times \mathcal{I} \to \mathcal{O}$ such that $\Delta(m, i) = (\text{Post}_{\mathcal{M}}(m, i), \text{Out}_{\mathcal{M}}(m, i))$ for all $(m, i) \in M \times \mathcal{I}$ if $\Delta(m, i)$ is defined. We naturally extend these two functions to any sequence of inputs $u \in \mathcal{I}^+$, denoted $\text{Post}^*_{\mathcal{M}}$ and $\text{Out}^*_{\mathcal{M}}$. In particular, for $u \in \mathcal{I}^+$, $\text{Post}^*_{\mathcal{M}}(m, u)$ is the state reached by $\mathcal{M}$ when reading u from m, while $\text{Out}^*_{\mathcal{M}}(m, u)$ is the last output in $\mathcal{O}$ produced by $\mathcal{M}$ when reading u. The subcript $\mathcal{M}$ is ommitted when $\mathcal{M}$ is clear from the context. Now, the language $L(\mathcal{M})$ of finite words in $(\mathcal{I}\mathcal{O})^*$ accepted by $\mathcal{M}$ is defined as $L(\mathcal{M}) = \{i_1 o_1 \ldots i_n o_n \mid \forall 1 \le j \le n,\ \text{Post}^*_{\mathcal{M}}(m_{\text{init}}, i_1 \ldots i_j)$ is defined and $o_j = \text{Out}^*_{\mathcal{M}}(m_{\text{init}}, i_1 \ldots i_j)\}$. The language $L_\omega(\mathcal{M})$ of infinite words accepted by $\mathcal{M}$ is the topological closure of $L(\mathcal{M})$: $L_\omega(\mathcal{M}) = \{w \in (\mathcal{I}\mathcal{O})^\omega \mid \text{Prefs}(w) \cap (\mathcal{I}\mathcal{O})^* \subseteq L(\mathcal{M})\}$.

The reactive synthesis problem A *specification* is a language $S \subseteq (\mathcal{I}\mathcal{O})^\omega$. The *reactive synthesis problem* (or just synthesis problem for short) is the problem of constructing, given a specification S, a Mealy machine $\mathcal{M}$ such that $L_\omega(\mathcal{M}) \subseteq S$ if it exists. Such a machine $\mathcal{M}$ is said to *realize* the specification S, also written $\mathcal{M} \models S$. We also say that S is *realizable* if some Mealy machine $\mathcal{M}$ realizes it. The induced decision problem is called the *realizability problem*.

It is well-known that if S is ω-regular (recognizable by, e.g., a parity automaton [33]) the realizability problem is decidable [1] and moreover, a Mealy machine realizing the specification can be effectively constructed. The realizability problem is 2EXPTIME-COMPLETE if S is given as an LTL formula [27] and EXPTIME-COMPLETE if S is given as a universal coBüchi automaton.

Theorem 1 ([7]). *The realizability problem for a specification S given as a universal coBüchi automaton $\mathcal{A}$ is* EXPTIME-C. *Moreover, if S is realizable and $\mathcal{A}$ has n states, then S is realizable by a Mealy machine with $2^{O(n \log_2 n)}$ states.*

We generalize this result to the following realizability problem which we describe first informally. Given a specification S and a preMealy machine $\mathcal{P}$, the goal is to decide whether $\mathcal{P}$ can be completed into a Mealy machine which realizes S. We now define this problem formally. Given two preMealy machines $\mathcal{P}_1, \mathcal{P}_2$, we write $\mathcal{P}_1 \preceq \mathcal{P}_2$ if $\mathcal{P}_1$ is a subgraph of $\mathcal{P}_2$ in the following sense: there exists an injective mapping Φ from the states of $\mathcal{P}_1$ to the states of $\mathcal{P}_2$ which preserves the initial state (s_0 is the initial state of $\mathcal{P}_1$ iff $\Phi(s_0)$ is the initial state of $\mathcal{P}_2$) and the transitions ($\Delta_{\mathcal{P}_1}(p, i) = (o, q)$ iff $\Delta_{\mathcal{P}_2}(\Phi(p), i) = (o, \Phi(q))$). As a consequence, $L(\mathcal{P}_1) \subseteq L(\mathcal{P}_2)$ and $L_\omega(\mathcal{P}_1) \subseteq L_\omega(\mathcal{P}_2)$. Given a preMealy machine $\mathcal{P}$, we say that a specification S *is $\mathcal{P}$-realizable* if there exists a Mealy machine $\mathcal{M}$ such that $\mathcal{P} \preceq \mathcal{M}$ and $\mathcal{M}$ realizes S. Note that if $\mathcal{P}$ is a (complete) Mealy machine, S is $\mathcal{P}$-realizable iff $\mathcal{P}$ realizes S. The next result is proved in [5]:

Theorem 2. *Given a universal co-Büchi automaton $\mathcal{A}$ with n states defining a specification $S = L^\forall(\mathcal{A})$ and a preMealy machine $\mathcal{P}$ with m states and n_h holes,* *deciding whether S is $\mathcal{P}$-realizable is* ExpTime-*hard and in* ExpTime *(in n and polynomial in m). Moreover, if S is $\mathcal{P}$-realizable, it is $\mathcal{P}$-realizable by a Mealy machine with $m + n_h 2^{O(n \log_2 n)}$ states. Hardness holds even if $\mathcal{P}$ has two states and $\mathcal{A}$ is a deterministic reachability automaton.*

3 Synthesis from safety specifications and examples

In this section, we present the learning framework we use to synthesise Mealy machines from examples, and safety specifications. Its generalization to any ω-regular specification is described in Sec. 4 and solved by reduction to safety specifications. It is a two-phase algorithm: (1) it generalizes the examples while maintaining realizability of the specification, and outputs a preMealy machine, (2) it completes the preMealy machine into a full Mealy machine.

Phase 1: Generalizing the examples This phase exploits the examples by generalizing them as much as possible while maintaining realizability of the specification. It outputs a preMealy machine which is consistent with the examples and realizes the specification, if it exists. It is an RPNI-like learning algorithm [21,20] which includes specific tests to maintain realizability of the specification. In particular, it first builds a tree-shaped preMealy machine whose accepted language is exactly the set of prefixes $\mathsf{Prefs}(E)$ of the given set of examples E, called a *prefix-tree acceptor* (PTA). Then, it tries to merge as many as possible states of the PTA. The strategy used to select a state to merge another given state with, is a parameter of the algorithm, and is called a *merging strategy* σ_G. Formally, a *merging* strategy σ_G is defined over 4-tuples $(\mathcal{M}, m, E, X)$ where $\mathcal{M}$ is a preMealy machine, m is a state of $\mathcal{M}$, E is a set of examples and X is subset of states of $\mathcal{M}$ (the candidate states to merge m with), and returns a state of X, i.e., $\sigma_G(\mathcal{M}, m, E, X) \in X$.

The pseudo-code is given by alg. 1. Initially, it tests whether the set of examples E is consistent[1] and if yes, checks if $\mathsf{PTA}(E)$ can be completed into a Mealy machine realizing the given specification S, thanks to Thm. 2. If that is the case, then it takes all prefixes of E as the set of examples, and enters a loop which consists in iteratively coarsening again and again some congruence $\sim$ over the states of $\mathsf{PTA}(E)$, by merging some of its classes. The congruence $\sim$ is initially the finest equivalence relation. It does the coarsening in a specific order: examples (which are states of $\mathsf{PTA}(E)$) are taken in length-lexicographic order. When entering the loop with example e, the algorithm computes at line 4 all the states, i.e., all the examples e' which have been processed already by the loop $(e' \prec_{ll} e)$ and whose current class can be merged with the class of e (predicate $\mathsf{Mergeable}(\mathsf{PTA}(E), \sim, e, e')$). State merging is a standard operation in automata learning algorithms which intuitively means that merging the $\sim$-class of e and the $\sim$-class of e', and propagating this merge to the descendants of e and e', does not result any conflict. The formal definition is in [5]. At line 5, it filters the previous set by keeping only the states which, when merged with e, produce a preMealy

---

[1] E is consistent if outputs uniquely depends on prefixes. Formally, it means for all prefixes $u \in \mathsf{Prefs}(E) \cap (\mathcal{IO})^* \mathcal{I}$, there is a unique output $\mathsf{o} \in \mathcal{O}$ s.t. $u\mathsf{o} \in \mathsf{Prefs}(E)$.

machine which can be completed into a Mealy machine realizing $\mathcal{S}$ (again by Thm. 2). If after the filtering there are still several candidates for merge, one of them is selected with the merging strategy σ_G and the equivalence relation is then coarsened via class merging (operation $\mathsf{MergeClass}(\mathsf{PTA}(E), \sim, e, e')$). At the end, the algorithm returns the quotient of $\mathsf{PTA}(E)$ by the computed Mealy-congruence. As a side remark, when $\mathcal{S}$ is universal, i.e. $\mathcal{S} = (\mathcal{IO})^\omega$, then it is realizable by *any* Mealy machine and therefore line 5 does not filter any of the candidates for merge. So, when $\mathcal{S}$ is universal, Algo 1 can be seen as an RPNI variant for learning preMealy machines.

Algorithm 1: $\mathrm{GEN}(E, \mathcal{S}, \sigma_G)$ – generalization algorithm

---

Input: A finite set of examples $E \subseteq (\mathcal{I}.\mathcal{O})^*$, a specification $\mathcal{S} \subseteq (\mathcal{I}.\mathcal{O})^\omega$ given
      as a deterministic safety automaton, a merging strategy σ_G
Output: A preMealy machine $\mathcal{M}$ s.t. $E \subseteq L(\mathcal{M})$ and $\mathcal{S}$ is $\mathcal{M}$-realizable, if it
      exists, otherwise UNREAL.

1   **if** E is not consistent or $\mathcal{S}$ is not $\mathsf{PTA}(E)$-realizable **then return** UNREAL
2 $E \leftarrow \mathsf{Prefs}(E) \cap (\mathcal{IO})^*$; $\sim \leftarrow \{(e, e) \mid e \in E\}$;   // $\sim = diag_E$
3   **for** $e \in E$ *in length-lexicographic order* $\preceq_{ll}$ **do**
4 $mergeCand \leftarrow \{e' \mid \mathsf{Mergeable}(\mathsf{PTA}(E), \sim, e, e') \wedge e' \prec_{ll} e\}$
5 $mergeCand \leftarrow \{e' \in mergeCand \mid \mathcal{S}$ is $\mathsf{MergeStates}(\mathsf{PTA}(E), \sim$
         $, e, e')-realizable\}$
6   **if** $mergeCand \neq \varnothing$ **then**
7 $e' \leftarrow \sigma_G(\mathcal{M}, e, mergeCand)$
8 $\sim \leftarrow \mathsf{MergeClass}(\mathsf{PTA}(E), \sim, e, e')$

9   **return** $\mathsf{PTA}(E)/_\sim$

Phase 2: completion of preMealy machines into Mealy machines As it only constructs the PTA and tries to merge its states, the generalization phase might not return a (complete) Mealy machine. In other words, the machine it returns might still contain some holes (missing transitions). The objective of this second phase is to complete those holes into a Mealy machine, while realizing the specification. More precisely, when a transition is not defined from some state m and some input $i \in \mathcal{I}$, the algorithm must select an output symbol $o \in \mathcal{O}$ and a state m' to transition to, which can be either an existing state or a new state to be created (in that case, we write $m' = \mathsf{fresh}$ to denote the fact that m' is a fresh state). In our implementation, if it is possible to reuse a state m' that was created during the generalization phase, it is favoured over other states, in order to exploit the examples. However, the algorithm for the completion phase we describe now does not depend on any particular strategy to pick states. Therefore, it is parameterized by a *completion strategy* σ_C, defined over all triples $(\mathcal{M}, m, i, X)$ where $\mathcal{M}$ is a preMealy machine with set of states M, (m, i) is a hole of $\mathcal{M}$, and $X \subseteq \mathcal{O} \times (M \cup \{\mathsf{fresh}\})$ is a list of candidate pairs (o, m'). It returns an element of X, i.e., $\sigma_C(\mathcal{M}, m, i, X) \in X$.

In addition to σ_C, the completion algorithm takes as input a preMealy machine $\mathcal{M}_0$ and a specification $\mathcal{S}$, and outputs a Mealy machine which $\mathcal{M}_0$-realizes $\mathcal{S}$, if it exists. The pseudo-code is given in Algo 2. Initially, it tests whether $\mathcal{S}$

is $\mathcal{M}_0$-realizable, otherwise it returns UNREAL. Then, it keeps on completing holes of $\mathcal{M}_0$. The computation of the list of output/state candidates is done at the loop of line 5. Note that the **for**-loop iterates over $M \cup \{\text{fresh}()\}$, where fresh() is a procedure that returns a fresh state not in M. The algorithm maintains the invariant that at any iteration of the **while**-loop, $\mathcal{S}$ is $\mathcal{M}$-realizable, thanks to the test at line 7, based on Thm. 2. Therefore, the list of candidates is necessarily non-empty. Amongst those candidates, a single one is selected and the transition on (m, i) is added to $\mathcal{M}$ accordingly at line 10.

Algorithm 2: COMP($\mathcal{M}_0,\mathcal{S},\sigma_C$): preMealy machine completion algorithm

Input: A preMealy machine $\mathcal{M}_0 = (M, m_{\text{init}}, \Delta)$, a specification $\mathcal{S} \subseteq (\mathcal{I}.\mathcal{O})^*$ given as a deterministic safety automaton, a completion strategy σ_C

Output: A (complete) Mealy machine $\mathcal{M}$ such that $\mathcal{S}$ is $\mathcal{M}_0$-realizable, otherwise UNREAL.

1 **if** $\mathcal{S}$ is not $\mathcal{M}_0$-realizable **then return** UNREAL
2 $\mathcal{M} \leftarrow \mathcal{M}_0$
3 **while** *there exists a hole* $(m, \mathsf{i}) \in M \times \mathcal{I}$ **do**
4      $candidates \leftarrow \varnothing$
5   **for** $(\mathsf{o}, m') \in \mathcal{O} \times (M \cup \{\text{fresh}()\})$ **do**
                                    // fresh() denotes a new state not in M
6          $\mathcal{M}_{\mathsf{o},m'} \leftarrow (M \cup \{m'\}, m_{\text{init}}, \Delta \cup \{(m, \mathsf{i}) \mapsto (\mathsf{o}, m')\})$
7   **if** $\mathcal{S}$ is $\mathcal{M}_{\mathsf{o},m'}$-*realizable* **then**
8              $candidates \leftarrow candidates \cup \{(\mathsf{o}, m')\}$

9      $(\mathsf{o}, m') \leftarrow \sigma_C(\mathcal{M}, m, \mathsf{i}, candidates)$
10     $(M, \Delta) \leftarrow (M \cup \{m'\}, \Delta \cup \{(m, \mathsf{i}) \mapsto (\mathsf{o}, m')\})$
11     $\mathcal{M} \leftarrow (M, m_{\text{init}}, \Delta)$

12 **return** $\mathcal{M}$

Two-phase synthesis algorithm from specifications and examples The two-phase synthesis algorithm for safety specifications and examples, called SYNTH-SAFE($E, \mathcal{S}, \sigma_G, \sigma_C$) works as follows: it takes as input a set of examples E, a specification $\mathcal{S}$ given as a deterministic safety automaton, a generalizing and completion strategies σ_G, σ_C respectively. It returns a Mealy machine $\mathcal{M}$ which realizes $\mathcal{S}$ and such that $E \subseteq L(\mathcal{M})$ if it exists. In a first steps, it calls GEN($E, \mathcal{S}, \sigma_G$). If this calls returns UNREAL, then SYNTHSAFE return UNREAL as well. Otherwise, the call to GEN returns a preMealy machine $\mathcal{M}_0$. In a second step, SYNTH-SAFE calls COMP($\mathcal{M}_0, \mathcal{S}, \sigma_C$). If this call returns UNREAL, so does SYNTH-SAFE, otherwise SYNTHSAFE returns the Mealy machine computed by COMP. The pseudo-code of SYNTHSAFE can be found in [5].

The completion procedure may not terminate for some completion strategies. It is because the completion strategy could for instance keep on selecting pairs of the form (o, m') where m' is a fresh state. However we prove that it always terminates for *lazy* completion strategies. A completion strategy σ_C is said to be *lazy* if it favours existing states, which formally means that if $X \setminus (\mathcal{O} \times \{\text{fresh}\}) \neq \varnothing$, then $\sigma_C(\mathcal{M}, m, \mathsf{i}, X) \notin \mathcal{O} \times \{\text{fresh}\}$. The 1st theorem states correctness and termination of the algorithm for lazy completion strategies (assuming the functions σ_G and σ_C are computable in worst-case exptime in the size of their inputs).

Theorem 3 (termination and correctness). *For all finite sets of examples $E \subseteq (\mathcal{I}.\mathcal{O})^*$, all specifications $\mathcal{S} \subseteq (\mathcal{I}.\mathcal{O})^\omega$ given as a deterministic safety automaton $\mathcal{A}$ with n states, all merging strategies σ_G and all completion strategies σ_C, if* SYNTHSAFE$(E, \mathcal{S}, \sigma_G, \sigma_C)$ *terminates then, it returns a Mealy machine $\mathcal{M}$ such that $E \subseteq L(\mathcal{M})$ and $\mathcal{M}$ realizes $\mathcal{S}$, if it exists, otherwise it returns UNREAL. Moreover,* SYNTHSAFE$(E, \mathcal{S}, \sigma_G, \sigma_C)$ *terminates if σ_C is lazy, in worst-case exponential time (polynomial in the size^2 of E and exponential in n).*

The proof of the latter theorem is a consequence of several results proved on the generalization and completion phases, and is given in [5].

A Mealy machine $\mathcal{T}$ is minimal if for all Mealy machine $\mathcal{M}$ such that $L(\mathcal{T}) = L(\mathcal{M})$, the number of states of $\mathcal{M}$ is at least that of $\mathcal{T}$. The next result, proved in [5], states that any minimal Mealy machine realizing a specification $\mathcal{S}$ can be returned by our synthesis algorithm, providing representative examples.

Theorem 4 (Mealy completeness). *For all specifications $\mathcal{S} \subseteq (\mathcal{I}.\mathcal{O})^\omega$ given as a deterministic safety automaton, for all minimal Mealy machines $\mathcal{M}$ realizing $\mathcal{S}$, there exists a finite set of examples $E \subseteq (\mathcal{I}.\mathcal{O})^*$, of size polynomial in the size of $\mathcal{M}$, such that for all generalizing strategies σ_G and completion strategies σ_C, and all sets of examples E' s.t. $E \subseteq E' \subseteq L(\mathcal{M})$,* SYNTHSAFE$(E', \mathcal{S}, \sigma_G, \sigma_C) = \mathcal{M}$.

The polynomial upper bound given in the statement of Theorem 4 is more precisely the following: the cardinality of E is $O(m + n^2)$ where n is the number of states of $\mathcal{M}$ while m is its number of transitions. Moreover, each example $e \in E$ has length $O(n^2)$. More details can be found in Remark 1 of [5].

4   Synthesis from ω-regular specifications and examples

We now consider the case where the specification $\mathcal{S}$ is given as universal coBüchi automaton, in Section 4. We consider this class of specifications as it is complete for ω-regular languages and allow for compact symbolic representations. Further in this section, we consider the case of LTL specifications.

Specifications given as universal coBüchi automata Our solution for ω-regular specifications relies on a reduction to the safety case treated in Sec. 3. It relies on previous works that develop so called Safraless algorithms for ω-regular reactive synthesis [24,29,18]. The main idea is to strengthen the (safety) acceptance condition of the automaton from coBüchi to K-coBüchi. It is complete for the plain synthesis problem (w/o examples) if K is large enough (in the worst-case exponential in the number of states of the automaton (e.g., see [18])). Moreover, it allows for incremental synthesis algorithms: if the specification defined by the automaton with a k-coBüchi acceptance condition is realizable, for $k \le K$, so is the specification defined by taking K-coBüchi acceptance. Here, as we also take examples into account, we need to slightly adapt the results. The next theorem is proved in [5] while the next lemma is immediate:

---

^{2} The size of E is the sum of the lengths of the examples of E.

Theorem 5. *Given a universal co-Büchi automaton $\mathcal{A}$ with n states defining a specification $\mathcal{S} = L^{\vee}(\mathcal{A})$ and a preMealy machine $\mathcal{P}$ with m states, we have that $\mathcal{S}$ is $\mathcal{P}$-realizable iff $\mathcal{S}' = L_K^{\vee}(\mathcal{A})$ is $\mathcal{P}$-realizable for $K = nm|\mathcal{I}|2^{O(n \log_2 n)}$.*

Lemma 1. *For all co-Büchi automata $\mathcal{A}$, for all preMealy machines $\mathcal{P}$, for all $k_1 \leq k_2$, we have that $L_{k_1}^{\vee}(\mathcal{A}) \subseteq L_{k_2}^{\vee}(\mathcal{A})$ and so if $L_{k_1}^{\vee}(\mathcal{A})$ is $\mathcal{P}$-realizable then $L_{k_2}^{\vee}(\mathcal{A})$ is $\mathcal{P}$-realizable. Furthermore for all $k \geq 0$, if $\mathcal{S}' = L_k^{\vee}(\mathcal{A})$ is $\mathcal{P}$-realizable then $\mathcal{S} = L^{\vee}(\mathcal{A})$ is $\mathcal{P}$-realizable.*

Thanks to the latter two results applied to $\mathcal{P} = \text{PTA}(E)$ for a set E of examples of size m, we can design an algorithm for synthesising Mealy machines from a specification defined by a universal coBüchi automaton $\mathcal{A}$ with n states and E: it calls SYNTHSAFE on the safety specification $L_k^{\vee}(\mathcal{A})$ and E for increasing values of k, until it concludes positively, or reach the bound $K = 2^{O(mn \log_2 mn)} + 1$. In the latter case, it returns UNREAL. However, to apply SYNTHSAFE properly, $L_k^{\vee}(\mathcal{A})$ must be represented by a deterministic safety automaton. This is possible as k-coBüchi automata are determinizable [18].

Determinization The determinization of k-co-Büchi automata $\mathcal{A}$ relies on a simple generalization of the subset construction: in addition to remembering the set of states that can be reached by a prefix of a run while reading an infinite word, the construction counts the maximal number of times a run prefix that reaches a given state q has visited states labelled with color 1 (remember that a run can visit at most k such states to be accepting). The states of the deterministic automaton are so-called *counting functions*, formally defined for a co-Büchi automaton $\mathcal{A} = (Q, q_{\text{init}}, \Sigma, \delta, d)$ and $k \in \mathbb{N}$, as the set noted $CF(\mathcal{A}, k)$ of functions $f : Q \to \{-1, 0, 1, \ldots, k, k+1\}$. If $f(q) = -1$ for some state q, it means that q is inactive (no run of $\mathcal{A}$ reach q on the current prefix). The initial counting function f_{init} maps all 1-colored initial states to 1, all 0-colored initial states to 0 and all other states to -1. We denote by $\mathcal{D}(\mathcal{A}, k) = (Q^{\mathcal{D}} = CF(\mathcal{A}, k), q_{\text{init}}^{\mathcal{D}} = f_{\text{init}}, \Sigma, \delta^{\mathcal{D}}, Q_{\text{usf}}^{\mathcal{D}})$ the deterministic automaton obtained by this determinization procedure. It is formally defined in [5]. We can now give algorithm SYNTHLEARN, in pseudo-code, as Algo 3.

Complexity considerations and improving the upper-bound As the automaton $\mathcal{D}(\mathcal{A}, k)$ is in the worst-case exponential in the size of the automaton $\mathcal{A}$, a direct application of Thm. 3 yields a doubly exponential time procedure. This complexity is a consequence of the fact that the $\mathcal{P}$-realizability problem is EXPTIME in the size of the deterministic automaton as shown in Thm. 2, and that the termination of the completion procedure is also worst-case exponential in the size of the deterministic automaton.

We show that we can improve the complexity of each call to SYNTHSAFE and obtain an optimal worst-case (single) exponential complexity. We provide an algorithm to check $\mathcal{P}$-realizability of a specification $\mathcal{S} = L_k^{\vee}(\mathcal{A})$ that runs in time singly exponential in the size of $\mathcal{A}$ and polynomial in k and the size of $\mathcal{P}$. Second, we provide a finer complexity analysis for the termination of the completion algorithm, which exhibits a worst case exponential time in $|\mathcal{A}|$. Those two improvements lead to an overall complexity of SYNTHLEARN which is expo-

---

Algorithm 3: SYNTHLEARN(E,$\mathcal{A}$,σ_G,σ_C) – synthesis algorithm from
ω-regular specification and examples by a reduction to safety

---

Input: A universal co-Büchi automaton $\mathcal{A}$ with n states, a finite set of
examples $E \subseteq (\mathcal{I}.\mathcal{O})^*$, a generalizing strategy σ_G and a completion
strategy σ_C.

Output: A Mealy machine $\mathcal{M}$ realizing $L^\forall(\mathcal{A})$ and such that $E \subseteq L(\mathcal{M})$ if it
exists, otherwise UNREAL.

1 $K \leftarrow nm|\mathcal{I}|2^{O(n \log_2 n)}$; $k \leftarrow 0$;   // m is the size of E

2 **while** $k \leq K$ **do**

3   **if** SYNTHSAFE($E, \mathcal{D}(\mathcal{A}, k), \sigma_C, \sigma_G$) $\neq$ UNREAL **then**

4   **return** SYNTHSAFE($E, \mathcal{D}(\mathcal{A}, k), \sigma_C, \sigma_G$)

5     $k \leftarrow k + 1$;

6 **return** *UNREAL*

---

nential in the size of the specification $\mathcal{A}$ and polynomial in the set of examples
E. This is provably worst-case optimal because for $E = \emptyset$ the problem is already
EXPTIME-COMPLETE. We explain next the first improvement, the upper-bound
for termination is provided in [5].

Checking $\mathcal{P}$-realizability of a specification $\mathcal{S} = L_k^\forall(\mathcal{A})$ To obtain a better
complexity, we exploit some structure that exists in the deterministic automaton
$\mathcal{D}(\mathcal{A}, k)$. First, the set of counting functions $CF(\mathcal{A}, k)$ forms a complete lattice
for the partial order $\preceq$ defined by $f_1 \preceq f_2$ if $f_1(q) \leq f_2(q)$ for all states q.
We denote by $f_1 \bigsqcup f_2$ the least upper-bound of f_1, f_2, and by $W_k^\mathcal{A}$ the set of
counting functions f such that the specification $L(\mathcal{D}(\mathcal{A}, k)[f])$ is realizable (i.e.
the specification defined by $\mathcal{D}(\mathcal{A}, k)$ with initial state f). It is known that $W_k^\mathcal{A}$
is downward-closed for $\preceq$ [18], because for all $f_1 \preceq f_2$, any machine realizing
$L(\mathcal{D}(\mathcal{A}, k)[f_2])$ also realizes $L(\mathcal{D}(\mathcal{A}, k)[f_1])$. Therefore, $W_k^\mathcal{A}$ can be represented
compactly by the antichain $\lceil W_k^\mathcal{A} \rceil$ of its $\preceq$-maximal elements. Now, the first
improvement is obtained thanks to the following result:

Lemma 2. *Given a preMealy $\mathcal{P} = (M, m_0, \Delta)$, a co-Büchi automata $\mathcal{A}$, and
$k \in \mathbb{N}$. For all states $m \in M$, we let $F^*(m) = \bigsqcup \{ f \mid \exists u \in (\mathcal{I}\mathcal{O})^* \cdot Post_\mathcal{P}^*(m_0, u) =
m \wedge Post_\mathcal{D}(f_0, u) = f \}$. Then, $L(\mathcal{D}(\mathcal{A}, k))$ is $\mathcal{P}$-realizable iff there does not exist
$m \in M$ such that $F^*(m) \notin W_k^\mathcal{A}$.*

It is easily shown that the operator F^* can be computed in PTIME. Thus, the
latter lemma implies that there is a poly-time algorithm in $|\mathcal{P}|, |\mathcal{A}|, k \in \mathbb{N}$, and
the size of $\lceil W_k^\mathcal{A} \rceil$ to check the $\mathcal{P}$-realizability of $L^\forall(\mathcal{A})$. Formal details in [5].

We end this subsection by summarizing the behavior of our synthesis algorithm for ω-regular specifications defined as universal co-Büchi automata.

Theorem 6. *Given a universal coBüchi automaton $\mathcal{A}$ and a set of examples E,
the synthesis algorithm SYNTHLEARN returns, if it exists, a Mealy machine $\mathcal{M}$
such that $E \subseteq L(\mathcal{M})$ and $L_\omega(\mathcal{M}) \subseteq L^\forall(\mathcal{A})$, in worst-case exponential time in
the size of $\mathcal{A}$ and polynomial in the size of E. Otherwise, it returns UNREAL.*

Specifications given as an LTL formula We are now in position to apply
Alg. 3 to a specification given as LTL formula φ. Indeed, thanks to the results

of the subsection above, to provide an algorithm for LTL specifications, we only need to translate φ into a universal co-Büchi automaton. This can be done according to the next lemma. It is well-known (see [24]), that given an LTL formula φ over two sets of atomic propositions $P_\mathcal{I}$ and $P_\mathcal{O}$, we can construct in exponential time a universal co-Büchi automaton $\mathcal{A}_\varphi$ such that $L^\forall(\mathcal{A}_\varphi) = [\varphi]$, i.e. $\mathcal{A}$ recognizes exactly the set of words $w \in (2^{P_\mathcal{I}}2^{P_\mathcal{O}})^\omega$ that satisfy φ. We then get the following theorem that gives the complexity of our synthesis algorithm for a set of examples E and an LTL formula φ, complexity which is provably worst-case optimal as deciding if $[\varphi]$ is realizable with $E = \emptyset$, i.e. the plain LTL realizability problem, is already 2ExpTime-Complete [27].

Theorem 7. *Given an LTL formula φ and a set of examples E, the synthesis algorithm* SynthLearn *returns a Mealy machine $\mathcal{M}$ such that $E \subseteq L(\mathcal{M})$ and $L_\omega(\mathcal{M}) \subseteq [\varphi]$ if it exists, in worst-case doubly exponential time in the size of φ and polynomial in the size of E. Otherwise it returns UNREAL.*

5 Implementation and Case study

We have implemented the algorithm SynthLearn of the previous section in a prototype tool, in Python, using the tool Acacia-Bonzai [11] to manipulate antichains of counting functions. We first explain the heuristics we have used to define state-merging and completion strategies, and then demonstrate how our implementation behaves on a case study whose goal is to synthesize the controller for an elevator. The interested reader can find in [5] other case studies, including a controller for an e-bike and two variations on mutual exclusion.

Merging and completion strategies implemented in our prototype Our tool implements a *merging* strategy σ_G where, given an example e that leads in the current preMealy machine to a state m and a set $\{m_1, m_2, \ldots, m_k\}$ of candidates for merging, as computed in line 7 of Algorithm 1, we choose state m_i with a $\preceq$-minimal counting function $F^*(m_i)$, as defined in Lemma 2. Intuitively, favouring minimal counting functions preserves as much as possible the set of behaviors that are possible after the example e.

Our tool also implements a *completion strategy* σ_C, where for every hole (m, i) of the preMealy machine $\mathcal{M}$ and out of the list of candidate pairs, selects an element which again favour states associated with $\preceq$-minimal counting functions. For more details, we refer the reader to [5].

Lift Controller Example We illustrate how to use our tool to construct a suitable controller for a two-floor elevator system.

Considering two floors is sufficient enough to illustrate most of the main difficulties of a more general elevator. Inputs of the controller are given by two atomic propositions b0 and b1, which are true whenever the button at floor 0 (resp. floor 1) is pressed by a user. Outputs are given by the atomic propositions f0 and f1, true whenever the elevator is at floor 0 (resp. floor 1); and ser, true whenever the elevator is *serving* the current floor (i.e. doors are opened). This controller should ensure the following core properties:

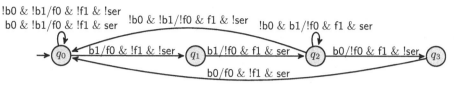

Fig. 2: Machine returned by our tool on the elevator specification w/o examples. Here, q_0, q_1, q_2, q_3 represents the states where f0 is served when required, where b1 is pending, where f1 is served, the state where b0 is pending respectively.

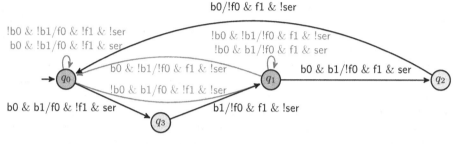

Fig. 3: Mealy machine returned by our tool on the elevator specification with additional examples. The preMealy machine obtained after generalizing the examples and before completion is highlighted in red. This took 3.10s to be generated.

1. **Functional Guarantee:** whenever a button of floor 0 (resp. floor 1) is pressed, the elevator must eventually *serve* floor 0 (resp. floor 1): G(b0 -> F (f0 & ser)) & G(b1 -> F (f1 & ser))
2. **Safety Guarantee:** The elevator is always at one floor exactly: G(f0<->!f1)
3. **Safety Guarantee:** The elevator cannot transition between two floors when doors are opened: G((f0 & ser) -> X(!f1)) & G((f1 & ser) -> X(!f0))
4. **Initial State:** The elevator should be in floor 0 initially: f0

Additionally, we make the following **assumption**: whenever a button of floor 0 (or floor 1) is pressed, it must remain pressed until the floor has been served, i.e., G(b0 -> (b0 W (f0 & ser))) & G(b1 -> (b1 W (f1 & ser))).

Before going into the details of this example, let us explain the methodology that we apply to use our tool on this example. We start by providing only the high level specification φ_{CORE} for the elevator given above. We obtain a first Mealy machine from the tool. We then observe the machine to identify prefix of behaviours that we are unhappy with, and for which we can provide better alternative decisions. Then we run the tool on φ_{CORE} and the examples that we have identified, and we get a new machine, and we proceed like that up to a point where we are satisfied with the synthesized Mealy machine.

Let us now give details. When our tool is provided with this specification without any examples, we get the machine depicted in fig. 2. This solution makes the controller switch between floor 0 and floor 1, sometimes unnecessarily. For instance, consider the trace s # {!b0 & !b1}{!f0 & f1 & !ser} # {!b0 & !b1}{f0 & !f1 & !ser}, where we let s = {!b0 & b1}{f0 & !f1 & !ser}

{!b0 & b1}{!f0 & f1 & ser}. Here, we note that the transition goes back to state q_0, where the elevator is at floor 0, when the elevator could have remained at floor 1 after serving floor 1. The methodology described above allows us to identify the following three examples:

1. The 1st trace states that after serving floor 1, the elevator must remain at floor 1 as b0 is false: s # {!b0 & !b1}{!f0 & f1 & !ser} # {!b0 & !b1}{!f0 & f1 & !ser}

2. The 2nd trace states that the elevator must remain at floor 0, as b1 is false: {!b0 & !b1}{f0 & !f1 & !ser} # {!b0 & !b1}{f0 & !f1 & !ser}

3. The 3rd trace ensures that after s, there is no unnecessary delay in serving floor 0 after floor 1 is served in s: s # {b0 & !b1}{!f0 & f1 & !ser} # {b0 & !b1}{f0 & !f1 & ser}

With those additional examples, our tool outputs the machine of fig. 3, which generalizes them and now ensures that moves of the elevator occur only when required. For example, the end of the first trace has been generalized into a loop on state q_1 ensuring that the elevator does not go to floor 0 from floor 1 unless b0 is pressed. We note that the number of examples provided here is much smaller than the theoretical (polynomial) upper bound proved in Theorem 4.

6   Conclusion

We have introduced *synthesis with a few hints*, which allows the user to guide synthesis using examples of expected executions of high quality solutions. Existing synthesis tools may provide unnatural solutions when fed with high-level specifications only. As providing complete specifications goes against the very goal of synthesis, we believe our algorithm has a greater potential in practice.

We have studied the computational complexity of problems that need to be solved during our synthesis procedure. We have proved our algorithm is *complete*: any Mealy machine $\mathcal{M}$ realizing a specification φ can be obtained from φ and a representative example set E, whose size is bounded polynomially in the size of $\mathcal{M}$. We have implemented our algorithm in a prototype tool that extends Acacia-Bonzai [11] with tailored state-merging learning algorithms. We have shown that only a small number of examples are necessary to obtain high quality machines from high-level LTL specifications only. The tool is not fully optimized yet. While this is sufficient to demonstrate the relevance of our approach, we will work on efficiency aspects of the implementation.

As future works, we will consider extensions of the user interface to interactively and concisely specify sets of (counter-)examples to solutions output by the tool. In the same line, an interesting future direction is to handle parametric examples (e.g. elevator with the number of floors given as parameter). This would require to provide a concise syntax to define parametric examples and to design efficient synthesis algorithm in this setting. We will also consider the possibility to formulate negative examples, as our theoretical results readily extend to this case and their integration in the implementation should be easy.

References

1. Abadi, M., Lamport, L., Wolper, P.: Realizable and unrealizable specifications of reactive systems. In: Automata, Languages and Programming, 16th International Colloquium, ICALP89, Stresa, Italy, July 11-15, 1989, Proceedings. Lecture Notes in Computer Science, vol. 372, pp. 1–17. Springer (1989)
2. Almagor, S., Kupferman, O., Velner, Y.: Minimizing expected cost under hard boolean constraints, with applications to quantitative synthesis. In: 27th International Conference on Concurrency Theory, CONCUR 2016, August 23-26, 2016, Québec City, Canada. LIPIcs, vol. 59, pp. 9:1–9:15. Schloss Dagstuhl - Leibniz-Zentrum für Informatik (2016)
3. Alur, R., Bodík, R., Dallal, E., Fisman, D., Garg, P., Juniwal, G., Kress-Gazit, H., Madhusudan, P., Martin, M.M.K., Raghothaman, M., Saha, S., Seshia, S.A., Singh, R., Solar-Lezama, A., Torlak, E., Udupa, A.: Syntax-guided synthesis. In: Dependable Software Systems Engineering, pp. 1–25 (2015)
4. Alur, R., Martin, M.M.K., Raghothaman, M., Stergiou, C., Tripakis, S., Udupa, A.: Synthesizing finite-state protocols from scenarios and requirements. In: Hardware and Software: Verification and Testing - 10th International Haifa Verification Conference, HVC 2014, Haifa, Israel, November 18-20, 2014. Proceedings. Lecture Notes in Computer Science, vol. 8855, pp. 75–91. Springer (2014)
5. Balachander, M., Filiot, E., Raskin, J.F.: Ltl reactive synthesis with a few hints (2023). https://doi.org/10.48550/ARXIV.2301.10485, https://arxiv.org/abs/2301.10485
6. Bloem, R., Chatterjee, K., Henzinger, T.A., Jobstmann, B.: Better quality in synthesis through quantitative objectives. In: Computer Aided Verification, 21st International Conference, CAV 2009, Grenoble, France, June 26 - July 2, 2009. Proceedings. Lecture Notes in Computer Science, vol. 5643, pp. 140–156. Springer (2009)
7. Bloem, R., Chatterjee, K., Jobstmann, B.: Graph games and reactive synthesis. In: Handbook of Model Checking, pp. 921–962. Springer (2018)
8. Bloem, R., Chockler, H., Ebrahimi, M., Strichman, O.: Synthesizing non-vacuous systems. In: Bouajjani, A., Monniaux, D. (eds.) Verification, Model Checking, and Abstract Interpretation. pp. 55–72. Springer International Publishing, Cham (2017)
9. Bohy, A., Bruyère, V., Filiot, E., Jin, N., Raskin, J.: Acacia+, a tool for LTL synthesis. In: Computer Aided Verification - 24th International Conference, CAV 2012, Berkeley, CA, USA, July 7-13, 2012 Proceedings. Lecture Notes in Computer Science, vol. 7358, pp. 652–657. Springer (2012)
10. Bruyère, V., Filiot, E., Randour, M., Raskin, J.: Meet your expectations with guarantees: Beyond worst-case synthesis in quantitative games. Inf. Comput. **254**, 259–295 (2017). https://doi.org/10.1016/j.ic.2016.10.011, https://doi.org/10.1016/j.ic.2016.10.011
11. Cadilhac, M., Pérez, G.A.: Acacia-bonsai: A modern implementation of downset-based LTL realizability. CoRR **abs/2204.06079** (2022). https://doi.org/10.48550/arXiv.2204.06079, https://doi.org/10.48550/arXiv.2204.06079
12. Damas, C., Lambeau, B., van Lamsweerde, A.: Scenarios, goals, and state machines: a win-win partnership for model synthesis. In: Proceedings of the 14th ACM SIGSOFT International Symposium on Foundations of Software Engineering, FSE 2006, Portland, Oregon, USA, November 5-11, 2006. pp. 197–207. ACM (2006)

13. D'Ippolito, N., Braberman, V.A., Piterman, N., Uchitel, S.: Synthesizing nonanomalous event-based controllers for liveness goals. ACM Trans. Softw. Eng. Methodol. **22**(1), 9:1–9:36 (2013). https://doi.org/10.1145/2430536.2430543, https://doi.org/10.1145/2430536.2430543

14. Dupont, P., Lambeau, B., Damas, C., van Lamsweerde, A.: The QSM algorithm and its application to software behavior model induction. Appl. Artif. Intell. **22**(1&2), 77–115 (2008). https://doi.org/10.1080/08839510701853200, https://doi.org/10.1080/08839510701853200

15. Duret-Lutz, A., Renault, E., Colange, M., Renkin, F., Gbaguidi, A., Schlehuber-Caissier, P., Medioni, T., Martin, A., Dubois, J., Gillard, C., Lauko, H.: From spot 2.0 to spot 2.10: What's new? CoRR **abs/2206.11366** (2022). https://doi.org/10.48550/arXiv.2206.11366, https://doi.org/10.48550/arXiv.2206.11366

16. Esparza, J., Kretínský, J., Raskin, J., Sickert, S.: From LTL and limit-deterministic Büchi automata to deterministic parity automata. In: Tools and Algorithms for the Construction and Analysis of Systems - 23rd International Conference, TACAS 2017, Held as Part of the European Joint Conferences on Theory and Practice of Software, ETAPS 2017, Uppsala, Sweden, April 22-29, 2017, Proceedings, Part I. Lecture Notes in Computer Science, vol. 10205, pp. 426–442 (2017)

17. Faymonville, P., Finkbeiner, B., Tentrup, L.: Bosy: An experimentation framework for bounded synthesis. In: Majumdar, R., Kuncak, V. (eds.) Computer Aided Verification - 29th International Conference, CAV 2017, Heidelberg, Germany, July 24-28, 2017, Proceedings, Part II. Lecture Notes in Computer Science, vol. 10427, pp. 325–332. Springer (2017). https://doi.org/10.1007/978-3-319-63390-9_17, https://doi.org/10.1007/978-3-319-63390-9_17

18. Filiot, E., Jin, N., Raskin, J.: An antichain algorithm for LTL realizability. In: Computer Aided Verification, 21st International Conference, CAV 2009, Grenoble, France, June 26 - July 2, 2009. Proceedings. Lecture Notes in Computer Science, vol. 5643, pp. 263–277. Springer (2009)

19. Filiot, E., Jin, N., Raskin, J.: Antichains and compositional algorithms for LTL synthesis. Formal Methods Syst. Des. **39**(3), 261–296 (2011). https://doi.org/10.1007/s10703-011-0115-3, https://doi.org/10.1007/s10703-011-0115-3

20. Giantamidis, G., Tripakis, S., Basagiannis, S.: Learning Moore machines from input-output traces. Int. J. Softw. Tools Technol. Transf. **23**(1), 1–29 (2021)

21. Heinz, J., de la Higuera, C., van Zaanen, M.: Grammatical Inference for Computational Linguistics. Synthesis Lectures on Human Language Technologies, Morgan & Claypool Publishers (2015). https://doi.org/10.2200/S00643ED1V01Y201504HLT028, https://doi.org/10.2200/S00643ED1V01Y201504HLT028

22. Kupferman, O.: On high-quality synthesis. In: Computer Science - Theory and Applications - 11th International Computer Science Symposium in Russia, CSR 2016, St. Petersburg, Russia, June 9-13, 2016, Proceedings. Lecture Notes in Computer Science, vol. 9691, pp. 1–15. Springer (2016)

23. Kupferman, O., Vardi, M.Y.: Vacuity detection in temporal model checking. In: Pierre, L., Kropf, T. (eds.) Correct Hardware Design and Verification Methods. pp. 82–98. Springer Berlin Heidelberg, Berlin, Heidelberg (1999)

24. Kupferman, O., Vardi, M.Y.: Safraless decision procedures. In: 46th Annual IEEE Symposium on Foundations of Computer Science (FOCS 2005), 23-25 October 2005, Pittsburgh, PA, USA, Proceedings. pp. 531–542. IEEE Computer Society (2005)

25. Meyer, P.J., Sickert, S., Luttenberger, M.: Strix: Explicit reactive synthesis strikes back! In: Computer Aided Verification - 30th International Conference, CAV 2018, Held as Part of the Federated Logic Conference, FloC 2018, Oxford, UK, July 14-17, 2018, Proceedings, Part I. Lecture Notes in Computer Science, vol. 10981, pp. 578–586. Springer (2018)
26. Natarajan, N., Simmons, D., Datha, N., Jain, P., Gulwani, S.: Learning natural programs from a few examples in real-time. In: Chaudhuri, K., Sugiyama, M. (eds.) The 22nd International Conference on Artificial Intelligence and Statistics, AISTATS 2019, 16-18 April 2019, Naha, Okinawa, Japan. Proceedings of Machine Learning Research, vol. 89, pp. 1714–1722. PMLR (2019), http://proceedings.mlr.press/v89/natarajan19a.html
27. Pnueli, A., Rosner, R.: On the synthesis of an asynchronous reactive module. In: Automata, Languages and Programming, 16th International Colloquium, ICALP89, Stresa, Italy, July 11-15, 1989, Proceedings. Lecture Notes in Computer Science, vol. 372, pp. 652–671. Springer (1989)
28. Raha, R., Roy, R., Fijalkow, N., Neider, D.: Scalable anytime algorithms for learning fragments of linear temporal logic. In: Fisman, D., Rosu, G. (eds.) Tools and Algorithms for the Construction and Analysis of Systems - 28th International Conference, TACAS 2022, Held as Part of the European Joint Conferences on Theory and Practice of Software, ETAPS 2022, Munich, Germany, April 2-7, 2022, Proceedings, Part I. Lecture Notes in Computer Science, vol. 13243, pp. 263–280. Springer (2022). https://doi.org/10.1007/978-3-030-99524-9_14, https://doi.org/10.1007/978-3-030-99524-9_14
29. Schewe, S., Finkbeiner, B.: Bounded synthesis. In: Automated Technology for Verification and Analysis, 5th International Symposium, ATVA 2007, Tokyo, Japan, October 22-25, 2007, Proceedings. Lecture Notes in Computer Science, vol. 4762, pp. 474–488. Springer (2007)
30. Singh, R., Gulwani, S.: Transforming spreadsheet data types using examples. In: Proceedings of the 43rd Annual ACM SIGPLAN-SIGACT Symposium on Principles of Programming Languages, POPL 2016, St. Petersburg, FL, USA, January 20 - 22, 2016. pp. 343–356 (2016). https://doi.org/10.1145/2837614.2837668, https://doi.org/10.1145/2837614.2837668
31. Solar-Lezama, A.: Program sketching. STTT 15(5-6), 475–495 (2013), https://doi.org/10.1007/s10009-012-0249-7
32. Solar-Lezama, A., Tancau, L., Bodík, R., Seshia, S.A., Saraswat, V.A.: Combinatorial sketching for finite programs. In: Shen, J.P., Martonosi, M. (eds.) Proceedings of the 12th International Conference on Architectural Support for Programming Languages and Operating Systems, ASPLOS 2006, San Jose, CA, USA, October 21-25, 2006. pp. 404–415. ACM (2006). https://doi.org/10.1145/1168857.1168907, https://doi.org/10.1145/1168857.1168907
33. Thomas, W.: Automata on infinite objects. In: Handbook of Theoretical Computer Science, Volume B: Formal Models and Sematics (1991)

Timed Automata Verification and Synthesis via Finite Automata Learning*

Ocan Sankur[✉]

Univ Rennes, Inria, CNRS, Rennes, France
ocan.sankur@cnrs.fr

Abstract. We present algorithms for model checking and controller synthesis of timed automata, seeing a timed automaton model as a parallel composition of a large finite-state machine and a relatively smaller timed automaton, and using compositional reasoning on this composition. We use automata learning algorithms to learn finite automata approximations of the timed automaton component, in order to reduce the problem at hand to finite-state model checking or to finite-state controller synthesis. We present an experimental evaluation of our approach.

1 Introduction

Timed automata [1] are a well-known formalism for modeling and verifying real-time systems. They can be used to model systems as finite automata, while using, in addition, clocks to impose timing constraints on the transitions. Using clock variables have advantages. They allow one to describe models that are expressive thanks to real-valued clock values; moreover, the use of specific clock variables enable optimizations such as sound and complete abstractions, also known as extrapolation operators [5]. Model checking algorithms have been developed and implemented in tools such as Uppaal [8], TChecker [28], PAT [50].

One approach for model checking timed automata is based on representing the set of clock values with *zones*, which are particular polyhedra, and using explicit enumeration on the discrete states. There has been extensive research on sound and complete abstractions on zones, which improved the performance of the model checking tools, and made it possible to handle models with more complex time constraints; see [11] for a survey. However this approach does not scale to models with large discrete spaces due to explicit enumeration. Several authors have developed algorithms to remedy this issue, and to attempt to adapt efficient model checking techniques finite-state systems to timed systems. Extensions of binary decision diagrams (BDD) with clock constraints have been considered both for continuous time [53,10,23] and discrete time [42,51]. Another approach is to use predicate abstraction on clock variables that enables efficient finite-state verification techniques based on BDDs or SAT solvers [17,16,46].

Controller synthesis is a related problem in which some transitions of the system are controllable and some are uncontrollable, and the objective is to

---

* This work was partially funded by ANR project Ticktac (ANR-18-CE40-0015).

S. Sankaranarayanan and N. Sharygina (Eds.): TACAS 2023, LNCS 13994, pp. 329–349, 2023.
https://doi.org/10.1007/978-3-031-30820-8_21

compute a control strategy which guarantees that all induced runs of the system satisfy a given specification; see *e.g.* [52]. This problem is formalized using *games*, and in the case of real-time systems, using timed games [39,4]. Zone-based algorithms have been developed to solve timed games and compute control strategies [14], and are available in the Uppaal TIGA tool [7]. These algorithms suffer from the same limitations as the zone-based model checking algorithms. Although they can be efficient on instances with small discrete state spaces, they do not scale well to large systems. An attempt was made to implement the counter-example guided abstraction refinement scheme to handle larger discrete state space in timed games in [44]. On the other hand, there are several efficient finite-state game solvers, based on BDDs and SAT solvers, which can efficiently handle relatively large state spaces [31], but cannot handle real time.

In this work, we introduce an approach that is applied both to model checking and controller synthesis of timed automata with the objective of combining the advantages of both timed automata and finite-state model checkers and game solvers. Our suggestion is to see the input model, without loss of generality, as a parallel composition between a finite-state machine $\mathcal{A}$, and a timed automaton $\mathcal{T}$. We specifically target instances where $\mathcal{A}$ is large, and $\mathcal{T}$ is relatively small but nontrivial. Note that this point of view was considered before in the verification of synchronous systems within a real-time environment [9]. As a novelty, for model checking, we apply a compositional reasoning rule on the product $\mathcal{A} \| \mathcal{T}$ by replacing the timed automaton $\mathcal{T}$ by a (small) deterministic finite automaton (DFA) H which represents the behaviors of $\mathcal{T}$. To automatically select the DFA H, we adapt the algorithm [43] to our setting, and use a DFA learning algorithm (such as L* [3], or TTT [29]) to find an appropriate DFA either to prove the specification or to reveal a counterexample.

Our approach enjoys the principle of *separation of concerns* in the following sense. A timed automaton model checker is used by the learning algorithm to answer *membership* and *equivalence queries* (see Section 2.2); these are answered without referring to $\mathcal{A}$, thus, by avoiding the large discrete state space. Therefore, the timed automaton model checker is used in this approach for what it is designed for: handling real-time constraints encoded in $\mathcal{T}$, not for dealing with excessive discrete state spaces. Once an appropriate DFA H is found by the learning algorithm, the system $\mathcal{A} \| H$ is model-checked using a finite-state model checker whose focus is to deal with large *discrete* state spaces. We can thus benefit from the best of the two worlds: a state-of-the-art model checker for timed automata, which is somewhat used here as a theory solver, and any finite-state model checker based on BDDs, SAT solvers, or even explicit-state enumeration.

The application of the learning-based compositional reasoning of [43] to controller synthesis is more involved. Our objective was to find a way to exploit efficient finite-state game solvers [31] in the context of timed automata even if this meant having an incomplete algorithm. We describe a setting where a one-sided abstraction is applied for controller synthesis by replacing the timed automaton component by a learned DFA. Contrarily to the model checking algorithm, our controller synthesis algorithm is sound but not complete, that is, the algorithm may fail although there exists a control strategy, while any control strategy that is output is correct. More precisely, we consider timed games in the form $\mathcal{G}\|\mathcal{T}$ where $\mathcal{G}$ is a finite-state game, and $\mathcal{T}$ is a timed automaton. We describe an algorithm that alternates between two phases. In the first phase, the goal is to find a DFA $\overline{H}$ that is an overapproximation of $\mathcal{T}$. Once this is found, we use a finite-state game solver on $\mathcal{G}\|\overline{H}$; if there is a control strategy, we prove that it can be applied in the original system $\mathcal{G}\|\mathcal{T}$. If not, then we obtain a counterstrategy $\mathfrak{S}$. We then switch to the second phase whose goal is to check whether the counterstrategy is spurious or not; and it does so by learning an underapproximation DFA $\underline{H}$ of $\mathcal{T}$, and checking whether $\mathfrak{S}$ induces runs that are all in $\underline{H}$. Accordingly, we either reject the instance or switch back to the first phase. As in the model checking algorithm, the timed automaton model checker is only used to answer queries independently from $\mathcal{G}$, and a finite-state game solver and a model checker are used to compute and analyze strategies in a discrete state-space.

To the best of our knowledge, apart from [44], we present the first algorithm that can solve timed games with large discrete state spaces. Although the algorithm applies to a subset of timed games and is not complete, we believe it is of utmost importance to make progress on the scalability of timed game solvers in order for these methods to be applied in convincing applications. Our paper makes an attempt in this direction.

We evaluate our algorithms in comparison with state-of-the-art tools and show that our approach is competitive with the existing tools, and can allow both model checking and synthesis to scale to larger models. The approach offers an alternative treatment of timed models, which might be applied in other settings.

We present the model checking algorithm in Section 2 which contains formal definitions, the description of the algorithm, and the experiments. Section 3 presents our contributions on the controller synthesis problem, and includes formal definitions, the description of the algorithm, and the experiments. In Section 4, we provide a broader discussion on related works, and present our conclusions and perspectives.

2   Compositional Model Checking

2.1   Preliminaries

Labeled Transition Systems and Finite Automata. We denote finite *labeled transition systems (LTS)* as tuples (Q, q^0, Σ, T) where Q is the set of states, $q^0 \in Q$ is the initial state, Σ is a finite alphabet, $T \subseteq Q \times \Sigma \cup \{\epsilon\} \times Q$ is the transition relation (ϵ labels silent transitions). Because we will consider synchronous product of LTSs, we will use silent transitions to define internal transitions not exposed for synchronization. A *finite automaton* is an LTS given with a set of accepting states $F \subseteq Q$, and is written (Q, q^0, Σ, T, F). A *run* of an automaton is a sequence $q_1 e_1 q_2 e_2 \ldots q_n$ where $q_1 = q^0$, $e_i = (q_i, \sigma_i, q_{i+1}) \in T$ for some $\sigma_i \in \Sigma \cup \{\epsilon\}$ for each $1 \leq i \leq n - 1$. The *trace* of the run is the sequence $\sigma_1 \sigma_2 \ldots \sigma_{n-1}$. An *accepting run* starts at q^0 and ends in F. The language of a finite automaton $\mathcal{A}$ is the set of the traces of all accepting runs of $\mathcal{A}$, and is denoted by $\mathcal{L}(\mathcal{A})$. We will consider *deterministic finite automata (DFA)* which do not have silent transitions, and have at most one edge for each label from each state.

The *parallel composition* of two automata $\mathcal{A}_i = (Q_i, q_i^0, \Sigma, T_i, F_i)$, $i \in \{1, 2\}$, defined on the same alphabet, is the automaton $\mathcal{A}_1 \parallel \mathcal{A}_2 = (Q, q^0, \Sigma, T, F)$ with $Q = Q_1 \times Q_2$, $q^0 = (q_1^0, q_2^0)$, $F = F_1 \times F_2$, and T contains $((q_1, q_2), \sigma, (q_1', q_2'))$ for all $(q_1, \sigma, q_1') \in T_1$, and $(q_2, \sigma, q_2') \in T_2$; and $((q_1, q_2), \epsilon, (q_1', q_2))$ for all $(q_1, \epsilon, q_1') \in T_1$, and $q_2 \in Q_2$; and symmetrically, $((q_1, q_2), \epsilon, (q_1, q_2'))$ for all $(q_2, \epsilon, q_2') \in T_2$, and $q_1 \in Q_1$.

Finite Automata Learning. We use finite automata learning algorithms such as L^* [3,45] and TTT [29]. In the *online* learning model, the learning algorithm interacts with a teacher in order to learn a deterministic finite automaton recognizing a hidden regular language known to the teacher. The algorithm can make two types of queries. A *membership query* consists in asking whether a given word belongs to the language, to which the teacher answers by yes or no. An *equivalence query* consists in creating a hypothesis automaton H, and asking the teacher whether H recognizes the language. The teacher either answers yes, or no and provides a counterexample word which is in the symmetric difference of $\mathcal{L}(H)$ and of the target language. Learning algorithms typically make a large number of membership queries, and a smaller number of equivalence queries.

Timed Automata. We fix a finite set of clocks $\mathcal{C}$. *Clock valuations* are the elements of $\mathbb{R}_{\geq 0}^{\mathcal{C}}$. For $R \subseteq \mathcal{C}$ and a valuation v, $v[R \leftarrow 0]$ is the valuation defined by $v[R \leftarrow 0](x) = v(x)$ for $x \in \mathcal{C} \setminus R$ and $v[R \leftarrow 0](x) = 0$ for $x \in R$. Given $d \in \mathbb{R}_{\geq 0}$ and a valuation v, $v + d$ is defined by $(v + d)(x) = v(x) + d$ for all $x \in \mathcal{C}$. We extend these operations to sets of valuations in the standard way. We write $\mathbf{0}$ for the valuation that assigns 0 to every clock.

We consider a clock named 0 which has the constant value 0, and let $\mathcal{C}_0 = \mathcal{C} \cup \{0\}$. An *atomic guard* is a formula of the form $x \bowtie k$, or $x - y \bowtie k$ where $x, y \in \mathcal{C}_0$, $k, l \in \mathbb{N}$, and $\bowtie \in \{<, \leq, >, \geq\}$. A *guard* is a conjunction of atomic guards. A valuation v satisfies a guard g, denoted $v \models g$, if all atomic guards are satisfied when each $x \in \mathcal{C}$ is replaced by $v(x)$. Let $\Phi_{\mathcal{C}}$ denote the set of guards for $\mathcal{C}$.

A *timed automaton* $\mathcal{T}$ is a tuple $(L, \ell_0, \Sigma, \text{Inv}, \mathcal{C}, E, F)$, where L is a finite set of locations, $\ell_0 \in L$ is the initial location, Σ is the alphabet, $\text{Inv} : L \to \Phi_{\mathcal{C}}$ the invariants, $\mathcal{C}$ is a finite set of clocks, $E \subseteq L \times \Sigma \times \Phi_{\mathcal{C}} \times 2^{\mathcal{C}} \times L$ is a set of edges. An edge $e = (\ell, g, \sigma, R, \ell')$ is also written as $\ell \xrightarrow{g, \sigma, R} \ell'$. $F \subseteq L$ is the set of accepting locations.

A *run* of $\mathcal{T}$ is a sequence $r = q_1 e_1 q_2 e_2 \ldots q_n$ where $q_i \in L \times \mathbb{R}_{\geq 0}^{\mathcal{C}}$, $q_1 = (\ell_0, \mathbf{0})$, and writing $q_i = (\ell, v)$ for each $1 \leq i \leq n$, we have $v \in \text{Inv}(\ell)$. If $i < n$, then either $e_i \in \mathbb{R}_{>0}$ and $v + e_i \in \text{Inv}(\ell)$, in which case $q_{i+1} = (\ell, v + e_i)$, or $e_i = (\ell, g, \sigma, R, \ell') \in E$, in which case $v \models g$ and $q_{i+1} = (\ell', v[R \leftarrow 0])$. The run is accepting if the last location is in F. The *trace* of the run r is the word $\sigma_0 \sigma_1 \ldots \sigma_n$ where σ_i is the label of edge e_i.

The *untimed language* of the timed automaton $\mathcal{T}$ is the set the traces of the accepting runs of $\mathcal{T}$, and is denoted by $\mathcal{L}(\mathcal{T})$.

A timed automaton is *label-deterministic* if at each location ℓ, for each label $\sigma \in \Sigma$, there is at most one transition leaving ℓ labelled by σ; in other terms, the finite automaton obtained by removing all clocks is deterministic.

We consider the parallel composition of a finite automaton $\mathcal{A} = (Q, q^0, \Sigma, T, F)$ and a timed automaton $\mathcal{T} = (L, \ell_0, \Sigma, \mathrm{Inv}, \mathcal{C}, E, F_\mathcal{T})$ which is a new timed automaton. Intuitively, a transition labeled by σ consists in an arbitrary number of silent transitions of $\mathcal{A}$, followed by a joint σ-transition of both components. The guard and the reset of the overall transition are those of the transition of $\mathcal{T}$. Formally, let $\mathcal{A} \| \mathcal{T} = (L', \ell'_0, \Sigma, \mathrm{Inv}', \mathcal{C}, E', F')$ with $L' = Q \times L$, $\mathrm{Inv}' : (q, \ell) \mapsto \mathrm{Inv}(\ell)$, $\ell'_0 = (q_0, \ell_0)$, and E' contains all edges of the form $((q, \ell), g, \sigma, R, (q', \ell'))$ such that $(\ell, g, \sigma, R, \ell') \in E$, and there exists a sequence $q = q_0, q_1, \ldots, q_k, q_{k+1} = q'$ of states of $\mathcal{A}$ such that $(q_0, \epsilon, q_1), \ldots, (q_{k-1}, \epsilon, q_k), (q_k, \sigma, q_{k+1})$ are transitions of $\mathcal{A}$. We let $F' = F \times F_\mathcal{T}$.

It follows from the definition of the parallel composition that $\mathcal{L}(\mathcal{A} \| \mathcal{T}) = \mathcal{L}(\mathcal{A}) \cap \mathcal{L}(\mathcal{T})$.

Target Timed Automata Instances. Our main motivation is to consider real-time systems that are modeled naturally as $\mathcal{A} \| \mathcal{T}$. Typically, $\mathcal{A}$ has a large (discrete) state space, and $\mathcal{T}$ is a relatively small timed automaton, but with potentially complex time constraints involving several clocks.

It should be clear however that any timed automaton $\mathcal{T}$ can be seen as such a product as follows. Let $\mathcal{A}$ be a finite automaton identical to $\mathcal{T}$ except that guards and resets are removed; and for each pair of guard g and reset r, a fresh label $\sigma_{g,r}$ is defined and added to each edge with the said guard and reset. Now, define the timed automaton $\mathcal{T}'$ as a single state with the same clocks as $\mathcal{T}$, with one self-loop for each pair (g, r): such an edge is labeled by $\sigma_{g,r}$, has guard g, and reset r. We have that $\mathcal{T}$ is isomorphic to $\mathcal{A} \| \mathcal{T}'$.

An example is given in Figure 1 which shows how a simple scheduling setting can be modeled in this way. Here, the finite automaton is simple and only stores the mapping from machines to the tasks they are executing. Typically, if the machines or the processes executing tasks have internal states, these could be modeled in $\mathcal{A}$ as well without altering the timed automaton.

2.2   Learning-Based Compositional Model Checking Algorithm

We present an algorithm for model checking the untimed language $\mathcal{L}(\mathcal{A} \| \mathcal{T})$.

Although it is known that the untimed language is regular [1], the size of the corresponding finite automaton can be exponential so a direct computation is not efficient. We will be looking for a finite automaton H which is an *overapproximation* of $\mathcal{T}$ i.e. $\mathcal{L}(\mathcal{T}) \subseteq \mathcal{L}(H)$. H stands for *hypothesis* made by the learning algorithm. We will in fact use the following lemma.

Lemma 1. *For all finite automata $\mathcal{A}$ and H, and timed automata $\mathcal{T}$ on common alphabet Σ, if $\mathcal{L}(\mathcal{T}) \subseteq \mathcal{L}(H)$, then $\mathcal{L}(\mathcal{A} \| \mathcal{T}) \subseteq \mathcal{L}(\mathcal{A} \| H)$.*

Finite automaton $\mathcal{A}$:

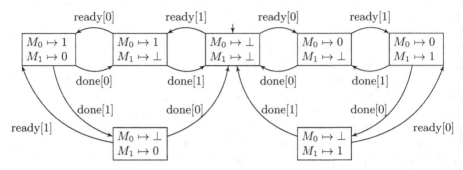

Timed automaton $\mathcal{T}$:

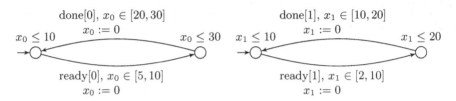

Fig. 1. Timed automaton $\mathcal{A}\|\mathcal{T}$ modeling a simple scheduling policy. The finite automaton $\mathcal{A}$ is given above and models a scheduler which schedules tasks (0 and 1) immediately when they become ready (ready[0] and ready[1]) on machines M_0 and M_1, using M_0 first if it is available. The timed automaton $\mathcal{T}$ is below, here, as a network of the timed automata, and models interarrival and computation times for each task.

In other terms, by replacing the timed automaton $\mathcal{T}$ by its overapproximation, we obtain an overapproximation of the compound system in terms of untimed language. So if a linear property can be established on $\mathcal{A}\|H$ for an appropriate H, then the property also holds on the original system.

Let us present the above property as a verification rule. Assuming that we want to establish $\mathcal{A}\|\mathcal{T} \subseteq \mathsf{Spec}$ for some language Spec, we have

$$\frac{\mathcal{L}(\mathcal{T}) \subseteq \mathcal{L}(H) \quad \mathcal{L}(\mathcal{A}\|H) \subseteq \mathsf{Spec}}{\mathcal{L}(\mathcal{A}\|\mathcal{T}) \subseteq \mathsf{Spec}.} \; \mathsf{Asym} \qquad (1)$$

Here, H serves as an *assumption* we make on $\mathcal{T}$ when verifying $\mathcal{A}$; so as in Lemma 1, we can use H instead of $\mathcal{T}$ during model checking. The rule (1) is well known as the assume-guarantee verification rule [19], and has been used in model checking finite-state systems as well as timed automata [35]. The assumption H can either be provided by the user, or automatically computed using automata learning as in [43]. Intuitively, the model checking algorithm we present in this section is an application of [43] to our specific case.

Figure 2 presents the overview of the algorithm. The membership queries of the learning algorithm are answered by the membership oracle; the equivalence query with conjecture H is answered by the inclusion oracle. When the conjecture H

passes the inclusion check, we model-check $H\|\mathcal{A}$. When this is successful, we stop and declare that the original system $\mathcal{A}\|\mathcal{T}$ satisfies the specification. Otherwise, a counterexample $w \in \mathcal{L}(\mathcal{A}\|H) \setminus \mathsf{Spec}$ was found, and we use a realizability check to see whether $w \in \mathcal{L}(\mathcal{T})$ (this is actually done by the membership oracle). If the answer is yes, then the counterexample is confirmed, and we stop. Otherwise, we inform the learning algorithm that w must be excluded, and continue the learning process.

Note that this algorithm can be used for any regular language specification Spec. We focus on safety properties in our experiments, presented next.

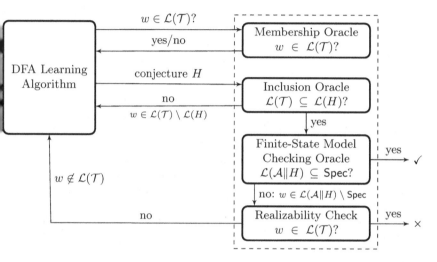

Fig. 2. The learning-based compositional model checking algorithm. The box on the left is a DFA learning algorithm, while the oracles answering the queries of the learning algorithm are shown on the right and correspond to the teacher.

2.3   Experiments

We built a prototype implementation of our algorithm in Scala, using the TTT automata learning algorithm [29] from the learnlib library [30], and the associated automatalib for manipulating finite automata[1]. We used the TChecker [28] model checker for implementing membership and inclusion oracles. For the latter, we complement H into H^c, and check the emptiness of the parallel composition of $\mathcal{T}$ with H^c. We use the NuSMV model checker for finite-state model checking.

The overall input consists in an SMV file describing $\mathcal{A}$, and of a TChecker timed automaton describing $\mathcal{T}$. We use define expressions in SMV to define the labels Σ, while TChecker allows us to tag each transition with a label.

---

[1] https://github.com/osankur/compRTMC/releases/tag/tacas23

Table 1. Model checking benchmarks. The column #Clk is the number of clocks; #C is the number of conjectures made by the DFA learning algorithm; #M is the number of membership queries; and |DFA| is the size of the final finite automaton learned. The safety specification holds on all models but those marked with *. In each cell, — means out of memory (8GB), and - means time out (30 minutes).

	#Clk	#C	#M	|DFA|	Compositional Time	Uppaal Time	nuXmv Time
Leader Election A	3	13	232	15	**157s**	—	—
Leader Election B	3	26	661	29	**198s**	—	—
Leader Election C	3	33	997	53	**149s**	—	-
Leader Election D	3				-	—	-
Leader Election (Stateless) A	3	13	232	15	15s	**6s**	—
Leader Election (Stateless) B	3	28	776	33	44s	**8s**	—
Leader Election (Stateless) C	3	33	997	53	17s	**6s**	-
Leader Election (Stateless) D *	3	134	6965	240	10m7s	**6s**	-
FTSP-abstract-2	2	3	54	8	**2s**	**2s**	-
FTSP-abstract-3	3	17	340	23	**47s**	7m8s	-
FTSP-abstract-4	4				-	-	-
STS-2	5				**7s**	19s	-
STS-3	6				-	-	-
Rt-broadcast A	4	49	1324	63	**59s**	-	87s
Rt-broadcast B	4	41	1100	63	101s	-	**90s**
Rt-broadcast C	4	21	590	39	**31s**	-	86s
Rt-broadcast D	4	27	901	52	**49s**	-	80s
Priority Scheduling 2 A	3	35	9859	49	34s	**1s**	7s
Priority Scheduling 2 B	3	29	1162	42	16s	—	**2s**
Priority Scheduling 3 C	4				-	—	**6s**
Priority Scheduling 3 D	4				-	—	**8s**
Priority Scheduling 3 E *	4				-	—	**11s**

We compare our algorithm on a set of benchmarks with the model checkers Uppaal [8] and nuXmv which has a timed automata model checker [16]. The former implements a zone-based enumerative algorithm, while the latter uses predicate abstraction through IC3IA. We describe some of the benchmarks here.

The leader election protocol is a distributed protocol that can recover from crashes [22], extended here with periodic activation times and crash durations. The first four rows of Table 1 correspond to the case where one of the processes crashes when its internal state enters an error state. Internal states are modeled using Boolean circuits from from the synthesis competition (SYNTCOMP) benchmarks. The stateless version is more abstract: there is no internal state model, and crashes can occur at any time. The letters A, B, C, D indicate different timed automaton models. Uppaal was more efficient at solving the stateless version but failed in the full version due to the large discrete state space. The compositional algorithm was effective in verifying all instances but the D case which required a large finite automaton to be learned. One can notice an overhead of the compositional algorithm in the stateless version due to the computation of the finite automaton H. This was particularly an issue in the stateless D case where Uppaal could find a counterexample trace faster; nuXmv was not able to solve these instances.

The flooding time synchronization protocol (FTSP) is a leader election algorithm for multi-hop wireless sensor networks used for clock synchronization [40], and has been the subject of formal verification before [41,34]. We consider the abstract model used in [48] for parameterized verification allowing one to verify the model for a large number of topologies. Our algorithm was faster for the model with 3 processes, although none of the tools scaled to 4 processes.

Overall, the experiments show that our algorithm is competitive with the state of the art tools; while it does not improve the performance uniformly on all considered benchmarks, it does allow us to solve instances that are not solvable by other tools, and sometimes to improve performance both compared to a zone-based approach (Uppaal) and SAT-based algorithms (nuXmv).

3 Compositional Controller Synthesis

3.1 Preliminaries

Games. A *finite safety game* is a pair $(\mathcal{G}, \mathsf{Bad})$ where $\mathcal{G}$ is an LTS $(Q_E \dot\cup Q_C, q_0, \Sigma, T)$ with the set of states given as a partition $Q_E \dot\cup Q_C$, namely, *Environment states* (Q_E), and *Controller states* (Q_C), and $\mathsf{Bad} \subseteq Q_E \dot\cup Q_C$ is an *objective*. The game is played between two players, namely, *Controller* and *Environment*. At each state $q \in Q_C$, Controller determines the successor by choosing an edge from q, and Environment determines the successor from states $q \in Q_E$. A *strategy* for Controller (resp. Environment) maps finite runs of $(Q_E \dot\cup Q_C, q_0, \Sigma, T)$ ending in Q_C (resp. Q_E) to an edge leaving the last state. A pair of strategies, one for each player, induces a unique infinite run from the initial state. A run is *winning* for Controller if it does not visit Bad; it is winning for Environment otherwise. A *winning strategy* for Controller is such that for all Environment strategies, the run induced by the two strategies is winning for Controller. Symmetrically, Environment has a winning strategy if for all Controller strategies, the induced run is winning. A strategy is *positional* (a.k.a. memoryless) if it only depends on the last state of the given run.

The parallel composition of $(\mathcal{G}, \mathsf{Bad})$ and a deterministic finite automaton $\mathcal{F} = (Q', q_0', \Sigma, T', F)$ on alphabet Σ is a new game whose LTS is $\mathcal{G}\|\mathcal{F}$ in which the Controller states are $Q_C \times Q'$, the Environment states are $Q_E \times Q'$, and the objective is $\mathsf{Bad} \times F$ (Notice that Controller thus has a safety objective).

Finite games were extended to the real-time setting as *timed games* [39,4]. A *timed game* is a timed automaton $\mathcal{T} = (L_E \dot\cup L_C, \ell_0, \Sigma, \mathrm{Inv}, \mathcal{C}, E, \mathsf{Bad})$ with the exception that its edges are labeled by $\Sigma \cup \{\epsilon\}$ (and not just by Σ as in the previous section), and the locations are partitioned as $L_E \dot\cup L_C$ into *Environment locations* and *Controller locations*. The semantics is defined by letting Environment choose the delay and the edge to be taken at locations L_E, while Controller choose these from L_C. Formally, a *strategy* for Environment (resp. Controller) is a function which associates a run that ends in L_E (resp. L_C) to a pair of delay and an edge enabled from the state reached after the delay. A run is winning for Controller if it does not visit Bad. A Controller (resp. Environment) strategy is *winning* for objective Bad if for all Environment (resp. Controller) strategies, the induced run from the initial state is winning (resp. not winning) for Controller. A run r is *compatible* with a strategy $\mathfrak{S}$ for Controller (resp. Environment) if there exists an Environment (resp. Controller) strategy $\mathfrak{S}'$ such that r is induced by $\mathfrak{S}, \mathfrak{S}'$.

The parallel composition of a finite safety game $(\mathcal{G}, \mathsf{Bad})$ and a timed automaton $\mathcal{T} = (L, \ell_0, \Sigma, \mathrm{Inv}, \mathcal{C}, E, F)$ on common alphabet Σ is the timed game $\mathcal{G}\|\mathcal{T}$ where Controller locations are $Q_C \times L$, and Environment locations are $Q_E \times L$.

Positional strategies exist both for reachability and safety objectives in finite and timed games. Both finite and timed games are known to be *determined* for reachability and safety objectives. For instance, if Controller does not have a winning strategy for the safety objective, then Environment has a strategy ensuring the reachability of Bad [39,4].

Target Timed Game Instances. We consider controller synthesis problems described as timed games in the form of $(\mathcal{G}\|\mathcal{T}, \mathsf{Bad} \times F)$ where $(\mathcal{G}, \mathsf{Bad})$ is a finite safety game, and $\mathcal{T}$ is a timed automaton. In addition, we assume that $\mathcal{G}\|\mathcal{T}$ is *Controller-silent*, defined as follows.

Definition 1. *The timed game $(\mathcal{G}\|\mathcal{T}, \mathsf{Bad} \times F)$ on alphabet Σ is Controller-silent if 1) all Controller transitions are silent; and 2) all Controller locations in $\mathcal{T}$ are urgent, that is, an invariant ensures that no time can elapse.*

Hence, we again separate the game $\mathcal{G}$ defined on a possibly large discrete state space while real-time constraints are separately given in $\mathcal{T}$.

The intuition behind the semantics is the following: because the game is played in $\mathcal{G}\|\mathcal{T}$ and $\mathcal{G}$ is Controller-silent, the timed automaton model $\mathcal{T}$ is only used to disallow some of the Environment transitions according to real-time constraints, while Controller's actions are instantaneous responses to Environment's actions and thus are unaffected by the constraints of $\mathcal{T}$. One can think of the timed automaton as some form of scheduler that schedules uncontrollable events in the system, so the order of these is determined by Environment. This assumption is restrictive; for instance, this excludes controller synthesis problems where the control strategy is to choose delays to execute some events. Nonetheless, this asymmetric view enables a one-sided abstraction framework presented in the next section, where Environment transitions are approximated by a DFA.

An example is given in Figure 3. The finite game drawn here only shows the structure of the game. It has, in addition, integer variables `rob_x`, `rob_y`, `obs_x`, `obs_y` encoding the positions of the robot and of the obstacle, and a Boolean variable `door` to encode the state of the door. The state e belongs to Environment, which can move the obstacle in any direction, close or open the door, or let the robot move by going to state c. The state c belongs to Controller. All its leaving transitions are silent, and correspond to moving the robot in four directions. These transitions have preconditions, not shown in the figure, that check whether the moves are possible, and have updates that modify the state variables. The timed automaton, given as a network of three timed automata, determine the timings of these events. One can notice, for example, that the

Finite game:

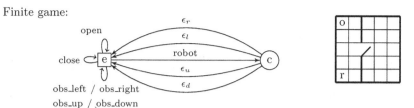

Timed automaton:

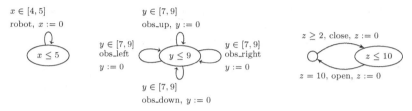

Fig. 3. The sketch of a timed game $\mathcal{G}\|\mathcal{T}$ modelling a planning problem. The finite game models a robot and an obstacle moving in a grid world as shown on top right. The cells r and o show, respectively, the initial positions of the robot and the obstacle. The robot cannot cross walls (shown in thick segments), and can only cross the door if it is open. Here four silent transitions were marked with $\epsilon_r, \epsilon_l, \epsilon_u, \epsilon_d$ for readability; in reality, these are all labeled by ϵ.

robot is moving faster than the obstacle, and that whenever the door is closed, it remains so for 10 time units.

3.2 One-Sided Abstraction

Thanks to the assumption we make on considered timed games, we show that by replacing $\mathcal{T}$ by a DFA H that is an overapproximation, we obtain an abstract game in which Controller strategies can be transferred to the original game. This is formalized in the next lemma (the proof is in the appendix).

Lemma 2. *Consider a Controller-silent timed game* $(\mathcal{G}\|\mathcal{T}, \mathsf{Bad} \times F)$, *and a complete DFA* H *with accepting states* F_H, *satisfying* $\mathcal{L}(\mathcal{T}) \subseteq \mathcal{L}(H)$.

- *If Controller wins* $(\mathcal{G}\|H, \mathsf{Bad} \times F_H)$, *then it wins* $(\mathcal{G}\|\mathcal{T}, \mathsf{Bad} \times F)$.
- *If Environment wins* $(\mathcal{G}\|\mathcal{T}, \mathsf{Bad} \times F)$, *then it wins* $(\mathcal{G}\|H, \mathsf{Bad} \times F_H)$, *and has a strategy in* $(\mathcal{G}\|H, \mathsf{Bad} \times F_H)$ *whose all compatible runs have traces in* $\mathcal{L}(\mathcal{T})$.

Note that in the above lemma, it is crucial that the game is Controller-silent. In fact, if Controller could take edges that synchronize with $\mathcal{T}$, then we may not be able to apply a strategy in $\mathcal{G}\|H$ to $\mathcal{G}\|\mathcal{T}$, since such a strategy may prescribe traces that are not accepted in $\mathcal{T}$. Moreover, if Controller locations are not urgent, we would not know how to select the delays when mapping the strategy to $\mathcal{G}\|\mathcal{T}$.

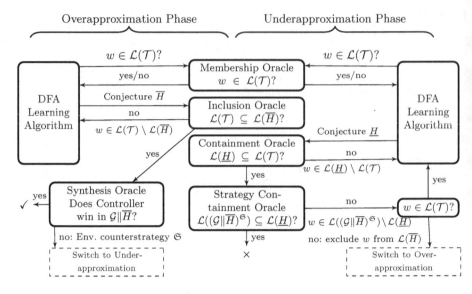

Fig. 4. The learning-based compositional controller synthesis algorithm for the input timed game $\mathcal{G}\|\mathcal{T}$, with $\mathcal{G}$ a Controller-silent finite game, and $\mathcal{T}$ a label-deterministic timed automaton. Two automata learning algorithms run in parallel to learn under- and over-approximations $\underline{H}$ and $\overline{H}$ such that $\underline{H} \subseteq \mathcal{L}(\mathcal{T}) \subseteq \overline{H}$.

3.3   Learning-Based Compositional Controller Synthesis Algorithm

We now present our compositional controller synthesis algorithm whose overview is given in Figure 4. The algorithm for controller synthesis is more involved than the model checking algorithm due to the alternating semantics for two players in games. It consists in two phases that alternate: the overapproximation phase, and the underapproximation phase. Each phase runs a DFA learning algorithm which is interrupted when we switch to the other phase, and continued when we switch back, until a decision is made. Together, both phases maintain two approximations, $\underline{H}$ and $\overline{H}$, such that $\mathcal{L}(\underline{H}) \subseteq \mathcal{L}(\mathcal{T}) \subseteq \mathcal{L}(\overline{H})$.

The objective of the overapproximation phase is to attempt to learn a DFA $\overline{H}$ satisfying $\mathcal{L}(\mathcal{T}) \subseteq \overline{H}$, and such that Controller wins in $\mathcal{G}\|\overline{H}$. The learning algorithm uses membership and inclusion oracles just like in Section 2.2. Once such a candidate DFA $\overline{H}$ is found, the synthesis oracle checks, using finite-state techniques, whether Controller has a winning strategy in $\mathcal{G}\|\overline{H}$. If this is the case, we stop and conclude that Controller wins in $\mathcal{G}\|\mathcal{T}$ by Lemma 2. Otherwise, Environment has a winning strategy $\mathfrak{S}$ in this game; and we switch to the underapproximation phase.

The goal of the underapproximation is to check whether the given Environment strategy $\mathfrak{S}$ can be proved to be spurious. Intuitively, we would like to check whether $\mathcal{L}((\mathcal{G}\|\overline{H})^{\mathfrak{S}}) \subseteq \mathcal{L}(\mathcal{T})$ and reject if this is the case. In fact, by Lemma 2, we know that a winning Environment strategy in $\mathcal{G}\|\mathcal{T}$ implies that there is such a strategy $\mathfrak{S}$. This is the source of incompleteness of our algorithm, since this condition is necessary but not sufficient for Environment to win; that is, the condition does not guarantee that Environment actually wins in $\mathcal{G}\|\mathcal{T}$.

While $\mathcal{L}((\mathcal{G}\|\overline{H})^{\mathfrak{S}}) \subseteq \mathcal{L}(\mathcal{T})$ can be checked with a timed automaton model checker (see *Checking Containment* below), this would mean exploring the large state space due to $\mathcal{G}$. Since we want to avoid using timed automata model checkers on such large instances, we rather learn an underapproximation $\underline{H}$ of $\mathcal{L}(\mathcal{T})$ using the membership and containment oracles, and use a finite-state model checker to check $\mathcal{L}((\mathcal{G}\|\overline{H})^{\mathfrak{S}}) \subseteq \mathcal{L}(\underline{H})$. Note that although the learning process does require inclusion checks of the form $\mathcal{L}(\underline{H}) \subseteq \mathcal{L}(\mathcal{T})$, this check is feasible with a timed automaton model checker since $\underline{H}$ is typically much smaller than $\mathcal{G}$. If the above check passes, then we reject the instance, that is, we declare the system not controllable. Otherwise, some trace w appears in $\mathcal{L}((\mathcal{G}\|\overline{H})^{\mathfrak{S}})$ but not in $\mathcal{L}(\underline{H})$. If $w \in \mathcal{L}(\mathcal{T})$, then we require that w be included in $\underline{H}$, and continue the learning process. Otherwise, $\mathfrak{S}$ is not valid since it induces w which is not in $\mathcal{L}(\mathcal{T})$. So we interrupt the current phase and switch back to the overapproximation phase requiring w to be removed from $\overline{H}$.

Membership and inclusion oracles are implemented with a timed automata model checker. Here, the synthesis oracle can be any finite game solver; we just need the capability of computing the controlled system $(\mathcal{G}\|\overline{H})^{\mathfrak{S}}$. Such a system is finite-state, so the strategy containment oracle can be implemented using a finite-state model checker (since $\underline{H}$ is deterministic and can thus be complemented). It remains to explain how the containment oracle is implemented.

Checking Containment $\mathcal{L}(\underline{H}) \subseteq \mathcal{L}(\mathcal{T})$. First, notice that, even with determinism assumptions on $\mathcal{T}$, the untimed language of the timed automaton complement of $\mathcal{T}$ is not the complement of $\mathcal{L}(\mathcal{T})$. To see this, consider a timed automaton with a single state which is both initial and accepting, a single clock x, and a self-loop with guard $x = 1$, labeled by σ. Then, both $\mathcal{L}(\mathcal{T})$ and $\mathcal{L}(\mathcal{T}^c)$ are the language σ^* where $\mathcal{T}^c$ denotes the timed automaton complement.

Nevertheless, assuming the label-determinism of $\mathcal{T}$, this check can be done by a simple adaptation of a zone-based exploration algorithm, as follows. Let us assume that accepting states are reachable from all states of $\underline{H}$, which can be ensured by a preprocessing step. We start exploring the timed automaton $\underline{H}\|\mathcal{T}$ using a zone-based exploration algorithm [11]. Consider any search node $((q_{\underline{H}}, q_{\mathcal{T}}), Z)$ encountered during the exploration algorithm, reachable by the trace w, where $(q_{\underline{H}}, q_{\mathcal{T}})$ is a location of $\underline{H}\|\mathcal{T}$, and Z a zone. The exploration algorithm generates all available successors for $\sigma \in \Sigma$. We make the following additional check: If there is $\sigma' \in \Sigma$ such that $q_{\underline{H}}$ has a successor by σ', but not $\mathcal{T}$ (either because there is no such edge, or because the guard of the unique edge labeled by σ' is not satisfied by Z), then we stop and return the trace $w\sigma' \in \mathcal{L}(\underline{H}) \setminus \mathcal{L}(\mathcal{T})$ as a counterexample to containment. If no such label can be found, the zone-based exploration will terminate and the algorithm confirms the containment.

As an alternative, one can use testing such as the Wp-method [36] to establish the containment, as it is customary in DFA learning. In this case, the answer is approximate in the sense that the conformance test can fail to detect that containment does not hold. However, this does not affect the soundness of the overall algorithm since it can only increase false negatives.

3.4 Experiments

Our tool accepts instances $\mathcal{G}\|\mathcal{T}$ where $\mathcal{G}$ is given as a Verilog module, and $\mathcal{T}$ as a TChecker timed automaton. Some of the inputs of the Verilog module are *uncontrollable* (chosen by Environment), some others are controllable (chosen by Controller). We use outputs of the Verilog module to define the synchronization labels Σ; while TChecker models tag each transition with such a label.

Table 2. The results of the controller synthesis experiments. The columns #Clks, #C, #M respectively show the number of clocks in the model, the numbers of conjectures and membership queries made by the compositional algorithm; while $|\overline{H}|$, $|\underline{H}|$ show the sizes of the DFAs learned by the two phases.

	#Clks	#C	#M	$|\overline{H}|$	$|\underline{H}|$	Time	Uppaal TIGA Time	Controllable
Scheduling genbuf A	3	50	2178	114		**26s**	—	yes
Scheduling genbuf B	3	40	1734	96		**15s**	—	yes
Scheduling genbuf C	3	45	1503	88		**4s**	—	yes
Scheduling counter64 D	3	54	2098	108		26s	**14s**	yes
Scheduling counter64 E	3	37	1454	83		**16s**	19s	yes
Scheduling counter64 F	3	19	21391	19	19	89s	**0s**	no
Planning genbuf A	2	2	17	4		**6s**	—	yes
Planning genbuf B	2	2	24	5		**9s**	—	yes
Planning genbuf C	2	9	1156	5	5	**266s**	—	no
Planning stateless D	2	3	50	9		**2s**	22s	yes
Planning stateless E	2	2	17	4		**2s**	4s	yes
Planning stateless F	2	8	973	5	5	10s	**2s**	no

Membership, inclusion, and containment queries are answered by TChecker. For the synthesis oracle, we used the game solver Abssynthe [12]. Abssynthe's input format is the and-inverter graphs format (AIG). For translating Verilog modules to AIG circuits, we use berkeley-abc and yosys. Abssynthe is able to compute the winning strategy $\mathfrak{S}$ for the winning player; it also computes the system controlled by $\mathfrak{S}$ in this case as an AIG circuit. The strategy containment oracle is implemented using NuSMV; since $\underline{H}$ is deterministic, one can complement it, and check whether the intersection with $(\mathcal{G}\|\overline{H})^{\mathfrak{S}}$ is empty.

The tool uses two Java threads to implement both learning phases, which are interrupted and continued while switching phases. Note that the very first learning step of $\overline{H}$ and $\underline{H}$ can be parallelized since the first underapproximation conjecture $\underline{H}$ does not depend on $\mathfrak{S}$.

We evaluate our algorithm with two classes of benchmarks (Table 2). The only tool to which we compare is Uppaal-TIGA [6] since Synthia [44] is not available anymore, and we are not aware of any other timed game solver.

In the scheduling benchmarks, there are two sporadic tasks that arrive nondeterministically, but constrained by the timed automaton. The controller must schedule these using two machines which have internal states, modeled either by a simple 8-bit counter, or by a genbuf circuit from the SYNTCOMP database. The scheduling duration depends on the internal state: some states require executing two external tasks, some others require executing three. The external task has a nondeterministic duration constrained by the timed automaton. The internal states change when a task is finalized. The controller loses if all machines are busy upon the arrival of a new task, or if it schedules a task on a busy machine. Uppaal TIGA was able to solve the counter models since they induce a smaller state space, but failed at the genbuf models. The compositional algorithm could efficiently handle these models. Uppaal was generally able to determine very quickly when the model is not controllable by finding a small counterstrategy, while the compositional algorithm had a overhead: it had to learn $\overline{H}$ and $\underline{H}$ before it can find and check the counterexample.

In the planning benchmarks, a robot and an obstacle is moving in a 6×6 grid (or 9×9 for the stateless case). Each agent can decide to move to an adjacent cell when they are scheduled, and the scheduling times are determined by a timed automaton. The goal of the robot is to avoid the obstacles. In the genbuf case, there are moreover internal states that can cause a glitch and prevent the agents from performing their moves, depending on their states. Uppaal TIGA was not able to manage the large state space unlike the compositional algorithm in this case, but both were able to solve the stateless case.

4   Conclusion

Related Works Perhaps the most closely related approach to our compositional model checking algorithm is trace abstraction refinement [25]. This was originally applied to program verification, and consists in building a network of finite automata that recognizes the program's control flow paths that are infeasible. One refines this language by model checking the control flow graph intersected with the complement of the automaton. Thus, the semantics of the variables of the program are abstractly represented by the finite automaton. This idea was applied to timed automata as well [54,15]. However, the generalization of the counterexamples which ensures convergence turns out to be less effective in timed automata. We attempted at obtaining an implementation, but could only confirm the poor performance for model checking timed automata as in [15] (we do not include these results here). It might be that simpler graph structures such as control flow graphs of programs are necessary for this approach to scale; further investigation is also necessary to study better generalization methods.

The learning-based compositional reasoning approach of [43] is also related to counter-example guided abstraction refinement (CEGAR) [18]. In fact, the automata learning algorithm builds an overapproximation of one of the components, and refines it as needed, guided by counterexamples. The difference is that, instead of using predicates, one uses automata to represent the overapproximation. A discussion can also be found in [43].

Learning algorithms for event-recording automata, a subset of timed automata were studied in [24]. The algorithm of [43] was extended for these automata in [35]. In the context of parameter synthesis with learning, parameterized systems were seen as a parallel composition of a non-parameterized component, and a parameterized component in [2].

Other approaches targeting the formal verification of real-time systems with large discrete state spaces include encodings of timed automata semantics in Boolean logic include [33,49]. An extension of and-inverter graphs were used in [20] that uses predicates to represent the state space of linear hybrid automata.

The abstract interpretation of games were studied in [27] that presents a theory allowing one to define under- and over-approximations. Abstraction-refinement algorithms based on counterexamples were given in [26,21]. These ideas were applied to timed games in [44]. Several abstraction-refinement and compositional algorithms were given in [12,13] for solving finite-state games given as Boolean circuits. The synthesis competition gathers every year researchers who present their game solvers [31,32].

Perspectives The algorithm we presented builds finite-state abstractions of real-time constraints, that it represents as DFA. The approach is well adapted when the interaction alphabet between $\mathcal{A}$ and $\mathcal{T}$ is small; this is the case, for instance, for distributed systems where the time constraints are used to describe the approximate period with which each process communicates with its neighbors; so the alphabet contains only a few symbols per process. Some of the benchmarks we considered are models of such systems. The approach is less convenient for time-intensive systems such as, say, job shop scheduling problems where a separate alphabet symbol is needed for each task.

As future work, we would like to understand when various abstraction schemes are efficient among the approach presented here, the predicate-abstraction approach, and zone-based state-space exploration. Currently, all algorithms fail in some benchmarks. Understanding the strengths of each algorithm might help designing a uniformly better solution. Currently, we can only verify linear properties; one might verify branching-time properties by learning automata with a stronger notion of equivalence such as bisimulation. In fact, an important limitation is due to learning being slow for large alphabets. Our setting could be extended to deal with large or symbolic alphabets *e.g.* [37,38].

For synthesis, our setting is currently restricted by the abstractions we use since when the algorithm rejects the instance, we cannot conclude whether the system is controllable or not. Using both the under- and overapproximations within the finite-state synthesis, for instance, using the three-valued abstraction approach [21] might allow us to render the approach complete, and to consider a larger class of timed games such as those that allow Controller to select nonzero delays.

Data Availability Statement Source codes, executables, and benchmark data are available as an artifact [47].

References

1. Rajeev Alur and David L. Dill. A theory of timed automata. *Theoretical Computer Science*, 126(2):183–235, 1994.
2. Étienne André and Shang-Wei Lin. Learning-based compositional parameter synthesis for event-recording automata. In Ahmed Bouajjani and Alexandra Silva, editors, *Formal Techniques for Distributed Objects, Components, and Systems*, pages 17–32, Cham, 2017. Springer International Publishing.
3. Dana Angluin. Learning regular sets from queries and counterexamples. *Information and Computation*, 75(2):87–106, 1987.
4. Eugene Asarin, Oded Maler, and Amir Pnueli. Symbolic controller synthesis for discrete and timed systems. In *Hybrid Systems II*, volume 999 of *LNCS*, pages 1–20. Springer, 1995.
5. Gerd Behrmann, Patricia Bouyer, Kim G. Larsen, and Radek Pelanek. Lower and upper bounds in zone-based abstractions of timed automata. *Int. J. Softw. Tools Technol. Transf.*, 8(3):204–215, June 2006.
6. Gerd Behrmann, Agnes Cougnard, Alexandre David, Emmanuel Fleury, Kim G Larsen, and Didier Lime. Uppaal-tiga: Time for playing games! In *International Conference on Computer Aided Verification*, pages 121–125. Springer, 2007.
7. Gerd Behrmann, Agnès Cougnard, Alexandre David, Emmanuel Fleury, Kim Guldstrand Larsen, and Didier Lime. UPPAAL-Tiga: Time for playing games! In *Proc. 19th International Conference on Computer Aided Verification (CAV'07)*, volume 4590 of *Lecture Notes in Computer Science*, pages 121–125. Springer, 2007.
8. Gerd Behrmann, Alexandre David, Kim Guldstrand Larsen, John Håkansson, Paul Pettersson, Wang Yi, and Martijn Hendriks. UPPAAL 4.0. In *Third International Conference on the Quantitative Evaluation of Systems (QEST 2006), 11-14 September 2006, Riverside, California, USA*, pages 125–126, 2006.
9. V. Bertin, E. Closse, M. Poize, J. Pulou, J. Sifakis, P. Venier, D. Weil, and S. Yovine. Taxys=esterel+kronos. a tool for verifying real-time properties of embedded systems. In *Proceedings of the 40th IEEE Conference on Decision and Control (Cat. No.01CH37228)*, volume 3, pages 2875–2880 vol.3, 2001.
10. Dirk Beyer, Claus Lewerentz, and Andreas Noack. Rabbit: A tool for BDD-based verification of real-time systems. In *Proc. 15th International Conference on Computer Aided Verification (CAV'03)*, volume 2725 of *Lecture Notes in Computer Science*, pages 122–125. Springer, 2003.
11. Patricia Bouyer, Paul Gastin, Frédéric Herbreteau, Ocan Sankur, and B. Srivathsan. Zone-based verification of timed automata: extrapolations, simulations and what next? In *20th International Conference on Formal Modeling and Analysis of Timed Systems (FORMATS 2022)*. Springer, 2022.
12. Romain Brenguier, Guillermo A. Pérez, Jean-François Raskin, and Ocan Sankur. Abssynthe: abstract synthesis from succinct safety specifications. In Krishnendu Chatterjee, Rüdiger Ehlers, and Susmit Jha, editors, *Proceedings 3rd Workshop on Synthesis (SYNT'14)*, volume 157 of *Electronic Proceedings in Theoretical Computer Science*, pages 100–116. Open Publishing Association, 2014.
13. Romain Brenguier, Guillermo A. Pérez, Jean-François Raskin, and Ocan Sankur. Compositional algorithms for succinct safety games. In Pavol Černý, Viktor Kuncak, and Madhusudan Parthasarathy, editors, *Proceedings Fourth Workshop on Synthesis (SYNT'15), San Francisco, CA, USA, 18th July 2015*, volume 202 of *Electronic Proceedings in Theoretical Computer Science*, pages 98–111. Open Publishing Association, 2016.

14. Franck Cassez, Alexandre David, Emmanuel Fleury, Kim Guldstrand Larsen, and Didier Lime. Efficient on-the-fly algorithms for the analysis of timed games. In *Proc. 16th International Conference on Concurrency Theory (CONCUR'05)*, volume 3653 of *Lecture Notes in Computer Science*, pages 66–80. Springer, 2005.

15. Franck Cassez, Peter Gjøl Jensen, and Kim Guldstrand Larsen. Verification and parameter synthesis for real-time programs using refinement of trace abstraction. *Fundam. Informaticae*, 178(1-2):31–57, 2021.

16. Alessandro Cimatti, Alberto Griggio, Enrico Magnago, Marco Roveri, and Stefano Tonetta. Extending nuxmv with timed transition systems and timed temporal properties. In *International Conference on Computer Aided Verification*, pages 376–386. Springer, 2019.

17. Alessandro Cimatti, Alberto Griggio, Sergio Mover, and Stefano Tonetta. IC3 modulo theories via implicit predicate abstraction. In *Proc. 20th International Conference on Tools and Algorithms for the Construction and Analysis of Systems (TACAS'14)*, volume 8413 of *Lecture Notes in Computer Science*, pages 46–61, 2014.

18. Edmund Clarke, Orna Grumberg, Somesh Jha, Yuan Lu, and Helmut Veith. Counterexample-guided abstraction refinement for symbolic model checking. *Journal of the ACM (JACM)*, 50(5):752–794, 2003.

19. Edmund M Clarke, Thomas A Henzinger, Helmut Veith, Roderick Bloem, et al. *Handbook of model checking*, volume 10. Springer, 2018.

20. Werner Damm, Henning Dierks, Stefan Disch, Willem Hagemann, Florian Pigorsch, Christoph Scholl, Uwe Waldmann, and Boris Wirtz. Exact and fully symbolic verification of linear hybrid automata with large discrete state spaces. *Science of Computer Programming*, 77(10):1122–1150, 2012.

21. Luca de Alfaro and Pritam Roy. Solving games via three-valued abstraction refinement. *Information and Computation*, 208(6):666–676, 2010. Special Issue: 18th International Conference on Concurrency Theory (CONCUR 2007).

22. Carole Delporte-Gallet, Stéphane Devismes, and Hugues Fauconnier. Robust stabilizing leader election. In Toshimitsu Masuzawa and Sébastien Tixeuil, editors, *Stabilization, Safety, and Security of Distributed Systems*, pages 219–233, Berlin, Heidelberg, 2007. Springer Berlin Heidelberg.

23. Rudiger Ehlers, Daniel Fass, Michael Gerke, and Hans-Jorg Peter. Fully symbolic timed model checking using constraint matrix diagrams. In *Proc. 31th IEEE Real-Time Systems Symposium (RTSS'10)*, pages 360–371. IEEE Computer Society Press, 2010.

24. Olga Grinchtein, Bengt Jonsson, and Martin Leucker. Learning of event-recording automata. *Theoretical Computer Science*, 411(47):4029–4054, 2010.

25. Matthias Heizmann, Jochen Hoenicke, and Andreas Podelski. Refinement of trace abstraction. In *International Static Analysis Symposium*, pages 69–85. Springer, 2009.

26. Thomas A Henzinger, Ranjit Jhala, and Rupak Majumdar. Counterexample-guided control. In *International Colloquium on Automata, Languages, and Programming*, pages 886–902. Springer, 2003.

27. Thomas A. Henzinger, Rupak Majumdar, Freddy Mang, and Jean-François Raskin. Abstract interpretation of game properties. In Jens Palsberg, editor, *Static Analysis*, pages 220–239, Berlin, Heidelberg, 2000. Springer Berlin Heidelberg.

28. Frédéric Herbreteau and Gérald Point. The TChecker tool and librairies. https://github.com/ticktac-project/tchecker.

29. Malte Isberner, Falk Howar, and Bernhard Steffen. The ttt algorithm: a redundancy-free approach to active automata learning. In *International Conference on Runtime Verification*, pages 307–322. Springer, 2014.
30. Malte Isberner, Falk Howar, and Bernhard Steffen. The open-source learnlib. In Daniel Kroening and Corina S. Păsăreanu, editors, *Computer Aided Verification*, pages 487–495, Cham, 2015. Springer International Publishing.
31. Swen Jacobs, Roderick Bloem, Romain Brenguier, Rüdiger Ehlers, Timotheus Hell, Robert Könighofer, Guillermo A Pérez, Jean-François Raskin, Leonid Ryzhyk, Ocan Sankur, et al. The first reactive synthesis competition (syntcomp 2014). *International journal on software tools for technology transfer*, 19(3):367–390, 2017.
32. Swen Jacobs, Guillermo A Perez, Remco Abraham, Veronique Bruyere, Michael Cadilhac, Maximilien Colange, Charly Delfosse, Tom van Dijk, Alexandre Duret-Lutz, Peter Faymonville, et al. The reactive synthesis competition (syntcomp): 2018-2021. *arXiv preprint arXiv:2206.00251*, 2022.
33. Roland Kindermann, Tommi Junttila, and Ilkka Niemela. Modeling for symbolic analysis of safety instrumented systems with clocks. In *Proc. 11th International Conference on Application of Concurrency to System Design (ACSD'11)*, pages 185–194. IEEE Computer Society Press, 2011.
34. Branislav Kusy and Sherif Abdelwahed. Ftsp protocol verification using spin. May 2006.
35. Shang-Wei Lin, Étienne André, Yang Liu, Jun Sun, and Jin Song Dong. Learning assumptions for compositional verification of timed systems. *Transactions on Software Engineering*, 40(2):137–153, mar 2014.
36. Gang Luo, G. von Bochmann, and A. Petrenko. Test selection based on communicating nondeterministic finite-state machines using a generalized wp-method. *IEEE Transactions on Software Engineering*, 20(2):149–162, 1994.
37. Oded Maler and Irini-Eleftheria Mens. Learning regular languages over large alphabets. In Erika Ábrahám and Klaus Havelund, editors, *Tools and Algorithms for the Construction and Analysis of Systems*, pages 485–499, Berlin, Heidelberg, 2014. Springer Berlin Heidelberg.
38. Oded Maler and Irini-Eleftheria Mens. A generic algorithm for learning symbolic automata from membership queries. In Luca Aceto, Giorgio Bacci, Giovanni Bacci, Anna Ingólfsdóttir, Axel Legay, and Radu Mardare, editors, *Models, Algorithms, Logics and Tools: Essays Dedicated to Kim Guldstrand Larsen on the Occasion of His 60th Birthday*, pages 146–169, Cham, 2017. Springer International Publishing.
39. Oded Maler, Amir Pnueli, and Joseph Sifakis. On the synthesis of discrete controllers for timed systems (an extended abstract). In *STACS*, pages 229–242, 1995.
40. Miklós Maróti, Branislav Kusy, Gyula Simon, and Ákos Lédeczi. The flooding time synchronization protocol. In *Proceedings of the 2Nd International Conference on Embedded Networked Sensor Systems*, SenSys '04, pages 39–49, New York, NY, USA, 2004. ACM.
41. A. I. McInnes. Model-checking the flooding time synchronization protocol. In *Control and Automation, 2009. ICCA 2009. IEEE International Conference on*, pages 422–429, Dec 2009.
42. Truong Khanh Nguyen, Jun Sun, Yang Liu, Jin Song Dong, and Yan Liu. Improved BDD-based discrete analysis of timed systems. In *Proc. 20th International Symposium on Formal Methods (FM'12)*, volume 7436, pages 326–340. Springer, 2012.

43. Corina S Păsăreanu, Dimitra Giannakopoulou, Mihaela Gheorghiu Bobaru, Jamieson M Cobleigh, and Howard Barringer. Learning to divide and conquer: applying the L* algorithm to automate assume-guarantee reasoning. *Formal Methods in System Design*, 32(3):175–205, 2008.
44. Hans-Jörg Peter, Rüdiger Ehlers, and Robert Mattmüller. Synthia: Verification and synthesis for timed automata. In *International Conference on Computer Aided Verification*, pages 649–655. Springer, 2011.
45. R.L. Rivest and R.E. Schapire. Inference of finite automata using homing sequences. *Information and Computation*, 103(2):299–347, 1993.
46. Victor Roussanaly, Ocan Sankur, and Nicolas Markey. Abstraction refinement algorithms for timed automata. In Isil Dillig and Serdar Tasiran, editors, *Computer Aided Verification (CAV'19)*, pages 22–40, Cham, 2019. Springer International Publishing.
47. Ocan Sankur. Artifact for the paper: Timed Automata Verification and Synthesis via Finite Automata Learning. https://doi.org/10.5281/zenodo.7487508, December 2022.
48. Ocan Sankur and Jean-Pierre Talpin. An abstraction technique for parameterized model checking of leader election protocols: Application to FTSP. In *Tools and Algorithms for the Construction and Analysis of Systems - 23rd International Conference, TACAS 2017, Held as Part of the European Joint Conferences on Theory and Practice of Software, ETAPS 2017, Uppsala, Sweden, April 22-29, 2017, Proceedings, Part I*, pages 23–40, 2017.
49. Sanjit A. Seshia and Randal E. Bryant. Unbounded, fully symbolic model checking of timed automata using boolean methods. In Warren A. Hunt and Fabio Somenzi, editors, *Computer Aided Verification*, pages 154–166, Berlin, Heidelberg, 2003. Springer Berlin Heidelberg.
50. Jun Sun, Yang Liu, Jin Song Dong, and Jun Pang. Pat: Towards flexible verification under fairness. In *Proceedings of the 21th International Conference on Computer Aided Verification (CAV'09)*, volume 5643 of *Lecture Notes in Computer Science*, pages 709–714. Springer, 2009.
51. Yann Thierry-Mieg. Symbolic model-checking using ITS-tools. In *Proc. 21st International Conference on Tools and Algorithms for the Construction and Analysis of Systems (TACAS'15)*, pages 231–237. Springer, 2015.
52. Wolfgang Thomas. On the synthesis of strategies in infinite games. In Ernst W. Mayr and Claude Puech, editors, *STACS 95*, pages 1–13, Berlin, Heidelberg, 1995. Springer Berlin Heidelberg.
53. Farn Wang. Symbolic verification of complex real-time systems with clock-restriction diagram. In *Proc. 21st International Conference on Formal Techniques for Networked and Distributed Systems (FORTE'01)*, volume 197 of *IFIP Conference Proceedings*, pages 235–250. Kluwer, 2001.
54. Weifeng Wang and Li Jiao. Trace abstraction refinement for timed automata. In Franck Cassez and Jean-François Raskin, editors, *Automated Technology for Verification and Analysis*, pages 396–410, Cham, 2014. Springer International Publishing.

Graphs/Probabilistic Systems

A Truly Symbolic Linear-Time Algorithm for SCC Decomposition

Casper Abild Larsen, Simon Meldahl Schmidt, Jesper Steensgaard,
Anna Blume Jakobsen, Jaco van de Pol[iD],
and Andreas Pavlogiannis[✉][iD]

Aarhus University, Aarhus, Denmark
{jaco,pavlogiannis}@cs.au.dk

Abstract. Decomposing a directed graph to its strongly connected components (SCCs) is a fundamental task in model checking. To deal with the state-space explosion problem, graphs are often represented *symbolically* using binary decision diagrams (BDDs), which have exponential compression capabilities. The theoretically-best symbolic algorithm for SCC decomposition is Gentilini et al's SKELETON algorithm, that uses $O(n)$ symbolic steps on a graph of n nodes. However, SKELETON uses $\Theta(n)$ symbolic objects, as opposed to (poly-)logarithmically many, which is the norm for symbolic algorithms, thereby relinquishing its symbolic nature. Here we present CHAIN, a new symbolic algorithm for SCC decomposition that also makes $O(n)$ symbolic steps, but further uses *logarithmic space*, and is thus *truly symbolic*. We then extend CHAIN to COLOREDCHAIN, an algorithm for SCC decomposition on *edge-colored graphs*, which arise naturally in model-checking a family of systems. Finally, we perform an experimental evaluation of CHAIN among other standard symbolic SCC algorithms in the literature. The results show that CHAIN is competitive on almost all benchmarks, and often faster, while it clearly outperforms all other algorithms on challenging inputs.

Keywords: Binary decision diagrams · Strongly connected components · Colored graphs

1 Introduction

Strongly connected components (SCCs) are one of the most elegant and widely applicable concepts of graph theory. They play a fundamental role in model checking for LTL and ω-regular properties, as most model-checking tasks reduce to locating cycles that traverse certain vertices in a graph [26], while strong fairness assumptions typically require an SCC decomposition at hand [21,31]. SCCs are also a key step to characterizing the attractor properties of systems, such as bottom SCCs in Markov Chains [2] and maximal end components in Markov Decision Processes [12]. From an algorithmic point of view, the simplest approach to SCC decomposition is by running a forward-backward reachability analysis

© The Author(s) 2023
S. Sankaranarayanan and N. Sharygina (Eds.): TACAS 2023, LNCS 13994, pp. 353–371, 2023.
https://doi.org/10.1007/978-3-031-30820-8_22

from each vertex, which results in $O(n^2)$ time on a graph of n vertices. The celebrated Tarjan's algorithm [28], and subsequently Dijkstra's algorithm [15] and Kosaraju-Sharir's algorithm [27] have reduced the complexity down to $O(n)$.

In the everyday practice of model checking, systems are represented as *symbolic*, rather than *explicit* graphs. One predominant symbolic representation is via (reduced/ordered) Binary Decision Diagrams (BDDs) [9], which are found at the core of many classic and modern model checkers [13,23,19,24,3]. BDDs can offer exponential compactness of the huge state space typically involved in the model-checking task, by succinctly encoding symmetries abundant in the represented system. On the other hand, this symbolic representation gives only coarse-grained efficient access to the graph. In particular, one can query for the image and preimage of a set of vertices with respect to the edge relation, which accounts for one *symbolic step*. Although the time for performing a symbolic step may vary, it is typically significantly larger than the time taken to perform elementary operations (e.g., incrementing a counter). As such, symbolic steps serve as the complexity measure of symbolic algorithms [8,18,11].

The simplest symbolic algorithm for SCC decomposition is the FWDBWD algorithm, which computes the SCC of a vertex u as the intersection of its forward and backward sets (as in the explicit setting). As this results in $O(n^2)$ time complexity, the algorithm is often too slow in practice. The key challenge towards efficient symbolic SCC algorithms is the seeming difficulty to traverse the input graph G in a depth-first fashion, which is the technical underpinning of the $O(n)$-time explicit SCC algorithms. Nevertheless, a series of improvements have been made in this direction: (i) a variant of FWDBWD was shown in [30] to run in time $O(\delta n)$, where δ is the diameter of G, and only becomes quadratic when $\delta = \Theta(n)$, (ii) the LOCKSTEP algorithm [7] has complexity $O(n \log n)$, while (iii) the SKELETON algorithm with complexity $O(n)$ is provably optimal [11]. Practical improvements based on heuristics have also been proposed [29,16,31].

One characteristic requirement for symbolic algorithms is that they operate in *logarithmic symbolic space*, i.e., they use logarithmically many objects, with the size of a single symbolic data structure (e.g., a BDD) counting as $O(1)$ [11]. Indeed, without this restriction, an algorithm could extract, and later analyze, an explicit representation of its input graph, thereby relinquishing its symbolic nature. Unfortunately, the theoretically optimal SKELETON algorithm uses $\Theta(n)$ space, thereby violating the logarithmic-space requirement. As such, we find that SKELETON is not truly symbolic, which also has a measurable effect: perhaps paradoxically, SKELETON is often the slowest algorithm in practice.

1.1 Our Contributions

The CHAIN algorithm. We present a new algorithm, CHAIN, for symbolically computing SCC decompositions. On input graph G with n vertices, CHAIN takes time $O(\sum_{S \in \mathrm{SCCs}(G)}(\delta(S) + 1)) = O(n)$, where $\mathrm{SCCs}(G)$ denotes the SCCs of G and $\delta(S)$ is the diameter of S. It is known that $\Omega(\sum_{S \in \mathrm{SCCs}(G)}(\delta(S) + 1))$ is also a lower bound for the problem [11], thus CHAIN is optimal. Moreover, CHAIN uses $O(\log n)$ symbolic data structures, thus being truly symbolic.

It is worth highlighting that CHAIN offers optimality while also being arguably the simplest among all symbolic SCC decomposition algorithms beyond FWDBWD. Indeed, CHAIN simply extends FWDBWD to accept as an argument a set of vertices K, among which to choose a pivot in the current recursive call. It is perhaps surprising that such a simple mechanism has been elusive for decades, as all previous efforts [30,7,17] relied on more elaborate procedures to either reduce or refine the $O(n^2)$ time bound. That being said, our new mechanism is somewhat insightful and with a non-trivial complexity analysis.

The COLOREDCHAIN algorithm. We extend CHAIN to COLOREDCHAIN for computing SCCs on edge-colored graphs, in which edges have colors, and SCCs are formed by restricting to monochromatic paths. Although a graph of p colors can be handled in $O(pn)$ time by breaking it to its monochromatic components and executing CHAIN on each of them, COLOREDCHAIN handles all colors simultaneously, thus benefiting from the symbolic compression of the edge relation across multiple colors. A similar approach was followed recently [6], by extending the standard LOCKSTEP algorithm [7] to colored graphs. However, the corresponding colored LOCKSTEP algorithm runs in time $O(pn \log n)$, as it inherits the $\log n$ factor from the basic LOCKSTEP algorithm.

Experimental evaluation. We implement and evaluate CHAIN in controlled, synthetic, and previously-used experimental settings. We find that CHAIN is never notably slower than other, standard algorithms, except when compared to LOCKSTEP on a few benchmarks. On the other hand, CHAIN is measurably faster than all other algorithms on demanding inputs. We further evaluate COLOREDCHAIN on colored Boolean Networks, used recently for the colored LOCKSTEP algorithm [6]. Our results indicate that COLOREDCHAIN is considerably faster than LOCKSTEP, making it a promising alternative for the analysis of Boolean networks.

2 Preliminaries

Here we set up our main notation on graphs, SCCs, and symbolic algorithms.

General notation. Given a natural number $\ell \in \mathbb{N}$, we let $[\ell] = \{1, 2, \ldots, \ell\}$.

Graphs. We consider (directed) graphs $G = (V, E)$, where V is a set of n vertices and $E \subseteq V \times V$ is a set of edges. Given a set $X \subseteq V$, the *restriction* of G on X is the graph $G[X] = (X, E \cap (X \times X))$. For a vertex v, we let $\mathrm{Pre}(v) = \{u : (u, v) \in E\}$ and $\mathrm{Post}(v) = \{u : (v, u) \in E\}$ denote the set of *preimage* and *image* of v under E, respectively. We lift this notation to sets of vertices X, by letting $\mathrm{Pre}(X) = \bigcup_{v \in X} \mathrm{Pre}(v)$ and $\mathrm{Post}(X) = \bigcup_{v \in X} \mathrm{Post}(v)$. A path from v to u in G is a sequence of vertices $P : v = w_1, w_2, \ldots, w_\ell = u$ such that, for each $i \in [\ell - 1]$, we have $(w_i, w_{i+1}) \in E$. The length of P is $|P| = \ell - 1$, while a single vertex v serves as a path of length 0. We denote by $v \rightsquigarrow u$ the existence of a path from v to u, and call u reachable from v if there is such a path in G. For a vertex $v \in V$, we let $\text{Fwd}(v)$ and $\text{Bwd}(v)$ denote the reflexive transitive closure of $\text{Post}(v)$ and $\text{Pre}(v)$, respectively. In other words, $\text{Fwd}(v)$ (resp., $\text{Bwd}(v)$) contains the vertices that are reachable from v (resp., can reach v). Given an additional set $X \subseteq V$, we let $\text{Fwd}(v, X)$ and $\text{Bwd}(v, X)$ denote the forward and backward, respectively, set of v in the graph $G[X]$. The distance from v to u is the length of the shortest path $v \rightsquigarrow u$, i.e., $d(v, u) = \min_{P:\, v \rightsquigarrow u} |P|$, where we take the minimum of an empty set to be ∞. The diameter of a set $X \subseteq V$ is $\delta(X) = \max_{v, u \in X, v \rightsquigarrow u} d(v, u)$, i.e., it is the maximum distance between any pair of vertices in X, provided that they are connected by a path.

Strongly connected components (SCCs). A set $X \subseteq V$ is strongly connected if, for every two vertices $v, u \in X$, we have $v \rightsquigarrow u$. A strongly connected component (SCC) of G is a maximal strongly connected set $S \subseteq V$. Given a vertex $v \in V$, we let $\text{SCC}(v)$ denote its SCC. We let $\text{SCCs}(G)$ denote the set of SCCs of G; note that $\text{SCCs}(G)$ induces a partitioning on V. A set $X \subseteq V$ is called *SCC-closed* if for every $S \in \text{SCCs}(G)$, we have either $S \subseteq X$ or $S \cap X = \emptyset$. In other words, for every $v \in X$, we have $\text{SCC}(v) \subseteq X$. We sometimes call $G[X]$ SCC-closed, to indicate that X is SCC-closed (in G).

Symbolic operations and complexity measures. We consider that graphs are represented *symbolically* using Binary Decision Diagrams (BDDs) [9]. The symbolic representation suggests that efficient access to the graph can only be carried out in a *coarse-grained* way. In particular, given a symbolically-represented set of vertices X, a *symbolic operation* on X is either $\text{Pre}(X)$ or $\text{Post}(X)$, and serves as the unit of time in measuring the time complexity of symbolic algorithms. As per standard, we also perform common set operations such as union, intersection, and difference, and use a specialized function $\text{Pick}(X)$ that returns an arbitrary vertex $u \in X$. This operation is natural in symbolic SCC algorithms, as typically one needs to identify a specific vertex u in order to output $\text{SCC}(u)$. In alignment with the symbolic time complexity, the symbolic space complexity of an algorithm is measured in number of (symbolic, or not) objects it uses. As symbolic representations usually allow (in the context they are designed for) large (and sometimes, even exponential) compression, we require symbolic algorithms to operate in logarithmic symbolic space [11].

3   The CHAIN Algorithm

In this section we present the main result of this paper: a new algorithm, called CHAIN, that runs in linear time and is truly symbolic (i.e., it uses $O(\log n)$ symbolic memory). In particular, we establish the following theorem.

Theorem 1. *Given a graph $G = (V, E)$ of n nodes CHAIN computes $\text{SCCs}(G)$ in $O(\sum_{S \in \text{SCCs}(G)}(\delta(S) + 1))$ symbolic time and $O(\log n)$ symbolic space.*

Note that $O(\sum_{S \in \text{SCCs}(G)}(\delta(S) + 1)) = O(n)$, as $\text{SCCs}(G)$ partition G, while for each $S \in \text{SCCs}(G)$ we have $\delta(S) \leq |S|$. It is worth observing that $O(\sum_{S \in \text{SCCs}(G)}(\delta(S) + 1))$ can, however, be much smaller than n: e.g., over cliques G, this bound becomes $O(1)$. On the other hand, it is known that $\Omega(\sum_{S \in \text{SCCs}(G)}(\delta(S)+1))$ is also a lower bound for the problem [11], hence Theorem 1 is tight. As was shown in [11], a more refined analysis of the SKELETON algorithm also achieves the time bound of Theorem 1. However, SKELETON suffers a linear space bound, and thus is not truly symbolic.

In the following, we first present CHAIN in detail in Section 3.1. It's correctness is relatively straightforward, and stated in Section 3.2. On the other hand, its complexity analysis is more involved, and is presented in Section 3.3.

3.1 Algorithm

Here we present CHAIN in detail, develop some intuition behind its time complexity, and illustrate its execution on a small example.

Algorithm 1: CHAIN

Input: A graph $G = (V, E)$, a vertex set $K \subseteq V$
1 **if** $V = \emptyset$ **then return**
2 **if** $K \neq \emptyset$ **then**   // Pick a pivot on the chain, if possible
3     $v = \text{Pick}(K)$
4 **else**
5     $v = \text{Pick}(V)$
6 $F = \emptyset$; Last $= \emptyset$; Layer $= \{v\}$; $S = \{v\}$
7 **while** Layer $\neq \emptyset$ **do**   // Compute $\text{Fwd}(v, V)$
8     $F = F \cup \text{Layer}$
9   Last $=$ Layer
10   Layer $= \text{Post}(\text{Layer}) \setminus F$
11 **while** $\text{Pre}(S) \cap F \nsubseteq S$ **do**   // Compute $\text{SCC}(v)$
12     $S = S \cup (\text{Pre}(S) \cap F)$
13 **output** S
14 CHAIN $(G[F \setminus S], \text{Last} \setminus S)$ // Recursive call on the forward set
15 CHAIN $(G[V \setminus F], \text{Pre}(S) \setminus F)$ // Recursive call on the rest
---

The CHAIN algorithm. Algorithm 1 presents CHAIN in pseudocode. The principle of operation of the algorithm is, perhaps, surprisingly simple. Given a $G = (V, E)$ and a pivot vertex v of G, the algorithm computes $\text{SCC}(v)$ in two phases, similarly to the standard FWDBWD algorithm. In particular:

1. The first phase computes $\text{Fwd}(v, V)$ (i.e., the forward set of v in V) as the least fixed point $F = \mu X.\{v\} \cup \text{Post}(X)$ (loop in Line 7).
2. The second phase outputs $\text{SCC}(v)$ by iteratively computing the least fixed point $S = \mu X.\{v\} \cup (\text{Pre}(X) \cap F)$ (loop in Line 11).
3. Finally, the computation proceeds recursively on the SCC-closed components $G[F \setminus S]$ and $G[V \setminus F]$ that partition $V \setminus S$ (Line 14 and Line 15).

However, in order to avoid the high complexity, CHAIN passes along each recursive call the K argument (initially $K = \emptyset$). This argument restricts the recursive call to pick its next pivot v such that $v \in K$; choosing the right set to pass as K makes the algorithm achieve its tight time complexity.

Conceptually, after $\mathrm{Fwd}(v, V)$ has been computed, the first recursive call (Line 14) chooses K to be the set of vertices that are of maximum distance from v (and not in $\mathrm{SCC}(v)$, as those are output in Line 13). On the other hand, the second recursive call (Line 15) chooses K to be the predecessors of $\mathrm{SCC}(v)$. Although the formal complexity analysis is somewhat involved (see Section 3.3), the key, high-level idea is as follows. When computing $\mathrm{Fwd}(v, V)$, the algorithm has taken a number of symbolic steps that is proportional to the maximum distance of a vertex from v. The chain of recursive calls starting in Line 14 and followed by all recursive calls in Line 15 until $\mathrm{Pre}(S) \cap F = \emptyset$, ensures that the algorithm will output all SCCs, in reverse order, along a maximal path from v to a vertex in $\mathrm{Fwd}(v, V) \setminus \mathrm{SCC}(v)$. This amortizes the high cost of computing $\mathrm{Fwd}(v, V)$ in the current call to the cost of outputting these SCCs in future calls, leading to only a constant factor increase in the overall complexity.

Besides viewing CHAIN as an augmentation of the FWDBWD algorithm with a restriction on pivots, the algorithm can also be seen as a simplification of the SKELETON algorithm [17]. Indeed, the computation of skeletons in the latter serves the exact purpose to force the recursion to output SCCs in the same order as in our chain argument above. As we show here, computing skeletons is redundant: dropping them makes the algorithm simpler, truly symbolic, while not sacrificing any of its time-complexity guarantees.

Example. Fig. 1 illustrates CHAIN on a graph $G = (V, E)$ (left). The tree T (right) represents the recursion of CHAIN as it outputs $\mathrm{SCCs}(G)$. We identify every vertex of T by a vertex $v \in V$ for which $\mathrm{SCC}(v)$ is computed in the corresponding step. We subscript variables of the algorithm with v to denote their value at that step. E.g., V_v denotes the vertex set in the recursive call that computed $\mathrm{SCC}(v)$, and F_v denotes the forward set computed after the loop of Line 7 has completed. The edges of T are labeled with the line that performed the respective recursive call.

The key observation for understanding the complexity of CHAIN is as follows. In the first step, the algorithm has paid the high cost of 5 symbolic steps to compute F_1, while its output is a small SCC of 2 vertices. However, the path $1 \xrightarrow{14} 6 \xrightarrow{15} 4 \xrightarrow{15} 3$ in T forms a chain from vertex 6, which is of maximum distance from 1, back to vertex 3 that is adjacent to $\mathrm{SCC}(1)$. The cost of computing F_1 can thus be amortized to outputting the SCCs along this chain (i.e., $\mathrm{SCC}(3)$, $\mathrm{SCC}(4)$, $\mathrm{SCC}(6)$), yielding only a linear overhead. As we prove in Section 3.3, this behavior is not accidental, but guaranteed in every recursive call.

3.2   Correctness

We start with the soundness of CHAIN, i.e., it only outputs SCCs of G.

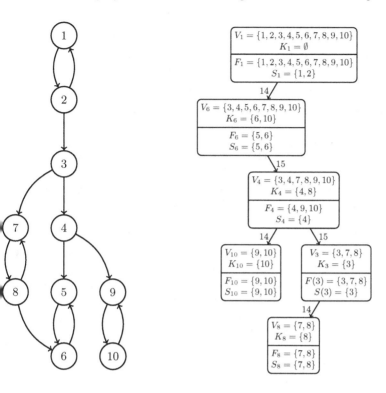

Fig. 1. An input graph (left), and the recursive computation of CHAIN (right).

Lemma 1. *In every call of* CHAIN, *Line 13 outputs an SCC of G.*

Proof. Consider any call to CHAIN on input $G' = (V', E'), K'$, with $K' \subseteq V'$. The algorithm first picks a vertex v from either V' or K', with $v \in S$, where S is the set outputted in Line 13. It is straightforward to see that, after the loop in Line 7 has executed, we have $F = \text{Fwd}(u, V')$, while after the loop in Line 11 has executed, we have $S = \text{Fwd}(u, V') \cap \text{Bwd}(u, V')$. It suffices to argue that G' is an SCC-closed subgraph of G, which implies that $S = \text{SCC}(v)$.

The statement is true initially, as $G' = G$. Now, assuming that the statement holds on some input $G' = (V', E'), K'$ we argue each of $G'[F \setminus S]$ and $G'[V' \setminus F]$, in Line 14 and Line 15, respectively, is SCC-closed. Indeed, F is closed under Post operations and thus SCC-closed. As S is an SCC of X, we have that $F \setminus S$ is also SCC closed. Since $F \setminus S$, S, and $V' \setminus F$ partition V', we have that $G'[V' \setminus F]$ is also SCC-closed. The desired result follows.   □

Lemma 2. CHAIN *outputs every SCC in* SCCs(G) *exactly once.*

Proof. The statement follows from the fact that, in every recursive call on input $G' = (V', E')$, the sets $F \setminus S$, S, and $V' \setminus F$ partition V'.   □

3.3   Complexity Analysis

We now present the (symbolic) time and space complexity analysis of CHAIN. For measuring time, we only count the number of $\text{Pre}(\cdot)$ and $\text{Post}(\cdot)$ operations.

Consider any input $G = (V, E)$, and let T be the recursion tree produced by the execution of CHAIN on G, as in Fig. 1. We will use lowercase (resp., uppercase) letters to refer to the vertices of G (resp., T), and we will subscript the variables of the algorithm with vertices of T (e.g., V_A) to refer to variables in the recursive call associated with the recursive step (at A). T has labeled directed edges $A \xrightarrow{f} B$, where $f \in \{14, 15\}$ denotes the line of the recursive call that made B a child of A in T. Without loss of generality, we consider that every vertex A of T corresponds to a recursive call with $V_A \neq \emptyset$.

Main complexity analysis. Consider an edge $A \xrightarrow{14} B$ in T, and the path $A \xrightarrow{14} B_1 \xrightarrow{15} B_2 \xrightarrow{15} \ldots \xrightarrow{15} B_k$, where B_k is the first vertex B for which $\text{Pre}(S_B) \setminus F_B = \emptyset$ in Line 15. Let $\text{Levels}(A)$ denote the number of iterations executing in Line 7, and note that $\text{Levels}(A) = \max_{u \in V_A} d(v_A, u)$. The crux of the complexity proof of CHAIN is the following lemma.

Lemma 3. $\text{Levels}(A) \leq \delta(\text{SCC}(v_A)) + 1 + \sum_{i \in [k]} (\delta(\text{SCC}(v_{B_i})) + 1)$.

Before we prove Lemma 3, we show how it leads to the complexity of Theorem 1. Given a vertex A of T, let $\mathcal{T}(A)$ denote the running time of CHAIN on the subtree of T rooted at A. Let $A \xrightarrow{14} B$ and $A \xrightarrow{15} C$ be the children of A, and the path $A \xrightarrow{14} B_1 \xrightarrow{15} B_2 \xrightarrow{15} \ldots \xrightarrow{15} B_k$ as defined above (thus $B_1 = B$). Then $\mathcal{T}(A)$ satisfies the following recurrence.

$$
\begin{aligned}
\mathcal{T}(A) &\leq \overbrace{\text{Levels}(v_A)}^{\text{loop in Line 7}} + \overbrace{\delta(\text{SCC}(v_A)) + 1}^{\text{loop in Line 11}} + \overbrace{\mathcal{T}(B)}^{\text{Line 14}} + \overbrace{1 + \mathcal{T}(C)}^{\text{Line 15}} \\
&\leq \sum_{i \in [k]} (\delta(\text{SCC}(v_{B_i})) + 1) + \delta(\text{SCC}(v_A)) + 1 \qquad \text{[Lemma 3]}\\
&\qquad + \delta(\text{SCC}(v_A)) + 1 + \mathcal{T}(B) + 1 + \mathcal{T}(C) \\
&= \sum_{i \in [k]} (\delta(\text{SCC}(v_{B_i})) + 1) + 2\delta(\text{SCC}(v_A)) + 3 + \mathcal{T}(B) + \mathcal{T}(C)
\end{aligned}
$$

For every i iterating in $\sum_{i \in [k]} (\delta(\text{SCC}(v_{B_i})) + 1)$, the vertex v_{B_i} will not appear in such a sum in any other vertex A' of T. Indeed assume towards contradiction that for some vertex B_i there are two vertices $A \neq A'$ and paths

$$
P : A \xrightarrow{14} B_1 \xrightarrow{15} B_2 \xrightarrow{15} \ldots \xrightarrow{15} B_i \quad \text{and} \quad P' : A' \xrightarrow{14} B'_1 \xrightarrow{15} B'_2 \xrightarrow{15} \ldots \xrightarrow{15} B'_i
$$

with $B'_i = B_i$. Due to the edge labels, none can be a sub-path of the other, which, in turn, contradicts the tree structure of T. Given such a vertex B_i, let $\mathcal{A}(B_i)$ denote its unique ancestor in T that appears as vertex A in the path P above.

The total running time of CHAIN on G is $\leq \sum_{B \in T}(3\delta(\text{SCC}(v_B))+4)$, obtained by counting for each vertex B of T (i) the $2\delta(\text{SCC}(v_B))+3$ symbolic operations from its own recursive call, plus (ii) $\delta(\text{SCC}(v_B))+1$ symbolic operations from the call at $\mathcal{A}(B)$. Hence the total number of symbolic steps is $O(\sum_{S \in \text{SCCs}(G)}(\delta(S)+1))$.

Proof of Lemma 3. We now turn our attention to the proof of Lemma 3. Consider again the path $A \xrightarrow{14} B_1 \xrightarrow{15} B_2 \xrightarrow{15} \ldots \xrightarrow{15} B_k$ of T as defined above. For simplicity of notation, let $v_i = v_{B_i}$, for $i \in [k]$. Clearly $\text{SCC}(v_i) \neq \text{SCC}(v_j)$ for $i \neq j$. We start with two simple lemmas.

Lemma 4. *For every* $i \in [k]$*, we have* $K_{B_i} \neq \emptyset$*.*

Proof. The statement holds for $i = 1$, since otherwise $\text{Last}_A \setminus S_A = \emptyset$, implying that $F_A \setminus S_A = V_{B_1} = \emptyset$, and thus B_1 would not be a vertex of T. The statement also holds for all $i > 1$, by construction of the path to B_k. □

Lemma 5. *For all* $i \in [k-1]$*, we have* $v_i \in \text{Fwd}(v_k)$*.*

Proof. The lemma follows from the more general statement that $v_i \in \text{Fwd}(v_{i+1})$. Indeed, by Lemma 4, we have that $v_{i+1} \in \text{Pre}(S_{B_i})$, while $S_{B_i} = \text{SCC}(v_i)$. □

We call a vertex u *critical* if it is the first vertex w in a path from v_A to v_k in V_A, such that $w \notin \text{SCC}(v_A)$. We further call a path $u \rightsquigarrow v_k$ *critical* if u is a critical vertex. In the example of Fig. 1, for the first call to CHAIN, where $v_A = 1$, vertex 3 is a critical vertex and the path $3 \to 4 \to 5 \to 6$ is a critical path. The following lemma captures the fact that every recursive call B_i is performed on a vertex set V_{B_i} that is adjacent to $\text{SCC}(v_A)$.

Lemma 6. *For all* $i \in [k]$*, the set* V_{B_i} *has a critical path.*

Proof. The proof follows induction on i. For $i = 1$, we have $V_{B_1} = \text{Fwd}(v_A, V_A) \setminus \text{SCC}(v_A)$. Since $A \xrightarrow{14} B_1$ in T, we have $\text{Fwd}(v_A, V_A) \setminus \text{SCC}(v_A) = V_{B_1} \neq \emptyset$, thus the statement holds for $i = 1$. Now assume that the statement holds for some $i \geq 1$, and we argue that it holds for $i + 1$. Take any critical path $P: u \rightsquigarrow v_k$ in V_{B_i}, and assume towards contradiction that P is not a path in $V_{B_{i+1}}$ (i.e., at least one vertex of P is outside $V_{B_{i+1}}$). Since $V_{B_{i+1}} = V_{B_i} \setminus \text{Fwd}(v_i, V_{B_i})$, we obtain that P has a vertex w with $w \in \text{Fwd}(v_i, V_{B_i})$, and hence $v_k \in \text{Fwd}(v_i)$. By Lemma 5, we also have $v_i \in \text{Fwd}(v_k)$, thus $\text{SCC}(v_i) = \text{SCC}(v_k)$, violating the choices of v_i. Thus $V_{B_{i+1}}$ has a critical path. □

Specifically for the case $i = k$, the following is a strengthening of Lemma 6, showing that $\text{SCC}(v_k)$ (only a subset of V_{B_k}) is also adjacent to $\text{SCC}(v_A)$.

Lemma 7. $\text{SCC}(v_k)$ *contains a critical vertex.*

Proof. By Lemma 6, we have a critical path $u \rightsquigarrow v_k$ in V_{B_k}. By construction, $(\text{Pre}(\text{SCC}(v_k)) \cap V_{B_k}) \setminus \text{SCC}(v_k) = \emptyset$, thus $u \in \text{SCC}(v_k)$. □

Let v_{k+1} be a critical vertex in $\mathrm{SCC}(v_k)$, whose existence is guaranteed by Lemma 7. Given a vertex $u \in V_A$, we write $\ell(u)$ for the distance of u from v_A in V_A. Note that $\mathrm{Levels}(A) = \ell(v_1)$. Observe that for all $u, v \in V_A$, if $u \in \mathrm{SCC}(v)$ then $\ell(u) - \ell(v) \leq \delta(\mathrm{SCC}(v))$. The following two lemmas relate the distances $\ell(v_i)$ with the diameters of SCCs, and lead to the proof of Lemma 3.

Lemma 8. *We have* $\ell(v_{k+1}) \leq \delta(\mathrm{SCC}(v_A)) + 1$.

Proof. By definition, there is a vertex $w \in \mathrm{Pre}(v_{k+1}) \cap \mathrm{SCC}(v_A)$. We have $\ell(w) \geq \ell(v_{k+1}) - 1$, while $\ell(w) \leq \delta(\mathrm{SCC}(v_A))$, hence $\ell(v_{k+1}) \leq \delta(\mathrm{SCC}(v_A)) + 1$.   □

Lemma 9. *For every* $i \in [k]$, *we have* $\ell(v_i) - \ell(v_{i+1}) \leq \delta(\mathrm{SCC}(v_i)) + 1$.

Proof. The statement holds trivially when $\ell(v_i) \leq \ell(v_{i+1})$. Now consider the case that $\ell(v_i) > \ell(v_{i+1})$. If $i = k$, then by our choice of v_{k+1}, we have $v_{i+1} \in \mathrm{SCC}(v_i)$, thus $\ell(v_i) - \ell(v_{i+1}) \leq \delta(\mathrm{SCC}(v_i))$. Now consider that $i < k$. By construction, there is a vertex $w \in \mathrm{SCC}(v_i) \cap \mathrm{Post}(v_{i+1})$. Then $\ell(v_i) - \ell(w) \leq \delta(\mathrm{SCC}(v_i))$, while $\ell(w) \leq \ell(v_{i+1}) + 1$, resulting in $\ell(v_i) - \ell(v_{i+1}) \leq \delta(\mathrm{SCC}(v_i)) + 1$.   □

Proof (of Lemma 3).

$$
\begin{aligned}
\mathrm{Levels}(A) = \ell(v_1) &= \sum_{i \in [k]} (\ell(v_i) - \ell(v_{i+1})) + \ell(v_{k+1}) && \text{[algebra]} \\
&\leq \sum_{i \in [k]} (\ell(v_i) - \ell(v_{i+1})) + \delta(\mathrm{SCC}(v_A)) + 1 && \text{[Lemma 8]} \\
&\leq \sum_{i \in [k]} (\delta(\mathrm{SCC}(v_i)) + 1) + \delta(\mathrm{SCC}(v_A)) + 1 && \text{[Lemma 9]}
\end{aligned}
$$

□

Space complexity. Finally, we address the $O(\log n)$ symbolic-space complexity of Theorem 1. CHAIN uses $O(1)$ symbolic sets in each recursive call. To achieve the $O(\log n)$ bound, it suffices to first follow the recursive call between Line 14 and Line 15 with the smaller graph input. This results in $O(\log n)$ pending recursive calls at any step of the execution, leading to storing $O(\log n)$ symbolic sets overall. Note that this requires a function $\mathrm{Count}(X)$ that returns the size of a symbolically represented set X. This is not a problem: BDDs are equipped with such operations, and their complexity is only linear in the size of the *representation* of X, even though X might be exponentially large.

4   Extension to Colored Graphs

In this section we turn our attention to colored graphs, where the edge relation is parameterized by colors, and SCCs are formed with respect to monochromatic components of the graph. Each edge color stands for a different binary relation, and all colors together allow to superpose several graphs on top of each other. Although each monochromatic graph could be represented in isolation, this superpositioning allows for an efficient symbolic representation, especially when the edge relations are highly similar. In turn, this asks for efficient symbolic algorithms that are able to exploit similarities between colors. Our study of this setting is inspired by the recent extension of LOCKSTEP to colored graphs [6].

4.1   Edge-Colored Graphs

Here we lift some of our graph notation from Section 2 to the colored setting.

Colored graphs. An edge-colored graph $G = (V, C, E)$ consists of a set of n vertices V, a set of p colors C, and an edge relation $E \subseteq V \times C \times V$. Given a color $c \in C$, we let $G_c = (V, E_c)$ be the *projection* of G on c, where $E_c = E \cap (V \times \{c\} \times V)$ restricts the edge relation to color c. Given two vertices $v, u \in V$, we write $v \overset{c}{\rightsquigarrow} u$ to denote that there is a path $v \rightsquigarrow u$ in G_c, and say that u is c-reachable from v in G. A *colored vertex set* is a set $X \subseteq V \times C$. The *restriction* of G on X is the colored graph $G[X] = (V', C', E')$, where (i) $V' = \{v : \exists c \in C.(v, c) \in X)\}$, (ii) $C' = \{c : \exists v \in V.(v, c) \in X\}$, and (iii) $E' = \{(u, c, v) : (u, c), (v, c) \in X\}$. Given such a set X, we let $\mathrm{Pre}(X) = \{(u, c) : \exists (v, c) \in X.(u, c, v) \in E\}$, and $\mathrm{Post}(X) = \{(u, c) : \exists (v, c) \in X.(v, c, u) \in E\}$. We call a set $\mathcal{V} \subseteq V \times C$ *degenerate* if for all $c \in \mathrm{Colors}$, we have $|\mathcal{V} \cap (V \times \{c\})| \leq 1$, i.e., $\mathcal{V}$ has at most one vertex per color. Given a degenerate set $\mathcal{V}$, we let $\mathrm{Fwd}(\mathcal{V}) = \{(v, c) : \exists (u, c) \in \mathcal{V} \text{ and } u \overset{c}{\rightsquigarrow} v\}$, i.e., it is the set of colored vertices reached by each colored vertex in $\mathcal{V}$. We similarly let $\mathrm{Bwd}(\mathcal{V}) = \{(v, c) : \exists (u, c) \in \mathcal{V} \text{ and } v \overset{c}{\rightsquigarrow} u\}$. Note that for degenerate sets, Fwd (Bwd) is the transitive closure of Post (Pre). Further, given a colored vertex set X, we let $\mathrm{Fwd}(\mathcal{V}, X)$ (resp., $\mathrm{Bwd}(\mathcal{V}, X)$) be the set of colored vertices reached by (resp., reaching) each colored vertex in $\mathcal{V}$ in the subgraph $G[X]$.

Colored SCCs. Given a colored graph $G = (V, C, E)$, a c-colored SCC of G is a pair $S = (R, c) \subseteq V \times \{c\}$ such that R is an SCC of G_c. Given a vertex $v \in V$ and a color $c \in C$, we write $\mathrm{SCC}(v, c)$ for the SCC of v in G_c. We let $\mathrm{SCCs}(G)$ denote the set of SCCs of G, and observe that $\mathrm{SCCs}(G)$ partitions $V \times C$. A set $X \subseteq V \times C$ is *SCC-closed* if for every color $c \in C$, the set $X \cap (V \times \{c\})$ is SCC closed in G_c. Given an SCC-closed set X, we will also call $G[X]$ SCC-closed. Given a degenerate set $\mathcal{V}$, we write $\mathrm{SCC}(\mathcal{V})$ for the set of SCCs $\{(R, c) : (v, c) \in \mathcal{V} \text{ and } R = \mathrm{SCC}(v) \text{ in } G_c\}$.

Symbolic operations. Similarly to the non-colored setting, we use symbolic operations $\mathrm{Pre}(X)$ and $\mathrm{Post}(X)$ on sets $X \subseteq V \times C$, which incur a unit time cost. We further perform unions, intersections and differences on subsets of $V \times C$, and use a specialized operation $\mathrm{Pick}(X)$ that returns an arbitrary pair $(v, c) \in X$. Finally, we consider at our disposal a function $\mathrm{Pivots}(X)$, that acts on sets $X \subseteq V \times C$ and returns a maximal degenerate subset of X containing one pair (v, c) per color c appearing in X. This operation can be performed by combining Pick with basic set operations, and has also appeared in other works [6].

4.2   The COLOREDCHAIN Algorithm

Here we present our extension of CHAIN for handling edge colored graphs.

Algorithm 2: COLOREDCHAIN

Input: A graph $G = (V, C, E)$, two colored vertex sets $X, K \subseteq V \times C$,

1 **if** $X = \emptyset$ **then return**
2 $\mathcal{V} = \text{Pivots}(K \cup (X \setminus (V \times \text{Colors}(K))))$ // A degenerate set of pivots
3 $F = \emptyset; \text{Last} = \emptyset; \text{Layer} = \mathcal{V}; S = \mathcal{V}$
4 **while** $\text{Layer} \neq \emptyset$ **do**   // Compute $\text{Fwd}(\mathcal{V}, X)$
5     $F = F \cup \text{Layer}$
6     $\text{Last} = \text{Layer} \cup (\text{Last} \setminus (V \times \text{Colors}(\text{Layer})))$
7     $\text{Layer} = \text{Post}(\text{Layer}) \setminus F$
8 **while** $\text{Pre}(S) \cap F \not\subseteq S$ **do**   // Compute $\text{SCC}(\mathcal{V})$
9     $S = S \cup (\text{Pre}(S) \cap F)$
10 **output** S
11 COLOREDCHAIN $(G[F \setminus S], F \setminus S, \text{Last} \setminus S)$
12 COLOREDCHAIN $(G[X \setminus F], X \setminus F, \text{Pre}(S) \setminus F)$

The COLOREDCHAIN algorithm. Algorithm 2 presents COLOREDCHAIN in pseudocode. The algorithm takes as input an edge-colored graph $G = (V, C, E)$, as well as two colored vertex sets X and K (initially $X = V \times \text{Colors}$ and $K = \emptyset$). In words, the current and future recursive steps will compute the colored SCCs of G that are subsets of X. The set K serves the same purpose as in the basic CHAIN algorithm, i.e., to restrict the set of vertices over which we select pivots in the current recursive call, towards the linear-time properties of the algorithm. The algorithm starts by selecting a degenerate set of pivots $\mathcal{V}$ in Line 2, with the goal to output each $\text{SCC}(v, c)$, for $(v, c) \in \mathcal{V}$ in the current recursive step. The pivot set is constructed to contain one pair (v, c) for every color c present in X. If c is also present in K, then the algorithm selects a pivot $(v, c) \in K$, otherwise, it chooses an arbitrary pivot from X. The algorithm then computes $\text{SCC}(\mathcal{V})$ as $\text{Fwd}(\mathcal{V}, X) \cap \text{Bwd}(\mathcal{V}, X)$, similarly to the non-colored case (where $\mathcal{V}$ is simply a non-colored vertex). In the i-th iteration of the loop of Line 4, the variable Last contains the vertices (u, c) that have maximum distance $\leq i$ from $(v, c) \in \mathcal{V}$. As these maximal distances might converge at different lengths for different colors, extra care is taken in Line 6 to maintain the converged colors in the next iteration. Finally, the algorithm outputs $\text{SCC}(\mathcal{V})$ (Line 10), and proceeds recursively on the disjoint subsets $F \setminus S$ and $X \setminus F$ (Line 11 and Line 12). The K argument is passed on each recursive call in the same way as in the CHAIN algorithm, so that, in effect, the time taken to compute F is amortized by the time to output colored SCCs in subsequent recursive calls (where now the amortization also takes place among colors). Observe that, in the special case of $p = 1$ color, COLOREDCHAIN operates identically to CHAIN.

Correctness and complexity. Due to the similarity of COLOREDCHAIN to CHAIN, we will only sketch the main arguments for its correctness and complexity. The key observation for correctness is that each recursive call processes an

SCC-closed subgraph of G. Indeed, given an SCC-closed colored vertex set X, for any vertex $(v, c) \in X$, we have $\mathrm{SCC}(v, c) = \mathrm{Fwd}(\{(v, c)\}, X) \cap \mathrm{Bwd}(\{(v, c)\}, X)$. Hence $S = \mathrm{SCC}(\mathcal{V})$ in Line 10. As $F \cup S$ is closed under Post operations and S is an SCC of X, we have $F \setminus S$ (and thus also $X \setminus F$) is SCC closed.

The complexity of COLOREDCHAIN is $O(\sum_{S \in \mathrm{SCCs}(G)}(\delta(S) + 1)) = O(pn)$, as every vertex v belongs to exactly one $\mathrm{SCC}(v, c)$ for each color $c \in C$. This bound follows from amortizing the number of iterations of the loop in Line 4 to the diameter of a color that converges last in the loop. Observe that the computation on the remaining colors comes "for free". This is the benefit of treating all colors symbolically (as opposed to each monochromatic graph G_c separately). The same observation holds for the while loop in Line 8.

5 Experiments

In this section we report our experimental evaluation of the new algorithms CHAIN and COLOREDCHAIN on three classes of benchmarks. We compared their performance to the standard algorithms FWDBWD [30], LOCKSTEP [7] (and its recent colored variant [6]) and SKELETON [17]. Our experiments were run on a Linux machine with 2.4GHz CPU speed and 60GB of memory (using 1 core).

5.1 Experiments on Synthetic Benchmarks

To better illustrate the behavior of the various algorithms, we start with a controlled setting of synthetic benchmarks.

Setup. We performed a controlled experiment on product graphs $G_k^i = \mathcal{L}_{k-i} \times \mathcal{C}_i$, where $\mathcal{L}_j$ (resp, $\mathcal{C}_j$) denotes a line graph (resp., cycle graph) of size 2^j. This setup follows [4]. Observe that G_k^i has 2^{k-i} SCCs, of size (and diameter) 2^i each. Our implementation is in C++ and based on the Sylvan BDD library [14]. Recall that the behavior of each algorithm depends on the non-determinism involved in the Pick operation, that returns an arbitrary vertex of a given vertex set. Sylvan returns the vertex with the smallest (binary encoded) ID. We generated two variants of this setting: one in which vertex IDs follow an incremental order in each graph component, and one in which they are uniformly random.

Results. Fig. 2 shows the number of symbolic steps per algorithm, for graphs G_{10}^i, $i \in \{0\} \cup [10]$. When the vertex encoding follows sequential IDs (left), FWDBWD exhibits its worst-case $\Theta(n^2)$ performance on graphs with many SCCs (i.e., small i) as it repeatedly Pick's pivots with large forward sets. As i increases, the number of SCCs decreases, and FWDBWD eventually terminates in the first call (for $i = 10$). On the other hand, the other algorithms exhibit almost identical, $O(n)$ performance. In particular, every recursive call of LOCKSTEP Pick's a vertex v whose backward set equals $\mathrm{SCC}(v)$; thus the algorithm convergences in a number of steps that is proportional to $\delta(\mathrm{SCC}(v))$, leading to $\Theta(n)$ performance. Finally, after the first call, SKELETON and CHAIN output SCCs in the

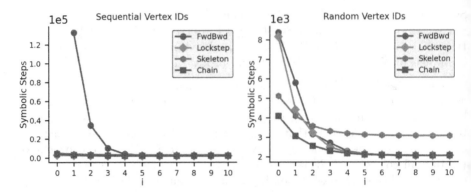

Fig. 2. Experimental results on product graphs $G_{10}^i = \mathcal{L}_{10-i} \times \mathcal{C}_i$.

reverse order of FwDBwD, performing in each step a number of symbolic steps that is proportional to the diameter of the SCC, like LOCKSTEP.

When the vertex encoding follows random IDs (right), every recursive call of FwDBwD and LOCKSTEP Pick's a pivot whose first component is roughly in the middle of the line segment that is processed in that call. Hence the two algorithms have similar performance, which follows $\Theta(n \log n)$ behavior for large lines (i.e., when i is small). On the other hand, SKELETON and CHAIN spend $O(\sum_{S \in \text{SCCs}(G)}(\delta(S) + 1))$ symbolic steps. Naturally, for larger lines, the two algorithms spend more steps for computing the forward sets of their pivots, a cost that is amortized in later recursive calls by a constant factor. Observe, however, that SKELETON pays a larger constant factor, as the construction of skeletons requires the forward sets to also be traversed backwards. This results in SKELETON having the worst performance relative to the other algorithms when the number of SCCs decreases (i.e., as i gets larger), as there are fewer recursive calls to amortize the high cost of skeleton computation. Finally, we remark that for small and large i, SKELETON constructs (in expectation) $\Theta(n)$ BDDs, hence this is a family of graphs exposing the non-symbolic nature of the algorithm.

5.2 Experiments on Uncolored Graphs

To better understand the performance of the various algorithms in the wild, we continue with their evaluation on standard model-checking benchmarks.

Setup. We considered benchmarks from the following categories:

- 1-safe Petri Net models from MCC, the Model Checking Contest [22].
- DiVinE models from BEEM, the Benchmark of Explicit Models [25].

In order to create equal experimental circumstances for all models, we used the language-independent model checker LTSmin [19] to generate the disjunctively partitioned symbolic transition relations for all these models. As symbolic representation, we chose the multi-core BDD package Sylvan [14]. We implemented all four algorithms of the previous section inside LTSmin. We disregarded graphs

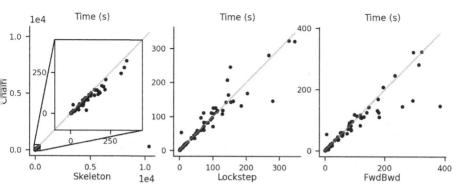

Fig. 3. Experimental results on PNML and DiVinE models.

of size $< 10^4$, as such graphs are handled more efficiently by explicit algorithms. This led to a pool of 101 benchmarks. We measured the average time (across three runs) each algorithm took on each benchmark, while discarding the overhead due to state-space generation.

Results. Fig. 3 shows the running times of CHAIN against SKELETON, LOCKSTEP and FWDBWD. Compared to the only other theoretically optimal algorithm SKELETON, CHAIN is almost always somewhat faster, with the exception of one benchmark on which CHAIN is an order of magnitude faster. When compared to LOCKSTEP, we find the two algorithms to be incomparable, with CHAIN being slower on some benchmarks but faster on others. Indeed, we expect that LOCKSTEP behaves adequately in most practical scenarios, while its $\log n$ slowdown (as demonstrated in Section 5.1) is witnessed only rarely. Finally, we find that CHAIN is measurably and consistently equally-or-better performing than FWDBWD.

5.3 Experiments on Colored Graphs

Finally, we turn our attention to colored graphs. We used models of discrete control systems representing Biological Genetic Networks [20]. In high level, a Boolean Network (BN) is defined by a set of Boolean variables $X = \{x_1, \ldots, x_k\}$ and update functions of the form $x_i := \varphi_i$, where each φ_i is a Boolean combination over variables X. State updates are performed by nondeterministic applications of the functions φ_i. In Colored Boolean Networks (CBNs), uninterpreted function symbols are used to represent uncertainty. For instance, $x_1 := x_2 \wedge f(x_3, x_4)$ represents that x_1 has a positive dependence on x_2 and an unknown dependence on x_3 and x_4. A single color corresponds to an assignment of Boolean functions to the uninterpreted function symbols. The set of colors is further restricted by constraints representing biological knowledge. This setting is inspired by its use to evaluate the recently introduced colored LOCKSTEP [6].

Setup. We implemented our new COLOREDCHAIN-algorithm in Scala, using JavaBDD (wrapping the classical BDD package BuDDy) with recommended

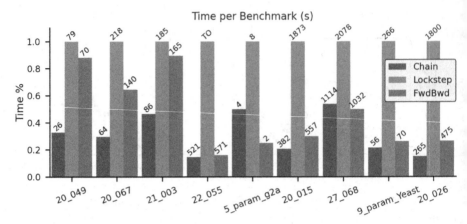

Fig. 4. Experimental results on colored graphs from AEON models (seconds).

settings. We also reimplemented colored LOCKSTEP from [6] (without preprocessing) and FWDBWD in Scala/JavaBDD. We used the CBNs coming from the GINsim Boolean network database [10], represented in the AEON format that supported the experiments in [6], accessed at [1]. We focused on benchmarks with $np \geq 10^4$, as the rest were run in < 0.2s by all algorithms. We remark that most of these CBNs generate huge graphs; for the purposes of our evaluation, we timed our experiments within 1h, which yielded a pool of 9 benchmarks.

Results. Fig. 4 shows the running time of each of the three algorithms. Perhaps surprisingly, LOCKSTEP is consistently the slowest and by a large margin. On the other hand, COLOREDCHAIN was always considerably faster than LOCKSTEP, and consistently the fastest algorithm overall. The two exceptions are on the CBNs 5_param_g2a and 27_068, where FWDBWD finished first in 2s and 1032s (as opposed to 4s and 1114s for COLOREDCHAIN). On the other hand, FWDBWD was considerably slower than COLOREDCHAIN in some CBNs (e.g., 20_049). Although a wider experimental setting is required for conclusive results, our evaluation indicates that COLOREDCHAIN is very effective in handling CBNs.

6 Conclusion

We have introduced CHAIN, a new, truly symbolic, and time-optimal algorithm for SCC decomposition. The simplicity of CHAIN makes it theoretically elegant, while our experimental evaluation demonstrates a potential for practical impact. Some opportunities for future research include introducing saturation techniques [31] to CHAIN, as well as specializing it to the computation of bottom SCCs, which have received special attention [5].

Acknowledgements. This work was supported in part by Villum Fonden (Project VIL42117).

References

1. AEON models repository (2022), https://github.com/sybila/biodivine-lib-par am-bn/tree/lmcs, Last accessed on 2022-10-01
2. Abraham, E., Jansen, N., Wimmer, R., Katoen, J.P., Becker, B.: DTMC model checking by SCC reduction. In: Proceedings of the 2010 Seventh International Conference on the Quantitative Evaluation of Systems. p. 37–46. QEST '10, IEEE Computer Society, USA (2010). https://doi.org/10.1109/QEST.2010.13
3. Amparore, E.G., Donatelli, S., Gallà, F.: starMC: an automata based CTL* model checker. PeerJ Comput. Sci. **8**, e823 (2022)
4. Barnat, J., Chaloupka, J., van de Pol, J.: Distributed algorithms for SCC decomposition. J. Log. Comput. **21**(1), 23–44 (2011)
5. Benes, N., Brim, L., Pastva, S., Safránek, D.: Computing bottom SCCs symbolically using transition guided reduction. In: Silva, A., Leino, K.R.M. (eds.) Computer Aided Verification, CAV 2021, Part I. LNCS, vol. 12759, pp. 505–528. Springer (2021). https://doi.org/10.1007/978-3-030-81685-8_24
6. Benes, N., Brim, L., Pastva, S., Safránek, D.: BDD-based algorithm for SCC decomposition of edge-coloured graphs. Logical Methods in Computer Science **18**(1) (2022). https://doi.org/10.46298/lmcs-18(1:38)2022
7. Bloem, R., Gabow, H.N., Somenzi, F.: An algorithm for strongly connected component analysis in n log n symbolic steps. Formal Methods in System Design **28**(1), 37–56 (2006)
8. Bloem, R., Ravi, K., Somenzi, F.: Efficient decision procedures for model checking of linear time logic properties. In: Proceedings of the 11th International Conference on Computer Aided Verification. p. 222–235. CAV '99, Springer (1999)
9. Bryant, R.E.: Symbolic Boolean manipulation with ordered binary-decision diagrams. ACM Comput. Surv. **24**(3), 293–318 (1992)
10. Chaouiya, C., Naldi, A., Thieffry, D.: Logical modelling of gene regulatory networks with GINsim. Bacterial Molecular Networks p. 463–479 (2012). https://doi.org/10.1007/978-1-61779-361-5_23
11. Chatterjee, K., Dvořák, W., Henzinger, M., Loitzenbauer, V.: Lower bounds for symbolic computation on graphs: Strongly connected components, liveness, safety, and diameter. In: Proc. 29th ACM-SIAM Symp. on Discrete Algorithms. p. 2341–2356. SODA '18, Soc. for Industrial and Applied Mathematics, USA (2018)
12. Chatterjee, K., Henzinger, M.: Faster and dynamic algorithms for maximal end-component decomposition and related graph problems in probabilistic verification. In: Proc. 22nd ACM-SIAM Symp. on Discrete Algorithms. p. 1318–1336. SODA '11, Society for Industrial and Applied Mathematics, USA (2011)
13. Cimatti, A., Clarke, E.M., Giunchiglia, E., Giunchiglia, F., Pistore, M., Roveri, M., Sebastiani, R., Tacchella, A.: Nusmv 2: An opensource tool for symbolic model checking. In: CAV. LNCS, vol. 2404, pp. 359–364. Springer (2002)
14. van Dijk, T., van de Pol, J.: Sylvan: multi-core framework for decision diagrams. Int. Journal on Software Tools for Technology Transfer **19**(6), 675–696 (2017)
15. Dijkstra, E.W.: A Discipline of Programming. Prentice Hall PTR, USA, 1st edn. (1997)
16. Fisler, K., Fraer, R., Kamhi, G., Vardi, M.Y., Yang, Z.: Is there a best symbolic cycle-detection algorithm? In: Proc. 7th IC on Tools and Algorithms for the Construction and Analysis of Systems. p. 420–434. TACAS 2001, Springer (2001)

17. Gentilini, R., Piazza, C., Policriti, A.: Computing strongly connected components in a linear number of symbolic steps. In: Proceedings of the Fourteenth Annual ACM-SIAM Symposium on Discrete Algorithms. p. 573–582. SODA '03, Society for Industrial and Applied Mathematics, USA (2003)

18. Hardin, R.H., Kurshan, R.P., Shukla, S.K., Vardi, M.Y.: A new heuristic for bad cycle detection using BDDs. Form. Methods Syst. Des. **18**(2), 131–140 (mar 2001). https://doi.org/10.1023/A:1008727508722

19. Kant, G., Laarman, A., Meijer, J., van de Pol, J., Blom, S., van Dijk, T.: LTSmin: High-performance language-independent model checking. In: TACAS. Lecture Notes in Computer Science, vol. 9035, pp. 692–707. Springer (2015)

20. Kauffman, S.A.: Metabolic stability and epigenesis in randomly constructed genetic nets. Journal of Theoretical Biology **22**(3), 437–67 (1969). https://doi.org/10.1016/0022-5193(69)90015-0

21. Kesten, Y., Pnueli, A., Raviv, L., Shahar, E.: Model checking with strong fairness. Formal Methods Syst. Des. **28**(1), 57–84 (2006)

22. Kordon, F., Garavel, H., Hillah, L., Paviot-Adet, E., Jezequel, L., Hulin-Hubard, F., Amparore, E.G., Beccuti, M., Berthomieu, B., Evrard, H., Jensen, P.G., Botlan, D.L., Liebke, T., Meijer, J., Srba, J., Thierry-Mieg, Y., van de Pol, J., Wolf, K.: MCC'2017 - the seventh model checking contest. Trans. Petri Nets Other Model. Concurr. **13**, 181–209 (2018)

23. Kwiatkowska, M.Z., Norman, G., Parker, D.: PRISM 4.0: Verification of probabilistic real-time systems. In: CAV. Lecture Notes in Computer Science, vol. 6806, pp. 585–591. Springer (2011)

24. Lomuscio, A., Qu, H., Raimondi, F.: MCMAS: an open-source model checker for the verification of multi-agent systems. Int. J. Softw. Tools Technol. Transf. **19**(1), 9–30 (2017)

25. Pelánek, R.: BEEM: benchmarks for explicit model checkers. In: SPIN. Lecture Notes in Computer Science, vol. 4595, pp. 263–267. Springer (2007)

26. Schwoon, S., Esparza, J.: A note on on-the-fly verification algorithms. In: TACAS. Lecture Notes in Computer Science, vol. 3440, pp. 174–190. Springer (2005)

27. Sharir, M.: A strong-connectivity algorithm and its applications in data flow analysis. Computers & Mathematics with Applications **7**(1), 67–72 (1981). https://doi.org/https://doi.org/10.1016/0898-1221(81)90008-0

28. Tarjan, R.: Depth-first search and linear graph algorithms. SIAM J. Comput. **1**(2), 146–160 (jun 1972). https://doi.org/10.1137/0201010

29. Wang, C., Bloem, R., Hachtel, G.D., Ravi, K., Somenzi, F.: Divide and compose: SCC refinement for language emptiness. In: Proceedings of the 12th International Conference on Concurrency Theory. p. 456–471. CONCUR '01, Springer-Verlag, Berlin, Heidelberg (2001)

30. Xie, A., Beerel, P.A.: Implicit enumeration of strongly connected components and an application to formal verification. IEEE Transactions on Computer-Aided Design of Integrated Circuits and Systems **19**(10), 1225–1230 (2000)

31. Zhao, Y., Ciardo, G.: Symbolic computation of strongly connected components and fair cycles using saturation. Innov. Syst. Softw. Eng. **7**(2), 141–150 (2011)

Transforming Quantified Boolean Formulas Using Biclique Covers

Oliver Kullmann[1]([⊠])[*] and Ankit Shukla[2]

[1] Swansea University, Swansea, UK
O.Kullmann@Swansea.ac.uk
[2] Johannes Kepler University, Austria
ankit.shukla@jku.at

Abstract. We introduce the *global conflict graph* of DQCNFs (dependency quantified conjunctive normal forms), recording clashes between clauses on such universal variables on which all existential variables depend (called "global variables"). The biclique covers of this graph correspond to the eligible clause-slices of the DQCNF which consider only the global variables. We show that all such slices yield satisfiability-equivalent variations. This opens the possibility to realise this slice using as few global variables as possible. We give basic theoretical results and first supporting experimental data.

Keywords: QBF solving, DQBF, 2QCNF, biclique cover problem, conflict graph, preprocessing, Horn clause-sets, minimal unsatisfiability

1 Introduction

The last two decades have seen enormous progress in quantified Boolean formula (QBF) theory and technology, as witnessed by the Handbook chapters [2,14]. Core areas are preprocessing techniques, result validation of the solvers, strategy extraction, and theoretical lower bounds. There are many applications in the areas of artificial intelligence, planning, two player gaming and synthesis; see the overview [25]. This progress is complemented by the annual QBF competition called QBFEval (see [21]). A special class of QBF, 2QBF, is used to model problems with simple quantifier structure (see [1,24] for basic references). In the other direction, the more expressive logic DQBF has also seen recent progress in this decade; see for example [13,26,3,12]. Here solving techniques from SAT and QBFs are generalised, including preprocessing, strategy extraction and circuit synthesis. We remind at the central complexity classes covered here: SAT is NP-complete, 2QBF is Π_2^P-complete, QBF is PSPACE-complete, and DQBF is NEXPTIME-complete. In our paper we rely on the CNF-structure, and thus we will use 2QCNF instead of 2QBF, and DQCNF instead of DQBF.

In our paper we present a new, at first sight astonishing, but essentially simple theoretical insight into general DQCNFs, which enables transformations

---

[*] Supported by EPSRC grant EP/S015523/1

S. Sankaranarayanan and N. Sharygina (Eds.): TACAS 2023, LNCS 13994, pp. 372–390, 2023.
https://doi.org/10.1007/978-3-031-30820-8_23

of problem instances, maintaining satisfiability-equivalence. We consider "global variables", universal variables on which *every* existential variable depends, and the corresponding "slice" of the CNF (the parts of the clauses using these variables). The main insight is that we can replace this global slice by any other global slice (using completely different variables and clauses), with the only condition that the conflict (clashing) patterns between global literals need to be maintained. These conflict patterns can be represented by bicliques in graphs, with one biclique corresponding to one variable with its positive and negative occurrences, establishing the two sides of the biclique (where all vertices from the two sides are connected). In this way the tools of the theory of biclique (edge) covers (and also biclique partitions) of graphs can be used to find "better" global slices. A natural first metric for "better" is to use fewer bicliques, and the corresponding decision problem, whether a graph has a biclique cover using at most a given number of bicliques, is the NP-complete Problem GT18 in the classical book [11]. The smallest number of bicliques needed to cover a graph is called the *biclique cover number*, or also the *bipartite dimension*. In our context there is a very natural alternative point of view of biclique-covers/partitions, namely representing bicliques by boolean variables in CNFs, and then instead of a biclique-cover we just have a CNF realising the graph, which means its conflict graph is the given graph; now "fewer bicliques" means "fewer variables". This has apparently been first explored in [18,10]. The potential applications of this new transformation (changing the global slice) are in preprocessing for solving, and also the proof complexity aspect seems very interesting — how much do such changes affect the complexity of the formula?

We now run through a simple example, which shows the main topic of the paper in a nutshell: Using graph theory connected to CNFs to lower the number of (certain) universal variables in a DQCNF.

1.1 Using fewer universal variables

Consider the DQCNF F with four universal and two existential variables

$$F := \forall x_1, x_2, x_3, x_4 \,\exists y_1(x_1, x_2, x_3)\, \exists y_2(x_1, x_2, x_3, x_4) : F,$$

where $F := (y_1 \vee x_2 \vee x_3) \wedge (\neg y_1 \vee x_1 \vee \neg x_2) \wedge (\neg y_2 \vee \neg x_1 \vee \neg x_2 \vee \neg x_3 \vee x_4) \wedge (y_2 \vee \neg x_4)$. The universal variables of F are x_1, x_2, x_3, x_4, the existential variables are y_1, y_2, with their dependencies shown in brackets. F has a solution: $y_1 = \neg x_2$, $y_2 = x_4$ (which makes all clauses tautologies). A central concept for this paper is that of a **global variable**, which is a universal variable such that all existential variables depend on it. The global variables of F are x_1, x_2, x_3. The sub-clauses given by the global variables yield the **global slice**, which is denoted by gsl(F) (switching from logical to clause-notation — the global slice is just a CNF-clause-set):

$$\mathrm{gsl}(F) = \big\{ \{x_2, x_3\}, \{x_1, \overline{x_2}\}, \{\overline{x_1}, \overline{x_2}, \overline{x_3}\}, \emptyset \big\}.$$

The second central concept of this paper is the **global conflict graph** gcg(F), which is the conflict graph of the global slice: the clauses are the vertices, and an edge connects clauses iff they have clashing literals:

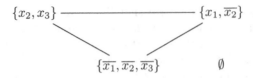

Note that indeed we have a *graph*, and there is only *one* edge between $\{x_2, x_3\}$ and $\{\overline{x_1}, \overline{x_2}, \overline{x_3}\}$ (not two). Now the basic insight of our paper (Corollary 2) is:

Any clause-set realising the conflict-graph
can be used instead of the (given) global slice.

Here by "realising" we just mean that the clause-set has the given conflict-graph. In our case, the triangle can be realised with just two variables x_1, x_2, yielding

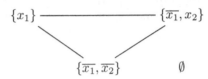

This triangle-realisation is Horn, minimally unsatisfiable, with one clause more than variables (we will show that this is always available). We obtain the new DQCNF F' (which is satisfiability-equivalent to F, also shown for comparison):

$$F = \forall\boxed{x_1, x_2, x_3,}x_4 \exists y_1(x_1, x_2, x_3) \exists y_2(x_1, x_2, x_3, x_4) : F$$

$$F = (y_1 \vee \underline{x_2 \vee x_3}) \wedge (\neg y_1 \vee \underline{x_1} \vee \neg x_2) \wedge (\neg y_2 \vee \underline{\neg x_1 \vee \neg x_2 \vee \neg x_3} \vee x_4) \wedge (y_2 \vee \neg x_4)$$

$$F' := \forall\boxed{x_1, x_2,}x_4 \exists y_1(x_1, x_2) \exists y_2(x_1, x_2, x_4) : F'$$

$$F' := (y_1 \vee \underline{x_1}) \wedge (\neg y_1 \vee \underline{\neg x_1 \vee x_2}) \wedge (\neg y_2 \vee \underline{\neg x_1 \vee \neg x_2} \vee x_4) \wedge (y_2 \vee \neg x_4),$$

where a solution now is $y_1 = \neg x_1$, $y_2 = x_4$. In general we are aiming at reducing the number of global variables, by using a smaller CNF-realisation of the global conflict graph. Since minimising the number of global variables is NP-hard, for this first study we only consider fixed predetermined replacement-schemes.

1.2   Overview

In Section 2 we present basic definitions related to logic and graph theory. Especially the conflict graph of clause-sets is given in Definition 1, and in Subsection 2.2 we discuss biclique-covers/partitions, and how they relate to conflict graphs (Lemma 1). Section 3 then discusses the semantics of global variables in DQC-NFs. Theorem 1 spells out the basic fact that global variables can be expanded (they can be eliminated by considering all assignments to them), and that the results are captured by independent (clash-free) sets of the global conflict graph. In Definition 7 we make precise what it means that one DQCNF is obtained from another one by replacing the global slice with an equivalent one, namely having the same global conflict graph, and being the same after removal of the global slices. Corollary 2 then says that such DQCNFs are satisfiability-equivalent.

In Section 4 we study the most basic realisations, "precise" and "imprecise" ones, the former realising *precisely* the number of given parallel edges in a given multigraph. We start in Subsection 4.1 by using "full clause-sets", which are clause-sets where all clauses contain the same variables. So these are (imprecise) realisations of complete graphs, and indeed contain optimal ones (always w.r.t. the number of variables). In Subsection 4.2 we consider the trivial realisations, where every clash is realised by one new variable with one positive and one negative occurrence. A new perspective on basic realisations by "singular variables", which occur in one sign only once, is then presented in Subsection 4.3. In Lemma 2 we give a simple generation process for the class of Horn minimally unsatisfiable clause-sets (HMUs), and, exploiting this, in Theorem 2 we show that every graph has a precise realisation by HMUs, computable in linear time. In Corollary 4 we obtain that every DQCNF with m clauses can be transformed in linear time into a satisfiability-equivalent one with only the global slice changed, so that now there are at most $m - 1$ global variables, using for each connected component of the global conflict graph a (variable-disjoint) HMU.

We now come to the experimental part of the paper. In Section 5 we present the first instance of a general scheme for generating 2QCNF, which are DQCNFs of the form $\forall X \exists Y : F$, where X is the set of global variables, and Y the set of existential variables. The general scheme starts with a graph G with m vertices, and chooses some realisation F of G. One chooses the number $C \geq 1$ of connected components of the (overall) global conflict graph, consisting of C vertex-disjoint copies of G, realised by C variable-disjoint copies of F. This yields altogether $C \cdot m$ clauses. On these Cm clauses finally the existential slice is created, with n variables, which makes altogether three parameters (C, m, n). For the graphs G we choose complete graphs, and for the realisations the trivial realisation, the (unique) HMU realisation, and the (optimum) log (full) realisation, considering only powers of two: $m = 2^p$. Finally for the existential slice we create random 3-CNFs. The basic question we want to explore is Hypothesis SIB: is using fewer global variables better for solving? We run two leading solvers on a selection of benchmark sets, which is presented in Section 6; see [19] for the benchmarks. To a large extend SIB is validated; we found only one parameter triple where the HMU-realisation could have some edge over the log-realisation, and present the finding. We conclude in Section 7 with future research directions.

2   Preliminaries

2.1   Logic

We have an infinite set of variables to start with; these variables can be used as universal or existential (boolean) variables in DQCNFs (see below), or just as plain (boolean) variables in clause-sets. We usually write v for a variable, using x for literals, with $\overline{x}$ the complement of a literal ("negation"). A clause C is a (finite) set of literals not containing clashing literals, that is, there is no $x \in C$ with $\overline{x} \in C$. Using $\overline{L} := \{\overline{x} : x \in L\}$ for a set L of literals, clash-freeness of clauses C means the condition $C \cap \overline{C} = \emptyset$. A clause-set F is a finite set of clauses. We use var(x) for the underlying variable of a literal x, var(C) := {var(x) : $x \in C$} for the set of variables occurring (positively or negatively) in a clause C, and var(F) := $\bigcup_{C \in F}$ var(C) for the set of variables occurring in F. As measures for clause-sets F we use (taking values in $\mathbb{N}_0 = \{x \in \mathbb{Z} : x \geq 0\}$):

1. $n(F) := |\mathrm{var}(F)| \in \mathbb{N}_0$ for the number of variables in F;
2. $c(F) := |F| \in \mathbb{N}_0$ for the number of clauses in F;
3. $\delta(F) := c(F) - n(F) \in \mathbb{Z}$ for the deficiency of F.

Since in general we can not avoid having clauses with multiplicity, and we want to name clauses, we also use *labelled clause-sets*, which are pairs (L, F), where L is the (finite) set of (clause-)labels, and F is a map with domain L, mapping every label $l \in L$ to a clause $F(l)$. An ordinary clause-set F is converted into a labelled clause-set by using F as the label-set, and using the identity on F as clause-map. A *DQCNF* is a 4-tuple $\boldsymbol{F} = (A, E, F, D)$, where

- A, E are disjoint sets of variables, the universal and the existential variables;
- F is a clause-set over $A \cup E$ (i.e., using literals with variables from A or E);
- D maps every existential variable v to $D(v) \subseteq A$ (the set of universal variables on which v depends; boolean variables have $D(v) = \emptyset$).

A *satisfying (total) assignment of* $\boldsymbol{F}$ is a map Φ with domain E, where $\Phi(v)$ is a boolean function over the variables $D(v)$, such that F after substitution via Φ becomes a tautology (over A), where F is understood as a CNF (a conjunction of clauses, where a clause is a disjunction of literals). A DQCNF $\boldsymbol{F}$ is *satisfiable* if it has a satisfying assignment, otherwise $\boldsymbol{F}$ is *unsatisfiable*. Two DQCNFs are *satisfiability-equivalent* if either both are satisfiable or both are unsatisfiable.

2.2   Graphs

We use $\binom{V}{2}$ to denote the set of 2-element subsets of a set V. A *graph* is a pair (V, E), with V the (finite) vertex-set, and $E \subseteq \binom{V}{2}$ the edge-set (undirected, no parallel edges or (self-)loops). More generally, a *multigraph* is a pair (V, E), with V as before, while $E : \binom{V}{2} \to \mathbb{N}_0$ maps every potential edge to its multiplicity (a natural number ≥ 0). An ordinary graph is converted into a multigraph by using the characteristic function of the edge-set. In the other direction, the underlying graph of a multigraph (V, E) has the edge $\{v, w\}$ iff $E(\{v, w\}) \geq 1$. We use $V(G)$ for the vertex-set of a (multi)graph G, and $E(G)$ for the edge-set of a graph G resp. for the edge-function of a multigraph G. An *independent set* $I \subseteq V(G)$ of a (multi)graph G has no edge $e \in E(G)$ with $e \subseteq I$ (resp. $E(G)(e) \subseteq I$). For the number of vertices we use $|V(G)| \in \mathbb{N}_0$, while for the number of edges we use $|E(G)| \in \mathbb{N}_0$, which for a multigraph G is defined as $|E(G)| := \sum_{e \in \binom{V(G)}{2}} E(G)(e)$, that is, as the sum of edge-multiplicities. K_n is the complete graph with $n \in \mathbb{N}_0$ vertices, that is, $V(K_n) = \{1, \ldots, n\}$ and $E(G) = \binom{V(G)}{2}$ (thus $|E(K_n)| = \frac{1}{2}n(n-1)$).

Definition 1. *Consider a labelled clause-set* (L, F). *The **conflict multigraph** $\text{cmg}(F)$ is the multigraph with vertex-set L, where the multiplicity of an edge $\{a, b\}$ (for labels $a, b \in L$) is $|F(a) \cap \overline{F(b)}|$, that is, the number of clashing literals between the clauses of a and b. The **conflict graph** $\text{cg}(F)$ is the underlying graph of $\text{cmg}(F)$. A labelled clause-set (L, F) **precisely-realises a multigraph** G, if $\text{cmg}(L, F) = G$, and **realises a graph** G, if $\text{cg}(L, F) = G$.*

We write "precisely-realise" instead of "precisely realise" to avoid grammatical ambiguity (as in "that precisely realises what I want").

A *biclique* in a multigraph G is a pair (A, B) of disjoint vertex sets $A, B \subseteq V(G)$, such that all $a \in A$ are adjacent with all $b \in B$. The corresponding characteristic function maps exactly the edges $\{a, b\}$ to 1 (all other edges to zero). A *biclique partition of* G is a family $((A_i, B_i))_{i \in I}$ of bicliques in G, such that the sum of characteristic functions equals the edge-function of G, while for a *biclique cover of* G that sum needs to be equal zero exactly for the non-edges. For graphs G a biclique represents the corresponding set of edges of G, and a biclique partition yields a partitioning of the edge-set, while a biclique cover has as its union the edge-set. For (multi)graphs G by $\mathbf{bcp}(G) \in \mathbb{N}_0$ resp. $\mathbf{bcc}(G) \in \mathbb{N}_0$ the minimum number of bicliques in a biclique partition resp. cover of G is denoted. For an overview on the complexity of computing $\text{bcp}(G)$ and $\text{bcc}(G)$ see [9,4,7]. That boolean clause-sets yield a natural environment for biclique partitions (and covers) was apparently first realised in [18]:

Lemma 1. *For a multigraph G the biclique partitions resp. biclique covers correspond, up to handling of degenerations, to precise-realisation resp. realisations of G by labelled clause-sets (Definition 1), with the bicliques corresponding to the variables and their positive and negative occurrences. $\text{bcp}(G)$ is the minimal number of variables in a precise-realisation of G, while $\text{bcc}(G)$ is the minimal number of variables in a realisation of G.*

We are mostly interested in (imprecise-)realisations, since we are interested in using realisations F with as few variables as possible (i.e., minimising $n(F)$), which is equivalent to maximising $\delta(F)$). However also precise-realisations can be of interest, since they are smaller in regards to the number of literal occurrences.

With the example from Subsection 1.1 we have already seen two different realisations of the triangle K_3 (thus using the label-set $\{1, 2, 3\}$), namely first using three variables in $\{1 \mapsto \{x_2, x_3\}, 2 \mapsto \{x_1, \overline{x_2}\}, 3 \mapsto \{\overline{x_1}, \overline{x_2}, \overline{x_3}\}\}$, corresponding to the biclique cover by the three bicliques $(\{2\}, \{3\}), (\{1\}, \{2, 3\}), (\{1\}, \{3\})$, and second using two variables in $\{1 \mapsto \{x_1\}, 2 \mapsto \{\overline{x_1}, x_2\}, 3 \mapsto \{\overline{x_1}, \overline{x_2}\}\}$, corresponding to the biclique cover by the two bicliques $(\{1\}, \{2, 3\}), (\{2\}, \{3\})$. The latter is a precise-realisation (the cover is a partition).

3   The global conflict graph

We now study the simplest type of universal variables of a DQCNF, called "global variables", which are the variables every existential variable depends on. In the final result, Corollary 2, we will see that concerning satisfiability (at all), all what matters about global variables is the clashes they create between the clauses.

Definition 2. *A **global variable** of a DQCNF $F = (A, E, F, D)$ is a universal variable, such that every existential variable depends on it. We denote the set of all global variables by* $\mathrm{gvar}(F) := \{v \in A : \forall w \in E : v \in D(w)\}$.

We note that the notion of a global variable does not depend on the clauses. A DQCNF might not have any global variable. For a 2QCNF the global variables are all the universal variables, i.e., $\mathrm{gvar}(A, E, F, D) = A$ (that is indeed the definition of 2QCNF). In order to access the clause-parts with global literals, we consider a DQCNF as "sliced up" by their variable-sets, for example for a QCNF $\exists X \forall Y \exists Z : F$ we have three natural slices, for X, Y, Z.

Definition 3. *For a DQCNF $F = (A, E, F, D)$ and some set $V \subseteq A \cup E$ of variables, the V-**slice** is the labelled clause-set (F, F_V) (using the clauses of F as labels), such that the clause of label $C \in F$ is $F_V(C) := C[V] := \{x \in C : \mathrm{var}(x) \in V\}$. The **global slice of** F is the $\mathrm{gvar}(F)$-slice, denoted by $\mathbf{gsl}(F)$.*

Combining Definition 1, 2, and 3, we obtain the "global conflict graph" as the conflict graph of the global slice:

Definition 4. *For a DQCNF $F = (A, E, F, D)$ the **global conflict graph** resp. **multigraph** is $\mathbf{gcg}(F) := \mathrm{cg}(\mathrm{gsl}(F))$ resp. $\mathbf{gcmg}(F) := \mathrm{cmg}(\mathrm{gsl}(F))$.*

The vertices of the global conflict (multi)graph are the clauses, with the edges corresponding to clashes between literals over global variables. Note that the realisations of the global conflict graph are the same as the realisations of the global conflict multigraph (for realisations, multiplicities of edges are irrelevant).

We need the ability to remove the global variables (obtaining another DQCNF) for which we introduce the following notation:

Definition 5. *For a DQCNF $F = (A, E, F, D)$ let $V := \mathrm{gvar}(F)$ be the set of global variables, while $V' := (A \cup E) \setminus V$ is the set of other variables. We define*

$$\mathrm{mgvar}(F) := (A \setminus V, E, \{C - V\}_{C \in F}, (D(v) \setminus V)_{v \in E}),$$

with "m" for "minus", which is the DQCNF obtained by removing the global variables from its universal variables (removing all literals with underlying global variable). Here $C - V := C[V']$ (removing all literals with variables from V).

The semantic contribution of global variables is captured by the global-clash-free sub-clause-sets and their related sub-DQCNFs:

Definition 6. *Consider a DQCNF $F = (A, E, F, D)$. A **globally-independent sub-clause-set of** F is a clause-set $F' \subseteq F$ which is an independent subset of $\mathrm{gcg}(F)$ (that is, the global variables of F are all pure variables, appearing only in one sign, in F'). A **globally-independent sub-DQCNF** is some $\mathrm{mgvar}(A, E, F', D)$ for some globally-independent sub-clause-set F'. Speaking of* *maximal globally-independent,* we restrict the $F' \subseteq F$ to maximal independent subsets of $\mathrm{gcg}(F)$. The set of all maximally globally-independent sub-DQCNFs is denoted by $\mathrm{gind}(\boldsymbol{F})$, and two DQCNF's $\boldsymbol{F}, \boldsymbol{F'}$ are called **gind-equivalent** if $\mathrm{gind}(\boldsymbol{F}) = \mathrm{gind}(\boldsymbol{F'})$.

We note that two gind-equivalent DQCNFs have the same existential variables, and that gind-equivalence is indeed an equivalence relation. We now come in Theorem 1 to the basic observation about the role played by global literals (literals whose underlying variables are global). Most basic is the insight that global variables are exactly the variables which always allow reducing the problem by substituting all possible truth values, which we illustrate by a simple example:

Example 1. Let $A := \{a\}$, $E := \{x\}$, $F := \{\{a, \overline{x}\}, \{\overline{a}, x\}\}$, $D_1 := (x \mapsto A)$, $D_2 := (x \mapsto \emptyset)$, and finally $\boldsymbol{F}_i := (A, E, F, D_i)$ for $i = 1, 2$. Less formally, we have two QCNFs: $\boldsymbol{F}_1 \triangleq \forall a \exists x : F$ and $\boldsymbol{F}_2 \triangleq \exists x \forall a : F$, where $F \triangleq a \leftrightarrow x$. Obviously $\boldsymbol{F}_1$ is satisfiable, with the unique solution $x \triangleq a$, while $\boldsymbol{F}_2$ is unsatisfiable.

We have $\mathrm{gvar}(\boldsymbol{F}_1) = \{a\}$, while $\mathrm{gvar}(\boldsymbol{F}_2) = \emptyset$. Substituting $a \mapsto 0$ into $\boldsymbol{F}_1$ or $\boldsymbol{F}_2$ yields in both cases the DQCNF $\boldsymbol{G}_0 = \exists x : \neg x$, while $a \mapsto 1$ yields $\boldsymbol{G}_1 = \exists x : x$. $\boldsymbol{G}_\varepsilon$ has the unique solution $x \triangleq \varepsilon$ for $\varepsilon \in \{0, 1\}$. For $\boldsymbol{F}_1$ we are then able to get a solution for x, since x depends on a, and thus we can select the appropriate solution from $\boldsymbol{G}_\varepsilon$, depending on the value ε. While x does not depend on a in $\boldsymbol{F}_2$, and thus we could only lift the solutions from $\boldsymbol{G}_{0,1}$ to $\boldsymbol{F}_2$ if they would be the same in both cases.

The vertices of the global conflict graphs of $\boldsymbol{F}_1, \boldsymbol{F}_2$ are the two clauses, which in $\boldsymbol{F}_1$ are connected by an edge, while in $\boldsymbol{F}_2$ they are isolated. So $\mathrm{gind}(\boldsymbol{F}_1) \triangleq \{\exists x : \neg x, \exists x : x\}$, while $\mathrm{gind}(\boldsymbol{F}_2) = \{\boldsymbol{F}_2\}$.

Theorem 1. *A DQCNF $\boldsymbol{F} = (A, E, F, D)$ is unsatisfiable iff there is some unsatisfiable maximal globally-independent sub-DQCNF of $\boldsymbol{F}$.*

Proof. We show the equivalent statement: $\boldsymbol{F}$ is satisfiable iff all maximal globally-independent sub-DQCNFs are satisfiable.

Let $V := \mathrm{gvar}(\boldsymbol{F})$. $\boldsymbol{F}$ is satisfiable iff for all boolean total assignments $\varphi : V \to \{0, 1\}$, after substitution of φ into $\boldsymbol{F}$, the resulting DQCNF $\varphi * \boldsymbol{F} := (A \backslash V, E, \varphi * F, (D(v) \backslash V)_{v \in E})$ is satisfiable, where $\varphi * F$ is the usual application of a partial assignment to a clause-set (removing all satisfied clauses, and removing the falsified literals from the remaining clauses): The direction from left to right holds for all partial assignments to universal variables, while the direction from right to left uses that the variables in V are global, and thus the boolean functions used in a satisfying assignment of a DQCNF can be made dependent on them. Now the clauses of $\varphi * F$ come from an independent subset of $\mathrm{gcg}(\boldsymbol{F})$, since an edge, that is a clash, would cause one of the two clauses involved to be satisfied. And for every maximal independent subset F' we can find $\varphi : V \to \{0, 1\}$ satisfying exactly all clauses in $F \backslash F'$, by setting all global literals occurring in F' to 1. Thus the maximal independent $F' \subseteq F$ cover exactly the relevant (maximal) cases of $\varphi * \boldsymbol{F}$, which shows the assertion. $\square$

Thus $\boldsymbol{F}$ is unsatisfiable iff $\mathrm{gind}(\boldsymbol{F})$ contains an unsatisfiable element:

Corollary 1. *Gind-equivalence implies sat-equivalence, that is, if for DQCNF* F, F' *holds* $\mathrm{gind}(F) = \mathrm{gind}(F')$, *then* F *is satisfiable iff* F' *is satisfiable.*

A sufficient condition for F, F' being gind-equivalent is that F' is obtained from F by replacing the global slice in such a way that the global conflict graph is maintained. The precise concept is captured by "global-conflict-graph-equivalence":

Definition 7. *Two DQCNFs* $F = (A, E, F, D)$, $F' = (A', E', F', D')$ *are* **gcg-equivalent** *if the following conditions hold:*

1. $\mathrm{mgvar}(F) = \mathrm{mgvar}(F')$.
2. *There is a bijection* $\sigma : F \to F'$, *which is an isomorphism from* $\mathrm{gcg}(F)$ *to* $\mathrm{gcg}(F')$, *such that for all* $C \in F$ *we have* $C - \mathrm{gvar}(F) = \sigma(C) - \mathrm{gvar}(F')$.

The first condition of Definition 7 says that after removal of the global variables, we have *exactly* the same DQCNFs, while the second condition says that the global literals inserted into the clauses of $\mathrm{mgvar}(F) = \mathrm{mgvar}(F')$ yield exactly the same conflict-pattern (and thus the same independent subsets).

Corollary 2. *Gcg-equivalence implies gind-equivalence. Thus two gcg-equivalent DQCNFs are sat-equivalent.*

In the following Section 4 we will consider the problem of constructing gcg-equivalences. This is just a study of graphs G and their (CNF-)realisations, since all what matters here is the global slice of a DQCNF, which is just a boolean CNF. Furthermore we only need to consider connected graphs, since every connected component of G can be handled separately.

4   Realisations

We now introduce the three most basic classes of realisations of multigraphs:

1. In Subsection 4.1 we consider clause-sets, where all clauses contain the same variables ("full clause-sets"). These realisations realise exactly complete graphs (all vertices connected to each other), and they contain the optimum realisation (always w.r.t. the number of variables), which we call *log-realisations* (of complete graphs).
2. In Subsection 4.2 we consider realisations, which as biclique-partitions/covers only contain bicliques which are single edges. In this way every multigraph is (trivially) precisely-realised, and we speak of *trivial realisations*.
3. In Subsection 4.3 we consider more generally realisations, which correspond to biclique-partitions/covers containing only claws (connecting one vertex with many). Here we get better bounds, and it is known that every connected graph with m vertices allows such a precise-realisations with $m - 1$ variables. Looking closer, one sees that these realisations actually encode unit-clause propagation, and thus the underlying class of clause-sets is the class of minimally unsatisfiable Horn clause-sets (which are special cases of MUs of deficiency 1). We call these realisations *HMU-realisations*.

These three representation-classes are based on three classes of clause-sets:

Definition 8. *For a clause-set F we introduce the following special cases of variables $v \in \mathrm{var}(F)$:*

1. *v is **full** if every clause contains v (positively or negatively);*
2. *v is **1-singular** if it occurs in both signs exactly once;*
3. *v is **singular** if it occurs in both signs, and in one sign exactly once.*

*A clause-set having only full resp. 1-singular resp. singular variables is a **full** resp. **totally 1-singular** resp. **totally singular clause-set.***

4.1   Full clause-sets

Any full clause-set F realises the complete graph $K_{c(F)}$ with $c(F)$ many vertices. Indeed the realisations of the complete graphs are exactly the hitting clause-sets (any two clauses clash; as DNFs also known as orthogonal or disjoint DNFs), and we will see in Corollary 5 another class of hitting clause-sets. For a complete graph K_m with $m \in \mathbb{N}$ vertices, it is well-known ([8]) that $\mathrm{bcc}(K_m) = \lceil \lg(m) \rceil$, where $\lg(m)$ is the binary logarithm of m. Such optimal realisations F are obtained from the canonical (full) clause-set with $n := \lceil \lg(m) \rceil$ many variables and 2^n clauses by selecting any m clauses.

In contrast to this we have the Theorem of Graham-Pollak ([15]), which states $\mathrm{bcp}(K_m) = m - 1$. Thus there exists a precise-realisation of K_m with deficiency 1 (which is optimal among *precise*-realisations), and in the already mentioned Corollary 5 we will see an example for that (the simplest example). More generally, in Subsection 4.2 we will indeed see that every nonempty connected graph has a minimally unsatisfiable precise-realisation F with $\delta(F) = 1$. We note that the above optimal logarithmic realisations by full clause-sets are minimally unsatisfiable iff m is a power of two (otherwise they are satisfiable); this could be repaired by removal of literal occurrences for the non-powers of two, but we have to leave this refinement to future work, and in this paper we only consider the cases $m = 2^n$.

4.2   Totally 1-singular clause-sets

Obviously, every multigraph G can be precisely-realised by a totally 1-singular clause-set F with $n(F) = |E(G)|$. For a connected G, these precise-realisations are minimally unsatisfiable iff G is a tree; these are exactly the marginal minimally unsatisfiable clause-sets of deficiency 1 (see Corollary 6). Otherwise they are satisfiable.

4.3   Totally singular MUs

It is well-known that every connected graph G with $m := |E(G)| \geq 1$ vertices has a claw-decomposition with $m - 1$ claws, and thus $\mathrm{bcp}(G) \leq m - 1$. Here a "claw" is a special biclique, with one side having exactly one vertex. The proof uses a elimination-sequence $v_1, \ldots, v_{m-1}$ of G, which removes one vertex after the other (including incident edges) such that always a (nonempty) connected graph is maintained. That is, $G_0 := G$, while $G_i := G_{i-1} - v_i$ for $i = 0, \ldots, m - 1$: the defining property of "elimination-sequence" is that each G_i is connected (and nonempty — eliminating the last vertex would yield a superfluous claw, with one side being empty). Here for a graph G and a vertex $v \in V(G)$ we define $G - v := (V(G) \setminus \{v\}, \{e \in E(G) : v \notin e\})$.

The existence of an elimination-sequence, and computing it in linear time in the size of the graph, can be accomplished as follows (this is well-known, see e.g. [6, Proposition 1.4.1], but for completeness we discuss it here):

(a) an elimination-sequence for a spanning tree of G (which can be computed in linear time) is an elimination-sequence for G;
(b) an elimination-sequence for a tree is a sequence removing one leaf after the other (these are the vertices of degree 1, that is, having exactly one neighbour); by a procedure similar to unit-clause propagation this can be accomplished in linear time as well.

A claw in a biclique-partition is a singular variable in the corresponding realisation. Thus we obtain that G has a totally singular realisation F with $m - 1$ variables (and m clauses, thus of deficiency 1). Now indeed the F constructed in this way are *exactly* the minimally unsatisfiable Horn clause-sets, and this correspondence, based on unit-clause propagation, we discuss in this subsection.

It is useful to introduce the following three classes of clause-sets:

- $\mathcal{MU}$ is the class of all minimally unsatisfiable clause-sets, that is, all unsatisfiable clause-sets F such that $F \setminus \{C\}$ is satisfiable for all $C \in F$.
- $\mathcal{HO}$ is the class of all Horn clause-sets, defined by the property that every clause contains at most one positive literal (i.e., all F such that for all $C \in F$ holds $|C \cap \mathrm{var}(C)| \leq 1$).
- $\mathcal{HMU} := \mathcal{HO} \cap \mathcal{MU}$ are the minimally unsatisfiable Horn clause-sets.

For a general overview on minimally unsatisfiable formulas see [17], while [5, Corollary 10] seems the first source for the fact that HMUs have deficiency 1.

Lemma 2. *The class $\mathcal{HMU}$ is generated by the following process (each step called a **singular positive unit-extension**):*

1. *Start with $\{\bot\}$.*
2. *For some F already created, choose a variable $v \notin \mathrm{var}(F)$ and some $\emptyset \neq F_0 \subseteq F$, and create a new clause-set $F' := \{\{v\}\} \cup (F \setminus F_0) \cup \{C \cup \{\overline{v}\} : C \in F_0\}$ (that is, add the unit-clause $\{v\}$, and add the literal $\overline{v}$ to the clauses of F_0).*

Proof. It is easy to see that all generated clause-sets are elements of $\mathcal{HMU}$. It remains to show that all $F \in \mathcal{HMU}$ can be generated; we show this by induction on $n(F)$. For $n(F) = 0$ we have $F = \{\bot\}$, which is the base case of the generation process. So assume $n(F) > 0$. F must contain a positive unit-clause $\{v\}$ (otherwise every clause would contain a negative literal, due to the Horn-property, and then setting all literals to 0 would be a satisfying assignment). Due to F being minimally unsatisfiable, there is no other clause than $\{v\}$ containing the positive literal v. Now setting v to 1 produces $F' \in \mathcal{HMU}$, where we can apply the induction hypothesis to F', and from F' by one step of singular positive unit-extension with v we obtain F. □

The following four properties of HMUs follow all easily from the generation process of Lemma 2 by induction:

Corollary 3. *Clause-sets $F \in \mathcal{HMU}$ have the following properties:*

1. *F is totally singular (indeed for every variable the positive literal occurs exactly once).*
2. *The number $n(F)$ of variables equals the number of singular unit-extensions applied, while $c(F) = n(F) + 1$. Thus F has deficiency 1 ($\delta(F) = 1$).*
3. *F has exactly one negative clause.*
4. *The conflict multigraph of F is a graph (at most one conflict between clauses).*

So HMUs precisely-realise nonempty connected graphs, and indeed they realise exactly those:

Theorem 2. *For every connected nonempty (finite) graph G one can construct in linear time (in the length of G, i.e., in $|V(G)| + |E(G)|$) an HMU precisely-realising G.*

Proof. For G compute an elimination-sequence $v_1, \ldots, v_{m-1}$ as explained at the beginning of the subsection, and use these vertices as variables for the generation process according to Lemma 2, where F_0 is the set of neighbours. □

The novelty of Theorem 2 from the graph-theoretical perspective lies in relating biclique partitions by claws with realisations by HMUs (note that realisation by any totally singular clause-set of deficiency 1 is trivial). The restriction to graphs (without parallel edges) is natural here, since our main interest is in imprecise-realisations (using as few variables as possible). A related result here for precise-realisations of multigraphs is given in [27], where it is shown (in graph-theoretical language), that for every graph G the multigraph G' with $V(G) = V(G')$, which has as many edges between vertices as is given by their distance in G, has a precise-realisation F with $\delta(F) \geq 1$; such an F yields a so-called "addressing" of G.

Corollary 4. *For each DQCNF F there is a gcg-equivalent F' such that the global slice of F' is a variable-disjoint union of HMUs.*

Recall that a "hitting clause-set" is a clause-set F such that every two (different) clauses clash; full clause-sets are a special case. In other words, hitting clause-sets are exactly the realisations of complete graphs.

Corollary 5. *The hitting HMUs are exactly those where for each singular unit-extension step $F_0 = F$ holds. For every $n \in \mathbb{N}_0$ there is up to isomorphism exactly one such clause-set, called S_n, with $n(S_n) = n$.*

Corollary 6. *The totally 1-singular HMUs are exactly those where for each singular unit-extension step $|F_0| = 1$ holds; they precisely-realise exactly all trees.*

5   A basic generator

The main target of this first experimental evaluation is the validation or refutation of the **Hypothesis SIB**: "Small Is Better" — the smaller the number of variables in the realisation, the easier to solve.

First, to generate test-instances, we take the simplest approach for our generator, focusing on generating 2QCNFs. For 2QCNFs, the global variables are all the universal variables (for more information, see Section 3), and thus the universal slice is the same as the global slice. The following is an example of 2QCNF in the standard QDIMACS form, with 6 variables and 4 clauses:

```
p cnf 6 4              # parameter line; nvars ncls
a 5 6 0                # universally quantified variables
e 1 2 3 4 0            # existentially quantified variables
-1 -3  4 |  5 0        #            |        0
-1 -2  3 | -5 0        # exist      | univ   0
 1 -2  5 |  6 0        # slice      | slice  0
 1  3 -4 | -6 0        #            |        0
```

For the presentation, existential literals precede the universal literals, using a separator "|". The existential slice is $\{\{-1, -3, 4\}, \{-1, -2, 3\}, \{1, -2, 5\}, \{1, 3, -4\}\}$, while the universal (global) slice is $\{\{5\}, \{-5\}, \{6\}, \{-6\}\}$. In Section 3 we considered the case of connected graphs. Real world instances have indeed a large number of connected (global) components, and so we are using $C \in \mathbb{N}$ many components. Altogether the parameters (C, p, n) specify the generated 2QCNF, where $p \in \mathbb{N}$ is the (binary log of the) number of vertices in a component, and $n \in \mathbb{N}$ is the total number of existential variables.

For the component-conflict-graph of the universal slice, we use the complete graph with $m := 2^p$ vertices (clauses), and $q := \frac{1}{2}m(m - 1)$ edges — this is the simplest case where we have an exponential separation between the optimum realisation and the HMU-realisation. So the total number of generated clauses is $C \cdot m$. In the above QDIMACS we have $C = 2$ and $p = 1$ (the smallest value to obtain a proper 2QCNF), thus $q = 1$. For the existential slice we choose a random 3-CNF with n variables and $C \cdot m$ clauses; note that components of the conflict graph do not play any role here. We use the three realisation from Section 4 (for each component, with m clauses):

- Trivial: q variables (Subsection 4.2; all clauses have length $m - 1$).
- HMU: $m - 1$ variables (S_{m-1} from Corollary 5; clause-lengths $1, \ldots, m - 1$).
- Log: a full clause-set with p variables (Subsection 4.1).

Example 2. Below we display a generated 2QCNF for all three realisations, with $(C, p, n) = (2, 2, 4)$. Thus $m = 2^2 = 4$ clauses per component, making $2 \cdot 4 = 8$ clauses in total. The existential slice is a uniform random 3-CNF with 4 variables and 8 clauses. For each component, the trivial realisation uses $q = \frac{1}{2} \cdot 4 \cdot 3 = 6$ variables, HMU uses 3 variables, and log uses 2 variables. Leftmost is the trivial realisation, then the HMU realisation, and finally the logarithmic realisation:

```
-1 -3 -4 |   5    6    7 0        -1 -3 -4 |  5    0              -1 -3 -4 | -5 -6 0
 1  2 -4 |  -5    8    9 0         1  2 -4 | -5  6 0               1  2 -4 | -5  6 0
-2  3  4 |  -6   -8   10 0        -2  3  4 | -5 -6    7 0         -2  3  4 |  5 -6 0
 1 -3  4 |  -7   -9  -10 0         1 -3  4 | -5 -6   -7 0          1 -3  4 |  5  6 0
 1  3  4 |  11   12   13 0         1  3  4 |  8    0               1  3  4 | -7 -8 0
 2  3  4 | -11   14   15 0         2  3  4 | -8  9 0               2  3  4 | -7  8 0
 1  2 -3 | -12  -14   16 0         1  2 -3 | -8 -9   10 0          1  2 -3 |  7 -8 0
 2  3 -4 | -13  -15  -16 0         2  3 -4 | -8 -9  -10 0          2  3 -4 |  7  8 0
```

6   Experimental results

We use two top-performing 2QCNF solvers, DepQBF [20] and CADET [23], based on the QBFEVAL 2020 competition results [22]. In order to avoid the known high variability on satisfiable instances, for this first experimental evaluation we only considered unsatisfiable instances (throwing away satisfiable instances). Recall that we use parameter values (C, p, n) according to Section 5. For each parameter value, we generated 1000 instances and report the results only on the unsatisfiable instances. In general we tried to select values such that the created benchmarks are of medium hardness, around at most one hour, considering all three realisations (trivial, HMU, logarithmic). Now it turned out that the trivial realisation caused mostly very hard instances, and so our selection process focuses on HMU and logarithmic realisations. We found in general Hypothesis SIB ("small is better") well validated: On all parameters considered, both solvers solved more instances with the logarithmic realisation and had a better average runtime than with the HMU-realisation. All the experiments were conducted on Intel(R) Xeon(R) E5-2620 v4 @ 2.10GHz CPUs with a time limit of 3600s and memory limit of 8 GB per instance. Memory usage for instance generation and solving processes of generated benchmarks was minimal (< 1 GB). The summary of the results is as follows, using rounded runtimes:

No.	Solver	C	p	n	#inst /1000	Solved instances triv	HMU	log	HMU time(s) mean	median	log time(s) mean	median
1.	D	10	4	8	1000	0	978	1000	280	82	32	23
	C					140	384	990	448	39	67	2
2.	D	10	4	10	500	0	167	500	1260	884	155	139
	C					7	23	236	303	10	637	146
3.	D	10	4	12	28	0	14	28	1530	1562	87	87
	C					0	3	19	774	56	458	70
4.	D	10	5	12	35	0	3	35	1788	1108	1911	1916
	C					3	4	5	721	232	1099	375
5.	D	12	4	12	384	0	70	384	1176	993	1125	930
	C					5	12	149	663	381	736	218
6.	D	14	4	11	1000	1	971	1000	301	92	294	172
	C					170	327	827	431	27	292	13

The solver column labelled with "D" refers to DepQBF, while "C" is CADET. The mean and median consider only instances solved by the corresponding solver.

For example for Row 1D, the HMU-mean 280 as well as the HMU-median 82 relates only to the runtimes on the 978 HMU-instances solved by DepQBF.

The table shows that the Hypothesis SIB is mostly validated for the $2 \cdot 6 = 12$ rows (only comparing HMU and log now). First there are 6 fully conforming rows, namely 1DC, 2D, 3D, 5D, and 6C, where more instances were solved for the log-realisation, and this also with better mean and median times. Then there are 4 mostly conforming rows 2C, 3C, 4D, and 5C, where we have also clearly more solved log-realisations, while mean or median could be better for HMU, but only for a small number of instances. This leaves two exceptional rows: 4C and 6D. We need to leave **4C** for more extensive experimentation: these instances were very hard for CADET, and the number of solved instances is too small for a statistical analysis. For the **6D** instances with $(C, p, n) = (14, 4, 11)$, the median solving time for the HMU realisation is better (92s versus 172s), and it solves nearly as many instances as the logarithmic realisation. However, the average solving time for the HMU realisation is worse than for the logarithmic realisation (301s versus 294s; timeouts are not included in these averages). This warrants further investigation, and the density plot (the second plot shows times $\leq 1000s$ only) can provide additional insight:

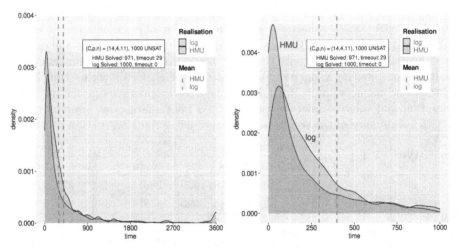

The mean values shown in the plots now include the 3600s timeout, which for HMU increases the mean to 397s. The second plot, which shows times $\leq$ 1000s, reveals that the HMU realisation solves several instances faster than the logarithmic realisation, but its performance deteriorates over time, with fewer and fewer instances solved. The first plot, which shows the overall picture, shows a spike for the HMU realisation at times $\leq 3600s$ at the tail end, indicating that 29 instances timed out (while the logarithmic realisation solved all instances). When the timeout is increased from 3600s to 18000s, the mean of the HMU realisation increases to 445s.

On these instances we could devise a portfolio strategy in which both HMU and logarithmic realisation instances run in parallel, while aborting HMU realisation relatively quickly — in this way one could achieve a faster average solving time overall. While this parameter triple is interesting, more investigation is required to understand the precise causes of this behaviour.

7   Conclusion and Outlook

We have introduced the global conflict graph of DQCNFs, which represents the clashes (conflicts) between global literals; for 2QCNFs the global literals are just the universal literals. We have shown that the corresponding global slice can be replaced by anything else which just reproduces the conflict graph. We then switched to investigating (CNF-)realisations of arbitrary graphs, concentrating on the three most basic classes, given by full clause-sets (complete graphs only), by variables occurring only twice, and by HMUs (Horn minimally unsatisfiable clause-sets). For the latter we showed that they can realise everything, and thus yield the upper bound $m - k$ on the number of global variables needed for any DQCNF with m clauses and k connected components of the conflict graph; such a transformation can be computed in linear time. We created then families of 2QCNF instances, with a relatively small number of connected components, and consisting of small complete graphs; together with any of the three basic realisations (full-log, trivial, HMU) this creates the universal slice, while the existential slice is given by a random 3-CNF. We investigated whether indeed in this setting fewer universal variables mean easier solving, and found that in general well supported. There are many future avenues for research and practice:

1. In a forthcoming paper we investigate the global conflict graph of *real-world instances* — when and how we can simplify the global slice (using several metrics), and what effect this has on solving time (for satisfiable and unsatisfiable instances). For the minimisation of the number of variables, naturally SAT-solving is employed.
2. The instances created for this first experimental evaluation can be generalised by a *general DQCNF generator*, which takes as input-parameters (a) graph families for the global conflict graphs, (b) realisation strategies to produce the global slice, and (c) some generator to create the DQCNF minus the global slice.
3. Especially interesting should be classes where an *exponential separation* between the best and an HMU-realisation exists. We have seen the example of complete graphs; a more complex class are the grid graphs ([16]).

Of course, insights into the behaviour of solvers is an important goal here.

On the *theory side*, a fundamental question here is to investigate which restricted classes of global conflict graphs still yield completeness for the respective complexity classes. Finally it seems natural to conjecture that allowing arbitrary transformations of the global slice can have a huge influence on various complexity issues, like proof-length in various calculi, and the complexities of strategy extraction.

References

1. Valeriy Balabanov, Jie-Hong Roland Jiang, Christoph Scholl, Alan Mishchenko, and Robert K. Brayton. 2QBF: Challenges and solutions. In Nadia Creignou and Daniel Le Berre, editors, *Theory and Applications of Satisfiability Testing - SAT 2016 - 19th International Conference, Bordeaux, France, July 5-8, 2016, Proceedings*, volume 9710 of *Lecture Notes in Computer Science*, pages 453–469. Springer, 2016. URL: https://doi.org/10.1007/978-3-319-40970-2_28, doi: 10.1007/978-3-319-40970-2_28.

2. Olaf Beyersdorff, Mikolás Janota, Florian Lonsing, and Martina Seidl. Quantified Boolean Formulas. In Armin Biere, Marijn Heule, Hans van Maaren, and Toby Walsh, editors, *Handbook of Satisfiability - Second Edition*, volume 336 of *Frontiers in Artificial Intelligence and Applications*, pages 1177–1221. IOS Press, 2021. doi: 10.3233/FAIA201015.

3. Joshua Blinkhorn, Tomás Peitl, and Friedrich Slivovsky. Davis and Putnam meet Henkin: Solving DQBF with resolution. In Chu-Min Li and Felip Manyà, editors, *Theory and Applications of Satisfiability Testing - SAT 2021 - 24th International Conference, Barcelona, Spain, July 5-9, 2021, Proceedings*, volume 12831 of *Lecture Notes in Computer Science*, pages 30–46. Springer, 2021. doi: 10.1007/978-3-030-80223-3_4.

4. Sunil Chandran, Davis Issac, and Andreas Karrenbauer. On the Parameterized Complexity of Biclique Cover and Partition. In Jiong Guo and Danny Hermelin, editors, *11th International Symposium on Parameterized and Exact Computation (IPEC 2016)*, volume 63 of *Leibniz International Proceedings in Informatics (LIPIcs)*, pages 11:1–11:13. Schloss Dagstuhl–Leibniz-Zentrum fuer Informatik, 2017. doi:10.4230/LIPIcs.IPEC.2016.11.

5. Gennady Davydov, Inna Davydova, and Hans Kleine Büning. An efficient algorithm for the minimal unsatisfiability problem for a subclass of CNF. *Annals of Mathematics and Artificial Intelligence*, 23(3-4):229–245, 1998. doi:10.1023/A: 1018924526592.

6. Reinhard Diestel. *Graph Theory*, volume 173 of *Graduate Texts in Mathematics*. Springer, New York, second edition, 2000. ISBN 0-387-98976-5. URL: http://www.esi2.us.es/~mbilbao/pdffiles/DiestelGT.pdf.

7. Alessandro Epasto and Eli Upfal. Efficient approximation for restricted biclique cover problems. *Algorithms*, 11(6):84, June 2018. doi:10.3390/a11060084.

8. Peter C. Fishburn and Peter L. Hammer. Bipartite dimensions and bipartite degrees of graphs. *Discrete Mathematics*, 160(1):127–148, 1996. doi:10.1016/0012-365X(95)00154-0.

9. Herbert Fleischner, Egbert Mujuni, Daniël Paulusma, and Stefan Szeider. Covering graphs with few complete bipartite subgraphs. *Theoretical Computer Science*, 410:2045–2053, 2009. doi:10.1016/j.tcs.2008.12.059.

10. Nicola Galesi and Oliver Kullmann. Polynomial time SAT decision, hypergraph transversals and the hermitian rank. In Holger H. Hoos and David G. Mitchell, editors, *Theory and Applications of Satisfiability Testing 2004*, volume 3542 of *Lecture Notes in Computer Science*, pages 89–104, Berlin, 2005. Springer. doi: 10.1007/11527695_8.

11. Michael R. Garey and David S. Johnson. *Computers and Intractability / A Guide to the Theory of NP-Completeness*. W.H. Freeman and Company, 1979.

12. Aile Ge-Ernst, Christoph Scholl, and Ralf Wimmer. Localizing quantifiers for DQBF. In Clark W. Barrett and Jin Yang, editors, *2019 Formal Methods in Computer Aided Design, FMCAD 2019, San Jose, CA, USA, October 22-25, 2019*, pages 184–192. IEEE, 2019. doi:10.23919/FMCAD.2019.8894269.
13. Karina Gitina, Ralf Wimmer, Sven Reimer, Matthias Sauer, Christoph Scholl, and Bernd Becker. Solving DQBF through quantifier elimination. In Wolfgang Nebel and David Atienza, editors, *Proceedings of the 2015 Design, Automation & Test in Europe Conference & Exhibition, DATE 2015, Grenoble, France, March 9-13, 2015*, pages 1617–1622. ACM, 2015. URL: http://dl.acm.org/citation.cfm?id=2757188.
14. Enrico Giunchiglia, Paolo Marin, and Massimo Narizzano. Reasoning with Quantified Boolean Formulas. In Armin Biere, Marijn Heule, Hans van Maaren, and Toby Walsh, editors, *Handbook of Satisfiability - Second Edition*, volume 336 of *Frontiers in Artificial Intelligence and Applications*, pages 1157–1176. IOS Press, 2021. doi:10.3233/FAIA201014.
15. Ronald L. Graham and H.O. Pollak. On the addressing problem for loop switching. *Bell System Technical Journal*, 50(8):2495–2519, 1971. doi:10.1002/j.1538-7305.1971.tb02618.x.
16. Krystal Guo, Tony Huynh, and Marco Macchia. The biclique covering number of grids. *The Electronic Journal of Combinatorics*, 26(4):P4.27, 2019. URL: https://www.combinatorics.org/ojs/index.php/eljc/article/view/v26i4p27/pdf.
17. Hans Kleine Büning and Oliver Kullmann. Minimal unsatisfiability and autarkies. In Armin Biere, Marijn J.H. Heule, Hans van Maaren, and Toby Walsh, editors, *Handbook of Satisfiability*, volume 185 of *Frontiers in Artificial Intelligence and Applications*, chapter 11, pages 339–401. IOS Press, February 2009. doi:10.3233/978-1-58603-929-5-339.
18. Oliver Kullmann. The combinatorics of conflicts between clauses. In Enrico Giunchiglia and Armando Tacchella, editors, *Theory and Applications of Satisfiability Testing 2003*, volume 2919 of *Lecture Notes in Computer Science*, pages 426–440, Berlin, 2004. Springer. doi:10.1007/978-3-540-24605-3_32.
19. Oliver Kullmann and Ankit Shukla. TransformingQBFusingBicliqueCovers_Tacas2022, January 2023. GitHub repository. URL: https://github.com/OKullmann/TransformingQBFusingBicliqueCovers_Tacas2022.
20. Florian Lonsing and Uwe Egly. Depqbf 6.0: A search-based QBF solver beyond traditional QCDCL. In Leonardo de Moura, editor, *Automated Deduction - CADE 26 - 26th International Conference on Automated Deduction, Gothenburg, Sweden, August 6-11, 2017, Proceedings*, volume 10395 of *Lecture Notes in Computer Science*, pages 371–384. Springer, 2017. doi:10.1007/978-3-319-63046-5_23.
21. Luca Pulina and Martina Seidl. The 2016 and 2017 QBF solvers evaluations (qbfeval'16 and qbfeval'17). *Artif. Intell.*, 274:224–248, 2019. doi:10.1016/j.artint.2019.04.002.
22. Luca Pulina, Martina Seidl, and Ankit Shukla. QBFeval'18–competitive evaluation of QBF solvers, 2018.
23. Markus N. Rabe and Sanjit A. Seshia. Incremental determinization. In Nadia Creignou and Daniel Le Berre, editors, *Theory and Applications of Satisfiability Testing - SAT 2016 - 19th International Conference, Bordeaux, France, July 5-8, 2016, Proceedings*, volume 9710 of *Lecture Notes in Computer Science*, pages 375–392. Springer, 2016. doi:10.1007/978-3-319-40970-2_23.

24. Markus N. Rabe, Leander Tentrup, Cameron Rasmussen, and Sanjit A. Seshia. Understanding and extending incremental determinization for 2QBF. In Hana Chockler and Georg Weissenbacher, editors, *Computer Aided Verification - 30th International Conference, CAV 2018, Held as Part of the Federated Logic Conference, FloC 2018, Oxford, UK, July 14-17, 2018, Proceedings, Part II*, volume 10982 of *Lecture Notes in Computer Science*, pages 256–274. Springer, 2018. `doi:10.1007/978-3-319-96142-2\_17`.
25. Ankit Shukla, Armin Biere, Luca Pulina, and Martina Seidl. A survey on applications of Quantified boolean formulas. In *31st IEEE International Conference on Tools with Artificial Intelligence, ICTAI 2019, Portland, OR, USA, November 4-6, 2019*, pages 78–84. IEEE, 2019. `doi:10.1109/ICTAI.2019.00020`.
26. Leander Tentrup and Markus N. Rabe. Clausal abstraction for DQBF. In Mikolás Janota and Inês Lynce, editors, *Theory and Applications of Satisfiability Testing - SAT 2019 - 22nd International Conference, SAT 2019, Lisbon, Portugal, July 9-12, 2019, Proceedings*, volume 11628 of *Lecture Notes in Computer Science*, pages 388–405. Springer, 2019. `doi:10.1007/978-3-030-24258-9\_27`.
27. Peter M. Winkler. Proof of the squashed cube conjecture. *Combinatorica*, 3(1):135–139, 1983. `doi:10.1007/BF02579350`.

Certificates for Probabilistic Pushdown Automata via Optimistic Value Iteration

Tobias Winkler[✉] and Joost-Pieter Katoen

RWTH Aachen University, Aachen, Germany
{tobias.winkler,katoen}@cs.rwth-aachen.de

Abstract. Probabilistic pushdown automata (pPDA) are a standard model for discrete probabilistic programs with procedures and recursion. In pPDA, many quantitative properties are characterized as least fixpoints of polynomial equation systems. In this paper, we study the problem of *certifying* that these quantities lie within certain bounds. To this end, we first characterize the polynomial systems that admit easy-to-check certificates for validating bounds on their least fixpoint. Second, we present a sound and complete Optimistic Value Iteration algorithm for computing such certificates. Third, we show how certificates for polynomial systems can be transferred to certificates for various quantitative pPDA properties. Experiments demonstrate that our algorithm computes succinct certificates for several intricate example programs as well as stochastic context-free grammars with $> 10^4$ production rules.

Keywords: Probabilistic Pushdown Automata · Probabilistic Model Checking · Certified Algorithms · Probabilistic Recursive Programs.

1 Introduction

Complex software is likely to contain bugs. This applies in particular to model checking tools. This is a serious problem, as the possibility of such bugs compromises the trust one can put in the verification results, rendering the process of formal modeling and analysis less useful. Ideally, the implementation of a model checker should be formally verified itself [15]. However, due to the great complexity of these tools, this is often out of reach in practice. *Certifying algorithms* [31] mitigate this problem by providing an *easy-to-check certificate* along with their regular output. This means that there exists a *verifier* that, given the input problem, the output, and the certificate, constructs a formal proof that the output is indeed correct. The idea is that the verifier is much simpler than the algorithm, and thus likely to be bug-free or even amenable to formal verification.

This paper extends the recent line of research on probabilistic certification [19,23,24,41] to *probabilistic pushdown automata* [13,30] (pPDA). pPDA and related models have applications in, amongst others, pattern recognition [39],

This work is supported by the DFG research training group 2236 UnRAVeL and the ERC advanced research grant 787914 FRAPPANT.

S. Sankaranarayanan and N. Sharygina (Eds.): TACAS 2023, LNCS 13994, pp. 391–409, 2023.
https://doi.org/10.1007/978-3-031-30820-8_24

$$X \rightarrow a \mid XYY \qquad x = \frac{1}{2}(1 + xy^2)$$

$$Y \rightarrow b \mid X \mid YY \qquad y = \frac{1}{3}(1 + x + y^2)$$

Fig. 1: Left: A stochastic context-free grammar (SCFG; e.g. [16]) and the associated positive polynomial system (PPS) which encodes the termination probabilities of each non-terminal, assuming production rules are taken uniformly at random. Right: The curves defined by the two equations. The least fixpoint (lfp) is $\approx (0.66, 0.70)$. The thin colored area to the top right of the lfp is the set of inductive, self-certifying upper bounds on the lfp.

computational biology [28], and speech recognition [25]. They are moreover a natural operational model for programs with procedures, recursion, and (discrete) probabilistic constructs such as the ability to flip coins. With the advent of *probabilistic programming* [32] as a paradigm for model-based machine learning [6], such programs have received lots of attention recently. Moreover, several efficient algorithms such as Hoare's quicksort with randomized pivot selection (e.g. [26]) are readily encoded as probabilistic recursive programs.

A pPDA can be seen as a purely probabilistic variant of a standard pushdown automaton: Instead of reading an input word, it takes its transitions randomly based on fixed probability distributions over successor states. Quantities of interest in pPDA include reachability probabilities [13], expected runtimes [8], variances [14], satisfaction probabilities of temporal logic formulas [47,42], and others (see [7] for an overview). pPDA are equivalent to *Recursive Markov Chains* [17]. In the past two decades there have been significant research efforts on efficient *approximative* algorithms for pPDA, especially a decomposed variant of *Newton iteration* [16,27,11,17,12,10,40] which provides guaranteed lower, and occasionally upper [10,12] bounds on key quantities. However, even though implementations might be complex [46], these algorithms are not certifying.

Our technique for certificate generation is a non-trivial extension of *Optimistic Value Iteration* [22] (OVI) to pPDA. In a nutshell, the idea of OVI is to compute *some* lower bound l on the solution—which can be done using an approximative iterative algorithm—and then *optimistically guess* an upper bound $u = l + \varepsilon$ and verify that the guess was correct. Prior to our paper, OVI had only been considered in Markov Decision Processes (MDP) [22] and Stochastic Games (SG) [1], where it is used to compute bounds on, e.g., maximal reachability probabilities. The upper bounds computed by OVI have a special property: They are *self-certifying* (also called *inductive* in our paper): Given the system and the bounds, one *can check very easily that the bounds are indeed correct.*

However, *pPDA are much more complicated than MDP or SG* for the following reasons: (i) pPDA may induce *infinite-state* Markov processes due to their unbounded stack; (ii) the analysis of pPDA requires solving *non-linear equa-*

tions; (iii) the complexity of basic decision problems is generally higher than in MDP/SG. For example, reachability in MDP is characterized as the *least fix-point* (lfp) of a piece-wise *linear* function that can be computed in PTIME via, e.g., LP solving. On the other hand, reachability in pPDA requires computing a fixed point of a *positive polynomial* function, leading to a PSPACE complexity bound [13]. See Figure 1 for an example.

Contributions. Despite the difficulties mentioned above, we show in this paper that the general idea of OVI can be extended to pPDA, yielding a practically feasible algorithm with good theoretical properties. More concretely:

Contribution 1 We present an OVI-style algorithm for computing inductive upper bounds of any desired precision $\varepsilon > 0$ on the lfp of a positive polynomial system. Compared to the existing OVI [22], the key novelty of our algorithm is to compute a certain *direction* v in which to guess, i.e., the guess is $u = l + \varepsilon v$ rather than $u = l + \varepsilon$. The direction v is an estimate of a certain *eigenvector*. This ensures that we eventually hit an inductive bound, even if the latter lie in a very "thin strip" as in Figure 1, and yields a *provably complete* algorithm that is guaranteed to find an inductive bound in finite time (under mild assumptions).

Contribution 2 We implement our algorithm in the software tool PRAY and compare the new technique to an out-of-the-box approach based on SMT solving, as well as to standard OVI with a simpler guessing heuristic.

Related Work. Certification of pPDA has not yet been addressed explicitly, but some existing technical results go in a similar direction. For instance, [17, Prop. 8.7] yields certificates for non-termination in SCFG, but they require an SCC decomposition for verification. *Farkas certificates* for MDP [19] are more closely related to our idea of certificates. They require checking a set of *linear* constraints. A symbolic approach to verify probabilistic recursive programs on the syntax level including inductive proof rules for upper bounds was studied in [35]. A higher-order generalization of pPDA was introduced in [29], and an algorithm for finding upper bounds inspired by the Finite Element method was proposed. Applications of PPS beyond the analysis of pPDA include the recent *factor graph grammars* [9] as well as obtaining approximate counting formulas for many classes of trees in the framework of *analytic combinatorics* [18]. Regarding software tools, PREMO [46] implements iterative algorithms for lower bounds in Recursive Markov Chains, but it supports neither certificates nor upper bounds.

Paper Outline. We review the relevant background information on PPS in Section 2. Section 3 presents our theoretical results on inductive upper bounds in PPS as well as the new Optimistic Value Iteration algorithm. In Section 4 we explain how inductive bounds in PPS are used to certify quantitative properties of pPPA. The experimental evaluation is in Section 5. We conclude in Section 6. A full version of this paper is available online [44].

2 Preliminaries

Notation for Vectors. All vectors in this paper are *column* vectors and are written in boldface, e.g., $\boldsymbol{u} = (u_1, \ldots, u_n)^T$. For vectors $\boldsymbol{u}, \boldsymbol{u}'$, we write $\boldsymbol{u} \leq \boldsymbol{u}'$ if $\boldsymbol{u}$ is *component-wise* less than or equal to $\boldsymbol{u}'$. Moreover, we write $\boldsymbol{u} < \boldsymbol{u}'$ if $\boldsymbol{u} \leq \boldsymbol{u}'$ and $\boldsymbol{u} \neq \boldsymbol{u}'$, and $\boldsymbol{u} \prec \boldsymbol{u}'$ if $\boldsymbol{u}$ is component-wise *strictly* smaller than $\boldsymbol{u}'$. The zero vector is denoted $\boldsymbol{0}$. The *max norm* of a vector $\boldsymbol{u}$ is $||\boldsymbol{u}||_\infty = \max_{1 \leq i \leq n} |u_i|$. We say that $\boldsymbol{u}$ is *normalized* if $||\boldsymbol{u}||_\infty = 1$.

Positive Polynomial Systems (PPS). Let $n \geq 1$ and $\boldsymbol{x} = (x_1, \ldots, x_n)^T$ be a vector of variables. An n-dimensional PPS is an equation system of the form

$$x_1 = f_1(x_1, \ldots, x_n) \quad \cdots \quad x_n = f_n(x_1, \ldots, x_n)$$

where for all $1 \leq i \leq n$, the function f_i is a *polynomial with non-negative real coefficients*. An example PPS is the system $x = \frac{1}{2}(1 + xy^2), y = \frac{1}{3}(1 + x + y^2)$ from Figure 1. We also use vector notation for PPS: $\boldsymbol{x} = \boldsymbol{f}(\boldsymbol{x}) = (f_1(\boldsymbol{x}), \ldots, f_n(\boldsymbol{x}))^T$.

We write $\overline{\mathbb{R}}_{\geq 0} = \mathbb{R}_{\geq 0} \cup \{\infty\}$ for the *extended non-negative reals*. By convention, for all $a \in \overline{\mathbb{R}}_{\geq 0}$, $a \leq \infty$, $a + \infty = \infty + a = \infty$, and $a \cdot \infty = \infty \cdot a$ equals 0 if $a = 0$ and ∞ otherwise. For $n \geq 1$, the partial order $(\overline{\mathbb{R}}_{\geq 0}^n, \leq)$ is a *complete lattice*, i.e., all subsets of $\overline{\mathbb{R}}_{\geq 0}^n$ have an infimum and a supremum. In particular, there exists a least element $\boldsymbol{0}$ and a greatest element $\boldsymbol{\infty} = (\infty, \ldots, \infty)^T$. Every PPS induces a *monotone* function $\boldsymbol{f} \colon \overline{\mathbb{R}}_{\geq 0}^n \to \overline{\mathbb{R}}_{\geq 0}^n$, i.e., $\boldsymbol{u} \leq \boldsymbol{v} \implies \boldsymbol{f}(\boldsymbol{u}) \leq \boldsymbol{f}(\boldsymbol{v})$. By the Knaster-Tarski fixpoint theorem, the set of fixpoints of $\boldsymbol{f}$ is also a complete lattice, and thus there exists a *least fixpoint* (lfp) denoted by $\mu\boldsymbol{f}$.

In general, the lfp $\mu\boldsymbol{f}$ is a vector which may contain ∞ as an entry. For instance, this happens in the PPS $x = x + 1$. A PPS $\boldsymbol{f}$ is called *feasible* if $\mu\boldsymbol{f} \prec \boldsymbol{\infty}$ (or equivalently, $\mu\boldsymbol{f} \in \mathbb{R}_{\geq 0}^n$). The Knaster-Tarski theorem also implies:

Lemma 1 (Inductive upper bounds). *For all $\boldsymbol{u} \in \overline{\mathbb{R}}_{\geq 0}^n$ it holds that*

$$\boldsymbol{f}(\boldsymbol{u}) \leq \boldsymbol{u} \quad \text{implies} \quad \mu\boldsymbol{f} \leq \boldsymbol{u} .$$

Such a vector $\boldsymbol{u}$ with $\boldsymbol{u} \prec \boldsymbol{\infty}$ is called inductive *upper bound.*

If $\boldsymbol{f}$ is feasible, then $\mu\boldsymbol{f}$ is obviously an inductive upper bound. The problem is that $\mu\boldsymbol{f}$ may be irrational even if $\boldsymbol{f}$ has rational coefficients only (see Example 1 below) and can thus not easily be represented exactly. In Section 3 we show under which conditions there exist *rational* inductive upper bounds $\boldsymbol{u} \in \mathbb{Q}_{\geq 0}^n$.

Problem statement of this paper

Given a feasible PPS $\boldsymbol{f}$, find a rational *inductive* upper bound $\boldsymbol{u} \geq \mu\boldsymbol{f}$.

A PPS is called *clean* if $\mu\boldsymbol{f} \succ \boldsymbol{0}$. Every PPS can be cleaned in linear time by identifying and removing the variables that are assigned 0 in the lfp [17,12].

Given a PPS $\boldsymbol{f}$ and a point $\boldsymbol{u} \in \mathbb{R}_{\geq 0}^n$, we define the *Jacobi matrix* of $\boldsymbol{f}$ at $\boldsymbol{u}$ as the $n \times n$-matrix $\boldsymbol{f}'(\boldsymbol{u})$ with coefficients $\boldsymbol{f}'(\boldsymbol{u})_{1 \leq i, j \leq n} = \frac{\partial}{\partial x_j} f_i(\boldsymbol{u})$.

Example 1. Consider the example PPS $\boldsymbol{f}_{ex}$ with variables $\boldsymbol{x} = (x, y)^T$:

$$x = f_1(x, y) = y + 0.1 \qquad y = f_2(x, y) = 0.2x^2 + 0.8xy + 0.1 .$$

The line and the hyperbola defined by these equations are depicted in Figure 2 on Page 7. The fixpoints of $\boldsymbol{f}_{ex}$ are the intersections of these geometric objects; in this case there are two. In particular, $\boldsymbol{f}_{ex}$ is feasible and its lfp is

$$\mu\boldsymbol{f}_{ex} = \left((27-\sqrt{229})/50 , (22-\sqrt{229})/50 \right)^T \approx (0.237 , 0.137)^T .$$

Therefore, $\boldsymbol{f}_{ex}$ is clean as $\mu\boldsymbol{f}_{ex} \succ \boldsymbol{0}$. The Jacobi matrix of $\boldsymbol{f}_{ex}$ is

$$\boldsymbol{f}'_{ex}(x, y) = \begin{pmatrix} \frac{\partial}{\partial x}f_1 & \frac{\partial}{\partial y}f_1 \\ \frac{\partial}{\partial x}f_2 & \frac{\partial}{\partial y}f_2 \end{pmatrix} = \begin{pmatrix} 0 & 1 \\ 0.4x + 0.8y & 0.8x \end{pmatrix} .$$

Note that the lfp $\mu\boldsymbol{f}_{ex}$ contains *irrational* numbers. In the above example, these irrational numbers could still be represented using square roots because the fixpoints of $\boldsymbol{f}_{ex}$ are the zeros of a quadratic polynomial. However, there are PPS whose lfp *cannot* be expressed using radicals, i.e., square roots and cubic roots, etc. [16]. This means that in general, there is no easy way to compute the lfp exactly. It is thus desirable to provide bounds, which we do in this paper.   △

Matrices and Eigenvectors. Let M be a real $n \times n$-matrix. We say that M is *non-negative* (in symbols: $M \geq 0$) if it has no negative entries. M is called *irreducible* if for all $1 \leq i, j \leq n$ there exists $0 \leq k < n$ such that $(M^k)_{i,j} \neq 0$. It is known that M is irreducible iff the directed graph $G_M = (\{1, \ldots, n\}, E)$ with $(i, j) \in E$ iff $M_{i,j} \neq 0$ is strongly connected. A *maximal irreducible submatrix* of M is a square submatrix induced by a strongly connected component of G_M. The *period* of a strongly connected M is the length of the shortest cycle in G_M. It is instructive to note that PPS $\boldsymbol{x} = \boldsymbol{f}(\boldsymbol{x})$ are generalizations of linear equation systems of the form $\boldsymbol{x} = M\boldsymbol{x} + \boldsymbol{c}$, with $M \geq 0$ and $\boldsymbol{c} \geq \boldsymbol{0}$. Moreover, note that for any PPS $\boldsymbol{f}$ it holds that $\boldsymbol{f}'(\boldsymbol{u}) \geq 0$ for all $\boldsymbol{u} \succ \boldsymbol{0}$.

An *eigenvector* of an $n \times n$-matrix M with eigenvalue $\lambda \in \mathbb{C}$ is a (complex) vector $\boldsymbol{v} \neq \boldsymbol{0}$ satisfying $M\boldsymbol{v} = \lambda\boldsymbol{v}$. There are at most n different eigenvalues. The *spectral radius* $\rho(M) \in \mathbb{R}_{\geq 0}$ is the largest absolute value of the eigenvalues of M. The following is a fundamental theorem about non-negative matrices:

Theorem 1 (Perron-Frobenius; e.g. [37]). *Let $M \geq 0$ be irreducible.*

(1) M has a strictly positive eigenvector $\boldsymbol{v} \succ \boldsymbol{0}$ with eigenvalue $\rho(M)$, the spectral radius of M, and all other eigenvectors $\boldsymbol{v}' \succ \boldsymbol{0}$ are scalar multiples of $\boldsymbol{v}$.

(2) The eigenvalues of M with absolute value $\rho(M)$ are exactly the h numbers $\rho(M), \xi\rho(M), \ldots, \xi^{h-1}\rho(M)$, where ξ is a primitive hth root of unity.

The *unique* eigenvector $\boldsymbol{v} \succ \boldsymbol{0}$ with $\|\boldsymbol{v}\|_\infty = 1$ of an irreducible non-negative matrix M is called the *Perron-Frobenius* eigenvector of M.

Strongly Connected Components. To each PPS $\boldsymbol{f}$ we associate a finite directed graph $G_{\boldsymbol{f}} = (\{x_1, \ldots, x_n\}, E)$, which, intuitively speaking, captures the dependency structure among the variables. Formally, $(x_i, x_j) \in E$ if the polynomial f_i *depends* on x_j, i.e., x_j appears in at least one term of f_i with a non-zero coefficient. This is equivalent to saying that the *partial derivative* $\frac{\partial}{\partial x_j} f_i$ is not the zero polynomial. We say that $\boldsymbol{f}$ is *strongly connected* if $G_{\boldsymbol{f}}$ is strongly connected, i.e., for each pair (x_i, x_j) of variables, there exists a path from x_i to x_j in $G_{\boldsymbol{f}}$. For instance, $\boldsymbol{f}_{ex}$ from Example 1 is strongly connected because the dependency graph has the edges $E = \{(x, y), (y, x), (y, y)\}$. Strong connectivity of PPS is a generalization of irreducibility of matrices; indeed, a matrix M is irreducible iff the PPS $\boldsymbol{x} = M\boldsymbol{x}$ is strongly connected. We often use the fact that $\boldsymbol{f}'(\boldsymbol{u})$ for $\boldsymbol{u} \succ \boldsymbol{0}$ is irreducible iff $\boldsymbol{f}$ is strongly connected.

PPS are usually analyzed in a decomposed fashion by considering the subsystems induced by the *strongly connected components* (SCCs) of $G_{\boldsymbol{f}}$ in bottom-up order [16]. Here we also follow this approach and therefore focus on strongly connected PPS. The following was proved in [17, Lem. 6.5] and later generalized in [12, Thm. 4.1] (also see remark below [12, Prop. 5.4] and [17, Lem. 8.2]):

Theorem 2 ([17,12]). *If $\boldsymbol{f}$ is feasible, strongly connected and clean, then for all $\boldsymbol{u} < \mu \boldsymbol{f}$, we have $\rho(\boldsymbol{f}'(\boldsymbol{u})) < 1$. As a consequence, $\rho(\boldsymbol{f}'(\mu \boldsymbol{f})) \leq 1$.*

Theorem 2 partitions all PPS $\boldsymbol{f}$ which satisfy its precondition into two classes: Either (1) $\rho(\boldsymbol{f}'(\mu \boldsymbol{f})) < 1$, or (2) $\rho(\boldsymbol{f}'(\mu \boldsymbol{f})) = 1$. In the next section we show that $\boldsymbol{f}$ admits non-trivial inductive upper bounds iff it is in class (1).

Example 2. Reconsider the PPS $\boldsymbol{f}_{ex}$ from Example 1. It can be shown that $\boldsymbol{v} = (1, \lambda_1)^T$ where $\lambda_1 \approx 0.557$ is an eigenvector of $\boldsymbol{f}'_{ex}(\mu \boldsymbol{f}_{ex})$ with eigenvalue λ_1. Thus by the Perron-Frobenius Theorem, $\rho(\boldsymbol{f}'_{ex}(\mu \boldsymbol{f}_{ex})) = \lambda_1 < 1$. As promised, there exist inductive upper bounds as can be seen in Figure 2. $\triangle$

3   Finding Inductive Upper Bounds in PPS

In this section, we are concerned with the following problem: Given a feasible, clean, and strongly connected PPS $\boldsymbol{f}$, find a vector $\boldsymbol{0} \prec \boldsymbol{u} \prec \infty$ such that $\boldsymbol{f}(\boldsymbol{u}) \leq \boldsymbol{u}$, i.e., an inductive upper bound on the lfp of $\boldsymbol{f}$ (see Lemma 1).

3.1   Existence of Inductive Upper Bounds

An important first observation is that *inductive upper bounds other than the exact lfp do not necessarily exist*. As a simple counter-example consider the 1-dimensional PPS $x = \frac{1}{2}x^2 + \frac{1}{2}$. If u is an inductive upper bound, then

$$\frac{1}{2}u^2 + \frac{1}{2} \leq u \implies u^2 - 2u + 1 \leq 0 \implies (u-1)^2 \leq 0 \implies u = 1,$$

and thus the only inductive upper bound is the exact lfp $u = 1$. Another example is the PPS $\tilde{\boldsymbol{f}}_{ex}$ from Figure 2. What these examples have in common is the

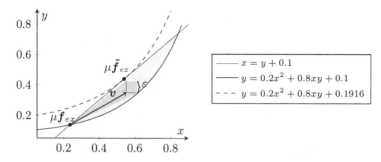

Fig. 2: The PPS $\boldsymbol{f}_{ex}$ corresponds to the solid red line and the solid blue curve. Its inductive upper bounds form the shaded area above the lfp $\mu\boldsymbol{f}_{ex}$. Lemma 2(4) ensures that one can fit the gray "cone" pointing in direction of the Perron-Frobenius eigenvector $\boldsymbol{v}$ inside the inductive region. The PPS $\tilde{\boldsymbol{f}}_{ex}$ which comprises the dashed curve and the solid line does not have any non-trivial inductive upper bounds. Note that the tangent lines at $\mu\tilde{\boldsymbol{f}}_{ex}$ are parallel to each other.

following property: Their derivative evaluated *at the lfp* is not invertible. Indeed, we have $\frac{\partial}{\partial x}(\frac{1}{2}x^2 + \frac{1}{2} - x) = x - 1$, and inserting the lfp $x = 1$ yields zero. The higher dimensional generalization of this property to arbitrary PPS $\boldsymbol{f}$ is that the Jacobi matrix of the function $\boldsymbol{f} - \boldsymbol{x}$ evaluated at $\mu\boldsymbol{f}$ is singular; note that this is precisely the matrix $\boldsymbol{f}'(\mu\boldsymbol{f}) - I$. Geometrically, this means that the tangent lines at $\mu\boldsymbol{f}$ are parallel, as can be seen in Figure 2 for the example PPS $\tilde{\boldsymbol{f}}_{ex}$. It should be intuitively clear from the figure that *inductive upper bounds only exist if the tangent lines are not parallel*. The next lemma makes this more precise:

Lemma 2 (Existence of inductive upper bounds). *Let $\boldsymbol{f}$ be a feasible, clean, and strongly connected PPS. Then the following are equivalent:*

(1) *The matrix $I - \boldsymbol{f}'(\mu\boldsymbol{f})$ is non-singular.*
(2) *The spectral radius of $\boldsymbol{f}'(\mu\boldsymbol{f})$ satisfies $\rho(\boldsymbol{f}'(\mu\boldsymbol{f})) < 1$.*
(3) *There exists $\boldsymbol{0} \prec \boldsymbol{u} \prec \infty$ s.t. $\boldsymbol{f}(\boldsymbol{u}) < \boldsymbol{u}$ (i.e. $\boldsymbol{u}$ is inductive but not a fixpoint).*
(4) *The matrix $\boldsymbol{f}'(\mu\boldsymbol{f})$ has a unique (normalized) eigenvector $\boldsymbol{v} \succ \boldsymbol{0}$ and there exist numbers $\delta_{max} > 0$ and $\varepsilon > 0$ s.t.*

$$\boldsymbol{f}(\mu\boldsymbol{f} + \delta \cdot \tilde{\boldsymbol{v}}) \quad \prec \quad \mu\boldsymbol{f} + \delta \cdot \tilde{\boldsymbol{v}}$$

holds for all $0 < \delta \le \delta_{max}$ and vectors $\tilde{\boldsymbol{v}} \ge \boldsymbol{v}$ with $||\boldsymbol{v} - \tilde{\boldsymbol{v}}||_\infty \le \varepsilon$.

The proof of Lemma 2 (see [44]) relies on a linear approximation of $\boldsymbol{f}$ via Taylor's familiar theorem as well as Theorems 1 and 2. Condition (4) of Lemma 2 means that there exists a "truncated cone"

$$Cone(\mu\boldsymbol{f}, \boldsymbol{v}, \varepsilon, \delta_{max}) \;=\; \{\, \mu\boldsymbol{f} + \delta\tilde{\boldsymbol{v}} \mid 0 \le \delta \le \delta_{max}, \tilde{\boldsymbol{v}} \ge \boldsymbol{v}, ||\tilde{\boldsymbol{v}} - \boldsymbol{v}||_\infty \le \varepsilon \,\}$$

which is entirely contained in the inductive region. The "tip" of the cone is located at the lfp $\mu\boldsymbol{f}$ and, the cone points in the direction of the Perron-Frobenius eigenvector v, as illustrated in Figure 2 (assuming $\delta_{max} = 1$ for simplicity). The length $\delta_{max} > 0$ and the radius $\varepsilon > 0$ of the cone depend on $\rho(f'(\mu f))$, but for us it suffices that they are non-zero. Note that this cone has non-empty interior and thus contains rational-valued vectors. The idea of our Optimistic Value Iteration is to *construct a sequence of guesses that eventually hits this cone.*

3.2   The Optimistic Value Iteration Algorithm

The basic idea of Optimistic Value Iteration (OVI) can be applied to monotone functions of the form $\phi \colon \mathbb{R}^n_{\geq 0} \to \mathbb{R}^n_{\geq 0}$ (in [22], ϕ is the Bellman operator of an MDP). Kleene's fixpoint theorem suggests a simple method for approximating the lfp $\mu\phi$ *from below:* Simply iterate ϕ starting at $\mathbf{0}$, i.e., compute the sequence $l_0 = \mathbf{0}$, $l_1 = \phi(l_0)$, $l_2 = \phi(l_1)$, etc.[1] In the context of MDP, this iterative scheme is known as *Value Iteration* (VI). VI is easy to implement, but it is difficult to decide when to stop the iteration. In particular, standard stopping criteria such as small absolute difference of consecutive approximations are formally unsound [20]. OVI and other algorithms [3,36] cope with this problem by computing not only a lower but also an *upper* bound on $\mu\phi$. In the case of OVI, an upper bound with absolute error $\leq \varepsilon$ is obtained as follows (we omit some details):

(1) Compute $l_k \leq \mu\phi$ such that $\|l_k - l_{k-1}\|_\infty \leq \tau$, for some (small) $\tau > 0$.
(2) Guess a candidate upper bound $u = l_k + \varepsilon$.
    (a) If $\phi(u) \leq u$ holds, i.e., u is inductive, then return u.
    (b) If not, *refine* u (see [22] for details). If the refined u is still not inductive, then go back to step (1) and try again with $0 < \tau' < \tau$.

We present our variant of OVI for PPS as Algorithm 1. The main differences to the above scheme are that (i) we do not insist on Kleene iteration for obtaining the lower bounds l, and (ii) we approximate the eigenvector v from condition (4) of Lemma 2 and compute the "more informed" guesses $u = l + \varepsilon v$, for various ε. *Refining the guesses* as original OVI does *is not necessary* (but see our remarks in Section 3.3 regarding floating point computations).

The functions `improveLowerBound` and `approxEigenvec` used in Algorithm 1 must satisfy the following contracts in order for the algorithm to be correct:

– The sequence $l_0 = \mathbf{0}$, $l_{i+1} = \texttt{improveLowerBound}(f, l_i)$ for $i \geq 0$, is a monotonically increasing sequence of rational vectors converging to μf.
– `approxEigenvec` must satisfy the following: Let $M \geq 0$ be an irreducible matrix with (normalized) Perron-Frobenius eigenvector $v \succ \mathbf{0}$. Then for all $\varepsilon > 0$, we require that there exists $\tau > 0$ such that $\|\texttt{approxEigenvec}(M, \tau) - v\|_\infty \leq \varepsilon$. In words, `approxEigenvec` approximates v up to arbitrarily small absolute error if the tolerance τ is chosen sufficiently small. Moreover, $\texttt{approxEigenvec}(M, \tau)$ returns a *rational* vector.

---

[1] In order for the Kleene seqence to converge to the lfp, i.e., $\lim_{k \to \infty} l_k = \mu\phi$, it suffices that ϕ is ω-continuous. This already implies monotonicity.

Algorithm 1: Optimistic Value Iteration (OVI) for PPS

    input   : strongly connected clean PPS f; maximum abs. error $\varepsilon \in \mathbb{Q}_{>0}$

    output   : a pair (l, u) of rational vectors s.t. $l \leq \mu f$, $f(u) \leq u$ (hence
                    $\mu f \leq u$), and $\|l - u\|_\infty \leq \varepsilon$

    termination : guaranteed if f is feasible and $I - f'(\mu f)$ is non-singular

1 $l \leftarrow \mathbf{0}$; $N \leftarrow 0$;

2 $\tau \leftarrow \varepsilon$;   `/* τ is the current tolerance */`

3 **while** true **do**

4      $l' \leftarrow$ improveLowerBound(f, l) ;   `/* e.g. Kleene or Newton update */`
        `/* guess and verify phase starts here`   `*/`

5   **if** $\|l - l'\|_\infty \leq \tau$ **then**

6          $v \leftarrow$ approxEigenvec$(f'(l), \tau)$;   `/* recall v is normalized */`

7   **for** k from 0 to N **do**

8              $u \leftarrow l + d^k \varepsilon \cdot v$;   `/* optimistic guess, d ∈ (0, 1) */`

9   **if** $f(u) \leq u$ **then**

10   **return** (l, u) ;   `/* guess was successful */`

11      $N \leftarrow N + 1$;

12      $\tau \leftarrow c \cdot \tau$;   `/* decrease tolerance for next guess, c ∈ (0, 1) */`

13    $l \leftarrow l'$;

In practice, both the Kleene and the Newton [16,17,12] update operator can be used to implement `improveLowerBound`. We outline a possible implementation of `approxEigenvec` further below in Section 3.3.

Example 3. Consider the following PPS f: $x = \frac{1}{4}x^2 + \frac{1}{8}$, $y = \frac{1}{4}xy + \frac{1}{4}y + \frac{1}{4}$. The table illustrates the execution of Algorithm 1 on f with $\varepsilon = 0.1$ and $c = 0.5$:

#	N	τ	l	l'	$\|l - l'\|_\infty$	v	u	$f(u) \leq u$
1	0	0.1	$(0, 0)$	$(0.4, 0.3)$	0.4			
2	0	0.1	$(0.4, 0.3)$	$(0.5, 0.4)$	0.1	$(1.0, 0.8)$	$(0.5, 0.38)$	✗
3	1	0.05	$(0.5, 0.4)$	$(0.55, 0.41)$	0.05	$(1.0, 0.9)$	$(0.6, 0.49)$	✓

The algorithm has to improve the lower bound 3 times (corresponding to the 3 lines of the table). After the second improvement, the difference between the current lower bound l_2 and the new bound l'_2 does not exceed the current tolerance $\tau_2 = 0.1$ and the algorithm enters the optimistic guessing stage. The first guess u_2 is not successful. The tolerance is then decreased to $\tau_3 = c \cdot \tau_2 = 0.05$ and the lower bound is improved to l'_3. The next guess u_3 is inductive. △

Theorem 3. *Algorithm 1 is correct: when invoked with a strongly connected clean PPS f and $\varepsilon \in \mathbb{Q}_{>0}$, then (if it terminates) it outputs a pair (l, u) of rational vectors s.t. $l \leq \mu f$, $f(u) \leq u$, and $\|l - u\|_\infty \leq \varepsilon$. Moreover, if f is feasible and $I - f'(\mu f)$ is non-singular, then the algorithm terminates.*

The proof of Theorem 3 (see [44]) crucially relies on condition (4) of Lemma 2 that assures the existence of a "truncated cone" of inductive bounds centered around the Perron-Frobenius eigenvector of $f'(\mu f)$ (see Figure 2 for an illustration). Intuitively, since the lower bounds l computed by the algorithm approach the lfp μf, the eigenvectors of $f'(l)$ approach those of $f'(\mu f)$. As a consequence, it is guaranteed that the algorithm eventually finds an eigenvector that intersects the cone. The inner loop starting on line 7 is needed because the "length" of the cone is a priori unknown; the purpose of the loop is to scale the eigenvector down so that it is ultimately small enough to fit inside the cone.

3.3 Considerations for Implementing OVI

As said earlier, there are at least two options for `improveLowerBound`: Kleene or Newton iteration. We now show that `approxEigenvec` can be effectively implemented as well. Further below we comment on floating point arithmetic.

Approximating the Eigenvector. A possible implementation of `approxEigenvec` relies on the *power iteration* method (e.g. [38, Thm. 4.1]). Given a square matrix M and an initial vector v_0 with $Mv_0 \neq 0$, power iteration computes the sequence $(v_i)_{i \geq 0}$ such that for $i > 0$, $v_i = Mv_{i-1}/\|Mv_{i-1}\|_\infty$.

Lemma 3. *Let $M \geq 0$ be irreducible. Then power iteration applied to $M + I$ and any $v_0 > 0$ converges to the Perron-Frobenius eigenvector $v \succ 0$ of M.*

The convergence rate of power iteration is determined by the ratio $|\lambda_2|/|\lambda_1|$ where λ_1 and λ_2 are eigenvalues of largest and second largest absolute value, respectively. Each time `approxEigenvec` is called in Algorithm 1, the result of the previous call to `approxEigenvec` may be used as initial approximation v_0.

Exact vs Floating Point Arithmetic. So far we have assumed exact arithmetic for the computations in Algorithm 1, but an actual implementation should use floating point arithmetic for efficiency. However, *this leads to unsound results*. More specifically, the condition $f(u) \leq u$ may hold in floating point arithmetic even though it is actually violated. As a remedy, we propose to nevertheless run the algorithm with floats, but then verify its output u with exact arbitrary-precision rational arithmetic. That is, we compute a rational number approximation $u_\mathbb{Q}$ of u and check $f(u_\mathbb{Q}) \leq u_\mathbb{Q}$ with exact arithmetic. If the check fails, we resort to the following refinement scheme which is an instance of the general k-induction principle for complete lattices from [5]: We iteratively check the conditions

$$f(u_\mathbb{Q} \sqcap f(u_\mathbb{Q})) \leq u_\mathbb{Q}, \quad f(u_\mathbb{Q} \sqcap f(u_\mathbb{Q} \sqcap f(u_\mathbb{Q}))) \leq u_\mathbb{Q}, \quad \text{and so on,}$$

where $\sqcap$ denotes pointwise minimum. If one of the checks is satisfied, then $\mu f \leq u_\mathbb{Q}$ [5]. This scheme often works well in practice (see Section 5). The original OVI from [22] uses a similar technique to refine its guesses.

4   Certificates for Probabilistic Pushdown Automata

This section shows how the results from Section 3 can be applied to pPDA. We introduce some additional notation. For finite sets A, $\mathcal{D}(A)$ denotes the set of *probability distributions* on A. In this section we often denote tuples without parentheses and commata, e.g., we may write ab rather than (a, b).

Definition 1 (pPDA [13]). *A probabilistic pushdown automaton (pPDA) is a triple $\Delta = (Q, \Gamma, P)$ where $Q \neq \emptyset$ is a finite set of states, $\Gamma \neq \emptyset$ is a finite stack alphabet, and $P \colon Q \times \Gamma \to \mathcal{D}(Q \times \Gamma^{\leq 2})$ is a probabilistic transition function.*

In the following, we often write $qZ \xrightarrow{p} r\alpha$ instead of $P(qZ)(r\alpha) = p$ [13]. Intuitively, $qZ \xrightarrow{p} r\alpha$ means that if the pPDA is in state q and Z is on top of the stack, then with probability p, the pPDA moves to state r, pops Z and pushes α on the stack. More formally, the semantics of a pPDA $\Delta = (Q, \Gamma, P)$ is a countably infinite Markov chain with state space $Q \times \Gamma^*$ and transition probability matrix M such that for all $q, r \in Q$, $Z \in \Gamma$, $\alpha \in \Gamma^{\leq 2}$, $\gamma \in \Gamma^*$, we have

$$M(qZ\gamma, r\alpha\gamma) = P(qZ)(r\alpha) , \qquad M(q\varepsilon, q\varepsilon) = 1 ,$$

and all other transition probabilities are zero. This Markov chain, where the initial state is fixed to qZ, is denoted $\mathcal{M}_\Delta^{qZ}$ (see Figure 3 for an example). As usual, one can formally define a probability measure $\mathbb{P}_\Delta^{qZ}$ on the infinite runs of $\mathcal{M}_\Delta^{qZ}$ via the standard cylinder construction (e.g., [2, Sec. 10]).

Consider a triple $qZr \in Q \times \Gamma \times Q$. We define the *return probability*[2] $[qZr]$ as the probability of reaching $r\varepsilon$ in the Markov chain $\mathcal{M}_\Delta^{qZ}$, i.e., $[qZr] = \mathbb{P}_\Delta^{qZ}(\Diamond\{r\varepsilon\})$, where $\Diamond\{r\varepsilon\}$ is the set of infinite runs of $\mathcal{M}_\Delta^{qZ}$ that eventually hit state $r\varepsilon$.

Theorem 4 (The PPS of return probabilities [13][3]). *Let $\Delta = (Q, \Gamma, P)$ be a pPDA and $(\langle qZr \rangle)_{qZr \in Q \times \Gamma \times Q}$ be variables. For each $\langle qZr \rangle$, define*

$$\langle qZr \rangle \;=\; \sum_{qZ \xrightarrow{p} sYX} p \cdot \sum_{t \in Q} \langle sYt \rangle \cdot \langle tXr \rangle \;+\; \sum_{qZ \xrightarrow{p} sY} p \cdot \langle sYr \rangle \;+\; \sum_{qZ \xrightarrow{p} r\varepsilon} p$$

and call the resulting PPS $\boldsymbol{f}_\Delta$. Then $\mu \boldsymbol{f}_\Delta = ([qZr])_{qZr \in Q \times \Gamma \times Q}$.

Example 4. Figure 3 shows a pPDA Δ_{ex} and the associated PPS $\boldsymbol{f}_{\Delta_{ex}}$. The least non-negative solution is $\langle qZq \rangle = 2 - \sqrt{2} \approx 0.586$ and $\langle qZr \rangle = \sqrt{2} - 1 \approx 0.414$ (and, of course, $\langle rZq \rangle = 0$, $\langle rZr \rangle = 1$). Thus by Theorem 4, the return probabilities are $[qZq] = 2 - \sqrt{2}$ and $[qZr] = \sqrt{2} - 1$.   △

The PPS $\boldsymbol{f}_\Delta$ is always feasible (because $\mu \boldsymbol{f}_\Delta \leq 1$). $\boldsymbol{f}_\Delta$ is neither necessarily strongly connected nor clean. Let $\hat{\boldsymbol{f}}_\Delta$ denote the cleaned up version of $\boldsymbol{f}_\Delta$.

---

[2] See [42] for an explanation of this terminology.

[3] We refer to [30, Sec. 3] for an intuitive explanation of the equations in $\boldsymbol{f}_\Delta$.

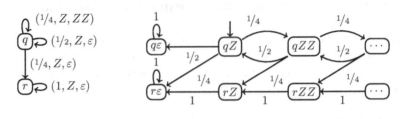

$$\langle qZq \rangle = {}^1/_4(\langle qZq \rangle\langle qZq \rangle + \langle qZr \rangle\langle rZq \rangle) + {}^1/_2 \qquad \langle rZq \rangle = 0$$
$$\langle qZr \rangle = {}^1/_4(\langle qZq \rangle\langle qZr \rangle + \langle qZr \rangle\langle rZr \rangle) + {}^1/_4 \qquad \langle rZr \rangle = 1$$

Fig. 3: Top left: The pPDA $\Delta_{ex} = (\{q, r\}, \{Z\}, P)$ where P comprises the transitions $qZ \xrightarrow{1/4} qZZ$, $qZ \xrightarrow{1/2} q\varepsilon$, $qZ \xrightarrow{1/4} r\varepsilon$, $rZ \xrightarrow{1} r\varepsilon$. Top right: A fragment of the *infinite* underlying Markov chain $\mathcal{M}_\Delta^{qZ}$, assuming initial configuration qZ. Bottom: The associated equation system from Theorem 4.

Proposition 1 (Basic Certificates for pPDA).   A basic certificate *for* $\Delta = (Q, \Gamma, P)$ *is a rational inductive upper bound* $\boldsymbol{u} \in \mathbb{Q}_{\geq 0}^{Q \times \Gamma \times Q}$ *on the lfp of the return probabilities system* $\boldsymbol{f}_\Delta$ *(see Thm. 4). They have the following properties:*

- *(Existence)* $\forall \varepsilon > 0$ *there exists a basic certificate* $\boldsymbol{u}$ *with* $\|\mu\boldsymbol{f}_\Delta - \boldsymbol{u}\|_\infty \leq \varepsilon$ *if all maximal irreducible submatrices* M *of* $\boldsymbol{f}'_\Delta(\mu\hat{\boldsymbol{f}}_\Delta)$ *satisfy* $\rho(M) < 1$.
- *(Complexity) Let* β *be the maximum number of bits used to encode any of the numerators and denominators of the fractions occurring in* $\boldsymbol{u} \in \mathbb{Q}_{\geq 0}^{Q \times \Gamma \times Q}$. *Then checking* $\boldsymbol{f}_\Delta(\boldsymbol{u}) \leq \boldsymbol{u}$, *i.e., whether* $\boldsymbol{u}$ *is basic certificate for* Δ, *can be done in time polynomial in* β *and the size of* Δ.

Existence of basic certificates follows from Lemma 2 applied to each SCC of the cleaned-up version of $\boldsymbol{f}_\Delta$ individually. However, note that in order to merely *check* the certificate, i.e., verify the inequality $\boldsymbol{f}(\boldsymbol{u}) \leq \boldsymbol{u}$, neither do SCCs need to be computed nor does the system has to be cleaned up.

Example 5. Reconsider the example pPDA and its associated (non-strongly connected) system of return probabilities from Figure 3. We verify that $\boldsymbol{u}_{qZq} = 3/5$ and $\boldsymbol{u}_{qZr} = 1/2$ (as well as $\boldsymbol{u}_{rZq} = 0, \boldsymbol{u}_{rZr} = 1$) is a basic certificate:

$$\frac{1}{4}\left(\frac{3}{5} \cdot \frac{3}{5} + \frac{1}{2} \cdot 0\right) + \frac{1}{2} = \frac{59}{100} \overset{\checkmark}{\leq} \frac{3}{5} \quad, \quad \frac{1}{4}\left(\frac{3}{5} \cdot \frac{1}{2} + \frac{1}{2} \cdot 1\right) + \frac{1}{4} = \frac{45}{100} \overset{\checkmark}{\leq} \frac{1}{2}.$$

Note that $[qZq] \approx 0.586 \leq 3/5 = 0.6$ and $[qZr] \approx 0.414 \leq 1/2 = 0.5$.   △

In the following we outline how a variety of key quantities associated with a pPDA can be verified using basic certificates.

Upper Bounds on Temporal Properties. We may use basic certificates to verify that a bad state r_{bad} is reached with low probability, e.g., at most $p = 0.01$. To this end, we remove the outgoing transitions of r_{bad} and add the transitions $r_{bad} Z \xrightarrow{1} r_{bad} \varepsilon$ for all $Z \in \Gamma$. Clearly, r_{bad} is reached with probability at most p from initial configuration qZ iff $[qZr_{bad}] \leq p$. The results of [13] imply that this idea can be generalized to *until*-properties of the form $\mathcal{C}_1 \mathcal{U} \mathcal{C}_2$, where $\mathcal{C}_1$ and $\mathcal{C}_2$ are *regular* sets of configurations.

Certificates for the Output Distribution. Once a pPDA reaches the empty stack, we say that it has *terminated*. When modeling procedural programs, this corresponds to returning from a program's main procedure. Assuming initial configuration qZ, the probability sub-distribution over the possible return values is then given by the return probabilities $\{[qZr] \mid r \in Q\}$. Missing probability mass models the probability of non-termination. Therefore, a basic certificate may be used to prove a point-wise upper bound on the output distribution as well as <u>non</u> *almost-sure termination* (AST). If a pPDA Δ is known to be AST, then we can also certify a lower bound on the output distribution: Suppose that u is a basic certificate for Δ and assume that Δ is AST from initial configuration qZ. Define $\varepsilon = \sum_{r \in Q} u_{qZr} - 1$. Then for all $r \in Q$, we have $u_{qZr} - \varepsilon \leq [qZr] \leq u_{qZr}$.

Example 6. The pPDA Δ_{ex} from Figure 3 is AST from initial configuration qZ, as the transition $qZ \xrightarrow{1/4} r\varepsilon$ is eventually taken with probability 1, and the stack is emptied certainly once r is reached. Using the basic certificate from Example 5 we can thus (correctly) certify that $0.5 \leq [qZq] \leq 0.6$ and $0.4 \leq [qZr] \leq 0.5$.

Certificates for Expected Rewards. pPDA may also be equipped with a reward function $Q \to \mathbb{R}_{\geq 0}$. It was shown in [14] that the expected reward accumulated during the run of a pPDA is the solution of a linear equation system whose coefficients depends on the numbers $[qZr]$. Given a basic certificate u, we obtain an equation system whose solution is an over-approximation of the true expected reward (see [44]). We may extend the basic certificate u by the solution of this linear system to make verification straightforward. Note that a program's *expected runtime* [8,35] is a special case of total expected reward.

5 Implementation and Experiments

Our Tool: PRAY. We implemented our algorithm in the prototypical Java-tool PRAY (Probabilistic Recursion AnalYzer) [43]. It supports two input formats: (i) Recursive probabilistic programs in a Java-like syntax (e.g. Figure 4); these programs are *automatically* translated to pPDA. (ii) Explicit PPS in the same syntax used by the tool PREMO [46]. The output of PRAY is a rational *inductive* upper bound on the lfp of the return probability PPS of the input program's pPDA model (a basic certificate), or on the lfp of the explicitly given PPS. The absolute precision ε is configurable. The implementation works as follows:

(1) It parses the input and, if the latter is a program, constructs a pPDA model and the associated PPS of return probabilities.

(2) It computes an SCC decomposition of the PPS under consideration using standard algorithms implemented in the JGRAPHT library [33].

(3) It applies Algorithm 1 to the individual SCC in reverse topological order using floating point arithmetic. Algorithm 1 is instantiated with Kleene iteration[4], the power iteration for approximating eigenvectors as outlined in Section 3.3, and constants $c = 0.1$, $d = 0.5$. We allow ≤ 10 guesses per SCC.

(4) If stage (3) is successful, the tool verifies the resulting floating point certificate using exact rational number arithmetic as described in Section 3.3.

Baselines. To the best of our knowledge, no alternative techniques for finding *inductive* upper bounds in PPS have been described explicitly in the literature. However, there is an (almost) out-of-the-box approach using an SMT solver: Given a PPS $x = f(x)$, compute some lower bound $l \leq \mu f$ using an iterative technique. Then query the SMT solver for a model (variable assignment) of the quantifier-free first-order logic formula $\varphi_f(x) = \bigwedge_{i=1}^n f_i(x) \leq x_i \wedge l_i \leq x_i \leq l_i + \varepsilon$ in the (decidable) theory of polynomial real arithmetic with inequality (aka QF_NRA in the SMT community). If such a model u exists, then clearly $\mu f \leq u$ and $||l - u||_\infty \leq \varepsilon$. If no model exists, then improve l and try again. We have implemented this approach using the state-of-the-art SMT solvers CVC5 [4] and Z3 [34], the winners of the 2022 SMT-COMP in the category QF_NRA[5].

As yet another baseline, we have also implemented a variant of OVI for PPS which is closer to the original MDP algorithm from [22]. In this variant, called "standard OVI" from now on, we compute the candidate u based on the *relative* update rule $u = (1 + \varepsilon)l$, where l is the current lower bound [22].

Research Questions. We aim to shed some light on the following questions: (A) How well does our algorithm scale? (B) Is the algorithm suitable for PPS with different characteristics, e.g., dense or sparse? (C) Is the requirement $\rho(f(\mu f)') < 1$ restrictive in practice? (D) How does our OVI compare to the baselines?

Benchmarks. To answer the above questions we run our implementation on two sets of benchmarks (Table 1 and Table 2, respectively). The first set consists of various example programs from the literature as well as a few new programs, which are automatically translated to pPDA. This translation is standard and usually takes not more than a few seconds. The programs golden, and-or (see Figure 4), virus, gen-fun are adapted from [35,8,42] and [32, Program 5.6], respectively. The source code of all considered programs is in [44]. We have selected only programs with possibly unbounded recursion depth which induce *infinite* Markov chains. The second benchmark set comprises explicit PPS from [46]. The instances brown, lemonde, negra, swbd, tiger, tuebadz, and wsj all encode SCFG

---

[4] In fact, we use the slightly optimized Gauss-Seidel iteration (see [45, Sec. 5.2]) which provides a good trade-off between ease of implementation and efficiency [45].

[5] https://smt-comp.github.io/2022/results

```
bool and() {                          bool or() {
    prob {                                prob {
        1//2: return                          1//2: return
            (1//2: true | 1//2: false);           (1//2: true | 1//2: false);
        1//2: {                               1//2: {
            if(!or()) return false;               if(and()) return true;
            else return or(); } } }               else return and(); } } }
```

Fig. 4: Program evaluating a random and-or tree [8]. The **prob**-blocks execute the contained statements with the respective probabilities (syntax inspired by Java's **switch**). Our tool automatically translates this program to a pPDA and computes a basic certificate (Proposition 1) witnessing that calling **and()** returns **true** and **false** with probability $\leq 382/657 \approx 0.58$ and $391/933 \approx 0.42$, resp.

from the area of language processing (see [46] for details). random is the return probability system of a randomly generated pPDA.

Summary of Results. We ran the experiments on a standard notebook. The approach based on CVC5 turns out to be not competitive (see [44]). We thus focus on Z3 in the following. Both PRAY and the Z3 approach handle most of the programs from Table 1 within a 10 minute time limit. The considered programs induce sparse PPS with 38 - 26,367 variables, and most of them have just a single SCC. Notably, the examples with greatest maximum SCC size are only solved by Z3. PRAY and Z3 need at most 95 and 31 seconds, respectively, for the instances where they succeed. In many cases (e.g., rw-5.01, golden, virus, brown, swbd), the resulting certificates formally disprove AST. For the explicit PPS in Table 2, PRAY solves all instances whereas Z3 only solves 3/8 within the time limit, and only finds the trivial solution 1. Most of these benchmarks contain dense high-degree polynomials, and our tool spends most time on performing exact arithmetic. Standard OVI (rightmost columns in Tables 1 and 2) solves strictly less instances than our eigenvector-based OVI. On some instances, Standard OVI is slightly faster (if it succeeds). However, on some larger benchmarks (brown, swbd) our variant runs $\approx 3\times$ faster.

Evaluation of Research Questions. (A) Scalability: Our algorithm succeeds on instances with maximum SCC size of up to 8,000 and number of terms over 50,000. PRAY solves all instances with a maximum SCC size of $\leq 1,000$ in less than 2 minutes per instance. For the examples where our algorithm does not succeed (e.g., escape100) it is mostly because it fails converting a floating point to a rational certificate. (B) PPS with different flavors: The problems in Table 1 (low degree and sparse, i.e., few terms per polynomials) and Table 2 (higher degree and dense) are quite different. A comparison to the SMT approach suggests that our technique might be especially well suited for dense problems with higher degrees. (C) Non-singularity: The only instance where our algorithm fails because of the non-singularity condition is the symmetric random walk rw-0.500. We therefore conjecture that this condition is often satisfied in practice. (D) Comparison with baselines: There is no clear winner. Some instances can only

Table 1: Experiments with PPS obtained from recursive probabilistic programs. Columns *vars* and *terms* display the number of variables and terms in the PPS. Columns *sccs* and scc_{max} indicate the number of non-trivial SCC and the size of the largest SCC. G is total number of guesses made by OVI (at least one guess per SCC). t_{tot} is the total runtime excluding the time for model construction. t_Q is the percentage of t_{tot} spent on exact rational arithmetic. D is the average number of decimal digits of the rational numbers in the certificate. The timeout (TO) was set to 10 minutes. Time is in ms. The absolute precision is $\varepsilon = 10^{-3}$.

benchmark	$|Q|$	$|P|$	$|\Gamma|$	vars	terms	sccs	scc_{max}	cert	G	D	t_Q	t_{tot}	$cert_{z3}$	D_{z3}	t_{z3}	$cert_{std}$	G_{std}	D_{std}	t_{std}
rw-0.499	18	29	5	38	45	1	12	✓	5	5	17%	163	✓	2	11	✓	4	5	59
rw-0.500	18	29	5	38	45	1	12	✗	10	-	-	7327	✓	2	10	✗	10	-	8083
rw-0.501	18	29	5	38	45	1	12	✓	5	4	6%	36	✓	13	12	✓	4	5	23
geom-offspring	24	40	5	52	80	4	24	✓	8	6	13%	15	✓	9	16	✓	8	6	14
golden	27	49	6	81	94	1	36	✓	1	5	30%	10	✓	7	14	✓	2	4	12
and-or	50	90	7	149	182	1	48	✓	2	4	26%	19	✓	12	15260	✓	2	4	19
gen-fun	85	219	7	202	327	1	16	✓	2	3	32%	22	✓	15	141	✓	2	3	21
virus	68	149	27	341	551	1	220	✓	1	5	38%	40	✓	7	139	✓	1	6	59
escape10	109	174	23	220	263	1	122	✓	1	4	5%	56	✓	7	48	✓	1	8	71
escape25	258	413	53	518	621	1	300	✓	1	5	17%	245	✓	7	15958	✓	1	9	172
escape50	508	813	103	1018	1221	1	600	✓	1	7	23%	653	✓	7	410	✗	1	-	400
escape75	760	1215	153	1522	1825	1	904	✓	2	9	10%	3803	✗	-	TO	✗	1	-	635
escape100	1009	1614	203	2020	2423	1	1202	✗	5	-	-	29027	✓	6	939	✗	1	-	901
escape200	2008	3213	403	4018	4821	1	2400	✗	6	-	-	83781	✗	-	TO	✗	1	-	2206
sequential5	230	490	39	1017	1200	10	12	✓	15	4	26%	103	✓	8	1074	✓	15	5	204
sequential7	572	1354	137	3349	3856	14	12	✓	21	5	27%	1049	✓	8	12822	✓	20	5	1042
sequential10	3341	8666	1036	26367	29616	20	12	✓	30	5	2%	100613	✓	8	453718	✓	30	6	101554
mod5	44	103	10	296	425	1	86	✓	1	5	39%	28	✓	9	34150	✗	2	-	178
mod7	64	159	14	680	1017	1	222	✓	1	6	69%	172	✓	7	443	✗	2	-	624
mod10	95	244	20	1574	2403	1	557	✗	1	-	-	675	✓	7	1245	✗	2	-	882

Table 2: Experiments with explicitly given PPS (setup as in Table 1).

benchmark	vars	terms	sccs	scc_{max}	cert	G	D	t_Q	t_{tot}	$cert_{z3}$	D_{z3}	t_{z3}	$cert_{std}$	G_{std}	D_{std}	t_{std}
brown	37	22866	1	22	✓	2	6	74%	3212	✗	-	TO	✓	2	8	9065
lemonde	121	32885	1	48	✓	2	5	97%	40738	✗	-	TO	✓	2	5	38107
negra	256	29297	1	149	✓	2	7	89%	10174	✓	1	37248	✓	1	7	8873
swbd	309	47578	1	243	✓	1	7	93%	18989	✗	-	TO	✓	1	8	67314
tiger	318	52184	1	214	✓	2	8	98%	94490	✓	1	17454	✓	1	8	90801
tuebadz	196	8932	2	168	✓	4	9	85%	2666	✓	1	15323	✓	3	9	2700
wsj	240	31170	1	194	✓	2	9	96%	30275	✗	-	TO	✓	2	9	29038
random	10000	20129	1	8072	✓	3	7	5%	17585	✗	-	TO	✓	4	8	16357

be solved by one tool or the other (e.g., escape100 and brown). However, PRAY often delivers more succinct certificates, i.e., the rational numbers have less digits. Moreover, z3 behaves *much less predictably* than PRAY.

6 Conclusion and Future Work

We have proposed using inductive bounds as certificates for various properties in probabilistic recursive models, and presented the first dedicated algorithm for computing such bounds. Our algorithm already scales to non-trivial problems. A remaining bottleneck is the need for exact rational arithmetic. This might be improved using appropriate rounding modes as in [21]. Additional future work includes certificates for *lower* bounds and termination.

Data availability statement The datasets generated during and/or analysed during the current study are available in the Zenodo repository [43].

References

1. Azeem, M., Evangelidis, A., Kretínský, J., Slivinskiy, A., Weininger, M.: Optimistic and topological value iteration for simple stochastic games. In: ATVA. Lecture Notes in Computer Science, vol. 13505, pp. 285–302. Springer (2022)
2. Baier, C., Katoen, J.: Principles of model checking. MIT Press (2008)
3. Baier, C., Klein, J., Leuschner, L., Parker, D., Wunderlich, S.: Ensuring the Reliability of Your Model Checker: Interval Iteration for Markov Decision Processes. In: CAV (1). Lecture Notes in Computer Science, vol. 10426, pp. 160–180. Springer (2017)
4. Barbosa, H., Barrett, C.W., Brain, M., Kremer, G., Lachnitt, H., Mann, M., Mohamed, A., Mohamed, M., Niemetz, A., Nötzli, A., Ozdemir, A., Preiner, M., Reynolds, A., Sheng, Y., Tinelli, C., Zohar, Y.: cvc5: A versatile and industrial-strength SMT solver. In: TACAS (1). Lecture Notes in Computer Science, vol. 13243, pp. 415–442. Springer (2022)
5. Batz, K., Chen, M., Kaminski, B.L., Katoen, J., Matheja, C., Schröer, P.: Latticed k-induction with an application to probabilistic programs. In: CAV (2). Lecture Notes in Computer Science, vol. 12760, pp. 524–549. Springer (2021)
6. Bishop, C.M.: Model-based machine learning. Philosophical Transactions of the Royal Society A: Mathematical, Physical and Engineering Sciences **371**(1984), 20120222 (2013)
7. Brázdil, T., Esparza, J., Kiefer, S., Kucera, A.: Analyzing probabilistic pushdown automata. Formal Methods Syst. Des. **43**(2), 124–163 (2013)
8. Brázdil, T., Kiefer, S., Kucera, A., Vareková, I.H.: Runtime analysis of probabilistic programs with unbounded recursion. J. Comput. Syst. Sci. **81**(1), 288–310 (2015)
9. Chiang, D., Riley, D.: Factor Graph Grammars. In: NeurIPS (2020)
10. Esparza, J., Gaiser, A., Kiefer, S.: Computing Least Fixed Points of Probabilistic Systems of Polynomials. In: STACS. LIPIcs, vol. 5, pp. 359–370. Schloss Dagstuhl - Leibniz-Zentrum für Informatik (2010)
11. Esparza, J., Kiefer, S., Luttenberger, M.: Convergence Thresholds of Newton's Method for Monotone Polynomial Equations. In: STACS. LIPIcs, vol. 1, pp. 289–300. Schloss Dagstuhl - Leibniz-Zentrum für Informatik, Germany (2008)
12. Esparza, J., Kiefer, S., Luttenberger, M.: Computing the Least Fixed Point of Positive Polynomial Systems. SIAM J. Comput. **39**(6), 2282–2335 (2010)
13. Esparza, J., Kucera, A., Mayr, R.: Model Checking Probabilistic Pushdown Automata. In: LICS. pp. 12–21. IEEE Computer Society (2004)
14. Esparza, J., Kucera, A., Mayr, R.: Quantitative Analysis of Probabilistic Pushdown Automata: Expectations and Variances. In: LICS. pp. 117–126. IEEE Computer Society (2005)
15. Esparza, J., Lammich, P., Neumann, R., Nipkow, T., Schimpf, A., Smaus, J.: A fully verified executable LTL model checker. In: CAV. Lecture Notes in Computer Science, vol. 8044, pp. 463–478. Springer (2013)
16. Etessami, K., Yannakakis, M.: Recursive Markov Chains, Stochastic Grammars, and Monotone Systems of Nonlinear Equations. In: STACS. Lecture Notes in Computer Science, vol. 3404, pp. 340–352. Springer (2005)

17. Etessami, K., Yannakakis, M.: Recursive Markov chains, stochastic grammars, and monotone systems of nonlinear equations. J. ACM **56**(1), 1:1–1:66 (2009)
18. Flajolet, P., Sedgewick, R.: Analytic Combinatorics. Cambridge University Press (2009)
19. Funke, F., Jantsch, S., Baier, C.: Farkas Certificates and Minimal Witnesses for Probabilistic Reachability Constraints. In: TACAS (1). Lecture Notes in Computer Science, vol. 12078, pp. 324–345. Springer (2020)
20. Haddad, S., Monmege, B.: Reachability in mdps: Refining convergence of value iteration. In: RP. Lecture Notes in Computer Science, vol. 8762, pp. 125–137. Springer (2014)
21. Hartmanns, A.: Correct Probabilistic Model Checking with Floating-Point Arithmetic. In: TACAS (2). Lecture Notes in Computer Science, vol. 13244, pp. 41–59. Springer (2022)
22. Hartmanns, A., Kaminski, B.L.: Optimistic value iteration. In: CAV (2). Lecture Notes in Computer Science, vol. 12225, pp. 488–511. Springer (2020)
23. Jantsch, S.: Certificates and Witnesses for Probabilistic Model Checking. Ph.D. thesis, Dresden University of Technology, Germany (2022)
24. Jantsch, S., Funke, F., Baier, C.: Minimal Witnesses for Probabilistic Timed Automata. In: ATVA. Lecture Notes in Computer Science, vol. 12302, pp. 501–517. Springer (2020)
25. Jurafsky, D., Wooters, C., Segal, J., Stolcke, A., Fosler, E., Tajchman, G.N., Morgan, N.: Using a stochastic context-free grammar as a language model for speech recognition. In: ICASSP. pp. 189–192. IEEE Computer Society (1995)
26. Karp, R.M.: An introduction to randomized algorithms. Discret. Appl. Math. **34**(1-3), 165–201 (1991)
27. Kiefer, S., Luttenberger, M., Esparza, J.: On the convergence of newton's method for monotone systems of polynomial equations. In: STOC. pp. 217–226. ACM (2007)
28. Knudsen, B., Hein, J.: Pfold: RNA secondary structure prediction using stochastic context-free grammars. Nucleic Acids Res. **31**(13), 3423–3428 (2003)
29. Kobayashi, N., Dal Lago, U., Grellois, C.: On the Termination Problem for Probabilistic Higher-Order Recursive Programs. Log. Methods Comput. Sci. **16**(4) (2020)
30. Kucera, A., Esparza, J., Mayr, R.: Model checking probabilistic pushdown automata. Log. Methods Comput. Sci. **2**(1) (2006)
31. McConnell, R.M., Mehlhorn, K., Näher, S., Schweitzer, P.: Certifying algorithms. Comput. Sci. Rev. **5**(2), 119–161 (2011)
32. van de Meent, J., Paige, B., Yang, H., Wood, F.: An Introduction to Probabilistic Programming. CoRR **abs/1809.10756** (2018)
33. Michail, D., Kinable, J., Naveh, B., Sichi, J.V.: Jgrapht - A java library for graph data structures and algorithms. ACM Trans. Math. Softw. **46**(2), 16:1–16:29 (2020)
34. de Moura, L.M., Bjørner, N.S.: Z3: an efficient SMT solver. In: TACAS. Lecture Notes in Computer Science, vol. 4963, pp. 337–340. Springer (2008)
35. Olmedo, F., Kaminski, B.L., Katoen, J., Matheja, C.: Reasoning about Recursive Probabilistic Programs. In: LICS. pp. 672–681. ACM (2016)
36. Quatmann, T., Katoen, J.: Sound Value Iteration. In: CAV (1). Lecture Notes in Computer Science, vol. 10981, pp. 643–661. Springer (2018)
37. Rothblum, U.G.: Nonnegative matrices and stochastic matrices. In: Hogben, L. (ed.) Handbook of Linear Algebra. CRC press (2006)
38. Saad, Y.: Numerical methods for large eigenvalue problems: revised edition. SIAM (2011)

39. Simistira, F., Katsouros, V., Carayannis, G.: Recognition of online handwritten mathematical formulas using probabilistic SVMs and stochastic context free grammars. Pattern Recognit. Lett. **53**, 85–92 (2015)
40. Stewart, A., Etessami, K., Yannakakis, M.: Upper Bounds for Newton's Method on Monotone Polynomial Systems, and P-Time Model Checking of Probabilistic One-Counter Automata. J. ACM **62**(4), 30:1–30:33 (2015)
41. Wimmer, S., von Mutius, J.: Verified Certification of Reachability Checking for Timed Automata. In: TACAS (1). Lecture Notes in Computer Science, vol. 12078, pp. 425–443. Springer (2020)
42. Winkler, T., Gehnen, C., Katoen, J.: Model Checking Temporal Properties of Recursive Probabilistic Programs. In: FoSSaCS. Lecture Notes in Computer Science, vol. 13242, pp. 449–469. Springer (2022)
43. Winkler, T., Katoen, J.: Artifcat Evaluation for TACAS '23 Paper: "Certificates for Probabilistic Pushdown Automata via Optimistic Value Iteration" (2023). `https://doi.org/10.5281/zenodo.7506305`
44. Winkler, T., Katoen, J.P.: Certificates for Probabilistic Pushdown Automata via Optimistic Value Iteration (2023). `https://doi.org/10.48550/ARXIV.2301.08657`
45. Wojtczak, D.: Recursive probabilistic models : efficient analysis and implementation. Ph.D. thesis, University of Edinburgh, UK (2009)
46. Wojtczak, D., Etessami, K.: PReMo : An Analyzer for Probabilistic Recursive Models. In: TACAS. Lecture Notes in Computer Science, vol. 4424, pp. 66–71. Springer (2007)
47. Yannakakis, M., Etessami, K.: Checking LTL properties of recursive markov chains. In: QEST. pp. 155–165. IEEE Computer Society (2005)

Probabilistic Program Verification via Inductive Synthesis of Inductive Invariants*

Kevin Batz[1]([✉])[iD], Mingshuai Chen[2]([✉])[iD], Sebastian Junges[3]([✉])[iD], Benjamin Lucien Kaminski[4]([✉])[iD], Joost-Pieter Katoen[1]([✉])[iD], and Christoph Matheja[5]([✉])[iD]

[1] RWTH Aachen University, Aachen, Germany
{kevin.batz,katoen}@cs.rwth-aachen.de
[2] Zhejiang University, Hangzhou, China
m.chen@zju.edu.cn
[3] Radboud University, Nijmegen, Netherlands
sebastian.junges@ru.nl
[4] Saarland University, Saarbrücken, Germany
and University College London, London, United Kingdom
kaminski@cs.uni-saarland.de
[5] Technical University of Denmark, Kgs. Lyngby, Denmark
chmat@dtu.dk

Abstract. Essential tasks for the verification of probabilistic programs include bounding expected outcomes and proving termination in finite expected runtime. We contribute a simple yet effective *inductive synthesis* approach for proving such *quantitative reachability properties* by generating *inductive invariants* on *source-code level*. Our implementation shows promise: It finds invariants for (in)finite-state programs, can beat state-of-the-art probabilistic model checkers, and is competitive with modern tools dedicated to invariant synthesis and expected runtime reasoning.

1 Introduction

Reasoning about reachability probabilities is a foundational task in the analysis of randomized systems. Such systems are (possibly infinite-state) *Markov chains*, which are typically described as *probabilistic programs* – imperative programs that may sample from probability distributions. We contribute a method for proving bounds on *quantitative properties* of probabilistic programs, which finds *inductive invariants* on *source-code level* by *inductive synthesis*. We discuss each of these ingredients below, present our approach with a running example in Sect. 2, and defer a detailed discussion of related work to Sect. 8.

1) *Quantitative Reachability Properties.* We aim to verify properties such as *"is the probability of reaching an error at most 1%?"* More generally, our technique proves bounds on the expected value of a probabilistic program terminating in designated states (see Sect. 2.1). Various verification problems are ultimately

---

* This research was funded by the ERC AdG FRAPPANT under grant No. 787914.

S. Sankaranarayanan and N. Sharygina (Eds.): TACAS 2023, LNCS 13994, pp. 410–429, 2023.
https://doi.org/10.1007/978-3-031-30820-8_25

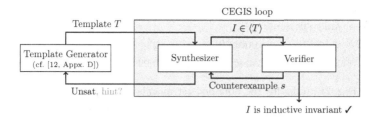

Fig. 1: Our CEGIS framework for synthesizing quantitative inductive invariants.

solved by bounding quantitative reachability properties (cf. [7,47]). Further examples of such problems include *"does a program terminate with finite expected runtime?"* and *"is the expected sum of program variables x and y at least one?"*

2) *Inductive Invariants.* An inductive invariant is a *certificate* that witnesses a certain quantitative reachability property. Quantitative (and qualitative) reachability are typically captured as least fixed points (cf. [52,47,7]). For upper bounds, this characterization makes it natural to search for a prefixed point – the inductive invariant – that, by standard fixed point theory [56], is greater than or equal to the least fixed point. Our invariants assign every state a quantity. If the initial state is assigned a quantity below the desired threshold, then the invariant certifies that the property in question holds. We detail quantitative inductive invariants in Sect. 2.2; we adapt our method to lower bound reasoning in Sect. 6.

3) *Source-Code Level.* We consider probabilistic programs over (potentially unbounded) integer variables that conceptually extend while-programs with coin flips, see e.g. Fig. 2.[6] We exploit the program structure to reason about infinite-state (and large finite-state) programs: We *never* construct a Markov chain but find *symbolic* inductive invariants (mapping from program states to nonnegative reals) on *source-code* level. We particularly discover inductive invariants that are piecewise linear, as they can often be verified efficiently.

4) *Inductive Synthesis.* Our approach to finding invariants, as sketched in Fig. 1, is inspired by *inductive synthesis* [4]: The inner loop (shaded box) is provided with a *template* T which may generate an infinite set $\langle T \rangle$ of instances. We then synthesize a template instance I that is an inductive invariant witnessing quantitative reachability, or determine that no such instance exists. We search for such instances in a *counterexample-guided inductive synthesis* (CEGIS) loop: The synthesizer constructs a candidate. (A tailored variant of) an off-the-shelf verifier either (i) decides that the candidate is a suitable inductive invariant or (ii) reports a counterexample state s back to the synthesizer. Upon termination (guaranteed for finite-state programs), the inner loop has either found an inductive invariant or the solver reports that the template T does not admit an inductive invariant.

Contributions. We show that inductive synthesis for verifying *quantitative reachability properties* by finding *inductive invariants* on *source-code level* is

---

[6] PRISM programs can be interpreted as an implicit `while(not error-state) {...}` program – see [40] for an explicit translation.

```
1:    fail := 0 ; sent := 0 ;
2:    while ( sent < 8 000 000  ∧  fail < 10 ) {
3:        { fail := 0 ; sent := sent + 1 } [ 0.999 ] { fail := fail + 1 }    }
```

Fig. 2: Model for the bounded retransmission protocol (BRP).

feasible: Our approach is sound for arbitrary probabilistic programs, and complete for finite-state programs. We implemented our simple yet powerful technique. The results are promising: Our CEGIS loop is sufficiently fast to support large templates and finds inductive invariants for various probabilistic programs and properties. It can prove, amongst others, upper and lower bounds on reachability probabilities and universal positive almost-termination [42]. Our implementation is competitive with three state-of-the-art tools – STORM [39], ABSYNTH [50], and EXIST [9] – on subsets of their benchmarks fitting our framework.

Applicability and Limitations. We consider programs with possibly unbounded nonnegative integer-valued variables and arbitrary affine expressions in quantitative specifications. As for other synthesis-based approaches, there are unrealizable cases – loops for which no piecewise linear invariant exists. But, if there is an invariant, our CEGIS loop often finds it within a few iterations.

2   Overview

We illustrate our approach using the bounded retransmission protocol (BRP) – a standard probabilistic model checking benchmark [38,28] – modeled by the probabilistic program in Fig. 2. The model attempts to transmit 8 million packets[7] over a lossy channel, where each packet is lost with probability 0.1%; if a packet is lost, we retry sending it; if any packet is lost in 10 consecutive sending attempts ($fail = 10$), the *entire* transmission fails; if all packets have been transmitted successfully ($sent = 8\,000\,000$), the transmission succeeds.

2.1   Reachability Probabilities and Loops

We aim to reason about the transmission-failure probability of BRP, i.e. the probability that the loop terminates in a target state t with $t(fail) = 10$ when started in initial program state s_0 with $s_0(fail) = s_0(sent) = 0$. One approach to determine this probability is to (i) construct an explicit-state Markov chain (MC) per Fig. 2, (ii) derive its Bellmann operator Φ [52], (iii) compute its least fixed point lfp Φ (a vector containing for <u>each</u> state the probability to reach t), e.g. using value iteration (cf. [7, Thm 10.15]), and finally (iv) evaluate lfp Φ at s_0.

The explicit-state MC of BRP has ca. 80 million states. We *avoid* building such large state spaces by computing a symbolic representation of Φ from the

---

[7] Large constants like the number of packets appear naturally in quantitative models of protocols and have a non-trivial impact on probabilities.

program. More formally, let S be the set of all states, `loop` the entire loop (ll. 2–3 in Fig. 2), `body` the loop's body (l. 3), and $[\![body]\!](s)(s')$ the probability of reaching state s' by executing `body` once on state s. Then the least fixed point of the `loop`'s Bellmann operator $\Phi \colon \left(S \to \mathbb{R}_{\geq 0}^{\infty}\right) \to \left(S \to \mathbb{R}_{\geq 0}^{\infty}\right)$, defined by

$$
\Phi(I) \;=\; \lambda s. \begin{cases} 1, & \text{if } s(\mathit{fail}) = 10 \;, \\[2mm] \displaystyle\sum_{s' \in S} [\![body]\!](s)(s') \cdot I(s'), & \begin{aligned} &\text{if } s(\mathit{sent}) < 8\,000\,000 \\ &\text{and } s(\mathit{fail}) < 10 \;, \end{aligned} \\[4mm] 0, & \text{otherwise} \;, \end{cases}
$$

captures the transmission-failure probability for the *entire* execution of `loop` and for *any* initial state, that is, $(\mathsf{lfp}\ \Phi)(s)$ is the probability of terminating in a target state when executing `loop` on s (even if `loop` would not terminate almost-surely). Intuitively, $\Phi(I)(s)$ maps to 1 if `loop` has terminated meeting the target condition transmission failure); and to 0 if `loop` has terminated otherwise (transmission success). If `loop` is still running (i.e. it has neither failed nor succeeded yet), then $\Phi(I)(s)$ maps to the expected value of I after executing `body` on state s.

2.2 Quantitative Inductive Invariants

Reachability probabilities are generally not computable for infinite-state probabilistic programs [43]. Even for finite-state programs the state-space explosion may prevent us from computing reachability probabilities exactly. However, it often suffices to know that the reachability probability is bounded from above by some threshold λ. For BRP, we hence aim to prove that $(\mathsf{lfp}\ \Phi)(s_0) \leq \lambda$.

We attack the above task by means of *(quantitative) inductive invariants*: a candidate for an inductive invariant is a mapping $I \colon S \to \mathbb{R}_{\geq 0}^{\infty}$. Intuitively, such a candidate I is *inductive* if the following holds: when assuming that $I(s)$ is (an over-approximation of) the probability to reach a target state upon termination of `loop` on s, then the probability to reach a target state after performing one more guarded loop iteration, i.e. executing `if ( sent < ... ) { body ; loop }` on s, must be *at most* $I(s)$. Formally, I is an inductive invariant[8] if

$$
\forall s \colon \quad \Phi(I)(s) \;\leq\; I(s) \qquad \text{which implies} \qquad \forall s \colon \quad \big(\mathsf{lfp}\ \Phi\big)(s) \;\leq\; I(s)
$$

by Park induction [51]. Hence, $I(s)$ bounds for each initial state s the exact reachability probability from above. If we are able to find an inductive I that is below λ for the initial state s_0 with $\mathit{fail} = \mathit{sent} = 0$, i.e. $I(s_0) \leq \lambda$, then we have indeed proven the upper bound λ on the transmission-failure probability of our BRP model. In a nutshell, our goal can be phrased as follows:

Goal: Find an inductive invariant I, i.e. an I with $\Phi(I) \leq I$, s.t. $I(s_0) \leq \lambda$.

---

[8] For an exposition of why it makes sense to speak of *invariants* even in a quantitative setting, [42, Sect. 5.1] relates quantitative invariants to invariants in Hoare logic.

2.3 Our CEGIS Framework for Synthesizing Inductive Invariants

While *finding* a safe inductive invariant I is challenging, *checking* whether a given candidate I is indeed inductive is easier: it is decidable for certain infinite-state programs (cf. [14, Sect. 7.2]), it may not require an explicit exploration of the whole state space, and it can be done efficiently for piecewise linear I. Hence, techniques that generate decent candidate expressions fast and then check their inductivity could enable the automatic verification of probabilistic programs with gigantic and even infinite state spaces.

In this paper, we test this hypothesis by developing the CEGIS framework depicted in Fig. 1 for incrementally synthesizing inductive invariants. A template generator generates parametrized templates for inductive invariants. The inner loop (shaded box in Fig. 1) then tries to solve for appropriate template-parameter instantiations. If it succeeds, an inductive invariant has been synthesized. Otherwise, the template provably cannot be instantiated into an inductive invariant. The inner loop then reports that back to the template generator (possibly with some hint on why it failed, see [12, Appx. D]) and asks for a refined template.

For our running example, we start with the template

$$T \;=\; [\mathit{fail} < 10 \wedge \mathit{sent} < 8\,000\,000] \cdot (\alpha \cdot \mathit{sent} + \beta \cdot \mathit{fail} + \gamma) \;+\; [\mathit{fail} = 10]\,, \quad (1)$$

where we use *Iverson brackets* for indicators, i.e. $[\varphi]\,(s) = 1$ if $s \models \varphi$ and 0 otherwise. T contains two kinds of variables: integer program variables $\mathit{fail}, \mathit{sent}$ and $\mathbb{Q}$-valued parameters α, β, γ. While the template is nonlinear, substituting α, β, γ with concrete values yields piecewise linear candidate invariants I. We ensure that those I are piecewise linear to render the repeated inductivity checks efficient. We construct only so-called *natural* templates T with Φ in mind, e.g. we want to construct only I such that $I(s) = 1$ when $s(\mathit{fail}) = 10$.

Our inner CEGIS loop checks whether there exists an assignment from these template variables to concrete values such that the resulting piecewise linear expression is an inductive invariant. Concretely, we try to determine whether there exist values for α, β, γ such that $T(\alpha, \beta, \gamma)$ is inductive. For that, we first guess values for α, β, γ, say all 0's, and ask a verifier whether the instantiated (and now piecewise linear) template $I = T(0,0,0)$ is indeed inductive. In our example, the verifier determines that I is *not* inductive: a counterexample is $s(\mathit{fail}) = 9$, $s(\mathit{sent}) = 7999999$. Intuitively, the probability to reach the target after one more loop iteration exceeds the value in I for this state, that is, $\Phi(I)(s) = 0.001 > 0 = I(s)$. From this counterexample, our synthesizer learns

$$\Phi(T)(s) \;=\; 0.001 \;\overset{!}{\leq}\; \alpha \cdot 7999999 + \beta \cdot 9 + \gamma \;=\; T(s)\,.$$

Observe that this learned lemma is linear in α, β, γ. The synthesizer will now keep "guessing" assignments to the parameters which are consistent with the learned lemmas until either no such parameter assignment exists anymore, or until it produces an *inductive* invariant $I = T(\ldots)$. In our running example, assuming $\lambda = 0.9$, after 6 lemmas, our synthesizer finds the inductive invariant I

$$[\mathit{fail} < 10 \wedge \mathit{sent} < 8 \cdot 10^6] \cdot (-\tfrac{9}{8 \cdot 10^7} \cdot \mathit{sent} + \tfrac{79\,991}{72 \cdot 10^7} \cdot \mathit{fail} + \tfrac{9}{10}) + [\mathit{fail} = 10] \quad (2)$$

$fail := 0\,;\ sent := 0\,;$

$\texttt{while}\,(\ sent < P\ \wedge\ fail < R\ \wedge\ P \leq 8\,000\,000\ \wedge\ R \geq 5\,)\,\{$

   $\{\,fail := 0\,;\ sent := sent + 1\,\}\,[\,0.99\,]\,\{\,fail := fail + 1\,\}$

$\}$

(a) A family of retransmission protocols

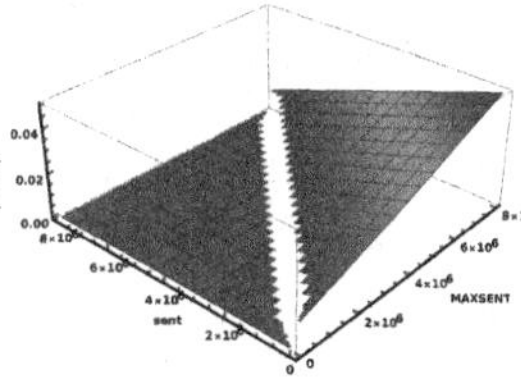

(b) Inductive invariant for $fail = 0$ and $R \geq 5$

Fig. 3: A bounded retransmission protocol family and piece of a matching invariant.

where indeed $I(s_0) \leq \lambda$ holds. For a tighter threshold λ, such simple templates do not suffice. For example, it is impossible to instantiate this template to an inductive invariant for $\lambda = 0.8$, even though 0.8 is an upper bound on the actual reachability probability. We therefore support *more general templates* of the form

$$T \ = \ \sum_i [B_i] \cdot (\alpha_i \cdot sent + \beta_i \cdot fail + \gamma_i) \ + \ [fail = 10] \ ,$$

where the B_i are (restricted) predicates over program and template variables which partition the state space. In particular, we allow for a template such as

$$\begin{aligned}
T \ = \ &[fail < 10 \wedge sent < \delta] \cdot (\alpha_1 \cdot sent + \beta_1 \cdot fail + \gamma_1) \ + \\
&[fail < 10 \wedge sent \geq \delta] \cdot (\alpha_2 \cdot sent + \beta_2 \cdot fail + \gamma_2) \ + \ [fail = 10]
\end{aligned} \tag{3}$$

However, such templates are challenging for the CEGIS loop. Thus, we additionally consider templates where the B_i's range only over program variables, e.g.

$$[fail < 10 \wedge sent < 4\,000\,000] \cdot (\ldots) \ + \ [fail < 10 \wedge sent \geq 4\,000\,000] \cdot (\ldots) \ + \ \ldots$$

Our partition refinement algorithms automatically produce these templates, without the need for user interaction.

    Finally, we highlight that we may use our approach for more general questions. For BRP, suppose we want to verify an upper bound $\lambda = 0.05$ on the probability of failing to transmit *all* packages for an *infinite set of models* (also called a *family*) with varying upper bounds on packets $1 \leq P \leq 8000000$ and retransmissions $R \geq 5$. This infinite set of models is described by the loop shown in Fig. 3a. Our approach fully automatically synthesizes the following inductive invariant I:

$$\begin{bmatrix} fail < R\ \wedge\ sent < P\ \wedge\ P < 8\,000\,000\ \wedge\ R \geq 5 \\ \wedge\ R > 1 + fail\ \wedge\ \frac{13067990199}{5280132671650} \cdot fail \leq \frac{5278689867}{211205306866000} \end{bmatrix} \cdot \begin{pmatrix} \frac{-19}{3820000040} \cdot sent \\ + \frac{19}{3820000040} \cdot P \\ + \frac{19500001}{1910000020} \end{pmatrix}$$

$+ \ \ldots$ (7 additional summands omitted)

The first summand of I is plotted in Fig. 3b. Since I overapproximates the probability of failing to transmit all packages for every state, I may be used to infer additional information about the reachability probabilities.

3 Formal Problem Statement

Before we state the precise invariant synthesis problem that we aim to solve, we summarize the essential concepts underlying our formalization.

Probabilistic Loops. We consider *single probabilistic loops* $\texttt{while}\,(\,\varphi\,)\,\{\,C\,\}$ whose *loop guard* φ and (loop-free) *body* C adhere to the grammar

$$C \;\longrightarrow\; \texttt{skip} \mid x := e \mid C\,;C \mid \{C\}\,[p]\,\{C\} \mid \texttt{if}\,(\varphi)\,\{C\}\,\texttt{else}\,\{C\}$$
$$\varphi \;\longrightarrow\; e < e \mid \neg\varphi \mid \varphi \wedge \varphi \qquad e \;\longrightarrow\; z \mid x \mid z\cdot e \mid e+e \,,$$

where $z \in \mathbb{Z}$ is a constant and x is from an arbitrary *finite* set Vars of $\mathbb{N}$-valued program variables. Program states in $S = \{\,s \mid s\colon \mathsf{Vars} \to \mathbb{N}\,\}$ map variables to natural numbers.[9] All statements are standard (cf. [47]). $\{C_1\}\,[p]\,\{C_2\}$ is a probabilistic choice which executes C_1 with probability $p \in [0,1] \cap \mathbb{Q}$ and C_2 with probability $1-p$. Fig. 2 (ll. 2–3) is an example of a probabilistic loop.

Expectations. In Sect. 2, we considered whether final states meet some target condition by assigning 0 or 1 to each final state. The assignment can be generalized to more general quantities in $\mathbb{R}_{\geq 0}^{\infty}$. We call such assignments f *expectations* [47] (think: random variable) and collect them in the set $\mathbb{E}$, i.e.

$$\mathbb{E} \;=\; \{\,f \mid f\colon S \to \mathbb{R}_{\geq 0}^{\infty}\,\}\,, \qquad \text{where} \quad f \preceq g \quad \text{iff} \quad \forall s \in S\colon f(s) \leq g(s)\,.$$

$\preceq$ is a partial order on $\mathbb{E}$ – necessary to sensibly speak about least fixed points.

Characteristic Functions. The expected behavior of a probabilistic loop for an expectation f is captured by an expectation transformer (namely the $\varPhi\colon \mathbb{E} \to \mathbb{E}$ of Sect. 2), called the loop's *characteristic function*. To focus on invariant synthesis, we abstract from the details[10] of constructing characteristic functions from probabilistic loops; our framework only requires the following key property:

Proposition 1 (Characteristic Functions). *For every loop* $\texttt{while}\,(\,\varphi\,)\,\{\,C\,\}$ *and expectation* f*, there exists a monotone function* $\varPhi_f\colon \mathbb{E} \to \mathbb{E}$ *such that*

$$\varPhi_f(I)(s) \;=\; \begin{cases} f(s), & \text{if } s \not\models \varphi\,, \\[4pt] \text{``expected value of } I \text{ after executing } C \text{ once on } s\text{''}, & \text{if } s \models \varphi\,, \end{cases}$$

and the least fixed point of $\varPhi_f$*, denoted* $\mathsf{lfp}\,\varPhi_f$*, satisfies*

$$\big(\mathsf{lfp}\,\varPhi_f\big)(s) \;=\; \text{``expected value of } f \text{ after executing } \texttt{while}\,(\,\varphi\,)\,\{\,C\,\} \text{ on } s\text{''}\,.$$

---

[9] Considering only unsigned integers does not decrease expressive power but simplifies the technical presentation (cf. [16, Sect. 11.2] for a detailed discussion). We statically ensure that for every assignment $x := e$, e always evaluates to some value in $\mathbb{N}$.

[10] We can (and our tool does) derive a symbolic representation of a loop's characteristic function from the program structure using a weakest-precondition-style calculus (cf. [47]); see [12, Appx. A] for details. If f maps only to 0 or 1, $\varPhi_f$ corresponds to the least fixed point characterization of reachability probabilities [7, Thm. 10.15].

Example 1. In our running example from Sect. 2.1, we chose as f the expression $fail = 10]$, which evaluates to 1 in every state s where $fail = 10$ and to 0 otherwise. The characteristic function $\Phi_f(I)$ of the loop in Fig. 2 is

$$\neg\varphi] \cdot [fail{=}10] \;+\; [\varphi] \cdot \big(0.999 \cdot I\,[sent/sent{+}1]\,[fail/0] + 0.001 \cdot I\,[fail/fail{+}1]\big),$$

where $\varphi = sent < 8\,000\,000 \wedge fail < 10$ is the loop guard and $I\,[x/e]$ denotes the (syntactic) substitution of variable x by expression e in expectation I – the latter is used to model the effect of assignments as in standard Hoare logic. $\triangleleft$

Inductive Invariants. For a probabilistic loop $\text{while}\,(\varphi)\,\{\,C\,\}$, and *pre-* and *post*expectations $g, f \in \mathbb{E}$, we aim to verify $\text{lfp}\,\Phi_f \preceq g$, i.e. that the expected value of f after termination of the loop is bounded from above by g. We discuss how to adapt our approach to expected runtimes and lower bounds in Sect. 6. Intuitively, f assigns a quantity to all *target* states reached upon termination. g assigns to all *initial states* a desired bound on the expected value of f after termination of the loop. By choosing $g(s) = \infty$ for certain s, we can make s so-to-speak "irrelevant". An $I \in \mathbb{E}$ is an *inductive invariant* proving $\text{lfp}\,\Phi_f \preceq g$ iff $\Phi_f(I) \preceq I$ and $I \preceq g$. Continuing our example, Eq. (2) on p. 5 shows an inductive invariant proving that $\text{lfp}\,\Phi_f \preceq g := [fail = 0 \wedge sent = 0] \cdot 0.9 + [\neg(fail = 0 \wedge sent = 0)] \cdot \infty$.

Our framework employs syntactic fragments of expectations on which the check $\Phi_f(I) \preceq I$ can be done symbolically by an SMT solver. As illustrated in Fig. 1, we use *templates* to further narrow down the invariant search space.

Templates. Let $\mathsf{TVars} = \{\alpha, \beta, \ldots\}$ be a countably infinite set of $\mathbb{Q}$-valued *template variables*. A *template valuation* is a function $\mathfrak{I}\colon \mathsf{TVars} \to \mathbb{Q}$ that assigns to each template variable a rational number. We will use the same expressions as in our programs except that we admit both rationals and template variables as coefficients. Formally, arithmetic and Boolean expressions E and B adhere to

$$E \;\longrightarrow\; r \mid x \mid r \cdot x \mid E + E \qquad B \;\longrightarrow\; E < E \mid \neg B \mid B \wedge B \,,$$

where $x \in \mathsf{Vars}$ and $r \in \mathbb{Q} \cup \mathsf{TVars}$. The set TExp of templates then consists of all

$$T \;=\; [B_1] \cdot E_1 + \ldots + [B_n] \cdot E_n \,,$$

for $n \geq 1$, where *the Boolean expressions B_i partition the state space*, i.e. for all template valuations $\mathfrak{I}$ and all states s, there is *exactly one* B_i such that $\mathfrak{I}, s \models B_i$. T is a *fixed-partition template* if additionally no B_i contains a template variable. Notice that templates are generally *not* linear (over $\mathsf{Vars} \cup \mathsf{TVars}$). Sect. 2 gives several examples of templates, e.g. Eq. (1).

Template Instances. We denote by $T\,[\mathfrak{I}]$ the *instance* of template T under $\mathfrak{I}$, i.e. the expression obtained from substituting every template variable α in T by its valuation $\mathfrak{I}(\alpha)$. For example, the expression in Eq. (2) on p. 5 is an instance of the template in Eq. (1) on p. 5. The set of all instances of template T is defined as $\langle T \rangle = \{\, T\,[\mathfrak{I}] \mid \mathfrak{I}\colon \mathsf{TVars} \to \mathbb{Q}\,\}$. We chose the shape of templates on purpose: To evaluate an instance $T\,[\mathfrak{I}]$ of a template T in a state s, it suffices to find the *unique* Boolean expression B_i with $\mathfrak{I}, s \models B_i$ and then evaluate the *single* linear arithmetic expression $E_i\,[\mathfrak{I}]$ in s. For fixed-partition templates, the selection of the right B_i does not even depend on the template evaluation $\mathfrak{I}$.

Piecewise Linear Expectations. Some template instances $T[\mathfrak{I}]$ do *not* represent expectations, i.e. they are not of type $S \to \mathbb{R}^{\infty}_{\geq 0}$, as they may evaluate to *negative numbers.* Template instances $T[\mathfrak{I}]$ that *do* represent expectations are *piecewise linear*; we collect such *well-defined* instances in the set LinExp. Formally,

Definition 1 (LinExp). *The set* LinExp *of* (piecewise) linear expectations *is* LinExp $= \{T[\mathfrak{I}] \mid T \in \mathsf{TExp}$ and $\mathfrak{I}\colon \mathsf{TVars} \to \mathbb{Q}$ and $\forall s \in S\colon T[\mathfrak{I}](s) \geq 0\}$.

We identify well-defined instances of templates in LinExp with the expectation in $\mathbb{E}$ that they represent, e.g. when writing the inductivity check $\varPhi_f(T[\mathfrak{I}]) \overset{?}{\preceq} (T[\mathfrak{I}])$.

Natural Templates. As suggested in Sect. 2.3, it makes sense to focus only on so-called *natural* templates. Those are templates that even have a chance of becoming inductive, as they take the loop guard φ and postexpectation f into account. Formally, a template T is *natural* (wrt. to φ and f) if T is of the form

$$T = \underbrace{[\neg\varphi \wedge B_1] \cdot E_1 + \ldots + [\neg\varphi \wedge B_n] \cdot E_n}_{\text{must be equivalent to } [\neg\varphi] \cdot f} + [B'_1] \cdot E'_1 + \ldots + [B'_m] \cdot E'_m \ .$$

We collect all natural templates in the set TnExp.

Formal Problem Statement. Throughout this paper, we fix an ambient single loop $\mathtt{while}\,(\,\varphi\,)\,\{\,C\,\}$, a postexpectation $f \in \mathsf{LinExp}$, and a preexpectation $g \in \mathsf{LinExp}$[11] such that $\mathsf{lfp}\,\varPhi_f(I) \preceq g$[12]. The set AdmInv of *admissible invariants* (i.e. those expectations that are both *inductive* and *safe*) is then given by

$$\mathsf{AdmInv} = \{\ \underbrace{I \in \mathsf{LinExp}}_{\text{well-definedness: } I \succeq 0}\ \mid\ \underbrace{\varPhi_f(I) \preceq I}_{\text{inductivity}}\ \text{and}\ \underbrace{I \preceq g}_{\text{safety}}\ \},$$

where the underbraces summarize the tasks for a verifier to decide whether a template instance I is an admissible inductive invariant. We require $\mathsf{lfp}\,\varPhi_f \preceq g$, so that AdmInv is not vacuously empty due to an unsafe bound g.

> **Formal problem statement**: Given a natural template T, find an instantiation $I \in \langle T \rangle \cap \mathsf{AdmInv}$ or determine that there is no such I.

Notice that AdmInv might be empty, even for safe g's, because generally one might need more complex invariants than piecewise linear ones [16]. However, there always exists an inductive invariant in LinExp if a loop can reach only finitely many states.[13] We call a loop $\mathtt{while}\,(\,\varphi\,)\,\{\,C\,\}$ *finite-state*, if only finitely many states satisfy the loop guard φ, i.e. if $S_\varphi = \{\,s \in S \mid s \models \varphi\,\}$ is finite.

Syntactic Characteristic Functions. We work with *linear* expectations $I, f \in \mathsf{LinExp}$, so that we can check inductivity $(\varPhi_f(I) \preceq I)$ symbolically (via SMT) without state space construction. In particular, we can construct a *syntactic counterpart* $\varPsi_f$ to $\varPhi_f$ that operates on *templates*. Intuitively, whether

---

[11] To enable declaring certain states as irrelevant, we additionally allow $E_i = \infty$ in the linear preexpectation $g = [B_1] \cdot E_1 + \ldots + [B_n] \cdot E_n$.

[12] We discuss in Sect. 6 how to reason about lower bounds $g \preceq \mathsf{lfp}\,\varPhi_f(I)$.

[13] Bluntly just choose as many pieces as there are states.

we evaluate Ψ_f on a (syntactic) template T and then instantiate the result with a valuation $\Im$, *or* we evaluate Φ_f on the (semantic) expectation $T[\Im]$ emerging from instantiating T with $\Im$ – the results will coincide if $T[\Im]$ is well-defined. Formally:

Proposition 2. *Given* while $(\varphi)\{C\}$ *and* $f \in$ LinExp, *one can effectively compute a mapping* $\Psi_f \colon$ TExp $\to$ TExp, *such that for all T and $\Im$*

$$T[\Im] \in \text{LinExp} \quad \text{implies} \quad \Psi_f(T)[\Im] = \Phi_f(T[\Im]) \ .$$

Moreover, Ψ_f *maps fixed-partition templates to fixed-partition templates.*

In Ex. 1, we have already constructed such a Ψ_f to represent Φ_f. The general construction is inspired by [14], but treats template variables as constants.

4   One-Shot Solver

One could address the template instantiation problem from Sect. 3 in one shot: encode it as an SMT query, ask a solver for a model, and infer from the model an admissible invariant. While this approach is infeasible in practice (as it involves quantification over S_φ), it inspires the CEGIS loop in Fig. 1.

Regarding the encoding, given a template T, we need a formula over TVars that is satisfiable if and only if there exists a template valuation $\Im$ such that $T[\Im]$ is an admissible invariant, i.e. $T[\Im] \in$ AdmInv. To get rid of program variables in templates, we denote by $T(s)$ the expression over TVars in which all *program* variables $x \in$ Vars have been substituted by $s(x)$.

Intuitively, we then encode that, for every state s, the expression $T(s)$ satisfies the three conditions of admissible invariants, i.e. well-definedness, inductivity, and safety. In particular, we use Prop. 2 to compute a template $\Psi_f(T)$ that represents the application of the characteristic function Φ_f to a candidate invariant, i.e. $\Phi_f(T[\Im])$ – a necessity for encoding inductivity.

Formally, we denote by $\text{Sat}(\phi)$ the set of all models of a first-order formula ϕ (with a fixed underlying structure), i.e. $\text{Sat}(\phi) = \{\Im \mid \Im \models \phi\}$. Then:

Theorem 1. *For every natural template $T \in$ TnExp and $f,g \in$ LinExp, we have*

$$\langle T \rangle \cap \text{AdmInv} \neq \emptyset$$

$$\text{iff} \quad \text{Sat}\big(\forall s \in S_\varphi \colon \underbrace{0 \leq T(s)}_{\textit{well-definedness}} \wedge \underbrace{\Psi_f(T)(s) \leq T(s)}_{\textit{inductivity}} \wedge \underbrace{T(s) \leq g(s)}_{\textit{safety}} \big) \neq \emptyset \ .$$

Notice that, for fixed-partition templates, the above encoding is particularly simple: $T(s)$ and $\Psi_f(T)(s)$ are equivalent to single linear arithmetic expressions over TVars; $g(s)$ is either a single expression or ∞ – in the latter case, we get an equisatisfiable formula by dropping the always-satisfied constraint $T(s) \leq g(s)$.

For general templates, one can exploit the partitioning to break it down into multiple inequalities, i.e. every inequality becomes a conjunction over implications of linear inequalities over the template variables TVars.

Example 2. Reconsider template T in Eq. (3) on p. 6 and assume a state s with $s(\textit{fail}) = 5$ and $s(\textit{sent}) = 2$. Then, we encode the well-definedness, $T(s) \geq 0$, as

$$\big(5 < 10 \wedge 2 < \delta \Rightarrow \alpha_1 \cdot 2 + \beta_1 \cdot 5 + \gamma_1 \geq 0\big) \wedge \big(5 < 10 \wedge 2 \geq \delta \Rightarrow \alpha_2 \cdot 2 + \beta_2 \cdot 5 + \gamma_2 \geq 0\big)$$

where the trivially satisfiable conjunct $5 = 10 \Rightarrow \mathtt{true}$ encoding the last summand, i.e. $[\textit{fail} = 10]$, has been dropped. ◁

The query in Thm. 1 involves (non-linear) mixed real and integer arithmetic with quantifiers – a theory that is undecidable in general. However, for finite-state loops and natural templates, one can replace the universal quantifier $\forall s$ by a finite conjunction $\bigwedge_{s \in S_\varphi}$ to obtain a (decidable) $\mathtt{QF\_LRA}$ formula.

Theorem 2. *The problem* $\langle T \rangle \cap \mathsf{AdmInv} \overset{?}{\neq} \emptyset$ *is decidable for finite-state loops and* $T \in \mathsf{TnExp}$. *If* T *is fixed-partition, it is decidable via linear programming.*

5   Constructing an Efficient CEGIS Loop

We now present a CEGIS loop (see inner loop of Fig. 1) in which a *synthesizer* and a *verifier* attempt to incrementally solve our problem statement (cf. p. 9).

5.1   The Verifier

We assume a verifier for checking $I \overset{?}{\in} \mathsf{AdmInv}$. For CEGIS, it is important to get some feedback whenever $I \notin \mathsf{AdmInv}$. To this end, we define:

Definition 2. *For a state* $s \in S$, *the set* $\mathsf{AdmInv}(s)$ *of* s-admissible invariants *is*

$$\mathsf{AdmInv}(s) = \{\, I \mid \underbrace{I(s) \geq 0}_{s\text{-well-defined}} \quad \text{and} \quad \underbrace{\Phi_f(I)(s) \leq I(s)}_{s\text{-inductive}} \quad \text{and} \quad \underbrace{I(s) \leq g(s)}_{s\text{-safe}} \,\} \,.$$

For a subset $S' \subseteq S$ *of states, we define* $\mathsf{AdmInv}(S') = \bigcap_{s \in S'} \mathsf{AdmInv}(s)$.

Clearly, if $I \notin \mathsf{AdmInv}$, then $I \notin \mathsf{AdmInv}(s)$ for some $s \in S$, i.e. state s is a *counterexample* to well-definedness, inductivity, or safety of I. We denote the set of all such counterexamples (to the claim $I \in \mathsf{AdmInv}$) by $\mathsf{CounterEx}_I$. We assume an effective (baseline) verifier for detecting counterexamples:

Definition 3. *A verifier is any function* $\mathsf{Verify} \colon \mathsf{LinExp} \to \{\mathtt{true}\} \cup S$ *such that*

1. $\mathsf{Verify}(I) = \mathtt{true}$ *if and only if* $I \in \mathsf{AdmInv}$, *and*
2. $\mathsf{Verify}(I) = s$ *implies* $s \in \mathsf{CounterEx}_I$.

Proposition 3 ([14]). *There exist effective verifiers.*

For example, one can implement an SMT-backed verifier using an encoding analogous to Thm. 1, where every model is a counterexample $s \in \mathsf{CounterEx}_I$:

$$I \notin \mathsf{AdmInv} \quad \text{iff} \quad \underbrace{\mathsf{Sat}\Big(\neg\big(0 \leq I \,\wedge\, \Phi_f(I) \leq I \,\wedge\, I \leq g\big)\Big) \neq \emptyset}_{\exists s \in S \colon\; I \notin \mathsf{AdmInv}(s)} \,.$$

Algorithm 1: Template-Instance Synthesizer for template T

---

1 $S' \leftarrow \emptyset$;
2 **while** $\mathsf{Synt}_T(S') \neq \mathsf{false}$ **do**
3      $I \leftarrow \mathsf{Synt}_T(S')$;
4      $result \leftarrow \mathsf{Verify}(I)$;
5   **if** $result = \mathsf{true}$ **then**
6         $\lfloor$ **return** I ;   /* Verifier returns true, we have $I \in \mathsf{AdmInv}$ */
7      $\lfloor$ $S' \leftarrow S' \cup \{result\}$;   /* $result$ is a counterexample */
8 **return** false ;   /* $\langle T \rangle \cap \mathsf{AdmInv} = \emptyset$ */

5.2 The Counterexample-Guided Inductive Synthesizer

A synthesizer must generate from a given template T instances $I \in \langle T \rangle$ which can be passed to a verifier for checking admissibility. To make an informed guess, our synthesizers can take a finite set of witnesses $S' \subseteq S$ into account:

Definition 4. *Let* $\mathsf{FinStates}$ *be the set of finite sets of states. A synthesizer for template* $T \in \mathsf{TnExp}$ *is any function* $\mathsf{Synt}_T \colon \mathsf{FinStates} \to \langle T \rangle \cup \{\mathsf{false}\}$ *such that*

1. *if* $\mathsf{Synt}_T(S') = I$, *then* $I \in \langle T \rangle \cap \mathsf{AdmInv}(S')$, *and*
2. $\mathsf{Synt}_T(S') = \mathsf{false}$ *if and only if* $\langle T \rangle \cap \mathsf{AdmInv}(S') = \emptyset$.

To build a synthesizer $\mathsf{Synt}_T(S')$ for finite sets of states $S' \subseteq S$, we proceed analogously to one-shot solving for finite-state loops (Thm. 2), i.e. we exploit

$$T[\mathfrak{I}] \in \mathsf{AdmInv}(S') \quad \text{iff} \quad \mathfrak{I} \models \bigwedge_{s \in S'} \underbrace{0 \leq T(s) \wedge \Psi_f(T)(s) \leq T(s) \wedge T(s) \leq g(s)}_{T[\mathfrak{I}] \in \mathsf{AdmInv}(s)} \ .$$

That is, our synthesizer may return any model $\mathfrak{I}$ of the above constraint system; it can be implemented as one SMT query. In particular, one can efficiently find such an $\mathfrak{I}$ for fixed-partition templates via linear programming.

Theorem 3 (Synthesizer Completeness). *For finite-state loops and natural templates* $T \in \mathsf{TnExp}$, *we have* $\mathsf{Synt}_T(S_\varphi) \in \mathsf{AdmInv}$ *or* $\langle T \rangle \cap \mathsf{AdmInv} = \emptyset$.

Using the synthesizer and verifier in concert is then intuitive as in Alg. 1. We incrementally ask our synthesizer to provide a candidate invariant I that is s-admissible for all states $s \in S'$. Unless the synthesizer returns false, we ask the verifier whether I is admissible. If yes, we return I; otherwise, we get a counterexample s and add it to S' before synthesizing the next candidate.

Remark 1. Without further restrictions, the verifier of Def. 3 may go into a *counterexample enumeration spiral*. In [12, Appx. C], we therefore discuss additional constraints that make this verifier act more cooperatively. $\triangleleft$

6   Generalization to Termination and Lower Bounds

We extend our approach to (i) proving *universal positive almost-sure termination* (UPAST) – termination in finite expected runtime on all inputs, see [42, Sect. 6] – by synthesizing piecewise linear upper bounds on expected runtimes, and to (ii) verifying *lower bounds* on possibly unbounded expected values.

UPAST. We leverage Kaminski et al.'s weakest-precondition-style calculus for reasoning about expected runtimes [44,45]:

Proposition 4. *For every loop* while $(\varphi)\{C\}$, *the monotone function*

$$\Theta\colon \quad \mathbb{E} \to \mathbb{E}, \qquad \Theta(I)(s) \;=\; 1 + \Phi_0(I)(s) \;,$$

obtained from Φ_0 *(cf. Prop. 1) satisfies*

$$\left(\mathsf{lfp}\; \Theta\right)(s) \;=\; \begin{array}{l} \text{``expected number of loop guard evaluations} \\ \qquad\qquad \text{when executing } \texttt{while}\,(\varphi)\,\{\,C\,\} \text{ on } s\text{''}\;. \end{array}$$

All properties of Φ_0 relevant to our approach carry over to Θ, thus enabling the synthesis of inductive invariants $I \in \mathsf{LinExp}$ satisfying $0 \preceq I$ and $\Theta(I) \preceq I$. Such I *upper-bound the expected number of loop iterations* [44] and, since expectations in LinExp never evaluate to infinity, I witnesses UPAST of the while-loop.

Lower Bounds. Consider the problem of verifying a lower bound $g \preceq \mathsf{lfp}\; \Phi_f$ for some loop $C' = \texttt{while}\,(\varphi)\,\{\,C\,\}$. It is straightforward to modify our CEGIS approach for synthesizing <u>*sub-invariants*</u>, i.e. $I \in \mathsf{LinExp}$ with $I \preceq \Phi_f(I)$. However, Hark et al. [36] showed that sub-invariants *do not necessarily lower-bound* $\mathsf{lfp}\; \Phi_f$; they hence proposed a more involved yet sound induction rule for lower bounds:

Theorem 4 (Adapted from Hark et al. [36]). *Let T be a natural template and $I \in \langle T \rangle$. If $0 \preceq I$, $I \preceq \Phi_f(I)$, and C' is UPAST, then*

$$\underbrace{\exists c \in \mathbb{R}_{\geq 0}\; \forall s \in S_\varphi\colon \quad \Phi_f\big(|I - I(s)|\big)(s) \;\leq\; c}_{I \;is\; \text{conditionally difference bounded (c.d.b.)}} \qquad implies \qquad I \preceq \mathsf{lfp}\; \Phi_f \;.$$

Akin to Prop. 2, given $T \in \mathsf{TnExp}$, we can *compute* $T' \in \mathsf{TnExp}$ s.t. for all $\mathfrak{I}$,

$$T\,[\mathfrak{I}] \;\in\; \mathsf{LinExp} \qquad implies \qquad T'\,[\mathfrak{I}] \;=\; \lambda s\text{.}\; \Phi_f\big(|T\,[\mathfrak{I}] - T\,[\mathfrak{I}]\,(s)|\big)(s) \;,$$

which facilitates the extension of our verifier and synthesizer (see Sect. 5) for encoding and checking conditional difference boundedness. Hence, we can employ our CEGIS framework for verifying $g \preceq \mathsf{lfp}\; \Phi_f$ by (i) proving UPAST of C' as demonstrated above and (ii) synthesizing a c.d.b. sub-invariant I with $g \preceq I$.

7   Empirical Evaluation

We have implemented a prototype of our techniques called CEGISPRO2[14]: CEGIS for PRObabilistic PROgrams. The tool is written in Python using pySMT [34]

---

[14] ⌗ https://github.com/moves-rwth/cegispro2

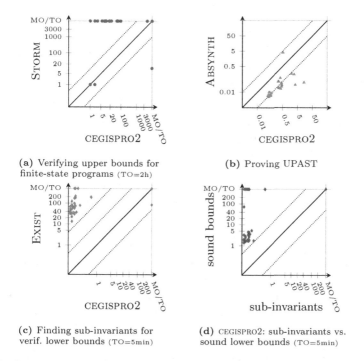

(a) Verifying upper bounds for finite-state programs (TO=2h)

(b) Proving UPAST

(c) Finding sub-invariants for verif. lower bounds (TO=5min)

(d) CEGISPRO2: sub-invariants vs. sound lower bounds (TO=5min)

Fig. 4: Performance of CEGISPRO2 vs. state-of-the-art tools on three verification tasks time in seconds, log-scaled; MO=8GB). Markers above the solid line depict benchmarks where CEGISPRO2 is faster (in different orders of magnitude marked by the dashed lines).

with Z3 [49] as the backend for SMT solving. CEGISPRO2 proves upper- or lower bounds on expected outcomes of a probabilistic program by synthesizing quantitative inductive invariants. We investigate the applicability and scalability of our approach with a focus on the expressiveness of piecewise linear invariants. Moreover, we compare with three state-of-the-art tools – STORM [39], ABSYNTH [50], and EXIST [9] – on subsets of their benchmarks fitting into our framework.

Template Refinement. We start with a fixed-partition template T_1 constructed automatically from the syntactic structure of the given loop (i.e. the loop guard and branches in the loop body, see e.g. Eq. (1)). If we learn that T_1 admits no admissible invariant, we generate a refined template T_2, and so on, until we find a template T_i with $\langle T_i \rangle \cap \mathsf{AdmInv} \neq \emptyset$ or realize that no further refinement is possible. We implemented three strategies for template refinement (including one producing non-fixed-partition templates); see [12, Appx. D] for details.

Finite-State Programs. Fig. 4a depicts experiments on verifying upper bounds on expected values of finite-state programs. For each benchmark, i.e. program and property with increasingly sharper bounds, we evaluate CEGISPRO2 on all template-refinement strategies (cf. [12, Appx. D]). We compare explicit- and symbolic-state engines of the probabilistic model checker STORM 1.6.3 [39] with exact arithmetic. STORM implements LP-based model checking (as in Sect. 4) but employs more efficient methods in its default configuration. Fig. 4a depicts the runtime of the best configuration. See detailed configurations in [12, Appx. E.1].

Results. (i) Our CEGIS approach synthesizes inductive invariants for a variety of programs. We mostly find *syntactically small* invariants with a *small number of counterexamples* compared to the state-space size (cf. [12, Tab. 2]). This indicates that piecewise linear inductive invariants can be sufficiently expressive for the verification of finite-state programs. The overall performance of CEGISPRO2 depends highly on the sharpness of the given thresholds. (ii) Our approach can outperform state-of-the-art *explicit- and symbolic-state* model checking techniques and can scale to huge state spaces. There are also simple programs where our method fails to find an inductive invariant (gridbig) or finds inductive invariants only for rather simple properties while requiring many counterexamples (gridsmall). Whether we need more sophisticated template refinements or whether these programs are not amenable to piecewise linear expectations is left for future work. (iii) There is no clear winner between the two fixed-partition template-refinement strategies (cf. [12, Tab. 2]). We further observe that the non-fixed-partition refinement is not competitive as significantly more time is spent in the synthesizer to solve formulae with Boolean structures. We thus conclude that searching for good fixed-partition templates in a separate outer loop (cf. Fig. 1) pays off.

Proving UPAST. Fig. 4b depicts experiments on proving UPAST of (possibly infinite-state) programs taken from [50] (restricted to N-valued, linear programs with flattened nested loops). We compare to the LP-based tool ABSYNTH [50] for computing upper bounds on expected runtimes. These benchmarks do not require template refinements. More details are given in [12, Appx. E.2].

Results. CEGISPRO2 can prove UPAST of various infnite-state programs from the literature using very few counterexamples. ABSYNTH mostly outperforms CEGISPRO2[15], which is to be expected as ABSYNTH is tailored to the computation of expected runtimes. Remarkably, the runtime bounds synthesized by CEGISPRO2 are often as tight as the bounds synthesized by ABSYNTH (cf. [12, Tab. 3]).

Verifying Lower Bounds. Fig. 4c depicts experiments aiming to verify lower bounds on expected values of (possibly infinite-state) programs taken from [9]. We compare to EXIST [9][16], which combines CEGIS with sampling- and ML-based techniques. However, EXIST synthesizes sub-invariants only, which might be unsound for proving lower bounds (cf. Sect. 6). Thus, for a fair comparison, Fig. 4c depicts experiments where *both* EXIST and CEGISPRO2 synthesize sub-invariants only, whereas in Fig. 4d, we compare CEGISPRO2 that finds sub-invariants only with CEGISPRO2 that *additionally* proves UPAST and c.d.b., thus obtaining sound lower bounds as per Thm. 4. No benchmark requires template refinements.

---

[15] ABSYNTH uses floating-point arithmetic whereas CEGISPRO2 uses exact arithmetic.
[16] EXIST supports parametric probabilities, which are not supported by our tool. We have instantiated these parameters with varying probabilities to enable a comparison.

Results. CEGISPRO2 is capable of verifying quantitative lower bounds and outperforms EXIST (on 30/32 benchmarks) for synthesizing sub-invariants. Additionally proving UPAST and c.d.b. naturally requires more time. A manual inspection reveals that, for most TO/MO cases in Fig. 4d, there is no c.d.b. sub-invariant. One soundness check times out, since we could not prove UPAST for that benchmark.

8   Related Work

We discuss related works in invariant synthesis, probabilistic model checking, and symbolic inference. ICE [33] is a template-based, cex.-guided technique for learning invariants. More inductive synthesis approaches are surveyed in [4,29].

Quantitative Invariant Synthesis. Apart from the discussed method [9], *constraint solving-based approaches* [30,26,46] aim to synthesize quantitative invariants for proving lower bounds over $\mathbb{R}$-valued program variables – arguably a simplification as it allows solvers to use (decidable) real arithmetic. In particular, [26] also obtains linear constraints from counterexamples ensuring certain validity conditions on candidate invariants. Apart from various technical differences, we identify three conceptual differences: (i) we support piecewise expectations which have been shown sufficiently expressive for verifying quantitative reachability properties; (ii) we focus on the integration of fast verifiers over efficiently decidable theories; and (iii) we do not need to *assume* termination or boundedness of expectations.

Various *martingale-based approaches*, such as [19,23,24,32,31,2,48], aim to synthesize quantitative invariants over $\mathbb{R}$-valued variables, see [55] for a recent survey. Most of these approaches yield invariants for proving almost-sure termination or bounding expected runtimes. ε-*decreasing supermartingales* [19,20] and *nonnegative repulsing supermartingales* [55] can upper-bound arbitrary reachability probabilities. In contrast, we synthesize invariants for proving upper- or lower bounds for more general quantities, i.e. expectations. [10] can prove bounds on expected values via symbolic reasoning and *Doob's decomposition*, which, however, requires user-supplied invariants and hints. [1] employs a CEGIS loop to train a neural network dedicated to learning a ranking supermartingale witnessing UPAST of (possibly continuous) probabilistic programs. They also use counterexamples provided by SMT solvers to guide the learning process.

The *recurrence solving-based approach* in [11] synthesizes nonlinear invariants encoding (higher-order) moments of program variables. However, the underlying algebraic techniques are confined to the sub-class of *prob-solvable loops*.

Probabilistic Model Checking. Symbolic probabilistic model checking focusses mostly on algebraic decision diagrams [6,3], representing the transition relation symbolically and using equation solving or value iteration [8,37,53] on that representation. PrIC3 [15] finds quantitative invariants by iteratively overapproximating k-step reachability. Alternative CEGIS approaches synthesize Markov chains [18] and probabilistic programs [5] that satisfy reachability properties.

Symbolic Inference. Probabilistic inference – in the finite-horizon case – employs weighted model counting via either decision diagrams annotated with probabilities as in DICE [41,40] or approximate versions by SAT/SMT-solvers [21,22,27,54,17]. PSI [35] determines symbolic representations of exact distributions. PRODIGY [25] decides whether a probabilistic loop agrees with an (invariant) specification.

Data-Availability Statement The datasets generated during and/or analysed during the current study are available in the Zenodo repository [13].

References

1. Abate, A., Giacobbe, M., Roy, D.: Learning probabilistic termination proofs. In: CAV (2). Lecture Notes in Computer Science, vol. 12760, pp. 3–26. Springer (2021)
2. Agrawal, S., Chatterjee, K., Novotný, P.: Lexicographic ranking supermartingales. PACMPL **2**(POPL), 34:1–34:32 (2018)
3. de Alfaro, L., Kwiatkowska, M.Z., Norman, G., Parker, D., Segala, R.: Symbolic model checking of probabilistic processes using MTBDDs and the Kronecker representation. In: TACAS. Lecture Notes in Computer Science, vol. 1785, pp. 395–410. Springer (2000)
4. Alur, R., Bodík, R., Dallal, E., Fisman, D., Garg, P., Juniwal, G., Kress-Gazit, H., Madhusudan, P., Martin, M.M.K., Raghothaman, M., Saha, S., Seshia, S.A., Singh, R., Solar-Lezama, A., Torlak, E., Udupa, A.: Syntax-guided synthesis. In: Dependable Software Systems Engineering, vol. 40, pp. 1–25. IOS Press (2015)
5. Andriushchenko, R., Ceska, M., Junges, S., Katoen, J.: Inductive synthesis for probabilistic programs reaches new horizons. In: TACAS (1). Lecture Notes in Computer Science, vol. 12651, pp. 191–209. Springer (2021)
6. Baier, C., Clarke, E.M., Hartonas-Garmhausen, V., Kwiatkowska, M.Z., Ryan, M.: Symbolic model checking for probabilistic processes. In: ICALP. Lecture Notes in Computer Science, vol. 1256, pp. 430–440. Springer (1997)
7. Baier, C., Katoen, J.: Principles of Model Checking. MIT Press (2008)
8. Baier, C., Klein, J., Leuschner, L., Parker, D., Wunderlich, S.: Ensuring the reliability of your model checker: Interval iteration for Markov decision processes. In: CAV (1). Lecture Notes in Computer Science, vol. 10426, pp. 160–180. Springer (2017)
9. Bao, J., Trivedi, N., Pathak, D., Hsu, J., Roy, S.: Data-driven invariant learning for probabilistic programs. In: CAV (1). Lecture Notes in Computer Science, vol. 13371, pp. 33–54. Springer (2022)
10. Barthe, G., Espitau, T., Fioriti, L.M.F., Hsu, J.: Synthesizing probabilistic invariants via Doob's decomposition. In: CAV (1). Lecture Notes in Computer Science, vol. 9779, pp. 43–61. Springer (2016)
11. Bartocci, E., Kovács, L., Stankovic, M.: Automatic generation of moment-based invariants for prob-solvable loops. In: ATVA. Lecture Notes in Computer Science, vol. 11781, pp. 255–276. Springer (2019)
12. Batz, K., Chen, M., Junges, S., Kaminski, B.L., Katoen, J., Matheja, C.: Probabilistic program verification via inductive synthesis of inductive invariants. CoRR **abs/2205.06152** (2022)
13. Batz, K., Chen, M., Junges, S., Kaminski, B.L., Katoen, J., Matheja, C.: CEGISPRO2: Artifact for paper "probabilistic program verification via inductive synthesis of inductive invariants" (2023). https://doi.org/10.5281/zenodo.7507921
14. Batz, K., Chen, M., Kaminski, B.L., Katoen, J., Matheja, C., Schröer, P.: Latticed k-induction with an application to probabilistic programs. In: CAV (2). Lecture Notes in Computer Science, vol. 12760, pp. 524–549. Springer (2021)

15. Batz, K., Junges, S., Kaminski, B.L., Katoen, J., Matheja, C., Schröer, P.: PrIC3: Property directed reachability for MDPs. In: CAV (2). Lecture Notes in Computer Science, vol. 12225, pp. 512–538. Springer (2020)
16. Batz, K., Kaminski, B.L., Katoen, J., Matheja, C.: Relatively complete verification of probabilistic programs: An expressive language for expectation-based reasoning. Proc. ACM Program. Lang. **5**(POPL), 1–30 (2021)
17. Belle, V., Passerini, A., van den Broeck, G.: Probabilistic inference in hybrid domains by weighted model integration. In: IJCAI. pp. 2770–2776. AAAI Press (2015)
18. Ceska, M., Hensel, C., Junges, S., Katoen, J.: Counterexample-guided inductive synthesis for probabilistic systems. Formal Aspects Comput. **33**(4-5), 637–667 (2021)
19. Chakarov, A., Sankaranarayanan, S.: Probabilistic program analysis with martingales. In: CAV. Lecture Notes in Computer Science, vol. 8044, pp. 511–526. Springer (2013)
20. Chakarov, A., Voronin, Y., Sankaranarayanan, S.: Deductive proofs of almost sure persistence and recurrence properties. In: TACAS. Lecture Notes in Computer Science, vol. 9636, pp. 260–279. Springer (2016)
21. Chakraborty, S., Fried, D., Meel, K.S., Vardi, M.Y.: From weighted to unweighted model counting. In: IJCAI. pp. 689–695. AAAI Press (2015)
22. Chakraborty, S., Meel, K.S., Mistry, R., Vardi, M.Y.: Approximate probabilistic inference via word-level counting. In: AAAI. pp. 3218–3224. AAAI Press (2016)
23. Chatterjee, K., Fu, H., Goharshady, A.K.: Termination analysis of probabilistic programs through Positivstellensatz's. In: CAV (1). Lecture Notes in Computer Science, vol. 9779, pp. 3–22. Springer (2016)
24. Chatterjee, K., Novotný, P., Zikelic, D.: Stochastic invariants for probabilistic termination. In: POPL. pp. 145–160. ACM (2017)
25. Chen, M., Katoen, J., Klinkenberg, L., Winkler, T.: Does a program yield the right distribution? Verifying probabilistic programs via generating functions. In: CAV (1). Lecture Notes in Computer Science, vol. 13371, pp. 79–101. Springer (2022)
26. Chen, Y., Hong, C., Wang, B., Zhang, L.: Counterexample-guided polynomial loop invariant generation by Lagrange interpolation. In: CAV (1). Lecture Notes in Computer Science, vol. 9206, pp. 658–674. Springer (2015)
27. Chistikov, D., Dimitrova, R., Majumdar, R.: Approximate counting in SMT and value estimation for probabilistic programs. Acta Informatica **54**(8), 729–764 (2017)
28. D'Argenio, P.R., Jeannet, B., Jensen, H.E., Larsen, K.G.: Reachability analysis of probabilistic systems by successive refinements. In: PAPM-PROBMIV. Lecture Notes in Computer Science, vol. 2165, pp. 39–56. Springer (2001)
29. Fedyukovich, G., Bodík, R.: Accelerating syntax-guided invariant synthesis. In: TACAS (1). Lecture Notes in Computer Science, vol. 10805, pp. 251–269. Springer (2018)
30. Feng, Y., Zhang, L., Jansen, D.N., Zhan, N., Xia, B.: Finding polynomial loop invariants for probabilistic programs. In: ATVA. Lecture Notes in Computer Science, vol. 10482, pp. 400–416. Springer (2017)
31. Fioriti, L.M.F., Hermanns, H.: Probabilistic termination: Soundness, completeness, and compositionality. In: POPL. pp. 489–501. ACM (2015)
32. Fu, H., Chatterjee, K.: Termination of nondeterministic probabilistic programs. In: VMCAI. Lecture Notes in Computer Science, vol. 11388, pp. 468–490. Springer (2019)

33. Garg, P., Löding, C., Madhusudan, P., Neider, D.: ICE: A robust framework for learning invariants. In: CAV. Lecture Notes in Computer Science, vol. 8559, pp. 69–87. Springer (2014)
34. Gario, M., Micheli, A.: PySMT: A solver-agnostic library for fast prototyping of SMT-based algorithms. In: SMT Workshop (2015)
35. Gehr, T., Misailovic, S., Vechev, M.T.: PSI: Exact symbolic inference for probabilistic programs. In: CAV (1). Lecture Notes in Computer Science, vol. 9779, pp. 62–83. Springer (2016)
36. Hark, M., Kaminski, B.L., Giesl, J., Katoen, J.: Aiming low is harder: Induction for lower bounds in probabilistic program verification. Proc. ACM Program. Lang. 4(POPL), 37:1–37:28 (2020)
37. Hartmanns, A., Kaminski, B.L.: Optimistic value iteration. In: CAV (2). Lecture Notes in Computer Science, vol. 12225, pp. 488–511. Springer (2020)
38. Helmink, L., Sellink, M.P.A., Vaandrager, F.W.: Proof-checking a data link protocol. In: TYPES. Lecture Notes in Computer Science, vol. 806, pp. 127–165. Springer (1993)
39. Hensel, C., Junges, S., Katoen, J., Quatmann, T., Volk, M.: The probabilistic model checker Storm. Int. J. Softw. Tools Technol. Transf. 24(4), 589–610 (2022)
40. Holtzen, S., Junges, S., Vazquez-Chanlatte, M., Millstein, T.D., Seshia, S.A., van den Broeck, G.: Model checking finite-horizon Markov chains with probabilistic inference. In: CAV (2). Lecture Notes in Computer Science, vol. 12760, pp. 577–601. Springer (2021)
41. Holtzen, S., van den Broeck, G., Millstein, T.D.: Scaling exact inference for discrete probabilistic programs. Proc. ACM Program. Lang. 4(OOPSLA), 140:1–140:31 (2020)
42. Kaminski, B.L.: Advanced Weakest Precondition Calculi for Probabilistic Programs. Ph.D. thesis, RWTH Aachen University, Germany (2019)
43. Kaminski, B.L., Katoen, J., Matheja, C.: On the hardness of analyzing probabilistic programs. Acta Inform. 56(3), 255–285 (2019)
44. Kaminski, B.L., Katoen, J., Matheja, C., Olmedo, F.: Weakest precondition reasoning for expected run-times of probabilistic programs. In: ESOP. Lecture Notes in Computer Science, vol. 9632, pp. 364–389. Springer (2016)
45. Kaminski, B.L., Katoen, J., Matheja, C., Olmedo, F.: Weakest precondition reasoning for expected runtimes of randomized algorithms. J. ACM 65(5), 30:1–30:68 (2018)
46. Katoen, J., McIver, A., Meinicke, L., Morgan, C.: Linear-invariant generation for probabilistic programs: Automated support for proof-based methods. In: SAS. Lecture Notes in Computer Science, vol. 6337, pp. 390–406. Springer (2010)
47. McIver, A., Morgan, C.: Abstraction, Refinement and Proof for Probabilistic Systems. Monographs in Computer Science, Springer (2005)
48. Moosbrugger, M., Bartocci, E., Katoen, J., Kovács, L.: Automated termination analysis of polynomial probabilistic programs. In: ESOP. Lecture Notes in Computer Science, vol. 12648, pp. 491–518. Springer (2021)
49. de Moura, L.M., Bjørner, N.S.: Z3: An efficient SMT solver. In: TACAS. Lecture Notes in Computer Science, vol. 4963, pp. 337–340. Springer (2008)
50. Ngo, V.C., Carbonneaux, Q., Hoffmann, J.: Bounded expectations: Resource analysis for probabilistic programs. In: PLDI. pp. 496–512. ACM (2018)
51. Park, D.: Fixpoint induction and proofs of program properties. Mach. Intell. 5 (1969)
52. Puterman, M.L.: Markov Decision Processes. Wiley Series in Probability and Statistics, Wiley (1994)

53. Quatmann, T., Katoen, J.: Sound value iteration. In: CAV (1). Lecture Notes in Computer Science, vol. 10981, pp. 643–661. Springer (2018)
54. Rabe, M.N., Wintersteiger, C.M., Kugler, H., Yordanov, B., Hamadi, Y.: Symbolic approximation of the bounded reachability probability in large Markov chains. In: QEST. Lecture Notes in Computer Science, vol. 8657, pp. 388–403. Springer (2014)
55. Takisaka, T., Oyabu, Y., Urabe, N., Hasuo, I.: Ranking and repulsing supermartingales for reachability in randomized programs. ACM Trans. Program. Lang. Syst. **43**(2), 5:1–5:46 (2021)
56. Tarski, A.: A lattice-theoretical fixpoint theorem and its applications. Pacific J. Math. **5**(2), 285–309 (1955)

Runtime Monitoring/Program Analysis

Industrial-Strength Controlled Concurrency Testing for C# Programs with COYOTE

Pantazis Deligiannis[1]([✉])([iD]), Aditya Senthilnathan[2], Fahad Nayyar[3]⋆,
Chris Lovett[1], and Akash Lal[2]

[1] Microsoft Research, Redmond, WA, USA
{pdeligia,clovett}@microsoft.com
[2] Microsoft Research, Bengaluru, India
{t-adityase,akashl}@microsoft.com
[3] Apple UK Ltd., London, UK
f_nayyar@apple.com

Abstract. This paper describes the design and implementation of the open-source tool COYOTE for testing concurrent programs written in the C# language. COYOTE provides algorithmic capabilities to explore the state-space of interleavings of a concurrent program, with deterministic repro for any bug that it finds. COYOTE encapsulates multiple ideas from the research community to offer state-of-the-art testing for C# programs, as well as an efficiently engineered implementation that has been shown robust enough to support industrial use.

1 Introduction

Testing programs with concurrency is a challenging problem for developers. Concurrency introduces non-determinism in the program, making bugs hard to find, re-produce and debug [25,43]. In fact, concurrency is one of the main reasons behind *flaky* tests [34] (tests that may pass or fail without any code changes), causing a significant engineering burden on development teams [31]. As concurrency, in the form of multi-threading or distributed systems, is fundamental to how we build modern systems, solutions are required to help developers test their concurrent code for correctness.

There are two important challenges with testing concurrent programs. First is the problem of *reproducibility* or *control*. By default, a programmer does not have control over how concurrent workers interleave during execution.[4] The only programmatic control is through enforcing synchronization, but that is usually not enough to guarantee that certain interleavings can be reproduced. The second challenge is the *state-space explosion* problem. A concurrent program, even with a fixed test input, can have many possible behaviors; in fact, there can be exponentially many interleavings in terms of the length of the execution.

⋆ Work was done while the author was at Microsoft Research.
[4] Concurrency comes in many forms: threads, tasks, actors, processes, etc. We use the term *workers* to abstractly refer to any of these forms.

© The Author(s) 2023
S. Sankaranarayanan and N. Sharygina (Eds.): TACAS 2023, LNCS 13994, pp. 433–452, 2023.
https://doi.org/10.1007/978-3-031-30820-8_26

One line of work that attempts to solve these challenges is *controlled concurrency testing* (CCT) [53]. This approach proposes taking over the scheduling of concurrent workers and then using algorithms, either randomized or systematic, for searching over the space of interleavings. The former (i.e., taking over scheduling) is typically an engineering challenge. It requires understanding the language runtime and building solutions that are efficient, robust and usable. The latter (i.e., searching over the space of interleavings) requires algorithmic and empirical insights on finding bugs, and it has been the main topic of many research publications (e.g., [43,42,55,32,54,10,40,13,53,16,41,48,19,56]). Both these aspects are essential for industrial adoption.

In this paper, we describe the design and implementation of the open-source tool COYOTE [7] for controlled concurrency testing of C# programs. COYOTE aims to make testing of concurrent programs as easy and natural as testing of sequential programs.

Usage COYOTE was released on GitHub on March 2020, and since then its release binaries have been downloaded from nuget.org over a million times. The project has extensive documentation as well as tutorials for developers [8]. COYOTE has been used internally in MICROSOFT for testing multiple different services of the AZURE cloud infrastructure. Through the use of lightweight telemetry [9], we have consistently seen over three million seconds of testing each month for the last 12 months, peaking at roughly 13 million seconds in a month. COYOTE testing has been invoked 71K times per month on average, reporting around 10K test failures per month on average.

COYOTE is also a testing backend for the P language [15], currently used in Amazon for the analysis of several core distributed systems [5]. A P program is compiled to a C# program and fed to COYOTE for testing.

Contributions This paper covers the design decisions that were necessary for supporting industrial usage. It is unreasonable to support *all* programs in a language as broad as C#, so the focus of COYOTE has been on the task asynchronous programming (TAP) model [38] that is the recommended and most common way of expressing concurrency and asynchrony in C#. COYOTE encapsulates multiple state-space exploration techniques from the literature in order to provide state-of-the-art testing to its users. COYOTE is also designed to be extensible, both in supporting other programming models (it already supports an actor programming model [4,12] and support for threads is straightforward), as well as other exploration strategies. This paper also describes a novel search technique specifically for TAP and its evaluation on industrial benchmarks.

Historical journey The origin of the COYOTE code base can be traced back to an earlier system called P# [11] that defined a restricted (domain-specific) programming model for communicating state machines. The P# system has since then evolved into an actor framework that is still supported by COYOTE, however COYOTE itself has generalized to focus on TAP, making it a very different tool compared to P#. Prior work with COYOTE has either focused on exploration strategies [48,40,39] or on applications [12,11,13], but not on the tool itself.

COYOTE is useful for practitioners looking for industrial-strength tools (for C#), as well as researchers interested in evaluating new exploration algorithms for concurrency testing. This paper hopes to inspire and inform the reader towards contributing new ideas, features, and case-studies to COYOTE.

2   The COYOTE Tool

The C# task asynchronous programming (TAP) model revolves around the Task type that is used to encapsulate parallel computation. One can spawn a new task to execute in parallel with its parent, wait on an existing task to finish, or query for the result of a task once it has finished. Furthermore, the C# language offers async and await keywords that make it very convenient to write efficient (non-blocking) programs [37]. Similar features are also mainstream in other languages such as Rust, Python, Javascript and Go, and even C++ has support for them. Their semantics are fairly standard so we avoid them for space constraints, and instead just illustrate using an example.

Fig. 1 shows a typical concurrency test that we will use as a running example in this paper. The RunTest method creates two parallel tasks t1 and t2, waits for them to finish and asserts some condition. A programmer can run this test as-is with COYOTE to find if the assertion can fail. There are two key points to note about this example. First, its behavior is interleaving dependent. The loop in SendMessages adds a string to the global list variable that is shared between the two tasks, so its final value will have a mix of strings of the form aN and bN, depending on the interleaving order. (This program has an unsynchronized access to list, but let us assume for simplicity that operations on List are atomic; in practice, one can guard these operations with locks). Second, while this code seemingly only has two tasks, at runtime it can have up to a 100 tasks created by the .NET runtime. The initial task created by SendMessages starts executing the async lambda code, but when it hits the await point, the runtime can (optionally) end the current task and spawn a new one to execute the rest of the code after the awaited expression finishes. (This "magic" happens when async methods get de-sugared by the C# compiler into state machines [52]. This transformation is what allows the code to be non-blocking.) Note that the await in this code can be hit 100 times (50 for each of the call to SendMessages). We will revisit the complexity imposed by such implicit tasks, both for the tool to take control (§4.1) and on space-space exploration later (§3.2); for now, we focus on the user experience.

COYOTE use is illustrated in Fig. 2. After the user compiles their C# program containing one or more tests, they invoke the coyote rewrite command-line tool to rewrite their binaries. This automatic rewriting adds instrumentation to the original code to provide the necessary hooks and metadata for COYOTE to control the (task-based) concurrency in the program (§3). Next, the user invokes the coyote test command-line tool to run their tests with the COYOTE

```
List⟨string⟩ list = new ( );                Task SendMessages (string prefix) {
                                              return Task.Run (async ( ) => {
async Task RunTest ( ) {                         for (int val = 0; val < 50; val++) {
   Task t1 = SendMessages ("a");                   list.Add (string.Concat (prefix, val));
   Task t2 = SendMessages ("b");                    await Task.Yield ( );
   await task.WhenAll (t1, t2);                   }
   Assert.True (predicate (list));             });
}                                            }
```

Fig. 1: Example test code in C# with concurrency.

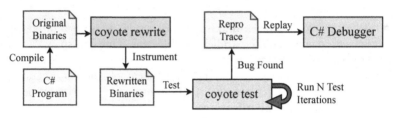

Fig. 2: Developer workflow when using COYOTE.

test engine. The engine runs each test repeatedly for a user-specified number of iterations until a bug (failed assertion or unhandled exception) is found. The engine uses the instrumented hooks to intercept the execution of all workers in the test, and *control* them to allow only a single worker to execute at a time. The exact choice of which worker to enable in each step is left to an *exploration strategy* (§3.2).

When a bug is found, COYOTE dumps out the sequence of all scheduling decisions taken in that test iteration. The user can replay the test failure using the `coyote replay` command, as many times as they like, with the C# debugger attached to step through the test deterministically.

Architecture, Extensibility The architecture of COYOTE is illustrated in Fig. 3. The test engine exposes an *instrumentation API* used for declaring the concurrency, and synchronization, used in the program (§3). For task-based programs, the experience is seamless because the rewriting engine takes care of adding calls to this API automatically (§4). One can also add a custom runtime to COYOTE. For instance, COYOTE supports an actor-based programming model (to code at the level of *actors* instead of tasks) [12]. The actor runtime, in this case, performs the necessary calls into the COYOTE test engine, again providing a seamless experience to users. For other programming models, say, a program using threads directly instead of tasks, these calls must either be inserted manually or a rewriting pass be added to COYOTE to add these calls automatically for threads. Exploration strategies are also defined by a simple interface that makes it easy to implement multiple techniques.

The test engine is roughly 11K lines of C# code, the rewriting engine and the actor runtime are 12K lines each, and COYOTE is overall 45K lines of code.

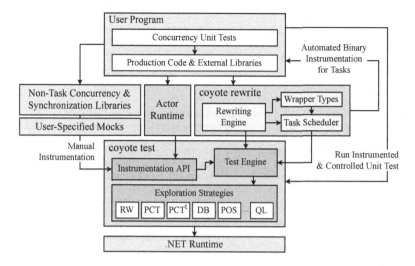

Fig. 3: The architecture of COYOTE.

COYOTE is heavily tested for robustness, with an additional 38K lines of code of unit tests.

Limitations, Requirements COYOTE requires a test to be deterministic modulo scheduling between workers. This implies that, for instance, the program should not take a branch based on the current system time, or read data from an external service or a file that may change outside the scope of the test. COYOTE also requires that tests be *idempotent*, that is, running the test twice has the same effect as running it once. This is because COYOTE runs a test multiple times without re-starting the hosting process. Idempotence is easy to guarantee by avoiding static variables. Violating these requirements can imply that replay will fail. These are minor requirements, with users seldom complaining about them in our experience so far.

A more significant requirement is that COYOTE be able to control all the concurrency created by a test. This may not happen when the program uses an unsupported programming model, or a library that cannot be rewritten because, say, it includes native code, which is outside the scope of `coyote rewrite`. COYOTE has partial defenses against this: when it detects concurrent activity outside its control, it tries to tolerate it by letting it finish on its own (§5), else throws an error to make the user aware.

COYOTE does not currently support the detection of *low-level data races*, i.e., unsynchronized memory accesses, which can indicate concurrency bugs. Race detection requires instrumentation at the level of individual memory accesses, which COYOTE avoids for engineering simplicity and lower maintenance costs. (COYOTE only instruments at the level of task APIs or synchronization operations.) Nonetheless, `coyote rewrite` is extensible, and the door is open for any contributor to take on this responsibility and implement race detection [22,49,23,51,50].

```
interface Instrumentation
    WorkerId OnWorkerCreated();              void OnWorkerPaused(WorkerId, 𝒫);
    void OnWorkerStarted(WorkerId);          void ScheduleNextWorker(WorkerId);
    void OnWorkerCompleted(WorkerId);        WorkerId GetCurrentWorkerId();
```

Fig. 4: The COYOTE test engine instrumentation API.

```
Task Run (Action lambda) {                  void WaitAll (IEnumerable(Task) tasks) {
    WorkerId id = OnWorkerCreated ( );           // Get the worker id associated with the current task.
    Task task = new Task (( ) => {               WorkerId id = GetCurrentWorkerId ( );
        // Control the executing task (worker).   // Pause the current (task) worker until all the specified
        OnWorkerStarted (id);                     // tasks have completed their execution. Invoking this
        lambda ( ); // Execute the task lambda.   // API also calls ScheduleNextWorker to schedule a
        OnWorkerCompleted (id);                   // worker that is not paused nor completed.
        ScheduleNextWorker (id);                  OnWorkerPaused (id, ( ) => tasks.All(t => t.IsCompleted));
    });                                           // At this point, Coyote guarantees that the predicate passed
    task.Start ( ); // Start the task concurrently. // to OnWorkerPaused above evaluates to true, hence all
    return task;                                  // tasks have completed and we can return.
}                                           }
```

Fig. 5: Example wrappers for task creation (left) and waiting (right) that call into the COYOTE test engine.

3   COYOTE Test Engine

3.1   Instrumentation API

Fig. 4 lists the core instrumentation API that must be called from the user program to provide the COYOTE test engine (CTE) with enough hooks for controlling its concurrency. CTE itself does not have a first-class understanding of TAP (or any programming model for that matter); all information about the program comes through this API, which allows us to keep CTE simple, and also allows easy addition of new programming models.

The instrumentation API takes inspiration from prior work [3] that demonstrated the generality of the API, even outside of C#, at capturing different programming models. Each worker created in the program must inform CTE when it is created (OnWorkerCreated), when it starts running (OnWorkerStarted), and when it completes (OnWorkerCompleted). A worker calls OnWorkerPaused with a predicate $\mathcal{P}$ to notify CTE that it has paused its execution and will become unblocked when $\mathcal{P}$ evaluates to *true*. For instance, when a worker pauses to acquire a lock, then $\mathcal{P}$ becomes *true* when the lock is released by some other worker. A worker calls ScheduleNextWorker to ask CTE to consider running a different worker. A worker calls GetCurrentWorkerId to ask CTE for its unique identifier.

Fig. 5 shows wrapper methods for task creation (Run) and waiting on the completion of a set of tasks (WaitAll). These methods implement the original semantics, but additionally call the instrumentation APIs to notify CTE. We show this only for illustrating the instrumentation APIs. In practice, the developer does not have to add these calls. §4 demonstrates how the COYOTE binary rewriting engine automatically inserts these calls to cover the broad TAP programming model. An approach that creates a substitute method for each TAP method does not scale. For actor-based programs, the COYOTE actor runtime takes care of calling the CTE without the need for binary rewriting.

Any time the program invokes CTE via one of these APIs (referred to as a *scheduling point* or *step*), CTE blocks the current worker, then looks at the list of workers that are enabled (by inspecting their pause-predicates, if any). It will then query the exploration strategy to select one worker from this list. The selected worker is unblocked (rest all workers remain blocked) and is allowed to execute until it hits a scheduling point again, at which point control goes into the CTE and the process repeats. This design, of *sequentializing* workers to execute only one-at-a-time is fairly standard in CCT tools [3].

3.2   Exploration Strategies

COYOTE decouples the concern of *how to control* workers from *how to explore* their interleavings. The latter is the responsibility of the exploration strategy, which is defined by a common interface. At its core, the interface has a single method that accepts a list of enabled workers and must return one of them. With most of the heavy lifting performed by CTE, exploration strategies are easy to implement; the largest one is only 400 lines of code. Furthermore, at the time the exploration strategy is invoked, all workers are in a blocked state (blocked by the CTE). Some strategies (like QL and POS; see below) require inspection of the program state. This can be done safely by the strategy without worrying about racing with the program's execution.

The *random walk* strategy (RW) picks an enabled worker uniformly at random in each step. This simple strategy has been shown to be effective in practice and argued as a necessary baseline for other strategies [53]. The PCT strategy [10] implements a priority-based scheduler. When a worker is created, it is assigned a new randomly-generated priority. At a scheduling point, PCT always picks the enabled worker that has the highest priority. In addition, at d times during an execution (called the *bug depth* parameter, which is supplied by a user-controlled configuration), PCT lowers the priority of the currently executing worker to be the smallest. These d priority lowering points are picked uniformly across the entire program execution. This priority-based nature helps PCT induce long delays in workers, unlike RW that switches back-and-forth between workers much more frequently.

Task-based PCT PCT was originally designed for multi-threaded programs. Later work observed its shortcomings for distributed systems and proposed the revised strategy called PCTCP [48]. We now discuss a novel adaptation of the idea behind PCTCP to TAP in a strategy called PCT^t.

Consider again the program of Fig. 1. Let us define the function *predicate* to check that the string a49 does not appear before b0 in list. For the assertion in this program to fail, an interleaving must essentially execute t1 to completion before t2 gets a chance. The chance of RW producing this interleaving is tiny:

around 1 in 2^{50}. If we imagine a thread-based scenario (ideal setting for PCT), where RunTest created two threads instead of tasks, then PCT (with $d = 0$) has 50% probability of hitting this bug. This is because if the first thread is assigned a higher priority, it will execute to completion before the second thread gets a chance to execute. However, PCT, with priorities-per-task, is unable to find this bug because of all the implicit tasks that get created at the await point (recall §2). Each time a new task is created, it gets a new randomly-generated priority. In effect, for this program, PCT behaves like RW.

PCTCP addresses this problem by constructing a partial order between workers, where two workers w_1 and w_2 are ordered if the programming model enforces that w_2 must only start after w_1 finishes. This partial order, constructed on-the-fly during program execution, is then decomposed into *chains*, which are totally-ordered subsets of the partial order. PCTCP then maintains priorities per chain, not per worker. When a new worker starts, it gets assigned to a chain (existing or a new one) and *inherits* the priority of the chain. PCTCP's effectiveness has only been demonstrated for distributed message-passing systems.

PCT^t adapts the concept of chains for TAP. On the explicit creation of a task (using Task.Run), it gets assigned to a new chain (hence, it gets a randomly-generated priority). If a task t yields control by executing Task.Yield, the continuation task is assigned to the same chain as t (hence, it inherits its priority). When a task t1 awaits another task t2 to complete, the continuation task of t1 is assigned to the chain of t2 because the continuation can only execute after t2 completes. (In reality, the continuation task is assigned to the chain of the task that completes t2, because t2 may have its own continuations created.) PCT^t recovers the benefits of PCT; in our running example, only two chains are created, and it can find the bug with a 50% probability.

Other strategies COYOTE also implements a strategy based on reinforcement-learning (QL) [40]. QL requires a partial hash (or fingerprint) of the program state and then *learns* a model that maximize the number of unique fingerprints seen during a test run. Increased coverage helps uncover more bugs. The partial order sampling (POS) strategy [56] uses information about which workers are *racing* with each other, i.e., they are about to access the same object (either a memory location or a synchronization object). POS uses a priority-based scheduler like PCT, but instead of lowering priority at d chosen points, POS keeps shuffling (i.e., re-assigning) priorities of racing workers at each step.

Other strategies available in COYOTE are delay bounding (DB) [19] and variants of RW that use a biased coin. These strategies can also be combined either in the same test iteration (run one strategy for certain number of steps, then switch to running another strategy) or across iterations (pick a different strategy, in a round-robin fashion, for each iteration).

Data non-determinism Exploration strategies also offer a means to generate unconstrained *boolean* or *integer* values. COYOTE exposes these APIs to developers, who can use them to express non-determinism in their program. An example is when testing for the robustness of a program against *faults*. In this case, the developer can non-deterministically choose to raise a fault (like an exception or return an error code) and check that their code can handle the fault correctly. Other examples are non-deterministically firing timeouts, non-deterministically choosing what method to call from a set of equivalent library methods, etc. Most exploration strategies resolve this non-determinism uniformly at random, with the exception of QL that tries to learn, alongside scheduling decisions, what return values are able to maximize program coverage.

Liveness checking In addition to catching safety violations (assertion failures and uncaught exceptions), COYOTE can also check liveness properties where, essentially, one asserts that every program run *eventually* makes *progress*. The definition of *progress* is programmable, using the concept of liveness monitors (variant of deterministic Büchi automata) borrowed from the P modeling language [15]. A violation of a liveness property is an infinite run where no progress is made. Testing cannot produce an infinite run, so instead COYOTE looks for a sufficiently long execution based on user-set thresholds [27,39]. Liveness properties are not rare. In fact, they are commonly asserted when testing distributed services to check that the service eventually completes every user request [12].

Any exploration strategy can be used for liveness checking, as long as it is *fair*, i.e., it does not contiguously starve an enabled worker for a long time. Unfairness can easily lead to liveness violations, but such violations are considered false positives because they cannot happen in practice as system scheduling is generally fair. RW is (probabilistically) fair, but PCT is not. COYOTE converts unfair strategies to fair ones by running them up to a certain number of scheduling steps and then switching to use RW.

4   Automation for C# Task Asynchronous Programs

The style of instrumentation shown in Fig. 5 is not practical because there are many ways in which lambdas and tasks can be created (some return a result on completion, some do not, and there are optimized variants of tasks like ValueTask [45], etc.). Imposing directly on the creation process would be very cumbersome. One must also be able to handle both explicit creation of tasks, as well as the implicit creation that happens at await points. After much trial-and-error, we arrived at an efficient solution that is simple and easy to maintain, even as C# itself evolves. We crucially rely on controlling task execution through a narrow lower layer of abstraction in the .NET runtime called the TaskScheduler [44]. We observed that whenever a task is created, it goes to the .NET *default* task scheduler, which is then responsible for executing the task on the .NET thread pool. This task scheduler can be subclassed, which we do as shown in Fig. 6 (right). Coyote.TaskScheduler offers a convenient place to call into the test engine, without requiring imposition on the creation of the task or its lambda. The job of rewriting then is to route tasks to this scheduler instead of the default task scheduler. We do this by defining simple wrapper methods for Task APIs, and rewriting the user C# binaries to call the wrapper methods instead of the original ones.

```
class Coyote.TaskWrapper                    class Coyote.TaskScheduler : TaskScheduler
  state                                       state
  | TestEngine engine                         | TestEngine engine
  | Coyote.TaskScheduler scheduler            | ThreadPool pool // Managed by Coyote.
  static Task Run(F func)                      void QueueTask(Task task)
  | task ← new Task(func)                      | id ← engine.OnWorkerCreated()
  | scheduler.QueueTask(task)                  | thread ← pool.GetNextAvailableThread()
  | return task                                | thread.Run(() → ExecuteTask(task, id))
  static void Wait(Task self)                  void ExecuteTask(Task task, WorkerId id)
  | id ← engine.GetCurrentWorkerId()           | engine.OnWorkerStarted(id)
  | P ← self.Status.IsCompleted                | base.RunInline(task) // Execute task inline.
  | engine.OnWorkerPaused(id, P)               | engine.OnWorkerCompleted(id)
  | self.Wait()                                | engine.ScheduleNextWorker(id)
```

Fig. 6: Wrapper methods for Task APIs (left) and the implementation of the
Coyote task scheduler (right).

Fig. 6 (left) illustrates static wrapper methods for Task.Run and Task.Wait.
Notice that on TaskWrapper.Run, no modification to the lambda (func) is required. A task gets created as usual, then gets enqueued to the Coyote task
scheduler, which, in turn, executes the task with appropriate calls to the test
engine (ExecuteTask). This solution piggybacks on the RunInline functionality
that the default scheduler also uses. The TaskWrapper.Wait method adds the
call to OnWorkerPaused.

What about implicitly created tasks? This required more digging into the
C# compiler to understand the compilation of async methods to state machines
[52]. Fortunately, all we required is to identify the point where continuation tasks
are created by these state machines, and instead call a wrapper method (similar
to TaskWrapper.Run) that enqueues the task to the Coyote task scheduler.

4.1   Binary Rewriting for C# Tasks

Binary rewriting is necessary to provide a push-button experience for Coyote
on TAP programs. In C#, code gets compiled into the Common Intermediate
Language (CIL) [17], which is an object-oriented machine-independent bytecode
language that can run on top of the .NET runtime in any supported operating
system (Windows, Linux and macOS). Each compiled C# program consists of
one or more CIL binaries. Each binary contains an *assembly*, which is a unit of
functionality implemented as a set of types (these can be exposed publicly to be
consumed by other assemblies). Each *type* might contain members such as fields
and methods, and so on.

We implemented the binary rewriting engine on top of Cecil [46], an open-
source .NET library that provides a rich API for rewriting CIL code. The rewriting engine architecture is illustrated in Fig. 7. The engine loads all program
binaries from disk to access the CIL assemblies in-memory, topologically sorts
them (to ensure that dependencies are processed first), and then traverses each
assembly (using the visitor pattern) to apply a sequence of CIL rewriting passes,
where each pass focuses on a different type of instrumentation.

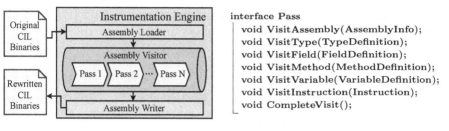

interface Pass
| void VisitAssembly(AssemblyInfo);
| void VisitType(TypeDefinition);
| void VisitField(FieldDefinition);
| void VisitMethod(MethodDefinition);
| void VisitVariable(VariableDefinition);
| void VisitInstruction(Instruction);
| void CompleteVisit();

Fig. 7: The architecture of the COYOTE rewriting engine (left). The interface of a CIL rewriting pass (right).

Each rewriting pass implements the COYOTE **Pass** interface, which is listed in Fig. 7. The rewriting engine visitor will traverse the CIL assembly and invoke the corresponding pass method for each encountered type, field, method signature, as well as each variable and instruction in each method body.

Built-in Rewriting Passes COYOTE implements and invokes in-order the following four passes: *type* rewriting pass, *task API* rewriting pass, *async* rewriting pass, and *inter-assembly invocation* rewriting pass. The type rewriting pass is responsible for replacing certain C# system library types in the user program with corresponding *drop-in-replacement* types that are implemented by COYOTE. The replacement types implement exactly the same interface as the original types, and invoke the original methods to maintain semantics, but are instrumented with callbacks to the COYOTE test engine. Some examples of replaced types are: (1) System.Threading.Monitor type, which implements the lock statement in C#, and (2) the System.Threading.Semaphore type that is another variant of a lock. The COYOTE versions of these types invoke the test engine to notify it when a worker acquires or releases a lock. These two are the synchronization primitives that COYOTE supports by default, in addition to Task APIs. Adding support for more synchronization requires adding another type rewriting pass.

The task API rewriting pass inserts calls to the Coyote.TaskWrapper wrapper type, as discussed earlier. The async rewriting pass is similar, except for wrapping APIs that create implicit tasks. Finally, the inter-assembly invocation rewriting pass is responsible for identifying invocations in the code that are made across CIL assembly boundaries, where the target assembly is not rewritten by COYOTE. COYOTE adds instrumentation to detect (and tolerate) *uncontrolled* concurrency (see §5).

New passes that implement the **Pass** interface can be easily integrated in the current pipeline of passes, allowing power users to extend coyote rewrite for custom rewriting (e.g., to support controlling a new synchronization type without having to manually use the COYOTE instrumentation API).

Design Considerations We decided to target CIL for instrumentation instead of doing it at the level of ASTs. This helps reduce the instrumentation scope because the CIL instruction set is much smaller than C# surface syntax.

Furthermore, CIL changes infrequently (last update was in 2012 [17]), and we can target pre-compiled binaries without access to their source code.

5   Additional Features

Partially-Controlled Exploration As mentioned in §2, COYOTE requires tests to be deterministic modulo the concurrency that it controls. This requirement can be broken when the test creates a worker without reporting it to the COYOTE test engine, which impacts the ability of COYOTE to reproduce an execution. This can happen when using APIs outside of the TAP programming model or by calling into a library that has not been rewritten. Partially-controlled exploration allows the controlled part of a program to be tested with high-coverage, even when interacting with an uncontrolled part. In fact, COYOTE recommends to developers that they should only rewrite their test binaries as well as the binaries of their production code, but leave the binaries of any external dependencies unmodified (to be handled by partially-controlled exploration).

During partially-controlled exploration, COYOTE will treat any un-rewritten binaries as "pass-through", and their methods are invoked *atomically* from the perspective of the tool. In this testing mode, COYOTE sequentializes the execution of the controlled workers, as usual, and if a controlled worker invokes a method in an un-rewritten binary, or waits on a task that was earlier returned by a method from a non-rewritten binary, or invokes an unsupported low-level C# concurrency API, then COYOTE detects this and invokes `ScheduleNextWorker` to explore a scheduling decision. Instead of immediately trying to choose a controlled worker to schedule, COYOTE uses a (tunable) heuristic that gives a chance to wait for the uncontrolled task or invocation to first complete, before trying to resolve the scheduling decision. This is important because instead of regressing coverage, it allows COYOTE to cover scenarios where completing the uncontrolled task or invocation first results in new states of the state space being available for exploration.

Setting `max-steps` Some tests can be potentially non-terminating, i.e., some executions of the test will go on forever. Non-termination comes naturally when a program has *spinloops* or *polling loops* (loops that keep going until some condition is met), or when they are unavoidable, as in consensus protocols like Paxos or Raft that cannot avoid the existence of infinite executions. `coyote test` provides the option of setting a bound on the length of a test iteration in terms of the number of scheduling points that it hits. This bound is supplied with the `max-steps` flag. The test engine keeps a count of the number of scheduling points in the current iteration. When it hits the max value, the test engine throws an exception in all of the workers (that would currently be blocked by the engine). This exception essentially kills the worker by propagating all the way up to the test harness, where it is caught by the engine. Once all workers are killed, the engine starts the next iteration.

This solution, of throwing an exception to kill a worker, only works when the worker does not catch the exception to try and resume the execution. All exceptions in C# must derive from the `System.Exception` type, and a construct like `catch(Exception)` will catch all exceptions. COYOTE gets around this problem by using a binary rewriting pass that edits all `catch` statements to disallow catching of COYOTE exceptions.

Thread-safety violations A *thread-safety violation* occurs in a program when it concurrently invokes some library API that is not designed to be thread safe. Prior work showed the prevalence of such errors in .NET programs when accessing data structures such as dictionaries and lists in the `System.Collections.Generic` namespace [33]. These data structures do not offer thread safe APIs. (In concurrent scenarios, one should instead use the data structures in `System.Collections.Concurrent` namespace.)

COYOTE offers the ability to catch such errors. It implements a rewriting pass that replaces such a data structure, say `Dictionary`, with a drop-in replacement type `WrapperDictionary`. The latter keeps tracks of concurrent (write-write or write-read) accesses and throws an exception when there are two such simultaneous accesses. The exception causes COYOTE to report a test failure.

Actor runtime COYOTE offers a library, inspired from the P# [11] line of work, that allows a developer to use actors to express concurrency in their program. Actors, when created, run concurrently with respect to other actors. They continue to be alive unless explicitly halted. Each actor has an inbox where it listens for messages from other actors and processes them in a FIFO order. Several production systems have been build with COYOTE's actor framework [12]. The actor runtime takes care of calling the test engine instrumentation APIs at the appropriate points, such as when creating an actor or sending a message to another actor. Hence, no rewriting is required. The COYOTE test engine treats tasks and actors the same way, allowing a developer to freely mix the two programming models, i.e., test programs that use both actors and tasks.

6   Evaluation

Our evaluation covers three experiments, each on a different set of benchmarks. Each benchmark is a concurrent program with a known bug. We measure the effectiveness of COYOTE by the number of times that it is able to hit the bug within a fixed number of test iterations. For each benchmark, we report its *degree of concurrency* (DoC), defined as the maximum number of simultaneously enabled workers, and the number of scheduling decisions (#SD), i.e., number of times the exploration strategy is invoked on average per test iteration.

The first experiment compares the performance of PCT^t against PCT on task-heavy programs. We took a proprietary production service of MICROSOFT, which we call PRODSERVICE. The service runs as part of the Azure platform; it is roughly $54K$ lines of C#, and is designed to be highly-concurrent for high throughput. The owning engineering team were routinely running COYOTE on multiple concurrency tests. We took an intermediate version of this service and

Table 1: Results on PRODSERVICE tests. Degree of concurrency varied from 5 to 16, and the number of scheduling decisions varied from 94 to 1054.

Test#	1	2	3	4	5	6	7	8	9	10	11	12	13	14	15	16	17	18	19	20	21
RW	1	1	✗	✗	✗	✗	✗	✗	1	4	✗	✗	✗	1	1	**1**	4	✗	**4**	✗	✗
PCT	46	3	✗	✗	✗	✗	✗	✗	30	17	2	1	**1**	1	2	✗	5	**1**	1	8	✗
PCT^t	119	159	49	2	5	5	11	8	43	59	8	11	✗	72	71	✗	50	✗	✗	45	1

Table 2: Results from testing buggy protocol implementations. Number of test iterations was set to 10K, except for FailureDetector and Paxos that used 100K iterations. PCT, PCT^t and DB use the bound $d = 10$.

				Exploration Strategies					
	Benchmarks	DoC	#SD	RW	PCT	PCT^t	DB	POS	QL
	ChainReplication	9	620	✗	**22**	13	1	✗	✗
	Chord	7	223	1715	557	1185	537	**2782**	1533
Protocols	FailureDetector	6	115	✗	**37**	1	11	2	1
	Paxos	11	217	✗	5	2	**10**	1	✗
	Raft	18	798	166	18	88	7	**204**	✗

ran all tests with RW, PCT and PCT^t, each with 1000 iterations each. There were a total of 111 tests, out of which 21 tests reported a failure (i.e., bug) with some strategy. The comparison is shown in Table 1. (We actually ran both PCT and PCT^t with multiple different values of the d parameter, and selected the best among them for each strategy; this value turned out to be $d = 10$ for both.)

Table 1 shows superior performance of PCT^t. It is able to find 17 test failures, compared to 13 for PCT and 9 for Random. Furthermore, on tests that failed with both PCT and PCT^t, the latter found the bug 9 times more often (geo mean). We observe that these tests created many tasks, roughly 277 tasks (geo mean) in each test iteration, which throws off PCT. With PCT^t, the number of chains was 6 times smaller (geo mean). Running these 21 tests for 1000 iterations each takes roughly 50 min (wall clock) on a 16 core AMD EPYC (2.6Ghz) VM, running Ubuntu 20.04 on Azure, when utilizing 14 threads on the machine to run tests in parallel.

The second experiment is on buggy protocol implementations from prior work [48,40], shown in Table 2. This experiment evaluates a wider range of strategies. Three schedulers (PCT, PCT^t and DB) find all the bugs, but none is a clear winner. A combination of schedulers is likely required for reliably finding bugs in a small number of iterations.

The final experiment is to show that COYOTE is indeed state-of-the-art by comparing against other tools. We did not find any other CCT tool for C#, so we instead took an established benchmark suite SCTBENCH [53] of C/C++ programs that use pthreads for concurrency, and manually ported some of them to C# (Table 3), replacing pthreads APIs with Task APIs. These benchmarks have potentially racy shared variables, so we implemented an experimental bi-

Table 3: Results on SCTBENCH with 10K test iterations. PCT uses the $d = 3$ and DB uses the $d = 5$ bound. Numbers in parenthesis report performance on the same benchmark-strategy pair from a different CCT tool (Maple) [56].

	Benchmarks	DoC	#SD	RW	PCT	DB	POS	QL
	bluetooth_dr...	2	18	598(628)	281(597)	**651**	610(847)	402
	deadlock01_bad	3	12	3132(3668)	994(1714)	1717	**4436**(3315)	2856
SCTBENCH	queue_bad	3	53	**10000**(9999)	8212(1415)	9387	9737(9999)	**10000**
	reorder_10_bad	52	238	✗(✗)	18(14)	✗	**2568**(308)	✗
	reorder_20_bad	111	515	✗(✗)	4(27)	✗	**2526**(1709)	✗
	reorder_5_bad	27	121	1(18)	36(110)	✗	**2591**(668)	34
	token_ring_bad	5	31	1305(1245)	1303(1717)	403	**1640**(1724)	1552
	twostage_bad	15	115	192(806)	146(1959)	6	**7440**(1212)	273

nary rewriting pass in COYOTE that adds scheduling points on heap accesses, to ease the porting exercise. A direct comparison with prior tools is difficult because there can still be subtle differences in how scheduling points get inserted. Regardless, we note that numbers for POS are roughly in agreement with its original paper [56] and numbers for PCT and RW are in agreement with a prior empirical study [53]. (Note that PCT^t is identical to PCT on these benchmarks because there are no task continuations.) Our implementation of POS performs better than the original one, but the original implementation is unavailable for us to make a more accurate assessment. This comparison is useful to ground COYOTE with respect to related work.

The code and scripts to run all the non-proprietary experiments from this paper are available as an artifact on Zenodo [14].

7   Related Work

The term *controlled concurrency testing* (CCT) was coined only recently [53] but it inherits its roots from *stateless model checking* (SMC) that was popularized by VERISOFT [24]. *Stateful* approaches require the ability to record the state of an executing program; this is hard to achieve for production code, consequently stateful checking tools [26,6] are often applied to models of code that are written in custom languages. SMC/CCT, on the other hand, only record the sequence of actions taken during an execution, making them the technique of choice for directly testing code written in commercial languages (like C#).

Research in SMC/CCT can further be classified in two categories. One category is of exhaustive techniques, where the goal is to explore the entire state-space of a program (in reality, it is the state-space of a fixed test that invokes a bounded workload on the program), and obtain a *verified* verdict. Exhaustive techniques are based on the notion of *partial order reduction* (POR) [24] that constructs equivalence classes of executions so that only one exploration per equivalence class is required [35]. Recently, this line of work has produced several tools, such as CDSCHECKER [47], GENMC [30], and NIDHUGG [2], that have demonstrated value in verifying concurrency primitives (e.g., latches, mutex implementations) and concurrent data structures, especially when considering weak memory behaviors [1,28,29].

The other category for SMC/CCT are techniques aimed towards *bug-finding*. These techniques are either bounded (i.e., aim to explore only a subset of the executions) or randomized or both. By lowering expectations (i.e., not insisting on covering the entire state-space), these techniques can be applied on larger systems. We have discussed several instances of these techniques throughout this paper. The first work that popularized bug-finding was the notion of context-bounded exploration [41]. COYOTE borrows heavily from this line of work on bug-finding techniques, which is evident in the set of exploration strategies that it supports. Implementing POR-based strategies is possible; the POS strategy already takes COYOTE in this direction. The absence of exhaustive techniques has (so far) not been felt by users of COYOTE, likely because the usage scenarios have neither focused on weak memory behaviors (more present in C/C++ rather than C#), nor on verifying concurrent data structures. Nonetheless, supporting POR-based techniques remains an important direction for future work.

Related to the idea of CCT for bug-finding are noise-injection-based techniques [21,20,18]. These techniques rely on perturbing the execution of a concurrent program by injecting *noise* such as sleep statements, which force the execution to explore alternative interleavings. Unlike CCT, no *control* is required on concurrent workers, hence these techniques have simpler engineering requirements. However, the tradeoff is that the loss of control implies that the ability to explore specific interleavings, such as what PCT requires, is reduced. The ANaConDA tool has successfully demonstrated noise-injection in an industrial setting [21]. It can be interesting to explore the use of noise injection to provide coverage in portions of code that are not controlled by COYOTE.

The CHESS tool [41], to the best of our knowledge, was the only other CCT tool to support C#. CHESS is currently not in a usable state. It was designed prior to the popularity of TAP in C#, thus had no special support for tasks. In terms of implementation, it occupied a different design space than COYOTE. It relied on interception of C# threading APIs and redirecting them to custom mocks. Maintenance of these mocks was an engineering cost. Furthermore, the interception technology relied on a framework [36] that also went out of support. This showcases that the complexity of supporting C# must be met with good engineering, built on stable frameworks. COYOTE is also more extensible, both in terms of programming frameworks, as well as exploration strategies.

Acknowledgements The authors would like to thank everyone who has contributed to COYOTE over the years. This includes many open-source contributors that have filed issues and fixes, as well as developers that have integrated COYOTE into their engineering process to provide valuable insights on what concurrency testing can and should do. We would especially like to thank Immad Naseer for his help with PRODSERVICE.

References

1. Abdulla, P.A., Atig, M.F., Jonsson, B., Lång, M., Ngo, T.P., Sagonas, K.: Optimal stateless model checking for reads-from equivalence under sequential consistency. Proc. ACM Program. Lang. **3**(OOPSLA), 150:1–150:29 (2019)
2. Abdulla, P.A., Atig, M.F., Jonsson, B., Ngo, T.P.: Dynamic partial order reduction under the release-acquire semantics (tutorial). In: Atig, M.F., Schwarzmann, A.A. (eds.) Networked Systems - 7th International Conference, NETYS 2019, Marrakech, Morocco, June 19-21, 2019, Revised Selected Papers. Lecture Notes in Computer Science, vol. 11704, pp. 3–18. Springer (2019)
3. Agarwal, U., Deligiannis, P., Huang, C., Jung, K., Lal, A., Naseer, I., Parkinson, M., Thangamani, A., Vedurada, J., Xiao, Y.: Nekara: Generalized concurrency testing. In: 36th IEEE/ACM International Conference on Automated Software Engineering, ASE 2021, Melbourne, Australia, November 15-19, 2021. pp. 679–691. IEEE (2021)
4. Agha, G.: Actors: A Model of Concurrent Computation in Distributed Systems. MIT Press, Cambridge, MA, USA (1986)
5. Amazon, Microsoft, Berkeley: P: Formal Modeling and Analysis of Distributed (Event-Driven) Systems. https://github.com/p-org/P (2022)
6. Andrews, T., Qadeer, S., Rajamani, S.K., Rehof, J., Xie, Y.: Zing: A model checker for concurrent software. In: Computer Aided Verification, 16th International Conference, CAV 2004, Boston, MA, USA, July 13-17, 2004, Proceedings. pp. 484–487 (2004)
7. Microsoft Research: Coyote: Fearless coding for reliable asynchronous software. https://github.com/microsoft/coyote (2020)
8. Microsoft Research: Coyote Documentation, Tutorials and References. https://microsoft.github.io/coyote/ (2022)
9. Microsoft Research: Telemetry in Coyote. https://microsoft.github.io/coyote/#get-started/telemetry/ (2022)
10. Burckhardt, S., Kothari, P., Musuvathi, M., Nagarakatte, S.: A randomized scheduler with probabilistic guarantees of finding bugs. In: ASPLOS. pp. 167–178 (2010)
11. Deligiannis, P., Donaldson, A.F., Ketema, J., Lal, A., Thomson, P.: Asynchronous programming, analysis and testing with state machines. In: PLDI. pp. 154–164 (2015)
12. Deligiannis, P., Ganapathy, N., Lal, A., Qadeer, S.: Building reliable cloud services using coyote actors. In: Curino, C., Koutrika, G., Netravali, R. (eds.) SoCC '21: ACM Symposium on Cloud Computing, Seattle, WA, USA, November 1 - 4, 2021. pp. 108–121. ACM (2021)
13. Deligiannis, P., McCutchen, M., Thomson, P., Chen, S., Donaldson, A.F., Erickson, J., Huang, C., Lal, A., Mudduluru, R., Qadeer, S., Schulte, W.: Uncovering bugs in distributed storage systems during testing (not in production!). In: FAST. pp. 249–262 (2016)
14. Deligiannis, P., Senthilnathan, A., Nayyar, F., Lovett, C., Lal, A.: Industrial-Strength Controlled Concurrency Testing for C# Programs with Coyote - Artifact (Nov 2022). https://doi.org/10.5281/zenodo.7311192, https://zenodo.org/record/7311192#.Y8ru2EHMJaa
15. Desai, A., Gupta, V., Jackson, E.K., Qadeer, S., Rajamani, S.K., Zufferey, D.: P: safe asynchronous event-driven programming. In: PLDI. pp. 321–332 (2013)
16. Desai, A., Qadeer, S., Seshia, S.A.: Systematic testing of asynchronous reactive systems. In: FSE. pp. 73–83 (2015)

17. Ecma International: ECMA-335, Common Language Infrastructure (CLI), 6th edition. https://www.ecma-international.org/publications-and-standards/standards/ecma-335/ (2012)
18. Edelstein, O., Farchi, E., Goldin, E., Nir, Y., Ratsaby, G., Ur, S.: Framework for testing multi-threaded java programs. Concurrency and Computation: Practice and Experience **15**(3-5), 485–499 (2003)
19. Emmi, M., Qadeer, S., Rakamaric, Z.: Delay-bounded scheduling. In: Proceedings of the 38th ACM SIGPLAN-SIGACT Symposium on Principles of Programming Languages, POPL 2011, Austin, TX, USA, January 26-28, 2011. pp. 411–422 (2011)
20. Fiedor, J., Hrubá, V., Krena, B., Letko, Z., Ur, S., Vojnar, T.: Advances in noise-based testing of concurrent software. Softw. Test. Verification Reliab. **25**(3), 272–309 (2015)
21. Fiedor, J., Muzikovská, M., Smrcka, A., Vasícek, O., Vojnar, T.: Advances in the ANaConDA framework for dynamic analysis and testing of concurrent C/C++ programs. In: Tip, F., Bodden, E. (eds.) Proceedings of the 27th ACM SIGSOFT International Symposium on Software Testing and Analysis, ISSTA 2018, Amsterdam, The Netherlands, July 16-21, 2018. pp. 356–359. ACM (2018)
22. Flanagan, C., Freund, S.N.: Atomizer: a dynamic atomicity checker for multi-threaded programs. In: Proceedings of the 31st ACM SIGPLAN-SIGACT Symposium on Principles of Programming Languages, POPL 2004, Venice, Italy, January 14-16, 2004. pp. 256–267 (2004)
23. Flanagan, C., Freund, S.N.: Fasttrack: efficient and precise dynamic race detection. In: Proceedings of the 2009 ACM SIGPLAN Conference on Programming Language Design and Implementation, PLDI 2009, Dublin, Ireland, June 15-21, 2009. pp. 121–133 (2009)
24. Godefroid, P.: Software model checking: The verisoft approach. Formal Methods in System Design **26**(2), 77–101 (2005)
25. Gray, J.: Why do computers stop and what can be done about it? In: Proceedings of the 5th Symposium on Reliability in Distributed Software and Database Systems. pp. 3–12. IEEE (1986)
26. Holzmann, G.: The SPIN Model Checker: Primer and Reference Manual. Addison-Wesley Professional, 1st edn. (2011)
27. Killian, C.E., Anderson, J.W., Jhala, R., Vahdat, A.: Life, death, and the critical transition: Finding liveness bugs in systems code (awarded best paper). In: Balakrishnan, H., Druschel, P. (eds.) 4th Symposium on Networked Systems Design and Implementation (NSDI 2007), April 11-13, 2007, Cambridge, Massachusetts, USA, Proceedings. USENIX (2007)
28. Kokologiannakis, M., Marmanis, I., Gladstein, V., Vafeiadis, V.: Truly stateless, optimal dynamic partial order reduction. Proc. ACM Program. Lang. **6**(POPL), 1–28 (2022)
29. Kokologiannakis, M., Raad, A., Vafeiadis, V.: Effective lock handling in stateless model checking. Proc. ACM Program. Lang. **3**(OOPSLA), 173:1–173:26 (2019)
30. Kokologiannakis, M., Vafeiadis, V.: Genmc: A model checker for weak memory models. In: Silva, A., Leino, K.R.M. (eds.) Computer Aided Verification - 33rd International Conference, CAV 2021, Virtual Event, July 20-23, 2021, Proceedings, Part I. Lecture Notes in Computer Science, vol. 12759, pp. 427–440. Springer (2021)
31. Lam, W., Godefroid, P., Nath, S., Santhiar, A., Thummalapenta, S.: Root causing flaky tests in a large-scale industrial setting. In: Zhang, D., Møller, A. (eds.) Proceedings of the 28th ACM SIGSOFT International Symposium on Software Testing and Analysis, ISSTA 2019, Beijing, China, July 15-19, 2019. pp. 101–111. ACM (2019)

32. Leesatapornwongsa, T., Hao, M., Joshi, P., Lukman, J.F., Gunawi, H.S.: SAMC: Semantic-aware model checking for fast discovery of deep bugs in cloud systems. In: OSDI. pp. 399–414 (2014)
33. Li, G., Lu, S., Musuvathi, M., Nath, S., Padhye, R.: Efficient scalable thread-safety-violation detection: finding thousands of concurrency bugs during testing. In: Brecht, T., Williamson, C. (eds.) Proceedings of the 27th ACM Symposium on Operating Systems Principles, SOSP 2019, Huntsville, ON, Canada, October 27-30, 2019. pp. 162–180. ACM (2019)
34. Luo, Q., Hariri, F., Eloussi, L., Marinov, D.: An empirical analysis of flaky tests. In: Cheung, S., Orso, A., Storey, M.D. (eds.) Proceedings of the 22nd ACM SIGSOFT International Symposium on Foundations of Software Engineering, (FSE-22), Hong Kong, China, November 16 - 22, 2014. pp. 643–653. ACM (2014)
35. Mazurkiewicz, A.W.: Trace theory. In: Brauer, W., Reisig, W., Rozenberg, G. (eds.) Petri Nets: Central Models and Their Properties, Advances in Petri Nets 1986, Part II, Proceedings of an Advanced Course, Bad Honnef, Germany, 8-19 September 1986. Lecture Notes in Computer Science, vol. 255, pp. 279–324. Springer (1986)
36. Microsoft: CCI: Common Compiler Infrastructure. https://github.com/microsoft/cci (2015)
37. Microsoft: Asynchronous programming in C#. https://docs.microsoft.com/en-us/dotnet/csharp/programming-guide/concepts/async/ (2019)
38. Microsoft: Task Asynchronous Programming Model. https://learn.microsoft.com/en-us/dotnet/csharp/programming-guide/concepts/async/task-asynchronous-programming-model (2022)
39. Mudduluru, R., Deligiannis, P., Desai, A., Lal, A., Qadeer, S.: Lasso detection using partial-state caching. In: FMCAD. pp. 84–91 (2017)
40. Mukherjee, S., Deligiannis, P., Biswas, A., Lal, A.: Learning-based controlled concurrency testing. Proc. ACM Programming Languages 4(OOPSLA), 230:1–230:31 (2020)
41. Musuvathi, M., Qadeer, S.: Iterative context bounding for systematic testing of multithreaded programs. In: Proceedings of the ACM SIGPLAN 2007 Conference on Programming Language Design and Implementation, San Diego, California, USA, June 10-13, 2007. pp. 446–455 (2007)
42. Musuvathi, M., Qadeer, S.: Fair stateless model checking. In: PLDI. pp. 362–371. ACM (2008)
43. Musuvathi, M., Qadeer, S., Ball, T., Basler, G., Nainar, P.A., Neamtiu, I.: Finding and reproducing Heisenbugs in concurrent programs. In: OSDI. pp. 267–280. USENIX (2008)
44. .Net Documentation: TaskScheduler Class. https://learn.microsoft.com/en-us/dotnet/api/system.threading.tasks.taskscheduler?view=net-6.0 (2022)
45. .Net Documentation: ValueTask Class. https://learn.microsoft.com/en-us/dotnet/api/system.threading.tasks.valuetask-1?view=net-6.0 (2022)
46. .NET Foundation: Mono.Cecil: inspect, modify and create .NET programs and libraries. https://github.com/jbevain/cecil (2022)
47. Norris, B., Demsky, B.: Cdschecker: checking concurrent data structures written with C/C++ atomics. In: Hosking, A.L., Eugster, P.T., Lopes, C.V. (eds.) Proceedings of the 2013 ACM SIGPLAN International Conference on Object Oriented Programming Systems Languages & Applications, OOPSLA 2013, part of SPLASH 2013, Indianapolis, IN, USA, October 26-31, 2013. pp. 131–150. ACM (2013)
48. Ozkan, B.K., Majumdar, R., Niksic, F., Befrouei, M.T., Weissenbacher, G.: Randomized testing of distributed systems with probabilistic guarantees. PACMPL 2(OOPSLA), 160:1–160:28 (2018)

49. Park, S., Lu, S., Zhou, Y.: Ctrigger: exposing atomicity violation bugs from their hiding places. In: Proceedings of the 14th International Conference on Architectural Support for Programming Languages and Operating Systems, ASPLOS 2009, Washington, DC, USA, March 7-11, 2009. pp. 25–36 (2009)
50. Savage, S., Burrows, M., Nelson, G., Sobalvarro, P., Anderson, T.E.: Eraser: A dynamic data race detector for multi-threaded programs. In: Proceedings of the Sixteenth ACM Symposium on Operating System Principles, SOSP 1997, St. Malo, France, October 5-8, 1997. pp. 27–37 (1997)
51. Sen, K.: Race directed random testing of concurrent programs. In: Proceedings of the ACM SIGPLAN 2008 Conference on Programming Language Design and Implementation, Tucson, AZ, USA, June 7-13, 2008. pp. 11–21 (2008)
52. Tepliakov, S.: Microsoft DevBlogs: Dissecting the async methods in C#. https://devblogs.microsoft.com/premier-developer/dissecting-the-async-methods-in-c/ (2017)
53. Thomson, P., Donaldson, A.F., Betts, A.: Concurrency testing using controlled schedulers: An empirical study. TOPC 2(4), 23:1–23:37 (2016)
54. Šimša, J., Bryant, R., Gibson, G.: dBug: Systematic testing of unmodified distributed and multi-threaded systems. In: SPIN. pp. 188–193. Springer-Verlag (2011)
55. Yang, J., Chen, T., Wu, M., Xu, Z., Liu, X., Lin, H., Yang, M., Long, F., Zhang, L., Zhou, L.: MODIST: Transparent model checking of unmodified distributed systems. In: NSDI. pp. 213–228 (2009)
56. Yuan, X., Yang, J., Gu, R.: Partial order aware concurrency sampling. In: Chockler, H., Weissenbacher, G. (eds.) Computer Aided Verification - 30th International Conference, CAV 2018, Held as Part of the Federated Logic Conference, FloC 2018, Oxford, UK, July 14-17, 2018, Proceedings, Part II. Lecture Notes in Computer Science, vol. 10982, pp. 317–335. Springer (2018)

Context-Sensitive Meta-Constraint Systems for Explainable Program Analysis

Kalmer Apinis(✉) and Vesal Vojdani

Institute of Computer Science, University of Tartu,
Narva mnt 18, EE-51009 Tartu, Estonia
{kalmera,vesal}@ut.ee

Abstract. We show how to generate a constraint system of symbolic expressions as part of an inter-procedural constraint-system–based program analysis such that any chosen slice of the intended analysis may be computed through the evaluation of the symbolic constraints. Thus, our method ensures that the computed expressions provide genuine explanations for the chosen analysis slice.The resulting system is then annotated with program location information, translated into closed-form expressions, and simplified to yield a human-readable justification for the analyzer's verdict. Justifications are given using program locations, constants from the program, abstract lattice operations, loops in the analysis, and computed results.

Keywords: Program analysis, Data-flow analysis, Constraint systems, Abstract domains, Explainability

1 Introduction

When a program analysis tool identifies a flaw in the program, it is often possible to produce a counterexample execution trace that is useful for debugging the program. As noted by the founders of model checking, "it is impossible to overestimate the importance of this feature" [13]. In contrast, when a sound analyzer verifies the absence of errors, it does not produce an equivalent human-readable artifact to explain this verdict. The challenge is to explain why a property holds along *all* possible executions of the program in a way that is understandable to users of the tool.

A simple example of explaining an invariant is seen in Fig. 1, where the code inspection of IntelliJ IDEA explains the reason for a boolean guard being always false. This is elegant, and we aim to generalize this idea to explain verdicts that rely on inductive invariants. IntelliJ does not explain more complicated analyses than simple constant propagation.

```
1 ▶   public class Main {
2 ▶       public static void main(String[] args) {
3             int x = 0;
4             while (x < 100) {
5                 x++;
6             }
7             if(x == 50) System.out.println("OK!");
8       }
9   }
```
Value Is Always False
Left operand is >= 100
Range is known from line #4

Fig. 1: Explanation in IntelliJ IDEA.

S. Sankaranarayanan and N. Sharygina (Eds.): TACAS 2023, LNCS 13994, pp. 453–472, 2023.
https://doi.org/10.1007/978-3-031-30820-8_27

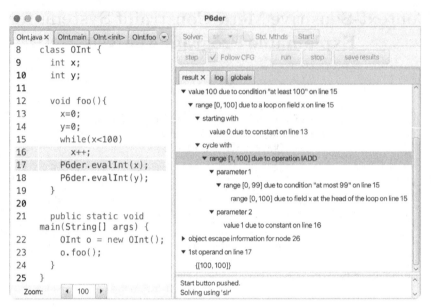

Fig. 2: Explanation generated for Interval Analysis by the Põder analyzer.

The usability aspects of sound static analyzers deserve more research attention, especially as decades of work have been put into the more technical aspects of analysis theory and tool design. Empirical studies suggest that poor explainability of analysis results is as serious an obstacle as false positives in preventing the wider adoption of static analysis tools [12, 22, 28]. We take a first step in this direction by providing a general framework for explaining abstract interpreters. We then instantiate this framework to generate explanations for interval analysis with widening and narrowing iterations. A prototype implementation of our approach is avaliable in the static analysis framework Põder[1]. In the Fig. 2 we see the results of Põder analyzing a Java bytecode program. On the right-hand side, the solved interval value of the field x on line 17 is shown together with reasoning on how the value was computed. The example program and its (interval) analysis is explained in Section 4 (Example 1); the justification is explained in Section 6.

Explanations for simple analyses can be useful in practice. In our previous work on static analysis for Linux device drivers [34], we spent countless hours determining why the analyzer claimed that a portion of the code is definitely unreachable. Rather than relying on ad-hoc methods to trace the computation of the analyzer, we aim to build an analyzer with explainability as a core consideration. We identify two desirable functional requirements that a framework for explainable static analysis should satisfy:

Result consistency. Computing explanations should not influence the result of the actual analysis.

[1] Avaliable via artifact[6] or bitbucket: https://bitbucket.org/kalmera/poder.

Explanation Consistency. The explanation should be semantically consistent with the result of the analysis.

The key contribution of this paper is a framework for explainable analysis that prioritizes explanation consistency. The analysis will operate with symbolic expressions, which can be directly translated into explanations, and crucially, the result of the analysis is based on evaluating these expressions. This ensures explanation consistency by construction.

The proposed method fits into the framework of A^2I (also called meta-abstract interpretation) described by Cousot et al. [18]. A simplified view of A^2I is that the analysis is divided into two instances of abstract interpretation: a meta-analysis and an underlying-analysis. The benefit of this approach is that one can reason about the soundness of the meta-analysis with the same formalism as the analysis itself. In our case, the meta-analysis generates analysis expressions and the underlying analysis evaluates them.

The structure of the paper. We introduce the formal setting in Section 2, and give abstract definitions for explainable analysis in Section 3. The main contribution is introduced via an example in Section 4 — transforming interval analysis to additionally gather interval expressions. Several examples are presented. The post-processing of generated expressions into closed form is shown in Section 5. In Section 6, we discuss our prototype implementation in Põder. Next, in Section 7 we discuss limitations of the current implementation and possibilities for applying our approach in various settings. Related work is described in Section 8, after which we conclude.

2   Data-flow Analysis

A *program* is a set of functions Fun containing main. Each function $f \in$ Fun is represented by its *Control Flow Graph* $(N_f, E_f, f_{begin}, f_{end})$ where N_f is a finite set of program points and $E_f \subseteq N_f \times L \times N_f$ is the set of labeled edges (u, l, v). Each function has a unique source f_{begin} and a unique sink f_{end}. The label set L represents program statements including (but not limited to) function calls as well as conditional guards. We assume that CFG nodes of distinct functions are distinct, so we can leave out subscripts from N_f and E_f.

A complete lattice $(D, \sqsubseteq)$ is a partial order that for each set $D' \subseteq D$ has a least upper bound $\bigsqcup D'$ [9]. We know that any complete lattice must have a unique least element $\bot := \bigsqcup \varnothing$ and a unique greatest element $\top := \bigsqcup D$.

A constraint system is a set of variables V where each variable $v \in V$ may be constrained using $(\sqsubseteq)$ by an expression f_v over variables V. The expression f_v is formalized as a function $(V \to D) \to D$. A (partial) mapping $\sigma : V \to D$ is a (partial) solution to a constraint system if for all variables v in the domain of σ it holds that $\sigma(v) \sqsupseteq f_v(\sigma)$.

Let S denote the set of all possible concrete program states. We can formulate the collecting semantics for the set of states reachable by the program, using the functional approach [33] to include states reachable through inter-procedurally valid paths only. The constraint system variable $[v, d]$ consists of a program point $v \in N_f$ together with sets of program states d, representing states at the beginning of the function f. For each $d \in 2^S = D$ we have constraints:

$$[f_{begin}, d] \supseteq d \qquad\qquad\qquad\qquad\qquad \forall f \in \mathsf{Fun}$$

$$[v, d] \supseteq [\![e]\!]([u, d]) \qquad\qquad\qquad\qquad \forall e = (u, l, v) \in E$$

$$[v, d] \supseteq \bigcup_{d' \in [u,d]} \mathsf{comb}_f(d', [f_{end}, \mathsf{enter}_f(d')]) \qquad \forall e = (u, x := f(\ldots), v) \in E$$

The value of a constraint system variable $[f_{begin}, d]$ is the set of states that reach the beginning of f with the assumption that the start of f can be reached in states d. Thus, the first constraint is trivial. For non–function-call edges a distributive transfer function $[\![\cdot]\!] : E \to (2^S \to 2^S)$ is applied which translates labels to transformations of program state sets. For calls to $f \in \mathsf{Fun}$ in edges $e = (u, x := f(\ldots), v) \in E$ two distributive functions are used: enter_e and comb_e. First, caller states are translated to callee starting states using $\mathsf{enter}_e : S \to S$, and then caller states together with called function end-states are translated to returning states using $\mathsf{comb}_e : S \to 2^S \to 2^S$.

Given the least partial solution σ, the set of reaching states for each program point u is the union of values of $\sigma[u, d]$ that $[\mathtt{main}_{end}, d_0]$ (recursively) depends on. Note that we prefer partial solutions over total solutions as we want to avoid unreachable contexts. Thus, we have for each CFG node the set of program states that this node may be reached with. We have proven partial correctness if erroneous states can not be reached. Reachable program state sets, however, are in general not practically computable. So instead of sets of states, we use a different complete lattice so that a single abstract value describes a whole set of concrete program states.

The correspondence of program states and the chosen complete lattice elements is formalized using a *description relation* $(\underline{\Delta}) \subset S \times D$ [32], i.e., we write $s \underline{\Delta} d$ if the program state $s \in S$ is described by the abstract state $d \in D$. We require that the least element $\bot$ should not describe any program state and the greatest element $\top$ must describe all concrete program states. The description relation must also reflect the ordering of the lattice: $s \underline{\Delta} d_1 \wedge d_1 \sqsubseteq d_2 \implies s \underline{\Delta} d_2$. For sound analysis we require an abstract version of semantics function that agrees with concrete semantics:

$$s \underline{\Delta} d \wedge s' \in [\![e]\!](\{s\}) \implies s' \underline{\Delta} [\![e]\!]^\sharp(d)$$

$$s \underline{\Delta} d \wedge s' \underline{\Delta} d' \wedge s'' \in \mathsf{comb}_f(s, s') \implies s'' \underline{\Delta} \mathsf{comb}_f^\sharp(d, d')$$

$$s \underline{\Delta} d \implies \mathsf{enter}_e(s) \underline{\Delta} \mathsf{enter}_e^\sharp(d)$$

For non-recursive programs, the most precise partial solution is computable if D does not contain infinite ascending chains. In the case of ascending chains, we can find a partial solution that is not necessarily the most precise [4]. Either

way, any partial solution is a sound over-approximation of the collecting semantics. Thus, we have proven partial correctness if the computed partial solution
does not contain any abstract state that describes a concrete error state.

As a side-note, if program graphs contain an equivalent of dynamic goto
instructions, full CFG-s might be impractically large. Then it is advantageous to
explore the CFG lazily starting from main_{begin}, for example, using the function
$\text{next}: N \to D \to 2^{L \times N}$ that gives for each node n and abstract state d the set of
reached nodes and their corresponding edge labels from n [33]. For manageable-
sized CFG-s, an off-the-shelf local solver can also be used in practice to produce
the partial solution [2, 31].

3 Meta-analysis for explanations

Data-flow analysis with finite number of constraint system variables can be succinctly formalized as a single vectorized constraint

$$\bar{x} \sqsupseteq F_p^\sharp(\bar{x}) \tag{1}$$

where a post-fixpoint of $F_p^\sharp$ contains true statements about the program p. In
general, there is no easy way to succinctly explain how a member of the vector
$\bar{x}$ is computed without expensive inspection of the function $F_p^\sharp$. Instead, we
propose to apply meta-abstract interpretation and split the analysis into two
constraints

$$\bar{y} \sqsupseteq G_p^\sharp(\bar{x})$$
$$\bar{x} \sqsupseteq E^\sharp(\bar{x}, \bar{y}) \tag{2}$$

where, first, the function $G_p^\sharp$ generates expressions and, second, the function $E^\sharp$
evaluates the generated expressions.

Definition 1 (Result & Explanation Consistency). *Let $\bar{x}_1$ be a solution of
System 1, and $(\bar{y}_2, \bar{x}_2)$ be a solution of System 2. We say the result is consistent
iff $\bar{x}_1 = \bar{x}_2$. And the explanation is consistent iff $\bar{x}_2 = E^\sharp(\bar{x}_2, \bar{y}_2)$. Jointly, these
properties ensure that $\bar{y}_2$ is a valid explanation for the computation of $\bar{x}_1$.*

The functions $G_p^\sharp$ and $E^\sharp$ must be implemented in a way that guarantees *result consistency* — explanation consistency is guaranteed by construction for
the least solution. As the resulting construction is in the form of a constraint
system, it may be combined with other constraint system based analyses into
a single constraint system. Thus, the analysis designer can choose to generate
explanations about the (sub-)analysis where it is considered beneficial.

One standard example of a complete lattice is the box domain — a mapping
from program variables to integer intervals. For this domain, the analysis produces bounds for integer variables that may be used to warn the user if array
accesses are not within bounds. In practice, however, programs use dynamic language features such as function pointers, dynamic memory, multi-threading, etc.

and more information must be stored in the domain than just intervals. Thus, we should also show how interval analysis can use and provide information to other analyses. In the next section, we propose a process to modify an analysis to that effect.

4   Transforming the box domain

We start with a functional approach [33] analysis where the domain D consists of an arbitrary "helper" analysis domain H and the box domain.

$$D = H \times (\text{Var} \to I)_\perp$$

The box domain can either be $\perp$, meaning that the program point is not reachable, or a function that maps program variables to inclusive integer intervals $[a, b]$. The lower (upper) bound a (b) can be an integer or negative (positive) infinity. We can assume that the lower bound is not larger than the upper bound. The lattice order is defined pointwise with the exception that $\perp$ is the least lattice element. For any context $d \in D$, the constraint for the analysis are the following:

$$[f_{begin}, d] \sqsupseteq d \qquad\qquad \forall f \in \text{Fun}$$
$$[v, d] \sqsupseteq [\![e]\!]^\sharp([u, d]) \qquad\qquad \forall e = (u, l, v) \in E$$
$$[v, d] \sqsupseteq \text{comb}_e^\sharp([u, d], [f_{end}, \text{enter}_e^\sharp([u, d])]) \quad \forall e = (u, x := f(\ldots), v) \in E$$

First, the starting point of the function is constrained by the value in the context. The second and third constraints deal with non-call edges and function call edges, respectively. The constraint system is analogous to the constraint system for concrete semantics with the exception that the argument of $\text{enter}^\sharp$ and the first argument of $\text{comb}^\sharp$ represent state sets instead of one particular state.

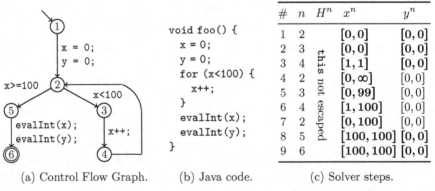

#	n	H^n	x^n	y^n
1	2		$[0, 0]$	$[0, 0]$
2	3		$[0, 0]$	$[0, 0]$
3	4		$[1, 1]$	$[0, 0]$
4	2	this not escaped	$[0, \infty]$	$[0, 0]$
5	3		$[0, 99]$	$[0, 0]$
6	4		$[1, 100]$	$[0, 0]$
7	2		$[0, 100]$	$[0, 0]$
8	5		$[100, 100]$	$[0, 0]$
9	6		$[100, 100]$	$[0, 0]$

```
void foo() {
    x = 0;
    y = 0;
    for (x<100) {
        x++;
    }
    evalInt(x);
    evalInt(y);
}
```

(a) Control Flow Graph.   (b) Java code.   (c) Solver steps.

Fig. 3: Interval analysis of a program with a loop.

Example 1. Consider the Java method `foo` in Fig. 3a and 3b. First, two fields are initialized to the value 0. The field x is incremented in the loop, but the field y is left as is. At the end, field values are printed using the `evalInt` method. We assume that the helper analysis may conclude that the object pointed to by this will not be visible to other threads. Until a reference to the object escapes to other threads, we can be sure that no other access to these fields can happen during the call to `foo`. Solving steps are shown in Fig. 3c, where the abstract values of fields x and y at program point m are referred to as x^m and y^m, respectively.

Thanks to the helper analysis, we know that the object pointed to by this will not be visible to other threads and, thus, we may consider fields x and y as local variables. At the final node, the value of x is 100 and y is zero. Bold font in Fig. 3c emphasizes a change to the solver variable. The analysis uses widening and narrowing [15] to reach the least partial solution in nine steps.

For novice program analysis tool users, seeing only the final result, it might not be clear how values for x and y are derived. Other users might complain that for iterations 4 to 7, the values for y and H are re-computed unnecessarily. In the following sections, we aim to remedy such issues.

4.1 A naive approach to adding expressions

To add interval expression information for each program point we, instead of D, use the domain D' consisting of the helper analysis domain, interval expressions, and interval values.

$$D' = H \times (\text{Var} \to \mathbb{E}^\sharp)_\perp \times (\text{Var} \to \mathbb{I})_\perp$$

For abstract expressions we use values in the form $\text{join}(S) \in \mathbb{E}^\sharp$ where $S \in 2^{\mathcal{E}}$ is a set of expressions defined using the following grammar:

$$\mathcal{E} ::= [N, D', \text{Var}] \mid \text{F}(\mathcal{E}^*) \mid \top$$

The ordering is defined as $\text{join}(X) \sqsubseteq \text{join}(Y) := \top \in Y \lor X \subseteq Y$. The variable $[n, d, x]$ (written as x^n in the examples where the context can be inferred) refers to the value of the program variable x in program point n in context d. Furthermore, an expression can be unknown ($\top$) or an n-ary function from the set F together with its argument expressions. It is assumed that F contains interval constants as nullary functions. The expression mapping $k \in \text{Var} \to \mathbb{E}^\sharp$ can be evaluated for each variable evaluation $\rho \in N \times D' \times \text{Var} \to \mathbb{I}$ using $[\![k]\!]_\mathcal{E}^\sharp(\rho) = \lambda x . [\![k(x)]\!]_\mathcal{E}^\sharp(\rho)$ where

$$[\![\text{join}(S)]\!]_\mathcal{E}^\sharp(\rho) = \bigsqcup \{[\![s]\!]_\mathcal{E}^\sharp(\rho) \mid s \in S\}$$
$$[\![\top]\!]_\mathcal{E}^\sharp(\rho) = [-\infty, \infty]$$
$$[\![f(s_1, \ldots, s_n)]\!]_\mathcal{E}^\sharp(\rho) = f([\![s_1]\!]_\mathcal{E}^\sharp(\rho), \ldots, [\![s_n]\!]_\mathcal{E}^\sharp(\rho))$$
$$[\![[n, d, x]]\!]_\mathcal{E}^\sharp(\rho) = \rho(n, d, x)$$

This analysis can be implemented directly using the functional approach, i.e., the previously discussed constraint system with the domain D' instead of D.

The transfer functions need to be extended such that the expressions perform the same operations as the analysis performs on the interval values.

#	n	H^n	x^n	y^n	$[\![x^n]\!]^\sharp_\mathcal{E}$	$[\![y^n]\!]^\sharp_\mathcal{E}$
1	2	this not escaped	$\mathbf{0 \sqcup x^4}$	$\mathbf{0 \sqcup y^4}$	$\mathbf{[0,0]}$	$\mathbf{[0,0]}$
2	3		$\mathbf{x^2 \sqcap [-\infty,99]}$	$\mathbf{y^2}$	$\mathbf{[0,0]}$	$\mathbf{[0,0]}$
3	4		$\mathbf{x^3+1}$	$\mathbf{y^3}$	$\mathbf{[1,1]}$	$\mathbf{[0,0]}$
4	2		$0 \sqcup x^4$	$0 \sqcup y^4$	$\mathbf{[0,\infty]}$	$[0,0]$
5	3		$x^2 \sqcap [-\infty,99]$	y^2	$\mathbf{[0,99]}$	$[0,0]$
6	4		x^3+1	y^3	$\mathbf{[1,100]}$	$[0,0]$
7	2		$0 \sqcup x^4$	$0 \sqcup y^4$	$\mathbf{[0,100]}$	$[0,0]$
8	5		$\mathbf{x^2 \sqcap [100,\infty]}$	$\mathbf{y^2}$	$\mathbf{[100,100]}$	$\mathbf{[0,0]}$
9	6		$\mathbf{x^5}$	$\mathbf{y^5}$	$\mathbf{[100,100]}$	$\mathbf{[0,0]}$

Fig. 4: Analysis of program in Fig. 3a using the domain D'.

Example 2. When analyzing the program form Fig. 3a using the domain D', we get the iterates shown in Fig. 4. The interval values stay the same w.r.t. analysis using D. In addition, we obtain an interval constraint system for integer program variables. The unknown x^n signifies the interval state of program variable x in the program point n. Note that without the helper analysis we would need to handle potential write operations from other threads. In general, we have gathered the information on how interval values are computed at each step, but the overview is still lacking. As the expressions refer to several variables, the correspondence and correctness may not be immediately apparent. Also, note that we have increased the amount of unnecessary re-computation (in non-bold font).

4.2 A more sophisticated approach to adding expressions

The naive approach has two downsides which we aim to overcome. First, we tackle the issue that a buggy analysis may output inconsistent expressions and interval values. Furthermore, a function would be analyzed for each expression and value at the start point, i.e., context, not only for each distinct value. This is excessive as the analyzed program can only access the numeric value — not the way values were computed — and therefore cannot behave differently based on it. Thus, we only store interval values as the context so that the expressions at the start of the function will have literal values.

We use three kinds of constraint system variables instead of triples to reduce unnecessary re-computation. First, helper analysis variables $[u,d]_1$ with values from the domain H which corresponds to the first components of $[u,d]$. Second, expression map variables $[u,d]_2$ with values from the domain $(\mathrm{Var} \to \mathbb{E}^\sharp)_\perp$, and finally, interval map variables $[u,d]_3$ with values from the domain $(\mathrm{Var} \to \mathrm{I})_\perp$. Interval values are computed from interval expression by evaluation as follows;

thus guaranteeing that they will agree w.r.t. the solution.

$$[v, d]_3 \sqsupseteq \lambda x. \, [\![[v, d]_2(x)]\!]^\sharp_\mathcal{E} (\lambda \, (u, d', y). \, [u, d']_3(y)) \qquad v \in N \wedge d \in D$$

The constraints for non-function-call labels for any $d \in D$ are as follows

$$[f_{begin}, (h, k)]_1 \sqsupseteq h \qquad\qquad\qquad\qquad \forall f \in \mathsf{Fun}$$
$$[f_{begin}, (h, k)]_2 \sqsupseteq k \qquad\qquad\qquad\qquad \forall f \in \mathsf{Fun}$$
$$([v, d]_1, [v, d]_2) \sqsupseteq [\![e]\!]^\sharp(([u, d]_1, [u, d]_3), d) \qquad \forall e = (u, l, v) \in E$$

Note that the transfer function does get the expression component as a parameter and does not contribute directly to the interval component. Also, the current calling context is passed on to the function so that it is able to reference variables for this context in the expression component. The calling context may not be used for any other purpose. In addition, we have constraints for any $d \in D$ and for function call edges $e = (u, x := f(\ldots), v) \in E$:

$$([v, d]_1, [v, d]_2) \sqsupseteq \text{let } h, k = \mathsf{enter}^\sharp_e([u, d]_1, [u, d]_3, d) \text{ in}$$
$$\text{let } d' = (h, \lambda x. \, [\![k(x)]\!]^\sharp_\mathcal{E} (\lambda \, (u, d', y). \, [u, d']_3(y))) \text{ in}$$
$$\mathsf{comb}^\sharp_e([u, d]_1, [u, d]_3, [f_{end}, d']_1, [f_{end}, d']_3, d, d')$$

Neither $\mathsf{enter}^\sharp_e$ nor $\mathsf{comb}^\sharp_e$ depend directly on the expression component and do not contribute directly to the interval component. In addition to the caller calling context, the new context is passed on to $\mathsf{comb}^\sharp_e$. We assume that the contexts are used only in the expression component to reference variables in the respective contexts. Thus, if the generation of expressions also does not depend on interval values, they will be computed alongside the helper analysis and do not add iteration steps.

The correctness condition of interval analysis with interval expression can be stated w.r.t. plain interval analysis: the produced expressions must evaluate to intervals that describe all possible states from the collecting semantics. I.e., for any state $s \in [v, c]$ in collecting semantics, we must ensure that it is described by the analysis $s \, \underline{\Delta} \, ([v, d]_1, [v, d]_3)$ where context are related $c \, \underline{\Delta} \, d$.

The above is ensured by the framework if the transfer functions are translated into corresponding symbolic expressions. Given an edge e, and the original sound abstract function $[\![e]\!]^\sharp_I$, we now need corresponding symbolic representations, $e^\sharp$. Ignoring detail, in order to ensure result consistency, it is sufficient for our symbolic transfer function to satisfy the condition that $[\![e^\sharp]\!]^\sharp_\mathcal{E}$ must compute the same result as $[\![e]\!]^\sharp_I$. Similar conditions can be given for inter-procedural analysis functions $\mathsf{enter}^\sharp$ and $\mathsf{comb}^\sharp$. The detailed sufficient conditions for result consistency are stated in the following lemmas.

Lemma 1 (Intra-Procedural Result Consistency). *Given for all $d \in D$ and $(u, e, v) \in E$ where $e^\sharp = [\![e]\!]^\sharp(([u, d]_1, [u, d]_3), d)_2$ only contains variables preceding program point u and context d such that its evaluation $[\![e^\sharp]\!]^\sharp_\mathcal{E} (\lambda\_.[u, d]_3)$ is equal to the original interval analysis $[\![e]\!]^\sharp_I([u, d]_1, [u, d]_3)$ —then the results of the original intra-procedural analysis and transformed analysis are consistent.*

#	n	H^n	x^n	y^n
1	2		$0 \sqcup x^4$	$0 \sqcup y^4$
2	3	not escaped	$x^2 \sqcap [-\infty, 99]$	y^2
3	4		$x^3 + 1$	y^3
4	5		$x^2 \sqcap [100, \infty]$	y^2
5	6		x^5	y^5

#	n	$[\![x^n]\!]_{\mathcal{E}}^{\sharp}$	$[\![y^n]\!]_{\mathcal{E}}^{\sharp}$
1	2	$[\![0 \sqcup x^4]\!]_{\mathcal{E}}^{\sharp}(\rho) = [0,0]$	$[\![0 \sqcup y^4]\!]_{\mathcal{E}}^{\sharp}(\rho) = [0,0]$
2	3	$[\![x^2 \sqcap [-\infty, 99]]\!]_{\mathcal{E}}^{\sharp}(\rho) = [0,0]$	$[\![y^2]\!]_{\mathcal{E}}^{\sharp}(\rho) = [0,0]$
3	4	$[\![x^3 + 1]\!]_{\mathcal{E}}^{\sharp}(\rho) = [1,1]$	$[\![y^3]\!]_{\mathcal{E}}^{\sharp}(\rho) = [0,0]$
4	2	$[0,0]\nabla[\![0 \sqcup x^4]\!]_{\mathcal{E}}^{\sharp}(\rho) = [0,\infty]$	$[\![0 \sqcup y^4]\!]_{\mathcal{E}}^{\sharp}(\rho) = [0,0]$
5	3	$[\![x^2 \sqcap [-\infty, 99]]\!]_{\mathcal{E}}^{\sharp}(\rho) = [0,99]$	$[\![y^2]\!]_{\mathcal{E}}^{\sharp}(\rho) = [0,0]$
6	4	$[\![x^3 + 1]\!]_{\mathcal{E}}^{\sharp}(\rho) = [1,100]$	$[\![y^3]\!]_{\mathcal{E}}^{\sharp}(\rho) = [0,0]$
7	2	$[0,\infty]\Delta[\![0 \sqcup x^4]\!]_{\mathcal{E}}^{\sharp}(\rho) = [0,100]$	$[\![0 \sqcup y^4]\!]_{\mathcal{E}}^{\sharp}(\rho) = [0,0]$
8	5	$[\![x^2 \sqcap [100, \infty]]\!]_{\mathcal{E}}^{\sharp}(\rho) = [100,100]$	$[\![y^2]\!]_{\mathcal{E}}^{\sharp}(\rho) = [0,0]$
9	6	$[\![x^5]\!]_{\mathcal{E}}^{\sharp}(\rho) = [100,100]$	$[\![y^5]\!]_{\mathcal{E}}^{\sharp}(\rho) = [0,0]$

Fig. 5: Example analysis of using separate components of the domain D'.

Lemma 2 (Inter-Procedural Result Consistency). *In addition to the assumptions of Lemma 1, we require that the generated function entry state $s^{\sharp} = enter_e^{\sharp}([u,d]_1, [u,d]_3, d)_2$ evaluates to the same value as in the original analysis, i.e., $[\![s^{\sharp}]\!]_{\mathcal{E}}(\lambda\_.[u,d]_3) = enter_{e,I}^{\sharp}([u,d]_1, [u,d]_3)$. Finally, the generated function return state $r^{\sharp} = comb_e^{\sharp}([u,d]_1, [u,d]_3, [f_{end}, d']_1, [f_{end}, d']_3, d, d')_2$ must evaluate to the same value as in the original analysis, i.e., $[\![r^{\sharp}]\!]_{\mathcal{E}}(\lambda\_.[u,d]_3) = comb_{e,I}^{\sharp}([u,d]_1, [u,d]_3, [f_{end}, d']_1, [f_{end}, d']_3)$. Then the results of the inter-procedu original analysis and transformed analysis are consistent.*

A demand-driven constraint system solver would alternate between generating and evaluating expressions, yielding online meta-abstract interpretation [18]. Offline meta-abstract interpretation could be achieved when the generation of expressions does not depend on or even query the results of the expressions' evaluations. A demand-driven constraint system solver could first generate all expressions and then, independently, evaluate them.

Example 3. The analysis of the running example using our most recent constraint system that separates the helper, expression, and interval components of D' is shown in Fig. 5. The analysis in this example produces expressions based on the helper analysis — interval values are not queried. Thus, we can first compute all object-escape information and interval expressions, and only then interval values. We have decreased the amount of unnecessary re-computation (in non-bold font), but clarity for the analysis user is still lacking. We note that we can eliminate unnecessary re-computation altogether by distributing interval computations of different program variables to separate constraint system unknowns [5].

$$[\![\mathrm{lfp}(f)]\!]_{\mathcal{E}}^{\sharp}(\rho) \sqsubseteq k(\Delta, k(\nabla, [\![f(\bot)]\!]_{\mathcal{E}}^{\sharp}(\rho))) \quad \text{where}$$

$$k(\square, x) := \begin{cases} k(\square, x \,\square\, [\![f(x)]\!]_{\mathcal{E}}^{\sharp}(\rho)), & \text{if } x \neq [\![f(x)]\!]_{\mathcal{E}}^{\sharp}(\rho) \\ x, & \text{otherwise} \end{cases}$$

Fig. 6: Over-approximating lfp using widening and narrowing.

5   Obtaining closed-form expressions

We saw from the previous example that the generated constraint system is not very clear. Thus, as a post-processing step, we may want to produce closed expressions $\mathcal{E}' \supset \mathbb{E}^{\sharp}$ that compute the respecting values. For that, we need to encode the least upper bounds as uninterpreted function calls (join $\in F$) and add the least fixpoint operator that takes a lambda expression as an argument.

$$\mathcal{E}' ::= [N, D', \mathrm{Var}] \mid F(\mathcal{E}'^{*}) \mid \top \mid \mathrm{lfp}(\lambda\, x.\, \mathcal{E}')$$

The extended expressions $\mathcal{E}'$ need not form a complete lattice as it is only used as output. Also, we need to note that the expressions we generate specifies the least (partial) solution of a constraint system, i.e., the smallest element of the lattice that over-approximates the concrete collecting semantics. And for that reason we make use of the least fixpoint expressions $\mathrm{lfp}(f)$, the meaning of which can be described as $[\![\mathrm{lfp}(f)]\!]_{\mathcal{E}}^{\sharp}(\rho) = \bigsqcup_{n \in \mathbb{N}} [\![f^{n}(\bot)]\!]_{\mathcal{E}}^{\sharp}(\rho)$. The least over-approximations are not computable in general, e.g., generic constraint system solvers also do not aim to compute the least fixpoint but some nontrivial fixpoint. For a domain with infinite ascending chains, a fixpoint can be computed using an ascending iteration using widening followed by a descending iteration using narrowing [15], as shown in Fig. 6. Though, for Noetherian domains, it suffices to have a single precise ascending iteration.

To get closed expressions, we need to inline constraints in such a way that recursion is captured using the fixpoint operator lfp. For that we define a substitution function $\mathsf{subst}(e, \rho)$ where $e \in \mathcal{E}'$ is an expression, $\rho \in (N \times D' \times \mathrm{Var}) \hookrightarrow \mathcal{E}'$ is a partial map from variables to expressions that are to be substituted.

$$\mathsf{subst}(\top, \rho) = \top$$
$$\mathsf{subst}(g(e_1, \ldots, e_n), \rho) = g(\mathsf{subst}(e_1, \rho), \ldots, \mathsf{subst}(e_n, \rho))$$
$$\mathsf{subst}(\mathrm{lfp}(\lambda\, x.\, e), \rho) = \mathrm{lfp}(\lambda\, x.\, \mathsf{subst}(e, \rho - \{x\}))$$

$$\mathsf{subst}([x], \rho) = \begin{cases} [x] & \text{if } x \notin \mathrm{dom}(\rho) \\ \begin{aligned} &\mathbf{let}\ e = \mathsf{subst}(\rho(x), \rho - \{x\})\ \mathbf{in} \\ &\mathbf{if}\ x \in \mathrm{FV}(e)\ \mathbf{then}\ \mathrm{lfp}(\lambda\, x.\, e)\ \mathbf{else}\ e \end{aligned} & \text{otherwise} \end{cases}$$

No further substitution is required in case the expression is $\top$. For function application, we recursively perform substitution in the arguments. For fixpoint expressions, we use recursion while decreasing the partial map ρ by the formal parameter x. For variables $[x]$, we first determine whether substitution is needed.

$$x^2 = 0 \sqcup ((x^2 \sqcap [-\infty, 99]) + 1)$$
$$x^6 = x^2 \sqcap [100, \infty] \tag{3}$$

$$x^6 = \mathrm{lfp}(\lambda z. 0 \sqcup (z \sqcap [-\infty, 99]) + 1) \sqcap [100, \infty] \tag{4}$$

$$y^6 = \mathrm{lfp}(\lambda z. 0 \sqcup z) = 0 \tag{5}$$

$$[\![x^6]\!]_{\mathcal{E}}^{\sharp}(\rho) = ((0 \triangledown [0,1]) \triangle [0, 100]) \sqcap [100, \infty] = [100, 100] \tag{6}$$

Fig. 7: Simplified interval expressions and evaluation for our running example.

We perform no substitution if x is not a key in ρ. If x maps to e' in ρ, we first perform the substitution in e' to obtain a closed form; however, we remove x from ρ to ensure termination. Next, if x is still free in the result of the recursive substitution e'', we return $\mathrm{lfp}(\lambda x. e'')$. If, however, x is not free in e'' we can, as an optimization, directly return e''.

The justification for using substitution for expressions is given in Lemma 3 that states that substitution retains the least solutions. Using widening and narrowing in conjunction with substitution is not predictable as widening and narrowing are not necessarily monotonic. However, any solution is still a sound over-approximation of the least solution.

Lemma 3. *Given a constraint system ρ with the least solution σ such that a constraint $x \sqsupseteq f_x$ in ρ implies that x maps to $[\![f_x]\!]_{\mathcal{E}}^{\sharp}(\sigma)$ in σ. Then for any subset of constraints $\rho' \subseteq \rho$ and expression e we have*

$$[\![subst(e, \rho')]\!]_{\mathcal{E}}^{\sharp}(\sigma - dom(\rho')) = [\![e]\!]_{\mathcal{E}}^{\sharp}(\sigma)$$

Proof. Using structural induction, the $\top$ case is trivial. Function application and fixpoint iteration cases are applications of the induction hypothesis if we can conclude that substituted variables will not be free after substitution. Similarly, the first case of $[x]$ is trivial. For the second case in $[x]$, we see that the evaluation of e using σ will be equal to the value $\sigma(x)$ and if x is not free in e then we have shown our goal. If, however, x is free in e then we can conclude that $\mathrm{lfp}(\lambda x. e)$ will be equal to $\sigma(x)$ as σ is the least solution.   □

Example 4. For our running example in Fig. 3a we have computed interval expressions for each program point in Fig. 5. Results shown in Fig. 7: inlining can produce (based on preference) recursive definitions for x^2 and x^6 (3) or a single non-recursive definition that uses the lfp operator (4). We see that the expression for y^6 can be simplified to constant zero (5). The evaluation of x^6 yields the expected result of exactly one hundred (6).

The function subst can be used to inline all constraints at once to generate a closed expression or, using some custom strategy, to generate a more compact constraint system. For using generated expressions to explain the resulting interval values in a user-friendly way, we may want to inline all variables except function or method calls. As a corollary of Lemma 3, we then have explanation consistency for the least solutions of the closed forms and the interval analysis.

```
2   void foo() {
3       x = 0;
4       y = 0;
5       for (x<100)
6           x += 1;
7       P6der.evalInt(x);
8       P6der.evalInt(y);
9   }
```

▾ value 100 due to condition "at least 100" on line 15
  ▾ range [0, 100] due to a loop on line 15 on field x
    starting with: value 0 due to constant on line 13
    ▾ cycle with:
      ▾ range [1, 100] due to operation IADD
        ▾ parameter 1:
          ▾ range [0, 99] due to condition "at most 99"
            range [0, 100] due to field x at line 15
        parameter 2: value 1 due to constant on line 16

Fig. 8: Reproduction of the explanation provided by Põder from Fig. 2.

Theorem 1 (Consistency Closed-Form Explanations). *For any program point $v \in N$ and any context $d \in D$, the inlined version of expression $[v, d]_2$ describes the least possible interval value of $[v, d]_3$, even if the computed interval is an over-approximation.*

6   Usability and Experimental implementation

Displaying analysis expressions to the user is a challenge. First, the size of the expressions might be overwhelming for non-trivial programs. Instead of asking the user to grasp the whole expression at once, we should formulate the expression in a way that can be followed step by step. Second, the syntax should be intuitively understandable but sufficiently precise. The terminology should be programmer centric such that it avoids unnecessarily theoretic and program analysis specific terms. This could be fine-tuned based on user studies. Third, the sub-expressions should relate to the analyzed source code in a clear fashion so that knowledge from the expression can be used to better understand the code.

To investigate these usability issues further, we prototyped the proposed analysis method in a new Java bytecode analyzer called Põder. The tool has a source-code view and a control-flow-graph view which may be inspected while stepping through the analysis. Analysis results are presented in a collapsible tree-view, which may be examined by selecting a line in the source-code or selecting a node in the CFG.

Fig. 2, at the start of the paper, is a screenshot of Põder after it has completed the analysis of the code from Fig. 3. For easier readability, we have reproduced this explanation in Fig. 8. When the line 17 from OInt.java is selected by the user, the value of the field x is shown as 100 on the right.

The full explanation of the value in field y, which was not updated in the loop, is "value 0 due to constant on line 14". We note that the loop has been optimized away as shown in Fig. 7. The full explanation of the value in field x is also shown in Fig. 8, even though initially the explanation of the value is partially collapsed at the level of "range [1,100] due to operation IADD". Leaving the loop is only possible with a value no less than 100. Before that, a loop is entered with a constant value of 0 and each cycle performs an addition operation. The second addend is the constant one while the first addend is the value

▾ range [0, +inf] due to loop in class OIntBad on field x.
    starting with: value 0 due to constant
  ▾ cycle with:
    ▾ range [1, +inf] due to operation IADD
      parameter 1: range [0, +inf] due to field x at the head of the loop in the class OIntBad.
      parameter 2: value 1 due to constant.

Fig. 9: Explanation for field x if this may escape.

of x at the head of the loop, satisfying the condition for entering the body, i.e., it is less than 100. Selecting a line from the explanation highlights its source in the source-code view. In the screenshot the line "range $[1, 100]$ due to operation IADD" is selected by the user, after which the source of the operation, at line 16, is highlighted in the source-code view.

Now let us consider other programs than our running example. Suppose we need to explain a value returned from a method call a = add(5,20). In that case, the explanation will list explanations of parameters, the returned range, and the line of the called method in the source code where the user can find the explanation of that method's return. Next, we look at the case where foo is called on an object that may be visible to other threads — this happens, e.g., when its reference is written to a static field. In such a general case, the analysis handles the object fields context- and flow-insensitively [30]. Thus, guard constraints will not have an effect and the result for field x is $[0, +\infty]$. Furthermore, because of flow-insensitivity, the loop materializes in the fields' value and not directly because of the loop in method foo. The generated explanation is given in Fig. 9.

7   Generalizability

The problem of explaining the absence of warnings is challenging, especially from a usability perspective. Our experimental implementation shows that generating explanations for simple inductive invariants is possible. We will now address questions of generalizability to larger programs and state-of-the-art analyses where one may require more fine-grained explanations of the computation and the employed domains are more complex.

Large Programs. While we have focused here on simpler programs where the explanation is brief and all related program points are close to each other. The implementation can handle inter-procedural explanations, and we include an inter-procedural example in the replication package. Explanations may thus span multiple different files, and the explanation tab allows convenient navigation between these files. The limitation of experimental implementation is that it lacks state-of-the-art abstractions for the analysis of real-world Java programs. As symbolic domains are employed by many real-world analyzers [11, 20, 25], the runtime overhead is not a significant bottleneck. Our method generalizes well to larger programs; the main difficulty is explaining more complex analyses.

Complicated Computations. State-of-the-art analyzers handle a wide array of programming languages features, such as dynamic memory allocation and thread

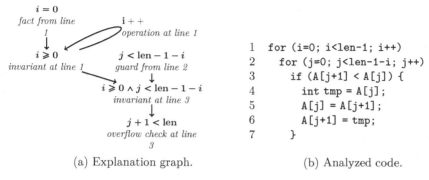

$i = 0$
*fact from line
1*
$\downarrow$
$i \geqslant 0$
invariant at line 1

$i++$
operation at line 1

$j < \mathrm{len} - 1 - i$
guard from line 2
$\downarrow$
$i \geqslant 0 \wedge j < \mathrm{len} - 1 - i$
invariant at line 3
$\downarrow$
$j + 1 < \mathrm{len}$
overflow check at line 3

```
1  for (i=0; i<len-1; i++)
2    for (j=0; j<len-1-i; j++)
3      if (A[j+1] < A[j]) {
4        int tmp = A[j];
5        A[j] = A[j+1];
6        A[j+1] = tmp;
7      }
```

(a) Explanation graph.   (b) Analyzed code.

Fig. 10: Bubble sort array bound example.

creation. The analysis is, therefore, built from a combination of domains [17]. Thus, a new abstract value is computed at each step, first, based on the computation for each individual domain, and then, refinement operations are applied (e.g., reduced products) and integrated with the previous state using more complex widening/narrowing operations that may interact with thresholds and counters.

While the general framework supports any granularity, obtaining more fine-grained explanations requires extending the explanation vocabulary with symbolic operations for low-level operators such as threshold widenings and reduced products. There are serious implementation and usability challenges to obtain readable explanations for complex computations. As we focused on how to explain simpler invariants to end users, we leave the issue of explaining more complex computations as an open problem in explainable static analysis.

Relational Domains. Filtering out relevant information happens naturally for pointwise domains such as the box domain. For each program variable, we collect only expressions that affect that variable. So, for justifying the value of a variable, we just need the expression for that variable. No such natural slicing occurs for relational domains where one program variable may depend on other program variables. Thus, the explanation of a relational value must filter out unnecessary information as a post-processing step taking into account the computed solution.

We have not yet worked out a general algorithm that generates arbitrary explanations for relational domains. However, as an example, consider a polyhedral analysis of the Bubble sort algorithm in Figure 10b, where we picked one specific bound condition $j + 1 < \mathrm{len}$ on line 3 to check. The hand-computed explanation is in Figure 10a, where the queried condition is explained using relevant parts of the invariant $i \geqslant 0 \wedge j < \mathrm{len} - 1 - i$ for line 3. The explanation of a part of an invariant may refer to other invariants, basic facts, or statements from the program, as seen on Figure 10a. We note that validity of the explanation is not trivial to see, but it nevertheless captures exactly how the analyzer inferred that the access is not outside the array bounds.

8   Related work

There has been work in recent years to address usability issues and improve the understandability of static analysis results [26, 28]. These mostly focus on explaining analysis warnings. Zhang et al. [35] present an interactive approach to eliminating false alarms of a sound race detection analysis by applying more aggressive and potentially unsound heuristics. Facts about the program inferred by the analyzer are translated into human-readable queries that the user can confirm or reject; however, the aim is not to explain *how* the results were computed, which is the emphasis of our work.

Combining abstract interpretation [15] and partial evaluation [24] has been considered to the effect of improving partial evaluation [14, 23]. As an alternative to generating constraints explicitly, partial evaluation can also be used in the context of constraint-based program analyses [3]. Though, partial evaluation does not allow direct inspection of the intermediate result and has, at times, unpredictable runtime behavior. In the context of partial evaluation of logic program analysis, improved precision and performance has been achieved [29] — though not with the goal of producing more explainable analyses. Recently, partial evaluation of Horn clauses has been used for control-flow refinement [19] to increase precision and make implicit control-flow explicit.

Cousot and Cousot [16] has described how sound program transformation can be formalized within abstract interpretation in a general uniform language-independent framework. The correctness of transformation is an orthogonal issue w.r.t. the goals of this paper. Most other applications of meta-analysis focus on reasoning and quantifying precision loss [10, 21], which is again orthogonal to the explainability of the fixpoint computation.

Another related approach has been the drive to generate proof objects, *witnesses*, as evidence for the verdict of the analyzer. For error verification, counterexample witnesses [8] may be generated based on the inspection of expression information to minimize the set of paths required to reach an error state. For correctness, analyzers can output their computed invariants, which can be validated by other analyzers [1, 7, 27]. Being able to produce some artifact as evidence for successful verification is also our goal, but we aim here for explanation that humans find understandable and convenient to navigate.

Finally, we note that symbolic domains [11, 20, 25] are also used to express properties about the program. Thus, these analyses use symbolic expressions over program variables that soundly over-approximate the program state. In contrast, we use expressions involving constraint system variables in order to reason about the constraint system itself and extract an explanation for the computation of the abstract values of program variables at a given program point.

9   Conclusion

The ability to produce counter-examples has been an important reason behind the tremendous success of software model checking. For developers to also see the value in *sound* analysis, more work is needed on explainability, so that a verdict that the program is safe can be trusted by our end users. We have taken a significant step in this direction, and characterized the challenges that lie ahead.

Using interval analysis as an example, we have presented a general scheme to write analyses that generate parts of the constraint system as an intermediate step. The generated constraint system can be transformed into a closed expression and simplified, e.g., to inline computations and even remove unnecessary loops. The closed expressions can be mapped onto user-friendly explanations of how the analysis results are computed, which we have integrated into a prototype tool for explainable program analysis.

Acknowledgments. We thank the reviewers for their thoughtful and constructive feedback. This work was supported by the Estonian Research Council grant PSG61 and the Estonian Centre of Excellence in IT (EXCITE), funded by the European Regional Development Fund.

References

1. Albert, E., Puebla, G., Hermenegildo, M.: Abstraction-carrying code. In: Logic for Programming, Artificial Intelligence, and Reasoning, pp. 380–397, Springer (2005), DOI: 10.1007/978-3-540-32275-7_25

2. Amato, G., Scozzari, F., Seidl, H., Apinis, K., Vojdani, V.: Efficiently intertwining widening and narrowing. Science of Computer Programming **120**, 1–24 (2016), DOI: 10.1016/j.scico.2015.12.005

3. Amtoft, T.: Partial Evaluation for Constraint-Based Program Analyses. Tech. rep., BRICS Report Series RS-99-45, Department of Computer Science, University of Aarhus (1999), DOI: 10.7146/brics.v6i45.20115

4. Apinis, K., Seidl, H., Vojdani, V.: How to combine widening and narrowing for non-monotonic systems of equations. ACM SIGPLAN Notices **48**(6), 377–386 (2013), DOI: 10.1145/2499370.2462190

5. Apinis, K., Vene, V., Vojdani, V.: Demand-driven interprocedural analysis for map-based abstract domains. Journal of Logical and Algebraic Methods in Programming **100**, 57–70 (2018), DOI: 10.1016/j.jlamp.2018.06.003

6. Apinis, K., Vojdani, V.: Context-Sensitive Meta-Constraint Systems for Explainable Program Analysis. Zenodo. (2023), DOI: 10.5281/zenodo.7560511, (Software artifact)

7. Beyer, D., Dangl, M., Dietsch, D., Heizmann, M.: Correctness witnesses: Exchanging verification results between verifiers. In: Proceedings of the 2016 24th ACM SIGSOFT International Symposium on Foundations of Software Engineering, pp. 326–337, FSE 2016, ACM (2016), DOI: 10.1145/2950290.2950351

8. Beyer, D., Dangl, M., Dietsch, D., Heizmann, M., Stahlbauer, A.: Witness validation and stepwise testification across software verifiers. In: Proceedings of the 2015 10th Joint Meeting on Foundations of Software Engineering, pp. 721–733, ESEC/FSE, ACM (Aug 2015), DOI: 10.1145/2786805.2786867

9. Birkhoff, G.: Lattice theory, vol. 25. American Mathematical Soc. (1940)

10. Campion, M., Dalla Preda, M., Giacobazzi, R.: Partial (In)Completeness in abstract interpretation: limiting the imprecision in program analysis. Proceedings of the ACM on Programming Languages **6**(POPL), 59:1–59:31 (Jan 2022), DOI: 10.1145/3498721

11. Chang, B.E., Leino, K.R.M.: Abstract interpretation with alien expressions and heap structures. In: VMCAI'05, LNCS, vol. 3385, pp. 147–163, Springer (2005), DOI: 10.1007/978-3-540-30579-8_11

12. Christakis, M., Bird, C.: What Developers Want and Need from Program Analysis: An Empirical Study. In: Proceedings of the 31st IEEE/ACM International Conference on Automated Software Engineering, pp. 332–343, ASE 2016, ACM (2016), DOI: 10.1145/2970276.2970347

13. Clarke, E.M., Emerson, E.A., Sifakis, J.: Model checking: Algorithmic verification and debugging. Commun. ACM **52**(11), 74–84 (nov 2009), DOI: 10.1145/1592761.1592781

14. Consel, C., Khoo, S.C.: Parameterized partial evaluation. ACM Transactions on Programming Languages and Systems **15**(3), 463–493 (Jul 1993), DOI: 10.1145/169683.174155

15. Cousot, P., Cousot, R.: Abstract Interpretation: A unified lattice model for static analysis of programs by construction or approximation of fixpoints. In: 4th ACM Symp. on Principles of Programming Languages (POPL'77), pp. 238–252, ACM Press (1977), DOI: 10.1145/512950.512973

16. Cousot, P., Cousot, R.: Systematic design of program transformation frameworks by abstract interpretation. ACM SIGPLAN Notices **37**(1), 178–190 (Jan 2002), DOI: 10.1145/565816.503290

17. Cousot, P., Cousot, R., Feret, J., Mauborgne, L., Miné, A., Monniaux, D., Rival, X.: Combination of abstractions in the astrée static analyzer. In: ASIAN'06, LNCS, vol. 4435, pp. 272–300, Springer (2006), DOI: 10.1007/978-3-540-77505-8_23

18. Cousot, P., Giacobazzi, R., Ranzato, F.: A2I: Abstract2 Interpretation. Proceedings of the ACM on Programming Languages **3**(POPL), 42:1–42:31 (Jan 2019), DOI: 10.1145/3290355

19. Doménech, J.J., Gallagher, J.P., Genaim, S.: Control-flow refinement by partial evaluation, and its application to termination and cost analysis. Theory and Practice of Logic Programming **19**(5-6), 990–1005 (2019), DOI: 10.1017/S1471068419000310

20. Gange, G., Navas, J.A., Schachte, P., Søndergaard, H., Stuckey, P.J.: An abstract domain of uninterpreted functions. In: VMCAI'05, LNCS, vol. 9583, pp. 85–103, Springer (2016), DOI: 10.1007/978-3-662-49122-5_4

21. Giacobazzi, R., Logozzo, F., Ranzato, F.: Analyzing program analyses. In: POPL '15, pp. 261–273, ACM Press (Jan 2015), DOI: 10.1145/2676726.2676987

22. Johnson, B., Song, Y., Murphy-Hill, E., Bowdidge, R.: Why Don't Software Developers Use Static Analysis Tools to Find Bugs? In: Proceedings of the 2013 International Conference on Software Engineering, pp. 672–681, ICSE '13, IEEE Press (2013), DOI: 10.1109/ICSE.2013.6606613

23. Jones, N.D.: Combining abstract interpretation and partial evaluation (brief overview). In: Van Hentenryck, P. (ed.) Static Analysis, pp. 396–405, LNCS, Springer, Berlin, Heidelberg (1997), DOI: 10.1007/BFb0032761

24. Jones, N.D., Gomard, C.K., Sestoft, P.: Partial evaluation and automatic program generation. Prentice-Hall (1993)

25. Miné, A.: Symbolic methods to enhance the precision of numerical abstract domains. In: VMCAI'06, LNCS, vol. 3855, pp. 348–363, Springer (2006), DOI: 10.1007/11609773_23

26. Nachtigall, M., Nguyen Quang Do, L., Bodden, E.: Explaining static analysis — A perspective. In: ASEW'19, pp. 29–32 (Nov 2019), DOI: 10.1109/ASEW.2019.00023

27. Necula, G.C.: Proof-carrying code. In: Proceedings of the 24th ACM SIGPLAN-SIGACT Symposium on Principles of Programming Languages, p. 106119, POPL '97, ACM (1997), DOI: 10.1145/263699.263712

28. Nguyen Quang Do, L., Bodden, E.: Explaining static analysis with rule graphs. IEEE Transactions on Software Engineering (Jan 2020), DOI: 10.1109/TSE.2020.2999534

29. Puebla, G., Albert, E., Hermenegildo, M.: Abstract Interpretation with Specialized Definitions. In: Yi, K. (ed.) Static Analysis, pp. 107–126, LNCS, Springer, Berlin, Heidelberg (2006), ISBN 978-3-540-37758-0, DOI: 10.1007/11823230_8

30. Seidl, H., Vene, V., Müller-Olm, M.: Global invariants for analyzing multithreaded applications. Proc. of the Estonian Academy of Sciences: Phys., Math. 52(4), 413–436 (2003), ISSN 1406-0086

31. Seidl, H., Vogler, R.: Three improvements to the top-down solver. In: Proceedings of the 20th International Symposium on Principles and Practice of Declarative Programming, PPDP '18, ACM (2018), DOI: 10.1145/3236950.3236967

32. Seidl, H., Wilhelm, R., Hack, S.: Compiler Design: Analysis and Transformation. Springer Science & Business Media (2012), DOI: 10.1007/978-3-642-17548-0

33. Sharir, M., Pnueli, A.: Two approaches to interprocedural data flow analysis. In: Muchnick, S., Jones, N. (eds.) Program Flow Analysis: Theory and Application, pp. 189–233, Prentice-Hall (1981)

34. Vojdani, V., Apinis, K., Rõtov, V., Seidl, H., Vene, V., Vogler, R.: Static race detection for device drivers: the goblint approach. In: Proceedings of the 31st IEEE/ACM International Conference on Automated Software Engineering, ASE 2016, pp. 391–402, ACM (2016), DOI: 10.1145/2970276.2970337

35. Zhang, X., Grigore, R., Si, X., Naik, M.: Effective interactive resolution of static analysis alarms. Proceedings of the ACM on Programming Languages 1(OOPSLA), 1–30 (Oct 2017), DOI: 10.1145/3133881

Explainable Online Monitoring of Metric Temporal Logic

Leonardo Lima[1]($\boxtimes$)[†], Andrei Herasimau[2], Martin Raszyk[3][†],

Dmitriy Traytel[1]($\boxtimes$)[†], and Simon Yuan[2]

[1] Department of Computer Science, University of Copenhagen, Copenhagen, Denmark
{leonardo,traytel}@di.ku.dk
[2] Department of Computer Science, ETH Zürich, Zurich, Switzerland
[3] DFINITY Foundation, Zurich, Switzerland

Abstract. Runtime monitors analyze system execution traces for policy compliance. Monitors for propositional specification languages, such as metric temporal logic (MTL), produce Boolean verdicts denoting whether the policy is satisfied or violated at a given point in the trace. Given a sufficiently complex policy, it can be difficult for the monitor's user to understand how the monitor arrived at its verdict. We develop an MTL monitor that outputs verdicts capturing why the policy was satisfied or violated. Our verdicts are proof trees in a sound and complete proof system that we design. We demonstrate that such verdicts can serve as explanations for end users by augmenting our monitor with a graphical interface for the interactive exploration of proof trees. As a second application, our verdicts serve as certificates in a formally verified checker we develop using the Isabelle proof assistant.

Keywords: metric temporal logic · runtime monitoring · explanations · proof system · formal verification · certification

1 Introduction

In runtime verification, monitoring is the task of analyzing an event stream produced by a running system for violations of specified policies. An online monitor for a propositional policy specification language, such as metric temporal logic (MTL), consumes the stream event-wise and gradually produces a stream of Boolean verdicts denoting the policy's satisfaction or violation at every point in the event stream. MTL monitors [3, 19, 24, 27, 33] use complex algorithms, whose correctness is not obvious, to efficiently arrive at the verdicts. Yet, users must rely on the algorithms being correct and correctly implemented, as the computed verdicts carry no information as to why the policy is satisfied or violated.

The two main approaches to increase the reliability of complex algorithm implementations are verification and certification. Formal verification using proof assistants or software verifiers is laborious and while it provides an ultimate level of trust, the user of a verified tool still gains no insight into why a specific, surely correct verdict was produced. In contrast, certification can yield both trust (especially when the certificate checker is itself formally verified) and insight, provided that the certificate is not only machine-checkable but also human-understandable.

[†] Lima and Traytel are supported by a Novo Nordisk Fonden start package grant (NNF20OC0063462). Raszyk's work was carried out during his past employment at ETH Zürich supported by the Swiss National Science Foundation grant Big Data Monitoring (167162). All authors thank David Basin for supporting this work.

S. Sankaranarayanan and N. Sharygina (Eds.): TACAS 2023, LNCS 13994, pp. 473–491, 2023.
https://doi.org/10.1007/978-3-031-30820-8_28

In this paper, we develop a certification approach to MTL monitoring: instead of Boolean verdicts, we require the monitor to produce checkable and understandable certificates. To this end, we develop a sound and complete local proof system (§2) for the satisfaction and violation of MTL policies. Following Cini and Francalanza [15], local means that a proof denotes the policy satisfaction on a given stream of events and not general MTL satisfiability (for any stream). Our proof system is an adaptation of Basin et al.'s [4] local proof system for LTL satisfiability on lasso words to MTL with past and bounded future temporal operators. A core design choice for our proof system was to remain close to the MTL semantics and thus to be understandable for users who reason about policies in terms of the semantics. Therefore, proof trees in our proof system, or rather their compact representation as proof objects (§3), serve as understandable certificates.

With the certificate format in place, we devise an algorithm that computes minimal (in terms of size) proof objects (§4). We implement the algorithm in OCaml and augment it with an interactive web application[1] to visualize and explore the computed proof objects (§5). Independently, we prove the soundness and completeness of our proof system and formally verify a proof checker using the Isabelle/HOL proof assistant. We extract OCaml code from this formalization and use it to check the correctness of the verdicts produced by our unverified algorithm. To ensure that our correct verdicts are also minimal, we develop a second formally verified but less efficient monitoring algorithm in Isabelle, which we use to compute the minimal proof object size when testing our unverified algorithm.

Finally, we demonstrate how our work provides explainable monitoring output through several examples (§6) and empirically evaluate our algorithm's performance in comparison to other monitors (§7). In summary, we make the following contributions:

- We develop a sound and complete local proof system for past and bounded future MTL that follows closely the semantics of the MTL operators.
- We develop and empirically evaluate an efficient algorithm to compute size-minimal proof objects representing proof trees in our proof system.
- We implement our algorithm in a new, publicly available monitoring tool EXPLANA-TOR2 [22] that includes a web front end and a formally verified proof object checker.

Related Work. We take the work by Basin et al. [4] on optimal proofs for LTL on lasso words as our starting point but change the setting from lasso words to streams of time-stamped events and the logic from LTL to MTL. Moreover, Basin et al. considered the offline path checking problem, whereas we tackle online monitoring here.

Parts of the work presented here are also described in two B.Sc. theses by Yuan [39] and Herasimau [16]. Yuan developed the MTL proof system we present here as well as a monitoring algorithm for computing optimal proofs based on dynamic programming (similarly to Basin et al.'s algorithm [4]). Herasimau formalized Yuan's development in Isabelle/HOL. We use his work as the basis for our formally verified checker. Here, we present a different algorithm that resembles the algorithms used by state-of-the-art monitors for metric first-order temporal logic [5, 29], which perform much better than dynamic programming algorithms for non-trivial metric interval bounds.

Basin et al.'s approach [4] is parameterized by a comparison relation on proof objects that specifies what the algorithm should optimize for. Yuan [39] discovers a flaw in the correctness claim for Basin et al.'s algorithm and corrects it by further restricting the

---

[1] `https://runtime-monitoring.github.io/explanator2`

$$i \vDash p \quad \text{iff } p \in \pi_i \;\Big|\; i \vDash \alpha \vee \beta \text{ iff } i \vDash \alpha \text{ or } i \vDash \beta \;\Big|\; i \vDash \bullet_I \alpha \text{ iff } i > 0 \text{ and } \tau_i - \tau_{i-1} \in I \text{ and } i - 1 \vDash \alpha$$

$$i \vDash \neg\alpha \quad \text{iff } i \nvDash \alpha \;\Big|\; i \vDash \alpha \wedge \beta \text{ iff } i \vDash \alpha \text{ and } i \vDash \beta \;\Big|\; i \vDash \bigcirc_I \alpha \text{ iff } \tau_{i+1} - \tau_i \in I \text{ and } i + 1 \vDash \alpha$$

$$i \vDash \alpha \, \mathcal{S}_I \, \beta \text{ iff } j \vDash \beta \text{ for some } j \le i \text{ with } \tau_i - \tau_j \in I \text{ and } k \vDash \alpha \text{ for all } j < k \le i$$

$$i \vDash \alpha \, \mathcal{U}_I \, \beta \text{ iff } j \vDash \beta \text{ for some } j \ge i \text{ with } \tau_j - \tau_i \in I \text{ and } k \vDash \alpha \text{ for all } i \le k < j$$

Fig. 1: Semantics of MTL for a fixed trace $\rho = \langle (\pi_i, \tau_i) \rangle_{i \in \mathbb{N}}$

supported comparisons. Herasimau [16] relaxes Yuan's requirements while formally verifying the correctness statement. Our algorithm minimizes the computed proof objects' size as this both simplifies the presentation and caters for a more efficient algorithm.

Formal verification of monitors is a timely topic. Some verified monitors were developed recently using proof assistants, e.g., VeriMon [29] and Vydra [28] in Isabelle and lattice-mtl [8] in Coq. Others leveraged SMT technology to increase their trustworthiness [12, 14]. To the best of our knowledge, we present the first verified checker for an online monitor's output, even though verified certifiers are standard practice in other areas such as distributed systems [35], model checking [37,38], and SAT solving [11,21].

Several monitors visualize their output [1,2,7,18,25,30]; some of these even present visually separate verdicts for different parts of the policy. Our work takes inspiration from these approaches, but goes deeper: our minimal proof trees characterize precisely how the verdicts for the different parts compose to a verdict for the overall policy.

Our work follows the "proof trees as explanations" paradigm and thereby joins a series of works on LTL [4,15,32], CFTL [13], and CTL [9]. Of these only Basin et al. [4] supports past operators and none support metric intervals. Two of the above works [9,15] use proof systems based on the unrolling equations for temporal operators instead of the operator's semantics, which we believe is suboptimal for understandability: users think about the operators in terms of their semantics and not in terms of unrolling equations.

Outside of the realm of temporal logics one can find the "proof trees as explanations" paradigm in regular expression matching [31] and in the database community [10].

Metric Temporal Logic. We briefly recall MTL's syntax and point-based semantics [6]. MTL formulas are built from atomic propositions (a, b, c, ...) via Boolean ($\wedge$, $\vee$, $\neg$) and metric temporal operators (previous $\bullet_I$, next $\bigcirc_I$, since $\mathcal{S}_I$, until $\mathcal{U}_I$), where $I = [l, r]$ is a non-empty interval of natural numbers with $l \in \mathbb{N}$ and $r \in \mathbb{N} \cup \{\infty\}$. We omit the interval when $l = 0$ and $r = \infty$. For the until operator $\mathcal{U}_{[l,r]}$, we require the interval to be bounded, i.e., $r \ne \infty$. Formulas are interpreted over streams of time-stamped events $\rho = \langle (\pi_i, \tau_i) \rangle_{i \in \mathbb{N}}$, also called traces. An event π_i is a set of atomic propositions that hold at the respective time-point i. Time-stamps τ_i are natural numbers that are required to be monotone (i.e., $i \le j$ implies $\tau_i \le \tau_j$) and progressing (i.e., for all τ there exists a time-point i with $\tau_i > \tau$). Note that consecutive time-points can have the same time-stamp. Figure 1 shows MTL's standard semantics for a formula φ at time-point i for a fixed trace ρ.

Fix a trace $\rho = \langle (\pi_i, \tau_i) \rangle_{i \in \mathbb{N}}$. The *earliest time-point* of a time-stamp τ on ρ is the smallest time-point i such that $\tau_i \ge \tau$ and is denoted as $\mathsf{ETP}_\rho(\tau)$. Similarly, the *latest time-point* of a time-stamp $\tau \ge \tau_0$ on ρ is the greatest time-point i such that $\tau_i \le \tau$ and is denoted as $\mathsf{LTP}_\rho(\tau)$. Whenever the trace ρ is fixed, we will only write $\mathsf{ETP}(\tau)$ and $\mathsf{LTP}(\tau)$.

2   Local Proof System

We introduce a local proof system for monitoring MTL formulas as the least relation satisfying the rules shown in Figure 2. It contains two mutually dependent judgments: $\vdash^+$

$$\frac{a \in \pi_i}{i \vdash^+ a} \, ap^+ \qquad \frac{i \vdash^- \alpha}{i \vdash^+ \neg\alpha} \, \neg^+ \qquad \frac{i \vdash^+ \alpha}{i \vdash^+ \alpha \vee \beta} \, \vee_L^+ \qquad \frac{i \vdash^+ \beta}{i \vdash^+ \alpha \vee \beta} \, \vee_R^+ \qquad \frac{i \vdash^+ \alpha \quad i \vdash^+ \beta}{i \vdash^+ \alpha \wedge \beta} \, \wedge^+$$

$$\frac{a \notin \pi_i}{i \vdash^- a} \, ap^- \qquad \frac{i \vdash^+ \alpha}{i \vdash^- \neg\alpha} \, \neg^- \qquad \frac{i \vdash^- \alpha}{i \vdash^- \alpha \wedge \beta} \, \wedge_L^- \qquad \frac{i \vdash^- \beta}{i \vdash^- \alpha \wedge \beta} \, \wedge_R^- \qquad \frac{i \vdash^- \alpha \quad i \vdash^- \beta}{i \vdash^- \alpha \vee \beta} \, \vee^-$$

$$\frac{j \leq i \quad \tau_i - \tau_j \in I \quad j \vdash^+ \beta \quad \forall k \in (j, i]. \, k \vdash^+ \alpha}{i \vdash^+ \alpha \, \mathcal{S}_I \, \beta} \, \mathcal{S}^+ \qquad \frac{i > 0 \quad \tau_i - \tau_{i-1} \in I \quad i - 1 \vdash^+ \alpha}{i \vdash^+ \bullet_I \alpha} \, \bullet^+$$

$$\frac{\mathsf{E}_i^{\mathsf{p}}([l,r]) \leq j \quad j \leq i \quad m = \mathsf{L}_i^{\mathsf{p}}([l,r]) \quad \tau_i - \tau_0 \geq l \quad j \vdash^- \alpha \quad \forall k \in [j, m]. \, k \vdash^- \beta}{i \vdash^- \alpha \, \mathcal{S}_{[l,r]} \, \beta} \, \mathcal{S}^-$$

$$\frac{j = \mathsf{E}_i^{\mathsf{p}}([l,r]) \quad m = \mathsf{L}_i^{\mathsf{p}}([l,r]) \quad \tau_i - \tau_0 \geq l \quad \forall k \in [j, m]. \, k \vdash^- \beta}{i \vdash^- \alpha \, \mathcal{S}_{[l,r]} \, \beta} \, \mathcal{S}_\infty^- \qquad \frac{\tau_i - \tau_0 < l}{i \vdash^- \alpha \, \mathcal{S}_{[l,r]} \, \beta} \, \mathcal{S}_{<l}^-$$

$$\frac{}{0 \vdash^- \bullet_I \alpha} \, \bullet_0^- \qquad \frac{i > 0 \quad i - 1 \vdash^- \alpha}{i \vdash^- \bullet_I \alpha} \, \bullet^- \qquad \frac{i > 0 \quad \tau_i - \tau_{i-1} < I}{i \vdash^- \bullet_I \alpha} \, \bullet_{<I}^- \qquad \frac{i > 0 \quad \tau_i - \tau_{i-1} > I}{i \vdash^- \bullet_I \alpha} \, \bullet_{>I}^-$$

$$\frac{i \leq j \quad \tau_j - \tau_i \in I \quad j \vdash^+ \beta \quad \forall k \in [i, j). \, k \vdash^+ \alpha}{i \vdash^+ \alpha \, \mathcal{U}_I \, \beta} \, \mathcal{U}^+ \qquad \frac{\tau_{i+1} - \tau_i \in I \quad i + 1 \vdash^+ \alpha}{i \vdash^+ \bigcirc_I \alpha} \, \bigcirc^+$$

$$\frac{m = \mathsf{E}_i^{\mathsf{f}}(I) \quad i \leq j \quad j \leq \mathsf{L}_i^{\mathsf{f}}(I) \quad j \vdash^- \alpha \quad \forall k \in [m, j]. \, k \vdash^- \beta}{i \vdash^- \alpha \, \mathcal{U}_I \, \beta} \, \mathcal{U}^- \qquad \frac{\tau_{i+1} - \tau_i < I}{i \vdash^- \bigcirc_I \alpha} \, \bigcirc_{<I}^-$$

$$\frac{m = \mathsf{E}_i^{\mathsf{f}}(I) \quad j = \mathsf{L}_i^{\mathsf{f}}(I) \quad \forall k \in [m, j]. \, k \vdash^- \beta}{i \vdash^- \alpha \, \mathcal{U}_I \, \beta} \, \mathcal{U}_\infty^- \qquad \frac{i + 1 \vdash^- \alpha}{i \vdash^- \bigcirc_I \alpha} \, \bigcirc^- \qquad \frac{\tau_{i+1} - \tau_i > I}{i \vdash^- \bigcirc_I \alpha} \, \bigcirc_{>I}^-$$

Fig. 2: Local proof system for MTL for a fixed trace $\rho = \langle (\pi_i, \tau_i) \rangle_{i \in \mathbb{N}}$

(for satisfaction proofs) and $\vdash^-$ (for violation proofs). A satisfaction (violation) proof describes the satisfaction (violation) of a formula at a given time-point on a fixed trace ρ. Each rule is suffixed by $^+$ or $^-$, indicating whether an operator has been satisfied or violated. Moreover, we define $\mathsf{E}_i^{\mathsf{p}}(I) := \mathsf{ETP}(\tau_i - r)$ and $\mathsf{L}_i^{\mathsf{p}}(I) := \min(i, \mathsf{LTP}(\tau_i - l))$ for $I = [l, r]$, which correspond to the earliest and latest time-point within the interval I, respectively, when formulas having $\mathcal{S}_I$ as their topmost operator are considered. In the definition of $\mathsf{L}_i^{\mathsf{p}}(I)$ we take the minimum to account for consecutive time-stamps with the same value. For formulas having $\mathcal{U}_I$ as their topmost operator, both definitions are mirrored, resulting in $\mathsf{E}_i^{\mathsf{f}}(I) := \max(i, \mathsf{ETP}(\tau_i + l))$ and $\mathsf{L}_i^{\mathsf{f}}(I) := \mathsf{LTP}(\tau_i + r)$.

The semantics of the MTL operators directly corresponds to the satisfaction rules ap^+, $\neg^+$, $\vee_L^+$, $\vee_R^+$, $\wedge^+$, $\mathcal{S}^+$, $\mathcal{U}^+$, $\bullet^+$, and $\bigcirc^+$. For instance, consider two time-points j and i such that $j \leq i$. The rule $\mathcal{S}^+$ is applied whenever the time-stamp difference $\tau_i - \tau_j$ belongs to the interval I, and there is a witness for a satisfaction proof of β in the form of $j \vdash^+ \beta$ together with a finite sequence of satisfaction proofs of α for all $k \in (j, i]$. The violation rules for the non-temporal operators ap^-, $\neg^-$, $\vee^-$, $\wedge_L^-$, $\wedge_R^-$ are dual to their satisfaction counterparts. On the other hand, the violation rules for the temporal operators $\bullet_I$, $\bigcirc_I$, $\mathcal{S}_I$, and $\mathcal{U}_I$ are derived by negating and rewriting their semantics. Consider $\mathcal{S}_I$ with $I = [l, r]$:

$$i \not\models \alpha \, \mathcal{S}_I \, \beta \, \leftrightarrow \, \left(\tau_i - \tau_0 \geq l \wedge \exists j \in (\mathsf{E}_i^{\mathsf{p}}(I), i]. \, j \not\models \alpha \wedge \forall k \in [j, \mathsf{L}_i^{\mathsf{p}}(I)]. \, k \not\models \beta \right) \vee \\ \left(\tau_i - \tau_0 \geq l \wedge \forall k \in [\mathsf{E}_i^{\mathsf{p}}(I), \mathsf{L}_i^{\mathsf{p}}(I)]. \, k \not\models \beta \right) \vee \tau_i - \tau_0 < l \quad (1)$$

The rules $\mathcal{S}^-$, $\mathcal{S}_\infty^-$, and $\mathcal{S}_{<l}^-$ correspond to the three disjuncts in Equation (1). We argue that these three cases intuitively represent different ways of violating a since operator. In the first disjunct, α is violated at some time-point after the interval starts and β is violated

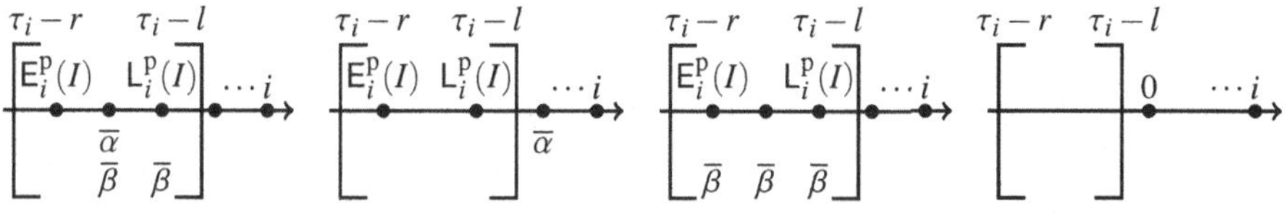

Fig. 3(a): $\mathcal{S}^-$ cases   Fig. 3(b): $\mathcal{S}^-_\infty$ case   Fig. 3(c): $\mathcal{S}^-_{<l}$ case

Fig. 3: Graphical representation of the violation cases for $\alpha\,\mathcal{S}_I\,\beta$ with $I = [l,r]$

from that time-point until the interval ends. Indeed, the violation proof $j \vdash^- \alpha$ is enough to dismiss all previous occurrences of a satisfaction of β. Moreover, if $l \neq 0$, i.e., if the interval does not include the current time-point, then α may be violated between the interval's end and the current time-point. Figure 3(a) shows both cases, where $\overline{\varphi}$ denotes a violation of φ. In the second disjunct, β is violated at every time-point inside the interval (Figure 3(b)). The third disjunct captures the special case at the beginning of the trace when the interval is located before the first time-point (Figure 3(c)). Next, we consider $\mathcal{U}_I$:

$$i \not\vDash \alpha\,\mathcal{U}_I\,\beta \;\leftrightarrow\; \big(\exists j \in [i, \mathsf{L}^{\mathrm{f}}_i(I)).\, j \not\vDash \alpha \wedge \forall k \in [\mathsf{E}^{\mathrm{f}}_i(I), j].\, k \not\vDash \beta\big) \vee \big(\forall k \in [\mathsf{E}^{\mathrm{f}}_i(I), \mathsf{L}^{\mathrm{f}}_i(I)].\, k \not\vDash \beta\big) \tag{2}$$

The rules $\mathcal{U}^-$ and $\mathcal{U}^-_\infty$ correspond to the two disjuncts in Equation (2). In the first disjunct, β is violated from the interval start until a time-point j at which also α is violated. Symmetrically to $\mathcal{S}^-$, we can dismiss all satisfactions of β after j because of the violation proof $j \vdash^- \alpha$. In the second disjunct, β is violated at every time-point inside the interval.

Theorem 1. *Fix an arbitrary trace $\rho = \langle(\pi_i, \tau_i)\rangle_{i \in \mathbb{N}}$. For any formula φ and $i \in \mathbb{N}$, we have $i \vdash^+ \varphi$ iff $i \vDash \varphi$ and $i \vdash^- \varphi$ iff $i \not\vDash \varphi$, i.e., the proof system is sound and complete.*

In other words, proof trees in our proof system contain all the necessary information to explain why a formula has been satisfied or violated on a given trace. A mechanically checked proof of the above statement can be found in our Isabelle formalization [22].

Example 1. Let $\rho = \langle(\{a,b,c\},1),(\{a,b\},3),(\{a,b\},3),(\{\cdot\},3),(\{a\},3),(\{a\},4)\rangle$ and $\varphi = a\,\mathcal{S}_{[1,2]}\,(b \wedge c)$. A proof of $5 \not\vDash \varphi$ has the following form:

$$\cfrac{\cfrac{a \notin \{\cdot\}}{3 \vdash^- a}\,ap^-\quad \cfrac{\cfrac{\cfrac{b \notin \{\cdot\}}{3 \vdash^- b}\,ap^-}{3 \vdash^- b \wedge c}\,\wedge^-_L \quad \cfrac{\cfrac{b \notin \{a\}}{4 \vdash^- b}\,ap^-}{4 \vdash^- b \wedge c}\,\wedge^-_L}{5 \vdash^- a\,\mathcal{S}_{[1,2]}\,(b \wedge c)}\,\mathcal{S}^-}$$

In ρ, only events with time-stamp 3 satisfy the interval conditions, resulting in $\mathsf{E}^{\mathrm{p}}_5(I) = 1$ and $\mathsf{L}^{\mathrm{p}}_5(I) = 4$, where $I = [1,2]$. (Time-points are zero-based.) Thus, the portion of the trace we are interested in is $\langle(\{a,b\},3),(\{a,b\},3),(\{\cdot\},3),(\{a\},3)\rangle$. Here, a is only violated at time-point 3, so our proof includes the witness $3 \vdash^- a$. From there until time-point $\mathsf{L}^{\mathrm{p}}_5(I) = 4$ the subformula $b \wedge c$ is violated, witnessed by $3 \vdash^- b$ and $4 \vdash^- b$. ∎

3 Proof Objects

To make proofs from our proof system explicit, we define an inductive syntax for satisfaction (sp) and violation (vp) proofs and call this representation *proof objects*. Proof objects allow us to easily compute with, modify and compare the size of proof trees. From now on, the term proof will be used for both proof tree and proof object.

$$\mathfrak{sp} = ap^+(\mathbb{N},\varSigma) \mid \neg^+(\mathfrak{vp}) \mid \vee_L^+(\mathfrak{sp}) \mid \vee_R^+(\mathfrak{sp}) \mid \wedge^+(\mathfrak{sp},\mathfrak{sp}) \mid \bullet^+(\mathfrak{sp}) \mid \bigcirc^+(\mathfrak{sp})$$
$$\mid \mathcal{S}^+(\mathfrak{sp},\overline{\mathfrak{sp}_\varnothing}) \mid \mathcal{U}^+(\mathfrak{sp},\overline{\mathfrak{sp}_\varnothing})$$
$$\mathfrak{vp} = ap^-(\mathbb{N},\varSigma) \mid \neg^-(\mathfrak{sp}) \mid \vee^-(\mathfrak{vp},\mathfrak{vp}) \mid \wedge_L^-(\mathfrak{vp}) \mid \wedge_R^-(\mathfrak{vp}) \mid \bullet^-(\mathfrak{vp}) \mid \bullet_{<I}^-(\mathbb{N})$$
$$\mid \bullet_{>I}^-(\mathbb{N}) \mid \bullet_0^- \mid \bigcirc^-(\mathfrak{vp}) \mid \bigcirc_{<I}^-(\mathbb{N}) \mid \bigcirc_{>I}^-(\mathbb{N}) \mid \mathcal{S}_{<I}^-(\mathbb{N}) \mid \mathcal{S}^-(\mathbb{N},\mathfrak{vp},\overline{\mathfrak{vp}_\varnothing})$$
$$\mid \mathcal{S}_\infty^-(\mathbb{N},\overline{\mathfrak{vp}_\varnothing}) \mid \mathcal{U}^-(\mathbb{N},\mathfrak{vp},\overline{\mathfrak{vp}_\varnothing}) \mid \mathcal{U}_\infty^-(\mathbb{N},\overline{\mathfrak{vp}_\varnothing})$$

Here, $\overline{\mathfrak{sp}}$ and $\overline{\mathfrak{vp}}$ denote finite non-empty sequences of $\mathfrak{sp}$ and $\mathfrak{vp}$ subproofs and $\overline{\mathfrak{sp}_\varnothing}$ and $\overline{\mathfrak{vp}_\varnothing}$ denote finite possibly empty sequences of $\mathfrak{sp}$ and $\mathfrak{vp}$ subproofs. We define $\mathfrak{p} = \mathfrak{sp} \uplus \mathfrak{vp}$ to be the disjoint union of satisfaction and violation proofs. Given a proof $p \in \mathfrak{p}$, we define $\mathbb{V}(p)$ to be $\top$ if $p \in \mathfrak{sp}$ and $\bot$ if $p \in \mathfrak{vp}$. Each constructor corresponds to a rule in our proof system. Each proof p has an associated time-point $\mathsf{tp}(p)$ for which it witnesses the satisfaction or violation. In some cases, $\mathsf{tp}(p)$ can be computed recursively from p's subproofs. For example, $\mathsf{tp}(\mathcal{S}^+(p,[q_1,\ldots,q_n]))$ is $\mathsf{tp}(q_n)$ if $n > 0$ and $\mathsf{tp}(p)$ otherwise. Similarly, $\mathsf{tp}(\mathcal{U}^+(p,[q_1,\ldots,q_n]))$ is $\mathsf{tp}(q_1)$ if $n > 0$ and $\mathsf{tp}(p)$ otherwise. Other cases, namely ap^+, ap^-, $\bullet_{<I}^-$, $\bullet_{>I}^-$, $\bigcirc_{<I}^-$, $\bigcirc_{>I}^-$, $\mathcal{S}_{<I}^-$, $\mathcal{S}^-$, and $\mathcal{S}_\infty^-$, explicitly store the associated time-points as an argument of type $\mathbb{N}$ because we cannot compute them from the respective subproofs. For example, $\mathsf{tp}(ap^+(j,a)) = j$ and $\mathsf{tp}(\mathcal{S}^-(j,q,[p_1,\ldots,p_n])) = j$.

Given a trace $\rho = \langle(\pi_i,\tau_i)\rangle_{i\in\mathbb{N}}$ and a formula φ, we call a proof p *valid* at $\mathsf{tp}(p)$, denoted by $p \vdash \varphi$, if p represents a valid proof according to the rules of our local proof system. Note that once again we leave the dependency on ρ implicit in $p \vdash \varphi$. Formally, validity $p \vdash \varphi$ is defined recursively, checking for each constructor that the corresponding rule has been correctly applied. For example, atomic proofs are valid if the mentioned atom is (not) contained in the trace at the specified time-points: $ap^+(i,a) \vdash a \leftrightarrow a \in \pi_i$ ($ap^-(i,a) \vdash a \leftrightarrow a \notin \pi_i$). Moreover, for $r = \mathcal{S}^+(p,[q_1,\ldots,q_n])$ we have

$$r \vdash \alpha \, \mathcal{S}_I \, \beta \leftrightarrow \mathsf{tp}(p) \leq \mathsf{tp}(r) \wedge \tau_{\mathsf{tp}(r)} - \tau_{\mathsf{tp}(p)} \in I \wedge$$
$$[\mathsf{tp}(q_1),\ldots,\mathsf{tp}(q_n)] = [\mathsf{tp}(p)+1,\mathsf{tp}(r)] \wedge p \vdash \beta \wedge (\forall k \in [1,n]. \, q_k \vdash \alpha).$$

Multiple valid proofs may exist for a time-point i and formula φ as we demonstrate next.

Example 2. The proof object representing the proof tree from Example 1 is $P_1 = \mathcal{S}^-(5,ap^-(3,a),[\wedge_L^-(ap^-(3,b)),\wedge_L^-(ap^-(4,b))])$. However, we could have argued differently, using the fact that c is violated at all time-points inside the interval. Then, $\mathcal{S}_\infty^-$ would be used instead to construct the proof $P_2 = \mathcal{S}_\infty^-(5,[\wedge_R^-(ap^-(1,c)),\wedge_R^-(ap^-(2,c)),$ $\wedge_R^-(ap^-(3,c)),\wedge_R^-(ap^-(4,c))])$, which is also a valid proof at $\mathsf{tp}(P_2) = 5$. In addition, $P_3 = \mathcal{S}^-(5,ap^-(3,a),[\wedge_L^-(ap^-(3,c)),\wedge_L^-(ap^-(4,c))])$ is another valid proof at $\mathsf{tp}(P_3) = 5$. It is structurally identical to P_1, but instead of using the violations of b as witnesses for time-points 3 and 4, it uses the violations of c. In fact, both b and c are violated at time-points 3 and 4, so we can use either to justify the violations of $b \wedge c$.

We now compare P_1, P_2, and P_3. The proof P_2 uses $\mathcal{S}_\infty^-$, so we must store a witness of the violation of $b \wedge c$ for each one of the 4 time-points inside the interval. The proofs P_1 and P_3 use $\mathcal{S}^-$, taking advantage of the violation proof $3 \vdash^- a$ that allows us to dismiss both $1 \vdash^+ a$ and $2 \vdash^+ a$. Formally, we define the size $|p|$ of a proof p to be the number of proof object constructors occurring in p. Then, $|P_1| = |P_3| = 6$, and $|P_2| = 9$. ∎

We are particularly interested in small proofs as they tend to be easier to understand. Given a trace ρ and a formula φ, a proof p is *minimal* at time-point i if and only if it is

ype $buf = \mathfrak{p}\ list \times \mathfrak{p}\ list$ **type** $buft = \mathfrak{p}\ list \times \mathfrak{p}\ list \times ((ts \times tp)\ list)$

ype $saux = \{\ ts_{zero} : ts\ option,\ \ ts\_tp_{in} : (ts \times tp)\ list,\ \ ts\_tp_{out} : (ts \times tp)\ list,$
       $s\_beta\_alphas_{in} : (ts \times \mathfrak{sp})\ slist,\ \ \ \ s\_beta\_alphas_{out} : (ts \times \mathfrak{sp})\ list,$
       $v\_alpha\_betas_{in} : (ts \times \mathfrak{vp})\ slist,\ \ \ \ \ v\_alphas_{out} \ \ \ \ \ \ \ \ : (ts \times \mathfrak{vp})\ slist,$
       $v\_betas_{in} \ \ \ \ \ \ : (ts \times \mathfrak{vp})\ list,\ \ \ \ \ \ \ v\_alphas\_betas_{out} : (ts \times \mathfrak{vp}\ option \times \mathfrak{vp}\ option)\ list\ \}$

ype $state = \mathsf{Pred}_S\ string \mid \mathsf{Neg}_S\ state \mid \mathsf{And}_S\ state\ state\ buf \mid \mathsf{Or}_S\ state\ state\ buf$
  | $\mathsf{Prev}_S\ \mathcal{I}\ state\ bool\ \mathfrak{p}\ (ts\ list) \mid \mathsf{Next}_S\ \mathcal{I}\ state\ bool\ (ts\ list)$
  | $\mathsf{Since}_S\ \mathcal{I}\ state\ state\ buft\ saux \mid \mathsf{Until}_S\ \mathcal{I}\ state\ buft\ uaux$

unction init :: $formula \Rightarrow state$ **function** eval :: $ts \times tp \Rightarrow atom\ set \Rightarrow state \Rightarrow \mathfrak{p}\ list \times state$

Fig. 4: Types of the monitor's state and evaluation functions

valid at i ($p \vdash \varphi$ and $\mathsf{tp}(p) = i$), and all other valid proofs q (at i) have greater or equal size ($q \vdash \varphi$ and $\mathsf{tp}(q) = i$ implies $|p| \leq |q|$). In our example, P_1 and P_3 are minimal.

4 Computing Minimal Proofs

Given an MTL formula φ, our (online) monitor incrementally processes a trace and for each time-point i it outputs a minimal proof of the satisfaction or violation of φ at i. The algorithm constructs this minimal proof of φ by combining minimal proofs of φ's immediate subformulas. To do this efficiently, the monitor maintains just enough information about the trace in its state so that it can guarantee to output minimal proofs. In case the monitored formula includes (bounded) future operators, the monitor's output may be delayed, such that a single event may trigger the output of multiple proofs at once. In this section, we describe our algorithm in detail and explain its correctness.

4.1 Monitor's State

Figure 4 shows the types of our algorithm's main functions init, which computes the monitor's initial state, and eval, which processes a time-stamped event while updating the monitor's state and producing a list of minimal proofs (satisfactions or violations) for an in-order (potentially empty) sequence of time-points. Our monitor's state (type *state* in Figure 4) has the same tree-like structure as the monitored MTL formula. Additionally, it stores operator-specific information for each Boolean and temporal operator. For example, in the state of $\alpha\ \mathcal{S}_I\ \beta$, we store the interval I, the states of the subformulas α and β, a buffer *buft* for proofs (and associated time-stamps) coming from the recursive evaluation of subformulas and the operator-specific data structures *saux*. Our monitor's overall structure is modeled after VERIMON [29], which has a similar interface (init and eval) and *state* type including the used buffers *buf* and *buft*. The main novelty is our design of the *saux* and *uaux* data structures, which store sufficient information to compute minimal proofs for formulas with topmost operator $\mathcal{S}$ and $\mathcal{U}$. Here, we only describe *saux* in detail.

The data structure *saux* for a formula $\varphi = \alpha\ \mathcal{S}_I\ \beta$ is a record consisting of nine fields. We will describe it next assuming that φ is being evaluated at the current time-point *cur*. Furthermore, some fields have the type *option*, which means they are of the form $\perp$ (if no value is available) or $\lfloor v \rfloor$ (storing the value v). The function THE retrieves the optional

```
1: procedure UPDATE_SAUX ([l,r],τ_cur,cur,p_1,p_2,saux)
2:     saux.ts_zero ← if saux.ts_zero = ⊥ then ⌊τ_cur⌋ else saux.ts_zero
3:     saux ← ADD_SUBPS (τ_cur,p_1,p_2,saux)
                ▷ update s_betas_alphas_in, s_betas_alphas_out, v_alphas_betas_out, and v_alphas_out
4:     if τ_cur < THE (saux.ts_zero) + l then
5:         saux.ts_tp_out ← APPEND (saux.ts_tp_out, [(τ_cur,cur)])
6:         return (S⁻_{<l}(cur), saux)
7:     else
8:         lr ← (if r = ∞ then THE (saux.ts_zero) else MAX (0,τ_cur − r), τ_cur − l)
9:         saux ← SHIFT_SAUX(lr,l,τ_cur,cur,saux)
10:        minimal_proof ← EVAL_SAUX(cur,saux)   ▷ extract proofs; pick one of minimal size
11:        return (minimal_proof, saux)
12:
13: procedure SHIFT_SAUX (lr,l,τ_cur,cur,saux)
14:     saux ← SHIFT_TS_TPS (lr,l,τ_cur,cur,saux)      ▷ update ts_tp_out and ts_tp_in
15:     saux ← SHIFT_SAT (lr,saux)          ▷ update s_beta_alphas_out and s_beta_alphas_in
16:     saux ← SHIFT_VIO (lr,saux) ▷ update v_alphas_betas_out, v_alpha_betas_in, and v_betas_in
17:     saux ← REMOVE_SAUX (lr,saux)   ▷ remove too old proofs (that fell out of the interval)
18:     return saux
```

Algorithm 1: State update algorithm for Since

value from $\lfloor v \rfloor$, i.e., THE $(\lfloor v \rfloor) = v$. The field ts_{zero} stores $\perp$ in the initial state, and after the first event arrives, it stores the first time-stamp $\lfloor \tau_0 \rfloor$. Fields $\mathsf{ts\_tp}_{in}$ and $\mathsf{ts\_tp}_{out}$ store lists of time-stamp-time-point pairs inside the interval (between $\mathsf{E}^{\mathsf{p}}_{cur}(I)$ and $\mathsf{L}^{\mathsf{p}}_{cur}(I)$) and after the interval (between $\mathsf{L}^{\mathsf{p}}_{cur}(I) + 1$ and cur), respectively. The other fields store satisfaction (prefix $\mathsf{s\_}$) or violation ($\mathsf{v\_}$) proofs. Specifically, $\mathsf{s\_beta\_alphas}_{in}$ stores $\mathcal{S}^+$ proofs inside and $\mathsf{s\_beta\_alphas}_{out}$ stores $\mathcal{S}^+$ proofs after the interval. Crucially, while $\mathsf{s\_beta\_alphas}_{out}$ is an ordinary list, $\mathsf{s\_beta\_alphas}_{in}$ has type *slist*, which is a variant of the list type that indicates that the stored proofs are sorted in ascending order (with respect to size). We maintain this invariant to optimize the number of proofs we must store, i.e., if a proof enters the interval, we can delete all larger proofs that entered the interval prior to it. In addition, we can quickly access the first proof of this list which necessarily has minimal size. On the other hand, $\mathsf{s\_beta\_alphas}_{out}$ must store all proofs because it is not possible to predict when and which of these proofs will enter the interval.

Furthermore, $\mathsf{v\_alpha\_betas}_{in}$ is the analogue of $\mathsf{s\_beta\_alphas}_{in}$ for $\mathcal{S}^-$ proofs with a violation of α inside the interval, and a sequence of violations of β until the end of the interval. Note that $\mathcal{S}^-$ proofs can also be constructed using a single violation proof of α that occurs after the interval, and these are instead stored in the also sorted list $\mathsf{v\_alphas}_{out}$. Moreover, $\mathcal{S}^-_\infty$ proofs require that β is violated at all time-points inside the interval, so $\mathsf{v\_betas}_{in}$ stores a suffix of β violations inside the interval. Finally, $\mathsf{v\_alphas\_betas}$ stores all α and β violations outside the interval, so all other components that store violation proofs inside the interval can be efficiently updated when the interval shifts.

4.2   State Update

Algorithm 1 shows the skeleton of our procedure for updating (and simultaneously evaluating) the state of a since operator. The state update for $\varphi = \alpha \, \mathcal{S}_I \, \beta$ is parametrized by the interval $I = [l, r]$, the current time-point cur and its time-stamp τ_{cur}, minimal proofs p_1 and p_2 (obtained recursively) for the subformulas α and β, respectively, and the current state $saux$. The procedure first checks if cur is the first time-point to arrive and initializes ts_{zero} accordingly (line 2). Next, we add the new subproofs to their destinations (ADD_SUBPS). For example, if $p_1 \in \mathsf{sp}$ then all proofs from s_betas_alphas$_{in}$ and s_betas_alphas$_{out}$ are extended with this additional satisfaction proof for α. In contrast, if $p_1 \in \mathsf{vp}$ then both s_betas_alphas lists are emptied and the violation of α is stored in v_alphas$_{out}$ and v_alphas_betas$_{out}$ instead. A similar case distinction happens for p_2. After storing the proofs, we handle the case where cur is a time-point at the beginning of the trace for which the past interval has not started yet (lines 4–6), which corresponds to the $\mathcal{S}_{<I}^-$ case depicted in Figure 3(b) on the right. Here, we add a new time-stamp-time-point pair to ts_tp$_{out}$ (line 5), and return the proof $\mathcal{S}_{<I}^-(cur)$ and the updated $saux$.

In the general case (when the interval has started), we compute the absolute time-stamp pair lr that constitute the boundaries of the past interval I relative to τ_{cur} (line 8). We use the absolute boundaries to identify a potential interval shift and move proofs in $saux$ from the out lists to the in lists accordingly (line 9). Lines 13–18 provide additional details in which order the various components are shifted. Lastly, we compute a minimal proof (line 10), performing a case distinction. If s_beta_alphas$_{in}$ is non-empty, then its head must be a minimal satisfaction proof. Otherwise, the formula is violated and a minimal violation proof is either the head of v_alpha_betas$_{in}$ or the head of v_alphas$_{out}$ (after adding a $\mathcal{S}^-$ constructor) or the application of $\mathcal{S}_\infty^-$ to v_betas$_{in}$ (provided that this suffix spans the entire interval which can be deduced by comparing the lengths of v_betas$_{in}$ and ts_tp$_{in}$). We extract these (at most three) candidates, compute their sizes, and pick one of minimal size. This minimal proof and the updated $saux$ are then returned (line 11).

Example 3. To illustrate how the state is updated, we once again consider the formula and trace introduced in Example 1. Figure 5 shows the $saux$ states of our algorithm and the produced minimal proof after processing every event. In every state, we only show the non-empty components. Initially, all components of the state are empty except for ts_{zero}, which is $\perp$. When the first event $(\{a,b,c\},1)$ arrives, the list ts_tp$_{out}$ is updated accordingly and a pair with time-stamp 1 and a $\mathcal{S}^+$ proof using the satisfactions of b and c is added to s_beta_alphas$_{out}$. This proof is clearly not valid for the current time-point 0, considering that the interval $[1,2]$ has not yet started, so the monitor outputs the trivial proof $\mathcal{S}_{<I}^-(0)$. The time-stamp of the first event moves inside the interval when the second event $(\{a,b\},3)$ arrives, and both ts_tp$_{out}$ and ts_tp$_{in}$ are updated accordingly. Furthermore, the algorithm extends the $\mathcal{S}^+$ proof previously stored in s_beta_alphas$_{out}$ by adding $ap^+(1,a)$ to the sequence of a satisfactions, after which the resulting proof is moved to s_beta_alphas$_{in}$. The algorithm also appends the proof $ap^-(1,c)$ to v_alphas_betas$_{out}$. Because s_beta_alphas$_{in}$ is not empty, the monitor outputs the first proof of this list.

In the next step, event $(\{a,b\},3)$ arrives and the monitor proceeds similarly, adding the proof $ap^+(2,a)$ to the $\mathcal{S}^+$ proof in s_beta_alphas$_{in}$. Aside from outputting the extended satisfaction proof, the algorithm also adds the proof $ap^-(2,c)$ to v_alphas_betas$_{out}$.

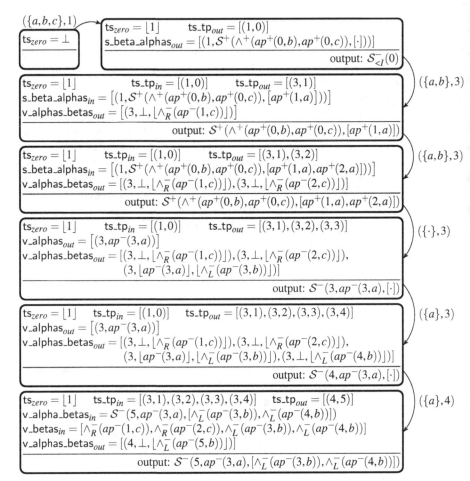

Fig. 5: The monitor's *saux* states when executing Example 1

When event $(\{\cdot\}, 3)$ arrives, the sequence of a satisfactions comes to an end, which indicates that the proofs in s_beta_alphas$_{in}$ and s_beta_alphas$_{out}$ are no longer valid nor useful. Hence, we clear both lists. In addition, the proof $ap^-(3, a)$ is stored in v_alphas$_{out}$, since the a violation happens after the interval. This subproof is also appended to v_alphas_betas$_{out}$ along with the violation of the conjunction $\wedge_L^-$. The algorithm then proceeds to construct a violation proof $\mathcal{S}^-(3, ap^-(3, a), [\cdot])$ using the subproof stored in v_alphas$_{out}$ and outputs it. When $(\{a\}, 3)$ arrives, the algorithm appends the proof $\wedge_L^-$ to v_alphas_betas$_{out}$ and again uses the same subproof stored in v_alphas$_{out}$ to construct $\mathcal{S}^-(4, ap^-(3, a), [\cdot])$. Note that this proof has an associated time-point of 4, which is the only distinction from the last proof that the monitor output.

Finally, when the last event $(\{a\}, 4)$ arrives, the interval shifts and ts_tp$_{in}$ and ts_tp$_{out}$ change accordingly. At this stage, the algorithm populates v_alpha_betas$_{in}$ and v_betas$_{in}$ with the subproofs stored in v_alphas_betas$_{out}$. In particular, it constructs and stores the proof $\mathcal{S}^-(5, ap^-(3, a), [\wedge_L^-(ap^-(3, b)), \wedge_L^-(ap^-(4, b))])$ in v_alpha_betas$_{in}$. Moreover, a

$\text{sorted}(\text{s\_beta\_alphas}_{in}) \land \text{sorted}(\text{v\_alpha\_betas}_{in}) \land \text{sorted}(\text{v\_alphas}_{out}) \land$

(1) $\forall (\tau, u) \in \text{s\_beta\_alphas}_{in}.$ $\exists p\, \bar{q}.\, u = \mathcal{S}^+(p, \bar{q}) \land u \vdash \alpha \, \mathcal{S}_I \, \beta \land \text{tp}(u) = cur \land \tau = \text{ts}(p)$

(2) $\forall (\tau, u) \in \text{s\_beta\_alphas}_{out}.$ $\exists p\, \bar{q}.\, u = \mathcal{S}^+(p, \bar{q}) \land u \vdash \alpha \, \mathcal{S} \, \beta \land \text{tp}(u) = cur \land \tau = \text{ts}(p)$

(3) $\forall (\tau, u) \in \text{v\_alpha\_betas}_{in}.$ $\exists p\, \bar{q}.\, u = \mathcal{S}^-(cur, p, \bar{q}) \land u \vdash \alpha \, \mathcal{S}_I \, \beta \land \tau = \text{ts}(p)$

(4) $\forall (\tau, p) \in \text{v\_alphas}_{out}.$ $\mathcal{S}^-(cur, p, []) \vdash \alpha \, \mathcal{S}_I \, \beta \land \tau = \text{ts}(p)$

(5) $\forall (\tau, p) \in \text{v\_betas\_suffix}_{in}.$ $\mathsf{E}^{\mathsf{p}}_{cur}(I) \leq \text{tp}(p) \leq \mathsf{L}^{\mathsf{p}}_{cur}(I) \land p \vdash \beta \land \neg \mathbb{V}(p) \land \tau = \text{ts}(p)$

(6) $\forall (\tau, p^*, q^*) \in \text{v\_alphas\_betas}_{out}.\ \exists i \in\,]\mathsf{L}^{\mathsf{p}}_{cur}(I), cur].\, \tau = \tau_i \land$
    $(p^* = \bot \lor (\exists p.\, \neg \mathbb{V}(p) \land p^* = \lfloor p \rfloor \land p \vdash \alpha)) \land (q^* = \bot \lor (\exists q.\, \neg \mathbb{V}(q) \land q^* = \lfloor q \rfloor \land q \vdash \beta))$

Fig. 6: The algorithm's invariant (soundness)

sequence of violations of the conjunction inside the interval is stored in v_betas$_{in}$. This sequence of violations fills the entire interval, so it is then used to construct the proof $\mathcal{S}^-_\infty(5, [\land^-_R(ap^-(1,c)), \land^-_R(ap^-(2,c)), \land^-_R(ap^-(3,c)), \land^-_R(ap^-(4,c))])$. The $\mathcal{S}^-$ proof corresponds precisely to the proof tree presented in Example 1, and the proof object P_1 in Example 2, whereas the $\mathcal{S}^-_\infty$ proof corresponds to the proof object P_2. Lastly, the size of these two proofs is computed, and the algorithm selects the $\mathcal{S}^-$ proof, since it is smaller (i.e., it includes fewer constructors).   ∎

4.3 Correctness

We now formally describe the invariant we maintain for *saux*. We write $\text{ts}(p)$ for the time-stamp associated with a proof, i.e., the time-stamp $\tau_{\text{tp}(p)}$ of the associated time-point $\text{tp}(p)$. We also use functional programming notations like λ-abstractions and the list map function. We define the predicate $\text{sorted}(seq) := (\forall (\tau_i, p_i), (\tau_j, p_j) \in seq.\ (i < j) \land$ $(j < \text{length}(seq)) \rightarrow \tau_i \leq \tau_j \land |p_i| \leq |p_j|)$ over a sequence of pairs of time-stamps and proofs and assume that every sequence below is monotone with respect to time-stamps ($i < j$ implies $\tau_i \leq \tau_j$). The fields ts_{zero}, ts_tp_{in} and ts_tp_{out} are characterized as follows:

$$\text{ts}_{zero} = \begin{cases} \bot & \text{iff } cur = -1 \\ \lfloor \tau_0 \rfloor & \text{iff } cur \geq 0 \end{cases} \qquad \begin{aligned} \text{ts\_tp}_{in} &= \text{map } (\lambda i.\ (\tau_i, i)) \ [\mathsf{E}^{\mathsf{p}}_{cur}(I), \mathsf{L}^{\mathsf{p}}_{cur}(I)] \\ \text{ts\_tp}_{out} &= \text{map } (\lambda i.\ (\tau_i, i)) \ ]\mathsf{L}^{\mathsf{p}}_{cur}(I), cur] \end{aligned}$$

The desired properties of the objects stored in other fields are given in Figure 6.

We describe each of the invariant's statements. In (1) a proof in s_beta_alphas$_{in}$ (which must be sorted) must have form $\mathcal{S}^+(p, \bar{q})$ and be a valid proof of $\alpha \, \mathcal{S}_I \, \beta$ at the current time-point, with time-stamp $\text{ts}(p)$. Next, (2) requires proofs to have the same form but instead be valid for a modified formula without the interval I. In this case, we can relax the timing constraint because these proofs will only be valid at a later time-point, namely once $\text{ts}(p)$ moves inside the interval. The statement (3) is precisely the same as (1), but for $\mathcal{S}^-$ proofs. In (4), each proof p in v_alphas$_{out}$ (which must too be sorted) must be a valid subproof of a $\mathcal{S}^-$ proof at the current time-point with time-stamp $\text{ts}(p)$. In (5), each subproof corresponding to the violation of β must be inside the interval with time-stamp $\text{ts}(p)$. The statement (6) specifies that outside the interval there is either a subproof of a violation of α or β or there are no such proofs. These statements formalize what must hold for the things stored in *saux*, which yields soundness. We briefly consider completeness,

Fig. 7: Visualization of Example 1

by answering the question of what must be stored, on the example of s_beta_alphas$_{in}$:

$$\forall p\, \bar{q}\, \tau.\, \mathcal{S}^+(p,\bar{q}) \vdash \alpha\, \mathcal{S}_I \beta \wedge \mathsf{tp}\left(\mathcal{S}^+(p,\bar{q})\right) = cur \wedge \tau = \mathsf{ts}(p) \rightarrow$$
$$\left(\exists p'\, \bar{q}'\, \tau'.\, |\mathcal{S}^+(p',\bar{q}')| \leq |\mathcal{S}^+(p,\bar{q})| \wedge \mathcal{S}^+(p',\bar{q}') \vdash \alpha\, \mathcal{S}_I \beta \wedge \tau' = \mathsf{ts}(p') \wedge \right.$$
$$\left. \tau' \geq \tau \wedge \mathsf{tp}\left(\mathcal{S}^+(p',\bar{q}')\right) = \mathsf{tp}\left(\mathcal{S}^+(p,\bar{q})\right) \wedge \left(\tau', \mathcal{S}^+(p',\bar{q}')\right) \in \mathsf{s\_beta\_alphas}_{in}\right)$$

In words: for any valid $\mathcal{S}^+$ proof for $\varphi = \alpha\, \mathcal{S}_I \beta$ at time-point cur, we must store in s_beta_alphas$_{in}$ another proof at most as large and old, that is also valid for φ at cur. Other fields of $saux$ have similar completeness statements and so have other state components.

Together, soundness and completeness ensure that given a formula, a trace, and a time-point i, our online monitoring algorithm will eventually output a valid minimal proof at i.

5   Implementation

We implement our algorithm in a new tool called EXPLANATOR2 [22]. The implementation amounts to around 4 000 lines of OCaml. In addition, a 6 900 lines long OCaml program is extracted from our Isabelle formalization consisting of 19 000 lines of definitions and proofs. The extracted program contains the proof object validity checker in the form of a function is_valid : $trace \rightarrow formula \rightarrow proof \rightarrow bool$, which effectively implements what we denote by $p \vdash \varphi$. Moreover, it also contains the minimality checker is_minimal : $trace \rightarrow formula \rightarrow proof \rightarrow bool$ that given a trace ρ, a formula φ, and a proof p computes a proof q for φ on ρ at time-point $\mathsf{tp}(p)$ with a minimal size using a verified dynamic programming algorithm and then checks that $|p| \leq |q|$. Note that q may differ from p because minimal proof objects are not unique. Herasimau [16] provides more details on the formalization and the dynamic programming algorithm. We used the verified validity and minimality checkers to thoroughly test our unverified algorithm. Our tool includes a command line option to enable the verified certification of its output, which slows down computation as the verified algorithm is rather inefficient but increases trustworthiness.

EXPLANATOR2 also includes a JavaScript web front end. To this end, we transpile the compiled OCaml bytecode to JavaScript using Js_of_ocaml [36]. The resulting JavaScript library runs in any web browser. We augment the library with an interactive visualization using React [17]. Figure 7 shows the visualization of our Example 1. On the left, the visualization shows the trace (from top to bottom) consisting of the atomic propositions (columns a, b, and c), the time-stamps (column TS) and associated time-points (column TP). The following columns show either the topmost operator of the different

$$
\cfrac{\cfrac{\vdots}{61 \vdash^+ r \wedge \neg q} \wedge^+ \quad \cfrac{\cfrac{q \in \{q\}}{56 \vdash^+ q} \, ap^+}{61 \vdash^+ \blacklozenge q} \blacklozenge^+}{\cfrac{61 \vdash^+ (r \wedge \neg q) \wedge \blacklozenge q}{61 \vdash^- \left((r \wedge \neg q) \wedge \blacklozenge q \right) \to \left(\left(\blacklozenge_{[0,3]} (p \vee q) \right) \mathcal{S} q \right)}} \wedge^+ \quad \cfrac{\cfrac{\cfrac{\vdots}{58,\ldots,61 \vdash^- p \vee q} \vee^-}{61 \vdash^- \blacklozenge_{[0,3]} (p \vee q)} \blacklozenge^- \quad \cfrac{q \notin \{r\}}{61 \vdash^- q} \, ap^-}{61 \vdash^- \left(\blacklozenge_{[0,3]} (p \vee q) \right) \mathcal{S} q} \mathcal{S}^-}{ } \to^-
$$

Fig. 8: Proof of φ_1's violation at time-point 61

subformulas or the atomic propositions of our monitored MTL formula $\varphi = a\, \mathcal{S}_{[1,2]}\, (b \wedge c)$. In particular, the column labeled with φ's topmost operator, namely $\mathcal{S}_{[1,2]}$, shows the Boolean verdicts that a traditional monitor would output. Users of EXPLANATOR2 can further inspect the Boolean verdicts by clicking on them. Figure 7 shows the visualization's state after clicking on φ's violation at time-point 5. The visualization highlights the time interval and the Boolean verdicts for subformulas that justify the verdict associated with the inspected formula and time-point. Furthermore, it shows the relevant violations of φ's subformulas a and $b \wedge c$: the subformula a is violated at time-point 3 and $b \wedge c$ is violated at time-points 3 and 4, which corresponds to a valid $\mathcal{S}^-$ proof. The user could continue the exploration by further clicking on the two $b \wedge c$ violations to find out that the tool used b violations to justify both. The visualization uses black circles to denote combinations of subformula and time-point that are relevant for at least one of φ's verdicts. The Boolean value for these relevant subformula verdicts is only revealed upon exploration.

6 Examples

We demonstrate how the minimal proofs produced by our monitor can be useful when trying to comprehend a satisfaction or violation of an MTL formula. To this end, we consider Timescales [34], a benchmark generator for MTL monitors. Timescales uses predefined MTL formulas that represent temporal patterns that commonly occur in real system designs [20]. It generates traces, in which the time-stamps are equal to their corresponding time-points. We selected the two most complex properties and generated their corresponding traces. At the end of both traces there is a violation of the pattern, and we use our approach to explain these violations. In addition to the operators presented in Figure 2, we extended our proof system and algorithm with the following operators: $\top$ (truth), $\bot$ (falsity), $\to$ (implies), $\leftrightarrow$ (iff), $\blacksquare_I$ (historically), $\square_I$ (always), $\blacklozenge_I$ (once), and $\lozenge_I$ (eventually).

Bounded Recurrence Between q and r. The bounded recurrence property specifies the following pattern: between events q and r there is at least one occurrence of event p every u time units. In MTL, this pattern is captured by the formula $\varphi_1 = (r \wedge \neg q \wedge \blacklozenge q) \to \left((\blacklozenge_{[0,u]} (p \vee q)) \mathcal{S} q \right)$. We set the bound $u = 3$, and we consider the trace $\langle \ldots, (\{q\}, 56), (\{\cdot\}, 57), (\{\cdot\}, 58), (\{\cdot\}, 59), (\{\cdot\}, 60), (\{r\}, 61) \rangle$, which is the portion pertinent to the proof. The formula φ_1 is violated at time-point 61 and the proof is shown in Figure 8.

To prove the violation of the implication (the formula's topmost operator) the subformula on the left (assumption) must be satisfied and the subformula on the right (conclusion) must be violated. For this reason, two subproofs are constructed. In the left subproof,

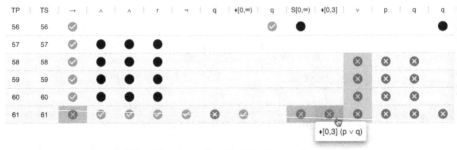

Fig. 9: Visualization of φ_1's violation at time-point 61

we can see that the subformula on the left is violated because both conjuncts $r \wedge \neg q$ and $\blacklozenge q$ are satisfied at time-point 61. This part of the formula enforces that: (i) r is satisfied (and q is not satisfied) at the current time-point; and (ii) q is satisfied at some point in the past. Note that (ii) corresponds exactly to $\blacklozenge q$. In the left subproof, we have $61 \vdash^+ r \wedge \neg q$ because r is satisfied and q is violated at time-point 61. Moreover, the proof $61 \vdash^+ \blacklozenge q$ uses the fact that q is satisfied at time-point 56, which is when the last q had arrived. Moving to the subproof $61 \vdash^- (\blacklozenge_{[0,3]} (p \vee q)) \mathcal{S} q$, the violation occurs because both subformulas are violated at time-point 61. The subproof $61 \vdash^- \blacklozenge_{[0,3]} (p \vee q)$ uses the violations of p and q in the last 3 time units $(58, \ldots, 61)$, whereas the proof $61 \vdash^- q$ indicates that q is not satisfied at the current time-point. This is sufficient to show that since the last q has arrived (at time-point 56), it is neither the case that a new sequence started (with a new occurrence of q) or that a sequence finished (with an occurrence of p) within 3 time units in the past.

Figure 9 shows our visualization of the above proof. Starting from $\rightarrow$, the columns show the topmost operators of φ_1's subformulas (including atomic propositions). For example, φ_1 is violated because the left subformula is satisfied (the first $\wedge$ column) and the right subformula is violated (column $\mathcal{S}_{[0,\infty)}$). All subformulas have a corresponding column and the order of the columns is such that immediate subformulas of a subformula appear further to the right. The same atomic proposition may occur in different subformulas, in which case there will be multiple columns showing the same proposition (but potentially different time-points of interest). Continuing our example, the right subproof from Figure 8 starts in column $\mathcal{S}_{[0,\infty)}$ in Figure 9. The formula $(\blacklozenge_{[0,3]} (p \vee q)) \mathcal{S} q$ is violated at time-point 61 because both subformulas are violated. In the visualization, we focus (by clicking) on the subformula $\blacklozenge_{[0,3]} (p \vee q)$ (displayed when hovering over the corresponding cell) and observe that it is violated because $p \vee q$ is violated at time-points $58, \ldots, 61$ (highlighted cells in the $\vee$ column). Also, the context of this subproof, i.e., all parent nodes in the proof tree, is highlighted. In this case, these are $\rightarrow$ and $\mathcal{S}_{[0,\infty)}$ at time-point 61. Even though it presents the exact same information as the proof tree, our interactive visualization makes the proofs easier to navigate, explore, and digest.

Bounded Response Between q and r. Closely related to the bounded recurrence, the bounded response property specifies the following pattern: between events q and r, event s must respond to event p within the interval $[l, u]$. In MTL, this pattern is specified by the formula $\varphi_2 = ((r \wedge \neg q) \wedge \blacklozenge q) \rightarrow (((s \rightarrow \blacklozenge_{[l,u]} p) \wedge \neg (\neg s \, \mathcal{S}_{[u,\infty)} p)) \mathcal{S} q)$. We consider the trace $\langle \ldots, (\{q\}, 58), (\{p\}, 59), (\{\cdot\}, 60), (\{\cdot\}, 61), (\{\cdot\}, 62), (\{\cdot\}, 63), (\{r\}, 64) \rangle$ and set $l = 0$ and $u = 3$. Figure 10 shows a violation proof for φ_2 at time-point 64.

$$\dfrac{\dfrac{p \in \{p\}}{59 \vdash^{+} p}\ ap^{+} \quad \dfrac{\dfrac{\vdots}{60,\dots,62 \vdash^{-} s}}{60,\dots,62 \vdash^{+} \neg s}\ \neg^{+}}{\dfrac{62 \vdash^{+} \neg s\ \mathcal{S}_{[3,\infty)}\ p}{\dfrac{62 \vdash^{-} \neg\left(\neg s\ \mathcal{S}_{[3,\infty)}\ p\right)}{\dfrac{62 \vdash^{-} \left(s \to \blacklozenge_{[0,3]} p\right) \wedge \neg\left(\neg s\ \mathcal{S}_{[3,\infty)}\ p\right)}{\dfrac{64 \vdash^{-} \left(\left(s \to \blacklozenge_{[0,3]} p\right) \wedge \neg\left(\neg s\ \mathcal{S}_{[3,\infty)}\ p\right)\right)\mathcal{S}\ q}{64 \vdash^{-} \left((r \wedge \neg q) \wedge \blacklozenge q\right) \to \left(\left(\left(s \to \blacklozenge_{[0,3]} p\right) \wedge \neg\left(\neg s\ \mathcal{S}_{[3,\infty)}\ p\right)\right)\mathcal{S}\ q\right)}\ \to^{-}}\ \dfrac{\vdots}{62,\dots,64 \vdash^{-} q}\ \mathcal{S}^{-}}\ \wedge_{R}^{-}}\ \neg^{-}}\ \mathcal{S}^{+}}$$

Fig. 10: Proof of φ_2's violation at time-point 64

TP	TS	$\to$	$\mathcal{S}[0,\infty)$	$\wedge$	$\to$	s	$\blacklozenge[0,3]$	p	$\neg$	$\mathcal{S}[3,\infty)$	$\neg$	s	p	q
59	59	✓												✓
60	60	✓			...					✓	✗			
61	61	✓								✓	✗			
62	62	✓		✗						✗	✓	✗		✗
63	63	✓									✓	✗		✗
64	64	✗	✗											✗

Fig. 11: Visualization of φ_2's violation at time-point 64

The implication's assumption in φ_2 is the same as the assumption in φ_1 (the *bounded recurrence* formula). We omit the corresponding subproof P from Figure 11 as it has the same structure as the subproof of the *bounded recurrence* example. (Yet, there are differences in the time-points.) The conclusion of φ_2 has the form $\alpha\ \mathcal{S}\ q$. It is violated at time-point 64 because α is violated at time-point 62, and from this point onward until the current time-point 64, q is always violated. According to our proof system, we only need to consider violations of q starting at time-point 62, because α is violated at that point. The formula $\alpha = \left(s \to \blacklozenge_{[0,3]} p\right) \wedge \neg\left(\neg s\ \mathcal{S}_{[3,\infty)}\ p\right)$ captures two properties: (i) if there is a response s then there must be a recent challenge p (i.e., p must be satisfied within the last 3 time units); (ii) there are no challenges p more than 3 time units in the past without a response s. In our proof, the violation of α is constructed using the violation of (ii). After applying the negation rule, the proof $62 \vdash^{+} \neg s\ \mathcal{S}_{[3,\infty)}\ p$ uses the fact that p is satisfied at time-point 59 and that s is violated at time-points 60, 61 and 62. In other words, there was no response s to the challenge p within the required time constraint. Figure 11 shows the visualization of this subproof. While the static image already helps with the intuition, we invite the reader to explore this and the previous example in our interactive visualization.

7 Performance

We empirically evaluate our tool by answering the following research question: How does EXPLANATOR2 scale with respect to the formula size when compared to other state-of-the-art monitoring tools? To this end, we reuse the evaluation setup of the MTL monitor

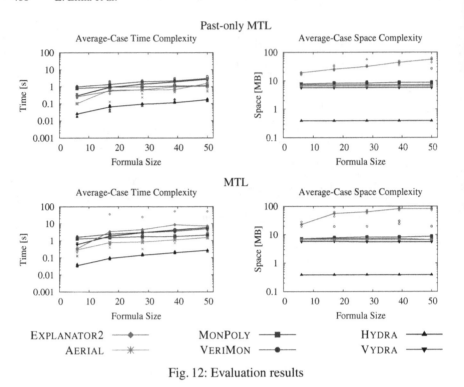

Fig. 12: Evaluation results

HYDRA [26]. We consider two different settings: (i) past-only MTL formulas; and (ii) MTL formulas (mixing past and future operators). For each setting we pseudo-randomly generate a trace with 100 000 events and collections of five different formulas for each size $s \in \{6, 17, \ldots, 50\}$. We measure the time and space usage of the EXPLANATOR2, HYDRA and VYDRA [27], AERIAL [3] MONPOLY [5], and VERIMON [29]. Our verified dynamic programming algorithm is not included because it times out (with a time-out of 200 seconds) even for the smallest formulas of size 6. The experiments were conducted on a computer with an AMD Ryzen 5 5600X CPU and 16GB of RAM. The results are presented in Figure 12. Each filled shape is an average of the measurements for the corresponding formula size. (Unfilled shapes show the individual runs, but are sometimes invisible.) The axes showing time and space usage measurements are of logarithmic scale.

Time-wise, EXPLANATOR2 outperforms MONPOLY and VERIMON (first-order monitors), and is on par with most of its competitors in the past-only setting. When we include future operators, EXPLANATOR2 performs worse than its competitors, although only by a narrow margin. However, we must consider that in contrast to the others our tool has a clear disadvantage: it produces checkable and understandable output instead of Boolean verdicts. Thus, these results reassure us that we do not compromise too much by providing this feature, and that our algorithm is indeed efficient. In terms of space usage, EXPLANATOR2 performs worse than other monitoring tools in both settings. This is hardly surprising, given that proofs can be huge (e.g., they may contain the entire trace).

8   Conclusion

We have developed an online MTL monitor that outputs detailed verdicts in the form of proof trees, which serve as both understandable explanations and checkable certificates. Our monitor incorporates a formally verified checker and an interactive visualization. Our empirical evaluation demonstrates the reasonable performance of our monitor, even though it provides a strictly more informative output than its competitors. Overall, we believe that our approach significantly improves the user experience when using an MTL monitor. In particular, the generated explanations provide insight into root causes of violations and can help with specification debugging. Another plausible application of explanations is teaching temporal logics to students and engineers.

As future work, we will lift our approach to the more expressive metric first-order temporal logic. The main challenge here is to incorporate parametric events and quantification. Moreover, we are interested in optimizing other aspects of the proofs than their size.

Data Availability Statement EXPLANATOR2 is available under the GNU Lesser General Public License v3.0 [22] and its interactive visualization is hosted on GitHub. Our artifact [23] contains the snapshot of the tool's source code at paper submission time along with instructions on how to run our test suite and to reproduce our evaluation.

References

1. Artho, C., Havelund, K., Honiden, S.: Visualization of concurrent program executions. In: COMPSAC 2007. pp. 541–546. IEEE Computer Society (2007). https://doi.org/10.1109/COMPSAC.2007.236
2. Bartocci, E., Ferrère, T., Manjunath, N., Nickovic, D.: Localizing faults in Simulink/Stateflow models with STL. In: Prandini, M., Deshmukh, J.V. (eds.) HSCC 2018. pp. 197–206. ACM (2018). https://doi.org/10.1145/3178126.3178131
3. Basin, D., Bhatt, B.N., Krstic, S., Traytel, D.: Almost event-rate independent monitoring. Formal Methods Syst. Des. **54**(3), 449–478 (2019). https://doi.org/10.1007/s10703-018-00328-3
4. Basin, D., Bhatt, B.N., Traytel, D.: Optimal proofs for linear temporal logic on lasso words. In: Lahiri, S.K., Wang, C. (eds.) ATVA 2018. LNCS, vol. 11138, pp. 37–55. Springer (2018). https://doi.org/10.1007/978-3-030-01090-4_3
5. Basin, D., Klaedtke, F., Müller, S., Zalinescu, E.: Monitoring metric first-order temporal properties. J. ACM **62**(2), 15:1–15:45 (2015). https://doi.org/10.1145/2699444
6. Basin, D., Klaedtke, F., Zalinescu, E.: Algorithms for monitoring real-time properties. Acta Informatica **55**(4), 309–338 (2018). https://doi.org/10.1007/s00236-017-0295-4
7. Baumeister, J., Finkbeiner, B., Gumhold, S., Schledjewski, M.: Real-time visualization of stream-based monitoring data. In: Dang, T., Stolz, V. (eds.) RV 2022. LNCS, vol. 13498, pp. 325–335. Springer (2022). https://doi.org/10.1007/978-3-031-17196-3_21
8. Chattopadhyay, A., Mamouras, K.: A verified online monitor for metric temporal logic with quantitative semantics. In: Deshmukh, J., Nickovic, D. (eds.) RV 2020. LNCS, vol. 12399, pp. 383–403. Springer (2020). https://doi.org/10.1007/978-3-030-60508-7_21
9. Chechik, M., Gurfinkel, A.: A framework for counterexample generation and exploration. Int. J. Softw. Tools Technol. Transf. **9**(5-6), 429–445 (2007). https://doi.org/10.1007/s10009-007-0047-9

10. Cheney, J., Chiticariu, L., Tan, W.C.: Provenance in databases: Why, how, and where. Found. Trends Databases **1**(4), 379–474 (2009). https://doi.org/10.1561/1900000006

11. Cruz-Filipe, L., Heule, M.J.H., Jr., W.A.H., Kaufmann, M., Schneider-Kamp, P.: Efficient certified RAT verification. In: de Moura, L. (ed.) CADE 26. vol. 10395, pp. 220–236. Springer (2017). https://doi.org/10.1007/978-3-319-63046-5_14

12. Dauer, J.C., Finkbeiner, B., Schirmer, S.: Monitoring with verified guarantees. In: Feng, L., Fisman, D. (eds.) RV 2021. LNCS, vol. 12974, pp. 62–80. Springer (2021). https://doi.org/10.1007/978-3-030-88494-9_4

13. Dawes, J.H., Reger, G.: Explaining violations of properties in control-flow temporal logic. In: Finkbeiner, B., Mariani, L. (eds.) RV 2019. LNCS, vol. 11757, pp. 202–220. Springer (2019). https://doi.org/10.1007/978-3-030-32079-9_12

14. Finkbeiner, B., Oswald, S., Passing, N., Schwenger, M.: Verified Rust monitors for Lola specifications. In: Deshmukh, J., Nickovic, D. (eds.) RV 2020. LNCS, vol. 12399, pp. 431–450. Springer (2020). https://doi.org/10.1007/978-3-030-60508-7_24

15. Francalanza, A., Cini, C.: Computer says no: Verdict explainability for runtime monitors using a local proof system. J. Log. Algebraic Methods Program. **119**, 100636 (2021). https://doi.org/10.1016/j.jlamp.2020.100636

16. Herasimau, A.: Formalizing Explanations for Metric Temporal Logic. B.Sc. thesis, ETH Zürich (2020)

17. Hunt, P., O'Shannessy, P., Smith, D., Coatta, T.: React: Facebook's functional turn on writing JavaScript. ACM Queue **14**(4), 40 (2016). https://doi.org/10.1145/2984629.2994373

18. Kallwies, H., Leucker, M., Schmitz, M., Schulz, A., Thoma, D., Weiss, A.: TeSSLa – an ecosystem for runtime verification. In: Dang, T., Stolz, V. (eds.) RV 2022. LNCS, vol. 13498, pp. 314–324. Springer (2022). https://doi.org/10.1007/978-3-031-17196-3_20

19. Kane, A., Chowdhury, O., Datta, A., Koopman, P.: A case study on runtime monitoring of an autonomous research vehicle (ARV) system. In: Bartocci, E., Majumdar, R. (eds.) RV 2015. LNCS, vol. 9333, pp. 102–117. Springer (2015). https://doi.org/10.1007/978-3-319-23820-3_7

20. Konrad, S., Cheng, B.H.C.: Real-time specification patterns. In: Roman, G., Griswold, W.G., Nuseibeh, B. (eds.) ICSE 2005. pp. 372–381. ACM (2005). https://doi.org/10.1145/1062455.1062526

21. Lammich, P.: Efficient verified (UN)SAT certificate checking. J. Autom. Reason. **64**(3), 513–532 (2020). https://doi.org/10.1007/s10817-019-09525-z

22. Lima, L., Herasimau, A., Raszyk, M., Traytel, D., Yuan, S.: The development repository of EXPLANATOR2. https://github.com/runtime-monitoring/explanator2 (2022)

23. Lima, L., Herasimau, A., Raszyk, M., Traytel, D., Yuan, S.: Artifact for "Explainable online monitoring of metric temporal logic" (2023). https://doi.org/10.5281/zenodo.7509199

24. Moosbrugger, P., Rozier, K.Y., Schumann, J.: R2U2: monitoring and diagnosis of security threats for unmanned aerial systems. Formal Methods Syst. Des. **51**(1), 31–61 (2017). https://doi.org/10.1007/s10703-017-0275-x

25. Nickovic, D., Lebeltel, O., Maler, O., Ferrère, T., Ulus, D.: AMT 2.0: qualitative and quantitative trace analysis with extended signal temporal logic. Int. J. Softw. Tools Technol. Transf. **22**(6), 741–758 (2020). https://doi.org/10.1007/s10009-020-00582-z

26. Raszyk, M.: Efficient, Expressive, and Verified Temporal Query Evaluation. Ph.D. thesis, ETH Zürich (2022). https://doi.org/10.3929/ethz-b-000553221

27. Raszyk, M., Basin, D., Krstic, S., Traytel, D.: Multi-head monitoring of metric temporal logic. In: Chen, Y., Cheng, C., Esparza, J. (eds.) ATVA 2019. LNCS, vol. 11781, pp. 151–170. Springer (2019). https://doi.org/10.1007/978-3-030-31784-3_9

28. Raszyk, M., Basin, D., Traytel, D.: Multi-head monitoring of metric dynamic logic. In: Hung, D.V., Sokolsky, O. (eds.) ATVA 2020. LNCS, vol. 12302, pp. 233–250. Springer (2020). https://doi.org/10.1007/978-3-030-59152-6_13

29. Schneider, J., Basin, D., Krstic, S., Traytel, D.: A formally verified monitor for metric first-order temporal logic. In: Finkbeiner, B., Mariani, L. (eds.) RV 2019. LNCS, vol. 11757, pp. 310–328. Springer (2019). https://doi.org/10.1007/978-3-030-32079-9_18

30. Schumann, J., Moosbrugger, P., Rozier, K.Y.: Runtime analysis with R2U2: A tool exhibition report. In: Falcone, Y., Sánchez, C. (eds.) RV 2016. LNCS, vol. 10012, pp. 504–509. Springer (2016). https://doi.org/10.1007/978-3-319-46982-9_35

31. Sulzmann, M., Lu, K.Z.M.: POSIX regular expression parsing with derivatives. In: Codish, M., Sumii, E. (eds.) FLOPS 2014. LNCS, vol. 8475, pp. 203–220. Springer (2014). https://doi.org/10.1007/978-3-319-07151-0_13

32. Sulzmann, M., Zechner, A.: Constructive finite trace analysis with linear temporal logic. In: Brucker, A.D., Julliand, J. (eds.) TAP 2012. LNCS, vol. 7305, pp. 132–148. Springer (2012). https://doi.org/10.1007/978-3-642-30473-6_11

33. Ulus, D.: Online monitoring of metric temporal logic using sequential networks. CoRR **abs/1901.00175** (2019). https://doi.org/10.48550/arxiv.1901.00175

34. Ulus, D.: Timescales: A benchmark generator for MTL monitoring tools. In: Finkbeiner, B., Mariani, L. (eds.) RV 2019. LNCS, vol. 11757, pp. 402–412. Springer (2019). https://doi.org/10.1007/978-3-030-32079-9_25

35. Völlinger, K.: Verifying the output of a distributed algorithm using certification. In: Lahiri, S.K., Reger, G. (eds.) RV 2017. LNCS, vol. 10548, pp. 424–430. Springer (2017). https://doi.org/10.1007/978-3-319-67531-2_29

36. Vouillon, J., Balat, V.: From bytecode to JavaScript: the Js_of_ocaml compiler. Softw. Pract. Exp. **44**(8), 951–972 (2014). https://doi.org/10.1002/spe.2187

37. Wimmer, S., Herbreteau, F., van de Pol, J.: Certifying emptiness of timed Büchi automata. In: Bertrand, N., Jansen, N. (eds.) FORMATS 2020. LNCS, vol. 12288, pp. 58–75. Springer (2020). https://doi.org/10.1007/978-3-030-57628-8_4

38. Wimmer, S., von Mutius, J.: Verified certification of reachability checking for timed automata. In: Biere, A., Parker, D. (eds.) TACAS 2020. LNCS, vol. 12078, pp. 425–443. Springer (2020). https://doi.org/10.1007/978-3-030-45190-5_24

39. Yuan, S.: Explaining Monitoring Verdicts for Metric Dynamic Logic. B.Sc. thesis, ETH Zürich (2019)

12th Competition on Software Verification — SV-COMP 2023

Competition on Software Verification and Witness Validation: SV-COMP 2023

Dirk Beyer

LMU Munich, Munich, Germany

Abstract. The 12th edition of the Competition on Software Verification (SV-COMP 2023) is again the largest overview of tools for software verification, evaluating 52 verification systems from 34 teams from 10 countries. Besides providing an overview of the state of the art in automatic software verification, the goal of the competition is to establish standards, provide a platform for exchange to developers of such tools, educate PhD students on reproducibility approaches and benchmarking, and provide computing resources to developers that do not have access to compute clusters. The competition consisted of 23 805 verification tasks for C programs and 586 verification tasks for Java programs. The specifications include reachability, memory safety, overflows, and termination. This year, the competition introduced a new competition track on witness validation, where validators for verification witnesses are evaluated with respect to their quality.

Keywords: Formal Verification · Program Analysis · Competition · Software Verification · Verification Tasks · Benchmark · C Language · Java Language · SV-Benchmarks · BENCHEXEC · COVERITEAM

1 Introduction

This report extends the series of competition reports (see footnote) by describing the results of the 2023 edition, but also explaining the process and rules, giving insights into some aspects of the competition (this time the focus is on the added validation track). The 12th Competition on Software Verification (SV-COMP, https://sv-comp.sosy-lab.org/2023) is the largest comparative evaluation ever in this area. The objectives of the competitions were discussed earlier (1-4 [16]) and extended over the years (5-6 [17]):

1. provide an overview of the state of the art in software-verification technology and increase visibility of the most recent software verifiers,
2. establish a repository of software-verification tasks that is publicly available for free use as standard benchmark suite for evaluating verification software,

---

This report extends previous reports on SV-COMP [10, 11, 12, 13, 14, 15, 16, 17, 18, 20]. Reproduction packages are available on Zenodo (see Table 3).
✉ dirk.beyer@sosy-lab.org

© The Author(s) 2023
S. Sankaranarayanan and N. Sharygina (Eds.): TACAS 2023, LNCS 13994, pp. 495–522, 2023.
https://doi.org/10.1007/978-3-031-30820-8_29

3. establish standards that make it possible to compare different verification tools, including a property language and formats for the results,
4. accelerate the transfer of new verification technology to industrial practice by identifying the strengths of the various verifiers on a diverse set of tasks,
5. educate PhD students and others on performing reproducible benchmarking, packaging tools, and running robust and accurate research experiments, and
6. provide research teams that do not have sufficient computing resources with the opportunity to obtain experimental results on large benchmark sets.

The SV-COMP 2020 report [17] discusses the achievements of the SV-COMP competition so far with respect to these objectives.

Related Competitions. There are many competitions in the area of formal methods [9], because it is well-understood that competitions are a fair and accurate means to execute a comparative evaluation with involvement of the developing teams. We refer to a previous report [17] for a more detailed discussion and give here only the references to the most related competitions [22, 58, 67, 74].

Quick Summary of Changes. While we try to keep the setup of the competition stable, there are always improvements and developments. For the 2023 edition, the following changes were made:

- The category for data-race detection was added (last year as demonstration, this year as regular category).
- New verification tasks were added, with an increase in C from 15 648 in 2022 to 23 805 in 2023.
- A new track was added that evaluates all validators for verification witnesses, which was discussed and approved by the jury in the 2022 community meeting in Munich, based on a proposal by two community members [37].

2   Organization, Definitions, Formats, and Rules

Procedure. The overall organization of the competition did not change in comparison to the earlier editions [10, 11, 12, 13, 14, 15, 16, 17, 18]. SV-COMP is an open competition (also known as comparative evaluation), where all verification tasks are known before the submission of the participating verifiers, which is necessary due to the complexity of the C language. The procedure is partitioned into the *benchmark submission* phase, the *training* phase, and the *evaluation* phase. The participants received the results of their verifier continuously via e-mail (for preruns and the final competition run), and the results were publicly announced on the competition web site after the teams inspected them.

Competition Jury. Traditionally, the competition jury consists of the chair and one member of each participating team; the team-representing members circulate every year after the candidate-submission deadline. This committee reviews the competition contribution papers and helps the organizer with resolving any disputes that might occur (cf. competition report of SV-COMP 2013 [11]). The

Table 1: Scoring schema for SV-COMP 2023 (unchanged from 2021 [18])

Reported result	Points	Description
UNKNOWN	0	Failure to compute verification result
FALSE correct	+1	Violation of property in program was correctly found and a validator confirmed the result based on a witness
FALSE incorrect	−16	Violation reported but property holds (false alarm)
TRUE correct	+2	Program correctly reported to satisfy property and a validator confirmed the result based on a witness
TRUE incorrect	−32	Incorrect program reported as correct (wrong proof)

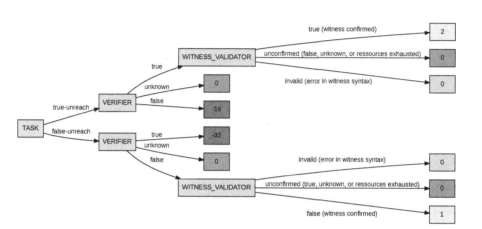

Fig. 1: Visualization of the scoring schema for the reachability property (unchanged from 2021 [18])

tasks of the jury were described in more detail in the report of SV-COMP 2022 [20]. The team representatives of the competition jury are listed in Table 5.

Scoring Schema and Ranking. The scoring schema of SV-COMP 2023 was the same as for SV-COMP 2021. Table 1 provides an overview and Fig. 1 visually illustrates the score assignment for the reachability property as an example. As before, the rank of a verifier was decided based on the sum of points (normalized for meta categories). In case of a tie, the rank was decided based on success run time, which is the total CPU time over all verification tasks for which the verifier reported a correct verification result. *Opt-out from Categories* and *Score Normalization for Meta Categories* was done as described previously [11, page 597].

License Requirements. Starting 2018, SV-COMP required that the verifier must be publicly available for download and has a license that

(i) allows reproduction and evaluation by anybody (incl. results publication),
(ii) does not restrict the usage of the verifier output (log files, witnesses), and
(iii) allows (re-)distribution of the unmodified verifier archive via SV-COMP repositories and archives.

Table 2: Publicly available components for reproducing SV-COMP 2023

Component	Fig. 3	Repository	Version
Verification Tasks	(a)	gitlab.com/sosy-lab/benchmarking/sv-benchmarks	svcomp23
Benchmark Definitions	(b)	gitlab.com/sosy-lab/sv-comp/bench-defs	svcomp23
Tool-Info Modules	(c)	github.com/sosy-lab/benchexec	3.16
Verifier Archives	(d)	gitlab.com/sosy-lab/sv-comp/archives-2023	svcomp23
Benchmarking	(e)	github.com/sosy-lab/benchexec	3.16
Witness Format	(f)	gitlab.com/sosy-lab/benchmarking/sv-witnesses	svcomp23
Continuous Integration	(f)	gitlab.com/sosy-lab/software/coveriteam	1.0

Table 3: Artifacts published for SV-COMP 2023

Content	DOI	Reference
Verification Tasks	10.5281/zenodo.7627783	[23]
Competition Results	10.5281/zenodo.7627787	[21]
Verifiers and Validators	10.5281/zenodo.7627829	[25]
Verification Witnesses	10.5281/zenodo.7627791	[24]
BENCHEXEC	10.5281/zenodo.7612021	[112]
COVERITEAM	10.5281/zenodo.7635975	[32]

Task-Definition Format 2.0. SV-COMP 2023 used the task-definition format in version 2.0. More details can be found in the report for Test-Comp 2021 [19].

Properties. Please see the 2015 competition report [13] for the definition of the properties and the property format. All specifications used in SV-COMP 2023 are available in the directory c/properties/ of the benchmark repository.

Categories. The (updated) category structure of SV-COMP 2023 is illustrated by Fig. 2. Category *C-FalsificationOverall* contains all verification tasks of *C-Overall* without *Termination* and *Java-Overall* contains all Java verification tasks. Compared to SV-COMP 2022, we added one new sub-category *ReachSafety-Hardware* to main category *ReachSafety*, sub-categories *ConcurrencySafety-MemSafety*, *ConcurrencySafety-NoOverflows*, and *ConcurrencySafety-NoDataRace-Main* (was demo in 2022) to main category *ConcurrencySafety*, main category *NoOverflows* was restructured, and finally we added *SoftwareSystems-DeviceDriversLinux64-MemSafety* to main category *SoftwareSystems*. The categories are also listed in Tables 8, 9, and 10, and described in detail on the competition web site (https://sv-comp.sosy-lab.org/2023/benchmarks.php).

Reproducibility. SV-COMP results must be reproducible, and consequently, all major components are maintained in public version-control repositories. The overview of the components is provided in Fig. 3, and the details are given in Table 2. We refer to the SV-COMP 2016 report [14] for a description of all components of the SV-COMP organization. There are competition artifacts at Zenodo (see Table 3) to guarantee their long-term availability and immutability.

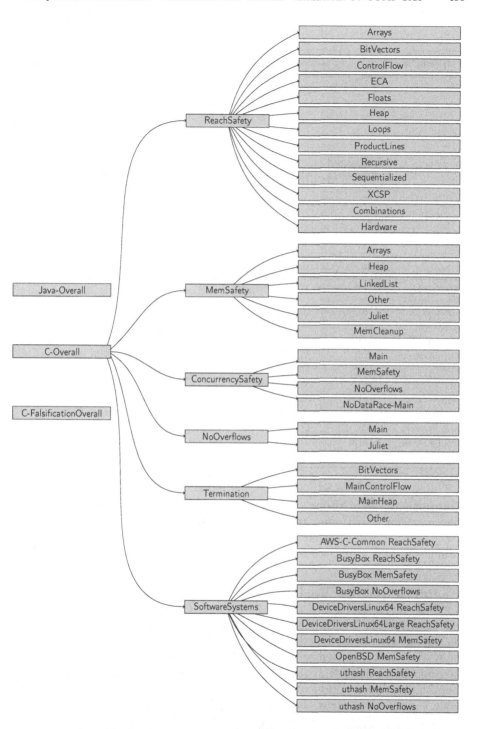

Fig. 2: Category structure for SV-COMP 2023

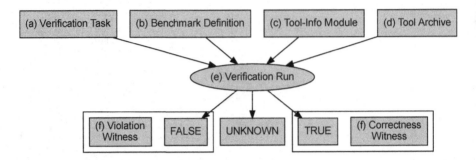

Fig. 3: Benchmarking components of SV-COMP and competition's execution flow (same as for SV-COMP 2020)

Table 4: Validation: Witness validators and witness linter

Validator	Reference	Jury Member	Affiliation
CPACHECKER	[26, 27, 29]	Henrik Wachowitz	LMU Munich, Germany
CPA-W2T	[28]	Henrik Wachowitz	LMU Munich, Germany
DARTAGNAN	[98]	Hernán Ponce de León	Huawei Dresden, Germany
CPROVER-W2T	[28]	Michael Tautschnig	Queen Mary U. of London, UK
GWIT	[75]	Falk Howar	TU Dortmund U., Germany
METAVAL	[35]	Martin Spiessl	LMU Munich, Germany
NITWIT	[115]	Jana (Philipp) Berger	RWTH Aachen, Germany
SYMBIOTIC-WITCH	[7]	Paulína Ayaziová	Masaryk U., Brno, Czechia
UAUTOMIZER	[26, 27]	Daniel Dietsch	U. of Freiburg, Germany
WIT4JAVA	[113]	Tong Wu	U. of Manchester, UK
WITNESSLINT		Martin Spiessl	LMU Munich, Germany

Competition Workflow. The workflow of the competition is described in the report for Test-Comp 2021 [19] (SV-COMP and Test-Comp use a similar workflow). For a description of how to reproduce single verification runs and a trouble-shooting guide, we refer to the previous report [20, Sect. 3].

3   Participating Verifiers and Validators

The participating verification systems are listed in Table 5. The table contains the verifier name (with hyperlink), references to papers that describe the systems, the representing jury member and the affiliation. The listing is also available on the competition web site at https://sv-comp.sosy-lab.org/2023/systems.php. Table 6 lists the algorithms and techniques that are used by the verification tools, and Table 7 gives an overview of commonly used solver libraries and frameworks.

Validation of Verification Results. The validation of the verification results was done by eleven validation tools (ten proper witness validators, and one

Table 5: Verification: Participating verifiers with tool references and representing jury members; [new] for first-time participants, [∅] for hors-concours participation

Participant	Ref.	Jury member	Affiliation
2LS	[39, 88]	Viktor Malík	BUT, Brno, Czechia
BRICK	[40]	Lei Bu	Nanjing U., China
BUBAAK [new]	[42]	Marek Chalupa	ISTA, Austria
CBMC	[46, 84]	Michael Tautschnig	Queen Mary U. London, UK
COASTAL[∅]	[109]	(hors concours)	–
CPA-BAM-BNB[∅]	[4, 111]	(hors concours)	–
CPA-BAM-SMG[∅]		(hors concours)	–
CPACHECKER	[33, 53]	Henrik Wachowitz	LMU Munich, Germany
CPALOCKATOR[∅]	[5, 6]	(hors concours)	–
CRUX[∅]	[57, 104]	(hors concours)	–
CSEQ[∅]	[51, 79]	(hors concours)	–
CVT-ALGOSEL[∅]	[30, 31]	(hors concours)	–
CVT-PARPORT[∅]	[30, 31]	(hors concours)	–
DARTAGNAN	[65, 97]	Hernán Ponce de León	Huawei Dresden, Germany
DEAGLE	[70]	Fei He	Tsinghua U., China
DIVINE[∅]	[8, 85]	(hors concours)	–
EBF	[3]	Fatimah Aljaafari	U. of Manchester, UK
ESBMC-INCR[∅]	[47, 50]	(hors concours)	–
ESBMC-KIND	[63, 64]	Rafael Sá Menezes	U. of Manchester, UK
FRAMA-C-SV	[36, 52]	Martin Spiessl	LMU Munich, Germany
GAZER-THETA[∅]	[1, 69]	(hors concours)	–
GDART	[93]	Falk Howar	TU Dortmund, Germany
GDART-LLVM [new]		Falk Howar	TU Dortmund, Germany
GOBLINT	[103, 110]	Simmo Saan	U. of Tartu, Estonia
GRAVES-CPA	[86]	Will Leeson	U. of Virginia, USA
GRAVES-PAR [new]		Hors Concurs	U. of Virginia, USA
INFER[∅]	[41, 82]	(hors concours)	–
JAVA-RANGER	[76, 106]	Soha Hussein	U. of Minnesota, USA
JAYHORN[∅]	[81, 105]	(hors concours)	–
JBMC	[48, 49]	Peter Schrammel	U. of Sussex / Diffblue, UK
JDART[∅]	[87, 92]	(hors concours)	–
KORN	[60, 61]	Gidon Ernst	LMU Munich, Germany
LAZY-CSEQ[∅]	[77, 78]	(hors concours)	–
LF-CHECKER [new]		Tong Wu	U. of Manchester, UK
LOCKSMITH	[99]	Vesal Vojdani	U. of Tartu, Estonia
MLB [new]		Lei Bu	Nanjing U., China
MOPSA [new]	[80, 91]	Raphaël Monat	Inria and U. of Lille, France
PESCO-CPA	[101, 102]	Cedric Richter	U. of Oldenburg, Germany
PICHECKER [new]	[107]	Jie Su	Xidian U., China
PINAKA[∅]	[45]	(hors concours)	–
PREDATORHP[∅]	[73, 96]	(hors concours)	–

(continues on next page)

Table 5: Competition candidates (continued)

Participant	Ref.	Jury member	Affiliation
SPF[∅]	[94, 100]	(hors concours)	–
SYMBIOTIC	[43, 44]	Marek Trtík	Masaryk U., Brno, Czechia
THETA	[108, 114]	Levente Bajczi	BME Budapest, Hungary
UAUTOMIZER	[71, 72]	Matthias Heizmann	U. of Freiburg, Germany
UGEMCUTTER	[62, 83]	Dominik Klumpp	U. of Freiburg, Germany
UKOJAK	[59, 95]	Frank Schüssele	U. of Freiburg, Germany
UTAIPAN	[56, 68]	Daniel Dietsch	U. of Freiburg, Germany
VERIABS	[2, 54]	Priyanka Darke	TCS, India
VERIABSL [new]	[55]	Priyanka Darke	TCS, India
VERIFUZZ	[89, 90]	Raveendra Kumar M.	TCS, India
VERIOOVER [new]		HaiPeng Qu	Ocean U. of China, China

Table 6: Algorithms and techniques that the participating verification systems used; [new] for first-time participants, [∅] for hors-concours participation

Verifier	CEGAR	Predicate Abstraction	Symbolic Execution	Bounded Model Checking	k-Induction	Property-Directed Reach.	Explicit-Value Analysis	Numeric. Interval Analysis	Shape Analysis	Separation Logic	Bit-Precise Analysis	ARG-Based Analysis	Lazy Abstraction	Interpolation	Automata-Based Analysis	Concurrency Support	Ranking Functions	Evolutionary Algorithms	Algorithm Selection	Portfolio
2LS				✓	✓		✓	✓			✓						✓			
BRICK	✓		✓	✓			✓									✓				
BUBAAK [new]			✓								✓					✓	✓			✓
CBMC			✓								✓					✓				
COASTAL [∅]			✓																	
CPA-BAM-BNB [∅]	✓	✓					✓					✓	✓	✓	✓					
CPA-BAM-SMG [∅]																				
CPACHECKER	✓	✓	✓	✓	✓		✓	✓			✓	✓	✓	✓	✓	✓	✓		✓	✓
CPALOCKATOR [∅]	✓	✓					✓					✓	✓	✓	✓	✓				
CRUX [∅]			✓																	
CSEQ [∅]			✓								✓					✓				
CVT-ALGOSEL [∅]	✓	✓	✓	✓	✓		✓	✓	✓		✓	✓	✓	✓	✓	✓	✓		✓	✓
CVT-PARPORT [∅]	✓	✓	✓	✓	✓		✓	✓	✓		✓	✓	✓	✓		✓	✓		✓	✓
DARTAGNAN			✓								✓					✓				
DEAGLE			✓								✓					✓				
DIVINE [∅]			✓				✓				✓					✓			✓	✓
EBF					✓															
ESBMC-INCR [∅]				✓	✓						✓					✓				
ESBMC-KIND				✓	✓				✓		✓					✓				

(continues on next page)

Table 6: Algorithms and techniques (continued)

Verifier	CEGAR	Predicate Abstraction	Symbolic Execution	Bounded Model Checking	k-Induction	Property-Directed Reach.	Explicit-Value Analysis	Numeric. Interval Analysis	Shape Analysis	Separation Logic	Bit-Precise Analysis	ARG-Based Analysis	Lazy Abstraction	Interpolation	Automata-Based Analysis	Concurrency Support	Ranking Functions	Evolutionary Algorithms	Algorithm Selection	Portfolio
FRAMA-C-SV							✓													
GAZER-THETA∅	✓	✓		✓			✓				✓	✓	✓	✓						✓
GDART			✓								✓									✓
GDART-LLVM new			✓								✓									
GOBLINT								✓								✓			✓	
GRAVES-CPA	✓	✓		✓	✓		✓	✓	✓		✓	✓	✓	✓		✓	✓		✓	✓
GRAVES-PAR new																				
INFER∅							✓	✓	✓											✓
JAVA-RANGER			✓								✓									
JAYHORN∅	✓	✓				✓	✓						✓	✓						
JBMC				✓							✓					✓				
JDART∅			✓								✓									✓
KORN			✓	✓			✓													✓
LAZY-CSEQ∅				✓							✓					✓				
LF-CHECKER new																				
LOCKSMITH																✓				
MLB new																				
MOPSA new								✓												
PESCO-CPA	✓	✓		✓	✓		✓	✓	✓		✓	✓	✓	✓		✓	✓		✓	✓
PICHECKER new	✓	✓									✓	✓		✓		✓			✓	
PINAKA∅				✓	✓						✓									
PREDATORHP∅									✓											
SPF∅			✓						✓							✓				
SYMBIOTIC			✓	✓				✓	✓		✓					✓				✓
THETA	✓	✓					✓				✓	✓		✓		✓			✓	✓
UAUTOMIZER	✓	✓									✓		✓	✓	✓	✓	✓		✓	✓
UGEMCUTTER	✓	✓									✓		✓	✓	✓	✓			✓	✓
UKOJAK	✓	✓									✓		✓	✓						
UTAIPAN	✓	✓					✓	✓			✓		✓	✓	✓				✓	✓
VERIABS	✓			✓	✓		✓	✓										✓	✓	✓
VERIABSL new	✓			✓	✓		✓	✓										✓	✓	✓
VERIFUZZ			✓					✓										✓		
VERIOOVER new																				

Table 7: Solver libraries and frameworks that are used as components in the participating verification systems (component is mentioned if used more than three times; [new] for first-time participants, [∅] for hors-concours participation)

Verifier	CPACHECKER	CPROVER	ESBMC	JPF	ULTIMATE	JAVASMT	MATHSAT	CVC4	SMTINTERPOL	z3	MINISAT	APRON
2LS		✓									✓	
BRICK										✓	✓	
BUBAAK [new]										✓		
CBMC		✓									✓	
COASTAL [∅]				✓								
CPA-BAM-BNB [∅]	✓					✓	✓					
CPA-BAM-SMG [∅]	✓					✓	✓					
CPACHECKER	✓					✓	✓					✓
CPALOCKATOR [∅]	✓					✓	✓					
CRUX [∅]										✓		
CSEQ [∅]		✓									✓	
CVT-ALGOSEL [∅]	✓	✓	✓		✓	✓	✓				✓	
CVT-PARPORT [∅]	✓	✓	✓		✓	✓	✓				✓	
DARTAGNAN						✓						
DEAGLE											✓	
DIVINE [∅]												
EBF			✓				✓					
ESBMC-INCR [∅]			✓				✓					
ESBMC-KIND			✓				✓					
FRAMA-C-SV												
GAZER-THETA [∅]												
GDART								✓		✓		
GDART-LLVM [new]										✓		
GOBLINT												✓
GRAVES-CPA	✓					✓	✓					
GRAVES-PAR [new]												
INFER [∅]												
JAVA-RANGER				✓								
JAYHORN [∅]												
JBMC		✓									✓	
JDART [∅]				✓				✓		✓		
KORN										✓		
LAZY-CSEQ [∅]		✓									✓	
LF-CHECKER [new]												
LOCKSMITH												

(continues on next page)

Table 7: Solver libraries and frameworks (continued)

Verifier	CPACHECKER	CPROVER	ESBMC	JPF	ULTIMATE	JAVASMT	MATHSAT	CVC4	SMTINTERPOL	z3	MINISAT	APRON
MLB [new]												
MOPSA [new]												✓
PESCO-CPA	✓					✓	✓					
PICHECKER [new]	✓					✓	✓		✓			
PINAKA [∅]												
PREDATORHP [∅]												
SPF [∅]				✓								
SYMBIOTIC										✓		
THETA												
UAUTOMIZER					✓		✓	✓	✓	✓		
UGEMCUTTER					✓		✓	✓	✓	✓		
UKOJAK					✓			✓	✓			
UTAIPAN					✓		✓	✓	✓	✓		
VERIABS	✓	✓								✓		✓
VERIABSL [new]	✓	✓								✓		✓
VERIFUZZ										✓		
VERIOOVER [new]												

witness linter for syntax checks), which are listed in Table 4, including references to literature. The ten witness validators are evaluated based on all verification witnesses that were produced in the verification track of the competition.

Hors-Concours Participation. As in previous years, we also included verifiers to the evaluation that did not actively compete or that should not occur in the rankings for some reasons (e.g., meta verifiers based on other competing tools, or tools for which the submitting teams were not sure if they show the full potential of the tool). These participations are called *hors concours*, as they cannot participate in rankings and cannot "win" the competition. Those verifiers are marked as 'hors concours' in Table 5 and others, and the names are annotated with a symbol ($^∅$).

4   Results of the Verification Track

The results of the competition represent the the state of the art of what can be achieved with fully automatic software-verification tools on the given benchmark set. We report the effectiveness (number of verification tasks that can be solved and correctness of the results, as accumulated in the score) and the efficiency (resource consumption in terms of CPU time and CPU energy). The results are presented in the same way as in last years, such that the improvements compared

Table 8: Verification: Quantitative overview over all regular results;

Participant	ReachSafety 9814 points 6138 tasks	MemSafety 4543 points 3202 tasks	ConcurrencySafety 5295 points 2865 tasks	NoOverflows 10200 points 6618 tasks	Termination 3103 points 1809 tasks	SoftwareSystems 5132 points 3173 tasks	FalsificationOverall 8689 points 21996 tasks	Overall 38644 points 23305 tasks	JavaOverall 827 points 586 tasks
2LS	3617	611	0	6570	**1183**	75	1884	9722	
BRICK									
BUBAAK ^{new}	4278	-4655	9	5005	195	**1589**	**4313**	2426	
CBMC	3497	1798	1185	6267	862	-711	2110	10886	
CPACHECKER	5535	**2612**	1744	4079	883	758	**4254**	14559	
DARTAGNAN			1268						
DEAGLE			**4744**						
DIVINE $^{\varnothing}$	2698	-354	-2	0	0	101	-573	1429	
EBF			-317						
ESBMC-INCR $^{\varnothing}$			480						
ESBMC-KIND	5183	2000	1162	6342	782	275	3507	13299	
FRAMA-C-SV				1522					
GDART-LLVM ^{new}									
GOBLINT	874		1591	5306		358		6397	
GRAVES-CPA	4868					-1186	3447	5258	
GRAVES-PAR ^{new}	-64	2179	118	-17785	590	-1337	-3063	-8217	
KORN									
LF-CHECKER ^{new}			1023						
LOCKSMITH									
MOPSA ^{new}	699	556		5671		**815**			
PESCO-CPA	**5576**					812	**4258**	14652	
PICHECKER ^{new}			552						
SYMBIOTIC	4786	**2620**	194	2407	930	**1604**	4026	12097	
THETA	1076		1286						
UAUTOMIZER	3997	2301	**2717**	**8639**	2105	476	4173	**19589**	
UGEMCUTTER			**2710**						
UKOJAK	2306	1526	0	**7305**	0	274	3092	8102	
UTAIPAN	3672	**2354**	2612	**8492**	0	412	4100	14514	
VERIABS	**6628**								
VERIABSL ^{new}	**6478**								
VERIFUZZ	1704					-500	**2305**		
VERIOOVER ^{new}									
GDART									652
JAVA-RANGER									400
JBMC									**667**
MLB ^{new}									495

Table 9: Verification: Quantitative overview over all hors-concours results; empty cells represent opt-outs, [new] for first-time participants, [∅] for hors-concours participation

Verifier	ReachSafety 8631 points 5400 tasks	MemSafety 5003 points 3321 tasks	ConcurrencySafety 1160 points 763 tasks	NoOverflows 685 points 454 tasks	Termination 4144 points 2293 tasks	SoftwareSystems 5898 points 3417 tasks	FalsificationOverall 5718 points 13355 tasks	Overall 25209 points 15648 tasks	JavaOverall 828 points 586 tasks
CVT-AlgoSel[∅]	-507		59						
CVT-ParPort[∅]	2033	2539	847	-3793	947	1421	3734	7212	
CPA-BAM-BnB[∅]						458			
CPA-BAM-SMG[∅]		2587				804			
CPALockator[∅]			-2720						
Crux[∅]	879				1316				
CSeq[∅]			-11702						
Divine[∅]	2698	-354	-2	0	0	101	-573	1429	
Esbmc-incr[∅]			480						
Gazer-Theta[∅]									
Infer[∅]	-56129			-5737	-77220	-25556			
Lazy-CSeq[∅]			-13840						
Pinaka[∅]	3387				-879	631			
PredatorHP[∅]		1926							
Coastal[∅]									-2816
JayHorn[∅]									220
JDart[∅]									382
Spf[∅]									182

to the last years are easy to identify. The results presented in this report were inspected and approved by the participating teams.

Quantitative Results. Tables 8 and 9 present the quantitative overview of all tools and all categories. Due to the large number of tools, we need to split the presentation into two tables, one for the verifiers that participate in the rankings (Table 8), and one for the hors-concours verifiers (Table 9). The head row mentions the category, the maximal score for the category, and the number of verification tasks. The tools are listed in alphabetical order; every table row lists the scores of one verifier. We indicate the top three candidates by formatting their scores in bold face and in larger font size. An empty table cell means that the verifier opted-out from the respective main category (perhaps participating in subcategories only, restricting the evaluation to a specific topic). More information (including interactive tables, quantile plots for every category, and also the raw data in XML format) is available on the competition web site (https://sv-comp.sosy-lab.org/2023/results) and in the results artifact (see Table 3).

Table 10: Verification: Overview of the top-three verifiers for each category; [new] for first-time participants, values for CPU time and energy rounded to two significant digits

Rank	Verifier	Score	CPU Time (in h)	CPU Energy (in kWh)	Solved Tasks	Unconf. Tasks	False Alarms	Wrong Proofs
ReachSafety								
1	VeriAbs	**6628**	150	1.6	3509	431		
2	VeriAbsL [new]	6478	120	1.1	3600	567		8
3	PeSCo-CPA	5576	79	0.84	3294	330	3	8
MemSafety								
1	Symbiotic	**2620**	1.4	0.018	304	0	2	
2	CPAchecker	2612	6.1	0.053	3053	0		
3	UTaipan	2354	34	0.33	1945	29		
ConcurrencySafety								
1	Deagle	**4744**	1.1	0.014	2545	27	1	
2	UAutomizer	2717	34	0.37	1498	18		
3	UGemCutter	2710	36	0.37	1495	13		
NoOverflows								
1	UAutomizer	**8639**	53	0.48	5407	62		
2	UTaipan	8492	55	0.51	5296	107		
3	UKojak	7305	32	0.26	4275	60		
Termination								
1	VeriFuzz	**2305**	21	0.26	1216	141		3
2	UAutomizer	2105	13	0.12	1196	9		
3	2ls	1183	3.7	0.029	1005	205		
SoftwareSystems								
1	Symbiotic	**1604**	0.80	0.011	1026	189		1
2	Bubaak [new]	1589	0.32	0.0036	432	206	1	
3	Mopsa [new]	815	12	0.16	1610	94		
FalsificationOverall								
1	Bubaak [new]	**4313**	36	0.39	5258	219	10	
2	PeSCo-CPA	4258	46	0.49	3800	150	7	
3	CPAchecker	4254	90	1.0	3677	99	4	
Overall								
1	UAutomizer	**19589**	250	2.5	13367	337		
2	PeSCo-CPA	14652	160	1.7	10372	497	9	8
3	CPAchecker	14559	220	2.5	10200	539	6	
JavaOverall								
1	Jbmc	**667**	0.34	0.0032	473	29		
2	GDart	652	3.0	0.026	477	9		
3	Mlb [new]	495	0.38	0.0036	336	95		

Table 10 reports the top three verifiers for each category. The run time (column 'CPU Time') and energy (column 'CPU Energy') refer to successfully solved verification tasks (column 'Solved Tasks'). We also report the number of tasks for which no witness validator was able to confirm the result (column 'Unconf. Tasks'). The columns 'False Alarms' and 'Wrong Proofs' report the number of verification

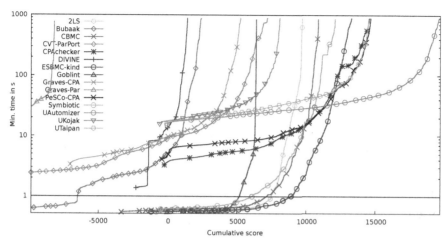

Fig. 4: Quantile functions for category *C-Overall*. Each quantile function illustrates the quantile (*x*-coordinate) of the scores obtained by correct verification runs below a certain run time (*y*-coordinate). More details were given previously [11]. A logarithmic scale is used for the time range from 1 s to 1000 s, and a linear scale is used for the time range between 0 s and 1 s.

tasks for which the verifier reported wrong results, i.e., reporting a counterexample when the property holds (incorrect FALSE) and claiming that the program fulfills the property although it actually contains a bug (incorrect TRUE), respectively.

Score-Based Quantile Functions for Quality Assessment. We use score-based quantile functions [11, 34] because these visualizations make it easier to understand the results of the comparative evaluation. The results archive (see Table 3) and the web site (https://sv-comp.sosy-lab.org/2023/results) include such a plot for each (sub-)category. As an example, we show the plot for category *C-Overall* (all verification tasks) in Fig. 4. A total of 13 verifiers participated in category *C-Overall*, for which the quantile plot shows the overall performance over all categories (scores for meta categories are normalized [11]). A more detailed discussion of score-based quantile plots, including examples of what insights one can obtain from the plots, is provided in previous competition reports [11, 14].

The winner of the competition, UAUTOMIZER, achieves the best cumulative score (graph for UAUTOMIZER has the longest width from $x = 0$ to its right end). Verifiers whose graphs start with a negative cumulative score produced wrong results.

New Verifiers. To acknowledge the verification systems that participate for the first or second time in SV-COMP, Table 11 lists the new verifiers (in SV-COMP 2022 or SV-COMP 2023). It is remarkable to see that first-time participants can win or almost win large categories: BUBAAK[new] is the best verifier for category *FalsificationOverall*, and BUBAAK[new] is the second-best and MOPSA[new] third-best in category *SoftwareSystems*. Figure 5 shows the growing interest in the competition over the years.

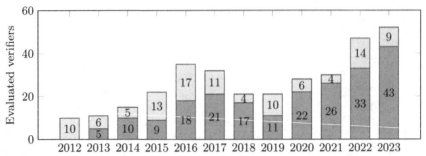

Fig. 5: Number of evaluated verifiers for each year (first-time participants on top)

Table 11: New verifiers in SV-COMP 2022 and SV-COMP 2023; column 'Sub-categories' gives the number of executed categories (including demo category *NoDataRace*), ^{new} for first-time participants, $^{\varnothing}$ for hors-concours participation

Verifier	Language	First Year	Sub-categories
Bubaak ^{new}	C	2023	40
GDart-Llvm ^{new}	C	2023	1
Graves-Par ^{new}	C	2023	40
LF-checker ^{new}	C	2023	3
Mopsa ^{new}	C	2023	32
PIChecker ^{new}	C	2023	1
VeriAbsL ^{new}	C	2023	13
VeriOover ^{new}	C	2023	1
Mlb ^{new}	Java	2023	1
CVT-AlgoSel $^{\varnothing}$	C	2022	18
CVT-ParPort $^{\varnothing}$	C	2022	35
CPA-BAM-SMG $^{\varnothing}$	C	2022	16
Crux $^{\varnothing}$	C	2022	20
Deagle	C	2022	1
Ebf	C	2022	1
Graves-CPA	C	2022	35
Infer $^{\varnothing}$	C	2022	25
Lart	C	2022	22
Locksmith	C	2022	1
Sesl	C	2022	6
Theta	C	2022	13
UGemCutter	C	2022	2
GDart	Java	2022	1

Computing Resources. The resource limits were the same as in the previous competitions [14], except for the upgraded operating system: Each verification run was limited to 8 processing units (cores), 15 GB of memory, and 15 min of CPU time. Witness validation was limited to 2 processing units, 7 GB of memory, and 1.5 min of CPU time for violation witnesses and 15 min of CPU time for correctness witnesses. The machines for running the experiments are part of a

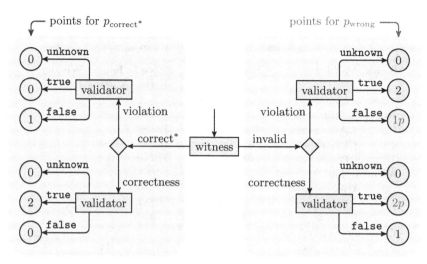

Fig. 6: Scoring schema for evaluation of validators; $p = -16$ for SV-COMP 2023; figure adopted from [37]

compute cluster that consists of 168 machines; each verification run was executed on an otherwise completely unloaded, dedicated machine, in order to achieve precise measurements. Each machine had one Intel Xeon E3-1230 v5 CPU, with 8 processing units each, a frequency of 3.4 GHz, 33 GB of RAM, and a GNU/Linux operating system (x86_64-linux, Ubuntu 22.04 with Linux kernel 5.15). We used BENCHEXEC [34] to measure and control computing resources (CPU time, memory, CPU energy) and VERIFIERCLOUD to distribute, install, run, and clean-up verification runs, and to collect the results. The values for time and energy are accumulated over all cores of the CPU. To measure the CPU energy, we used CPU ENERGY METER [38] (integrated in BENCHEXEC [34]).

One complete verification execution of the competition consisted of 490 858 verification runs in 91 run sets (each verifier on each verification task of the selected categories according to the opt-outs), consuming 1 114 days of CPU time and 299 kWh of CPU energy (without validation). Witness-based result validation required 4.59 million validation runs in 1 527 run sets (each validator on each verification task for categories with witness validation, and for each verifier), consuming 877 days of CPU time. Each tool was executed several times, in order to make sure no installation issues occur during the execution. Including these preruns, the infrastructure managed a total of 2.78 million verification runs in 560 run sets (verifier × property) consuming 13.8 years of CPU time, and 35.9 million validation runs in 11 532 run sets (validator × verifier × property) consuming 17.8 years of CPU time. This means that also the load of the experiment infrastructure increased and was larger than ever before.

Table 12: Validation of violation witnesses: Overview of the top-three verifiers for each category; values for CPU time and energy rounded to two significant digits

Rank	Validator	Score	CPU Time (in h)	Solved Tasks	False Alarms	Wrong Proofs
ReachSafety						
1	UAutomizer	**62966**	99	12 196		
2	CProver-w2t	49545	16	18 903	2	
3	CPAchecker	33938	92	17 770	12	
MemSafety						
1	UAutomizer	**31156**	49	5 680		
2	CPAchecker	9013	40	16 881	7	
3	CPA-w2t	1241	0.76	327		
ConcurrencySafety						
1	Dartagnan	**9777**	44	6 520	14	
2	CPAchecker	2658	14	3 466	28	
3	UAutomizer	912	1.2	263		
NoOverflows						
1	UAutomizer	**74933**	150	23 142		
2	CProver-w2t	61848	6.3	13 450		
3	CPAchecker	28600	5.0	2 747		
Termination						
1	UAutomizer	**3017**	7.6	1 052		
2	CPAchecker	423	19	3 113		
3	MetaVal	0	0	0		
SoftwareSystems						
1	Symbiotic-Witch	**3304**	0.55	846	1	
2	UAutomizer	2468	29	3 579		
3	CPAchecker	1620	14	2 475		
Overall						
1	UAutomizer	**127030**	330	45 912		
2	CPAchecker	52851	180	46 452	47	
3	Symbiotic-Witch	35851	65	38 644	10	

5   Results of the Witness-Validation Track

The validation of verification results, in particular, verification witnesses, becomes more and more important for various reasons: verification witnesses justify and help to understand and interpret a verification result, they serve as exchange object for intermediate results, and they allow to make use of imprecise verification techniques (e.g., via machine learning). A case study on the quality of the results of witness validators [37] suggested that validators for verification results should also undergo a periodical comparative evaluation and proposed a scoring schema for witness-validation results. SV-COMP 2023 evaluated 10 validators on more than 100 000 verification witnesses.

Table 13: Validation of correctness witnesses: Overview of the top-three verifiers for each category; values for CPU time and energy rounded to two significant digits

Rank	Validator	Score	CPU Time (in h)	Solved Tasks	False Alarms	Wrong Proofs
ReachSafety						
1	UAUTOMIZER	**21499**	350	16 768		
2	CPACHECKER	17816	220	16 437		
3	METAVAL	-89088	320	14 217		**16**
MemSafety						
1	UAUTOMIZER	**18219**	710	16 247		
2	METAVAL	0	0	0		
3	missing validator	0	0	0		
ConcurrencySafety						
1	UAUTOMIZER	**12994**	140	10 232		
2	missing validator	0	0	0		
3	missing validator	0	0	0		
NoOverflows						
1	UAUTOMIZER	**65478**	390	37 419		
2	CPACHECKER	27151	14	3 082		
3	METAVAL	0	0	0		
Termination						
1	**missing validator**	**0**	0	0		
2	missing validator	0	0	0		
3	missing validator	0	0	0		
SoftwareSystems						
1	CPACHECKER	**3147**	36	6 124		
2	UAUTOMIZER	3027	300	17 385		
3	METAVAL	-121312	600	18 148		**232**
Overall						
1	UAUTOMIZER	**930491**	900	98 051		
2	CPACHECKER	30076	280	25 643		
3	METAVAL	-165166	910	32 365		**248**

Scoring Schema for Validation Track. The score of a validator in a sub-category is computed as

$$score = \left(\frac{p_{\text{correct}^*}}{|\text{correct}^*|} + q \cdot \frac{p_{\text{wrong}}}{|\text{wrong}|} \right) \cdot \frac{|\text{correct}^*| + |\text{wrong}|}{2}$$

where the points in p_{correct^*} and p_{wrong} are determined according to the schema in Fig. 6 and then normalized using the normalization schema that SV-COMP uses for meta categories [11, page 597], except for the factor q, which gives a higher weight to wrong witnesses. Wrong witnesses are witnesses that do not agree with the expected verification verdict. Witnesses that agree with the expected verification verdict cannot be automatically treated as correct because we do not yet have an established way to determine this. Therefore, we call this class of witnesses correct*. Further details are given in the proposal [37]. This schema relates to each base category from the verification track a meta category that consists of two sub-categories, one with the correct* and one with the wrong witnesses.

Tables 12 and 13 show the rankings of the validators. False alarms in Table 12 are claims of a validator that the program contains a bug described by a given violation witness although the program is correct (the validator confirms a wrong violation witness). Wrong proofs in Table 13 are claims of a validator that the program is correct according to invariants in a given correctness witness although the program contains a bug (the validator confirms a wrong correctness witness). The scoring schema significantly punishes results that confirm a wrong verification witness, as visible for validator METAVAL in Table 13.

Table 13 shows that there are categories that are supported by less than three validators ('missing validators'). This reveals a remarkable gap in software-verification research:

> There are verification results that cannot be independently confirmed, according to the state of the art in software verification.

6   Conclusion

The 12th edition of the Competition on Software Verification (SV-COMP 2023) again increased the number of participating systems and gave the largest ever overview over software-verification tools, with 52 participating verification systems (incl. 9 new verifiers and 18 hors-concours; see Fig. 5 for the participation numbers and Table 5 for the details). For the first time, a thorough comparative evaluation of 10 validation tools was performed; the validation tools were assessed in a similar manner as in the verification track, using a community-agreed scoring schema [37] which is derived from the scoring schema of the verification track. The number of verification tasks in SV-COMP 2023 was significantly increased to 23 805 in the C category. The high quality standards of the TACAS conference are ensured by a competition jury, with a member from each actively participating team. We hope that the broad overview of verification tools stimulates the further advancements of software verification, and in particular, the validation track showed some open problems that should be addressed.

Data-Availability Statement. The verification tasks and results of the competition are published at Zenodo, as described in Table 3. All components and data that are necessary for reproducing the competition are available in public version repositories, as specified in Table 2. For easy access, the results are presented also online on the competition web site https://sv-comp.sosy-lab.org/2023/results. The main results were reproduced in an independent reproduction study [66].

Funding Statement. This project was funded in part by the Deutsche Forschungsgemeinschaft (DFG) — 418257054 (Coop).

Acknowledgements. We thank Marcus Gerhold and Arnd Hartmanns for their reproduction study [66] on SV-COMP 2023.

References

1. Ádám, Zs., Sallai, Gy., Hajdu, Á.: GAZER-THETA: LLVM-based verifier portfolio with BMC/CEGAR (competition contribution). In: Proc. TACAS (2). pp. 433–437. LNCS 12652, Springer (2021). https://doi.org/10.1007/978-3-030-72013-1_27
2. Afzal, M., Asia, A., Chauhan, A., Chimdyalwar, B., Darke, P., Datar, A., Kumar, S., Venkatesh, R.: VERIABS: Verification by abstraction and test generation. In: Proc. ASE. pp. 1138–1141 (2019). https://doi.org/10.1109/ASE.2019.00121
3. Aljaafari, F., Shmarov, F., Manino, E., Menezes, R., Cordeiro, L.: EBF 4.2: Black-Box cooperative verification for concurrent programs (competition contribution). In: Proc. TACAS (2). LNCS 13994, Springer (2023)
4. Andrianov, P., Friedberger, K., Mandrykin, M.U., Mutilin, V.S., Volkov, A.: CPA-BAM-BNB: Block-abstraction memoization and region-based memory models for predicate abstractions (competition contribution). In: Proc. TACAS. pp. 355–359. LNCS 10206, Springer (2017). https://doi.org/10.1007/978-3-662-54580-5_22
5. Andrianov, P., Mutilin, V., Khoroshilov, A.: CPALOCKATOR: Thread-modular approach with projections (competition contribution). In: Proc. TACAS (2). pp. 423–427. LNCS 12652, Springer (2021). https://doi.org/10.1007/978-3-030-72013-1_25
6. Andrianov, P.S.: Analysis of correct synchronization of operating system components. Program. Comput. Softw. **46**, 712–730 (2020). https://doi.org/10.1134/S0361768820080022
7. Ayaziová, P., Strejček, J.: SYMBIOTIC-WITCH 2: More efficient algorithm and witness refutation (competition contribution). In: Proc. TACAS (2). LNCS 13994, Springer (2023)
8. Baranová, Z., Barnat, J., Kejstová, K., Kučera, T., Lauko, H., Mrázek, J., Ročkai, P., Štill, V.: Model checking of C and C++ with DIVINE 4. In: Proc. ATVA. pp. 201–207. LNCS 10482, Springer (2017). https://doi.org/10.1007/978-3-319-68167-2_14
9. Bartocci, E., Beyer, D., Black, P.E., Fedyukovich, G., Garavel, H., Hartmanns, A., Huisman, M., Kordon, F., Nagele, J., Sighireanu, M., Steffen, B., Suda, M., Sutcliffe, G., Weber, T., Yamada, A.: TOOLympics 2019: An overview of competitions in formal methods. In: Proc. TACAS (3). pp. 3–24. LNCS 11429, Springer (2019). https://doi.org/10.1007/978-3-030-17502-3_1
10. Beyer, D.: Competition on software verification (SV-COMP). In: Proc. TACAS. pp. 504–524. LNCS 7214, Springer (2012). https://doi.org/10.1007/978-3-642-28756-5_38
11. Beyer, D.: Second competition on software verification (Summary of SV-COMP 2013). In: Proc. TACAS. pp. 594–609. LNCS 7795, Springer (2013). https://doi.org/10.1007/978-3-642-36742-7_43
12. Beyer, D.: Status report on software verification (Competition summary SV-COMP 2014). In: Proc. TACAS. pp. 373–388. LNCS 8413, Springer (2014). https://doi.org/10.1007/978-3-642-54862-8_25
13. Beyer, D.: Software verification and verifiable witnesses (Report on SV-COMP 2015). In: Proc. TACAS. pp. 401–416. LNCS 9035, Springer (2015). https://doi.org/10.1007/978-3-662-46681-0_31
14. Beyer, D.: Reliable and reproducible competition results with BENCHEXEC and witnesses (Report on SV-COMP 2016). In: Proc. TACAS. pp. 887–904. LNCS 9636, Springer (2016). https://doi.org/10.1007/978-3-662-49674-9_55

15. Beyer, D.: Software verification with validation of results (Report on SV-COMP 2017). In: Proc. TACAS. pp. 331–349. LNCS 10206, Springer (2017). https://doi.org/10.1007/978-3-662-54580-5_20

16. Beyer, D.: Automatic verification of C and Java programs: SV-COMP 2019. In: Proc. TACAS (3). pp. 133–155. LNCS 11429, Springer (2019). https://doi.org/10.1007/978-3-030-17502-3_9

17. Beyer, D.: Advances in automatic software verification: SV-COMP 2020. In: Proc. TACAS (2). pp. 347–367. LNCS 12079, Springer (2020). https://doi.org/10.1007/978-3-030-45237-7_21

18. Beyer, D.: Software verification: 10th comparative evaluation (SV-COMP 2021). In: Proc. TACAS (2). pp. 401–422. LNCS 12652, Springer (2021). https://doi.org/10.1007/978-3-030-72013-1_24

19. Beyer, D.: Status report on software testing: Test-Comp 2021. In: Proc. FASE. pp. 341–357. LNCS 12649, Springer (2021). https://doi.org/10.1007/978-3-030-71500-7_17

20. Beyer, D.: Progress on software verification: SV-COMP 2022. In: Proc. TACAS (2). pp. 375–402. LNCS 13244, Springer (2022). https://doi.org/10.1007/978-3-030-99527-0_20

21. Beyer, D.: Results of the 12th Intl. Competition on Software Verification (SV-COMP 2023). Zenodo (2023). https://doi.org/10.5281/zenodo.7627787

22. Beyer, D.: Software testing: 5th comparative evaluation: Test-Comp 2023. In: Proc. FASE. LNCS , Springer (2023)

23. Beyer, D.: SV-Benchmarks: Benchmark set for software verification and testing (SV-COMP 2023 and Test-Comp 2023). Zenodo (2023). https://doi.org/10.5281/zenodo.7627783

24. Beyer, D.: Verification witnesses from verification tools (SV-COMP 2023). Zenodo (2023). https://doi.org/10.5281/zenodo.7627791

25. Beyer, D.: Verifiers and validators of the 12th Intl. Competition on Software Verification (SV-COMP 2023). Zenodo (2023). https://doi.org/10.5281/zenodo.7627829

26. Beyer, D., Dangl, M., Dietsch, D., Heizmann, M.: Correctness witnesses: Exchanging verification results between verifiers. In: Proc. FSE. pp. 326–337. ACM (2016). https://doi.org/10.1145/2950290.2950351

27. Beyer, D., Dangl, M., Dietsch, D., Heizmann, M., Stahlbauer, A.: Witness validation and stepwise testification across software verifiers. In: Proc. FSE. pp. 721–733. ACM (2015). https://doi.org/10.1145/2786805.2786867

28. Beyer, D., Dangl, M., Lemberger, T., Tautschnig, M.: Tests from witnesses: Execution-based validation of verification results. In: Proc. TAP. pp. 3–23. LNCS 10889, Springer (2018). https://doi.org/10.1007/978-3-319-92994-1_1

29. Beyer, D., Friedberger, K.: Violation witnesses and result validation for multithreaded programs. In: Proc. ISoLA (1). pp. 449–470. LNCS 12476, Springer (2020). https://doi.org/10.1007/978-3-030-61362-4_26

30. Beyer, D., Kanav, S.: CoVeriTeam: On-demand composition of cooperative verification systems. In: Proc. TACAS. pp. 561–579. LNCS 13243, Springer (2022). https://doi.org/10.1007/978-3-030-99524-9_31

31. Beyer, D., Kanav, S., Richter, C.: Construction of verifier combinations based on off-the-shelf verifiers. In: Proc. FASE. pp. 49–70. Springer (2022). https://doi.org/10.1007/978-3-030-99429-7_3

32. Beyer, D., Kanav, S., Wachowitz, H.: Coveriteam Release 1.0. Zenodo (2023). https://doi.org/10.5281/zenodo.7635975

33. Beyer, D., Keremoglu, M.E.: CPACHECKER: A tool for configurable software verification. In: Proc. CAV. pp. 184–190. LNCS 6806, Springer (2011). https://doi.org/10.1007/978-3-642-22110-1_16

34. Beyer, D., Löwe, S., Wendler, P.: Reliable benchmarking: Requirements and solutions. Int. J. Softw. Tools Technol. Transfer **21**(1), 1–29 (2019). https://doi.org/10.1007/s10009-017-0469-y

35. Beyer, D., Spiessl, M.: METAVAL: Witness validation via verification. In: Proc. CAV. pp. 165–177. LNCS 12225, Springer (2020). https://doi.org/10.1007/978-3-030-53291-8_10

36. Beyer, D., Spiessl, M.: The static analyzer FRAMA-C in SV-COMP (competition contribution). In: Proc. TACAS (2). pp. 429–434. LNCS 13244, Springer (2022). https://doi.org/10.1007/978-3-030-99527-0_26

37. Beyer, D., Strejček, J.: Case study on verification-witness validators: Where we are and where we go. In: Proc. SAS. pp. 160–174. LNCS 13790, Springer (2022). https://doi.org/10.1007/978-3-031-22308-2_8

38. Beyer, D., Wendler, P.: CPU ENERGY METER: A tool for energy-aware algorithms engineering. In: Proc. TACAS (2). pp. 126–133. LNCS 12079, Springer (2020). https://doi.org/10.1007/978-3-030-45237-7_8

39. Brain, M., Joshi, S., Kröning, D., Schrammel, P.: Safety verification and refutation by k-invariants and k-induction. In: Proc. SAS. pp. 145–161. LNCS 9291, Springer (2015). https://doi.org/10.1007/978-3-662-48288-9_9

40. Bu, L., Xie, Z., Lyu, L., Li, Y., Guo, X., Zhao, J., Li, X.: BRICK: Path enumeration-based bounded reachability checking of C programs (competition contribution). In: Proc. TACAS (2). pp. 408–412. LNCS 13244, Springer (2022). https://doi.org/10.1007/978-3-030-99527-0_22

41. Calcagno, C., Distefano, D., O'Hearn, P.W., Yang, H.: Compositional shape analysis by means of bi-abduction. ACM **58**(6), 26:1–26:66 (2011). https://doi.org/10.1145/2049697.2049700

42. Chalupa, M., Henzinger, T.: BUBAAK: Runtime monitoring of program verifiers (competition contribution). In: Proc. TACAS (2). LNCS 13994, Springer (2023)

43. Chalupa, M., Strejček, J., Vitovská, M.: Joint forces for memory safety checking. In: Proc. SPIN. pp. 115–132. Springer (2018). https://doi.org/10.1007/978-3-319-94111-0_7

44. Chalupa, M., Řechtáčková, A., Mihalkovič, V., Zaoral, L., Strejček, J.: SYMBIOTIC 9: String analysis and backward symbolic execution with loop folding (competition contribution). In: Proc. TACAS (2). pp. 462–467. LNCS 13244, Springer (2022). https://doi.org/10.1007/978-3-030-99527-0_32

45. Chaudhary, E., Joshi, S.: PINAKA: Symbolic execution meets incremental solving (competition contribution). In: Proc. TACAS (3). pp. 234–238. LNCS 11429, Springer (2019). https://doi.org/10.1007/978-3-030-17502-3_20

46. Clarke, E.M., Kröning, D., Lerda, F.: A tool for checking ANSI-C programs. In: Proc. TACAS. pp. 168–176. LNCS 2988, Springer (2004). https://doi.org/10.1007/978-3-540-24730-2_15

47. Cordeiro, L.C., Fischer, B.: Verifying multi-threaded software using SMT-based context-bounded model checking. In: Proc. ICSE. pp. 331–340. ACM (2011). https://doi.org/10.1145/1985793.1985839

48. Cordeiro, L.C., Kesseli, P., Kröning, D., Schrammel, P., Trtík, M.: JBMC: A bounded model checking tool for verifying Java bytecode. In: Proc. CAV. pp. 183–190. LNCS 10981, Springer (2018). https://doi.org/10.1007/978-3-319-96145-3_10

49. Cordeiro, L.C., Kröning, D., Schrammel, P.: JBMC: Bounded model checking for Java bytecode (competition contribution). In: Proc. TACAS (3). pp. 219–223. LNCS 11429, Springer (2019). https://doi.org/10.1007/978-3-030-17502-3_17

50. Cordeiro, L.C., Morse, J., Nicole, D., Fischer, B.: Context-bounded model checking with ESBMC 1.17 (competition contribution). In: Proc. TACAS. pp. 534–537. LNCS 7214, Springer (2012). https://doi.org/10.1007/978-3-642-28756-5_42

51. Coto, A., Inverso, O., Sales, E., Tuosto, E.: A prototype for data race detection in CSEQ 3 (competition contribution). In: Proc. TACAS (2). pp. 413–417. LNCS 13244, Springer (2022). https://doi.org/10.1007/978-3-030-99527-0_23

52. Cuoq, P., Kirchner, F., Kosmatov, N., Prevosto, V., Signoles, J., Yakobowski, B.: Frama-C. In: Proc. SEFM. pp. 233–247. Springer (2012). https://doi.org/10.1007/978-3-642-33826-7_16

53. Dangl, M., Löwe, S., Wendler, P.: CPACHECKER with support for recursive programs and floating-point arithmetic (competition contribution). In: Proc. TACAS. pp. 423–425. LNCS 9035, Springer (2015). https://doi.org/10.1007/978-3-662-46681-0_34

54. Darke, P., Agrawal, S., Venkatesh, R.: VERIABS: A tool for scalable verification by abstraction (competition contribution). In: Proc. TACAS (2). pp. 458–462. LNCS 12652, Springer (2021). https://doi.org/10.1007/978-3-030-72013-1_32

55. Darke, P., Chimdyalwar, B., Agrawal, S., Venkatesh, R., Chakraborty, S., Kumar, S.: VERIABSL: Scalable verification by abstraction and strategy prediction (competition contribution). In: Proc. TACAS (2). LNCS 13994, Springer (2023)

56. Dietsch, D., Heizmann, M., Klumpp, D., Schüssele, F., Podelski, A.: ULTIMATE TAIPAN 2023 (competition contribution). In: Proc. TACAS (2). LNCS 13994, Springer (2023)

57. Dockins, R., Foltzer, A., Hendrix, J., Huffman, B., McNamee, D., Tomb, A.: Constructing semantic models of programs with the software analysis workbench. In: Proc. VSTTE. pp. 56–72. LNCS 9971, Springer (2016). https://doi.org/10.1007/978-3-319-48869-1_5

58. Dross, C., Furia, C.A., Huisman, M., Monahan, R., Müller, P.: Verifythis 2019: A program-verification competition. Int. J. Softw. Tools Technol. Transf. 23(6), 883–893 (2021). https://doi.org/10.1007/s10009-021-00619-x

59. Ermis, E., Hoenicke, J., Podelski, A.: Splitting via interpolants. In: Proc. VMCAI. pp. 186–201. LNCS 7148, Springer (2012). https://doi.org/10.1007/978-3-642-27940-9_13

60. Ernst, G.: A complete approach to loop verification with invariants and summaries. Tech. Rep. arXiv:2010.05812v2, arXiv (January 2020). https://doi.org/10.48550/arXiv.2010.05812

61. Ernst, G.: KORN: Horn clause based verification of C programs (competition contribution). In: Proc. TACAS (2). LNCS 13994, Springer (2023)

62. Farzan, A., Klumpp, D., Podelski, A.: Sound sequentialization for concurrent program verification. In: Proc. PLDI. pp. 506–521. ACM (2022). https://doi.org/10.1145/3519939.3523727

63. Gadelha, M.Y.R., Monteiro, F.R., Cordeiro, L.C., Nicole, D.A.: ESBMC v6.0: Verifying C programs using k-induction and invariant inference (competition contribution). In: Proc. TACAS (3). pp. 209–213. LNCS 11429, Springer (2019). https://doi.org/10.1007/978-3-030-17502-3_15

64. Gadelha, M.Y., Ismail, H.I., Cordeiro, L.C.: Handling loops in bounded model checking of C programs via k-induction. Int. J. Softw. Tools Technol. Transf. 19(1), 97–114 (February 2017). https://doi.org/10.1007/s10009-015-0407-9

65. Gavrilenko, N., Ponce de León, H., Furbach, F., Heljanko, K., Meyer, R.: BMC for weak memory models: Relation analysis for compact SMT encodings. In: Proc. CAV. pp. 355–365. LNCS 11561, Springer (2019). https://doi.org/10.1007/978-3-030-25540-4_19

66. Gerhold, M., Hartmanns, A.: Reproduction report for SV-COMP 2023. Tech. rep., University of Twente (2023). https://doi.org/10.48550/arXiv.2303.06477

67. Giesl, J., Mesnard, F., Rubio, A., Thiemann, R., Waldmann, J.: Termination competition (termCOMP 2015). In: Proc. CADE. pp. 105–108. LNCS 9195, Springer (2015). https://doi.org/10.1007/978-3-319-21401-6_6

68. Greitschus, M., Dietsch, D., Podelski, A.: Loop invariants from counterexamples. In: Proc. SAS. pp. 128–147. LNCS 10422, Springer (2017). https://doi.org/10.1007/978-3-319-66706-5_7

69. Hajdu, Á., Micskei, Z.: Efficient strategies for CEGAR-based model checking. J. Autom. Reasoning **64**(6), 1051–1091 (2020). https://doi.org/10.1007/s10817-019-09535-x

70. He, F., Sun, Z., Fan, H.: DEAGLE: An SMT-based verifier for multi-threaded programs (competition contribution). In: Proc. TACAS (2). pp. 424–428. LNCS 13244, Springer (2022). https://doi.org/10.1007/978-3-030-99527-0_25

71. Heizmann, M., Barth, M., Dietsch, D., Fichtner, L., Hoenicke, J., Klumpp, D., Naouar, M., Schindler, T., Schüssele, F., Podelski, A.: ULTIMATE AUTOMIZER 2023 (competition contribution). In: Proc. TACAS (2). LNCS 13994, Springer (2023)

72. Heizmann, M., Hoenicke, J., Podelski, A.: Software model checking for people who love automata. In: Proc. CAV. pp. 36–52. LNCS 8044, Springer (2013). https://doi.org/10.1007/978-3-642-39799-8_2

73. Holík, L., Kotoun, M., Peringer, P., Šoková, V., Trtík, M., Vojnar, T.: PREDATOR shape analysis tool suite. In: Hardware and Software: Verification and Testing. pp. 202–209. LNCS 10028, Springer (2016). https://doi.org/10.1007/978-3-319-49052-6

74. Howar, F., Jasper, M., Mues, M., Schmidt, D.A., Steffen, B.: The RERS challenge: Towards controllable and scalable benchmark synthesis. Int. J. Softw. Tools Technol. Transf. **23**(6), 917–930 (2021). https://doi.org/10.1007/s10009-021-00617-z

75. Howar, F., Mues, M.: GWIT (competition contribution). In: Proc. TACAS (2). pp. 446–450. LNCS 13244, Springer (2022). https://doi.org/10.1007/978-3-030-99527-0_29

76. Hussein, S., Yan, Q., McCamant, S., Sharma, V., Whalen, M.: JAVA RANGER: Supporting string and array operations (competition contribution). In: Proc. TACAS (2). LNCS 13994, Springer (2023)

77. Inverso, O., Tomasco, E., Fischer, B., La Torre, S., Parlato, G.: LAZY-CSEQ: A lazy sequentialization tool for C (competition contribution). In: Proc. TACAS. pp. 398–401. LNCS 8413, Springer (2014). https://doi.org/10.1007/978-3-642-54862-8_29

78. Inverso, O., Tomasco, E., Fischer, B., Torre, S.L., Parlato, G.: Bounded verification of multi-threaded programs via lazy sequentialization. ACM Trans. Program. Lang. Syst. **44**(1), 1:1–1:50 (2022). https://doi.org/10.1145/3478536

79. Inverso, O., Trubiani, C.: Parallel and distributed bounded model checking of multi-threaded programs. In: Proc. PPoPP. pp. 202–216. ACM (2020). https://doi.org/10.1145/3332466.3374529

80. Journault, M., Miné, A., Monat, R., Ouadjaout, A.: Combinations of reusable abstract domains for a multilingual static analyzer. In: Proc. VSTTE. pp. 1–18. LNCS 12031, Springer (2019)

81. Kahsai, T., Rümmer, P., Sanchez, H., Schäf, M.: JAYHORN: A framework for verifying Java programs. In: Proc. CAV. pp. 352–358. LNCS 9779, Springer (2016). https://doi.org/10.1007/978-3-319-41528-4_19

82. Kettl, M., Lemberger, T.: The static analyzer INFER in SV-COMP (competition contribution). In: Proc. TACAS (2). pp. 451–456. LNCS 13244, Springer (2022). https://doi.org/10.1007/978-3-030-99527-0_30

83. Klumpp, D., Dietsch, D., Heizmann, M., Schüssele, F., Ebbinghaus, M., Farzan, A., Podelski, A.: ULTIMATE GEMCUTTER and the axes of generalization (competition contribution). In: Proc. TACAS (2). pp. 479–483. LNCS 13244, Springer (2022). https://doi.org/10.1007/978-3-030-99527-0_35

84. Kröning, D., Tautschnig, M.: CBMC: C bounded model checker (competition contribution). In: Proc. TACAS. pp. 389–391. LNCS 8413, Springer (2014). https://doi.org/10.1007/978-3-642-54862-8_26

85. Lauko, H., Ročkai, P., Barnat, J.: Symbolic computation via program transformation. In: Proc. ICTAC. pp. 313–332. Springer (2018). https://doi.org/10.1007/978-3-030-02508-3_17

86. Leeson, W., Dwyer, M.: GRAVES-CPA: A graph-attention verifier selector (competition contribution). In: Proc. TACAS (2). pp. 440–445. LNCS 13244, Springer (2022). https://doi.org/10.1007/978-3-030-99527-0_28

87. Luckow, K.S., Dimjasevic, M., Giannakopoulou, D., Howar, F., Isberner, M., Kahsai, T., Rakamaric, Z., Raman, V.: JDART: A dynamic symbolic analysis framework. In: Proc. TACAS. pp. 442–459. LNCSS 9636, Springer (2016). https://doi.org/10.1007/978-3-662-49674-9_26

88. Malík, V., Schrammel, P., Vojnar, T., Nečas, F.: 2LS: Arrays and loop unwinding (competition contribution). In: Proc. TACAS (2). LNCS 13994, Springer (2023)

89. Metta, R., Medicherla, R.K., Chakraborty, S.: BMC+FUZZ: Efficient and effective test generation. In: Proc. DATE. pp. 1419–1424. IEEE (2022). https://doi.org/10.23919/DATE54114.2022.9774672

90. Metta, R., Yeduru, P., Karmarkar, H., Medicherla, R.K.: VERIFUZZ 1.4: Checking for (non-)termination (competition contribution). In: Proc. TACAS (2). LNCS 13994, Springer (2023)

91. Monat, R., Ouadjaout, A., Miné, A.: MOPSA-C: Modular domains and relational abstract interpretation for C programs (competition contribution). In: Proc. TACAS (2). LNCS 13994, Springer (2023)

92. Mues, M., Howar, F.: JDART: Portfolio solving, breadth-first search and SMT-Lib strings (competition contribution). In: Proc. TACAS (2). pp. 448–452. LNCS 12652, Springer (2021). https://doi.org/10.1007/978-3-030-72013-1_30

93. Mues, M., Howar, F.: GDART (competition contribution). In: Proc. TACAS (2). pp. 435–439. LNCS 13244, Springer (2022). https://doi.org/10.1007/978-3-030-99527-0_27

94. Noller, Y., Păsăreanu, C.S., Le, X.B.D., Visser, W., Fromherz, A.: Symbolic PATHFINDER for SV-COMP (competition contribution). In: Proc. TACAS (3). pp. 239–243. LNCS 11429, Springer (2019). https://doi.org/10.1007/978-3-030-17502-3_21

95. Nutz, A., Dietsch, D., Mohamed, M.M., Podelski, A.: ULTIMATE KOJAK with memory safety checks (competition contribution). In: Proc. TACAS. pp. 458–460. LNCS 9035, Springer (2015). https://doi.org/10.1007/978-3-662-46681-0_44

96. Peringer, P., Šoková, V., Vojnar, T.: PREDATORHP revamped (not only) for interval-sized memory regions and memory reallocation (competition contribution). In: Proc. TACAS (2). pp. 408–412. LNCS 12079, Springer (2020). https://doi.org/10.1007/978-3-030-45237-7_30

97. Ponce-De-Leon, H., Haas, T., Meyer, R.: DARTAGNAN: Leveraging compiler optimizations and the price of precision (competition contribution). In: Proc. TACAS (2). pp. 428–432. LNCS 12652, Springer (2021). https://doi.org/10.1007/978-3-030-72013-1_26

98. Ponce-De-Leon, H., Haas, T., Meyer, R.: DARTAGNAN: Smt-based violation witness validation (competition contribution). In: Proc. TACAS (2). pp. 418–423. LNCS 13244, Springer (2022). https://doi.org/10.1007/978-3-030-99527-0_24

99. Pratikakis, P., Foster, J.S., Hicks, M.: LOCKSMITH: Practical static race detection for C. ACM Trans. Program. Lang. Syst. 33(1) (January 2011). https://doi.org/10.1145/1889997.1890000

100. Păsăreanu, C.S., Visser, W., Bushnell, D.H., Geldenhuys, J., Mehlitz, P.C., Rungta, N.: Symbolic PATHFINDER: integrating symbolic execution with model checking for Java bytecode analysis. Autom. Software Eng. 20(3), 391–425 (2013). https://doi.org/10.1007/s10515-013-0122-2

101. Richter, C., Hüllermeier, E., Jakobs, M.C., Wehrheim, H.: Algorithm selection for software validation based on graph kernels. Autom. Softw. Eng. 27(1), 153–186 (2020). https://doi.org/10.1007/s10515-020-00270-x

102. Richter, C., Wehrheim, H.: PESCo: Predicting sequential combinations of verifiers (competition contribution). In: Proc. TACAS (3). pp. 229–233. LNCS 11429, Springer (2019). https://doi.org/10.1007/978-3-030-17502-3_19

103. Saan, S., Schwarz, M., Erhard, J., Pietsch, M., Seidl, H., Tilscher, S., Vojdani, V.: GOBLINT: Autotuning thread-modular abstract interpretation (competition contribution). In: Proc. TACAS (2). LNCS 13994, Springer (2023)

104. Scott, R., Dockins, R., Ravitch, T., Tomb, A.: CRUX: Symbolic execution meets SMT-based verification (competition contribution). Zenodo (February 2022). https://doi.org/10.5281/zenodo.6147218

105. Shamakhi, A., Hojjat, H., Rümmer, P.: Towards string support in JAYHORN (competition contribution). In: Proc. TACAS (2). pp. 443–447. LNCS 12652, Springer (2021). https://doi.org/10.1007/978-3-030-72013-1_29

106. Sharma, V., Hussein, S., Whalen, M.W., McCamant, S.A., Visser, W.: JAVA RANGER: Statically summarizing regions for efficient symbolic execution of Java. In: Proc. ESEC/FSE. pp. 123–134. ACM (2020). https://doi.org/10.1145/3368089.3409734

107. Su, J., Yang, Z., Xing, H., Yang, J., Tian, C., Duan, Z.: PICHECKER: A POR and interpolation-based verifier for concurrent programs (competition contribution). In: Proc. TACAS (2). LNCS 13994, Springer (2023)

108. Tóth, T., Hajdu, A., Vörös, A., Micskei, Z., Majzik, I.: THETA: A framework for abstraction refinement-based model checking. In: Proc. FMCAD. pp. 176–179 (2017). https://doi.org/10.23919/FMCAD.2017.8102257

109. Visser, W., Geldenhuys, J.: COASTAL: Combining concolic and fuzzing for Java (competition contribution). In: Proc. TACAS (2). pp. 373–377. LNCS 12079, Springer (2020). https://doi.org/10.1007/978-3-030-45237-7_23

110. Vojdani, V., Apinis, K., Rõtov, V., Seidl, H., Vene, V., Vogler, R.: Static race detection for device drivers: The Goblint approach. In: Proc. ASE. pp. 391–402. ACM (2016). https://doi.org/10.1145/2970276.2970337

111. Volkov, A.R., Mandrykin, M.U.: Predicate abstractions memory modeling method with separation into disjoint regions. Proceedings of the Institute for System Programming (ISPRAS) 29, 203–216 (2017). https://doi.org/10.15514/ISPRAS-2017-29(4)-13

112. Wendler, P., Beyer, D.: sosy-lab/benchexec: Release 3.16. Zenodo (2023). https://doi.org/10.5281/zenodo.7612021

113. Wu, T., Schrammel, P., Cordeiro, L.: WIT4JAVA: A violation-witness validator for Java verifiers (competition contribution). In: Proc. TACAS (2). pp. 484–489. LNCS 13244, Springer (2022). https://doi.org/10.1007/978-3-030-99527-0_36

114. Ádám, Z., Bajczi, L., Dobos-Kovács, M., Hajdu, A., Molnár, V.: THETA: Portfolio of cegar-based analyses with dynamic algorithm selection (competition contribution). In: Proc. TACAS (2). pp. 474–478. LNCS 13244, Springer (2022). https://doi.org/10.1007/978-3-030-99527-0_34

115. J. Švejda, Berger, P., Katoen, J.P.: Interpretation-based violation witness validation for C: NITWIT. In: Proc. TACAS. pp. 40–57. LNCS 12078, Springer (2020). https://doi.org/10.1007/978-3-030-45190-5_3

Symbiotic-Witch 2: More Efficient Algorithm and Witness Refutation*
(Competition Contribution)

Paulína Ayaziová and Jan Strejček[✉]

Masaryk University, Brno, Czech Republic
{xayaziov,strejcek}@fi.muni.cz

Abstract. The new version of the witness validator Symbiotic-Witch follows more precisely the (fixed version of the) semantics of verification witnesses. This makes the tool more efficient as it can benefit from sink nodes. Further, the tool can now refute a witness. To sum up, Symbiotic-Witch 2 can confirm or refute violation witnesses of *reachability safety*, *memory safety*, *memory cleanup*, and *overflow* properties of sequential C programs.

1 Witness Validation Approach

The basic principle of the witness validator Symbiotic-Witch 2 remains the same as in the previous version of the tool [1], i.e., it symbolically executes [9] the given program along execution paths specified by the corresponding witness. The substantial differences were induced by a more precise interpretation of violation witnesses and by the commmunity decision to support witness refutation.

We originally thought that every node of a witness automaton has an implicit self-loop that can be taken under each program instruction. After SV-COMP 2022, we learnt that the implicit self-loop of a node q can be used only by edges of *control flow automata (CFA)* that are "either

(a) not matched by the source-code guard of any other outgoing transition of q or

(b) are matched by the source-code guard of some other outgoing transition of q that also matches a successor CFA edge." [5]

This definition is problematic in particular because it refers to CFA and there is no standardized translation of C programs to CFA. Especially the case (b) heavily depends on the granularity of constructed CFA as it refers to adjacent edges. As the semantics of verification witnesses has to be unambiguous, we have convinced the community that the case (b) should be removed from the semantics. Still, the case (a) is viable and it considerably reduces the applicability of implicit self-loops.

---

* This work has been supported by the Czech Science Foundation grant GA23-06506S.

S. Sankaranarayanan and N. Sharygina (Eds.): TACAS 2023, LNCS 13994, pp. 523–528, 2023.
https://doi.org/10.1007/978-3-031-30820-8_30

SYMBIOTIC-WITCH 2 works as follows. It reads a given violation witness and the corresponding program. The program is symbolically executed and every state of symbolic execution is accompanied by the set of witness automaton nodes that are reached by the executed program path. Note that these sets are dramatically smaller than in the previous version of our tool due to the more precise semantics of implicit self-loops. If the set does not contain any node except sink nodes, the symbolic execution of the corresponding path is stopped. This brings a significant speed up compared to the previous version of our tool where this situation cannot happen.

Another significant difference to the previous version is the handling of state-space guards of a given witness. Consider a symbolic execution state and the associated set of witness automata nodes. Further, assume that the next instruction processed by the symbolic execution matches the source-code guards of some automata edges leading from the set of nodes. For each state-space guard of these edges, we create a fork of symbolic execution and restrict the next symbolic execution state to satisfy the state-space guard. The set of nodes accompanying the restricted symbolic execution state contains only target nodes of the edges with the enforced state-space guard. Note that the previous version of our validator ignores state-space guards unless the witness automaton contains a single path from the entry node to the violation node.

If the symbolic execution detects a violation of the considered property and the tracked set of witness automata nodes contains a violation node, the witness is confirmed. The witness is refuted if

- the symbolic execution ends without finding a property violation represented by the witness and
- there was no execution path unexplored due to the limitations of the employed symbolic executor (e.g., our executor based on KLEE [6] cannot handle symbolic floats and thus it instantiates them with a concrete value and ignores executions with other values) and
- the witness uses only source-code guards supported by our tool (see below).

The witness automata use various attributes to specify source-code guards (saying which instructions correspond to a given witness automaton edge) and state-space guards (restrictions on program states). SYMBIOTIC-WITCH 2 supports only selected attributes for source-code guards, namely the line number of executed instructions, the information whether *true* or *false* branch is taken, and the information about entering a function or returning from a function. Regarding the state-space guard, our tool uses only the return values of the __VERIFIER_nondet_* functions. The limited support of attributes means that our tool can misinterpret a given witness automaton, i.e., it can consider some execution path to be represented by the automaton even if it is not, and vice versa. In practice, this is not a big issue as many verification tools produce violation witnesses with only the supported attributes and some other tools use unsupported attributes to provide additional information (like offset of an instruction in the source code) that typically do not change the represented set of execution paths.

2   Software Architecture

The tool SYMBIOTIC-WITCH 2 is integrated to the SYMBIOTIC framework [7] and it can be roughly divided into two components. The first component is a set of python scripts (many of them shared with other SYMBIOTIC tools) that preprocess the code. More precisely, they set the options for optimisations and CLANG sanitizer depending on the considered property, translates the given C program into LLVM intermediate representation via CLANG, and links necessary function definitions.

The second component called WITCH-KLEE takes the preprocessed program and the witness, and it runs the actual witness validation. WITCH-KLEE is derived from the symbolic executor JETKLEE, which is a fork of KLEE [6] used in the SYMBIOTIC framework. WITCH-KLEE employs RAPIDXML for parsing witnesses in the GraphML format [5] and Z3 [10] as the SMT solver in symbolic execution.

Both components of SYMBIOTIC-WITCH 2 run on LLVM 10.0.1.

3   Strengths and Weaknesses

On the positive side, SYMBIOTIC-WITCH 2 can efficiently handle violation witnesses providing return values of `__VERIFIER_nondet_*` functions as well as those describing execution paths by taken branches.

Further, if SYMBIOTIC-WITCH 2 confirms a witness containing only attributes supported by the tool, then the witness is indeed valid. If SYMBIOTIC-WITCH 2 confirms a witness with some attributes not supported by the tool, then the program really violates the considered property and this violation can, but does not have to be represented by the witness. If SYMBIOTIC-WITCH 2 refutes a witness, then this witness is indeed invalid. The only exception is the case when the program contains some inner nondeterminism that is lost by the translation to LLVM. For example, consider a program that contains a test `f(x) < g(x)`. Due to the C standard, the functions `f(x)` and `g(x)` can be evaluated in any order. If a violation witness prescribes one order of evaluation and CLANG translates the program such that the functions are evaluated in the opposite order, then the witness can be refuted even if it is correct. We can construct such a witness, but we have not yet come across any of these in practice. We plan to extend our tool with a check for this kind of inner nondeterminism in order to guarantee the correctness of refutation answers.

Our tool also has some weaknesses. Some of them come from the fact that we do not support all possible attributes of witnesses. We decided not to invest more effort to support other attributes as we expect the witness format to be revised soon due to detected issues in its semantics. In spite of this, the tool correctly confirmed 35536 and refuted 3108 violation witnesses of SV-COMP 2023. On the negative side, the tool also confirmed 10 witnesses of memory safety violation marked as invalid. Nine of these incorrect validation results stem from two verification tasks where our symbolic executor reported a `valid-memtrack` violation while the tasks are marked *true* for this property.

SYMBIOTIC-WITCH 2 struggles to evaluate two specific classes of witnesses. The first class are the witnesses for the programs in the ECA subcategory. These generated artificial programs are hard to compile and optimize. Thus, our tool sometimes runs out of time during the code preprocessing phase.

The second class are the witnesses that contain edges describing declarations and initializations of global variables (e.g., some witnesses produced by Ultimate Automizer [8]). Our algorithm processes these declarations and initializations in a separate step and starts the symbolic execution of a given program (and thus also the witness tracking) in the function `main`. This means that the witness tracking cannot pass any witness edge representing instructions that are not reachable from `main`. Hence, SYMBIOTIC-WITCH 2 can refute some witnesses of the second class even if it finds the property violations they represent. This issue can be seen as another consequence of the fact that the semantics of witnesses is formulated over CFA and the translation of C programs to CFA is not given.

4   Tool Setup and Configuration

The archive with SYMBIOTIC-WITCH 2 is available in the SV-COMP archives. To run the validator, use the command

```
./symbiotic [--prp <prop>] [--32 | --64] --witness-check <witness> <prg>
```

where `<witness>` is a violation witness in the GraphML format, `<prg>` is the corresponding C program, and `<prop>` is the considered property. The property can be supplied as a `.prp` file or one of the following shortcuts: `no-overflow`, `valid-memsafety`, or `valid-memcleanup`. The default property is unreachability of the function `reach_error()`. The switches `--32` and `--64` specify the considered architecture, 64-bit being the default.

Both components of the tool are also available on GitHub with build instructions in the respective `README.md` files. To start validation, build each component separately, add the path to the built `witch-klee` executable to `$PATH` and run SYMBIOTIC as previously described.

5   Software Project and Contributors

SYMBIOTIC-WITCH 2 has been developed at Faculty of Informatics, Masaryk University by Paulína Ayaziová under the guidance of Jan Strejček. The tool is available under the MIT license and all used tools and libraries (LLVM, KLEE, Z3, RAPIDXML, SYMBIOTIC) are also available under open-source licenses that comply with SV-COMP's policy for the reproduction of results. The source code of WITCH-KLEE (the competing version tagged SV-COMP23) can be found at:

https://github.com/ayazip/witch-klee

The source code of the respective version of SYMBIOTIC is available at:

https://github.com/staticafi/symbiotic/tree/witch-klee

Data Availability Statement. All data of SV-COMP 2023 are archived as described in the competition report [3] and available on the competition web site. This includes the verification tasks, results, witnesses, scripts, and instructions for reproduction. The version of Symbiotic-Witch 2 used in the competition is archived together with other participating tools [4] or separately [2].

References

1. Ayaziová, P., Chalupa, M., Strejček, J.: Symbiotic-Witch: A Klee-based violation witness checker (competition contribution). In: Fisman, D., Rosu, G. (eds.) Tools and Algorithms for the Construction and Analysis of Systems - 28th International Conference, TACAS 2022, Held as Part of the European Joint Conferences on Theory and Practice of Software, ETAPS 2022, Munich, Germany, April 2-7, 2022, Proceedings, Part II. Lecture Notes in Computer Science, vol. 13244, pp. 468–473. Springer (2022), https://doi.org/10.1007/978-3-030-99527-0_33
2. Ayaziová, P., Strejček, J.: Symbiotic-Witch 2. Zenodo (2023). https://doi.org/10.5281/zenodo.7630406
3. Beyer, D.: Competition on software verification and witness validation: SV-COMP 2023. In: Proc. TACAS (2). LNCS , Springer (2023)
4. Beyer, D.: Verifiers and validators of the 12th Intl. Competition on Software Verification (SV-COMP 2023). Zenodo (2023). https://doi.org/10.5281/zenodo.7627829
5. Beyer, D., Dangl, M., Dietsch, D., Heizmann, M., Lemberger, T., Tautschnig, M.: Verification witnesses. ACM Trans. Softw. Eng. Methodol. 31(4), 57:1–57:69 (2022). https://doi.org/10.1145/3477579, https://doi.org/10.1145/3477579
6. Cadar, C., Dunbar, D., Engler, D.R.: KLEE: Unassisted and automatic generation of high-coverage tests for complex systems programs. In: OSDI. pp. 209–224. USENIX Association (2008), http://www.usenix.org/events/osdi08/tech/full_papers/cadar/cadar.pdf
7. Chalupa, M., Mihalkovič, V., Řechtáčková, A., Zaoral, L., Strejček, J.: Symbiotic 9: String analysis and backward symbolic execution with loop folding (competition contribution). In: Fisman, D., Rosu, G. (eds.) Tools and Algorithms for the Construction and Analysis of Systems - 28th International Conference, TACAS 2022, Held as Part of the European Joint Conferences on Theory and Practice of Software, ETAPS 2022, Munich, Germany, April 2-7, 2022, Proceedings, Part II. Lecture Notes in Computer Science, vol. 13244, pp. 462–467. Springer (2022), https://doi.org/10.1007/978-3-030-99527-0_32
8. Heizmann, M., Chen, Y., Dietsch, D., Greitschus, M., Hoenicke, J., Li, Y., Nutz, A., Musa, B., Schilling, C., Schindler, T., Podelski, A.: Ultimate Automizer and the search for perfect interpolants - (competition contribution). In: Beyer, D., Huisman, M. (eds.) Tools and Algorithms for the Construction and Analysis of Systems - 24th International Conference, TACAS 2018, Held as Part of the European Joint Conferences on Theory and Practice of Software, ETAPS 2018, Thessaloniki, Greece, April 14-20, 2018, Proceedings, Part II. Lecture Notes in Computer Science, vol. 10806, pp. 447–451. Springer (2018), https://doi.org/10.1007/978-3-319-89963-3_30
9. King, J.C.: Symbolic execution and program testing. Communications of ACM 19(7), 385–394 (1976), https://doi.org/10.1145/360248.360252
10. de Moura, L.M., Bjørner, N.: Z3: an efficient SMT solver. In: TACAS 2008. LNCS, vol. 4963, pp. 337–340. Springer (2008), https://doi.org/10.1007/978-3-540-78800-3_24

2LS: Arrays and Loop Unwinding
(Competition Contribution)

Viktor Malík[3][*][⊠], František Nečas[3], Peter Schrammel[1,2],
and Tomáš Vojnar[3]

[1]Diffblue Ltd., Oxford, UK
[2]University of Sussex, Sussex, UK
[3]Brno University of Technology, FIT, Brno, Czech Republic [**]
imalik@fit.vut.cz

Abstract 2LS is a C program analyser built upon the CPROVER infrastructure that can verify and refute program assertions, memory safety, and termination. Until now, one of the main drawbacks of 2LS was its inability to verify most programs with arrays. This paper introduces a new abstract domain in 2LS for reasoning about the contents of arrays. In addition, we introduce an improved approach to loop unwinding, a crucial component of the 2LS' verification algorithm, which particularly enables finding proofs and counterexamples for programs working with dynamic memory.

1 Overview

2LS is a static analysis and verification tool for sequential C programs. At its core, it uses the kIkI algorithm (k-invariants and k-induction) [2], which integrates bounded model checking, k-induction, and abstract interpretation into a single, scalable framework. kIkI relies on incremental SAT solving in order to find proofs and refutations of assertions, as well as to perform (non)termination analysis [3].

One of the core mechanisms of kIkI is incremental loop unwinding. However, the original unwinding approach that 2LS used was not compatible with the memory model developed in [6]. Hence, in the first part of this paper, we introduce a new approach to loop unwinding [9] that supports programs manipulating dynamic memory and hence allows 2LS to verify programs that could not be handled before.

The abstract interpretation part of kIkI features multiple abstract domains for reasoning about various data structures in programs. In particular, the competition version of 2LS uses the interval domain for numerical values and our custom heap domain for describing the shape of the heap. A common data structure that 2LS could not handle in the past are arrays. Therefore, in the second part of this paper, we introduce a new array abstract domain capable of reasoning about the content of arrays.

Architecture. The architecture of 2LS has been described in previous competition contributions [10,7,8]. In brief, 2LS is built upon the CPROVER infrastructure [4] and thus uses *GOTO programs* as the internal program representation. The analysed program is first translated into a single static assignment (SSA) form. Then, inductive invariants in various abstract domains are computed for the program's loops. Last, the SSA form and the invariants are bit-blasted into a propositional formula and given to a SAT solver which is used to reason about the program's properties.

---

[*] Jury member

[**] The Czech authors were supported by the Czech Science Foundation project 23-06506S, the FIT BUT project FIT-S-23-8151, and the Horizon Europe project CHESS (id 101087529).

S. Sankaranarayanan and N. Sharygina (Eds.): TACAS 2023, LNCS 13994, pp. 529–534, 2023.
https://doi.org/10.1007/978-3-031-30820-8_31

Software Project. 2LS is implemented in C++ and it is maintained by Peter Schrammel and Viktor Malík with contributions by the community. The competition version uses Glucose 4.0 as its back-end SAT solver. 2LS competes in all C categories except Concurrency. See the previous competition report [8] for details on executing 2LS.

2   Loop Unwinding of Heap-Manipulating Programs

Whenever the kIkI algorithm is not able to verify or refute the program's properties for the given unwinding level, it incrementally unwinds the loops in order to compute a stronger invariant or to explore additional reachable program states [2]. 2LS' original unwinder unrolls the loops directly at the level of the program's SSA form. However, this approach is not compatible with the encoding of pointer operations that 2LS uses [6]. Hence, for this year's competition version of 2LS, we introduce a new approach to loop unwinding which overcomes these limitations and allows to verify heap-manipulating programs using k-induction and BMC.

Memory model in 2LS. Each call of `malloc` is replaced by a finite number of so-called *abstract dynamic objects* that over-approximate the (possibly unbounded) set of concrete dynamic objects allocated by that call. Subsequently, the conversion of pointer-dereferencing operations to the SSA form is based on a static *points-to* analysis which computes for each pointer p the set of memory objects that p can be dereferenced into. Reads and writes to memory through p are then encoded using a case-split of objects which p can point to in the program location of the given memory operation [6].

The points-to analysis is performed on the *GOTO program* (control-flow graph) prior to generating the SSA form. This approach poses a problem for the original unwinder when dealing with allocations inside loops. Each new unwinding of a loop may introduce a new call to `malloc`, effectively introducing new abstract dynamic objects. Such additions invalidate the previously computed points-to analysis since pointers may now also point to the new objects and, thus, operations via pointers must be re-encoded.

Unwinding in the GOTO programs. Our new approach to loop unwinding unrolls the loops in the *GOTO program* representation instead of the SSA form. This allows us to update the set of abstract dynamic objects in the program as well as to compute the points-to analysis anew based on the newly introduced objects [9]. In order to facilitate verification in 2LS, there are multiple transformations that need to be done after the loops of the *GOTO program* are unwound. First, the k-induction algorithm of 2LS requires a special unwinding approach. Many state-of-the-art unwinders, including the unwinder from CPROVER that we use, copy the loop body and place it before the original loop (i.e., the unwound loop bodies are outside the loop). On the contrary, 2LS requires all of the unwindings to be included in a single loop, i.e., the backwards edge of the not-yet-unwound part must go to the beginning of the topmost unwinding (instead of going to the top of the not-yet-unwound part) [2]. Hence, we must appropriately reconnect the backwards edges to fulfil this requirement and make our approach usable with the current algorithms of 2LS. Second, assertions inside the unwound loop bodies may be assumed to hold as they were verified in the previous iteration of the kIkI algorithm. Hence, 2LS converts such assertions into assumptions. We reflect this approach inside our new unwinding algorithm, cf. [9] for details.

Combining the two approaches. The proposed approach, while being sound when handling dynamic memory, introduces a noticeable performance degradation. Unwinding of loops in the *GOTO program* changes a great part of the generated SSA form which decreases the benefits of incremental SAT solving. To overcome this issue, we only enable the new unwinder when necessary, i.e., when dynamic memory is used in the analysed program. In addition, in our future work, we plan to improve our new unwinder to fully leverage incremental solving.

3 Array Domain

The core algorithm of 2LS, $kIkI$, uses abstract interpretation to infer k-inductive invariants in various abstract domains. The computed invariants are used to verify or refute the program's properties. Since the verification approach of 2LS is based on translating the program into a first-order formula to reason about its properties, the abstract domains in 2LS are required to have the form of a *template*—a parametrised, quantifier-free, first-order formula describing a relevant program property. 2LS already supports a handful of domains, such as the interval domain [2], a shape domain [6], or ranking domains [3] for termination analysis, however, a domain for describing the content of arrays has been missing, which limited usability of 2LS on programs manipulating array structures. In this section, we propose such a domain.

In the literature, there exists a number of works on abstract domains for arrays. To exploit the 2LS' seamless combination of abstract domains, we found that perhaps the most suitable approach to draw inspiration from is [5], where each array is split into several parts, called *segments*, and a separate invariant is computed for every segment. The segment invariant can be computed in any domain supported by 2LS, usually selected based on the data type of the array elements (e.g., the interval domain for numerical values or the shape domain for pointers). In the rest of this section, we describe different aspects of our proposed domain. In all of the below parts, we assume that we compute a loop invariant of an array a. We use N_a to denote the number of elements of a.

Array Segmentation. First, let us assume that we know the set of array indices, so-called *segment borders*, for an array a which we denote B_a (see below on the way this set is obtained). When splitting a into segments, we distinguish two situations:

1. Indices from B_a cannot be totally ordered. In such a case, we create multiple segmentations, one for each $b \in B_a$:

$$\{0\}\ S_1^b\ \{b\}\ S_2^b\ \{b+1\}\ S_3^b\ \{N_a\}. \tag{1}$$

2. Indices from B_a can be totally ordered s.t. $b_1 \leq \cdots \leq b_n$. In such a case, we create a single segmentation for the entire a:

$$\{0\}\ S_1\ \{b_1\}\ S_2\ \{b_1+1\}\ S_3\ \{b_2\}\ \ldots\ \{b_n\}\ S_{2n}\ \{b_n+1\}\ S_{2n+1}\ \{N_a\}. \tag{2}$$

A single array segment S denoted $\{b_l\}\ S\ \{b_u\}$ represents an abstraction of the elements of a between the indices b_l (inclusive) and b_u (exclusive). For each S, we define two special variables: (1) the *segment element variable* $elem^S$ being an abstraction of the array elements contained in S and (2) the *segment index variable* idx^S being an abstraction of the indices of the array elements contained in S.

Array Template. Having the set of program arrays Arr and the set of segments S^a for each $a \in Arr$, we define the array domain template as:

$$\mathcal{T}^A \equiv \bigwedge_{a \in Arr} \bigwedge_{S \in S^a} \left(G^S \Rightarrow \mathcal{T}^{in}(elem^S) \right) \tag{3}$$

where $\mathcal{T}^{in}$ is the inner domain template (over the inner elements of S abstracted by $elem^S$) and G^S is the conjunction of guards associated with the segment S. The purpose of G^S is to make sure that the inner invariant is limited to the elements of the given segment $\{b_l\}$ S $\{b_u\}$. In particular, G^S is a conjunction of several guards:

$$b_l \leq idx^S < b_u \wedge 0 \leq idx^S < N_a \wedge elem^S = a[idx^S] \tag{4}$$

where the first conjunct ensures that the segment index variable stays between the segment borders, the second conjunct makes sure that the segment index variable stays between the array borders (since segment borders are generic expressions, they may lie outside of the array), and the last conjunct binds the segment element variable to the segment index variable. Using the above template, 2LS is able to compute a different invariant for each segment. For example, for a typical array iteration loop, this would allow 2LS to infer a different invariant for the part of the array that has already been traversed than for the part of the array that is still to be visited.

Computing Array Segment Borders. Since 2LS requires the template formula to be fixed at the beginning of the analysis, the set of segments must be pre-computed. The main idea of our approach is that the segment borders should be closely related to the expressions that are used to access array elements in the analysed program. Therefore, we perform a static *array index analysis* which collects the set of all expressions occurring as array access indices (i.e., inside the square bracket operators). Once the analysis is complete, for each array a, we determine the set of its segment borders by taking the set of all index expressions used to write into a in the corresponding loop.

4   Strengths and Weaknesses

For general strengths and weaknesses of 2LS, we refer to the previous competition contribution [8]. The two major improvements described in the previous sections, increase the number of programs correctly verified by this year's version of 2LS. The new loop unwinding approach allows us to use the BMC part of the kIkI algorithm for programs manipulating dynamic memory, which particularly enables us to find counterexamples occurring in higher loop iterations, as well as verify such programs for which the initially computed invariant is not sufficiently strong and the loops can be unwound completely. This is most notable in the heap-related categories (*MemSafety-Heap*, *MemSafety-LinkedLists*, and *ReachSafety-Heap*) where the number of the *correct true* and the *correct false* results increased from 110 to 177 and from 51 to 82, respectively. The new array domain allowed us to score points in array-related categories, which was not possible before (e.g., 2LS correctly solved 17 tasks in *ReachSafety-Arrays* compared to 2 from the previous years, which 2LS managed by chance)[1].

Still, there remains a number of limitations. The array domain is rather simple and cannot verify many array-manipulating programs. In addition, as we described earlier, the new unwinder cannot make use of incremental SAT solving efficiently.

5   Data-Availablitity Statement

2LS is publicly available from https://www.github.com/diffblue/2ls, under a BSD-style license. The competition version is based on version 0.9.6 and the archive used in the competition is available from https://doi.org/10.5281/zenodo.7467706 or from the collection of all verifiers and validators participating in SV-COMP 2023 [1].

References

1. Beyer, D.: Verifiers and validators of the 12th Intl. Competition on Software Verification (SV-COMP 2023). Zenodo (2023). https://doi.org/10.5281/zenodo.7627829
2. Brain, M., Joshi, S., Kroening, D., Schrammel, P.: Safety Verification and Refutation by k-Invariants and k-Induction. In: Proc. of SAS'15. LNCS, vol. 9291. Springer (2015)
3. Chen, H.Y., David, C., Kroening, D., Schrammel, P., Wachter, B.: Bit-Precise Procedure-Modular Termination Proofs. TOPLAS **40** (2017)
4. Clarke, E.M., Kroening, D., Lerda, F.: A Tool for Checking ANSI-C Programs. In: Proc. of TACAS'04. LNCS, vol. 2988. Springer (2004)
5. Cousot, P., Cousot, R., Logozzo, F.: A parametric segmentation functor for fully automatic and scalable array content analysis. In: Proceedings of the 38th. p. 105–118. POPL '11, Association for Computing Machinery, New York, NY, USA (2011). https://doi.org/10.1145/1926385.1926399
6. Malík, V., Hruška, M., Schrammel, P., Vojnar, T.: Template-Based Verification of Heap-Manipulating Programs. In: Proc. of FMCAD'18. IEEE (2018)
7. Malík, V., Martiček, Š., Schrammel, P., Srivas, M., Vojnar, T., Wahlang, J.: 2LS: Memory Safety and Non-termination (Competition Contrib.). In: Proc. of TACAS'18. Springer (2018)
8. Malík, V., Schrammel, P., Vojnar, T.: 2ls: Heap analysis and memory safety. In: Proc. of TACAS'20. pp. 368–372. Springer International Publishing (2020)
9. Nečas, F.: Program Loop Unwinding in the 2LS Framework. Bachelor's thesis, Brno University of Technology (2022), https://www.fit.vut.cz/study/thesis/24719/
10. Schrammel, P., Kroening, D.: 2LS for Program Analysis (Competition Contribution). In: Proc. of TACAS'16. LNCS, vol. 9636. Springer (2016)

---

[1] A number of tasks was last-minute disqualified from SV-COMP 2023 due to past-deadline changes which were often related to the tasks being added to new categories (e.g., *NoOverflows*) rather than actual modifications of the tasks or their verdicts. Hence, we present results from the entire benchmark instead of the (limited) competition benchmark set as those results are more representative and can be better compared to the previous year's results.

BUBAAK:
Runtime Monitoring of Program Verifiers*
(Competition Contribution)

Marek Chalupa$^{(\boxtimes)}$ [ID]** and Thomas A. Henzinger [ID]

Institute of Science and Technology Austria (ISTA), Klosterneuburg, Austria
mchalupa@ista.ac.at

Abstract. The main idea behind BUBAAK is to run multiple program analyses in parallel and use *runtime monitoring* and *enforcement* to observe and control their progress in real time. The analyses send information about (un)explored states of the program and discovered invariants to a *monitor*. The monitor processes the received data and can force an analysis to stop the search of certain program parts (which have already been analyzed by other analyses), or to make it utilize a program invariant found by another analysis.

At SV-COMP 2023, the implementation of data exchange between the monitor and the analyses was not yet completed, which is why BUBAAK only ran several analyses in parallel, without any coordination. Still, BUBAAK won the meta-category *FalsificationOverall* and placed very well in several other (sub)-categories of the competition.

1 Verification Approach

Runtime monitoring (RM) [1] is a lightweight approach to observing the executions of software systems and analyzing their behavior. The system, for simplicity take a single program, is executed and observed to obtain a *trace* of events. The observed events carry information about (a subset of) actions that have been performed by the program like accesses to memory, calls of functions, or writing a text to the standard output. The trace is analyzed by the *monitor* that outputs verdicts, be it verdicts about some correctness property of the program or, e.g., information about resource consumption. *Runtime enforcement* [12] goes a step further and allows the monitor to alter the behavior of the program upon seeing some event or detecting a certain (usually faulty) behavior of the program.

RM is traditionally applied as a complementary method to static analysis to find bugs in computer programs. In BUBAAK, we use RM to do monitoring and enforcement of the *verifiers* instead of the analyzed program itself. The verifiers are manually modified to emit events about their internal actions, for example, that they have reached some part of the analyzed code or that they have discovered an invariant. The monitor gathers and analyzes these events and can decide to command a verifier to stop a search of some parts of a program or to take into account an invariant found by another verifier.

---

* This work was supported by the ERC-2020-AdG 10102009 grant.
** Jury member

S. Sankaranarayanan and N. Sharygina (Eds.): TACAS 2023, LNCS 13994, pp. 535–540, 2023.
https://doi.org/10.1007/978-3-031-30820-8_32

2   BUBAAK at SV-COMP 2023

At SV-COMP 2023 [2], the verifiers that we used are based on *forward* and *backward symbolic execution*.

(Forward) symbolic execution (SE) [14] is well-known for being efficient in searching for bugs. It aims to explore every feasible execution path of the analyzed program by building the so-called *symbolic execution tree*. Such an approach must fail if the SE tree is infinite or very large, in which case we talk about the *path explosion problem*. There are ways how to *prune* the SE tree from paths that are known to exclude buggy behavior, e.g., using interpolation [13].

Backward symbolic execution (BSE) [11] is a form of SE that searches the program backwards from error locations towards the initial locations. It has been shown [11] that BSE is equivalent to *k-induction* [16], another popular but incomplete verification technique. The incompleteness of BSE (*k*-induction) is caused by the lack of information about reachable states. This deficiency can be tackled by providing (often trivial) invariants that supplement the missing information [5]. These invariants can be computed externally before running BSE, or they can be computed on the fly [5,4,11]. One of the on-the-fly methods is *loop folding* and the resulting technique is called BSELF [11].

SE and BSE(LF) are well suited for analyzing safety properties, but are not suited for analyzing the termination of programs. To analyse this property, we have developed a new algorithm that has not been published yet and that we dubbed *TIIP: termination with inductive invariants with progress*. This algorithm runs SE, searching for non-terminating executions by remembering and comparing program states visited at loop headers. At the same time, it tries to incrementally (using a procedure similar to loop folding) compute an *inductive invariant with progress* for each visited loop. This invariant, if found, gives a pre-condition for the loop termination.

At SV-COMP 2023, we run in parallel two SE instances and one BSELF instance when checking properties *unreach-call* and *no-overflow*, SE and TIIP when checking *termination*, and just SE for memory safety properties. Using multiple SE instances at the same time makes sense because we use different verifiers (see Section 3) and their SE implementations support different features.

Because all the algorithms that we use are based on symbolic execution, the enforcement done by the monitor would effectively do a pruning of SE and BSE trees. Unfortunately, we have not managed to sufficiently debug this pruning and therefore it was disabled in the competition. As a result, BUBAAK at SV-COMP 2023 only runs analyses in parallel without any coordination.

3   Software Architecture

The high-level scheme of BUBAAK for SV-COMP 2023 is shown in Figure 1. BUBAAK takes as input C files and the property file. Internally, it compiles and links the input files into a single LLVM bitcode file [7] which is also instrumented using UBSAN sanitizer [18] if the checked property is *no-overflow*. Then, verifiers are spawned according to the given property. All verifiers run in parallel

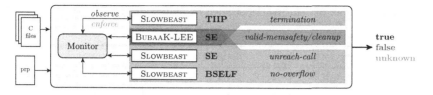

Fig. 1. The setup of BUBAAK at SV-COMP 2023. The colors indicate the properties that were checked by the different tools and algorithms.

(when there is more of them). At SV-COMP 2023, we used SLOWBEAST for SE, BSELF, and TIIP, and BUBAAK-LEE as another instance of SE[1].

SLOWBEAST [17] is a symbolic executor written in Python. It supports checking properties *unreach-call* and *no-verflow* with SE, BSE, and BSELF, and *termination* with TIIP. The tool has no or only a very limited support for properties *no-data-race*, *valid-memsafety*, and *valid-memcleanup*.

BUBAAK-LEE is a fork of symbolic executor KLEE [9] which is implemented in C++ and the current version is a merge of the upstream KLEE and JETKLEE (the fork of KLEE used in the tool SYMBIOTIC [10]) with additional modifications. These modifications mostly concern modeling standard C functions but include also partial support for 128-bit wide integers and support for global variables with external linkage. BUBAAK-LEE implements SE without any SE tree pruning and can check for all SV-COMP properties except for *no-data-race*.

Both symbolic executors use Z3 [15] as the SMT solver. The features they support differ significantly, though. For example, SLOWBEAST supports, apart from BSE(LF) and TIIP, symbolic floating-point computations, threaded programs, and incremental solving, while it does not support symbolic pointers and addresses which are features supported by BUBAAK-LEE.

The monitor is currently a part of the control scripts written in Python and at SV-COMP 2023 it monitors only the standard (error) output of the tools as monitoring anything else is redundant until the implementation of data exchange between verifiers and the monitor is finished. The only enforcement that it does at SV-COMP 2023 is terminating the analysis entirely.

Differences to SYMBIOTIC The tool SYMBIOTIC [10] also uses SLOWBEAST and a fork of KLEE, and therefore a discussion on differences between BUBAAK and SYMBIOTIC is in place. The version of SLOWBEAST used in SYMBIOTIC is outdated while BUBAAK uses the most up-to-date version (at the time of writing the paper) where a substantial part of the code has been rewritten and that contains new features including the implementation of TIIP. The relation between BUBAAK-LEE and JETKLEE is mentioned earlier in this section.

Other differences between BUBAAK and SYMBIOTIC exist: BUBAAK does not use any pre-analyses, slicing, and instrumentation (apart from the instrumenta-

---

[1] Because these verifiers do not compete at SV-COMP 2023 on their own, this does not make BUBAAK a meta-verifier.

Table 1. Number of benchmarks decided by individual verifiers per property.

Property	Total	BUBAAK-LEE	SLOWBEAST
unreach-call	3263	2952	311
valid-memsafety/cleanup	3401	3401	0
termination	1417	739	678
no-overflow	4716	4399	317

tion by UBSAN for the property *no-overflow*, but there SYMBIOTIC uses its own instrumentation), and it runs the verifiers in parallel, while SYMBIOTIC uses a sequential composition [10].

4   Strengths and Weaknesses

The combination of SE and BSELF has been previously shown to be promising [11] because SE can quickly analyse many programs and BSELF then solves hard safe instances were SE found no bug or was unable to enumerate all paths. Running TIIP in parallel with pure SE has similar advantages. Still, all of SE, BSELF, and TIIP can be computationally very demanding as the number of executions they must search may be enormous and/or their exploration may involve lots of non-trivial queries to the SMT solver.

Running multiple verifiers in parallel reduces the wall-time while eating CPU time rapidly, which may be a disadvantage in SV-COMP. A remedy for this should be finishing the data exchange support between verifiers, which will allow to avoid burning CPU time on duplicate tasks.

5   Results of BUBAAK at SV-COMP 2023

The results of BUBAAK were highly influenced by bugs in the implementation. The tool had 41 wrong answers, 31 of these caused by a mistake in parsing of the output of BUBAAK-LEE (25 for the property *valid-memcleanup* and 6 for the property *termination*). The rest of wrong answers (10) were caused by miscellaneous bugs. After normalizing scores, these 41 wrong answers resulted in loosing almost 10000 points in the overall score.

Also, BSELF did not decide a single benchmark because of a mistake in command line arguments when invoking it. Therefore, running SLOWBEAST was useful mainly in the category *Termination* where TIIP was able to solve roughly half of the decided benchmarks (in the rest of cases, BUBAAK-LEE successfully enumerated all execution paths). The numbers of decided benchmarks are summarized in Table 1.

Overall, BUBAAK won the category *Falsification-Overall* which confirms that SE is very good in finding bugs. The tool also scored silver in the category *SoftwareSystems* where it was also the leading tool in several sub-categories.

Data Availability Statement. The version of BUBAAK that competed at SV-COMP 2023 is available at Zenodo [3,6]. The source code of BUBAAK is available at github [8].

References

1. Bartocci, E., Falcone, Y., Francalanza, A., Reger, G.: Introduction to runtime verification. In: RV'18, pp. 1–33. Springer International Publishing (2018). https://doi.org/10.1007/978-3-319-75632-5_1
2. Beyer, D.: Competition on software verification and witness validation: SV-COMP 2023. In: Proc. TACAS (2). LNCS , Springer (2023)
3. Beyer, D.: Verifiers and validators of the 12th Intl. Competition on Software Verification (SV-COMP 2023). Zenodo (2023). https://doi.org/10.5281/zenodo.7627829
4. Beyer, D., Dangl, M.: Software verification with PDR: an implementation of the state of the art. In: TACAS'20. LNCS, vol. 12078, pp. 3–21. Springer (2020). https://doi.org/10.1007/978-3-030-45190-5_1
5. Beyer, D., Dangl, M., Wendler, P.: Boosting k-induction with continuously-refined invariants. In: CAV'15. LNCS, vol. 9206, pp. 622–640. Springer (2015). https://doi.org/10.1007/978-3-319-21690-4_42
6. BUBAAK artifact. Zenodo (2022). https://doi.org/10.5281/zenodo.7468631
7. LLVM. https://llvm.org, accessed 2023-02-17
8. BUBAAK repository. https://gitlab.com/mchalupa/bubaak (2022)
9. Cadar, C., Dunbar, D., Engler, D.R.: KLEE: Unassisted and automatic generation of high-coverage tests for complex systems programs. In: OSDI'08. pp. 209–224. USENIX Association (2008), http://www.usenix.org/events/osdi08/tech/full_papers/cadar/cadar.pdf
10. Chalupa, M., Mihalkovič, V., Řechtáčková, A., Zaoral, L., Strejček, J.: Symbiotic 9: String analysis and backward symbolic execution with loop folding - (competition contribution). In: TACAS'22. LNCS, vol. 13244, pp. 462–467. Springer (2022). https://doi.org/10.1007/978-3-030-99527-0_32
11. Chalupa, M., Strejček, J.: Backward symbolic execution with loop folding. In: SAS'21. LNCS, vol. 12913, pp. 49–76. Springer (2021). https://doi.org/10.1007/978-3-030-88806-0_3
12. Falcone, Y., Mariani, L., Rollet, A., Saha, S.: Runtime failure prevention and reaction. In: Lectures on Runtime Verification - Introductory and Advanced Topics, LNCS, vol. 10457, pp. 103–134. Springer (2018). https://doi.org/10.1007/978-3-319-75632-5_4
13. Jaffar, J., Navas, J.A., Santosa, A.E.: Unbounded symbolic execution for program verification. In: Runtime Verification, pp. 396–411. Springer (2012). https://doi.org/10.1007/978-3-642-29860-8_32
14. King, J.C.: Symbolic execution and program testing. Communications of ACM 19(7), 385–394 (1976). https://doi.org/10.1145/360248.360252
15. de Moura, L.M., Bjørner, N.: Z3: an efficient SMT solver. In: TACAS'08. LNCS, vol. 4963, pp. 337–340. Springer (2008). https://doi.org/10.1007/978-3-540-78800-3_24
16. Sheeran, M., Singh, S., Stålmarck, G.: Checking safety properties using induction and a SAT-solver. In: FMCAD'00. LNCS, vol. 1954, pp. 108–125. Springer (2000). https://doi.org/10.1007/3-540-40922-X_8
17. SLOWBEAST repository. https://gitlab.com/mchalupa/slowbeast (2022)
18. UBSan, https://clang.llvm.org/docs/UndefinedBehaviorSanitizer.html, accessed 2023-02-17

EBF 4.2: Black-Box Cooperative Verification for Concurrent Programs

(Competition Contribution)

Fatimah Aljaafari[1,2](✉), Fedor Shmarov [1], Edoardo Manino [1],
Rafael Menezes [1], and Lucas C. Cordeiro [1]

[1] Department of Computer Science, The University of Manchester, Manchester M13 9PL, UK
fatimahaljaafari@gmail.com
[2] Department of Computer Networks & Communications, CCSIT, King Faisal University,
Al Hassa 31982, SA

Abstract. Combining different verification and testing techniques together could, at least in theory, achieve better results than each individual one on its own. The challenge in doing so is how to take advantage of the strengths of each technique while compensating for their weaknesses. *EBF* 4.2 addresses this challenge for concurrency vulnerabilities by creating Ensembles of Bounded model checkers and gray-box Fuzzers. In contrast with portfolios, which simply run all possible techniques in parallel, *EBF* strives to obtain closer cooperation between them. This goal is achieved in a black-box fashion. On the one hand, the model checkers are forced to provide seeds to the fuzzers by injecting additional vulnerabilities in the program under test. On the other hand, off-the-shelf fuzzers are forced to explore different interleavings by adding lightweight instrumentation and systematically re-seeding them.

1 Overview

Finding vulnerabilities in concurrent programs presents the combined challenge of exploring the search space of program inputs and execution schedules, or *interleavings*. Recently, there have been attempts at solving complex verification problems by combining different techniques into hybrid verification tools [1,2,3].

More generally, these attempts belong to a larger trend in automated software analysis called *cooperative verification* [4,5]. In this paradigm, the main idea is implementing some form of communication interface between different tools (i.e., a common information exchange format), which allows the exchange of partial results (artifacts). In this way, we can harness the strengths of multiple verification techniques and solve more complex problems [6,7,8].

In *EBF* [9], we are the first to implement a cooperative approach that combines Bounded Model Checking (BMC) and concurrency-aware Gray-Box Fuzzing (GBF) for finding vulnerabilities in concurrent C programs. In order to simplify the communication interface between the cooperating tools, we adopt a *black-box* design philosophy where verification artifacts are implicitly shared via appropriate transformation and instrumentation of the program under test (PUT). The advantage of this design philosophy is its universality: in fact, *EBF* can incorporate any BMC or GBF tool that takes a C program as input.

S. Sankaranarayanan and N. Sharygina (Eds.): TACAS 2023, LNCS 13994, pp. 541–546, 2023.
https://doi.org/10.1007/978-3-031-30820-8_33

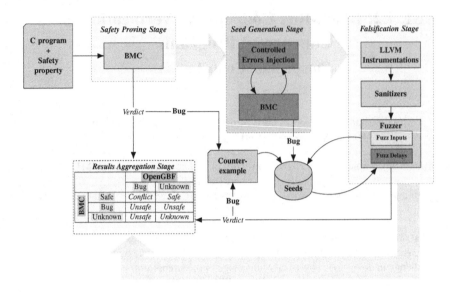

Fig. 1: The workflow of *EBF 4.2* comprises four stages (dashed rectangles). The safety proving and seed generation stages use a BMC tool. The falsification stage uses our *OpenGBF* tool. The result aggregation stage generates a verification verdict and counter-example (if any). Areas of improvement over *EBF 4.0* [9] are shown in blue.

More specifically, *EBF 4.2* expands the cooperative verification capabilities of previous versions of *EBF*. First, we introduce a new seed generation module for the GBF. This module works by injecting additional vulnerabilities in critical areas of the PUT, and then using a BMC engine to generate program inputs that trigger them. These inputs represent higher quality seeds for the fuzzer than randomly-generated ones. Second, we propose an improved light-weight instrumentation based on the Clang/LLVM toolchain that turns any compatible off-the-shelf GBF into a concurrency-aware fuzzer. We do so by injecting fuzzer-controlled delays in the PUT, which implicitly force the exploration of different interleavings.

2   Architecture

Figure 1 illustrates the workflow of *EBF*, which comprises four verification stages: safety proving, seed generation, falsification and results aggregation. Each of these stages take a concurrent C program and a given safety property as an input.

Safety Proving Stage. During this stage, *EBF* calls the BMC engine with the given inputs. The BMC tool produces one of the three possible *verdicts*: *Safe* if the model checker deems the PUT safe with respect to the given property, *Bug* if a vulnerability is detected, or *Unknown* encompassing a variety of different outcomes including reaching a timeout, running out of memory, or crashing unexpectedly. If the BMC tool finds a bug, it generates a counter-example – a sequence of program inputs and a thread schedule leading to the vulnerability. The input values are stored for later use as a seed.

Seed Generation Stage. This is a new feature of *EBF 4.2*, which harnesses the strength of BMC in resolving complex path conditions. For instance, the branch `if (x*x -2*x +1 == 0)` may be extremely difficult for the fuzzer to explore. *EBF* tackles this issue by repeatedly injecting the error statement `assert(0)` in each conditional branch of the PUT (similar to the approach in [2]). Then, each transformed program (which contains one unique error statement) is independently verified with the BMC tool. If the BMC reaches the error within a timeout, *EBF* converts the resulting counter-example into a fuzzing seed. The seed generation process continues until all injected errors have been detected or the stage timeout has been reached. The seeds we collect during this stage greatly improve the fuzzer performance in the next stage.

Falsification Stage. During this stage, *EBF* checks whether the PUT contains any vulnerabilities by fuzzing its inputs and thread interleavings. Due to the current lack of open-source GBF tools for concurrent programs [9], *EBF* uses our own concurrency-aware gray-box fuzzer *OpenGBF*. Its implementation extends *AFL++*, a state-of-the-art GBF for single-threaded programs, by introducing the following concurrency-aware lightweight instrumentation in the PUT.

First, *OpenGBF* injects delays after each instruction at the *LLVM* intermediate representation level. The value of these delays (typically several micro-seconds) is controlled by the fuzzer and implicitly forces the execution of different thread interleavings. Second, *OpenGBF* inserts functions for recording all the information needed for witness generation: assumption values, thread ID, variable names, and function names. Third, *OpenGBF* supports the use of *UndefinedBehaviorSanitizer* [10], *AddressSanitizer* [11] and *ThreadSanitizer* [12] for the detection of vulnerabilities that cannot be expressed as reachability errors (e.g., buffer overflows, thread leaks).

Results Aggregation Stage. Finally, *EBF* aggregates the outcomes of the *Safety Proving* and the *Falsification* stages as depicted in the table in Fig. 1. The majority of cases are straightforward: if one of the tools produces an inconclusive verdict (i.e., *Unknown*), then *EBF* relies on the decision provided by the other tool. However, if *OpenGBF* finds a bug in the PUT that is deemed to be safe by BMC, *EBF* reports a *Conflict*. In this case extra information can be obtained from the counter-example produced by the fuzzer.

3 Strengths and Weaknesses

EBF 4.2 participated in the *ConcurrencySafety* category of *SV-COMP 2023*, which comprises four subcategories: *ConcurrencySafety-Main, NoDataRace-Main, ConcurrencySafety-NoOverflows* and *ConcurrencySafety-MemSafety*.

Regarding the *ConcurrencySafety-Main* subcategory, *EBF 4.2* provided 357 correct results out of 692, with only 1 incorrect false and the rest unknown. More in detail, *EBF* correctly identified 67 safe benchmarks and 249 unsafe benchmarks, thus highlighting the *EBF* strengths in bug-finding. In addition, *EBF* labeled an extra 41 benchmarks as unsafe, which were not confirmed by the witness validator. Among these benchmarks, there are 10 verification tasks (beginning with *goblint-regression/28-race_reach_**) where only two tools can find bugs: *EBF* and *Infer* [13]. At the same time, we hypothesise that the counter-examples provided by *EBF* are more trustworthy than those provided by *Infer* for these 10 tasks. This is because *EBF* is very conservative in its bug-finding claims, with 290 correct false outcomes, 41 unconfirmed, and only 1 incorrect. In contrast, *Infer* produces 330 correct false outcomes and 331 incorrect ones.

Regarding the *NoDataRace-Main* subcategory, *EBF 4.2* only offered partial support for data race detection by enabling *ThreadSanitizer* inside *OpenGBF*. Unfortunately, the BMC engine we used in this year's competition, *ESBMC*, does not yet maintain full support of this safety property. As a consequence, *EBF* provided only 199 correct verification verdicts out of 904, of which 112 were correct true and 87 correct false. At the same time, *EBF* also reported 46 incorrect verdicts (23 incorrect true and 23 incorrect false), which resulted in a negative score for this subcategory.

Regarding the *ConcurrencySafety-NoOverflows* and *ConcurrencySafety-MemSafety* subcategories, *EBF 4.2* did provide support for detecting arithmetic overflows and memory safety violations by enabling *UndefinedBehaviorSanitizer* and *AddressSanitizer*. However, we did not succeed in providing an implementation that was compliant with the competition standards in time.

As a result, *EBF* did not feature in these subcategories.

4   Tool Setup and Configuration

In order to use *EBF*[3], the user must set the architecture (32 or 64-bit) with flag −a, the property file path with flag −p, the benchmark file paths, and run the following command from the *EBF* root directory:

```
./scripts/RunEBF.py [-h]  [-a {32,64}]  [-p PROPERTY_FILE]
                                [benchmark]
```

Furthermore, there are optional flags that can be enabled (e.g., set the time and memory limit for each engine). In SV-COMP 2023 we divided the allotted 15 minutes of CPU time per verification task across the verification stages inside *EBF 4.2* as follows: $400s$ for the safety proving stage, $120s$ for the seed generation stage, $240s$ for the falsification stage, and the remaining $140s$ were allocated for the results aggregation, counter-example generation and potential execution overheads.

5   Software Project

We released *EBF* 4.2 under the MIT License, and its code is publicly available on GitHub[4]. All dependencies and installation instructions are listed in the repository README.md.

---

[3] https://gitlab.com/sosy-lab/sv-comp/archives-2023/-/blob/main/2023/ebf.zip

[4] https://github.com/fatimahkj/EBF

Data-Availability Statement

The tool and all necessary files are available on Zenodo [14][15].

Acknowledgment

The authors would like to thank Dr. Mustafa A. Mustafa for his constant support. The work in this paper is partially funded by the Engineering and Physical Sciences Research Council (EPSRC) grants EP/T026995/1, EP/V000497/1, EU H2020 ELEGANT 957286, and Soteria project awarded by the UK Research and Innovation for the Digital Security by Design (DSbD) Programme.

References

1. Ognawala, S., Hutzelmann, T., Psallida, E., Pretschner, A.: Improving function coverage with munch: A hybrid fuzzing and directed symbolic execution approach. In: SAC. (2018) 1475–1482
2. Alshmrany, K.M., Menezes, R.S., Gadelha, M.R., Cordeiro, L.C.: Fusebmc: A white-box fuzzer for finding security vulnerabilities in c programs. FASE (2020)
3. Chowdhury, A.B., Medicherla, R.K., Venkatesh, R.: Verifuzz: Program aware fuzzing. In: International Conference on Tools and Algorithms for the Construction and Analysis of Systems, Springer, Cham (2019) 244–249
4. Beyer, D., Wehrheim, H.: Verification artifacts in cooperative verification: Survey and unifying component framework. In Margaria, T., Steffen, B., eds.: Leveraging Applications of Formal Methods, Verification and Validation: Verification Principles, Cham, Springer International Publishing (2020) 143–167
5. Beyer, D., Spiessl, M., Umbricht, S.: Cooperation between automatic and interactive software verifiers. In Schlingloff, B.H., Chai, M., eds.: Software Engineering and Formal Methods, Cham, Springer International Publishing (2022) 111–128
6. Stephens, N., Grosen, J., Salls, C., Dutcher, A., Wang, R., Corbetta, J., Shoshitaishvili, Y., Kruegel, C., Vigna, G.: Driller: Augmenting fuzzing through selective symbolic execution. In: NDSS. Volume 16. (2016) 1–16
7. Yun, I., Lee, S., Xu, M., Jang, Y., Kim, T.: {QSYM}: A practical concolic execution engine tailored for hybrid fuzzing. In: USENIX). (2018) 745–761
8. Li, J., Zhao, B., Zhang, C.: Fuzzing: a survey. Cybersecurity 1(1) (2018) 1–13
9. Aljaafari, F.K., Menezes, R., Manino, E., Shmarov, F., Mustafa, M.A., Cordeiro, L.C.: Combining bmc and fuzzing techniques for finding software vulnerabilities in concurrent programs. IEEE Access 10 (2022) 121365–121384
10. Zannoni, E.: Improving application security with undefinedbehaviorsanitizer (ubsan) and gcc. Accessed: 2022-11-01.
11. Serebryany, K., Bruening, D., Potapenko, A., Vyukov, D.: Addresssanitizer: A fast address sanity checker. In: USENIX, USA (2012) 28
12. Serebryany, K., Iskhodzhanov, T.: Threadsanitizer: Data race detection in practice. In: WBIA. (2009) 62–71
13. Kettl, M., Lemberger, T.: The static analyzer Infer in SV-COMP (competition contribution). In: Proc. TACAS (2). LNCS 13244, Springer (2022) 451–456
14. Aljaafari, F.: Ebf a participated version in sv-comp 2023. Zenodo (2023)
15. Beyer, D.: Verifiers and validators of the 12th Intl. Competition on Software Verification (SV-COMP 2023). Zenodo (2023)

GOBLINT: Autotuning Thread-Modular Abstract Interpretation
(Competition Contribution)

Simmo Saan[1]([envelope])[*][ORCID], Michael Schwarz[2][ORCID], Julian Erhard[2][ORCID],
Manuel Pietsch[2], Helmut Seidl[2][ORCID], Sarah Tilscher[2], and Vesal Vojdani[1][ORCID]

[1] University of Tartu, Tartu, Estonia
{simmo.saan,vesal.vojdani}@ut.ee
[2] Technische Universität München, Garching, Germany
{m.schwarz,julian.erhard,m.pietsch,helmut.seidl,sarah.tilscher}@tum.de

Abstract. The static analyzer GOBLINT is dedicated to the analysis
of multi-threaded C programs by abstract interpretation. It provides
multiple techniques for increasing analysis precision, e.g., configurable
context-sensitivity and a wide range of numerical analyses. As a rule
of thumb, more precise analyses decrease scalability, while not always
necessary for solving the task at hand. Therefore, GOBLINT has been
enhanced with *autotuning* which, based on syntactical criteria, adapts
analysis configuration to the given program such that *relevant* precision
is obtained with acceptable effort.

1 Verification Approach

GOBLINT is a static analysis framework for C programs based on abstract interpretation [6]. It features scalable thread-modular analysis of concurrent programs on top of flow- and context-sensitive interprocedural analysis. The analysis
is specified as a side-effecting constraint system [2], which can conveniently express flow-insensitive invariants as well as flow-sensitive information per program
point [16] and is solved using a local generic solver [15]. Here, we detail some
recent SV-COMP–related advances in GOBLINT. The previous competition tool
paper [11] provides further details on the general approach.

New abstract domains have been added to enhance precision. In addition to
interval analysis of integer variables, GOBLINT now performs interval analysis of
floating-point variables following Miné [9], and maintains congruence information [7]. Furthermore, the APRON library [8] has been integrated for relational
analysis. GOBLINT includes novel approaches to relational analysis of concurrent
programs [14], inferring relations between jointly-protected global variables.

In the previous tool paper, we suggested dynamically tailoring GOBLINT to
the program under analysis. This can increase precision, by activating analyses
that are more expensive yet offer crucial precision, and also decrease resource

---

[*] Jury member

© The Author(s) 2023
S. Sankaranarayanan and N. Sharygina (Eds.): TACAS 2023, LNCS 13994, pp. 547–552, 2023.
https://doi.org/10.1007/978-3-031-30820-8_34

usage, by deactivating redundant analyses. To this end, we have implemented analysis configuration *autotuning* based on cheap *syntactic* heuristics on the program, before the analysis begins. The particular features have been chosen according to how expert users might configure GOBLINT for a given program. Measurements of program size (e.g. number of functions, loops, variables) are taken into account to limit slowdown on larger programs.

GOBLINT provides a multitude of concurrency-related analyses (e.g. races, symbolic locking patterns, thread joins [14, 16]) that have no use in single-threaded programs which abound in SV-COMP. Hence, all such analyses are now automatically deactivated for programs that never create any threads.

GOBLINT implements a wide variety of numerical abstract domains, but most are not necessary for every program, thus, offering many possibilities for auto-tuning. Interval information is omitted in calling contexts of recursive functions to avoid an explosion of contexts in which they are to be analyzed. While the congruence domain is generally active on small programs, for medium-sized programs it is only enabled for functions involving the modulo operator, either directly or indirectly (up to fixed depth in the call stack). If the program uses enums, then an integer domain for sets of enumeration values is activated. Octagon analysis is enabled for those local variables which occur most often in linear expressions and conditions. Interval and octagon widening thresholds are extracted from conditional expressions containing constants. Such thresholds are especially useful for flow-insensitive analysis of global variables in multi-threaded programs, since no narrowing is performed on flow-insensitive invariants.

Loop unrolling is a well-known technique to increase the precision of static analysis. GOBLINT now unrolls loops up to their static bounds or feasible unrolled code size. Loops which contain memory allocation, thread creation, or error function calls, are prioritized since unique heap locations and threads are key to maintaining analysis precision.

Schwarz et al. [13] enhanced GOBLINT with a suite of concurrent value analyses and evaluated their precision. Following their observations, we use the cheap yet sufficiently precise *Protection-Based Reading*. Data-race detection was made more precise using *may-happen-in-parallel* analysis [14], to filter out spurious races with threads that have already been joined or have not yet been created.

2   Software Architecture

GOBLINT is implemented in OCAML and uses an updated fork of CIL [10] as its parser frontend for the C language. It depends on APRON [8] for relational analyses. No other major libraries or external tools are required.

GOBLINT employs a modular architecture [1] where a combination of analyses can be selected at runtime. Analyses are defined through their abstract domains and transfer functions, which can communicate with other analyses using predefined queries and events. The combined analyses together with the control-flow graphs of the functions yield a side-effecting constraint system [2], which is solved using a local generic solver [15]. The solution is post-processed to determine the verdict and construct a witness.

3   Strengths and Weaknesses

GOBLINT focuses on *sound* static analysis which is confirmed by the competition: our tool does not produce any incorrect results. A major limitation of our approach is that, due to over-approximation, the tool can only prove the absence of bugs, but not their presence. Thus, when GOBLINT flags a potential violation, it answers "unknown" in the competition.

In SV-COMP 2023, *NoDataRace* became an official category and existing *ConcurrencySafety* reachability tasks were newly included into it. This is where GOBLINT really shines: it proves 652 out of 783 programs race-free, thereby winning the category. Overall, the strengths and weaknesses of GOBLINT w.r.t. categories remain the same as described in our previous tool paper. Therefore, we describe here the impact of autotuning, based on our own preliminary comparative evaluation. Unlike official SV-COMP evaluation, we used a 1 GB memory limit, which is sufficient for most tasks GOBLINT can solve, and no witness validators.

As noted above, the majority of SV-COMP programs across all categories are single-threaded, thus, the greatest improvement comes from disabling all concurrency analyses in those cases. This yields a notable reduction in runtime and memory usage as shown in table 1, improving overall efficiency without compromising precision.

The second greatest improvement is due to the use of relational analysis with octagons. Although this incurs a runtime penalty, it increases the number of correct verdicts notably. The improvement is especially visible in *NoOverflows*, where it yields 104 additional correct results. We also confirmed that the automatic selection of octagon variables is better than tracking all variables: our selection yields more correct verdicts (due to fewer timeouts) while successfully avoiding an unnecessarily large performance penalty.

Autotuning along the other axes is not as impactful. Nevertheless, each leads to GOBLINT being able to solve tasks it could not otherwise. Hence, a small increase in score is achieved, justifying their use. Although disabling unnecessary

Table 1. Reduction in resource usage due to disabling all concurrency analyses for single-threaded programs, as reported by BENCHEXEC using ordinary least squares (OLS) regression.

Tasks	unreach-call		no-overflows	
	CPU time	Memory	CPU time	Memory
Correct only	16%	4%	5%	0%
All	5%	8%	16%	6%

concurrency analyses reduces resource usage, overall this performance improvement is canceled out by the simultaneous use of expensive analyses enabled by autotuning, such as octagons. Thus, GOBLINT can solve more tasks while retaining the same level of overall efficiency observed in previous editions of the competition [3].

Many future opportunities for autotuning exist: GOBLINT implements a number of concurrent value analyses offering different tradeoffs between time and precision [13, 14], but only used the fastest and least precise of these in SV-COMP. If appropriate heuristics for using the more involved analyses are identified, autotuning could enable these when they are likely to yield a benefit. Autotuning could be extended to supply a sequence of configurations, increasing in precision, for a portfolio of analyses, instead of relying on the autotuning to immediately pick the most appropriate configuration. While the current autotuning in GOBLINT is hand-crafted, machine learning may provide additional improvements.

4   Tool Setup and Configuration

GOBLINT version `svcomp23-0-g4f5dcf38f` participated in SV-COMP 2023 [4, 12]. It is available in both binary (Ubuntu 22.04) and source code form at our GitHub repository under the `svcomp23` tag.[3] The only runtime dependency is APRON [8]. Instructions for building from source can be found in the README.

Both the tool-info module and the benchmark definition for SV-COMP are named `goblint`. They correspond to running the tool as follows:

```
./goblint --conf conf/svcomp23.json \
          --set ana.specification property.prp input.c
```

GOBLINT participated in the following categories: *ReachSafety, Concurrency-Safety, NoOverflows, SoftwareSystems* and *Overall*, while opting-out from *MemSafety, Termination* and *SoftwareSystems-*-MemSafety*.

5   Software Project and Contributors

GOBLINT development takes place on GitHub,[4] while related publications are listed on its website.[5] It is an MIT-licensed joint project of the Technische Universität München (Chair of Formal Languages, Compiler Construction, Software Construction) and University of Tartu (Laboratory for Software Science).

Acknowledgements. This work was supported by Deutsche Forschungsgemeinschaft (DFG) – 378803395/2428 CONVEY and the Estonian Centre of Excellence in IT (EXCITE), funded by the European Regional Development Fund. We would like to thank everyone who has contributed to GOBLINT over the years, especially the students who contributed various autotunable analyses.

---

[3] https://github.com/goblint/analyzer/releases/tag/svcomp23
[4] https://github.com/goblint/analyzer
[5] https://goblint.in.tum.de

Data Availability. All data of SV-COMP 2023 are archived as described in the competition report [4] and available on the competition web site. This includes the verification tasks, results, witnesses, scripts, and instructions for reproduction. The version of Goblint as used in the competition is archived together with other participating tools [5] and individually [12] on Zenodo.

Bibliography

[1] Apinis, K.: Frameworks for analyzing multi-threaded C. Ph.D. thesis, Technische Universität München (2014)

[2] Apinis, K., Seidl, H., Vojdani, V.: Side-Effecting Constraint Systems: A Swiss Army Knife for Program Analysis. In: APLAS '12, pp. 157–172, Springer (2012), DOI: 10.1007/978-3-642-35182-2_12

[3] Beyer, D.: Progress on software verification: SV-COMP 2022. In: TACAS '22, pp. 375–402, Springer (2022), DOI: 10.1007/978-3-030-99527-0_20

[4] Beyer, D.: Competition on software verification and witness validation: SV-COMP 2023. In: Proc. TACAS (2), LNCS , Springer (2023)

[5] Beyer, D.: Verifiers and validators of the 12th Intl. Competition on Software Verification (SV-COMP 2023). Zenodo (2023), DOI: 10.5281/zenodo.7627829

[6] Cousot, P., Cousot, R.: Abstract interpretation: a unified lattice model for static analysis of programs by construction or approximation of fixpoints. In: POPL '77, pp. 238–252 (1977), DOI: 10.1145/512950.512973

[7] Granger, P.: Static analysis of arithmetical congruences. International Journal of Computer Mathematics **30**(3-4), 165–190 (1989), DOI: 10.1080/00207168908803778

[8] Jeannet, B., Miné, A.: APRON: A library of numerical abstract domains for static analysis. In: CAV '09, pp. 661–667 (2009), DOI: 10.1007/978-3-642-02658-4_52

[9] Miné, A.: Relational abstract domains for the detection of floating-point run-time errors. In: ESOP '04, pp. 3–17, Springer (2004), DOI: 10.1007/978-3-540-24725-8_2

[10] Necula, G.C., McPeak, S., Rahul, S.P., Weimer, W.: CIL: Intermediate language and tools for analysis and transformation of C programs. In: CC '02, pp. 213–228, Springer (2002), DOI: 10.1007/3-540-45937-5_16

[11] Saan, S., Schwarz, M., Apinis, K., Erhard, J., Seidl, H., Vogler, R., Vojdani, V.: Goblint: Thread-modular abstract interpretation using side-effecting constraints. In: TACAS '21, pp. 438–442 (2021), DOI: 10.1007/978-3-030-72013-1_28

[12] Saan, S., Schwarz, M., Erhard, J., Pietsch, M., Seidl, H., Tilscher, S., Vojdani, V.: Goblint at SV-COMP 2023 (Nov 2022), DOI: 10.5281/zenodo.7467093, tool artifact

[13] Schwarz, M., Saan, S., Seidl, H., Apinis, K., Erhard, J., Vojdani, V.: Improving thread-modular abstract interpretation. In: SAS '21, pp. 359–383, Springer (2021), DOI: 10.1007/978-3-030-88806-0_18

[14] Schwarz, M., Saan, S., Seidl, H., Erhard, J., Vojdani, V.: Clustered relational thread-modular abstract interpretation with local traces. In: ESOP '23, Springer (2023)

[15] Seidl, H., Vogler, R.: Three improvements to the top-down solver. Mathematical Structures in Computer Science p. 1–45 (2022), DOI: 10.1017/S0960129521000499

[16] Vojdani, V., Apinis, K., Rõtov, V., Seidl, H., Vene, V., Vogler, R.: Static Race Detection for Device Drivers: The Goblint Approach. In: ASE '16, pp. 391–402, ACM (2016), DOI: 10.1145/2970276.2970337

Java Ranger: Supporting String and Array Operations in Java Ranger (Competition Contribution)⋆

⋆⋆Soha Hussein⋆ ⋆ ⋆[1](✉) ⓘ, Qiuchen Yan[1](✉), Stephen McCamant[1](✉),
Vaibhav Sharma[1](✉) ⓘ, and Michael W. Whalen[1](✉) ⓘ

University of Minnesota, Minneapolis, MN, USA
{soha,yanxx297,smccaman,vaibhav,mwwhalen}@umn.edu

Abstract. Java Ranger is a path-merging tool for Java Programs. It identifies branching regions of code and summarizes them by generating a disjunctive logical constraint that describes the behavior of the code region. Previously, Java Ranger showed that a reduction of 70% of execution paths is possible when used to merge branching regions of code that support numeric constraints.

In this paper, we describe the support of two additional features since participation in SV-COMP 2020: symbolic array and symbolic string operations. Finally, we present a preliminary evaluation of the effect of the structure of the disjunctive constraint on the solver's performance. Results suggest that certain constraint structures can speed up the performance of Java Ranger.

1 Introduction

Path-merging [1,7,8] is a technique that speeds up the execution of Dynamic Symbolic Execution (DSE) by collapsing paths within code regions into a disjunctive logical constraint. Java Ranger (JR) [12] is a path-merging tool for Java Programs. It summarizes symbolic branches during execution. JR generates the disjunctive logical constraint for a code region predicated on a symbolic branch by using a sequence of transformations. For example, JR alternates between substituting values for local variables in its summary and inlining method summaries to eliminate dynamically dispatched method invocations. See [11] for more information.

2 Path Merging Extensions and Results

Despite handling many of the Java language features, in SV-COMP 2020 [10] JR did not support symbolically executing string functions. It also did not sum-

---

⋆ The research described in this paper has been supported in part by the National Science Foundation under grant 1563920, and Google Summer of Code.

⋆⋆ Jury member

⋆ Lecturer on a Leave of Absence Ain Shams University, Cairo, Egypt
soha.hussien@cis.asu.edu.eg

S. Sankaranarayanan and N. Sharygina (Eds.): TACAS 2023, LNCS 13994, pp. 553–558, 2023.
https://doi.org/10.1007/978-3-031-30820-8_35

marize `arrayload` and `arraystore` statements that exist outside a code region predicated on a symbolic branch. For example, if a and i are symbolic integers, JR could summarize a region of the form: $if(a)$ $\{myval = arr[i]...\}$ But not: $myval = arr[i]$. More precisely, the newly introduced features to JR include:

1. **Summarizing Array Creation of Symbolic Size**: to support the creation of symbolic-sized single and multi-dimensional arrays, we bound the symbolic size to several values, and we executed the program on each concrete value.
2. **Summarizing ArrayLoad and ArrayStore**: to support the arrayload and the arraystore of a symbolic index, we create a disjunctive constraint that describes possible valuations. This constraint is then pushed on the path condition. For example: for a symbolic index i and an array arr of size 3, we encode arrayload of the form $myval = arr[i]$ as

$$myval := \text{ite}(i == 0, arr[0], \text{ite}(i == 1, arr[1], arr[2]))$$

Similarly, we encode the arraystore of the form $arr[i] = myval$ as

$$arr[0]_{new} := \text{ite}(i == 0, myval, arr[0]_{old})$$
$$\wedge \ arr[1]_{new} := \text{ite}(i == 1, myval, arr[1]_{old})$$
$$\wedge \ arr[2]_{new} := \text{ite}(i == 2, myval, arr[2]_{old})$$

where $arr[i]_{old}$, and $arr[i]_{new}$ indicate the old and the new values of the array arr at index i.
3. **Symbolically Executing Symbolic Strings**: We added support to some basic string operations for the `String` package and the `StringBuilder` package; this includes but is not limited to `charAt`, `concat`, `contains`, `endsWith`, `equals`, `indexOf`, `length`, `replace`, `startsWith`, `isEmpty` and `substring`.

2.1   Run Configuration

In addition to JR configurations used in SV-COMP 2020 [10], we used the below configurations for turning on the added features.:

- **symbolic.jrarrays=true**: to enable the above array features.
- **symbolic.strings=true**: to enable executing symbolic string
- **symbolic.string_dp=z3str3**: to use Z3's default string theory.
- **symbolic.string_dp_timeout_ms=3000**: for timeout on the string queries.

2.2   Results

To understand the value of the JR's extensions above, we evaluated the old JR tool [9] from SV-COMP 2020, which had no support for symbolic arrays nor symbolic strings, to JR's version participating in 2023. We ran both versions on the verification tasks used in SV-COMP 2023. Results in Tb. 1 show an increased number of correctly solved tasks from 429 to 475, but more importantly, a significant reduction in incorrect results from 97 to zero. These improved

	JR 2020	JR 2023
number of tasks	587	
total correct	429	475
correct true	220	200
correct false	209	275
total incorrect	97	0
incorrect true	97	0
incorrect false	0	0
Score	-2455	400

Table 1: results of JR's version participating in 2020 versus the improved 2023 version

scores show the importance and significance of the added support.

Unfortunately, however, because the current version of JR has no support for witness generation, all correctly reached false verdicts were not included in the SV-COMP 2023 score [2], which resulted in JR scoring 400 points instead of 675. In the future, we plan to extend JR to support witness generation.

3   Formula Structure in Path-Merged String Constraints

Fig. 1 shows `loopCharAt`: an SV-COMP 2023 verification task [3] (from an example of Avgerinos et al. [1]) that can dramatically benefit from path-merging. The task accepts a symbolic string `arg`, and checks each character to see if it is the letter 'B'. If so it increments `counter`. The assertion fails if the value of the counter can be 121. For a symbolic string of length n,

```
public static void loopCharAt(String arg) {
  int counter = 0;
  for (int i = 0; i < arg.length(); i++) {
    char myChar = arg.charAt(i);
    if (myChar == 'B') counter++;
  }
  assert (counter != 121);
}
```

Fig. 1: loopCharAt Example

this code has 2^n execution paths, since each character can be B or not B independently. But applying path merging to the `if` statement leads to a single execution path for a given length string. While JR sees this expected asymptotic benefit (one path per string length), reaching the assertion failure takes more than 2 hours, well beyond the competition time limit. Most time is spent in the solver, so we investigated whether changing the syntax of the query could improve performance.

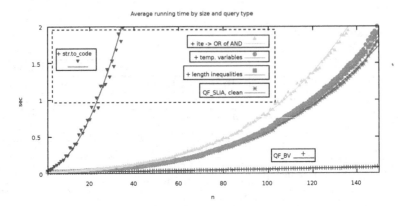

Fig. 2: Average running time by size and query type

Each query generated from the satisfiability of the assert statement asks whether an n-character string can contain 121 (or more generally, k) B characters; this query is satisfiable if $0 \leq k \leq n$. We used a script to generate variations of the query for different values of n and k, and different semantically equivalent ways of expressing the constraints. We then measured the time to solve the queries using Z3 4.8.15 with the seq string solver, on an Intel i7-3770 workstation running Ubuntu 20.04. The choice of k appeared to have little effect on performance, so we report the results of averaging over runs with $0 \leq k \leq n+1$. Figure 2 shows how the running time grows with n, and that the query style has a large impact on performance.

We describe the query styles in order of increasing overhead. Because no complex string operations are needed, an equivalent query can be expressed in a simple bit-vector (QF_BV) logic. This was by far the fastest, and the only style where the running time appears to grow linearly with n. The remaining styles use a logic of strings and integers (QF_SLIA), and we started with the constraint style that seemed most natural to write by hand ("clean") and sequentially added complexities to make the constraints increasingly similar to those JR produces. All these QF_SLIA styles appear to slow down as a cubic polynomial in n, as illustrated by the best-fit lines. Two features of JR's queries had little effect on performance: expressing the string length with a series of inequalities (in JR these come from the loop), and introducing a temporary variable corresponding to each update of the counter. A modest but measurable slowdown came from expressing the effect of the merged region with OR and AND operations, instead of the functional if-then-else operator. A final dramatic slowdown came from constraining the value of each character via its character code (= (str.to_code (str.at s 0)) 66) (natural because Java's char is an integer type) instead of as a one-character string (= (str.at s 0) "B"). These results suggest that this verification task could become feasible in 15 minutes if either JR or solvers can transform the slow-to-solve forms into fast-to-solve ones.

4   Data-Availability Statement

Java Ranger is developed at the University of Minnesota. It is continuously maintained on GitHub [6]. Readers interested in the reproducibility of Java Ranger results in the competition an artifact can be found here [5,4].

References

1. Avgerinos, T., Rebert, A., Cha, S.K., Brumley, D.: Enhancing symbolic execution with veritesting. In: ICSE. pp. 1083–1094. ACM, New York, NY, USA (2014)
2. Beyer, D.: Results of the 12th Intl. Competition on Software Verification (SV-COMP 2023). Zenodo (2023). https://doi.org/10.5281/zenodo.7627787
3. Beyer, D.: SV-Benchmarks: Benchmark set for software verification and testing (SV-COMP 2023 and Test-Comp 2023). Zenodo (2023). https://doi.org/10.5281/zenodo.7627783
4. Beyer, D.: Verifiers and validators of the 12th Intl. Competition on Software Verification (SV-COMP 2023). Zenodo (2023). https://doi.org/10.5281/zenodo.7627829
5. Hussein, S., Yan, Q., Sharma, V., McCamant, S., Whalen, M., Visser, W.: Java ranger artifact for sv-comp2023 (2023). https://doi.org/10.5281/zenodo.7467038
6. Java Ranger, https://github.com/vaibhavbsharma/java-ranger, accessed: 2022-12-17
7. Kuznetsov, V., Kinder, J., Bucur, S., Candea, G.: Efficient state merging in symbolic execution. In: PLDI. pp. 193–204. ACM, New York, NY, USA (2012)
8. Sen, K., Necula, G., Gong, L., Choi, W.: MultiSE: Multi-path symbolic execution using value summaries. In: ESEC/FSE. pp. 842–853. ACM (2015)
9. Sharma, V., Hussein, S., Whalen, M., McCamant, S., Visser, W.: Artifact for sv-comp2020 verifiers including java ranger's (2020). https://doi.org/10.5281/zenodo.3630205
10. Sharma, V., Hussein, S., Whalen, M.W., McCamant, S., Visser, W.: Java Ranger at SV-COMP 2020 (competition contribution). In: Biere, A., Parker, D. (eds.) Tools and Algorithms for the Construction and Analysis of Systems. pp. 393–397. Springer International Publishing, Cham (2020)
11. Sharma, V., Hussein, S., Whalen, M.W., McCamant, S., Visser, W.: Java Ranger: Statically summarizing regions for efficient symbolic execution of Java. In: ESEC/FSE. p. 123–134. ACM, New York, NY, USA (2020)
12. Sharma, V., Whalen, M.W., McCamant, S., Visser, W.: Veritesting challenges in symbolic execution of Java. SIGSOFT Softw. Eng. Notes **42**(4), 1–5 (Jan 2018)

KORN—Software Verification with Horn Clauses (Competition Contribution)

Gidon Ernst[(✉)]⋆

LMU Munich, Munich, Germany
gidon.ernst@lmu.de

Abstract. KORN is a software verifier that infers correctness certificates and violation witnesses sutomatically using state-of-the-art Horn-clause solvers, such as Z3 and Eldarica. The solvers are used in a portfolio together with cheap random sampling where the latter can be very effective at finding counterexamples. KORN perfomend best in the Recursive sub-category of SV-COMP 2023.

Keywords: Software Verification · Horn Clauses · Loop Contracts

1 Verification Approach

KORN is a verifier for C programs that is based on a translation into systems of constrained Horn clauses [5,12]. Therein, each program location is abstracted by a second-order predicate over the program variables which are active at that point. The system of Horn clauses has a (second-order) solution if and only if the program is correct. Horn clauses encodings are a convenient intermediate representation that is linear in the size of the program and that is inherently modular, such that loops, procedure contracts, and non-local control flow like gotos and labels can be easily abstracted (see Sect. 3 wrt. category Recursive).

KORN uses state-of-the-art solvers to determine the satisfiability of the generated Horn clause system (cf. Sect. 2), specifically for SV-COMP it uses Z3 [6] and Eldarica [15]. Both solvers generate evidence for correctness of a given program in terms of models that describe how the unknown predicates need to be instantiated. Moreover, Eldarica can generate counterexample traces, and KORN instruments the Horn clause system to get the concrete values returned by the __VERIFIER_nondet_*() functions on an error path. For these reasons, KORN tends to produce detailed correctness and violation witnesses.

The different solvers have different strengths and weaknesses. To that end, KORN implements a portfolio approach with several sequential stages. The configuration for SV-COMP 2023 [2] is as follows, where the specific timeouts for the individual tools are chosen heuristically based on prior experiments:

1. Initially, 10s of random sampling with small values is performed. It picks for each input value uniformly between number 0, and values of 2, 5, and 10 bits respectively, possibly with a sign. Absense of too large values avoids

---

⋆ Jury Member

ⓒ The Author(s) 2023
S. Sankaranarayanan and N. Sharygina (Eds.): TACAS 2023, LNCS 13994, pp. 559–564, 2023.
https://doi.org/10.1007/978-3-031-30820-8_36

very long running loops when the counter is nondeterministic. There is no particular justification for the sampling scheme, but it is effective.

2. Next, Z3 is executed on the verification problem, translated from C to Horn clauses for 20s. Usually, Z3 finds solutions very quickly if it succeeds at all, specifically on those benchmarks where Z3 succeeds but not Eldarica.

3. Finally, Eldarica is executed for the remaining time. From past experience, it should be slightly better in comparison to Z3 in the long run on this specific set of tasks [10]. The generated invariants from Eldarica tend to be simpler and avoid the existential quantifiers often introduced by Z3, which improves witness generation. To prevent spurious counterexamples, KORN reports a violations only if it can be confirmed by executing the program natively.

KORN is overall similar to SeaHorn [13] but it operates on the C source level instead of LLVM. KORN aims at a rather different design point, namely to favor simplicity over features, therefore offering a good platform for experiments. Eldarica has its own C frontend that supports a different set of features, recently published as TRICERA [11]. Here the main distinction is that KORN uses a large block encoding, such that the verification conditions closely reflect the structure of the program. KORN offers a second verification approach with loop contracts [16,14,7]. This was the original motivation to develop the tool, and neither SeaHorn nor TRICERA supports this feature, albeit it was not used for SV-COMP because it offers no advantages [10] and because the encoding of loop contracts into loop invariants would require quantifiers in the witnesses format.

2   Software Architecture

KORN is mainly written in the JVM language Scala.[1] The front-end uses a custom parser, generated with jFlex and Beaver. The random sampler relies on native execution which links the benchmark task with a C file __VERIFIER_random.c that implements the _VERIFIER_nondet_* functions. Verification conditions are generated in the fragment of SMT-LIB of the HORN logic.[2] KORN can invoke any compliant solver as a backend either using its standard input or a file to communicate the verification task. There is explicit support for Z3 [12], Eldarica [15] to pass e.g. timeouts with tool-specific options or to produce models resp. counterexamples. Currently, KORN use the theories of integers and arrays.

In order to produce SV-COMP correctness witnesses, KORN can read the models generated by the backend-solvers, and translate them back into C expressions. The correctness witnesses produced currently are derived from the invariants that are reported back by the Horn solvers (get-model resp. -ssol flag of Eldarica). Violation witnesses are either read off the output of Eldarica (-cex flag), or from the output of the random sampler, as a sequence of nondeterministic choices. When a counterexample is found, a test harness is compiled to confirm whether reach_error() is in fact called.

---

[1] https://scala-lang.org
[2] https://chc-comp.github.io/format.html

3 Discussion: Strengths and Weaknesses

KORN supports a substantial fraction of the C language, with the greatest limitation being the lack of support for dynamic data structures (see website for a detailed account), which means that currently any task which requires a memory model is out of scope. The translation supports most control structures, including `goto` and labels. With respect to solving verification tasks, KORN inherits the strenths and limitations of the underlying solvers. Tasks that for which invariants and procedure contracts are expressible in linear integer arithmetic are typically proved quickly by the solvers, whereas they struggle on tasks with arrays and quantified invariants. Honoring these aspects, KORN participated in four categories, `ControlFlow`, `Loops`, `Recursive`, `XCSP` for property `ReachSafety`.

The theoretical approach used by KORN is sound and complete relative to the solver capabilities. KORN produced no incorrect result in SV-COMP 2023, but there are circumstances which could lead to wrong verdicts. With respect to C semantics, KORN currently makes the following trade-offs:

- Integer types are treated as unbounded and arithmetic overflows are not modeled at all. This affects a single task, `nla-digbench/geo1-u.c`, which contains an error caused by an unsigned integer overflow. This error is fortunately caught by random sampling— KORN would otherwise wrongly prove this task safe. We aim to experiment with a bitvector encoding eventually, which would allow KORN to tackle tasks involving bitwise operations.
- Arrays are currently modeled as value types. Benchmarks in which tracking aliases is relevant may not be solved correctly, but that does not occur in the categories in which KORN participates.
- By confirming counterexamples via native execution, each bug reported is necessarily a true bug. This safety net catches two incorrect error verdicts on `loops-crafted/theatreSquare.c` and `recursive/Primes.c`, the reason for this unsoundness is under investigation. However, counterexample confirmation prevents KORN from rightfully reporting 50 error verdicts found by Z3 in category `XCSP` which are missed by Eldarica († in Sect. 1). It is unclear how to get usable counterexample traces from Z3 to resolve this dilemma.
- Differently from most other SV-COMP tools, KORN fixes the evaluation order of function arguments to be right-to-left which matches the order typically used by C compilers. This is not faithful to C semantics as KORN potentially misses bugs due to side-effects for some specific evaluation order.

The random sampler is very effective—in SV-COMP 2023 it discovered all 210 violations reported by KORN, of which 204 are found within 2 seconds. Sampling of small *non-zero* values is crucial, e.g., `Ackermann02.c` falsifies with input vector `[2,0]`; using all zero inputs still finds 57 of these 210 violations.

A key strength of Horn clause encodings is that they are inherently modular. This means that loops and recursion are abstracted by invariants resp. pre-/postcondition pairs. The latter enable KORN to significantly outperform all other tools in category `Recursive`. Plausible explanations are that classic state-space exploration techniques struggle to abstract call stacks or maybe that

Table 1. Comparison of official results (number of tasks solved) in comparison to result of the best-scoring other tool in that category and post-competition experiments after fixing an issue with the submitted KORN verifier archive which did not run Eldarica at all. # Tasks is the number of tasks supported by KORN vs. category size. The result marked by † is without counterexample confirmation. The official results can be found at https://sv-comp.sosy-lab.org/2023/results/results-verified/

| | | SV-COMP 2023 | | | | | Post-Comp. | |
| | # tasks | best scoring competitor | | | KORN | | | |
Category	supp./all	tool	true	false	true	false	true	false
ControlFlow	19/ 22	CVT-ParPort	15	7	12	7	12	7
Loops	641/ 685	VeriAbs	386	185	80	178	**288**	178
Recursive	57/ 59	UAutomizer	20	18	27	25	27	25
XCSP	109/ 114	CBMC	54	50	46	0	46	† 50

techniques developed for loops like k-induction have simply not been adapted well to recursive procedures. For Horn clause encodings on the other hand both abstractions are uniform and solvers are largely agnostic to the purpose of predicates. As a downside of enforcing modular proofs, KORN is currently unable to compete in category Arrays, where finding the quantified invariants is hard but state-space exploration succeeds on tasks with fixed loop bounds.

Unfortunately, in the 2023 competition, Eldarica did not run at all due to some unknown problem with the verifier archive, such that KORN terminated way too early and missed out on many results. Table 1 presents results from re-running the evaluation on the competition hardware. This produces 208 additional proofs from Eldarica in category Loops with a hypothetical score of 755 wrt. 323 in SV-COMP 2023, albeit the actual score would be lower than that because usually not all witnesses are confirmed.

4   Software Project, Configuration & Participation

The implementation of KORN is available at https://github.com/gernst/korn under the MIT license, installation instructions are part of the README. The SV-COMP 2023 submission was packaged from commit 8e968dd and shows version 0.4. The included solvers are Z3 4.11.2 64 bit (default configuration) and Eldarica v2.0.8 (using -portfolio). The command line in SV-COMP 2023 is

```
./run -write -model -witness witness.graphml -confirm \
      -random 10 -timeout 20 -z3 -timeout 900 -eld:portfolio <file.c>
```

Participation: ControlFlow, Loops, Recursive, XCSP for ReachSafety.

Contributors. KORN is developed and maintained by the author. G. Alexandru [1] and J. Blau have contributed insights to approach of loop contracts [7].

Data Availability Statement

The tool archive packaged for SV-COMP 2023 is part of the official tools artifact [4] and also available separately [9]. The official competition results [3] are complemented with our post-competition evaluation, based on commit 92e6732 and are available at [8].

References

1. Alexandru, G.: Specifying loops with contracts (2019), Bachelor's Thesis, LMU Munich
2. Beyer, D.: Competition on software verification and witness validation: SV-COMP 2023. In: Proc. TACAS (2). LNCS , Springer (2023)
3. Beyer, D.: Results of the 12th Intl. Competition on Software Verification (SV-COMP 2023). Zenodo (2023). https://doi.org/10.5281/zenodo.7627787
4. Beyer, D.: Verifiers and validators of the 12th Intl. Competition on Software Verification (SV-COMP 2023). Zenodo (2023). https://doi.org/10.5281/zenodo.7627829
5. Bjørner, N., Gurfinkel, A., McMillan, K., Rybalchenko, A.: Horn clause solvers for program verification. In: Fields of Logic and Computation II, pp. 24–51. Springer (2015)
6. Bjørner, N., McMillan, K., Rybalchenko, A.: On solving universally quantified Horn clauses. In: International Static Analysis Symposium. pp. 105–125. Springer (2013)
7. Ernst, G.: Loop verification with invariants and summaries. In: Proc. of Verification, Model-Checking, and Abstract Interpretation (VMCAI). LNCS, vol. 13182. Springer (2022)
8. Ernst, G.: Korn post-competition evaluation. Zenodo (2023). https://doi.org/10.5281/zenodo.7647533
9. Ernst, G.: Korn tool archive as submitted to SV-COMP 2023. Zenodo (2023). https://doi.org/10.5281/zenodo.7647511
10. Ernst, G.: A complete approach to loop verification with invariants and summaries (2020), https://arxiv.org/abs/2010.05812, draft
11. Esen, Z., Rümmer, P.: TriCera: Verifying C Programs Using the Theory of Heaps. In: Formal Methods in Computer-aided Design (FMCAD). p. 380 (2022)
12. Gurfinkel, A., Bjørner, N.: The science, art, and magic of Constrained Horn Clauses. In: 2019 21st International Symposium on Symbolic and Numeric Algorithms for Scientific Computing (SYNASC). pp. 6–10. IEEE (2019)
13. Gurfinkel, A., Kahsai, T., Komuravelli, A., Navas, J.A.: The seahorn verification framework. In: Computer Aided Verification. pp. 343–361. Springer (2015)
14. Hehner, E.C.: Specified blocks. In: Working Conference on Verified Software: Theories, Tools, and Experiments. pp. 384–391. Springer (2005)
15. Hojjat, H., Rümmer, P.: The Eldarica Horn solver. In: 2018 Formal Methods in Computer Aided Design (FMCAD). pp. 1–7. IEEE (2018)
16. Tuerk, T.: Local reasoning about while-loops. VSTTE **2010**, 29 (2010)

Mopsa-C: Modular Domains and Relational Abstract Interpretation for C Programs (Competition Contribution)

Raphaël Monat[1]*(✉) , Abdelraouf Ouadjaout[2] , and Antoine Miné[3]

[1] Univ. Lille, Inria, CNRS, Centrale Lille, UMR 9189 CRIStAL, F-59000 Lille, France
[2] Grenoble, France
[3] LIP6, Sorbonne Université, F-75005, Paris, France

Abstract. Mopsa is a multilanguage static analysis platform relying on abstract interpretation.
It is able to analyze C, Python, and programs mixing these two languages; we focus on the C analysis here. It provides a novel way to combine abstract domains, in order to offer extensibility and cooperation between them, which is especially beneficial when relational numerical domains are used. The analyses are currently flow-sensitive and fully context-sensitive. We focus only on proving programs to be correct, as our analyses are designed to be sound and terminating but not complete. We present our first participation to SV-Comp, where Mopsa earned a bronze medal in the *SoftwareSystems* category.

Keywords: Static analysis · Abstract interpretation · Competition on Software Verification · SV-Comp

1 Verification Approach: the Mopsa platform

Mopsa is an open-source static analysis platform relying on abstract interpretation [4]. The implementation of Mopsa aims at exploring new perspectives for the design of static analyzers. Mopsa has a triple objective:

– To allow developers to define abstract domains in a modular fashion – that is, as independently of each other as possible. In particular, this means that each abstract domain can easily be enabled or disabled to customize an analysis.
– To allow different abstract domains to cooperate and communicate in a relational way. Previous analyzers were able to combine domains in tree-shaped structures [5, Fig. 1]. Mopsa allows sharing between abstract domains, meaning schematically that the domains can be combined into an acyclic graph.
– To support the analysis of multiple languages while reusing existing abstractions. Mopsa is able to analyze C [16], Python [13], and multilanguage Python/C programs [14]. The Michelson smart contract language is being added [1]. Other safe analyzers, such as Astrée [5], Frama-C [6], Goblint [19], and TAJS [8] are specialized in analyzing a single language.

---

* Jury member
A. Ouadjaout—Unaffiliated.

S. Sankaranarayanan and N. Sharygina (Eds.): TACAS 2023, LNCS 13994, pp. 565–570, 2023.
https://doi.org/10.1007/978-3-031-30820-8_37

These aims are achieved through a dynamic expression rewriting mechanism, and a unified signature for abstract domains and iterators. Journault et al. [9] describe the core Mopsa principles, and Monat [12, Chapter 3] provides an in-depth introduction to Mopsa's design.

The C analysis which we rely on for this competition is based on the work of Ouadjaout and Miné [16]. The analysis works by induction on the syntax, is fully context- and flow-sensitive, and committed to be sound. It targets complete programs that have not been modified: Mopsa can be seamlessly integrated in standard build systems (such as make), it supports main functions with symbolic arguments, and it includes precise stubs for most of the standard C library. Our benchmarks analyses include, for instance, several tools from coreutils.

Mopsa is written in 50,000 lines of OCaml code [21], and relies on the Clang frontend to parse C programs. It relies on the Apron library [7] to handle relational numerical abstract domains.

2   Software Architecture: the SV-Comp driver

By default, the C analysis of Mopsa detects all the runtime errors that may happen in the analyzed program (NULL pointer dereferences, integer overflows, ...), while SV-Comp tasks focus on a specific property at a time (reachability of a function, validity of memory accesses, ...). We thus created an SV-Comp specific driver. It takes as input the task description (program, property, data model). It runs increasingly precise C analyses defined in Mopsa until the property of interest is proved or the most precise analysis is reached. Each analysis result is postprocessed by the driver to check if the property is proved.

An analysis configuration defines the set of domains used, as well as their parameters allowing modifications of the precision-efficiency ratio. The four increasingly precise configurations we use are the following:

– Conf. 1 is the base analysis relying on intervals and cells (a field-sensitive, low-level memory abstraction able to handle type-puning, pointer casts, C unions, ...) [11]. Global structures having up to 5 fields are precisely initialized.
– Conf. 2 additionally enables the string length domain [10], which precisely tracks the position of the first 0 in byte arrays. Static struct initialization is done precisely for structures having up to 50 fields.
– Conf. 3 adds a polyhedra abstract domain. This includes tracking numerical relations between string lengths and scalar variables.[4] It relies on a static packing heuristic [5] to achieve a good precision-scalability tradeoff.
– Conf. 4 adds a congruence abstract domain, delayed widenings, and widening with thresholds.

A schematic representation of the domains used in these analyses is shown in Figure 1. The SV-Comp driver is written in 250 lines of Python code.

---

[4] In this case, Mopsa's ability to share abstract domain comes in handy. With a tree, we would have to "linearize" the domains and put either cells or string length on top of the other. This makes reduction more difficult (e.g., Astrée uses a global reduction system on the whole tree, while we can use local reductions between two domains).

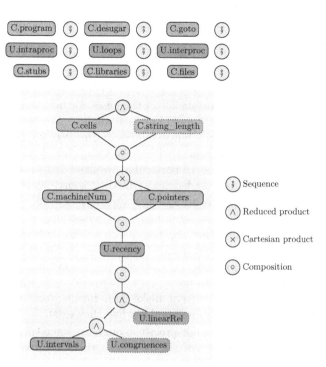

Fig. 1. Configurations for Mopsa-C analyses used in SV-Comp. Dotted rectangles indicate optionally enabled domains. "U.*" domains are shared between the analysis of different languages, while the others are C-specific. The sequence operator lets the domain on the left handle the analysis of a given statement: if it cannot, the analysis continues with the domain on the right. The composition operator allows multiple domains to share the same underlying domain. Products let both domains analyze the given statement. In the case of a reduced product, a reduction operation is applied after the analysis of a statement.

Conf.	Tasks proved correct		Tasks yielding timeout	
1	5695		279	
2	6433	(+738)	365	(+86)
3	6885	(+452)	1844	(+1479)
4	6909	(+24)	2009	(+165)

Fig. 2. Results of the increasingly precise analyses (21220 tasks in total, 12636 correctness tasks). Conf. 2 is able to prove 738 tasks correct in addition to the 5695 proved by conf. 1, although 86 tasks reach the resource limits when analyzed by conf. 1 and 2. Mopsa yields unknown in the analysis of the other tasks.

3   Strengths and Weaknesses

Mopsa participated in all categories targeting reachability, memory safety and overflow properties: *ReachSafety, MemSafety, NoOverflows* and *SoftwareSys-*

tems. It did not compete in the datarace and termination categories. The competition report [2] details all results.

Mopsa relies on over-approximations to guarantee soundness and termination of its analyses. As such, Mopsa scales well on SV-Comp benchmarks: the successive analyses described in Section 1 yield a result within the allocated resources in 91% of the tasks (and 98.5% of the cases for our cheapest analysis). We show the detailed precision benefits of each analysis for the benchmarks in Figure 2. Thanks to Mopsa's scalability and commitment to soundness, we have been able to discover and fix defects within SV-Comp benchmarks which were not discovered by previous tools. In particular, we fixed 164 task definitions, as well as 23 programs with unintended issues in their source code.[5] Mopsa is especially competitive in the *SoftwareSystems* category, focusing on verifying real software systems: it ranked third for our first participation.

Our approach is scalable but not complete: we can only prove programs correct. In other cases, we cannot decide if the issues we found are real bugs or false alarms: we return "unknown" in all these cases to avoid yielding incorrect results. Thus, we can only obtain points on correctness verification tasks, which represents around 58% of the current tasks. Our future work includes finding approaches to exhibit real counterexamples when they exist.

In addition, our analyses are not precise enough for some small but intricate benchmarks (for exemple, on arrays). In particular, the current version of Mopsa does not support partitioning the abstract state into different ones to improve its precision. We plan to add this classic feature for SV-Comp's next edition. For an over-approximating analyzer, Mopsa is nevertheless quite precise: Mopsa is able to prove around 8% more tasks than Goblint [19, 20] (the leading state-of-the-art abstract interpreter running in SV-Comp).

Finally, the SV-Comp driver we built does not extract precise witnesses from the analyses. Indeed, the case of invariant generation for loops defined in functions called in different contexts seems open for now: Saan [18] observed that complex, interprocedural witnesses do not help the witness verifiers. However, the trivial correctness witnesses we generate are validated in 96.4% of the cases.

4   Software Project and Contributors

Mopsa is currently available on Gitlab[17], and released under an open-source license (GNU LGPL v3). Mopsa was originally developed at LIP6, Sorbonne Université following an ERC Consolidator Grant award to Antoine Miné. Mopsa is now developed in other places, including Inria, Airbus, and Nomadic Labs. We thank Matthieu Journault for being one of the initial contributors to Mopsa. This first participation to SV-Comp has spurred a lot of interesting discussions within our development team, and lead to 20 bugfixes and new features.

---

[5] We also added contributed to the benchmarks used in SV-Comp, by adding tasks to check overflows from the Juliet Benchmarks (6156 new tasks); and reviewing 12 merge requests from the community.

Data-Availability Statement The exact version of Mopsa that participated in SV-Comp 2023, and our specific driver are available as a Zenodo archive [15]. A global tool archive is also available [3].

Acknowledgements. We thank Simmo Saan for his precious advice on how to start integrating our tool within SV-Comp.

References

1. Bau, G., Miné, A., Botbol, V., Bouaziz, M.: Abstract interpretation of michelson smart-contracts. In: ACM SOAP, pp. 36–43 (2022)
2. Beyer, D.: Competition on software verification and witness validation: SV-COMP 2023. In: Proc. TACAS (2), LNCS , Springer (2023)
3. Beyer, D.: Verifiers and validators of the 12th Intl. Competition on Software Verification (SV-COMP 2023) (2023), https://doi.org/10.5281/zenodo.7627829
4. Cousot, P., Cousot, R.: Abstract interpretation: A unified lattice model for static analysis of programs by construction or approximation of fixpoints. In: POPL, pp. 238–252 (1977)
5. Cousot, P., Cousot, R., Feret, J., Mauborgne, L., Miné, A., Monniaux, D., Rival, X.: Combination of abstractions in the Astrée static analyzer. In: ASIAN, pp. 272–300 (2006)
6. Cuoq, P., Kirchner, F., Kosmatov, N., Prevosto, V., Signoles, J., Yakobowski, B.: Frama-C - A software analysis perspective. In: SEFM, pp. 233–247 (2012)
7. Jeannet, B., Miné, A.: Apron: A library of numerical abstract domains for static analysis. In: CAV, pp. 661–667, Springer (2009)
8. Jensen, S.H., Møller, A., Thiemann, P.: Type analysis for JavaScript. In: SAS, pp. 238–255 (2009)
9. Journault, M., Miné, A., Monat, R., Ouadjaout, A.: Combinations of reusable abstract domains for a multilingual static analyzer. In: VSTTE, pp. 1–18 (2019)
10. Journault, M., Miné, A., Ouadjaout, A.: Modular static analysis of string manipulations in C programs. In: SAS, pp. 243–262 (2018)
11. Miné, A.: Field-sensitive value analysis of embedded C programs with union types and pointer arithmetics. In: LCTES (2006)
12. Monat, R.: Static Type and Value Analysis by Abstract Interpretation of Python Programs with Native C Libraries. Ph.D. thesis, Sorbonne Université, France (2021)
13. Monat, R., Ouadjaout, A., Miné, A.: Static type analysis by abstract interpretation of python programs. In: ECOOP, pp. 1–29 (2020)
14. Monat, R., Ouadjaout, A., Miné, A.: A multilanguage static analysis of python programs with native C extensions. In: SAS, pp. 323–345 (2021)
15. Monat, R., Ouadjaout, A., Miné, A.: Mopsa-C: Modular Domains and Relational Abstract Interpretation for C Programs (Artefact) (Dec 2022), https://doi.org/10.5281/zenodo.7467136
16. Ouadjaout, A., Miné, A.: A library modeling language for the static analysis of C programs. In: SAS, pp. 223–247 (2020)
17. Ouadjaout, A., Monat, R., Miné, A., Journault, M.: Mopsa (2022), URL https://gitlab.com/mopsa/mopsa-analyzer
18. Saan, S.: Witness generation for data-flow analysis. https://comserv.cs.ut.ee/home/files/saan_computerscience_2020.pdf (2020)

19. Saan, S., Schwarz, M., Apinis, K., Erhard, J., Seidl, H., Vogler, R., Vojdani, V.: Goblint: Thread-modular abstract interpretation using side-effecting constraints - (competition contribution). In: TACAS (2021)
20. Saan, S., Schwarz, M., Erhard, J., Pietsch, M., Seidl, H., Tilscher, S., Vojdani, V.: GOBLINT: Autotuning thread-modular abstract interpretation (competition contribution). In: Proc. TACAS (2), LNCS , Springer (2023)
21. The OCaml Developers: Ocaml (2020), URL https://github.com/ocaml/ocaml

PIChecker: A POR and Interpolation based Verifier for Concurrent Programs (Competition Contribution)⋆

Jie Su [ID], Zuchao Yang [ID], Hengrui Xing [ID], Jiyu Yang [ID],
Cong Tian [ID][✉]⋆⋆, and Zhenhua Duan [ID]

ICTT and ISN Lab, Xidian University, Xi'an 710071, China
{jsu_3,mujueke,morui,jiyuy2024}@stu.xidian.edu.cn,
{ctian,zhhduan}@mail.xidian.edu.cn

Abstract. PIChecker is a tool for verifying reachability properties of concurrent C programs. It moderates the trace-space explosion problem, aggravated by thread alternation, through utilizing the PC-DPOR and C-Intp techniques. The PC-DPOR technique constructs a constrained dependency graph to refine dependencies between transitions. With this basis, the inherent imprecision of the dependence over-approximation can be overcome. Thereby, many redundant equivalent traces are prevented from being explored. On the other hand, the C-Intp technique performs conditional interpolation to confine the reachable regions of states, so that infeasible conditional branches which occur more frequently in concurrent verification tasks could be pruned automatically. We have implemented the above techniques on top of the open-source program analysis framework CPAchecker.

Keywords: Partial-Order Reduction · Interpolation · Concurrent Program · Model Checking

1 Verification Approach

Program synthesis[11] and verification[5] are two ways to improve the quality of software. In this paper, we propose a tool, namely PIChecker, that utilizes the PC-DPOR [9] and C-Intp [8] techniques to verify the reachability properties of concurrent programs. These techniques work in two different ways, equivalent trace class partitioning and infeasible conditional branch pruning, to reduce the search space in model checking.

The PC-DPOR technique addresses the problem that the coarse dependency approximation of transitions used in many POR [6] approaches significantly increases the number of equivalent trace classes to be explored. In order to reduce

---

⋆ This research is supported by the National Natural Science Foundation of China (No. 62192734, No. 61732013 and No. 62172322).
⋆⋆ The corresponding author.

S. Sankaranarayanan and N. Sharygina (Eds.): TACAS 2023, LNCS 13994, pp. 571–576, 2023.
https://doi.org/10.1007/978-3-031-30820-8_38

unnecessary exploration, the PC-DPOR technique constructs a *constrained dependency graph* (CDG) to refine the dependencies between transitions, where the edges in a CDG represent the dependency constraints that transitions from different threads depend on each other. The first configuration in Fig. 1 combines this technique with BDD-based reachability analysis to explore the reachable state-space of a concurrent program. At each state s, if there are *isolated transitions* which have no connection with the nodes of other threads in the CDG, then only one reachable successor state s' corresponding to an isolated transition will be explored (i.e., the enabled transitions of other threads will be pruned). We have proved that the prioritized exploration strategy for isolated transition still provides full coverage of all program behaviors[9]. This prioritized exploration continues until a *checking state* without any successor of isolated transition is reached. Thereafter, the dependency between any two different transitions t and t' at a checking state can be dynamically determined by checking whether their dependency constraint holds at the checking state. If the constraint does not hold (i.e., t is independent of t' at the current checking state), then only one of the execution orders $t \cdot t'$ and $t' \cdot t$ will be explored. With the basis of CDG, the inherent imprecision of traditional dependence over-approximation is overcome and many redundant equivalent traces can be saved from being explored.

On the other hand, the C-Intp technique focuses on pruning the infeasible conditional branches that may be explored in traditional abstraction-refinement iterations [7] when predicates are insufficient. At each state s, besides the reachability check of error locations, the C-Intp technique also inspects whether there exists any path that contains infeasible conditional branches. If so, the C-Intp technique will treat such a path as another form of spurious path, and additional constraints, namely *conditional interpolants*, will be generated by performing conditional interpolation on these additional spurious paths. Thereafter, infeasible conditional branches can be pruned by introducing these constraints into the reachable regions of states. In order to improve the efficiency of satisfiability checking and Craig interpolation [4] steps performed by C-Intp, the generated conditional interpolants are utilized to shorten the interpolation paths. To do so, *the shortest C-Intp formula chains* which contain only the formulas that affect decision-making are constructed at each choice point to perform the interpolations. With the conditional interpolants and shorter interpolation paths, a sufficient amount of predicates can be generated efficiently, and more attention can be paid to the analysis of feasible paths.

2   Software Architecture

PIChecker is developed on top of CPAchecker with the PC-DPOR and C-Intp extensions. By taking the strength of the CPA concept, PIChecker uses different configurations as shown in Fig. 1 to cover as many concurrent programs as possible. Within the verification time-bound, the verification for a given program starts by executing the first configuration that combines the PC-DPOR technique and BDD-based reachability analysis. If a counterexample is reported,

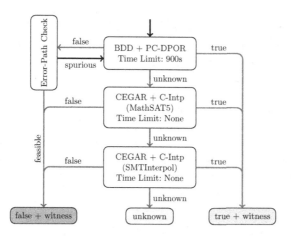

Fig. 1. The verification flow that combines the PC-DPOR and C-Intp strategies.

the feasibility of this error path will be checked since the BDD-based reachability analysis in `CPAchecker` currently only supports the representation of integer variable values and other states in waitlist will continue to be explored if the counterexample is spurious. If the execution of the first configuration terminates unexpectedly within 900s, the verification will continue by using the other two CEGAR + C-Intp based configurations with different back-end solvers. In that case, the second configuration with the `MathSAT5` will be chosen firstly. If its execution also aborts abnormally because the `MathSAT5` solver fails to perform interpolation on the shortest C-Intp formula chains generated by the C-Intp approach, the last configuration with the `SMTInterpol` solver will finally be utilized if the time cost is still within the bound.

3   Strengths and Weakness

Compared to `CPAchecker` which conservatively approximates the independence of transitions by checking whether a transition only accesses local variables [2], the use of CDG in `PIChecker` can improve the precision of estimating the dependencies of enabled transitions at reachable states. Therefore, the exploration of more traces in the same equivalent class can be avoided by utilizing `PIChecker`. In addition, different from most of the abstraction-refinement approaches that generate only a few number of predicates at the end of each iteration, the two CEGAR + C-Intp based configurations can effectively generate a sufficient amount of conditional interpolants within a single round of iteration by performing the conditional interpolation technique at conditional branches. Thus, the exploration of many infeasible conditional branches can be avoided. For the sake of clarifying the improvement from `PIChecker` more clearly, a comparison between `PIChecker` and `CPAchecker`, on checking the `unreach-call` property under the category `ConcurrencySafety` in SV-COMP 2023, is made. The results indicate that PIChecker succeeds to verify 394 out of 665 verification tasks, which is more than 375 of CPAchecker. Further, for the 372 tasks that can be verified by the both tools, the average time and memory costs of PIChecker (37.49s, 672.15MB) only account for 56.58% and 61.71% of the corresponding overheads consumed by CPAchecker (66.27s, 1089.19MB), respectively.

In order to guarantee the correctness of verification results, some conservative strategies are adopted by the three configurations. For example, when the program statement corresponding to a transition contains non-deterministic function calls (e.g., 'x = __VERIFIER_nondet_int();'), the PC-DPOR technique conservatively considers it to be dependent on other transitions if they access the same shared variables. These strategies may significantly reduce the verification efficiency.

4   Tool Setup and Configuration

PIChecker is built on the CPAchecker codebase and is publicly available[1]. It contains all the dependent libraries and requires a Java 11 Runtime Environment. In SV-COMP 2023, PIChecker only participates in the ConcurrencySafety category and checks the unreach-call property[2]. Before verifying a program, all files from the submitted archive must be extracted into the same folder. Executing PIChecker on a task can be done in the same way as executing any other CPAchecker configuration by running: scripts/cpa.sh -svcomp23-pichecker -timelimit <TIME_LIMIT> [-spec <SPEC_FILE>] <SOURCE_FILE>. The experimental statistics and verification results are written in output/Statistics.txt. Moreover, human readable counterexamples output/Counterexample.%d.txt will be generated if the reachability property does not hold. For more instructions, please refer to README.md and INSTALL.md.

5   Software Project and Contributors

Based on the open-source tool CPAchecker [3], PIChecker has been developed by Jie Su, Zuchao Yang, Hengrui Xing, Jiyu Yang from the ICTT Lab in Xidian University under the supervision of Cong Tian and Zhenhua Duan. We thank Dirk Beyer and his team for their original contributions to CPAchecker. PIChecker is licensed under the Apache 2.0, and it also contains the copyright of CPAchecker.

Data Availability Statement. All data of SV-COMP 2023 are archived as described in the competition report[1] and available on the competition web site. This includes the verification tasks, results, witnesses, scripts, and instructions for reproduction. The version of PIChecker used in the competition is archived on Zenodo [10] and also in its own artifact at GitLab.

---

[1] PIChecker repository: https://gitlab.com/Lapulatos/pichecker.git
[2] The benchmark definition of PIChecker: https://gitlab.com/sosy-lab/sv-comp/bench-defs/-/blob/main/benchmark-defs/pichecker.xml

References

1. Beyer, D.: Competition on software verification and witness validation: SV-COMP 2023. In: Proc. TACAS (2). LNCS , Springer (2023)
2. Beyer, D., Friedberger, K.: A Light-Weight Approach for Verifying Multi-Threaded Programs with CPAchecker. arXiv preprint arXiv:1612.04983 (2016). https://doi.org/10.4204/EPTCS.233.6
3. Beyer, D., Keremoglu, M.E.: CPACHECKER: A Tool for Configurable Software Verification. In: Proceedings of the 23rd International Conference on Computer Aided Verification. pp. 184–190. CAV'11, Springer Berlin Heidelberg, Berlin, Heidelberg (2011). https://doi.org/10.1007/978-3-642-22110-1_16
4. Craig, W.: Three uses of the Herbrand-Gentzen theorem in relating model theory and proof theory. The Journal of Symbolic Logic **22**(3), 269–285 (1957)
5. Fetzer, J.H.: Program verification: The very idea. Communications of the ACM **31**(9), 1048–1063 (1988)
6. Godefroid, P.: Partial-order methods for the verification of concurrent systems: an approach to the state-explosion problem. Springer (1996)
7. Henzinger, T.A., Jhala, R., Majumdar, R., Sutre, G.: Lazy abstraction. In: Proceedings of the 29th ACM SIGPLAN-SIGACT Symposium on Principles of Programming Languages. pp. 58–70. POPL'02, Association for Computing Machinery, New York, NY, USA (2002). https://doi.org/10.1145/503272.503279
8. Jie, S., Cong, T., Zhenhua, D.: Conditional Interpolation: Making Concurrent Program Verification More Effective. In: Proceedings of the 29th ACM Joint Meeting on European Software Engineering Conference and Symposium on the Foundations of Software Engineering. pp. 144–154. ESEC/FSE'21, Association for Computing Machinery, New York, NY, USA (2021). https://doi.org/10.1145/3468264.3468602
9. Jie, S., Cong, T., Zuchao, Y., Jiyu, Y., Bin, Y., Zhenhua, D.: Prioritized Constraint-Aided Dynamic Partial-Order Reduction. In: Proceedings of the 37th IEEE/ACM International Conference on Automated Software Engineering. ASE'22, Association for Computing Machinery, New York, NY, USA (2022). https://doi.org/10.1145/3551349.3561159
10. Jie, S., Zuchao, Y., Hengrui, X., Jiyu, Y., Cong, T., Zhenhua, D.: PIChecker for SV-COMP 2023 (Dec 2022). https://doi.org/10.5281/zenodo.7471378
11. Mengfei, Y., Bin, G., Zhenhua, D., Zhi, J., Naijun, Z., Yunwei, D.: Intelligent program synthesis framework and key scientific problems for embedded software. Chinese Space Science and Technology **42**(4), 1 (2022)

Ultimate Automizer and the CommuHash Normal Form
(Competition Contribution)

Matthias Heizmann[(✉)], Max Barth, Daniel Dietsch, Leonard Fichtner, Jochen Hoenicke, Dominik Klumpp, Mehdi Naouar, Tanja Schindler, Frank Schüssele, and Andreas Podelski

University of Freiburg, Freiburg im Breisgau, Germany
heizmann@informatik.uni-freiburg.de

Abstract. The verification approach of ULTIMATE AUTOMIZER utilizes SMT formulas. This paper presents techniques to keep the size of the formulas small. We focus especially on a normal form, called CommuHash normal form that was easy to implement and had a significant impact on the runtime of our tool.

1 Verification Approach

ULTIMATE AUTOMIZER (in the following called AUTOMIZER) is a software verifier that combines a CEGAR scheme and trace abstraction [6] to check safety and liveness properties.

AUTOMIZER's algorithm begins by transforming an input program to a program automaton whose transitions are labelled with formulas representing the effects of a statement (or multiple statements), whose accepting states correspond to error locations of the input program, and whose structure is equal to the structure of the control-flow graph of the input program. This program automaton recognizes a language, where every word is a sequence of statements that leads to an error location. If the language is empty, we can conclude that the program is safe. If the language is not empty, our algorithm picks a word from the language and checks whether it is *feasible* (i.e., the sequence of statements corresponds to an execution of the program) or *infeasible*. If the word is feasible we have found an actual counterexample. If it is infeasible we compute a proof of infeasibility for this sequence of statements. Afterwards we generalize this sequence of statements to a new automaton that accepts sequences of statements whose infeasibility can be shown by the very same proof. We then subtract the automaton with the language of infeasible words from the program automaton and obtain a new automaton that represents a smaller language, with which we continue the refinement loop. An important benefit of this approach is that because we perform the refinement step purely with automata operations, we never have to mix infeasibility proofs from different iterations.

This basic approach has not changed since the last competition. In the next section we explain improvements for the handling of SMT formulas.

S. Sankaranarayanan and N. Sharygina (Eds.): TACAS 2023, LNCS 13994, pp. 577–581, 2023.
https://doi.org/10.1007/978-3-031-30820-8_39

2   SMT formulas in Ultimate

The ULTIMATE program analysis framework on which ULTIMATE AUTOMIZER is built upon, uses SMT formulas to represent the effect of program statements and to represent sets of states. We call formulas that represent sets of states *state assertions*. State assertions play a major role in the verification approach of AUTOMIZER. The infeasibility proof that we infer for each infeasible sequence of states is a sequence of state assertions and in the generalization step of the overall verification algorithm we have to check thousands of Hoare triples of the form $\{\varphi\} st \{\psi\}$, where φ and ψ are state assertions from infeasibility proofs. In order to check these Hoare triples, we reduce the validity problem for Hoare triples to a satisfiability problem for SMT formulas and let an SMT solver decide the satisfiability. The costs for the overall verification algorithm would be dominated by the costs for these satisfiability checks if we would not take additional actions to keep the size of the SMT formulas low.

We infer the sequence of state assertions by Craig interpolation or by a symbolic execution (via strongest post and weakest precondition) that is supported by unsatisfiable cores [3]. In the latter case the state assertions are usually quantified and we try to get rid of these quantifiers by applying several quantifier elimination techniques. These quantifier elimination techniques make the formulas simpler for SMT solvers but increase their size.

Our most powerful technique for reducing the size of formulas is an algorithm [4] that removes subformulas if the removal does not change the models of the formula. This algorithm however is itself costly because it calls an SMT solver for each subformula.

In order to also reduce the size of formulas without additional SMT solver calls, we utilize the following optimizations whenever we construct a formula.

- We apply the laws for annulment (e.g., $X \lor true$ becomes $true$), identity (e.g., $X \land X$ becomes X), idempotency (e.g., $x + 0$ becomes x), double negation (e.g., $\neg\neg X$ becomes X), and complement (e.g., $X \land \neg X$ becomes $false$).
- We compute the result for all operations on literals (e.g., $5 \le 7\%2$ becomes $false$).
- We represent all integer and bitvector terms as polynomials. All terms that cannot be converted to polynomials become "variables" of the polynomial (e.g., $2 \cdot select(a, k) + 3 \cdot (x\%256) + 4$).
- For inequalities over integers and equalities over bitvectors and integers, we move monomials to the side of the relation where it can occur with a positive coefficient. (e.g., $2x - 3y = 0$ becomes $2x = 3y$).
- We work only with inequalities that open to the right. I.e., we transform $>$ to $<$, $\ge$ to $\le$, *sgt* to *slt*, *sge* to *sle*, *ugt* to *ult*, and *uge* to *ule*.

3   The CommuHash Normal Form

An effect of the quantifier elimination techniques and the optimizations mentioned above is that we construct formulas in many places of our code. A side-effect of this is that we get formulas that have subformulas that differ only in the order of the parameters of a commutative operator. E.g., we saw formulas like, e.g., $i = k \vee k \neq i$ or $a[i + k] = a[k + i]$. For both formulas the logical equivalence to $true$ would have been detected if the operands of the commutative operations $+$ and $=$ would not have occurred in different orders. To minimize this problem we define a normal form that we call CommuHash Normal Form (CHNF). This normal form utilizes the fact that in ULTIMATE every formula has a 32-bit hash code. We say that an SMT formula is in *CommuHash Normal Form* if for every subformula with a commutative operator the operands are sorted according to their hash code in ascending order. To ensure that every formula is in CHNF ULTIMATE sorts the parameters whenever we construct a term whose operand is one of the following SMT operators: `=`, `distinct`, `and`, `or`, `xor`, `+`, `*`, `bvadd`, `bvmul`, `bvand`, `bvor`, `bvxor`.

In order to evalutate the effect of the CommuHash Normal Form we conducted an experiment in which we compared the default version of ULTIMATE AUTOMIZER to a version in which we disabled the sorting of parameters. We ran both versions on the benchmarks of the MemSafety category. In this category we typically have to deal with large formulas because the state assertions of proofs have to encode alias information about the program's pointers. We ran both versions on all 3440 benchmarks of the category. The CPU was an AMD Ryzen Threadripper 3970X, the time limit was 90s, the memory limit was 8000 MB and for each benchmark two CPU cores were used. In each run there were no incorrect results. The run without CHNF produced 1347 correct results, the run with CHNF produced 1439 correct results. Figure 1 shows a comparison of the runtimes for each benchmark in which at least one setting produced a result. We see that on average the run with CHNF needs less time. In fact on average the speedup is 31%.

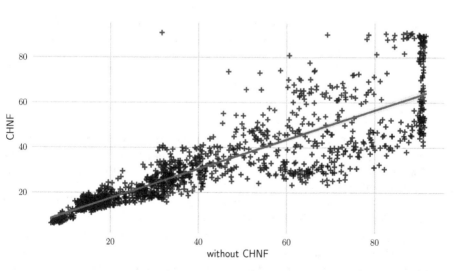

Fig. 1: Comparison of the runtime with and without CHNF

4   Project, Setup and Configuration

AUTOMIZER is a part of the open-source program analysis framework ULTI-MATE[1]. Both are written in Java and licensed under LGPLv3. We use version 0.2.3 of AUTOMIZER [5] for SV-COMP, which requires Java 11 and Python 3.6. The release 0.2.3 contains binaries for AUTOMIZER and the SMT solvers Z3, CVC4, and MATHSAT, as well as the Python wrapper script Ultimate.py. The Python script provides an interface to the competition environment, in particular to the BENCHEXEC[2] tool-info module ultimateautomizer.py. AUTOMIZER also participates as witness validator and can validate violation [2] or correctness witnesses [1]. We participate in all categories [3] as verifier, but our witness validator does not yet support concurrency witnesses. Hence, our validator does not participate in ConcurrencySafety [4].

AUTOMIZER can be run by calling

```
./Ultimate.py --spec prop.prp --file input.c --architecture
    32bit|64bit --full-output [--validate witness.graphml]
```

where prop.prp is the SV-COMP property file, input.c is the C file that should be analyzed, 32bit or 64bit is the architecture of the input file, and --full-output enables writing of verbose output to stdout. The witness that should be validated is specified with --validate. If AUTOMIZER generates a result, a witness is written to the file witness.graphml. AUTOMIZER's output is always written to the file Ultimate.log.

References

1. Beyer, D., Dangl, M., Dietsch, D., Heizmann, M.: Correctness witnesses: exchanging verification results between verifiers. In: Zimmermann, T., Cleland-Huang, J., Su, Z. (eds.) Proceedings of the 24th ACM SIGSOFT International Symposium on Foundations of Software Engineering, FSE 2016, Seattle, WA, USA, November 13-18, 2016. pp. 326–337. ACM (2016), https://doi.org/10.1145/2950290.2950351
2. Beyer, D., Dangl, M., Dietsch, D., Heizmann, M., Stahlbauer, A.: Witness validation and stepwise testification across software verifiers. In: Nitto, E.D., Harman, M., Heymans, P. (eds.) Proceedings of the 2015 10th Joint Meeting on Foundations of Software Engineering, ESEC/FSE 2015, Bergamo, Italy, August 30 - September 4, 2015. pp. 721–733. ACM (2015), https://doi.org/10.1145/2786805.2786867
3. Dietsch, D., Heizmann, M., Musa, B., Nutz, A., Podelski, A.: Craig vs. newton in software model checking. In: Bodden, E., Schäfer, W., van Deursen, A., Zisman, A. (eds.) Proceedings of the 2017 11th Joint Meeting on Foundations of Software Engineering, ESEC/FSE 2017, Paderborn, Germany, September 4-8, 2017. pp. 487–497. ACM (2017), https://doi.org/10.1145/3106237.3106307

---

[1] https://github.com/ultimate-pa/ultimate
[2] https://github.com/sosy-lab/benchexec
[3] Specified by uautomizer.xml at https://github.com/sosy-lab/sv-comp.
[4] Specified by uautomizer-validate-*-witnesses.xml.

4. Dillig, I., Dillig, T., Aiken, A.: Small formulas for large programs: On-line constraint simplification in scalable static analysis. In: Cousot, R., Martel, M. (eds.) Static Analysis - 17th International Symposium, SAS 2010, Perpignan, France, September 14-16, 2010. Proceedings. Lecture Notes in Computer Science, vol. 6337, pp. 236–252. Springer (2010), https://doi.org/10.1007/978-3-642-15769-1_15

5. Heizmann, M., Dietsch, D., Klumpp, D., Schüssele, F., Podelski, A.: Ultimate Automizer SV-COMP 2023 Competition Contribution (Dec 2022), https://doi.org/10.5281/zenodo.7480181

6. Heizmann, M., Hoenicke, J., Podelski, A.: Software model checking for people who love automata. In: Sharygina, N., Veith, H. (eds.) Computer Aided Verification - 25th International Conference, CAV 2013, Saint Petersburg, Russia, July 13-19, 2013. Proceedings. Lecture Notes in Computer Science, vol. 8044, pp. 36–52. Springer (2013), https://doi.org/10.1007/978-3-642-39799-8_2

Ultimate Taipan and Race Detection in Ultimate
(Competition Contribution)

Daniel Dietsch[*] , Matthias Heizmann , Dominik Klumpp[⊠] ,
Frank Schüssele , and Andreas Podelski

University of Freiburg, Freiburg im Breisgau, Germany
klumpp@informatik.uni.freiburg.de

Abstract. ULTIMATE TAIPAN integrates trace abstraction with algebraic program analysis on path programs. TAIPAN supports data race checking in concurrent programs through a reduction to reachability checking. Though the subsequent verification is not tuned for data race checking, the results are encouraging.

1 Verification Approach

ULTIMATE TAIPAN [6,7] verifies programs using an approach based on trace abstraction [8]. The program is represented as a control flow automaton: Letters correspond to program statements, accepting states correspond to error locations, and accepted words are *error traces*. The verification consists of proving that all error traces are *infeasible* (they cannot be executed). To this end, TAIPAN picks an error trace from the control flow automaton, and computes the corresponding *path program*, i.e., the projection of the program on the statements in the trace. TAIPAN then uses *symbolic interpretation with fluid abstractions* [6], a variant of algebraic program analysis, to prove correctness of this path program. If this fails, the algorithm falls back to an interpolation-based method to prove correctness of the trace itself. In either case, the resulting predicates are used to build a Floyd/Hoare-automaton [8] that accepts a regular language of infeasible traces. This automaton is subtracted from the program's control flow automaton, yielding a refined abstraction. TAIPAN repeats this procedure in a loop until it finds a feasible error trace (the program is incorrect) or the abstraction is empty (all error traces are infeasible, the program is correct).

For concurrent programs, TAIPAN performs a *naïve sequentialization*, and considers the interleaving product of all threads as a (nondeterministic) sequential program. Verification then proceeds on this program as it would for any other sequential program. Note that this also affects the notion of *path program*, i.e., path programs are also just sequential programs.

TAIPAN is part of the ULTIMATE framework, and uses the same front-end as other ULTIMATE tools. C programs are first translated to the intermediate verification language Boogie [10], the resulting Boogie program is converted into a control flow automaton, which is then verified. The translation from C to

---

[*] Jury Member: Daniel Dietsch

S. Sankaranarayanan and N. Sharygina (Eds.): TACAS 2023, LNCS 13994, pp. 582–587, 2023.
https://doi.org/10.1007/978-3-031-30820-8_40

Boogie models heap and stack memory through Boogie arrays (associative maps), where pointers correspond to indices. To simplify the subsequent verification, any variables, arrays and structures that are guaranteed to never be accessed through a pointer are instead translated to corresponding Boogie variables.

2   From Data Races to Reachability

Since SV-COMP'22, TAIPAN can check for data races in concurrent programs. A program written in C contains a data race if there are two different threads, *(i)* one thread writes to a memory location and the other thread writes to or reads from the same memory location, *(ii)* at least one of the accesses is not atomic, and *(iii)* neither access *happens-before* the other. The C standard [9], section 5.1.2.4, gives the precise definition. Data races constitute undefined behaviour.

ULTIMATE supports data race checking through a reduction to reachability. This reduction is implemented as part of our translation from C to our custom Boogie dialect. Contrary to C, data races do not constitute undefined behaviour in our Boogie dialect. The semantics prescribes that "simple" Boogie statements – (nondeterministic) assignments and **assume** statements – execute atomically. We consider all interleavings of these atomic statements, i.e., we assume sequential consistency. Hence the correctness of the generated Boogie programs is well-defined, even if the input C program has undefined behaviour. Any verification algorithm for concurrent programs can be applied to the resulting Boogie program, including the algorithm implemented by TAIPAN.

The reduction to reachability proceeds as follows. For every global variable x, we introduce a fresh Boolean global variable **race_x**, which tracks read and write accesses to x. By comparing the current value of **race_x** to some value it previously held, we can detect if x has been accessed since. We call an atomic Boogie statement that represents a C statement or an evaluation step for a C expression an *action*. Let **<read(x)>** denote an action that reads the value of x, and let **<write(x)>** denote an action that assigns a new value to x. Our translation wraps such actions in data race detection code as shown in the following listings, where **tmp** is a boolean, thread-local variable.

```
race_x := true;
<read(x)>
assert race_x == true;
```

```
havoc tmp; // nondeterministic assignment
race_x := tmp;
<write(x)>
assert race_x == tmp;
```

For an action a, we call the sequence of Boogie statements that results from this wrapping *block(a)*. Note that a is always contained in *block(a)*. Our translation ensures that if an action a is part of an atomic block (delimited by __VERIFIER_atomic_*), then the entire *block(a)* falls inside that atomic block.

For two actions a and b, we say that *block(b) can interrupt block(a)* if there exists a program execution that executes *block(a)* up to and including the action a, then fully executes *block(b)*, and then continues to execute the remaining assert statement of *block(a)*. Hence, a *block(a)* can interrupt *block(b)* or vice versa if and only if at least one of the actions a or b is not atomic, and neither *happens-before* [9] the other.

For an action a, the assert statement in $block(a)$ cannot fail, unless there is an action b such that *(i)* $block(b)$ can interrupt $block(a)$, and *(ii)* a and b both access the same variable x. For instance, let a be an action that writes to x, and let b be an action that reads from x. In the following example, $block(b)$ can interrupt $block(a)$ and the last assert statement can fail because false can be chosen as value of tmp.

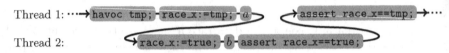

Thread 1: ···→ `havoc tmp; race_x:=tmp;` a →`assert race_x==tmp;` →···

Thread 2:   →`race_x:=true;` b `assert race_x==true;`

Based on the definition of data races we distinguish three cases for the actions a and b:

two reads: The assert statements cannot fail for any interleaving because both blocks set race_x to the same value. The fact that this value is true has no significance; it only matters that the value is fixed.

a read r and a write w: If $block(w)$ can interrupt $block(r)$, the assert statement for r can fail if $block(w)$ assigns tmp (and consequently, race_x) to false. Similarly, if $block(r)$ can interrupt $block(w)$, the assert statement for w can fail (again, if tmp has value false).

two writes w_1, w_2: If some $block(w_i)$ can interrupt $block(w_{3-i})$, the assert statement for w_{3-i} can fail (the blocks may assign different values to race_x).

From this case distinction we conclude that in the translated Boogie program, an assert statement added for data race detection can fail if and only if the original C program contains a data race.

Our encoding is independent of the synchronization mechanisms used to rule out data races. Whether the program uses __VERIFIER_atomic_*, pthread mutexes, or directly implements locking mechanisms, no special handling is needed. Our implementation supports not only (primitive) global variables, but also data on the heap (accessed through pointers) as well as off-heap structures and arrays. In such cases, instead of a Boolean variable race_x, more complicated data structures are needed. We mirror the data layout with Boolean fields: For every data array, there exists a corresponding Boolean array, for every structure, there is a corresponding structure with Boolean-valued fields, etc.

This handling of complex data types also allows us to deal with aliasing issues: ULTIMATE models memory as an associative array mem : [Pointer]Int, with pointers as indices. Our race detection encoding creates a corresponding boolean-valued associative array race_mem : [Pointer]Boolean. The instrumentation for an access to a memory location through a pointer p then manipulates the entry race_mem[p]. If pointers p and q point to the same memory location ℓ at runtime, then race_mem[p] and race_mem[q] refer to the same array entry. Hence, if there is a data race on ℓ, one of the generated assert statements can fail.

3   Strengths and Weaknesses

Our encoding of data races is independent of the subsequent verification algorithm. We have employed this encoding since SV-COMP 2022 [2], for TAIPAN as well as in the ULTIMATE tools AUTOMIZER and GEMCUTTER (ULTIMATE KOJAK currently does not support concurrency).

We inherit limitations of the respective verification algorithms. TAIPAN is unable to prove correctness of programs with an unbounded (or very high) number of threads. The NoDataRace category contains many such programs. Overall, the ULTIMATE tools perform competitively in the NoDataRace-Main category, with AUTOMIZER, GEMCUTTER and TAIPAN reaching 4th, 5th and 6th place, respectively. In comparison with last year's performance in the demo category (4th, 1st and 2nd place), a major factor seems to be the large number of new correct benchmarks, where we do not perform as well yet. Perhaps some tuning of the subsequent verification algorithms to the detection of data races can lead to improvements in the future.

The presented encoding of data races as reachability is compositional, and independent of the number of threads that are running concurrently: We always add a single assertion per access, in contrast to some other methods [4].

One limitation of our implementation is that, from a feasible trace that ends in an assertion violation, it is not always immediately clear which accesses have a data race. In order to support violation witnesses for data races in future editions of SV-COMP, a more detailed analysis of the trace will be needed.

Our performance suffers in some cases due to a large amount of instrumentation, e.g. in benchmarks where large structs are copied: Currently, we handle each byte in the struct separately. In the future, we hope to improve the implementation to (i) handle reads and writes of large memory chunks more efficiently, (ii) detect more situations in which a concurrent access can be easily ruled out, and no instrumentation is needed, and (iii) making parts of the generated data race detection code atomic, thus reducing the number of interleavings.

4   Architecture, Setup, Configuration, and Project

ULTIMATE TAIPAN is part of ULTIMATE[1], a program analysis framework written in Java and licensed under LGPLv3[2]. TAIPAN version 0.2.2-2329fc70 requires Java 11 and Python 3.6. The submitted .zip archive contains the Linux version of TAIPAN, binaries of the required SMT solvers[3], and a Python wrapper script. TAIPAN is invoked with

    ./Ultimate.py --spec <p> --file <f> --architecture <a> --full-output

where <p> is an SV-COMP property file, <f> is an input C file, <a> is the data model (32bit or 64bit), and --full-output enables verbose output to stdout. A violation or correctness witness may be written to the file witness.graphml. The benchmarking tool BENCHEXEC [3] supports TAIPAN through the tool-info module ultimatetaipan.py[4]. TAIPAN participates in all categories, as declared in its SV-COMP benchmark definition file utaipan.xml[5].

---

[1] ultimate.informatik.uni-freiburg.de and github.com/ultimate-pa/ultimate

[2] www.gnu.org/licenses/lgpl-3.0.en.html

[3] Z3 (github.com/Z3Prover/z3), CVC4 (cvc4.github.io/) and MATHSAT (mathsat.fbk.eu)

[4] github.com/sosy-lab/benchexec/blob/main/benchexec/tools/ultimatetaipan.py

[5] gitlab.com/sosy-lab/sv-comp/bench-defs/-/blob/main/benchmark-defs/utaipan.xml

Data Availability ULTIMATE TAIPAN can be found in the archive of all verifiers and validators participating in SV-COMP'23 [1]. Additionally, the `.zip` archive containing only TAIPAN is available online[6] and on Zenodo [5].

References

1. Beyer, D.: Verifiers and validators of the 12th Intl. Competition on Software Verification (SV-COMP 2023). Zenodo (2023). https://doi.org/10.5281/zenodo.7627829
2. Beyer, D.: Progress on software verification: SV-COMP 2022. In: TACAS (2). Lecture Notes in Computer Science, vol. 13244, pp. 375–402. Springer (2022). https://doi.org/10.1007/978-3-030-99527-0_20
3. Beyer, D., Löwe, S., Wendler, P.: Reliable Benchmarking: Requirements and Solutions. Int. J. Softw. Tools Technol. Transf. **21**(1), 1–29 (2019). https://doi.org/10.1007/s10009-017-0469-y
4. Coto, A., Inverso, O., Sales, E., Tuosto, E.: A prototype for data race detection in cseq 3 - (competition contribution). In: TACAS (2). Lecture Notes in Computer Science, vol. 13244, pp. 413–417. Springer (2022). https://doi.org/10.1007/978-3-030-99527-0_23
5. Dietsch, D., Heizmann, M., Klumpp, D., Schüssele, F., Podelski, A.: Ultimate Taipan SV-COMP 2023 Competition Contribution. Zenodo (Dec 2022). https://doi.org/10.5281/zenodo.7480186
6. Dietsch, D., Heizmann, M., Nutz, A., Schätzle, C., Schüssele, F.: Ultimate Taipan with Symbolic Interpretation and Fluid Abstractions - (Competition Contribution). In: TACAS (2). Lecture Notes in Computer Science, vol. 12079, pp. 418–422. Springer (2020). https://doi.org/10.1007/978-3-030-45237-7_32
7. Greitschus, M., Dietsch, D., Podelski, A.: Loop invariants from counterexamples. In: SAS. Lecture Notes in Computer Science, vol. 10422, pp. 128–147. Springer (2017). https://doi.org/10.1007/978-3-319-66706-5_7
8. Heizmann, M., Hoenicke, J., Podelski, A.: Refinement of Trace Abstraction. In: SAS. Lecture Notes in Computer Science, vol. 5673, pp. 69–85. Springer (2009). https://doi.org/10.1007/978-3-642-03237-0_7
9. ISO: ISO/IEC 9899:2011 Information technology — Programming languages — C. International Organization for Standardization, Geneva, Switzerland (2011)
10. Leino, K.R.M.: This is Boogie 2 (June 2008), https://www.microsoft.com/en-us/research/publication/this-is-boogie-2-2/

---

[6] gitlab.com/sosy-lab/sv-comp/archives-2023/-/blob/main/2023/utaipan.zip

VeriAbsL: Scalable Verification by Abstraction and Strategy Prediction (Competition Contribution)

Priyanka Darke[1],[*]([✉])(iD), Bharti Chimdyalwar[1],
Sakshi Agrawal[1], Shrawan Kumar[1], R. Venkatesh[1], and Supratik Chakraborty[2](iD)

[1] TCS Research, Pune, India
priyanka.darke@tcs.com
[2] Indian Institute of Technology, Bombay, India

Abstract. We present VeriAbsL, a reachability verifier that performs verification in three stages. First, it slices the input code using a combination of two slicers, then it verifies the slices using *predicted* strategies, and at last, it composes the result of verifying the individual slices. We introduce a novel *shallow slicing* technique that uses variable reference information of the program, and data and control dependencies of the entry function to generate slices. We also introduce a novel *strategy prediction* technique that uses machine learning to predict a strategy. It uses boolean features to describe a program to a neural network that predicts a strategy. We use the portfolio of VeriAbs, a reachabiltiy verifier with manually defined strategies. In SV-COMP 2023, VeriAbsL verified 227^3 more programs than VeriAbs, and 475^3 programs that VeriAbs could not verify.

1 Verification Approach

It is folklore in automated software verification that no single verification technique is good enough to verify all programs of interest. This limitation led to the advent of strategy selection-based verifiers that use predefined verification strategies [4]. A strategy is a sequence of verification techniques applied to a program, where each technique is bounded by a heuristically defined time limit. In this paper, we present a strategy prediction-based reachability verifier for C programs called VeriAbsL. It verifies a program in stages using a portfolio of two slicing, and ten verification techniques. First, it slices a program using a sequence of slicers. Then it uses a few syntactic and semantic features of the slice to predict a strategy and verify the slice. Lastly, it composes the result of verifying each slice. VeriAbsL uses a sequential combination of two slicers, a *slicer-analyzer* [7], and a novel *shallow slicer* or SSLICER. SSLICER is applied to programs that could not be sliced by the slicer-analyzer. The slicer-analyzer is more efficient than SSLICER, but applies to a smaller class of programs as explained in Section 1.2. Let a program P be sliced into n slices. A strategy prediction module extracts the features of each slice P_i, $1 \le i \le n$, and predicts a strategy for it using a neural network. The program P is safe if each slice P_i is safe, and P is unsafe if any slice P_i is unsafe. If program P cannot be sliced, then a

---

* P. Darke—Jury member
3 Without witness validation.

S. Sankaranarayanan and N. Sharygina (Eds.): TACAS 2023, LNCS 13994, pp. 588–593, 2023.
https://doi.org/10.1007/978-3-031-30820-8_41

strategy is predicted for P itself. Fig. 1 shows the architecture of VeriAbsL. As shown VeriAbsL uses the portfolio of a *strategy selection*-based verifier called VeriAbs [7].

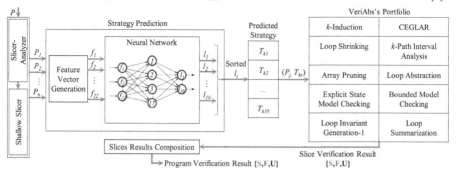

Fig. 1. VeriAbsL Architecture (S: Program Safe, F: Property Fails, U: Unknown)

1.1   Strategy Prediction using Machine Learning (ML)

Despite the advantages of sequencing multiple verification techniques in a strategy, experimental evidence indicates that each strategy works well for only a class of programs. When a new class is encountered, experts define a new strategy and update the strategy-selection algorithm of the verifier. This is a tedious task. In order to automate it, recently ML-based verifiers have been used with partial success [5]. VeriAbsL is one such verifier. It uses a simple ML-based approach explained as follows.

Feature Vector Generation. VeriAbsL uses a feature vector $\boldsymbol{f}$ of 22 boolean features that describe a few semantic, or syntactic constructs of the input slice P_j. For example, a boolean feature $f_i \in \boldsymbol{f}$ if set to *true* can indicate the presence of arrays in the input code, and *false* can indicate that no arrays are used. These features are computed using a light-weight static analysis, and derived from those presented in [8].

Neural Network. VeriAbsL uses a three layered neural network with multi-class classification, one class for each of the ten techniques in our portfolio. It has 22, 17, and 10 neurons in the respective layers. It was trained using ReLU for the hidden layer and softmax for the output layer, as activation functions, and with the mean-squared error loss function. It translates an input feature vector $\boldsymbol{f}$ representing program slice P_j into likelihoods of success l_i, $1 \leq i \leq 10$, of the corresponding verification techniques T_i in the portfolio for slice P_j. Each output node of the neural network n_i represents one verification technique T_i and the value l_i generated by the network at that node n_i is a heuristic measure of the relative likelihood that technique T_i will successfully verify/disprove the property for slice P_j within 900 seconds.

Strategy Prediction. A strategy $(T_{k_1},...,T_{k_{10}})$, $1 \leq k_r \leq 10$, $1 \leq r \leq 10$, is created by sorting the relative likelihoods of success l_i of each verification technique T_i in the decreasing order. The techniques T_i are invoked in that order to verify slice P_j.

Experimental Results. The neural network in VeriAbsL was trained on 800 randomly selected SV-COMP 2022 ReachSafety benchmarks. At SV-COMP 2023 out of all 6138 benchmarks, VeriAbsL verified 227 more programs in 4.4% lesser time than

VeriAbs[4] and verified 475 programs that VeriAbs could not verify[3]. This was because VeriAbsL predicted useful techniques early in its strategies, while VeriAbs selected unsuitable strategies and ran out of time. Further the randomly selected training data did not contain any benchmarks from three ReachSafety sub-categories namely Combinations, ProductLines, and Hardware. VeriAbsL verified 72 more programs than VeriAbs in these 3 sub-categories demonstrating that strategy-prediction in VeriAbsL generalizes to programs for which it was not trained. VeriAbsL ran out of time for 248 programs verified by VeriAbs because the randomly selected training data did not contain any sample corresponding to two techniques, namely VAJRA [6] and Counter-Example Guided Loop Abstraction Refinement (CEGLAR) [4], needed to verify the 248 programs. Thus they were always predicted late. Further VeriAbsL verified 1047 and 543 more benchmarks compared to the other ML-based strategy prediction tools, GRAVES [11] and PESCO [12], respectively.

Strengths and Weaknesses of Strategy Prediction. VeriAbsL can verify more programs than VeriAbs in spite of the same portfolio because it uses ML for strategy prediction. Also VeriAbsL demonstrates that a small set of boolean features can be used successfully to verify programs, while other successful verifiers predict a strategy using graph based learning methods [12]. Further VeriAbsL does not incorporate a feedback mechanism that can penalize a technique if it cannot verify a program. Such a feedback mechanism can improve its efficiency and accuracy.

1.2   Shallow Slicer

SSLICER is a generalization of the slicer-analyzer presented in [7] and like the latter, aims for a scalable slicing with respect to calls in entry function *main*. But unlike the slicer-analyzer, SSLICER allows multiple calls in *main* to (1) refer to the same global variable, (2) transitively invoke the same function, or (3) have transitive dependence on the same data element or control structure in *main*.

SSLICER partitions the program functions directly or indirectly called from *main* into n sets $F_1...F_n$ such that the following conditions, termed as *partition-independence*, are satisfied: (1) Each partition F_i contains at least one function directly called from *main*. (2) Each partition F_i contains functions which are either directly or transitively called from *main*. (3) All functions transitively called from function $f \in F_i$ also belong to F_i, the same partition as f. Thus if $T(f)$ is the set of functions transitively called from f, then $\forall i, 1 \leq i \leq n, \forall f \in F_i, T(f) \subseteq F_i$. (4) No two functions $f \in F_i$ and $g \in F_j$ belonging to different partitions transitively call the same function or refer to the same global variable. Let $V(F_i)$ be the set of global variables referred to by functions in set F_i then $\forall i,j \mid 1 \leq i \leq n, 1 \leq j \leq n, i \neq j \implies (V(F_i) \cap V(F_j) = \emptyset)$ (5) Let $main_i$ be the function generated when a program containing only one function, the function *main*, is sliced (using known slicing techniques [9]) with respect to calls to functions in set F_i which are directly called from *main*. Then functions of no other set $F_j, i \neq j$, should refer to the variables used in $main_i$. Thus $\forall i,j \mid 1 \leq i \leq n, 1 \leq j \leq n, i \neq j \implies (V(main_i) \cap V(F_j) = \emptyset)$ (6) n is the largest possible natural number satisfying the above conditions.

---

[4] The competition score of VeriAbs is greater than VeriAbsL because of 8 incorrect results produced due to bugs in the implementation of a technique predicted by VeriAbsL. This technique was not executed for these 8 programs by VeriAbs.

A slice P_i corresponding to each set F_i is generated. The set of functions in slice P_i is given by $main_i \cup F_i$. To create the slice, call graph and referred variables information is computed using call-trees, and a light-weight flow-insensitive pointer analysis. We assume that function $main$ itself is not a part of any recursive call chain, and does not specify the assertions directly.

```
main(){
    if(a&&b)f1();        main(){
    f2();                    if(a&&b)f1();
    if(b)  f5();             f2();                  main(){
}                        }                              if(b)  f5();
f1() { f3(); }           f1() { f3(); }             }
f2() { f4(); }           f2() { f4(); }             f5() { d++; }
f3() { c++; }            f3() { c++; }
f4() { a++; }            f4() { a++; }                 (c) Slice 2
f5() { d++; }
                             (b) Slice 1
    (a) Input Code
```

Fig. 2. Example

Example. Consider the program presented in Fig. 2a. In this example functions called from $main$ can be initially partitioned into three sets {f1, f3}, {f2, f4,} and {f5} as f1 calls f3, f2 calls f4, and f5 does not refer to any function or variable that other functions refer to. But function f4 refers to variable a. If a program containing only the body of function $main$ shown in Fig. 2a were to be sliced with respect to the call to f1 in $main$ then it would refer to variable a. Function f1 belongs to the first partition and f4 to the second. To satisfy the fifth condition of *partition-independence* functions f1 and f4 must belong to a single partition. Thus finally there are two partitions - {f1, f2, f3, f4}, and {f5}. The slices created for the first and second partitions are shown in Figures 2b and 2c respectively. Notice that since function f5 does not refer to variable b in its body, it need not be merged with the other partition even though the body of sliced $main$ in Fig. 2c refers to variable b.

Experimental Results. We compare the performances of VeriAbsL with (1) *slicer-analyzer*, and (2) *slicer-analyzer* and SSLICER, on all 6138 benchmarks of the Reach-Safety category of SV-COMP 2023. The first configuration generated slices for 671 programs while the second generated slices for 1369 programs showing better applicability. Further, due to SSLICER, VeriAbsL terminated its analysis for 42 more programs, showing improved scalability, and its portfolio could verify 4 additional programs.

1.3 Software Project, Architecture, and Setup

The Foundations of Computing research group at TCS Research [1] has developed VeriAbsL. It is written in Perl, Java and Python. It uses TCS's program analysis framework [10] for static analysis, and TensorFlow libraries [2] for learning. VeriAbsL uses VeriAbs's portfolio [7], except VAJRA [6] because it is not supported on Ubuntu 22.04 LTS. VeriAbsL participated in the Reach-Safety category at SV-COMP 2023, and is available at [3]. The installation instructions are in `VeriAbsL/INSTALL.txt`, the BenchExec[5] wrapper script for the tool is `veriabsl.py`, and the benchmark definition file is `veriabsl.xml`. On successful verification, VeriAbsL generates a witness in the current working directory as `witness.graphml`. A sample command to verify property given in file `reach-safety.prp` for a program, given in `a.c`, of a 32-bit (or 64-bit) architecture is as follows: `VeriAbsL/scripts/veriabs -32|64 --property-file reach-safety.prp a.c`

---

[5] https://github.com/sosy-lab/benchexec

2   Data-Availability Statement

VeriAbsL is available as part of SV-COMP 2023 verifier repository at `https://gitlab.com/sosy-lab/sv-comp/archives-2023/-/blob/main/2023/veriabsl.zip`. For any queries please contact the authors at veriabs.tool@tcs.com.

References

1. Foundations of Computing Group at TCS Research. `https://www.tcs.com/what-we-do/research`.
2. TensorFlow. `https://www.tensorflow.org/`.
3. VeriAbsL Tool Archive. `https://gitlab.com/sosy-lab/sv-comp/archives-2023/-/blob/main/2023/veriabsl.zip`.
4. M. Afzal, A. Asia, A. Chauhan, B. Chimdyalwar, P. Darke, A. Datar, S. Kumar, and R Venkatesh. VeriAbs: Verification by Abstraction and Test Generation. In *ASE*, pages 1138–1141, 2019.
5. Dirk Beyer. Progress on software verification: SV-COMP 2022. In Dana Fisman and Grigore Rosu, editors, *Tools and Algorithms for the Construction and Analysis of Systems - 28th International Conference, TACAS 2022, Held as Part of the European Joint Conferences on Theory and Practice of Software, ETAPS 2022, Munich, Germany, April 2-7, 2022, Proceedings, Part II*, volume 13244 of *Lecture Notes in Computer Science*, pages 375–402. Springer, 2022.
6. Supratik Chakraborty, Ashutosh Gupta, and Divyesh Unadkat. Verifying array manipulating programs with full-program induction. In *International Conference on Tools and Algorithms for the Construction and Analysis of Systems (TACAS)*, pages 22–39. Springer, 2020.
7. P. Darke, S. Agrawal, and R. Venkatesh. VERIABS: A Tool for Scalable Verification by Abstraction (Competition Contribution). In *Proc. TACAS (2)*, LNCS 12652. Springer, 2021.
8. Yulia Demyanova, Thomas Pani, Helmut Veith, and Florian Zuleger. Empirical software metrics for benchmarking of verification tools. In Jens Knoop and Uwe Zdun, editors, *Software Engineering 2016*, pages 67–68, Bonn, 2016. Gesellschaft für Informatik e.V.
9. Mark Harman and Robert M. Hierons. An overview of program slicing. *Software Focus*, 2(3):85–92, 2001.
10. S. Khare, S. Saraswat, and S. Kumar. Static program analysis of large embedded code base: an experience. In *ISEC*, pages 99–102, 2011.
11. Will Leeson and Matthew B. Dwyer. Graves-cpa: A graph-attention verifier selector (competition contribution). In Dana Fisman and Grigore Rosu, editors, *Tools and Algorithms for the Construction and Analysis of Systems*, pages 440–445, Cham, 2022. Springer International Publishing.
12. Cedric Richter, Eyke Hüllermeier, Marie-Christine Jakobs, and Heike Wehrheim. Algorithm selection for software validation based on graph kernels, 2020. `https://link.springer.com/article/10.1007/s10515-020-00270-x`.
13. Cedric Richter and Heike Wehrheim. Pesco: Predicting sequential combinations of verifiers. In Dirk Beyer, Marieke Huisman, Fabrice Kordon, and Bernhard Steffen, editors, *Tools and Algorithms for the Construction and Analysis of Systems*, pages 229–233, Cham, 2019. Springer International Publishing.

VeriFuzz 1.4: Checking for (Non-)termination (Competition Contribution)

Ravindra Metta[ID], Prasanth Yeduru[ID], Hrishikesh Karmarkar[ID], and
Raveendra Kumar Medicherla[*][✉][ID]

TCS Research, Tata Consultancy Services, Pune, India
{r.metta,prasanth.yeduru,hrishikesh.karmarkar,raveendra.kumar}@tcs.com

Abstract. In VeriFuzz 1.4, we implemented two new techniques for checking Non-termination and Termination. VeriFuzz 1.4 won the Termination category of SV-COMP 2023.

1 Approach for Non-termination and Termination

VeriFuzz 1.2.0 [4,10,11] is a framework to automatically generate test cases, and lacks the ability to prove properties such as *termination*. Given a program P and *termination* as the property, a tool needs to either provide a witness for Non-termination of P, or give a *true* verdict if P always terminates. Therefore, we developed two techniques: one for *proving* Non-termination and one for checking termination with a *high confidence*, which are described below.

1.1 Technique for Non-termination Checking

For SV-COMP 2023, we implemented a variant of FuzzNT [7], a sound technique for proving Non-termination arising due to infinite loops. FuzzNT takes as input a C program P and a corpus of test inputs T generated using the Coverage Guided Fuzzer of VeriFuzz 1.2. Each test input $t \in T$ is a sequence of values to be supplied to P via *nondet()* calls. We illustrate the key steps of FuzzNT using the program P (Listing 1.1), adopted from the code that caused the SSL non-termination [13]. Note that P terminates on the test input $t = \langle 1 : j = 129, 4 : i == 1, 5 : j = 5, 4 : i == 3 \rangle$. Given such a test input, FuzzNT transforms P into a Path Specific Program (PSP) P' (Listing 1.2), by replacing each nondet() call in P with the corresponding value in the test input, if any, as described in [7]. If multiple values in the test input correspond to a nondet() call in P, FuzzNT picks the first value among them to replace the nondet() call. For example, in t, both $i == 1$ and $i == 3$ correspond to the nondet() call on Line 4 in Listing 1.1. So, as shown on Line 4 of Listing 1.2, this nondet() call is replaced with $i == 1$. Notice that P' has only one feasible execution path, which does not terminate. P' is then supplied to an abstract interpretation based safety checker, which checks if P' does not terminate. If the check succeeds, then P' is non-terminating and

---

* Jury member

S. Sankaranarayanan and N. Sharygina (Eds.): TACAS 2023, LNCS 13994, pp. 594–599, 2023.
https://doi.org/10.1007/978-3-031-30820-8_42

| Listing 1.1. Program P | Listing 1.2. Program P' |

```
1  i=1; j=nondet();
2  while(j!=1) {
3      i=i+1;
4      if (i==nondet()) exit(0);
5      j=nondet(); }
```

```
1  i=1; j=129;
2  while(j!=1) {
3      i=i+1;
4      if (i==1) exit(0);
5      j=5; }
```

hence P is also non-terminating, and a proof of Non-termination is generated for P in the form of a witness automaton. These steps are repeated until either a non-terminating execution is discovered, or test inputs are exhausted.

1.2   Variant of FuzzNT implemented in VeriFuzz 1.4

The version of FuzzNT in [7] uses Frama-C [14] for the abstract interpretation based Non-termination check. However, we noticed that Frama-C's abstract interpretation does not precisely model termination semantics of standard library functions like *abort()*. This leads to Frama-C incorrectly identifying some terminating programs as non-terminating. Further, we could not bundle Frama-C with FuzzNT due to the installation dependencies and it is unavailable in the Competition Environment of SV-COMP 2023. Therefore, we implemented a variant of FuzzNT using the C Bounded Model Checker [5], as described below.

Given a program P, we begin by checking if P terminates as described in Section 1.3. If this check could not identify the termination of P, then we generate PSPs for P using VeriFuzz 1.2 (described in Section 1.1). Next CBMC is run on each generated PSP, say P', with a small loop unwind bound, say k, and check for CBMC's built-in unwinding assertion, which checks if all loops within P' iterate at most k times. If this check succeeds, then P' is a terminating program. If this check fails, then there exists an input for which some loop in P' iterates more than k times. We then iteratively increase k and repeat the termination check until a large enough k such as $10,000$. In our experiments, we observed that while CBMC does not scale to such a large unwinding of P, it does scale to large unwindings of the PSPs of P, as they admit much fewer behaviours than P. If the check fails even at $10,000$ for P', it is likely to be non-terminating. We then generate a witness automaton for P using P', classifying P as non-terminating.

1.3   Technique for termination

To check if a given a program P terminates on all inputs, we designed an unsound, but high confidence, incremental verification technique based on Bounded Model Checking (CBMC). This technique works in two phases. *Phase-1* is the same as CBMC's own termination check. In this, we begin by unwinding all the loops in P for a small number of iterations, such as 2. Then, using CBMC's built-in loop unwinding assertion check, we verify if all loops terminate within this small unwinding, say k. If this check is successful, then all loops in P terminate within k iterations and hence P itself terminates, and we return *TRUE* to declare P to be terminating. If the check fails for any loop, then that loop can iterate more than k times. So, we increment k, and repeat the check. This approach suffers from two limitations. (1) As k grows larger, BMC suffers from scalability issues, and (2) if P has a feasible non-terminating path, then the check for a higher k repeats forever. To overcome these limitations, we stop *Phase-1* and return *UNKNOWN* as soon as k reaches a threshold value (pre-configured for SV-COMP 2023). We then proceed to *Phase-2*, described below.

In *Phase-2*, we try to find a small model for the termination property of P, by *guessing* a small range R of the inputs (viz. nondet() calls), such that if P terminates for all inputs in R, then P is *highly likely* to terminate for all its inputs. To guess this R, we learnt a Decision Tree (DT) model on a training data of less than 10% of SV-COMP benchmarks, based on program features and sample execution traces. We are working on formalizing this approach via ranking functions [6].

We then run the incremental verification from *Phase-1*, but by bounding the nondet() values to those in R. This bounding allows CBMC's backend solvers such as Z3 to scale to a larger loop unwind K ($\sim 100,000$ in our experiments). If all loops in P terminate within at most K iterations given the R-bounding, then we assume that P is *highly likely* to terminate on all inputs even without R-bounding. Therefore, if this *bounded value check* concludes that P terminates, then we return *TRUE* to declare P to be terminating, else we return *UNKNOWN* and invoke the non-termination check described in Section 1.2.

2   Software Architecture

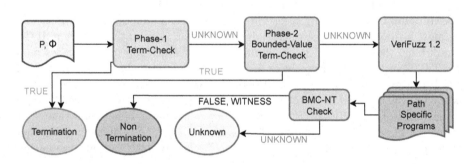

Fig. 1. VeriFuzz 1.4 architecture

Figure 1 shows the architecture of VeriFuzz 1.4. Here P is the input program, and ϕ is the termination property. The process-blocks *Phase-1 Term-Check* and *Phase-2 Bounded-Value Term-Check*, together constitute our two phased termination check described in Section 1.3. If both Phase-1 and Phase-2 return UNKNOWN, we then execute the Non-termination check described in Section 1.2. That is, we first generate PSPs using *VeriFuzz 1.2*, and search for a likely non-terminating PSP, say P'. If we find such a P', we generate a witness automaton and return *FALSE* (to report non-termination). Else, all the above steps must have returned *UNKNOWN*, and VeriFuzz 1.4 is unable to decide if P is terminating or non-terminating, and hence returns *UNKNOWN*.

In Figure 1, VeriFuzz 1.2 is built using PRISM [8] program analysis framework, AFL [16], and CBMC v5.67.0 [1] with Z3 4.8.15 [12] and Glucose Syrup [2] as the backend SMT and SAT solvers respectively. The DT model used in Phase-2 of the termination check (see Section 1.3) is trained offline using booster trees [3]. The rest of VeriFuzz 1.4 is implemented in C++ and Python.

3   Strengths and Weaknesses

Out of 1043 Termination tasks in SV-COMP 2023, our two phase technique correctly solved 865. Some of these, such as termination-crafted/easy2-2.c and termination-dietlibc/atoi.c, contain loops that iterate arbitrarily large number of times. Hence, while BMC fails to conclude their termination, our approach succeeds as it limits the number of loop iterations by restricting the inputs to a small range. Tasks, such as termination-restricted-15/Sunset.c, terminate within the value ranges guessed during Phase-2, but do not terminate for some inputs that lie outside the ranges. Thus, we wrongly reported them to be terminating.

Out of 766 Non-termination tasks, our Non-termination technique correctly solved 351. Of these, tasks such as systemc/pipeline.cil-1.c , have complex control and data dependencies, which could not be solved by approaches such as those in UAutomizer [9] and Symbiotic [15]. But, the PSPs of these programs, generated by our technique, were much simpler to check for non-termination and hence our technique succeeded on them. However, within the given time limits, if all the PSPs we generated happen to be terminating, then our technique fails to identify the non-termination. Our results on tasks locks/test_locks_14-2.c and termination-restricted-15/Ex02.c demonstrate this behaviour. Another weakness is that our technique currently does not handle programs with recursion. We are currently developing new techniques that address these weaknesses.

4   Tool Configuration and Setup

VeriFuzz 1.4 is available at git@gitlab.com:sosy-lab/sv-comp/archives-2023.git. To install and run the tool, follow the instructions in the `README.txt`. The benchexec tool-info module is `verifuzz.py` and the benchmark definition file is `verifuzz.xml`. A sample run command is as follows: `./scripts/verifuzz.py --propertyFile` *termination.prp example.c*. In SV-COMP 2023, VeriFuzz opts to participate in Termination, ReachSafety, and Overflow categories.

5   Software Project and Contributors

VeriFuzz is developed and maintained by the authors at TCS Research. We thank everyone who has contributed to the development of VeriFuzz and the tools AFL, PRISM, CBMC, Glucose Syrup, and Z3. Contact: verifuzz.tool@tcs.com.

6   Data-Availability Statement

VeriFuzz 1.4 is available as part of SV-COMP 2023 verifier repository at https://gitlab.com/sosy-lab/sv-comp/archives-2023/-/blob/main/2023/verifuzz.zip. For any queries, please contact the authors at verifuzz.tool@tcs.com.

References

1. C Bounded Model Checker. https://github.com/diffblue/cbmc
2. Audemard, G., Simon, L.: On the glucose SAT solver. Int. J. Artif. Intell. Tools pp. 1840001:1–1840001:25 (2018). https://doi.org/10.1142/S0218213018400018
3. Chen T., G.C.: Xgboost: A scalable tree boosting system. In: KDD. pp. 785–794 (2016). https://doi.org/10.1145/2939672.2939785
4. Chowdhury, A.B., Medicherla, R.K., Venkatesh, R.: Verifuzz: Program aware fuzzing - (competition contribution). In: TACAS. pp. 244–249 (2019). https://doi.org/10.1007/978-3-030-17502-3_22
5. Clarke E., Kroening D., L.F.: A tool for checking ansi-c programs. In: TACAS. pp. 168–176 (2004). https://doi.org/10.1007/978-3-540-24730-2_15
6. Giacobbe, M., Kroening, D., Parsert, J.: Neural termination analysis. In: ESEC/FSE. pp. 633–645 (2022). https://doi.org/10.1145/3540250.3549120
7. Karmarkar, H., Medicherla, R., Metta, R., Yeduru, P.: FuzzNT: Checking for program non-termination. In: ICSME. pp. 409–413 (2022). https://doi.org/10.1109/ICSME55016.2022.00049
8. Khare, S., Saraswat, S., Kumar, S.: Static program analysis of large embedded code base: an experience. In: ISEC. pp. 99–102 (2011). https://doi.org/10.1145/1953355.1953368
9. Matthias, H.: Uautomizer (2022), https://gitlab.com/sosy-lab/sv-comp/archives-2022/raw/svcomp22/2022/uautomizer.zip
10. Metta, R., Medicherla, R.K., Chakraborty, S.: BMC+Fuzz: Efficient and Effective Test Generation. In: DATE. pp. 1419–1424 (2022). https://doi.org/10.23919/DATE54114.2022.9774672
11. Metta, R., Medicherla, R.K., Karmarkar, H.: VeriFuzz: Good Seeds for Fuzzing (Competition Contribution). In: FASE. pp. 341–346 (2022). https://doi.org/10.1007/978-3-030-99429-7_20
12. Moura, L.M.d., Bjørner, N.: Z3: An Efficient SMT Solver. In: TACAS. pp. 337–340 (2008). https://doi.org/10.1007/978-3-540-78800-3_24
13. OpenSSL: Fix possible infinite loop in BN_mod_sqrt(). https://github.com/openssl/openssl/commit/3118eb64934499d93db3230748a452351d1d9a65 (2022)
14. Patrick, B., et al.: The dogged pursuit of bug-free C programs: the Frama-C software analysis platform. Commun. ACM pp. 56–68 (2021). https://doi.org/10.1145/3470569
15. Viktor, M.: 2LS (2022), https://github.com/diffblue/2ls
16. Zalewski, M.: American Fuzzy Lop. http://lcamtuf.coredump.cx/afl/

Author Index

A

Abdulla, Parosh Aziz I-588
Abdulla, Parosh I-105
Aggarwal, Saksham I-666
Agrawal, Sakshi II-588
Albert, Elvira I-448
Aljaafari, Fatimah II-541
Amir, Guy I-607
Anand, Ashwani II-211
Andreotti, Bruno I-367
Apinis, Kalmer II-453
Atig, Mohamad Faouzi I-588
Atig, Mohamed Faouzi I-105
Avigad, Jeremy II-74
Ayaziová, Paulína II-523

B

Bach, Jakob I-407
Bajwa, Ali I-308
Balachander, Mrudula II-309
Banerjee, Anindya II-133
Barbosa, Haniel I-367
Barrau, Florian II-3
Barth, Max II-577
Bassan, Shahaf I-187
Batz, Kevin II-410
Bentkamp, Alexander II-74
Beutner, Raven I-145
Beyer, Dirk II-152, II-495
Biere, Armin I-426
Blanchette, Jasmin II-111
Bonakdarpour, Borzoo I-29, I-66
Bouma, Jelle II-19
Bruyère, Véronique I-271

C

Cadilhac, Michaël II-192
Chadha, Rohit I-308

D

Chakraborty, Supratik II-588
Chalupa, Marek II-535
Chatterjee, Krishnendu I-3
Chen, Mingshuai II-410
Chien, Po-Chun II-152
Chimdyalwar, Bharti II-588
Chin, Wei-Ngan I-569
Cimatti, Alessandro II-3
Cooper, Martin C. I-167
Cordeiro, Lucas C. II-541
Corfini, Sara II-3
Correas, Jesús I-448
Corsi, Davide I-607
Cortes, João II-55
Cristoforetti, Luca II-3

D

Darke, Priyanka II-588
de Gouw, Stijn II-19
de la Banda, Alejandro Stuckey I-666
de Pol, Jaco van II-353
Deligiannis, Pantazis II-433
Denis, Xavier II-93
Di Natale, Marco II-3
Dietsch, Daniel II-577, II-582
Dimitrova, Rayna II-251
Doveri, Kyveli I-290
Duan, Zhenhua II-571

E

Erhard, Julian II-547
Ernst, Gidon II-559
Etman, L. F. P. II-44
Eugster, Patrick I-126

F

Fang, Wenji II-11
Farinelli, Alessandro I-607

Fedyukovich, Grigory   II-270
Fichtner, Leonard   II-577
Filiot, Emmanuel   II-309
Finkbeiner, Bernd   I-29, I-145
Fokkink, W. J.   II-44
Fuchs, Tobias   I-407
Furbach, Florian   I-588

G
Ganty, Pierre   I-290
Godbole, Adwait A.   I-588
Goorden, M. A.   II-44
Gordillo, Pablo   I-448
Griggio, Alberto   II-3
Guo, Xingwu   I-208
Gupta, Ashutosh   I-105
Gutierrez, Julian   I-666

H
Hadži-Đokić, Luka   I-290
Hahn, Ernst Moritz   I-527
Hamza, Ameer   II-270
Harel, David   I-607
Hartmanns, Arnd   I-469
Havlena, Vojtěch   I-249
Heim, Philippe   II-251
Heisinger, Maximilian   I-426
Heizmann, Matthias   II-577, II-582
Hendi, Yacoub G.   I-588
Hendriks, D.   II-44
Henzinger, Thomas A.   I-3, II-535
Herasimau, Andrei   II-473
Heule, Marijn J. H.   I-329, I-348, I-389
Hoenicke, Jochen   II-577
Hofkamp, A. T.   II-44
Hsu, Tzu-Han   I-29, I-66
Huang, Xuanxiang   I-167
Hussein, Soha   II-553

I
Iser, Markus   I-407

J
Jaber, Nouraldin   II-289
Jacobs, Swen   II-289
Jakobsen, Anna Blume   II-353
Jansen, Nils   I-508
Jongmans, Sung-Shik   II-19

Jourdan, Jacques-Henri   II-93
Junges, Sebastian   I-469, I-508, II-410

K
Kaminski, Benjamin Lucien   II-410
Karmarkar, Hrishikesh   II-594
Katoen, Joost-Pieter   II-391, II-410
Katz, Guy   I-187, I-208, I-607
Kiesl-Reiter, Benjamin   I-329, I-348
Klumpp, Dominik   II-577, II-582
Kobayashi, Naoki   I-227
Kokologiannakis, Michalis   I-85
Konnov, Igor   I-126
Korovin, Konstantin   I-647
Kovács, Laura   I-647
Krishna, S.   I-105
Krishna, Shankara N.   I-588
Kukovec, Jure   I-126
Kulkarni, Milind   II-289
Kullmann, Oliver   II-372
Kumar, Shrawan   II-588

L
Lachnitt, Hanna   I-367
Lal, Akash   II-433
Larsen, Casper Abild   II-353
Lechner, Mathias   I-3
Lee, Nian-Ze   II-152
Lefaucheux, Engel   I-47
Lengál, Ondřej   I-249
Lester, Martin Mariusz   II-173
Li, Jianwen   II-36
Li, Yong   I-249
Lima, Leonardo   II-473
Lovett, Chris   II-433
Lynce, Inês   II-55

M
Malík, Viktor   II-529
Mallik, Kaushik   II-211
Manino, Edoardo   II-541
Manquinho, Vasco   II-55
Marmanis, Iason   I-85
Marques-Silva, Joao   I-167
Marzari, Luca   I-607
Matheja, Christoph   II-410
McCamant, Stephen   II-553
Medicherla, Raveendra Kumar   II-594
Meggendorfer, Tobias   I-489

Melham, Tom I-549
Menezes, Rafael II-541
Metta, Ravindra II-594
Meyer, Roland I-628
Michaelson, Dawn I-348
Miné, Antoine II-565
Mir, Ramon Fernández II-74
Monat, Raphaël II-565
Moormann, L. II-44
Morgado, Antonio I-167

N

Nagasamudram, Ramana II-133
Naouar, Mehdi II-577
Naumann, David A. II-133
Nayak, Satya Prakash II-211
Nayyar, Fahad II-433
Nečas, František II-529

O

Osama, Muhammad I-684
Otoni, Rodrigo I-126
Ouadjaout, Abdelraouf II-565
Ouaknine, Joël I-47

P

Pai, Rekha I-549
Park, Seung Hoon I-549
Pavlogiannis, Andreas II-353
Pérez, Guillermo A. I-271, II-192
Perez, Mateo I-527
Pietsch, Manuel II-547
Planes, Jordi I-167
Podelski, Andreas II-577, II-582
Pu, Geguang II-36
Purser, David I-47

Q

Quatmann, Tim I-469

R

Raskin, Jean-François II-309
Raszyk, Martin II-473
Reeves, Joseph E. I-329
Reger, Giles I-647
Reijnen, F. F. H. II-44

Reniers, M. A. II-44
Román-Díez, Guillermo I-448
Rooda, J. E. II-44
Rubio, Albert I-448

S

Saan, Simmo II-547
Samanta, Roopsha II-289
Sánchez, César I-29, I-66
Sankur, Ocan II-28, II-329
Schewe, Sven I-527
Schiffelers, R. R. H. II-44
Schindler, Tanja II-577
Schmidt, Simon Meldahl II-353
Schmuck, Anne-Kathrin II-211
Schoisswohl, Johannes I-647
Schrammel, Peter II-529
Schreiber, Dominik I-348
Schulz, Stephan II-111
Schüssele, Frank II-577, II-582
Schwarz, Michael II-547
Seidl, Helmut II-547
Seidl, Martina I-426
Senthilnathan, Aditya II-433
Sharifi, Mohammadamin I-47
Sharma, Vaibhav II-553
Sharygina, Natasha I-126
Sheinvald, Sarai I-66
Shmarov, Fedor II-541
Shukla, Ankit II-372
Šmahlíková, Barbora I-249
Somenzi, Fabio I-527
Song, Yahui I-569
Spengler, Stephan I-588
Staquet, Gaëtan I-271
Steensgaard, Jesper II-353
Strejček, Jan II-523
Su, Jie II-571
Subercaseaux, Bernardo I-389

T

Thomas, Bastien II-28
Thuijsman, S. B. II-44
Tian, Cong II-571
Tilscher, Sarah II-547
Tonetta, Stefano II-3

Traytel, Dmitriy   II-473
Trivedi, Ashutosh   I-527
Tuppe, Omkar   I-105
Turrini, Andrea   I-249

V

Vafeiadis, Viktor   I-85
van Beek, D. A.   II-44
van de Mortel-Fronczak, J. M.   II-44
van der Sanden, L. J.   II-44
van der Vegt, Marck   I-508
Venkatesh, R   II-588
Verbakel, J. J.   II-44
Viswanathan, Mahesh   I-308
Vogel, J. A.   II-44
Vojdani, Vesal   II-453, II-547
Vojnar, Tomáš   II-529
Voronkov, Andrei   I-647
Vukmirović, Petar   II-111

W

Wagner, Christopher   II-289
Wang, Yuning   II-229
Weininger, Maximilian   I-469
Whalen, Michael W.   I-348, II-553
Wies, Thomas   I-628
Wijs, Anton   I-684

Winkler, Tobias   II-391
Wojtczak, Dominik   I-527
Wolff, Sebastian   I-628
Wu, Minchao   I-227

X

Xiao, Shengping   II-36
Xing, Hengrui   II-571

Y

Yan, Qiuchen   II-553
Yang, Jiyu   II-571
Yang, Luke   I-666
Yang, Zuchao   II-571
Yeduru, Prasanth   II-594
Yerushalmi, Raz   I-607
Yuan, Simon   II-473

Z

Zhang, Chengyu   II-36
Zhang, Hongce   II-11
Zhang, Min   I-208
Zhang, Minjian   I-308
Zhang, Yueling   I-208
Zhou, Ziwei   I-208
Zhu, He   II-229
Žikelić, Đorđe   I-3

Printed in the United States
by Baker & Taylor Publisher Services